Constitutional Law

AN INTEGRATED APPROACH

RICHARD D. FRIEDMAN

ALENE AND ALLAN F. SMITH PROFESSOR OF LAW
UNIVERSITY OF MICHIGAN LAW SCHOOL

JULIAN DAVIS MORTENSON

JAMES G. PHILLIPP PROFESSOR OF LAW
UNIVERSITY OF MICHIGAN LAW SCHOOL

DOCTRINE AND PRACTICE SERIES™

FOUNDATION
PRESS

© 2021 LEG, Inc. d/b/a West Academic
  444 Cedar Street, Suite 700
  St. Paul, MN 55101
  1-877-888-1330

Printed in the United States of America

ISBN: 978-1-64020-258-0

To Steve, Barbara, Phyllis, and Brad, from a lucky little brother, with love and gratitude for a lifetime web of love and support. RDF

To Jo Ann Davis and Peter Mortenson, who always said to go for it. JDM

Preface

We are pleased to present this textbook for an introductory course on Constitutional Law.

One of our principal aims in creating this book was to facilitate flexibility in instruction. Our own approaches to the course differ substantially, and we expect that instructors will find that the book lends itself to being used in a variety of ways. Some, for example, might want to begin with Chapter I, which provides a survey of American constitutional history through the New Deal. Others may skip that chapter, perhaps dipping back into it as needed through the course, and start with the *Heller* case or Frederick Douglass's speech at the Scottish Debating Society. Still others may start even further along in the book. Whatever approach the instructor uses, it will not feel as if the course is being taught "against the grain" of the book.

Another of our aims has been leanness. We hesitate to say brevity, because Constitutional Law textbooks are never short, but we have zealously sought to eliminate unnecessary bloat. We believe this will ease the burden on students and also allow instructors to cover more material without feeling rushed. Where we have presented questions in the text, we have tried to make them focused, and ones that can readily be used in class discussion.

We have also attempted to maintain throughout the book a strong historical consciousness, which we believe is useful in most areas of law but absolutely essential in Constitutional Law. This orientation is most apparent in the historical survey, but it underlies subsequent chapters as well, which are organized by subject matter.

Because this is a textbook and not a document repository, we have taken numerous measures to present textual materials in a clear, clean, simplified manner. We usually do not present full citations of cases, except in the heading of principal cases. (Even without citations, all the cases are easy to find online, for those who may be interested.) If we present only the name of a case, or only the name and a date, it is a decision by the United States Supreme Court; when we cite decisions by other courts, we do indicate the name of the court. In some cases, where we omit a decision's first reference to a prior case and the decision then referred to the earlier case by a shorter name, we use the full name in the first mention that we include, without so indicating by brackets. In general, where we omit text and insert material in brackets to fill in the gap, we have let the brackets indicate the omission, without need for ellipses. Sometimes, for visual appeal, we alter the presentation of texts in various ways, without so indicating. For example, we sometimes italicize or otherwise format headings within a text, or break up long passages into separate paragraphs. Sometimes, where a footnote contains only a citation that we think is worth presenting, we move the citation into the body of the text. Where a passage has multiple individual citations to subsections of one statute, we sometimes replace those with a single citation at the end of the passage to the overarching section. In some relatively short passages, we drop section headings. If the repeated use of "sometimes" in this paragraph indicates that we have not always been consistent, we revert to our purpose to emphasize clarity and simplicity; we do not believe that we have ever sacrificed substantive accuracy.

Footnote numbers (or, in a few cases, characters) are as in the original texts. Where we have written footnotes of our own, they are indicated by calls in lower-case letters.

No doubt we have made mistakes along the way, and there is room for improvement. We welcome comments, to Rich at rdfrdman@umich.edu and to Julian at jdmorten@umich.edu.

We gratefully acknowledge the following persons and entities for permission to use excerpts from the indicated materials, in order of their appearance in the book: Michael McConnell (his 1997 Harvard Law Review article, Institutions and Interpretation: A Critique of City of Boerne v. Flores); Maryland Law Review (John Hart Ely's 1978 article, Toward a Representation-Reinforcing Mode of Judicial Review); our colleague Nick Bagley (his 2019 Michigan Law Review article, The Procedure Fetish); Michael James and Adam Burgos (their entry, Race, in the Stanford Encyclopedia of Philosophy); MIT Press (David Hollinger's 2005 Daedalus article, The One Drop Rule and the One Hate Rule); the UCLA Civil Rights Project (the 2014 study by Gary Orfield, Erica Frankenberg, et al., Brown at 60: Great Progress, a Long Retreat and an Uncertain Future); our colleague James Boyd White (his book, Keeping Law Alive); Harvard University Press (John Hart Ely's book, Democracy and Distrust: A Theory of Judicial Review); The Roanoke Times (a 2017 article by Laurence Hammack on the Virginia Military Institute).

We also have many people to thank, for various forms of guidance and assistance along the way. With apologies to any we may have omitted in error, we particularly appreciate help from Alex DiLalla, Joanna Friedman, Jeff Gurley, Lori Hale, Laura Harlow, Amy Jiang, Margaret Klocinski, Rachel Kreager, William Lang, Leah Litman, Emily Liu, Seth Mayer, Lindsey Young Mortenson, Virginia Neisler, Alexandra Noll, Juliet Norris-Clay, Anne Joseph O'Connell, Kyle Patel, Carmelo Anthony, Karen Pritula, Seth Quidachay-Swan, Stacey Rzeszut, Annie Sloan, Christina van Wagenen, Sophia Weaver, Lauren Wilson, Solomon F. Worlds, Anna Venguer, and Lauren Yu. And we also thank each other. We have enjoyed working together, we have learned from one another, and we are confident that the book is much better than if either of us had been foolish enough to try to write it on his own.

RICH FRIEDMAN
JULIAN DAVIS MORTENSON

March 2021

Summary of Contents

Table of Contents

Table of Cases

*Principal cases are in bold. Except where otherwise indicated, all cases
are decisions of the Supreme Court of the United States.*

The Constitution of the United States

Preamble

We the People of the United States, in Order to form a more perfect Union, establish Justice, insure domestic Tranquility, provide for the common defence, promote the general Welfare, and secure the Blessings of Liberty to ourselves and our Posterity, do ordain and establish this Constitution for the United States of America.

Article I

§ 1. All legislative Powers herein granted shall be vested in a Congress of the United States, which shall consist of a Senate and House of Representatives.

§ 2. The House of Representatives shall be composed of Members chosen every second Year by the People of the several States, and the Electors in each State shall have the Qualifications requisite for Electors of the most numerous Branch of the State Legislature.

No Person shall be a Representative who shall not have attained to the age of twenty five Years, and been seven Years a Citizen of the United States, and who shall not, when elected, be an Inhabitant of that State in which he shall be chosen.

Representatives and direct Taxes shall be apportioned among the several States which may be included within this Union, according to their respective Numbers, which shall be determined by adding to the whole Number of free Persons, including those bound to Service for a Term of Years, and excluding Indians not taxed, three fifths of all other Persons. The actual Enumeration shall be made within three Years after the first Meeting of the Congress of the United States, and within every subsequent Term of ten Years, in such Manner as they shall by Law direct. The Number of Representatives shall not exceed one for every thirty Thousand, but each State shall have at Least one Representative; and until such enumeration shall be made, the State of New Hampshire shall be entitled to chuse three, Massachusetts eight, Rhode Island and Providence Plantations one, Connecticut five, New York six, New Jersey four, Pennsylvania eight, Delaware one, Maryland six, Virginia ten, North Carolina five, South Carolina five, and Georgia three.

When vacancies happen in the Representation from any State, the Executive Authority thereof shall issue Writs of Election to fill such Vacancies.

The House of Representatives shall chuse their Speaker and other Officers; and shall have the sole Power of Impeachment.

§ 3. The Senate of the United States shall be composed of two Senators from each State, chosen by the Legislature thereof, for six Years; and each Senator shall have one Vote.

Immediately after they shall be assembled in Consequence of the first Election, they shall be divided as equally as may be into three Classes. The Seats of the Senators of the first Class shall be vacated at the Expiration of the second Year, of the second Class at the Expiration of the fourth Year, and of the third Class at the Expiration of the sixth Year, so that one third may be chosen every second Year; and if Vacancies happen by Resignation, or otherwise, during the Recess of the Legislature of any State, the Executive thereof may make temporary Appointments until the next Meeting of the Legislature, which shall then fill such Vacancies.

No Person shall be a Senator who shall not have attained to the Age of thirty Years, and been nine Years a Citizen of the United States, and who shall not, when elected, be an Inhabitant of that State for which he shall be chosen.

The Vice President of the United States shall be President of the Senate but shall have no Vote, unless they be equally divided.

The Senate shall chuse their other Officers, and also a President pro tempore, in the Absence of the Vice President, or when he shall exercise the Office of President of the United States.

The Senate shall have the sole Power to try all Impeachments. When sitting for that Purpose, they shall be on Oath or Affirmation. When the President of the United States is tried the Chief Justice shall preside: And no Person shall be convicted without the Concurrence of two thirds of the Members present.

Judgment in Cases of Impeachment shall not extend further than to removal from Office, and disqualification to hold and enjoy any Office of honor, Trust or Profit under the United States: but the Party convicted shall nevertheless be liable and subject to Indictment, Trial, Judgment and Punishment, according to Law.

§ 4. The Times, Places and Manner of holding Elections for Senators and Representatives, shall be prescribed in each State by the Legislature thereof; but the Congress may at any time by Law make or alter such Regulations, except as to the Places of chusing Senators.

The Congress shall assemble at least once in every Year, and such Meeting shall be on the first Monday in December, unless they shall by Law appoint a different Day.

§ 5. Each House shall be the Judge of the Elections, Returns and Qualifications of its own Members, and a Majority of each shall constitute a Quorum to do Business; but a smaller Number may adjourn from day to day, and may be authorized to compel the Attendance of absent Members, in such Manner, and under such Penalties as each House may provide.

Each House may determine the Rules of its Proceedings, punish its Members for disorderly Behaviour, and, with the Concurrence of two thirds, expel a Member.

Each House shall keep a Journal of its Proceedings, and from time to time publish the same, excepting such Parts as may in their Judgment require Secrecy; and the Yeas and Nays of the Members of either House on any question shall, at the Desire of one fifth of those Present, be entered on the Journal.

Neither House, during the Session of Congress, shall, without the Consent of the other, adjourn for more than three days, nor to any other Place than that in which the two Houses shall be sitting.

§ 6. The Senators and Representatives shall receive a Compensation for their Services, to be ascertained by Law, and paid out of the Treasury of the United States. They shall in all Cases, except Treason, Felony and Breach of the Peace, be privileged from Arrest during their Attendance at the Session of their respective Houses, and in going to and returning from the same; and for any Speech or Debate in either House, they shall not be questioned in any other Place.

No Senator or Representative shall, during the Time for which he was elected, be appointed to any civil Office under the Authority of the United States, which shall have been created, or the Emoluments whereof shall have been encreased during such time; and no Person holding any Office under the United States, shall be a Member of either House during his Continuance in Office.

§ 7. All Bills for raising Revenue shall originate in the House of Representatives; but the Senate may propose or concur with amendments as on other Bills.

Every Bill which shall have passed the House of Representatives and the Senate, shall, before it become a law, be presented to the President of the United States: If he approve he shall sign it, but if not he shall return it, with his Objections to that House in which it shall have originated, who shall enter the Objections at large on their Journal, and proceed to reconsider it. If after such Reconsideration two thirds of that House shall agree to pass the Bill, it shall be sent, together with the Objections, to the other House, by which it shall likewise be reconsidered, and if approved by two thirds of that House, it shall become a Law. But in all such Cases the Votes of both Houses shall be determined by Yeas and Nays, and the Names of the Persons voting for and against the Bill shall be entered on the Journal of each House respectively. If any Bill shall not be returned by the President within ten Days (Sundays excepted) after it shall have been presented to him, the Same shall be a Law, in like Manner as if he had signed it, unless the Congress by their Adjournment prevent its Return, in which Case it shall not be a Law.

Every Order, Resolution, or Vote to which the Concurrence of the Senate and House of Representatives may be necessary (except on a question of Adjournment) shall be presented to the President of the United States; and before the Same shall take Effect, shall be approved by him, or being disapproved by him, shall be repassed by two thirds of the Senate and House of Representatives, according to the Rules and Limitations prescribed in the Case of a Bill.

§ 8. The Congress shall have Power

[1]   To lay and collect Taxes, Duties, Imposts and Excises, to pay the Debts and provide for the common Defence and general Welfare of the United States; but all Duties, Imposts and Excises shall be uniform throughout the United States;

[2]   To borrow Money on the credit of the United States;

[3]   To regulate Commerce with foreign Nations, and among the several States, and with the Indian Tribes;

[4]   To establish an uniform Rule of Naturalization, and uniform Laws on the subject of Bankruptcies throughout the United States;

[5]   To coin Money, regulate the Value thereof, and of foreign Coin, and fix the Standard of Weights and Measures;

[6]   To provide for the Punishment of counterfeiting the Securities and current Coin of the United States;

[7]   To establish Post Offices and post Roads;

[8]   To promote the Progress of Science and useful Arts, by securing for limited Times to Authors and Inventors the exclusive Right to their respective Writings and Discoveries;

[9]   To constitute Tribunals inferior to the supreme Court;

[10] To define and punish Piracies and Felonies committed on the high Seas, and Offences against the Law of Nations;

[11] To declare War, grant Letters of Marque and Reprisal, and make Rules concerning Captures on Land and Water;

[12] To raise and support Armies, but no Appropriation of Money to that Use shall be for a longer Term than two Years;

[13] To provide and maintain a Navy;

[14] To make Rules for the Government and Regulation of the land and naval Forces;

[15] To provide for calling forth the Militia to execute the Laws of the Union, suppress Insurrections and repel Invasions;

[16] To provide for organizing, arming, and disciplining, the Militia, and for governing such Part of them as may be employed in the Service of the United States, reserving to the States respectively, the Appointment of the Officers, and the Authority of training the Militia according to the discipline prescribed by Congress;

[17] To exercise exclusive Legislation in all Cases whatsoever, over such District (not exceeding ten Miles square) as may, by Cession of Particular States, and the Acceptance of Congress, become the Seat of the Government of the United States, and to exercise like Authority over all Places purchased

by the Consent of the Legislature of the State in which the Same shall be, for the Erection of Forts, Magazines, Arsenals, dock Yards and other needful Buildings;—And

[18]   To make all Laws which shall be necessary and proper for carrying into Execution the foregoing Powers and all other Powers vested by this Constitution in the Government of the United States, or in any Department or Officer thereof.

§ 9. The Migration or Importation of such Persons as any of the States now existing shall think proper to admit, shall not be prohibited by the Congress prior to the Year one thousand eight hundred and eight, but a Tax or duty may be imposed on such Importation, not exceeding ten dollars for each Person.

The Privilege of the Writ of Habeas Corpus shall not be suspended, unless when in Cases of Rebellion or Invasion the public Safety may require it.

No Bill of Attainder or ex post facto Law shall be passed.

No Capitation, or other direct, Tax shall be laid, unless in Proportion to the Census of Enumeration herein before directed to be taken.

No Tax or Duty shall be laid on Articles exported from any State.

No Preference shall be given by any Regulation of Commerce or Revenue to the Ports of one State over those of another: nor shall Vessels bound to, or from, one State, be obliged to enter, clear or pay Duties in another.

No Money shall be drawn from the Treasury, but in Consequence of Appropriations made by Law; and a regular Statement and Account of the Receipts and Expenditures of all public Money shall be published from time to time.

No Title of Nobility shall be granted by the United States: And no Person holding any Office of Profit or Trust under them, shall, without the Consent of the Congress, accept of any present, Emolument, Office, or Title, of any kind whatever, from any King, Prince or foreign State.

§ 10. No State shall enter into any Treaty, Alliance, or Confederation; grant Letters of Marque and Reprisal; coin Money; emit Bills of Credit; make any Thing but gold and silver Coin a Tender in Payment of Debts; pass any Bill of Attainder, ex post facto Law, or Law impairing the Obligation of Contracts, or grant any Title of Nobility.

No State shall, without the Consent of the Congress, lay any Imposts or Duties on Imports or Exports, except what may be absolutely necessary for executing it's inspection Laws: and the net Produce of all Duties and Imposts, laid by any State on Imports or Exports, shall be for the Use of the Treasury of the United States; and all such Laws shall be subject to the Revision and Controul of the Congress.

No State shall, without the Consent of Congress, lay any Duty of Tonnage, keep Troops, or Ships of War in time of Peace, enter into any Agreement or Compact with another State, or with a foreign Power, or engage in War, unless actually invaded, or in such imminent Danger as will not admit of delay.

Article II

§ 1. The executive Power shall be vested in a President of the United States of America. He shall hold his Office during the Term of four Years, and, together with the Vice President, chosen for the same Term, be elected, as follows:

Each State shall appoint, in such Manner as the Legislature thereof may direct, a Number of Electors, equal to the whole Number of Senators and Representatives to which the State may be entitled in the Congress: but no Senator or Representative, or Person holding an Office of Trust or Profit under the United States, shall be appointed an Elector.

The Electors shall meet in their respective States, and vote by Ballot for two Persons, of whom one at least shall not be an Inhabitant of the same State with themselves. And they shall make a List of all the Persons voted for, and of the Number of Votes for each; which List they shall sign and certify, and transmit sealed to the Seat of the Government of the United States, directed to the President of the Senate. The President of the Senate shall, in the Presence of the Senate and House of Representatives, open all the Certificates, and the Votes shall then be counted. The Person having the greatest Number of Votes shall be the President, if such Number be a Majority of the whole Number of Electors appointed; and if there be more than one who have such Majority, and have an equal Number of Votes, then the House of Representatives shall immediately chuse by Ballot one of them for President; and if no Person have a Majority, then from the five highest on the List the said House shall in like Manner chuse the President. But in chusing the President, the Votes shall be taken by States, the Representatives from each State having one Vote; a quorum for this Purpose shall consist of a Member or Members from two thirds of the States, and a Majority of all the States shall be necessary to a Choice. In every Case, after the Choice of the President, the Person having the greatest Number of Votes of the Electors shall be the Vice President. But if there should remain two or more who have equal Votes, the Senate shall chuse from them by Ballot the Vice President.

The Congress may determine the Time of chusing the Electors, and the Day on which they shall give their Votes; which Day shall be the same throughout the United States.

No Person except a natural born Citizen, or a Citizen of the United States, at the time of the Adoption of this Constitution, shall be eligible to the Office of President; neither shall any person be eligible to that Office who shall not have attained to the Age of thirty five Years, and been fourteen Years a Resident within the United States.

In Case of the Removal of the President from Office, or of his Death, Resignation, or Inability to discharge the Powers and Duties of the said Office, the Same shall devolve on the Vice President, and the Congress may by Law provide for the Case of Removal, Death, Resignation or Inability, both of the President and Vice President, declaring what Officer shall then act as President, and such Officer shall act accordingly, until the Disability be removed, or a President shall be elected.

The President shall, at stated Times, receive for his Services, a Compensation, which shall neither be encreased nor diminished during the Period for which he shall have been elected, and he shall not receive within that Period any other Emolument from the United States, or any of them.

Before he enter on the Execution of his Office, he shall take the following Oath or Affirmation:—"I do solemnly swear (or affirm) that I will faithfully execute the Office of President of the United States, and will to the best of my Ability, preserve, protect and defend the Constitution of the United States."

§ 2. The President shall be Commander in Chief of the Army and Navy of the United States, and of the Militia of the several States, when called into the actual Service of the United States; he may require the Opinion, in writing, of the principal Officer in each of the executive Departments, upon any Subject relating to the Duties of their respective Offices, and he shall have Power to Grant Reprieves and Pardons for Offences against the United States, except in Cases of Impeachment.

He shall have Power, by and with the Advice and Consent of the Senate, to make Treaties, provided two thirds of the Senators present concur; and he shall nominate, and by and with the Advice and Consent of the Senate, shall appoint Ambassadors, other public Ministers and Consuls, Judges of the supreme Court, and all other Officers of the United States, whose Appointments are not herein otherwise provided for, and which shall be established by Law: but the Congress may by Law vest the Appointment of such inferior Officers, as they think proper, in the President alone, in the Courts of Law, or in the Heads of Departments.

The President shall have Power to fill up all Vacancies that may happen during the Recess of the Senate, by granting Commissions which shall expire at the End of their next Session.

§ 3. He shall from time to time give to the Congress Information on the State of the Union, and recommend to their Consideration such Measures as he shall judge necessary and expedient; he may, on extraordinary Occasions, convene both Houses, or either of them, and in Case of Disagreement between them, with Respect to the Time of Adjournment, he may adjourn them to such Time as he shall think proper; he shall receive Ambassadors and other public Ministers; he shall take Care that the Laws be faithfully executed, and shall Commission all the Officers of the United States.

§ 4. The President, Vice President and all Civil Officers of the United States, shall be removed from Office on Impeachment for and Conviction of, Treason, Bribery, or other high Crimes and Misdemeanors.

Article III

§ 1. The judicial Power of the United States, shall be vested in one supreme Court, and in such inferior Courts as the Congress may from time to time ordain and establish. The Judges, both of the supreme and inferior Courts, shall hold their Offices during good Behaviour, and shall, at stated Times, receive for their Services, a Compensation, which shall not be diminished during their Continuance in Office.

§ 2. The judicial Power shall extend to all Cases, in Law and Equity, arising under this Constitution, the Laws of the United States, and Treaties made, or which shall be made, under their Authority;—to all Cases affecting Ambassadors, other public ministers and Consuls;—to all Cases of admiralty and maritime Jurisdiction;—to Controversies to which the United States shall be a Party;—to Controversies between two or more States;—between a State and Citizens of another State;—between Citizens of different States;—between Citizens of the same State claiming Lands under Grants of different States, and between a State, or the Citizens thereof, and foreign States, Citizens or Subjects.

In all Cases affecting Ambassadors, other public Ministers and Consuls, and those in which a State shall be Party, the supreme Court shall have original Jurisdiction. In all the other Cases before mentioned, the supreme Court shall have appellate Jurisdiction, both as to Law and Fact, with such Exceptions, and under such Regulations as the Congress shall make.

The Trial of all Crimes, except in Cases of Impeachment, shall be by Jury; and such Trial shall be held in the State where the said Crimes shall have been committed; but when not committed within any State, the Trial shall be at such Place or Places as the Congress may by Law have directed.

§ 3. Treason against the United States, shall consist only in levying War against them, or in adhering to their Enemies, giving them Aid and Comfort. No Person shall be convicted of Treason unless on the Testimony of two Witnesses to the same overt Act, or on Confession in open Court.

The Congress shall have Power to declare the Punishment of Treason, but no Attainder of Treason shall work Corruption of Blood, or Forfeiture except during the Life of the Person attainted.

Article IV

§ 1. Full Faith and Credit shall be given in each State to the public Acts, Records, and judicial Proceedings of every other State. And the Congress may by general Laws prescribe the Manner in which such Acts, Records and Proceedings shall be proved, and the Effect thereof.

§ 2. The Citizens of each State shall be entitled to all Privileges and Immunities of Citizens in the several States.

A Person charged in any State with Treason, Felony, or other Crime, who shall flee from Justice, and be found in another State, shall on Demand of the executive Authority of the State from which he fled, be delivered up, to be removed to the State having Jurisdiction of the Crime.

No Person held to Service or Labour in one State, under the Laws thereof, escaping into another, shall, in Consequence of any Law or Regulation therein, be discharged from such Service or Labour, but shall be delivered up on Claim of the Party to whom such Service or Labour may be due.

§ 3. New States may be admitted by the Congress into this Union; but no new State shall be formed or erected within the Jurisdiction of any other State; nor any State be formed by the Junction of two or more States, or Parts of States, without the Consent of the Legislatures of the States concerned as well as of the Congress.

The Congress shall have Power to dispose of and make all needful Rules and Regulations respecting the Territory or other Property belonging to the United States; and nothing in this Constitution shall be so construed as to Prejudice any Claims of the United States, or of any particular State.

§ 4. The United States shall guarantee to every State in this Union a Republican Form of Government, and shall protect each of them against Invasion; and on Application of the Legislature, or of the Executive (when the Legislature cannot be convened) against domestic Violence.

Article V

The Congress, whenever two thirds of both Houses shall deem it necessary, shall propose Amendments to this Constitution, or, on the Application of the Legislatures of two thirds of the several States, shall call a Convention for proposing Amendments, which, in either Case, shall be valid to all Intents and Purposes, as Part of this Constitution, when ratified by the Legislatures of three fourths of the several States, or by Conventions in three fourths thereof, as the one or the other Mode of Ratification may be proposed by the Congress; Provided that no Amendment which may be made prior to the Year One thousand eight hundred and eight shall in any Manner affect the first and fourth Clauses in the Ninth Section of the first Article; and that no State, without its Consent, shall be deprived of its equal Suffrage in the Senate.

Article VI

All Debts contracted and Engagements entered into, before the Adoption of this Constitution, shall be as valid against the United States under this Constitution, as under the Confederation.

This Constitution, and the Laws of the United States which shall be made in Pursuance thereof; and all Treaties made, or which shall be made, under the Authority of the United States, shall be the supreme Law of the Land; and the

Judges in every State shall be bound thereby, any Thing in the Constitution or Laws of any state to the Contrary notwithstanding.

The Senators and Representatives before mentioned, and the Members of the several State Legislatures, and all executive and judicial Officers, both of the United States and of the several States, shall be bound by Oath or Affirmation, to support this Constitution; but no religious Test shall ever be required as a Qualification to any Office or public Trust under the United States.

Article VII

The Ratification of the Conventions of nine States, shall be sufficient for the Establishment of this Constitution between the States so ratifying the same.

Amendment I

Congress shall make no law respecting an establishment of religion, or prohibiting the free exercise thereof; or abridging the freedom of speech, or of the press; or the right of the people peaceably to assemble, and to petition the Government for a redress of grievances.

Amendment II

A well regulated Militia, being necessary to the security of a free State, the right of the people to keep and bear Arms, shall not be infringed.

Amendment III

No Soldier shall, in time of peace be quartered in any house, without the consent of the Owner, nor in time of war, but in a manner to be prescribed by law.

Amendment IV

The right of the people to be secure in their persons, houses, papers, and effects, against unreasonable searches and seizures, shall not be violated, and no Warrants shall issue, but upon probable cause, supported by Oath or affirmation, and particularly describing the place to be searched, and the persons or things to be seized.

Amendment V

No person shall be held to answer for a capital, or otherwise infamous crime, unless on a presentment or indictment of a Grand Jury, except in cases arising in the land or naval forces, or in the Militia, when in actual service in time of War or public danger; nor shall any person be subject for the same offence to be twice put in jeopardy of life or limb; nor shall be compelled in any criminal case to be a witness against himself, nor be deprived of life, liberty, or property, without due process of law; nor shall private property be taken for public use, without just compensation.

Amendment VI

In all criminal prosecutions, the accused shall enjoy the right to a speedy and public trial, by an impartial jury of the State and district wherein the crime shall have been committed, which district shall have been previously ascertained by law, and to be informed of the nature and cause of the accusation; to be confronted with the witnesses against him; to have compulsory process for obtaining witnesses in his favor, and to have the Assistance of Counsel for his defence.

Amendment VII

In Suits at common law, where the value in controversy shall exceed twenty dollars, the right of trial by jury shall be preserved, and no fact tried by a jury, shall be otherwise re examined in any Court of the United States, than according to the rules of the common law.

Amendment VIII

Excessive bail shall not be required, nor excessive fines imposed, nor cruel and unusual punishments inflicted.

Amendment IX

The enumeration in the Constitution, of certain rights, shall not be construed to deny or disparage others retained by the people.

Amendment X

The powers not delegated to the United States by the Constitution, nor prohibited by it to the States, are reserved to the States respectively, or to the people.

Amendment XI

The Judicial power of the United States shall not be construed to extend to any suit in law or equity, commenced or prosecuted against one of the United States by Citizens of another State, or by Citizens or Subjects of any Foreign State.

Amendment XII

The Electors shall meet in their respective states, and vote by ballot for President and Vice President, one of whom, at least, shall not be an inhabitant of the same state with themselves; they shall name in their ballots the person voted for as President, and in distinct ballots the person voted for as Vice-President, and they shall make distinct lists of all persons voted for as President, and of all persons voted for as Vice-President, and of the number of votes for each, which lists they shall sign and certify, and transmit sealed to the seat of the government of the United States, directed to the President of the Senate;—The President of the Senate shall, in the presence of the Senate and House of Representatives, open all the certificates and the votes shall then be counted;—The person having the greatest number of votes for President, shall be the President, if such number be a majority of the whole number of Electors appointed; and if no person have such majority, then from the persons having the highest numbers not exceeding three on the list of those voted for as President, the House of Representatives shall choose immediately, by ballot, the President. But in choosing the President, the votes shall be taken by states, the representation from each state having one vote; a quorum for this purpose shall consist of a member or members from two thirds of the states, and a majority of all the states shall be necessary to a choice. And if the House of Representatives shall not choose a President whenever the right of choice shall devolve upon them, before the fourth day of March next following, then the Vice-President shall act as President, as in the case of the death or other constitutional disability of the President.—The person having the greatest number of votes as Vice-President, shall be the Vice-President, if such number be a majority of the whole number of Electors appointed, and if no person have a majority, then from the two highest numbers on the list, the Senate shall choose the Vice-President; a quorum for the purpose shall consist of two thirds of the whole number of Senators, and a majority of the whole number shall be necessary to a choice. But no person constitutionally ineligible to the office of President shall be eligible to that of Vice-President of the United States.

Amendment XIII

§ 1. Neither slavery nor involuntary servitude, except as a punishment for crime whereof the party shall have been duly convicted, shall exist within the United States, or any place subject to their jurisdiction.

§ 2. Congress shall have power to enforce this article by appropriate legislation.

Amendment XIV

§ 1. All persons born or naturalized in the United States, and subject to the jurisdiction thereof, are citizens of the United States and of the State wherein they reside. No State shall make or enforce any law which shall abridge the privileges or immunities of citizens of the United States; nor shall any State deprive any person of life, liberty, or property, without due process of law; nor deny to any person within its jurisdiction the equal protection of the laws.

§ 2. Representatives shall be apportioned among the several States according to their respective numbers, counting the whole number of persons in each State, excluding Indians not taxed. But when the right to vote at any election for the choice of electors for President and Vice President of the United States, Representatives in Congress, the Executive and Judicial officers of a State, or the members of the Legislature thereof, is denied to any of the male inhabitants of such State, being twenty one years of age, and citizens of the United States, or in any way abridged, except for participation in rebellion, or other crime, the basis of representation therein shall be reduced in the proportion which the number of such male citizens shall bear to the whole number of male citizens twenty one years of age in such State.

§ 3. No person shall be a Senator or Representative in Congress, or elector of President and Vice President, or hold any office, civil or military, under the United States, or under any State, who, having previously taken an oath, as a member of Congress, or as an officer of the United States, or as a member of any State legislature, or as an executive or judicial officer of any State, to support the Constitution of the United States, shall have engaged in insurrection or rebellion against the same, or given aid or comfort to the enemies thereof. But Congress may by a vote of two thirds of each House, remove such disability.

§ 4. The validity of the public debt of the United States, authorized by law, including debts incurred for payment of pensions and bounties for services in suppressing insurrection or rebellion, shall not be questioned. But neither the United States nor any State shall assume or pay any debt or obligation incurred in aid of insurrection or rebellion against the United States, or any claim for the loss or emancipation of any slave; but all such debts, obligations and claims shall be held illegal and void.

§ 5. The Congress shall have power to enforce, by appropriate legislation, the provisions of this article.

Amendment XV

§ 1. The right of citizens of the United States to vote shall not be denied or abridged by the United States or by any State on account of race, color, or previous condition of servitude.

§ 2. The Congress shall have power to enforce this article by appropriate legislation.

Amendment XVI

The Congress shall have power to lay and collect taxes on incomes, from whatever source derived, without apportionment among the several States, and without regard to any census or enumeration.

Amendment XVII

The Senate of the United States shall be composed of two Senators from each State, elected by the people thereof, for six years; and each Senator shall have one vote. The electors in each State shall have the qualifications requisite for electors of the most numerous branch of the State legislatures.

When vacancies happen in the representation of any State in the Senate, the executive authority of such State shall issue writs of election to fill such vacancies: Provided, That the legislature of any State may empower the executive thereof to make temporary appointments until the people fill the vacancies by election as the legislature may direct.

This amendment shall not be so construed as to affect the election or term of any Senator chosen before it becomes valid as part of the Constitution.

Amendment XVIII

§ 1. After one year from the ratification of this article the manufacture, sale, or transportation of intoxicating liquors within, the importation thereof into, or the exportation thereof from the United States and all territory subject to the jurisdiction thereof for beverage purposes is hereby prohibited.

§ 2. The Congress and the several States shall have concurrent power to enforce this article by appropriate legislation.

§ 3. This article shall be inoperative unless it shall have been ratified as an amendment to the Constitution by the legislatures of the several States, as provided in the Constitution, within seven years from the date of the submission hereof to the States by the Congress.

Amendment XIX

The right of citizens of the United States to vote shall not be denied or abridged by the United States or by any State on account of sex.

Congress shall have power to enforce this article by appropriate legislation.

Amendment XX

§ 1. The terms of the President and Vice President shall end at noon on the 20th day of January, and the terms of Senators and Representatives at noon on the 3d day of January, of the years in which such terms would have ended if this article had not been ratified; and the terms of their successors shall then begin.

§ 2. The Congress shall assemble at least once in every year, and such meeting shall begin at noon on the 3d day of January, unless they shall by law appoint a different day.

§ 3. If, at the time fixed for the beginning of the term of the President, the President elect shall have died, the Vice President elect shall become President. If a President shall not have been chosen before the time fixed for the beginning of his term, or if the President elect shall have failed to qualify, then the Vice President elect shall act as President until a President shall have qualified; and the Congress may by law provide for the case wherein neither a President elect nor a Vice President elect shall have qualified, declaring who shall then act as President, or the manner in which one who is to act shall be selected, and such person shall act accordingly until a President or Vice President shall have qualified.

§ 4. The Congress may by law provide for the case of the death of any of the persons from whom the House of Representatives may choose a President whenever the right of choice shall have devolved upon them, and for the case of the death of any of the persons from whom the Senate may choose a Vice President whenever the right of choice shall have devolved upon them.

§ 5. Sections 1 and 2 shall take effect on the 15th day of October following the ratification of this article.

§ 6. This article shall be inoperative unless it shall have been ratified as an amendment to the Constitution by the legislatures of three fourths of the several States within seven years from the date of its submission.

Amendment XXI

§ 1. The eighteenth article of amendment to the Constitution of the United States is hereby repealed.

§ 2. The transportation or importation into any State, Territory, or possession of the United States for delivery or use therein of intoxicating liquors, in violation of the laws thereof, is hereby prohibited.

§ 3. This article shall be inoperative unless it shall have been ratified as an amendment to the Constitution by conventions in the several States, as provided in the Constitution, within seven years from the date of the submission hereof to the States by the Congress.

Amendment XXII

§ 1. No person shall be elected to the office of the President more than twice, and no person who has held the office of President, or acted as President, for more than two years of a term to which some other person was elected President shall be elected to the office of the President more than once. But this article shall not apply to any person holding the office of President when this article was proposed by the Congress, and shall not prevent any person who may be holding the office of President, or acting as President, during the term within which this article becomes operative from holding the office of President or acting as President during the remainder of such term.

§ 2. This article shall be inoperative unless it shall have been ratified as an amendment to the Constitution by the legislatures of three fourths of the several states within seven years from the date of its submission to the states by the Congress.

Amendment XXIII

§ 1. The District constituting the seat of government of the United States shall appoint in such manner as the Congress may direct:

A number of electors of President and Vice President equal to the whole number of Senators and Representatives in Congress to which the District would be entitled if it were a state, but in no event more than the least populous state; they shall be in addition to those appointed by the states, but they shall be considered, for the purposes of the election of President and Vice President, to be electors appointed by a state; and they shall meet in the District and perform such duties as provided by the twelfth article of amendment.

§ 2. The Congress shall have power to enforce this article by appropriate legislation.

Amendment XXIV

§ 1. The right of citizens of the United States to vote in any primary or other election for President or Vice President, for electors for President or Vice President, or for Senator or Representative in Congress, shall not be denied or abridged by the United States or any state by reason of failure to pay any poll tax or other tax.

§ 2. The Congress shall have power to enforce this article by appropriate legislation.

Amendment XXV

§ 1. In case of the removal of the President from office or of his death or resignation, the Vice President shall become President.

§ 2. Whenever there is a vacancy in the office of the Vice President, the President shall nominate a Vice President who shall take office upon confirmation by a majority vote of both Houses of Congress.

§ 3. Whenever the President transmits to the President pro tempore of the Senate and the Speaker of the House of Representatives his written declaration that he is unable to discharge the powers and duties of his office, and until he transmits to them a written declaration to the contrary, such powers and duties shall be discharged by the Vice President as Acting President.

§ 4. Whenever the Vice President and a majority of either the principal officers of the executive departments or of such other body as Congress may by law provide, transmit to the President pro tempore of the Senate and the Speaker of the House of Representatives their written declaration that the President is unable to discharge the powers and duties of his office, the Vice President shall immediately assume the powers and duties of the office as Acting President.

Thereafter, when the President transmits to the President pro tempore of the Senate and the Speaker of the House of Representatives his written declaration that no inability exists, he shall resume the powers and duties of his office unless the Vice President and a majority of either the principal officers of the executive department or of such other body as Congress may by law provide, transmit within four days to the President pro tempore of the Senate and the Speaker of the House of Representatives their written declaration that the President is unable to discharge the powers and duties of his office. Thereupon Congress shall decide the issue, assembling within forty eight hours for that purpose if not in session. If the Congress, within twenty one days after receipt of the latter written declaration, or, if Congress is not in session, within twenty one days after Congress is required to assemble, determines by two thirds vote of both Houses that the President is unable to discharge the powers and duties of his office, the Vice President shall continue to discharge the same as Acting President; otherwise, the President shall resume the powers and duties of his office.

Amendment XXVI

§ 1. The right of citizens of the United States, who are 18 years of age or older, to vote, shall not be denied or abridged by the United States or any state on account of age.

§ 2. The Congress shall have the power to enforce this article by appropriate legislation.

Amendment XXVII

No law varying the compensation for the services of the Senators and Representatives shall take effect until an election of Representatives shall have intervened.

Constitutional Law

AN INTEGRATED APPROACH

CHAPTER I

Constitutional History from the Beginning to the New Deal

A. Before the Constitution

The first human inhabitants of what is now the United States were, of course, Native Americans, who had extensive forms of political organization; the Iroquois League, for example, had already been organized by the 16th century. The earliest European settlements were by the Spaniards, in Florida in the mid-16th century. But the developments that most clearly played a role in American constitutional development occurred in the English colonies.

The first permanent English colony was Jamestown, founded in Virginia in 1607. This was a commercial venture, established by the Virginia Company of London, which had been granted a royal charter to establish settlements along much of what is now the eastern seaboard of the United States. At first, the colony was governed by a president and council appointed by the king; after a few years, the Company took over the power of appointment. In 1619— the same year in which enslaved Africans were first brought to Virginia—the Company attempted to encourage greater migration by establishing the first true representative legislature in the Americas, known as the House of Burgesses. The Company failed in 1624, and King James I made Virginia a royal colony, with a governor appointed by the king. A few years later, the House of Burgesses was reconstituted, and it retained legislative power over the colony almost without interruption until independence.

In 1620, a group of Separatists from the Church of England who had gone to the Netherlands to escape religious persecution decided to move as a group to the New World. The Separatists joined in England with a group to whom they referred as "Strangers," who did not share their religious orientation but were drawn to America for other reasons. Together with seamen and servants, they all sailed from Plymouth on the *Mayflower*. The Virginia Company of London had given this group—who ultimately became known as the Pilgrims—a patent to settle in the northern part of the vast area that was then known as Virginia. Eventually, though, they decided to settle further north, in what is now Plymouth, Massachusetts.

While they were still in the harbor, dissension arose. According to a later account by a Separatist leader named William Bradford, some of the Strangers suggested that because the settlement would be outside of the authorized territory, "when they came a shore they would use their own libertie; for none had power to command them." According to Bradford, the rest of the group believed that if these potential dissenters were persuaded to agree affirmatively to a system of governance, that accord "might be as firme as any patent, and in some respects more sure." Eventually, if the sources are to be believed, all or virtually all of the adult males on board—other than some seamen and perhaps a couple of servants—signed what became known as *The Mayflower Compact*; what cajolery was necessary to reach this result, we do not know.

WORTH NOTING

There were, as best we can tell, 41 signers of the compact. All told, there were 102 passengers on the Mayflower, 74 male and 28 female; approximately 18 of the females were adults, all but one of those being wives of male passengers.

The Mayflower Compact

1620

In the name of God, Amen. We whose names are underwritten, the loyal subjects of our dread Sovereign Lord King James, by the Grace of God of Great Britain, France and Ireland, King, Defender of the Faith, etc.

Having undertaken, for the Glory of God and advancement of the Christian Faith and Honour of our King and Country, a Voyage to plant the First Colony in the Northern Parts of Virginia, do by these presents solemnly and mutually in the presence of God and one of another, Covenant and Combine ourselves together into a Civil Body Politic, for our better ordering and preservation and furtherance of the ends aforesaid; and by virtue hereof to enact, constitute and frame such just and equal Laws, Ordinances, Acts, Constitutions and Offices, from time to time, as shall be thought most meet and convenient for the general good of the Colony, unto which we promise all due submission and obedience. In witness whereof we have hereunder subscribed our names at Cape Cod, the 11th of November, in the year of the reign of our Sovereign Lord King James, of England, France and Ireland the eighteenth, and of Scotland the fifty-fourth. Anno Domini 1620.

FOR DISCUSSION Was the Mayflower Compact a legitimate source of legal authority? Did it accomplish anything that could not have been accomplished without it? Was it binding on anybody who did not sign it—in particular on (a) any adults who were given an opportunity to sign but did not? (b) adults who were present but not given an opportunity to sign? (c) children who were on board? (d) unborn descendants of those on board? What did the reference to "equal Laws" mean?

The Mayflower Compact was considered the cornerstone of the governance of the Plymouth Plantation colony until it merged with Massachusetts Bay in 1691.

While we will not work through each of the American colonies, it is worth examining one more to emphasize how distinct were their several paths to statehood. William Penn was the son of an admiral who was close to King Charles II, but he was a convert to Quakerism whose agitation landed him twice in jail. In 1681, after his father's death and with persecution of Quakers accelerating, he and the King reached a remarkable deal: The King granted Penn a huge tract of land in America (with the consent of the prior owner, the King's brother, the future King James II), making him the largest private landowner in the world. In return, Penn promised to pay the Crown one-fifth of all the gold and silver mined there—a bad deal for the King, because there was none—and to release the King from a debt of £16,000 that he had owed Penn's father. Moreover, Penn held out the hope, appealing to the King, that English Quakers would now make a mass migration to the new world. As sole proprietor—with all the powers that would ordinarily belong to the Crown except for the power to declare war, subject to the proviso that the laws had to be in harmony with those of England—Penn drew up a "Frame of Government" in

1682. This was a remarkably far-sighted document, not only providing a form of representative government but also including protection of liberties, including absolute freedom of worship. Penn replaced the first Frame three times over the next two decades; his last iteration, issued in 1701, served as the constitution of Pennsylvania until independence. William Penn and his successors were known as the Proprietors of the province, or colony; John Penn, one of William's grandsons, also served as governor in the years leading up to independence.

IN SIGHTS As British political theorist and parliamentarian Edmund Burke later wrote, "The settlement of our colonies was never pursued upon any regular plan; by they were formed, grew, and flourished, as accidents, the nature of the climate, or the dispositions of private men happened to operate."

There were significant differences among the colonies in demography and religious orientation. For example, Puritans dominated the largest early migration to Massachusetts Bay; New York had a large Dutch population because the Netherlands had been the first colonial power; and settlers from many countries in northern and western Europe, as well as Quakers, tended to go to Pennsylvania because it was famously receptive. There were large economic differences as well. The typical farm in the north was a small one, often worked by a single family; large plantations dominated the south. And of course the most significant difference between north and south was that the southern economy was heavily and directly dependent on chattel slavery; although slavery was not prohibited anywhere in the colonies until after they declared independence, it was far more important and widespread in the south than in the north.

And yet there were significant political similarities among the colonies. Most of them had been founded as either corporate or proprietary colonies, but unlike Pennsylvania most became Crown colonies by the middle of the 18th century, with governors appointed by the English monarch. Governance followed the English model. Typically, a colony had a council, which was appointed by the governor and acted in part as a court, as well as an elected assembly. There was an ongoing contest for power between the governor and the assembly, but the assembly—with the power of the purse and the ability to make laws for the colony—grew steadily in strength. "By the 1760s," two noted constitutional historians have written, "the assemblies represented the colonists far more re-sponsively than Parliament spoke for the English people."

In the first half of the 18th century, Parliament rarely legislated on the internal affairs of the colonies. It did pass laws attempting to tie the colonies' trade to the mother country, but these were often ignored. And the Board of Trade reviewed colonial legislation that might impinge on imperial mercantile policies. It vetoed hundreds of such statutes, but left thousands alone. The over-all policy of the English government to the colonies was later character-ized by Edmund Burke as one of "wise and salutary neglect"—but with Britain paying for defense of the colonies.

WORTH NOTING

In general, the colo-nies thrived; they had a total population of about a quarter million in 1700, and about 1.17 million by 1750 (when the population of Britain was about 6.5 million); the population continued to grow briskly in succeeding decades.

In 1754, representatives of seven northern colonies met at the Albany Congress, a brainchild of Benjamin Franklin, to discuss matters of common interest, including relations with the Indian tribes and defense against the French. The Congress unani-mously approved a plan outlined by Franklin, proposing a government made up of a President-General appointed by the crown and a Grand Council chosen by the colonial assemblies. The general government would raise money from the colonies, which would be represented in the Council in proportion to their contributions, and would take responsibility for Indian relations, military pre-paredness, and other matters of common concern. The proposal was roundly rejected both by the colonies and by the British government.

The Seven Years War (1756–63) between France and Great Britain es-tablished British domination throughout eastern North America. While the colonists fought alongside the British, the conflict drastically changed the trans-Atlantic relationship. Smuggling had become more than an irritant to the British. More significantly, imperial authorities felt that the colonists should pay a fair share of the immense cost of the war; the American view tended to be that Britain had fought for its own interests and should bear the burden, especially given that the colonies were not represented in Parliament.

The first significant conflict arose over the petition of customs officers in Massachusetts for open-ended "writs of assistance," which would give broad search authority. James Otis, who had been Advocate-General of the colony, resigned his position and led the fight against granting the authority. A young John Adams was present and took detailed notes when Otis argued against the writs in proceedings before the Superior Court of Massachusetts in 1761; Adams later termed the speech "the first scene of the first act of opposition to the arbitrary claims of Great Britain. Then and there, the child Independence was born." According to Adams's notes, Otis's speech contained this arresting passage: "As to acts of parliament. An act against the Constitution is void; an Act against natural Equity is void; and if an act of Parliament should be made, in the very words of this petition, it would be void. The Executive Courts [i.e., the courts of justice, as opposed to a legislature or "general court"] must pass such acts into disuse."

FOR DISCUSSION What do you suppose Otis meant, by his reference to the Constitution? On what basis would a court be justified in concluding that an Act of Parliament ran counter to it, or to "natural equity"?

The British Parliament passed a Sugar Act in 1764, imposing a tariff on molasses imported from the French sugar islands. New England merchants were affronted by the idea of paying any tax. Soon after, Parliament passed a Currency Act in an attempt to prevent the issuance of paper money; this led opponents in Massachusetts to establish the first known Committee of Correspondence, an attempt to rally and coordinate opposition across the colonies. Transient though it was, this may be considered to be the first significant step towards union among the colonies; in the following years, committees of correspondence, with participants appointed by the colonial legislatures, became a more established and significant feature of the colonial political scene.

In 1765, Parliament passed a Stamp Act, requiring revenue stamps on legal documents and printed matter. This law generated widespread disobedience in the colonies. The Massachusetts Assembly sent a circular letter to its counterparts in the other colonies, suggesting that they "consult together on the present circumstances of the colonies." Representatives of eight colonies and of various counties in New York gathered in October in New York for what has been labeled the Stamp Act Congress. Officials in England recognized the significance of this gathering, but too late to do anything about it. After two weeks, the Congress issued a Declaration of Rights and Grievances, though the individual delegates were unwilling to sign it. The Declaration objected to the Stamp Act—which indeed soon became unenforceable as a result of colonists' unwillingness to comply—but went far beyond. It included the following passages:

1st. That his majesty's subjects in these colonies, owe the same allegiance to the crown of Great Britain that is owing from his subjects born within the realm, and all due subordination to that august body, the parliament of Great Britain.

2d. That his majesty's liege subjects in these colonies are entitled to all the inherent rights and privileges of his natural born subjects within the kingdom of Great Britain.

3d. That it is inseparably essential to the freedom of a people, and the undoubted rights of Englishmen, that no taxes should be imposed on them, but with their own consent, given personally, or by their representatives. . . .

4th. That the people of these colonies are not, and from their local circumstances, cannot be represented in the house of commons in Great Britain.

5th. That the only representatives of the people of these colonies are persons chosen therein, by themselves; and that no taxes ever have been, or can be constitutionally imposed on them, but by their respective legislatures.

FOR DISCUSSION

In a 1764 pamphlet called *The Rights of the British Colonies Asserted and Proved*, Otis argued that, in addition to having their own legislatures, the colonies should be "represented in some proportion to their number and estates in the grand legislature of the nation," and that doing so "would firmly unite all parts of the British empire in the greater peace and prosperity, and render it invulnerable and perpetual." This idea of expanding the British Parliament to include direct representation for the colonies seems not to have gained significant support on either side of the Atlantic. Indeed, as you can see, the Declaration of Rights and Grievances of the Stamp Act Congress rejected it out of hand. Why do you suppose Otis's idea did not gain more traction?

Parliament repealed the Stamp Act but simultaneously asserted, in the Declaratory Act of 1766, that it "had, hath, and of right ought to have, full power and authority to make laws and statutes of sufficient force and validity to bind the colonies and people of America . . . in all cases whatsoever." Soon Parliament passed a broader set of levies known as the Townshend duties, which generated widespread protests in the colonies, especially because part of the revenue was to be used for the salaries of judges and other colonial officials—who had previously been dependent on appropriations by the assemblies. Ultimately, most of these duties were repealed; the one on tea, however, remained. A period of relative calm followed, broken by passage of the Tea Act of 1773, which raised the duty on tea modestly but was designed to give the financially distressed East India Company a monopoly over tea imported to North America. There followed the Boston Tea Party, in which a band of locals boarded ships in Boston harbor and dumped huge quantities of tea into the water. Parliament responded by passing the Coercive Acts—often referred to by colonists as the Intolerable Acts—which closed the port of Boston, concentrated power in the hands of royal officials, and allowed soldiers and others accused of certain crimes to be remanded to England for trial.

In the spring of 1774, members of the Virginia House of Burgesses—which had been dissolved by the governor after protesting Parliament's Boston Port Act—met at the Raleigh Tavern in Williamsburg and issued a call for a Continental Congress. Delegates from twelve colonies attended the Congress, which met in September and October in Philadelphia. Some of the delegates had been sent by their respective assemblies; in other cases, the committees of correspondence or hurriedly assembled conventions had chosen them. The Congress rejected a proposal by Patrick Henry that the delegates vote as individuals; they were instead instructed representatives of their respective colonies, and voted by delegation.

FOR DISCUSSION

Henry's proposal was considered a radical one. Why, do you suppose?

Despite rejecting a proposal for a plan of Union that resembled the Albany Plan of nearly two decades before, the Congress took four bold measures.

First, it endorsed the Suffolk Resolves, a set of resolutions adopted in Suffolk County, Massachusetts (which includes Boston). Ridden to Philadelphia by the designated horseman, Paul Revere, the Resolves declared that the Intolerable Acts were "gross infractions of those rights to which we are justly entitled by the laws of nature, the British constitution, and the charter of the province" and called for a provincial government free of royal control until such time as the Acts should be repealed. Second, the Congress adopted another Declaration of Rights and Grievances, which contained ominous language saying that "Americans cannot submit" to the "grievous acts and measures" taken by the British government, but that "for the present" they were resolved only to pursue peaceful measures. Third, in accordance with that Declaration, the Congress adopted Articles of Association, a detailed plan for boycotting British goods. Finally, and perhaps most significantly, the Congress agreed that there should be a Second Continental Congress if, as the delegates expected, circumstances required. Invitations were sent to several British colonies that had not been represented at the First Congress: Georgia, Quebec, Saint John's Island, Nova Scotia, East Florida, and West Florida. None of these sent delegates to the Second Congress except, belatedly, Georgia, which had not sent delegates to the First Congress in part because it was hoping for British cooperation on its Indian frontier.

The situation further deteriorated in the spring of 1775. The royal governor of Massachusetts sent troops to capture military supplies that the Massachusetts militia had stored in Concord. They exchanged fire with a few militiamen at Lexington, were repelled by a larger force in Concord, and harassed all the way back to Boston. Militia companies from the New England colonies gathered around Boston and laid siege to the British troops there.

The Second Continental Congress met in Philadelphia, beginning on May 10, 1775. George Bancroft, the great 19th century historian, vividly described the status of the Congress:

> Whom did they represent? and what were their functions? They were committees from twelve colonies, deputed to consult on measures of conciliation, with no means of resistance to oppression beyond a voluntary agreement for the suspension of importations from Great Britain. They formed no confederacy; they were not an executive government; they were not even a legislative body. They owed the use of a hall for their sessions to the courtesy of the carpenters of the city; there was not a foot of land on which they had the right to execute their decisions; and they had not one civil officer to carry out their commands, nor the power to appoint one. Nor was one soldier enlisted, nor one officer commissioned in their name. They had no treasury; and neither authority to lay a tax, nor to borrow money.

They had been elected, in part at least, by tumultuary assemblies, or bodies which had no recognised legal existence; they were intrusted with no powers but those of counsel; most of them were held back by explicit or implied instructions; and they represented nothing more solid than the unformed opinion of an unformed people.

And yet the Congress responded to the situation by taking on many of the functions of a government; indeed, unlike its predecessor, it remained in session practically continuously (though not always in Philadelphia) until it was succeeded six years later. In June, it constituted the Continental Army, based on the militia companies surrounding Boston. To affirm that the struggle was not a regional one, Congress appointed George Washington—a Virginian who had been a delegate to the First Continental Congress—as commander-in-chief. A week later it authorized the issuance of paper currency, to be backed up by each of the states. This currency helped finance the war, but eventually it became virtually worthless, in part because of effective counterfeiting by the British.

On July 6, 1775, Congress adopted a Declaration of the Causes and Ne-cessity of Taking up Arms, drafted by the relatively hawkish Thomas Jefferson and the more dovish John Dickinson. The Declaration, which referred to "the united colonies of North America," was in large part a historical narration and another list of grievances. Among these were the extended use in customs cases of courts not following the common-law model of trial by jury; provisions for remand of those accused of certain crimes to England; dissolution of Virginia's House of Burgesses; the closing of Boston; and, most prominently, the assertion by Parliament—none of whose members had been chosen in the colonies—of complete legislative power over the colonies, in the Declaratory Act of 1766. The Declaration professed loyalty to the King—for the time being:

> [W]e mean not to dissolve that union which has so long and so happily subsisted between us, and which we sincerely wish to see restored.—Necessity has not yet driven us into that desperate mea-sure . . . .

The previous day, reflecting both its ambivalence and its respect for Dickinson, Congress had unanimously adopted the so-called Olive Branch petition, which emphasized the ties the colonists felt with the mother country "with all devo-tion that principle and affection can inspire." But the King refused to accept the petition, in part because the Americans—having been rebuffed in their attempt to persuade Quebec to join them—had instead made an ill-fated invasion of what would eventually become Canada. The King issued a proclamation that the colonies were in a state of "open and avowed rebellion."

From then the momentum to independence grew, spurred in large part by Parliament's passage in December 1775 of the Prohibitory Act, which provided that American ports should be blockaded and declared that American ships were to be treated as enemy vessels subject to forfeiture, and by publication the next month of Thomas Paine's pamphlet *Common Sense*. On May 4, 1776, Rhode Island's legislature declared independence. On May 15, the Virginia Convention—a sort of rump legislature—instructed its delegates to Congress to propose independence. Several delegations were under instructions that precluded them from voting for independence, but over the next several weeks the situation rapidly changed.

In June, Congress voted to postpone a decision on independence for three weeks, but meanwhile to appoint a committee to draft a statement explaining the decision to declare independence, if in fact Congress took that step. The Committee reported back its draft, of which Jefferson was the principal author, on June 28. On July 1, Congress, as a committee of the whole, approved Virginia's resolution for independence—nine states in favor, two (Pennsylvania and South Carolina) against, one (Delaware) divided equally, and one (New York) abstaining because it had not yet been authorized to vote for independence. The next day, the resolution was presented to Congress itself. Vote switches in the Pennsylvania and South Carolina delegations and the arrival of Caesar Rodney, a pro-independence delegate from Delaware, just as the vote was starting, led those three delegations to favor independence; New York continued to abstain. After debate, the Congress adopted a modified form of the committee's draft declaration on July 4. Among the passages deleted was a long, passionate castigation of the slave trade; Jefferson—the draftsman, a slave holder, and often rather hypocritical—resented the excision. There has been considerable debate about who, if anybody, signed the Declaration on July 4. It is clear that at least some signatures (including those of the New York delegation, which had finally received new instructions) were not added until August 2.

Declaration of Independence

1776

In CONGRESS, July 4, 1776

The unanimous Declaration of the thirteen united States of America

When in the Course of human events it becomes necessary for one people to dissolve the political bands which have connected them with another and to assume among the powers of the earth, the separate and equal station to which the Laws of Nature and of Nature's God entitle them, a decent respect to the opinions of mankind requires that they should declare the causes which impel them to the separation.

WORTH NOTING

Here and below, note that "united" is not capitalized even though "States" is. What's the signifi-cance of that?

FOR DISCUSSION

On what basis do the signers of the Declaration believe that "the Laws of Nature and of Nature's God entitle" the people of America to political status, as a people, separate from and equal to that of Great Britain?

We hold these truths to be self-evident, that all men are created equal, that they are endowed by their Creator with certain unalienable Rights, that among these are Life, Liberty and the pursuit of Happiness.—That to secure these rights, Governments are instituted among Men, deriving their just powers from the consent of the governed,

In this paragraph, the Declaration is making, at least in part, a series of descriptive statements. Do you believe they are accurate?

What did the signers mean in saying that "all men are created equal"? Why did they regard that proposition as a "self-evident" truth? Who was included within the term "men"?

FOR DISCUSSION

—That whenever any Form of Government becomes destructive of these ends, it is the Right of the People to alter or to abolish it, and to institute new Government, laying its foundation on such principles and organizing its powers in such form, as to them shall seem most likely to effect their Safety and Happiness.

Prudence, indeed, will dictate that Governments long established should not be changed for light and transient causes; and accordingly all experience hath shewn that mankind are more disposed to suffer, while evils are sufferable, than to right themselves by abolishing the forms to which they are accustomed. But when

FOR DISCUSSION Do you agree with this assertion of the right to abolish government? Who are "the People" for this purpose, and how are they to decide whether the conditions warranting such a transformation are present?

a long train of abuses and usurpations, pursuing invariably the same Object evinces a design to reduce them under absolute Despotism, it is their right, it is their duty, to throw off such Government, and to provide new Guards for their future security.—Such has been the patient sufferance of these Colonies; and such is now the necessity which constrains them to alter their former Systems of Government. The history of the present King of Great Britain is a history of repeated injuries and usurpations, all having in direct object the establishment of an absolute Tyranny over these States. To prove this, let Facts be submitted to a candid world.

He has refused his Assent to Laws, the most wholesome and necessary for the public good.

He has forbidden his Governors to pass Laws of immediate and pressing importance, unless suspended in their operation till his Assent should be obtained; and when so suspended, he has utterly neglected to attend to them.

He has refused to pass other Laws for the accommodation of large districts of people, unless those people would relinquish the right of Representation in the Legislature, a right inestimable to them and formidable to tyrants only.

He has called together legislative bodies at places unusual, uncomfortable, and distant from the depository of their Public Records, for the sole purpose of fatiguing them into compliance with his measures.

He has dissolved Representative Houses repeatedly, for opposing with manly firmness his invasions on the rights of the people.

He has refused for a long time, after such dissolutions, to cause others to be elected, whereby the Legislative Powers, incapable of Annihilation, have returned to the People at large for their exercise; the State remaining in the mean time exposed to all the dangers of invasion from without, and convulsions within.

He has endeavoured to prevent the population of these States; for that purpose obstructing the Laws for Naturalization of Foreigners; refusing to pass others to encourage their migrations hither, and raising the conditions of new Appropriations of Lands.

He has obstructed the Administration of Justice by refusing his Assent to Laws for establishing Judiciary Powers.

He has made Judges dependent on his Will alone for the tenure of their offices, and the amount and payment of their salaries.

He has erected a multitude of New Offices, and sent hither swarms of Officers to harass our people and eat out their substance.

He has kept among us, in times of peace, Standing Armies without the Consent of our legislatures.

He has affected to render the Military independent of and superior to the Civil Power.

He has combined with others to subject us to a jurisdiction foreign to our constitution, and unacknowledged by our laws; giving his Assent to their Acts of pretended Legislation:

For quartering large bodies of armed troops among us:

For protecting them, by a mock Trial from punishment for any Murders which they should commit on the Inhabitants of these States:

For cutting off our Trade with all parts of the world:

For imposing Taxes on us without our Consent:

For depriving us in many cases, of the benefit of Trial by Jury:

For transporting us beyond Seas to be tried for pretended offences:

For abolishing the free System of English Laws in a neighbouring Province, establishing therein an Arbitrary government, and enlarging its Boundaries so as to render it at once an example and fit instrument for introducing the same absolute rule into these Colonies:

For taking away our Charters, abolishing our most valuable Laws and altering fundamentally the Forms of our Governments:

For suspending our own Legislatures, and declaring themselves invested with power to legislate for us in all cases whatsoever.

He has abdicated Government here, by declaring us out of his Protection and waging War against us.

He has plundered our seas, ravaged our coasts, burnt our towns, and destroyed the lives of our people.

He is at this time transporting large Armies of foreign Mercenaries to compleat the works of death, desolation, and tyranny, already begun with circumstances of Cruelty & Perfidy scarcely paralleled in the most barbarous ages, and totally unworthy the Head of a civilized nation.

He has constrained our fellow Citizens taken Captive on the high Seas to bear Arms against their Country, to become the executioners of their friends and Brethren, or to fall themselves by their Hands.

He has excited domestic insurrections amongst us, and has endeavoured to bring on the inhabitants of our frontiers, the merciless Indian Savages whose known rule of warfare, is an undistinguished destruction of all ages, sexes and conditions.

In every stage of these Oppressions We have Petitioned for Redress in the most humble terms: Our repeated Petitions have been answered only by repeated injury. A Prince, whose character is thus marked by every act which may define a Tyrant, is unfit to be the ruler of a free people.

Nor have we been wanting in attentions to our British brethren. We have warned them from time to time of attempts by their legislature to extend an unwarrantable jurisdiction over us. We have reminded them of the circumstances of our emigration and settlement here. We have appealed to their native justice and magnanimity, and we have conjured them by the ties of our common kindred to disavow these usurpations, which would inevitably interrupt our connections and correspondence. They too have been deaf to the voice of justice and of consanguinity. We must, therefore, acquiesce in the necessity, which denounces our Separation, and hold them, as we hold the rest of mankind, Enemies in War, in Peace Friends.

We, therefore, the Representatives of the united States of America, in General Congress, Assembled, appealing to the Supreme Judge of the world for the rectitude of our intentions, do, in the Name, and by Authority of the good People of these Colonies, solemnly publish and declare, That these united

Colonies are, and of Right ought to be Free and Independent States, that they are Absolved from all Allegiance to the British Crown, and that all political connection between them and the State of Great Britain, is and ought to be totally dissolved; and that as Free and Independent States, they have full Power to levy War, conclude Peace, contract Alliances, establish Commerce, and to do all other Acts and Things which Independent States may of right do.—And for the support of this Declaration, with a firm reliance on the protection of Divine Providence, we mutually pledge to each other our Lives, our Fortunes, and our sacred Honor.

> JOHN HANCOCK
>
> [There follow the signatures of 55 other delegates, organized by delegation, though the names of the delegations are not included.]

Questions for Consideration After Reading the Declaration

(1) Assuming that a *Declaration* of Independence was necessary to achieve independence, this document is much more than that; it appears to be an attempt at persuasion. Who is its intended audience?

(2) Assuming one accepts the legitimacy of the Declaration, how many independent nations resulted? If one, what was its name?

(3) The Declaration certainly makes King George III out to be a bad king and a bad guy. But Massachusetts probably could have stated an impressive sounding list of complaints against George W. Bush or Donald J. Trump, and Idaho could probably have done the same with respect to Barack Obama or Joe Biden. Does the Declaration make a persuasive case that it is "necessary" for the American colonies to "dissolve" the political bands that have connected America to Great Britain? Do you believe the Declaration is a complete statement of the reasons that actually motivated the decision to assert independence?

(4) In 1789, Franklin wrote, with reference to the Albany Plan discussed on pp. 5:

> On Reflection it now seems probable, that if the foregoing Plan or some thing like it, had been adopted and carried into Execution, the subsequent Separation of the Colonies from the Mother Country might not so soon have happened, nor the Mischiefs suffered on both sides have occurred, perhaps during another

Century. For the Colonies, if so united, would have really been,
as they then thought themselves, sufficient to their own Defence,
and being trusted with it, as by the Plan, an Army from Britain,
for that purpose would have been unnecessary: The Pretences
for framing the Stamp-Act would not then have existed, nor the
other Projects for drawing a Revenue from America to Britain
by Acts of Parliament, which were the Cause of the Breach, and
attended with such terrible Expence of Blood and Treasure: so
that the different Parts of the Empire might still have remained in
Peace and Union.

Was he right? Would that have been a good thing or a bad one? Is it imaginable that as late as the 21st century a nation in North America would be
independent of Great Britain but remain in close political association with it?

Rather soon after the Declaration, each of the states adopted a constitution. But what of the "united States"? On June 12, 1776, a day after appointing
the committee that drafted the Declaration, Congress appointed another committee to draft a plan for a confederation of the prospective states. Not until
November 1777 did Congress approve a draft of Articles of Confederation to
be sent to the states for ratification. Beginning in July 1778, as states approved
the Articles, their respective Congressional delegations signed them. The last
holdout, Maryland, did not approve until February 1781, because of disputes
with other states over western land claims. Its delegates signed the Articles on
March 1, 1781, and at that point the Continental Congress became the Congress of the Confederation.

Here is the text of the Articles, edited down somewhat.

Articles of Confederation

To all to whom these Presents shall come, we the undersigned Delegates
of the States affixed to our Names send greeting.

Articles of Confederation and perpetual Union between the States of
New Hampshire, Massachusetts-bay, Rhode Island and Providence Planta-
tions, Connecticut, New York, New Jersey, Pennsylvania, Delaware, Maryland,
Virginia, North Carolina, South Carolina and Georgia.

Article I. The Stile of this Confederacy shall be "The United States of America."

Article II. Each state retains its sovereignty, freedom, and independence, and every power, jurisdiction, and right, which is not by this Confederation expressly delegated to the United States, in Congress assembled.

Article III. The said States hereby severally enter into a firm league of friendship with each other, for their common defense, the security of their liberties, and their mutual and general welfare, binding themselves to assist each other, against all force offered to, or attacks made upon them, or any of them, on account of religion, sovereignty, trade, or any other pretense whatever.

Article IV. The better to secure and perpetuate mutual friendship and intercourse among the people of the different States in this Union, the free inhabitants of each of these States, paupers, vagabonds, and fugitives from justice excepted, shall be entitled to all privileges and immunities of free citizens in the several States; and the people of each State shall have free ingress and regress to and from any other State, and shall enjoy therein all the privileges of trade and commerce, subject to the same duties, impositions, and restrictions as the inhabitants thereof respectively, provided that such restrictions shall not extend so far as to prevent the removal of property imported into any State, to any other State, of which the owner is an inhabitant; provided also that no imposition, duties or restriction shall be laid by any State, on the property of the United States, or either of them.

If any person guilty of, or charged with, treason, felony, or other high misdemeanor in any State, shall flee from justice, and be found in any of the United States, he shall, upon demand of the Governor or executive power of the State from which he fled, be delivered up and removed to the State having jurisdiction of his offense.

Full faith and credit shall be given in each of these States to the records, acts, and judicial proceedings of the courts and magistrates of every other State.

Article V. For the most convenient management of the general interests of the United States, delegates shall be annually appointed in such manner as the legislatures of each State shall direct, to meet in Congress on the first Monday in November, in every year, with a power reserved to each State to recall its delegates, or any of them, at any time within the year, and to send others in their stead for the remainder of the year. . . .

In determining questions in the United States in Congress assembled, each State shall have one vote.

Freedom of speech and debate in Congress shall not be impeached or questioned in any court or place out of Congress, and the members of Congress shall be protected in their persons from arrests or imprisonments, during the time of their going to and from, and attendance on Congress, except for treason, felony, or breach of the peace.

Article VI. No State, without the consent of the United States in Congress assembled, shall send any embassy to, or receive any embassy from, or enter into any conference, agreement, alliance or treaty with any King, Prince or State; nor shall any person holding any office of profit or trust under the United States, or any of them, accept any present, emolument, office or title of any kind whatever from any King, Prince or foreign State; nor shall the United States in Congress assembled, or any of them, grant any title of nobility.

No two or more States shall enter into any treaty, confederation or alliance whatever between them, without the consent of the United States in Congress assembled, specifying accurately the purposes for which the same is to be entered into, and how long it shall continue.

No State shall lay any imposts or duties, which may interfere with any stipulations in treaties, entered into by the United States in Congress assembled, with any King, Prince or State, in pursuance of any treaties already proposed by Congress, to the courts of France and Spain.

No vessel of war shall be kept up in time of peace by any State, except such number only, as shall be deemed necessary by the United States in Congress assembled, for the defense of such State, or its trade; nor shall any body of forces be kept up by any State in time of peace, except such number only, as in the judgement of the United States in Congress assembled, shall be deemed requisite to garrison the forts necessary for the defense of such State; but every State shall always keep up a well-regulated and disciplined militia, sufficiently armed and accoutered, and shall provide and constantly have ready for use, in public stores, a due number of filed pieces and tents, and a proper quantity of arms, ammunition and camp equipage.

No State shall engage in any war without the consent of the United States in Congress assembled, unless such State be actually invaded by enemies, or shall have received certain advice of a resolution being formed by some nation of Indians to invade such State, and the danger is so imminent as not to admit of a delay till the United States in Congress assembled can be consulted. . . .

Article VIII. All charges of war, and all other expenses that shall be incurred for the common defense or general welfare, and allowed by the United States in Congress assembled, shall be defrayed out of a common treasury, which shall be supplied by the several States in proportion to the value of all land within each State, granted or surveyed for any person, as such land and the buildings and improvements thereon shall be estimated according to such mode as the United States in Congress assembled, shall from time to time direct and appoint.

The taxes for paying that proportion shall be laid and levied by the authority and direction of the legislatures of the several States within the time agreed upon by the United States in Congress assembled.

Article IX. The United States in Congress assembled, shall have the sole and exclusive right and power of determining on peace and war, except in the cases mentioned in the sixth article—of sending and receiving ambassadors—entering into treaties and alliances, provided that no treaty of commerce shall be made whereby the legislative power of the respective States shall be restrained from imposing such imposts and duties on foreigners, as their own people are subjected to, or from prohibiting the exportation or importation of any species of goods or commodities whatsoever—of establishing rules for deciding in all cases, what captures on land or water shall be legal, and in what manner prizes taken by land or naval forces in the service of the United States shall be divided or appropriated—of granting letters of marque and reprisal in times of peace—appointing courts for the trial of piracies and felonies committed on the high seas and establishing courts for receiving and determining finally appeals in all cases of captures, provided that no member of Congress shall be appointed a judge of any of the said courts.

The United States in Congress assembled shall also be the last resort on appeal in all disputes and differences now subsisting or that hereafter may arise between two or more States concerning boundary, jurisdiction or any other causes whatever; which authority shall always be exercised in the manner following. . . .

WORTH NOTING

The Articles go into great detail, omitted here, on the process of congressional adjudication in disputes between states.

The United States in Congress assembled shall also have the sole and exclusive right and power of regulating the alloy and value of coin struck by their own authority, or by that of the respective States—fixing the standards of weights and measures throughout the United States—regulating the trade and managing all affairs with the Indians, not members of any of the States, provided that the legislative right of any State within its own limits be not infringed or violated—establishing or regulating post offices from one State to another, throughout all the United States, and exacting such postage on the papers passing through the same as may be requisite to defray the expenses of the said office—appointing all officers of the land forces, in the service of the United States, excepting regimental officers—appointing all the officers of the naval forces, and commissioning all officers whatever in the service of the United States—making rules for the government and regulation of the said land and naval forces, and directing their operations.

The United States in Congress assembled shall have authority to appoint a committee, to sit in the recess of Congress, to be denominated "A Committee of the States", and to consist of one delegate from each State; and to appoint such other committees and civil officers as may be necessary for managing the general affairs of the United States under their direction—to appoint one of their members to preside, provided that no person be allowed to serve in the office of president more than one year in any term of three years; to ascertain the necessary sums of money to be raised for the service of the United States, and to appropriate and apply the same for defraying the public expenses—to borrow money, or emit bills on the credit of the United States, transmitting every half-year to the respective States an account of the sums of money so borrowed or emitted—to build and equip a navy—to agree upon the number of land forces, and to make requisitions from each State for its quota, in proportion to the number of white inhabitants in such State; which requisition shall be binding. . . .

The United States in Congress assembled shall never engage in a war, nor grant letters of marque or reprisal in time of peace, nor enter into any treaties or alliances, nor coin money, nor regulate the value thereof, nor ascertain the sums and expenses necessary for the defense and welfare of the United States, or any of them, nor emit bills, nor borrow money on the credit of the United States, nor appropriate money, nor agree upon the number of vessels of war, to be built or purchased, or the number of land or sea forces to be raised, nor appoint a commander in chief of the army or navy, unless nine States assent to the same: nor shall a question on any other point, except for adjourning from day to day be determined, unless by the votes of the majority of the United States in Congress assembled.

The Congress of the United States shall have power to adjourn to any time within the year, and to any place within the United States, so that no period of adjournment be for a longer duration than the space of six months, and shall publish the journal of their proceedings monthly, except such parts thereof relating to treaties, alliances or military operations, as in their judgement require secrecy. . . .

Article X. The Committee of the States, or any nine of them, shall be authorized to execute, in the recess of Congress, such of the powers of Congress as the United States in Congress assembled, by the consent of the nine States, shall from time to time think expedient to vest them with; provided that no power be delegated to the said Committee, for the exercise of which, by the Articles of Confederation, the voice of nine States in the Congress of the United States assembled be requisite.

Article XI. Canada acceding to this confederation, and adjoining in the measures of the United States, shall be admitted into, and entitled to all the advantages of this Union; but no other colony shall be admitted into the same, unless such admission be agreed to by nine States.

Article XII. All bills of credit emitted, monies borrowed, and debts contracted by, or under the authority of Congress, before the assembling of the United States, in pursuance of the present confederation, shall be deemed and considered as a charge against the United States, for payment and satisfaction whereof the said United States, and the public faith are hereby solemnly pledged.

Article XIII. Every State shall abide by the determination of the United States in Congress assembled, on all questions which by this confederation are submitted to them. And the Articles of this Confederation shall be inviolably observed by every State, and the Union shall be perpetual; nor shall any alteration at any time hereafter be made in any of them; unless such alteration be agreed to in a Congress of the United States, and be afterwards confirmed by the legislatures of every State. . . .

Questions for Consideration After Reading the Articles

(1) Did adoption of the Articles constitute the United States as a nation? What portions of the Articles themselves might lead you to answer this question affirmatively? What portions might lead you to answer negatively?

(2) However you might answer the first question, clearly the Articles were at least a significant step on the path toward nationhood. What portions do you regard as their greatest accomplishments? What were their most significant limitations and weaknesses?

The United States had some notable achievements during the period of the Confederation Congress. The war was brought to a successful military conclusion with the battle of Yorktown in October 1781 and to a successful diplomatic conclusion by the 1783 Treaty of Paris, which was ratified the next year. The treaty recognized not only American independence but also American control over a large body of land, bounded on the south by the Ohio River and on the west by the Mississippi, beyond the accepted borders of the states. One by one, reluctantly, the states gave up their claims to this land, which had been a source of considerable conflict among them. The territory therefore belonged to the United States as a whole. The Land Ordinance of 1785 devised a system of public surveying for this land, dividing much of it into townships six miles square. The Northwest Ordinance of 1787 provided a mechanism for this large area—which covers all the modern states of Ohio, Michigan, Indiana, Illinois, and Wisconsin, as well as part of Minnesota—to be organized into territories that would eventually become states. The ordinance also contained a guarantee of various civil rights, including trial by jury and religious tolerance. And it prohibited slavery in the territory (though indentured servitude was allowed).

But there were serious problems as well. Congress was not in complete control of foreign policy; Georgia skirmished with the Spanish, who had regained control of all of Florida after the Revolution, and some states fought and made treaties with Indian tribes. Congress was unable to pay the national debt, including debts to veterans. The Continental currency had become virtually worthless, in part because Congress was able to raise far less money from the states than it demanded or believed it needed. Economic depression led to a wave of foreclosures, and so too to considerable resistance on the part of debtors, which briefly erupted into violence in western Massachusetts in 1786, in Shays's Rebellion. State legislatures passed various forms of debtor relief measures, including moratoria on foreclosures and the issuance of inflationary paper money. States also passed various sorts of protective legislation—for example, favoring their own citizens' vessels and limiting access to their ports—that effectively created a continuous trade war.

B. Adoption of the Constitution

In January 1786—at least in part at the instigation of James Madison, who had already taken some local initiatives on interstate cooperation—the Virginia Assembly issued a call for the states to send delegates to a convention to "consider how far a uniform system in their commercial intercourse and regulations might be necessary to their common interest and permanent harmony." Five states sent a total of twelve delegates to the convention, which was held in September at Annapolis, Maryland. The delegates recognized that the poor turnout limited their ability to attain any substantive accomplishments. But at the suggestion of Alexander Hamilton, a delegate from New York, they adopted a resolution recommending the calling of a second convention, which would be able to "devise such . . . provisions as shall appear to them necessary to render the constitution of the Federal Government adequate to the exigencies of the Union."

The Annapolis resolution was presented in February 1787 to Congress, which soon after called for delegates appointed by the states to convene in Philadelphia on May 14 "for the sole and express purpose of revising the Articles of Confederation" and proposing "such alterations and provisions therein" as would "when agreed to in Congress and confirmed by the states render the federal constitution adequate to the exigencies of Government & the preservation of the Union." George Washington agreed to attend as a delegate from Virginia, which boosted the convention's credibility. Ultimately twelve states sent delegates—Rhode Island refused to do so—but because of travel difficulties the Convention did not have a quorum for business until May 25.

At the outset, the Convention unanimously elected Washington as its president. Madison came to the sessions early, sat near the front, and took extensive notes. These remain perhaps the most important record of the proceedings, which were conducted in secret. The Convention nearly broke up more than once, and some delegates departed in protest over the proceedings. In July, Hamilton was left as the only member of the New York delegation; under the rules of the Convention, the state needed at least two delegates to vote, but Hamilton was allowed to remain and speak. In all, 55 men participated at one point or another in the Convention, never all at once; ultimately, those who remained were able to resolve their differences well enough that 39 of 42 signed the final document.

Near the beginning of the Convention, Governor Edmund Randolph of Virginia presented a plan, largely drafted by Madison, that ignored the instructions to the Convention by proposing an entirely new system of government—a bicameral legislature, with representation in both houses to be proportional to population, and separate legislative and judicial branches.

FOR DISCUSSION

Suppose you are a delegate of a small state to the Constitutional Convention. You would like your state to be part of an American Union, but you are afraid that it might be swamped by larger states with potentially conflicting interests. What protections might you seek? And if you are a delegate of a large state, pleased to have extra influence but eager to keep the smaller states in the Union, what might your attitude be?

When the Convention published its draft Constitution, opponents argued that the delegates had exceeded their authority by proposing a brand-new constitution instead of limiting themselves to proposals for amending the Articles of Confederation. During the ensuing debates, one Federalist responded to this attack with a homey analogy:

FOR DISCUSSION

> [S]uppose sir, your house although the timber were new and strong, yet for the want of workmanship in the builders, it was so illy proportioned and disjointed, as to threaten to totter to pieces and crush your family under its ruins, notwithstanding which you thought it might be altered or amended, and therefore called a number of Carpenters to examine it, and report to you the necessary alterations; but these architects on a thorough examination, were of opinion, that the only way to save the family from ruin, was to take the house entirely down and re-build it, and in pursuit of this opinion, they thought it but their duty to report to you a plan for the execution of it; they could not see any evil in the proposal as it still remained with you to adopt it or reject it.—The object in view was the preservation of your family, if they erred in judgment, it was not a criminal error as they had left you at liberty to make your opinion.—After these men had so faithfully discharged their consciences, if you should rail at them, and tell them that they were usurpurs, that they aragantly assumed a power of prescribing a rule for the government of your conduct, and had exceeded the limits of their authority, would not your neighbours call you a mad-man?

A Friend to Good Government, Poughkeepsie Country Journal (April 15, 1788). Do you find this response convincing?

Regardless of whether Randolph's proposal was *ultra vires*, the small states strongly objected to its substance. William Paterson of New Jersey proposed an alternative that would adhere to the structure of the Articles, while enhancing Congressional powers somewhat. The Convention agreed to move towards a stronger national government—scuttling the Articles—but the issue of representation continued to be divisive. Ultimately, in July, the Convention adopted a compromise that had been proposed by Roger Sherman of Connecticut: a lower house allotted according to population and an upper house in which the states were represented equally.

FOR DISCUSSION

Reynolds v. Sims (1964) held that each house of a state legislature must be apportioned according to population. There has never been a serious prospect that the same rule would be applied to the United States Senate—or to the allocation of Presidential electors. Why, do you suppose?

Among the other compromises crafted by the Convention were ones concerning the extent of Congress's power, the nature of the office of the Presidency, and the treatment of slavery and of the enslaved population for purposes of taxation and representation. The Constitution was signed on September 17, 1787. Eleven days later, Congress resolved to transmit it to the state legislatures for submission to conventions in each state, pursuant to the terms of Article VII of the new Constitution itself.

In some of the states, ratification was not controversial. In others, it was bitterly contested; in Massachusetts, for example, the convention approved ratification by a vote of 187–168. New Hampshire was the ninth state to ratify, on June 21, 1788, by a 57–47 vote, allowing the Constitution to go into effect among the states that had ratified. But it had no chance to succeed without the participation of Virginia, the largest state, and of New York, one of the most pivotal. Virginia ratified by 89–79 on June 25. To support the New York ratification effort, Madison, Hamilton, and John Jay wrote a series of essays, later published as *The Federalist*. Here is one example.

CROSS REFERENCE

See pp. 34–38 for more on the Constitution's treatment of slavery.

The Federalist No. 51 (James Madison)

February 8, 1788

To the People of the State of New York:

TO WHAT expedient, then, shall we finally resort, for maintaining in practice the necessary partition of power among the several departments, as laid down in the Constitution? The only answer that can be given is, that as all these exterior provisions are found to be inadequate, the defect must be supplied, by so contriving the interior structure of the government as that its several constituent parts may, by their mutual relations, be the means of keeping each other in their proper places. Without presuming to undertake a full development of this important idea, I will hazard a few general observations, which may perhaps place it in a clearer light, and enable us to form a more correct judgment of the principles and structure of the government planned by the convention.

In order to lay a due foundation for that separate and distinct exercise of the different powers of government, which to a certain extent is admitted on all hands to be essential to the preservation of liberty, it is evident that each department should have a will of its own; and consequently should be so constituted that the members of each should have as little agency as possible in the appointment of the members of the others. Were this principle rigorously adhered to, it would require that all the appointments for the supreme executive, legislative, and judiciary magistracies should be drawn from the same fountain of authority, the people, through channels having no communication whatever with one another. Perhaps such a plan of constructing the several departments would be less difficult in practice than it may in contemplation appear. Some difficulties, however, and some additional expense would attend the execution of it. Some deviations, therefore, from the principle must be admitted. In the constitution of the judiciary department in particular, it might be inexpedient to insist rigorously on the principle: first, because peculiar qualifications being essential in the members, the primary consideration ought to be to select that mode of choice which best secures these qualifications; secondly, because the permanent tenure by which the appointments are held in that department, must soon destroy all sense of dependence on the authority conferring them.

It is equally evident, that the members of each department should be as little dependent as possible on those of the others, for the emoluments annexed to their offices. Were the executive magistrate, or the judges, not independent of the legislature in this particular, their independence in every other would be merely nominal.

But the great security against a gradual concentration of the several powers in the same department, consists in giving to those who administer each department the necessary constitutional means and personal motives to resist encroachments of the others. The provision for defense must in this, as in all other cases, be made commensurate to the danger of attack. Ambition must be made to counteract ambition. The interest of the man must be connected with the constitutional rights of the place. It may be a reflection on human nature, that such devices should be necessary to control the abuses of government. But what is government itself, but the greatest of all reflections on human nature? If men were angels, no government would be necessary. If angels were to govern men, neither external nor internal controls on government would be necessary. In framing a government which is to be administered by men over men, the great difficulty lies in this: you must first enable the government to control the governed; and in the next place oblige it to control itself. A dependence on the people is, no doubt, the primary control on the government; but experience has taught mankind the necessity of auxiliary precautions. This policy of supplying, by opposite and rival interests, the defect of better motives, might be traced through the whole system of human affairs, private as well as public. . . .

But it is not possible to give to each department an equal power of self-defense. In republican government, the legislative authority necessarily predominates. The remedy for this inconveniency is to divide the legislature into different branches; and to render them, by different modes of election and different principles of action, as little connected with each other as the nature of their common functions and their common dependence on the society will admit. It may even be necessary to guard against dangerous encroachments by still further precautions. As the weight of the legislative authority requires that it should be thus divided, the weakness of the executive may require, on the other hand, that it should be fortified. An absolute negative on the legislature appears, at first view, to be the natural defense with which the executive magistrate should be armed. But perhaps it would be neither altogether safe nor alone sufficient. On ordinary occasions it might not be exerted with the requisite firmness, and on extraordinary occasions it might be perfidiously abused. May not this defect of an absolute negative be supplied by some qualified connection between this weaker department and the weaker branch of the stronger department, by which the latter may be led to support the constitutional rights of the former, without being too much detached from the rights of its own department?

If the principles on which these observations are founded be just, as I persuade myself they are, and they be applied as a criterion to the several State constitutions, and to the federal Constitution it will be found that if the latter does not perfectly correspond with them, the former are infinitely less able to bear such a test.

There are, moreover, two considerations particularly applicable to the federal system of America, which place that system in a very interesting point of view.

First. In a single republic, all the power surrendered by the people is submitted to the administration of a single government; and the usurpations are guarded against by a division of the government into distinct and separate departments. In the compound republic of America, the power surrendered by the people is first divided between two distinct governments, and then the portion allotted to each subdivided among distinct and separate departments. Hence a double security arises to the rights of the people. The different governments will control each other, at the same time that each will be controlled by itself.

Second. It is of great importance in a republic not only to guard the society against the oppression of its rulers, but to guard one part of the society against the injustice of the other part. Different interests necessarily exist in different classes of citizens. If a majority be united by a common interest, the rights of the minority will be insecure.

There are but two methods of providing against this evil: the one by creating a will in the community independent of the majority—that is, of the society itself; the other, by comprehending in the society so many separate descriptions of citizens as will render an unjust combination of a majority of the whole very improbable, if not impracticable. The first method prevails in all governments possessing an hereditary or self-appointed authority. This, at best, is but a precarious security; because a power independent of the society may as well espouse the unjust views of the major, as the rightful interests of the minor party, and may possibly be turned against both parties. The second method will be exemplified in the federal republic of the United States. Whilst all authority in it will be derived from and dependent on the society, the society itself will be broken into so many parts, interests, and classes of citizens, that the rights of individuals, or of the minority, will be in little danger from interested combinations of the majority. In a free government the security for civil rights must be the same as that for religious rights. It consists in the one case in the multiplicity of interests, and in the other in the multiplicity of sects. The degree of security in both cases will depend on the number of interests and sects; and this may be presumed to depend on the extent of country and number of people comprehended under the same government. . . .

In a society under the forms of which the stronger faction can readily unite and oppress the weaker, anarchy may as truly be said to reign as in a state of nature, where the weaker individual is not secured against the violence of the stronger; and as, in the latter state, even the stronger individuals are prompted, by the uncertainty of their condition, to submit to a government which may protect the weak as well as themselves; so, in the former state, will the more powerful factions or parties be gradually induced, by a like motive, to wish for a government which will protect all parties, the weaker as well as the more powerful.

It can be little doubted that if the State of Rhode Island was separated from the Confederacy and left to itself, the insecurity of rights under the popular form of government within such narrow limits would be displayed by such reiterated oppressions of factious majorities that some power altogether independent of the people would soon be called for by the voice of the very factions whose misrule had proved the necessity of it. In the extended republic of the United States, and among the great variety of interests, parties, and sects which it embraces, a coalition of a majority of the whole society could seldom take place on any other principles than those of justice and the general good; whilst there being thus less danger to a minor from the will of a major party, there must be less pretext, also, to provide for the security of the former, by introducing into the government a will not dependent on the latter, or, in other words, a will independent of the society itself. It is no less certain than it is important, notwithstanding the contrary opinions which have been entertained, that the larger the society, provided it lie within a practical sphere, the more duly capable it will be of self-government. And happily for the republican cause, the practicable sphere may be carried to a very great extent, by a judicious modification and mixture of the federal principle.

PUBLIUS

FOR DISCUSSION It is sometimes said that the federal government is composed of three "coequal branches." What does this mean? Does it reflect Madison's view? Do you accept Madison's rationale for division of the legislature?

Not everyone thought the draft Constitution was so great. Twenty-one members of the losing side in the Pennsylvania ratification convention, for example, signed a declaration of principles designed to appeal to their allies and persuadables alike in other states. They had a lot of criticisms; some of them are reproduced below.

The Address and Reasons of Dissent of the Minority of the [Ratification] Convention of the State of Pennsylvania to their Constituents

December 18, 1787

Our objections are comprised under three general heads of dissent, viz.:

[1.] We dissent, first, because it is the opinion of the most celebrated writers on government, and confirmed by uniform experience, that a very extensive territory cannot be governed on the principles of freedom, otherwise than by a confederation of republics, possessing all the powers of internal government; but united in the management of their general, and foreign concerns. . . .

[2.] We dissent, secondly, because the powers vested in Congress by this constitution must necessarily annihilate and absorb the legislative, executive, and judicial powers of the several states, and produce from their ruins one consolidated government, which from the nature of things will be *an iron-handed despotism*, as nothing short of the supremacy of despotic sway could connect and govern these United States under one government. . . . That the new government will not be a confederacy of states, as it ought, but one consolidated government founded upon the destruction of the several governments of the states, we shall now show.

The powers of Congress under the new constitution are complete and unlimited over the *purse* and the *sword*, and are perfectly independent of, and supreme over, the state governments; whose intervention in these great points is entirely destroyed. By virtue of their power of taxation, Congress may command the whole, or any part of the property of the people. They may impose what imposts upon commerce; they may impose what land taxes, poll taxes, excises, duties on all written instruments, and duties on every other article that they may judge proper; in short, every species of taxation, whether of an external or internal nature is comprised in section the 8th, of Article the 1st, viz.: "The Congress shall have power to lay and collect taxes, duties, imposts, and excises, to pay the debts, and provide for the common defence and general welfare of the United States."

As there is no one article of taxation reserved to the state governments, the Congress may monopolize every source of revenue, and thus indirectly demolish the state governments, for without funds they could not exist. The taxes, duties, and excises imposed by Congress may be so high as to render it impracticable to levy further sums on the same articles; but whether this should be the case or not, if the state governments should presume to impose taxes, duties, or excises, on the same articles with Congress, the latter may abrogate and repeal the laws whereby they are imposed, upon the allegation that they interfere with the due collection of their taxes, duties, or excises. . . .

And the supremacy of the laws of the United States is established by Article 6th, viz.: "That this constitution and the laws of the United States, which shall be made in pursuance thereof, and *all treaties* made, or which shall be made, under the authority of the United States, shall be the *supreme law* of the *land;* and *the judges in every state shall be bound thereby; any thing in the constitution or laws of any state to the contrary notwithstanding.*" . . . In our opinion, "pursuant to the constitution" will be coextensive with the *will* and *pleasure* of Congress, which, indeed, will be the only limitation of their powers. . . .

In short, consolidation pervades the whole constitution. It begins with an annunciation that such was the intention. The main pillars of the fabric correspond with it, and the concluding paragraph is a confirmation of it. The preamble begins with the words, "We the people of the United States," which is the style of a compact between individuals entering into a state of society, and not that of a confederation of states. . . . Thus we have fully established the position, that the powers vested by this constitution in Congress will effect a consolidation of the states under one government, which even the advocates of this constitution admit could not be done without the sacrifice of all liberty.

3. We dissent, thirdly, because . . . the legislature of a free country should be so formed as to have a competent knowledge of its constituents, and enjoy

their confidence. To produce these essential requisites, the representation ought to be fair, equal, and sufficiently numerous, to possess the same interests, feelings, opinions, and views, which the people themselves would possess were they all assembled; and so numerous as to prevent bribery and undue influence, and so responsible to the people, by frequent and fair elections, as to prevent their neglecting or sacrificing the views and interests of their constituents, to their own pursuits.

We will now bring the legislature under this constitution to the test of the foregoing principles, which will demonstrate, that it is deficient in every essential quality of a just and safe representation.

The house of representatives is to consist of 65 members; that is one for about every 50,000 inhabitants, to be chosen every two years. Thirty-three members will form a quorum for doing business, and 17 of these, being the majority, determine the sense of the house. The senate, the other constituent branch of the legislature, consists of 26 members, being *two* from each state. . . .

How inadequate and unsafe a representation! Inadequate, because the sense and views of 3 or 4 millions of people diffused over so extensive a territory comprising such various climates, products, habits, interests, and opinions cannot be collected in so small a body; and besides, it is not a fair and equal representation of the people even in proportion to its number, for the smallest state has as much weight in the senate as the largest, and from the smallness of the number to be chosen for both branches of the legislature; and from the mode of election and appointment, which is under the control of Congress; and from the nature of the thing, men of the most elevated rank in life will alone be chosen. The other orders in the society, such as farmers, traders, and mechanics, who all ought to have a competent number of their best-informed men in the legislature, will be totally unrepresented.

The representation is unsafe because in the exercise of such great powers and trusts, it is so exposed to corruption and undue influence, by the gift of the numerous places of honor and emolument, at the disposal of the executive; by the arts and address of the great and designing; and by direct bribery.

The representation is moreover inadequate and unsafe, because of the long terms for which it is appointed, and the mode of its appointment, by which Congress may not only control the choice of the people, but may so manage as to divest the people of this fundamental right, and become self-elected. . . .

As this government will not enjoy the confidence of the people, but be executed by force, it will be a very expensive and burthensome government. The standing army must be numerous, and as a further support, it will be the policy of this government to multiply officers in every department: judges, collectors, tax gatherers, excisemen, and the whole host of revenue officers will swarm over the land, devouring the hard earnings of the industrious, like the locusts of old, impoverishing and desolating all before them.

We have not noticed the smaller, nor many of the considerable blemishes, but have confined our objections to the great and essential defects; the main pillars of the constitution, which we have shown to be inconsistent with the liberty and happiness of the people, as its establishment will annihilate the state governments, and produce one consolidated government, that will eventually and speedily issue in the supremacy of despotism. . . .

FOR DISCUSSION

What was the Pennsylvania Dissenters' biggest fear? Were they right to worry about it? Should their view of how to interpret the Constitution matter when we think about the original understanding? Or should their claims be ignored given that they were not only on the losing side, but engaged in an active propaganda project? (Were they the only ones involved in a propaganda project?)

Other critics emphasized different reasons to oppose the Constitution. The practice of slavery in colonial America goes back to at least the 1500s. Formal introduction of the institution under English law is typically dated to 1619, when Dutch traders sold some twenty enslaved Africans to residents of Jamestown, Virginia. As ratified in 1789, the U.S. Constitution did not use the word "slavery." But it actually said quite a bit about America's peculiar institution. The following provisions are often referred to as the Constitution's "slavery clauses":

- *Slave Trade Guarantee*—"The Migration or Importation of such Persons as any of the States now existing shall think proper to admit shall not be prohibited by the Congress prior to the Year one thousand eight hundred and eight, but a Tax or duty may be imposed on such Importation, not exceeding ten dollars for each Person." U.S. Const., Art. I, § 9, cl. 1.

- *Fugitive Slave Clause*—"No person held to service or labour in one state, under the laws thereof, escaping into another, shall, in consequence of any law or regulation therein, be discharged from such service or labour, but shall be delivered up on claim of the party to whom such service or labour may be due." U.S. Const., Art. IV, § 2, cl. 3.

- *Three-Fifths Clause*—"Representatives and direct Taxes shall be apportioned among the several States which may be included within this Union, according to their respective Numbers, which shall be determined by adding to the whole Number of free Persons, including those bound to Service for a Term of Years, and excluding Indians not taxed, three fifths of all other Persons." U.S. Const., Art. I, § 2, cl. 3.

Each of these clauses speaks in some way to the institution of slavery. Can you see how?

The slavery clauses were the result of an elaborate and hotly-debated compromise during the drafting of the Constitution. During the debates at the 1787 Constitutional Convention, James Madison observed that slavery was perhaps the most important fault line in national politics:

> It seemed now to be pretty well understood that the real difference of interests [in national politics] lay, not between the large & small [states] but between the N. & Southn. States. The institution of slavery & its consequences formed the line of discrimination. There were 5 States on the South, 8 on the Northn. side of this line.

Madison's comments came during a debate about the structure of state representation in the Senate. But the regional divide he described surfaced most explicitly during the debates on the slavery clauses themselves.

Opponents of these provisions did not mince words. During a debate about how to calculate state populations—an enormously significant issue for purposes of representation in the House of Representatives—Pennsylvania delegate Gouverneur Morris made the following observations, as later summarized in James Madison's notes of the proceedings:

> He never would concur in upholding domestic slavery. It was a nefarious institution—It was the curse of heaven on the States where

it prevailed. Compare the free regions of the Middle States, where a rich & noble cultivation marks the prosperity & happiness of the people, with the misery & poverty which overspread the barren wastes of Va. Maryd. & the other States having slaves. (Travel thro' ye whole Continent & you behold the prospect continually varying with the appearance & disappearance of slavery. . . .[)]

> Upon what principle is it that the slaves shall be computed in the representation? Are they men? Then make them Citizens & let them vote? Are they property? Why then is no other property included [for purpose of calculating representation in the House]? The Houses in this City (Philada.) are worth more than all the wretched slaves which cover the rice swamps of South Carolina. . . . The admission of slaves into the Representation when fairly explained comes to this: that the inhabitant of Georgia and S. C. who goes to the Coast of Africa, and in defiance of the most sacred laws of humanity tears away his fellow creatures from their dearest connections & dam[n]s them to the most cruel bondages, shall have more votes in a Govt. instituted for protection of the rights of mankind, than the Citizen of Pa or N. Jersey who views with a laudable horror, so nefarious a practice. He would add that Domestic slavery is the most prominent feature in the aristocratic countenance of the proposed Constitution. The vassalage of the poor has ever been the favorite offspring of Aristocracy.

It quickly became clear, however, that some Southern states viewed the slavery clauses—or something like them—as non-negotiable. Later that month, discussing the question of whether to prohibit the slave trade, one of the South Carolina Pinckneys[a] drew a typically stark line in the sand, saying: "South Carolina can never receive the plan if it prohibits the slave trade. In every proposed extension of the powers of Congress, that State has expressly & watchfully excepted that of meddling with the importation of negroes." The next day, he[b] amplified on this view:

> If slavery be wrong, it is justified by the example of all the world. He cited the case of Greece Rome & other antient States; the sanction

---

[a]   There were two Pinckneys at the Convention. They were both named Charles. One had been a general in the Revolutionary War; the speaker here was probably the other one.

[b]   Assuming that the Pinckney quoted just above wasn't the General.

given by France England, Holland & other modern States. In all ages one half of mankind have been slaves. If the S. States were let alone they will probably of themselves stop importations. He wd. himself as a Citizen of S. Carolina vote for it. An attempt to take away the right as proposed will produce serious objections to the Constitution which he wished to see adopted.

His cousin was even more emphatic, asserting that even if the South Carolina delegates signed and supported a Constitution that did not protect the institution of slavery, "it would be of no avail towards obtaining the assent of their Constituents," because "S. Carolina & Georgia cannot do without slaves."

The writing was on the wall, at least for anyone who prioritized national union. Oliver Ellsworth was a delegate from Connecticut, a state that had recently adopted a plan of gradual emancipation. His observations on the question of the slave trade may represent something like a moderate middle [!?] on the question of slavery more generally:

Mr. Elseworth was for . . . let[ting] every State import what it pleases. The morality or wisdom of slavery are considerations belonging to the States themselves—What enriches a part enriches the whole, and the States are the best judges of their particular interest. The old confederation had not meddled with this point, and he did not see any greater necessity for bringing it within the policy of the new one.

This was a classic federalist solution: the national government should neither prohibit nor require slavery, but instead leave the question for each individual state to decide. And that's what happened. As North Carolina delegate Hugh Williamson put it: "both in opinion & practice he was, against slavery; but [he] thought it more in favor of humanity, from a view of all circumstances, to let in S-C & Georgia on those terms, than to exclude them from the Union." In the end, even Gouverneur Morris—speaker in the first excerpt above—signed the draft Constitution.

FOR DISCUSSION

Massachusetts delegate Elbridge Gerry "thought we [should have] nothing to do with the conduct of the States as to Slaves, but ought to be careful not to give any sanction to it." Does the "compromise" represented by the slavery clauses achieve this goal?

Compare, in this respect, another author's comment on the slave trade guarantee in Art. I, § 9, cl. 1:

> The doctrine of slavery is unpopular in this country and contrary to the sentiments of the more sensible part of the people. Nevertheless . . . it cannot be got rid of at one stroke. The interests of the Southern States are immediately involved in it. Their system of business cannot be altered at once without ruin. In this circumstance, the Constitution does everything which a constitution could reasonably do. It provides for the interest of the Southern States, and, at the same time, manifests to the world that slavery is inconsistent with the views and sentiments of this country, which error will be reformed as soon as it can be done consistent with the interest of the people.

A Letter from a Gentleman in a Neighbouring State, to a Gentleman in this City, 3 DHRC 390 (Oct. 31, 1787).

Assume that the slave states would not have ratified the Constitution without these clauses, or something like them. Would you have voted to ratify the Constitution with these clauses as the price of national union? The following materials may bear on your answer.

During the ratification debates, some opponents of the constitution argued that the Constitution's accommodation of slavery was reason enough to reject it. It's often said that we shouldn't impose our own modern moral judgments on the past. What would the following authors say about that?

Consider Arms, Malachi Maynard, & Samuel Field, Dissent to the Massachusetts Convention

Hampshire Gazette (April 16, 1788)

. . . It is a standing law in the kingdom of Heaven, "Do unto others as ye would have others do unto you." This is the royal law—this we often hear inculcated upon others. But had we [voted in favor of ratifying the Constitution], could we have claimed to ourselves that consistent line of conduct, which marks the path of every honest man? Should we not rather have been guilty of a contumelious repugnancy, to what we profess to believe is equitable and just? . . .

Where is the man, who under the influence of sober dispassionate reasoning, and not void of natural affection, can lay his hand upon his heart and say, I am willing my sons and my daughters should be torn from me and doomed to perpetual slavery? We presume that man is not to be found amongst us: And yet we think the consequence is fairly drawn, that this is what every man ought to be able to say, who voted for this constitution. . . . Notwithstanding this we will practise this upon those who are destitute of the power of repulsion. . . .

If we could once make it our own case, we should soon discover what distress & anxiety, what poignant feelings it would produce in our own breasts, to have our infants torn from the bosoms of their tender mothers—indeed our children of all ages, from infancy to manhood, arrested from us by a banditti of lawless ruffians, in defiance of all the laws of humanity, and carried to a country far distant, without any hopes of their return—attended likewise with the cutting reflection, that they were likely to undergo all those indignities, those miseries, which are the usual concomitants of slavery.

Indeed when we consider the depredations committed in Africa, the cruelties exercised towards the poor captivated inhabitants of that country on their passage to this—crowded by droves into the holds of ships, suffering what might naturally be expected would result from scanty provisions, and inelastic infectious air, and after their arrival, drove like brutes from market to market, branded on their naked bodies with hot irons, with the initial letters of their masters names—fed upon the entrails of beasts like swine in the slaughter-yard of a butcher; and many other barbarities, of which we have documents well authenticated: then put to the hardest of labour, and to perform the vilest of drudges—their master (or rather usurpers) by far less kind and benevolent to them, than to their horses and their hounds. . . .

When we hear those barbarities pled for—When we see them voted for, (as in the late [Ratification] Convention at Boston) when we see them practised by those who denominate themselves Christians, we are presented with something truely heterogeneous—something monstrous indeed! . . .

This practice of enslaving mankind is in direct opposition to a fundamental maxim of truth, on which our state constitution is founded, viz. "All men are born free and equal." This is our motto. We have said it—we cannot go back. . . .

"Phileleutheros"

Hampshire Gazette (June 4, 1788)

. . . If we cannot connect with the southern states without giving countenance to blood and carnage, and all kinds of fraud and injustice, I say let them go—Often do we see unhappy convicts led forth to execution for only taking the property of another—The Congress by the new Constitution are to make laws for the punishment of piracy and murder upon the high seas—But all this seems only to respect white people—the Africans may be pirated, hacked and tortured, and all with impunity.

> "Is there not?" sure there is, "some chosen curse,
> Some hidden thunder in the stores of heaven,
> Red with uncommon wrath, to blast the men.
> Who sport with lives and drain out human blood?"[c]

Despite serious opposition on various grounds, including some of those canvassed above, New York's convention ratified the Constitution by a 30–27 vote on July 26, 1788, but with a recommendation that a bill of rights be added to it. The following month, the North Carolina convention refused ratification. Rhode Island, still obdurate, meanwhile refused even to hold a convention. But with all the other states in the fold, Congress in September set in motion the machinery for putting the new government into place pursuant to Article VII of the Constitution.

March 4, 1789, was designated as the date for the First Congress to meet, and in theory for the first Presidential term to begin, but neither House had a quorum until April. Presidential electors were chosen in January and cast their votes in February. Only ten states participated in the election; in addition to North Carolina and Rhode Island, New York, still ambivalent despite the designation of New York City as the new government's capital, refused to designate electors. All 69 electors who participated cast one of their two votes for Washington, and he was therefore chosen as President; John Adams received 34 votes, easily the second highest total, and so he was chosen as Vice President. Each of them took their oaths in April 1789, and the government was in

---

[c]   "Phileleutheros" is quoting from Joseph Addison's *Cato: A Tragedy* (1713).

place. On November 21, North Carolina ratified the Constitution, and finally, on May 29, 1790, so did Rhode Island, by a 34–32 vote.

FOR DISCUSSION

Was the Constitution legitimate when it was adopted? Could it have been justified as an amendment—a total amendment, to be sure—of the Articles, pursuant to the resolution authorizing the Philadelphia convention? Who might have had a claim to be injured by implementation of the new system? If the Constitution was not legitimate when it was adopted, when (if ever) did it become legitimate, and why?

How should we think about the ratification of the Constitution: as an agreement of the states, as an agreement of "the People," or in some other way? Here are discussions from two cases—first, one of the great early landmarks of American constitutional law; and second, a more recent case addressing an important question of governmental structure.

In *McCulloch v Maryland*, the State of Maryland attempted to enforce a tax on the Second Bank of the United States. The Court, per Chief Justice John Marshall, unanimously held the tax unconstitutional; in doing so, it held that creation of the Bank was a valid exercise of Congressional power.

CROSS REFERENCE   *McCulloch* is presented more fully at pp. 356–368.

McCulloch v. Maryland

Supreme Court of the United States, 1819.
17 U.S. (4 Wheat.) 316.

. . . In discussing this question, the counsel for the State of Maryland have deemed it of some importance, in the construction of the constitution, to consider that instrument, not as emanating from the people, but as the act of sovereign and independent States. [According to the Court's reporter, counsel for Maryland said that the Constitution is "a compact between the States, and all the powers which are not expressly relinquished by it, are reserved to the States."] The powers of the general government, it has been said, are delegated by the States, who alone are truly sovereign; and must be exercised in subordination to the States, who alone possess supreme dominion. It would be

difficult to sustain this proposition. The Convention which framed the constitution was indeed elected by the State legislatures. But the instrument, when it
came from their hands, was a mere proposal, without obligation, or pretensions
to it. It was reported to the then existing Congress of the United States, with
a request that it might "be submitted to a Convention of Delegates, chosen in
each State by the people thereof, under the recommendation of its Legislature,
for their assent and ratification." This mode of proceeding was adopted; and by
the Convention, by Congress, and by the State Legislatures, the instrument
was submitted to the people. They acted upon it in the only manner in which
they can act safely, effectively and wisely, on such a subject, by assembling in
Convention. It is true, they assembled in their several States—and where else
should they have assembled? No political dreamer was ever wild enough to think
of breaking down the lines which separate the States, and of compounding
the American people into one common mass. Of consequence, when they act,
they act in their States. But the measures they adopt do not, on that account,
cease to be the measures of the people themselves, or become the measures of
the state governments.

From these Conventions, the constitution derives its whole authority. The
government proceeds directly from the people; is "ordained and established,"
in the name of the people; and is declared to be ordained, "in order to form a
more perfect union, establish justice, insure domestic tranquillity, and secure
the blessings of liberty to themselves and to their posterity." The assent of the
States, in their sovereign capacity, is implied, in calling a Convention, and thus
submitting that instrument to the people. But the people were at perfect liberty to accept or reject it; and their act was final. It required not the affirmance,
and could not be negatived, by the State governments. The constitution, when
thus adopted, was of complete obligation, and bound the State sovereignties.

It has been said, that the people had already surrendered all their powers
to the State sovereignties, and had nothing more to give. But, surely, the question whether they may resume and modify the powers granted to government,
does not remain to be settled in this country. Much more might the legitimacy
of the general government be doubted, had it been created by the States. The
powers delegated to the State sovereignties were to be exercised by themselves,
not by a distinct and independent sovereignty, created by themselves. To the
formation of a league, such as was the confederation, the State sovereignties
were certainly competent. But when, "in order to form a more perfect union,"
it was deemed necessary to change this alliance into an effective government,

possessing great and sovereign powers, and acting directly on the people, the necessity of referring it to the people, and of deriving its powers directly from them, was felt and acknowledged by all. The government of the Union, then (whatever may be the influence of this fact on the case), is, emphatically and truly, a government of the people. In form, and in substance, it emanates from them. Its powers are granted by them, and are to be exercised directly on them, and for their benefit. . . .

In *U.S. Term Limits v. Thornton* (1995), an amendment to the Arkansas constitution prohibited the name of an otherwise-eligible candidate for the House of Representatives from appearing on the general election ballot if that candidate had already served three terms in the House; a similar provision applied to Senate candidates who had served two terms in that body. Numerous parties brought a challenge to this provision. A 5–4 majority of the Court, per Justice John Paul Stevens, held it unconstitutional.

Part of the disagreement between the majority and the dissenters concerned how to view the scope of state authority to regulate matters related to federal elections. In the majority's view, such power existed only to the extent authorized by, or pursuant to, the Constitution. In the dissent's view, such power should be considered part of the general body of powers reserved to the states by the absence of any contrary provision in the Constitution, with the reservation confirmed by the Tenth Amendment. And that disagreement in turn stemmed from disagreement concerning the fundamental nature of the relationship created by the Constitution among the national government, the states, and the people. Although concurring opinions are usually printed before dissents, it makes sense here to present excerpts from Justice Thomas's dissent before excerpts from Justice Kennedy's concurring opinion.

U.S. Term Limits, Inc. v. Thornton

Supreme Court of the United States, 1995.
514 U.S. 779.

JUSTICE STEVENS delivered the opinion of the Court.

. . . With respect to setting qualifications for service in Congress, no such right existed before the Constitution was ratified. The contrary argument overlooks the revolutionary character of the Government that the Framers conceived. Prior to the adoption of the Constitution, the States had joined together under the Articles of Confederation. In that system, "the States retained most of their sovereignty, like independent nations bound together only by treaties." *Wesberry v. Sanders* (1964). After the Constitutional Convention convened, the Framers were presented with, and eventually adopted a variation of, "a plan not merely to amend the Articles of Confederation but to create an entirely new National Government with a National Executive, National Judiciary, and a National Legislature." *Id.* In adopting that plan, the Framers envisioned a uniform national system, rejecting the notion that the Nation was a collection of States, and instead creating a direct link between the National Government and the people of the United States. In that National Government, representatives owe primary allegiance not to the people of a State, but to the people of the Nation. As Justice Story observed, each Member of Congress is "an officer of the union, deriving his powers and qualifications from the constitution, and neither created by, dependent upon, nor controllable by, the states. . . . Those officers owe their existence and functions to the united voice of the whole, not of a portion, of the people." Representatives and Senators are as much officers of the entire Union as is the President. States thus "have just as much right, and no more, to prescribe new qualifications for a representative, as they have for a president. . . . It is no original prerogative of state power to appoint a representative, a senator, or president for the union." *Ibid.*[16]

We believe that the Constitution reflects the Framers' general agreement with the approach later articulated by Justice Story. For example, Art. I, § 5, cl. 1, provides: "Each House shall be the Judge of the Elections, Returns and

[16] The Constitution's provision for election of Senators by the state legislatures, see Art. I, § 3, cl. 1, is entirely consistent with this view. The power of state legislatures to elect Senators comes from an express delegation of power from the Constitution, and thus was not at all based on some aspect of original state power. Of course, with the adoption of the Seventeenth Amendment, state power over the election of Senators was eliminated, and Senators, like Representatives, were elected directly by the people.

Qualifications of its own Members." The text of the Constitution thus gives the representatives of all the people the final say in judging the qualifications of the representatives of any one State. For this reason, the dissent falters when it states that "the people of Georgia have no say over whom the people of Massachusetts select to represent them in Congress."

Two other sections of the Constitution further support our view of the Framers' vision. First, consistent with Story's view, the Constitution provides that the salaries of representatives should "be ascertained by Law, and paid out of the Treasury of the United States," Art. I, § 6, rather than by individual States. The salary provisions reflect the view that representatives owe their allegiance to the people, and not to the States. Second, the provisions governing elections reveal the Framers' understanding that powers over the election of federal officers had to be delegated to, rather than reserved by, the States. It is surely no coincidence that the context of federal elections provides one of the few areas in which the Constitution expressly requires action by the States, namely that "[t]he Times, Places and Manner of holding Elections for Senators and Representatives, shall be prescribed in each State by the Legislature thereof." Art. I, § 4, cl. 1. This duty parallels the duty under Article II that "Each State shall appoint, in such Manner as the Legislature thereof may direct, a Number of Electors." Art. II, § 1, cl. 2. These Clauses are express delegations of power to the States to act with respect to federal elections.

This conclusion is consistent with our previous recognition that, in certain limited contexts, the power to regulate the incidents of the federal system is not a reserved power of the States, but rather is delegated by the Constitution. Thus, we have noted that "[w]hile, in a loose sense, the right to vote for representatives in Congress is sometimes spoken of as a right derived from the states, . . . this statement is true only in the sense that the states are authorized by the Constitution, to legislate on the subject as provided by § 2 of Art. I." *United States v. Classic* (1941).

In short, as the Framers recognized, electing representatives to the National Legislature was a new right, arising from the Constitution itself. The Tenth Amendment thus provides no basis for concluding that the States possess reserved power to add qualifications to those that are fixed in the Constitution. Instead, any state power to set the qualifications for membership in Congress must derive not from the reserved powers of state sovereignty, but rather from the delegated powers of national sovereignty. In the absence of any constitutional delegation to the States of power to add qualifications to those enumerated in the Constitution, such a power does not exist. . . .

Justice Thomas, with whom The Chief Justice, Justice O'Connor, and Justice Scalia join, dissenting.

. . . Because the majority fundamentally misunderstands the notion of "reserved" powers, I start with some first principles. Contrary to the majority's suggestion, the people of the States need not point to any affirmative grant of power in the Constitution in order to prescribe qualifications for their representatives in Congress, or to authorize their elected state legislators to do so. . . .

Our system of government rests on one overriding principle: All power stems from the consent of the people. To phrase the principle in this way, however, is to be imprecise about something important to the notion of "reserved" powers. The ultimate source of the Constitution's authority is the consent of the people of each individual State, not the consent of the undifferentiated people of the Nation as a whole.

The ratification procedure erected by Article VII makes this point clear. The Constitution took effect once it had been ratified by the people gathered in convention in nine different States. But the Constitution went into effect only "between the States so ratifying the same," Art. VII; it did not bind the people of North Carolina until they had accepted it. In Madison's words, the popular consent upon which the Constitution's authority rests was "given by the people, not as individuals composing one entire nation, but as composing the distinct and independent States to which they respectively belong." The Federalist No. 39. Accord, Debates in the Several State Conventions on the Adoption of the Federal Constitution (J. Elliot 2d ed. 1876) (remarks of James Madison at the Virginia Convention).[1]

When they adopted the Federal Constitution, of course, the people of each State surrendered some of their authority to the United States (and hence

---

[1] The ringing initial words of the Constitution—"We the People of the United States"—convey something of the same idea. (In the Constitution, after all, "the United States" is consistently a plural noun. See Art. I, § 9, cl. 8; Art. II, § 1, cl. 7; Art. III, § 2, cl. 1; Art. III, § 3, cl. 1; cf. Amar, Of Sovereignty and Federalism, 96 Yale L.J. 1425, 1455 (1987) (noting this fact, though reaching other conclusions).) The Preamble that the Philadelphia Convention approved before sending the Constitution to the Committee of Style is even clearer. It began: "We the people of the States of New-Hampshire, Massachusetts, Rhode-Island and Providence Plantations, Connecticut, New-York, New-Jersey, Pennsylvania, Delaware, Maryland, Virginia, North-Carolina, South-Carolina, and Georgia. . . ." Records of the Federal Convention of 1787. Scholars have suggested that the Committee of Style adopted the current language because it was not clear that all the States would actually ratify the Constitution. M. Farrand, The Framing of the Constitution of the United States (1913). In this instance, at least, I agree with the majority that the Committee's edits did not work a substantive change in the Constitution.

to entities accountable to the people of other States as well as to themselves). They affirmatively deprived their States of certain powers, see, *e.g.*, Art. I, § 10, and they affirmatively conferred certain powers upon the Federal Government, see, *e.g.*, Art. I, § 8. Because the people of the several States are the only true source of power, however, the Federal Government enjoys no authority beyond what the Constitution confers: The Federal Government's powers are limited and enumerated. In the words of Justice Black: "The United States is entirely a creature of the Constitution. Its power and authority have no other source." *Reid v. Covert* (1957) (plurality opinion).

. . . As far as the Federal Constitution is concerned, then, the States can exercise all powers that the Constitution does not withhold from them. The Federal Government and the States thus face different default rules: Where the Constitution is silent about the exercise of a particular power—that is, where the Constitution does not speak either expressly or by necessary implication— the Federal Government lacks that power and the States enjoy it.

These basic principles are enshrined in the Tenth Amendment, which declares that all powers neither delegated to the Federal Government nor pro- hibited to the States "are reserved to the States respectively, or to the people." With this careful last phrase, the Amendment avoids taking any position on the division of power between the state governments and the people of the States: It is up to the people of each State to determine which "reserved" powers their state government may exercise. But the Amendment does make clear that powers reside at the state level except where the Constitution removes them from that level. All powers that the Constitution neither delegates to the Federal Govern- ment nor prohibits to the States are controlled by the people of each State. . . .

In short, the notion of popular sovereignty that undergirds the Con- stitution does not erase state boundaries, but rather tracks them. The people of each State obviously did trust their fate to the people of the several States when they consented to the Constitution; not only did they empower the gov- ernmental institutions of the United States, but they also agreed to be bound by constitutional amendments that they themselves refused to ratify. See Art. V (providing that proposed amendments shall take effect upon ratification by three-quarters of the States). At the same time, however, the people of each State retained their separate political identities. As Chief Justice Marshall put it, "[n]o political dreamer was ever wild enough to think of breaking down the lines which separate the States, and of compounding the American people into one common mass." *McCulloch.* . . .

In short, while the majority is correct that the Framers expected the selection process to create a "direct link" between Members of the House of Representatives and the people, the link was between the Representatives from each State and the people of that State; the people of Georgia have no say over whom the people of Massachusetts select to represent them in Congress. This arrangement must baffle the majority, whose understanding of Congress would surely fit more comfortably within a system of nationwide elections. But the fact remains that when it comes to the selection of Members of Congress, the people of each State have retained their independent political identity. As a result, there is absolutely nothing strange about the notion that the people of the States or their state legislatures possess "reserved" powers in this area. . . .

JUSTICE KENNEDY, concurring.

I join the opinion of the Court.

The majority and dissenting opinions demonstrate the intricacy of the question whether or not the Qualifications Clauses are exclusive. In my view, however, it is well settled that the whole people of the United States asserted their political identity and unity of purpose when they created the federal system. The dissent's course of reasoning suggesting otherwise might be construed to disparage the republican character of the National Government, and it seems appropriate to add these few remarks to explain why that course of argumentation runs counter to fundamental principles of federalism.

Federalism was our Nation's own discovery. The Framers split the atom of sovereignty. It was the genius of their idea that our citizens would have two political capacities, one state and one federal, each protected from incursion by the other. The resulting Constitution created a legal system unprecedented in form and design, establishing two orders of government, each with its own direct relationship, its own privity, its own set of mutual rights and obligations to the people who sustain it and are governed by it. It is appropriate to recall these origins, which instruct us as to the nature of the two different governments created and confirmed by the Constitution.

A distinctive character of the National Government, the mark of its legitimacy, is that it owes its existence to the act of the whole people who created it. It must be remembered that the National Government, too, is republican in essence and in theory. John Jay insisted on this point early in The Federalist Papers, in his comments on the government that preceded the one formed by the Constitution.

> To all general purposes we have uniformly been one people; each individual citizen everywhere enjoying the same national rights, privileges, and protection. . . .

> A strong sense of the value and blessings of union induced the people, at a very early period, to institute a federal government to preserve and perpetuate it. They formed it almost as soon as they had a political existence. . . .

The Federalist No. 2.

Once the National Government was formed under our Constitution, the same republican principles continued to guide its operation and practice. As James Madison explained, the House of Representatives "derive[s] its powers from the people of America," and "the operation of the government on the people in their individual capacities" makes it "a national government," not merely a federal one. *Federalist* No. 39. The Court confirmed this principle in *McCulloch*, when it said: "The government of the Union, then, . . . is, emphatically, and truly, a government of the people. In form and in substance it emanates from them. Its powers are granted by them, and are to be exercised directly on them, and for their benefit." . . .

In one sense it is true that "the people of each State retained their separate political identities," for the Constitution takes care both to preserve the States and to make use of their identities and structures at various points in organizing the federal union. It does not at all follow from this that the sole political identity of an American is with the State of his or her residence. It denies the dual character of the Federal Government which is its very foundation to assert that the people of the United States do not have a political identity as well, one independent of, though consistent with, their identity as citizens of the State of their residence. . . .

Of course, because the Framers recognized that state power and identity were essential parts of the federal balance, the Constitution is solicitous of the prerogatives of the States, even in an otherwise sovereign federal province. The Constitution uses state boundaries to fix the size of congressional delegations, Art. I, § 2, cl. 3, ensures that each State shall have at least one representative, *ibid.*, grants States certain powers over the times, places, and manner of federal elections (subject to congressional revision), Art. I, § 4, cl. 1, requires that when the President is elected by the House of Representatives, the delegations from each State have one vote, Art. II, § 1, cl. 3, and Amdt. 12, and allows States to appoint electors for the President, Art. II, § 1, cl. 2. Nothing in the Constitution or The Federalist Papers, however, supports the idea of state interference with the most basic relation between the National Government and its citizens, the selection of legislative representatives. . . .

There can be no doubt, if we are to respect the republican origins of the Nation and preserve its federal character, that there exists a federal right of citizenship, a relationship between the people of the Nation and their National Government, with which the States may not interfere. Because the Arkansas enactment intrudes upon this federal domain, it exceeds the boundaries of the Constitution.

For Discussion

(1) Suppose that in December 1789 the people of North Carolina had second thoughts. By the same process by which they had just elected one convention, they elected another, and this convention passed a resolution seceding from the Union. Would that resolution have been valid? Do the excerpts we have read cast any light on that issue?

(2) In most, if not all, states, the ballot presents the names of the candidates for President rather than the names of the candidates for elector, whom the people of the state actually choose on Election Day. Many states have statutes imposing penalties on electors who fail to vote for the designated candidate for President. Are such statutes valid? See *Chiafolo v. Washington* (2020). Does *Thornton* provide guidance?

Read the Constitution as it was originally adopted, *supra* pp. xlv–lxv and be prepared to discuss the following questions. If this exercise seems a bit like a review of high school civics, the effect is intentional. Far from being deep or difficult, most of these questions are clear-cut—unlike the questions that will most consume us, many of them can be answered readily from the text of the Constitution itself, and you should be able to answer some of them even before reading the Constitution. But before we go on to the tough questions it is important to be familiar with the text of the Constitution and with the fundamentals and some of the details of our constitutional structure. Indeed, Sandy Levinson, a leading contemporary constitutional scholar, has argued vigorously that "hard wiring" issues of structure and process, like some of those posed below, are among the most important ones of American constitutional law. Though much has changed since 1789, it is notable that much has remained the same, and that many significant matters are prescribed rather clearly by the text of the Constitution. We will also find that some of these seemingly straightforward questions suggest more difficult issues.

Some Questions About Constitutional Structure

The Lawmaking Process

(1) Congress, tired of spending most of its time in the budget process and eager to facilitate long-range military planning, enacts a five-year appropriation bill. Constitutional?

(2) Consider the following:

(a) On August 1, Congress passes and sends to the President a bill declaring the Carrier Dome a national shrine. The President takes the bill with him on vacation in Hawaii. On August 14 he vetoes it. Congress goes out of session on August 16. Is the bill law?

(b) Now suppose that Congress adjourns on August 6. Is the bill law?

(c) Now suppose that the President vetoes the bill on August 5 and that on August 6 the House votes to override the veto by 290–138, and the Senate by 62–35. Is the bill law?

(3) When the President addresses a Joint Session of Congress, who sits behind him? Why them?

(4) The proposed Equal Rights Amendment passed each house of Congress by a two-thirds vote. Did it at that point become part of the Constitution?

(5) President Lincoln signed the 13th Amendment. Was this necessary? President Franklin Roosevelt signed the resolution declaring war against Japan. Was this necessary?

Allocation of Power Within the Federal Government

(6) Suppose you would very much like to be a federal judge. What must happen for that to occur? If you get your wish, in what ways might you lose your job?

(7) Suppose the Senate advises and consents to the appointment of a Supreme Court nominee by a vote of 58–42, but the House passes a resolution disapproving it. What happens?

(8) What constitutional provision would you cite to justify President Obama's use of armed force in Libya without prior Congressional approval?

(9) Congress, concerned that the Supreme Court is unable to keep up with its workload, increases the Court's membership from nine to eleven. Constitutional? What if Congress's motive was to pack the Court with Justices more to its and the President's liking? Could Congress reduce the membership of the Court from nine to seven?

The Scope of Federal Powers

(10) The first President Bush vetoed a budget bill passed by Congress for the District of Columbia because it would provide funding for abortion. Previously, the entire Criminal Code of the District of Columbia was prescribed by Congress. By what authority does Congress legislate on such matters? Could Congress do the same for New Jersey? In what article and section of the Constitution would you look to find an answer to this question?

(11) Congress, concerned about the quality of justice in state courts, passes a law giving the federal courts concurrent jurisdiction with the state courts over any lawsuits in which the amount in controversy exceeds $1,000,000. Constitutional?

(12) In 1972, the California Supreme Court held that the death penalty violated both the federal and California constitutions. Could the United States Supreme Court review that decision?

Restraints on the States; Individual Rights and Liberties

(13) Wisconsin, deciding that a two-house legislature is wasteful, abolishes its Senate. Constitutional?

(14) Delaware is concerned about the high incidence of traffic accidents on its roads. By an act of its legislature, Delaware sets a statewide speed limit of 50 m.p.h. Suppose the National Highway Transportation Safety Administration is given general authority by Congress to make such regulations as it believes will expedite commerce on the Interstate Highway System. The NHTSA provides that the speed limit on all the interstates shall be 55 m.p.h. What is the legal speed limit on I-95 in Delaware?

(15) Virginia enacts a substantial tax on exports from the state, and makes it enforceable in actions brought before its justices of the peace. In such an enforcement action, what defense might be raised by an exporter who failed to pay the tax? Should the justice of the peace uphold that defense? What

if the same tax law, also enforceable before state justices of the peace, had been passed by Congress?

(16) Michigan and Ontario enter into an agreement coordinating police activity along the Detroit River. Constitutional?

C. Early Years of the Republic

1. Establishing the Federal Courts

The Constitution prescribed the creation of a Supreme Court, but left its form undefined. It also authorized, but did not clearly require, the creation of lower federal courts. The new Congress—which included 20 members who had been delegates to the Constitutional Convention—promptly turned its attention to these matters. While only eleven states were participating in the new government, Congress passed the First Judiciary Act on September 24, 1789. The Act accomplished numerous objectives.

First, it set up the Supreme Court, with a Chief Justice and five Associates, and established its jurisdiction. Why an even number of justices? The Act divided the nation into three circuits, and the anticipation was that two Justices would come from, and be assigned to, each circuit; of course, Congress could have created three seats for each circuit, but that might have struck it as wasteful.

Second, the Act set up a system of lower courts. Each state was constituted into one or more judicial districts, with a single judge for each district. The district courts were given jurisdiction over relatively small matters. Jurisdiction over more significant matters—as well as appellate jurisdiction over the district courts—was assigned to circuit courts. A circuit court consisted of two Supreme Court justices and the district judges from within that circuit. The jurisdiction of circuit courts included cases of diverse citizenship involving at least $500. (The jurisdictional threshold for federal diversity cases has been raised periodically over the years, and now stands at $75,000.) Between them, the district and circuit courts had jurisdiction over federal criminal matters— but there was no general grant of jurisdiction over civil cases arising under the laws of the United States.

For Discussion

(1) What do you suppose was to happen with cases arising under the laws of the United States?

(2) Is the jurisdictional threshold constitutional?

Third, the Act established various housekeeping rules for the courts. Some of those remain to the present day. For example, the first sentence of § 5, the All-Writs Act, which grants the federal courts power to grant writs "necessary for the exercise of their respective jurisdictions, and agreeable to the principles and usages of law," remains in substance as 28 U.S.C. § 1651(a). And § 34, the Rules of Decision Act, prescribed that

> the laws of the several states, except where the constitution, treaties or statutes of the United States shall otherwise require or provide, shall be regarded as rules of decision in trials at common law in the courts of the United States in cases where they apply.

Except for the substitution of "civil actions" for "trials at common law" and punctuation and capitalization changes, this provision remains as 28 U.S.C. § 1652.

FOR DISCUSSION   Duff, a citizen of New York, owns a private road in that state. Plunkett, a Pennsylvanian, is injured while walking across that road and brings an action against Duff in federal court in New York. Under New York law, Duff would not be liable for ordinary negligence; under the law as applied in most states, he would be. What law should the federal court apply? *Compare Erie R. Co. v. Tompkins* (1938) with *Swift v. Tyson* (1842).

Fourth, the statute established a United States Attorney for each judicial district.

2.   The Early Amendments—and the Latest

The 1215 Magna Carta and the 1689 English Bill of Rights were totemic bulwarks of liberty, both in English legal tradition and among the American revolutionaries. Those charters guaranteed individual rights such as due process, trial by jury, the right to petition government, and a prohibition on cruel and unusual punishment. Magna Carta and the English Bill of Rights also specified certain guarantees of collective self-governance, such as regular parliamentary elections, a prohibition on a standing army without legislative approval, and parliamentary immunity. Some of these guarantees were incorporated into the Constitution as drafted in Philadelphia—but many of them, including most of those relating to individual freedom, were not. During the national ratification debates that ensued, the Constitution's critics often focused on the omission of a bill of rights. Thomas Jefferson, for example, wrote James Madison from Paris (where he was serving as Ambassador) to warn that "a bill of rights is what the people are entitled to against every government on earth, general or particular, & what no just government should refuse, or rest on inferences." Consider the following perspectives on this question.

A Countryman II

New Haven Gazette (Nov. 22, 1787)

No bill of rights ever yet bound the supreme power longer than the honeymoon of a new married couple, unless the rulers were interested in preserving the rights; and in that case they have always been ready enough to declare the rights and to preserve them when they were declared. The famous English Magna Charta is but an act of Parliament, which every subsequent Parliament has had just as much constitutional power to repeal and annul as the Parliament which made it had to pass it at first. But the security of the nation has always been that their government was so formed that at least one branch of their legislature must be strongly interested to preserve the rights of the nation.

The Address and Reasons of Dissent of the Minority of the [Ratification] Convention of the State of Pennsylvania to their Constituents

December 18, 1787

[T]he construction of this [draft] constitution . . . would of itself, necessarily produce a despotism, and that not by the usual gradations, but with the celerity that has hitherto only attended revolutions effected by the sword. To establish the truth of this position, a cursory investigation of the principles and form of this constitution will suffice. The first consideration that this review suggests is the omission of a BILL OF RIGHTS ascertaining and fundamentally establishing those unalienable and personal rights of men, without the full, free, and secure enjoyment of which there can be no liberty, and over which it is not necessary for a good government to have the control. The principal of which are the rights of conscience, personal liberty by the clear and unequivocal establishment of the writ of *habeas corpus*, jury trial in criminal and civil cases, by an impartial jury of the vicinage or county; with the common law proceedings, for the safety of the accused in criminal prosecutions; and the liberty of the press, that scourge of tyrants, and the grand bulwark of every other liberty and privilege; the stipulation heretofore made in favor of them in the state constitutions are entirely superseded by this constitution.

The Federalist No. 84 (Alexander Hamilton)

Summer 1788

The most considerable of the remaining objections [to the draft Constitution] is that the plan of the convention contains no bill of rights. . . .

It has been several times truly remarked that bills of rights are, in their origin, stipulations between kings and their subjects, abridgements of prerogative in favor of privilege, reservations of rights not surrendered to the prince. Such was MAGNA CHARTA, obtained by the barons, sword in hand, from King John. . . . It is evident, therefore, that, according to their primitive signification, they have no application to constitutions professedly founded upon the power of the people, and executed by their immediate representatives and servants. Here, in strictness, the people surrender nothing; and as they retain every thing they have no need of particular reservations. . . .

I go further, and affirm that bills of rights, in the sense and to the extent in which they are contended for, are not only unnecessary in the proposed Constitution, but would even be dangerous. They would contain various exceptions to powers not granted; and, on this very account, would afford a colorable pretext to claim more than were granted. For why declare that things shall not be done which there is no power to do? Why, for instance, should it be said that the liberty of the press shall not be restrained, when no power is given by which restrictions may be imposed? I will not contend that such a provision would confer a regulating power; but it is evident that it would furnish, to men disposed to usurp, a plausible pretense for claiming that power. They might urge with a semblance of reason . . . that the provision against restraining the liberty of the press afforded a clear implication, that a power to prescribe proper regulations concerning it was intended to be vested in the national government. . . .

On the subject of the liberty of the press, as much as has been said, I cannot forbear adding a remark or two: in the first place, I observe, that there is not a syllable concerning it in the constitution of this State [i.e., New York]; in the next, I contend, that whatever has been said about it in that of any other State, amounts to nothing. What signifies a declaration, that "the liberty of the press shall be inviolably preserved"? What is the liberty of the press? Who can give it any definition which would not leave the utmost latitude for evasion? I hold it to be impracticable; and from this I infer, that its security, whatever fine declarations may be inserted in any constitution respecting it, must altogether depend on public opinion, and on the general spirit of the people and of the government. And here, after all, as is intimated upon another occasion, must we seek for the only solid basis of all our rights.

Letter from James Madison to Thomas Jefferson

October 17, 1788

My own opinion has always been in favor of a bill of rights; provided that it be so framed as not to imply powers not meant to be included in the enumeration. At the same time I have never thought the omission a material defect, nor been anxious to supply it even by subsequent amendment, for any other reason than that it is anxiously desired by others. I have favored it because I suppose it might be of use, and if properly executed could not be of disservice.

I have not viewed it in an important light—

1. Because I conceive that in a certain degree . . . the rights in question are reserved by the manner in which the federal powers are granted.

2. Because there is great reason to fear that a positive declaration of some of the most essential rights could not be obtained in the requisite latitude. I am sure that the rights of conscience in particular, if submitted to public definition would be narrowed much more than they are ever likely to be by an assumed power. One of the objections in New England was that the

Constitution by prohibiting religious tests, opened a door for Jews Turks & infidels.

3.   Because the limited powers of the federal Government and the jealousy of the subordinate Governments, afford a security which has not existed in the case of the State Governments, and exists in no other.

4.   Because experience proves the inefficiency of a bill of rights on those occasions when its controul is most needed. Repeated violations of these parchment barriers have been committed by overbearing majorities in every State. In Virginia I have seen the bill of rights violated in every instance where it has been opposed to a popular current. . . .

Wherever the real power in a government lies, there is the danger of oppression. In our Governments the real power lies in the majority of the Community, and the invasion of private rights is chiefly to be apprehended, not from acts of Government contrary to the sense of its constituents, but from acts in which the Government is the mere instrument of the major number of the Constituents. This is a truth of great importance, but not yet sufficiently attended to. . . . Wherever there is an interest and power to do wrong, wrong will generally be done, and not less readily by a powerful & interested party than by a powerful and interested prince. . . .

What use then it may be asked can a bill of rights serve in popular Governments? I answer the [two] following . . .

1.   The political truths declared in that solemn manner acquire by degrees the character of fundamental maxims of free Government, and as they become incorporated with the national sentiment, counteract the impulses of interest and passion.

2.   Altho it be generally true as above stated that the danger of oppression lies in the interested majorities of the people rather than in usurped acts of the Government, yet there may be occasions on which the evil may spring from the latter source; and on such, a bill of rights will be good ground for an appeal to the sense of the community. . . .

Supposing a bill of rights to be proper . . . I am inclined to think that absolute restrictions in cases that are doubtful, or where emergencies may overrule them, ought to be avoided. The restrictions however strongly marked on paper will never be regarded when opposed to the decided sense of the public, and after repeated violations in extraordinary cases they will lose even their ordinary efficacy. Should a Rebellion or insurrection alarm the people as well as the Government, and a suspension of the Hab[eas] Corp[us] be dictated by the alarm, no written prohibitions on earth would prevent the measure. . . . The best security ag[ain]st these evils is to remove the pretext for them.

Whoever had the best of this argument, the need for a bill of rights was a political fact. In several state conventions, support for the Constitution was qualified by demands that a Bill of Rights be added; indeed, the New York convention made this point an express part of its ratifying resolution. After reciting a long list of rights that bear a strong resemblance to the amendments later adopted, the New York delegates' ratifying resolution concluded:

> Under these impressions and declaring that the rights aforesaid cannot be abridged or violated, . . . [a]nd in confidence that the Amendments which shall have been proposed to the said Constitution will receive an early and mature Consideration: We the said Delegates, in the Name and in the behalf of the People of the State of New York Do by these presents Assent to and Ratify the said Constitution. In full Confidence nevertheless that until a Convention shall be called and convened for proposing Amendments to the said Constitution, the Militia of this State will not be continued in Service out of this State for a longer term than six weeks without the Consent of the Legislature thereof. . .

FOR DISCUSSION Why do you think the New York delegates included the last sentence quoted?

The First Congress promptly acted to satisfy the demands. On June 8, 1789, Madison introduced in the House a set of proposed amendments. Seventeen were passed by the House, but these were whittled down. On September 25—a day after approval of the Judiciary Act—Congress approved twelve and passed them on to the states, explicitly referring to the fact that several of the conventions had, "at the time of their adopting the Constitution, expressed a desire, in order to prevent misconstruction or abuse of its powers, that further declaratory and restrictive clauses should be added." The third through the twelfth were ratified in relatively short order, and constitute the First through Tenth Amendments to the Constitution—what we now refer to as the Bill of Rights.

The first of the proposed amendments, dealing with apportionment of the House of Representatives, failed to be ratified; apparently Madison forgot the basic lawyering principle that one should always put one's strongest point first. The second of the proposals—which provided that "No law varying the compensation for the services of the Senators and Representatives shall take effect, until an election of Representatives shall have intervened"—has had a much more interesting history. It was ratified by six states in the years immediately following its proposal, but then lay fallow. In 1873, Ohio, in protest against a retroactive Congressional pay raise, passed a ratifying resolution. And then the amendment returned to dormancy. In 1982, Gregory Watson, an undergraduate at the University of Texas at Austin, wrote a term paper contending that ratification was still a live possibility. He later recounted that he got a C because the teacher said that he had not made a viable case that the amendment was still pending. Undeterred, Watson embarked on a letter-writing campaign in support of the amendment. Ultimately, in 1992, a 38th state (Alabama) ratified the amendment, and it is now generally regarded as the Twenty-Seventh Amendment to the Constitution.

FOR DISCUSSION

Should Madison's proposal be accepted as the Twenty-Seventh amendment? If the amendment process is supposed to determine a strong degree of consensus across the American public, does the history of its ratification suffice?

Now suppose that in 1798 New Jersey adopted two statutes, one adopting the Church of England as the established church of the state, and the other prohibiting the possession of any handgun. It may seem strange, but the federal Constitution would have had nothing to say about either of these statutes. Despite some textual ambiguity, it was generally understood that the Bill of Rights applied only to the *federal* government. And the Court so held in 1833:

Barron v. City of Baltimore

Supreme Court of the United States, 1833.
32 U.S. (7 Pet.) 243.

Chief Justice Marshall delivered the opinion of the court.

[Barron owned a valuable wharf in Baltimore harbor. He contended that actions taken by the city, including regrading of streets, resulted in large deposits of sand and earth near the wharf, making it unusable by ships and so rendering it virtually worthless.]

. . . The plaintiff in error contends, that [the case] comes within that clause in the fifth amendment to the constitution, which inhibits the taking of private property for public use, without just compensation. He insists, that this amendment being in favor of the liberty of the citizen, ought to be so construed as to restrain the legislative power of a state, as well as that of the United States. If this proposition be untrue, the court can take no jurisdiction of the cause.

The question thus presented is, we think, of great importance, but not of much difficulty.

The constitution was ordained and established by the people of the United States for themselves, for their own government, and not for the government of the individual states. Each state established a constitution for itself, and in that constitution, provided such limitations and restrictions on the powers of its particular government, as its judgment dictated. The people of the United States framed such a government for the United States as they supposed best adapted to their situation and best calculated to promote their interests. The powers they conferred on this government were to be exercised by itself; and the limitations on power, if expressed in general terms, are naturally, and, we think, necessarily, applicable to the government created by the instrument. They are limitations of power granted in the instrument itself; not of distinct governments, framed by different persons and for different purposes.

If these propositions be correct, the fifth amendment must be understood as restraining the power of the general government, not as applicable to the states. In their several constitutions, they have imposed such restrictions on their respective governments, as their own wisdom suggested; such as they deemed most proper for themselves. It is a subject on which they judge exclusively, and with which others interfere no further than they are supposed to have a common interest.

The counsel for the plaintiff in error insists, that the constitution was intended to secure the people of the several states against the undue exercise of power by their respective state governments; as well as against that which might be attempted by their general government. In support of this argument he relies on the inhibitions contained in the tenth section of the first article.

We think, that section affords a strong, if not a conclusive, argument in support of the opinion already indicated by the court.

The preceding section contains restrictions which are obviously intended for the exclusive purpose of restraining the exercise of power by the departments of the general government. Some of them use language applicable only to congress; others are expressed in general terms. The third clause, for example, declares, that "no bill of attainder or *ex post facto* law shall be passed." No language can be more general; yet the demonstration is complete, that it applies solely to the government of the United States. In addition to the general arguments furnished by the instrument itself, some of which have been already suggested, the succeeding section, the avowed purpose of which is to restrain state legislation, contains in terms the very prohibition. It declares, that "no state shall pass any bill of attainder or *ex post facto* law." This provision, then, of the ninth section, however comprehensive its language, contains no restriction on state legislation.

The ninth section having enumerated, in the nature of a bill of rights, the limitations intended to be imposed on the powers of the general government, the tenth proceeds to enumerate those which were to operate on the state legislatures. These restrictions are brought together in the same section, and are by express words applied to the states. "No state shall enter into any treaty," &c. Perceiving, that in a constitution framed by the people of the United States, for the government of all, no limitation of the action of government on the people would apply to the state government, unless expressed in terms, the restrictions contained in the tenth section are in direct words so applied to the states.

It is worthy of remark, too, that these inhibitions generally restrain state legislation on subjects intrusted to the general government, or in which the people of all the states feel an interest.

A state is forbidden to enter into any treaty, alliance or confederation. If these compacts are with foreign nations, they interfere with the treaty-making power, which is conferred entirely on the general government; if with each other, for political purposes, they can scarcely fail to interfere with the general purpose and intent of the constitution. To grant letters of marque and reprisal, would lead directly to war; the power of declaring which is expressly given to congress. To coin money is also the exercise of a power conferred on congress. It would be tedious to recapitulate the several limitations on the powers of the states which are contained in this section. They will be found, generally, to restrain state legislation on subjects intrusted to the government of the Union, in which the citizens of all the states are interested. In these alone, were the whole people concerned. The question of their application to states is not left to construction. It is averred in positive words.

If the original constitution, in the ninth and tenth sections of the first article, draws this plain and marked line of discrimination between the limitations it imposes on the powers of the general government, and on those of the state; if, in every inhibition intended to act on state power, words are employed, which directly express that intent; some strong reason must be assigned for departing from this safe and judicious course, in framing the amendments, before that departure can be assumed.

We search in vain for that reason. Had the people of the several states, or any of them, required changes in their constitutions; had they required additional safe-guards to liberty from the apprehended encroachments of their particular governments; the remedy was in their own hands, and could have been applied by themselves. . . .

[I]t is universally understood, it is a part of the history of the day, that the great revolution which established the constitution of the United States, was not effected without immense opposition. Serious fears were extensively entertained, that those powers which the patriot statesmen, who then watched over the interests of our country, deemed essential to union, and to the attainment of those invaluable objects for which union was sought, might be exercised in a manner dangerous to liberty. In almost every convention by which the constitution was adopted, amendments to guard against the abuse of power were recommended. These amendments demanded security against the apprehended encroachments of the general government not against those of the local governments.

In compliance with a sentiment thus generally expressed, to quiet fears thus extensively entertained, amendments were proposed by the required majority in congress, and adopted by the states. These amendments contain no expression indicating an intention to apply them to the state governments. This court cannot so apply them.

We are of opinion, that the provision in the fifth amendment to the constitution, declaring that private property shall not be taken for public use, without just compensation, is intended solely as a limitation on the exercise of power by the government of the United States, and is not applicable to the legislation of the states.

The Eleventh Amendment was passed in response to the Supreme Court's first significant decision, *Chisholm v. Georgia* (1793). Chisholm, executor of the estate of one Farquhar and likewise a citizen of South Carolina, sued Georgia in the Supreme Court under the Court's original jurisdiction for payments due for goods supplied to the state during the Revolution. The state declined to appear, claiming that as a sovereign it was immune from suits absent its consent. The Court disagreed—and, in response, for the first time the Constitution was amended to nullify an unpopular Supreme Court decision. Read the Amendment.

Despite its rather narrow terms, the Eleventh Amendment has been held to assert broad immunity of the states from individuals' suits for damages brought without their consent. There are two large loopholes, however: First, actions for injunctive relief may be brought against state officers. *Ex parte Young,* 209 U.S. 123 (1908). Second, Congress may abrogate the immunity when acting under certain of its powers, principally those granted under amendments enacted after passage of the 11th. (A smaller loophole is that the Amendment says nothing about actions brought by the federal government.) Despite these exceptions, the Amendment is a significant limitation on federal power—indeed, perhaps greater than the more publicity-generating limitations that occupy more time in a typical constitutional law class. A significant percentage of all workers is employed by states, and therefore unable to bring individual actions enforcing much of the body of federal protective legislation.

 CROSS REFERENCE The Eleventh Amendment is discussed in greater detail below, pp. 633–634.

Finally, the Twelfth Amendment was passed in response to a great national crisis. The first two Presidential elections were uncontested, with Washington being named on every elector's ballot and John Adams easily coming in second, and so being elected Vice President. By 1796, a party system had begun to form, and Adams won a close election over Jefferson.

The election of 1796 was orderly. But the election of 1800 was not. This time Jefferson, representing the Democratic-Republican party, won a close presidential contest over John Adams, whose Federalists were by now badly divided. Both Jefferson and Aaron Burr were named on the ballot of every Democratic-Republican elector; various stories are told about why the plan to leave Burr's name off one ballot never came off.

FOR DISCUSSION

Jefferson had the second highest number of electoral votes in the 1796 election, more than the second highest Federalist, Thomas Pinckney. And so Jefferson, by now a bitter rival of Adams, became Vice President. Is that result a problem?

In any event, the election was thrown into the House of Representatives—the old House, still controlled by Federalists, many of whom preferred Burr to Jefferson. Ultimately, after 36 ballots, the deadlock was broken, largely because Alexander Hamilton threw his support to Jefferson over Burr, whom he found less trustworthy. This election marked the first time the opposition took over the Presidency. It was done peacefully in the end—a significant achievement—but the chaos was disturbing, and the Twelfth Amendment was adopted in direct response. Read it, in conjunction with Article II.

Some Questions About the Presidential Election Process

(1) Vermont has one Representative. How many electoral votes does it have? How many electoral votes did the District of Columbia have in 1804?

(2) George W. Bush won 271 of 538 electoral votes in the 2000 election. Suppose the Green ticket rather than the Republican one had won Wyoming. What would have happened then?

(3) In the 2000 campaign, Republicans insisted that Dick Cheney should be considered an inhabitant of Wyoming and not of Texas. Democrats did not strenuously object, perhaps because of fear that Republicans would contend that Hillary Clinton, who was running for the Senate, was not an

inhabitant of New York. What would have been the consequence if Cheney were considered an inhabitant of Texas, Bush's home state? If Clinton were not considered an inhabitant of New York? If these matters were in dispute, who would have decided them?

(4) Does the Constitution require that a state have a winner-take-all election for the state's Presidential electors?

3.   Assertion of the Power of Judicial Review

a.   The Neutrality Controversy

One of the first significant acts of the new Supreme Court was to say no to George Washington. As the wars between revolutionary France and much of the rest of Europe intensified, some very difficult questions of international law began to emerge for the young American republic—especially regarding the United States' legal obligations toward each side of the European conflict. On July 18, 1793, the Secretary of State, Thomas Jefferson, wrote to the members of the Court as follows:

PHILADELPHIA, July 18, 1793.

GENTLEMEN:

The war which has taken place among the powers of Europe produces frequent transactions within our ports and limits, on which questions arise of considerable difficulty, and of greater importance to the peace of the United States. These questions depend for their solution on the construction of our treaties, on the laws of nature and nations, and on the laws of the land, and are often presented under circumstances *which do not give a cognisance of them to the tribunals of the country.* Yet their decision is so little analogous to the ordinary functions of the executive, as to occasion much embarrassment and difficulty to them.

The President therefore would be much relieved if he found himself free to refer questions of this description to the opinions of the judges of the Supreme Court of the United States, whose knowledge of the subject would secure us against errors dangerous to the peace of the United States, and their authority insure the respect of all parties.

He has therefore asked the attendance of such of the judges as could be collected in time for the occasion, to know, in the first place, their opinion, whether the public may, with propriety, be availed of *their advice on these questions?* And if they may, to present, for their advice, the abstract questions which have already occurred, or may soon occur, from which they will themselves strike out such as any circumstances might, in their opinion, forbid them to pronounce on. I have the honour to be with sentiments of the most perfect respect, gentlemen.

Your most obedient and humble servant,

THOS. JEFFERSON.

Attached to the letter was a series of 29 questions—some in multiple parts—dealing with matters of treaty interpretation and international law. Here, just to give a flavor, are the first and the last:

1.   Do the treaties between the United States and France give to France or her citizens a *right*, when at war with a power with whom the United States are at peace, to fit out originally in and from the ports of the United States vessels armed for war, with or without commission? . . .

29.   May an armed vessel belonging to any of the belligerent powers follow *immediately* merchant vessels, enemies, departing from our ports, for the purpose of making prizes of them? If not, how long ought the former to remain, after the latter have sailed? And what shall be considered as the place of departure, from which the time is to be counted? And how are the facts to be ascertained?

Two days later, the Court replied, asking the administration to wait til the absent Brethren were in place. Take your time, Washington responded. On August 8, the Justices sent this letter to Washington:

PHILADELPHIA, 8th August, 1793.

SIR:

We have considered the previous question stated in a letter written by your direction to us by the Secretary of State on the 18th of last month, [regarding] the lines of separation drawn by the Constitution between the three departments of the government. These being in certain respects checks upon each other, and our being judges of a court in the last resort, are considerations which afford strong arguments against the propriety of our extra-judicially deciding the questions alluded to, especially as the power given by the Constitution to the President, of calling on the heads of departments for opinions, seems to have been *purposely* as well as expressly united to the *executive* departments.

We exceedingly regret every event that may cause embarrassment to your administration, but we derive consolation from the reflection that your judgment will discern what is right, and that your usual prudence, decision, and firmness will surmount every obstacle to the preservation of the rights, peace, and dignity of the United States.

We have the honour to be, with perfect respect, sir, your most obedient and most humble servants.

Did the Court get this one right? What is gained and what is lost by its abstemious view? Is there a textual basis in the Constitution for its decision? What does the separation of powers have to do with it? What does the fact that the Court is a court of last resort have to do with it? Could Washington have taken his questions to another federal court? (And if that court had given him answers, what would happen then?) Would it have been different if Washington had only propounded one question? Compare *Opinions of the Justices to the Senate*, 802 N.E.2d 565 (Mass. 2004):

FOR DISCUSSION

> Under Part II, c. 3, art. 2, of the Constitution of the Commonwealth [of Massachusetts], . . . "[e]ach branch of the legislature, as well as the governor or the council, shall have authority to require the opinions of the justices of the supreme judicial court, upon important questions of law, and upon solemn occasions." "[A] solemn occasion exists 'when the Governor or either branch of the Legislature, having some action in view, has serious doubts as to their power and authority to take such action, under the Constitution, or under existing statutes.' " *Answer of the Justices*, 364 Mass. 838 (1973), quoting *Answer of the Justices*, 148 Mass. 623 (1889).

The constitutional provision to which the Massachusetts justices refer traces back to the constitution of 1780, of which John Adams was the principal author.

---

b.   *Marbury v. Madison*

Contrast the Court's response to President Washington with its response a decade later to a litigant named William Marbury. As we will later see in more depth, infra at pp. 257–258, John Adams had appointed Marbury to a position as justice of the peace shortly before Adams left the presidency. The new Secretary of State, James Madison, refused to deliver Marbury's commission, so Marbury brought an action for a writ of mandamus in the Supreme Court to compel Madison to do so.

In the famous case of *Marbury v. Madison* (1803), the Supreme Court interpreted the Judiciary Act of 1789 as granting the Court statutory jurisdiction to issue the writ. But it also interpreted Article III of the Constitution as prohibiting Congress from granting such jurisdiction. Chief Justice John Marshall wrote the Court's unanimous opinion, and thought the question that resulted—"whether an act, repugnant to the constitution, can become the law of the land"—was, "happily, not of an intricacy proportioned to its interest." There were only two alternatives, with "no middle ground." Either the legislation is superior, in which case constitutions are "absurd attempts," or the Constitution is superior, in which case legislation repugnant to the Constitution "is not law." Unsurprisingly, Marshall chose the first option, and he drew the corollary that the legislation did not bind the courts "as if it was a law". The eventual holding of the case was that the Court did not have jurisdiction to grant the writ of mandamus that Marbury sought.

Thinking together about *Marbury* and the Justices' 1793 response to President Washington, it appears that: (1) if a question of constitutional law is properly presented in the context of a case properly before a court, the court will resolve the question (at least if that resolution is necessary for decision of the case), but (2) a court, at least in the federal system, should not resolve a constitutional question *unless* it is properly presented in the context of a live case.

FOR DISCUSSION

Does the fixation on a viable case make sense? The Supreme Court's practice and its own Rule 10 indicate clearly that the principal determining factor in its decision whether to review a case is not whether the decision below was correct; rather, in most cases, the principal factor is whether the court below decided a significant federal question in conflict with decisions of other courts; in other words, the Supreme Court's principal function is deciding unsettled questions of federal law that may arise repeatedly. Why then does it matter whether the question is presented in the context of a live case?

William Marbury and his fellow nominees to the District of Columbia court were not the only "midnight judges" that the lame-duck Federalists sought to install in 1801. From the beginning, Supreme Court Justices had complained about circuit riding. On February 13, 1801, just nineteen days before it expired, the Sixth Congress passed a law that relieved them of the duty and established a new set of circuit judges. With the aid of a friendly Senate, President Adams filled many of these positions. A year later, on March 8, 1802, the Republican Congress repealed the 1801 act. That knocked the circuit judges out of a job. A few weeks later, Congress passed a new Judiciary Act that provided for a more limited degree of circuit riding. But could the repealer of March 8 have been valid? In *Stuart v. Laird* (1803), decided just six days after *Marbury*, the Court did not fully answer that question, but it signaled that it would not interfere with the legislation. The case did not involve a complaint by one of the judges who had been removed; rather, it was filed by a losing litigant whose case was begun in the original circuit court, transferred to the court created by the 1801 act, and then transferred back after the 1802 repealer. Per Justice Paterson (Marshall not expressing a public opinion, because he had sat on the case below), the Court said:

> Congress have constitutional authority to establish from time to time such inferior tribunals as they may think proper, and to transfer a cause from one such tribunal to another. In this last particular, there are no words in the constitution to prohibit or restrain the exercise of legislative power.

Another reason presented for reversal, Justice Paterson wrote, was

> that the judges of the supreme court have no right to sit as circuit judges, not being appointed as such, or in other words, that they ought to have distinct commissions for that purpose. To this objection, which is of recent date, it is sufficient to observe, that practice and acquiescence under it for a period of several years, commencing with the organization of the judicial system, afford an irresistible answer, and have indeed fixed the construction. It is a contemporary interpretation of the most forcible nature. This practical exposition is too strong and obstinate to be shaken or controlled. Of course, the question is at rest, and ought not now to be disturbed.

Ultimately, in 1869, Congress ended altogether the requirement that the justices ride circuit. They are, however, still entitled to sit with the lower courts if they so choose, and Chief Justice William Rehnquist occasionally did sit as a trial judge, with a helper judge alongside, so that he could get a feel for trial courts.

D. National and State Powers Before the Civil War

1. The Bank Issue

We have examined two major accomplishments of the First Congress—the Judiciary Act of 1789 and proposal of the Bill of Rights. A third was the creation of the first Bank of the United States.

The Bank was the brainchild of the Secretary of the Treasury, Alexander Hamilton. There were only three banks in the nation at the time, and a great multiplicity of currencies. Hamilton hoped that a great national bank would help create a more stable financial system and provide an efficient mechanism for the national government to borrow money, to hold funds, and to make payments. The Bank was a private corporation chartered by Congress for 20 years, with the United States owning 20% of the stock (which it purchased by borrowing from the Bank itself!), and the rest raised from private investors. The law provided that bills issued by the Bank could be used to pay debts owed to the United States, and that no other bank would be granted this privilege. In general, the northern mercantile class favored creation of the Bank, while the Southern agrarian interests opposed it. In the House, James Madison was one of the leaders of the opposition. Nevertheless, in part because Hamilton agreed to support moving the nation's capital to the south, both Houses passed the bill and presented it to President Washington.

Washington had doubts about the constitutionality of the bill, and—recognizing that he could not get advice from the Supreme Court—asked Attorney General Edmund Randolph and Secretary of State Thomas Jefferson for their opinions. Both advised him that it was unconstitutional. Struck by the force of their arguments, Washington invited Hamilton to respond. A week later, Hamilton did, and two days after that Washington signed the bill. Here are excerpts from the Jefferson and Hamilton opinions.

Thomas Jefferson, Opinion on the Constitutionality of a National Bank

February 15, 1791

The bill for establishing a National Bank undertakes among other things:

1. To form the subscribers into a corporation.

2. To enable them in their corporate capacities to receive grants of land; and so far is against the laws of *Mortmain.*

WORTH NOTING Jefferson was referring here to traditional doctrine prohibiting perpetual ownership of land by entities.

3. To make alien subscribers capable of holding lands; and so far is against the laws of *Alienage.*

4. To transmit these lands, on the death of a proprietor, to a certain line of successors; and so far changes the course of *Descents.*

5. To put the lands out of the reach of forfeiture or escheat; and so far is against the laws of *Forfeiture* and *Escheat.*

6. To transmit personal chattels to successors in a certain line; and so far is against the laws of *Distribution.*

7. To give them the sole and exclusive right of banking under the national authority; and so far is against the laws of *Monopoly.*

8. To communicate to them a power to make laws paramount to the laws of the States: for so they must be construed, to protect the institution from the control of the State legislatures; and so, probably, they will be construed.

I consider the foundation of the Constitution as laid on this ground: That "all powers not delegated to the United States by the Constitution, nor prohibited by it to the States, are reserved to the States or to the people." To take a single step beyond the boundaries thus specially drawn around the

WORTH NOTING Jefferson is quoting what we now know as the 10th amendment, which was not yet a part of the Constitution; it was ratified on December 15 of that year.

powers of Congress, is to take possession of a boundless field of power, no longer susceptible of any definition.

The incorporation of a bank, and the powers assumed by this bill, have not, in my opinion, been delegated to the United States by the Constitution.

I.   They are not among the powers specially enumerated: for these are:

1st.   A power to lay taxes for the purpose of paying the debts of the United States; but no debt is paid by this bill, nor any tax laid. Were it a bill to raise money, its origination in the Senate would condemn it by the Constitution.

2d.   "To borrow money." But this bill neither borrows money nor ensures the borrowing it. The proprietors of the bank will be just as free as any other money holders to lend or not to lend their money to the public. . . .

3d.   To "regulate commerce with foreign nations, and among the States, and with the Indian tribes." To erect a bank, and to regulate commerce, are very different acts. He who erects a bank, creates a subject of commerce in its bills; so does he who makes a bushel of wheat, or digs a dollar out of the mines; yet neither of these persons regulates commerce thereby. To make a thing which may be bought and sold, is not to prescribe regulations for buying and selling. Besides, if this was an exercise of the power of regulating commerce, it would be void, as extending as much to the internal commerce of every State as to its external. . . . Accordingly the bill does not propose the measure as a regulation of trade, but as "productive of considerable advantages to trade." Still less are these powers covered by any other of the special enumerations.

II.   Nor are they within either of the general phrases, which are the two following:—

1.   To lay taxes to provide for the general welfare of the United States, that is to say, "to lay taxes for *the purpose* of providing for the general welfare." For the laying of taxes is the *power* and the general welfare the *purpose* for which the power is to be exercised. They are not to lay taxes *ad libitum [as much as desired] for any purpose they please;* but only *to pay the debts or provide for the welfare of the Union.* In like manner, they are not *to do anything they please* to provide for the general welfare, but only to *lay taxes* for that purpose. To consider the latter phrase, not as describing the purpose of the first, but as giving a distinct and independent power to do any act they please, which might be for the good of the Union, would render all the preceding and subsequent enumerations of power completely useless.

It would reduce the whole instrument to a single phrase, that of instituting a Congress with power to do whatever would be for the good of the United States; and, as they would be the sole judges of the good or evil, it would be also a power to do whatever evil they please.

It is an established rule of construction where a phrase will bear either of two meanings, to give it that which will allow some meaning to the other parts of the instrument, and not that which would render all the others useless. Certainly no such universal power was meant to be given them. It was intended to lace them up straitly within the enumerated powers, and those without which, as means, these powers could not be carried into effect. It is known that the very power now proposed *as a means* was rejected as *an end* by the Convention which formed the Constitution. A proposition was made to them to authorize Congress to open canals, and an amendatory one to empower them to incorporate. But the whole was rejected, and one of the reasons for rejection urged in debate was, that then they would have a power to erect a bank, which would render the great cities, where there were prejudices and jealousies on the subject, adverse to the reception of the Constitution.

2. The second general phrase is "to make all laws *necessary* and proper for carrying into execution the enumerated powers." But they can all be carried into execution without a bank. A bank therefore is not *necessary,* and consequently not authorized by this phrase.

It has been urged that a bank will give great facility or convenience in the collection of taxes. Suppose this were true: yet the Constitution allows only the means which are *"necessary,"* not those which are merely "convenient" for effecting the enumerated powers. If such a latitude of construction be allowed to this phrase as to give any non-enumerated power, it will go to every one, for there is not one which ingenuity may not torture into a *convenience* in some instance *or other* to *some one* of so long a list of enumerated powers. . . . Therefore it was that the Constitution restrained them to the *necessary* means, that is to say, to those means without which the grant of power would be nugatory. . . .

Perhaps, indeed, bank bills may be a more *convenient* vehicle than treasury orders. But a little *difference* in the degree of *convenience,* cannot constitute the necessity which the constitution makes the ground for assuming any non-enumerated power. . . .

The negative of the President is the shield provided by the Constitution to protect against the invasions of the legislature: 1. The right of the Executive. 2.

Of the Judiciary. 3. Of the States and state legislatures. The present is the case of a right remaining exclusively with the states, and consequently one of those intended by the Constitution to be placed under its protection.

It must be added, however, that unless the President's mind on a view of everything which is urged for and against this bill is tolerably clear that it is unauthorized by the Constitution; if the pro and the con hang so even as to balance his judgment, a just respect for the wisdom of the legislature would naturally decide the balance in favor of their opinion. It is chiefly for cases where they are clearly misled by error, ambition, or interest, that the Constitution has placed a check in the negative of the President.

Alexander Hamilton, Opinion on the Constitutionality of a National Bank

February 23, 1791

The Secretary of the Treasury having perused with attention the papers containing the opinions of the Secretary of State and Attorney General concerning the constitutionality of the bill for establishing a National Bank proceeds according to the order of the President to submit the reasons which have induced him to entertain a different opinion. . . .

In entering upon the argument it ought to be premised that the objections of the Secretary of State and Attorney General are founded on a general denial of the authority of the United States to erect corporations. The latter indeed expressly admits that if there be anything in the bill which is not warranted by the Constitution, it is the clause of incorporation.

Now it appears to the Secretary of the Treasury that this *general principle* is *inherent* in the very *definition* of *Government* and *essential* to every step of the progress to be made by that of the United States: namely—that every power vested in a Government is in its nature *sovereign* and includes by *force* of the *term* a right to employ all the *means* requisite and fairly *applicable* to the attainment of the *ends* of such power; and which are not precluded by restrictions & exceptions specified in the Constitution, or not immoral, or not contrary to the essential ends of political society.

This principle in its application to Government in general would be admitted as an axiom. And it will be incumbent upon those who may incline to deny it to *prove* a distinction; and to shew that a rule which in the general system of things is essential to the preservation of the social order is inapplicable to the United States.

The circumstances that the powers of sovereignty are in this country divided between the national and state governments does not afford the distinction required. It does not follow from this that each of the *portions* of powers delegated to the one or to the other is not sovereign *with regard to its proper objects*. It will only *follow* from it that each has sovereign power as to *certain things*, and not as to *other things*. . . .

If it would be necessary to bring proof to a proposition so clear as that which affirms that the powers of the federal government, *as to its objects*, are sovereign, there is a clause of its Constitution which would be decisive. It is that which declares that the Constitution and the laws of the United States made in pursuance of it, and all treaties made or which shall be made under their authority shall be the supreme law of the land. The power which can create the *Supreme law* of the land, in any case, is doubtless sovereign *as to such case*. . . .

The first of [the] arguments [raised by Jefferson and Randolph against a federal power to create corporations] is that the foundation of the Constitution is laid on this ground "that all powers not delegated to the United States by the Constitution nor prohibited to it by the States are reserved to the States or to the people," whence it is meant to be inferred that Congress can in no case exercise any power not included in those enumerated in the Constitution. And it is affirmed that the power of erecting a corporation is not included in any of the enumerated powers.

The main proposition here laid down, in its true signification, is not to be questioned. It is nothing more than a consequence of this republican maxim, that all government is a delegation of power. But how much is delegated in each case is a question of fact to be made out by fair reasoning & construction upon the particular provisions of the Constitution—taking as guides the general principles & general ends of government.

It is not denied that there are *implied* as well as *express* powers, and that the former are as effectually delegated as the latter. And for the sake of accuracy it shall be mentioned that there is another class of powers which may be properly denominated *resulting* powers. It will not be doubted that if the United States should make a conquest of any of the territories of its neighbors, they would possess sovereign jurisdiction over the conquered territory. This would rather be a result from the whole mass of the powers of the government & from the nature of political society, than a consequence of either of the powers specially enumerated.

But be this as it may, it furnishes a striking illustration of the general doctrine contended for. It shews an extensive case in which a power of erecting corporations is either implied in or would result from some or all of the powers vested in the National Government. The jurisdiction acquired over such conquered territory would certainly be competent to every species of legislation. . . .

[A] power of erecting a corporation may as well be *implied* as any other thing; it may as well be employed as an *instrument* or *mean* of carrying into execution any of the specified powers as any other instrument or mean whatever. The only question must be, in this as in every other case, whether the mean to be employed, or in this instance the corporation to be erected, has a natural relation to any of the acknowledged objects or lawful ends of the government. Thus a corporation may not be erected by Congress for superintending the police of the city of Philadelphia because they are not authorized to *regulate* the *police* of that city; but one may be erected in relation to the collection of the taxes, or to the trade with foreign countries, or to the trade between the states, or with the Indian Tribes, because it is the province of the federal government to regulate those objects & because it is incident to a general *sovereign* or *legislative power* to *regulate* a thing to employ all the means which relate to its regulation to the *best & greatest advantage.*

A strange fallacy seems to have crept into the manner of thinking & reasoning upon the subject. Imagination appears to have been unusually busy concerning it. An incorporation seems to have been regarded as some great, independent, substantive thing—as a political end of peculiar magnitude & moment; whereas it is truly to be considered as a *quality, capacity,* or *mean* to an end. . . .

To this mode of reasoning respecting the right of employing all the means requisite to the execution of the specified powers of the government, it is objected that none but *necessary* & proper means are to be employed, & the Secretary of State maintains that no means are to be considered as *necessary* but those without which the grant of the power would be *nugatory.* Nay so far does he go in his restrictive interpretation of the word as even to make the case of *necessity* which shall warrant the constitutional exercise of the power to depend on *casual & temporary* circumstances, an idea which alone refutes the construction. The *expediency* of exercising a particular power, at a particular time, must indeed depend on *circumstances;* but the constitutional right of exercising it must be uniform & invariable—the same today as tomorrow.

All the arguments therefore against the constitutionality of the bill derived from the accidental existence of certain state-banks, institutions which *happen* to exist today, & for ought that concerns the government of the United States, may disappear tomorrow, must not only be rejected as fallacious, but must be viewed as demonstrative that there is a *radical* source of error in the reasoning.

It is essential to the being of the national government that so erroneous a conception of the meaning of the word *necessary* should be exploded.

It is certain that neither the grammatical nor popular sense of the term requires that construction. According to both, *necessary* often means no more than *needful, requisite, incidental, useful,* or *conducive* to. It is a common mode of expression to say that it is *necessary* for a government or a person to do this or that thing when nothing more is intended or understood than that the interests of the government or person require, or will be promoted, by the doing of this or that thing. The imagination can be at no loss for exemplification of the use of the word in this sense.

And it is the true one in which it is to be understood as used in the Constitution. The whole turn of the clause containing it indicates that it was the intent of the convention by that clause to give a liberal latitude to the exercise of the specified powers. . . . To understand the word as the Secretary of State does would be to depart from its obvious & popular sense, and to give it a *restrictive* operation; an idea never before entertained. It would be to give it the same force as if the word *absolutely* or *indispensably* had been prefixed to it.

Such a construction would beget endless uncertainty & embarrassment. The cases must be palpable & extreme in which it could be pronounced with certainty that a measure was absolutely necessary, or one without which the exercise of a given power would be nugatory. There are few measures of any government which would stand so severe a test. To insist upon it would be to make the criterion of the exercise of any implied power a *case of extreme necessity;* which is rather a rule to justify the overleaping of the bounds of constitutional authority than to govern the ordinary exercise of it. . . .

The practice of the government is against the rule of construction advocated by the Secretary of State. Of this the act concerning light houses, beacons, buoys & public piers is a decisive example. This doubtless must be referred to *interpretation of "necessary" has not been applied strictly about other powers.*

↓

regulating trade

the power of regulating trade, and is fairly relative to it. But it cannot be af-firmed that the exercise of that power, in this instance, was strictly necessary; or that the power itself would be *nugatory* without that of regulating establish-ments of this nature.

This restrictive interpretation of the word *necessary* is also contrary to this sound maxim of construction: namely, that the powers contained in a constitu-tion of government, especially those which concern the general administration of the affairs of a country, its finances, trade, defence, etc. ought to be construed liberally in advancement of the public good. This rule does not depend on the particular form of a government or on the particular demarkation of the bound-aries of its powers, but on the nature and objects of government itself. The means by which national exigencies are to be provided for, national inconveniencies obviated, national prosperity promoted, are of such infinite variety, extent and complexity, that there must, of necessity, be great latitude of discretion in the selection & application of those means. Hence, consequently, the necessity & propriety of exercising the authorities intrusted to a government on principles of liberal construction. . . .

In order to do "what is best" the clause needs to be construc-ted broadly since "best" provides so many limitless instances

It is no valid objection to the doctrine to say that it is calculated to extend the powers of the general government throughout the entire sphere of state legislation. The same thing has been said and may be said with regard to every exercise of power by *implication* or *construction*. The moment the literal meaning is departed from, there is a chance of error and abuse. And yet an adherence to the letter of its powers would at once arrest the motions of the government. . . .

Need a balance between the demanding literal interpretation + broad implication

It shall now be endeavored to be shewn that there is a power to erect [a cor-poration] of the kind proposed by the bill. . . . [I]t remains to shew the relation of such an institution to one or more of the specified powers of the government.

Accordingly it is affirmed that it has a relation more or less direct to the power of collecting taxes; to that of borrowing money; to that of regulating trade between the states; and to those of raising, supporting & maintaining fleets & armies. To the two former, the relation may be said to be *immediate*.

And, in the last place, it will be argued that it is, *clearly*, within the provi-sion which authorizes the making of all *needful* rules & *regulations* concerning the *property* of the United States, as the same has been practiced upon by the government.

A Bank relates to the collection of taxes in two ways; *indirectly*, by in-creasing the quantity of circulating medium & quickening circulation, which facilitates the means of paying—*directly,* by creating a *convenient species* of *medium* in which they are to be paid.

A Bank has a direct relation to the power of borrowing money, because it is a usual and in sudden emergencies an essential instrument in the obtaining of loans to government.

A nation is threatened with a war. Large sums are wanted, on a sudden, to make the requisite preparations. Taxes are laid for the purpose, but it requires time to obtain the benefit of them. Anticipation is indispensable. If there be a bank, the supply can at once be had; if there be none loans from individuals must be sought. The progress of these is often too slow for the exigency; in some situations they are not practicable at all. Frequently, when they are, it is of great consequence to be able to anticipate the product of them by advances from a bank. . . .

The institution of a bank has also a natural relation to the regulation of trade between the states: in so far as it is conducive to the creation of a convenient medium of *exchange* between them, and to the keeping up a full circulation by preventing the frequent displacement of the metals in reciprocal remittances. Money is the very hinge on which commerce turns. And this does not mean merely gold & silver; many other things have served the purpose with different degrees of utility. Paper has been extensively employed. . . .

There is a sort of evidence on this point arising from an aggregate view of the Constitution, which is of no inconsiderable weight. The very general power of laying & collecting taxes & appropriating their proceeds—that of borrowing money indefinitely—that of coining money & regulating foreign coins—that of making all needful rules and regulations respecting the property of the United States—these powers combined, as well as the reason & nature of the thing speak strongly [about] this language: That it is the manifest design and scope of the Constitution to vest in Congress all the powers requisite to the effectual administration of the finances of the United States. As far as concerns this object, there appears to be no parsimony of power. . . .

Little less than a prohibitory clause can destroy the strong presumptions which result from the general aspect of the government. Nothing but demonstration should exclude the idea that the power exists.

In all questions of this nature the practice of mankind ought to have great weight against the theories of individuals.

The fact, for instance, that all the principal commercial nations have made use of trading corporations or companies for the purposes of *external commerce* is a satisfactory proof that the establishment of them is an incident to the regulation of that commerce. . . .

———————————————

The first Bank's 20-year charter expired in 1811, while Madison—who, as you may recall, led opposition to the original charter in the House—was President. The charter was not renewed. But in the War of 1812, the nation experienced severe inflation, and the Government found its ability to borrow seriously impaired. In 1816, Congress chartered a new Bank, also for 20 years. Madison, still President, signed the bill. He had explained his change of heart on the constitutional question the previous year:

> [T]he question of the constitutional authority of the Legislature to establish an incorporated bank [has been] precluded in my judgment by repeated recognitions under varied circumstances of the validity of such an institution in acts of the legislative, executive, and judicial branches of the Government, accompanied by indications, in different modes, of a concurrence of the general will of the nation.

What do you think Madison is referring to here?

In 1817, the Bank opened a branch in Maryland. The next year, the Maryland legislature passed a statute requiring any bank operating in the state but not chartered by it to pay a stamp tax on notes issued by the bank. (The Bank of the United States was the only one meeting this description.) The head of the Maryland branch, James McCulloch, refused to pay the tax. The statute allowed for an "informer" to bring an action against a bank violating the statute, and one did that. The Maryland Court of Appeals, the state's highest court, upheld the statute, and McCulloch appealed to the United

CROSS REFERENCE We've seen some of *McCulloch* already, pp. 41–43, and will see more below, pp. 356–368.

States Supreme Court. In a unanimous opinion by Marshall, the Supreme Court held that the United States had constitutional power to establish the Bank, and that Maryland could not constitutionally tax it. Marshall's opinion makes arguments on the first issue much like Hamilton's.

In 1832, Congress sent President Andrew Jackson a bill to extend the charter of the Bank for fifteen years. The purpose of the early attempt to re-charter the Bank was to put the President in a dilemma. He had made clear his distaste for the Bank, but its proponents believed that if he dared to veto the bill in the middle of the campaign he would endanger his chance for re-election. Jackson was not one to shrink from a fight.

WORTH NOTING

Jackson's veto message was drafted largely by his Attorney General, Roger Taney.

President Andrew Jackson, Veto Message on Bill to Recharter the Second Bank of the United States

WASHINGTON, July 10, 1832.

To the Senate. . . .

A bank of the United States is in many respects convenient for the Government and useful to the people. Entertaining this opinion, and deeply impressed with the belief that some of the powers and privileges possessed by the existing bank are unauthorized by the Constitution, subversive of the rights of the States, and dangerous to the liberties of the people, I felt it my duty at an early period of my Administration to call the attention of Congress to the practicability of organizing an institution combining all its advantages and obviating these objections. I sincerely regret that in the act before me I can perceive none of those modifications of the bank charter which are necessary, in my opinion, to make it compatible with justice, with sound policy, or with the Constitution of our country. . . .

The powers, privileges, and favors bestowed upon [the Bank] in the original charter, by increasing the value of the stock far above its par value, operated as a gratuity of many millions to the stockholders. . . . The act before me proposes another gratuity to the holders of the same stock, and in many cases to the same men, of at least seven millions more. . . . It is not our own citizens only who are to receive the bounty of our Government. More than eight millions of the stock of this bank are held by foreigners. By this act the American Republic proposes virtually to make them a present of some millions of dollars.

For these gratuities to foreigners and to some of our own opulent citizens the act secures no equivalent whatever. . . .

I can not perceive the justice or policy of this course. If our Government must sell monopolies, it would seem to be its duty to take nothing less than their full value, and if gratuities must be made once in fifteen or twenty years let them not be bestowed on the subjects of a foreign government nor upon a designated and favored class of men in our own country. . . .

If we must have a bank with private stockholders, every consideration of sound policy and every impulse of American feeling admonishes that it should be purely American. Its stockholders should be composed exclusively of our own citizens, who at least ought to be friendly to our Government and willing to support it in times of difficulty and danger. . . .

It is maintained by the advocates of the bank that its constitutionality in all its features ought to be considered as settled by precedent and by the decision of the Supreme Court. To this conclusion I can not assent. Mere precedent is a dangerous source of authority, and should not be regarded as deciding questions of constitutional power except where the acquiescence of the people and the States can be considered as well settled. So far from this being the case on this subject, an argument against the bank might be based on precedent. One Congress, in 1791, decided in favor of a bank; another, in 1811, decided against it. One Congress, in 1815, decided against a bank; another, in 1816, decided in its favor. Prior to the present Congress, therefore, the precedents drawn from that source were equal. If we resort to the States, the expressions of legislative, judicial, and executive opinions against the bank have been probably to those in its favor as 4 to 1. There is nothing in precedent, therefore, which, if its authority were admitted, ought to weigh in favor of the act before me.

If the opinion of the Supreme Court covered the whole ground of this act, it ought not to control the coordinate authorities of this Government. The Congress, the Executive, and the Court must each for itself be guided by its own opinion of the Constitution. Each public officer who takes an oath to support the Constitution swears that he will support it as he understands it, and not as it is understood by others. It is as much the duty of the House of Representatives, of the Senate, and of the President to decide upon the constitutionality of any bill or resolution which may be presented to them for passage or approval as it is of the supreme judges when it may be brought before them for judicial decision. The opinion of the judges has no more authority over Congress than the opinion of Congress has over the judges, and on that point the President is independent of both. The authority of the Supreme Court must not, therefore, be permitted to control the Congress or the Executive when acting in their legislative capacities, but to have only such influence as the force of their reasoning may deserve.

WORTH NOTING

Jackson points out that the *McCulloch* Court asserted that the degree of necessity was a legislative question rather than a judicial one.

But in the case relied upon the Supreme Court have not decided that all the features of this corporation are compatible with the Constitution.

The principle here affirmed is that the "degree of its necessity," involving all the details of a banking institution, is a question exclusively for legislative consideration. A bank is constitutional, but it is the province of the Legislature to determine whether this or that particular power, privilege, or exemption is "necessary and proper" to enable the bank to discharge its duties to the Government, and from their decision there is no appeal to the courts of justice. Under the decision of the Supreme Court, therefore, it is the exclusive province of Congress and the President to decide whether the particular features of this act are necessary and proper in order to enable the bank to perform conveniently and efficiently the public duties assigned to it as a fiscal agent, and therefore constitutional, or unnecessary and improper, and therefore unconstitutional.

Without commenting on the general principle affirmed by the Supreme Court, let us examine the details of this act in accordance with the rule of legislative action which they have laid down. It will be found that many of the powers and privileges conferred on it can not be supposed necessary for the purpose for which it is proposed to be created, and are not, therefore, means necessary to attain the end in view, and consequently not justified by the Constitution. [Jackson quotes a section of the incorporating act providing that Congress would not establish any other banks for twenty years and notes that the pending bill would add another fifteen years of exclusivity.]

If Congress possessed the power to establish one bank, they had power to establish more than one if in their opinion two or more banks had been "necessary" to facilitate the execution of the powers delegated to them in the Constitution. If they possessed the power to establish a second bank, it was a power derived from the Constitution to be exercised from time to time, and at any time when the interests of the country or the emergencies of the

Government might make it expedient. It was possessed by one Congress as well as another, and by all Congresses alike, and alike at every session. But the Congress of 1816 have taken it away from their successors for twenty years, and the Congress of 1832 proposes to abolish it for fifteen years more. It can not be "necessary" or "proper" for Congress to barter away or divest themselves of any of the powers vested in them by the Constitution to be exercised for the public good. It is not "necessary" to the efficiency of the bank, nor is it "proper" in relation to themselves and their successors. They may properly use the discretion vested in them, but they may not limit the discretion of their successors. This restriction on themselves and grant of a monopoly to the bank is therefore unconstitutional. . . .

The Government of the United States have no constitutional power to purchase lands within the States except "for the erection of forts, magazines, arsenals, dockyards, and other needful buildings," and even for these objects only "by the consent of the legislature of the State in which the same shall be." By making themselves stockholders in the bank and granting to the corporation the power to purchase lands for other purposes they assume a power not granted in the Constitution and grant to others what they do not themselves possess. It is not necessary to the receiving, safe-keeping, or transmission of the funds of the Government that the bank should possess this power, and it is not proper that Congress should thus enlarge the powers delegated to them in the Constitution. . . .

The Government is the only "proper" judge where its agents should reside and keep their offices, because it best knows where their presence will be "necessary." It can not, therefore, be "necessary" or "proper" to authorize the bank to locate branches where it pleases to perform the public service, without consulting the Government, and contrary to its will. The principle laid down by the Supreme Court concedes that Congress can not establish a bank for purposes of private speculation and gain, but only as a means of executing the delegated powers of the General Government. By the same principle a branch bank can not constitutionally be established for other than public purposes. The power which this act gives to establish two branches in any State, without the injunction or request of the Government and for other than public purposes, is not "necessary" to the due execution of the powers delegated to Congress. . . .

It is maintained by some that the bank is a means of executing the constitutional power "to coin money and regulate the value thereof." Congress have established a mint to coin money and passed laws to regulate the value thereof. The money so coined, with its value so regulated, and such foreign coins as Congress may adopt are the only currency known to the Constitution. But if they have other power to regulate the currency, it was conferred to be exercised by themselves, and not to be transferred to a corporation. If the bank be established for that purpose, with a charter unalterable without its consent, Congress have parted with their power for a term of years, during which the Constitution is a dead letter. It is neither necessary nor proper to transfer its legislative power to such a bank, and therefore unconstitutional. . . .

If our power over means is so absolute that the Supreme Court will not call in question the constitutionality of an act of Congress the subject of which "is not prohibited, and is really calculated to effect any of the objects intrusted to the Government," although, as in the case before me, it takes away powers expressly granted to Congress and rights scrupulously reserved to the States, it becomes us to proceed in our legislation with the utmost caution. . . . That a bank of the United States, competent to all the duties which may be required by the Government, might be so organized as not to infringe on our own delegated powers or the reserved rights of the States I do not entertain a doubt. Had the Executive been called upon to furnish the project of such an institution, the duty would have been cheerfully performed. . . .

ANDREW JACKSON.

The next year, after his re-election, Jackson decided to take aggressive action against the Bank. By statute, the Secretary of the Treasury controlled the placement of the Government's deposits. Jackson told Secretary William Duane to remove the Government's deposits from the Bank. To his surprise, Duane refused, and so Jackson removed him. He then made a recess appointment of Taney, the most committed Bank opponent in the Cabinet, to the Treasury position. Taney removed the deposits, which crippled the Bank. When the Senate reconvened, it rejected Taney's nomination. Characteristically loyal, Jackson nominated Taney to a

WORTH NOTING The United States had no central bank from Jackson's time until the creation of the Federal Reserve System in 1913. The Fed has become a largely—but not completely! (see Ron Paul, *End the Fed* (2009))—accepted feature of American governance.

Supreme Court seat in 1835, but the Senate again refused. When Marshall died later that year, Jackson tried again, nominating Taney to be Chief Justice. Early in 1836, a divided Senate confirmed the nomination. Taney served until his death in 1864. Meanwhile the charter of the Bank expired in 1836; it continued for five years as a private bank before failing in 1841.

2.   The Nullification Crisis and Its Precursors

In 1798, the Federalist-dominated Congress passed the notorious Alien and Sedition Acts in an attempt to stifle dissent. The Democratic-Republican opposition responded with fury. The Kentucky legislature adopted a set of resolutions drafted by Thomas Jefferson, the first of which asserted:

> 1.   *Resolved*, That the several states composing the United States of America are not united on the principle of unlimited submission to their general government; but that, by compact, under the style and title of a Constitution for the United States, and of amendments thereto, they constituted a general government for special purposes, delegated to that government certain definite powers, reserving, each state to itself, the residuary mass of right to their own self-government; and that whensoever the general government assumes undelegated powers, its acts are unauthoritative, void, and of no force; that to this compact each state acceded as a state, and is an integral party; that this government, created by this compact, was not made the exclusive or final judge of the extent of the powers delegated to itself, since that would have made its discretion, and not the Constitution, the measure of its powers; but that, as in all other cases of compact among powers having no common judge, *each party has an equal right to judge for itself, as well of infractions as of the mode and measure of redress.*

Virginia adopted a similar set of resolutions, drafted by James Madison. No other state followed, but the so-called "Principles of '98" gained a foothold in American constitutional debate. For instance, in 1814, the Massachusetts legislature adopted a resolution declaring that "[w]henever the national compact is violated, and the citizens of this State are oppressed by cruel and unauthorized laws, this Legislature is bound to interpose its power, and wrest from the oppressor its victim."

Far more significantly, in 1832, South Carolina adopted an Ordinance of Nullification, prompted by two federal tariff acts that it regarded as unduly onerous and unfairly favorable to northern states. The Nullification Ordinance declared that both Congress's so-called "Tariff of Abominations" of 1828 and a sucessor tariff of 1832 had "violated the true meaning and intent" of the Constitution and were therefore "null, void, and no law, nor binding upon this State, its officers or citizens." In response, President Jackson issued a proclamation that was drafted by his Secretary of State Edward Livingston. Characteristically, he pulled no punches:

> I consider . . . the power to annul a law of the United States, assumed by one State, *incompatible with the existence of the Union, contradicted expressly by the letter of the Constitution, unauthorized by its spirit, inconsistent with every principle on which It was founded, and destructive of the great object for which it was formed.*

Just before Jackson's second term began, he persuaded Congress to enact the so-called Force Bill of 1833 to compel South Carolina's compliance with the tariff acts. One of the statute's provisions gave the President temporary authority to use military force where necessary to overcome resistance to the execution of federal law. Not long afterwards, Congress passed a compromise tariff reducing some of the most bitterly-opposed exactions, and South Carolina repealed the nullification ordinance. And so the crisis passed—although the dispute about constitutional structure remained unresolved, and would re-emerge in far more virulent form a quarter century later.

3.   The Commerce Power

Marshall's opinion in *McCulloch* did not elaborate very much on any particular Congressional power. His opinion in *Gibbons v. Ogden* (1824) articulated a broad conception of Congress's power under the Commerce Clause, allowing it to regulate not only things moving *in* commerce but also matters that *affect* interstate commerce.

 Gibbons is presented below, pp. 379–387.

While *Gibbons* thus paved the way for the Commerce Clause to develop into the greatest source of national power, Congress did not actually regulate commerce aggressively for many years to come.

The principal importance of the Commerce Clause during this period was as a limitation on the power of the states. This doctrine—to which the curious name Dormant Commerce Clause has been attached—had roots in a suggestion by Marshall in *Gibbons* that Congress's power under the Clause is exclusive:

> It has been contended by the counsel for the appellant, that, as the word "to regulate" implies in its nature, full power over the thing to be regulated, it excludes, necessarily, the action of all others that would perform the same operation on the same thing. That regulation is designed for the entire result, applying to those parts which remain as they were, as well as to those which are altered. It produces a uniform whole, which is as much disturbed and deranged by changing what the regulating power designs to leave untouched, as that on which it has operated. There is great force in this argument, and the Court is not satisfied that it has been refuted.

The next two cases offer early examples of the doctrine that emerged.

Willson v. Black Bird Creek Marsh Company

Supreme Court of the United States, 1829.
27 U.S. 245.

[The Black Bird Creek Marsh Company was incorporated by an 1822 statute of Delaware and authorized to build a dam across Black Bird Creek, which it did. The creek was a navigable stream, with the tide flowing through it for some distance, but it passed through a deep marsh. Willson and his colleagues owned a sloop, the Sally, licensed and enrolled pursuant to federal law, which collided with and damaged the dam. The Company sued for trespass, seeking $20,000 in damages. The owners of the Sally contended, among other points, that the dam had been "wrongfully erected," because the creek was "a public and common navigable creek, in the nature of a highway, in which the tides have always flowed and reflowed; in which there was, and of right ought to have been, a certain common and public way," and that therefore they had a right to sail the sloop where the alleged trespass occurred. The Company won in state court, and the sloop owners sought review in the United States Supreme Court.]

MR CHIEF JUSTICE MARSHALL delivered the opinion of the Court.

. . . The Act of Assembly by which the plaintiffs were authorized to construct their dam shows plainly that this is one of those many creeks, passing through a deep level marsh adjoining the Delaware, up which the tide flows for some distance. The value of the property on its banks must be enhanced by excluding the water from the marsh, and the health of the inhabitants probably improved. Measures calculated to produce these objects, provided they do not come into collision with the powers of the General Government, are undoubtedly within those which are reserved to the States. But the measure authorised by this act stops a navigable creek, and must be supposed to abridge the rights of those who have been accustomed to use it. But this abridgement, unless it comes in conflict with the Constitution or a law of the United States, is an affair between the government of Delaware and its citizens of which this Court can take no cognizance.

The counsel for the plaintiffs in error insist that it comes in conflict with the power of the United States "to regulate commerce with foreign nations and among the several States." If Congress had passed any act which bore upon the case, any act in execution of the power to regulate commerce the object of which was to control State legislation over those small navigable creeks into which the tide flows, and which abound throughout the lower country of the middle and southern States, we should feel not much difficulty in saying that a State law coming in conflict with such act would be void. But Congress has passed no such act. The repugnancy of the law of Delaware to the Constitution is placed entirely on its repugnancy to the power to regulate commerce with for-eign nations and among the several States—a power which has not been so exercised as to affect the question. We do not think that the Act empowering the Black Bird Creek Marsh Company to place a dam across the creek can, under all the circumstances of the case, be considered as repugnant to the power to regulate commerce in its dormant State, or as being in conflict with any law passed on the subject. There is no error, and the judgment is affirmed.

FOR DISCUSSION Is this opinion consistent with Marshall's suggestion in *Gibbons* that the federal government has exclusive power to regulate interstate commerce?

The License Cases

Supreme Court of the United States, 1847.
46 U.S. (5 How.) 504.

Mr. Chief Justice Taney.

. . . The justices of this court do not . . . altogether agree in the principles upon which these cases are decided, and I therefore proceed to state the grounds upon which I concur in affirming the judgments. . . . Each of the cases has arisen upon State laws, passed for the purpose of discouraging the use of ardent spirits within their respective territories, by prohibiting their sale in small quantities, and without licenses previously obtained from the State authorities. . . .

[I]n the Rhode Island and Massachusetts cases, . . . the question is how far a State may regulate or prohibit the sale of ardent spirits, the importation of which from foreign countries has been authorized by Congress. Is such a law a regulation of foreign commerce, or of the internal traffic of the State?

It is unquestionably no easy task to mark by a certain and definite line the division between foreign and domestic commerce, and to fix the precise point, in relation to every important article, where the paramount power of Congress terminates, and that of the State begins. The constitution itself does not attempt to define these limits. They cannot be determined by the laws of Congress or the States, as neither can by its own legislation enlarge its own powers, or restrict those of the other. And as the constitution itself does not draw the line, the question is necessarily one for judicial decision, and depending altogether upon the words of the constitution.

This question came directly before the court for the first time in the case of *Brown v. The State of Maryland* [(1827), per Chief Justice Marshall]. And the court there held that an article authorized by a law of Congress to be imported continued to be a part of the foreign commerce of the country while it remained in the hands of the importer for sale, in the original bale, package, or vessel in which it was imported; that the authority given to import necessarily carried with it the right to sell the imported article in the form and shape in which it was imported, and that no State, either by direct assessment or by requiring a license from the importer before he was permitted to sell, could impose and burden upon him or the property imported beyond what the law of Congress had itself imposed; but that when the original package was broken up for use or for retail by the importer, and also when the commodity had passed from his hands into the hands of a purchaser, it ceased to be an import, or a part of foreign commerce, and became subject to the laws of the State, and might be taxed for State purposes, and the sale regulated by the State, like any other property. . . .

Adopting, therefore, the rule as laid down in *Brown v. The State of Maryland*, I proceed to apply it to the cases of Massachusetts and Rhode Island. The laws of Congress regulating foreign commerce authorize the importation of spirits, distilled liquors, and brandy, in casks or vessels not containing less than a certain quantity, specified in the laws upon this subject. . . .

It has . . . been suggested, that, if a State deems the traffic in ardent spirits to be injurious to its citizens, and calculated to introduce immorality, vice, and pauperism into the State, it may constitutionally refuse to permit its importation, notwithstanding the laws of Congress; and that a State may do this upon the same principles that it may resist and prevent the introduction of disease, pestilence, or pauperism from abroad. But it must be remembered that disease, pestilence, and pauperism are not subjects of commerce, although sometimes among its attendant evils. They are not things to be regulated and trafficked in, but to be prevented, as far as human foresight or human means can guard against them. But spirits and distilled liquors are universally admitted to be subjects of ownership and property, and are therefore subjects of exchange, barter, and traffic, like any other commodity in which a right of property exists. And Congress, under its general power to regulate commerce with foreign nations, may prescribe what article of merchandise shall be admitted, and what excluded; and may therefore admit, or not, as it shall deem best, the importation of ardent spirits. And inasmuch as the laws of Congress authorize their importation, no State has a right to prohibit their introduction.

But I do not understand the law of Massachusetts or Rhode Island as interfering with the trade in ardent spirits while the article remains a part of foreign commerce, and is in the hands of the importer for sale, in the cask or vessel in which the laws of Congress authorize it to be imported. These State laws act altogether upon the retail or domestic traffic within their respective borders. They act upon the article after it has passed the line of foreign commerce, and become a part of the general mass of property in the State. These laws may, indeed, discourage imports, and diminish the price which ardent spirits would otherwise bring. But although a State is bound to receive and to permit the sale by the importer of any article of merchandise which Congress authorizes to be imported, it is not bound to furnish a market for it, nor to abstain from the passage of any law which it may deem necessary or advisable to guard the health or morals of its citizens, although such law may discourage importation, or diminish the profits of the importer, or lessen the revenue of the general government. And if any State deems the retail and internal traffic in ardent spirits injurious to its citizens, and calculated to produce idleness, vice, or debauchery, I see nothing in the constitution of the United States to prevent it from regulating and restraining the traffic, or from prohibiting it altogether, if it thinks proper. . . .

And as these laws of Massachusetts and Rhode Island are not repugnant to the constitution of the United States, and do not come in conflict with any law of Congress passed in pursuance of its authority to regulate commerce with foreign nations and among the several States, there is no ground upon which this court can declare them to be void.

FOR DISCUSSION

In a passage omitted above, Taney asserts that the framers knew "that a multitude of minor regulations must be necessary, which Congress amid its great concerns could never find time to consider and provide." In Taney's view, what check (if any) is there on state legislation that might be of limited significance but harmful to interstate commerce?

Note also *Cooley v. Board of Wardens* (1851), which upheld a Pennsylvania statute that required all ships over a prescribed size either to hire a local pilot or to pay a fee when entering or leaving the port of Philadelphia. Justice Curtis's opinion for the Court took a more flexible and functional stance than prior cases had:

> Now the power to regulate commerce, embraces a vast field, containing not only many, but exceedingly various subjects, quite unlike in their nature; some imperatively demanding a single uniform rule, operating equally on the commerce of the United States in every port; and some, like the subject now in question, as imperatively demanding that diversity, which alone can meet the local necessities of navigation.
>
> Either absolutely to affirm, or deny that the nature of this power requires exclusive legislation by Congress, is to lose sight of the

nature of the subjects of this power, and to assert concerning all of them, what is really applicable but to a part. Whatever subjects of this power are in their nature national, or admit only of one uniform system, or plan of regulation, may justly be said to be of such a nature as to require exclusive legislation by Congress. That this cannot be affirmed of laws for the regulation of pilots and pilotage is plain.

E. Slavery Before the Civil War

During the 19th century, Northern revulsion against slavery steadily increased. Most Northerners disclaimed any intention of ending slavery in the slave-holding states of the South. But there were exceptions. One of the most eloquent and intellectually forceful assertions of the constitutional basis for emancipation came from Frederick Douglass, who had himself escaped from slavery to freedom in the North.

Frederick Douglass, Debate at the Scottish Anti-Slavery Society, The Constitution of the United States: Is it Pro-Slavery or Anti-Slavery?

(March 26, 1860)

. . . The real question between the parties differing at this point in America may be fairly stated thus:—"Does the United States constitution guarantee to any class or description of people in that country the right to enslave or hold as property any other class or description of people in that country?" . . .

FOR DISCUSSION

Does Douglass correctly frame the "real question"?

What is the constitution? It is no vague, indefinite, floating, unsubstantial something, called, according to any man's fancy, now a weasel and now a whale. But it is something substantial. It is a plainly written document; not in Hebrew nor in Greek, but in English, beginning with a preamble, fitted out with articles, sections, provisions, and clauses, defining the rights, powers, and duties to be secured, claimed, and exercised under its authority. It is not even like the British constitution. It is not made up of enactments of parliament, decisions of courts, and the established usages of the government. The American constitution is a written instrument, full and complete in itself. No court, no congress, no legislature, no combination in the country can add one word to it, or take one word from it. . . . It is a great national enactment, done by the people, and can only be altered, amended, or changed in any way, shape, or form by the people who enacted it. . . .

It should also be borne in mind that the intentions of those who framed the constitution, be they good or bad, be they for slavery or against slavery, are to be respected so far, and so far only, as they have succeeded in getting these intentions expressed in the written instrument itself. . . . It would be the wildest of absurdities, and would lead to the most endless confusions and mischiefs, if, instead of looking to the written instrument itself for its meaning, it were attempted to make us go in search of what could be the secret motives and dishonest intentions of some of the men who might have taken part in writing or adopting it. It was what they said that was adopted by the people; not what they were ashamed or afraid to say, or really omitted to say. It was not what they tried, nor what they concealed; it was what they wrote down, not what they kept back, that the people adopted. It was only what was declared upon its face that was adopted—not their secret understandings, if there were any such understandings.

Bear in mind, also, . . . that the framers of the constitution, the men who wrote the constitution, sat with closed doors in the city of Philadelphia while they wrote it. They sat with closed doors, and this was done purposely, that nothing but the result, the pure result of their labours should be seen, and that that result might stand alone and be judged of on its own merits, and adopted on its own merits, without any influence being exerted upon them by the debates. . . .

Again, where would be the advantage of a written constitution, I pray you, if, after we have it written, instead of looking to its plain, common sense reading, we should go in search of its meaning to the secret intentions of the individuals who may have had something to do with writing the paper? What will the people of America a hundred years hence, care about the intentions of the men who framed the constitution of the United States? These men were for a day—for a generation, but the constitution is for ages; and, a hundred years hence, the very names of the men who took part in framing that instrument will, perhaps, be blotted out or forgotten. . . .

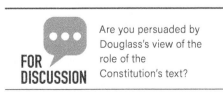

FOR DISCUSSION Are you persuaded by Douglass's view of the role of the Constitution's text?

[Douglass reads the three-fifths clause of art. I, § 2; art. I, § 8, cl. 15; art. I, § 9, cl. 1; and art. IV, § 2, cl. 3.] Here then are the provisions of the constitution which the most extravagant defenders of slavery have ever claimed to guarantee the right of property in man. These are the provisions which have been [fraudulently] pressed into the service of the human fleshmongers of America; let us look at them just as they stand, one by one.

You will notice there is not a word said there about "slave-trade," not a word said there about "slave insurrections;" not a word there about "three-fifths representation of slaves;" not a word there which any man outside of America, and who had not been accustomed to claim these particular provisions of the Constitution, would ever suspect had the remotest reference to slavery. *I deny utterly that these provisions of these constitution guarantee, or were intended to guarantee, in any shape or form, the right of property in man in the United States.*

But let us grant, for the sake of argument, *that the first of these provisions, referring to the basis of representation and taxation, does refer to slaves.*

We are not compelled to make this admission, for it might fairly apply, and indeed was intended to apply, to aliens and others, living in the United States, but who were not naturalised. But giving the provision the very worst construction—that it applies to slaves—what does it amount to?

I answer—and see you bear it in mind, for it shows the disposition of the constitution to slavery—I take the very worst aspect, and admit all that is claimed or that can be admitted consistently with truth; and I answer that this very provision, supposing it refers to slaves, is in itself a downright disability imposed upon the slave system of America, *one which deprives the slaveholding States of at least two-fifths of their natural basis of representation.* Therefore, instead of encouraging slavery, the constitution encourages freedom, by *holding out to every slaveholding State the inducement of an increase of two-fifths of political power by becoming a free State.*

So much for the three-fifths clause; taking it at its worst, it still leans to freedom, not to slavery; for be it remembered that, the constitution nowhere forbids a black man to vote. No "white," no "black," no "slaves," no "slaveholder"—nowhere in the instrument are any of these words to be found.

FOR DISCUSSION

Is Douglass correct that the three-fifths clause encourages freedom? If so, what is the legal significance of this?

I come to the next, that which it is said *guarantees the continuance of the African slave-trade* for twenty years. I will also take that for just what my opponent alleges it to have been, although the constitution does not warrant any such conclusion. But . . . let us suppose it did, and what follows?

Why, this—that this part of the constitution of the United States *expired by its own limitation no fewer than fifty two years ago.* My opponent is just fifty-two years too late in seeking the dissolution of the Union on account of this clause, for it expired as far back as 1808. . . . I ask is the constitution of the United States to be condemned to everlasting infamy because of what was done fifty-two years ago?

But there is still more to be said about this provision of the constitution. At the time the constitution was adopted, the slave trade was regarded as the jugular vein of slavery itself, and it was thought that slavery would die with the death of the slave trade. . . . The fathers who framed the American constitution supposed [likewise] that in making provision for the abolition of the African slave-trade they were making provision for the abolition of slavery itself, and they incorporated this clause in the constitution, not to perpetuate the traffic in human flesh, but to bring that unnatural traffic to an end. Outside of the Union the slave-trade could be carried on to an indefinite period; but the men who framed the constitution, and who proposed its adoption, *said to the slave States*—If you would purchase the privileges of this Union, you must consent that the humanity of this nation shall lay its hand upon this traffic at least in twenty years after the adoption of the constitution. So much for the African slave-trade clause. . . .

FOR DISCUSSION Is Douglass able to draw an argument of any constitutional significance from the fact that the Constitution authorized Congress to abolish the importation of slaves beginning in 1808?

But there is one other provision called the "Fugitive Slave Provision." It is called so by those who wish it to subserve the interests of slavery. . . . To whom does it apply if not to slaves? I answer that *it applied at the time of its adoption to a very numerous class of persons in America; and I have the authority of no less a person* than Daniel Webster that it was intended to apply to that class of men—a class of persons known in America as "Redemptioners."

There was quite a number of them at that day, who had been taken to America precisely as coolies have been taken to the West Indies. They entered into a contract to serve and labour so long for so much money, and the children born to them in that condition were also held as bound to "service and labour." It also applies "*indentured apprentices*," and to *persons* taking upon themselves an obligation to "serve and labour." The constitution says that the party shall be delivered up to whom such service and labour may be due.

Why, sir, due!

FOR DISCUSSION

Are you persuaded by Douglass's reading of this provision of art. IV, § 2?

In the first place this very clause of that provision makes it utterly impossible that it *can* apply to slaves. There is nothing *due* from the slave to his master in the way of service or labour. He is unable to show a contract. The thing implies an arrangement, an understanding, by which, for an equivalent, I will do for you so much, if you will do for me, or have done for me, so much.

The constitution says he will be delivered up to whom any service or labour shall be due. Due!

A slave owes nothing to any master; he can owe nothing to any master. In the eye of the law he is a chattel personal, to all intents, purposes, and constructions whatever. Talk of a horse owing something to his master, or a sheep, or a wheel-barrow! Perfectly ridiculous! The idea that a slave can owe anything!

I tell you what I would do if . . . I were a judge, and a slave was brought before me under this provision of the constitution, and the master should insist upon my sending him back to slavery, I should inquire how the slave was bound to serve and labour for him. I would point him to this same constitution, and tell him that I read in that constitution the great words of your own Magna Charta—"No person shall be deprived of life, liberty, or property without the process of law"—and I ought to know by what contract, how this man contracted an obligation, or took upon himself to serve and labour for you. And if he could not show that, I should dismiss the case and restore the man to his liberty. And I would do quite right, according to the constitution.

I admit nothing in favour of slavery when liberty is at stake; when I am called upon to argue on behalf of liberty I will range throughout the world, I am at perfect liberty by forms of law and by the roles of hermeneutics to range through the whole universe of God in proof of an innocent purpose, in proof of a good thing; but if you want to prove a bad thing, if you want to accomplish a bad and violent purpose, you must show it is so named in the bond. This is a sound legal rule. . . .

Slavery is not among [the objects stated in the preamble to the Constitution]; the objects are union, defence, welfare, tranquillity, justice, and liberty. Now, if the two last—to say nothing of the defence—if the two last purposes declared were reduced to practice, slavery would go reeling to its grave as if smitten with a bolt from heaven.

Let but the American people be true to their own constitution, true to the purposes set forth in that constitution, and we will have no need of a dissolution of the Union—we will have a dissolution of slavery all over that country.

But it has been said that negroes are not included in the benefits sought under this [preamble] declaration of purposes. . . . The constitution says "We the people;" the language is "we the people;" not we the white people, not we the citizens, not we the privileged class, not we the high, not we the low, not we of English extraction, not we of French or of Scotch extraction, but "we the people;" not we the horses, sheep, and swine, and wheelbarrows, but we the human inhabitants; and unless you deny that negroes are people, they are included within the purposes of this government.

They were there, and if we the people are included, negroes are included; they have a right, in the name of the constitution of the United States, to demand their liberty. This, I undertake to say, is the conclusion of the whole matter—*that the constitutionality of slavery can be made out only by discrediting the plain, common sense reading of the constitution itself* . . . .

For Discussion

(1) How might you respond to Douglass's argument that the Constitution itself rendered slavery unlawful?

(2) Consider what the constitutional status would be, at the time Douglass spoke, of the following:

  (a) a South Carolina statute abolishing slavery in the state.

  (b) a federal statute providing: "Neither slavery nor involuntary servitude, except as a punishment for crime whereof the party shall have been duly convicted, shall exist within the United States, or any place subject to their jurisdiction."

1. The Fugitive Slave Controversy

If the people held as slaves had always remained within the slave-holding states, the specifically national aspects of the slavery question might not ever have created a national crisis—or at least the crisis likely would have come later, and had a different shape. But the South was not hermetically sealed; sometimes enslaved people escaped to liberty, and sometimes the people enslaving them moved to different states. And so the institution of slavery threatened the continuance of the Union. Fundamentally, of course, the dispute was based on deep disagreement about the morality of slavery. But it played out in debates over the nature of federalism.

Reread Art. IV, § 2, cl. 3 of the Constitution, the Fugitive Slave Clause. In 1793, Congress passed a Fugitive Slave Law in an attempt to enforce this clause. Section 3 of the statute provided that if "a person held to labor" should escape into another part of the nation, the master or his agent was "empowered to seize or arrest" the fugitive, take him before any federal judge within the state, "or before any magistrate of a county, city, or town corporate, wherein such seizure or arrest shall be made"; on proof satisfactory to the judge or magistrate, "either by oral testimony or affidavit," that in fact the person seized owed service to the claimant, "it shall be the duty of such Judge or magistrate to give a certificate" allowing removal of the fugitive.

Over time, resistance to the return of fugitive slaves intensified in the North. In 1826, Pennsylvania passed a "personal liberty law," similar to statutes enacted by other Northern states, entitled "an act to give effect to the provisions of the constitution of the United States, relative to fugitives from labor, for the protection of free people of color, and to prevent kidnapping." Section 1 of the statute made it a felony to use "force or violence" to remove from the Commonwealth "any negro or mulatto" with the intention of causing the person to be detained as a slave. Subsequent sections of the statue provided procedures, somewhat more elaborate than those prescribed by the federal statute, under which a judge might issue a certificate for removal; a first warrant had to issue, which had to be supported by an affidavit completed by the claimant in his home state, and then the judge would hold another proceeding to determine whether the certificate of removal should issue.

Margaret Morgan's parents were enslaved in Maryland. Although never formally emancipated, they lived virtually as free people. Margaret was never claimed as a slave while in Maryland. In 1832, she moved with her free-born husband and their children to Pennsylvania; she had at least one more child there. In 1837, Edward Prigg, together with Nathan Beemis, the original owner's son-in-law, attempted to get a certificate for Morgan's removal. The justice of the peace refused, at least in part because of doubt as to Morgan's status. Prigg, Beemis, and two others then forcibly removed the entire family. After lengthy negotiations, Maryland agreed to extradite Prigg alone to Pennsylvania for trial under § 1 of the 1826 Act. Prigg was convicted, and appealed to the United States Supreme Court. With only Justice McLean dissenting, the Court reversed the conviction. *Prigg v. Pennsylvania* (1842). Atypically for the era, seven justices wrote opinions. The lead opinion was by Justice Story—a Massachusetts man, and no friend to slavery, but above all else a committed nationalist.

Near the beginning, Story's opinion in *Prigg* contained this remarkable passage:

FOR DISCUSSION

> Before proceeding to discuss the very important and interesting questions involved in this record, it is fit to say, that the cause has been conducted in the court below, and has been brought here by the co-operation and sanction, both of the state of Maryland, and the state of Pennsylvania, in the most friendly and courteous spirit, with a view to have those questions finally disposed of by the adjudication of this court; so that the agitations on this subject, in both states, which have had a tendency to interrupt the harmony between them, may subside, and the conflict of opinion be put at rest. It should also be added, that the statute of Pennsylvania of 1826, was (as has been suggested at the bar) passed with a view of meeting the supposed wishes of Maryland on the subject of fugitive slaves; and that, although it has failed to produce the good effects intended in its practical construction, the result was unforeseen and undesigned.

Does this reflect arrogance? Naiveté? The ability of law, and lawyers, to defuse passion-generating issues and handle them in a civil way?

Prigg and Maryland argued that the 1826 Pennsylvania statute was not valid—either because it was contrary to Article IV, or because it conflicted with the 1793 statute, or because the 1793 statute occupied the field. Story held that, by virtue of the constitutional language itself, slaveholders could recapture an escapee from chattel bondage without need for judicial process:

> [W]e have not the slightest hesitation in holding, that under and in virtue of the constitution, the owner of a slave is clothed with entire

authority, in every state in the Union, to seize and recapture his slave, whenever he can do it, without any breach of the peace or any illegal violence. In this sense, and to this extent, this clause of the constitution may properly be said to execute itself, and to require no aid from legislation, state or national.

Questions

(1) Does Story's conclusion seem to be a proper reading of the constitutional text?

(2) Can you think of a modern analogue to the power of recapture that Story articulates?

But Story went further. Pennsylvania claimed that the federal act was unconstitutional because it did not fall within the scope of any of Congress's enumerated powers. The Court held that the federal act was constitutional:

If, indeed, the constitution guaranties the right, and if it requires the delivery upon the claim of the owner (as cannot well be doubted), the natural inference certainly is, that the national government is clothed with the appropriate authority and functions to enforce it. The fundamental principle, applicable to all cases of this sort, would seem to be, that where the end is required, the means are given; and where the duty is enjoined, the ability to perform it is contemplated to exist, on the part of the functionaries to whom it is intrusted.

Questions

Was that the correct decision? If it is correct, what does that say about the sources of Congressional power under the Constitution? If Congress did *not* have authority to pass the statute, then what would the effect of the constitutional language be?

The Court then posed the question "whether the power of legislation upon this subject is exclusive in the national government, or concurrent in the states, until it is exercised by congress," and held that the power was exclusive:

It is scarcely conceivable, that the slave-holding states would have been satisfied with leaving to the legislation of the non-slave-holding states, a power of regulation, in the absence of that of congress, which would or might practically amount to a power to destroy the rights of the owner. If the argument, therefore, of a concurrent power in the states to act upon the subject-matter, in the absence of legislation by congress, be well founded; then, if congress had never acted at all, or if the act of congress should be repealed, without providing a substitute, there would be a resulting authority in each of the states to regulate the whole subject, at its pleasure, and to dole out its own remedial justice, or withhold it, at its pleasure, and according to its own views of policy and expediency.

Questions

Does that seem right? What would happen until such time as Congress legislated? Is this an area requiring—or capable of—nationwide uniformity? Could the Court have held the Pennsylvania statute unconstitutional on narrower grounds?

At the same time, Story did not mean that states lacked the power to return people who had escaped slavery, as a matter of their "general police power"—that is, the overall supervisory power that the states possess to act for the welfare of the state:

We entertain no doubt whatsoever, that the states, in virtue of their general police power, possess full jurisdiction to arrest and restrain runaway slaves, and remove them from their borders, and otherwise to secure themselves against their depredations and evil example, as they certainly may do in cases of idlers, vagabonds and paupers. The rights of the owners of fugitive slaves are in no just sense interfered with, or regulated, by such a course; and in many cases, the operations of this police power, although designed generally for other purposes, for protection, safety and peace of the state, may essentially promote and aid the interests of the owners. But such regulations can never be permitted to interfere with, or to obstruct, the just rights of the owner to reclaim his slave, derived from the constitution of the

United States, or with the remedies prescribed by congress to aid
and enforce the same.

Question

How does this square with the holding that Congress has exclusive jurisdiction
to pass legislation enforcing the constitutional clause?

After all this, it might surprise you to learn that, according to his son,
Story later spoke of *Prigg* as a "triumph of freedom." Its claim on that score is
attributable to passages absolving state officials from the responsibility of participating in the return of fugitives from slavery:

> The clause is found in the national constitution, and not in that
> of any state. It does not point out any state functionaries, or any state
> action, to carry its provisions into effect. The states cannot, therefore, be compelled to enforce them; and it might well be deemed an
> unconstitutional exercise of the power of interpretation, to insist,
> that the states are bound to provide means to carry into effect the
> duties of the national government, nowhere delegated or intrusted
> to them by the constitution. On the contrary, the natural, if not the
> necessary, conclusion is, that the national government, in the absence
> of all positive provisions to the contrary, is bound, through its own
> proper departments, legislative, judicial or executive, as the case may
> require, to carry into effect all the rights and duties imposed upon it
> by the constitution. . . .
>
> We hold the [federal] act to be clearly constitutional, in all
> its leading provisions, and, indeed, with the exception of that part
> which confers authority upon state magistrates, to be free from reasonable doubt and difficulty, upon the grounds already stated. As to
> the authority so conferred upon state magistrates, while a difference
> of opinion has existed, and may exist still, on the point, in different
> states, whether state magistrates are bound to act under it, none is
> entertained by this court, that state magistrates may, if they choose,
> exercise that authority, unless prohibited by state legislation.

Questions

Does this passage—which appears to be dictum*—declare part of the federal law unconstitutional? Is it correct?*

Some Northern states took up the invitation, prohibiting state officials from participating in the return of people who had escaped slavery. This hampered enforcement of the 1793 act, and so led to Southern pressure for a strengthened federal statute. One was passed as the critical component of the Compromise of 1850. The North got some significant benefits from the Compromise, including the admission of California as a free state and abolition of the slave trade in Washington, D.C. But the new Fugitive Slave Act was a very one-sided statute designed to make it easy for the claimant to secure the return of the alleged slave, and virtually impossible for the latter to resist. The statute also set up a system of federal commissioners in each district to provide a ready mechanism for issuing warrants of removal; this was an early instance of a federal bureaucracy spread across the nation.

The 1850 Act generated fierce resistance in the North. In one incident, Sherman Booth, an abolitionist in Wisconsin, led a mob that freed Joshua Glover, who had escaped from slavery, been captured, and was being held in federal custody. A federal marshal, Stephen Ableman, arrested Booth. But a justice of the Wisconsin Supreme Court issued a writ of habeas corpus, instructing Ableman to release Booth, on the ground that the 1850 Act was unconstitutional and that Booth was therefore being held illegally. While Ableman complied, the full court affirmed the single justice's order, and Ableman sought review in the United States Supreme Court. Meanwhile, Booth was tried and convicted in federal court of interfering with the 1850 Act, and then imprisoned; he was actually held by the sheriff of Milwaukee County. He went back to the state supreme court for another writ of habeas corpus, and again he won it; from this decision, the United States sought review in the United States Supreme Court. The two cases were heard together.

In *Ableman v. Booth* (1859), Chief Justice Taney wrote for a unanimous Court reversing the Wisconsin Supreme Court. His reasoning began from the premise that, if the Wisconsin courts were deemed to have the power they exercised in this case, "no offence against the laws of the United States [could] be punished by their own courts, without the permission and according to the judgment of the courts of the State in which the party happens to be imprisoned." Taney then wrote:

> The importance which the framers of the Constitution attached to . . . a tribunal [capable of resolving interstate conflicts], for the purpose of preserving internal tranquillity, is strikingly manifested by the clause which gives this court jurisdiction over the sovereign States which compose this Union, when a controversy arises between them. Instead of reserving the right to seek redress for injustice from another State by their sovereign powers, they have bound themselves to submit to the decision of this court, and to abide by its judgment. And it is not out of place to say, here, that experience has demonstrated that this power was not unwisely surrendered by the States; for in the time that has already elapsed since this Government came into existence, several irritating and angry controversies have taken place between adjoining States, in relation to their respective boundaries, and which have sometimes threatened to end in force and violence, but for the power vested in this court to hear them and decide between them. . . .
>
> We do not question the authority of State court, or judge, who is authorized by the laws of the State to issue the writ of habeas corpus, to issue it in any case where the party is imprisoned within its territorial limits, provided it does not appear, when the application is made, that the person imprisoned is in custody under the authority of the United States. The court or judge has a right to inquire, in this mode of proceeding, for what cause and by what authority the prisoner is confined within the territorial limits of the State sovereignty. . . .
>
> Now, it certainly can be no humiliation to the citizen of a republic to yield a ready obedience to the laws as administered by the constituted authorities. On the contrary, it is among his first and highest duties as a citizen, because free government cannot exist without it. Nor can it be inconsistent with the dignity of a sovereign State to observe faithfully, and in the spirit of sincerity and truth, the compact into which it voluntarily entered when it became a State of this Union. On the contrary, the highest honor of sovereignty is untarnished faith. And certainly no faith could be more deliberately and solemnly pledged than that which every State has plighted to the

other States to support the Constitution as it is, in all its provisions, until they shall be altered in the manner which the Constitution itself prescribes.

For Discussion

(1) What do you make of the fact that *Ableman* was unanimous? That it was written by Taney? Bear these questions in mind as you read *Scott v. Sandford*, below.

(2) It appears that Milwaukee County was providing jailing services for the federal government. The federal government could not require it to do so. What, then, was wrong with the state supreme court's order releasing Booth from the custody of the county sheriff?

2. The Mobility and Expansion of Slavery

The Missouri Compromise of 1820 admitted Maine as a free state and Missouri as a slave state, and prohibited slavery in the unorganized territory of the Great Plains, the former Louisiana Territory (other than Missouri itself) north of the parallel 36°30' north. In 1854, however, the Kansas-Nebraska Act, sponsored by Senator Stephen Douglas of Illinois, repealed that prohibition, providing instead for determination of the slavery question by a vote of the people—popular sovereignty—in the newly organized territories of Kansas and Nebraska. Northern outrage over the new law led to formation of the Republican Party, based on opposition to expansion of slavery. "Bleeding Kansas" became a flashpoint of the conflict, as partisans on both sides moved there to try to affect the outcome; ultimately, Kansas was admitted as a free state in January 1861.

COURSE THEME

Over the course of the nineteenth century, the national debate over slavery became closely tied to the problem of westward expansion. Slaveholders wanted slavery to be allowed in new territories, to preserve the economic viability of the institution, to protect slaveholding interests in the Senate, and to facilitate their own mobility. Naturally, opponents of slavery resisted expansion.

Slaveholders sometimes moved out of their states. One example was John Emerson, an army doctor, who purchased an enslaved man named Dred Scott in Missouri and traveled with him, first to the state of Illinois and then to Fort Snelling in the federal Wisconsin Territory—where Scott was allowed to marry. Illinois was part of the territory declared free by the Northwest Ordinance of 1787, and it was admitted as a free state in 1819. The Missouri Compromise had prescribed that the part of Wisconsin Territory that included Fort Snelling was free. Had Scott sued while in the North, he could presumably have secured his freedom. But he did not. Indeed, after Emerson was transferred back to Missouri, he left the Scotts up North; when he later sent for them, they traveled by themselves more than a thousand miles down the Mississippi to rejoin him, with a daughter born along the way.

After Emerson's death, Scott sued for his freedom in Missouri state court. He relied on a well-established Missouri doctrine known as "once free, always free," which would have required the courts to apply Illinois law and free Scott from slavery. In *Scott v. Emerson* (1852), however, the Missouri Supreme Court overruled its own longstanding precedent and denied Scott's petition for emancipation. The court reasoned:

> It is a humiliating spectacle, to see the courts of a State confiscating the property of her own citizens by the command of a foreign law. . . . On almost three sides the State of Missouri is surrounded by free soil. If one of our slaves touch that soil with his master's assent, he becomes entitled to his freedom. . . .

> Times are not now as they were when the former decisions on this subject were made[, requiring application of Illinois law under circumstances like these]. Since then not only individuals but States have been possessed with a dark and fell spirit in relation to slavery, whose gratification is sought in the pursuit of measures, whose inevitable consequences must be the overthrow and destruction of our government.

Missouri Chief Justice Gamble dissented on the ground that the court's refusal to apply "once free, always free" violated stare decisis: "I regard the question as conclusively settled [in Scott's favor], by repeated adjudications of this court."

As Scott's prospects in the Missouri courts dried up, he filed a federal action against John Sanford, Emerson's brother-in-law and the executor of his estate. (Sanford's name was misspelled in the United States Reports—a fitting legacy.) Scott based his claim to federal jurisdiction on diversity of citizenship: Sanford was a New Yorker, and Scott claimed to be a citizen of Missouri. After losing in Circuit Court on the basis of substantive Missouri law, Scott appealed to the United States Supreme Court.

The Supreme Court heard oral argument on the case twice, because "differences of opinion were found to exist among the members of the court" after the first argument. In the end, it ruled by a vote of 7–2, with Justices McLean and Curtis dissenting, that Scott remained enslaved. All nine justices wrote separate opinions, but Chief Justice Taney's opinion took the lead and in some respects spoke for a majority of the Court. In the words of Charles Evans Hughes, a 20th-century Chief Justice, the case was the greatest "self-inflicted wound" in the Court's history; it brought on the Court such intense contempt from the North that decades passed before the Court recovered its public standing.

Taney could have decided on narrow grounds by relying on "choice of law" precedent to apply Missouri law, under which Scott's northern sojourn did not set him free. But Taney decided to resolve broader issues, apparently hoping that he might settle the ongoing political conflict over slavery.

Scott v. Sandford

Supreme Court of the United States, 1857.
60 U.S. (19 How.) 393.

Opinion.

This case was brought up, by writ of error, from the Circuit Court of the United States for the district of Missouri. It was an action of trespass *vi et armis* instituted in the Circuit Court by Scott against Sandford. . . .

The declaration of Scott contained three counts: one, that Sandford had assaulted the plaintiff; one, that he had assaulted Harriet Scott, his wife; and one, that he had assaulted Eliza Scott and Lizzie Scott, his children. . . . At the times mentioned in the plaintiff's declaration, the defendant, claiming to be owner as aforesaid, laid his hands upon said plaintiff, Harriet, Eliza, and Lizzie, and imprisoned them, doing in this respect, however, no more than what he might lawfully do if they were of right his slaves at such times. . . .

Mr. Chief Justice Taney delivered the opinion of the court.

. . . There are two leading questions presented by the record:

1.   Had the Circuit Court of the United States jurisdiction to hear and determine the case between these parties? And

2.   If it had jurisdiction, is the judgment it has given erroneous or not?

The plaintiff in error, who was also the plaintiff in the court below, was, with his wife and children, held as slaves by the defendant, in the State of Missouri; and he brought this action in the Circuit Court of the United States for that district, to assert the title of himself and his family to freedom.

[I. Jurisdiction]

The declaration . . . contains the averment necessary to give the court jurisdiction; that he and the defendant are citizens of different States; that is, that he is a citizen of Missouri, and the defendant a citizen of New York.

WORTH NOTING Since Scott did not bring a federal claim, the only possible basis for Article III jurisdiction was diversity of citizenship. See U.S. Const, Art. III, Sec. 2 ("The judicial Power shall extend to . . . Controversies between . . . Citizens of different States").

The defendant pleaded in abatement to the jurisdiction of the court, that the plaintiff was not a citizen of the State of Missouri, as alleged in his declaration, being a negro of African descent, whose ancestors were of pure African blood, and who were brought into this country and sold as slaves. . .

The question is simply this: Can a negro, whose ancestors were imported into this country, and sold as slaves, become a member of the political community formed and brought into existence by the Constitution of the United States, and as such become entitled to all the rights, and privileges, and immunities, guaranteed by that instrument to the citizen? One of which rights is the privilege of suing in a court of the United States in the cases specified in the Constitution.

It will be observed, that the plea applies to that class of persons only whose ancestors were negroes of the African race, and imported into this country, and sold and held as slaves. The only matter in issue before the court, therefore, is, whether the descendants of such slaves, when they shall be emancipated, or who are born of parents who had become free before their birth, are citizens of a State, in the sense in which the word citizen is used in the Constitution of the United States. And this being the only matter in dispute on the pleadings, the court must be understood as speaking in this opinion of that class only, that is, of those persons who are the descendants of Africans who were imported into this country, and sold as slaves.

The situation of this population was altogether unlike that of the Indian race. The latter, it is true, formed no part of the colonial communities, and never amalgamated with them in social connections or in government. But although they were uncivilized, they were yet a free and independent people, associated together in nations or tribes, and governed by their own laws. . . . [T]hey may, without doubt, like the subjects of any other foreign Government, be naturalized by the authority of Congress, and become citizens of a State, and of the United States. . . .

The words "people of the United States" and "citizens" are synonymous terms, and mean the same thing. They both describe the political body who, according to our republican institutions, form the sovereignty, and who hold the power and conduct the Government through their representatives. . . .

The question before us is, whether the class of persons described in the plea in abatement compose a portion of this people, and are constituent members of this sovereignty? We think they are not, and that they are not included, and were not intended to be included, under the word "citizens" in the Constitution, and can therefore claim none of the rights and privileges which that instrument provides for and secures to citizens of the United States. On the contrary, they were at that time considered as a subordinate and inferior class of beings, who had been subjugated by the dominant race, and, whether emancipated or not, yet remained subject to their authority, and had no rights or privileges but such as those who held the power and the Government might choose to grant them.

It is not the province of the court to decide upon the justice or injustice, the policy or impolicy, of these laws. The decision of that question belonged to the political or law-making power; to those who formed the sovereignty and framed the Constitution. The duty of the court is, to interpret the instrument they have framed, with the best lights we can obtain on the subject, and to administer it as we find it, according to its true intent and meaning when it was adopted.

In discussing this question, we must not confound the rights of citizenship which a State may confer within its own limits, and the rights of citizenship as a member of the Union. . . . Each State may still confer [the rights of citizenship] upon an alien, or anyone it thinks proper, or upon any class or description of persons, yet he would not be a citizen in the sense in which that word is used in the Constitution of the United States. . . . nor entitled to sue as such in one of its courts, nor to the privileges and immunities of a citizen in the other States. The rights which he would acquire would be . . . restricted to the State which gave them. . . . It is very clear, therefore, that no State can, by any act or law of its own, passed since the adoption of the Constitution, introduce a new member into the political community created by the Constitution of the United States. It cannot make him a member of this community by making him a member of its own. . . . And, for the same reason, it cannot introduce any person or description of persons who were not intended to be embraced in this new political family which the Constitution brought into existence, but were intended to be excluded from it. . . .

It becomes necessary, therefore, to determine who were citizens of the several States when the Constitution was adopted. And in order to do this, we must recur to the Governments and institutions of the thirteen colonies, when they separated from Great Britain and formed new sovereignties, and took their places in the family of independent nations. . . .

In the opinion of the court, the legislation and histories of the times, and the language used in the Declaration of Independence, show, that neither the class of persons who had been imported as slaves, nor their descendants, whether they had become free or not, were then acknowledged as a part of the people, nor intended to be included in the general words used in that memorable instrument. It is difficult at this day to realize the state of public opinion in relation to that unfortunate race, which prevailed in the civilized and enlightened portions of the world at the time of the Declaration of Independence, and when the Constitution of the United States was framed and adopted. But the public history of every European nation displays it in a manner too plain to be mistaken.

They had for more than a century before been regarded as beings of an inferior order, and altogether unfit to associate with the white race, either in social or political relations; and so far inferior, that they had no rights which the white man was bound to respect; and that the negro might justly and lawfully be reduced to slavery for his benefit. He was bought and sold, and treated as an ordinary article of merchandise and traffic, whenever a profit could be made by it. This opinion was at that time fixed and universal in the civilized portion of the white race. . . .

And in no nation was this opinion more firmly fixed or more uniformly acted upon than by the English Government and English people. They not only seized them on the coast of Africa, and sold them or held them in slavery for their own use; but they took them as ordinary articles of merchandise to every country where they could make a profit on them, and were far more extensively engaged in this commerce than any other nation in the world.

The opinion thus entertained and acted upon in England was naturally impressed upon the colonies they founded on this side of the Atlantic. And, accordingly, a negro of the African race was regarded by them as an article of property, and held, and bought and sold as such, in every one of the thirteen colonies which united in the Declaration of Independence, and afterwards formed the Constitution of the United States. The slaves were more or less numerous in the different colonies, as slave labor was found more or less profitable. But no one seems to have doubted the correctness of the prevailing opinion of the time. . . .

The language of the Declaration of Independence is equally conclusive:

> . . . We hold these truths to be self-evident: that all men are created equal; that they are endowed by their Creator with certain unalienable rights; that among them is life, liberty, and the pursuit of happiness; that to secure these rights, Governments are instituted, deriving their just powers from the consent of the governed.

The general words above quoted would seem to embrace the whole human family, and if they were used in a similar instrument at this day would be so understood. But it is too clear for dispute, that the enslaved African race were not intended to be included, and formed no part of the people who framed and adopted this declaration; for if the language, as understood in that day, would embrace them, the conduct of the distinguished men who framed the Declaration of Independence would have been utterly and flagrantly inconsistent with the principles they asserted; and instead of the sympathy of mankind, to which they so confidently appealed, they would have deserved and received universal rebuke and reprobation. . . .

[T]here are two clauses in the Constitution which point directly and specifically to the negro race as a separate class of persons, and show clearly that they were not regarded as a portion of the people or citizens of the Government then formed. . . . [T]hese two provisions show, conclusively, that neither the description of persons therein referred to, nor their descendants, were embraced in any of the other provisions of the Constitution; for certainly these two clauses were not intended to confer on them or their posterity the blessings of liberty, or any of the personal rights so carefully provided for the citizen. . . .

CROSS REFERENCE Taney here discusses the Slave Trade Clause and the Fugitive Slave Clause. For more on each, see pp. 34–107 and pp. 97–107.

Indeed, when we look to the condition of this race in the several States at the time, it is impossible to believe that these rights and privileges were intended to be extended to them.

It is very true, that in that portion of the Union where the labor of the negro race was found to be unsuited to the climate and unprofitable to the master, but few slaves were held at the time of the Declaration of Independence; and when the Constitution was adopted, it had entirely worn out in one of them, and measures had been taken for its gradual abolition in several others. But this change had not been produced by any change of opinion in relation to this race; but because it was discovered, from experience, that slave labor was unsuited to the climate and productions of these States: for some of the States, where it had ceased or nearly ceased to exist, were actively engaged in the slave trade, procuring cargoes on the coast of Africa, and transporting them for sale to those parts of the Union where their labor was found to be profitable, and suited to the climate and productions. And this traffic was openly carried on, and fortunes accumulated by it, without reproach from the people of the States where they resided. And it can hardly be supposed that, in the States where it was then countenanced in its worst form—that is, in the seizure and transportation—the people could have regarded those who were emancipated as entitled to equal rights with themselves.

And we may here again refer, in support of this proposition, to the plain and unequivocal language of the laws of the several States, some passed after the Declaration of Independence and before the Constitution was adopted, and some since the Government went into operation.

We need not refer, on this point, particularly to the laws of the present slaveholding States. . . . They have continued to treat them as an inferior class, and to subject them to strict police regulations, drawing a broad line of distinction between the citizen and the slave races, and legislating in relation to them upon the same principle which prevailed at the time of the Declaration of Independence. As relates to these States, it is too plain for argument, that they have never been regarded as a part of the people or citizens of the State, nor supposed to possess any political rights which the dominant race might not withhold or grant at their pleasure. . . .

And if we turn to the legislation of the States where slavery had worn out, or measures taken for its speedy abolition, we shall find the same opinions and principles equally fixed and equally acted upon.

Thus, Massachusetts, in 1786, passed a law . . . [that] forbids the marriage of any white person with any negro, Indian, or mulatto, and inflicts a penalty of fifty pounds upon any one who shall join them in marriage; and declares all such marriage absolutely null and void, and degrades thus the unhappy issue of the marriage by fixing upon it the stain of bastardy. And this mark of degradation was renewed, and again impressed upon the race, in the careful and deliberate preparation of their revised code published in 1836. . . .

So, too, in Connecticut. We refer more particularly to the legislation of this State, because it was not only among the first to put an end to slavery within its own territory, but was the first to fix a mark of reprobation upon the African slave trade. . . . The first step taken by Connecticut upon this subject was as early as 1774, when it passed an act forbidding the further importation of slaves into the State. But the section containing the prohibition is introduced by the following preamble:

> And whereas the increase of slaves in this State is injurious to the poor, and inconvenient.

This recital would appear to have been carefully introduced, in order to prevent any misunderstanding of the motive which induced the Legislature to pass the law, and places it distinctly upon the interest and convenience of the white population—excluding the inference that it might have been intended in any degree for the benefit of the other. . . .

And still further pursuing its legislation, we find that in the same statute passed in 1774, which prohibited the further importation of slaves into the State, there is also a provision by which any negro, Indian, or mulatto servant, who was found wandering out of the town or place to which he belonged, without a written pass such as is therein described, was made liable to be seized by any one, and taken before the next authority to be examined and delivered up to his master—who was required to pay the charge which had accrued thereby. And a subsequent section of the same law provides, that if any free negro shall travel without such pass, and shall be stopped, seized, or taken up, he shall pay all charges arising thereby. And this law was in full operation when the Constitution of the United States was adopted, and was not repealed till 1797. So that up to that time free negroes and mulattoes were associated with servants and slaves in the police regulations established by the laws of the State.

And again, in 1833, Connecticut passed another law, which made it penal to set up or establish any school in that State for the instruction of persons of the African race not inhabitants of the State, or to instruct or teach in any such school or institution, or board or harbor for that purpose, any such person, without the previous consent in writing of the civil authority of the town in which such school or institution might be. . . .

It would be impossible to enumerate and compress in the space usually allotted to an opinion of a court, the various laws, marking the condition of this race, which were passed from time to time after the Revolution, and before and since the adoption of the Constitution of the United States. . . .

The legislation of the States therefore shows, in a manner not to be mistaken, the inferior and subject condition of that race at the time the Constitution was adopted, and long afterwards, throughout the thirteen States by which that instrument was framed; and it is hardly consistent with the respect due to these States, to suppose that they regarded at that time, as fellow-citizens and members of the sovereignty, a class of beings whom they had thus stigmatized. . . . More especially, it cannot be believed that the large slaveholding States regarded them as included in the word citizens, or would have consented to a Constitution which might compel them to receive them in that character from another State. . . .

To all this mass of proof we have still to add, that . . . [t]he conduct of the Executive Department of the [federal] Government has been in perfect harmony upon this subject with this course of legislation. The question was brought officially before the late William Wirt, when he was the Attorney General of the United States, in 1821, and he decided that the words "citizens of the United States" were used in the acts of Congress in the same sense as in the Constitution; and that free persons of color were not citizens, within the meaning of the Constitution and laws; and this opinion has been confirmed by that of the late Attorney General, Caleb Cushing, in a recent case, and acted upon by the Secretary of State, who refused to grant passports to them as "citizens of the United States."

But it is said that a person may be a citizen, and entitled to that character, although he does not possess all the rights which may belong to other citizens; as, for example, the right to vote, or to hold particular offices; and that yet, when he goes into another State, he is entitled to be recognized there as a citizen, although the State may measure his rights by the rights which it allows to persons of a like character or class resident in the State, and refuse to him the full rights of citizenship.

This argument overlooks the language of the provision in the Constitution of which we are speaking.

Undoubtedly, a person may be a citizen, that is, a member of the community who form the sovereignty, although he exercises no share of the political power, and is incapacitated from holding particular offices. Women and minors, who form a part of the political family, cannot vote; and when a property qualification is required to vote or hold a particular office, those who have not the necessary qualification cannot vote or hold the office, yet they are citizens. So, too, a person may be entitled to vote by the law of the State, who is not a citizen even of the State itself. And in some of the States of the Union foreigners not naturalized are allowed to vote. And the State may give the right to free negroes and mulattoes, but that does not make them citizens of the State, and still less of the United States. And the provision in the Constitution giving privileges and immunities in other States, does not apply to them. . . .

No one, we presume, supposes that any change in public opinion or feeling, in relation to this unfortunate race, in the civilized nations of Europe or in this country, should induce the court to give to the words of the Constitution a more liberal construction in their favor than they were intended to bear when the instrument was framed and adopted. Such an argument would be altogether inadmissible in any tribunal called on to interpret it. If any of its provisions are deemed unjust, there is a mode prescribed in the instrument itself by which it may be amended; but while it remains unaltered, it must be construed now as it was understood at the time of its adoption. . . . Any other rule of construction would abrogate the judicial character of this court, and make it the mere reflex of the popular opinion or passion of the day. This court was not created by the Constitution for such purposes. Higher and graver trusts have been confided to it, and it must not falter in the path of duty. . . .

[U]pon a full and careful consideration of the subject, the court is of opinion, that, upon the facts stated in the plea in abatement, Dred Scott was not a citizen of Missouri within the meaning of the Constitution of the United States, and not entitled as such to sue in its courts; and, consequently, that the Circuit Court had no jurisdiction of the case. . . .

For Discussion

(1) Much of this discussion is clearly *originalist*, in that it purports to be based on an understanding of the original meaning of the Constitution. But what kind of originalism is it? Is it *textualist*? Is it based on the *intent of the Framers*? Is it based on the *public meaning* of the text—that is, on what a reader at the time, familiar with publicly known events and issues, would understand the language to mean?

(2) Is the originalist portion of the opinion persuasive? If so, how do we cope with the fact that the result now appears intolerable? Does this suggest that sometimes conscientious constitutional interpretation will lead to unfortunate results, which we must accept, pending amendment, as the price of constitutionalism? Or should it force us to reconsider a too-comfortable distinction between law and morality?

(3) If the originalist portion of the opinion is *not* persuasive, is the problem that originalism is the wrong approach to resolving the issue presented? Or is Taney's argument a bad implementation of originalism? And if the latter, does that cast doubt on one of the arguments offered in support of originalism, that it is less subject to manipulation than interpretive approaches not rooted in original meaning?

(4) Suppose you agree with Taney that as of the time of the Constitution free descendants of slaves were not deemed to be citizens of any state, within the meaning of the constitutional language. Is it constitutionally significant that—as Taney seems willing to concede—attitudes had substantially changed by the time the Court decided this case?

[II. Emancipation—Federal Law]

We are aware that . . . some of the members of the court [doubt] whether [the question of jurisdiction just discussed] is legally before the court upon this writ of error[. But even] if that plea is regarded as waived, or out of the case upon any other ground, . . . the question as to the jurisdiction of the Circuit Court is [still] presented on the face of the bill of exception itself, taken by the plaintiff at the trial[. F]or he admits that he and his wife were born slaves, but endeavors to make out his title to freedom and citizenship by showing that they were taken by their owner to certain places, hereinafter mentioned, where slavery could not by law exist, and that they thereby became free, and upon their return to Missouri became citizens of that State.

Now, if the removal of which he speaks did not give them their freedom, then by his own admission he is still a slave; and whatever opinions may be entertained in favor of the citizenship of a free person of the African race, no one supposes that a slave is a citizen of the State or of the United States. If, therefore, the acts done by his owner did not make them free persons, he is still a slave, and certainly incapable of suing in the character of a citizen.

The principle of law is too well settled to be disputed, that a court can give no judgment for either party, where it has no jurisdiction; and if, upon the showing of Scott himself, it appeared that he was still a slave, the case ought to have been . . . dismissed by the Circuit Court for want of jurisdiction in that court. . . .

We proceed, therefore, to inquire whether the facts relied on by the plaintiff entitled him to his freedom. . . . In considering this part of the controversy, two questions arise:

1. Was he, together with his family, free in Missouri by reason of the stay in the territory of the United States hereinbefore mentioned?

And 2. If they were not, is Scott himself free by reason of his removal to Rock Island, in the State of Illinois, as stated in the above admissions?

We proceed to examine the first question.

The act of Congress, upon which the plaintiff relies, declares that slavery and involuntary servitude, except as a punishment for crime, shall be forever prohibited in all that part of the territory ceded by France, under the name of

Louisiana, which lies north of thirty-six degrees thirty minutes north latitude, and not included within the limits of Missouri. And the difficulty which meets us at the threshold of this part of the inquiry is, whether Congress was authorized to pass this law under any of the powers granted to it by the Constitution; for if the authority is not given by that instrument, it is the duty of this court to declare it void and inoperative, and incapable of conferring freedom upon any one who is held as a slave under the laws of any one of the States. . . .

WORTH NOTING

The statute referenced by the Court embodied the so-called Missouri Compromise of 1820. The compromise was intended to settle ongoing controversy about the expansion of slavery by admitting Maine as a free state, admitting Missouri as a slave state, and prohibiting slavery in most of the remaining Louisiana Purchase: "That in all that territory ceded by France to the United States, which lies north of thirty-six degrees thirty minutes north latitude, slavery and involuntary servitude shall be, and are hereby, forever prohibited." This covered an enormous swath of territory, including much or all of what is now Montana, Wyoming, Colorado, Kansas, Nebraska, North and South Dakota, Minnesota, and Iowa.

This brings us to examine by what provision of the Constitution the present Federal Government, under its delegated and restricted powers, is authorized to acquire territory outside of the original limits of the United States, and what powers it may exercise therein over the person or property of a citizen of the United States, while it remains a Territory, and until it shall be admitted as one of the States of the Union. . . .

The power to expand the territory of the United States by the admission of new States is plainly given; and in the construction of this power by all the departments of the Government, it has been held to authorize the acquisition of territory, not fit for admission at the time, but to be admitted as soon as its population and situation would entitle it to admission. It is acquired to become a State, and not to be held as a colony and governed by Congress with absolute authority. . . .

WORTH NOTING

Article IV, § 3 of the Constitution provides:

1: New States may be admitted by the Congress into this Union. . . .

2: The Congress shall have Power to dispose of and make all needful Rules and Regulations respecting the Territory or other Property belonging to the United States.

But until [the] time [of the Territory's admission as a state] arrives, it is undoubtedly necessary that some Government should be established, in order to organize society, and to protect the inhabitants in their persons and property; . . . it was not only within the scope of [Congress's] powers, but it was its duty to pass such laws. . . .

The form of government to be established necessarily rested in the discretion of Congress. . . . But [the] Territory being a part of the United States, the Government and the citizen both enter it under the authority of the Constitution, with their respective rights defined and marked out; and the Federal Government can exercise no power over his person or property, beyond what that instrument confers, nor lawfully deny any right which it has reserved.

A reference to a few of the provisions of the Constitution will illustrate this proposition.

For example, no one, we presume, will contend that Congress can make any law in a Territory respecting the establishment of religion, or the free exercise thereof, or abridging the freedom of speech or of the press, or the right of the people of the Territory peaceably to assemble, and to petition the Government for the redress of grievances. Nor can Congress deny to the people the right to keep and bear arms, nor the right to trial by jury, nor compel any one to be a witness against himself in a criminal proceeding.

These powers, and others, in relation to rights of person, which it is not necessary here to enumerate, are, in express and positive terms, denied to the General Government [by the text of the Constitution]; and the rights of private property have been guarded with equal care. Thus the rights of property are united with the rights of person, and placed on the same ground by the fifth amendment to the Constitution, which provides that no person shall be deprived of life, liberty, and property, without due process of law. And an act of Congress which deprives a citizen of the United States of his liberty or property, merely because he came himself or brought his property into a particular Territory of the United States, and who had committed no offence against the laws, could hardly be dignified with the name of due process of law. . . .

It seems, however, to be supposed, that there is a difference between property in a slave and other property, and that different rules may be applied to it in expounding the Constitution of the United States. And the laws and usages of nations, and the writings of eminent jurists upon the relation of master and slave and their mutual rights and duties, and the powers which Governments may exercise over it, have been dwelt upon in the argument.

But in considering the question before us, it must be borne in mind that there is no law of nations standing between the people of the United States and their Government, and interfering with their relation to each other. The powers of the Government, and the rights of the citizen under it, are positive and practical regulations plainly written down. The people of the United States have delegated to it certain enumerated powers, and forbidden it to exercise others. It has no power over the person or property of a citizen but what the citizens of the United States have granted. And no laws or usages of other nations, or reasoning of statesmen or jurists upon the relations of master and slave, can enlarge the powers of the Government, or take from the citizens the rights they have reserved. And if the Constitution recognizes the right of property of the master in a slave, and makes no distinction between that description of property and other property owned by a citizen, no tribunal, acting under the authority of the United States, whether it be legislative, executive, or judicial, has a right to draw such a distinction, or deny to it the benefit of the provisions and guarantees which have been provided for the protection of private property against the encroachments of the Government.

Now, as we have already said in an earlier part of this opinion, upon a different point, the right of property in a slave is distinctly and expressly affirmed in the Constitution. The right to traffic in it, like an ordinary article of merchandise and property, was guarantied to the citizens of the United States, in every State that might desire it, for twenty years. And the Government in express terms is pledged to protect it in all future time, if the slave escapes from his owner. This is done in plain words—too plain to be misunderstood. And no word can be found in the Constitution which gives Congress a greater power over slave property, or which entitles property of that kind to less protection that property of any other description. The only power conferred is the power coupled with the duty of guarding and protecting the owner in his rights.

Upon these considerations, it is the opinion of the court that the act of Congress which prohibited a citizen from holding and owning property of this kind in the territory of the United States north of the line therein mentioned, is not warranted by the Constitution, and is therefore void; and that neither Dred Scott himself, nor any of his family, were made free by being carried into this territory; even if they had been carried there by the owner, with the intention of becoming a permanent resident. . . .

For Discussion

(1) Ultimately, which provision of the Constitution does Taney hold the Missouri Compromise violated?

(2) Which of the above parts of Taney's opinion—the one dealing with citizenship or the one dealing with Congressional power—do you think had greater contemporary significance?

[III. Emancipation—State Law]

We have so far examined the case, as it stands under the Constitution of the United States, and the powers thereby delegated to the Federal Government.

But there is another point in the case which depends on State power and State law. And it is contended, on the part of the plaintiff, that he is made free by being taken to Rock Island, in the State of Illinois, independently of his residence in the territory of the United States; and being so made free, he was not again reduced to a state of slavery by being brought back to Missouri.

Our notice of this part of the case will be very brief; for the principle on which it depends was decided in this court, upon much consideration, in the case of *Strader v. Graham* (1851). In that case, the slaves had been taken from Kentucky to Ohio, with the consent of the owner, and afterwards brought back to Kentucky. And this court held that their *status* or condition, as free or slave, depended upon the laws of Kentucky, when they were brought back into that State, and not of Ohio; and that this court had no jurisdiction to revise the judgment of a State court upon its own laws. This was the point directly before the court, and the decision that this court had not jurisdiction turned upon it, as will be seen by the report of the case.

So in this case. As Scott was a slave when taken into the State of Illinois by his owner, and was there held as such, and brought back in that character, his *status*, as free or slave, depended on the laws of Missouri, and not of Illinois. . . .

* * *

Upon the whole, therefore, it is the judgment of this court, that it appears by the record before us that the plaintiff in error is not a citizen of Missouri, in the sense in which that word is used in the Constitution; and that the Circuit Court of the United States, for that reason, had no jurisdiction in the case, and could give no judgment in it. Its judgment for the defendant must, consequently, be reversed, and a mandate issued, directing the suit to be dismissed for want of jurisdiction.

Mr. Justice Daniel.

. . . The correct conclusions upon the question here considered would seem to be these: That in the establishment of the several communities now the States of this Union, and in the formation of the Federal Government, the African was not deemed politically a person. He was regarded and owned in every State in the Union as *property* merely, and as such was not and could not be a party or an actor, much less a *peer* in any compact or form of government established by the States or the United States. . . . That so far as rights and immunities appertaining to citizens have been defined and secured by the Constitution and laws of the United States, the African race is not and never was recognized either by the language or purposes of the former. . . .

Mr. Justice Catron.

. . . Congress cannot do indirectly what the Constitution prohibits directly. If the slaveholder is prohibited from going to the Territory with his slaves, who are parts of his family in name and in fact, it will follow that men owning lawful property in their own States, carrying with them the equality of their State to enjoy the common property, may be told, you cannot come here with your slaves, and he will be held out at the border. By this subterfuge, owners of slave property, to the amount of thousand of millions, might be almost as effectually excluded from removing into the Territory of Louisiana north of thirty-six degrees thirty minutes, as if the law declared that owners of slaves, as a class, should be excluded, even if their slaves were left behind. . . .

[T]he act of 1820, known as the Missouri compromise, violates the most leading feature of the Constitution—a feature on which the Union depends, and which secures to the respective States and their citizens and entire EQUALITY of rights, privileges, and immunities. . . .

Mr. Justice McLean dissenting.

. . . There is no averment in this plea which shows or conduces to show an inability in the plaintiff to sue in the Circuit Court. . . . It has never been held necessary, to constitute a citizen . . . , that he should have the qualifications of an elector. Females and minors may sue in the Federal courts, and so may any individual who has a permanent domicil in the State under whose laws his rights are protected, and to which he owes allegiance. . . .

In the argument, it was said that a colored citizen would not be an agreeable member of society. This is more a matter of taste than of law. Several of the States have admitted persons of color to the right of suffrage, and in this view have recognized them as citizens; and this has been done in the slave as well as the free States. On the question of citizenship, it must be admitted that we have not been very fastidious. Under the late treaty with Mexico, we have made citizens of all grades, combinations, and colors. The same was done in the admission of Louisiana and Florida. No one ever doubted, and no court ever held, that the people of these Territories did not become citizens under the treaty. They have exercised all the rights of citizens, without being naturalized under the acts of Congress. . . .

Our independence was a great epoch in the history of freedom; and while I admit the Government was not made expecially for the colored race, yet many of them were citizens of the New England States, and exercised, the rights of suffrage when the Constitution was adopted, and it was not doubted by any intelligent person that its tendencies would greatly ameliorate their condition. . . .

I think the judgment of the court below should be reversed.

MR. JUSTICE CURTIS dissenting.

. . . To determine whether any free persons, descended from Africans held in slavery, were citizens of the United States under the Confederation, and consequently at the time of the adoption of the Constitution of the United States, it is only necessary to know whether any such persons were citizens of either of the States under the Confederation, at the time of the adoption of the Constitution.

Of this there can be no doubt. At the time of the ratification of the Articles of Confederation, all free native-born inhabitants of the States of New Hampshire, Massachusetts, New York, New Jersey, and North Carolina, though descended from African slaves, were not only citizens of those States, but such of them as had the other necessary qualifications possessed the franchise of electors, on equal terms with other citizens. . . . The fourth of the fundamental articles of the Confederation was as follows: "The free inhabitants of each of these States, paupers, vagabonds, and fugitives from justice, excepted, shall be entitled to all the privileges and immunities of free citizens in the several States." . . .

Did the Constitution of the United States deprive [free persons of African descent] or their descendants of citizenship?

That Constitution was ordained and established by the people of the United States, through the action, in each State, or those persons who were qualified by its laws to act thereon, in behalf of themselves and all other citizens of that State. In some of the States, as we have seen, colored persons were among those qualified by law to act on this subject. These colored persons were not only included in the body of "the people of the United States," by whom the Constitution was ordained and established, but in at least five of the States they had the power to act, and doubtless did act, by their suffrages, upon the question of its adoption. It would be strange, if we were to find in that instrument anything which deprived of their citizenship any part of the people of the United States who were among those by whom it was established. . . .

WORTH NOTING

Curtis also responded to the argument that, if free persons of African descent who were citizens of their state were thereby made citizens of the United States, then the Privileges and Immunities Clause of Art. IV, § 2, would give them a right to vote and hold offices in other states. That argument, he said, was based on the false premise that any citizen is entitled to all the privileges of any other citizen in the state; in fact, states could make such distinctions as they saw fit in (for example) which citizens could vote.

I dissent, therefore, from that part of the opinion of the majority of the court, in which it is held that a person of African descent cannot be a citizen of the United States; and I regret I must go further, and dissent . . . from [their view] on the constitutionality of the act of Congress commonly called the Missouri compromise act, and the grounds and conclusions announced in their opinion. . . .

[T]he position, that a prohibition to bring slaves into a Territory deprives any one of his property without due process of law, [will not] bear examination. It must be remembered that this restriction on the legislative power is not peculiar to the Constitution of the United States; it was borrowed from *Magna Charta;* was brought to America by our ancestors, as part of their inherited liberties, and has existed in all the States, usually in the very words of the great charter. It existed in every political community in America in 1787, when the ordinance prohibiting slavery north and west of the Ohio was passed. And if a prohibition of slavery in a Territory in 1820 violated this principle of *Magna Charta*, the ordinance of 1787[, which prohibited slavery in the Northwest Territories,] also violated it. . . . I think I may at least say, if the Congress did then violate *Magna Charta* by the ordinance, no one discovered that violation. . . .

For these reasons, I am of opinion that so much of the several acts of Congress as prohibited slavery and involuntary servitude within that part of the Territory of Wisconsin lying north of thirty-six degrees thirty minutes north latitude, and west of the river Mississippi, were constitutional and valid laws.

WORTH NOTING

The remaining four justices also wrote separate opinions. Justice Wayne defended the decision to reach the merits even though the Court decided there was no jurisdiction. Justice Nelson asserted that the law of Missouri controlled, and that Scott lost under it. Justice Grier wrote briefly, concurring in Nelson's opinion, and also, for practical purposes, in Taney's. Justice Campbell wrote at length, emphasizing state control over slavery and characterizing the Constitution as "a federal compact among the States establishing a limited Government."

F. The Civil War

1. Secession

Notwithstanding the *Scott v. Sandford* decision, the emerging Republican Party continued to insist that slavery should not be expanded into the territories. Lincoln won the Presidency in 1860 by carrying all 18 free states and none of the 15 slave states. Many southerners became convinced that under Republican domination the Federal government would infringe on their constitutional rights. By the time of Lincoln's inauguration on March 4, 1861, seven Southern states had seceded. South Carolina, which had asserted its right to nullify federal law in the 1832–33 tariff crisis, led the way.

Declaration of the Immediate Causes Which Induce and Justify the Secession of South Carolina from the Federal Union

December 24, 1860

The State of South Carolina having resumed her separate and equal place among nations, deems it due to herself, to the remaining United States of America, and to the nations of the world, that she should declare the immediate causes which have led to this act.

In the year 1765, that portion of the British Empire embracing Great Britain, undertook to make laws for the government of that portion composed of the thirteen American Colonies. A struggle for the right of self-government ensued, which resulted, on the 4th of July, 1776, in a Declaration by the Colonies, "that they are, and of right ought to be, FREE AND INDEPENDENT STATES; and that, as free and independent States, they have full power to levy war, conclude peace, contract alliances, establish commerce, and to do all other acts and things which independent States may of right do."

They further solemnly declared that whenever any "form of government becomes destructive of the ends for which it was established, it is the right of the people to alter or abolish it, and to institute a new government." Deeming the Government of Great Britain to have become destructive of these ends, they declared that the Colonies "are absolved from all allegiance to the British Crown, and that all political connection between them and the State of Great Britain is, and ought to be, totally dissolved."

In pursuance of this Declaration of Independence, each of the thirteen States proceeded to exercise its separate sovereignty; adopted for itself a Constitution, and appointed officers for the administration of government in all its departments—Legislative, Executive and Judicial. For purposes of defense, they united their arms and their counsels; and, in 1778, they entered into a League known as the Articles of Confederation, whereby they agreed to entrust the administration of their external relations to a common agent, known as the Congress of the United States, expressly declaring, in the first Article "that each State retains its sovereignty, freedom and independence, and every power, jurisdiction and right which is not, by this Confederation, expressly delegated to the United States in Congress assembled."

Under this Confederation the war of the Revolution was carried on, and on the 3rd of September, 1783, the contest ended, and a definite Treaty was signed by Great Britain, in which she acknowledged the independence of the Colonies in the following terms:

ARTICLE I—His Britannic Majesty acknowledges the said United States, viz: New Hampshire, Massachusetts Bay, Rhode Island and Providence Plantations, Connecticut, New York, New Jersey, Pennsylvania, Delaware, Maryland, Virginia, North Carolina, South Carolina and Georgia, to be FREE, SOVEREIGN AND INDEPENDENT STATES; that he treats with them as such; and for himself, his heirs and successors, relinquishes all claims to the government, propriety and territorial rights of the same and every part thereof.

Thus were established the two great principles asserted by the Colonies, namely: the right of a State to govern itself; and the right of a people to abolish a Government when it becomes destructive of the ends for which it was instituted. And concurrent with the establishment of these principles, was the fact, that each Colony became and was recognized by the mother Country a FREE, SOVEREIGN AND INDEPENDENT STATE.

In 1787, Deputies were appointed by the States to revise the Articles of Confederation, and on 17th September, 1787, these Deputies recommended for the adoption of the States, the Articles of Union, known as the Constitution of the United States.

The parties to whom this Constitution was submitted, were the several sovereign States; they were to agree or disagree, and when nine of them agreed the compact was to take effect among those concurring; and the General Government, as the common agent, was then invested with their authority. If only nine of the thirteen States had concurred, the other four would have remained as they then were—separate, sovereign States, independent of any of the provisions of the Constitution. In fact, two of the States did not accede to the Constitution until long after it had gone into operation among the other eleven; and during that interval, they each exercised the functions of an independent nation. . . .

We hold that the Government thus established is subject to the two great principles asserted in the Declaration of Independence; and we hold further, that the mode of its formation subjects it to a third fundamental principle, namely: the law of compact. We maintain that in every compact between two or more parties, the obligation is mutual; that the failure of one of the contracting parties to perform a material part of the agreement, entirely releases the obligation of the other; and that where no arbiter is provided, each party is remitted to his own judgment to determine the fact of failure, with all its consequences.

In the present case, that fact is established with certainty. We assert that fourteen of the States have deliberately refused, for years past, to fulfill their constitutional obligations, and we refer to their own Statutes for the proof.

The Constitution of the United States, in its fourth Article, provides as follows: "No person held to service or labor in one State, under the laws thereof, escaping into another, shall, in consequence of any law or regulation therein, be discharged from such service or labor, but shall be delivered up, on claim of the party to whom such service or labor may be due." This stipulation was so material to the compact, that without it that compact would not have been made. The greater number of the contracting parties held slaves, and they had previously evinced their estimate of the value of such a stipulation by making it a condition in the Ordinance for the government of the territory ceded by Virginia, which now composes the States north of the Ohio River. The same article of the Constitution stipulates also for rendition by the several States of fugitives from justice from the other States.

The General Government, as the common agent, passed laws to carry into effect these stipulations of the States. For many years these laws were executed. But an increasing hostility on the part of the non-slaveholding States to the institution of slavery, has led to a disregard of their obligations, and the laws of the General Government have ceased to effect the objects of the Constitution. The States of Maine, New Hampshire, Vermont, Massachusetts, Connecticut, Rhode Island, New York, [New Jersey,] Pennsylvania, Illinois, Indiana, Michigan, Wisconsin and Iowa, have enacted laws which either nullify the Acts of Congress or render useless any attempt to execute them. . . . Thus the constituted compact has been deliberately broken and disregarded by the non-slaveholding States, and the consequence follows that South Carolina is released from her obligation. . . .

The right of property in slaves was recognized by giving to free persons distinct political rights, by giving them the right to represent, and burthening them with direct taxes for three-fifths of their slaves; by authorizing the importation of slaves for twenty years; and by stipulating for the rendition of fugitives from labor.

We affirm that these ends for which this Government was instituted have been defeated, and the Government itself has been made destructive of them by the action of the non-slaveholding States. Those States have assumed the right of deciding upon the propriety of our domestic institutions; and have denied the rights of property established in fifteen of the States and recognized by the Constitution; they have denounced as sinful the institution of slavery; they have permitted open establishment among them of societies, whose avowed object is to disturb the peace and to eloign the property of the citizens of other States. They have encouraged and assisted thousands of our slaves to leave their homes; and those who remain, have been incited by emissaries, books and pictures to servile insurrection.

For twenty-five years this agitation has been steadily increasing, until it has now secured to its aid the power of the common Government. Observing the *forms* of the Constitution, a sectional party has found within that Article establishing the Executive Department, the means of subverting the Constitution itself. A geographical line has been drawn across the Union, and all the States north of that line have united in the election of a man to the high office of President of the United States, whose opinions and purposes are hostile to slavery. He is to be entrusted with the administration of the common Government, because he has declared that that "Government cannot endure permanently half slave, half free," and that the public mind must rest in the belief that slavery is in the course of ultimate extinction.

This sectional combination for the submersion of the Constitution, has been aided in some of the States by elevating to citizenship, persons who, by the supreme law of the land, are incapable of becoming citizens; and their votes have been used to inaugurate a new policy, hostile to the South, and destructive of its beliefs and safety.

On the 4th day of March next, this party will take possession of the Government. It has announced that the South shall be excluded from the common territory, that the judicial tribunals shall be made sectional, and that a war must be waged against slavery until it shall cease throughout the United States.

The guaranties of the Constitution will then no longer exist; the equal rights of the States will be lost. The slaveholding States will no longer have the power of self-government, or self-protection, and the Federal Government will have become their enemy.

Sectional interest and animosity will deepen the irritation, and all hope of remedy is rendered vain, by the fact that public opinion at the North has invested a great political error with the sanction of more erroneous religious belief.

We, therefore, the People of South Carolina, by our delegates in Convention assembled, appealing to the Supreme Judge of the world for the rectitude of our intentions, have solemnly declared that the Union heretofore existing between this State and the other States of North America, is dissolved, and that the State of South Carolina has resumed her position among the nations of the world, as a separate and independent State; with full power to levy war, conclude peace, contract alliances, establish commerce, and to do all other acts and things which independent States may of right do.

Adopted December 24, 1860

In a last-ditch effort to save the Union, what was left of the 36th Congress approved—with three votes to spare in the House and none in the Senate—and passed on to the states a proposed constitutional amendment known as the Corwin Amendment, though the original drafter was Lincoln's nominee for Secretary of State, Senator William Seward. The proposal read as follows:

No amendment shall be made to the Constitution which will authorize or give to Congress the power to abolish or interfere, within any State, with the domestic institutions thereof, including that of persons held to labor or service by the laws of said State.

FOR DISCUSSION

What would the constitutional effect of this amendment have been had it been ratified?

Three states passed resolutions in 1861 ratifying this proposed amendment.

President Abraham Lincoln, First Inaugural Address

March 4, 1861

Fellow-Citizens of the United States:

. . . Apprehension seems to exist among the people of the Southern States that by the accession of a Republican Administration their property and their peace and personal security are to be endangered. There has never been any reasonable cause for such apprehension. Indeed, the most ample evidence to the contrary has all the while existed and been open to their inspection. It is found in nearly all the published speeches of him who now addresses you. I do but quote from one of those speeches when I declare that—

> I have no purpose, directly or indirectly, to interfere with the institution of slavery in the States where it exists. I believe I have no lawful right to do so, and I have no inclination to do so.

. . . I add, too, that all the protection which, consistently with the Constitution and the laws, can be given will be cheerfully given to all the States when lawfully demanded, for whatever cause—as cheerfully to one section as to another.

There is much controversy about the delivering up of fugitives from service or labor. . . . It is scarcely questioned that [the Fugitive Slave Clause of Article IV] was intended by those who made it for the reclaiming of what we call fugitive slaves; and the intention of the lawgiver is the law. All members of Congress swear their support to the whole Constitution—to this provision as much as to any other. To the proposition, then, that slaves whose cases come within the terms of this clause "shall be delivered up" their oaths are unanimous. Now, if they would make the effort in good temper, could they not with nearly equal unanimity frame and pass a law by means of which to keep good that unanimous oath?

There is some difference of opinion whether this clause should be enforced by national or by State authority, but surely that difference is not a very material one. If the slave is to be surrendered, it can be of but little consequence to him or to others by which authority it is done. And should anyone in any case be content that his oath shall go unkept on a merely unsubstantial controversy as to how it shall be kept?

Again: In any law upon this subject ought not all the safeguards of liberty known in civilized and humane jurisprudence to be introduced, so that a free man be not in any case surrendered as a slave? And might it not be well at the same time to provide by law for the enforcement of that clause in the Constitution which guarantees that "the citizens of each State shall be entitled to all privileges and immunities of citizens in the several States"? . . .

I now enter upon the same task [as my predecessors] for the brief constitutional term of four years under great and peculiar difficulty. A disruption of the Federal Union, heretofore only menaced, is now formidably attempted.

I hold that in contemplation of universal law and of the Constitution the Union of these States is perpetual. Perpetuity is implied, if not expressed, in the fundamental law of all national governments. It is safe to assert that no government proper ever had a provision in its organic law for its own termination. Continue to execute all the express provisions of our National Constitution, and the Union will endure forever, it being impossible to destroy it except by some action not provided for in the instrument itself.

Again: If the United States be not a government proper, but an association of States in the nature of contract merely, can it, as a contract, be peaceably unmade by less than all the parties who made it? One party to a contract may violate it—break it, so to speak—but does it not require all to lawfully rescind it?

Descending from these general principles, we find the proposition that in legal contemplation the Union is perpetual confirmed by the history of the Union itself. The Union is much older than the Constitution. It was formed, in fact, by the Articles of Association in 1774. It was matured and continued by the Declaration of Independence in 1776. It was further matured, and the faith of all the then thirteen States expressly plighted and engaged that it should be perpetual, by the Articles of Confederation in 1778. And finally, in 1787, one of the declared objects for ordaining and establishing the Constitution was "to *form a more perfect Union*."

But if destruction of the Union by one or by a part only of the States be lawfully possible, the Union is *less* perfect than before the Constitution, having lost the vital element of perpetuity.

It follows from these views that no State upon its own mere motion can lawfully get out of the Union; that *resolves* and *ordinances* to that effect are legally void, and that acts of violence within any State or States against the authority of the United States are insurrectionary or revolutionary, according to circumstances.

I therefore consider that in view of the Constitution and the laws the Union is unbroken, and to the extent of my ability, I shall take care, as the Constitution itself expressly enjoins upon me, that the laws of the Union be faithfully executed in all the States. Doing this I deem to be only a simple duty on my part, and I shall perform it so far as practicable unless my rightful masters, the American people, shall withhold the requisite means or in some authoritative manner direct the contrary. I trust this will not be regarded as a menace, but only as the declared purpose of the Union that it *will* constitutionally defend and maintain itself.

In doing this there needs to be no bloodshed or violence, and there shall be none unless it be forced upon the national authority. The power confided to me will be used to hold, occupy, and possess the property and places belonging to the Government and to collect the duties and imposts; but beyond what may be necessary for these objects, there will be no invasion, no using of force against or among the people anywhere. Where hostility to the United States in any interior locality shall be so great and universal as to prevent competent resident citizens from holding the Federal offices, there will be no attempt to force obnoxious strangers among the people for that object. While the strict legal right may exist in the Government to enforce the exercise of these offices, the attempt to do so would be so irritating and so nearly impracticable withal that I deem it better to forego for the time the uses of such offices.

The mails, unless repelled, will continue to be furnished in all parts of the Union. So far as possible the people everywhere shall have that sense of perfect security which is most favorable to calm thought and reflection. . . .

Before entering upon so grave a matter as the destruction of our national fabric, with all its benefits, its memories, and its hopes, would it not be wise to ascertain precisely why we do it? Will you hazard so desperate a step while there is any possibility that any portion of the ills you fly from have no real existence? Will you, while the certain ills you fly to are greater than all the real ones you fly from, will you risk the commission of so fearful a mistake?

All profess to be content in the Union if all constitutional rights can be maintained. Is it true, then, that any right plainly written in the Constitution has been denied? I think not. Happily, the human mind is so constituted that no party can reach to the audacity of doing this. Think, if you can, of a single instance in which a plainly written provision of the Constitution has ever been denied. If by the mere force of numbers a majority should deprive a minority of any clearly written constitutional right, it might in a moral point of view justify revolution; certainly would if such right were a vital one. But such is not our case. . . . [N]o organic law can ever be framed with a provision specifically applicable to every question which may occur in practical administration. No foresight can anticipate nor any document of reasonable length contain express provisions for all possible questions. Shall fugitives from labor be surrendered by national or by State authority? The Constitution does not expressly say. *May* Congress prohibit slavery in the Territories? The Constitution does not expressly say. *Must* Congress protect slavery in the Territories? The Constitution does not expressly say.

From questions of this class spring all our constitutional controversies, and we divide upon them into majorities and minorities. If the minority will not acquiesce, the majority must, or the Government must cease. There is no other alternative, for continuing the Government is acquiescence on one side or the other. If a minority in such case will secede rather than acquiesce, they make a precedent which in turn will divide and ruin them, for a minority of their own will secede from them whenever a majority refuses to be controlled by such minority. For instance, why may not any portion of a new confederacy a year or two hence arbitrarily secede again, precisely as portions of the present Union now claim to secede from it? All who cherish disunion sentiments are now being educated to the exact temper of doing this. . . .

Plainly the central idea of secession is the essence of anarchy. A majority held in restraint by constitutional checks and limitations, and always changing easily with deliberate changes of popular opinions and sentiments, is the only true sovereign of a free people. Whoever rejects it does of necessity fly to anarchy or to despotism. Unanimity is impossible. The rule of a minority, as a permanent arrangement, is wholly inadmissible; so that, rejecting the majority principle, anarchy or despotism in some form is all that is left.

FOR DISCUSSION How might a pro-secessionist respond to Lincoln's argument that any new confederacy would itself be subject to secession?

I do not forget the position assumed by some that constitutional questions are to be decided by the Supreme Court, nor do I deny that such decisions must be binding in any case upon the parties to a suit as to the object of that suit, while they are also entitled to very high respect and consideration in all parallel cases by all other departments of the Government. And while it is obviously possible that such decision may be erroneous in any given case, still the evil effect following it, being limited to that particular case, with the chance that it may be overruled and never become a precedent for other cases, can better be borne than could the evils of a different practice. At the same time, the candid citizen must confess that if the policy of the Government upon vital questions affecting the whole people is to be irrevocably fixed by decisions of the Supreme Court, the instant they are made in ordinary litigation between parties in personal actions the people will have ceased to be their own rulers, having to that extent practically resigned their Government into the hands of that eminent tribunal. Nor is there in this view any assault upon the court or the judges. It is a duty from which they may not shrink to decide cases properly brought before them, and it is no fault of theirs if others seek to turn their decisions to political purposes.

One section of our country believes slavery is *right* and ought to be extended, while the other believes it is *wrong* and ought not to be extended. This is the only substantial dispute. The fugitive-slave clause of the Constitution and the law for the suppression of the foreign slave trade are each as well enforced, perhaps, as any law can ever be in a community where the moral sense of the people imperfectly supports the law itself. The great body of the people abide by the dry legal obligation in both cases, and a few break over in each. This, I think, can not be perfectly cured, and it would be worse in both cases *after* the separation of the sections than before. The foreign slave trade, now imperfectly suppressed, would be ultimately revived without restriction in one section, while fugitive slaves, now only partially surrendered, would not be surrendered at all by the other. . . .

This country, with its institutions, belongs to the people who inhabit it. Whenever they shall grow weary of the existing Government, they can exercise their *constitutional* right of amending it or their *revolutionary* right to dismember or overthrow it. I can not be ignorant of the fact that many worthy and patriotic citizens are desirous of having the National Constitution amended. . . . I understand a

FOR DISCUSSION

Does Lincoln give away the legal issue when he speaks of the revolutionary right of the people to overthrow or dismember the government?

proposed amendment to the Constitution—which amendment, however, I have not seen—has passed Congress, to the effect that the Federal Government shall never interfere with the domestic institutions of the States, including that of persons held to service. To avoid misconstruction of what I have said, I depart from my purpose not to speak of particular amendments so far as to say that, holding such a provision to now be implied constitutional law, I have no objection to its being made express and irrevocable. . . .

In your hands, my dissatisfied fellow-countrymen, and not in *mine*, is the momentous issue of civil war. The Government will not assail you. You can have no conflict without being yourselves the aggressors. You have no oath registered in heaven to destroy the Government, while I shall have the most solemn one to "preserve, protect, and defend it."

I am loath to close. We are not enemies, but friends. We must not be enemies. Though passion may have strained it must not break our bonds of affection. The mystic chords of memory, stretching from every battlefield and patriot grave to every living heart and hearthstone all over this broad land, will yet swell the chorus of the Union, when again touched, as surely they will be, by the better angels of our nature.

Lincoln inserted the last paragraph at the suggestion of Seward. Seward offered a draft:

> I close. We are not we must not be aliens or enemies but fellow countrymen and brethren. Although passion has strained our bonds of affection too hardly they must not, I am sure they will not be broken. The mystic chords which proceeding from so many battle fields and so many patriot graves pass through all the hearts and all the hearths in this broad continent of ours will yet again harmonize in their ancient music when breathed upon by the guardian angel of the nation.

WORTH NOTING

That was not bad—but Lincoln marked it up, and note how he made it both tighter and more graceful.

On April 12, 1861, forces of the new Confederacy fired on Fort Sumter, a federal installation in Charleston harbor. Three days later, Lincoln issued a proclamation calling for 75,000 volunteers, and calling a special session of Congress for July 4. Four more Southern states seceded within several weeks after the attack on Fort Sumter. But four slave states—Taney's Maryland, Delaware, Missouri, and Lincoln's native state, Kentucky, remained loyal. (Lincoln reportedly said, "I hope to have God on my side, but I must have Kentucky.")

2.   War Powers Under Lincoln

a.   The Use of Force

On April 19, 1861, Lincoln issued a Proclamation of Blockade against Southern ports. The blockade proclamation, which was issued without congressional authorization, approved the seizure by private ships of other vessels attempting to travel to and from Confederate ports. In *The Prize Cases* (1863), the Supreme Court upheld the validity of the blockade by a 5–4 vote, relying in part on statutory authorization enacted after the blockade was announced.

 CROSS REFERENCE   The *Prize Cases* decision is presented at pp. 845–849.

b.   Suspension of Habeas Corpus

Washington, D.C., was surrounded by slave-holding territory. Virginia, just across the Potomac, seceded. Maryland did not, but many of its residents sympathized with the South—indeed, at one point the Governor of the state and the mayor of Baltimore refused to allow federal troops to pass through—and it was a hotbed of insurrectionary activity.

On April 27, 1861, Lincoln wrote Winfield Scott, Commanding General of the Army, as follows:

> You are engaged in repressing an insurrection against the laws of the United States. If at any point on or in the vicinity of the military line which is now used between the city of Philadelphia via Perryville, Annapolis City and Annapolis Junction you find resistance which renders it necessary to suspend the writ of habeas corpus for the public safety, you personally or through the officer in command at the point where resistance occurs are authorized to suspend that writ.

That same day, Scott re-delegated "a like authority" to three Departmental commanders in the prescribed area.

General Robert Patterson, who was serving as commander of the Department of Pennsylvania, Delaware and Maryland, issued a suspension order pursuant to this authority. John Merryman, who had allegedly cut telegraph wires and recruited soldiers for the Confederacy, was arrested by military authorities. He sought a writ of habeas corpus from the Circuit Justice—Roger Taney. As Taney summarized the situation, *Ex parte Merryman*, 17 F. Cas. 144 (1861),

> under these circumstances, a military officer, stationed in Pennsylvania, without giving any information to the district attorney, and without any application to the judicial authorities, assumes to himself the judicial power in the district of Maryland; undertakes to decide what constitutes the crime of treason or rebellion; what evidence (if indeed he required any) is sufficient to support the accusation and justify the commitment; and commits the party, without a hearing, even before himself, to close custody, in a strongly garrisoned fort, to be there held, it would seem, during the pleasure of those who committed him.

After quoting the Fourth, Fifth, and Sixth Amendments, Taney wrote:

> These great and fundamental laws, which congress itself could not suspend, have been disregarded and suspended, like the writ of habeas corpus, by a military order, supported by force of arms. Such is the case now before me, and I can only say that if the authority which the constitution has confided to the judiciary department and judicial officers, may thus, upon any pretext or under any circumstances, be usurped by the military power, at its discretion, the people of the United States are no longer living under a government of laws, but every citizen holds life, liberty and property at the will and pleasure of the army officer in whose military district he may happen to be found.
>
> In such a case, my duty was too plain to be mistaken. I have exercised all the power which the constitution and laws confer upon me, but that power has been resisted by a force too strong for me to overcome. It is possible that the officer who has incurred this grave responsibility may have misunderstood his instructions, and exceeded the authority intended to be given him; I shall, therefore, order all the proceedings in this case, with my opinion, to be filed and recorded in the circuit court of the United States for the district of Maryland, and direct the clerk to transmit a copy, under seal, to the president of the United States. It will then remain for that high officer, in fulfillment

of his constitutional obligation to 'take care that the laws be faithfully executed,' to determine what measures he will take to cause the civil process of the United States to be respected and enforced.

The military officers under Lincoln's command disregarded Taney's order. Lincoln authorized several other suspensions of habeas corpus before Congress, in 1863, gave him statutory authority to do so.

Questions

Was the 1861 suspension legitimate? Was the executive branch's disregard of Taney's order legitimate?

---

c.   Military Tribunals

One of the most legally vexing aspects of the Civil War was the way the internal nature of the conflict pressed on traditional distinctions under the law of war, in particular those relating to the distinctions among citizen, combatant, and civilian. The following case is one of the era's best known explorations of that problem.

Ex Parte Milligan

Supreme Court of the United States, 1866.
71 U.S. (4 Wall.) 2.

Mr. Justice Davis delivered the opinion of the court.

On the 10th day of May, 1865, Lambdin P. Milligan presented a petition to the Circuit Court of the United States for the District of Indiana, to be discharged from an alleged unlawful imprisonment. The case made by the petition is this: Milligan is a citizen of the United States; has lived for twenty years in Indiana; and, at the time of the grievances complained of, was not, and never had been in the military or naval service of the United States. On the 5th day of October, 1864, while at home, he was arrested by order of General Alvin P. Hovey, commanding the military district of Indiana; and has ever since been kept in close confinement.

On the 21st day of October, 1864, he was brought before a military commission, convened at Indianapolis, by order of General Hovey, tried on certain charges and specifications; found guilty, and sentenced to be hanged; and the sentence ordered to be executed on Friday, the 19th day of May, 1865.

On the 2d day of January, 1865, after the proceedings of the military commission were at an end, the Circuit Court of the United States for Indiana met at Indianapolis and empanelled a grand jury, who were charged to inquire whether the laws of the United States had been violated; and, if so, to make presentments. The court adjourned on the 27th day of January, having, prior thereto, discharged from further service the grand jury, who did not find any bill of indictment or make any presentment against Milligan for any offence whatever; and, in fact, since his imprisonment, no bill of indictment has been found or presentment made against him by any grand jury of the United States.

Milligan insists that said military commission had no jurisdiction to try him upon the charges preferred, or upon any charges whatever; because he was a citizen of the United States and the State of Indiana, and had not been, since the commencement of the late Rebellion, a resident of any of the States whose citizens were arrayed against the government, and that the right of trial by jury was guaranteed to him by the Constitution of the United States. . . .

The importance of the main question presented by this record cannot be overstated; for it involves the very framework of the government and the fundamental principles of American liberty.

During the late wicked Rebellion, the temper of the times did not allow that calmness in deliberation and discussion so necessary to a correct conclusion of a purely judicial question. *Then*, considerations of safety were mingled with the exercise of power; and feelings and interests prevailed which are happily terminated. *Now* that the public safety is assured, this question, as well as all others, can be discussed and decided without passion or the admixture of any element not required to form a legal judgment. We approach the investigation of this case, fully sensible of the magnitude of the inquiry and the necessity of full and cautious deliberation. . . .

The controlling question in the case is this: Upon the *facts* stated in Milligan's petition, and the exhibits filed, had the military commission mentioned in it *jurisdiction*, legally, to try and sentence him? Milligan, not a resident of one of the rebellious states, or a prisoner of war, but a citizen of Indiana for twenty years past, and never in the military or naval service, is, while at his home, arrested by the military power of the United States, imprisoned, and, on certain criminal charges preferred against him, tried, convicted, and sentenced to be hanged by a military commission, organized under the direction of the military commander of the military district of Indiana. Had this tribunal the *legal* power and authority to try and punish this man? . . .

Time has proven the discernment of our ancestors; for even these provisions [the jury-trial clause of the original Constitution, and the Fourth, Fifth, and Sixth Amendments], expressed in such plain English words, that it would seem the ingenuity of man could not evade them, are *now*, after the lapse of more than seventy years, sought to be avoided. Those great and good men foresaw that troublous times would arise, when rulers and people would become restive under restraint, and seek by sharp and decisive measures to accomplish ends deemed just and proper; and that the principles of constitutional liberty would be in peril, unless established by irrepealable law. The history of the world had taught them that what was done in the past might be attempted in the future. The Constitution of the United States is a law for rulers and people, equally in war and in peace, and covers with the shield of its protection all classes of men, at all times, and under all circumstances. No doctrine, involving more pernicious consequences, was ever invented by the wit of man than that any of its provisions can be suspended during any of the great exigencies of government. Such a doctrine leads directly to anarchy or despotism, but the theory of necessity on which it is based is false; for the government, within the Constitution, has all the powers granted to it, which are necessary to preserve its existence; as has been happily proved by the result of the great effort to throw off its just authority.

Have any of the rights guaranteed by the Constitution been violated in the case of Milligan? and if so, what are they?

Every trial involves the exercise of judicial power; and from what source did the military commission that tried him derive their authority? Certainly no part of judicial power of the country was conferred on them; because the Constitution expressly vests it "in one supreme court and such inferior courts as the Congress may from time to time ordain and establish," and it is not pretended that the commission was a court ordained and established by Congress. They cannot justify on the mandate of the President; because he is controlled by law, and has his appropriate sphere of duty, which is to execute, not to make, the laws; and there is "no unwritten criminal code to which resort can be had as a source of jurisdiction."

But it is said that the jurisdiction is complete under the "laws and usages of war."

It can serve no useful purpose to inquire what those laws and usages are, whence they originated, where found, and on whom they operate; they can never be applied to citizens in states which have upheld the authority of the government, and where the courts are open and their process unobstructed. This court has judicial knowledge that in Indiana the Federal authority was always unopposed, and its courts always open to hear criminal accusations and redress grievances; and no usage of war could sanction a military trial there for any offence whatever of a citizen in civil life, in nowise connected with the military service. Congress could grant no such power; and to the honor of our national legislature be it said, it has never been provoked by the state of the country even to attempt its exercise. One of the plainest constitutional provisions was, therefore, infringed when Milligan was tried by a court not ordained and established by Congress, and not composed of judges appointed during good behavior. . . .

It is claimed that martial law covers with its broad mantle the proceedings of this military commission. The proposition is this: that in a time of war the commander of an armed force (if in his opinion the exigencies of the country demand it, and of which he is to judge), has the power, within the lines of his military district, to suspend all civil rights and their remedies, and subject citizens as well as soldiers to the rule of *his will*; and in the exercise of his lawful authority cannot be restrained, except by his superior officer or the President of the United States.

If this position is sound to the extent claimed, then when war exists, foreign or domestic, and the country is subdivided into military departments for mere convenience, the commander of one of them can, if he chooses, within his limits, on the plea of necessity, with the approval of the Executive, substitute military force for and to the exclusion of the laws, and punish all persons, as he thinks right and proper, without fixed or certain rules.

The statement of this proposition shows its importance; for, if true, republican government is a failure, and there is an end of liberty regulated by law. . . . This nation, as experience has proved, cannot always remain at peace, and has no right to expect that it will always have wise and humane rulers, sincerely attached to the principles of the Constitution. Wicked men, ambitious of power, with hatred of liberty and contempt of law, may fill the place once occupied by Washington and Lincoln; and if this right is conceded, and the calamities of war again befall us, the dangers to human liberty are frightful to contemplate. . . .

It is essential to the safety of every government that, in a great crisis, like the one we have just passed through, there should be a power somewhere of suspending the writ of *habeas corpus*. . . . Unquestionably, there is then an exigency which demands that the government, if it should see fit in the exercise of a proper discretion to make arrests, should not be required to produce the persons arrested in answer to a writ of *habeas corpus*. The Constitution goes no further. It does not say after a writ of *habeas corpus* is denied a citizen, that he shall be tried otherwise than by the course of the common law; if it had intended this result, it was easy by the use of direct words to have accomplished it. The illustrious men who framed that instrument were guarding the foundations of civil liberty against the abuses of unlimited power; they were full of wisdom, and the lessons of history informed them that a trial by an established court, assisted by an impartial jury, was the only sure way of protecting the citizen against oppression and wrong. Knowing this, they limited the suspension to one great right, and left the rest to remain forever inviolable. But, it is insisted that the safety of the country in time of war demands that this broad claim for martial law shall be sustained. If this were true, it could be well said that a country, preserved at the sacrifice of all the cardinal principles of liberty, is not worth the cost of preservation. Happily, it is not so.

It will be borne in mind that this is not a question of the power to proclaim martial law, when war exists in a community and the courts and civil authorities are overthrown. Nor is it a question what rule a military commander, at the head of his army, can impose on states in rebellion to cripple their resources and quell the insurrection. The jurisdiction claimed is much more extensive. The necessities of the service, during the late Rebellion, required that the loyal states should be placed within the limits of certain military districts and commanders appointed in them; and, it is urged, that this, in a military sense, constituted them the theater of military operations; and, as in this case, Indiana had been and was again threatened with invasion by the enemy, the occasion was furnished to establish martial law. The conclusion does not follow from the premises. If armies were collected in Indiana, they were to be employed in another locality, where the laws were obstructed and the national authority disputed. On *her* soil there was no hostile foot; if once invaded, that invasion was at an end, and with it all pretext for martial law. Martial law cannot arise from a *threatened* invasion. The necessity must be actual and present; the invasion real, such as effectually closes the courts and deposes the civil administration.

It is difficult to see how the *safety* of the country required martial law in Indiana. If any of her citizens were plotting treason, the power of arrest could secure them, until the government was prepared for their trial, when the courts were open and ready to try them. It was as easy to protect witnesses before a civil as a military tribunal; and as there could be no wish to convict, except on sufficient legal evidence, surely an ordained and establish court was better able to judge of this than a military tribunal composed of gentlemen not trained to the profession of the law.

It follows, from what has been said on this subject, that there are occasions when martial rule can be properly applied. If, in foreign invasion or civil war, the courts are actually closed, and it is impossible to administer criminal justice according to law, *then*, on the theatre of active military operations, where war really prevails, there is a necessity to furnish a substitute for the civil authority, thus overthrown, to preserve the safety of the army and society; and as no power is left but the military, it is allowed to govern by martial rule until the laws can have their free course. As necessity creates the rule, so it limits its duration; for, if this government is continued *after* the courts are reinstated, it is a gross usurpation of power. Martial rule can never exist where the courts are open, and in the proper and unobstructed exercise of their jurisdiction. It is also confined to the locality of actual war. . . .

If the military trial of Milligan was contrary to law, then he was entitled, on the facts stated in his petition, to be discharged from custody. . . .

But it is insisted that Milligan was a prisoner of war, and, therefore, excluded from the privileges of the statute. It is not easy to see how he can be treated as a prisoner of war, when he lived in Indiana for the past twenty years, was arrested there, and had not been, during the late troubles, a resident of any of the states in rebellion. If in Indiana he conspired with bad men to assist the enemy, he is punishable for it in the courts of Indiana; but, when tried for the offence, he cannot plead the rights of war; for he was not engaged in legal acts of hostility against the government, and only such persons, when captured, are prisoners of war. If he cannot enjoy the immunities attaching to the character of a prisoner of war, how can he be subject to their pains and penalties? . . .

THE CHIEF JUSTICE delivered the following opinion [concurring in the result].

. . . We think that Congress had power, though not exercised, to authorize the military commission which was held in Indiana. . . .

Congress has the power not only to raise and support and govern armies but to declare war. It has, therefore, the power to provide by law for carrying on war. This power necessarily extends to all legislation essential to the prosecution of war with vigor and success, except such as interferes with the command of the forces and the conduct of campaigns. That power and duty belong to the President as commander-in-chief. Both these powers are derived from the Constitution, but neither is defined by that instrument. Their extent must be determined by their nature, and by the principles of our institutions.

The power to make the necessary laws is in Congress; the power to execute in the President. Both powers imply many subordinate and auxiliary powers. Each includes all authorities essential to its due exercise. But neither can the President, in war more than in peace, intrude upon the proper authority of Congress, nor Congress upon the proper authority of the President. Both are servants of the people, whose will is expressed in the fundamental law. Congress cannot direct the conduct of campaigns, nor can the President, or any commander under him, without the sanction of Congress, institute tribunals for the trial and punishment of offences, either of soldiers or civilians, unless in cases of a controlling necessity, which justifies what it compels, or at least insures acts of indemnity from the justice of the legislature.

We by no means assert that Congress can establish and apply the laws of war where no war has been declared or exists.

Where peace exists the laws of peace must prevail. What we do maintain is, that when the nation is involved in war, and some portions of the country are invaded, and all are exposed to invasion, it is within the power of Congress to determine in what states or district such great and imminent public danger exists as justifies the authorization of military tribunals for the trial of crimes and offences against the discipline or security of the army or against the public safety.

In Indiana, for example, at the time of the arrest of Milligan and his co-conspirators, it is established by the papers in the record, that the state was a military district, was the theatre of military operations, had been actually invaded, and was constantly threatened with invasion. It appears, also, that a powerful secret association, composed of citizens and others, existed within the state, under military organization, conspiring against the draft, and plotting insurrection, the liberation of the prisoners of war at various depots, the seizure of the state and national arsenals, armed cooperation with the enemy, and war against the national government.

We cannot doubt that, in such a time of public danger, Congress had power, under the Constitution, to provide for the organization of a military commission, and for trial by that commission of persons engaged in this conspiracy. The fact that the Federal courts were open was regarded by Congress as a sufficient reason for not exercising the power; but that fact could not deprive Congress of the right to exercise it. Those courts might be open and undisturbed in the execution of their functions, and yet wholly incompetent to avert threatened danger, or to punish, with adequate promptitude and certainty, the guilty conspirators.

In Indiana, the judges and officers of the courts were loyal to the government. But it might have been otherwise. In times of rebellion and civil war it may often happen, indeed, that judges and marshals will be in active sympathy with the rebels, and courts their most efficient allies.

We have confined ourselves to the question of power. It was for Congress to determine the question of expediency. And Congress did determine it. That body did not see fit to authorize trials by military commission in Indiana, but by the strongest implication prohibited them. . . .

MARTIAL LAW PROPER . . . is called into action by Congress, or temporarily, when the action of Congress cannot be invited, and in the case of justifying or excusing peril, by the President, in times of insurrection or invasion, or of civil or foreign war, within districts or localities where ordinary law no longer adequately secures public safety and private rights.

We think that the power of Congress, in such times and in such localities, to authorize trials for crimes against the security and safety of the national forces, may be derived from its constitutional authority to raise and support armies and to declare war, if not from its constitutional authority to provide for governing the national forces.

We have no apprehension that this power, under our American system of government, in which all official authority is derived from the people, and exercised under direct responsibility to the people, is more likely to be abused than the power to regulate commerce, or the power to borrow money. And we are unwilling to give our assent by silence to expressions of opinion which seem to us calculated, though not intended, to cripple the constitutional powers of the government, and to augment the public dangers in times of invasion and rebellion.

Mr. Justice Wayne, Mr. Justice Swayne, and Mr. Justice Miller concur with me in these views.

FOR DISCUSSION

In June 1942, eight Nazi saboteurs, all of whom were German-born but two of whom were United States citizens, landed in the United States, planning to destroy various war-related facilities. They wore full or partial military uniforms, to entitle them to prisoner-of-war status should they be captured. After the landings, however, they disposed of the uniforms and traveled in civilian clothes, in violation of the law of war. The plan fell apart almost immediately, in part because two of the men turned themselves in to the FBI (which did not believe them at first). The remaining six were quickly captured. All eight were tried by a military commission, authorized by the President, which promptly sentenced them to death. (The sentences of the two who had turned themselves in were commuted to life imprisonment, and they were deported after the war). The Supreme Court met in special session in July 1942 to determine whether this proceeding was valid. Was it valid, with respect to the citizen defendants? With respect to the non-citizens? Was it distinguishable from *Milligan*? See *Ex parte Quirin* (1942), p. 850.

---

3.   Emancipation

Of Lincoln's personal antipathy toward slavery there could be no doubt. "If slavery is not wrong, nothing is wrong," he wrote in a letter in 1864. "I can not remember when I did not so think, and feel." But at the outset of the Civil War he did not believe that he had authority to end slavery anywhere. And he did not regard the war as one against slavery. On the contrary, he famously said, "If I could save the Union without freeing any slave I would do it, and if I could save the Union by freeing all the slaves I would do it. And if I could save it by freeing some and leaving others alone, I would also do that."

Recall that at his inauguration Lincoln endorsed the Corwin Amendment, which would have entrenched the states' right to permit slavery. Moreover, early in his Administration he forbade his generals to effect military emancipation, and he overruled his Secretary of War's proposal to arm freed slaves. But contexts often change rapidly during wartime. "I claim not to have controlled events," Lincoln wrote in that same 1864 letter, "but confess plainly that events have controlled me."

In August 1861, Lincoln signed the First Confiscation Act, which authorized the seizure of property—including the freeing of slaves—used in the
rebellion. In March 1862, he signed a statute forbidding Union Army officers
to return fugitives from slavery. On April 10, he signed a joint resolution providing in principle that

> the United States ought to coöperate with any State which may adopt
> gradual abolishment of slavery, giving to such State pecuniary aid, to
> be used by such State in its discretion, to compensate for the incon-
> veniences, public and private, produced by such change of system.

Six days later he signed a statute that actually put into effect a system of compensated emancipation in the District of Columbia, which turned out to be
the only place in the nation where slave holders were compensated by law for
emancipation of their slaves. On June 19, he signed another statute that prohibited slavery in United States territories—thus effectively defying the *Scott
v. Sandford* decision. (Had a case arisen, a Supreme Court stocked with Republicans no doubt would have upheld the statute.) In July, Lincoln signed the
Second Confiscation Act, which freed anyone enslaved by individuals active
in the rebellion.

Then, after the Union victory at Antietam, by now—at least as he
claimed—convinced of the military necessity, Lincoln issued the following
proclamation.

Preliminary Emancipation Proclamation

(September 22, 1862)

I, Abraham Lincoln, President of the United States of America, and
Commander-in-chief of the Army and Navy thereof, do hereby proclaim and
declare that hereafter, as heretofore, the war will be prosecuted for the object
of practically restoring the constitutional relation between the United States
and each of the States, and the people thereof, in which States that relation is
or may be suspended or disturbed.

That it is my purpose, upon the next meeting of Congress, to again recommend the adoption of a practical measure tendering pecuniary aid to the
free acceptance or rejection of all slave States, so-called, the people whereof

may not then be in rebellion against the United States, and which States may then have voluntarily adopted, or thereafter may voluntarily adopt, immediate or gradual abolishment of slavery within their respective limits; and that the efforts to colonize persons of African descent, with their consent, upon this continent or elsewhere, with the previously obtained consent of the governments existing there, will be continued.

That on the first day of January, in the year of our Lord one thousand eight hundred and sixty-three, all persons held as slaves within any State, or designated part of a State, the people whereof shall then be in rebellion against the United States, shall be then, thenceforward, and forever free; and the Executive Government of the United States, including the military and naval authority thereof, will recognize and maintain the freedom of such persons, and will do no act or acts to repress such persons, or any of them, in any efforts they may make for their actual freedom.

That the Executive will, on the first day of January aforesaid, by proclamation, designate the States and parts of States, if any, in which the people thereof respectively shall then be in rebellion against the United States, and the fact that any State, or the people thereof, shall on that day be in good faith represented in the Congress of the United States, by members chosen thereto at elections wherein a majority of the qualified voters of such State shall have participated, shall, in the absence of strong countervailing testimony, be deemed conclusive evidence that such State, and the people thereof, are not then in rebellion against the United States.

That attention is hereby called to an Act of Congress entitled [the Second Confiscation Act], approved July 17, 1862, and which sections are in the words and figures following:

> Sec. 9. And be it further enacted, That all slaves of persons who shall hereafter be engaged in rebellion against the government of the United States, or who shall in any way give aid or comfort thereto, escaping from such persons and taking refuge within the lines of the army; and all slaves captured from such persons or deserted by them and coming under the control of the government of the United States; and all slaves of such persons found on [or] being within any place occupied by rebel forces and afterwards occupied by the forces of the United States, shall be deemed captives of war, and shall be forever free of their servitude and not again held as slaves.

... And the Executive will in due time recommend that all citizens of the United States who shall have remained loyal thereto throughout the rebellion shall (upon the restoration of the constitutional relation between the United States and their respective States and people, if that relation shall have been suspended or disturbed) be compensated for all losses by acts of the United States, including the loss of slaves.

In witness whereof I have hereunto set my hand and caused the seal of the United States to be affixed. . . .

ABRAHAM LINCOLN.

By the President:

WILLIAM H. SEWARD, Secretary of State.

One hundred days later, on January 1, 1863, Lincoln issued the promised final proclamation. Designating eight states (Arkansas, Texas, Mississippi, Alabama, Florida, Georgia, South Carolina, and North Carolina) and parts of two others (Louisiana and Virginia) as being in rebellion, he declared "that all persons held as slaves within said designated States, and parts of States, are, and henceforward shall be free." Lincoln asserted that this was "a fit and necessary war measure for suppressing [the] rebellion" and closed by saying:

And upon this act, sincerely believed to be an act of justice, warranted by the Constitution, upon military necessity, I invoke the considerate judgment of mankind, and the gracious favor of Almighty God.

The next excerpt is taken from a pamphlet published between the time of the two proclamations by

FOR DISCUSSION

What argument might support Lincoln's assertion that the emancipation was justified as a matter of military necessity? Are you persuaded?

Benjamin Curtis, who had retired at age 47 from the Supreme Court shortly after *Scott v. Sandford* and returned to private practice in Boston.

Benjamin R. Curtis, Executive Power

(1862)

I do not understand it to be the purpose of the President to incite a part of the inhabitants of the United States to rise in insurrection against valid laws; but that by virtue of some power which he possesses, he proposes to annul those laws, so that they are no longer to have any operation. . . .

What is the source of these vast powers? Have they any limit? Are they derived from, or are they utterly inconsistent with, the Constitution of the United States?

The only supposed source or measure of these vast powers appears to have been designated by the President, in his reply to the address of the Chicago clergymen, in the following words: "Understand, I raise no objection against it on legal or constitutional grounds; for, *as commander-in-chief of the army and navy, in time of war, I suppose I have a right to take any measure, which may best subdue the enemy.*" This is a clear and frank declaration of the opinion of the President respecting the origin and extent of the power he supposes himself to possess; and, so far as I know, *no source of these powers other than the authority of commander-in-chief in time of war, has ever been suggested.* . . .

It must be obvious to the meanest capacity, that if the President of the United States has an *implied* constitutional right, as commander-in-chief of the army and navy in time of war, to disregard any one positive prohibition of the Constitution, or to exercise any one power not delegated to the United States by the Constitution, because, in his judgment, he may thereby "best subdue the enemy," he has the same right, for the same reason, to disregard each and every provision of the Constitution, and to exercise all power, *needful, in his opinion,* to enable him "best to subdue the enemy."

It has never been doubted that the power to abolish slavery within the States was not delegated to the United States by the Constitution, but was re-served to the States. If the President, as commander-in-chief of the army and navy in time of war, may, by an executive decree, exercise this power to abolish slavery in the States, which power was reserved to the States, because he is of opinion that he may thus "best subdue the enemy," what other power, reserved to the States or to the people, may not be exercised by the President, for the same reason, that he is of opinion he may thus best subdue the enemy? And if so, what distinction can be made between powers not delegated to the United

States at all, and powers which, though thus delegated, are conferred by the Constitution upon some department of the government other than the executive?

Indeed, the proclamation of September 24, 1862, followed by the orders of the war department, intended to carry it into practical effect, are manifest assumptions, by the President, of powers delegated to the Congress and to the judicial department of the government. It is a clear and undoubted prerogative of Congress alone, to define all offences, and to affix to each some appropriate and not cruel or unusual punishment. But this proclamation and these orders create new offences, not known to any law of the United States. "Discouraging enlistments," and "any disloyal practice," are not offences known to any law of the United States. . . .

WORTH NOTING

The proclamation to which Curtis refers subjected rebels and persons aiding them to martial law and suspended habeas corpus with respect to persons arrested during the rebellion by military authority.

The necessary result of [the] interpretation of the Constitution [implied by the President's conduct] is, that, in time of war, the President has any and all power, which he may deem it necessary to exercise, to subdue the enemy; and that every private and personal right of individual security against mere executive control, and every right reserved to the States or the people, rests merely upon executive discretion.

But the military power of the President is derived solely from the Constitution; and it is as sufficiently defined there as his purely civil power. . . . He is the general-in-chief; and as such, in prosecuting war, may do what generals in the field are allowed to do within the sphere of their actual operations, *in subordination to the laws of their country, from which alone they derive their authority.* . . .[*]

If it were admitted that a commanding general in the field might do whatever in his discretion might be necessary to subdue the enemy, he could levy

---

[*] The case of *Mitchel vs. Harmony* (13 How. 115), presented for the decision of the Supreme Court of the United States, the question of the extent of the right of a commanding general in the field to appropriate private property to the public service, and it was decided that such an appropriation might be made, in case it should be rendered necessary by an immediate and pressing danger or urgent necessity existing at the time, and not admitting of delay, but not otherwise. . . . It may safely be said that neither of the very eminent counsel by whom that case was argued, and that no judge before whom it came, had then advanced to the conception that a commanding general may lawfully take any measure which may best subdue the enemy. The wagons, mules, and packages seized by General Donophon, in that case, were of essential service in his brilliant and successful attack on the lines of Chihuahua. But this did not save him from being liable to their owner as a mere wrongdoer, under the Constitution and laws of the United States.

contributions to pay his soldiers; he could force conscripts into his service; he could drive out of the entire country all persons not desirous to aid him;—in short, he would be the absolute master of the country for the time being. No one has ever supposed—no one will now undertake to maintain—that the commander-in-chief, in time of war, has any such lawful authority as this.

What, then, is his authority over the persons and property of citizens? I answer, that, over all persons enlisted in his forces he has military power and command; that over all persons and property *within the sphere of his actual operations in the field*, he may lawfully exercise such restraint and control as the successful prosecution of his particular military enterprise may, in his honest judgment, absolutely require; and upon such persons as have committed offences against any article of war, he may, through appropriate military tribunals, inflict the punishment prescribed by law. *And there his lawful authority ends.*

The military power over citizens and their property is a power to *act*, not a power to prescribe rules for *future* action. It springs from present pressing emergencies, and is limited by them. It cannot assume the functions of the statesman or legislator, and make provision for future or distant arrangements by which persons or property may be made subservient to military uses. It is the physical force of an army in the field, and may control whatever is so near as to be actually reached by that force, in order to remove obstructions to its exercise.

But when the military commander controls the persons or property of citizens, who are beyond the sphere of his actual operations in the field when he makes laws to govern their conduct, he becomes a legislator. . . . [W]hether his edicts are clothed in the form of proclamations, or of military orders, by whatever name they may be called, they are laws. If he have the legislative power, conferred on him by the people, it is well. If not, he usurps it. He has no more lawful authority to hold all the *citizens* of the entire country, outside of the sphere of his actual operations in the field, amenable to his military edicts, than he has to hold all the *property* of the country subject to his military requisitions. He is not the military commander of the *citizens* of the United States, but of its *soldiers*. . . .

What then is to be done? Are we to cease our utmost efforts to save our country, because its chief magistrate seems to have fallen, for the time being, into what we believe would be fatal errors if persisted in by him and acquiesced in by ourselves? Certainly not. Let the people but be right, and no President can long be wrong; nor can he effect any fatal mischief if he should be.

The sober second thought of the people has yet a controlling power. Let this gigantic shadow, which has been evoked out of the powers of the commander-in-chief, once be placed before the people, so that they can see clearly its proportions and its mien, and it will dissolve and disappear like the morning cloud before the rising sun.

The people yet can and will take care, by legitimate means, without disturbing any principle of the Constitution, or violating any law, or relaxing any of their utmost efforts for their country's salvation, that their will, embodied in the Constitution, shall be obeyed. If it needs amendment, they will amend it themselves. They will suffer nothing to be added to it, or taken from it, by any other power than their own. If they should, neither the government itself, nor any right under it, will any longer be theirs.

G.　Reconstruction

In the Union's view, the states had never left the Union. But clearly they had not played a role in its governance, and the Confederate governments could not be used as the basis for resuming the seceding states' roles in the Union. This problem created theoretical as well as practical difficulties.

1.　West Virginia

In one state, Virginia, reconstruction began even while most of the state was under Confederate control. The northern and western portions of the state, where the enslaved population was much smaller, were largely hostile to secession. After the state as a whole adopted an ordinance of secession, voters in that loyalist area, by a series of votes, declared the ordinance invalid and set up a rival legislature, purportedly governing the whole state, which for a time sent representatives to Congress. This loyalist legislature consented to the division of the state, and so a new state of West Virginia was created in 1863. Then, not wanting to create a precedent that would make readmission of the Southern states too easy, Congress had second thoughts about the legitimacy of the rump legislature, and Virginia's seats were declared vacant until 1870.

2.　Presidential Reconstruction Under Lincoln

Lincoln, with the election of 1864 in mind, was eager to restore the Southern states to the Union, and bring the war to a close, as quickly as possible.

In December 1863, he adopted a moderate program, the Ten Percent Plan, to govern reconstruction in Confederate territories that had come under Union control: If 10% of the number of voters from 1860 swore allegiance to the Union, then voters in the state would be authorized, under Presidential supervision, to form a new state constitution. Lincoln required, as a condition of Presidential recognition, that the new constitution abolish slavery. Lincoln ultimately recognized new governments in four states—Louisiana, Arkansas, Tennessee, and Virginia. But by the time of his death Congress had refused to seat the members of Congress elected from those states.

Meanwhile, Congress passed the Wade-Davis Bill, which would have required for readmission of each rebellious state an "ironclad oath" by a majority of voters in the state that they had never voluntarily supported the Confederacy. Lincoln had both theoretical and practical difficulties with the bill: It treated the Southern states as having left the Union, which of course Lincoln maintained had never happened, and he regarded the plan as impractically stringent, likely not to be satisfied in any state. And so he pocket vetoed it. When Lincoln was assassinated, the question of what the standards would be for restoring the rebellious states to their full rights in Congress remained unresolved.

3. The Thirteenth Amendment and the Civil Rights Act of 1866

The Senate passed the Thirteenth Amendment, by a 38–6 margin, in April 1864, but the House declined to do so. Lincoln made nationwide abolition of slavery a plank in the 1864 campaign of the Republican Party, renamed the National Union Party for that election. On January 31, 1865, the House passed the amendment by a 119–56 vote, and the next day Lincoln—contrary to precedent for constitutional amendments—signed it. Read the Amendment.

The chief Confederate army surrendered at Appomattox on April 9, virtually ending the Civil War. On April 15, Lincoln died. The new President was Andrew Johnson. Johnson had been a Democratic Senator from Tennessee and was the only member of the Senate from the Confederate states to continue participation in the Union Congress during the war. In 1862, Lincoln appointed him military governor of Tennessee. He was considered a savvy political choice in 1864 to broaden the appeal of the President's party. Like Lincoln, Johnson pursued a strategy for reconstruction—he preferred to call it "restoration"—that a majority of Congress regarded as too lenient. But, also like Lincoln, he actively promoted adoption of the Thirteenth Amendment; indeed, he pressured the state legislatures that he recognized to adopt it.

FOR DISCUSSION

At the time the Thirteenth Amendment was ratified, Congress did not recognize representatives of any of the Confederate states, including those that voted to ratify. Does this present a problem for the Amendment's validity?

On December 18, Secretary of State Seward declared that the Thirteenth Amendment had been ratified by legislatures in 27 of the 36 states and was part of the Constitution. Eight of the 27 were from former Confederate states—including the loyalist Virginia legislature and seven that had been recognized by one President or the other.

In immediate response to the abolition of slavery, legislatures of the southern states passed the so-called Black Codes, intended to maintain the subjugation of the freedmen. These took various forms. Some, for example, punished given conduct more severely for black defendants than for whites; others imposed racial restrictions on travel and the ability to contract.

On April 9, 1866, over President Johnson's veto, Congress passed the Civil Rights Act of 1866. This was the first major piece of legislation in American history passed over the President's veto. Section 1 of the Act read:

> *Be it enacted* by the Senate and House of Representatives of the United States of America in Congress assembled, That all persons born in the United States and not subject to any foreign power, excluding Indians not taxed, are hereby declared to be citizens of the United States; and such citizens, of every race and color, without regard to any previous condition of slavery or involuntary servitude, except as a punishment for crime whereof the party shall have been duly convicted, shall have the same right, in every State and Territory in the United States, to make and enforce contracts, to sue, be parties, and give evidence, to inherit, purchase, lease, sell, hold, and convey real and personal property, and to full and equal benefit of all laws and proceedings for the security of person and property, as is enjoyed by

white citizens, and shall be subject to like punishment, pains, and penalties, and to none other, any law, statute, ordinance, regulation, or custom, to the contrary notwithstanding.

FOR DISCUSSION

Suppose you are counsel to President Johnson. He is inclined to veto the Civil Rights Act of 1866 and would like to raise constitutional arguments against it. What arguments might he make? What counter-arguments might you expect?

The essence of the "same right" language of this statute remains in force, as 42 U.S.C. § 1981(a):

All persons within the jurisdiction of the United States shall have the same right in every State and Territory to make and enforce contracts, to sue, be parties, give evidence, and to the full and equal benefit of all laws and proceedings for the security of persons and property as is enjoyed by white citizens, and shall be subject to the like punishment, pains, penalties, taxes, licenses, and exactions of every kind, and to no other.

FOR DISCUSSION

A private home developer makes clear that its policy is to refuse to sell to African-Americans. Does § 1981(a) by its terms prohibit that discrimination? If so, is the statute valid under the Constitution as it stood in 1867? What if the developer refuses to sell to Mexican-Americans? See *Jones v. Alfred H. Mayer Co.* (1968).

4.   The Reconstruction Acts

From the time of Johnson's veto of the Civil Rights Act of 1866, he and Congress were in bitter opposition. The Radical wing of the Republican party— those who were most inclined to impose stringent conditions for readmission of the Southern states—gained considerable force in the 1866 elections. Just before the term of the old Congress expired, it passed a dramatic statute, the first Reconstruction Act of 1867. This Act recited that "no legal State governments nor adequate protection for life or property now exists" in ten of the rebel states (Tennessee excepted). It divided those states into five military districts, each to be governed by a general assigned by the President. That officer would have the discretion to displace civil courts by military tribunals. The statute further provided a mechanism for each of the ten states to gain readmission to Congress and remove itself from military rule: The state would have to hold a convention of delegates chosen in an election at which all adult males could vote, except those disqualified by reason of felony or participation in the rebellion. The convention would have to frame a state constitution in conformity with the Constitution of the United States and providing for similarly universal male suffrage, and the constitution would have to be ratified by the voters of the state and approved by Congress. And finally, the state legislature created by that constitution would have to ratify the Fourteenth Amendment, as part of the Constitution of the United States.

Johnson vetoed the Act, but it was passed over his veto.

For Discussion

(1) Does the premise behind the First Reconstruction Act of 1867 suggest that ratification of the Thirteenth Amendment was invalid?

(2) Given that votes of states acting pursuant to this statute were necessary for ratification of the Fourteenth Amendment, was ratification of that Amendment valid?

(3) Apart from these concerns, was the statute substantively valid?

Mississippi v. Johnson

Supreme Court of the United States, 1867.
71 U.S. 475.

THE CHIEF JUSTICE delivered the opinion of the court.

A motion was made, some days since, in behalf of the State of Mississippi, for leave to file a bill in the name of the State, praying this court perpetually to enjoin and restrain Andrew Johnson, President of the United States, and E.

O. C. Ord, general commanding in the District of Mississippi and Arkansas, from executing, or in any manner carrying out [the first Reconstruction Act and a supplemental act, relating to registration of voters.]

The Attorney-General objected to the leave asked for, upon the ground that no bill which makes a President a defendant, and seeks an injunction against him to restrain the performance of his duties as President, should be allowed to be filed in this court. . . . The single point which requires consideration is this: Can the President be restrained by injunction from carrying into effect an act of Congress alleged to be unconstitutional?

It is assumed by the counsel for the State of Mississippi, that the President, in the execution of the Reconstruction Acts, is required to perform a mere ministerial duty. In this assumption there is, we think, a confounding of the terms ministerial and executive, which are by no means equivalent in import.

A ministerial duty, the performance of which may, in proper cases, be required of the head of a department, by judicial process, is one in respect to which nothing is left to discretion. It is a simple, definite duty, arising under conditions admitted or proved to exist, and imposed by law. The case of *Marbury v. Madison, Secretary of State* (1803), furnishes an illustration. A citizen had been nominated, confirmed, and appointed a justice of the peace for the District of Columbia, and his commission had been made out, signed, and sealed. Nothing remained to be done except delivery, and the duty of delivery was imposed by law on the Secretary of State. It was held that the performance of this duty might be enforced by *mandamus* issuing from a court having jurisdiction. So, in the case of *Kendall, Postmaster-General, v. Stockton & Stokes* (1839), an act of Congress had directed the Postmaster-General to credit Stockton & Stokes with such sums as the Solicitor of the Treasury should find due to them; and that officer refused to credit them with certain sums, so found due. It was held that the crediting of this money was a mere ministerial duty, the performance of which might be judicially enforced.

In each of these cases nothing was left to discretion. There was no room for the exercise of judgment. The law required the performance of a single specific act; and that performance, it was held, might be required by *mandamus*.

Very different is the duty of the President in the exercise of the power to see that the laws are faithfully executed, and among these laws the acts named in the bill. By the first of these acts he is required to assign generals to command in the several military districts, and to detail sufficient military force to enable such officers to discharge their duties under the law. By the supplementary act, other duties are imposed on the several commanding generals, and these duties must necessarily be performed under the supervision of the President as commander-in-chief. The duty thus imposed on the President is in no just sense ministerial. It is purely executive and political.

FOR DISCUSSION Does the discretionary-ministerial distinction make sense as a basis for deciding whether the judiciary may restrain the executive branch? Does the executive have discretion in enforcing an unconstitutional statute?

An attempt on the part of the judicial department of the government to enforce the performance of such duties by the President might be justly characterized, in the language of Chief Justice Marshall, as "an absurd and excessive extravagance."

It is true that in the instance before us the interposition of the court is not sought to enforce action by the Executive under constitutional legislation, but to restrain such action under legislation alleged to be unconstitutional. But we are unable to perceive that this circumstance takes the case out of the general principles which forbid judicial interference with the exercise of Executive discretion. . . .

The Congress is the legislative department of the government; the President is the executive department. Neither can be restrained in its action by the judicial department; though the acts of both, when performed, are, in proper cases, subject to its cognizance. The impropriety of such interference will be clearly seen upon consideration of its possible consequences.

Suppose the bill filed and the injunction prayed for allowed. If the President refuse obedience, it is needless to observe that the court is without power to enforce its process. If, on the other hand, the President complies with the order of the court and refuses to execute the acts of Congress, is it not clear that a collision may occur between the executive and legislative departments of the government? May not the House of Representatives impeach the President for such refusal? And in that case could this court interfere, in behalf of the President, thus endangered by compliance with its mandate, and restrain by injunction

FOR DISCUSSION Is the Court's discussion of a three-branch impasse persuasive? What would you expect the Court in modern days to say about it?

the Senate of the United States from sitting as a court of impeachment? Would the strange spectacle be offered to the public world of an attempt by this court to arrest proceedings in that court?

These questions answer themselves.

It is true that a State may file an original bill in this court. And it may be true, in some cases, that such a bill may be filed against the United States. But we are fully satisfied that this court has no jurisdiction of a bill to enjoin the President in the performance of his official duties; and that no such bill ought to be received by us.

It has been suggested that the bill contains a prayer that, if the relief sought cannot be had against Andrew Johnson, as President, it may be granted against Andrew Johnson as a citizen of Tennessee. But it is plain that relief as against the execution of an act of Congress by Andrew Johnson, is relief against its execution by the President. A bill praying an injunction against the execution of an act of Congress by the incumbent of the presidential office cannot be received, whether it describes him as President or as a citizen of a State.

The motion for leave to file the bill is, therefore, DENIED.

Mississippi lost, having made the President the defendant. Georgia set its sights lower, suing the Secretary of War (Edwin Stanton), the general-in-chief of the army (Ulysses Grant), and the military commandant of its district (John Pope) for an injunction against enforcement of the Reconstruction Act. It fared no better, however; for in *Georgia v. Stanton* (1868), the Court dismissed the suit for lack of jurisdiction, holding that the matter presented a political question:

> [A] case must be presented appropriate for the exercise of judicial power; the rights in danger, as we have seen, must be rights of persons or property, not merely political rights, which do not belong to the jurisdiction of a court, either in law or equity. . . .
>
> [W]e are called upon to restrain the defendants, who represent the executive authority of the government, from carrying into execution certain acts of Congress, inasmuch as such execution would annul, and totally abolish the existing State government of Georgia, and establish another and different one in its place; in other words, would overthrow and destroy the corporate existence of the State, by

depriving it of all the means and instrumentalities whereby its existence might, and, otherwise would, be maintained. . . .

That these matters, both as stated in the body of the bill, and, in the prayers for relief, call for the judgment of the court upon political questions, and, upon rights, not of persons or property, but of a political character, will hardly be denied. For the rights for the protection of which our authority is invoked, are the rights of sovereignty, of political jurisdiction, of government, of corporate existence as a State, with all its constitutional powers and privileges. No case of private rights or private property infringed, or in danger of actual or threatened infringement, is presented by the bill, in a judicial form, for the judgment of the court.

It is true, the bill, in setting forth the political rights of the State, and of its people to be protected, among other matters, avers, that Georgia owns certain real estate and buildings therein, State capitol, and executive mansion, and other real and personal property; and that putting the acts of Congress into execution, and destroying the State, would deprive it of the possession and enjoyment of its property. But, it is apparent, that this reference to property and statement concerning it, are only by way of showing one of the grievances resulting from the threatened destruction of the State, and in aggravation of it, not as a specific ground of relief. . . .

The comments near the end of this excerpt suggest that the result might have been different had the party challenging the Reconstruction Acts complained about a specific deprivation of liberty or property. William McCardle brought exactly such a complaint. A newspaper publisher in Mississippi, he was thrown in jail by the military governor for writing articles deemed incendiary. He sought but failed to gain his release in federal court in Mississippi through a habeas corpus petition. When the United States Supreme Court held that it had jurisdiction to hear his appeal, *Ex parte McCardle* (1868), it appeared that the validity of the Reconstruction Acts would be determined at last. McCardle's case was argued on the merits in March 1868, with the arguments concluding on March 9. The Court considered the case at conference on March 21 but voted to postpone decision, because both houses of Congress had passed a bill repealing the provision of the 1867 statute that gave the Court jurisdiction. The President vetoed the bill, as expected, but on March 27 Congress overrode the veto. The Court then unanimously held that it did not have jurisdiction over the case. *Ex parte McCardle* (1869).

For Discussion

(1) Putting aside for the moment the fact that the 1868 statute was applied in *McCardle* to a pending case that had already been argued in the Supreme Court, was its repeal of Supreme Court jurisdiction constitutional? On what provision of the Constitution do you suppose the statute was based? Are there any limits to the ability of Congress to deny jurisdiction to the Supreme Court? What is the effect of such a denial?

(2) Could the 1868 statute be validly applied to a case pending in the Supreme Court? Should the Court have been willing to strain to construe the statute as not applying to pending cases? Compare *Hamdan v. Rumsfeld* (2006).

The Supreme Court never did rule on the constitutional validity of the governance system created by the Reconstruction Acts.

5. The Impeachment of Johnson

On March 3, 1867, the outgoing Congress passed—over Johnson's veto—the Tenure of Office Act, providing that the President could not, absent the advice and consent of the Senate, remove an officer appointed by a prior President. The President could suspend the officer while the

 CROSS REFERENCE Do you believe the Tenure of Office Act was valid? Congressional attempts to restrain the removal power are further considered pp. 773–812.

Senate was out of session, however. The Act was passed largely to protect Stanton, the Secretary of War. Johnson did suspend Stanton, but when the Senate returned it refused to give consent. Johnson, at least arguably in violation of the Act, attempted on February 21, 1868, to remove Stanton and appoint a new interim Secretary. Three days later, the House impeached Johnson. Ultimately, he escaped conviction by one vote in the Senate.

FOR DISCUSSION What do you suppose was the real impulse behind the impeachment of Johnson?

6. Adoption and Initial Judicial Construction of the Fourteenth and Fifteenth Amendments

Read the Fourteenth and Fifteenth Amendments, each of which was passed after the Civil War. Together with the Thirteenth Amendment, which abolished slavery, they are known as the "Reconstruction Amendments." Over time, the Fourteenth Amendment in particular transformed American constitutional law; it will be the focus of a considerable portion of our attention for the remainder of the course. While the Amendment was proposed in significant part to ensure that the Civil Rights Act of 1866 would not be held unconstitutional, it went beyond that purpose; indeed, Congress began working on it before the Civil Rights Act was passed.

The Fourteenth Amendment in particular quickly became—as it has remained—a source of deep and contentious debate. Those who favored a relatively broad interpretation argued that their opponents were failing to give the hard-won guarantees of the Amendment their natural implications. Those who favored relatively narrow interpretation argued that the Amendment was never intended to give the judiciary the equivalent of a veto power over a broad swath of social and economic legislation. We will begin with the *Slaughter-House Cases*, the Supreme Court's first judicial construction of the Reconstruction Era amendments. We will then read more recent discussions of the drafting of the Fourteenth Amendment, focusing on two issues that remain of central importance: the meaning of § 1 and the scope of the enforcement power under § 5.

a. Privileges or Immunities of Citizens

In *Barron v. Baltimore*, the Supreme Court held that the Bill of Rights did not apply to the states. Did the Fourteenth Amendment change that rule? The Reconstruction-era court gave an initial answer in *The*

CROSS REFERENCE An excerpt from *Barron* is presented at pp. 61–64.

Slaughter-House Cases (1873). The Court's discussion focused principally on the amendment's "privileges or immunities" clause, but its discussion ranged across all three Reconstruction Amendments. The underlying litigation was triggered by a state-enforced monopoly on butcher's services in the City of New Orleans. Tired of finding animal remains from upstream slaughterhouses in their drinking water, city leadership sought relief from the state legislature, which chartered the Crescent City Live-Stock Landing and Slaughter-House Company. The Company was authorized to run a Grand Slaughterhouse at the southern edge of the city, and was given a 25-year monopoly within a prescribed 1154-square-mile area that included New Orleans. The Company was expected not to do the slaughtering itself but to provide space and facilities for butchers for prescribed fees. Over four hundred butchers brought suit to prevent the monopoly. The Supreme Court held that the Fourteenth Amendment did not bar the monopoly:

WORTH NOTING

The butchers were represented by John A. Campbell, a former Justice of the Supreme Court who had resigned after his home state of Alabama seceded.

The Slaughter-House Cases

Supreme Court of the United States, 1873.
83 U.S. 36.

Mr. Justice Miller, now, April 14th, 1873, delivered the opinion of the court. . . .

. . . The power here exercised by the legislature of Louisiana is, in its essential nature, one which has been, up to the present period in the constitutional history of this country, always conceded to belong to the States, however it may *now* be questioned in some of its details. "Unwholesome trades, slaughter-houses, operations offensive to the senses, the deposit of powder, the application of steam power to propel cars, the building with combustible materials, and the burial of the dead, may all," says Chancellor [James] Kent, "be interdicted by law, in the midst of dense masses of population, on the general and rational principle, that every person ought so to use his property as not to injure his neighbors; and that private interests must be made subservient to the general interests of the community." This is called the police power; and it is declared by Chief

Justice Shaw that it is much easier to perceive and realize the existence and sources of it than to mark its boundaries, or prescribe limits to its exercise. . . .

The plaintiffs in error . . . allege that the statute is a violation of the Constitution of the United States in . . . [t]hat it abridges the privileges and immunities of citizens of the United States. . . .

[O]n the most casual examination of the language of [the Reconstruction] amendments, no one can fail to be impressed with the one pervading purpose found in them all, lying at the foundation of each, and without which none of them would have been even suggested; we mean the freedom of the slave race, the security and firm establishment of that freedom, and the protection of the newly-made freeman and citizen from the oppressions of those who had formerly exercised unlimited dominion over him. It is true that only the fifteenth amendment, in terms, mentions the negro by speaking of his color and his slavery. But it is just as true that each of the other articles was addressed to the grievances of that race, and designed to remedy them as the fifteenth.

We do not say that no one else but the negro can share in this protection. Both the language and spirit of these articles are to have their fair and just weight in any question of construction. . . . But what we do say, and what we wish to be understood is, that in any fair and just construction of any section or phrase of these amendments, it is necessary to look to the purpose which we have said was the pervading spirit of them all, the evil which they were designed to remedy, and the process of continued addition to the Constitution, until that purpose was supposed to be accomplished, as far as constitutional law can accomplish it. . . .

Was it the purpose of the fourteenth amendment, by the simple declaration that no State should make or enforce any law which shall abridge the privileges and immunities of *citizens of the United States*, to transfer the security and protection of all the civil rights which we have mentioned, from the States to the Federal government? And where it is declared that Congress shall have the power to enforce that article, was it intended to bring within the power of Congress the entire domain of civil rights heretofore belonging exclusively to the States? . . .

[S]uch a construction followed by the reversal of the judgments of the Supreme Court of Louisiana in these cases, would constitute this court a perpetual censor upon all legislation of the States, on the civil rights of their own citizens, with authority to nullify such as it did not approve as consistent with those rights, as they existed at the time of the adoption of this amendment. . . . We are convinced that no such results were intended by the Congress which proposed these amendments, nor by the legislatures of the States which ratified them. . . .

But lest it should be said that no such privileges and immunities are to be found if those we have been considering are excluded, we venture to suggest some which owe their existence to the Federal government, its National character, its Constitution, or its laws. One of these is well described in the case of *Crandall v. Nevada* (1868). It is said to be the right of the citizen of this great country, protected by implied guarantees of its Constitution,

> to come to the seat of government to assert any claim he may have upon that government, to transact any business he may have with it, to seek its protection, to share its offices, to engage in administering its functions. He has the right of free access to its seaports, through which all operations of foreign commerce are conducted, to the sub-treasuries, land offices, and courts of justice in the several States. . . .

Another privilege of a citizen of the United States is to demand the care and protection of the Federal government over his life, liberty, and property when on the high seas or within the jurisdiction of a foreign government. Of this there can be no doubt, nor that the right depends upon his character as a citizen of the United States. The right to peaceably assemble and petition for redress of grievances, the privilege of the writ of *habeas corpus*, are rights of the citizen guaranteed by the Federal Constitution. The right to use the navigable waters of the United States, however they may penetrate the territory of the several States, all rights secured to our citizens by treaties with foreign nations, are dependent upon citizenship of the United States, and not citizenship of a State. One of these privileges is conferred by the very article under consideration. It is that a citizen of the United States can, of his own volition, become a citizen of any State of the Union by a *bona fide* residence therein, with the same rights as other citizens of that State. To these may be added the rights secured by the thirteenth and fifteenth articles of amendment, and by the other clause of the fourteenth, next to be considered.

But it is useless to pursue this branch of the inquiry, since we are of opinion that the rights claimed by these plaintiffs in error, if they have any existence, are not privileges and immunities of citizens of the United States within the meaning of the clause of the fourteenth amendment under consideration. . . .

MR. JUSTICE FIELD, dissenting:

. . . The act of Louisiana presents the naked case, unaccompanied by any public considerations, where a right to pursue a lawful and necessary calling, previously enjoyed by every citizen, and in connection with which a thousand persons were daily employed, is taken away and vested exclusively for twenty-five years, for an extensive district and a large population, in a single corporation, or its exercise is for that period restricted to the establishments of the corporation, and there allowed only upon onerous conditions. . . .

The question presented is, therefore, . . . nothing less than the question whether the recent amendments to the Federal Constitution protect the citizens of the United States against the deprivation of their common rights by State legislation. In my judgment the fourteenth amendment does afford such protection, and was so intended by the Congress which framed and the States which adopted it. . . .

The amendment . . . assumes that there are such privileges and immunities which belong of right to citizens as such, and ordains that they shall not be abridged by State legislation. If this inhibition . . . only refers, as held by the majority of the court in their opinion, to such privileges and immunities as were before its adoption specially designated in the Constitution or necessarily implied as belonging to citizens of the United States, it was a vain and idle enactment, which accomplished nothing, and most unnecessarily excited Congress and the people on its passage. With privileges and immunities thus designated or implied no State could ever have interfered by its laws, and no new constitutional provision was required to inhibit such interference. . . .

What, then, are the privileges and immunities which are secured against abridgment by State legislation?

In the first section of the Civil Rights Act Congress has given its interpretation to these terms, or at least has stated some of the rights which, in its judgment, these terms include; it has there declared that they include the right

> to make and enforce contracts, to sue, be parties and give evidence,
> to inherit, purchase, lease, sell, hold, and convey real and personal
> property, and to full and equal benefit of all laws and proceedings
> for the security of person and property.

That act, it is true, was passed before the fourteenth amendment, but the amendment was adopted, as I have already said, to obviate objections to the act. . . .

Accordingly, after its ratification, Congress re-enacted the act under the belief that whatever doubts may have previously existed of its validity, they were removed by the amendment.

The terms, privileges and immunities, are not new in the amendment; they were in the Constitution before the amendment was adopted. . . . [Justice Washington's interpretation in *Coryell*] appears to me to be a sound construction of the clause in question. The privileges and immunities designated are those *which of right belong to the citizens of all free governments.* Clearly among these must be placed the right to pursue a lawful employment in a lawful manner, without other restraint than such as equally affects all persons. In the discussions in Congress upon the passage of the Civil Rights Act repeated reference was made to this language of Mr. Justice Washington. . . .

So fundamental has this privilege of every citizen to be free from disparaging and unequal enactments, in the pursuit of the ordinary avocations of life, been regarded, that few instances have arisen where the principle has been so far violated as to call for the interposition of the courts. But whenever this has occurred, with the exception of the present cases from Louisiana, which are the most barefaced and flagrant of all, the enactment interfering with the privilege of the citizen has been pronounced illegal and void. . . .

I am authorized by The Chief Justice, Mr. Justice Swayne, and Mr. Justice Bradley, to state that they concur with me in this dissenting opinion.

Mr. Justice Bradley, also dissenting:

. . . If a State legislature should pass a law prohibiting the inhabitants of a particular township, county, or city, from tanning leather or making shoes, would such a law violate any privileges or immunities of those inhabitants as citizens of the United States, or only their privileges and immunities as citizens of that particular State? Or if a State legislature should pass a law of caste, making all trades and professions, or certain enumerated trades and professions, hereditary, so that no one could follow any such trades or professions except that which was pursued by his father, would such a law violate the privileges and immunities of the people of that State as citizens of the United States, or only as citizens of the State? Would they have no redress but to appeal to the courts of that particular State?

. . . [I]n my judgment, the right of any citizen to follow whatever lawful employment he chooses to adopt (submitting himself to all lawful regulations) is one of his most valuable rights, and one which the legislature of a State cannot invade, whether restrained by its own constitution or not. . . .

Mr. Justice Swayne, dissenting:

. . . Fairly construed [the Reconstruction] amendments may be said to rise to the dignity of a new Magna Charta. . . . "The privileges and immunities" of a citizen of the United States include, among other things, the fundamental rights of life, liberty, and property, and also the rights which pertain to him by reason of his membership of the Nation. . . .

It is objected that the power conferred is novel and large. The answer is that the novelty was known and the measure deliberately adopted. . . . By the Constitution, as it stood before the war, ample protection was given against oppression by the Union, but little was given against wrong and oppression by the States. That want was intended to be supplied by this amendment. . . .

Most commentators agree that the practical upshot of *The Slaughter-House Cases* was basically to eviscerate the Privileges or Immunities Clause. This holding has been harshly criticized, not so much because of its practical impact as because it is demonstrably faithless to the understanding of the Amendment's ratifiers. The classic study concludes, on the basis of an exhaustive study of the legislative theory, that

> it is clear that Republicans thought the Fourteenth Amendment protected freedom of speech and of the press and other basic constitutional rights. Their statements on this question alone are sufficient to dispel the notion that the amendment in general and the privileges or immunities clause in particular protected only the right to equality under state law. . . . The [competing] hypothesis that the amendment . . . . only provided for equality in certain rights under state law is simply refuted by the evidence that Republicans thought the amendment protected absolute rights to freedom of speech, to assemble, to bear arms, and to due process that states could not abridge.

Michael Kent Curtis, *No State Shall Abridge: The Fourteenth Amendment and the Bill of Rights* (1986). Notably, the Supreme Court has since come close to stipulating that this criticism is correct. In *McDonald v. City of Chicago* (2010), the plaintiff asked the court to revisit the *Slaughter-House* holding. Although the majority declined to do so on stare decisis grounds, it noted that "many legal scholars dispute the correctness of the narrow Slaughter-House interpretation" and made a point of specifically quoting one commentator's stark summary of the modern consensus: " 'Virtually no serious modern scholar—left, right, and center—thinks that [the *Slaughter-House* interpretation] is a plausible reading of the Amendment.' "

 CROSS REFERENCE
For more context and a longer excerpt from *McDonald*, see pp. 1314–1330.

If you are convinced that *Slaughter-House* read the Privileges or Immunities Clause incorrectly, then what would a proper reading be? That it made the entire Bill of Rights applicable to the states? (The Supreme Court has never so held, and some states have long maintained a system allowing prosecution of felonies without grand jury presentment or indictment, which would be required if the Fifth Amendment applied to them.) Do you think the Clause was meant to give the federal judiciary the power to invalidate laws like the one at stake in *Slaughter-House*?

b.   Equal Protection Clause

Slaughter-House also rejected the butchers' attempt to invoke the Fourteenth Amendment's equal protection clause. The majority spoke ambivalently about the reach of the Clause. It acknowledged that the protections of the Reconstruction Amendments might apply in a proper case "though the party interested may not be of African descent." But, in light of the "pervading purpose" of the Amendments, and the fact that "the evil to be remedied" by the equal protection clause was "the existence of laws in the States where the newly emancipated negroes resided, which discriminated with gross injustice and hardship against them as a class," the Court added:

> We doubt very much whether any action of a State not directed by way of discrimination against the negroes as a class, or on account of their race, will ever be held to come within the purview of this provision. It is so clearly a provision for that race and that emergency, that a strong case would be necessary for its application to any other. . . . We find no such case in the one before us, and do not deem

it necessary to go over the argument again, as it may have relation to this particular clause of the amendment.

In dissent, Justice Bradley showed no such ambivalence:

> It is futile to argue that none but persons of the African race are intended to be benefited by this amendment. They may have been the primary cause of the amendment, but its language is general, embracing all citizens, and I think it was purposely so expressed.

> The mischief to be remedied was not merely slavery and its incidents and consequences; but that spirit of insubordination and disloyalty to the National government which had troubled the country for so many years in some of the States, and that intolerance of free speech and free discussion which often rendered life and property insecure, and led to much unequal legislation. The amendment was an attempt to give voice to the strong National yearning for that time and that condition of things, in which American citizenship should be a sure guaranty of safety, and in which every citizen of the United States might stand erect on every portion of its soil, in the full enjoyment of every right and privilege belonging to a freeman, without fear of violence or molestation. . . .

What about cases where the victims of inequality *were* African-American? The Supreme Court faced that issue in *U.S. v. Cruikshank* (1875). More than a hundred years later, the Supreme Court described the factual background:

> In that case, the Court reviewed convictions stemming from the infamous Colfax Massacre in Louisiana on Easter Sunday 1873. Dozens of blacks, many unarmed, were slaughtered by a rival band of armed white men. Cruikshank himself allegedly marched unarmed African-American prisoners through the streets and then had them summarily executed. Ninety-seven men were indicted for participating in the massacre, but only nine went to trial. Six of the nine were acquitted of all charges; the remaining three were acquitted of murder but convicted under the Enforcement Act of 1870 for banding and conspiring together to deprive their victims of various constitutional rights."

McDonald v. City of Chicago (2010). The Supreme Court reversed those convictions in the following opinion.

United States v. Cruikshank

Supreme Court of the United States, 1875.
92 U.S. 542.

Mr. Chief Justice Waite delivered the opinion of the court.

This case . . . presents for our consideration an indictment . . . based upon sect. 6 of the Enforcement Act of May 31, 1870. That section is as follows:

> That if two or more persons shall band or conspire together, or go in disguise upon the public highway, or upon the premises of another, with intent to violate any provision of this act, or to injure, oppress, threaten, or intimidate any citizen, with intent to prevent or hinder his free exercise and enjoyment of any right or privilege granted or secured to him by the constitution or laws of the United States, or because of his having exercised the same, such persons shall be held guilty of felony. . . .

To bring this case under the operation of the statute . . . , it must appear that the right, the enjoyment of which the conspirators intended to hinder or prevent, was one granted or secured by the constitution or laws of the United States. If it does not so appear, the criminal matter charged has not been made indictable by any act of Congress. . . .

The [indictment] charge[s] the intent to have been to deprive the citizens named, they being in Louisiana, "of their respective several lives and liberty of person without due process of law." This is nothing else than alleging a conspiracy to falsely imprison or murder citizens of the United States, being within the territorial jurisdiction of the State of Louisiana. . . .

The fourteenth amendment prohibits a State from depriving any person of life, liberty, or property, without due process of law; but this adds nothing to the rights of one citizen as against another. It simply furnishes an additional guaranty against any encroachment by the States upon the fundamental rights which belong to every citizen as a member of society. As was said by Mr. Justice Johnson in *Bank of Columbia v. Okely* (1819), it secures "the individual from the arbitrary exercise of the powers of government, unrestrained by the established principles of private rights and distributive justice." These counts in the indictment do not call for the exercise of any of the powers conferred by this provision in the amendment.

The [indictment also charges] . . . that the defendants conspired to prevent certain citizens of the United States, being within the State of Louisiana, from enjoying the equal protection of the laws of the State and of the United States.

The fourteenth amendment prohibits a State from denying to any person within its jurisdiction the equal protection of the laws; but this provision does not, any more than the one which precedes it, and which we have just considered, add any thing to the rights which one citizen has under the Constitution against another. The equality of the rights of citizens is a principle of republicanism. Every republican government is in duty bound to protect all its citizens in the enjoyment of this principle, if within its power. That duty was originally assumed by the States; and it still remains there. . . .

[Other] counts state the intent of the defendants to have been to hinder and prevent the citizens named, being of African descent, and colored, "in the free exercise and enjoyment of their several and respective right and privilege to vote at any election to be thereafter by law had and held by the people in and of the said State of Louisiana . . . ." The right to vote in the States comes from the States; but the right of exemption [from racial discrimination under the Fifteenth Amendment] comes from the United States.

Inasmuch, therefore, as it does not appear in these counts that the intent of the defendants was to prevent these parties from exercising their right to vote on account of their race, &c., it does not appear that it was their intent to interfere with any right granted or secured by the constitution or laws of the United States. We may suspect that race was the cause of the hostility; but it is not so averred. This is material to a description of the substance of the offence, and cannot be supplied by implication. Every thing essential must be charged positively, and not inferentially. . . .

We are, therefore, of the opinion that [the indictment does] not show that it was the intent of the defendants, by their conspiracy, to hinder or prevent the enjoyment of any right granted or secured by the Constitution. . . .

MR. JUSTICE CLIFFORD dissenting.

I concur that the judgment in this case should be arrested, but for reasons quite different from those given by the court. . . . Vague and indefinite allegations of the kind [in this indictment] are not sufficient to inform the accused in a criminal prosecution of the nature and cause of the accusation against him, within the meaning of the sixth amendment of the Constitution. . . .

Certain other causes for arresting the judgment are assigned in the record, which deny the constitutionality of the Enforcement Act; but, having come to the conclusion that the indictment is insufficient, it is not necessary to consider that question.

FOR DISCUSSION

Was *Cruikshank* correctly decided? If not, why not? What federal right did the defendants allegedly conspire to prevent their victims from exercising?

While *Cruikshank* held that private individuals could not violate the Equal Protection Clause, the Supreme Court soon returned to the issue of equal protection in a number of cases involving state defendants. Easily the most important among them was its decision in *Plessy v. Ferguson* (1896), which gave wide constitutional latitude to apartheid-style segregation (colloquially known as the "Jim Crow" system) throughout the former slaveholding South—and less pervasive forms of discrimination throughout the rest of the country as well.

CROSS REFERENCE   *Plessy* is presented at pp. 973–982.

c.   Enforcement Power

All three of the Reconstruction Amendments include a provision that Congress has "power to enforce" the amendment "by appropriate legislation." See U.S. Const., 13th Amdt. § 2; 14th Amdt. § 5; 15th Amdt. § 2. In 1875, Congress relied on its enforcement authority under the Thirteenth and Fourteenth Amendments to pass a major Civil Rights Act. In § 1, the Act provided that all persons within the jurisdiction of the United States shall be entitled to the full and equal enjoyment of the accommodations, advantages, facilities, and privileges of inns, public conveyances on land or water, theatres, and other places of public amusement, subject only to the conditions and limitations established by law and applicable alike to citizens of every race and color, regardless of any previous condition of servitude.

Section 2 of the Act provided a private cause of action for violations of § 1, and also made violations of that section a misdemeanor.

The Civil Rights Cases of 1883 consolidated several cases involving denial to African-Americans of accommodation in an inn, in theaters, an opera house, and a railroad car. The key question was whether the Reconstruction Amendments authorized Congress to pass the statute. The Court rejected the claim that the Fourteenth Amendment enforcement authority was a basis for the statute, on the ground that the Fourteenth Amendment's substantive protections applied only to state action and not to private actors. And it rejected the claim of enforcement authority under the Thirteenth Amendment, on the ground that the wrongs addressed by the Act could not be considered "incidents or elements of slavery."

 The *Civil Rights Cases* are presented at pp. 608–612.

If the courts conclude that one of the Reconstruction Amendments does not reach particular conduct, should that preclude Congress from invoking that Amendment's enforcement power to prohibit the same conduct? Here are two competing historical accounts. First is Justice Kennedy's opinion for the majority in *City of Boerne v. Flores* (1997). That case concerned the validity of the federal Religious Freedom Restoration Act ("RFRA"), which attempted to protect a broader conception of the free exercise of religion than the one recognized by the Supreme Court.

 Other portions of *Boerne* are presented at pp. 621–630.

City of Boerne v. Flores

United States Supreme Court, 1997.

521 U.S. 507.

. . . The Joint Committee on Reconstruction of the 39th Congress began drafting what would become the Fourteenth Amendment in January 1866. The objections to the Committee's first draft of the Amendment, and the rejection of the draft, have a direct bearing on the central issue of defining Congress' enforcement power. In February, Republican Representative John Bingham of Ohio reported the following draft amendment to the House of Representatives on behalf of the Joint Committee:

> The Congress shall have power to make all laws which shall be necessary and proper to secure to the citizens of each State all privileges and immunities of citizens in the several States, and to all persons in the several States equal protection in the rights of life, liberty, and property.

The proposal encountered immediate opposition, which continued through three days of debate. Members of Congress from across the political spectrum criticized the Amendment, and the criticisms had a common theme: The proposed Amendment gave Congress too much legislative power at the expense of the existing constitutional structure. Democrats and conservative Republicans argued that the proposed Amendment would give Congress a power to intrude into traditional areas of state responsibility, a power inconsistent with the federal design central to the Constitution. Some radicals, like their brethren "unwilling that Congress shall have any such power . . . to establish uniform laws throughout the United States upon . . . the protection of life, liberty, and property," also objected that giving Congress primary responsibility for enforcing legal equality would place power in the hands of changing congressional majorities.

As a result of these objections having been expressed from so many different quarters, the House voted to table the proposal until April. The congressional action was seen as marking the defeat of the proposal. . . . The Amendment in its early form was not again considered. Instead, the Joint Committee began drafting a new article of Amendment, which it reported to Congress on April 30, 1866.

Section 1 of the new draft Amendment imposed self-executing limits on the States. Section 5 prescribed that "[t]he Congress shall have power to enforce, by appropriate legislation, the provisions of this article." Under the revised Amendment, Congress' power was no longer plenary but remedial.

FOR DISCUSSION What does Justice Kennedy mean by saying that congressional power under the revised draft "was no longer plenary but remedial"?

Congress was granted the power to make the substantive constitutional prohibitions against the States effective. Representative Bingham said the new draft would give Congress "the power . . . to protect by national law the privileges and immunities of all the citizens of the Republic . . . whenever the same shall be abridged or denied by the unconstitutional acts of any State." Representative Stevens described the new draft Amendment as "allow[ing] Congress to correct the unjust legislation of the States." The revised Amendment proposal did not raise the concerns expressed earlier regarding broad congressional power to prescribe uniform national laws with respect to life, liberty, and property. After revisions not relevant here, the new measure passed both Houses and was ratified in July 1868 as the Fourteenth Amendment. . . .

The design of the Fourteenth Amendment has proved significant also in maintaining the traditional separation of powers between Congress and the Judiciary. The first eight Amendments to the Constitution set forth self-executing prohibitions on governmental action, and this Court has had primary authority to interpret those prohibitions. The Bingham draft, some thought, departed from that tradition by vesting in Congress primary power to interpret and elaborate on the meaning of the new Amendment through legislation. . . . As enacted, the Fourteenth Amendment confers substantive rights against the States which, like the provisions of the Bill of Rights, are self-executing. The power to interpret the Constitution in a case or controversy remains in the Judiciary.

Justice Kennedy's rendition of the history is sharply contested by Michael McConnell, a leading originalist scholar (and for a time a federal appellate judge) as well as a supporter of RFRA.

Michael McConnell, Institutions and Interpretation: A Critique of City of Boerne v. Flores

111 Harv. L. Rev. 153 (1997)

. . . The historical evidence presented in the *Boerne* opinion proves only that Congress was not intended to have authority to pass general legislation determining what the privileges and immunities of citizens should be. It does not support the more extreme claim that Congress lacks independent interpretive authority. . . .

The Court explained that [the April] proposal was approved because "[u]nder the revised Amendment, Congress' power was no longer plenary but remedial. Congress was granted the power to make the substantive constitutional prohibitions against the States effective." . . . It is far from clear that Congress would have had "plenary" power to promulgate rights under the February draft, and it is unlikely that the change to which the Court referred carried the meaning the Court ascribed to it. Moreover, the Court failed to note that the political climate—and not just the language of the proposed amendment—had changed between February and April: President Andrew Johnson had vetoed the Civil Rights bill, thereby radicalizing the moderates and increasing the urgency of action on an amendment. . . .

There are six differences between the two drafts. The pertinent question, which the *Boerne* Court failed to address, is how any of these changes diminished the power of Congress. Two of the changes (switching the verb in Section Five from "secure" to "enforce" and changing the standard of review from "necessary and proper" to "appropriate") were mere changes in nomenclature, with no substantive significance. The change from "privileges and immunities of citizens in the several States," which was lifted from the Comity Clause of Article IV, Section 2, to "privileges or immunities of the citizens of the United States," was later to provide the basis for emasculating the Amendment in the *Slaughter-House Cases*. Although no public explanation was given at the time, this modification probably was inspired by Bingham's theory that the rights subsumed by the language "privileges and immunities" ceased to be subject to the vicissitudes of

FOR DISCUSSION

What would it mean for "privileges and immunities" to no longer be subject to the vicissitudes of state law?

state law and could now be enforced by the federal government on behalf of all citizens.

Three changes warrant more extended discussion. First, the April draft made the substantive provisions of the Amendment self-executing, and thus ensured that the Privileges or Immunities Clause, the Equal Protection Clause, and the Due Process Clause (as well as the provisions of Sections Two, Three, and Four) would continue to apply to the states even if Congress ceased to support them. Representative Giles Hotchkiss of New York, who proposed this change, stated that civil rights should be "secured by a constitutional amendment that legislation cannot override." Although this change enhanced judicial power, it left congressional power as it was under the February draft. Hotchkiss stated that the "laws of Congress" would continue to be the primary instrument "for the enforcement of these rights"—a sentiment shared by nearly all the participants in this decision.

Another potentially important change was to cast the substantive protections of Section One in terms of prohibitions on the states ("No state shall. . .") rather than as rights inhering in individuals. Although this change is significant for the question of "state action," it has no bearing on interpretation of the provisions of the Bill of Rights, including the Free Exercise Clause, which by their nature apply only to state action.

The final change was to break the concept of "equal protection in the rights of life, liberty, and property" into two clauses, one forbidding denial of "equal protection of the laws" and the other forbidding deprivation of "life, liberty, or property without due process of law." As legal historian Earl Maltz has shown, this change was the key to relieving the concerns expressed by moderate Republicans about the February proposal. Under the February proposal, Congress was authorized to make laws to secure to all persons in the several states "equal protection in the rights of life, liberty, and property." [Two Republican opponents of the February version] expressly stated that their criticism did not apply to the Privileges or Immunities Clause, which was the expected vehicle for incorporation of the Bill of Rights. The target of the revised Amendment was the problem of an open-ended equal protection provision. Under the new formulation, Congress was stripped of any power it might have had under the February draft to provide direct protection for life, liberty, and property; Congress could only remedy or prevent state violations of equal protection or due process. Congress's power to enforce preexisting constitutional rights, such as the freedom of religion, was not affected by the change.

It is not clear whether this modification represented a real change or a mere clarification. Bingham's conception of the Amendment—both before and after its revision—was that it would provide federal protection for preexisting constitutional rights. The Privileges or Immunities clause was unobjectionable because it referred to a fixed set of civil rights defined by some combination of the Bill of Rights and longstanding practice (usually common law). . . .

The Court's reading of this history is distorted by its unsupported (and in my opinion unsupportable) assumption that any statement that rejects the pure substantive interpretation, or that uses remedial language, must be read as rejecting an independent interpretive role for Congress. . . . [T]he Court concluded that "Congress' power was no longer plenary but remedial." That is true, if by "remedial" one means that the authority of Congress must be triggered by a wrongful act of the state. . . . But such statements provide no support for the claim that Congress's power is "remedial" in the sense that the definition of "unjust" or "unconstitutional" state acts must be judicial.

Thus, the history of the Fourteenth Amendment supports the Court's conclusion that Congress was not vested with plenary "substantive" authority to determine the content of protected rights under Section Five. Rather, Congress was limited to enforcing rights established by the Fourteenth Amendment itself. This limitation was an important protection for the states, because it ensured that neither Congress nor the courts could go beyond the rights enshrined in the Constitution itself. Congress could not supersede ordinary state tort, contract, property, or criminal laws under the guise of providing (equal) "protection." But nothing in that history suggests that Congress was expected to be limited to enforcing judicially decreed conceptions of those rights.

For Discussion

(1) What is the significance of the debate between Kennedy and McConnell? Who do you think has the better of it?

(2) Consider again: On the basis of what you know, do you believe the Fourteenth Amendment was intended to make applicable against the states ("incorporate") the Bill of Rights, in whole or in part? If so, what portion or portions of the Amendment would have this effect?

7. The End of Reconstruction

The 1875 Civil Rights Act was in a sense the last hurrah of Reconstruction, for by then Northern enthusiasm for protecting the rights and interests of African-Americans had waned considerably. The Presidential election of 1876 created a legal and political impasse that made the election of 2000—and in some ways even the election of 2020 (insurrection excepted)—appear smooth and easy. Congress, faced with disputes as to the results in three states, referred the matter to an Electoral Commission, composed of five members of each house of Congress and five members of the Supreme Court. The anticipation was that the members would be divided by party, with one of the Justices being independent. But the supposed independent, Joseph Bradley, joined with the Republicans on every key vote, awarding the Republican candidate, Rutherford

FOR DISCUSSION Was it proper for the Supreme Court justices to sit on the Electoral Commission? What do you suppose would have happened if this dispute had occurred today?

B. Hayes, just enough electoral votes to secure election. The report of the Commission still had to be accepted by Congress, and Hayes was able to end Democratic resistance by promising to remove federal troops from the South. This is generally regarded as the end of Reconstruction.

H. The Advent of the Regulatory Age

To be sure, there had always been regulation and administrative apparatuses at every level of government. See, *e.g.*, Jerry L. Mashaw, *Creating the Administrative Constitution: The Lost One Hundred Years of American Administrative Law* (2012); William J. Novak, *The People's Welfare: Law and Regulation in Nineteenth-Century America* (1996); Julian Davis Mortenson & Nick Bagley, *Delegation at the Founding*, 121 Colum. L. Rev. 277 (2021). But the intensity of regulation at the federal, state, and local levels increased greatly in the last quarter of the 19th century, prompting a correspondingly burgeoning docket of litigation over its constitutional validity. The *Slaughter-House Cases* notwithstanding, the Supreme Court frequently invoked the Due Process Clause of the Fourteenth Amendment to invalidate state legislation that in the Court's view violated individual liberty. And as the Federal government expanded its regulatory reach, a key question became the scope of its power under the

Commerce Clause. Discord over these issues set the stage for a constitutional crisis in the 1930s.

 **COURSE THEME**

By the end of the 19th century, the existential issues that had threatened the Union had been resolved, and—as indicated by the result in *Plessy v. Ferguson*—the reforming fervor that led to the Reconstruction Amendments had abated. The principal issue for constitutional law over the next several decades became the extent to which governments could regulate economic matters.

1.   Substantive Due Process

We saw the idea of substantive due process at least suggested in *Scott v. Sandford*, and it was invoked by the dissenters in the *Slaughter-House Cases* as well. But the *Slaughter-House* majority leaned hard the other way, indicating that such holdings would be an abuse of judicial authority. Three years later, *Munn v. Illinois* (1876), pp. 1347–1352, held that a state could regulate the rates to be charged by grain elevators. Drawing on law reaching back at least to the 17th century, Chief Justice Waite wrote, "Common carriers exercise a sort of public office, and have duties to perform in which the public

 Defined Term

The term *substantive due process* is oxymoronic—process is usually contrasted to substance. And it is also anachronistic, because the cases during this period did not use it. Nevertheless, it is the standard term for the phenomenon we are going to examine: the judiciary using the Due Process Clause of the Fourteenth Amendment (and to some extent the corresponding clause of the Fifth Amendment) to hold some laws invalid as substantive impairments of liberty.

is interested. Their business is, therefore, 'affected with a public interest' . . . ." Grain elevators, like railroads and other utilities, were deemed to be within this doctrine. Over time, however, the negative implication of this statement became salient: If a business was *not* deemed "affected with a public interest," then it was not subject to close regulation by the state, especially with respect to matters such as price.

Indeed, another doctrine took hold, the idea of freedom (or liberty) of contract. Recall that Art. I, § 10, of the Constitution forbids states to "pass any Law impairing the Obligation of Contracts." That means, in essence (and with some qualification, as we will see) that the state cannot undo a contract already made. But the doctrine of freedom of contract is different. It means that, in some contexts, the state cannot control the making of *future* contracts. The doctrine received its first full expression in *Allgeyer v. Louisiana* (1897), in which the Court held unanimously that the state could not forbid citizens and businesses in the state from entering into a contract for marine insurance with an out-of-state company that had not appointed an in-state agent. Justice Rufus Peckham wrote:

> The "liberty" mentioned in that amendment means not only the right of the citizen to be free from the mere physical restraint of his person, as by incarceration, but the term is deemed to embrace the right of the citizen to be free in the enjoyment of all his faculties, to be free to use them in all lawful ways, to live and work where he will, to earn his livelihood by any lawful calling, to pursue any livelihood or avocation, and for that purpose to enter into all contracts which may be proper, necessary, and essential to his carrying out to a successful conclusion the purposes above mentioned.

Question

What question-begging is embedded in Justice Peckham's statement?

The next year, in *Holden v. Hardy* (1898), the Court pointed in the other direction. With only Justices Brewer and Peckham dissenting, the Court upheld a Utah statute that limited the working hours of miners and smelters to eight hours per day, "except in cases of emergency, where life or property is in imminent danger." After quoting *Allgeyer*, Justice Brown's opinion for the Court said:

> This right of contract, however, is itself subject to certain limitations which the State may lawfully impose in the exercise of its police powers. While this power is inherent in all governments, it has doubtless been greatly expanded in its application during the past century, owing to an enormous increase in the number of occupations which are dangerous, or so far detrimental to the health of employees as to demand special precautions for their wellbeing and protection, or the safety of adjacent property. While . . . the police power cannot

be put forward as an excuse for oppressive and unjust legislation, it may be lawfully resorted to for the purpose of preserving the public health, safety or morals, or the abatement of public nuisances, and a large discretion "is necessarily vested in the legislature to determine not only what the interests of the public require, but what measures are necessary for the protection of such interests." *Lawton v. Steele*. . . .

This power, legitimately exercised, can neither be limited by contract nor bartered away by legislation. . . .

Upon the principles above stated, we think the act in question may be sustained as a valid exercise of the police power of the State. The enactment does not profess to limit the hours of all workmen, but merely those who are employed in underground mines or in the smelting, reduction or refining of ores or metals. These employments, when too long pursued, the legislature has judged to be detrimental to the health of the employees, and, so long as there are reasonable grounds for believing that this is so, its decision upon this subject cannot be reviewed by the Federal courts.

While the general experience of mankind may justify us in believing that men may engage in ordinary employment more than eight hours per day without injury to their health, it does not follow that labor for the same length of time is innocuous when carried on beneath the surface of the earth, where the operative is deprived of fresh air and sunlight and is frequently subjected to foul atmosphere and a very high temperature or to the influence of noxious gases generated by the processes of refining or smelting. . . .

The legislature has also recognized the fact, which the experience of legislators in many states has corroborated, that the proprietors of these establishments and their operatives do not stand upon an equality, and that their interests are, to a certain extent, conflicting. . . . In other words, the proprietors lay down the rules, and the laborers are practically constrained to obey them. In such cases self-interest is often an unsafe guide, and the legislature may properly interpose its authority.

While *Allgeyer* and *Holden* can be reconciled with each other analytically, they indicate the considerable tension that marked the doctrine from the start. That tension became more evident in *Lochner v. New York* (1905), which held by a 5–4 vote that a maximum-hours law for bakers violated the constitutional freedom of contract. *Lochner* is often taken to symbolize the entire era—a fact that, ironically, appears to be attributable neither to the importance of the case nor to the quality of Justice Peckham's majority opinion, but rather to Justice Holmes's dissent. Justice Harlan also wrote a dissent.

 CROSS REFERENCE *Lochner* is presented pp. 1334–1346.

It bears emphasis that *Lochner* was just one case among many, and the results were often difficult to reconcile with each other, depending in large part on the particular context at issue and on the membership of the Court. Consider, for example, *Muller v. Oregon* (1908), decided three years after *Lochner. Muller*, presented more fully at pp. 1352–1354, upheld a state statute limiting female workers "in any mechanical establishment or factory or laundry" to ten hours of work per day. Justice Brewer's opinion for a unanimous Court declared:

> That woman's physical structure and the performance of maternal functions place her at a disadvantage in the struggle for subsistence is obvious. This is especially true when the burdens of motherhood are upon her. Even when they are not, by abundant testimony of the medical fraternity continuance for a long time on her feet at work, repeating this from day to day, tends to injurious effects upon the body, and as healthy mothers are essential to vigorous offspring, the physical well-being of woman becomes an object of public interest and care in order to preserve the strength and vigor of the race.

Muller is also notable as a landmark in Supreme Court lawyering. Louis Brandeis was counsel for Oregon. Brandeis was probably the leading progressive lawyer of the day. He was also a remarkable nerd, who routinely chose industrial reports for summer reading. His opinions often

 WORTH NOTING Brandeis later became the first Jewish Supreme Court justice. When he was nominated in 1916, he faced fierce opposition because many members of the legal establishment regarded him as a dangerous radical. In fact, seven former presidents of the American Bar Association (including former President Taft) described him as "not a fit person to be a member of the Supreme Court of the United States."

reflected this orientation, and so did his very long brief in the *Muller* case, which was a pioneering instance of what is now often referred to as a "Brandeis brief." The submission was chock-full not only to references to labor statutes from around the world, but also to sociological data—and Justice Brewer's opinion for the Court took note:

> It may not be amiss, in the present case, before examining the constitutional question, to notice the course of legislation, as well as expressions of opinion from other than judicial sources. In the brief filed by Mr. Louis D. Brandeis for the defendant in error is a very copious collection of all these matters, an epitome of which is found in the margin."

A footnote gathered many of Brandeis's references to domestic and foreign statutes limiting women's working hours as well as "extracts from over ninety reports of committees, bureaus of statistics, commissioners of hygiene, inspectors of factories," before adding:

> Perhaps the general scope and character of all these reports may be summed up in what an inspector for Hanover says: "The reasons for the reduction of the working day to ten hours—(a) the physical organization of women, (b) her maternal functions, (c) the rearing and education of the children, (d) the maintenance of the home—are all so important and so far reaching that the need for such reduction need hardly be discussed."

FOR DISCUSSION The data submitted by Brandeis had not been presented to the lower courts. Was it proper for the Court to draw conclusions from it? Suppose Brandeis were on the bench instead of at the bar. Would it have been appropriate for him to do the same research on his own in preparing his opinion? Would it have been appropriate for him to call up the inspector from Hanover to get an opinion on the effects on women of long working hours? Compare Allison Orr Larsen, *The Trouble With Amicus Facts,* 100 Va. L. Rev. 1757 (2014).

In 1913, Oregon followed up its hours-limitation success by passing a statute limiting hours of both men and women in manufacturing establishments or mills to ten hours per day, except for emergencies, and with a proviso that employees could work up to three extra hours per day so long as they were paid time and a half. Once again, Brandeis was retained to represent the state in resisting a challenge to its statute, and he prepared a "brief" of 900 pages. (Under current rules, he would have been limited to 15,000 words.) But then he was appointed to the Supreme Court, and Felix Frankfurter took the case over from him. With Brandeis recused, the state won by a 5–3 margin. *Bunting v. Oregon* 426 (1917). Justice McKenna's opinion for the Court was a striking example of judicial deference to the legislature:

> [W]e need not cast about for reasons for the legislative judgment. We are not required to be sure of the precise reasons for its exercise, or be convinced of the wisdom of its exercise. It is enough for our decision if the legislation under review was passed in the exercise of an admitted power of government; and that it is not as complete as it might be, not as rigid in its prohibitions as it might be, gives, perhaps, evasion too much play, is lighter in its penalties than it might be, is no impeachment of its legality. This may be a blemish, giving opportunity for criticism and difference in characterization, but the constitutional validity of legislation cannot be determined by the degree of exactness of its provisions or remedies. New policies are usually tentative in their beginnings, advance in firmness as they advance in acceptance. They do not at a particular moment of time spring full—perfect in extent or means—from the legislative brain. Time may be necessary to fashion them to precedent customs and conditions, and as they justify themselves or otherwise they pass from militancy to triumph or from question to repeal.

And how did the *Bunting* Court deal with *Lochner*? By ignoring it.

More generally, the Progressive Era also featured a wave of constitutional amendments. The Sixteenth authorized a federal income tax, effectively nullifying a decision that had made one impractical. The Seventeenth made a significant change in constitutional structure by providing that Senators should be chosen by popular election rather than by state legislators. The Eighteenth, the only amendment to the Constitution to be subsequently repealed (by the Twenty-First), created a nationwide prohibition on "the manufacture, sale, or transportation of intoxicating liquors." And the Nineteenth, culminating a long political struggle, guaranteed women the right to vote both in state and federal elections. Read these Amendments.

Six years after *Bunting*, the Court invalidated a minimum wage law for women by a 5–3 vote, with Frankfurter again arguing in favor of the statute and Brandeis again recused. *Adkins v. Children's Hospital* (1923). Justice Sutherland's opinion for the majority relied heavily on *Lochner*, and after quoting a statement from *Muller* on differences between men and women, said:

> In view of the great—not to say revolutionary—changes which have taken place since that utterance, in the contractual, political, and civil status of women, culminating in the Nineteenth Amendment, it is not unreasonable to say that these differences have now come almost, if not quite, to the vanishing point.

Two conservative justices, Edward Sanford and Chief Justice Taft, dissented. And so did Holmes, who wrote:

> It will need more than the Nineteenth Amendment to convince me that there are no differences between men and women, or that legislation cannot take those differences into account. I should not hesitate to take them into account if I thought it necessary to sustain this Act. But after *Bunting v. Oregon*, I had supposed that it was not necessary, and that *Lochner v. New York* would be allowed a deserved repose.

2. Federal Power Under the Commerce Clause

In 1887, Congress passed the Interstate Commerce Act, providing the federal government's initial extensive foray into regulation of interstate rail transportation. In 1890, it passed the Sherman Antitrust Act, which remains the cornerstone of federal antitrust law. Section 1 of the Act prohibits "combinations . . . in restraint of trade or commerce among the several States, or with foreign nations." Section 2 prohibits monopolization of "any part of the trade or commerce among the several States, or with foreign nations." The first great test of the Act came in *U.S. v. E.C. Knight Co.* (1895). The case concerned the Sugar Trust, a combination of sugar manufacturing companies accused of violating both sections 1 and 2. Writing for eight members of the

 E.C. Knight is presented at pp. 389–394.

Court, Chief Justice Fuller held that the Act should not be construed to reach the alleged activities, because manufacturing was not in itself commerce, and

because the control over manufacture only affected commerce in sugar "incidentally and indirectly." Justice Harlan dissented.

 Recall that in *Gibbons v. Ogden*, pp. 379–387, Marshall defined Congressional power under the Commerce Clause in expansive terms. But Congress did not seriously test the extent of the power until near the end of the nineteenth century. Instead, Commerce Clause doctrine focused on the extent to which the Clause limited state power. Most often, the Supreme Court treated the Clause as setting up mutually exclusive spheres of power: To hold that a state could legislate in a given manner necessarily implied that the law was not a regulation of interstate commerce within the meaning of the Clause. For this doctrine to achieve politically tolerable results, it had to be based on a relatively narrow conception of commerce.

While *E.C. Knight* took a highly constrained view of federal commerce power, the Court sometimes adopted doctrines permitting federal regulations effectively to target in-state activity. In *Champion v. Ames (The Lottery Case)* (1903), Justice Harlan wrote for a Court that voted 5–4 to uphold a federal statute that prohibited interstate shipment of lottery tickets. While the dissenters thought that lottery tickets were not articles of commerce, the majority held that Congress could in effect stand astride state lines and determine what articles were permitted to pass. In *Houston, East & West Texas Railway Co. v. United States (The Shreveport Rate Case)* (1914), the Court held that the Interstate Commerce Commission could determine freight rates for an intrastate railroad route as part of a larger effort to regulate the interstate trade. And in *Stafford v. Wallace* (1922), the Court built on its decision in *Swift & Co. v. United States* (1905) to held that Congress could authorize the Secretary of Agriculture to regulate the nation's stockyards. Even though the regulated activity was local when taken in isolation, the Court concluded that stockyards functioned as a "throat" in a continuous "stream of commerce" and therefore susceptible to federal regulation.

 Champion is presented at pp. 401–407.

 Shreveport is presented at pp. 395–398.

 Stafford is presented at pp. 398–401.

That said, the categorical line advanced by *E.C. Knight* still retained force. In *Hammer v. Dagenhart* (1918), the Court struck down the federal Child Labor Act of 1916. Relying on the logic of *Champion*, Congress had sought to suppress exploitative labor practices by banning the shipment in

Hammer is presented at pp. 407–413.

interstate commerce of any goods that had been produced with child labor. In a 5–4 decision that remained a political hot point for two decades, the Court struck down the statute as in effect an improper regulation of local production.

A postscript to *Hammer* is noteworthy. Congress responded by passing the Child Labor Tax Act of 1919, which imposed an excise tax of 10% on the profits of any company that knowingly engaged in conduct prohibited by the statute that *Hammer* had invalidated. In *Bailey v. Drexel Furniture Co.* (1922), the Supreme Court held the new statute invalid as well; although in form the new law was styled as a tax, the majority regarded it as really a penalty for violations of a regulatory requirement. Justice Clarke dissented without opinion, a practice that was fairly common in those days; the other *Hammer* dissenters joined Taft's opinion.

Bailey is presented at pp. 481–484.

The economic crisis of the 1930s would force the Court to consider how doctrines governing federal power should be applied to Congressional legislation of unprecedented reach. Before we proceed further, however, read the 20th and 21st amendments to the Constitution—both adopted in 1933.

I. Crisis and Transformation in the New Deal Era

In the last section, we saw how the doctrinal areas of substantive due process (as it is now called) and the Interstate Commerce Clause became contested ground during the first decades of the twentieth century. Contest turned into crisis in the 1930s, as Congress and state legislatures responded aggressively to the Great Depression, and their enactments came under scrutiny of the Supreme Court.

In the spring of 1930, just as the nation was descending into the Depression, Prof. Felix Frankfurter summarized the prior decade of constitutional adjudication:

> Since 1920, the Court has invalidated more legislation than in fifty years preceding. Views that were antiquated twenty-five years ago have been resurrected in decisions nullifying minimum-wage laws for women in industry, a standard-weight-bread law to protect buyers from short weights and honest bakers from unfair competition, a law fixing the resale price of theater tickets by ticket scalpers in New York, laws controlling exploitation of the unemployed by employment agencies and many tax laws. . . . Merely as a matter of arithmetic, this is an impressive mortality rate.

In that same year, President Herbert Hoover named two moderate justices who moved the Court substantially to the left of where it had been. Charles Evans Hughes had been one of the leading figures of the Progressive Era, serving as Governor of New York, Associate Justice of the Supreme Court, and Secretary of State before returning to private practice. Perhaps surprisingly, his nomination as Chief Justice generated substantial opposition in the Senate, among those who focused more on his recent career as a corporate lawyer rather than on his distinguished record of public service. To fill another vacancy, Hoover first nominated John J. Parker, Jr., of North Carolina, a judge of the United States Court of Appeals for the Fourth Circuit. But the Senate rejected him, largely because of resistance from unions and the National Association for the Advancement of the Colored People, based on statements he had made that seemed hostile to their interests. It is an open question whether Parker would have served those interests better than Hoover's second nominee for the position, Owen J. Roberts. Roberts was a capable lawyer from Philadelphia who had achieved some renown as counsel to a committee investigating the Teapot Dome scandal. The Senate confirmed his nomination smoothly, on the assumption that he was a progressive. He was indeed more progressive than Sanford, but he came to the Court without a clearly defined judicial philosophy.

Four members of the Court—James McReynolds, Willis Van Devanter, George Sutherland, and Pierce Butler—were markedly conservative, meaning that in contested cases they would usually vote to invalidate exercises of governmental power. Three members—Holmes, Brandeis, and Harlan Fiske Stone—were progressive, or liberal, meaning that they were more likely to vote to permit such exercises of power. In January 1932, Hughes, with great reluctance, told Holmes, who had turned 90 ten months before, that it was time to retire. Holmes did so immediately, and Hoover replaced him with the nation's most celebrated state court judge, Benjamin N. Cardozo. Cardozo turned out to be a liberal justice, and so the change did not alter the ideological balance of the Court. Hughes and Roberts were moderates, meaning that if both of them joined the liberals they would form a majority, but the conservatives would prevail if either of them joined that side. In most contexts, Roberts was more likely to join the conservatives.

1. State Power and Individual Liberties

The impact of the new Justices soon became apparent. See, *e.g.*, *O'Gorman & Young, Inc. v. Hartford Fire Insurance Co.* (1931) (upholding, 5–4, a New Jersey law regulating the commissions paid by fire insurers to their agents). But see, *e.g.*, *New State Ice Co. v. Liebmann* (1932) (invalidating, 6–2, an Oklahoma statute that had the effect of creating local monopolies by forbidding any person to manufacture or distribute ice without satisfying a licensing commission of the need for additional supply). We present here two important cases from 1934, one because it contains classic discussions of how the Constitution should be interpreted, especially in times of distress, and the other because it signaled a major shift in the Court's approach to determining the constitutionality of economic regulations.

Home Building & Loan Association v. Blaisdell

Supreme Court of the United States, 1934.
290 U.S. 398.

MR. CHIEF JUSTICE HUGHES delivered the opinion of the Court.

SUMMARY OF THE FACTS

In April 1933, Minnesota passed a Mortgage Moratorium Law to relieve the state's hard-pressed farmers and homeowners. For the duration of the emergency, but in no event past May 1935, this statute authorized state courts to postpone foreclosures and to extend redemption periods. The Blaisdells

> applied for and got relief under the statute, allowing them to hold onto their property, which was their home with additional rooms that they rented out; they alleged that the amount owed on their mortgage, which they could not pay, was much less than the reasonable value of the property. Their property had been foreclosed and sold to the Building & Loan Association, the mortgagee, but the trial court extended the period in which they could redeem it from one year to three, so long as they made prescribed monthly payments. The Building & Loan claimed that the law violated the obligation-of-contracts clause of Art. I, § 10, of the Constitution.

. . . In determining whether the provision for this temporary and conditional relief exceeds the power of the State by reason of the clause in the Federal Constitution prohibiting impairment of the obligations of contracts, we must consider the relation of emergency to constitutional power, the historical setting of the contract clause, the development of the jurisprudence of this Court in the construction of that clause, and the principles of construction which we may consider to be established.

Emergency does not create power. Emergency does not increase granted power or remove or diminish the restrictions imposed upon power granted or reserved. The Constitution was adopted in a period of grave emergency. Its grants of power to the Federal Government and its limitations of the power of the States were determined in the light of emergency, and they are not altered by emergency. What power was thus granted and what limitations were thus imposed are questions which have always been, and always will be, the subject of close examination under our constitutional system.

While emergency does not create power, emergency may furnish the occasion for the exercise of power. "Although an emergency may not call into life a power which has never lived, nevertheless emergency may afford a reason for the exertion of a living power already enjoyed." *Wilson v. New* (1917). The constitutional question presented in the light of an emergency is whether the power possessed embraces the particular exercise of it in response to particular conditions. Thus, the war power of the Federal Government is not created by the emergency of war, but it is a power given to meet that emergency. It is a power to wage war successfully, and thus it permits the harnessing of the entire energies of the people in a supreme co-operative effort to preserve the nation. But even the war power does not remove constitutional limitations safeguarding essential liberties. [Here, the Court cited *Milligan* among other decisions.]

When the provisions of the Constitution, in grant or restriction, are specific, so particularized as not to admit of construction, no question is presented. Thus, emergency would not permit a State to have more than two Senators in the Congress, or permit the election of President by a general popular vote without regard to the number of electors to which the States are respectively entitled, or permit the States to "coin money" or to "make anything but gold and silver coin a tender in payment of debts." But, where constitutional grants and limitations of power are set forth in general clauses, which afford a broad outline, the process of construction is essential to fill in the details. That is true of the contract clause. The necessity of construction is not obviated by the fact that the contract clause is associated in the same section with other and more specific prohibitions. Even the grouping of subjects in the same clause may not require the same application to each of the subjects, regardless of differences in their nature. . . .

To ascertain the scope of the constitutional prohibition, we examine the course of judicial decisions in its application. . . . The inescapable problems of construction have been: What is a contract? What are the obligations of contracts? What constitutes impairment of these obligations? What residuum of power is there still in the States, in relation to the operation of contracts, to protect the vital interests of the community? . . .

Not only is the constitutional provision qualified by the measure of control which the State retains over remedial processes, but the State also continues to possess authority to safeguard the vital interests of its people. . . . Not only are existing laws read into contracts in order to fix obligations as between the parties, but the reservation of essential attributes of sovereign power is also read into contracts as a postulate of the legal order. The policy of protecting contracts against impairment presupposes the maintenance of a government by virtue of which contractual relations are worth while—a government which retains adequate authority to secure the peace and good order of society. This principle of harmonizing the constitutional prohibition with the necessary residuum of state power has had progressive recognition in the decisions of this Court. . . .

The question is not whether the legislative action affects contracts incidentally, or directly or indirectly, but whether the legislation is addressed to a legitimate end and the measures taken are reasonable and appropriate to that end. Another argument, which comes more closely to the point, is that the state power may be addressed directly to the prevention of the enforcement of contracts only when these are of a sort which the Legislature in its discretion may denounce as being in themselves hostile to public morals, or public health, safety, or welfare, or where the prohibition is merely of injurious practices; that interference with the enforcement of other and valid contracts according to appropriate legal procedure, although the interference is temporary and for a public purpose, is not permissible. This is but to contend that in the latter case the end is not legitimate in the view that it cannot be reconciled with a fair interpretation of the constitutional provision.

Undoubtedly, whatever is reserved of state power must be consistent with the fair intent of the constitutional limitation of that power. The reserved power cannot be construed so as to destroy the limitation, nor is the limitation to be construed to destroy the reserved power in its essential aspects. They must be construed in harmony with each other. This principle precludes a construction which would permit the State to adopt as its policy the repudiation of debts or the destruction of contracts or the denial of means to enforce them. But it does not follow that conditions may not arise in which a temporary restraint of enforcement may be consistent with the spirit and purpose of the constitutional provision and thus be found to be within the range of the reserved power of the State to protect the vital interests of the community. It cannot be maintained that the constitutional prohibition should be so construed as to prevent limited and temporary interpositions with respect to the enforcement of contracts if made necessary by a great public calamity such as fire, flood, or earthquake. The reservation of state power appropriate to such extraordinary conditions may be deemed to be as much a part of all contracts as is the reservation of state power to protect the public interest in the other situations to which we have referred. And, if state power exists to give temporary relief from the enforcement of contracts in the presence of disasters due to physical causes such as fire, flood, or earthquake, that power cannot be said to be nonexistent when the urgent public need demanding such relief is produced by other and economic causes. . . .

It is manifest from this review of our decisions that there has been a growing appreciation of public needs and of the necessity of finding ground for a rational compromise between individual rights and public welfare. The settlement and consequent contraction of the public domain, the pressure of a constantly increasing density of population, the interrelation of the activities of our people and the complexity of our economic interests, have inevitably led to an increased use of the organization of society in order to protect the very bases of individual opportunity. Where, in earlier days, it was thought that only the concerns of individuals or of classes were involved, and that those of the State itself were touched only remotely, it has later been found that the fundamental interests of the State are directly affected; and that the question is no longer merely that of one party to a contract as against another, but of the use of reasonable means to safeguard the economic structure upon which the good of all depends.

It is no answer to say that this public need was not apprehended a century ago, or to insist that what the provision of the Constitution meant to the vision of that day it must mean to the vision of our time. If by the statement that what the Constitution meant at the time of its adoption it means to-day, it is intended to say that the great clauses of the Constitution must be confined to the interpretation which the framers, with the conditions and outlook of their time, would have placed upon them, the statement carries its own refutation. It was to guard against such a narrow conception that Chief Justice Marshall uttered the memorable warning: "We must never forget, that it is a *constitution* we are expounding" (*McCulloch*); "a constitution intended to endure for ages to come, and, consequently, to be adapted to the various *crises* of human affairs." When we are dealing with the words of the Constitution, said this Court in *Missouri v. Holland* (1920), 'we must realize that they have called into life a being the development of which could not have been foreseen completely by the most gifted of its begetters. . . . The case before us must be considered in the light of our whole experience and not merely in that of what was said a hundred years ago.'

Nor is it helpful to attempt to draw a fine distinction between the intended meaning of the words of the Constitution and their intended application. . . . With a growing recognition of public needs and the relation of individual right to public security, the court has sought to prevent the perversion of the clause through its use as an instrument to throttle the capacity of the States to protect their fundamental interests. This development is a growth from the seeds which the fathers planted. . . . The principle of this development is, as we have seen, that the reservation of the reasonable exercise of the protective power of the State is read into all contracts. . . .

Applying the criteria established by our decisions, we conclude:

1.   An emergency existed in Minnesota which furnished a proper occasion for the exercise of the reserved power of the State to protect the vital interests of the community. . . .

2.   The legislation was addressed to a legitimate end; that is, the legislation was not for the mere advantage of particular individuals but for the protection of a basic interest of society.

3.   In view of the nature of the contracts in question—mortgages of unquestionable validity—the relief afforded and justified by the emergency, in order not to contravene the constitutional provision, could only be of a character appropriate to that emergency, and could be granted only upon reasonable conditions.

4.   The conditions upon which the period of redemption is extended do not appear to be unreasonable. . . . As already noted, the integrity of the mortgage indebtedness is not impaired; interest continues to run; the validity of the sale and the right of a mortgagee-purchaser to title or to obtain a deficiency judgment, if the mortgagor fails to redeem within the extended period, are maintained; and the conditions of redemption, if redemption there be, stand as they were under the prior law. The mortgagor during the extended period is not ousted from possession, but he must pay the rental value of the premises as ascertained in judicial proceedings and this amount is applied to the carrying of the property and to interest upon the indebtedness. The mortgagee-purchaser during the time that he cannot obtain possession thus is not left without compensation for the withholding of possession.

Also important is the fact that mortgagees, as is shown by official reports of which we may take notice, are predominantly corporations, such as insurance companies, banks, and investment and mortgage companies. These, and such individual mortgagees as are small investors, are not seeking homes or the opportunity to engage in farming. Their chief concern is the reasonable protection of their investment security. It does not matter that there are, or may be, individual cases of another aspect. The Legislature was entitled to deal with the general or typical situation. The relief afforded by the statute has regard to the interest of mortgagees as well as to the interest of mortgagors. The legislation seeks to prevent the impending ruin of both by a considerate measure of relief. . . .

5.   The legislation is temporary in operation. It is limited to the exigency which called it forth. While the postponement of the period of redemption

from the foreclosure sale is to May 1, 1935, that period may be reduced by the order of the court under the statute, in case of a change in circumstances, and the operation of the statute itself could not validly outlast the emergency or be so extended as virtually to destroy the contracts.

We are of the opinion that the Minnesota statute as here applied does not violate the contract clause of the Federal Constitution. Whether the legislation is wise or unwise as a matter of policy is a question with which we are not concerned.

What has been said on that point is also applicable to the contention presented under the due process clause. Nor do we think that the statute denies to the appellant the equal protection of the laws. The classification which the statute makes cannot be said to be an arbitrary one. The judgment of the Supreme Court of Minnesota is affirmed. . . .

Mr. Justice Sutherland, dissenting.

Few questions of greater moment than that just decided have been submitted for judicial inquiry during this generation. He simply closes his eyes to the necessary implications of the decision who fails to see in it the potentiality of future gradual but ever-advancing encroachments upon the sanctity of private and public contracts. . . .

A provision of the Constitution, it is hardly necessary to say, does not admit of two distinctly opposite interpretations. It does not mean one thing at one time and an entirely different thing at another time. If the contract impairment clause, when framed and adopted, meant that the terms of a contract for the payment of money could not be altered *in invitum* [by force of law, irrespective of consent] by a state statute enacted for the relief of hardly pressed debtors to the end and with the effect of postponing payment or enforcement during and because of an economic or financial emergency, it is but to state the obvious to say that it means the same now. This view, at once so rational in its application to the written word, and so necessary to the stability of constitutional principles, though from time to time challenged, has never, unless recently, been put within the realm of doubt by the decisions of this court. . . .

Chief Justice Taney, in *Scott v. Sandford*, said that, while the Constitution remains unaltered, it must be construed now as it was understood at the time of its adoption; that it is not only the same in words but the same in meaning, "and as long as it continues to exist in its present form, it speaks not only in the same words, but with the same meaning and intent with which it spoke when it came from the hands of its framers, and was voted on and adopted by the people of the United States. Any other rule of construction would abrogate the judicial character of this court, and make it the mere reflex of the popular opinion or passion of the day." . . .

The provisions of the Federal Constitution, undoubtedly, are pliable in the sense that in appropriate cases they have the capacity of bringing within their grasp every new condition which falls within their meaning.[1] But, their meaning is changeless; it is only their application which is extensible. Constitutional grants of power and restrictions upon the exercise of power are not flexible as the doctrines of the common law are flexible. These doctrines, upon the principles of the common law itself, modify or abrogate themselves whenever they are or whenever they become plainly unsuited to different or changed conditions. . . .

The whole aim of construction, as applied to a provision of the Constitution, is to discover the meaning, to ascertain and give effect to the intent of its framers and the people who adopted it. The necessities which gave rise to the provision, the controversies which preceded, as well as the conflicts of opinion which were settled by its adoption, are matters to be considered to enable us to arrive at a correct result. The history of the times, the state of things existing when the provision was framed and adopted should be looked to in order to ascertain the mischief and the remedy. As nearly as possible we should place ourselves in the condition of those who framed and adopted it. And, if the meaning be at all doubtful, the doubt should be resolved, wherever reasonably possible to do so, in a way to forward the evident purpose with which the provision was adopted.

An application of these principles to the question under review removes any doubt, if otherwise there would be any, that the contract impairment clause denies to the several states the power to mitigate hard consequences resulting to debtors from financial or economic exigencies by an impairment of the obligation of contracts of indebtedness. A candid consideration of the history and circumstances which led up to and accompanied the framing and adoption of this clause will demonstrate conclusively that it was framed and adopted with

---

[1] In such cases it is no more necessary to modify constitutional rules to govern new conditions than it is to create new words to describe them. The commerce clause is a good example. When that was adopted, its application was necessarily confined to the regulation of the primitive methods of transportation then employed; but railroads, automobiles, and aircraft automatically were brought within the scope and subject to the terms of the commerce clause the moment these new means of transportation came into existence, just as they were at once brought within the meaning of the word "carrier," as defined by the dictionaries.

the specific and studied purpose of preventing legislation designed to relieve debtors *especially* in time of financial distress. Indeed, it is not probable that any other purpose was definitely in the minds of those who composed the framers' convention or the ratifying state conventions which followed, although the restriction has been given a wider application . . . .

WORTH NOTING Justice Sutherland's opinion here includes a long historical discussion, which you may assume is persuasive as to the intent of the Framers.

If it be possible by resort to the testimony of history to put any question of constitutional intent beyond the domain of uncertainty, the foregoing leaves no reasonable ground upon which to base a denial that the clause of the Constitution now under consideration was meant to foreclose state action impairing the obligation of contracts *primarily and especially* in respect of such action aimed at giving relief to debtors *in time of emergency*. And, if further proof be required to strengthen what already is inexpugnable, such proof will be found in the previous decisions of this court. . . .

WORTH NOTING Here, Justice Sutherland discussed precedent at considerable length.

. . . The present exigency is nothing new. From the beginning of our existence as a nation, periods of depression, of industrial failure, of financial distress, of unpaid and un-payable indebtedness, have alternated with years of plenty. The vital lesson that expenditure beyond income begets poverty, that public or private extravagance, financed by promises to pay, either must end in complete or partial repudiation or the promises be fulfilled by self-denial and painful effort, though constantly taught by bitter experience, seems never to be learned; and the attempt by legislative devices to shift the misfortune of the debtor to the shoulders of the creditor without coming into conflict with the contract impairment clause has been persistent and oft-repeated.

The defense of the Minnesota law is made upon grounds which were discountenanced by the makers of the Constitution and have many times been rejected by this Court. That defense should not now succeed because it constitutes an effort to overthrow the constitutional provision by an appeal to facts and circumstances identical with those which brought it into existence. With due regard for the processes of logical thinking, it legitimately cannot be urged that conditions which produced the rule may now be invoked to destroy it. . . .

The Minnesota statute either impairs the obligation of contracts or it does not. If it does not, the occasion to which it relates becomes immaterial, since then the passage of the statute is the exercise of a normal, unrestricted, state power and requires no special occasion to render it effective. If it does, the emergency no more furnishes a proper occasion for its exercise than if the emergency were nonexistent. And so, while, in form, the suggested distinction seems to put us forward in a straight line, in reality it simply carries us back in a circle, like bewildered travelers lost in a wood, to the point where we parted company with the view of the state court.

If what has now been said is sound, as I think it is, we come to what really is the vital question in the case: Does the Minnesota statute constitute an impairment of the obligation of the contract now under review?

In answering that question, we must first of all distinguish the present legislation from those statutes which, although interfering in some degree with the terms of contracts, or having the effect of entirely destroying them, have nevertheless been sustained as not impairing the obligation of contracts in the constitutional sense. Among these statutes are such as affect the remedy *merely*. . . .

It is quite true also that "the reservation of essential attributes of sovereign power is also read into contracts"; and that the Legislature cannot "bargain away the public health or the public morals." General statutes to put an end to lotteries, the sale or manufacture of intoxicating liquors, the maintenance of nuisances, to protect the public safety, etc., although they have the indirect effect of absolutely destroying private contracts previously made in contemplation of a continuance of the state of affairs then in existence but subsequently prohibited, have been uniformly upheld as not violating the contract impairment clause. The distinction between legislation of that character and the Minnesota statute, however, is readily observable. It may be demonstrated by an example. A, engaged in the business of manufacturing intoxicating liquor within a state, makes a contract, we will suppose, with B to manufacture and deliver at a stipulated price and at some date in the future a quantity of whisky. Before the day arrives for the performance of the contract, the state passes a law prohibiting the manufacture and sale of intoxicating liquor. The contract immediately falls because its performance has ceased to be lawful. . . .

By such legislation the obligation is not impaired in the constitutional sense. The contract is frustrated—it disappears in virtue of an implied condition to that effect read into the contract itself. [Here, by contrast, this] contract was lawful when made; and it has never been anything else. What the Legislature has done is to pass a statute which does not have the effect of frustrating the contract by rendering its performance unlawful, but one which, at the election of one of the parties, postpones for a time the effective enforcement of the contractual obligation, notwithstanding the obligation, under the exact terms of the contract, remains lawful and possible of performance after the passage of the statute as it was before. . . .

We come back, then, directly, to the question of impairment. As to that, the conclusion reached by the court here seems to be that the relief afforded by the statute does not contravene the constitutional provision because it is of a character appropriate to the emergency and allowed upon what are said to be reasonable conditions. . . .

[W]hether the statute operated directly upon the contract or indirectly by modifying the remedy, its effect was to extend the period of redemption absolutely for a period of sixteen days, and conditionally for a period of two years. That this brought about a substantial change in the terms of the contract reasonably cannot be denied. [And however reasonable the] contingencies may be, the statute denies appellant for a period of two years the ownership and possession of the property—an asset which, in any event, is of substantial character, and which possibly may turn out to be of great value. The statute, therefore, is not merely a modification of the remedy; it effects a material and injurious change in the obligation. The legally enforceable right of the creditor when the statute was passed was, at once upon default of redemption, to become the fee-simple owner of the property. . . .

A statute which materially delays enforcement of the mortgagee's contractual right of ownership and possession does not modify the remedy merely; it destroys, for the period of delay, *all* remedy so far as the enforcement of *that* right is concerned. The phrase "obligation of a contract" in the constitutional sense imports a legal duty to perform the specified obligation of that contract, not to substitute and perform, against the will of one of the parties, a different, albeit equally valuable, obligation. And a state, under the contract impairment clause, has no more power to accomplish such a substitution than has one of the parties to the contract against the will of the other. . . .

I quite agree with the opinion of the Court that whether the legislation under review is wise or unwise is a matter with which we have nothing to do. Whether it is likely to work well or work ill presents a question entirely irrelevant to the issue. The only legitimate inquiry we can make is whether it is constitutional. If it is not, its virtues, if it have any, cannot save it; if it is, its faults cannot be invoked to accomplish its destruction. If the provisions of the Constitution be not upheld when they pinch as well as when they comfort, they may as well be abandoned. Being unable to reach any other conclusion than that the Minnesota statute infringes the constitutional restriction under review, I have no choice but to say so.

I am authorized to say that MR. JUSTICE VAN DEVANTER, MR. JUSTICE McREYNOLDS, and MR. JUSTICE BUTLER concur in this opinion.

WORTH NOTING

"My dear Sutherland," wrote Brandeis on the proofs of Sutherland's dissent. "This is one of the great opinions in American constitutional law. Regretfully, I adhere to my error." Was Brandeis's assessment of the opinion correct? Was he right to adhere to his "error"?

Nebbia v. New York

Supreme Court of the United States, 1934.
291 U.S. 502.

MR. JUSTICE ROBERTS delivered the opinion of the Court.

The Legislature of New York established by chapter 158 of the Laws of 1933, a Milk Control Board with power, among other things to "fix minimum and maximum . . . retail prices to be charged by . . . stores to consumers for consumption off the premises where sold." The Board fixed nine cents as the price to be charged by a store for a quart of milk. Nebbia, the proprietor of a grocery store in Rochester, sold two quarts and a 5-cent loaf of bread for 18 cents; and was convicted for violating the Board's order. At his trial he asserted the statute and order contravene the equal protection clause and the due process clause of the Fourteenth Amendment, and renewed the contention in successive appeals to the county court and Court of Appeals. Both overruled his claim and affirmed the conviction.

The question for decision is whether the Federal Constitution prohibits a state from so fixing the selling price of milk. We first inquire as to the occasion for the legislation and its history.

During 1932 the prices received by farmers for milk were much below the cost of production. The decline in prices during 1931 and 1932 was much greater than that of prices generally. The situation of the families of dairy producers had become desperate and called for state aid similar to that afforded the unemployed, if conditions should not improve. . . .

[A joint legislative committee was created to investigate the milk industry and conducted an extensive inquiry, culminating in a lengthy and detailed report.] The conscientious effort and thoroughness exhibited by the report lend weight to the committee's conclusions.

In part those conclusions are:

1.   Milk is an essential item of diet. It cannot long be stored. . . . Failure of producers to receive a reasonable return for their labor and investment over an extended period threaten a relaxation of vigilance against contamination.

2.   The production and distribution of milk is a paramount industry of the state, and largely affects the health and prosperity of its people. Dairying yields fully one-half of the total income from all farm products. . . . Curtailment or destruction of the dairy industry would cause a serious economic loss to the people of the state.

3.   In addition to the general price decline, other causes for the low price of milk include a periodic increase in the number of cows and in milk production, the prevalence of unfair and destructive trade practices in the distribution of milk, leading to a demoralization of prices in the metropolitan area and other markets, and the failure of transportation and distribution charges to be reduced in proportion to the reduction in retail prices for milk and cream. . . .

The Legislature adopted chapter 158 as a method of correcting the evils, which the report of the committee showed could not be expected to right themselves through the ordinary play of the forces of supply and demand, owing to the peculiar and uncontrollable factors affecting the industry. . . .

[The] question is whether, in the light of the conditions disclosed, the enforcement of [the act] denied the appellant the due process secured to him by the Fourteenth Amendment. . . .

Under our form of government the use of property and the making of contracts are normally matters of private and not of public concern. The general rule is that both shall be free of governmental interference. But neither property rights, *e.g., Munn v. Illinois* (1877), nor contract rights, *e.g., Allgeyer v. Louisiana* (1897), are absolute; for government cannot exist if the citizen may at will use his property to the detriment of his fellows, or exercise his freedom of contract to work them harm. Equally fundamental with the private right is that of the public to regulate it in the common interest. . . .

Thus has this court from the early days affirmed that the power to promote the general welfare is inherent in government. Touching the matters committed to it by the Constitution the United States possesses the power, as do the states in their sovereign capacity touching all subjects jurisdiction of which is not surrendered to the federal government, as shown by the quotations above given. These correlative rights, that of the citizen to exercise exclusive dominion over property and freely to contract about his affairs, and that of the state to regulate the use of property and the conduct of business, are always in collision. No exercise of the private right can be imagined which will not in some respect, however slight, affect the public; no exercise of the legislative prerogative to regulate the conduct of the citizen which will not to some extent abridge his liberty or affect his property. But subject only to constitutional restraint the private right must yield to the public need.

The Fifth Amendment, in the field of federal activity, and the Fourteenth, as respects state action, do not prohibit governmental regulation for the public welfare. They merely condition the exertion of the admitted power, by securing that the end shall be accomplished by methods consistent with due process. And the guaranty of due process, as has often been held, demands only that the law shall not be unreasonable, arbitrary, or capricious, and that the means selected shall have a real and substantial relation to the object sought to be attained. It results that a regulation valid for one sort of business, or in given circumstances, may be invalid for another sort, or for the same business under other circumstances, because the reasonableness of each regulation depends upon the relevant facts.

The reports of our decisions abound with cases in which the citizen, individual or corporate, has vainly invoked the Fourteenth Amendment in resistance to necessary and appropriate exertion of the police power.

The court has repeatedly sustained curtailment of enjoyment of private property, in the public interest. The owner's rights may be subordinated to the needs of other private owners whose pursuits are vital to the paramount interests of the community. The state may control the use of property in various ways; may prohibit advertising bill boards except of a prescribed size and location, or their use for certain kinds of advertising; may in certain circumstances authorize encroachments by party walls in cities; may fix the height of buildings, the character of materials, and methods of construction, the adjoining area which must be left open, and may exclude from residential sections offensive trades, industries and structures likely injuriously to affect the public health or safety; or may establish zones within which certain types of buildings or businesses are permitted and others excluded. . . . [Citations omitted.]

Laws passed for the suppression of immorality, in the interest of health, to secure fair trade practices, and to safeguard the interests of depositors in banks, have been found consistent with due process.[24] These measures not only affected the use of private property, but also interfered with the right of private contract. Other instances are numerous where valid regulation has restricted the right of contract, while less directly affecting property rights.[25]

The Constitution does not guarantee the unrestricted privilege to engage in a business or to conduct it as one pleases. Certain kinds of business may be prohibited;[26] and the right to conduct a business, or to pursue a calling, may

---

[24]   [See, *e.g.,* a string of cases] [f]orbidding transmission of lottery tickets; transportation of prize fight films; the shipment of adulterated food; transportation of women for immoral purposes; transportation of intoxicating liquor; requiring the public weighing of grain; regulating the size and weight of loaves of bread; regulating the size and character of packages in which goods are sold; regulating sales in bulk of a stock in trade; sales of stocks and bonds; requiring fluid milk offered for sale to be tuberculin tested; regulating sales of grain by actual weight, and abrogating exchange rules to the contrary; subjecting state banks to assessments for a state depositors' guarantee fund.

[25]   [See, *e.g.,* a string of cases] [p]rescribing hours of labor in particular occupations; prohibiting child labor; forbidding night work by women; reducing hours of labor for women; fixing the time for payment of seamen's wages; of wages of railroad employees; regulating the redemption of store orders issued for wages; regulating the assignment of wages; requiring payment for coal mined on a fixed basis other than that usually practiced; establishing a system of compulsory workmen's compensation.

[26]   [See, *e.g.,* a string of cases prohibiting] [s]ales of stock or grain on margin; the conduct of pool and billiard rooms by aliens; the conduct of billiard and pool rooms by anyone; the sale of liquor; the business of soliciting claims by one not an attorney; manufacture or sale of oleomargarine; hawking and peddling of drugs or medicines; forbidding any other than a corporation to engage in the business of receiving deposits, or any other than corporations to do a banking business.

be conditioned.[27] Regulation of a business to prevent waste of the state's resources may be justified. And statutes prescribing the terms upon which those conducting certain businesses may contract, or imposing terms if they do enter into agreements, are within the state's competency.[29] . . .

The milk industry in New York has been the subject of long-standing and drastic regulation in the public interest. The legislative investigation of 1932 was persuasive of the fact that for this and other reasons unrestricted competition aggravated existing evils and the normal law of supply and demand was insufficient to correct maladjustments detrimental to the community. . . . In the light of the facts the order appears not to be unreasonable or arbitrary, or without relation to the purpose to prevent ruthless competition from destroying the wholesale price structure on which the farmer depends for his livelihood, and the community for an assured supply of milk.

But we are told that because the law essays to control prices it denies due process. Notwithstanding the admitted power to correct existing economic ills by appropriate regulation of business . . . the appellant urges that . . . the public control of rates or prices is *per se* unreasonable and unconstitutional, save as applied to businesses affected with a public interest. [He further claims] that a business so affected is one in which property is devoted to an enterprise of a sort which the public itself might appropriately undertake, or one whose owner relies on a public grant or franchise for the right to conduct the business, or in which he is bound to serve all who apply; in short, such as is commonly called a public utility; or a business in its nature a monopoly. The milk industry, it is said, possesses none of these characteristics, and, therefore, not being affected with a public interest, its charges may not be controlled by the state. . . .

The true interpretation of [our prior precedents] is claimed to be that only property voluntarily devoted to a known public use is subject to regulation as to rates. But obviously [the business owners in those earlier cases] had not voluntarily dedicated their business to a public use. They intended only to conduct it as private citizens, and they insisted that they had done nothing which gave the public an interest in their transactions or conferred any right of regulation.

---

[27]   [See, *e.g.*, a string of cases regulating] [p]hysicians; dentists; employment agencies; public weighers of grain; real estate brokers; insurance agents; insurance companies; the sale of cigarettes; the sale of spectacles; private detectives; grain brokers; business of renting automobiles to be used by the renter upon the public streets.

[29]   [See, *e.g.*, a string of cases regulating] [c]ontracts of carriage; agreements substituting relief or insurance payments for actions for negligence; affecting contracts of insurance; contracts for sale of real estate; contracts for sale of farm machinery; bonds for performance of building contracts.

The statement that one has dedicated his property to a public use is, therefore, merely another way of saying that if one embarks in a business which public interest demands shall be regulated, he must know regulation will ensue. . . .

It is clear that there is no closed class or category of businesses affected with a public interest, and the function of courts in the application of the Fifth and Fourteenth Amendments is to determine in each case whether circumstances vindicate the challenged regulation as a reasonable exertion of governmental authority or condemn it as arbitrary or discriminatory. The phrase "affected with a public interest" can, in the nature of things, mean no more than that an industry, for adequate reason, is subject to control for the public good. In several of the decisions of this court wherein the expressions "affected with a public interest," and "clothed with a public use," have been brought forward . . . , it has been admitted that they are not susceptible of definition and form an unsatisfactory test of the constitutionality of legislation directed at business practices or prices. These decisions must rest, finally, upon the basis that the requirements of due process were not met because the laws were found arbitrary in their operation and effect. But there can be no doubt that upon proper occasion and by appropriate measures the state may regulate a business in any of its aspects, including the prices to be charged for the products or commodities it sells. . . .

So far as the requirement of due process is concerned, and in the absence of other constitutional restriction, a state is free to adopt whatever economic policy may reasonably be deemed to promote public welfare, and to enforce that policy by legislation adapted to its purpose. The courts are without authority either to declare such policy, or, when it is declared by the legislature, to override it. If the laws passed are seen to have a reasonable relation to a proper legislative purpose, and are neither arbitrary nor discriminatory, the requirements of due process are satisfied. . . . Times without number we have said that the Legislature is primarily the judge of the necessity of such an enactment, that every possible presumption is in favor of its validity, and that though the court may hold views inconsistent with the wisdom of the law, it may not be annulled unless palpably in excess of legislative power. . . .

The Constitution does not secure to any one liberty to conduct his business in such fashion as to inflict injury upon the public at large, or upon any substantial group of the people. Price control, like any other form of regulation, is unconstitutional only if arbitrary, discriminatory, or demonstrably irrelevant to the policy the Legislature is free to adopt, and hence an unnecessary and unwarranted interference with individual liberty. . . .

MR. JUSTICE MCREYNOLDS, joined by JUSTICES VAN DEVANTER, MR. JUSTICE SUTHERLAND, and MR. JUSTICE BUTLER, dissenting.

. . . [W]e are told [the committee found that] the number of dairy cows had been increasing and that favorable prices for milk bring more cows. For two years notwithstanding low prices the per capita consumption had been falling. "The obvious cause is the reduced buying power of consumers." Notwithstanding the low prices, farmers continued to produce a large surplus of wholesome milk for which there was no market. . . .

The exigency is of the kind which inevitably arises when one set of men continue to produce more than all others can buy. The distressing result to the producer followed his ill-advised but voluntary efforts. Similar situations occur in almost every business. . . . The argument advanced here would support general prescription of prices for farm products, groceries, shoes, clothing, all the necessities of modern civilization, as well as labor, when some Legislature finds and declares such action advisable and for the public good. This Court has declared that a state may not by legislative fiat convert a private business into a public utility. [Citations omitted.] And if it be now ruled that one dedicates his property to public use whenever he embarks on an enterprise which the Legislature may think it desirable to bring under control, this is but to declare that rights guaranteed by the Constitution exist only so long as supposed public interest does not require their extinction. To adopt such a view, of course, would put an end to liberty under the Constitution. . . .

The painstaking effort [in earlier cases] to point out that certain businesses like ferries, mills, etc., were subject to legislative control at common law and then to show that warehousing at Chicago occupied like relation to the public would have been pointless if "affected with a public interest" only means that the public has serious concern about the perpetuity and success of the undertaking. That is true of almost all ordinary business affairs. Nothing in the opinion lends support, directly or otherwise to the notion that in times of peace a legislature may fix the price of ordinary commodities—grain, meat, milk, cotton, etc. . . .

[P]lainly, I think, this Court must have regard to the wisdom of the enactment. At least, we must inquire concerning its purpose and decide whether the means proposed have reasonable relation to something within legislative power—whether the end is legitimate, and the means appropriate. If a statute to prevent conflagrations, should require householders to pour oil on their roofs as a means of curbing the spread of fire when discovered in the neighborhood, we could hardly uphold it. Here, we find direct interference with guaranteed rights defended upon the ground that the purpose was to promote the public welfare by increasing milk prices at the farm. Unless we can affirm that the end proposed is proper and the means adopted have reasonable relation to it, this action is unjustifiable. . . .

An end although apparently desirable cannot justify inhibited means. . . . The Legislature cannot lawfully destroy guaranteed rights of one man with the prime purpose of enriching another, even if for the moment, this may seem advantageous to the public. And the adoption of any 'concept of jurisprudence' which permits facile disregard of the Constitution as long interpreted and respected will inevitably lead to its destruction. Then, all rights will be subject to the caprice of the hour; government by stable laws will pass. . . .

Bear in mind that Roberts wrote his broad opinion upholding state regulation in *Nebbia* free of any of the external pressure that was brought to bear on the Court three years later. Nevertheless, in *Railroad Retirement Board v. Alton R.R. Co.* (1935), he joined the four conservatives to invalidate the Railroad Retirement Act, passed by the New Deal Congress, in part on the ground that it violated the Fifth Amendment's due process clause.[d] Requiring retirement for railroad employees at age 65, the statute set up a pension scheme financed by compulsory contributions from both the carriers and their employees. Roberts, writing for the majority, found a plethora of reasons why various facets of it were invalid. For example, morale did not seem likely to be improved by allowing a pension to all employees at 65, whatever the duration of their service; nor would the economy likely be aided by allowing a pension to all employees, even those younger than 65, retiring after 30 years of service. Hughes, joined by the three liberals, dissented. He was willing to admit that the inclusion in the act of allowances for employees already retired was arbitrary, but the other choices made by Congress were reasonable ones; any program, he pointed out, would present anomalies.

---

[d]   Some of these materials are adapted from Richard Friedman, *Switching Time and Other Thought Experiments: The Hughes Court and Constitutional Transformation*, 142 U. Pa. L. Rev. 1891 (1994).

Of much greater political significance, the next year the Court invalidated by the same 5–4 vote a New York statute that set a minimum wage for women. *Morehead v. New York* ex rel. *Tipaldo* (1936). Recall that in *Adkins v. Children's Hospital* (1923), the Court had invalidated such a statute. Liberals hoped, however, that in an environment that changed greatly—politically, economically, and, given *Nebbia*, judicially—the Court would take a different view. The state attempted to distinguish *Adkins* on narrow grounds; the statute involved in *Adkins* had set the wage based on living costs necessary for health and, unlike the New York statute, did not take into account the reasonable value of the services. Stone, writing a dissent for the other two liberals and himself, said that *Adkins* should be overruled. Hughes dissented separately, without going quite as far, but leaving no doubt about his disdain for *Adkins*. Roberts, according to an account he later provided, found the ground of distinction offered by the state unpersuasive and said he would join any opinion that was based on the fact that the state had not asked for *Adkins* to be overruled and on the view that the two cases were not materially distinguishable. Apparently catering to Roberts, Butler began his opinion for the majority in that way. But, apparently in response to Stone, he added a portion expressing continued adherence to the principle of *Adkins*. And yet Roberts did not object.

For Discussion

(1) Citing *Nebbia*, Hughes's dissent argued that freedom of contract "is a qualified and not an absolute right," and that the question whether a statute invalidly encroaches on that freedom depends on whether the restraint is "arbitrary and capricious" rather than "reasonably required in order appropriately to serve the public interest." Butler's opinion for the majority never cited *Nebbia*. Why do you suppose that Roberts joined the majority?

(2) Butler wrote for the majority that "any measure that deprives employers and adult women of freedom to agree on wages, leaving employers and men employees free to do so, is necessarily arbitrary."

Hughes responded:

> The Legislature finds that the employment of women and minors in trade and industry in the state of New York at wages unreasonably low and not fairly commensurate with the value of the services rendered is a matter of vital public concern; that many women and minors are not, as a class, upon a level of equality in

bargaining with their employers in regard to minimum fair wage standards, and that "freedom of contract," as applied to their re-lations with employers, is illusory; that, by reason of the necessity of seeking support for themselves and their dependents, they are forced to accept whatever wages are offered, and that, judged by any reasonable standard, wages in many instances are fixed by chance and caprice, and the wages accepted are often found to bear no relation to the fair value of the service. . . .

In the factual brief, statistics are presented showing the in-creasing number of wage-earning women, and that women are in industry and in other fields of employment because they must support themselves and their dependents. Data are submitted, from reports of the Women's Bureau of the United States De-partment of Labor, showing such discrepancies and variations in wages paid for identical work as to indicate that no relationship exists between the value of the services rendered and the wages paid. It also appears that working women are largely unorganized, and that their bargaining power is relatively weak. . . . Thus, the failure of overreaching employers to pay to women the wages commensurate with the value of services rendered has imposed a direct and heavy burden upon the taxpayers.

Between Butler and Hughes, who do you think was right on this point?

Tipaldo prompted a furious reaction, spreading far beyond the liberal camp. Meeting in convention the following week, the Republican party adopted a platform urging legislation (including minimum wage laws) to protect wom-en and children laborers—pointedly adding that such laws were "within the Constitution as it now stands." Alf Landon, soon to be the party's presidential nominee, went so far as to say that he would favor a constitutional amendment authorizing minimum wage legislation if necessary.

2. Federal Power

Franklin Roosevelt's New Deal stretched federal power in new directions, and this inevitably led to conflict with the Supreme Court.

In January 1935, in *Panama Refining Co. v. Ryan* (1935), with only Car-dozo dissenting, the Court invalidated one provision of the National Industrial Recovery Act of 1933 that authorized the President to bar the shipment in in-terstate commerce of "hot oil"—that is, oil produced or withdrawn from storage in excess of state limitations. The decision was a narrow one, based on the perception that Congress had made an uncontrolled delegation of power to the President. Hughes, writing for the majority, expressed particular concern that the statute did not state a standard or policy to guide or limit the President, nor did it require him to make formal findings justifying his action.

Litigation in the so-called *Gold Clause Cases* was far more closely followed, because their potential consequences were so immediate and so enormous. In 1934, Congress, in an attempt to combat disastrous deflation, had lowered the value of the dollar against gold. But many contracts, both public and private, had specified that payment would be in a set amount of gold or in the currency equivalent. If this "gold clause" were given effect, a debtor whose income was in devalued dollars would have to discharge the obligation in pre-devaluation dollars. Even before devaluation, in 1933, Congress passed a resolution declaring the gold clause void against public policy. But the validity of that resolution would remain in doubt until the Supreme Court acted.

The cases presenting the issue created tremendous tension in early 1935, and it appears that the President—for the first time in history—was prepared (at least in anticipation) to disobey an order of the Supreme Court. But by a 5–4 vote—Hughes writing for the majority against the four conservatives—the Court declined to grant relief for those claiming under the clause. Two of the cases involved private contracts, and for the majority this was relatively easy:

> Contracts, however express, cannot fetter the constitutional authority of the Congress. . . . To subordinate the exercise of the federal authority to the continuing operation of previous contracts would be to place, to this extent, the regulation of interstate commerce in the hands of private individuals . . . .

Norman v. Baltimore & Ohio R.R. (1935). But one of the cases involved a federal obligation—a $10,000 bond with a gold clause—that the owner had not presented until after devaluation. *Perry v. United States* (1935). The Court emphatically held that the government's power over the monetary system did not entitle it to abrogate its own promise. But then, in a surprising turn, Hughes wrote that Perry had "not shown, or attempted to show, that in relation to buying power he has sustained any loss whatever." Indeed, payment of the amount Perry demanded would be "an unjust enrichment," and so there were no actual damages. Victory for the Government. "[T]he impending moral and legal chaos is appalling," wrote McReynolds in dissent. He closed his oral presentation by proclaiming: "As for the Constitution, it does not seem too much to say that it is gone. Shame and humiliation are upon us now!"

FOR DISCUSSION

Suppose that before the *Blaisdell* decision in January 1934, President Roosevelt had unveiled a proposal to pack the Court with six additional members, and that the debate over the plan lasted until after the *Gold Clause* decisions. Would it not have been obvious that the votes of Hughes and Roberts in *Blaisdell*, *Nebbia*, and the *Gold Clause Cases* resulted from the political pressure created by the President's plan and, with respect to the *Gold Clause Cases*, by the thumping Democratic victory in the 1934 elections?

The *Gold Clause Cases* were virtually the only major victory the Court gave the Roosevelt Administration before 1937. We have already seen the due process side of the *Alton* case, which invalidated the Railroad Retirement Act. Justice Roberts's opinion for the majority also held that the Act "really and essentially related solely to the social welfare of the worker" rather than to the regulation of interstate commerce. Joined by the liberals, Chief Justice Hughes dissented from this holding as well; they believed that, by improving morale and avoiding superannuation, the Act might reasonably improve the efficiency of the railroads, and that in any event Congress could decide that "industry should take care of its human wastage, whether that is due to accident [as in workers' compensation laws] or age."

Three weeks after *Alton*, the Court unanimously decided against the government in the "Sick Chicken" case, *Schechter Poultry Corp. v. United States* (1935). Section 3 of the National Industrial Recovery Act (NIRA) had authorized the President, on application by a trade group, to promulgate a "code of fair competition" for a particular industry. These codes, given

CROSS REFERENCE *Schechter* is presented at pp. 414–420.

the force of law, could specify unfair trade practices, prescribe wages, hours, and other employment conditions for the industry, and require collective bargaining. Writing for the Court, Hughes drew on his decision in *Panama Refining* to hold that this system—symbolized by the famous Blue Eagle of the National Recovery Administration—was improper delegation. Brandeis, who decades before had written a book called *The Curse of Bigness*, joined the opinion. Even Cardozo, who had dissented in *Panama Refining*, agreed with the conclusion.

In a separate concurrence joined by Stone, Cardozo wrote that Section 3's del-egation "is not canalized within banks that keep it from overflowing. It is unconfined and vagrant." Not limited to a single act or defined by a standard, it provided "a roving commission to inquire into evils and upon discovery cor-rect them." If this conception should prevail, Congress could transfer its entire power over commerce to the Executive. "This," Cardozo concluded, "is dele-gation running riot."

For Discussion

(1) Suppose you were a lawyer in the New Deal Administration, working on the bill that became the NIRA. You foresaw the delegation problem. Could you have given any advice that might have avoided it?

(2) The Communications Act of 1934 created the Federal Communications Commission (FCC) and authorized it to promulgate regulations that en-couraged the larger and more effective use of radio "in the public interest, convenience, or necessity." The Commission adopted regulations provid-ing, in general, that no licenses could be granted to stations or applicants having specified relationships with radio networks. Were these regulations adopted pursuant to invalid delegation? The Supreme Court has sometimes said that there must be an "intelligible principle" governing delegation. Is there one here? *National Broadcasting Co. v. United States* (1943).

But neither Hughes nor Cardozo stopped with discussion of delegation. The defendants in *Schechter*, slaughterhouse operators in Brooklyn, had been convicted of violating various sections of the Live Poultry Code, among them the wage and hours provisions; one of the counts charged them with having sold an unfit chicken. Both Hughes and Cardozo concluded that these activities were beyond Congress's reach under the commerce power. That the Schechters purchased virtually all their chickens from out of state was irrelevant, Hughes explained, for the interstate movement ended when the chickens were brought to their slaughterhouses. Since the regulated transactions were therefore not in interstate commerce, the question then became whether they could be fairly considered to "affect" it. In deciding this question, Hughes claimed that, though "[t]he precise line can be drawn only as individual cases arise," "there is a neces-sary and well-established distinction between direct and indirect effects." And here, Hughes did not find such a direct relationship. He rejected out of hand the macro-economic argument that the effect of general wage stimulation on the national economy provided a sufficient nexus between the labor provisions and interstate commerce. Cardozo, far from indicating disagreement, declared that on the commerce question "little can be added to the opinion of the court." Although he asserted that "[t]he law is not indifferent to considerations of degree," this was an argument against the code. His test was in terms of the hard words "immediacy" and "directness": "To find immediacy or directness here," he declared, "is to find it almost everywhere."

The same day as *Schechter*, the Supreme Court handed down its decisions in two other cases that held much public interest. Like *Schechter*, both decisions held against the Administration, and both were unanimous. One of them was *Humphrey's Executor v. United States* (1935), which upheld a statute that prevented the President from removing a member of the Federal Trade Commission except for cause. The other, *Louisville Joint Stock Land Bank v. Radford* (1935), written by Brandeis,

 CROSS REFERENCE   *Humphrey's Executor* is presented at pp. 776–778.

held invalid a federal debtor-relief statute that was enacted under the bankruptcy power but that swept more broadly than the statute upheld in *Blaisdell*. The triple blow gave May 27, 1935, the enduring name "Black Monday." Roosevelt criticized the Court sharply, referring at a press conference to its "horse-and-buggy age" conception of the Constitution. This comment brought a startlingly hostile reaction, even from liberals, and Roosevelt did not follow up on it; careful to avoid raising an unnecessary issue, he thereafter kept a virtual public silence on the Court until well after the election of 1936.

Meanwhile, in its January 1936 decision in *United States v. Butler*, the Court held invalid central provisions of the Agricultural Adjustment Act of

CROSS REFERENCE   *Butler* is quoted on p. 267 and further discussed on pp. 489–490.

1933, which remained a popular statute and a cornerstone of the New Deal. Aiming to restore farm prices hard hit by the Depression to the levels they had occupied between 1909 and 1914, the Act operated simply and boldly. The government, through the Agricultural Adjustment Administration (AAA), boosted market prices by renting cultivable land, by purchasing surpluses, and by making straight-out benefit payments to farmers in return for agreements not to produce. The funds to operate this program for any particular commodity were raised by a tax on the processors of that commodity. In court, the Administration justified the Act on the basis not of the Commerce Clause, but of the clause authorizing Congress "to lay and collect taxes, . . . to pay the debts and provide for the . . . general Welfare of the United States."

Roberts, writing for the Court in an opinion joined by Hughes as well as the conservative foursome, rejected this argument. The statute's taxes and appropriations, he held, were "but means to an unconstitutional end." The federal government had no authority to regulate agriculture, and participation in the AAA program could not truly be considered voluntary—the threatened loss of benefits strong-armed farmers into participation. "This is coercion by economic pressure," Roberts wrote. "The asserted power of choice is illusory." Even if the program of benefits were not coercive, moreover, it would still be unconstitutional; since Congress could not enforce its commands on the farmer directly, it could not "indirectly accomplish these ends by taxing and spending to purchase compliance." Stone, joined by the other two liberals, wrote a bitter and forceful dissent. He contended that the Act could not be deemed coercive, asserting that "[t]hreat of loss, not hope of gain, is the essence of economic coercion," and pointing out that a substantial minority of farmers declined to participate in the program. And he contended that what the Court condemned as "purchased regulation" was merely the appropriate imposition of conditions on a public expenditure.

Significantly, though *Butler* was an immediate defeat for the exercise of federal power, it laid the seeds for future expansions. The true meaning of the General Welfare Clause had never been definitively resolved. Madison had contended that Congress could tax and spend only in the exercise of other powers granted it; on the other hand, Hamilton, seconded by the later writings of Story, had contended that the grant was of a distinct substantive power limited only by the conception of "the General Welfare." In *Butler*, at the urging of Hughes, Roberts emphatically endorsed the Hamilton-Story interpretation. For more on that, see p. 490.

For Discussion

(1) Which view of the General Welfare Clause do you believe is most persuasive?

(2) Do you believe that the offer of payments to farmers in return for promises not to produce was coercive?

(3) Assuming it was not coercive, should the Act have been held invalid as "purchased regulation"?

The Court delivered one more blow in the spring of 1936. On May 18, Roberts joined the four conservatives in holding unconstitutional the Bituminous Coal Conservation Act of 1935. See *Carter v. Carter Coal Co.* (1936). Part of the Act used a complex tax-and-rebate mechanism to regulate labor conditions in bituminous coal mines. The majority, per Sutherland, held

 CROSS REFERENCE *Carter* is presented at pp. 420–426.

that these provisions were unconstitutional as a regulation of mining, which, of course, as a form of production had long been held to be a local activity rather than part of interstate commerce. Without considering the constitutionality of another portion of the Act—marketing provisions that regulated interstate coal prices—the majority held that the marketing provisions could not be severed from the labor provisions, and that the entire statute was therefore unenforceable. Hughes and the three liberals, by contrast, thought the marketing provisions were clearly constitutional, and enough to uphold the statute's tax provisions and resolve the case. The liberals therefore did not address the labor provisions. Writing separately, Hughes expressed the view that one of the labor provisions, which gave private parties the ability to negotiate wage and hours standards binding throughout the industry, was unconstitutional on various grounds; in one conclusory sentence, he asserted that it went beyond any proper regulation of commerce.

3.   1937

Roosevelt won a huge landslide in November 1936, losing only in Maine and Vermont. The Democrats won large majorities in both houses. Pursuant to the 20th amendment, Roosevelt was inaugurated for his second term on January 20, 1937.

On February 5, Roosevelt revealed a proposal to add one member of the Supreme Court, up to a maximum of six, for each Justice who did not retire within six months of his 70th birthday. While Roosevelt presented the plan as an attempt to improve the efficiency of the Court, nearly everyone realized that the plan was a blatant attempt to pack the Court with Justices with ideologies compatible with those of the President. Roosevelt began the battle in an extraordinarily powerful position. But the longer the plan sat in the Senate Judiciary Committee, the stronger resistance became. Meanwhile, the Court itself altered the political equation by issuing a flurry of significant liberal decisions.

The first decision was the most important in political terms. In December 1936, the Court had heard argument in *West Coast Hotel v. Parrish*—another case involving a minimum wage statute for women under state law. Justice Stone was ill, and at conference the Justices divided evenly; Justice Roberts, who had voted with the conservatives in

 West Coast Hotel is presented at pp. 1356–1359.

Tipaldo, now switched sides, for mysterious reasons. Because Stone's views were well known, the Court held the case until his return, which occurred after the Court-packing battle began. When finally issued on March 29, the decision upheld the Washington statute against due process challenge, with the four conservative justices dissenting. Chief Justice Hughes's opinion for the majority relied heavily on *Nebbia*'s declaration that regulations of private contracts satisfied due process so long as they "have a reasonable relation to a proper legislative purpose, and are neither arbitrary nor discriminatory." The same day, the Court issued several pro-Government decisions, giving it the name "White Monday."

 Was the Court's decision in *West Coast Hotel* revolutionary? If *Tipaldo* had not been decided the year before, would it have been surprising?

Two weeks later, on April 12, the Court upheld the National Labor Relations Act by a 5–4 vote in three companion cases, most notably *National Labor Relations Board v. Jones & Laughlin Steel Corp* (1937). All three cases involved manufacturing companies; in each case, the held that labor relations in the workplace affected commerce sufficiently to justify regulation under the Commerce Clause.

 Jones & Laughlin and its companions are presented at pp. 427–432.

The Court's decisions—especially *West Coast Hotel*—sapped some of the strength from the President's drive for Court-packing. That drive suffered a double blow on May 18. First, Justice Van Devanter announced that he would retire in June, giving the President at least one vacancy to fill immediately without packing the Court. (While Van Devanter had already been eager to retire, Congress cut pensions for retiring Justices a few years earlier. On March 1, 1937, however, Congress passed a new law allowing Justices to retire at full pay.) Second, the Senate Judiciary Committee voted 10–8 to issue an adverse report on the President's bill. When the Committee issued its report on June 14, the majority castigated the proposal as "a needless, futile and utterly dangerous abandonment of constitutional principle . . . without precedent or justification." Lest there be any doubt of where it stood, the majority declared that the bill "should be so emphatically rejected that its parallel will never again be present-ed to the free representatives of a free people."

Meanwhile, on May 24, the Court issued a pair of decisions rejecting chal-lenges to the Social Security Act of 1935. In the first, the Court held 7–2—with only McReynolds and Butler dissenting—that the payment of old-age benefits under the Act was a valid exercise of Congress's power under the General Wel-fare Clause. *Helvering v. Davis* (1937). Referring to Roberts's dictum in *United States v. Butler* adopting a broad con-ception of that power, Cardozo wrote for the majority: "We will not resur-rect the contest. It is now settled by decision." As for the contention that the benefit payments were too particular to be part of the "general welfare," Cardozo wrote that the "nation-wide calam-ity" had shown "the solidarity of interests" of all the people, in this case in preventing fear of the poor house "when journey's end is near."

CROSS REFERENCE   *Helvering* is presented at pp. 491–492.

FOR DISCUSSION   Are you persuaded that payments to aged individuals for them to use as they see fit is an expenditure in sup-port of the "general welfare" of the nation?

In the second case, the Court upheld the Social Security Act's more intricate unemployment relief pro-gram. *Steward Machine Co. v. Davis* (1937). Title IX of the Act levied a tax on employers but credited up to 90% of it for amounts contributed instead to qualifying state unemployment

CROSS REFERENCE   *Steward* is presented at pp. 492–494.

funds. Such contributions were paid over to a trust fund maintained by the Secretary of Treasury and were withdrawn by the states for unemployment compensation. The aim of this scheme was to encourage the states to set up their own unemployment programs without fear of placing themselves at a competitive disadvantage against other states that chose to do nothing. Again writing for the Court, Cardozo rejected the argument that the plan constituted improper coercion of the states.

The Social Security cases were the last major decisions of the Court's term. By now, many liberals were convinced that there was no need for Court-packing. Joseph T. Robinson, the Senate Majority Leader, still hoped to be nominated to a new vacancy, and some of his Senate colleagues were disposed to help him. But Robinson died suddenly on July 14, and Roosevelt soon realized that he had no hope of pushing even a modified bill through the Senate. That fall, his first appointee to the Court, Sen. Hugo Black of Alabama, took his seat in place of Van Devanter. This effectively moved the idcological center of the Court to the left of Roberts; Hughes did not dissent once during the 1937–38 term of the Court. Sutherland retired in 1938, and from then on, for more than three decades, the ideological center of the Court was to the left of the political center of the nation.

4.　Denouement

a.　Individual Rights

In April 1938, the Court decided *United States v. Carolene Products Co.* (1938). The decision upheld a federal statute banning the shipment in interstate

 Carolene Products is presented at pp. 956–959 and pp. 1179–1181.

commerce of "filled milk," a product in which milk or milk products were blended with non-milk oils or fats. With Van Devanter and Sutherland no longer on the Court, there was not much doubt about the outcome; indeed, only McReynolds dissented.

Among other objections to the Act, Carolene challenged the congressional judgment that filled milk was "an adulterated article of food, injurious to the public health." That conclusion was indeed debatable; one view of the statute was that it was a successful attempt at protection by the dairy industry against cheaper competition. The Court was unmoved. Even in the absence of a legislative report, Justice Stone wrote, "the existence of facts supporting the legislative judgment is to be presumed, for regulatory legislation affecting ordinary commercial transactions is not to be pronounced unconstitutional unless, in the light of the facts made known or generally assumed, it is of such a character as to preclude the assumption that it rests upon some rational basis within the knowledge and experience of the legislators."

At this point, Stone dropped footnote 4 to his opinion, which over time became far more celebrated than the opinion itself:

> There may be narrower scope for operation of the presumption of constitutionality when legislation appears on its face to be within a specific prohibition of the Constitution, such as those of the first ten amendments, which are deemed equally specific when held to be embraced within the Fourteenth. . . .

> It is unnecessary to consider now whether legislation which restricts those political processes which can ordinarily be expected to bring about repeal of undesirable legislation is to be subjected to more exacting judicial scrutiny under the general prohibitions of the Fourteenth Amendment than are most other types of legislation. . . .

> Nor need we enquire whether similar considerations enter into the review of statutes directed at particular religious, or national, or racial minorities; whether prejudice against discrete and insular minorities may be a special condition, which tends seriously to curtail the operation of those political processes ordinarily to be relied upon to protect minorities, and which may call for a correspondingly more searching judicial inquiry.

Stone tacked on the first paragraph of the footnote in an attempt to meet an objection stated by Hughes to the first draft, which suggested that "different considerations" might apply in different contexts. Hughes thought this unduly complicated matters. "Are the 'considerations' different," he asked Stone, "or does the difference lie not in the *test* but in the nature of the right invoked?" He illustrated with one of the cases that Stone had cited, the Chief's own recent opinion in *Lovell v. Griffin* (1938), a First Amendment case; there, he said, "the legislative action . . . is directly opposed to the constitutional guaranty and for that reason has no presumption to support it." Stone replied that his focus had been on questions where the only guarantee invoked was the general one of due process. In an attempt to appease the Chief, though, he added the first paragraph, citing *Lovell* and another First Amendment opinion written by Hughes. This was not what Hughes intended, and it gives the footnote a rather awkward appearance. But the essence of the footnote, placed in the context of the text to which it is attached, remains: In some contexts, courts should be much less inclined to indulge a presumption of validity than when they are reviewing the "ordinary commercial transactions."

For Discussion

(1) Is there a basis for making a distinction like the one drawn in Footnote Four? If so, did the Court identify the circumstances that might justify more exacting scrutiny?

(2) Why do you suppose Stone incorporated this footnote, which was completely unnecessary for resolution of the case?

Later in the book, we will devote substantial attention to the question of when (and how) the Court should apply the more exacting type of scrutiny indicated by Footnote 4. For now, however, we will just note how *un*-exacting the Court became with respect to regulations of the commercial marketplace. A classic illustration, from a Court still dominated by New Dealers a couple of decades later, is *Williamson v. Lee Optical Co.* (1955). In that case, the court considered a statute that, among other restrictions, required a prescription from an optometrist or ophthamologist before an optician could fit old lenses into new frames.

Williamson is presented at pp. 961–963.

While recognizing that the legislation might be "needless and wasteful," the Court held that it was "for the legislature, not the courts, to balance the advantages and disadvantages" of the requirement.

b.   The Commerce Power

The New Deal Court continued to take an expansive view of Congress's power under the Commerce Clause. The two most significant cases from the period shortly after the Court-packing crisis were *United States v. Darby* (1941) and *Wickard v. Filburn* (1942). In *Darby*, the Court overruled *Hammer v. Dagenhart* and upheld the Fair Labor Standards Act of 1938, which set wage and hours requirements for employees in businesses affecting commerce, including workers in production. In *Wickard*, the Court upheld a regulation that effectively limited how much wheat a farmer could consume

 CROSS REFERENCE

Darby and *Wickard* are presented at pp. 434–438 and pp. 439–443, respectively.

on the farm. These decisions raised the question of whether the Court would ever again hold that a federal statute exceeded Congress's power over commerce; it did not do so until 1995.

The constitutional framework that emerged from the historical developments we have traced remains familiar, in its overall outlines, in the current day. The national government has broad powers to regulate the national economy. States similarly have broad leeway to regulate their local commercial matters, including private economic relations. And yet on other issues, most notably when it comes to protecting politically vulnerable groups and guaranteeing certain rights, the principles adumbrated in Footnote 4 of *Carolene Products* lead courts to more actively constrain governmental actors. Much of constitutional law since the New Deal has concerned these matters.

The rest of this book is organized along thematic, rather than chronological, lines. Here are some of the more significant constitutional developments over the last three-quarters of a century.

- The Supreme Court took an active role in limiting racial discrimination; *Brown v. Board of Education* is the most notable decision in this area.

- The Court developed a large body of doctrine applying principles of equal protection of law outside the context of racial discrimination, most notably in the area of sex discrimination.

- The Court also protected what it regarded as fundamental rights of personal autonomy. Most notable in this line are decisions on abortion, same-sex intimacy, and same-sex marriages.

- The scope of national powers remained virtually unlimited by constitutional constraints until 1995; since then, there has been a modest retrenchment.

- Separation-of-powers issues—including the President's military, appointment, and removal powers—have remained both salient and highly contentious.

 TEST YOUR KNOWLEDGE: To assess your understanding of the material in this chapter, **click here** to take a quiz.

CHAPTER II

Interpreting the Constitution

A. Interpreting the Constitution—How?

One way to classify your first-year courses is by the dominant source of law in each class. Some—typically torts, property, and contracts—teach rules that mostly come from the common law. In these classes, the game is to navigate complicated and ambiguous judicial precedent without much reference to other texts that might provide a rule of decision. Other classes—such as legislation and regulation—teach rules that mostly come from statutes and regulations. In these classes, the game is to apply some piece of officially promulgated text to a real-world scenario: does a sign reading "no vehicles in the park" prohibit ambulances during an emergency? Precedent of course plays a role in the latter process, but textual interpretation and legislative history are at least as fundamental to the inquiry. Criminal law and civil procedure classes can sit in different places along this spectrum, depending on how heavily your professor's syllabus weights common law and constitutional issues versus the Model Penal Code and codifications of civil procedure rules.

Judged by these lights, constitutional law occupies a funny middle ground. Certainly as a formal matter, the underlying source of authority is a legal instrument called the Constitution of the United States, and the formal statement of a court's conclusion is that some particular constitutional clause "means" something as applied to a particular context. That said, you'll see that the actual practice of constitutional interpretation is harder to pin down. That's partly because the actual constitutional text is incredibly sparse. On many questions, there's just not much to work with when it comes to the traditional moves of statutory interpretation. Constitutional interpretation, moreover, has had hundreds of years to elaborate precedential solutions to the document's textual ambiguities, which means that the actual practice of applying the rules in a new case often doesn't involve much attention to what the text itself actually says. (Query whether this is appropriate.) And yet even in the areas of constitutional law where on-point caselaw is plentiful, it is at least potentially and at least sometimes a valid move for lawyers to invoke the underlying text, drafting and ratification history, or political custom and tradition as a counterargument to the logical implications of existing precedent.

So constitutional law calls on us to apply a wide range of interpretive tools. On one hand, we will be doing a great deal of common-law-style precedential analysis, often without much focus on the actual document's underlying text. On the other hand, many issues will require us to pay serious attention to the questions of text, legislative history, and political implementation that loom large when interpreting statutes. At the same time, do not lose sight of a deeper tension. On one hand, constitutional law is definitely a species of law; there are numerous questions on which, at any given time, most knowledgeable observers would agree. But on the other hand, it would be foolish to deny that judicial or even political ideology can often play an important role in constitutional interpretation.

District of Columbia v. Heller is a useful introduction to the range of tools deployed in modern constitutional interpretation, partly because it essentially announces a personal right (to bear arms outside of the context of a regulated militia) that had previously been rejected by the Supreme Court. In the course of debating whether this was appropriate, both the majority and the principal dissent worked carefully through many of the sources of meaning that typically inform constitutional interpretation.

District of Columbia v. Heller

Supreme Court of the United States, 2008.
554 U.S. 570.

Justice Scalia delivered the opinion of the Court.

We consider whether a District of Columbia prohibition on the possession of usable handguns in the home violates the Second Amendment to the Constitution.

I

The District of Columbia generally prohibits the possession of handguns. It is a crime to carry an unregistered firearm, and the registration of handguns is prohibited. Wholly apart from that prohibition, no person may carry a handgun without a license, but the chief of police may issue licenses for 1-year periods. District of Columbia law also requires residents to keep their lawfully owned firearms, such as registered long guns, "unloaded and dissembled or bound by a trigger lock or similar device" unless they are located in a place of business or are being used for lawful recreational activities.

Respondent Dick Heller is a D.C. special police officer authorized to carry a handgun while on duty at the Thurgood Marshall Judiciary Building. He applied for a registration certificate for a handgun that he wished to keep at home, but the District refused. He thereafter filed a lawsuit in the Federal District Court for the District of Columbia seeking, on Second Amendment grounds, to enjoin the city from enforcing the bar on the registration of handguns, the licensing requirement insofar as it prohibits the carrying of a firearm in the home without a license, and the trigger-lock requirement insofar as it prohibits the use of "functional firearms within the home." The District Court dismissed respondent's complaint. The Court of Appeals for the District of Columbia Circuit, construing his complaint as seeking the right to render a firearm operable and carry it about his home in that condition only when necessary for self-defense, reversed. It held that the Second Amendment protects an individual right to possess firearms and that the city's total ban on handguns, as well as its requirement that firearms in the home be kept nonfunctional even when necessary for self-defense, violated that right. The Court of Appeals directed the District Court to enter summary judgment for respondent. We granted certiorari.

II

We turn first to the meaning of the Second Amendment.

A

The Second Amendment provides: "A well regulated Militia being necessary to the security of a free State, the right of the people to keep and bear Arms, shall not be infringed." In interpreting this text, we are guided by the principle that "[t]he Constitution was written to be understood by the voters; its words and phrases were used in their normal and ordinary as distinguished from technical meaning." *United States v. Sprague* (1931); see also *Gibbons v. Ogden* (1824). Normal meaning may of course include an idiomatic meaning, but it excludes secret or technical meanings that would not have been known to ordinary citizens in the founding generation.

The two sides in this case have set out very different interpretations of the Amendment. Petitioners and today's dissenting Justices believe that it protects only the right to possess and carry a firearm in connection with militia service. Respondent argues that it protects an individual right to possess a firearm unconnected with service in a militia, and to use that arm for traditionally lawful purposes, such as self-defense within the home.

The Second Amendment is naturally divided into two parts: its prefatory clause and its operative clause. The former does not limit the latter grammatically, but rather announces a purpose. The Amendment could be rephrased, "Because a well regulated Militia is necessary to the security of a free State, the right of the people to keep and bear Arms shall not be infringed." . . .

Logic demands that there be a link between the stated purpose and the command. The Second Amendment would be nonsensical if it read, "A well regulated Militia, being necessary to the security of a free State, the right of the people to petition for redress of grievances shall not be infringed." That requirement of logical connection may cause a prefatory clause to resolve an ambiguity in the operative clause ("The separation of church and state being an important objective, the teachings of canons shall have no place in our jurisprudence." The preface makes clear that the operative clause refers not to canons of interpretation but to clergymen.) But apart from that clarifying function, a prefatory clause does not limit or expand the scope of the operative clause. . . . Therefore, while we will begin our textual analysis with the operative clause, we will return to the prefatory clause to ensure that our reading of the operative clause is consistent with the announced purpose.

1.   Operative Clause.

   a.   *"Right of the People."*

The first salient feature of the operative clause is that it codifies a "right of the people." The unamended Constitution and the Bill of Rights use the phrase "right of the people" two other times, in the First Amendment's Assembly-and-Petition Clause and in the Fourth Amendment's Search-and-Seizure Clause. The Ninth Amendment uses very similar terminology ("The enumeration *"the people" → individuals*

in the Constitution, of certain rights, shall not be construed to deny or disparage others retained by the people"). All three of these instances unambiguously refer to individual rights, not "collective" rights, or rights that may be exercised only through participation in some corporate body.

Three provisions of the Constitution refer to "the people" in a context other than "rights"—the famous preamble ("We the people"), § 2 of Article I (providing that "the people" will choose members of the House), and the Tenth Amendment (providing that those powers not given the Federal Government remain with "the States" or "the people"). Those provisions arguably refer to "the people" acting collectively—but they deal with the exercise or reservation of powers, not rights. Nowhere else in the Constitution does a "right" attributed to "the people" refer to anything other than an individual right. . . .

We start therefore with a strong presumption that the Second Amendment right is exercised individually and belongs to all Americans.

    b.   *"Keep and bear Arms."*

We move now from the holder of the right—"the people"—to the substance of the right: "to keep and bear Arms."

Before addressing the verbs "keep" and "bear," we interpret their object: "Arms." The 18th-century meaning is no different from the meaning today. The 1773 edition of Samuel Johnson's dictionary defined "arms" as "weapons of offence, or armour of defence." *Dictionary of the English Language* (4th ed.). Timothy Cunningham's important 1771 legal dictionary defined "arms" as "any thing that a man wears for his defence, or takes into his hands, or useth in wrath to cast at or strike another." . . .

Some have made the argument, bordering on the frivolous, that only those arms in existence in the 18th century are protected by the Second Amendment. We do not interpret constitutional rights that way. Just as the First Amendment protects modern forms of communications, *e.g., Reno v. American Civil Liberties Union* (1997) [(the internet)], and the Fourth Amendment applies to modern forms of search, *e.g., Kyllo v. United States* (2001) [(thermal imaging)], the Second Amendment extends, prima facie, to all instruments that constitute bearable arms, even those that were not in existence at the time of the founding.

We turn to the phrases "keep arms" and "bear arms." Johnson defined "keep" as, most relevantly, "[t]o retain; not to lose," and "[t]o have in custody." Webster defined it as "[t]o hold; to retain in one's power or possession." No party has apprised us of an idiomatic meaning of "keep Arms." Thus, the most natural reading of "keep Arms" in the Second Amendment is to "have weapons." . . .

At the time of the founding, as now, to "bear" meant to "carry." See Johnson; Webster; T. Sheridan, *A Complete Dictionary of the English Language* (1796); *Oxford English Dictionary* (1989) (hereinafter Oxford). When used with "arms," however, the term has a meaning that refers to carrying for a particular purpose—confrontation. [But] it in no way connotes participation in a structured military organization.

From our review of founding-era sources, we conclude that this natural meaning was also the meaning that "bear arms" had in the 18th century. In numerous instances, "bear arms" was unambiguously used to refer to the carrying of weapons outside of an organized militia. The most prominent examples are those most relevant to the Second Amendment: nine state constitutional provisions written in the 18th century or the first two decades of the 19th, which enshrined a right of citizens to "bear arms in defense of themselves and the state" or "bear arms in defense of himself and the state." It is clear from those formulations that "bear arms" did not refer only to carrying a weapon in an organized military unit. . . .

Petitioners justify their limitation of "bear arms" to the military context by pointing out the unremarkable fact that it was often used in that context. . . . Other legal sources frequently used "bear arms" in nonmilitary contexts. . . . [Additional cites omitted.] Justice Stevens points to a study by *amici* supposedly showing that the phrase "bear arms" was most frequently used in the military context. See Linguists' Brief. Of course, as we have said, the fact that the phrase was commonly used in a particular context does not show that it is limited to that context, and, in any event, we have given many sources where the phrase was used in nonmilitary contexts. Moreover, the study's collection appears to include (who knows how many times) the idiomatic phrase "bear arms against," which is irrelevant. . . .

Finally, Justice Stevens suggests that "keep and bear Arms" was some sort of term of art, presumably akin to "hue and cry" or "cease and desist." (This suggestion usefully evades the problem that there is no evidence whatsoever to support a military reading of "keep arms.") Justice Stevens believes that the unitary meaning of "keep and bear Arms" is established by the Second Amendment's calling it a "right" (singular) rather than "rights" (plural). There is nothing to this. State constitutions of the founding period routinely grouped multiple (related) guarantees under a singular "right," and the First Amendment protects the "right [singular] of the people peaceably to assemble, and to petition the Government for a redress of grievances." And even if "keep and bear Arms" were a unitary phrase, we find no evidence that it bore a military meaning. . . .

  c. Meaning of the Operative Clause.

  Putting all of these textual elements together, we find that they guarantee the individual right to possess and carry weapons in case of confrontation. This meaning is strongly confirmed by the historical background of the Second Amendment. We look to this because it has always been widely understood that the Second Amendment, like the First and Fourth Amendments, codified a *pre-existing* right. The very text of the Second Amendment implicitly recognizes the pre-existence of the right and declares only that it "shall not be infringed." . . .

  Between the Restoration and the Glorious Revolution, the Stuart Kings Charles II and James II succeeded in using select militias loyal to them to suppress political dissidents, in part by disarming their opponents. . . . These experiences caused Englishmen to be extremely wary of concentrated military forces run by the state and to be jealous of their arms. They accordingly obtained an assurance from William and Mary, in the Declaration of Right (which was codified as the English Bill of Rights), that Protestants would never be disarmed: "That the Subjects which are Protestants, may have Arms for their Defence suitable to their Conditions, and as allowed by Law." 1 W. & M., c. 2, § 7 (1689). This right has long been understood to be the predecessor to our Second Amendment. . . .

[margin annotation: This right has long been understood his. predecessor]

  There seems to us no doubt, on the basis of both text and history, that the Second Amendment conferred an individual right to keep and bear arms. Of course the right was not unlimited, just as the First Amendment's right of free speech was not, see, *e.g.*, *United States v. Williams* (2008). Thus, we do not read the Second Amendment to protect the right of citizens to carry arms for *any sort* of confrontation, just as we do not read the First Amendment to protect the right of citizens to speak for *any purpose*. Before turning to limitations upon the individual right, however, we must determine whether the prefatory clause of the Second Amendment comports with our interpretation of the operative clause.

[margin annotation: Like any other right in Const. it doesn't say it is unlimited]

2. Prefatory Clause.

  The prefatory clause reads: "A well regulated Militia, being necessary to the security of a free State. . . ."

a.   *"Well-Regulated Militia."*

In *United States v. Miller* (1939), we explained that "the Militia comprised all males physically capable of acting in concert for the common defense." That definition comports with founding-era sources. . . . [T]he adjective "well-regulated" implies nothing more than the imposition of proper discipline and training. See Johnson (1619) ("Regulate": "To adjust by rule or method"). . . .

b.   *"Security of a Free State."*

. . . There are many reasons why the militia was thought to be "necessary to the security of a free state." *See* Story, *Commentaries on the Constitution of the United States* (1833). First, of course, it is useful in repelling invasions and suppressing insurrections. Second, it renders large standing armies unnecessary—an argument that Alexander Hamilton made in favor of federal control over the militia. The Federalist No. 29. Third, when the able-bodied men of a nation are trained in arms and organized, they are better able to resist tyranny.

3.   Relationship between Prefatory Clause and Operative Clause

We reach the question, then: Does the preface fit with an operative clause that creates an individual right to keep and bear arms? It fits perfectly, once one knows the history that the founding generation knew and that we have described above. That history showed that the way tyrants had eliminated a militia consisting of all the able-bodied men was not by banning the militia but simply by taking away the people's arms, enabling a select militia or standing army to suppress political opponents. . . .

It is therefore entirely sensible that the Second Amendment's prefatory clause announces the purpose for which the right was codified: to prevent elimination of the militia. The prefatory clause does not suggest that preserving the militia was the only reason Americans valued the ancient right; most undoubtedly thought it even more important for self-defense and hunting. But the threat that the new Federal Government would destroy the citizens' militia by taking away their arms was the reason that right—unlike some other English rights—was codified in a written Constitution. . . .

C

Justice Stevens relies on the drafting history of the Second Amendment—the various proposals in the state conventions and the debates in Congress. It is dubious to rely on such history to interpret a text that was widely understood to codify a pre-existing right, rather than to fashion a new one. . . .

D

We now address how the Second Amendment was interpreted from immediately after its ratification through the end of the 19th century. As we will show, virtually all interpreters of the Second Amendment in the century after its enactment interpreted the Amendment as we do.

Everyone has interpreted it this way

↓

protect individual right (not militia right)

1.   Post-ratification Commentary

Three important founding-era legal scholars interpreted the Second Amendment in published writings. All three understood it to protect an individual right unconnected with militia service. [The majority discusses commentary by St. George Tucker, William Rawle, and Joseph Story.]

2.   Pre-Civil War Case Law

The 19th-century cases that interpreted the Second Amendment universally support an individual right unconnected to militia service. [The majority discusses a number of pre-Civil War decisions.]

3.   Post-Civil War Legislation.

. . . Blacks were routinely disarmed by Southern States after the Civil War. Those who opposed these injustices frequently stated that they infringed blacks' constitutional right to keep and bear arms. Needless to say, the claim was not that blacks were being prohibited from carrying arms in an organized state militia. . . .

Congress enacted the Freedmen's Bureau Act on July 16, 1866. Section 14 stated:

> [T]he right . . . to have full and equal benefit of all laws and proceedings concerning personal liberty, personal security, and the acquisition, enjoyment, and disposition of estate, real and personal, including the constitutional right to bear arms, shall be secured to and enjoyed by all the citizens . . . without respect to race or color, or previous condition of slavery . . . .

The understanding that the Second Amendment gave freed blacks the right to keep and bear arms was reflected in congressional discussion of the bill, with even an opponent of it saying that the founding generation "were for every man bearing his arms about him and keeping them in his house, his castle, for his own defense." Cong. Globe, 39th Cong., 1st Sess. (1866) (Sen. Davis).

***

E

[handwritten: Precedent analysis → No precedent forecloses]

We now ask whether any of our precedents forecloses the conclusions we have reached about the meaning of the Second Amendment. [Discussion of some early opinions omitted.]

Justice Stevens places overwhelming reliance upon this Court's decision in *United States v. Miller* (1939). . . . And what is, according to Justice Stevens, the holding of *Miller* that demands such obeisance? That the Second Amendment "protects the right to keep and bear arms for certain military purposes, but that it does not curtail the Legislature's power to regulate the nonmilitary use and ownership of weapons." *Post.*

[handwritten: miller does not apply they were saying that type of weapon wasn't protected]

Nothing so clearly demonstrates the weakness of Justice Stevens' case. *Miller* did not hold that and cannot possibly be read to have held that. The judgment in the case upheld against a Second Amendment challenge two men's federal indictment for transporting an unregistered short-barreled shotgun in interstate commerce, in violation of the National Firearms Act. It is entirely clear that the Court's basis for saying that the Second Amendment did not apply was *not* that the defendants were "bear[ing] arms" not "for . . . military purposes" but for "nonmilitary use," *post.* Rather, it was that the *type of weapon at issue* was not eligible for Second Amendment protection:

> In the absence of any evidence tending to show that the possession or use of a [short-barreled shotgun] at this time has some reasonable relationship to the preservation or efficiency of a well regulated militia, we cannot say that the Second Amendment guarantees the right to keep and bear *such an instrument.*

Miller (emphasis added). "Certainly," the Court continued, "it is not within judicial notice that this weapon is any part of the ordinary military equipment or that its use could contribute to the common defense." Beyond that, the opinion provided no explanation of the content of the right. . . . *Miller* stands only for

*[handwritten: *]* the proposition that the Second Amendment right, whatever its nature, extends only to certain types of weapons.

It is particularly wrongheaded to read *Miller* for more than what it said, because the case did not even purport to be a thorough examination of the

Second Amendment. . . . The defendants made no appearance in the case, nei-ther filing a brief nor appearing at oral argument; the Court heard from no one but the Government (reason enough, one would think, not to make that case the beginning and the end of this Court's consideration of the Second Amendment). . . . As for the text of the Court's opinion itself, that discusses *none* of the history of the Second Amendment. It assumes from the prologue that the Amendment was designed to preserve the militia (which we do not dispute), and then reviews some historical materials dealing with the nature of the militia, and in particular with the nature of the arms their members were expected to possess. Not a word (*not a word*) about the history of the Second Amendment. This is the mighty rock upon which the dissent rests its case. . . .

We conclude that nothing in our precedents forecloses our adoption of the original understanding of the Second Amendment.

III

Like most rights, the right secured by the Second Amendment is not un-limited. From Blackstone through the 19th-century cases, commentators and courts routinely explained that the right was not a right to keep and carry any weapon whatsoever in any manner whatsoever and for whatever purpose. . . . Although we do not undertake an exhaustive historical analysis today of the full scope of the Second Amendment, nothing in our opinion should be taken to cast doubt on longstanding prohibitions on the possession of firearms by fel-ons and the mentally ill, or laws forbidding the carrying of firearms in sensitive places such as schools and government buildings, or laws imposing conditions and qualifications on the commercial sale of arms.

We also recognize another important limitation on the right to keep and carry arms. *Miller* said, as we have explained, that the sorts of weapons protect-ed were those "in common use at the time." We think that limitation is fairly supported by the historical tradition of prohibiting the carrying of "dangerous and unusual weapons." . . .

It may be objected that if weapons that are most useful in military ser-vice—M-16 rifles and the like—may be banned, then the Second Amendment right is completely detached from the prefatory clause. But as we have said, the conception of the militia at the time of the Second Amendment's ratification was the body of all citizens capable of military service, who would bring the sorts of lawful weapons that they possessed at home to militia duty. It may well be true today that a militia, to be as effective as militias in the 18th century, would require sophisticated arms that are highly unusual in society at large. Indeed, it may be true that no amount of small arms could be useful against modern-day bombers and tanks. But the fact that modern developments have limited the degree of fit between the prefatory clause and the protected right cannot change our interpretation of the right.

IV

We turn finally to the law at issue here. . . . The handgun ban amounts to a prohibition of an entire class of "arms" that is overwhelmingly chosen by American society for that lawful purpose. The prohibition extends, moreover, to the home, where the need for defense of self, family, and property is most acute. . . .

Few laws in the history of our Nation have come close to the severe restriction of the District's handgun ban. . . . It is no answer to say, as petitioners do, that it is permissible to ban the possession of handguns so long as the possession of other firearms (*i.e.*, long guns) is allowed. It is enough to note, as we have observed, that the American people have considered the handgun to be the quintessential self-defense weapon. . . . Whatever the reason, handguns are the most popular weapon chosen by Americans for self-defense in the home, and a complete prohibition of their use is invalid.

We must also address the District's requirement (as applied to respondent's handgun) that firearms in the home be rendered and kept inoperable at all times. This makes it impossible for citizens to use them for the core lawful purpose of self-defense and is hence unconstitutional.

* * *

Justice Breyer moves on to make a broad jurisprudential point: He criticizes us for declining to establish a level of scrutiny for evaluating Second Amendment restrictions. . . . After an exhaustive discussion of the arguments for and against gun control, Justice Breyer arrives at his interest-balanced answer: Because handgun violence is a problem, because the law is limited to an urban area, and because there were somewhat similar restrictions in the founding period (a false proposition that we have already discussed), the interest-balancing inquiry results in the constitutionality of the handgun ban. QED. . . .

The Second Amendment is . . . the very *product* of an interest-balancing by the people—which Justice Breyer would now conduct for them anew. And whatever else it leaves to future evaluation, it surely elevates above all other interests the right of law-abiding, responsible citizens to use arms in defense of hearth and home. . . .

In sum, we hold that the District's ban on handgun possession in the home violates the Second Amendment, as does its prohibition against rendering any lawful firearm in the home operable for the purpose of immediate self-defense. Assuming that Heller is not disqualified from the exercise of Second Amendment rights, the District must permit him to register his handgun and must issue him a license to carry it in the home. . . .

JUSTICE STEVENS, with whom JUSTICE SOUTER, JUSTICE GINSBURG, and JUSTICE BREYER join, dissenting.

The question presented by this case is not whether the Second Amendment protects a "collective right" or an "individual right." Surely it protects a right that can be enforced by individuals. But a conclusion that the Second Amendment protects an individual right does not tell us anything about the scope of that right.

Guns are used to hunt, for self-defense, to commit crimes, for sporting activities, and to perform military duties. The Second Amendment plainly does not protect the right to use a gun to rob a bank; it is equally clear that it *does* encompass the right to use weapons for certain military purposes. Whether it also protects the right to possess and use guns for nonmilitary purposes like hunting and personal self-defense is the question presented by this case. The text of the Amendment, its history, and our decision in *United States v. Miller* (1939), provide a clear answer to that question.

The Second Amendment was adopted to protect the right of the people of each of the several States to maintain a well-regulated militia. It was a response to concerns raised during the ratification of the Constitution that the power of Congress to disarm the state militias and create a national standing army posed an intolerable threat to the sovereignty of the several States. Neither the text of the Amendment nor the arguments advanced by its proponents evidenced the slightest interest in limiting any legislature's authority to regulate private civilian uses of firearms. Specifically, there is no indication that the Framers of the Amendment intended to enshrine the common-law right of self-defense in the Constitution.

In 1934, Congress enacted the National Firearms Act, the first major federal firearms law. Sustaining an indictment under the Act, this Court held that, "[i]n the absence of any evidence tending to show that possession or use of a 'shotgun having a barrel of less than eighteen inches in length' at this time has some reasonable relationship to the preservation or efficiency of a well regulated militia, we cannot say that the Second Amendment guarantees the right to keep and bear such an instrument." *Miller.* The view of the Amendment we took in *Miller*—that it protects the right to keep and bear arms for certain military purposes, but that it does not curtail the Legislature's power to regulate the nonmilitary use and ownership of weapons—is both the most natural reading of the Amendment's text and the interpretation most faithful to the history of its adoption.

Since our decision in *Miller*, hundreds of judges have relied on the view of the Amendment we endorsed there;[2] we ourselves affirmed it in 1980. *See Lewis v. United States* (1980). No new evidence has surfaced since 1980 supporting the view that the Amendment was intended to curtail the power of Congress to regulate civilian use or misuse of weapons. Indeed, a review of the drafting history of the Amendment demonstrates that its Framers *rejected* proposals that would have broadened its coverage to include such uses. . . .

Even if the textual and historical arguments on both sides of the issue were evenly balanced, respect for the well-settled views of all of our predecessors on this Court, and for the rule of law itself, would prevent most jurists from endorsing such a dramatic upheaval in the law. As Justice Cardozo observed years ago, the "labor of judges would be increased almost to the breaking point if every past decision could be reopened in every case, and one could not lay one's own course of bricks on the secure foundation of the courses laid by others who had gone before him." *The Nature of the Judicial Process* (1921). . . .

I

. . . Three portions of [the Second Amendment] text merit special focus: the introductory language defining the Amendment's purpose, the class of persons encompassed within its reach, and the unitary nature of the right that it protects.

"A well regulated Militia, being necessary to the security of a free State"

The preamble to the Second Amendment makes three important points. It identifies the preservation of the militia as the Amendment's purpose; it explains that the militia is necessary to the security of a free State; and it recognizes

---

[2]   Until the Fifth Circuit's decision in *United States v. Emerson*, 270 F.3d 203 (2001), every Court of Appeals to consider the question had understood *Miller* to hold that the Second Amendment does not protect the right to possess and use guns for purely private, civilian purposes. [Citing cases.]

that the militia must be "well regulated." In all three respects it is comparable to provisions in several State Declarations of Rights that were adopted roughly contemporaneously with the Declaration of Independence. Those state provisions highlight the importance members of the founding generation attached to the maintenance of state militias; they also underscore the profound fear shared by many in that era of the dangers posed by standing armies. . . .

The parallels between the Second Amendment and these state declarations, and the Second Amendment's omission of any statement of purpose related to the right to use firearms for hunting or personal self-defense, is especially striking in light of the fact that the Declarations of Rights of Pennsylvania and Vermont did expressly protect such civilian uses at the time. . . . The contrast between those two declarations and the Second Amendment reinforces the clear statement of purpose announced in the Amendment's preamble. It confirms that the Framers' single-minded focus in crafting the constitutional guarantee "to keep and bear Arms" was on military uses of firearms, which they viewed in the context of service in state militias.

The preamble thus both sets forth the object of the Amendment and informs the meaning of the remainder of its text. Such text should not be treated as mere surplusage, for "[i]t cannot be presumed that any clause in the constitution is intended to be without effect." *Marbury v. Madison* (1803).

The Court today tries to denigrate the importance of this clause of the Amendment by beginning its analysis with the Amendment's operative provision. . . . Without identifying any language in the text that even mentions civilian uses of firearms, the Court proceeds to "find" its preferred reading in what is at best an ambiguous text, and then concludes that its reading is not foreclosed by the preamble. Perhaps the Court's approach to the text is acceptable advocacy, but it is surely an unusual approach for judges to follow.

"The right of the people"

The centerpiece of the Court's textual argument is its insistence that the words "the people" as used in the Second Amendment must have the same meaning, and protect the same class of individuals, as when they are used in the First and Fourth Amendments. . . . But the Court *itself* reads the Second Amendment to protect a "subset" significantly narrower than the class of persons protected by the First and Fourth Amendments; when it finally drills down on the substantive meaning of the Second Amendment, the Court limits the protected class to "law-abiding, responsible citizens." . . .

The Court also overlooks the significance of the way the Framers used the phrase "the people" in these constitutional provisions. In the First Amendment, no words define the class of individuals entitled to speak, to publish, or to worship; in that Amendment it is only the right peaceably to assemble, and to petition the Government for a redress of grievances, that is described as a right of "the people." These rights contemplate collective action. While the right peaceably to assemble protects the individual rights of those persons participating in the assembly, its concern is with action engaged in by members of a group, rather than any single individual. . . .

Similarly, the words "the people" in the Second Amendment refer back to the object announced in the Amendment's preamble. They remind us that it is the collective action of individuals having a duty to serve in the militia that the text directly protects and, perhaps more importantly, that the ultimate purpose of the Amendment was to protect the States' share of the divided sovereignty created by the Constitution. . . .

"To keep and bear Arms"

Although the Court's discussion of these words treats them as two "phrases"—as if they read "to keep" and "to bear"—they describe a unitary right: to possess arms if needed for military purposes and to use them in conjunction with military activities. . . .

The term "bear arms" is a familiar idiom; when used unadorned by any additional words, its meaning is "to serve as a soldier, do military service, fight." Oxford English Dictionary (1989). . . . Had the Framers wished to expand the meaning of the phrase "bear arms" to encompass civilian possession and use, they could have done so by the addition of phrases such as "for the defense of themselves," as was done in the Pennsylvania and Vermont Declarations of Rights. The *unmodified* use of "bear arms," by contrast, refers most naturally to a military purpose, as evidenced by its use in literally dozens of contemporary texts. [citing Brief of Amici Professors of Linguistics and English.] The absence of any reference to civilian uses of weapons tailors the text of the Amendment to the purpose identified in its preamble. But when discussing these words, the Court simply ignores the preamble. . . .

This reading is confirmed by the fact that the clause protects only one right, rather than two. It does not describe a right "to keep Arms" and a separate right "to bear Arms." Rather, the single right that it does describe is both a duty and a right to have arms available and ready for military service, and to use them for military purposes when necessary. Different language surely would have been used to protect nonmilitary use and possession of weapons from regulation if such an intent had played any role in the drafting of the Amendment.

* * *

. . . Even if the meaning of the text were genuinely susceptible to more than one interpretation, the burden would remain on those advocating a departure from the purpose identified in the preamble and from settled law to come forward with persuasive new arguments or evidence. The textual analysis offered by respondent and embraced by the Court falls far short of sustaining that heavy burden.[14] And the Court's emphatic reliance on the claim "that the Second Amendment . . . codified a *pre-existing* right" is of course beside the point because the right to keep and bear arms for service in a state militia was also a pre-existing right.

Indeed, not a word in the constitutional text even arguably supports the Court's overwrought and novel description of the Second Amendment as "elevat[ing] above all other interests" "the right of law-abiding, responsible citizens to use arms in defense of hearth and home." . . .

WORTH NOTING

Justice Stevens gives an extended account of the history of the drafting of the Second Amendment. The original Constitution balanced fear of a national standing army against recognition that an inadequately trained militia would be insufficient for national defense. The 1787 Convention therefore adopted a compromise: Congress had power to call the militia into national service (in which case the President would act as its Commander in Chief), and to provide for organizing, arming, and disciplining it, but the States retained the right to appoint its officers and to train it in accordance with the discipline prescribed by Congress. Art. I, § 8, cls. 15–16, Art. II, § 2. But then concern arose in numerous states that Congress might disarm the militia. Several proposed amendments were offered to address this problem, and some of those "would have unambiguously protected civilian uses of firearms." But James Madison, principal drafter of the Second Amendment, rejected those and instead modeled the Amendment on the "distinctly military Virginia proposal."

---

14   The Court's atomistic, word-by-word approach to construing the Amendment calls to mind the parable of the six blind men and the elephant, famously set in verse by John Godfrey Saxe. *The Poems of John Godfrey Saxe* (1873). In the parable, each blind man approaches a single elephant; touching a different part of the elephant's body in isolation, each concludes that he has learned its true nature. One touches the animal's leg, and concludes that the elephant is like a tree; another touches the trunk and decides that the elephant is like a snake; and so on. Each of them, of course, has fundamentally failed to grasp the nature of the creature.

III

Although it gives short shrift to the drafting history of the Second Amendment, the Court dwells at length on four other sources: the 17th-century English Bill of Rights; Blackstone's *Commentaries on the Laws of England*; postenactment commentary on the Second Amendment; and post-Civil War legislative history.[28] All of these sources shed only indirect light on the question before us, and in any event offer little support for the Court's conclusion. [Lengthy discussion of these sources omitted.]

IV

. . . The Amendment played little role in any legislative debate about the civilian use of firearms for most of the 19th century, and it made few appearances in the decisions of this Court. . . . Thus, for most of our history, the invalidity of Second-Amendment-based objections to firearms regulations has been well settled and uncontroversial. Indeed, the Second Amendment was not even mentioned in either full House of Congress during the legislative proceedings that led to the passage of the 1934 Act [regulating gun possession, which gave rise to *United States v. Miller* (1939)]. Yet enforcement of that law produced the judicial decision that confirmed the status of the Amendment as limited in reach to military usage.

[In *United States v. Miller,*] the Court unanimously concluded that the Second Amendment did not apply to the possession of a firearm that did not have "some reasonable relationship to the preservation or efficiency of a well regulated militia." The key to that decision did not, as the Court belatedly suggests, *ante*, turn on the difference between muskets and sawed-off shotguns; it turned, rather, on the basic difference between the military and nonmilitary use and possession of guns. Indeed, if the Second Amendment were not limited in its coverage to military uses of weapons, why should the Court in *Miller* have suggested that some weapons but not others were eligible for Second Amendment protection? If use for self-defense were the relevant standard, why did the Court not inquire into the suitability of a particular weapon for self-defense purposes?

---

[28]   The Court's fixation on the last two types of sources is particularly puzzling, since both have the same characteristics as postenactment legislative history, which is generally viewed as the least reliable source of authority for ascertaining the intent of any provision's drafters.

Perhaps in recognition of the weakness of its attempt to distinguish *Miller*, the Court argues in the alternative that *Miller* should be discounted because of its decisional history. . . . [A]s our decision in *Marbury v. Madison*, in which only one side appeared and presented arguments, demonstrates, the absence of adversarial presentation alone is not a basis for refusing to accord *stare decisis* effect to a decision of this Court. . . . The majority cannot seriously believe that the *Miller* Court did not consider any relevant evidence; the majority simply does not approve of the conclusion the *Miller* Court reached on that evidence. Standing alone, that is insufficient reason to disregard a unanimous opinion of this Court, upon which substantial reliance has been placed by legislators and citizens for nearly 70 years.

V

. . . The Court properly disclaims any interest in evaluating the wisdom of the specific policy choice challenged in this case, but it fails to pay heed to a far more important policy choice—the choice made by the Framers themselves. The Court would have us believe that over 200 years ago, the Framers made a choice to limit the tools available to elected officials wishing to regulate civilian uses of weapons, and to authorize this Court to use the common-law process of case-by-case judicial lawmaking to define the contours of acceptable gun control policy. Absent compelling evidence that is nowhere to be found in the Court's opinion, I could not possibly conclude that the Framers made such a choice.

For these reasons, I respectfully dissent.

JUSTICE BREYER, with whom JUSTICE STEVENS, JUSTICE SOUTER, and JUSTICE GINSBURG join, dissenting.

[T]he protection the [Second] Amendment provides is not absolute[: t]he Amendment permits government to regulate the interests that it serves. . . . In this opinion I shall . . . show that the District's law is consistent with the Second Amendment even if that Amendment is interpreted as protecting a wholly separate interest in individual self-defense. That is so because the District's regulation, which focuses upon the presence of handguns in high-crime urban areas, represents a permissible legislative response to a serious, indeed life-threatening, problem.

Thus I here assume that one objective (but, as the majority concedes, not the *primary* objective) of those who wrote the Second Amendment was to help assure citizens that they would have arms available for purposes of self-defense.

Even so, a legislature could reasonably conclude that the law will advance goals of great public importance, namely, saving lives, preventing injury, and reducing crime. . . .

[C]olonial history itself offers important examples of the kinds of gun regulation that citizens would then have thought compatible with the "right to keep and bear arms," whether embodied in Federal or State Constitutions, or the background common law. And those examples include substantial regulation of firearms in urban areas, including regulations that imposed obstacles to the use of firearms for the protection of the home. . . .

Boston, Philadelphia, and New York City, the three largest cities in America during that period, all restricted the firing of guns within city limits to at least some degree. . . . Furthermore, several towns and cities (including Philadelphia, New York, and Boston) regulated, for fire-safety reasons, the storage of gunpowder, a necessary component of an operational firearm. . . . Boston's law in particular impacted the use of firearms in the home very much as the District's law does today. Boston's gunpowder law imposed a £10 fine upon "any Person" who "shall take into any Dwelling-House, Stable, Barn, Out-house, Ware-house, Store, Shop, or other Building, within the Town of Boston, any Fire-Arm, loaded with, or having Gun-Powder." . . . Even assuming, as the majority does, that this law included an implicit self-defense exception, it would nevertheless have prevented a homeowner from keeping in his home a gun that he could immediately pick up and use against an intruder. . . .

I therefore begin by asking a process-based question: How is a court to determine whether a particular firearm regulation (here, the District's restriction on handguns) is consistent with the Second Amendment? What kind of constitutional standard should the court use? How high a protective hurdle does the Amendment erect?

The question matters. The majority is wrong when it says that the District's law is unconstitutional "[u]nder any of the standards of scrutiny that we have applied to enumerated constitutional rights." How could that be? It certainly would not be unconstitutional under, for example, a "rational basis" standard, which requires a court to uphold regulation so long as it bears a "rational relationship" to a "legitimate governmental purpose." *Heller v. Doe* (1993). . . .

I would simply adopt . . . an interest-balancing inquiry explicitly. The fact that important interests lie on both sides of the constitutional equation suggests that review of gun-control regulation is not a context in which a court should effectively presume either constitutionality (as in rational-basis review) or unconstitutionality (as in strict scrutiny). Rather, "where a law significantly implicates competing constitutionally protected interests in complex ways," the Court generally asks whether the statute burdens a protected interest in a way or to an extent that is out of proportion to the statute's salutary effects upon other important governmental interests. . . .

The majority's methodology is, in my view, substantially less transparent than mine. At a minimum, I find it difficult to understand the reasoning that seems to underlie certain conclusions that it reaches. . . .

I am similarly puzzled by the majority's list, in Part III of its opinion, of provisions that in its view would survive Second Amendment scrutiny. These consist of (1) "prohibitions on carrying concealed weapons"; (2) "prohibitions on the possession of firearms by felons"; (3) "prohibitions on the possession of firearms by . . . the mentally ill"; (4) "laws forbidding the carrying of firearms in sensitive places such as schools and government buildings"; and (5) government "conditions and qualifications" attached "to the commercial sale of arms." Why these? Is it that similar restrictions existed in the late 18th century? The majority fails to cite any colonial analogues. And even were it possible to find analogous colonial laws in respect to all these restrictions, why should these colonial laws count, while the Boston loaded-gun restriction (along with the other laws I have identified) apparently does not count?

At the same time the majority ignores a more important question: Given the purposes for which the Framers enacted the Second Amendment, how should it be applied to modern-day circumstances that they could not have anticipated? Assume, for argument's sake, that the Framers did intend the Amendment to offer a degree of self-defense protection. Does that mean that the Framers also intended to guarantee a right to possess a loaded gun near swimming pools, parks, and playgrounds? That they would not have cared about the children who might pick up a loaded gun on their parents' bedside table? That they (who certainly showed concern for the risk of fire, see *supra*) would have lacked concern for the risk of accidental deaths or suicides that readily accessible loaded handguns in urban areas might bring? Unless we believe that they intended future generations to ignore such matters, answering questions such as the questions in this case requires judgment—judicial judgment exercised within a framework for constitutional analysis that guides that judgment and which makes its exercise transparent. One cannot answer those questions by combining inconclusive historical research with judicial *ipse dixit*. . . .

For these reasons, I conclude that the District's measure is a proportionate, not a disproportionate, response to the compelling concerns that led the District to adopt it. . . . With respect, I dissent.

The following excerpt offers one justice's reflections on the process of constitutional interpretation. Is it consistent with the way the debate proceeded between the majority and the dissenters in *Heller*?

Justice David H. Souter, Harvard Commencement Remarks

May 27, 2010

[A] particular sort of criticism . . . is frequently aimed at the more controversial Supreme Court decisions: criticism that the court is making up the law, that the court is announcing constitutional rules that cannot be found in the Constitution, and that the court is engaging in activism to extend civil liberties. . . .

The charges of lawmaking and constitutional novelty seem to be based on an impression of the Constitution, and on a template for deciding constitutional claims, that go together something like this. A claim is made in court that the government is entitled to exercise a power, or an individual is entitled to claim the benefit of a right, that is set out in the terms of some particular provision of the Constitution. The claimant quotes the provision and provides evidence of facts that are said to prove the entitlement that is claimed. Once they have been determined, the facts on their face either do or do not support the claim. If they do, the court gives judgment for the claimant; if they don't, judgment goes to the party contesting the claim. On this view, deciding constitutional cases should be a straightforward exercise of reading fairly and viewing facts objectively.

There are, of course, constitutional claims that would be decided just about the way this fair reading model would have it. If one of today's 21-year-old college graduates claimed a place on the ballot for one of the United States Senate seats open this year, the claim could be disposed of simply by showing the person's age, quoting the constitutional provision that a senator must be at least 30 years old, and interpreting that requirement to forbid access to the ballot to someone who could not qualify to serve if elected. No one would be apt to respond that lawmaking was going on, or object that the age requirement did not say anything about ballot access. The fair reading model would describe pretty much what would happen. But cases like this do not usually come to court, or at least the Supreme Court. And for the ones that do get there, for the cases that tend to raise the national blood pressure, the fair reading model has only a tenuous connection to reality.

Even a moment's thought is enough to show why it is so unrealistic. The Constitution has a good share of deliberately open-ended guarantees, like rights to due process of law, equal protection of the law, and freedom from unreasonable searches. These provisions cannot be applied like the requirement for 30-year-old senators; they call for more elaborate reasoning to show why very general language applies in some specific cases but not in others, and over time the various examples turn into rules that the Constitution does not mention.

But this explanation hardly scratches the surface. The reasons that constitutional judging is not a mere combination of fair reading and simple facts extend way beyond the recognition that constitutions have to have a lot of general language in order to be useful over long stretches of time. Another reason is that the Constitution contains values that may well exist in tension with each other, not in harmony. Yet another reason is that the facts that determine whether a constitutional provision applies may be very different from facts like a person's age or the amount of the grocery bill; constitutional facts may require judges to understand the meaning that the facts may bear before the judges can figure out what to make of them. And this can be tricky. . . .

[T]he Constitution is no simple contract, not because it uses a certain amount of open-ended language that a contract draftsman would try to avoid, but because its language grants and guarantees many good things, and good things that compete with each other and can never all be realized, all together, all at once. . . .

[T]he First Amendment, [for example,] includes the familiar words that "Congress shall make no law . . . abridging the freedom of speech, or of the press." [And yet the court has not held] that the words "no law" allowed of no exception and meant that the rights of expression were absolute. [Justice Souter here describes the famous *Pentagon Papers* case, *New York Times v. United States* (1971), in which the Supreme Court rejected the government's request for a court order forbidding the publication of classified documents about the Vietnam War.] The court's majority decided only that the government had not met a high burden of showing facts that could justify [such] a prior restraint, and particular members of the court spoke of examples that might have turned the case around, to go the other way. Threatened publication of something like the D-Day invasion plans could have been enjoined; Justice Brennan mentioned a publication that would risk a nuclear holocaust in peacetime.

Even the First Amendment, then, expressing the value of speech and publication in the terms of a right as paramount as any fundamental right can be, does not quite get to the point of an absolute guarantee. It fails because the Constitution has to be read as a whole, and when it is, other values crop up in potential conflict with an unfettered right to publish, the value of security for the nation and the value of the president's authority in matters foreign and military. The explicit terms of the Constitution, in other words, can create a conflict of approved values, and the explicit terms of the Constitution do not resolve that conflict when it arises. The guarantee of the right to publish is unconditional in its terms, and in its terms the power of the government to govern is plenary. A choice may have to be made, not because language is vague but because the Constitution embodies the desire of the American people, like most people, to have things both ways. We want order and security, and we want liberty. And we want not only liberty but equality as well. These paired desires of ours can clash, and when they do a court is forced to choose between them, between one constitutional good and another one. The court has to decide which of our approved desires has the better claim, right here, right now, and a court has to do more than read fairly when it makes this kind of choice. And choices like the ones that the justices envisioned in the Papers case make up much of what we call law.

Let me ask a rhetorical question. Should the choice and its explanation be called illegitimate law making? Can it be an act beyond the judicial power when a choice must be made and the Constitution has not made it in advance in so many words? You know my answer. So much for the notion that all of constitutional law lies there in the Constitution waiting for a judge to read it fairly. . . .

Let me, like the lawyer that I am, sum up the case I've tried to present this afternoon. The fair reading model fails to account for what the Constitution actually says, and it fails just as badly to understand what judges have no choice but to do. . . . These are reasons enough to show how egregiously it misses the point to think of judges in constitutional cases as just sitting there reading constitutional phrases fairly and looking at reported facts objectively to produce their judgments. Judges have to choose between the good things that the Constitution approves, and when they do, they have to choose, not on the basis of measurement, but of meaning.

. . . But there is one thing more. I have to believe that something deeper is involved, and that behind most dreams of a simpler Constitution there lies a basic human hunger for the certainty and control that the fair reading model seems to promise. And who has not felt that same hunger? Is there any one of us who has not lived through moments, or years, of longing for a world without ambiguity, and for the stability of something unchangeable in human institutions? I don't forget my own longings for certainty, which heartily resisted the pronouncement of Justice Holmes, that certainty generally is illusion and repose is not our destiny.

But I have come to understand that he was right, and by the same token I understand that I differ from the critics I've described not merely in [respect to the right answer in particular cases]. Where I suspect we differ most fundamentally is in my belief that in an indeterminate world I cannot control, it is still possible to live fully in the trust that a way will be found leading through the uncertain future. And to me, the future of the Constitution as the Framers wrote it can be staked only upon that same trust. If we cannot share every intellectual assumption that formed the minds of those who framed the charter, we can still address the constitutional uncertainties the way they must have envisioned, by relying on reason, by respecting all the words the Framers wrote, by facing facts, and by seeking to understand their meaning for living people.

That is how a judge lives in a state of trust, and I know of no other way to make good on the aspirations that tell us who we are, and who we mean to be, as the people of the United States.

D.H.S.

B.   Interpreting the Constitution—Who?

There are a lot of ways to think about who gets to interpret the Constitution. The simplest answer is: everyone! It's not like any of us are forbidden to think about what the document means. But this "who" question is really after something more fundamental about the people and institutions doing the interpreting, and the authority and legitimacy with which they speak.

As you read the following materials, it's worth focusing on two key issues. First, the question of who gets final say. If the Supreme Court
rules that some immigration policy is unconstitutional, must the executive branch stop implementing it even if the President disagrees?
When a district court tells the governor of Alabama to desegregate the
public schools, does the governor have to obey? When the President
and Congress disagree about the constitutionality of a statute banning the use of military force, which interpretation is legally controlling?

A second question focuses on the process of interpretation itself. Does constitutional interpretation look different depending on whether it's being done by the states
or the federal government? Do the courts, the legislature, and the executive branch
have access to different sources of political meaning? Are there any decisions about
the Constitution that only the political branches have the legitimacy to make? These
questions often intersect in the same case as part of the complex jostling—both in
and out of the courts—among government entities with competing ambitions and
agendas, all of them appealing to the Constitution as a key source of both legal and
political legitimation.

1.   Judicial Review

Marbury v. Madison (1803) is one of the most famous decisions in American history; indeed, you may have learned about it in high school. The case
formally announced the principle of judicial review—*i.e.*, the power of courts
to hold that a law violates the Constitution. For many students, this statement
seems either trivial ("I mean, I can declare a statute unconstitutional too . . .")
or obvious ("It's the *Supreme* Court, right?"). As we'll see, the theoretical problem is a good bit more complicated than that. The historical claim that *Marbury*
broke new ground is also trickier than the civics class version of the story. As the
following materials suggest, while this principle was not then a feature of the
British constitutional system, it was hardly a novelty in American legal thinking.

William Blackstone, Commentaries on the Laws of England

6th ed. 1780

The power and jurisdiction of [the English] parliament . . . is so transcendent and absolute, that it cannot be confined, either for causes or persons,
within any bounds. . . . It hath sovereign and uncontrollable authority in making,
confirming, enlarging, restraining, abrogating, repealing, reviving, and expounding of laws, concerning matters of all possible denominations, ecclesiastical, or

temporal, civil, military, maritime, or criminal: this being the place where that absolute despotic power, which must in all governments reside somewhere, is entrusted by the constitution of these kingdoms. All mischief and grievances, operations and remedies, that transcend the ordinary course of the laws, are within the reach of this extraordinary tribunal. It can regulate, or new-model the succession to the crown. . . . It can alter the established religion of the land. . . . It can change and create afresh even the constitution of the kingdom and of parliaments themselves. . . . It can, in short, do every thing that is not naturally impossible; and therefore some have not scrupled to call its power by a figure rather too bold, the omnipotence of parliament. True it is, that what the parliament doth, no authority on earth can undo.

[I]f the parliament will positively enact a thing to be done which is unreasonable, I know of no power that can control it: and the [standard arguments for judicial review] do none of them prove, that where the main of the object of a statute is unreasonable the judges are at liberty to reject it; for that were to set the judicial power above that of the legislature, which would be subversive of all government. [T]here is no court that has power to defeat the legislature, when couched in such evident and express words, as leave no doubt whether it was the intent of the legislature or no.

Oliver Ellsworth, Speech at the Connecticut Ratifying Convention

7 January 1788

This constitution defines the extent of the powers of the general government. If the general legislature should at any time overleap their limits, the judicial department is a constitutional check. If the United States go beyond their powers, if they make a law which the constitution does not authorise, it is void; and the judicial power, the national judges, who to secure their impartiality are to be made independent, will declare it to be void. On the other hand, if the states go beyond their limits, if they make a law which is an usurpation upon the general government, the law is void, and upright independent judges will declare it to be so. Still however, if the United States and the individual states will quarrel, if they want to fight, they may do it, and no frame of government can possibly prevent it. It is sufficient for this Constitution, that, so far from laying them under a necessity of contending, it provides every reasonable check against it.

Brutus XII

New York Journal
7 February 1788

It is to be observed, that the supreme court has the power, in the last resort, to determine all questions that may arise in the course of legal discussion, on the meaning and construction of the constitution. This power they will hold under the constitution, and independent of the legislature. The latter can no more deprive the former of this right, than either of them, or both of them together, can take from the president, with the advice of the senate, the power of making treaties, or appointing ambassadors.

[I]f the legislature pass laws, which, in the judgment of the court, they are not authorised to do by the constitution, the court will not take notice of them; for it will not be denied, that the constitution is the highest or supreme law. And the courts are vested with the supreme and uncontroulable power, to determine, in all cases that come before them, what the constitution means; they cannot, therefore, execute a law, which, in their judgment, opposes the constitution, unless we can suppose they can make a superior law give way to an inferior.

The legislature, therefore, will not go over the limits by which the courts may adjudge they are confined. And there is little room to doubt but that they will come up to those bounds, as often as occasion and opportunity may offer, and they may judge it proper to do it. For as on the one hand, they will not readily pass laws which they know the courts will not execute, so on the other, we may be sure they will not scruple to pass such as they know they will give effect, as often as they may judge it proper. From these observations it appears, that the judgment of the judicial, on the constitution, will become the rule to guide the legislature in their construction of their powers.

Now let's consider *Marbury* itself, and begin by engaging it as an actual dispute that involved contested facts, contested law, and some highly motivated litigants.

POLITICAL BACKDROP

Marbury v. Madison was decided after an electoral earthquake that radically redistributed power among parties at the national level. In fact, the specific legal dispute presented by the case was directly related to the losing Federalist party's lame duck effort to entrench its power in the judiciary before turning over the reins of political power to the Democratic Republicans. When the Federalist plaintiff suing the Democratic-Republican cabinet member found out that the Court's opinion was written by its Federalist Chief Justice, do you think he expected the result that actually emerged?

In the election of 1800, the Democratic-Republican candidate Thomas Jefferson defeated the Federalist incumbent John Adams in the race for the presidency. The Democratic-Republican party also won decisive majorities in both the House and Senate, and swept state level races around the country. In the last days of the outgoing Congress, the lame duck Federalists cooked up a scheme to limit the damage their political opponents could do after taking office. Most famously, they created a string of new federal appeals court judgeships and confirmed sixteen lifetime appointments to fill them—the "midnight judges." The Federalists also created 42 justices of the peace for the District of Columbia, a position that had a fixed term of five years.

Question

Was this term limitation constitutional?

Outgoing President Adams nominated William Marbury and others for positions as justices of the peace, and the Senate confirmed them. The commissions were signed and sealed on the last full day of the Adams Administration by John Marshall, who had already begun to serve as Chief Justice—but was still, rather amazingly from a modern-day perspective, doing mop-up duty as Secretary of State. In the rush, Marshall's brother James (who was acting as the delivery agent) left some of the commissions behind. As the new President, Thomas Jefferson, later wrote,

> [T]he midnight appointments of peace for [the] Alexandria [side of D.C.] . . . were signed and sealed by [Adams], but not delivered. I found them on the table of the department of State, on my entrance

into the office, and I forbade their delivery. Marbury [was] named in one of them.

Marbury and others brought an action against the new Secretary of State, James Madison, in the Supreme Court to compel delivery. Because the new Democratic-Republican Congress passed legislation that prevented the Court from sitting in 1802, the Court did not consider Marbury's case until 1803. Over the course of two days, the Court heard evidence from three State Department clerks and the Attorney General. Madison did not appear; among the many remarkable features of *Marbury v. Madison* (1803) is that it was decided by default.

The structure of the opinion of (by now unambiguously) Chief Justice Marshall for a unanimous Court is notable. The eventual holding of the case was that the Court did not have jurisdiction to grant the writ of mandamus that Marbury sought—but first, Marshall decided the merits. He held that the appointment was completed when the President signed the commission; placing the seal on the commission and delivering it were mere ministerial acts of the Secretary.

Questions

Does this make sense? What would have happened if the President signed the commission in the privacy of his office and immediately had second thoughts?

Furthermore, given that the legislation made tenure of the office for a fixed term of years, the President could not undo the appointment.

WORTH NOTING

In *Myers v. United States* (1926), some of Marshall's dicta in this part of the opinion were disapproved because the *Myers* majority thought them inconsistent with the original understanding. The *Myers* decision held that Congress could not make the President's power to remove a postmaster subject to approval by the Senate, and also indicated that the Tenure of Office Act, which had purported to limit Andrew Johnson's power of removal in this manner with respect to department heads, was unconstitutional. *Myers* was itself in turn qualified by *Humphrey's Executor v. United States* (1935), which upheld a statute providing that a member of the Federal Trade Commission could not be removed except for good cause. *Myers* and *Humphrey's Executor*, along with other materials on the removal power, are presented more fully at pp. 773–812.

Thus, Marshall held that Marbury had a right to the commission, and so the law must provide him with a remedy; otherwise, the government of the United States could not be termed "a government of laws, and not of men," and "[I]f this obloquy is to be cast on the jurisprudence of our country, it must arise from the peculiar character of the case." Nor did Madison's official role give him immunity. While recognizing that conduct committed to executive discretion might create a nonjusticiable "political question," the Court held that in this case Madison had been assigned a specific, ministerial duty. Furthermore, mandamus was an appropriate remedy.

WORTH NOTING The distinction between political questions and ministerial duties often became contentious; in *Mississippi v. Johnson* (1867), presented at pp. 160–163, the Court distinguished *Marbury* on this point.

But could mandamus issue from the Supreme Court? Here, Marshall made a rather dubious interpretation of a portion of Section 13 of the Judiciary Act of 1789, holding that the Act authorized mandamus as a matter of original jurisdiction in a case of this sort. Section 13 provided in part:

> The Supreme Court shall also have appellate jurisdiction from the circuit courts and courts of the several states, in the cases herein after specially provided for; and shall have power to issue writs of prohibition to the district courts, when proceeding as courts of admiralty and maritime jurisdiction, and writs of mandamus, in cases warranted by the principles and usages of law, to any courts appointed, or persons holding office, under the authority of the United States.

From there, he turned to reach a debatable interpretation of Article III to conclude that the grant of such jurisdiction is contrary to the Constitution; the Constitution's allocation of original and appellate jurisdiction, he said, were meant to be airtight, so Congress could not grant one type of jurisdiction when the Constitution granted the other. (Marshall's argument in this portion of the opinion was subsequently undercut, in part by Marshall himself. *Cohens v. Virginia* (1821).)

The question that Marshall believed resulted—"whether an act, repugnant to the constitution, can become the law of the land"—was, "happily, not of an intricacy proportioned to its interest." There were only two alternatives, with "no middle ground." Either the legislation is superior, in which case constitutions are "absurd attempts," or the Constitution is superior, in which case legislation repugnant to the Constitution "is not law." Guess which Marshall chose. Given that the legislation was not valid, and so "not law," would it nevertheless bind the courts "as if it was a law"? Guess again.

Part of Marshall's argument was textual. It "is too extravagant to be maintained" that a case arising under the Constitution (and so within the federal judicial power as defined by Art. III) could be decided without examining the Constitution itself. Also, federal judges must swear to decide cases "agreeably to the constitution"—although Marshall did not mention that all state and federal officials are likewise required, by Art. VI, cl. 3, to support the Constitution. Marshall also emphasized his conception of the judicial function:

> So if a law be in opposition to the constitution; if both the law and the constitution apply to a particular case, so that the court must either decide that case conformably to the law, disregarding the constitution; or conformably to the constitution, disregarding the law; the court must determine which of these conflicting rules governs the case. This is of the very essence of judicial duty. If then the courts are to regard the constitution; and the constitution is superior to any ordinary act of the legislature; the constitution, and not such ordinary act, must govern the case to which they both apply.

Thus, Marshall proclaimed, "It is emphatically the province and the duty of the judicial department to say what the law is."

So in the end, *Marbury*, after asserting that the Secretary of State had acted wrongfully, and after asserting judicial power to hold an Act of Congress unconstitutional, did not order anybody to do anything—other than instructing the clerk to dismiss the case for lack of jurisdiction.

For Discussion

(1) Do you think that the *Marbury* decision's famous "province and duty" language was asserting a power lying exclusively within the province of the courts, or only judicial competence to perform this function? What would justify the exclusivity assertion? The competence assertion? Consider in conjunction with these questions that elsewhere in the opinion Marshall declares that the Constitution is "a rule for the government of courts as well as of the legislature," and that at the very close of the opinion he says that "courts, as well as other departments, are bound by that instrument."

(2) Consider also in this context *Cooper v. Aaron* (1958). This was a decision in a case brought to desegregate the public schools of Little Rock, Arkansas on the basis of the rule announced in *Brown v. Board of Education* (1954). Little Rock became the epicenter of "massive resistance" to *Brown* after the Governor dispatched units of the Arkansas National Guard to the grounds of Central High School and forcibly prevented nine African-American students from entering. After resolving the legal issues in the case against the state actors, the Court—in an opinion that was highly unusual in form, signed by all nine members of the Court—said:

> [W]e should answer the premise of the actions of the Governor and Legislature that they are not bound by our holding in the *Brown* case. It is necessary only to recall some basic constitutional propositions which are settled doctrine.
>
> Article VI of the Constitution makes the Constitution the "supreme Law of the Land." In 1803, Chief Justice Marshall, speaking for a unanimous Court, referring to the Constitution as "the fundamental and paramount law of the nation," declared in the notable case of *Marbury v. Madison* that "[i]t is emphatically the province and duty of the judicial department to say what the law is." This decision declared the basic principle that the federal judiciary is supreme in the exposition of the law of the Constitution, and that principle has ever since been respected by this Court and the Country as a permanent and indispensable feature of our constitutional system.

It follows that the interpretation of the Fourteenth Amendment enunciated by this Court in the *Brown* case is the supreme law of the land, and Art. VI of the Constitution makes it of binding effect on the States "any Thing in the Constitution or Laws of any State to the Contrary notwithstanding." Every state legislator and executive and judicial officer is solemnly committed by oath taken pursuant to Art. VI, cl. 3, "to support this Constitution." Chief Justice Taney, speaking for a unanimous Court in 1859, said that this requirement reflected the framers' "anxiety to preserve [the Constitution] in full force, in all its powers, and to guard against resistance to or evasion of its authority, on the part of a State. . . ." *Ableman v. Booth* (1859).

Was this passage an accurate reading of *Marbury*? Is it correct in principle?

(3) In contrast to *Cooper*, consider Abraham Lincoln's thoughts on the *Scott v. Sandford* case, pp. 109–127. Before the decision had even come down, he wrote notes for a speech, addressing the "creed" that "[w]hatever decision the Supreme Court makes on any constitutional question, must be obeyed, and enforced by all the departments of the federal government":

[I]t is not the full scope of this creed, that if the Supreme Court, having the particular question before them, shall decide that Dred Scott is a slave, the executive department must enforce the decision against Dred Scott—If this were it's [*sic!*] full scope, it is presumed, no one would controvert its correctness—But . . . [t]he creed . . . has a broader scope; and what is it? It is this; that so soon as the Supreme Court decides that Dred Scott is a slave, the whole community must decide that not only Dred Scott, but that all persons in like condition, are rightfully slaves.

On June 26, 1857, he elaborated on these views in public, responding to a speech two weeks before by Stephen Douglas:

We believe, as much as Judge Douglas, (perhaps more) in obedience to, and respect for the judicial department of government. We think its decisions on Constitutional questions, when fully settled, should control not only the particular cases decided, but the general policy of the country, subject to be disturbed only by amendments of the Constitution as provided in that instrument itself. More than this would be revolution. But we think the Dred Scott decision is erroneous. We know the court that made it, has often over-ruled its own decisions, and we shall do what we can to have it to over-rule this. We offer no resistance to it.

Judicial decisions are of greater or less authority as precedents, according to circumstances. That this should be so, accords both with common sense, and the customary understanding of the legal profession.

If this important decision had been made by the unanimous concurrence of the judges, and without any apparent partisan bias, and in accordance with legal public expectation, and with the steady practice of the departments throughout our history, and had been in no part, based on assumed historical facts which are not really true; or, if wanting in some of these, it had been before the court more than once, and had there been affirmed and re-affirmed through a course of years, it then might be, perhaps would be, factious, nay, even revolutionary, to not acquiesce in it as a precedent.

But when, as it is true we find it wanting in all these claims to the public confidence, it is not resistance, it is not factious, it is not even disrespectful, to treat it as not having yet quite established a settled doctrine for the country.

What does Lincoln mean when he says, "We offer no resistance to it?" Does he articulate appropriate standards for when respect should be paid to a Supreme Court decision? See pp. 282–284 for further discussion of *Cooper* and the Lincoln-Douglas exchange.

(4) Does the logic of Marshall's opinion in *Marbury* indicate that in a properly presented case a lower federal court or a state court might be obligated to declare an act of Congress unconstitutional? If so, is that troublesome?

(5) Now consider whether even Marshall's competence assertion is justified. The superiority of the Constitution seems unquestionable. And Marshall is certainly correct that the courts (any court, not merely the Supreme Court) must, in deciding a case, determine what the law is. But does it necessarily follow from those two points that the courts must determine whether a particular governmental action in fact violates the Constitution? Put another way, can courts be foreclosed from making determinations of this type by decisions made elsewhere?

Consider that we often accept this kind of foreclosure as a matter of course: The federal courts, including the Supreme Court, are bound by the interpretations made by the highest court of a state as to the law of that state; lower courts are bound by the legal interpretations of the higher courts; and even Marshall seemed to concede that in a limited realm the constitutional validity of officials' actions should be considered nonjusticiable "political questions." Is it therefore plausible to hold that when a political entity, or at least the national legislature, takes a given action, the courts should treat the entity—the members of which are also sworn to support the Constitution—as having made a determination, binding on the courts, that the Constitution permits that action?

What problems does such self-governance—a feature of some constitutional systems—raise? Compare them to the problems raised by judicial review—which appears both to be "countermajoritarian" and to depend on a form of self-governance, self-restraint by the judges themselves. At this early point in your study of constitutional law, which set of problems do you believe is greater? Consider this question in reading the materials below and as we proceed through the course.

2. The Counter-Majoritarian Difficulty

a. The Difficulty Defined

Marbury v. Madison (1803) was the first Supreme Court decision to strike down a federal statute as unconstitutional, thereby formally asserting the power of judicial review. Notwithstanding some revisionist accounts,[a] the evidence (including materials presented at pp. 254–256) suggests that the Founders did generally anticipate that the Constitution would authorize some sort of judicial review. If that's right, then why did Chief Justice Marshall argue the point at such length in *Marbury v. Madison*? It could be because of the politically delicate posture of judicial review as such: after all, *Marbury* itself saw a group of unelected, life-tenured judges strike down a democratically enacted statute on the basis of a plausible but hardly knock-down interpretation of sparse constitutional text.

The twentieth-century scholar Alexander Bickel had a good name for the source of this delicacy. He called it the "counter-majoritarian difficulty." He explained:

> The root difficulty is that judicial review is a counter-majoritarian force in our system. There are various ways of sliding over this ineluctable reality. [Chief Justice] Marshall did so when he spoke [in *Marbury*] of enforcing, in behalf of "the people," the limits they have ordained for the institutions of a limited government. . . . But the

[a] See, *e.g.* Larry Kramer, *The People Themselves: Popular Constitutionalism and Judicial Review* (2004). Certainly the position was not without dissenters and critics. As late as 1798, Supreme Court Justice Samuel Chase was emphasizing that he would not "giv[e] an opinion, at this time, whether this Court has jurisdiction to decide that any law made by Congress, contrary to the Constitution of the United States, is void." *Calder v. Bull* (1798).

word "people" so used is an abstraction. Not necessarily a meaning-less or a pernicious one by any means . . . , but nonrepresentational, an abstraction obscuring the reality that when the Supreme Court declares unconstitutional a legislative act or the action of an elected executive, it thwarts the will of representatives of the actual people of the here and now; it exercises control, not in behalf of the prevailing majority, but against it. That, without mystic overtones, is what actu-ally happens. It is an altogether different kettle of fish, and it is the reason the charge can be made that judicial review is undemocratic.

[handwritten margin note: Supreme Court declares that a leg act/action of an elected rep is unconstitutional]

Alexander Bickel, *The Least Dangerous Branch* (2d ed. 1986). The counter-ma-joritarian difficulty is often seen as the hardest theoretical problem of American constitutional law.

[handwritten margin note: Elected Rep = congress majority]

For Discussion ?

Which of the following is the most troubling from the perspective of the count-er-majoritarian difficulty? Which is least troubling? Why? *[handwritten: By majority]*

(a) A federal judge rules that a federal statute violates the U.S. Constitution. *[handwritten: Not elected +tenured — would not reflect will of majority states]*

(b) A federal judge rules that a state statute violates the U.S. Constitution. *[handwritten: Not elected + tenured]*

(c) A state judge rules that a federal statute violates the U.S. Constitution. *[handwritten: they are elected]*

(d) A state judge rules that a state statute violates the U.S. Constitution. *[handwritten: + they are elected half of the time — would not reflect will of majority states]*

The basic problem is that Americans understand their system as one of representative democracy. How do unelected federal judges dare, then, to over-ride the political process and thwart the will of a democratic majority? This is a favorite theme of those who find themselves on the losing end of constitutional disputes; they may suspect that the judicial majority was actually motivated by *?* the same policy preferences that failed to win in the political arena. Dissenting from a Supreme Court decision that struck down a same-sex marriage ban, Justice Antonin Scalia emphasized that the democratic difficulty was rooted,

not only in the small size of the Supreme Court, but also in its demographi-
cally unrepresentative makeup:

> Judges are selected precisely for their skill as lawyers; whether
> they reflect the policy views of a particular constituency is not (or
> should not be) relevant. Not surprisingly then, the Federal Judiciary
> is hardly a cross-section of America. Take, for example, this Court,
> which consists of only nine men and women, all of them successful
> lawyers who studied at Harvard or Yale Law School. Four of the nine
> are natives of New York City. Eight of them grew up in east- and
> west-coast States. Only one hails from the vast expanse in-between.
> Not a single Southwesterner or even, to tell the truth, a genuine West-
> erner (California does not count). Not a single evangelical Christian
> (a group that comprises about one quarter of Americans), or even a
> Protestant of any denomination. . . .
>
> [T]o allow the policy question of same-sex marriage to be con-
> sidered and resolved by a select, patrician, highly unrepresentative
> panel of nine is to violate a principle even more fundamental than
> no taxation without representation: no social transformation without
> representation. . . .

Obergefell v. Hodges (2015). Some judges do seem to worry less about this problem when they find themselves on the winning side. In *Bush v. Gore* (2000), for
example, the Supreme Court ordered Florida to stop its statutory recount process during a challenge to the presidential election in that state. When critics
called the decision not just wrong but democratically illegitimate, Scalia liked
to respond by telling them to "get over it."

Of course, we are none of us consistent; the larger point is that the practice of allowing a small group of life-tenured, unelected judges to overrule
decisions made by national or even local democratic majorities should make
us all at least a little nervous. The fear, at bottom, is that judges will use their
power of judicial review to make an essentially *political* intervention into the
democratic process, spiking democratic decisions that don't match their own
personal policy preferences. Think in this respect of how frequently media reports identify which political party appointed a judge whose decision makes
the news, particularly in politically charged cases.

In principle, if judges interpret a law faithlessly (or at least, in a way that most voters don't like), one way to solve the problem is to amend the law and correct the outcome. Even assuming that the judges would listen the second time around, though, this is often simply not viable when the law in question is the Constitution. That's because the process for amending the Constitution is so cumbersome that for decades it has been standard practice to call the document "effectively unamendable." See U.S. Const., Art. V (requiring approval by three-quarters of the states). To be sure, there are counter-examples: The citizenship holding of *Scott v. Sandford* was effectively overruled by the 14th Amendment; the 16th Amendment nullified a decision that had made a federal income tax inconsequential; and the 26th Amendment gave 18-year-olds a constitutional right to vote beyond the bounds the Supreme Court had recently set. But the infrequency of the phenomenon indicates its difficulty.

So then, what *is* the answer? How do judges justify participating in such a system, and why do we—commentators and citizens alike—respect their decisions? It's constitutional law's version of the theodicy problem, intertwining skepticism of judicial review with challenges to the very existence of constitutional obligations as such. What are some of the answers that have emerged from centuries of gnawing on this bone?

b.   Judicial Duty and the Mechanistic Solution

One possible justification for judicial review is that, as Marshall put it in *Marbury v. Madison*, it is "the very essence of judicial duty" to decide what the law is. And given that the Constitution is supreme law, judges are simply required to give it force over whatever subsidiary laws the political organs of government might produce. In effect, the judges might say: "Don't blame us for doing our job." A well-known 20th century expression of this view appeared in Justice Owen Roberts's opinion for the Court in *United States v. Butler* (1936):

> When an act of Congress is appropriately challenged in the courts as not conforming to the constitutional mandate, the judicial branch of the Government has only one duty—to lay the article of the Constitution which is invoked beside the statute which is challenged and to decide whether the latter squares with the former. All the court does, or can do, is to announce its considered judgment upon the question.

In an extreme variant of this justification, the act of legal interpretation is such a technocratic exercise that it involves no more judgment (and therefore no more possibility of abuse) than the act of doing trigonometry. On this view, it's a category mistake to talk about a counter-majoritarian difficulty: the law is created by the people; the judges simply apply the law. This view was richly represented at the Founding, and has often re-emerged since. Consider the following examples:

> The national judges are no more than the mouth that pronounces the words of the law, mere passive beings, incapable of moderating either its force or rigor.
>
> Baron de Montesquieu, *The Spirit of the Laws* (1748)

> In every criminal cause the judge should reason syllogistically. The Major should be the general law; the Minor the conformity of the action, or its opposition to the laws; the Conclusion, liberty or punishment. If the judge be obliged by the imperfection of the laws, or chuses to make any other, or more syllogisms than this, it will be an introduction to uncertainty.
>
> Cesare Beccaria, *On Crimes and Punishments* (1764)

> Judges and justices are servants of the law, not the other way around. Judges are like umpires. Umpires don't make the rules; they apply them. The role of an umpire and a judge is critical. They make sure everybody plays by the rules. But it is a limited role. Nobody ever went to a ball game to see the umpire. Judges have to have the humility to recognize that they operate within a system of precedent, shaped by other judges equally striving to live up to the judicial oath.
>
> Judge John Roberts, Senate Confirmation Hearings for the Chief Justiceship (2005)

Of course, not everyone agrees that legal interpretation is essentially mechanical. Recall Justice Souter's characterization of the Constitution as being "a pantheon of values," and consider also these views:

> All new laws, though penned with the greatest technical skill, and passed on the fullest and most mature deliberation, are considered as more or less obscure and equivocal, until their meaning be liquidated and ascertained by a series of particular discussions and adjudications.

Besides the obscurity arising from the complexity of objects, and the imperfection of the human faculties, the medium through which the conceptions of men are conveyed to each other, adds a fresh embarrassment. The use of words is to express ideas. Perspicuity therefore requires not only that the ideas should be distinctly formed, but that they should be expressed by words distinctly and exclusively appropriated to them.

But no language is so copious as to supply words and phrases for every complex idea, or so correct as not to include many equivocally denoting different ideas. Hence it must happen, that however accurately objects may be discriminated in themselves, and however accurately the discrimination may be considered, the definition of them may be rendered inaccurate by the inaccuracy of the terms in which it is delivered. And this unavoidable inaccuracy must be greater or less, according to the complexity and novelty of the objects defined.

Publius, *The Federalist*, No. 37 (1788) (James Madison)

c.   The Dead-Hand Problem with the Mechanistic Solution

Beyond such doubts about the mechanical model's descriptive accuracy, there is a deeper problem with relying on syllogisms as a solution to the counter-majoritarian difficulty. Forget the problem of unaccountable judges; what if the very document that they're interpreting fails any reasonable test of democratic legitimacy? "We must never forget," John Marshall wrote in *McCulloch v. Maryland* (1819), "that it is a constitution we are expounding," and one "intended to endure for ages to come." But perhaps that in itself is a problem.

Even if you ignore the race, gender, and wealth restrictions on voting during the Founding era, the democratic status of the Constitution as a restriction on present-day decisionmaking is uncertain at best. Just ask Thomas Jefferson:

The question whether one generation of men has a right to bind another, seems never to have been started either on this or our side of the water. Yet it is a question of such consequences as not only to merit decision, but place also, among the fundamental principles of every government. . . .

I set out on this ground, which I suppose to be self evident, "that the earth belongs in usufruct to the living": that the dead have neither powers nor rights over it. . . . Then no man can, by natural right, oblige the lands he occupied, or the persons who succeed him in that occupation, to the paiment of debts contracted by him. . . .

On similar ground it may be proved that no society can make a perpetual constitution, or even a perpetual law. The earth belongs always to the living generation. They may manage it then, and what proceeds from it, as they please, during their usufruct. . . . The constitution and the laws of their predecessors extinguished then in their natural course with those who gave them being. This could preserve that being till it ceased to be itself, and no longer. . . . If it be enforced longer, it is an act of force, and not of right.

Letter to James Madison (Sept. 6, 1789). Jefferson is talking about what is known as the dead-hand problem, as in "the dead hand of the past." Why should we even care about—much less be bound by—the political commitments of a long-dead social elite?

WORTH NOTING

The phrase "dead hand" is an old one. Mortmain (literally, "dead hand") refers to the inalienable ownership of real estate by a legal institution; statutes of 1279 and 1290 were intended to limit the practice. The plot of *The Merchant of Venice* turns in part on such restrictions imposed on Portia's marriage options by her father's will. See Act I, Scene 2, Lines 23–26 ("O me, the word 'choose!' I may neither choose whom I would nor refuse whom I dislike; so is the will of a living daughter curbed by the will of a dead father").

d.   Odysseus and the Deeper "We"

The start of an answer to the dead-hand problem might start with a famous story from Homer's *Odyssey*, which has long served as a parable for pre-commitment and self-control. At one point during Odysseus's long travels throughout the Mediterranean, the magician Circe warns him about two monsters called Sirens, whose singing is so enchanting that travelers within earshot make decisions contrary to their own enduring interests—unless those interests include straying too close to the Sirens and becoming "a great heap of . . . bones." Circe advises Odysseus to plug his men's ears with wax so that they cannot hear— but Odysseus himself may have the pleasure of listening, so long as he has the sailors tie him to the mast. "If you beg and pray the men to unloose you," Circe instructs, "then they must bind you faster." Odysseus follows the advice. Sure enough, he is so entranced by the singing that he implores his men to set him free. But they tie him tighter and row faster until the danger is past.

This idea of making commitments that serve our own enduring long-run interests—even at the expense of tempting attractions in the short run—is at the heart of many defenses of judicial review. On this theory, We the People make certain Odyssean commitments in our most sober moments—to equality, even when it's inconvenient; to certain kinds of localism, even when it's inefficient; and so on—and then we authorize the judiciary, as our faithful agents, to implement those commitments even when we later insist that we've changed our mind. The more romantic versions of these defenses of judicial review stray into the metaphysics of nationhood. On this view, the democratic People is a transcendent entity that extends over time and that is capable of meaningfully binding its future self—just like Odysseus does, in advance of facing Sirens who he knows will tempt him to act against his own best judgment.

The best-known argument for privileging such constitutional decision-making despite the dead-hand problem is probably Bruce Ackerman's. He suggests that day-to-day (and even year-to-year) political decisionmaking at the local and national level alike is less truly democratic, because most of us are not seriously engaged with the process by which those decisions are generated. Constitutional commitments, on the other hand, require such effort and focus over such a sustained period of time that they really do represent an Odyssean commitment rather than just another run-of-the-mill choice about which island to check out next:

> Above all else, [we must] distinguish between two different decisions that may be made in a democracy. The first is a decision by the American people; the second, by their government. Decisions by the People occur rarely, and under special constitutional conditions. Before gaining the authority to make supreme [constitutional] law in the name of the People, a movement's partisans must, first, convince an extraordinary number of their fellow citizens to take their proposed initiative with a seriousness they do not normally accord to politics; second, they must allow their opponents a fair opportunity to organize their forces; third, they must convince a majority of their fellow Americans to support their initiative as its merits are discussed, time

and again, in the deliberative fora provided for "higher lawmaking." It is only then that a political movement earns the enhanced legitimacy the dualist Constitution accords to decisions made by the People. Decisions made by the government[, by contrast,] occur daily. . . ."

Bruce Ackerman, *We The People: Foundations* 6 (1991).

FOR DISCUSSION

Suppose you are a law professor and Ackerman is your student. He has just handed in a paper containing the passage quoted here from his book. What comments do you have? What questions?

e. Some Things Are More Important than Majoritarian Democracy

Here's another way to defend judicial review against charges of countermajoritarianism: simply accept the claim, and remind yourself that democracy isn't the only value we care about. It may not even be the most important. Human rights quintessentially belong to the individual rather than to the group—they are, indeed, good precisely *against* the group. Tyranny of the majority is no theoretical abstraction; it's a demonstrable and often shameful threat to individual liberty, as our own history of chattel slavery and the "Jim Crow" system of apartheid powerfully demonstrate.

In this regard, consider James Madison's perspective at the Constitutional Convention. Discussing the proposed presidential veto, he said: "We must introduce the Checks, which will destroy the measures of an interested majority" precisely in order to secure "the safety of a minority in Danger of oppression from an unjust and interested majority." *Federalist* No. 10 famously expands on the kinds of minorities he had in mind:

> From the protection of different and unequal faculties of acquiring property, the possession of different degrees and kinds of property immediately results; and from the influence of these on the sentiments and views of the respective proprietors, ensues a division of the society into different interests and parties. The latent causes of faction are thus sown in the nature of man; and we see them everywhere brought into different degrees of activity, according to the different circumstances of civil society.

A zeal for different opinions concerning religion, concerning government, and many other points, as well of speculation as of practice; an attachment to different leaders ambitiously contending for pre-eminence and power; or to persons of other descriptions whose fortunes have been interesting to the human passions, have, in turn, divided mankind into parties, inflamed them with mutual animosity, and rendered them much more disposed to vex and oppress each other than to co-operate for their common good. . . .

But the most common and durable source of factions has been the various and unequal distribution of property. Those who hold and those who are without property have ever formed distinct interests in society. Those who are creditors, and those who are debtors, fall under a like discrimination. A landed interest, a manufacturing interest, a mercantile interest, a moneyed interest, with many lesser interests, grow up of necessity in civilized nations, and divide them into different classes, actuated by different sentiments and views. The regulation of these various and interfering interests forms the principal task of modern legislation, and involves the spirit of party and faction in the necessary and ordinary operations of the government.

James Madison, by the way, was a slaveholder. Which in a way underscores the obvious question: why should we trust the judges to make the right decision? Won't they be as subject to biases, factionalism, self-interest, and short-sightedness as the electorate? There is a hint of an answer in Federalist No. 10 itself, in which Madison refers to the virtues of a selection process for national officials that would "refine and enlarge the public views, by passing them through the medium of a chosen body of citizens, whose wisdom may best discern the true interest of their country, and whose patriotism and love of justice will be least likely to sacrifice it to temporary or partial considerations." Later

FOR DISCUSSION

Has Madison forgotten any significant sources of social division? When he was behind closed doors at the Constitutional Convention, do you remember what he called the most important divide in national politics? See p. 35. Why doesn't he mention that source of faction here?

commentators have pointed to additional sources of judicial discipline—some potentially conflicting with one another!—including the scholarly orientation of judges, the professional norms of the legal profession, the non-electoral means of selection, the pressure of popular disapproval, and the protection of life tenure.

If the courts are to protect minority rights, they must sometimes go contrary to popular opinion; indeed, one might conclude that if the courts are not willing to do that, not only would there be no counter-majoritarian difficulty but there would be no need for the courts to exercise the power of review at all, because we already have a full set of political institutions designed to respond to the public will. And yet popular opinion clearly provides significant constraints on what the Supreme Court does—some would say rightly so. It is not surprising, for example, that the Court's landmark rulings providing protection against discrimination in the public schools, of abortion rights, and of a right to same-sex marriage came in 1954, 1972, and 2015, respectively, and not, say, 20 years earlier—when each would have been essentially unthinkable. Indeed, "[o]n issue after contentious issue—abortion, affirmative action, gay rights, and the death penalty, to name a few—the Supreme Court has rendered decisions that meet with popular approval and find support in the latest Gallup Poll." Barry Friedman, *The Will of the People: How Public Opinion Has Influenced the Supreme Court and Shaped the Meaning of the Constitution* (2009).

FOR DISCUSSION Imagine the Supreme Court strikes down a city ordinance that bans either guns or abortions—take your pick. If the ruling is nationally popular, does that mean the counter-majoritarian difficulty is irrelevant?

Note that this might raise the question of whether judicial review actually protects minorities at all, at least for their own sake. Derrick Bell, for example, suggests that while "[r]acial justice—or its appearance—may from time to time be counted among the interests deemed important by the courts," it is a rule of thumb for Court watchers that "[t]he interest of blacks in achieving racial equality will be accommodated only when it converges with the interests of whites." Derrick Bell, Brown v. Board of Education *and the Interest-Convergence Dilemma*, 93 Harv. L. Rev. 518 (1979); see pp. 1006–1007 infra. Either way, the *quis custodiet ipsos custodes* ("who guards the guardians?") anxiety persists. Indeed, it remains one of the most powerful tropes in judicial politics to this day.

FOR DISCUSSION So, are you for counter-majoritarianism or against it?

f.   Representation Reinforcement

One theme in the Court's occasional ruminations on the problem is often called the "representation reinforcement" theory. On this theory, the Court sometimes suggests, maybe counter-majoritarianism in particular cases can actually enhance and protect democracy in the longer run. Best known in the individual rights context—but occasionally appearing even in federalism and separation of powers cases—this argument might serve as a particularly elegant solution to the counter-majoritarian difficulty. That's because it reframes judicial review as a constitutional feature that is (at least sometimes) fundamentally *in service* of majoritarianism and *protective* of "true" representative democracy.

On the "representation reinforcement" account, judicial review is at its most appropriate when it is putting an end to political decisions that interfere with—perhaps even stifle—the political process. Think here of restrictions on speech, on organization, on voting, or on citizens' ability to identify which political unit is responsible for a given policy. See *United States v. Carolene Products* (1938), pp. 224–226, 956–959, 1179–1181 (suggesting that "legislation which restricts those political processes which can ordinarily be expected to bring about repeal of undesirable legislation" might be "subjected to more exacting judicial scrutiny"). Think also, perhaps, of an elaborate and extended system of disenfranchisement in which certain groups are simply frozen out of the coalition building that usually lets everyone get what they want *some*times. See *ibid.* (hinting that "prejudice against discrete and insular minorities may be a special condition, which tends seriously to curtail the operation of those political processes ordinarily to be relied upon to protect minorities, and which may call for a correspondingly more searching judicial inquiry").

John Hart Ely offered the most extended scholarly exploration of this instinct, which judicial opinions typically leave somewhat fuzzy. He argues that judicial review is democratically legitimate even if counter-majoritarian with respect to any particular issue, so long as it is principally deployed to repair "malfunctions" in the democratic process itself:

> Our government cannot fairly be said to be "malfunctioning" simply because it sometimes generates outcomes with which we disagree, however strongly (and claims that it is reaching results with which "the people" really disagree—or would if they "understood"—are likely to be little more than self-deluding projections).

In representative democracy, value determinations are to be made by our elected representatives, and if in fact most of us disapprove we can kick them out of office.

Malfunction occurs whenever the process cannot be trusted, whenever: (1) the in's are choking off the channels of political change to ensure they will stay in and the out's will stay out, or (2) though no one is actually denied a voice or a vote, an effective majority, with the necessary and understandable cooperation of its representatives, is systematically advantaging itself at the expense of one or more minorities whose reciprocal support it does not need and thereby effectively denying them the protection afforded other groups by a representative system.

Obviously our elected representatives are the last persons we should trust with identification of either of these situations. Appointed judges, however, are comparative outsiders in our governmental system: they are largely removed from the political hurly-burly and need worry about continuance in office only very obliquely. This does not give them some special pipeline to the genuine values of the American people; in fact it goes far to ensure they will not have one. It does, however, put them in a position objectively to assess claims—though no one could suppose it will not be full of judgment calls—that either by clogging the channels of change or by acting as accessories to simple majority tyranny, our elected representatives in fact are not representing the interests of those that the system presumes and presupposes they are.

John Hart Ely, *Toward a Representation-Reinforcing Mode of Judicial Review*, 37 Md. L. Rev. 486 (1978).

FOR DISCUSSION

How do we know which kinds of rights protect democracy? How far into the future would Ely want us to look in deciding whether the political process is broken, or whether the losing groups just happen to be coming out on the short end for the time being?

---

g.   Letting Sleeping Dogs Lie

What if there is no knock-down philosophical defense of the criticism that judicial review is illegitimately counter-majoritarian? Is there any other reason to stick with it? Edmund Burke might have thought so. In his view, when you have a complex system that basically works, it's not always wise to tear out important pieces of it when they don't match up to the rational application of your philosophical principles. Here's what Burke had to say about the Rube Goldberg contraption often known as the English "constitution":

> [F]rom Magna Charta to the Declaration of Right, it has been the uniform policy of our constitution to claim and assert our liberties, as an entailed inheritance derived to us from our forefathers, and to be transmitted to our posterity; as an estate specially belonging to the people of this kingdom without any reference whatever to any other more general or prior right. . . .

> This policy appears to me to be . . . the happy effect of following nature, which is wisdom without reflection, and above it. . . . By a constitutional policy, working after the pattern of nature, we receive, we hold, we transmit our government and our privileges, in the same manner in which we enjoy and transmit our property and our lives. The institutions of policy, the goods of fortune, the gifts of Providence, are handed down, to us and from us, in the same course and order. . . . Thus, . . . in what we improve, we are never wholly new; in what we retain we are never wholly obsolete. . . .

> All your sophisters cannot produce any thing better adapted to preserve a rational and manly freedom than the course that we have pursued, who have chosen our nature rather than our speculations, our breasts rather than our inventions, for the great conservatories and magazines of our rights and privileges.

Edmund Burke, *Reflections on the Revolution in France* (1790) (not liking it). Burke might say that the best reason to stick with judicial review is that we have a whole system that has built up around the expectation that we have judicial review. Circular? Probably. But—and yes, this is a wildly imperfect analogy—so is driving on the right side of the road.

3.   Interpretation Outside the Courts

The drama over judicial review should not obscure the extent to which other political actors have persistently claimed an entitlement to interpret the Constitution, perhaps even independently of the courts. The first set of materials in this sub-section discuss versions of what is often called departmentalism: the claim that—at least in some contexts and under some circumstances—the political branches' authority to interpret the Constitution is equivalent to that of the judiciary. The second grouping outlines some of the principles that the political branches have suggested should guide this interpretation.

CROSS REFERENCE Recall, for example, Andrew Jackson's veto of the Bank bill on constitutional grounds, pp. 82–86, and Lincoln's response to *Scott v. Sandford*, pp. 262–263.

a.   Departmentalism

As a theory of constitutional interpretation, "departmentalism" proceeds from a deceptively simple observation: the Constitution creates a structural parallelism among the three federal branches, simultaneously creating, empowering, and restricting each one of them alike. In performing its own function, each is therefore of course not just permitted but required to interpret the underlying constitutional document. From those propositions is said to flow the conclusion that no single branch gets to claim interpretive supremacy: structurally parallel means constitutionally co-equal. There are weaker and stronger versions, however, and their implications vary widely. See if you can spot different versions of the claim in the materials that follow.

Thomas Jefferson, Letter to William Jarvis

28 September 1820

You seem to consider the judges as the ultimate arbiters of all constitutional questions; a very dangerous doctrine indeed, and one which would place us under the despotism of an oligarchy. Our judges are as honest as other men, and not more so. They have, with others, the same passions for party, for power, and the privilege of their corps. . . . Their power [is] the more dangerous as they are in office for life, and not responsible, as the other functionaries are, to the elective control. The Constitution has erected no such single tribunal, knowing that to whatever hands confided, with the corruptions of time and party, its members would become despots. It has more wisely made all the departments co-equal and co-sovereign within themselves. . . . When the legislative or executive functionaries act unconstitutionally, they are responsible to the people in their elective capacity. The exemption of the judges from that is quite dangerous enough. I know of no safe depository of the ultimate powers of the society, but the people themselves.

In vetoing a bill that would have re-chartered the Bank of the United States for a new term, Andrew Jackson argued that the bank was unconstitutional as proposed. Critics claimed that this reason was precluded by the Supreme Court's decision 13 years earlier in *McCulloch v. Maryland*. Partway through a long defense of his veto more generally, Jackson responded with the following argument:

 CROSS REFERENCE For more on the Jackson veto, see pp. 82–86.

President Andrew Jackson, Veto Message

10 July 1832

It is maintained by the advocates of the bank that its constitutionality in all its features ought to be considered as settled by precedent and by the decision of the Supreme Court. To this conclusion I cannot assent. . . . If the opinion of the Supreme Court covered the whole ground of this act, it ought not to control the coordinate authorities of this Government. The Congress, the Executive, and the Court must each for itself be guided by its own opinion of the Constitution. Each public officer who takes an oath to support the Constitution swears that he will support it as he understands it, and not as it is understood by others. It is as much the duty of the House of Representatives, of the Senate, and of the President to decide upon the constitutionality of any bill or resolution which may be presented to them for passage or approval as it is of the supreme judges when it may be brought before them for judicial decision. The opinion of the judges has no more authority over Congress than the opinion of Congress has over the judges, and on that point the President is independent of both. The authority of the Supreme Court must not, therefore, be permitted to control the Congress or the Executive when acting in their legislative capacities, but to have only such influence as the force of their reasoning may deserve.

In *Scott v. Sandford* (1857), presented at pp. 109–127, the Supreme Court held that Congress had no power to ban slavery in the Territories. This holding had significant implications for Congressional power to regulate slavery more generally. In his First Inaugural Address, Lincoln reiterated his long-asserted belief that *Scott v. Sandford* had not actually settled the matter:

 CROSS REFERENCE Portions of the Inaugural Address discussing secession are presented on pp. 133–138.

President Abraham Lincoln, First Inaugural Address

March 4, 1861

I do not forget the position assumed by some that constitutional questions are to be decided by the Supreme Court, nor do I deny that such decisions must be binding in any case upon the parties to a suit as to the object of that suit, while they are also entitled to very high respect and consideration in all parallel cases by all other departments of the Government. And while it is obviously possible that such decision may be erroneous in any given case, still the evil effect following it, being limited to that particular case, with the chance that it may be overruled and never become a precedent for other cases, can better be borne than could the evils of a different practice. At the same time, the candid citizen must confess that if the policy of the Government upon vital questions affecting the whole people is to be irrevocably fixed by decisions of the Supreme Court, the instant they are made in ordinary litigation between parties in personal actions the people will have ceased to be their own rulers, having to that extent practically resigned their Government into the hands of that eminent tribunal. Nor is there in this view any assault upon the court or the judges. It is a duty from which they may not shrink to decide cases properly brought before them, and it is no fault of theirs if others seek to turn their decisions to political purposes.

The next two documents offer two modern expressions of departmentalism. After you've read them both, ask yourself whether Ed Meese would support Newt Gingrich's proposal.

Attorney General Edwin Meese, The Law of the Constitution

Address, Tulane University
1986

Tonight I would like to . . . consider a distinction that is essential to maintaining our limited form of government. That is the necessary distinction between the Constitution and constitutional law. The two are not synonymous.

What, then, is this distinction?

The Constitution is—to put it simply but, one hopes, not simplistically—the Constitution. It is a document of our most fundamental law. It begins "We the People of the United States, in Order to form a more perfect Union . . ." and ends up, some 6,000 words later, with the 26th Amendment. It creates the institutions of our government, it enumerates the powers those institutions may wield, and it cordons off certain areas into which government may not enter. . . .

Constitutional law, on the other hand, is that body of law which has resulted from the Supreme Court's adjudications involving disputes over constitutional provisions or doctrines. To put it a bit more simply, constitutional law is what the Supreme Court says about the Constitution in its decisions resolving the cases and controversies that come before it.

And in its limited role of offering judgment, the Court has had a great deal to say. In almost two hundred years, it has produced nearly 500 volumes of reports of cases. While not all these opinions deal with constitutional questions, of course, a good many do. This stands in marked contrast to the few, slim paragraphs that have been added to the original Constitution as amendments. So, in terms of sheer bulk, constitutional law greatly overwhelms the Constitution. But in substance, it is meant to support and not overwhelm the Constitution whence it is derived. . . .

The answers the Court gives are very important to the stability of the law so necessary for good government. But as constitutional historian Charles Warren once noted, what's most important to remember is that "however the Court may interpret the provisions of the Constitution, it is still the Constitution which is the law, not the decisions of the Court." By this, of course, Charles Warren did not mean that a constitutional decision by the Supreme Court lacks the character of law. Obviously it does have binding quality: It binds the parties in a case and also the executive branch for whatever enforcement is necessary. But such a decision does not establish a "supreme Law of the Land" that is binding on all persons and parts of government, henceforth and forevermore. . . .

[A]lthough the point may seem obvious, there have been those down through our history—and especially, it seems, in our own time—who have denied the distinction between the Constitution and constitutional law. Such denial usually has gone hand in hand with an affirmation—that constitutional decisions are on a par with the Constitution in the sense that they, too, are "the supreme Law of the Land," from which there is no appeal.

Perhaps the most well-known instance of this denial occurred during the most important crisis in our political history. In 1857, in the *Dred Scott* case, the Supreme Court struck down the Missouri Compromise by declaring that Congress could not prevent the extension of slavery into the territories and that blacks could not be citizens and thus eligible to enjoy the constitutional privileges of citizenship. This was a constitutional decision, for the Court said that the right of whites to possess slaves was a property right affirmed in the Constitution.

This decision sparked the greatest political debate in our history. In the 1858 Senate campaign in Illinois, Stephen Douglas went so far in his defense of *Dred Scott* as to equate the decision with the Constitution. [H]e said, "The Constitution has created that Court to decide all Constitutional questions in the last resort, and when such decisions have been made, they become the law of the land." It plainly was Douglas's view that constitutional decisions by the Court were authoritative, controlling and final, binding on all persons and parts of government the instant they are made—from then on.

Lincoln, of course, disagreed. And in his response to Douglas we can see the nuances and subtleties, and the correctness, of the position that makes most sense in a constitutional democracy like ours—a position that seeks to maintain the important function of judicial review while at the same time upholding the right of the people to govern themselves through the democratic branches of government.

Lincoln said that insofar as the Court "decided in favor of Dred Scott's master and against Dred Scott and his family"—the actual parties in the case—he did not propose to resist the decision. But Lincoln went on to say: "We nevertheless do oppose [the *Scott v. Sandford* decision] as a political rule which shall be binding on the voter, to vote for nobody who thinks it wrong, which shall be binding on the members of Congress or the President to favor no measure that does not actually concur with the principles of the decision." . . .

Thus, not only can the Supreme Court respond to its previous constitutional decisions and change them, as it did in *Brown* and has done on many other occasions. So can the other branches of government, and, through them, the American people. As we know, Lincoln himself worked to overturn *Dred Scott* through the executive branch. The Congress joined him in this effort. Fortunately, *Dred Scott*—the case—lived a very short life.

Once we understand the distinction between constitutional law and the Constitution, once we see that constitutional decisions need not be seen as the last words in constitutional construction, once we comprehend that these decisions do not necessarily determine future public policy—once we see all of this, we can grasp a correlative point: that constitutional interpretation is not the business of the Court only, but also and properly, the business of all branches of government.

The Supreme Court, then, is not the only interpreter of the Constitution. Each of the three coordinate branches of government created and empowered by the Constitution—the executive and legislative no less than the judicial—has a duty to interpret the Constitution in the performance of its official functions. In fact, every official takes an oath precisely to that effect. . . .

Judicial review of Congressional and executive actions for their constitutionality have played a major role throughout our political history. The exercise of this power produces constitutional law. And in this task even the courts themselves have on occasion been tempted to think that the law of their decisions is on a par with the Constitution.

Some thirty years ago, in the midst of great racial turmoil, our highest Court seemed to succumb to this very temptation. By a flawed reading of our

Constitution and *Marbury v. Madison*, and an even more faulty syllogism of legal reasoning, the Court in a 1958 case called *Cooper v. Aaron* appeared to arrive at conclusions about its own power that would have shocked men like John Marshall and Joseph Story. In this case the Court proclaimed that the constitutional decision it had reached that day was nothing less than "the supreme law of the land." Obviously the decision was binding on the parties in the case; but the implication that everyone would have to accept its judgments uncritically, that it was a decision from which there could be no appeal, was astonishing; the language recalled what Stephen Douglas said about *Dred Scott*.

In one fell swoop, the Court seemed to reduce the Constitution to the status of ordinary constitutional law, and to equate the judge with the lawgiver. Such logic assumes, as Charles Evans Hughes once quipped, that the Constitution is "what the judges say it is." The logic of *Cooper v. Aaron* was, and is, at war with the Constitution, at war with the basic principles of democratic government, and at war with the very meaning of the rule of law. . . .

––––––––––––

In 2012, former Speaker of the House Newt Gingrich ran for president. Before the South Carolina primary, he said that "[i]f the court makes a fundamentally wrong decision, the president can in fact ignore it." He elaborated:

> I fully expect as president that there will be several occasions when [the Supreme Court and I] will collide. The first one, which is actually foreign policy, the *Boumediene* decision which extends American legal rights to enemy combatants on the battlefield is such an outrageous extension of the court in to the commander in chief's role. I will issue an instruction on the opening day, first day I'm sworn in, I will issue an executive order to the national security apparatus that it will not enforce *Boumediene* and it will regard it as null and void because it is an absurd extension of the Supreme Court in to the commander in chief's [authority].

Gingrich implied that he would take a similar position with respect to *Roe v. Wade*, and he invoked Lincoln's stance on *Dred Scott*. *Newt Gingrich: I Would Ignore Supreme Court as President*, The Guardian, Jan. 18, 2012 (noting also that Pres. George W. Bush's Attorney General, Michael Mukasey, had said that a President selectively ignoring Supreme Court decisions would make the U.S. a banana republic).

b.   Interpretive Method in the Political Branches

The question of the political branches' authority to interpret the Constitution independent of the courts is complicated, to say the least. But don't make the mistake of thinking that an independent interpretation of the Constitution necessarily translates into a completely free hand. At least sometimes, constitutional culture, political reputation, and professional norms of the legal profession can exert a disciplining function for the political branches similar to the one they play in the judiciary. Read the following excerpt from the 2010 Department of Justice guidelines for promulgating authoritative legal interpretations within the executive branch. Do they strike you as a puppet show?

Memorandum for Attorneys of the Office of Legal Counsel Re: Best Practices for OLC Legal Advice and Written Opinions

David J. Barron, Acting Attorney General,
Office of Legal Counsel, Department of Justice
2010

By delegation, the Office of Legal Counsel (OLC) exercises the Attorney General's authority under the Judiciary Act of 1789 to provide the President and executive agencies with advice on questions of law. . . .

Certain fundamental principles guide all aspects of the Office's work. As noted above, OLC's central function is to provide, pursuant to the Attorney General's delegation, controlling legal advice to Executive Branch officials in furtherance of the President's constitutional duties to preserve, protect, and defend the Constitution, and to "take Care that the Laws be faithfully executed." To fulfill this function, OLC must provide advice based on its best understanding of what the law requires—not simply an advocate's defense of the contemplated action or position proposed by an agency or the Administration. Thus, in rendering legal advice, OLC seeks to provide an accurate and honest appraisal of applicable law, even if that appraisal will constrain the Administration's or an agency's pursuit of desired practices or policy objectives. This practice is critically important to the Office's effective performance of its assigned role, particularly because it is frequently asked to opine on issues of first impression that are unlikely to be resolved by the courts—a circumstance in which OLC's advice may effectively be the final word on the controlling law.

[R]egardless of the Office's ultimate legal conclusions, it should strive to ensure that it candidly and fairly addresses the full range of relevant legal sources and significant arguments on all sides of a question. . . .

On any issue involving a constitutional question, OLC's analysis should focus on traditional sources of constitutional meaning, including the text of the Constitution, the historical record illuminating the text's meaning, the Constitution's structure and purpose, and judicial and Executive Branch precedents interpreting relevant constitutional provisions. Particularly where the question relates to the authorities of the President or other executive officers or the allocation of powers between the Branches of the Government, precedent and historical practice are often of special relevance. On other questions of interpretation, OLC's analysis should be guided by the texts of the relevant documents, and should use traditional tools of construction in interpreting those texts. Because OLC is part of the Executive Branch, its analyses may also reflect the institutional traditions and competencies of that branch of the Government. For example, OLC opinions should consider and ordinarily give great weight to any relevant past opinions of Attorneys General and the Office. The Office should not lightly depart from such past decisions, particularly where they directly address and decide a point in question, but as with any system of precedent, past decisions may be subject to reconsideration and withdrawal in appropriate cases and through appropriate processes.

Finally, OLC's analyses may appropriately reflect the fact that its responsibilities also include facilitating the work of the Executive Branch and the objectives of the President, consistent with the law. As a result, unlike a court, OLC will, where possible and appropriate, seek to recommend lawful alternatives to Executive Branch proposals that it decides would be unlawful. Notwithstanding this aspect of OLC's mission, however, its legal analyses should always be principled, forthright, as thorough as time permits, and not designed merely to advance the policy preferences of the President or other officials.

C. Interpreting the Constitution—When?

Not every violation of the Constitution can be fixed by the courts. This is partly a practical point. But it's also a doctrinal one. A whole array of judicially-developed doctrines of restraint serve to limit the courts to what might be described as the right kind of intervention in the right kind of dispute. The contours of these limits began to emerge at least as far back as 1793, when the

Supreme Court declined to satisfy the Washington Administration's request for an advisory opinion on treaty obligations. See pp. 66–68. Both academic commentators and the Court itself often suggest that these essentially self-imposed limitations are motivated by the kinds of legitimacy concerns that emerge from the tension between judicial review and the counter-majoritarian difficulty. Taken from that perspective, these "justiciability" doctrines may serve as a safety valve—a way for the Court to keep its nose out of places where it may not belong.

 An advanced course in federal courts will cover all of this material and more in great detail. What follows is merely an introduction to some of the key justiciability doctrines that can lead courts to avoid intervening in some disputes without reaching a holding on whether the Constitution has actually been violated.

1. Political Questions

When we speak colloquially about a "political question," we usually mean an issue where the Constitution does not constrain the range of political choices—*i.e.*, a policy question left entirely to the political process. How much should the defense budget be in a given year? How high should the corporate tax rate be? The Constitution has nothing to say about these issues, leaving them to the political process to decide. This might be the sense in which *Marbury* used the term "political question," p. 259.

But over time—and one can already detect the change in *Georgia v. Stanton* (1867)—the term has also gained a more specific meaning as a matter of technical doctrine. Where a given case is deemed to present a "political question" in the strict doctrinal sense, it means that while the Constitution might well impose legal restraints on the policy choice in question, the courts will not assess or even discuss those restraints given the circumstances of the case. Alexander Bickel called political question doctrine "the culmination of any progression of devices for withholding the ultimate constitutional judgment of the Supreme Court." Certainly many political question cases present both the promise and the peril of justiciability requirements in particularly sharp form. As you read the following excerpts, see if you can understand why.

 Stanton is presented at pp. 163–164.

Alexander Bickel, The Passive Virtues

from *The Least Dangerous Branch* (1962)

[J]udicial review is the principled process of enunciating and applying certain enduring values of our society. [T]he root idea is that the process is justified only if it injects into representative government something that is not already there, and that is principle. . . .

A neutral principle . . . is an intellectually coherent statement of the reason for a result which in like cases will produce a like result, whether or not it is immediately agreeable or expedient. [T]he demand for neutral principles is . . . . that the Court rest judgment only on principles that will be capable of application across the board and without compromise, in all relevant cases in the foreseeable future: absolute application of absolute—even if sometimes flexible—principles. The flexibility, if any, must be built into the principle itself, in equally principled fashion. Thus a neutral principle is a rule of action that will be authoritatively enforced without adjustment or concession and without let-up. If it sometimes hurts, nothing is better proof of its validity. . . .

[But no] society, certainly not a large and heterogeneous one, can fail in time to explode if it is deprived of the arts of compromise, if it knows no ways of muddling through. No good society can be unprincipled; and no viable society can be principle-ridden. . . . Most often, . . . and as often as not in matters of the widest and deepest concern, . . . both requirements exist most imperatively side by side: guiding principle and expedient compromise. . . . Our democratic system of government exists in this Lincolnian tension between principle and expediency, and within it judicial review must play its role. . . .

The essentially important fact, so often missed [in discussions of judicial review], is that the Court wields a threefold power. It may strike down legislation as inconsistent with principle. It may validate . . . legislation as consistent with principle. *Or it may do neither.* It may do neither, and therein lies the secret of its ability to maintain itself in the tension between principle and expediency. . . .

When the Court . . . stays its hand, and makes clear that it is staying its hand and not legitimating, then the political processes are given relatively free play. . . . But in withholding constitutional judgment, the Court does not necessarily forsake an educational function, nor does it abandon principle. It seeks merely to elicit the correct answers to certain prudential questions that . . . lie in the path of ultimate issues of principle. To this end, the Court has, over the years, developed an almost inexhaustible arsenal of techniques and devices. . . .

All the while the issue of principle remains in abeyance and ripens. "The most important thing we do," said [Justice] Brandeis, "is not doing." . . .

The culmination of any progression of devices for withholding the ultimate constitutional judgment of the Supreme Court—and in a sense their sum—is the doctrine of political questions. . . . Such is the foundation, in both intellect and instinct, of the political-question doctrine: the Court's sense of lack of capacity, compounded in unequal parts of (a) the strangeness of the issue and its intractability to principled resolution, (b) the sheer momentousness of it, which tends to unbalance judicial judgment; (c) the anxiety, not so much that the judicial judgment will be ignored, as that perhaps it should but will not be; (d) finally . . . , the inner vulnerability, the self-doubt of an institution which is electorally irresponsible and has no earth to draw strength from.

As a general matter, the courts narrowed political question doctrine in the second half of the 20th century. One indication of this is that, while there was no serious thought that the Supreme Court would attempt to resolve the chaotic Presidential election of 1876, a majority of the Court showed no such reluctance in 2000. *Bush v. Gore* (2000) (enjoining Florida's recount). Significant decisions from prior years giving force to the doctrine include:

- *Luther v. Borden* (1849) (deeming to be a political question the United States's obligation under Art. IV, § 4, to guarantee a republican form of government to every state).

- *Coleman v. Miller* (1939) (deeming to be political questions whether a state's ratification of a constitutional amendment was effective notwithstanding the state's earlier rejection of the same amendment, and whether a proposed amendment could no longer be ratified because of the lapse of time since its proposal).

WORTH NOTING

The *Coleman* Court was equally divided as to whether a third question should be deemed political: whether the Lieutenant Governor of a state, who had cast the deciding vote in the state's senate for ratification of a constitutional amendment, should be considered part of the legislature for purposes of the amendment process.

- *Colegrove v. Green* (1948) (plurality asserting that "the Constitution has conferred upon Congress exclusive authority to secure fair representation by the States in the popular House, and left to that House determination whether States have fulfilled their [constitutional] responsibility").

Colegrove was effectively nullified in *Baker v. Carr* (1962), which held that the constitutionality of unequal representation in a state's General Assembly was not a political question. And later that decade, the Court held that the House of Representatives could not exclude a Member on any grounds other than the standing qualifications expressly stated in the Constitution—specifically rejecting the claim that the case should be dismissed as a political question. *Powell v. McCormack* (1969).

But political question doctrine is far from dead. *Nixon v. United States* (1993) held non-justiciable the question of whether the Senate had properly tried the impeachment of a federal judge by appointing a committee to hear the evidence and report to the full body. More recently, a closely divided Court held that the constitutionality of political gerrymanders in electoral districting presents a political question not for resolution by the courts. *Rucho v. Common Cause* (2019).

Zivotofsky v. Clinton offers a recent summary of political question doctrine, with particular reference to the foreign affairs context. As you read it, think about how the considerations deployed by the majority, concurrences, and dissent might apply to other kinds of questions as well.

Zivotofsky v. Clinton

Supreme Court of the United States, 2012.
566 U.S. 189.

CHIEF JUSTICE ROBERTS delivered the opinion of the Court.

Congress enacted a statute providing that Americans born in Jerusalem may elect to have "Israel" listed as the place of birth on their passports. The State Department declined to follow that law, citing its longstanding policy of not taking a position on the political status of Jerusalem. When sued by an American who invoked the statute, the Secretary of State argued that the courts lacked authority to decide the case because it presented a political question. The Court of Appeals so held.

We disagree. The courts are fully capable of determining whether this statute may be given effect, or instead must be struck down in light of authority conferred on the Executive by the Constitution.

I

A

In 2002, Congress enacted the Foreign Relations Authorization Act, Fiscal Year 2003. Section 214 of the Act is entitled "United States Policy with Respect to Jerusalem as the Capital of Israel." The first two subsections express Congress's "commitment" to relocating the United States Embassy in Israel to Jerusalem. The third bars funding for the publication of official Government documents that do not list Jerusalem as the capital of Israel. The fourth and final provision, § 214(d), is the only one at stake in this case. Entitled "Record of Place of Birth as Israel for Passport Purposes," it provides that "[f]or purposes of the registration of birth, certification of nationality, or issuance of a passport of a United States citizen born in the city of Jerusalem, the Secretary shall, upon the request of the citizen or the citizen's legal guardian, record the place of birth as Israel."

The State Department's Foreign Affairs Manual states that "[w]here the birthplace of the applicant is located in territory disputed by another country, the city or area of birth may be written in the passport." The manual specifically directs that passport officials should enter "JERUSALEM" and should "not write Israel or Jordan" when recording the birthplace of a person born in Jerusalem on a passport.

Section 214(d) sought to override this instruction by allowing citizens born in Jerusalem to have "Israel" recorded on their passports if they wish. In signing the Foreign Relations Authorization Act into law, President George W. Bush stated his belief that § 214 "impermissibly interferes with the President's constitutional authority to conduct the Nation's foreign affairs and to supervise the unitary executive branch." He added that if the section is "construed as mandatory," then it would "interfere with the President's constitutional authority to formulate the position of the United States, speak for the Nation in international affairs, and determine the terms on which recognition is given to foreign states." He concluded by emphasizing that "U.S. policy regarding

Jerusalem has not changed." The President made no specific reference to the passport mandate in § 214(d).

B

Petitioner Menachem Binyamin Zivotofsky was born in Jerusalem on October 17, 2002, shortly after § 214(d) was enacted. Zivotofsky's parents were American citizens and he accordingly was as well, by virtue of congressional enactment. 8 U.S.C. § 1401(c). Zivotofsky's mother filed an application for a consular report of birth abroad and a United States passport. She requested that his place of birth be listed as "Jerusalem, Israel" on both documents. U.S. officials informed Zivotofsky's mother that State Department policy prohibits recording "Israel" as Zivotofsky's place of birth. Pursuant to that policy, Zivotofsky was issued a passport and consular report of birth abroad listing only "Jerusalem."

Zivotofsky's parents filed a complaint on his behalf against the Secretary of State. Zivotofsky sought a declaratory judgment and a permanent injunction ordering the Secretary to identify his place of birth as "Jerusalem, Israel" in the official documents. . . .

The District Court . . . found that the case was not justiciable. . . . The D.C. Circuit affirmed. It reasoned that the Constitution gives the Executive the exclusive power to recognize foreign sovereigns, and that the exercise of this power cannot be reviewed by the courts. Therefore, "deciding whether the Secretary of State must mark a passport . . . as Zivotofsky requests would necessarily draw [the court] into an area of decisionmaking the Constitution leaves to the Executive alone." The D.C. Circuit held that the political question doctrine prohibits such an intrusion by the courts, and rejected any suggestion that Congress's decision to take "a position on the status of Jerusalem" could change the analysis. . . .

Zivotofsky petitioned for certiorari, and we granted review.

II

. . . In general, the Judiciary has a responsibility to decide cases properly before it, even those it "would gladly avoid." *Cohens v. Virginia* (1821). Our precedents have identified a narrow exception to that rule, known as the "political question" doctrine. We have explained that a controversy "involves a political question . . . where there is 'a textually demonstrable constitutional commitment of the issue to a coordinate political department; or a lack of judicially discoverable and manageable standards for resolving it.'" *Nixon v. United States*

(1993) (quoting *Baker v. Carr* (1962)). In such a case, we have held that a court lacks the authority to decide the dispute before it.

The lower courts ruled that this case involves a political question because deciding Zivotofsky's claim would force the Judicial Branch to interfere with the President's exercise of constitutional power committed to him alone. The District Court understood Zivotofsky to ask the courts to "decide the political status of Jerusalem." This misunderstands the issue presented. Zivotofsky does not ask the courts to determine whether Jerusalem is the capital of Israel. He instead seeks to determine whether he may vindicate his statutory right, under § 214(d), to choose to have Israel recorded on his passport as his place of birth.

For its part, the D.C. Circuit treated the two questions as one and the same. That court concluded that "[o]nly the Executive—not Congress and not the courts—has the power to define U.S. policy regarding Israel's sovereignty over Jerusalem," and also to "decide how best to implement that policy." Because the Department's passport rule was adopted to implement the President's "exclusive and unreviewable constitutional power to keep the United States out of the debate over the status of Jerusalem," the validity of that rule was itself a "nonjusticiable political question" that "the Constitution leaves to the Executive alone." Indeed, the D.C. Circuit's opinion does not even mention § 214(d) until the fifth of its six paragraphs of analysis, and then only to dismiss it as irrelevant: "That Congress took a position on the status of Jerusalem and gave Zivotofsky a statutory cause of action . . . is of no moment to whether the judiciary has [the] authority to resolve this dispute. . . ."

The existence of a statutory right, however, is certainly relevant to the Judiciary's power to decide Zivotofsky's claim. The federal courts are not being asked to supplant a foreign policy decision of the political branches with the courts' own unmoored determination of what United States policy toward Jerusalem should be. Instead, Zivotofsky requests that the courts enforce a specific statutory right. To resolve his claim, the Judiciary must decide if Zivotofsky's interpretation of the statute is correct, and whether the statute is constitutional. This is a familiar judicial exercise.

Moreover, because the parties do not dispute the interpretation of § 214(d), the only real question for the courts is whether the statute is constitutional. At least since *Marbury v. Madison* (1803), we have recognized that when an Act of Congress is alleged to conflict with the Constitution, "[i]t is emphatically the province and duty of the judicial department to say what the law is."

That duty will sometimes involve the "[r]esolution of litigation challenging the constitutional authority of one of the three branches," but courts cannot avoid their responsibility merely "because the issues have political implications." *INS v. Chadha* (1983).

In this case, determining the constitutionality of § 214(d) involves deciding whether the statute impermissibly intrudes upon Presidential powers under the Constitution. If so, the law must be invalidated and Zivotofsky's case should be dismissed for failure to state a claim. If, on the other hand, the statute does not trench on the President's powers, then the Secretary must be ordered to issue Zivotofsky a passport that complies with § 214(d). Either way, the political question doctrine is not implicated. "No policy underlying the political question doctrine suggests that Congress or the Executive . . . can decide the constitutionality of a statute; that is a decision for the courts." *Id.*

The Secretary contends that "there is 'a textually demonstrable constitutional commitment' " to the President of the sole power to recognize foreign sovereigns and, as a corollary, to determine whether an American born in Jerusalem may choose to have Israel listed as his place of birth on his passport. *Nixon, supra.* Perhaps. But there is, of course, no exclusive commitment to the Executive of the power to determine the constitutionality of a statute. The Judicial Branch appropriately exercises that authority, including in a case such as this, where the question is whether Congress or the Executive is "aggrandizing its power at the expense of another branch." *Freytag v. Commissioner* (1991); *see, e.g., Myers v. United States* (1926) (finding a statute unconstitutional because it encroached upon the President's removal power); *Bowsher v. Synar* (1986) (finding a statute unconstitutional because it "intruded into the executive function"); *Morrison v. Olson* (1988) (upholding a statute's constitutionality against a charge that it "impermissibly interfere[d] with the President's exercise of his constitutionally appointed functions").

Our precedents have also found the political question doctrine implicated when there is " 'a lack of judicially discoverable and manageable standards for resolving' " the question before the court. *Nixon, supra* (quoting *Baker, supra*). Framing the issue as the lower courts did, in terms of whether the Judiciary may decide the political status of Jerusalem, certainly raises those concerns. They dissipate, however, when the issue is recognized to be the more focused one of the constitutionality of § 214(d). Indeed, both sides offer detailed legal arguments regarding whether § 214(d) is constitutional in light of powers committed to the Executive, and whether Congress's own powers with respect to passports must be weighed in analyzing this question.

For example, the Secretary reprises on the merits her argument on the political question issue, claiming that the Constitution gives the Executive the exclusive power to formulate recognition policy. She roots her claim in the Constitution's declaration that the President shall "receive Ambassadors and other public Ministers." According to the Secretary, "[c]enturies-long Executive Branch practice, congressional acquiescence, and decisions by this Court" confirm that the "receive Ambassadors" clause confers upon the Executive the exclusive power of recognition. . . .

For his part, Zivotofsky argues that, far from being an exercise of the recognition power, § 214(d) is instead a "legitimate and permissible" exercise of Congress's "authority to legislate on the form and content of a passport." He points the Court to Professor Louis Henkin's observation that " 'in the competition for power in foreign relations,' Congress has 'an impressive array of powers expressly enumerated in the Constitution.' " Zivotofsky suggests that Congress's authority to enact § 214(d) derives specifically from its powers over naturalization, U.S. Const., Art. I, § 8, cl. 4, and foreign commerce, id., § 8, cl. 3. According to Zivotofsky, Congress has used these powers to pass laws regulating the content and issuance of passports since 1856. . . .

Recitation of these arguments—which sound in familiar principles of constitutional interpretation—is enough to establish that this case does not "turn on standards that defy judicial application." *Baker.* Resolution of Zivotofsky's claim demands careful examination of the textual, structural, and historical evidence put forward by the parties regarding the nature of the statute and of the passport and recognition powers. This is what courts do. The political question doctrine poses no bar to judicial review of this case. . . .

The judgment of the Court of Appeals for the D.C. Circuit is vacated, and the case is remanded for further proceedings consistent with this opinion.

It is so ordered.

JUSTICE SOTOMAYOR, with whom JUSTICE BREYER joins as to Part I, concurring in part and concurring in the judgment.

. . . I concur in the Court's conclusion that this case does not present a political question. I write separately, however, because I understand the inquiry required by the political question doctrine to be more demanding than that suggested by the Court.

I

The political question doctrine speaks to an amalgam of circumstances in which courts properly examine whether a particular suit is justiciable—that is, whether the dispute is appropriate for resolution by courts. The doctrine is "essentially a function of the separation of powers," *Baker v. Carr* (1962), which recognizes the limits that Article III imposes upon courts and accords appropriate respect to the other branches' exercise of their own constitutional powers.

In *Baker*, this Court identified six circumstances in which an issue might present a political question:

(1) "a textually demonstrable constitutional commitment of the issue to a coordinate political department";

(2) "a lack of judicially discoverable and manageable standards for resolving it";

(3) "the impossibility of deciding without an initial policy determination of a kind clearly for nonjudicial discretion";

(4) "the impossibility of a court's undertaking independent resolution without expressing lack of the respect due coordinate branches of government";

(5) "an unusual need for unquestioning adherence to a political decision already made"; or

(6) "the potentiality of embarrassment from multifarious pronouncements by various departments on one question."

Baker established that "[u]nless one of these formulations is inextricable from the case at bar, there should be no dismissal for nonjusticiability." But *Baker* left unanswered when the presence of one or more factors warrants dismissal, as well as the interrelationship of the six factors and the relative importance of each in determining whether a case is suitable for adjudication.

In my view, the *Baker* factors reflect three distinct justifications for withholding judgment on the merits of a dispute. When a case would require a court to decide an issue whose resolution is textually committed to a coordinate political department, as envisioned by *Baker*'s first factor, abstention is warranted because the court lacks authority to resolve that issue. See, *e.g., Nixon v. United States* (1993) (holding nonjusticiable the Senate's impeachment procedures in light of Article I's commitment to the Senate of the " 'sole Power to try all Impeachments' "); see also *Marbury v. Madison* (1803) ("By the constitution of the United States, the president is invested with certain important political powers, in the exercise of which he is to use his own discretion, and is accountable only to his country in his political character, and to his own conscience"). In such cases, the Constitution itself requires that another branch resolve the question presented.

The second and third *Baker* factors reflect circumstances in which a dispute calls for decisionmaking beyond courts' competence. " 'The judicial Power' created by Article III, § 1, of the Constitution is not *whatever* judges choose to do," but rather the power "to act in the manner traditional for English and American courts." *Vieth v. Jubelirer* (2004) (plurality opinion). That traditional role involves the application of some manageable and cognizable standard within the competence of the Judiciary to ascertain and employ to the facts of a concrete case. When a court is given no standard by which to adjudicate a dispute, or cannot resolve a dispute in the absence of a yet-unmade policy determination charged to a political branch, resolution of the suit is beyond the judicial role envisioned by Article III. See, *e.g., Gilligan v. Morgan* (1973) ("[I]t is difficult to conceive of an area of governmental activity in which the courts have less competence" than "[t]he complex, subtle, and professional decisions as to the composition, training, equipping, and control of a military force"). This is not to say, of course, that courts are incapable of interpreting or applying somewhat ambiguous standards using familiar tools of statutory or constitutional interpretation. But where an issue leaves courts truly rudderless, there can be "no doubt of [the] validity" of a court's decision to abstain from judgment. *Ibid.*

The final three *Baker* factors address circumstances in which prudence may counsel against a court's resolution of an issue presented. Courts should be particularly cautious before forgoing adjudication of a dispute on the basis that judicial intervention risks "embarrassment from multifarious pronouncements by various departments on one question," would express a "lack of the respect due coordinate branches of government," or because there exists an "unusual need for unquestioning adherence to a political decision already made." We have repeatedly rejected the view that these thresholds are met whenever a court is called upon to resolve the constitutionality or propriety of the act of another branch of Government. A court may not refuse to adjudicate a dispute merely because a decision "may have significant political overtones" or affect "the conduct of this Nation's foreign relations," *Japan Whaling Assn. v. American Cetacean Soc.* (1986). Nor may courts decline to resolve a controversy within their traditional competence and proper jurisdiction simply because the question is difficult, the consequences weighty, or the potential real for conflict with the policy preferences of the political branches. The exercise of such authority is among the "gravest and most delicate dut[ies] that this Court is called on to perform," *Blodgett v. Holden* (1927) (Holmes, J., concurring), but it is the role assigned to courts by the Constitution. . . .

Rare occasions implicating *Baker*'s final factors, however, may present an " 'unusual case' " unfit for judicial disposition. *Baker v. Carr* (1961) (quoting the argument of Daniel Webster in *Luther v. Borden* (1849)). Because of the respect due to a coequal and independent department, for instance, courts properly resist calls to question the good faith with which another branch attests to the authenticity of its internal acts. See, *e.g., Field v. Clark* (1892) (deeming "forbidden by the respect due to a coordinate branch of the government" "[j]udicial action" requiring a belief in a "deliberate conspiracy" by the Senate and House of Representatives "to defeat an expression of the popular will"). Likewise, we have long acknowledged that courts are particularly ill suited to intervening in exigent disputes necessitating unusual need for "attributing finality to the action of the political departments," *Coleman v. Miller* (1939), or creating acute "risk [of] embarrassment of our government abroad, or grave disturbance at home," *Baker.* Finally, it may be appropriate for courts to stay their hand in cases implicating delicate questions concerning the distribution of political authority between coordinate branches until a dispute is ripe, intractable, and incapable of resolution by the political process. See *Goldwater v. Carter* (1979) (Powell, J., concurring in judgment) [(concluding that President's power to terminate treaties can at least sometimes present such a political question)]. Abstention merely reflects that judicial intervention in such cases is "legitimate only in the last resort," and is disfavored relative to the prospect of accommodation between the political branches. . . .

To be sure, it will be the rare case in which *Baker*'s final factors alone render a case nonjusticiable. But our long historical tradition recognizes that such exceptional cases arise, and due regard for the separation of powers and the judicial role envisioned by Article III confirms that abstention may be an appropriate response.

II

. . . Largely for the reasons set out by the Court, I agree that the Court of Appeals misapprehended the nature of its task. In two respects, however, my understanding of the political question doctrine might require a court to engage in further analysis beyond that relied upon by the Court.

First, the Court appropriately recognizes that petitioner's claim to a statutory right is "relevant" to the justiciability inquiry required in this case. In order to evaluate whether a case presents a political question, a court must first identify with precision the issue it is being asked to decide. Here, petitioner's suit claims that a federal statute provides him with a right to have "Israel" listed as his place of birth on his passport and other related documents. To decide that question, a court must determine whether the statute is constitutional, and therefore mandates the Secretary of State to issue petitioner's desired passport, or unconstitutional, in which case his suit is at an end. Resolution of that issue is not one "textually committed" to another branch; to the contrary, it is committed to this one. In no fashion does the question require a court to review the wisdom of the President's policy toward Jerusalem or any other decision committed to the discretion of a coordinate department. For that reason, I agree that the decision below should be reversed.

That is not to say, however, that no statute could give rise to a political question. It is not impossible to imagine a case involving the application or even the constitutionality of an enactment that would present a nonjusticiable issue. Indeed, this Court refused to determine whether an Ohio state constitutional provision offended the Republican Guarantee Clause, Art. IV, § 4, holding that "the question of whether that guarantee of the Constitution has been disregarded presents no justiciable controversy." *Ohio ex rel. Davis v. Hildebrant* (1916). A similar result would follow if Congress passed a statute, for instance, purporting to award financial relief to those improperly "tried" of impeachment offenses. To adjudicate claims under such a statute would require a court to resolve the very same issue we found nonjusticiable in *Nixon.* Such examples are atypical, but they suffice to show that the foreclosure altogether of political question analysis in statutory cases is unwarranted.

Second, the Court suggests that this case does not implicate the political question doctrine's concern with issues exhibiting " 'a lack of judicially discoverable and manageable standards,' " because the parties' arguments rely on textual, structural, and historical evidence of the kind that courts routinely consider. But that was equally true in *Nixon,* a case in which we found that "the use of the word 'try' in the first sentence of the Impeachment Trial Clause lacks sufficient precision to afford any judicially manageable standard of review of the Senate's actions." We reached that conclusion even though the parties' briefs focused upon the text of the Impeachment Trial Clause, "the Constitution's drafting history," "contemporaneous commentary," "the unbroken practice of the Senate for 150 years," contemporary dictionary meanings, "Hamilton's Federalist essays," and the practice in the House of Lords prior to ratification. Such evidence was no more or less unfamiliar to courts than that on which the parties rely here.

In my view, it is not whether the evidence upon which litigants rely is common to judicial consideration that determines whether a case lacks judicially discoverable and manageable standards. Rather, it is whether that evidence in fact provides a court a basis to adjudicate meaningfully the issue with which it is presented. The answer will almost always be yes, but if the parties' textual, structural, and historical evidence is inapposite or wholly unilluminating, rendering judicial decision no more than guesswork, a case relying on the ordinary kinds of arguments offered to courts might well still present justiciability concerns.

In this case, however, the Court of Appeals majority found a political question solely on the basis that this case required resolution of an issue "textually committed" to the Executive Branch. Because there was no such textual commitment, I respectfully concur in the Court's decision to reverse the Court of Appeals.

JUSTICE ALITO, concurring in the judgment.

. . . Under our case law, determining the constitutionality of an Act of Congress may present a political question, but I do not think that the narrow question presented here falls within that category. Delineating the precise dividing line between the powers of Congress and the President with respect to the contents of a passport is not an easy matter, but I agree with the Court that it does not constitute a political question that the Judiciary is unable to decide.

JUSTICE BREYER, dissenting.

I join Part I of Justice Sotomayor's opinion. As she points out, *Baker v. Carr* (1962) set forth several categories of legal questions that the Court had previously held to be "political questions" inappropriate for judicial determination. . . . Justice Sotomayor adds that the circumstances in which these prudential considerations lead the Court not to decide a case otherwise properly before it are rare. I agree. But in my view we nonetheless have before us such a case. Four sets of prudential considerations, *taken together*, lead me to that conclusion.

First, the issue before us arises in the field of foreign affairs. (Indeed, the statutory provision before us is a subsection of a section that concerns the relation between Jerusalem and the State of Israel. See § 214 of the Foreign Relations Authorization Act, Fiscal Year 2003 ("United States Policy with Respect to Jerusalem as the Capital of Israel").) The Constitution primarily delegates the foreign affairs powers "to the political departments of the government, Executive and Legislative," not to the Judiciary. And that fact is not surprising. Decisionmaking in this area typically is highly political. It is "delicate" and "complex." It often rests upon information readily available to the Executive Branch and to the intelligence committees of Congress, but not readily available to the courts. It frequently is highly dependent upon what Justice Jackson called "prophecy." And the creation of wise foreign policy typically lies well beyond the experience or professional capacity of a judge. At the same time, where foreign affairs is at issue, the practical need for the United States to speak "with one voice and ac[t] as one," is particularly important. See *United States v. Pink* (1942) (Frankfurter, J., concurring).

The result is a judicial hesitancy to make decisions that have significant foreign policy implications, as reflected in the fact that many of the cases in which the Court has invoked the political-question doctrine have arisen in this area, *e.g.*, cases in which the validity of a treaty depended upon the partner state's constitutional authority, *Doe v. Braden* (1854), or upon its continuing existence, *Terlinden v. Ames* (1902); cases concerning the existence of foreign states, governments, belligerents, and insurgents, *Oetjen v. Central Leather Co.* (1918); and cases concerning the territorial boundaries of foreign states, *Foster v. Neilson* (1829).

Second, if the courts must answer the constitutional question before us, they may well have to evaluate the foreign policy implications of foreign policy decisions. . . . Were the statutory provision undisputedly concerned only with purely administrative matters (or were its enforcement undisputedly to involve only major foreign policy matters), judicial efforts to answer the constitutional question might not involve judges in trying to answer questions of foreign policy. But in the Middle East, administrative matters can have implications that extend far beyond the purely administrative. Political reactions in that region can prove uncertain. And in that context it may well turn out that resolution of the constitutional argument will require a court to decide how far the statute, in practice, reaches beyond the purely administrative, determining not only whether but also the extent to which enforcement will interfere with the President's ability to make significant recognition-related foreign policy decisions. . . .

A judge's ability to evaluate opposing claims of this kind is minimal. At the same time, a judicial effort to do so risks inadvertently jeopardizing sound foreign policy decisionmaking by the other branches of Government. How, for example, is this Court to determine whether, or the extent to which, the continuation of the adjudication that it now orders will itself have a foreign policy effect?

Third, the countervailing interests in obtaining judicial resolution of the constitutional determination are not particularly strong ones. Zivotofsky does not assert the kind of interest, *e.g.,* an interest in property or bodily integrity, which courts have traditionally sought to protect. Nor, importantly, does he assert an interest in vindicating a basic right of the kind that the Constitution grants to individuals and that courts traditionally have protected from invasion by the other branches of Government. And I emphasize this fact because the need for judicial action in such cases can trump the foreign policy concerns that I have mentioned. As Professor Jaffe pointed out many years ago, "Our courts would not refuse to entertain habeas corpus to test the constitutionality of the imprisonment of an alleged Chinese agent even if it were clear that his imprisonment was closely bound up with our relations to the Chinese government." Cf. *Boumediene v. Bush* (2008).

The interest that Zivotofsky asserts, however, is akin to an ideological interest. . . . And insofar as an individual suffers an injury that is purely ideological, courts have often refused to consider the matter, leaving the injured party to look to the political branches for protection. This is not to say that Zivotofsky's claim is unimportant or that the injury is not serious or even that it is purely ideological. . . .

Fourth, insofar as the controversy reflects different foreign policy views among the political branches of Government, those branches have nonjudicial methods of working out their differences. The Executive and Legislative

Branches frequently work out disagreements through ongoing contacts and relationships, involving, for example, budget authorizations, confirmation of personnel, committee hearings, and a host of more informal contacts, which, taken together, ensure that, in practice, Members of Congress as well as the President play an important role in the shaping of foreign policy. Indeed, both the Legislative Branch and the Executive Branch typically understand the need to work each with the other in order to create effective foreign policy. In that understanding, those related contacts, and the continuous foreign policy-related relationship lies the possibility of working out the kind of disagreement we see before us. . . .

With respect, I dissent.

For Discussion

(1) Writing in 1976, when the force of political-question doctrine appeared to be at an ebb, Louis Henkin raised doubts about whether there actually is a "doctrine requiring abstention from judicial review of 'political questions,'" in which "the courts [are thought to] say to the petitioner in effect: 'Although you may indeed be aggrieved by an action of government, although the action may indeed do violence to the Constitution, it involves a political question which is not justiciable, not given to us to review'":

> The cases which are supposed to have established the political question doctrine required no such extra-ordinary abstention from judicial review; they called only for the ordinary respect by the courts for the political domain. Having reviewed, the Court refused to invalidate the challenged actions because they were within the constitutional authority of President or Congress. In no case did the Court have to use the phrase "political question," and when it did, it was using it in a different sense, saying in effect: "We have reviewed your claims and we find that the action complained of . . . is within the powers granted by the Constitution to the political branches. The act complained of violates no constitutional limitation on that power, either because the Constitution imposes no relevant limitations, or because the action is amply within the limits prescribed. We give effect to what the political branches have done because they had political authority under the Constitution to do it."

Note that Henkin's argument here is doctrinal. That is, he's not saying there *shouldn't* be a political question doctrine; he's saying there *isn't* one—or at least, not one that is any different from a straight decision on the merits.

To assess the implications of this thesis, consider *Rucho v. Common Cause* (2019). Even though the 5–4 majority accepted that excessive partisanship in districting is "incompatible with democratic principles," the Court still held that equal protection and First Amendment challenges to political gerrymandering present such a judicially unmanageable question as to defy resolution by the courts":

> Unable to claim that the Constitution requires proportional representation outright, plaintiffs inevitably ask the courts to make their own political judgment about how much representation particular political parties deserve—based on the votes of their supporters—and to rearrange the challenged districts to achieve that end. But federal courts are not equipped to apportion political power as a matter of fairness, nor is there any basis for concluding that they were authorized to do so.

Rucho. Judging by *Rucho*, is Henkin right? Can you see a difference between the majority's view that political gerrymandering presents a nonjusticiable political question and the view that such gerrymandering does not violate the Constitution? If you see a difference, how would you describe it? Is it a practical difference, a theoretical difference, or both? See generally *Vieth v. Jubelirer* (2004) (Kennedy, J., concurring in the judgment) ("I would not foreclose all possibility of judicial relief if some limited and precise rationale were found to correct an established violation of the Constitution in some redistricting cases.").

(2)   Do you support or oppose a true political question doctrine? Why?

2. Standing

Suppose you bring a suit in federal court seeking an injunction against a governmental action that you regard as blatantly illegal. The court asks, "But how does this affect *you*?" If you respond that you are offended to see the government acting so improperly, the court is likely to say something like this: "Article III of the Constitution does not authorize federal courts to address generalized grievances. Unless you show that you've been injured in an individualized way, and that a court order could make things better, you have no standing to complain."

As we turn to the "standing" doctrine that underlies this response, be forewarned that it's not a terribly satisfying area of the law. A description offered by Judge William Fletcher of the federal Ninth Circuit remains as true now as when written in 1988:

> The structure of standing law in the federal courts has long been criticized as incoherent. It has been described as "permeated with sophistry," as "a word game played by secret rules," and more recently as a largely meaningless "litany" recited before "the Court . . . chooses up sides and decides the case." This unhappy state of affairs does not result from the unimportance of standing doctrine. If anything, the contrary is true.

William A. Fletcher, *The Structure of Standing*, 98 Yale L. J. 221 (1988). Note that Fletcher is making two points. First, the doctrine is frustrating and often self-contradictory. Second, the doctrine is extremely important. As the next case suggests, he's right on both counts.

As you read the standing cases, try to decide whether you think the values served by the doctrine are worth the tangled analysis that it often serves up.

Lujan v. Defenders of Wildlife

Supreme Court of the United States, 1992.
504 U.S. 555.

JUSTICE SCALIA delivered the opinion of the Court with respect to Parts I, II, III-A, and IV, and an opinion with respect to Part III-B, in which THE CHIEF JUSTICE, JUSTICE WHITE, and JUSTICE THOMAS join.

I

SUMMARY OF THE FACTS

The Endangered Species Act of 1973 (ESA) requires the Secretary of the Interior to designate endangered and threatened species and to define their critical habitats. Section 7(a)(2) of the Act requires each Federal agency to consult

> with the Secretary to "insure that any action authorized, funded, or carried out by such agency" is not likely to jeopardize any endangered or threatened species or critically impair its habitat. In 1986, reversing a position taken by their predecessors in 1978, the Secretaries of the Interior and of Commerce promulgated a joint regulation that exempted actions taken in foreign nations from the § 7(a)(2) consultation requirement.

Shortly thereafter, respondents, organizations dedicated to wildlife conservation and other environmental causes, filed this action against the Secretary of the Interior, seeking a declaratory judgment that the new regulation is in error as to the geographic scope of § 7(a)(2) and an injunction requiring the Secretary to promulgate a new regulation restoring the initial interpretation. . . .

II

While the Constitution of the United States divides all power conferred upon the Federal Government into "legislative Powers," Art. I, § 1, "[t]he executive Power," Art. II, § 1, and "[t]he judicial Power," Art. III, § 1, it does not attempt to define those terms. To be sure, it limits the jurisdiction of federal courts to "Cases" and "Controversies," but an executive inquiry can bear the name "case" (the Hoffa case) and a legislative dispute can bear the name "controversy" (the Smoot-Hawley controversy).

Obviously, then, the Constitution's central mechanism of separation of powers depends largely upon common understanding of what activities are appropriate to legislatures, to executives, and to courts. . . . One of [the] landmarks, setting apart the "Cases" and "Controversies" that are of the justiciable sort referred to in Article III . . . is the doctrine of standing. . . . [T]he core component of standing is an essential and unchanging part of the case-or-controversy requirement of Article III. See, *e.g., Allen v. Wright* (1984).

Over the years, our cases have established that the irreducible constitutional minimum of standing contains three elements. First, the plaintiff must have suffered an "injury in fact"—an invasion of a legally protected interest which is (a) concrete and particularized,[1] and (b) "actual or imminent, not 'conjectural' or 'hypothetical.'" Second, there must be a causal connection between the injury and the conduct complained of—the injury has to be "fairly . . . trace[able]" to the challenged action of the defendant, and not . . . th[e] result

---

[1] By particularized, we mean that the injury must affect the plaintiff in a personal and individual way.

[of] the independent action of some third party not before the court." Third, it must be "likely," as opposed to merely "speculative," that the injury will be "redressed by a favorable decision."

The party invoking federal jurisdiction bears the burden of establishing these elements. . . . When the suit is one challenging the legality of government action or inaction, the nature and extent of facts that must be averred (at the summary judgment stage) or proved (at the trial stage) in order to establish standing depends considerably upon whether the plaintiff is himself an object of the action (or forgone action) at issue. If he is, there is ordinarily little question that the action or inaction has caused him injury, and that a judgment preventing or requiring the action will redress it.

When, however, as in this case, a plaintiff's asserted injury arises from the government's allegedly unlawful regulation (or lack of regulation) of *someone else*, much more is needed. In that circumstance, causation and redressability ordinarily hinge on the response of the regulated (or regulable) third party to the government action or inaction—and perhaps on the response of others as well. The existence of one or more of the essential elements of standing "depends on the unfettered choices made by independent actors not before the courts and whose exercise of broad and legitimate discretion the courts cannot presume either to control or to predict," and it becomes the burden of the plaintiff to adduce facts showing that those choices have been or will be made in such manner as to produce causation and permit redressability of injury. Thus, when the plaintiff is not himself the object of the government action or inaction he challenges, standing is not precluded, but it is ordinarily "substantially more difficult" to establish.

III

We think the Court of Appeals failed to apply the foregoing principles in denying the Secretary's motion for summary judgment. Respondents had not made the requisite demonstration of (at least) injury and redressability.

A

Respondents' claim to injury is that the lack of consultation with respect to certain funded activities abroad "increas[es] the rate of extinction of endangered and threatened species." Complaint ¶ 5. Of course, the desire to use or observe an animal species, even for purely esthetic purposes, is undeniably a cognizable interest for purpose of standing. See, *e.g., Sierra Club v. Morton* (1972). "But the 'injury in fact' test requires more than an injury to a cognizable interest. It requires that the party seeking review be himself among the injured." To survive the Secretary's summary judgment motion, respondents had to submit affidavits or other evidence showing, through specific facts, not only that listed species were in fact being threatened by funded activities abroad, but also that one or more of respondents' members would thereby be "directly" affected apart from their " 'special interest' in th[e] subject."

With respect to this aspect of the case, the Court of Appeals focused on the affidavits of two Defenders' members—Joyce Kelly and Amy Skilbred. Ms. Kelly stated that she traveled to Egypt in 1986 and "observed the traditional habitat of the endangered [N]ile crocodile there and intend[s] to do so again, and hope[s] to observe the crocodile directly," and that she "will suffer harm in fact as the result of [the] American . . . role . . . in overseeing the rehabilitation of the Aswan High Dam on the Nile . . . and [in] develop[ing] . . . Egypt's . . . Master Water Plan." Ms. Skilbred averred that she traveled to Sri Lanka in 1981 and "observed th[e] habitat" of "endangered species such as the Asian elephant and the leopard" at what is now the site of the Mahaweli project funded by the Agency for International Development (AID), although she "was unable to see any of the endangered species"; "this development project," she continued, "will seriously reduce endangered, threatened, and endemic species habitat including areas that I visited[, which] may severely shorten the future of these species"; that threat, she concluded, harmed her because she "intend[s] to return to Sri Lanka in the future and hope[s] to be more fortunate in spotting at least the endangered elephant and leopard." When Ms. Skilbred was asked at a subsequent deposition if and when she had any plans to return to Sri Lanka, she reiterated that "I intend to go back to Sri Lanka," but confessed that she had no current plans: "I don't know [when]. There is a civil war going on right now. I don't know. Not next year, I will say. In the future."

We shall assume for the sake of argument that these affidavits contain facts showing that certain agency-funded projects threaten listed species—though that is questionable. They plainly contain no facts, however, showing how damage to the species will produce "imminent" injury to Mses. Kelly and Skilbred. That the women "had visited" the areas of the projects before the projects commenced proves nothing. As we have said in a related context, " 'Past exposure to illegal conduct does not in itself show a present case or controversy regarding injunctive relief . . . if unaccompanied by any continuing, present adverse effects.' " *Los Angeles v. Lyons* (1983). And the affiants' profession of an "inten[t]" to return to the places they had visited before—where they will pre-sumably, this time, be deprived of the opportunity to observe animals of the endangered species—is simply not enough. Such "some day" inten-tions—without any description of concrete plans, or indeed even any specification of *when* the some day will be—do not support a finding of the "actual or imminent" injury that our cases require. . . .

 CROSS REFERENCE *Lyons*, which held that a person who had been choked uncon-scious by an L.A. police officer had no standing to seek an injunction against the police department's chokehold policy, is presented on pp. 315–320.

Besides relying upon the Kelly and Skilbred affidavits, respondents pro-pose a series of novel standing theories. The first, inelegantly styled "ecosystem nexus," proposes that any person who uses *any part* of a "contiguous ecosystem" adversely affected by a funded activity has standing even if the activity is lo-cated a great distance away. This approach, as the Court of Appeals correctly observed, is inconsistent with our opinion in *Lujan v. National Wildlife Feder-ation* (1990), which held that a plaintiff claiming injury from environmental damage must use the area affected by the challenged activity and not an area roughly "in the vicinity" of it. . . . To say that the Act protects ecosystems is not to say that the Act creates (if it were possible) rights of action in persons who have not been injured in fact, that is, persons who use portions of an ecosystem not perceptibly affected by the unlawful action in question.

Respondents' other theories are called, alas, the "animal nexus" approach, whereby anyone who has an interest in studying or seeing the endangered ani-mals anywhere on the globe has standing; and the "vocational nexus" approach, under which anyone with a professional interest in such animals can sue. Under these theories, anyone who goes to see Asian elephants in the Bronx Zoo, and anyone who is a keeper of Asian elephants in the Bronx Zoo, has standing to sue because the Director of the Agency for International Development (AID) did not consult with the Secretary regarding the AID-funded project in Sri Lanka. This is beyond all reason. Standing is not "an ingenious academic exer-cise in the conceivable," but as we have said requires, at the summary judgment stage, a factual showing of perceptible harm. It is clear that the person who observes or works with a particular animal threatened by a federal decision is facing perceptible harm, since the very subject of his interest will no longer exist. It is even plausible—though it goes to the outermost limit of plausibility—to think that a person who observes or works with animals of a particular species in the very area of the world where that species is threatened by a federal decision is facing such harm, since some animals that might have been the subject of his interest will no longer exist. It goes beyond the limit, however, and into pure speculation and fantasy, to say that anyone who observes or works with an endangered species, anywhere in the world, is appreciably harmed by a single project affecting some portion of that species with which he has no more specific connection.

B

Besides failing to show injury, respondents failed to demonstrate redressability. Instead of attacking the separate decisions to fund particular projects allegedly causing them harm, respondents chose to challenge a more generalized level of Government action (rules regarding consultation), the invalidation of which would affect all overseas projects. This programmatic approach has obvious practical advantages, but also obvious difficulties insofar as proof of causation or redressability is concerned. . . .

The most obvious problem in the present case is redressability. Since the agencies funding the projects were not parties to the case, the District Court could accord relief only against the Secretary: He could be ordered to revise his regulation to require consultation for foreign projects. But this would not remedy respondents' alleged injury unless the funding agencies were bound by the Secretary's regulation, which is very much an open question. . . . When the Secretary promulgated the regulation at issue here, he thought it was binding on the agencies. The Solicitor General, however, has repudiated that position here, and the agencies themselves apparently deny the Secretary's authority. . . .

A further impediment to redressability is the fact that the agencies generally supply only a fraction of the funding for a foreign project. AID, for example, has provided less than 10% of the funding for the Mahaweli project. Respondents have produced nothing to indicate that the projects they have named will either be suspended, or do less harm to listed species, if that fraction is eliminated. [I]t is entirely conjectural whether the nonagency activity that affects respondents will be altered or affected by the agency activity they seek to achieve. There is no standing.

IV

The Court of Appeals found that respondents had standing for an additional reason: because they had suffered a "procedural injury." The so-called "citizen-suit" provision of the ESA provides, in pertinent part, that "any person may commence a civil suit on his own behalf . . . to enjoin any person, including the United States . . . who is alleged to be in violation of any provision of this chapter." 16 U.S.C. § 1540(g). The court held that, because § 7(a)(2) requires interagency consultation, the citizen-suit provision creates a "procedural righ[t]" to consultation in all "persons"—so that *anyone* can file suit in federal court to challenge the Secretary's (or presumably any other official's) failure to follow the assertedly correct consultative procedure, notwithstanding his or her inability to allege any discrete injury flowing from that failure.

To understand the remarkable nature of this holding one must be clear about what it does *not* rest upon: This is not a case where plaintiffs are seeking to enforce a procedural requirement the disregard of which could impair a separate concrete interest of theirs (*e.g.,* the procedural requirement for a hearing prior to denial of their license application, or the procedural requirement for an environmental impact statement before a federal facility is constructed next door to them).[7] Nor is it simply a case where concrete injury has been suffered by many persons, as in mass fraud or mass tort situations. Nor, finally, is it the unusual case in which Congress has created a concrete private interest in the outcome of a suit against a private party for the government's benefit, by providing a cash bounty for the victorious plaintiff. Rather, the court held that the injury-in-fact requirement had been satisfied by congressional conferral upon *all* persons of an abstract, self-contained, noninstrumental "right" to have the Executive observe the procedures required by law. We reject this view.

We have consistently held that a plaintiff raising only a generally available grievance about government—claiming only harm to his and every citizen's interest in proper application of the Constitution and laws, and seeking relief that

---

[7] There is this much truth to the assertion that "procedural rights" are special: The person who has been accorded a procedural right to protect his concrete interests can assert that right without meeting all the normal standards for redressability and immediacy. Thus, under our case law, one living adjacent to the site for proposed construction of a federally licensed dam has standing to challenge the licensing agency's failure to prepare an environmental impact statement, even though he cannot establish with any certainty that the statement will cause the license to be withheld or altered, and even though the dam will not be completed for many years. (That is why we do not rely, in the present case, upon the Government's argument that, even if the other agencies were obliged to consult with the Secretary, they might not have followed his advice.) What respondents' "procedural rights" argument seeks, however, is quite different from this: standing for persons who have no concrete interests affected—persons who live (and propose to live) at the other end of the country from the dam.

no more directly and tangibly benefits him than it does the public at large—does not state an Article III case or controversy. For example, in *Fairchild v. Hughes* (1922), we dismissed a suit challenging the propriety of the process by which the Nineteenth Amendment was ratified. Justice Brandeis wrote for the Court:

> [This is] not a case within the meaning of . . . Article III. . . . Plaintiff has [asserted] only the right, possessed by every citizen, to require that the Government be administered according to law and that the public moneys be not wasted. Obviously this general right does not entitle a private citizen to institute in the federal courts a suit. . . .

. . . More recent cases are to the same effect. In *United States v. Richardson* (1974), we dismissed for lack of standing a taxpayer suit challenging the Government's failure to disclose the expenditures of the Central Intelligence Agency, in alleged violation of the constitutional requirement, Art. I, § 9, cl. 7, that "a regular Statement and Account of the Receipts and Expenditures of all public Money shall be published from time to time." We held that such a suit rested upon an impermissible "generalized grievance," and was inconsistent with "the framework of Article III" because "the impact on [plaintiff] is plainly undifferentiated and 'common to all members of the public.'" . . .

Whether the courts were to act on their own, or at the invitation of Congress, in ignoring the concrete injury requirement described in our cases, they would be discarding a principle fundamental to the separate and distinct constitutional role of the Third Branch—one of the essential elements that identifies those "Cases" and "Controversies" that are the business of the courts rather than of the political branches. "The province of the court," as Chief Justice Marshall said in *Marbury v. Madison* (1803), "is, solely, to decide on the rights of individuals." Vindicating the *public* interest (including the public interest in Government observance of the Constitution and laws) is the function of Congress and the Chief Executive.

The question presented here is whether the public interest in proper administration of the laws (specifically, in agencies' observance of a particular, statutorily prescribed procedure) can be converted into an individual right by a statute that denominates it as such, and that permits all citizens (or, for that matter, a subclass of citizens who suffer no distinctive concrete harm) to sue. If the concrete injury requirement has the separation-of-powers significance we have always said, the answer must be obvious: To permit Congress to convert the undifferentiated public interest in executive officers' compliance with the law into an "individual right" vindicable in the courts is to permit Congress to transfer from the President to the courts the Chief Executive's most important constitutional duty, to "take Care that the Laws be faithfully executed," Art. II, § 3. . . .

JUSTICE KENNEDY, with whom JUSTICE SOUTER joins, concurring in part and concurring in the judgment.

Although I agree with the essential parts of the Court's analysis, I write separately to make several observations.

I agree with the Court's conclusion in Part III-A that, on the record before us, respondents have failed to demonstrate that they themselves are "among the injured." *Sierra Club v. Morton* (1972). . . . While it may seem trivial to require that Mses. Kelly and Skilbred acquire airline tickets to the project sites or announce a date certain upon which they will return, this is not a case where it is reasonable to assume that the affiants will be using the sites on a regular basis, nor do the affiants claim to have visited the sites since the projects commenced. With respect to the Court's discussion of respondents' "ecosystem nexus," "animal nexus," and "vocational nexus" theories, I agree that on this record respondents' showing is insufficient to establish standing on any of these bases. I am not willing to foreclose the possibility, however, that in different circumstances a nexus theory similar to those proffered here might support a claim to standing. See *Japan Whaling Assn. v. American Cetacean Society* (1986) ("[R]espondents . . . undoubtedly have alleged a sufficient 'injury in fact' in that the whale watching and studying of their members will be adversely affected by continued whale harvesting").

In light of the conclusion that respondents have not demonstrated a concrete injury here sufficient to support standing under our precedents, I would not reach the issue of redressability that is discussed by the plurality in Part III-B.

I also join Part IV of the Court's opinion with the following observations. As Government programs and policies become more complex and far reaching, we must be sensitive to the articulation of new rights of action that do not have clear analogs in our common-law tradition. . . . In my view, Congress has the power to define injuries and articulate chains of causation that will give rise to a case or controversy where none existed before, and I do not read the Court's opinion to suggest a contrary view. In exercising this power, however, Congress must at the very least identify the injury it seeks to vindicate and relate the injury to the class of persons entitled to bring suit. The citizen-suit provision of the Endangered Species Act does not meet these minimal requirements, because while the statute purports to confer a right on "any person . . . to enjoin . . . the United States and any other governmental instrumentality or agency . . . who is alleged to be in violation of any provision of this chapter," it does not of its own force establish that there is an injury in "any person" by virtue of any "violation."

The Court's holding that there is an outer limit to the power of Congress to confer rights of action is a direct and necessary consequence of the case and controversy limitations found in Article III. [T]he party bringing suit must show that the action injures him in a concrete and personal way. This requirement is not just an empty formality. It preserves the vitality of the adversarial process by assuring both that the parties before the court have an actual, as opposed to professed, stake in the outcome, and that "the legal questions presented . . . will be resolved, not in the rarified atmosphere of a debating society, but in a concrete factual context conducive to a realistic appreciation of the consequences of judicial action." In addition, the requirement of concrete injury confines the Judicial Branch to its proper, limited role in the constitutional framework of Government. . . .

With these observations, I concur in Parts I, II, III-A, and IV of the Court's opinion and in the judgment of the Court. . . .

Justice Stevens concurred in the judgment in *Lujan* because he agreed with the Government on the merits that § 7(a)(2) does not apply to activities in foreign countries. On the standing question, he believed that the Court should not "demean the importance of the interest that particular individuals may have in observing any species or its habitat" and that imminence "should be measured by the timing and likelihood of the threatened environmental harm," not by the time until an interested person might visit a habitat. He also believed the claimed harms were redressable, because agencies would presumably comply with an interpretation of § 7(a)(2).

Justice Blackmun, joined by Justice O'Connor, dissented. He believed that the Kelly and Skilbred affidavits were enough to avoid a summary ruling with respect to their interests. He disagreed with the plurality with respect to redressability on several grounds, among them that the respondents had raised a genuine issue of fact that federal agencies could mitigate harm that foreign projects would cause endangered species.

WORTH NOTING

City of Los Angeles v. Lyons

Supreme Court of the United States, 1983.
461 U.S. 95.

JUSTICE WHITE delivered the opinion of the Court.

The issue here is whether respondent Lyons satisfied the prerequisites for seeking injunctive relief in the federal district court.

I

This case began on February 7, 1977, when respondent, Adolph Lyons, filed a complaint for damages, injunction, and declaratory relief in the United States District Court for the Central District of California. The defendants were the City of Los Angeles and four of its police officers.

The complaint alleged that on October 6, 1976, at 2 a.m., Lyons was stopped by the defendant officers for a traffic or vehicle code violation and that although Lyons offered no resistance or threat whatsoever, the officers, without provocation or justification, seized Lyons and applied a "chokehold"—either the "bar arm control" hold or the "carotid-artery control" hold or both—rendering him unconscious and causing damage to his larynx.

Counts I through IV of the complaint sought damages against the officers and the City. Count V, with which we are principally concerned here, sought a preliminary and permanent injunction against the City barring the use of the control holds. That count alleged that the city's police officers, "pursuant to the authorization, instruction and encouragement of defendant City of Los Angeles, regularly and routinely apply these choke holds in innumerable situations where they are not threatened by the use of any deadly force whatsoever" . . . .

Lyons has failed to demonstrate a case or controversy with the City that would justify the equitable relief sought. Lyons' standing to seek the injunction requested depended on whether he was likely to suffer future injury from the use of the chokeholds by police officers. Count V of the complaint alleged the traffic stop and choking incident five months before. That Lyons may have been illegally choked by the police on October 6, 1976, while presumably affording Lyons standing to claim damages against the individual officers and perhaps against the City, does nothing to establish a real and immediate threat that he would again be stopped for a traffic violation, or for any other offense, by an officer or officers who would illegally choke him into unconsciousness without any provocation or resistance on his part. . . .

In order to establish an actual controversy in this case, Lyons would have had not only to allege that he would have another encounter with the police but also to make the incredible assertion either, (1) that *all* police officers in Los Angeles *always* choke any citizen with whom they happen to have an encounter, whether for the purpose of arrest, issuing a citation or for questioning or, (2) that the City ordered or authorized police officers to act in such manner. . . .[8]

[E]ven assuming that Lyons would again be stopped for a traffic or other violation in the reasonably near future, it is untenable to assert, and the complaint made no such allegation, that strangleholds are applied by the Los Angeles police to every citizen who is stopped or arrested regardless of the conduct of the person stopped. We cannot agree that the "odds" that Lyons would not only again be stopped for a traffic violation but would also be subjected to a choke-hold without any provocation whatsoever are sufficient to make out a federal case for equitable relief. We note that five months elapsed between October 6, 1976, and the filing of the complaint, yet there was no allegation of further unfortunate encounters between Lyons and the police. . . .

Nothing in [the City's] policy, contained in a Police Department manual, suggests that the chokeholds, or other kinds of force for that matter, are authorized absent some resistance or other provocation by the arrestee or other suspect. On the contrary, police officers were instructed to use chokeholds only when lesser degrees of force do not suffice and then only "to gain control of a suspect who is violently resisting the officer or trying to escape."

Our conclusion is that . . . the District Court was quite right in dismissing Count V. . . . Absent a sufficient likelihood that he will again be wronged in a similar way, Lyons is no more entitled to an injunction than any other citizen of Los Angeles; and a federal court may not entertain a claim by any or all citizens who no more than assert that certain practices of law enforcement officers are unconstitutional. This is not to suggest that such undifferentiated claims should not be taken seriously by local authorities. Indeed, the interest

---

[8]   As previously indicated, Lyons alleged that he feared he would be choked in any future encounter with the police. The reasonableness of Lyons' fear is dependent upon the likelihood of a recurrence of the allegedly unlawful conduct. It is the *reality* of the threat of repeated injury that is relevant to the standing inquiry, not the plaintiff's subjective apprehensions. The emotional consequences of a prior act simply are not a sufficient basis for an injunction absent a real and immediate threat of future injury by the defendant. Of course, emotional upset is a relevant consideration in a damages action.

of an alert and interested citizen is an essential element of an effective and fair government, whether on the local, state or national level.[10] A federal court, however, is not the proper forum to press such claims unless the requirements for entry and the prerequisites for injunctive relief are satisfied. . . .

[W]ithholding injunctive relief does not mean that the "federal law will exercise no deterrent effect in these circumstances." If Lyons has suffered an injury barred by the Federal Constitution, he has a remedy for damages under § 1983. Furthermore, those who deliberately deprive a citizen of his constitutional rights risk conviction under the federal criminal laws. Beyond these considerations the state courts need not impose the same standing or remedial requirements that govern federal court proceedings. The individual states may permit their courts to use injunctions to oversee the conduct of law enforcement authorities on a continuing basis. But this is not the role of a federal court absent far more justification than Lyons has proffered in this case.

The judgment of the Court of Appeals is accordingly reversed.

Justice Marshall, with whom Justice Brennan, Justice Blackmun and Justice Stevens join, dissenting.

The District Court found that the City of Los Angeles authorizes its police officers to apply life-threatening chokeholds to citizens who pose no threat of violence, and that respondent, Adolph Lyons, was subjected to such a chokehold. The Court today holds that a federal court is without power to enjoin the enforcement of the City's policy, no matter how flagrantly unconstitutional it may be. Since no one can show that he will be choked in the future, no one—not even a person who, like Lyons, has almost been choked to death—has standing to challenge the continuation of the policy. The City is free to continue the policy indefinitely as long as it is willing to pay damages for the injuries and deaths that result. I dissent from this unprecedented and unwarranted approach to standing. . . .

---

[10]   The City's Memorandum Suggesting a Question of Mootness informed the Court that the use of the control holds had become "a major civic controversy" and that in April and May of 1982 "a spirited, vigorous, and at times emotional debate" on the issue took place. The result was the current moratorium on the use of the holds.

I

A

Respondent Adolph Lyons is a 24-year-old Negro male who resides in Los Angeles. According to the uncontradicted evidence in the record, at about 2:30 A.M. on October 6, 1976, Lyons was pulled over to the curb by two officers of the Los Angeles Police Department (LAPD) for a traffic infraction because one of his taillights was burned out. The officers greeted him with drawn revolvers as he exited from his car. Lyons was told to face his car and spread his legs. He did so. He was then ordered to clasp his hands and put them on top of his head. He again complied. After one of the officers completed a pat-down search, Lyons dropped his hands, but was ordered to place them back above his head, and one of the officers grabbed Lyons' hands and slammed them onto his head. Lyons complained about the pain caused by the ring of keys he was holding in his hand. Within five to ten seconds, the officer began to choke Lyons by applying a forearm against his throat. As Lyons struggled for air, the officer handcuffed him, but continued to apply the chokehold until he blacked out. When Lyons regained consciousness, he was lying face down on the ground, choking, gasping for air, and spitting up blood and dirt. He had urinated and defecated. He was issued a traffic citation and released. . . .

B

Although the City instructs its officers that use of a chokehold does not constitute deadly force, since 1975 no less than 16 persons have died following the use of a chokehold by an LAPD police officer. Twelve have been Negro males.[3] . . .

It is undisputed that chokeholds pose a high and unpredictable risk of serious injury or death. Chokeholds are intended to bring a subject under control by causing pain and rendering him unconscious. Depending on the position of the officer's arm and the force applied, the victim's voluntary or involuntary reaction, and his state of health, an officer may inadvertently crush the victim's larynx, trachea, or thyroid. The result may be death caused by either cardiac arrest or asphyxiation. An LAPD officer described the reaction of a person to being choked as "do[ing] the chicken," in reference apparently to the reactions

---

[3]   Thus in a City where Negro males constitute 9% of the population, they have accounted for 75% of the deaths resulting from the use of chokeholds. In addition to his other allegations, Lyons alleged racial discrimination in violation of the Equal Protection Clause of the Fourteenth Amendment. . . .

of a chicken when its neck is wrung. The victim experiences extreme pain. His face turns blue as he is deprived of oxygen, he goes into spasmodic convulsions, his eyes roll back, his body wriggles, his feet kick up and down, and his arms move about wildly.

Although there has been no occasion to determine the precise contours of the City's chokehold policy, the evidence submitted to the District Court provides some indications. LAPD training officer Terry Speer testified that an officer is authorized to deploy a chokehold whenever he *"feels* that there's about to be a bodily attack made on him." (Emphasis added.) A training bulletin states that "[c]ontrol holds . . . allow officers to subdue *any* resistance by the suspects." (Emphasis added.) In the proceedings below the City characterized its own policy as authorizing the use of chokeholds "to gain control of a suspect who is violently resisting the officer *or trying to escape,"* to "subdue *any* resistance by suspects," and to permit an officer, "where . . . resisted, but *not necessarily threatened with serious bodily harm or death,* . . . to subdue a suspect who forcibly resists an officer." (Emphasis added.)

The training given LAPD officers provides additional revealing evidence of the City's chokehold policy. Officer Speer testified that in instructing officers concerning the use of force, the LAPD does not distinguish between felony and misdemeanor suspects. Moreover, the officers are taught to maintain the chokehold until the suspect goes limp, despite substantial evidence that the application of a chokehold invariably induces a "flight or flee" syndrome, producing an *involuntary* struggle by the victim which can easily be misinterpreted by the officer as willful resistance that must be overcome by prolonging the chokehold and increasing the force applied. In addition, officers are instructed that the chokeholds can be safely deployed for up to three or four minutes. Robert Jarvis, the City's expert who has taught at the Los Angeles Police Academy for the past twelve years, admitted that officers are never told that the bar-arm control can cause death if applied for just two seconds. Of the nine deaths for which evidence was submitted to the District Court, the average duration of the choke where specified was approximately 40 seconds. . . .

III

Since Lyons' claim for damages plainly gives him standing, and since the success of that claim depends upon a demonstration that the City's chokehold policy is unconstitutional, it is beyond dispute that Lyons has properly invoked the District Court's authority to adjudicate the constitutionality of the City's chokehold policy. The dispute concerning the constitutionality of that policy plainly presents a "case or controversy" under Article III. The Court nevertheless holds that a federal court has no power under Article III to adjudicate Lyons' request, in the same lawsuit, for injunctive relief with respect to that very policy. . . .

By fragmenting the standing inquiry and imposing a separate standing hurdle with respect to each form of relief sought, the decision today departs significantly from this Court's traditional conception of the standing requirement and of the remedial powers of the federal courts. We have never required more than that a plaintiff have standing to litigate a claim. Whether he will be entitled to obtain particular forms of relief should he prevail has never been understood to be an issue of standing. In determining whether a plaintiff has standing, we have always focused on his personal stake in the outcome of the controversy, not on the issues sought to be litigated or the "precise nature of the relief sought." . . .

VI

The Court's decision removes an entire class of constitutional violations from the equitable powers of a federal court. It immunizes from prospective equitable relief any policy that authorizes persistent deprivations of constitutional rights as long as no individual can establish with substantial certainty that he will be injured, or injured again, in the future. . . . Under the view expressed by the majority today, if the police adopt a policy of "shoot to kill," or a policy of shooting one out of ten suspects, the federal courts will be powerless to enjoin its continuation. The federal judicial power is now limited to levying a toll for such a systematic constitutional violation.

Massachusetts v. Environmental Protection Agency

Supreme Court of the United States, 2007.
549 U.S. 497.

JUSTICE STEVENS delivered the opinion of the Court.

. . . Calling global warming "the most pressing environmental challenge of our time," a group of States, local governments, and private organizations alleged in a petition for certiorari that the Environmental Protection Agency

(EPA) has abdicated its responsibility under the Clean Air Act to regulate the emissions of four greenhouse gases, including carbon dioxide. Specifically, petitioners asked us to answer two questions concerning the meaning of § 202(a)(1) of the Act: whether EPA has the statutory authority to regulate greenhouse gas emissions from new motor vehicles; and if so, whether its stated reasons for refusing to do so are consistent with the statute. . . .

I

Section 202(a)(1) of the Clean Air Act . . . provides:

> The [EPA] Administrator shall by regulation prescribe (and from time to time revise) in accordance with the provisions of this section, standards applicable to the emission of any air pollutant from any class or classes of new motor vehicles or new motor vehicle engines, which in his judgment cause, or contribute to, air pollution which may reasonably be anticipated to endanger public health or welfare. . . .

The Act defines "air pollutant" to include "any air pollution agent or combination of such agents, including any physical, chemical, biological, radioactive . . . substance or matter which is emitted into or otherwise enters the ambient air." "Welfare" is also defined broadly: among other things, it includes "effects on . . . weather . . . and climate." . . .

II

On October 20, 1999, a group of 19 private organizations filed a rulemaking petition asking EPA to regulate "greenhouse gas emissions from new motor vehicles under § 202 of the Clean Air Act." [In response to the petition,] the White House sought "assistance in identifying the areas in the science of climate change where there are the greatest certainties and uncertainties" from the National Research Council, asking for a response "as soon as possible." The result was a 2001 report [from the NRC] conclud[ing] that "[g]reenhouse gases are accumulating in Earth's atmosphere as a result of human activities, causing surface air temperatures and subsurface ocean temperatures to rise. Temperatures are, in fact, rising."

On September 8, 2003, EPA entered an order denying the rulemaking petition. The Agency gave two reasons for its decision: [First,] EPA believed

. . . that greenhouse gases cannot be "air pollutants" within the meaning of the Act. . . . [Second, e]ven assuming that it had authority over greenhouse gases, EPA explained in detail why it would refuse to exercise that authority. The Agency began by recognizing that the concentration of greenhouse gases has dramatically increased as a result of human activities, and acknowledged the attendant increase in global surface air temperatures. EPA nevertheless gave controlling importance to the NRC Report's statement that a causal link between the two " 'cannot be unequivocally established.' " Given that residual uncertainty, EPA concluded that regulating greenhouse gas emissions would be unwise. . . .

Petitioners, now joined by intervenor States and local governments, sought review of EPA's order in the United States Court of Appeals for the District of Columbia Circuit. . . .

IV

Article III of the Constitution limits federal-court jurisdiction to "Cases" and "Controversies." Those two words confine "the business of federal courts to questions presented in an adversary context and in a form historically viewed as capable of resolution through the judicial process." *Flast v. Cohen* (1968). It is therefore familiar learning that no justiciable "controversy" exists when parties seek adjudication of a political question, *Luther v. Borden* (1849), when they ask for an advisory opinion, *Hayburn's Case* (1792), or when the question sought to be adjudicated has been mooted by subsequent developments, *California v. San Pablo & Tulare R. Co.* (1893). This case suffers from none of these defects.

The parties' dispute turns on the proper construction of a congressional statute, a question eminently suitable to resolution in federal court. Congress has moreover authorized this type of challenge to EPA action. See 42 U.S.C. § 7607(b) [(authorizing judicial review of agency action that has been "unlawfully withheld")]. That authorization is of critical importance to the standing inquiry: "Congress has the power to define injuries and articulate chains of causation that will give rise to a case or controversy where none existed before." *Lujan* (Kennedy, J., concurring in part and concurring in judgment). "In exercising this power, however, Congress must at the very least identify the injury it seeks to vindicate and relate the injury to the class of persons entitled to bring suit." *Ibid.* We will not, therefore, "entertain citizen suits to vindicate the public's nonconcrete interest in the proper administration of the laws." *Id.*

[Margin note: ESA says general injury.]

EPA maintains that because greenhouse gas emissions inflict widespread harm, the doctrine of standing presents an insuperable jurisdictional obstacle. We do not agree. At bottom, "the gist of the question of standing" is whether petitioners have "such a personal stake in the outcome of the controversy as to assure that concrete adverseness which sharpens the presentation of issues upon which the court so largely depends for illumination." *Baker v. Carr* (1962). . . .

[Margin note: Concrete stake in issue. Rule]

To ensure the proper adversarial presentation, *Lujan* holds that a litigant must demonstrate that it has suffered a concrete and particularized injury that is either actual or imminent, that the injury is fairly traceable to the defendant, and that it is likely that a favorable decision will redress that injury. However, a litigant to whom Congress has "accorded a procedural right to protect his concrete interests,"—here, the right to challenge agency action unlawfully withheld—"can assert that right without meeting all the normal standards for redressability and immediacy." When a litigant is vested with a procedural right, that litigant has standing if there is some possibility that the requested relief will prompt the injury-causing party to reconsider the decision that allegedly harmed the litigant.

[Margin note: Rule Lujan. Exception → vested w/ procedural right creates standing if there is some possibility that relief will cause injuring party to reconsider decision that caused harm]

Only one of the petitioners needs to have standing to permit us to consider the petition for review. See *Rumsfeld v. Forum for Academic and Institutional Rights, Inc.* (2006). We stress here . . . the special position and interest of Massachusetts. It is of considerable relevance that the party seeking review here is a sovereign State and not, as it was in *Lujan*, a private individual.

Well before the creation of the modern administrative state, we recognized that States are not normal litigants for the purposes of invoking federal jurisdiction. As Justice Holmes explained in *Georgia v. Tennessee Copper Co.* (1907), a case in which Georgia sought to protect its citizens from air pollution originating outside its borders:

[Margin note: Injury to MA → pollution to their territory]

> . . . This is a suit by a State for an injury to it in its capacity of *quasi*-sovereign. In that capacity the State has an interest independent of and behind the titles of its citizens, in all the earth and air within its domain. It has the last word as to whether its mountains shall be stripped of their forests and its inhabitants shall breathe pure air.

Just as Georgia's independent interest "in all the earth and air within its domain" supported federal jurisdiction a century ago, so too does Massachusetts' well-founded desire to preserve its sovereign territory today. Cf. *Alden v. Maine* (1999) (observing that in the federal system, the States "are not relegated to the role of mere provinces or political corporations, but retain the dignity, though not the full authority, of sovereignty"). That Massachusetts does in fact own a great deal of the "territory alleged to be affected" only reinforces the conclusion that its stake in the outcome of this case is sufficiently concrete to warrant the exercise of federal judicial power.

. . . Congress has moreover recognized a concomitant procedural right to challenge the rejection of its rulemaking petition as arbitrary and capricious. § 7607(b)(1). Given that procedural right and Massachusetts' stake in protecting its quasi-sovereign interests, the Commonwealth is entitled to special solicitude in our standing analysis.

With that in mind, it is clear that petitioners' submissions as they pertain to Massachusetts have satisfied the most demanding standards of the adversarial process. EPA's steadfast refusal to regulate greenhouse gas emissions presents a risk of harm to Massachusetts that is both "actual" and "imminent." *Lujan*. There is, moreover, a "substantial likelihood that the judicial relief requested" will prompt EPA to take steps to reduce that risk. *Duke Power Co. v. Carolina Environmental Study Group, Inc.* (1978).

The Injury

The harms associated with climate change are serious and well recognized. . . . That these climate-change risks are "widely shared" does not minimize Massachusetts' interest in the outcome of this litigation. See *Federal Election Comm'n v. Akins* (1998) ("[W]here a harm is concrete, though widely shared, the Court has found 'injury in fact'"). According to petitioners' unchallenged affidavits, global sea levels rose somewhere between 10 and 20 centimeters over the 20th century as a result of global warming. These rising seas have already begun to swallow Massachusetts' coastal land. Because the Commonwealth "owns a substantial portion of the state's coastal property," it has alleged a particularized injury in its capacity as a landowner. The severity of that injury will only increase over the course of the next century: If sea levels continue to rise as predicted, one Massachusetts official believes that a significant fraction of coastal property will be "either permanently lost through inundation or temporarily lost through periodic storm surge and flooding events." Remediation costs alone, petitioners allege, could run well into the hundreds of millions of dollars.

Causation

EPA does not dispute the existence of a causal connection between man-made greenhouse gas emissions and global warming. At a minimum, therefore, EPA's refusal to regulate such emissions "contributes" to Massachusetts' injuries.

EPA nevertheless maintains that its decision not to regulate greenhouse gas emissions from new motor vehicles contributes so insignificantly to petitioners' injuries that the Agency cannot be haled into federal court to answer for them. For the same reason, EPA does not believe that any realistic possibility exists that the relief petitioners seek would mitigate global climate change and remedy their injuries. That is especially so because predicted increases in greenhouse gas emissions from developing nations, particularly China and India, are likely to offset any marginal domestic decrease.

But EPA overstates its case. Its argument rests on the erroneous assumption that a small incremental step, because it is incremental, can never be attacked in a federal judicial forum. Yet accepting that premise would doom most challenges to regulatory action. Agencies, like legislatures, do not generally resolve massive problems in one fell regulatory swoop. See *Williamson v. Lee Optical of Okla., Inc.* (1955). They instead whittle away at them over time, refining their preferred approach as circumstances change and as they develop a more nuanced understanding of how best to proceed. That a first step might be tentative does not by itself support the notion that federal courts lack jurisdiction to determine whether that step conforms to law.

And reducing domestic automobile emissions is hardly a tentative step. Even leaving aside the other greenhouse gases, the United States transportation sector emits an enormous quantity of carbon dioxide into the atmosphere—according to [one] affidavit, more than 1.7 billion metric tons in 1999 alone. That accounts for more than 6% of worldwide carbon dioxide emissions. To put this in perspective: Considering just emissions from the transportation sector, which represent less than one-third of this country's total carbon dioxide emissions, the United States would still rank as the third-largest emitter of carbon dioxide in the world, outpaced only by the European Union and China. Judged by any standard, U.S. motor-vehicle emissions make a meaningful contribution to greenhouse gas concentrations and hence, according to petitioners, to global warming.

The Remedy

While it may be true that regulating motor-vehicle emissions will not by itself *reverse* global warming, it by no means follows that we lack jurisdiction to decide whether EPA has a duty to take steps to *slow* or *reduce* it. . . . A reduction in domestic emissions would slow the pace of global emissions increases, no matter what happens elsewhere. . . .

In sum—at least according to petitioners' uncontested affidavits—the rise in sea levels associated with global warming has already harmed and will continue to harm Massachusetts. The risk of catastrophic harm, though remote, is nevertheless real. That risk would be reduced to some extent if petitioners received the relief they seek. We therefore hold that petitioners have standing to challenge EPA's denial of their rulemaking petition. . . .

WORTH NOTING

On the merits, the Court concluded that the EPA had not offered a "reasoned explanation" for refusing to decide whether greenhouse gases contribute to climate change," and so it remanded the case to the agency for reconsideration.

CHIEF JUSTICE ROBERTS, with whom JUSTICE SCALIA, JUSTICE THOMAS, and JUSTICE ALITO join, dissenting.

. . . I would reject these challenges as nonjusticiable. Such a conclusion involves no judgment on whether global warming exists, what causes it, or the extent of the problem. Nor does it render petitioners without recourse. This Court's standing jurisprudence simply recognizes that redress of grievances of the sort at issue here "is the function of Congress and the Chief Executive," not the federal courts. *Lujan v. Defenders of Wildlife* (1992). . . .

I

. . . [P]etitioners bear the burden of alleging an injury that is fairly traceable to the Environmental Protection Agency's failure to promulgate new motor vehicle greenhouse gas emission standards, and that is likely to be redressed by the prospective issuance of such standards.

Before determining whether petitioners can meet this familiar test, however, the Court changes the rules. It asserts that "States are not normal litigants for the purposes of invoking federal jurisdiction," and that given "Massachusetts' stake in protecting its quasi-sovereign interests, the Commonwealth is entitled to *special solicitude* in our standing analysis." Relaxing Article III standing requirements because asserted injuries are pressed by a State, however, has no basis in our jurisprudence, and support for any such "special solicitude" is conspicuously absent from the Court's opinion. . . . What is more, the Court's reasoning falters on its own terms. The Court asserts that Massachusetts is entitled to "special solicitude" due to its "quasi-sovereign interests," but then applies our Article III standing test to the asserted injury of the Commonwealth's loss of coastal property. See *ante* (concluding that Massachusetts "has alleged a particularized injury *in its capacity as a landowner*"). . . .

II

. . . When the Court actually applies the three-part test, it focuses . . . on the Commonwealth's asserted loss of coastal land as the injury in fact. If petitioners rely on loss of land as the Article III injury, however, they must ground the rest of the standing analysis in that specific injury. That alleged injury must be "concrete and particularized" and "distinct and palpable." Central to this concept of "particularized" injury is the requirement that a plaintiff be affected in a "personal and individual way," and seek relief that "directly and tangibly benefits him" in a manner distinct from its impact on "the public at large." . . .

The very concept of global warming seems inconsistent with this particularization requirement. Global warming is a phenomenon "harmful to humanity at large," and the redress petitioners seek is focused no more on them than on the public generally—it is literally to change the atmosphere around the world.

If petitioners' particularized injury is loss of coastal land, it is also that injury that must be "actual or imminent, not conjectural or hypothetical," "real and immediate," and "certainly impending."

As to "actual" injury, the Court observes that "global sea levels rose somewhere between 10 and 20 centimeters over the 20th century as a result of global warming" and that "[t]hese rising seas have already begun to swallow Massachusetts' coastal land." [One] of petitioners' declarations . . . states that "a rise in sea level due to climate change is occurring on the coast of Massachusetts, in the metropolitan Boston area," but [offers] no elaboration. [A]side from [that] single conclusory statement, there is nothing in petitioners' 43 standing declarations and accompanying exhibits to support an inference of actual loss of Massachusetts coastal land from 20th-century global sea level increases. It is pure conjecture.

The Court's attempts to identify "imminent" or "certainly impending" loss of Massachusetts coastal land fares no better. One of petitioners' declarants predicts global warming will cause sea level to rise by 20 to 70 centimeters *by the year 2100.* . . . But . . . accepting a century-long time horizon and a series of compounded estimates renders requirements of imminence and immediacy utterly toothless. "Allegations of possible future injury do not satisfy the requirements of Art. III. A threatened injury must be *certainly impending* to constitute injury in fact." *Whitmore v. Arkansas* (1990).

III

Petitioners' reliance on Massachusetts's loss of coastal land as their injury in fact for standing purposes creates insurmountable problems for them with respect to causation and redressability. To establish standing, petitioners must show a causal connection between that specific injury and the lack of new motor vehicle greenhouse gas emission standards, and that the promulgation of such standards would likely redress that injury. As is often the case, the questions of causation and redressability overlap. And importantly, when a party is challenging the Government's allegedly unlawful regulation, or lack of regulation, of a third party, satisfying the causation and redressability requirements becomes "substantially more difficult." . . .

The Court ignores the complexities of global warming, and does so by now disregarding the "particularized" injury it relied on in step one, and using the dire nature of global warming itself as a bootstrap for finding causation and redressability. First, it is important to recognize the extent of the emissions at issue here. Because local greenhouse gas emissions disperse throughout the atmosphere and remain there for anywhere from 50 to 200 years, it is global emissions data that are relevant. According to one of petitioners' declarations, domestic motor vehicles contribute about 6 percent of global carbon dioxide emissions and 4 percent of global greenhouse gas emissions. The amount of global emissions at issue here is smaller still; § 202(a)(1) of the Clean Air Act covers only *new* motor vehicles and *new* motor vehicle engines, so petitioners' desired emission standards might reduce only a fraction of 4 percent of global emissions.

This gets us only to the relevant greenhouse gas emissions; linking them to global warming and ultimately to petitioners' alleged injuries next requires consideration of further complexities. As EPA explained in its denial of petitioners' request for rulemaking, predicting future climate change necessarily involves a complex web of economic and physical factors including: our ability to predict future global anthropogenic emissions of [greenhouse gases] and aerosols; the fate of these emissions once they enter the atmosphere (e.g., what percentage are absorbed by vegetation or are taken up by the oceans); the impact of those emissions that remain in the atmosphere on the radiative properties of the atmosphere; changes in critically important climate feedbacks (e.g., changes in cloud cover and ocean circulation); changes in temperature characteristics (e.g., average temperatures, shifts in daytime and evening temperatures); changes in other climatic parameters (e.g., shifts in precipitation, storms); and ultimately the impact of such changes on human health and welfare (e.g., increases or decreases in agricultural productivity, human health impacts).

Petitioners are never able to trace their alleged injuries back through this complex web to the fractional amount of global emissions that might have been limited with EPA standards. In light of the bit-part domestic new motor vehicle greenhouse gas emissions have played in what petitioners describe as a 150-year global phenomenon, and the myriad additional factors bearing on petitioners' alleged injury—the loss of Massachusetts coastal land—the connection is far too speculative to establish causation.

IV

Redressability is even more problematic. To the tenuous link between petitioners' alleged injury and the indeterminate fractional domestic emissions at issue here, add the fact that petitioners cannot meaningfully predict what will come of the 80 percent of global greenhouse gas emissions that originate outside the United States. . . . No matter, the Court reasons, because *any* decrease in domestic emissions will "slow the pace of global emissions increases, no matter what happens elsewhere." Every little bit helps, so Massachusetts can sue over any little bit.

The Court's sleight of hand is in failing to link up the different elements of the three-part standing test. What must be *likely* to be redressed is the particular injury in fact. The injury the Court looks to is the asserted loss of land. The Court contends that regulating domestic motor vehicle emissions will reduce carbon dioxide in the atmosphere, *and therefore* redress Massachusetts's injury. But even if regulation *does* reduce emissions—to some indeterminate degree, given events elsewhere in the world—the Court never explains why that makes it *likely* that the injury in fact—the loss of land—will be redressed. Schoolchildren know that a kingdom might be lost "all for the want of a horse-shoe nail," but "likely" redressability is a different matter. The realities make it pure conjecture to suppose that EPA regulation of new automobile emissions will *likely* prevent the loss of Massachusetts coastal land.

V

. . . The constitutional role of the courts . . . is to decide concrete cases—not to serve as a convenient forum for policy debates. . . . Perhaps the Court recognizes as much. How else to explain its need to devise a new doctrine of state standing to support its result? The good news is that the Court's "special solicitude" for Massachusetts limits the future applicability of the diluted standing requirements applied in this case. The bad news is that the Court's self-professed relaxation of those Article III requirements has caused us to transgress "the proper—and properly limited—role of the courts in a democratic society."

WORTH NOTING Justice Scalia—joined by the Chief Justice, Justice Thomas, and Justice Alito—wrote a separate dissent on the merits.

I respectfully dissent.

3. Ripeness and Mootness

We won't spend much time on ripeness and mootness, but they are sometimes crucial. Start by contrasting them to standing doctrine. The question of standing focuses on the *plaintiff.* To ask whether there is standing in a case is to ask whether the person challenging the government's action has suffered the right kind of injury. The doctrines of ripeness and mootness, by contrast, focus on the *claim.* If a claim is unripe, that means that it is too early in the nascent dispute for the court to be sure that a decision is necessary or even meaningfully possible. If the claim is moot, that means that it is now too late for the court's decision to make any difference, typically because the facts have changed since the claim was filed.

For an example of a ripeness problem, imagine that Brother and Sister are quarreling. Sister says, "I'm thinking about doing something that you're *really* going to hate." Brother runs to their parents to ask for help. They roll their eyes and say, "We don't even know what she has in mind, let alone whether there's any chance she'd actually do it." This is essentially an objection that Brother's claim isn't ripe. The parents just don't have enough information about the threat to be able to formulate a useful order without a bunch of guesswork. Until the threat to Brother's interests comes into sharper focus, all they can really say is: "Don't do anything wrong." To be clear, many parents might be totally comfortable saying exactly that! But courts are a different story. The judiciary just isn't in the business of issuing such general admonishments in the abstract without much more concrete background on which to rule, and without knowing whether there will in fact be a "case or controversy" that will require resolution.

A typical real-world example of ripeness analysis comes when the government announces a policy plan or a legal interpretation, and someone files suit to challenge it before the implications of that announcement show any sign of being applied to the challenger. Compare, *e.g.*, *National Park Hospitality Assoc. v. Dep't of Interior* (2003) (newly announced legal interpretation unripe before the agency applies it to anyone) and *Poe v. Ullman* (1961) (pre-enforcement challenge to criminal statute unripe where the statute has virtually never been enforced) with, *e.g.*, *Steffel v. Thompson* (1974) (pre-enforcement challenge to ban on distributing pamphlets was ripe).

Now mootness. Brother and Sister are quarreling again. This time, Brother grabs a book that Sister will need for homework later that evening. Sister runs to their parents, yelling "Make him give it back!" While she's looking for them, Brother puts the book back on her desk. By the time her parents know what's going on, she already has it back. Brother has already done exactly what Sister wants them to *make* him do. So they throw up their hands and say, "Honestly. He already gave it back. There's nothing for us to do!" This is basically a mootness instinct.

One way mootness arises in the real world is when a regulation gets rewritten during the pendency of a lawsuit challenging it. *Cf. City of Mesquite v. Aladdin's Castle Inc.* (1982) (repealing a law does not moot the challenge to that law where the repeal is accompanied by a statement of intent to re-enact it). Courts often ask whether new developments like these are really just "voluntary cessation" of the alleged violation. If the answer is yes, then the litigation may not be considered moot, and the plaintiff may continue to seek injunctive relief. Compare *Princeton University v. Schmid* (1982) (case mooted by defendant's repeal of the challenged regulations) and *Preiser v. Newkirk* (1975) (inmate's challenge to his transfer to a maximum security prison mooted by his transfer back to a lower security facility) with *Friends of the Earth, Inc. v. Laidlaw Environmental Services* (2000) (rejecting mootness defense even though the defendant had stopped the challenged activity, because defendant still held a license for the activity). If the plaintiff has already asserted a viable damages claim, the court may allow that claim to proceed even though injunctive relief is no longer on the table. *Cf. New York State Rifle & Pistol Assn., Inc. v. City of New York* (2020). Also, courts sometimes apply an exception to mootness doctrine if a constitutional violation is "capable of repetition, yet evading review." *E.g. Roe v. Wade* (1973) (challenge to abortion restrictions was not moot even though plaintiff was no longer pregnant, because a "pregnancy will [typically] come to term before the usual appellate process is complete").

For Discussion

(1) A white plaintiff contends that Davis State Medical School, while purporting to operate a valid "holistic" admissions program, has in fact set aside 16 of the 100 seats in its entering class for applicants belonging to designated racial minorities; under prevailing constitutional doctrine, this would be invalid. (For more on the substantive equal protection merits, see *Regents of the University of California v. Bakke* (1978), p. 1113.) Should a federal court entertain the action if the plaintiff is

   (a) a journalist with no intention of going to medical school?

   (b) a high school junior who intends to go to medical school?

   (c) a graduate of a higher-ranking medical school, whose application to Davis was rejected?

   (d) an applicant to the current class, whose test scores indicate that he would have no chance of admission even if he qualified for the set-aside?

   (e) a rejected applicant to the current class, whose test scores suggest that he would have been admitted if he qualified for the set-aside, but who presumably would not have been admitted if there had been no set-aside?

   (f) the applicant ranking highest on the wait list who was not admitted to the current class?

(2) Suppose that the plaintiff is the one described above in 1(f), that the court does take jurisdiction, and that it enters a preliminary injunction requiring the medical school to admit him. After the plaintiff begins his last semester,

while the case is still in litigation, the school announces that even if it wins the litigation it will allow him to graduate. What then? See *DeFunis v. Odegaard* (1974).

D. State Action

COURSE THEME For the most part, the restrictions of the Constitution apply only to governments, state or federal, or to individuals who play a role in government. That is, the Constitution does not tell private persons what they must or may not do; so far as it is concerned, for example, a private citizen is free to discriminate on racial grounds in whom she invites to dinner or allows to room in her house or even makes retail sales to. We speak of this principle by referring to a "state action" limit on the scope of constitutional prohibitions. See *The Civil Rights Cases* (1883), presented at pp. 608–612. The one apparent exception is the Thirteenth Amendment, which uses notably absolute language in proclaiming that "[n]either slavery nor involuntary servitude . . . shall exist within the United States." See *Clyatt v. United States* (1905) ("The prohibitions of the 14th and 15th Amendments are largely upon the acts of the states; but the 13th Amendment names no party or authority, but simply forbids slavery and involuntary servitude.").

The state action requirement is often pretty easy to analyze: Either the government did it, or it didn't. But sometimes the question gets more complicated. Contentious cases often follow this pattern: A private entity engages in behavior that would violate the Constitution if the state were to take it, and either the private entity exercises such comprehensive control that it resembles the state, or its conduct is in some way facilitated by the state. Should that facilitation be considered state action sufficient to create a violation? Should the entity be deemed to be a state actor with respect to the conduct at issue?

Consider, for example, the classic case of *Burton v. Wilmington Parking Authority* (1961). The city of Wilmington, Delaware set up and provided some financing for a tax-exempt corporation, the Wilmington Parking Authority, for the purpose of operating parking facilities in the city. On the ground floor of a garage owned by the Authority was a restaurant, the Eagle Coffee Shoppe. The restaurant was privately owned; it was merely a tenant of the Authority, which provided heating, gas, and water services and maintained the property. The restaurant refused to serve African-Americans. Burton, a would-be customer who was refused service because of his race, sued the restaurant and the

Authority for injunctive and declaratory relief under the Fourteenth Amendment. (The 1964 Civil Rights Act was still a few years from passage.) Who should win?

 As you think about *Burton* and read the following cases, ask: Why does constitutional analysis start with the question of whether a deprivation of rights was perpetrated by the government, rather than with the question of how that deprivation affects the victim? What would the world look like if we didn't generally require state action? And where do you draw the line between government facilitation of private choice and government responsibility for the consequences that predictably follow?

Marsh v. Alabama

Supreme Court of the United States. 1946.
326 U.S. 501.

MR. JUSTICE BLACK delivered the opinion of the Court.

In this case we are asked to decide whether a State, consistently with the First and Fourteenth Amendments, can impose criminal punishment on a person who undertakes to distribute religious literature on the premises of a company-owned town contrary to the wishes of the town's management.

The town, a suburb of Mobile, Alabama, known as Chickasaw, is owned by the Gulf Shipbuilding Corporation. Except for that it has all the characteristics of any other American town. The property consists of residential buildings, streets, a system of sewers, a sewage disposal plant and a "business block" on which business places are situated. A deputy of the Mobile County Sheriff, paid by the company, serves as the town's policeman. Merchants and service establishments have rented the stores and business places on the business block and the United States uses one of the places as a post office from which six carriers deliver mail to the people of Chickasaw and the adjacent area. The town and the surrounding neighborhood, which can not be distinguished from the Gulf property by anyone not familiar with the property lines, are thickly settled, and according to all indications the residents use the business block as their regular shopping center. To do so, they now, as they have for many years, make use of a company-owned paved street and sidewalk located alongside the store fronts in order to enter and leave the stores and the post office. Intersecting company-owned roads at each end of the business block lead into a four-lane public highway which runs parallel to the business block at a distance of thirty feet. There is nothing to stop highway traffic from coming onto the business block and upon arrival a traveler may make free use of the facilities available there. In short the town and its shopping district are accessible to and freely used by the public in general and there is nothing to distinguish them from any other town and shopping center except the fact that the title to the property belongs to a private corporation.

Appellant, a Jehovah's Witness, came onto the sidewalk we have just described, stood near the post-office and undertook to distribute religious literature. In the stores the corporation had posted a notice which read as follows: "This Is Private Property, and Without Written Permission, No Street, or House Vendor, Agent or Solicitation of Any Kind Will Be Permitted." Appellant was warned that she could not distribute the literature without a permit and told that no permit would be issued to her. She protested that the company rule could not be constitutionally applied so as to prohibit her from distributing religious writings. When she was asked to leave the sidewalk and Chickasaw she declined. The deputy sheriff arrested her and she was charged in the state court with violating [a provision of the] Alabama Code which makes it a crime to enter or remain on the premises of another after having been warned not to do so. Appellant contended that to construe the state statute as applicable to her activities would abridge her right to freedom of press and religion contrary to the First and Fourteenth Amendments to the Constitution. This contention was rejected and she was convicted. The Alabama Court of Appeals affirmed the conviction, holding that the statute as applied was constitutional because the title to the sidewalk was in the corporation and because the public use of the sidewalk had not been such as to give rise to a presumption under Alabama law of its irrevocable dedication to the public. . . .

Had the title to Chickasaw belonged not to a private but to a municipal corporation and had appellant been arrested for violating a municipal ordinance rather than a ruling by those appointed by the corporation to manage a company-town it would have been clear that appellant's conviction must be reversed. Under our decision in *Lovell v. Griffin* (1938), and others which have followed that case, neither a state nor a municipality can completely bar the distribution of literature containing religious or political ideas on its streets, sidewalks and public places or make the right to distribute dependent on a flat license tax or permit to be issued by an official who could deny it at will. We have also held that an ordinance completely prohibiting the dissemination of ideas on the city streets can not be justified on the ground that the municipality holds legal title to them. *Jamison v. Texas* (1943). . . . From these decisions it is clear that had the people of Chickasaw owned all the homes, and all the stores, and all the streets, and all the sidewalks, all those owners together could not have set up a municipal government with sufficient power to pass an ordinance completely barring the distribution of religious literature.

Our question then narrows down to this: Can those people who live in or come to Chickasaw be denied freedom of press and religion simply because a single company has legal title to all the town? For it is the state's contention that the mere fact that all the property interests in the town are held by a single company is enough to give that company power, enforceable by a state statute, to abridge these freedoms.

We do not agree that the corporation's property interests settle the question. The State urges in effect that the corporation's right to control the inhabitants of Chickasaw is coextensive with the right of a homeowner to regulate the conduct of his guests. We can not accept that contention. Ownership does not always mean absolute dominion. The more an owner, for his advantage, opens up his property for use by the public in general, the more do his rights become circumscribed by the statutory and constitutional rights of those who use it. Thus, the owners of privately held bridges, ferries, turnpikes and railroads may not operate them as freely as a farmer does his farm. Since these facilities are built and operated primarily to benefit the public and since their operation is essentially a public function, it is subject to state regulation. . . . Had the corporation here owned the segment of the four-lane highway which runs parallel to the "business block" and operated the same under a State franchise, doubtless no one would have seriously contended that the corporation's property interest in the highway gave it power to obstruct through traffic or to discriminate against interstate commerce. And even had there been no express franchise but mere acquiescence by the State in the corporation's use of its property as a segment of the four-lane highway, operation of all the highway, including the segment owned by the corporation, would still have been performance of a public function and discrimination would certainly have been illegal.

We do not think it makes any significant constitutional difference as to the relationship between the rights of the owner and those of the public that here the State, instead of permitting the corporation to operate a highway, permitted it to use its property as a town, operate a "business block" in the town and a street and sidewalk on that business block. Whether a corporation or a municipality owns or possesses the town the public in either case has an identical interest in the functioning of the community in such manner that the channels of communication remain free. . . .

Many people in the United States live in company-owned towns.[5] These people, just as residents of municipalities, are free citizens of their State and country. Just as all other citizens they must make decisions which affect the welfare of community and nation. To act as good citizens they must be informed. In order to enable them to be properly informed their information must be uncensored. There is no more reason for depriving these people of the liberties guaranteed by the First and Fourteenth Amendments than there is for curtailing these freedoms with respect to any other citizen.

When we balance the Constitutional rights of owners of property against those of the people to enjoy freedom of press and religion, as we must here, we remain mindful of the fact that the latter occupy a preferred position. . . . In our view the circumstance that the property rights to the premises where the deprivation of liberty, here involved, took place, were held by others than the public, is not sufficient to justify the State's permitting a corporation to govern a community of citizens so as to restrict their fundamental liberties and the enforcement of such restraint by the application of a State statute. . . .

MR. JUSTICE JACKSON took no part in the consideration or decision of this case.

MR. JUSTICE FRANKFURTER, concurring.

. . . A company-owned town gives rise to a net-work of property relations. As to these, the judicial organ of a State has the final say. But a company-owned town is a town. In its community aspects it does not differ from other towns. These community aspects are decisive in adjusting the relations now before us, and more particularly in adjudicating the clash of freedoms which the Bill of Rights was designed to resolve—the freedom of the community to regulate its life and the freedom of the individual to exercise his religion and to disseminate his ideas. Title to property as defined by State law controls property relations; it cannot control issues of civil liberties which arise precisely because a company town is a town as well as a congeries of property relations. And similarly the

---

[5]   In the bituminous coal industry alone, approximately one-half of the miners in the United States lived in company-owned houses in the period from 1922–23. . . .

technical distinctions on which a finding of "trespass" so often depends are too tenuous to control decision regarding the scope of the vital liberties guaranteed by the Constitution. . . .

MR. JUSTICE REED, joined by CHIEF JUSTICE STONE and JUSTICE BURTON, dissenting.

. . . What the present decision establishes as a principle is that one may remain on private property against the will of the owner and contrary to the law of the state so long as the only objection to his presence is that he is exercising an asserted right to spread there his religious views. This is the first case to extend by law the privilege of religious exercises beyond public places or to private places without the assent of the owner. . . .

Both Federal and Alabama law permit, so far as we are aware, company towns. By that we mean an area occupied by numerous houses, connected by passways, fenced or not, as the owners may choose. These communities may be essential to furnish proper and convenient living conditions for employees on isolated operations in lumbering, mining, production of high explosives and large-scale farming. The restrictions imposed by the owners upon the occupants are sometimes galling to the employees and may appear unreasonable to outsiders. Unless they fall under the prohibition of some legal rule, however, they are a matter for adjustment between owner and licensee, or by appropriate legislation.

Alabama has a statute generally applicable to all privately owned premises. [Justice Reed quotes the Alabama trespass statute, which made it a crime to remain, "without legal cause or good excuse," on the premises of another after being asked to leave.]

Appellant was distributing religious pamphlets on a privately owned passway or sidewalk thirty feet removed from a public highway of the State of Alabama and remained on these private premises after an authorized order to get off. We do not understand from the record that there was objection to appellant's use of the nearby public highway and under our decisions she could rightfully have continued her activities a few feet from the spot she insisted upon using. An owner of property may very well have been willing for the public to use the private passway for business purposes and yet have been unwilling to furnish space for street trades or a location for the practice of religious exhortations by itinerants. The passway here in question was not put to any different use than other private passways that lead to privately owned areas, amusement places, resort hotels or other businesses. There had been no dedication of the sidewalk to the public use, express or implied. Alabama so decided and we understand that this Court accepts that conclusion. Alabama, also, decided that appellant violated by her activities the above quoted state statute.

The Court calls attention to the fact that the owners of public utilities, bridges, ferries, turnpikes and railroads are subject to state regulation of rates and are forbidden to discriminate against interstate commerce. This is quite true but we doubt if the Court means to imply that the property of these utilities may be utilized, against the companies' wishes, for religious exercises of the kind in question. A state does have the moral duty of furnishing the opportunity for information, education and religious enlightenment to its inhabitants, including those who live in company towns, but it has not heretofore been adjudged that it must commandeer, without compensation, the private property of other citizens to carry out that obligation. . . .

Our Constitution guarantees to every man the right to express his views in an orderly fashion. An essential element of "orderly" is that the man shall also have a right to use the place he chooses for his exposition. The rights of the owner, which the Constitution protects as well as the right of free speech, are not outweighed by the interests of the trespasser, even though he trespasses in behalf of religion or free speech. . . . Appellant, as we have said, was free to engage in such practices on the public highways, without becoming a trespasser on the company's property.

Georgia v. McCollum

Supreme Court of the United States, 1992.
505 U.S. 42.

JUSTICE BLACKMUN delivered the opinion of the Court.

. . .

I

On August 10, 1990, a grand jury sitting in Dougherty County, Ga., returned a six-count indictment charging respondents with aggravated assault and simple battery. The indictment alleged that respondents beat and assaulted Jerry and Myra Collins. Respondents are white; the alleged victims are

African-Americans. Shortly after the events, a leaflet was widely distributed in the local African-American community reporting the assault and urging community residents not to patronize respondents' business.

Before jury selection began, the prosecution moved to prohibit respondents from exercising peremptory challenges in a racially discriminatory manner. The State explained that it expected to show that the victims' race was a factor in the alleged assault. . . . Observing that 43 percent of the county's population is African-American, the State contended that, if a statistically representative panel is assembled for jury selection, 18 of the potential 42 jurors would be African-American. With 20 peremptory challenges, respondents therefore would be able to remove all the African-American potential jurors. Relying on *Batson v. Kentucky* (1986), the Sixth Amendment, and the Georgia Constitution, the State sought an order providing that, if it succeeded in making out a prima facie case of racial discrimination by respondents, the latter would be required to articulate a racially neutral explanation for peremptory challenges.

The trial judge denied the State's motion . . . . The issue was certified for immediate appeal.

The Supreme Court of Georgia, by a 4-to-3 vote, affirmed the trial court's ruling. The court acknowledged that in *Edmonson v. Leesville Concrete Co.* (1991) this Court had found that the exercise of a peremptory challenge in a racially discriminatory manner "would constitute an impermissible injury" to the excluded juror. The court noted, however, that *Edmonson* involved private civil litigants, not criminal defendants. "Bearing in mind the long history of jury trials as an essential element of the protection of human rights," the court "decline[d] to diminish the free exercise of peremptory strikes by a criminal defendant." . . .

II

Over the last century, in an almost unbroken chain of decisions, this Court gradually has abolished race as a consideration for jury service. In *Strauder v. West Virginia* (1880), the Court invalidated a state statute providing that only white men could serve as jurors. While stating that a defendant has no right to a "petit jury composed in whole or in part of persons of his own race," the Court held that a defendant does have the right to be tried by a jury whose members are selected by nondiscriminatory criteria. . . .

In *Swain v. Alabama* (1965), the Court was confronted with the question whether an African-American defendant was denied equal protection by the State's exercise of peremptory challenges to exclude members of his race from the petit jury. Although the Court rejected the defendant's attempt to establish an equal protection claim premised solely on the pattern of jury strikes in his own case, it acknowledged that proof of systematic exclusion of African-Americans through the use of peremptories over a period of time might establish such a violation.

In *Batson v. Kentucky* (1986), the Court discarded *Swain's* evidentiary formulation. The *Batson* Court held that a defendant may establish a prima facie case of purposeful discrimination in selection of the petit jury based solely on the prosecutor's exercise of peremptory challenges at the defendant's trial. . . . Last Term this Court applied the *Batson* framework in two other contexts. In *Powers v. Ohio* (1991), it held that in the trial of a white criminal defendant, a prosecutor is prohibited from excluding African-American jurors on the basis of race. In *Edmonson*, the Court decided that in a civil case, private litigants cannot exercise their peremptory strikes in a racially discriminatory manner. . . .

III

A

The majority in *Powers* recognized that "*Batson* 'was designed "to serve multiple ends," ' only one of which was to protect individual defendants from discrimination in the selection of jurors."

As long ago as *Strauder*, this Court recognized that denying a person participation in jury service on account of his race unconstitutionally discriminates against the excluded juror. While "[a]n individual juror does not have a right to sit on any particular petit jury, . . . he or she does possess the right not to be excluded from one on account of race." *Powers*. Regardless of who invokes the discriminatory challenge, there can be no doubt that the harm is the same—in all cases, the juror is subjected to open and public racial discrimination.

But "[t]he harm from discriminatory jury selection extends beyond that inflicted on the defendant and the excluded juror to touch the entire community." *Batson* . . . . The need for public confidence is especially high in cases involving race-related crimes. In such cases, emotions in the affected community will inevitably be heated and volatile. Public confidence in the integrity of the criminal justice system is essential for preserving community peace in trials involving race-related crimes. . . .

B

The fact that a defendant's use of discriminatory peremptory challenges harms the jurors and the community does not end our equal protection inquiry. Racial discrimination, although repugnant in all contexts, violates the Constitution only when it is attributable to state action. See *Moose Lodge No. 107 v. Irvis* (1972). Thus, the second question that must be answered is whether a criminal defendant's exercise of a peremptory challenge constitutes state action for purposes of the Equal Protection Clause.

Until *Edmonson,* the cases decided by this Court that presented the problem of racially discriminatory peremptory challenges involved assertions of discrimination by a prosecutor, a quintessential state actor. In *Edmonson,* by contrast, the contested peremptory challenges were exercised by a private defendant in a civil action. In order to determine whether state action was present in that setting, the Court in *Edmonson* used the analytical framework summarized in *Lugar v. Edmondson Oil Co.* (1982).[7]

The first inquiry is "whether the claimed [constitutional] deprivation has resulted from the exercise of a right or privilege having its source in state authority." "There can be no question" that peremptory challenges satisfy this first requirement, as they "are permitted only when the government, by statute or decisional law, deems it appropriate to allow parties to exclude a given number of persons who otherwise would satisfy the requirements for service on the petit jury." *Edmonson.* As in *Edmonson,* a Georgia defendant's right to exercise peremptory challenges and the scope of that right are established by a provision of state law.

The second inquiry is whether the private party charged with the deprivation can be described as a state actor. In resolving that issue, the Court in *Edmonson* found it useful to apply three principles: (1) "the extent to which the actor relies on governmental assistance and benefits"; (2) "whether the actor is performing a traditional governmental function"; and (3) "whether the injury caused is aggravated in a unique way by the incidents of governmental authority."

---

[7]   The Court in *Lugar* held that a private litigant is appropriately characterized as a state actor when he "jointly participates" with state officials in securing the seizure of property in which the private party claims to have rights.

As to the first principle, the *Edmonson* Court found that the peremptory challenge system, as well as the jury system as a whole, "simply could not exist" without the "overt, significant participation of the government." . . . In light of these procedures, the defendant in a Georgia criminal case relies on "governmental assistance and benefits" that are equivalent to those found in the civil context in *Edmonson*. "By enforcing a discriminatory peremptory challenge, the Court 'has . . . elected to place its power, property and prestige behind the [alleged] discrimination.' " *Edmonson*.

In regard to the second principle, the Court in *Edmonson* found that peremptory challenges perform a traditional function of the government: "Their sole purpose is to permit litigants to assist the government in the selection of an impartial trier of fact." And, as the *Edmonson* Court recognized, the jury system in turn "performs the critical governmental functions of guarding the rights of litigants and 'ensur[ing] continued acceptance of the laws by all of the people.' " These same conclusions apply with even greater force in the criminal context because the selection of a jury in a criminal case fulfills a unique and constitutionally compelled governmental function. . . . Cf. *West v. Atkins* (1988) (private physician hired by State to provide medical care to prisoners was state actor because doctor was hired to fulfill State's constitutional obligation to attend to necessary medical care of prison inmates). The State cannot avoid its constitutional responsibilities by delegating a public function to private parties. Cf. *Terry v. Adams* (1953) (private political party's determination of qualifications for primary voters held to constitute state action).

Finally, the *Edmonson* Court indicated that the courtroom setting in which the peremptory challenge is exercised intensifies the harmful effects of the private litigant's discriminatory act and contributes to its characterization as state action. These concerns are equally present in the context of a criminal trial. Regardless of who precipitated the jurors' removal, the perception and the reality in a criminal trial will be that the court has excused jurors based on race, an outcome that will be attributed to the State.[8]

Respondents nonetheless contend that the adversarial relationship between the defendant and the prosecution negates the governmental character of the peremptory challenge. Respondents rely on *Polk County v. Dodson* (1981), in which a defendant sued, under 42 U.S.C. § 1983, the public defender who

---

[8]   Indeed, it is common practice not to reveal the identity of the challenging party to the jurors and potential jurors, thus enhancing the perception that it is the court that has rejected them. . . .

represented him. The defendant claimed that the public defender had violated his constitutional rights in failing to provide adequate representation. This Court determined that a public defender does not qualify as a state actor when engaged in his general representation of a criminal defendant.

Polk County did not hold that the adversarial relationship of a public defender with the State precludes a finding of state action—it held that this adversarial relationship prevented the attorney's public employment from *alone* being sufficient to support a finding of state action. Instead, the determination whether a public defender is a state actor for a particular purpose depends on the nature and context of the function he is performing. For example, in *Branti v. Finkel* (1980), this Court held that a public defender, in making personnel decisions on behalf of the State, is a state actor who must comply with constitutional requirements. And the *Polk County* Court itself noted, without deciding, that a public defender may act under color of state law while performing certain administrative, and possibly investigative, functions.

The exercise of a peremptory challenge differs significantly from other actions taken in support of a defendant's defense. In exercising a peremptory challenge, a criminal defendant is wielding the power to choose a quintessential governmental body—indeed, the institution of government on which our judicial system depends. Thus, as we held in *Edmonson,* when "a government confers on a private body the power to choose the government's employees or officials, the private body will be bound by the constitutional mandate of race neutrality."

Lastly, the fact that a defendant exercises a peremptory challenge to further his interest in acquittal does not conflict with a finding of state action. Whenever a private actor's conduct is deemed "fairly attributable" to the government, it is likely that private motives will have animated the actor's decision. Indeed, in *Edmonson,* the Court recognized that the private party's exercise of peremptory challenges constituted state action, even though the motive underlying the exercise of the peremptory challenge may be to protect a private interest.

[The Court also held that the prosecutors had standing to raise the constitutional challenge and that the defendants had no constitutional right to exercise peremptories without regard to *Batson*.]

Chief Justice Rehnquist, who had dissented in *Edmonson*, wrote a brief concurrence, saying he continued to think the case was wrongly decided but that it controlled on the state-action question, and so he joined the opinion of the Court.

WORTH NOTING

Justice Thomas, who had not been on the Court when *Edmonson* was decided, concurred in the judgment. He believed he would have shared the *Edmonson* dissenters' views, but he agreed that the case was controlling. He wrote separately to express his "general dissatisfaction" with the *Batson* line. "I am certain," he said, "that black criminal defendants will rue the day that this Court ventured down this road that inexorably will lead to the elimination of peremptory strikes." He also noted that the NAACP Legal Defense and Educational Fund, Inc., had "submitted a brief arguing, in all sincerity, that 'whether white defendants can use peremptory challenges to purge minority jurors presents quite different issues from whether a minority defendant can strike majority group jurors,'" and he commented that "it is difficult to see how the result could be different if the defendants here were black."

JUSTICE O'CONNOR, dissenting.

The Court reaches the remarkable conclusion that criminal defendants being prosecuted by the State act on behalf of their adversary when they exercise peremptory challenges during jury selection. The Court purports merely to follow precedents, but our cases do not compel this perverse result. To the contrary, our decisions specifically establish that criminal defendants and their lawyers are not government actors when they perform traditional trial functions.

I

. . . The critical but straightforward question this case presents is whether criminal defendants and their lawyers, when exercising peremptory challenges as part of a defense, are state actors. . . . What our cases require, and what the Court neglects, is a realistic appraisal of the relationship between defendants and the government that has brought them to trial.

We discussed that relationship in *Polk County v. Dodson* (1981), which held that a public defender does not act "under color of state law" for purposes of 42 U.S.C. § 1983 "when performing a lawyer's traditional functions as counsel to a defendant in a criminal proceeding." We began our analysis by explaining that a public defender's obligations toward her client are no different than the obligations of any other defense attorney. . . .

We went on to stress the inconsistency between our adversarial system of justice and theories that would make defense lawyers state actors. "In our system," we said, "a defense lawyer characteristically opposes the designated representatives of the State." . . . Moreover, we pointed out that the independence of defense attorneys from state control has a constitutional dimension. . . . Implicit in this right "is the assumption that counsel will be free of state control. There can be no fair trial unless the accused receives the services of an effective and independent advocate." Thus, the defense's freedom from state authority is not just empirically true, but is a constitutionally mandated attribute of our adversarial system.

Because this Court deems the "under color of state law" requirement that was not satisfied in *Dodson* identical to the Fourteenth Amendment's state action requirement, see *Lugar*, the holding of *Dodson* simply cannot be squared with today's decision. In particular, *Dodson* cannot be explained away as a case concerned exclusively with the employment status of public defenders. The *Dodson* Court reasoned that public defenders performing traditional defense functions are not state actors because they occupy the same position as other defense attorneys in relevant respects. This reasoning followed on the heels of a critical determination: Defending an accused "is essentially a private function," not state action. The Court's refusal to acknowledge *Dodson*'s initial holding, on which the entire opinion turned, will not make that holding go away.

The Court also seeks to evade *Dodson*'s logic by spinning out a theory that defendants and their lawyers transmogrify from government adversaries into state actors when they exercise a peremptory challenge, and then change back to perform other defense functions. *Dodson*, however, established that even though public defenders might act under color of state law when carrying out administrative or investigative functions outside a courtroom, they are not vested with state authority "when performing a lawyer's traditional functions as counsel to a defendant in a criminal proceeding." Since making peremptory challenges plainly qualifies as a "traditional function" of criminal defense lawyers, . . . *Dodson* forecloses the Court's functional analysis.

Even aside from our prior rejection of it, the Court's functional theory fails. "[A] State normally can be held responsible for a private decision only when it has exercised coercive power or has provided such significant encouragement . . . that the choice must in law be deemed to be that of the State." *Blum v. Yaretsky* (1982). Thus, a private party's exercise of choice allowed by state law does not amount to state action for purposes of the Fourteenth Amendment so long as "the initiative comes from [the private party] and not from the State." *Jackson v. Metropolitan Edison Co.* (1974). See *Flagg Bros., Inc. v. Brooks* (1978) (State not responsible for a decision it "permits but does not compel"). The government in no way influences the defense's decision to use a peremptory challenge to strike a particular juror. . . .

Certainly, *Edmonson v. Leesville Concrete Co.* did not render *Dodson* and its realistic approach to the state action inquiry dead letters. The *Edmonson* Court distinguished *Dodson* by saying: "In the ordinary context of civil litigation in which the government is not a party, an adversarial relation does not exist between the government and a private litigant. In the jury selection process, the government and private litigants work for the same end." While the nonpartisan administrative interests of the State and the partisan interests of private litigants may not be at odds during civil jury selection, the same cannot be said of the partisan interests of the State and the defendant during jury selection in a criminal trial. A private civil litigant opposes a private counterpart, but a criminal defendant is by design in an adversarial relationship with the government. Simply put, the defendant seeks to strike jurors predisposed to convict, while the State seeks to strike jurors predisposed to acquit. The *Edmonson* Court clearly recognized this point when it limited the statement that "an adversarial relation does not exist between the government and a private litigant" to "the ordinary context of *civil litigation in which the government is not a party*" (emphasis added). . . .

II

What really seems to bother the Court is the prospect that leaving criminal defendants and their attorneys free to make racially motivated peremptory challenges will undermine the ideal of nondiscriminatory jury selection we espoused in *Batson*. The concept that the government alone must honor constitutional dictates, however, is a fundamental tenet of our legal order, not an obstacle to be circumvented. This is particularly so in the context of criminal trials, where we have held the prosecution to uniquely high standards of conduct. . . .

Considered in purely pragmatic terms, moreover, the Court's holding may fail to advance nondiscriminatory criminal justice. . . . As *amicus* NAACP Legal Defense and Educational Fund explained in this case:

> The ability to use peremptory challenges to exclude majority race jurors may be crucial to empaneling a fair jury. In many cases an African American, or other minority defendant, may be faced with a jury array in which his racial group is underrepresented to some

degree, but not sufficiently to permit challenge under the Fourteenth Amendment. The only possible chance the defendant may have of having any minority jurors on the jury that actually tries him will be if he uses his peremptories to strike members of the majority race.

In a world where the outcome of a minority defendant's trial may turn on the misconceptions or biases of white jurors, there is cause to question the implications of this Court's good intentions.

That the Constitution does not give federal judges the reach to wipe all marks of racism from every courtroom in the land is frustrating, to be sure. But such limitations are the necessary and intended consequence of the Fourteenth Amendment's state action requirement. Because I cannot accept the Court's conclusion that government is responsible for decisions criminal defendants make while fighting state prosecution, I respectfully dissent.

JUSTICE SCALIA, dissenting.

. . . Barely a year [after *Edmonson*], we witness its reduction to the terminally absurd: A criminal defendant, in the process of defending himself against the state, is held to be acting on behalf of the state. Justice O'Connor demonstrates the sheer inanity of this proposition (in case the mere statement of it does not suffice), and the contrived nature of the Court's justifications. I see no need to add to her discussion, and differ from her views only in that I do not consider *Edmonson* distinguishable in principle—except in the principle that a bad decision should not be followed logically to its illogical conclusion.

. . .

FOR DISCUSSION

Under the First Amendment, the city may not eject you from the town square for saying "I dislike the American government." Imagine instead that you are in your neighbor's yard. You tell her, "I dislike the American government." She says, "No one with those views can stay on my property," and she calls the police to eject you. Is she violating the First Amendment? If the police force you to leave, have they violated the First Amendment?

TEST YOUR KNOWLEDGE: To assess your understanding of the material in this chapter, **click here** to take a quiz.

CHAPTER III

Federalism: Distribution of Authority Between the National Government and the States

A. Congressional Power

1. The Enumeration Principle

The 1776 Declaration of Independence asserted that the former colonies were "Free and Independent States" possessing "full Power . . . to do all . . . Acts and Things which Independent States may of right do." That kind of plenary governance power is sometimes referred to by the curious term "police power," which means the general authority to regulate for the public's safety, health, welfare, and morals. Despite some puzzling instances of early state legislatures asking the Continental Congress for permission to take domestic measures, by the 1780s it was basically uncontested that the individual states did not need any grant of authority from the national Constitution to exercise full governing authority within their respective territories.

The federal government stands on a very different footing from the states: it only has the powers granted to it by the Constitution, which created it. And those powers are enumerated with particularity, rather than as an open-ended provision that simply authorizes the federal government to enact laws that promote the general welfare. To be clear: Congress is certainly entitled to *pursue* the general welfare—but only insofar as its actions are authorized under one or more specific grants of power in the Constitution itself, most of which are located in Article I, § 8. At times, judicial interpretation of the enumerated powers has been so generous as to almost amount to a police power in practice—but even then, courts made sure to justify a governmental action by invoking one or more particular enumerated powers. The Founders themselves disagreed about the wisdom and implementation of this enumeration strategy, and Americans have been arguing about both its theory and its practice ever since.

For some early light on the nature and scope of congressional power, let's look at some documents from the debates on ratification of the Constitution.

James Wilson, Speech at the Philadelphia State House

6 October 1787

It will be proper . . . to mark the leading discrimination between the state constitutions and the Constitution of the United States.

When the people established the powers of legislation under their separate [state] governments, they invested their representatives with every right and authority which they did not in explicit terms reserve; and therefore upon every question, respecting the jurisdiction of the [state] house of assembly, if the frame of government is silent, the jurisdiction is efficient and complete.

But in delegating federal powers, another criterion was necessarily introduced, and the congressional authority is to be collected, not from tacit implication, but from the positive grant expressed in the instrument of union. Hence it is evident, that in the former case everything which is not reserved is given, but in the latter the reverse of the proposition prevails, and everything which is not given, is reserved.

A Citizen of New York [John Jay], An Address to the People of the State of New York

15 April 1788

Complaints are also made that the proposed Constitution is not accompanied by a bill of rights; and yet they who make these complaints, know and are content that no bill of rights accompanied the Constitution of this State. In days and countries where Monarchs and their subjects were frequently disputing about prerogative and privileges, the latter often found it necessary, as it were to run out the line between them, and oblige the former to admit by solemn acts, called bills of rights, that certain enumerated rights belonged to the people, and were not comprehended in the royal prerogative. But thank

God we have no such disputes—we have no Monarchs to contend with, or demand admissions from—the proposed Government is to be the government of the people—all its officers are to be their officers, and to exercise no rights but such as the people commit to them.

James Bowdoin, Speech at the Massachusetts Ratifying Convention

23 January 1788

There have been many objections offered against the constitution: and of these the one most strongly urged has been, the great power vested in Congress. If we consider the objects of the power, they are numerous and important; and as human foresight cannot extend to many of them; and all of them are in the womb of futurity, the quantum of the power cannot be estimated. . . .

But however that may be, this is certain, that . . . the commercial and political happiness, the liberty and property, the peace, safety and general welfare, both internal and external, of each and all the States, depend on that power: which as it must be applied to a vast variety of objects, and to cases and exigencies beyond the ken of human prescience, must be very great; and which cannot be limited without endangering the publick safety.

It will be and has been said, this great power may be abused; and instead of protecting, may be employed by Congress in oppressing their constituents. A possibility of abuse, as it may be affirmed of all delegated power whatever, is by itself no sufficient reason for withholding the delegation. . . .

Federal Farmer XII–XIII

23 January 1788
25 January 1788

To erect a federal republic, [t]he states, as such, must unite under a federal head, and delegate to it powers to make and execute laws in certain enumerated cases, under certain restrictions. . . . All these enumerated powers we must examine and contemplate in all their extent and various branches, and then reflect, that the federal head will have full power to make all laws whatever respecting them; and for carrying into full effect all powers vested in the union, in any department, or officers of it, by the constitution, in order to see the full extent of the federal powers, which will be supreme, and exercised by that head at pleasure, conforming to the few limitations mentioned in the constitution. Indeed, I conceive, it is impossible to see them in their full extent at present: we see vast undefined powers lodged in a weak organization, but cannot, by the enquiries of months and years, clearly discern them in all their numerous branches. These powers in feeble hands, must be tempting objects for ambition and a love of power and fame.

The Federalist No. 45 (James Madison)

Independent Journal
26 January 1788

The powers delegated by the proposed Constitution to the federal government, are few and defined. Those which are to remain in the State governments are numerous and indefinite. The former will be exercised principally on external objects, as war, peace, negotiation, and foreign commerce; with which last the power of taxation will, for the most part, be connected. The powers reserved to the several States will extend to all the objects which, in the ordinary course of affairs, concern the lives, liberties, and properties of the people, and the internal order, improvement, and prosperity of the State.

The operations of the federal government will be most extensive and important in times of war and danger; those of the State governments, in times of peace and security. As the former periods will probably bear a small proportion to the latter, the State governments will here enjoy another advantage over the federal government. The more adequate, indeed, the federal powers may be rendered to the national defense, the less frequent will be those scenes of danger which might favor their ascendancy over the governments of the particular States.

A Farmer

Philadelphia Freeman's Journal
16 April 1788

The peculiar advantages and distinctive properties of a federal republic are, that each state or member of the confederation may be fully adequate for every local purpose, that it may subsist in a small territory, that the people may have a common interest, possess a competent knowledge of the resources and expenditures of their own particular government, that their immediate representatives in the state governments will know and be known by the citizens, will have a common interest with them, and must bear a part of all the burdens which they may lay upon the people, that they will be responsible to the people, and may be dismissed by them at pleasure. . . .

The perfection of a federal republic consists in drawing the proper line between those objects of sovereignty which are of a general nature, and which ought to be vested in the federal government, and those which are of a more local nature and ought to remain with the particular governments; any rule that can be laid down for this must vary according to the situation and circumstances of the confederating states; yet still this general rule will hold good, viz. that all that portion of sovereignty which involve the common interest of all the confederating states, and which cannot be exercised by the states in their individual capacity without endangering the liberty and welfare of the whole, ought to be vested in the general government, reserving such a proportion of sovereignty in the state governments as would enable them to exist alone, if the general government should fail either by violence or with the common consent of the confederates[.]

2.   The Necessary & Proper Clause

We will consider each of the most important congressional powers separately, but for an overall perspective we will begin at the end of the long list in Article I, § 8: a grand catchall known as the Necessary and Proper Clause:

> The Congress shall have Power . . . [t]o make all Laws which shall
> be necessary and proper for carrying into Execution the foregoing
> Powers, and all other Powers vested by this Constitution in the

> Government of the United States, or in any Department or Officer thereof.
>
> Art I, § 8, cl. 18.

This may have been the most controversial enumerated power in the entire Constitution. What follows is some commentary from the Ratification debates, and then a John Marshall opinion that remains one of the most important discussions not only of the Necessary and Proper Clause but of the very nature of Congressional power.

Brutus V

New York Journal
13 December 1787

It is a rule in construing a law to consider the objects the legislature had in view in passing it, and to give it such an explanation as to promote their intention. The same rule will apply in explaining a constitution.

The great objects then are declared in this preamble in general and indefinite terms to be to provide for the common defence, promote the general welfare, and an express power being vested in the legislature to make all laws which shall be necessary and proper for carrying into execution all the powers vested in the general government. The inference is natural that the legislature will have an authority to make all laws which they shall judge necessary for the common safety, and to promote the general welfare. This amounts to a power to make laws at discretion: No terms can be found more indefinite than these, and it is obvious, that the legislature alone must judge what laws are proper and necessary for the purpose. . . .

Were I to enter into the detail, it would be easy to shew how [the Necessary and Proper Clause] in its operation, would totally destroy all the powers of the individual states. But this is not necessary for those who will think for themselves. . . . I shall only remark, that this power, given to the federal legislature, directly annihilates all the powers of the state legislatures.

The Federalist No. 44 (James Madison)

New York Packet
25 January 1788

Few parts of the Constitution have been assailed with more intemperance than [the Necessary and Proper Clause]; yet on a fair investigation of it, no part can appear more completely invulnerable. Without the SUBSTANCE of this power, the whole Constitution would be a dead letter. Those who object to the article, therefore, as a part of the Constitution, can only mean that the FORM of the provision is improper. . . .

Had the convention attempted a positive enumeration of the powers necessary and proper for carrying their other powers into effect, the attempt would have involved a complete digest of laws on every subject to which the Constitution relates . . . . Had the Constitution been silent on this head, there can be no doubt that all the particular powers requisite as means of executing the general powers would have resulted to the government, by unavoidable implication. No axiom is more clearly established in law, or in reason, than that wherever the end is required, the means are authorized; wherever a general power to do a thing is given, every particular power necessary for doing it is included.

If it be asked what is to be the consequence, in case the Congress shall misconstrue this part of the Constitution, and exercise powers not warranted by its true meaning, I answer, the same as if they should misconstrue or enlarge any other power vested in them. . . . In the first instance, the success of the usurpation will depend on the executive and judiciary departments, which are to expound and give effect to the legislative acts; and in the last resort a remedy must be obtained from the people who can, by the election of more faithful representatives, annul the acts of the usurpers.

The Bank Controversy

McCulloch v. Maryland concerned an attempt by Maryland to tax a branch of the Second Bank of the United States. Created by an 1816 Act of Congress, the Bank had established a branch in Baltimore. In 1818, the Maryland legis-

CROSS REFERENCE For further background on the historical controversies concerning the First and Second Banks of the United States, see pp. 71–87.

lature enacted a law purporting to tax any in-state branches of a bank that it had not chartered; the Bank of the United States was the only one that met this description.

McCulloch v. Maryland

Supreme Court of the United States, 1819.
17 U.S. (4 Wheat.) 316.

MARSHALL, C. J., delivered the opinion of the court.

In the case now to be determined, the defendant, a sovereign State, denies the obligation of a law enacted by the legislature of the Union, and the plaintiff, on his part, contests the validity of an act which has been passed by the legislature of that State. The constitution of our country, in its most interesting and vital parts, is to be considered; the conflicting powers of the government of the Union and of its members, as marked in that constitution, are to be discussed; and an opinion given, which may essentially influence the great operations of the government. No tribunal can approach such a question without a deep sense of its importance, and of the awful responsibility involved in its decision. . . .

The first question made in the cause is—has Congress power to incorporate a bank? It has been truly said, that this can scarcely be considered as an open question, entirely unprejudiced by the former proceedings of the nation respecting it. The principle now contested was introduced at a very early period of our history, has been recognised by many successive legislatures, and has been acted upon by the judicial department, in cases of peculiar delicacy, as a law of undoubted obligation.

It will not be denied, that a bold and daring usurpation might be resisted, after an acquiescence still longer and more complete than this. But it is conceived, that a doubtful question, one on which human reason may pause, and the human judgment be suspended, in the decision of which the great principles of liberty are not concerned, but the respective powers of those who are equally the representatives of the people, are to be adjusted; if not put at rest by the practice of the government, ought to receive a considerable impression from that practice. An exposition of the constitution, deliberately established by legislative acts, on the faith of which an immense property has been advanced, ought not to be lightly disregarded.

The power now contested was exercised by the first Congress elected under the present constitution. The bill for incorporating the Bank of the United States did not steal upon an unsuspecting legislature, and pass unobserved. Its principle was completely understood, and was opposed with equal zeal and ability. After being resisted, first, in the fair and open field of debate, and afterwards, in the executive cabinet, with as much persevering talent as any measure has ever experienced, and being supported by arguments which convinced minds as pure and as intelligent as this country can boast, it became a law. The original act was permitted to expire; but a short experience of the embarrassments to which the refusal to revive it exposed the government, convinced those who were most prejudiced against the measure of its necessity, and induced the passage of the present law. It would require no ordinary share of intrepidity, to assert that a measure adopted under these circumstances, was a bold and plain usurpation, to which the constitution gave no countenance. . . .

> **CROSS REFERENCE** Here Marshall, at the instance of Maryland's lawyers, took up the theoretical question of whether the Constitution should be considered as "emanating from the people" or as "the act of sovereign and independent states." For his argument on this point, adopting the former view, see pp. 41–43.

This government is acknowledged by all, to be one of enumerated powers. The principle, that it can exercise only the powers granted to it, would seem too apparent, to have required to be enforced by all those arguments, which its enlightened friends, while it was depending before the people, found it necessary to urge. That principle is now universally admitted. But the question respecting the extent of the powers actually granted, is perpetually arising, and will probably continue to arise, so long as our system shall exist. In discussing these questions, the conflicting powers of the general and State governments must be brought into view, and the supremacy of their respective laws, when they are in opposition, must be settled. . . .

Among the enumerated powers, we do not find that of establishing a bank or creating a corporation. But there is no phrase in the instrument which, like the articles of confederation, excludes incidental or implied powers; and which requires that everything granted shall be expressly and minutely described. Even the 10th amendment, which was framed for the purpose of quieting the excessive jealousies which had been excited, omits the word "expressly," and declares only, that the powers "not delegated to the United States, nor prohibited to the States, are reserved to the States or to the people;" thus leaving the question, whether the particular power which may become the subject of contest, has been delegated to the one government, or prohibited to the other, to depend on a fair construction of the whole instrument. The men who drew and adopted this amendment had experienced the embarrassments resulting from the insertion of this word in the articles of confederation, and probably omitted it, to avoid those embarrassments.

WORTH NOTING The Articles of Confederation had included a much stricter counterpart to the Tenth Amendment, providing that "[e]ach state retains its sovereignty, freedom, and independence, and every power, jurisdiction, and right, which is not by this Confederation *expressly* delegated to the United States, in Congress assembled." Arts. of Confed., art. 2 (emphasis added).

A constitution, to contain an accurate detail of all the subdivisions of which its great powers will admit, and of all the means by which they may be carried into execution, would partake of the prolixity of a legal code, and could scarcely be embraced by the human mind. It would, probably, never be understood by the public. Its nature, therefore, requires, that only its great outlines should be marked, its important objects designated, and the minor ingredients which compose those objects, be deduced from the nature of the objects themselves. That this idea was entertained by the framers of the American constitution, is not only to be inferred from the nature of the instrument, but from the language. Why else were some of the limitations, found in the 9th section of the 1st article, introduced? It is also, in some degree, warranted, by their having omitted to use any restrictive term which might prevent its receiving a fair and just interpretation. In considering this question, then, we must never forget that it is *a constitution* we are expounding.

Although, among the enumerated powers of government, we do not find the word "bank" or "incorporation," we find the great powers, to lay and collect taxes; to borrow money; to regulate commerce; to declare and conduct a war;

and to raise and support armies and navies. The sword and the purse, all the external relations, and no inconsiderable portion of the industry of the nation, are intrusted to its government. . . . [I]t may with great reason be contended, that a government, entrusted with such ample powers, on the due execution of which the happiness and prosperity of the nation so vitally depends, must also be entrusted with ample means for their execution. The power being given, it is the interest of the nation to facilitate its execution. It can never be their interest, and cannot be presumed to have been their intention, to clog and embarrass its execution, by withholding the most appropriate means.

Throughout this vast republic, from the St. Croix to the Gulph of Mexico, from the Atlantic to the Pacific, revenue is to be collected and expended, armies are to be marched and supported. The exigencies of the nation may require, that the treasure raised in the north should be transported to the south, *that* raised in the east, conveyed to the west, or that this order should be reversed. Is that construction of the constitution to be preferred, which would render these operations difficult, hazardous and expensive? Can we adopt that construction (unless the words imperiously require it), which would impute to the framers of that instrument, when granting these powers for the public good, the intention of impeding their exercise, by withholding a choice of means? If, indeed, such be the mandate of the constitution, we have only to obey; but that instrument does not profess to enumerate the means by which the powers it confers may be executed; nor does it prohibit the creation of a corporation, if the existence of such a being be essential, to the beneficial exercise of those powers. It is, then, the subject of fair inquiry, how far such means may be employed . . . .

The power of creating a corporation, though appertaining to sovereignty, is not, like the power of making war, or levying taxes, or of regulating commerce, a great substantive and independent power, which cannot be implied as incidental to other powers, or used as a means of executing them. It is never the end for which other powers are exercised, but a means by which other objects are accomplished. No contributions are made to charity, for the sake of an incorporation, but a corporation is created to administer the charity; no seminary of learning is instituted, in order to be incorporated, but the corporate character is conferred to subserve the purposes of education. No city was ever built, with the sole object of being incorporated, but is incorporated as affording the best means of being well governed. The power of creating a corporation is never used for its own sake, but for the purpose of effecting something else. No sufficient reason is, therefore, perceived, why it may not pass as incidental to those powers which are expressly given, if it be a direct mode of executing them.

But the constitution of the United States has not left the right of Congress to employ the necessary means, for the execution of the powers conferred on the government, to general reasoning. To its enumeration of powers is added, that of making "all laws which shall be necessary and proper, for carrying into execution the foregoing powers, and all other powers vested by this constitution, in the government of the United States, or in any department thereof."

The counsel for the State of Maryland have urged various arguments, to prove that this clause, though, in terms, a grant of power, is not so, in effect; but is really restrictive of the general right, which might otherwise be implied, of selecting means for executing the enumerated powers. . . .

[T]he argument on which most reliance is placed, is drawn from that peculiar language of this clause. Congress is not empowered by it to make all laws, which may have relation to the powers conferred on the government, but such only as may be *"necessary and proper"* for carrying them into execution. The word *"necessary"* is considered as controlling the whole sentence, and as limiting the right to pass laws for the execution of the granted powers, to such as are indispensable, and without which the power would be nugatory. That it excludes the choice of means, and leaves to Congress, in each case, that only which is most direct and simple.

Is it true, that this is the sense in which the word "necessary" is always used? Does it always import an absolute physical necessity, so strong, that one thing to which another may be termed necessary, cannot exist without that other? We think it does not. If reference be had to its use, in the common affairs of the world, or in approved authors, we find that it frequently imports no more than that one thing is convenient, or useful, or essential to another. To employ the means necessary to an end, is generally understood as employing any means calculated to produce the end, and not as being confined to those single means, without which the end would be entirely unattainable.

Such is the character of human language, that no word conveys to the mind, in all situations, one single definite idea; and nothing is more common than to use words in a figurative sense. Almost all compositions contain words, which, taken in their rigorous sense, would convey a meaning different from that which is obviously intended. It is essential to just construction, that many words which import something excessive, should be understood in a more mitigated sense—in that sense which common usage justifies. The word "necessary" is of this description. It has not a fixed character, peculiar to itself. It admits of all degrees of comparison; and is often connected with other words, which increase or diminish the impression the mind receives of the urgency it imports. A thing may be necessary, very necessary, absolutely or indispensably necessary. To no mind would the same idea be conveyed by these several phrases.

The comment on the word is well illustrated by the passage cited at the bar, from the 10th section of the 1st article of the constitution. It is, we think, impossible to compare the sentence which prohibits a State from laying "imposts, or duties on imports or exports, except what may be *absolutely* necessary for executing its inspection laws," with that which authorizes Congress "to make all laws which shall be necessary and proper for carrying into execution" the powers of the general government, without feeling a conviction, that the convention understood itself to change materially the meaning of the word "necessary," by prefixing the word "absolutely." This word, then, like others, is used in various senses; and, in its construction, the subject, the context, the intention of the person using them, are all to be taken into view.

Let this be done in the case under consideration. The subject is the execution of those great powers on which the welfare of a nation essentially depends. It must have been the intention of those who gave these powers, to insure, so far as human prudence could insure, their beneficial execution. This could not be done, by confiding the choice of means to such narrow limits as not to leave it in the power of Congress to adopt any which might be appropriate, and which were conducive to the end. This provision is made in a constitution, intended to endure for ages to come, and consequently, to be adapted to the various *crises* of human affairs. To have prescribed the means by which government should, in all future time, execute its powers, would have been to change, entirely, the character of the instrument, and give it the properties of a legal code. It would have been an unwise attempt to provide, by immutable rules, for exigencies which, if foreseen at all, must have been seen dimly, and which can be best provided for as they occur. To have declared, that the best means shall not be used, but those alone, without which the power given would be nugatory, would have been to deprive the legislature of the capacity to avail itself of experience, to exercise its reason, and to accommodate its legislation to circumstances.

If we apply this principle of construction to any of the powers of the government, we shall find it so pernicious in its operation that we shall be compelled to discard it. . . .

So, with respect to the whole penal code of the United States: whence arises the power to punish, in cases not prescribed by the constitution? All admit, that the government may, legitimately, punish any violation of its laws; and yet, this is not among the enumerated powers of Congress. The right to enforce the observance of law, by punishing its infraction, might be denied, with the more plausibility, because it is expressly given in some cases. Congress is empowered "to provide for the punishment of counterfeiting the securities and current coin of the United States," and "to define and punish piracies and felonies committed on the high seas, and offences against the law of nations." The several powers of Congress may exist, in a very imperfect state, to be sure, but they may exist and be carried into execution, although no punishment should be inflicted, in cases where the right to punish is not expressly given.

Take, for example, the power "to establish post offices and post roads." This power is executed, by the single act of making the establishment. But, from this has been inferred the power and duty of carrying the mail along the post road, from one post office to another. And from this implied power, has again been inferred the right to punish those who steal letters from the post office, or rob the mail. It may be said, with some plausibility, that the right to carry the mail, and to punish those who rob it, is not indispensably necessary to the establishment of a post office and post road. This right is indeed essential to the beneficial exercise of the power, but not indispensably necessary to its existence.

So [too] of the punishment of the crimes of stealing or falsifying a record or process of a Court of the United States, or of perjury in such court. To punish these offences, is certainly conducive to the due administration of justice. But courts may exist, and may decide the causes brought before them, though such crimes escape punishment. . . . If the word "necessary" means "needful," "requisite," "essential," "conducive to," in order to let in [such] power of punishment for the infraction of law; why is it not equally comprehensive, when required to authorize the use of means which facilitate the execution of the powers of government, without the infliction of punishment? . . .

But the argument which most conclusively demonstrates the error of the construction contended for by the counsel for the State of Maryland, is founded on the intention of the Convention, as manifested in the whole clause. To waste time and argument in proving that, without it, Congress might carry its powers into execution, would be not much less idle, than to hold a lighted taper to the sun. As little can it be required to prove, that in the absence of this clause, Congress would have some choice of means. That it might employ those which, in its judgment, would most advantageously effect the object to be accomplished. That any means adapted to the end, any means which tended directly to the execution of the constitutional powers of the government, were in themselves constitutional. This clause, as construed by the State of Maryland, would abridge, and almost annihilate, this useful and necessary right of the legislature to select its means. That this could not be intended, is, we should think, had it not been already controverted, too apparent for controversy.

We think so for the following reasons: 1st. The clause is placed among the powers of Congress, not among the limitations on those powers. 2nd. Its terms purport to enlarge, not to diminish the powers vested in the government. It purports to be an additional power, not a restriction on those already granted. No reason has been, or can be assigned, for thus concealing an intention to narrow the discretion of the national legislature, under words which purport to enlarge it. The framers of the constitution wished its adoption, and well knew that it would be endangered by its strength, not by its weakness. Had they been capable of using language which would convey to the eye one idea, and, after deep reflection, impress on the mind, another, they would rather have disguised the grant of power, than its limitation. If, then, their intention had been, by this clause, to restrain the free use of means which might otherwise have been implied, that intention would have been inserted in another place, and would have been expressed in terms resembling these. "In carrying into execution the foregoing powers, and all others," &c., "no laws shall be passed but such as are necessary and proper." Had the intention been to make this clause restrictive, it would unquestionably have been so in form as well as in effect.

The result of the most careful and attentive consideration bestowed upon this clause is, that if it does not enlarge, it cannot be construed to restrain the powers of Congress, or to impair the right of the legislature to exercise its best judgment in the selection of measures to carry into execution the constitutional powers of the government. If no other motive for its insertion can be suggested, a sufficient one is found in the desire to remove all doubts respecting the right to legislate on that vast mass of incidental powers which must be involved in the constitution, if that instrument be not a splendid bauble.

We admit, as all must admit, that the powers of the government are limited, and that its limits are not to be transcended. But we think the sound construction of the constitution must allow to the national legislature that discretion, with respect to the means by which the powers it confers are to be carried into execution, which will enable that body to perform the high duties assigned to it, in the manner most beneficial to the people. Let the end be legitimate, let it be within the scope of the constitution, and all means which are appropriate, which are plainly adapted to that end, which are not prohibited, but consist with the letter and spirit of the constitution, are constitutional.

That a corporation must be considered as a means not less usual, not of higher dignity, not more requiring a particular specification than other means, has been sufficiently proved. . . . If a corporation may be employed, indiscriminately with other means, to carry into execution the powers of the government, no particular reason can be assigned for excluding the use of a bank, if required for its fiscal operations. To use one, must be within the discretion of Congress, if it be an appropriate mode of executing the powers of government. That it is a convenient, a useful, and essential instrument in the prosecution of its fiscal operations, is not now a subject of controversy. All those who have been concerned in the administration of our finances, have concurred in representing its importance and necessity; and so strongly have they been felt, that statesmen of the first class, whose previous opinions against it had been confirmed by every circumstance which can fix the human judgment, have yielded those opinions to the exigencies of the nation. . . .

But were its necessity less apparent, none can deny its being an appropriate measure; and if it is, the degree of its necessity, as has been very justly observed, is to be discussed in another place.

Should Congress, in the execution of its powers, adopt measures which are prohibited by the constitution; or should Congress, under the pretext of executing its powers, pass laws for the accomplishment of objects not entrusted to the government; it would become the painful duty of this tribunal, should a case requiring such a decision come before it, to say, that such an act was not the law of the land. But where the law is not prohibited, and is really calculated to effect any of the objects entrusted to the government, to undertake here to inquire into the degree of its necessity, would be to pass the line which circumscribes the judicial department, and to tread on legislative ground. This court disclaims all pretensions to such a power.

After this declaration, it can scarcely be necessary to say, that the existence of State banks can have no possible influence on the question. No trace is to be found in the constitution, of an intention to create a dependence of the government of the Union on those of the States, for the execution of the great powers assigned to it. Its means are adequate to its ends; and on those means alone was it expected to rely for the accomplishment of its ends. To impose on it the necessity of resorting to means which it cannot control, which another government may furnish or withhold, would render its course precarious, the result of its measures uncertain, and create a dependence on other governments, which might disappoint its most important designs, and is incompatible with the language of the constitution. But were it otherwise, the choice of means implies a right to choose a national bank in preference to State banks, and Congress alone can make the election.

After the most deliberate consideration, it is the unanimous and decided opinion of this Court, that the act to incorporate the Bank of the United States is a law made in pursuance of the constitution, and is a part of the supreme law of the land. . . . It being the opinion of the Court, that the act incorporating the bank is constitutional; and that the power of establishing a branch in the State of Maryland might be properly exercised by the bank itself, we proceed to inquire—

2. *Whether the State of Maryland may, without violating the constitution, tax that branch?*

That the power of taxation is one of vital importance; that it is retained by the States; that it is not abridged by the grant of a similar power to the government of the Union; that it is to be concurrently exercised by the two governments—are truths which have never been denied.

But such is the paramount character of the constitution, that its capacity to withdraw any subject from the action of even this power, is admitted. . . . [T]he same paramount character would seem to restrain, as it certainly may restrain, a State from such other exercise of this power, as is in its nature incompatible with, and repugnant to, the constitutional laws of the Union. A law, absolutely repugnant to another, as entirely repeals that other as if express terms of repeal were used.

On this ground, the counsel for the bank place its claim to be exempted from the power of a State to tax its operations. There is no express provision for the case, but the claim has been sustained on a principle which so entirely pervades the constitution, is so intermixed with the materials which compose it, so interwoven with its web, so blended with its texture, as to be incapable of being separated from it, without rending it into shreds. This great principle is, that the constitution and the laws made in pursuance thereof are supreme; that they control the constitution and laws of the respective States, and cannot be controlled by them.

In a different part of the opinion, Marshall said:

> If any one proposition could command the universal assent of mankind, we might expect it would be this—that the government of the Union, though limited in its powers, is supreme within its sphere of action. This would seem to result, necessarily, from its nature. It is the government of all; its powers are delegated by all; it represents all, and acts for all. Though any one State may be willing to control its operations, no State is willing to allow others to control them. The nation, on those subjects on which it can act, must necessarily bind its component parts. But this question is not left to mere reason: the people have, in express terms, decided it, by saying, "this constitution, and the laws of the United States, which shall be made in pursuance thereof," "shall be the supreme law of the land," and by requiring that the members of the State legislatures, and the officers of the executive and judicial departments of the States, shall take the oath of fidelity to it. The government of the United States, then, though limited in its powers, is supreme; and its laws, when made in pursuance of the constitution, form the supreme law of the land, "anything in the constitution or laws of any State to the contrary notwithstanding."

WORTH NOTING

From this, which may be almost termed an axiom, other propositions are deduced as corollaries, on the truth or error of which, and on their application to this case, the cause has been supposed to depend. These are,

1st. That a power to create implies a power to preserve:

2d. That a power to destroy, if wielded by a different hand, is hostile to, and incompatible with these powers to create and to preserve:

3d. That where this repugnancy exists, that authority which is supreme must control, not yield to that over which it is supreme. . . .

It is of the very essence of supremacy, to remove all obstacles to its action within its own sphere, and so to modify every power vested in subordinate governments, as to exempt its own operations from their own influence. This effect need not be stated in terms. It is so involved in the declaration of supremacy, so necessarily implied in it, that the expression of it could not make it more certain. We must, therefore, keep it in view, while construing the constitution. . . .

If we apply the principle for which the State of Maryland contends, to the constitution, generally, we shall find it capable of changing totally the character of that instrument. We shall find it capable of arresting all the measures of the government, and of prostrating it at the foot of the States. The American people have declared their constitution and the laws made in pursuance thereof, to be supreme; but this principle would transfer the supremacy, in fact, to the States. If the States may tax one instrument, employed by the government in the execution of its powers, they may tax any and every other instrument. They may tax the mail; they may tax the mint; they may tax patent-rights; they may tax the papers of the custom-house; they may tax judicial process; they may tax all the means employed by the government, to an excess which would defeat all the ends of government. This was not intended by the American people. They did not design to make their government dependent on the States. . . .

It has also been insisted that . . . [e]very argument which would sustain the right of the general government to tax banks chartered by the States, will equally sustain the right of the States to tax banks chartered by the general government. But the two cases are not on the same reason. The people of all the States have created the general government, and have conferred upon it the general power of taxation. The people of all the States, and the States themselves, are represented in Congress, and, by their representatives, exercise this power. When they tax the chartered institutions of the States, they tax their constituents, and these taxes must be uniform. But when a State taxes the operations of the government of the United States, it acts upon institutions created not by their own constituents, but by people over whom they claim no control. It acts upon the measures of a government created by others as well as themselves, for the benefit of others in common with themselves. The difference is that which always exists, and always must exist, between the action of the whole on a part, and the action of a part on the whole—between the laws of a government declared to be supreme, and those of a government which, when in opposition to those laws, is not supreme. . . .

For a classic cinematic analogy to Marshall's view of the relation between federal and state power, see Marv Newland, *Bambi Meets Godzilla* (1969).

The Court has bestowed on this subject its most deliberate consideration. The result is a conviction that the States have no power, by taxation or otherwise, to retard, impede, burden, or in any manner control, the operations of the constitutional laws enacted by Congress to carry into execution the powers vested in the general government. This is, we think, the unavoidable consequence of that supremacy which the constitution has declared. We are unanimously of opinion, that the law passed by the legislature of Maryland, imposing a tax on the Bank of the United States, is unconstitutional and void. . . .

For Discussion

(1) Does *McCulloch's* interpretation of the Necessary and Proper Clause reduce the enumeration principle to a pleasant fiction? And if so, does that mean that it must be wrong? For an argument that the bare fact of constitutionally enumerated powers doesn't require that those powers be construed as collectively conveying something less than the police power, see Richard Primus, *The Limits of Enumeration*, 124 Yale L. J. 576. (2014). Imagine, for example, a constitution that enumerated only two legislative powers: the power to regulate anything on weekdays, and the power to regulate anything on weekends.

(2) If there were no Necessary and Proper Clause, would the result of *McCulloch* have changed? How, if at all, would its analysis have changed?

(3) What is Marshall's answer to the question of whether the federal government and its instrumentalities are immune from state taxation? Can you think of any reasonable alternatives? Consider these possibilities:

    (a) A state may impose a tax on the federal government or its instrumentalities if and only if the tax is reasonable.

    (b) A state may impose a tax on the federal government or its instrumentalities if and only if the tax is non-discriminatory.

    (c) Congress may immunize the federal government or its instrumentalities from state taxation, but only by expressly stating so.

    (d) The federal government is immune from state taxation, but instrumentalities created by the government are immune only if they are an integral part of the government.

While adopting an extremely broad view of federal power, the *McCulloch* decision seemed careful to ground its technical holding on specific textual provisions expressly enumerated in Article I, § 8. Now let's examine two late-nineteenth century cases that revisit the enumeration principle in the immigration context. As you read the discussion, consider whether you read them as applications of *McCulloch* or as departures from it.

Both cases arose from a series of congressional statutes passed in response to the fears of many Americans that—in the words of Justice Stephen Field, who hailed from California—the western portion of the nation would be "overrun" by "vast hordes" of Chinese immigrants:

> The discovery of gold in California in 1848, as is well known, was followed by a large immigration thither from all parts of the world, attracted not only by the hope of gain from the mines, but from the great prices paid for all kinds of labor. The news of the discovery penetrated China, and laborers came from there in great numbers. . . . Not being accompanied by families, except in rare instances, their expenses were small; and they were content with the simplest fare, such as would not suffice for our laborers and artisans. The competition between them and our people was for this reason altogether in their favor, and the consequent irritation, proportionately deep and bitter, was followed, in many cases, by open conflicts, to the great disturbance of the public peace.

> The differences of race added greatly to the difficulties of the situation. [T]hey remained strangers in the land, residing apart by themselves, and adhering to the customs and usages of their own country. It seemed impossible for them to assimilate with our people, or to make any change in their habits or modes of living. As they grew in numbers each year the people of the coast saw, or believed they saw, in the facility of immigration, and in the crowded millions of China, where population presses upon the means of subsistence, great danger that at no distant day that portion of our country would be overrun by them, unless prompt action was taken to restrict their immigration. The people there accordingly petitioned earnestly for protective legislation.

Chae Chan Ping v. United States (1889).

Among the enactments that resulted were the Page Act of 1875, which invoked concerns about forced labor to effectively prohibit the immigration of women from East Asia, and the Chinese Exclusion Act of 1882, which pro-hibited the immigration of Chinese laborers for ten years. These laws did not affect the status of Chinese immigrants already in the United States. In *Chae Chan Ping*, the appellant was a Chinese citizen who lived in San Francisco from 1875 to 1887. He then returned temporarily to China, first obtaining a certificate—duly issued by the collector of the port of San Francisco pursuant to the 1882 Exclusion Act—that legally entitled him to return. When he attempted to return the next year, however, he discovered a serious problem. Just one week earlier, Congress had passed the Scott Act of 1888, which prohib-ited the return of Chinese laborers who sought re-entry to the United States. The Act explicitly nullified certificates of the type issued to Chae Chan Ping. The Supreme Court upheld this legislation, in a unanimous opinion by Justice Field. Addressing the question of whether Congress had power to enact the law, he wrote:

> . . . That the government of the United States, through the action of the legislative department, can exclude aliens from its territory is a proposition which we do not think open to controversy. Jurisdiction over its own territory to that extent is an incident of every independent nation. It is a part of its independence. If it could not exclude aliens it would be to that extent subject to the control of another power. . . . The powers to declare war, make treaties, suppress insurrection, repel invasion, regulate foreign commerce, secure republican governments to the states, and admit subjects of other nations to citizenship, are all sovereign powers, restricted in their exercise only by the constitution itself and considerations of public policy and justice which control, more or less, the conduct of all civilized nations. . . .
>
> To preserve its independence, and give security against foreign aggression and encroachment, is the highest duty of every nation, and to attain these ends nearly all other considerations are to be subordi-nated. It matters not in what form such aggression and encroachment come, whether from the foreign nation acting in its national character, or from vast hordes of its people crowding in upon us. The govern-ment, possessing the powers which are to be exercised for protection and security, is clothed with authority to determine the occasion on which the powers shall be called forth; and its determinations, so

far as the subjects affected are concerned, are necessarily conclusive upon all its departments and officers. . . .

The power of exclusion of foreigners being an incident of sovereignty belonging to the government of the United States as a part of those sovereign powers delegated by the constitution, the right to its exercise at any time when, in the judgment of the government, the interests of the country require it, cannot be granted away or restrained on behalf of any one. . . . Whatever license, therefore, Chinese laborers may have obtained, previous to the [Scott Act of 1888], to return to the United States [is] revocable at any time. . . .

FOR DISCUSSION According to the Court, which provision of the Constitution authorizes the Scott Act of 1888?

As the Exclusion Act of 1882 was about to expire, Congress passed the Geary Act of 1892, which extended the exclusion for another ten years. The Geary Act also required any Chinese laborer already in the United States to apply to the local collector of internal revenue for a certificate establishing, with the testimony of "at least one credible white witness," that he was a lawful resident of the U.S. at the time the Act was passed. Failure to obtain this certificate within a year of the bill's enactment would subject the laborer to arrest and deportation. In *Fong Yue Ting v. United States* (1893), the Court upheld this provision by a 6–3 vote. Justice Gray, for the majority, wrote:

> In the recent case of *Nishimura Ekiu v. United States*, the court, in sustaining the action of the executive department, putting in force an act of congress for the exclusion of aliens, said:
>
> > It is an accepted maxim of international law that every sovereign nation has the power, as inherent in sovereignty, and essential to self-preservation, to forbid the entrance of foreigners within its dominions, or to admit them only in such cases and upon such conditions as it may see fit to prescribe. In the United States this power is vested in the national government [and] may be exercised either through treaties made by the president and senate or through statutes enacted by congress.

. . . The statements of leading commentators on the law of nations are to the same effect. Vattel says:

> Every nation has the right to refuse to admit a foreigner into the country, when he cannot enter without putting the nation in evident danger, or doing it a manifest injury. What it owes to itself, the care of its own safety, gives it this right; and, in virtue of its natural liberty, it belongs to the nation to judge whether its circumstances will or will not justify the admission of the foreigner . . . . Thus, also, it has a right to send them elsewhere, if it has just cause to fear that they will corrupt the manners of the citizens; that they will create religious disturbances, or occasion any other disorder, contrary to the public safety. In a word, it has a right, and is even obliged, in this respect, to follow the rules which prudence dictates.

Vattel, The Laws of Nature. [The Court goes on to cite other major treatises, international law precedent, and British law on the same point.]

The right to exclude or to expel all aliens, or any class of aliens, absolutely or upon certain conditions, in war or in peace, being an inherent and inalienable right of every sovereign and independent nation, essential to its safety, its independence, and its welfare, the question now before the court is whether the manner in which congress has exercised this right in [the Geary Act of 1892] is consistent with the constitution.

The United States are a sovereign and independent nation, and are vested by the constitution with the entire control of international relations, and with all the powers of government necessary to maintain that control, and to make it effective. The only government of this country which other nations recognize or treat with is the government of the Union, and the only American flag known throughout the world is the flag of the United States.

The constitution of the United States speaks with no uncertain sound upon this subject. That instrument, established by the people of the United States as the fundamental law of the land, has conferred upon the president the executive power; has made him the commander in chief of the army and navy; has authorized him, by and with the consent of the senate, to make treaties, and to appoint ambassadors, public ministers, and consuls; and has made it his duty to take care that the laws be faithfully executed. The constitution has granted to congress the power to regulate commerce with foreign nations, including the entrance of ships, the importation of goods, and the bringing of persons into the ports of the United States; to establish a uniform rule of naturalization; to define and punish piracies and felonies committed on the high seas, and offenses against the law of nations; to declare war, grant letters of marque and reprisal, and make rules concerning captures on land and water; to raise and support armies, to provide and maintain a navy, and to make rules for the government and regulation of the land and naval forces; and to make all laws necessary and proper for carrying into execution these powers, and all other powers vested by the constitution in the government of the United States, or in any department or officer thereof. And the several states are expressly forbidden to enter into any treaty, alliance, or confederation; to grant letters of marque and reprisal; to enter into any agreement or compact with another state, or with a foreign power; or to engage in war, unless actually invaded, or in such imminent danger as will not admit of delay.

In exercising the great power which the people of the United States, by establishing a written constitution as the supreme and paramount law, have vested in this court, of determining, whenever the question is properly brought before it, whether the acts of the legislature or of the executive are consistent with the constitution, it behooves the court to be careful that it does not undertake to pass upon political questions, the final decision of which has been committed by the constitution to the other departments of the government.

Justice Gray then quoted the legitimate-ends, appropriate-means language of *McCulloch*.

Chief Justice Fuller, Justice Field, and his nephew Justice Brewer each wrote in dissent. They all drew a sharp distinction between laws (like the Scott Act of 1888) that excluded subjects of foreign nations and those (like the Geary Act) that provided for deportation of people already in the United States. While recognizing that Congress had the power to deport subjects of enemy nations, Justice Field wrote that

> in no other instance has the deportation of friendly aliens been advocated as a lawful measure by any department of our Government. And it will surprise most people to learn that any such dangerous and despotic power lies in our Government—a power which will authorize it to expel at pleasure, in time of peace, the whole body of friendly foreigners of any country domiciled herein by its permission; a power which can be brought into exercise whenever it may suit the pleasure of Congress. . . . Is it possible that Congress can, at its pleasure, in disregard of the guaranties of the Constitution, expel at any time the Irish, German, French, and English who may have taken up their residence here on the invitation of the Government, while we are at peace with the countries from which they came, simply on the ground that they have not been naturalized?

Each of the three dissenters also concluded that the Geary Act violated the due-process rights of the persons subject to the deportation orders. According to the majority's theory, Justice Field wrote, "Congress might have ordered executive officers to take the Chinese laborers to the ocean, and put them into a boat, and set them adrift, or to take them to the borders of Mexico, and turn them loose there, and in both cases without any means of support. Indeed, it might have sanctioned towards these laborers the most shocking brutality conceivable."

For Discussion

(1) According to the Court, which provision of the Constitution authorizes the Geary Act of 1892?

(2) What does it mean for a power to be "enumerated"? If some unmentioned authority is fairly implied in some specific textual grant of power, does that count as an enumeration? Is it possible for a power to be implicitly enumerated? When Congress relies on the Necessary & Proper Clause, is it using an enumerated power?

(3) In *National Federation of Independent Businesses v. Sebelius* (2012), presented at pp. 525–588, the Supreme Court held that a key element of the Affordable Care Act could not be justified as an exercise of congressional power under the Necessary & Proper Clause. The Court observed

that "[i]f no enumerated power authorizes Congress to pass a certain law, that law may not be enacted, even if it would not violate any of the express prohibitions in the Bill of Rights or elsewhere in the Constitution. . . ." Is this statement about enumerated powers consistent with *Chae Chan Ping*? With *Fong Yue Ting*? If so, how? If not, what does that mean?

3. The Commerce Clause

The Commerce Clause is probably the most important regulatory authority granted in Article I:

> The Congress shall have Power . . . [t]o regulate Commerce with foreign Nations, and among the several States, and with the Indian Tribes.
>
> Art. I, § 8, cl. 3.

The clause authorizes Congress to regulate three different kinds of activity: commerce that takes place with foreign countries, commerce that takes place among the several states, and commerce that takes place with Native American tribes. Most of the time, bare references to "the Commerce Clause" have the second category in mind—that is to say, commerce "among the several States"—and that will be our focus.

This unit will explore the origins, historical development, and present application of the Commerce Clause. By the end of this sequence of cases, you should have a good understanding of what kinds of regulatory authority are included in this authorization "to regulate Commerce . . . among the several states." You should also have a better sense for why this provision—which could have been interpreted relatively narrowly—has always been understood to authorize a wide array of regulations that go far beyond merely dictating the terms of a market transaction.

a. Commerce Clause—the Framework

Among the most significant defects of the Articles of Confederation, the lack of a single supreme regulatory authority over the nation's commerce ranked high on just about everyone's agenda. Indeed, it was little short of a disaster—giving rise to obstructive legislation by the states, confusion among producers, distributors, and consumers of goods, and a generally debilitating state of affairs for the American economy. Even many opponents of the Constitution agreed that it was a pressing priority to create commerce authority at the national level; they just thought it could and should have been done by amending the Articles of Confederation.

But what did the power "to regulate Commerce" mean? The 1824 decision in *Gibbons v. Ogden*, the Supreme Court's first extensive discussion of the power, is foundational because of the analytical structure it produced. Textually speaking, the Court could have adopted a very narrow reading of Congress's commerce authority—perhaps as creating only the power to dictate the terms on which interstate transactions could be completed. In keeping with the robustly nationalist tendencies of Marshall and his Court, however, that's not what *Gibbons* did. Rather, it created a framework for Commerce Clause analysis that recognized two quite distinct and equally valid realms of congressional commerce regulation. First, the regulation of the actual conduct of interstate commerce. Second, the regulation of at least some things that *affect* interstate commerce or other states in a legally relevant way. To put it mildly, these categories are not self-defining. But they structure the debates over commerce authority in a framework that has persisted to the present day.

The story of the case itself began in 1808, when the New York Legislature gave Chancellor Robert Livingston and Robert Fulton—one a politically well-connected money man and the other an engineer and inventor—an exclusive franchise to operate steamboats "within" the state; the franchise was meant to encourage them to develop a practical steamboat, and they succeeded. In 1815, their assignee, John Livingston, sold Aaron Ogden, a former Governor of New Jersey, a license to operate a steamboat between New York City and New Jersey. Thomas Gibbons later began operating two steamboat ferries on the same route. Ogden got an injunction from the New York Court of Chancery, per Chancellor James Kent—probably the leading American legal scholar of the era—preventing Gibbons from operating. Meanwhile, though, Gibbons had gotten licenses for the boats under the federal Coasting Act of 1793. He moved to dissolve the injunction on the basis of these licenses. Kent refused. He wrote that the 1793 statute

> provides for the enrolling and licensing ships and vessels to be employed in the coasting trade and fisheries. Without being enrolled and licensed, they are not entitled to the privileges of American vessels,

but must pay the same fees and tonnage as foreign vessels, and if they have on board articles of foreign growth or manufacture, or distilled spirits, they are liable to forfeiture. . . . The act of Congress referred to never meant to determine the right of property, or the use or enjoyment of it, under the laws of the states. Any person in the assumed character of owner, may obtain the enrolment and license required, but it will still remain for the laws and courts of the several states to determine the right and title of such assumed owner, or of some other person, to navigate the vessel. The license only gives to the vessel an American character, while the right of the individual procuring the license to use the vessel as against another individual setting up a distinct and exclusive right, remains precisely as it did before. . . . However unquestionable the right and title to a specific chattel may be, and from whatever source that title may be derived, the use and employment of it must, as a general rule, be subject to the laws and regulations of the state. . . .

The only limitation upon such a general discretion and power of control, is the occurrence of the case when the exercise of it would impede or defeat the operation of some lawful measure, or be absolutely repugnant to some constitutional law of the Union. When laws become repugnant to each other, the supreme or paramount law must and will prevail. There can be no doubt of the fitness and necessity of this result, in every mind that entertains a just sense of its duty and loyalty. Suppose there was a provision in the act of Congress that all vessels, duly licensed, should be at liberty to navigate, for the purpose of trade and commerce, over all the navigable bays, harbors, rivers and lakes within the several states, any law of the states creating particular privileges as to any particular class of vessels to the contrary notwithstanding, the only question that could arise in such a case would be, whether the law was constitutional. If that was to be granted or decided in favor of the validity of the law, it would certainly, in all courts and places, overrule and set aside the state grant.

But at present we have no such case, and there is no ground to infer any such supremacy or intention from the act regulating the coasting trade. There is no collision between the act of Congress and the acts of this state creating the steam-boat monopoly. The one requires all vessels to be licensed, to entitle them to the privileges of American vessels, and the others confer on particular individuals the exclusive right to navigate steam-boats, without, however, interfering with or questioning the requisition of the license. . . . The suggestion that the laws of the two governments are repugnant to each other upon this point appears to be new, and without any foundation. The acts granting exclusive privileges to Livingston and Fulton were all passed subsequent to the act of Congress; and it must have struck every one, at the time, to have been perfectly idle to pass such laws, conferring such privileges, if a coasting license, which was to be obtained as a matter of course, and with as much facility as the flag of the United States could be procured and hoisted, was sufficient to interpose and annihilate the force and authority of those laws.

Gibbons appealed to the Court for the Trial of Impeachments and Correction of Errors, which affirmed on similar grounds:

The term "license" seems not to be used in the sense imputed to it by the counsel for the appellant: that is, a permit to trade; or as giving a right of transit. Because it is perfectly clear, that such a vessel, coasting from one state to another, would have exactly the same right to trade, and the same right of transit, whether she had the coasting license or not. She does not, therefore, derive her right from the license; the only effect of which is, to determine her national character, and the rate of duties which she is to pay.

Whatever may be the abstract right of Congress, to pass laws for regulating trade, which might come in collision, and conflict with the exclusive privilege granted by this state, it is sufficient, now, for the protection of the respondent, that the statute of the United States relied on by the appellant, is not of that character.

Whether Congress have the power to authorize the coasting trade to be carried on, in vessels propelled by steam, so as to give a paramount right, in opposition to the special license given by this state, is a question not yet presented to us. No such act of Congress yet exists, and it will be time enough to discuss that question when it arises.

Gibbons, represented by Daniel Webster, then appealed to the United States Supreme Court.

Gibbons v. Ogden

Supreme Court of the United States, 1824.
22 U.S. (9 Wheat.) 1.

Mr. Chief Justice Marshall delivered the opinion of the Court, and, after stating the case, proceeded as follows:

The appellant contends that this decree is erroneous, because the laws which purport to give the exclusive privilege it sustains, are repugnant to the constitution and laws of the United States. They are said to be repugnant [t]o that clause in the constitution which authorizes Congress to regulate commerce. . . .

This instrument contains an enumeration of powers expressly granted by the people to their government. It has been said that these powers ought to be construed strictly. But why ought they to be so construed? Is there one sentence in the constitution which gives countenance to this rule? In the last of the enumerated powers, that which grants, expressly, the means for carrying all others into execution, Congress is authorized "to make all laws which shall be necessary and proper" for the purpose. But this limitation on the means which may be used, is not extended to the powers which are conferred; nor is there one sentence in the constitution, which has been pointed out by the gentlemen of the bar, or which we have been able to discern, that prescribes this rule. We do not, therefore, think ourselves justified in adopting it. . . .

We know of no rule for construing the extent of such powers, other than is given by the language of the instrument which confers them, taken in connexion with the purposes for which they were conferred.

The words are, "Congress shall have power to regulate commerce with foreign nations, and among the several States, and with the Indian tribes."

The subject to be regulated is commerce; and our constitution being, as was aptly said at the bar, one of enumeration, and not of definition, to ascertain the extent of the power, it becomes necessary to settle the meaning of the word. The counsel for the appellee would limit it to traffic, to buying and selling, or the interchange of commodities, and do not admit that it comprehends navigation. This would restrict a general term, applicable to many objects, to one of its significations. Commerce, undoubtedly, is traffic, but it is something more: it is intercourse. It describes the commercial intercourse between nations, and parts of nations, in all its branches, and is regulated by prescribing rules for carrying on that intercourse. The mind can scarcely conceive a system for regulating commerce between nations, which shall exclude all laws concerning navigation, which shall be silent on the admission of the vessels of the one nation into the ports of the other, and be confined to prescribing rules for the conduct of individuals, in the actual employment of buying and selling, or of barter.

If commerce does not include navigation, the government of the Union has no direct power over that subject, and can make no law prescribing what shall constitute American vessels, or requiring that they shall be navigated by American seamen. Yet this power has been exercised from the commencement of the government, has been exercised with the consent of all, and has been understood by all to be a commercial regulation. All America understands, and has uniformly understood, the word "commerce," to comprehend navigation. It was so understood, and must have been so understood, when the constitution was framed. The power over commerce, including navigation, was one of the primary objects for which the people of America adopted their government, and must have been contemplated in forming it. The convention must have used the word in that sense, because all have understood it in that sense; and the attempt to restrict it comes too late.

If the opinion that "commerce," as the word is used in the constitution, comprehends navigation also, requires any additional confirmation, that additional confirmation is, we think, furnished by the words of the instrument itself.

It is a rule of construction, acknowledged by all, that the exceptions from a power mark its extent; for it would be absurd, as well as useless, to except from a granted power, that which was not granted—that which the words of the grant could not comprehend. If, then, there are in the constitution plain exceptions from the power over navigation, plain inhibitions to the exercise of that power in a particular way, it is a proof that those who made these exceptions, and prescribed these inhibitions, understood the power to which they applied as being granted. The 9th section of the 1st article declares, that "no preference shall be given, by any regulation of commerce or revenue, to the ports of one State over those of another." [T]he most obvious preference which can be given to one port over another, in regulating commerce, relates to navigation.

But the subsequent part of the sentence is still more explicit. It is, "nor shall vessels bound to or from one State, be obliged to enter, clear, or pay duties, in another." These words have a direct reference to navigation.

The universally acknowledged power of the government to impose embargoes, must also be considered as showing, that all America is united in that construction which comprehends navigation in the word commerce. [Indeed, embargoes] are sometimes resorted to without a view to war, and with a single view to commerce.

The word used in the constitution, then, comprehends, and has been always understood to comprehend, navigation within its meaning; and a power to regulate navigation, is as expressly granted, as if that term had been added to the word "commerce."

To what commerce does this power extend? The constitution informs us, to commerce "with foreign nations, and among the several States, and with the Indian tribes."

It has, we believe, been universally admitted, that these words comprehend every species of commercial intercourse between the United States and foreign nations. No sort of trade can be carried on between this country and any other, to which this power does not extend. It has been truly said, that commerce, as the word is used in the constitution, is a unit, every part of which is indicated by the term. If this be the admitted meaning of the word, in its application to foreign nations, it must carry the same meaning throughout the sentence, and remain a unit, unless there be some plain intelligible cause which alters it.

The subject to which the power is next applied, is to commerce "among the several States." The word "among" means intermingled with. A thing which is among others, is intermingled with them. Commerce among the States, cannot stop at the external boundary line of each State, but may be introduced into the interior.

It is not intended to say that these words comprehend that commerce, which is completely internal, which is carried on between man and man in a State, or between different parts of the same State, and which does not extend to or affect other States. Such a power would be inconvenient, and is certainly unnecessary.

Comprehensive as the word "among" is, it may very properly be restricted to that commerce which concerns more States than one. The phrase is not one which would probably have been selected to indicate the completely interior traffic of a State, because it is not an apt phrase for that purpose; and the enumeration of the particular classes of commerce, to which the power was to be extended, would not have been made, had the intention been to extend the power to every description. The enumeration presupposes something not enumerated; and that something, if we regard the language or the subject of the sentence, must be the exclusively internal commerce of a State. The genius and character of the whole government seem to be, that its action is to be applied to all the external concerns of the nation, and to those internal concerns which affect the States generally; but not to those which are completely within a particular State, which do not affect other States, and with which it is not necessary to interfere, for the purpose of executing some of the general powers of the government. The completely internal commerce of a State, then, may be considered as reserved for the State itself.

But, in regulating commerce with foreign nations, the power of Congress does not stop at the jurisdictional lines of the several States. It would be a very useless power, if it could not pass those lines. The commerce of the United States with foreign nations, is that of the whole United States. Every district has a right to participate in it. The deep streams which penetrate our country in every direction, pass through the interior of almost every State in the Union, and furnish the means of exercising this right. If Congress has the power to regulate it, that power must be exercised whenever the subject exists. If it exists within the States, if a foreign voyage may commence or terminate at a port within a State, then the power of Congress may be exercised within a State.

This principle is, if possible, still more clear, when applied to commerce "among the several States." They either join each other, in which case they are separated by a mathematical line, or they are remote from each other, in which case other States lie between them. What is commerce "among" them; and how is it to be conducted? Can a trading expedition between two adjoining States, commence and terminate outside of each? And if the trading intercourse be between two States remote from each other, must it not commence in one, terminate in the other, and probably pass through a third? Commerce among the States must, of necessity, be commerce with the States. In the regulation of trade with the Indian tribes, the action of the law, especially when the constitution was made, was chiefly within a State. The power of Congress, then, whatever it may be, must be exercised within the territorial jurisdiction of the several States. The sense of the nation on this subject, is unequivocally manifested by the provisions made in the laws for transporting goods, by land, between Baltimore and Providence, between New-York and Philadelphia, and between Philadelphia and Baltimore.

We are now arrived at the inquiry—What is this power?

It is the power to regulate; that is, to prescribe the rule by which commerce is to be governed. This power, like all others vested in Congress, is complete in itself, may be exercised to its utmost extent, and acknowledges no limitations, other than are prescribed in the constitution. These are expressed in plain terms, and do not affect the questions which arise in this case, or which have been discussed at the bar. If, as has always been understood, the sovereignty of Congress, though limited to specified objects, is plenary as to those objects, the power over commerce with foreign nations, and among the several States, is vested in Congress as absolutely as it would be in a single government, having in its constitution the same restrictions on the exercise of the power as are found in the constitution of the United States. The wisdom and the discretion of Congress, their identity with the people, and the influence which their constituents possess at elections, are, in this, as in many other instances, as that, for example, of declaring war, the sole restraints on which they have relied, to secure them from its abuse. They are the restraints on which the people must often rely solely, in all representative governments.

The power of Congress, then, comprehends navigation, within the limits of every State in the Union; so far as that navigation may be, in any manner, connected with "commerce with foreign nations, or among the several States, or with the Indian tribes." It may, of consequence, pass the jurisdictional line of New-York, and act upon the very waters to which the prohibition now under consideration applies.

But it has been urged with great earnestness [by respondent], that, although the power of Congress to regulate commerce with foreign nations, and among the several States, be co-extensive with the subject itself, and have no other limits than are prescribed in the constitution, yet the States may severally exercise the same power, within their respective jurisdictions. . . . In discussing the question, whether this power is still in the States, in the case under consideration, we may dismiss from it the inquiry, whether it is surrendered by the mere grant to Congress, or is retained until Congress shall exercise the power. We may dismiss that inquiry, because it has been exercised, and the regulations which Congress deemed it proper to make, are now in full operation.

The sole question is, can a State regulate commerce with foreign nations and among the States, while Congress is regulating it? . . . It is obvious, that the government of the Union, in the exercise of its express powers, that, for example, of regulating commerce with foreign nations and among the States, may use means that may also be employed by a State, in the exercise of its acknowledged powers; that, for example, of regulating commerce within the State.

WORTH NOTING

Here, Marshall discusses state inspection and health laws, which he says do not find their source in a power over commerce but constitute "a portion of that immense mass of legislation, which embraces every thing within the territory of a State, not surrendered to the general government: all which can be most advantageously exercised by the States themselves."

In our complex system, presenting the rare and difficult scheme of one general government, whose action extends over the whole, but which possesses only certain enumerated powers; and of numerous State governments, which retain and exercise all powers not delegated to the Union, contests respecting power must arise. [Since] in exercising the power of regulating their own purely internal affairs, whether of trading or police, the States may sometimes enact laws, the validity of which depends on their interfering with, and being contrary to, an act of Congress passed in pursuance of the constitution, the Court will enter upon the inquiry, whether the laws of New-York, as expounded by the highest tribunal of that State, have, in their application to this case, come into collision with an act of Congress, and deprived a citizen of a right to which that act entitles him.

Should this collision exist, it will be immaterial whether those laws were passed in virtue of a concurrent power "to regulate commerce with foreign nations and among the several States," or, in virtue of a power to regulate their domestic trade and police. In one case and the other, the acts of New-York must yield to the law of Congress; and the decision sustaining the privilege they confer, against a right given by a law of the Union, must be erroneous.

[The court then turns to a close analysis of the Federal Coasting Trade Act of 1793 in order to decide whether the restrictive New York statute "collides" with it.]

The first section [of the federal Act] declares, that vessels . . . enrolled as described in that act, and having a license in force, as is by the act required, "and no others, shall be deemed ships or vessels of the United States, entitled to the privileges of ships or vessels employed in the coasting trade."

This section seems to the Court to contain a positive enactment, the vessels it describes shall be entitled to the privileges of ships or vessels employed in the coasting trade. These privileges cannot be separated from the trade, and cannot be enjoyed, unless the trade may be prosecuted. The grant of the privilege is an idle, empty form, conveying nothing, unless it convey the right to which the privilege is attached, and in the exercise of which its whole value consists. To construe these words otherwise than as entitling the ships or vessels described, to carry on the coasting trade, would be, we think, to disregard the apparent intent of the act. . . .

The license [issued to Gibbons pursuant to the federal Act] must be understood to be what it purports to be, a legislative authority to the steamboat Bellona, "to be employed in carrying on the coasting trade, for one year from this date."

It has been denied that these words authorize a voyage from New-Jersey to New-York. It is true, that no ports are specified; but it is equally true, that the words used are perfectly intelligible, and do confer such authority as unquestionably, as if the ports had been mentioned. The coasting trade is a term well understood. The law has defined it; and all know its meaning perfectly. The act describes, with great minuteness, the various operations of a vessel engaged in it; and it cannot, we think, be doubted, that a voyage from New-Jersey to New-York, is one of those operations. . . .

[T]he act of a State inhibiting the use of [the coastal waters] to any vessel having a license under the act of Congress, comes, we think, in direct collision with that act. . . .

Powerful and ingenious minds, taking, as postulates, that the powers expressly granted to the government of the Union, are to be contracted by construction, into the narrowest possible compass, and that the original powers of the States are retained, if any possible construction will retain them, may, by a course of well digested, but refined and metaphysical reasoning, founded on these premises, explain away the constitution of our country, and leave it, a magnificent structure, indeed, to look at, but totally unfit for use. They may so entangle and perplex the understanding, as to obscure principles, which were before thought quite plain, and induce doubts where, if the mind were to pursue its own course, none would be perceived. In such a case, it is peculiarly necessary to recur to safe and fundamental principles to sustain those principles, and when sustained, to make them the tests of the arguments to be examined.

MR. JUSTICE JOHNSON [concurring].

The judgment entered by the Court in this cause, has my entire approbation; but having adopted my conclusions on views of the subject materially different from those of my brethren, I feel it incumbent on me to exhibit those views. . . .

The great and paramount purpose [of the Constitution], was to unite [the nation's] mass of wealth and power, for the protection of the humblest individual. . . .

The strong sympathies, rather than the feeble government, which bound the States together during a common war [*i.e.*, the American Revolution], dissolved on the return of peace; and the very principles which gave rise to the war of the revolution, began to threaten the confederacy with anarchy and ruin. The States had resisted a tax imposed by the parent state [*i.e.*, Great Britain], and now reluctantly submitted to, or altogether rejected, the moderate demands of the [new American] confederation. Every one recollects the painful and threatening discussions, which arose on the subject of the five per cent duty [proposed by the Continental Congress in 1783]. Some States rejected it altogether; others insisted on collecting it themselves; scarcely any acquiesced without reservations, which deprived it altogether of the character of a national measure; and at length, some repealed the laws by which they had signified their acquiescence.

For a century the States had submitted, with murmurs, to the commercial restrictions imposed by [Great Britain]; and now, finding themselves in the unlimited possession of those powers over their own commerce, which they had so long been deprived of, and so earnestly coveted, that selfish principle which, well controlled, is so salutary, and which, unrestricted, is so unjust and tyrannical, guided by inexperience and jealousy, began to show itself in iniquitous laws and impolitic measures, from which grew up a conflict of commercial regulations, destructive to the harmony of the States, and fatal to their commercial interests abroad.

This was the immediate cause, that led to the forming of a convention. . . . And the plain and direct import of the words of the grant [under the Commerce Clause], is consistent with this general understanding. . . . The power of a sovereign state over commerce . . . amounts to nothing more than a power to limit and restrain it at pleasure. And since the power to prescribe the limits to its freedom, necessarily implies the power to determine what shall remain unrestrained, it follows, that the power must be exclusive. . . .

When speaking of the power of Congress over navigation, I do not regard it as a power incidental to that of regulating commerce; I consider it as the thing itself; inseparable from it as vital motion is from vital existence. Commerce, in its simplest signification, means an exchange of goods; but in the advancement of society, labour, transportation, intelligence, care, and various mediums of exchange, become commodities, and enter into commerce; the subject, the vehicle, the agent, and their various operations, become the objects of commercial regulation. Ship building, the carrying trade, and propagation of seamen, are such vital agents of commercial prosperity, that the nation which could not legislate over these subjects, would not possess power to regulate commerce. . . .

It has been contended, that the grants of power to the United States over any subject, do not, necessarily, paralyze the arm of the States, or deprive them of the capacity to act on the same subject. [But] although one grant of power over commerce, should not be deemed a total relinquishment of power over the subject, but amounting only to a power to assume, still the power of the States must be at an end, so far as the United States have, by their legislative act, taken the subject under their immediate superintendence. . . .

It would be in vain to deny the possibility of a clashing and collision between the measures of the two governments. The line cannot be drawn with sufficient distinctness between the municipal powers of the one, and the commercial powers of the other. In some points they meet and blend so as scarcely to admit of separation. Hitherto the only remedy has been applied which the case admits of; that of a frank and candid co-operation for the general good. Witness the laws of Congress requiring its officers to respect the inspection laws of the States, and to aid in enforcing their health laws; that which surrenders to the States the superintendence of pilotage, and the many laws passed to permit a tonnage duty to be levied for the use of their ports. Other instances could be cited, abundantly. . . .

For Discussion

(1) What does the Court actually hold? If you were to write a simple, narrow opinion reaching the same result that the Court did, what might you say?

(2) If you were to write a simple opinion reaching the opposite result, what might you say?

i.   Commerce Clause Framework—Command-and-Control Regulation

The Commerce Clause framework established by *Gibbons v. Ogden* persists to the present day. Just about every development in the doctrine since then can be seen as an elaboration on one of the two categories recognized by *Gibbons*: regulation of things "in" interstate commerce, and regulation of things that "affect" other states or interstate commerce itself. It might have been hard for Chief Justice Marshall to predict how this framework would evolve in response to the sheer growth of federal regulation over time.

The Supreme Court did not seriously test the extent of this power until near the end of the nineteenth century. Instead, Commerce Clause doctrine mainly focused on the extent to which the Clause limited *state* power. Most often, the nineteenth-century Court treated the Clause as setting up mutually exclusive state and federal spheres: to hold that a state could regulate some activity implied that the activity was not part of interstate commerce within the meaning of the Clause. For this doctrine to achieve plausible results, it had to be based on a relatively narrow conception of commerce. For example, regulations of production—manufacturing, agriculture, and mining—were not considered regulations of commerce. *E.g., Kidd v. Pearson* (1888) ("No distinction is more popular to the common mind or more clearly expressed in economic and political literature than that between manufactures and commerce.").

 See subchapters H and I of Chapter I for more on the growth of the regulatory state.

 For more on this "dormant commerce clause" doctrine, see pp. 88–94 and pp. 649–694.

In 1887, Congress passed the Interstate Commerce Act, its first extensive foray into regulation of interstate rail transportation. In 1890, it passed
the Sherman Antitrust Act, which remains the cornerstone of federal antitrust
law to this day. Section 1 of the Sherman Act prohibits "combination[s] in restraint of trade or commerce among the several States, or with foreign nations."
Section 2 makes it illegal to "monopolize any part of the trade or commerce
among the several States, or with foreign nations." The first great test of the Act
concerned the Sugar Trust, a combination of sugar manufacturing companies
accused of violating both §§ 1 and 2. The claim was based on the purchase by
the American Sugar Refining Company, based in New York and New Jersey,
of four sugar refiners in Pennsylvania—a move that gave it "nearly complete
control" of the U.S. market in refined sugar. The United States brought suit
under the Sherman Act, seeking cancellation of the transaction.

United States v. E.C. Knight Co.

Supreme Court of the United States, 1895.
156 U.S. 1.

MR. CHIEF JUSTICE FULLER . . . delivered the opinion of the court.

. . . The fundamental question is whether, conceding that the existence of a
monopoly in manufacture is established by the evidence, that monopoly can be
directly suppressed under the act of Congress in the mode attempted by this bill.

It cannot be denied that the power of a State to protect the lives, health,
and property of its citizens, and to preserve good order and the public morals,
"the power to govern men and things within the limits of its dominion," is a
power originally and always belonging to the States, not surrendered by them
to the general government, nor directly restrained by the Constitution of the
United States, and essentially exclusive. The relief of the citizens of each State
from the burden of monopoly and the evils resulting from the restraint of trade
among such citizens was left with the States to deal with. . . .

On the other hand, the power of Congress to regulate commerce among
the several States is also exclusive. . . . and if a law passed by a State in the
exercise of its acknowledged powers comes into conflict with that will, the Congress and the State cannot occupy the position of equal opposing sovereignties,
because the Constitution declares its supremacy, and that of the laws passed

in pursuance thereof; and that which is not supreme must yield to that which is supreme. . . . That which belongs to commerce is within the jurisdiction of the United States, but that which does not belong to commerce is within the jurisdiction of the police power of the State. *Gibbons v. Ogden*. . . .

The argument is that the power to control the manufacture of refined sugar is a monopoly over a necessary of life, to the enjoyment of which by a large part of the population of the United States interstate commerce is indispensable, and that, therefore, the general government, in the exercise of the power to regulate commerce, may repress such monopoly directly, and set aside the instruments which have created it. But this argument cannot be confined to necessaries of life merely, and must include all articles of general consumption.

Doubtless the power to control the manufacture of a given thing involves, in a certain sense, the control of its disposition, but this is a secondary, and not the primary, sense; and, although the exercise of that power may result in bringing the operation of commerce into play, it does not control it, and affects it only incidentally and indirectly. Commerce succeeds to manufacture, and is not a part of it. The power to regulate commerce is the power to prescribe the rule by which commerce shall be governed, and is a power independent of the power to suppress monopoly. But it may operate in repression of monopoly whenever that comes within the rules by which commerce is governed, or whenever the transaction is itself a monopoly of commerce.

It is vital that the independence of the commercial power and of the police power, and the delimitation between them, however sometimes perplexing, should always be recognized and observed, for, while the one furnishes the strongest bond of union, the other is essential to the preservation of the autonomy of the States as required by our dual form of government; and acknowledged evils, however grave and urgent they may appear to be, had better be borne, than the risk be run, in the effort to suppress them, of more serious consequences by resort to expedients of even doubtful constitutionality.

It will be perceived how far-reaching the proposition is that the power of dealing with a monopoly directly may be exercised by the general government whenever interstate or international commerce may be ultimately affected. The regulation of commerce applies to the subjects of commerce, and not to matters of internal police. Contracts to buy, sell, or exchange goods to be transported among the several States, the transportation and its instrumentalities, and articles bought, sold, or exchanged for the purposes of such transit among the

States, or put in the way of transit, may be regulated; but this is because they form part of interstate trade or commerce. The fact that an article is manufactured for export to another State does not of itself make it an article of interstate commerce, and the intent of the manufacturer does not determine the time when the article or product passes from the control of the State and belongs to commerce. . . .

In *Gibbons v. Ogden* . . . and other cases often cited, the state laws, which were held inoperative, were instances of direct interference with, or regulations of, interstate or international commerce; yet in *Kidd v. Pearson* (1888) the refusal of a State to allow articles [there, intoxicating liquors] to be manufactured within her borders, even for export, was held not to directly affect external commerce; and state legislation which, in a great variety of ways, affected interstate commerce and persons engaged in it, has been frequently sustained because the interference was not direct.

Contracts, combinations, or conspiracies to control domestic enterprise in manufacture, agriculture, mining, production in all its forms, or to raise or lower prices or wages, might unquestionably tend to restrain external as well as domestic trade, but the restraint would be an indirect result, however inevitable, and whatever its extent, and such result would not necessarily determine the object of the contract, combination, or conspiracy. . . . Slight reflection will show that, if the national power extends to all contracts and combinations in manufacture, agriculture, mining, and other productive industries, whose ultimate result may affect external commerce, comparatively little of business operations and affairs would be left for state control.

It was in the light of well-settled principles that the [Sherman Act], was framed. . . . Aside from the provisions applicable where congress might exercise municipal power[—*i.e.,* in the federal territories and the District of Columbia—] what the law struck at was combinations, contracts, and conspiracies to monopolize trade and commerce among the several States or with foreign nations. [B]ut the contracts and acts of the defendants related exclusively to the acquisition of the Philadelphia refineries and the business of sugar refining in Pennsylvania, and bore no direct relation to commerce between the States or with foreign nations. The object was manifestly private gain in the manufacture of the commodity, but not through the control of interstate or foreign commerce.

It is true that the bill alleged that the products of these refineries were sold and distributed among the several States, and that all the companies were engaged in trade or commerce with the several States and with foreign nations; but this was no more than to say that trade and commerce served manufacture to fulfill its function. Sugar was refined for sale, and sales were probably made at Philadelphia for consumption, and undoubtedly for resale by the first purchasers throughout Pennsylvania and other States, and refined sugar was also forwarded by the companies to other States for sale. Nevertheless it does not follow that an attempt to monopolize, or the actual monopoly of, the manufacture was an attempt, whether executory or consummated, to monopolize commerce, even though, in order to dispose of the product, the instrumentality of commerce was necessarily invoked. There was nothing in the proofs to indicate any intention to put a restraint upon trade or commerce, and the fact, as we have seen, that trade or commerce might be indirectly affected, was not enough to entitle complainants to a decree. . . .

FOR DISCUSSION

In the majority's view, what is the general standard for determining whether a given subject matter is within the reach of the commerce power? Why did the majority think the charged acts were beyond that reach?

MR. JUSTICE HARLAN, dissenting.

. . . "The object," the court below said, "in purchasing the Philadelphia refineries was to obtain a greater influence or *more perfect control over the business* of refining *and selling* sugar *in this country*." This characterization of the object for which this stupendous combination was formed is properly accepted in the opinion of the court as justified by the proof. I need not, therefore, analyze the evidence upon this point. . . .

The Constitution which enumerates the powers committed to the nation for objects of interest to the people of all the States should not . . . be subjected to an interpretation so rigid, technical, and narrow that those objects cannot be accomplished. [In *Gibbons v. Ogden,*] the principle was announced that the objects for which a power was granted to Congress, especially when those objects are expressed in the constitution itself, should have great influence in determining the extent of any given power. . . .

"Commerce, as the word is used in the Constitution, is a unit," and "cannot stop at the external boundary line of each State, but may be introduced into the interior." *Gibbons.* . . . It is the settled doctrine of this court that interstate commerce embraces something more than the mere physical transportation of articles of property, and the vehicles or vessels by which such transportation is effected. . . . In *Kidd v. Pearson* (1888), it was said that "the buying and selling and the transportation *incidental thereto* constitute commerce." Interstate commerce does not, therefore, consist in transportation simply. It includes the purchase and sale of articles that are intended to be transported from one State to another—every species of commercial intercourse among the states and with foreign nations. . . .

[T]here is a trade among the several States which is distinct from that carried on within the territorial limits of a State. The regulation and control of the former are committed by the national Constitution to Congress. Commerce among the States, as this court has declared, is a unit, and in respect of *that* commerce this is one country, and we are one people. It may be regulated by rules applicable to every part of the United States, and state lines and state jurisdiction cannot interfere with the enforcement of such rules. The jurisdiction of the general government extends over every foot of territory within the United States. Under the power with which it is invested, Congress may remove unlawful obstructions, of whatever kind, to the free course of trade among the States. In so doing it would not interfere with the "autonomy of the States," because the power thus to protect interstate commerce is expressly given by the people of all the States. . . .

In committing to Congress the control of commerce with foreign nations and among the several States, the Constitution did not define the means that may be employed to protect the freedom of commercial intercourse and traffic established for the benefit of all the people of the Union. . . . It gives to Congress, in express words, authority to enact all laws necessary and proper for carrying into execution the power to regulate commerce; and whether an act of Congress, passed to accomplish an object to which the general government is competent, is within the power granted, must be determined by the rule announced [in] *McCulloch v. Maryland* (1819).

The end proposed to be accomplished by the [Sherman Act] is the protection of trade and commerce among the States against unlawful restraints. Who can say that that end is not legitimate, or is not within the scope of the Constitution? The means employed are the suppression, by legal proceedings, of combinations, conspiracies, and monopolies which, by their inevitable and admitted tendency, improperly restrain trade and commerce among the States. Who can say that such means are not appropriate to attain the end of freeing commercial intercourse among the States from burdens and exactions imposed upon it by combinations which, under principles long recognized in this country, as well as at the common law, are illegal and dangerous to the public welfare? What clause of the Constitution can be referred to which prohibits the means thus prescribed in the act of Congress? . . .

In my judgment, the general government is not placed by the Constitution in such a condition of helplessness that it must fold its arms and remain inactive while capital combines, under the name of a corporation, to destroy competition, not in one State only, but throughout the entire country, in the buying and selling of articles—especially the necessaries of life—that go into commerce among the States. . . . For the reasons stated, I dissent from the opinion and judgment of the court.

Toward the end of its opinion, the *E.C. Knight* majority made a point of observing that "[t]here was nothing . . . to indicate" that the defendants had "any intention to put a restraint upon trade or commerce" when they formed the sugar monopoly. Three decades later, the Supreme Court gave force to the unstated implication. An Arkansas coal company filed suit against the United Mine Workers, claiming that a union strike violated § 1 of the Sherman Act by restraining interstate commerce. In *United Mine Workers of America v. Coronado Coal Co. (Coronado I)* (1922), the Court reversed a judgment for the defendants and remanded for a retrial to determine whether the effect on commerce had been intentional. The case ultimately came back up to the Court, which held:

> The mere reduction in the supply of an article to be shipped in interstate commerce by the illegal or tortious prevention of its manufacture or production is ordinarily an indirect and remote obstruction to that commerce. But when the intent of those unlawfully preventing the manufacture or production is shown to be to restrain or control the supply entering and moving in interstate commerce, or the price of it in interstate markets, their action is a direct violation of the Anti-Trust Act. . . .
>
> We think there was substantial evidence at the second trial in this case tending to show that the purpose of the destruction of the mines was to stop the production of nonunion coal and prevent its shipment to markets of other states than Arkansas, where it would

by competition tend to reduce the price of the commodity and affect injuriously the maintenance of wages for union labor in competing mines, and that the direction by the District Judge to return a verdict for the defendants other than the International Union was erroneous.

Coronado Coal Co. v. United Mine Workers (*Coronado II*) (1925). On this reasoning, two otherwise identical acts might be treated differently for Commerce Clause purposes based solely on the different intentions of the respective actors. Does this make sense?

"The Shreveport Rate Cases" (Houston, East & West Texas Railway Company v. United States)

Supreme Court of the United States (1914).
234 U.S. 342.

Mr. Justice Hughes delivered the opinion of the court:

. . . Shreveport, Louisiana, is about 40 miles from the Texas state line, and 231 miles from Houston, Texas, on the [railroad] line of the Houston, East & West Texas and Houston & Shreveport Companies (which are affiliated in interest); it is 189 miles from Dallas, Texas, on the line of the Texas & Pacific. Shreveport competes with both [Texas] cities for the trade of the intervening territory.

SUMMARY OF THE FACTS

The Interstate Commerce Commission, a federal agency, issued an order finding that the railroad companies were charging unreasonably high freight rates for shipments from Shreveport to points in Texas, thereby discriminating against traffic from Louisiana. The ICC prescribed maximum rates for the interstate routes, but these were higher per mile than the maximums set by the Railroad Commission of Texas for intrastate transport of freight. Accordingly, the ICC also directed the railroads not to set rates for their *intra*state traffic that would discriminate against interstate traffic from Shreveport. The commerce court upheld the order, which it interpreted to relieve the railroads from complying with the state maximums; they could eliminate the discrimination by charging for both intrastate and interstate traffic up to the limits set by the ICC.

The invalidity of the order in this aspect is challenged upon [the ground that] Congress is impotent to control the intrastate charges of an interstate carrier even to the extent necessary to prevent injurious discrimination against interstate traffic. . . .

It is unnecessary to repeat what has frequently been said by this court with respect to the complete and paramount character of the power confided to Congress to regulate commerce among the several States. It is of the essence of this power that, where it exists, it dominates. Interstate trade was not left to be destroyed or impeded by the rivalries of local government. The purpose was to make impossible the recurrence of the evils which had overwhelmed the Confederation, and to provide the necessary basis of national unity by insuring "uniformity of regulation against conflicting and discriminating state legislation." By virtue of the comprehensive terms of the grant, the authority of Congress is at all times adequate to meet the varying exigencies that arise, and to protect the national interest by securing the freedom of interstate commercial intercourse from local control. *Gibbons v. Ogden.* . . .

Congress is empowered to regulate—that is, to provide the law for the government of interstate commerce; to enact "all appropriate legislation" for its "protection and advancement," *The Daniel Ball* (1870) [(upholding a federal license tax on travel on the Grand River in Michigan, as applied to a steamer carrying goods "destined for other states")]; to adopt measures "to promote its growth and insure its safety," *Mobile County v. Kimball* (1880) [(dicta in case involving state regulation of harbor)]; "to foster, protect, control, and restrain," *Second Employers' Liability Cases* (1912) [(upholding Federal Employer's Liability Act, which made railroads liable to employees for personal injury caused by a coworker)]. Its authority, extending to these interstate carriers as instruments of interstate commerce, necessarily embraces the right to control their operations in all matters having such a close and substantial relation to interstate traffic that the control is essential or appropriate to the security of that traffic, to the efficiency of the interstate service, and to the maintenance of conditions under which interstate commerce may be conducted upon fair terms and without molestation or hindrance. As it is competent for Congress to legislate to these ends, unquestionably it may seek their attainment by requiring that the agencies of interstate commerce shall not be used in such manner as to cripple, retard, or destroy it.

The fact that carriers are instruments of intrastate commerce, as well as of interstate commerce, does not derogate from the complete and paramount authority of Congress over the latter, or preclude the Federal power from being exerted to prevent the intrastate operations of such carriers from being made a means of injury to that which has been confided to Federal care. Wherever the interstate and intrastate transactions of carriers are so related that the government of the one involves the control of the other, it is Congress, and not the State, that is entitled to prescribe the final and dominant rule, for otherwise Congress would be denied the exercise of its constitutional authority, and the State, and not the Nation, would be supreme within the national field. . . .

While these decisions sustaining the Federal power relate to measures adopted in the interest of the safety of persons and property, they illustrate the principle that Congress, in the exercise of its paramount power, may prevent the common instrumentalities of interstate and intrastate commercial intercourse from being used in their intrastate operations to the injury of interstate commerce. This is not to say that Congress possesses the authority to regulate the internal commerce of a State, as such, but that it does possess the power to foster and protect interstate commerce, and to take all measures necessary or appropriate to that end, although intrastate transactions of interstate carriers may thereby be controlled.

This principle is applicable here. We find no reason to doubt that Congress is entitled to keep the highways of interstate communication open to interstate traffic upon fair and equal terms. . . . It is immaterial, so far as the protecting power of Congress is concerned, that the discrimination arises from intrastate rates, as compared with interstate rates. . . . Nor can the attempted exercise of state authority alter the matter, where Congress has acted, for a state may not authorize the carrier to do that which Congress is entitled to forbid and has forbidden. . . . It is also clear that, in removing the injurious discriminations against interstate traffic arising from the relation of intrastate to interstate rates, Congress is not bound to reduce the latter below what it may deem to be a proper standard fair to the carrier and to the public. Otherwise, it could prevent the injury to interstate commerce only by the sacrifice of its judgment as to interstate rates. . . .

Having this power, Congress could provide for its execution through the aid of a subordinate body; and we conclude that the order of the Commission now in question cannot be held invalid upon the ground that it exceeded the authority which Congress could lawfully confer. . . .

The decree of the Commerce Court is affirmed in each case.

Mr. Justice Lurton and Mr. Justice Pitney dissent [without opinion].

Stafford v. Wallace

Supreme Court of the United States, 1922.
258 U.S. 495.

These cases involve the constitutionality of the Packers and Stockyards Act of 1921 . . . so far as that act provides for the supervision by federal authority of the business of the commission men and of the live stock dealers in the great stockyards of the country. . . .

[T]he appellants aver that they are members of the Chicago Live Stock Exchange . . . and that they bring their bill for all of them who may choose to join and take the benefit of the litigation. . . . It was conceded that, of all the live stock coming into the Chicago stockyards and going out, only a small percentage, less than 10 per cent., is shipped from or to Illinois. . . .

Mr. Chief Justice Taft, after making the foregoing statement of the case, delivered the opinion of the Court.

. . . The Packers and Stockyards Act of 1921 seeks to regulate the business of the packers done in interstate commerce and forbids them to engage in unfair, discriminatory, or deceptive practices in such commerce, or to . . . establish a monopoly in the business. . . .

The act requires that all rates and charges for services and facilities in the stockyards and all practices in connection with the live stock passing through the yards shall be just, reasonable, nondiscriminatory, and nondeceptive. . . . The Secretary is given power to make rules and regulations to carry out the provisions, to fix rates, or a minimum or maximum thereof, and to prescribe how every packer, stockyard owner, commission man, and dealer shall keep accounts. [In accordance with that authority,] the Secretary . . . has announced proposed rules and regulations, prescribing the form of rate schedules, the required reports, including daily accounts of receipts, sales, and shipments, forbidding misleading reports to depress or enhance prices, prescribing proper feed and care of live stock, and forbidding a commission man to sell live stock to another in whose business he is interested, without disclosing such interest to his principal.

The object to be secured by the act is the free and unburdened flow of live stock from the ranges and farms of the West and the Southwest through the great stockyards and slaughtering centers on the borders of that region, and thence in the form of meat products to the consuming cities of the country in the Middle West and East, or, still, as live stock, to the feeding places and fattening farms in the Middle West or East for further preparation for the market.

The chief evil feared is the monopoly of the packers, enabling them unduly and arbitrarily to lower prices to the shipper, who sells, and unduly and arbitrarily to increase the price to the consumer, who buys. Congress thought that the power to maintain this monopoly was aided by control of the stockyards. Another evil, which it sought to provide against by the act, was exorbitant charges, duplication of commissions, deceptive practices in respect of prices, in the passage of the live stock through the stockyards, all made possible by collusion between the stockyards management and the commission men, on the one hand, and the packers and dealers, on the other. . . .

. . . The only [constitutional] question here is whether the business done in the stockyards, between the receipt of the live stock in the yards and the shipment of them therefrom, is a part of interstate commerce, or is so associated with it as to bring it within the power of national regulation. . . .

The stockyards are not a place of rest or final destination. Thousands of head of live stock arrive daily by carload and trainload lots, and must be promptly sold and disposed of and moved out, to give place to the constantly flowing traffic that presses behind. The stockyards are but a throat through which the current flows, and the transactions which occur therein are only incident to this current from the West to the East, and from one state to another. Such transactions cannot be separated from the movement to which they contribute and necessarily take on its character. The commission men are essential in making the sales, without which the flow of the current would be obstructed, and this, whether they are made to packers or dealers. The dealers are essential to the sales to the stock farmers and feeders.

The sales are not in this aspect merely local transactions. They create a local change of title, it is true, but they do not stop the flow; they merely change the private interests in the subject of the current, not interfering with, but, on the contrary, being indispensable to, its continuity. The origin of the live stock is in the West; its ultimate destination, known to, and intended by, all engaged in the business, is in the Middle West and East, either as meat products or stock for feeding and fattening. This is the definite and well-understood course of business. The stockyards and the sales are necessary factors in the middle of this current of commerce.

[In *Swift v. United States* (1905), a Sherman Act enforcement action brought against many of the same packers targeted by the 1921 Packers and Stockyards Act,] the court said:

> Commerce among the states is not a technical legal conception, but a practical one, drawn from the course of business. When cattle are sent for sale from a place in one state, with the expectation that they will end their transit, after purchase, in another, and when in effect they do so, with only the interruption necessary to find a purchaser at the stockyards, and when this is a typical, constantly recurring course, the current thus existing is a current of commerce among the states, and the purchase of the cattle is a part and incident of such commerce. What we say is true at least of such a purchase by residents in another state from that of the seller and of the cattle.

The application of the commerce clause of the Constitution in the *Swift* Case was the result of the natural development of interstate commerce under modern conditions. It was the inevitable recognition of the great central fact that such streams of commerce from one part of the country to another, which are ever flowing, are in their very essence the commerce among the states and with foreign nations, which historically it was one of the chief purposes of the Constitution to bring under national protection and control. This court declined to defeat this purpose in respect of such a stream and take it out of complete national regulation by a nice and technical inquiry into the noninterstate character of some of its necessary incidents and facilities, when considered alone and without reference to their association with the movement of which they were an essential but subordinate part. . . .

It is manifest that Congress framed the Packers and Stockyards Act in keeping with the principles announced and applied in the opinion in the *Swift* Case. . . . The language of the law shows that what Congress had in mind primarily was to prevent . . . conspiracies [like those charged in *Swift*] by supervision of the agencies which would be likely to be employed in it. If

Congress could provide for punishment or restraint of such conspiracies after their formation through the Anti-Trust Law as in the *Swift* Case, certainly it may provide regulation to prevent their formation. . . . Thus construed and applied, we think the act clearly within Congressional power and valid.

MR. JUSTICE MCREYNOLDS dissents [without opinion].

MR. JUSTICE DAY did not sit in these cases and took no part in their decision.

ii.   Commerce Clause Framework—Border Controls

Just as water wants to run downhill, Congress wants to regulate. And just as water seeps through the floorboards, Congress finds loopholes and drafting tricks to work around legal barriers to its regulatory goals. So when the Supreme Court tells Congress that it can't regulate wages by doing X, Congress will often try to regulate wages by doing Y instead. You'll see examples of this throughout our federalism and enumeration discussions. But let's start with one specific workaround that emerged in the early twentieth century: If Congress couldn't directly regulate intrastate commercial activity, what about denying access to interstate customers for any commercial actor who didn't play by Congress's rules? For any business that depended on the national market, that might create a well-nigh irresistible financial incentive to follow Congress's instructions. The next two cases explore the formal mechanics of this legislative tactic, and the functional reasons that eventually led the pre-New-Deal Court to reject it.

Champion v. Ames ("The Lottery Case")

Supreme Court of the United States, 1903.
188 U.S. 321.

MR. JUSTICE HARLAN delivered the opinion of the court:

SUMMARY OF THE FACTS

The defendant in *Champion* was accused of conspiring to violate a federal statute that prohibited the interstate shipment of "any paper, certificate, or instrument purporting to be or represent a ticket, chance, share, or interest in or dependent upon the event of a lottery." According to the indictment, the defendant and his confederates transported tickets in the Pan-American Lottery from Texas to California. Based in Paraguay, the lottery offered a prize of $32,000; whole tickets sold for $2, and eighth tickets for 25 cents. Champion appealed from an unsuccessful attempt to secure dismissal of the indictment.

. . . The appellant insists that the carrying of lottery tickets from one State to another State by an express company engaged in carrying freight and packages from State to State, . . . does not constitute, and cannot by any act of Congress be legally made to constitute, *commerce* among the States . . . ; [and] consequently, that Congress cannot make it an offense to cause such tickets to be carried from one State to another.

The Government insists that express companies, when engaged, for hire, in the business of transportation from one State to another, are instrumentalities of commerce among the States; that the carrying of lottery tickets from one state to another is commerce which Congress may regulate; and that as a means of executing the power to regulate interstate commerce Congress may make it an offense against the United States to cause lottery tickets to be carried from one State to another. . . .

[Our prior cases] show that commerce among the States embraces navigation, intercourse, communication, traffic, the transit of persons, and the transmission of messages by telegraph. They also show that the power to regulate commerce among the several States is vested in Congress as absolutely as it would be in a single government, having in its constitution the same restrictions on the exercise of the power as are found in the Constitution of the United States; that such power is plenary, complete in itself, and may be exerted by Congress to its utmost extent, subject *only* to such limitations as the Constitution imposes upon the exercise of the powers granted by it; and that in determining the character of the regulations to be adopted Congress has a large discretion which is not to be controlled by the courts, simply because, in their opinion, such regulations may not be the best or most effective that could be employed. . . .

It was said in argument that lottery tickets are not of any real or substantial value in themselves, and therefore are not subjects of commerce. If that were conceded to be the only legal test as to what are to be deemed subjects of the commerce that may be regulated by Congress, we cannot accept as accurate the broad statement that such tickets are of no value. Upon their face they showed that the lottery company offered a large capital prize, to be paid to the holder of the ticket winning the prize at the drawing advertised to be held at Asuncion, Paraguay. Money was placed on deposit in different banks in the United States to be applied by the agents representing the lottery company to the prompt payment of prizes. These tickets were the subject of traffic; they could have been sold; and the holder was assured that the company would pay to him the amount of the prize drawn.

That the holder might not have been able to enforce his claim in the courts of any country making the drawing of lotteries illegal, and forbidding the circulation of lottery tickets, did not change the fact that the tickets issued by the foreign company represented so much money payable to the person holding them and who might draw the prizes affixed to them. Even if a holder did not draw a prize, the tickets, before the drawing, had a money value in the market among those who chose to sell or buy lottery tickets. In short, a lottery ticket is a subject of traffic, and is so designated in the act of 1895.

We are of opinion that lottery tickets are subjects of traffic, and therefore are subjects of commerce, and the regulation of the carriage of such tickets from state to state, at least by independent carriers, is a regulation of commerce among the several states.

But it is said that the statute in question does not regulate the carrying of lottery tickets from state to state[. Rather,] by punishing those who cause them to be so carried Congress in effect prohibits such carrying[. And] in respect of the carrying from one state to another of articles or things that are, in fact, or according to usage in business, the subjects of commerce, the authority given Congress was not to *prohibit*, but only to *regulate*. This view was earnestly pressed at the bar by learned counsel, and must be examined.

It is to be remarked that the Constitution does not define what is to be deemed a legitimate regulation of interstate commerce. In *Gibbons v. Ogden* it was said that the power to regulate such commerce is the power to prescribe the rule by which it is to be governed. . . .

In determining whether regulation may not under some circumstances properly take the form or have the effect of prohibition, the nature of the interstate traffic which the act of May 2, 1895, [sought] to suppress cannot be overlooked. When enacting that statute Congress no doubt shared the views upon the subject of lotteries heretofore expressed by this court. In *Phalen v. Virginia* (1850), after observing that the suppression of nuisances injurious to public health or morality is among the most important duties of Government, this court said: "Experience has shown that the common forms of gambling are comparatively innocuous when placed in contrast with the widespread pestilence of lotteries. The former are confined to a few persons and places, but the latter infests the whole community; it enters every dwelling; it reaches every class; it preys upon the hard earnings of the poor; it plunders the ignorant and simple." . . .

If a state, when considering legislation for the suppression of lotteries within its own limits, may properly take into view the evils that inhere in the raising of money, in that mode, why may not Congress, invested with the power to regulate commerce among the several states, provide that such commerce shall not be polluted by the carrying of lottery tickets from one state to another? In this connection it must not be forgotten that the power of Congress to regulate commerce among the states is plenary, is complete in itself, and is subject to no limitations except such as may be found in the Constitution. What provision in that instrument can be regarded as limiting the exercise of the power granted? What clause can be cited which, in any degree, countenances the suggestion that one may, of right, carry or cause to be carried from one state to another that which will harm the public morals? . . .

Congress . . . does not assume to interfere with traffic or commerce in lottery tickets carried on exclusively within the limits of any state, but has in view only commerce of that kind among the several states. It has not assumed to interfere with the completely internal affairs of any state, and has only legislated in respect of a matter which concerns the people of the United States. As a state may, for the purpose of guarding the morals of its own people, forbid all sales of lottery tickets within its limits, so Congress, for the purpose of guarding the people of the United States against the "widespread pestilence of lotteries" and to protect the commerce which concerns all the states, may prohibit the carrying of lottery tickets from one state to another.

In legislating upon the subject of the traffic in lottery tickets, as carried on through interstate commerce, Congress only supplemented the action of those states—perhaps all of them—which, for the protection of the public morals, prohibit the drawing of lotteries, as well as the sale or circulation of lottery tickets, within their respective limits. It said, in effect, that it would not permit the declared policy of the states, which sought to protect their people against the mischiefs of the lottery business, to be overthrown or disregarded by the agency of interstate commerce. We should hesitate long before adjudging that an evil of such appalling character, carried on through interstate commerce, cannot be met and crushed by the only power competent to that end. We say competent to that end, because Congress alone has the power to occupy, by legislation, the whole field of interstate commerce. . . .

It is said, however, that if, in order to suppress lotteries carried on through interstate commerce, Congress may exclude lottery tickets from such commerce, that principle leads necessarily to the conclusion that Congress may arbitrarily exclude from commerce among the states any article, commodity, or thing, of whatever kind or nature, or however useful or valuable, which it may choose, no matter with what motive, to declare shall not be carried from one state to another. It will be time enough to consider the constitutionality of such legislation when we must do so. The present case does not require the court to declare the full extent of the power that Congress may exercise in the regulation of commerce among the states. . . . The whole subject is too important, and the questions suggested by its consideration are too difficult of solution, to justify any attempt to lay down a rule for determining in advance the validity of every statute that may be enacted under the commerce clause. . . .

The judgment is affirmed.

Mr. Chief Justice Fuller, with whom concur Mr. Justice Brewer, Mr. Justice Shiras, and Mr. Justice Peckham, dissenting:

. . . That the purpose of Congress in this enactment was the suppression of lotteries cannot reasonably be denied. That purpose is avowed in the title of the act, and is its natural and reasonable effect, and by that its validity must be tested.

The power of the state to impose restraints and burdens on persons and property in conservation and promotion of the public health, good order, and prosperity is a power originally and always belonging to the states, not surrendered by them to the General Government, nor directly restrained by the Constitution of the United States, and essentially exclusive, and the suppression of lotteries as a harmful business falls within this power, commonly called, of police.

It is urged, however, that because Congress is empowered to regulate commerce between the several states, it, therefore, may suppress lotteries by prohibiting the carriage of lottery matter. Congress may, indeed, make all laws necessary and proper for carrying the powers granted to it into execution, and doubtless an act prohibiting the carriage of lottery matter would be necessary and proper to the execution of a power to suppress lotteries; but that power belongs to the states and not to Congress. To hold that Congress has general police power would be to hold that it may accomplish objects not entrusted to the General Government, and to defeat the operation of the 10th Amendment, declaring that "the powers not delegated to the United States by the Constitution, nor prohibited by it to the states, are reserved to the states respectively, or to the people."

. . . But apart from the question of *bona fides*, this act cannot be brought within the power to regulate commerce among the several states, unless lottery tickets are articles of commerce, and, therefore, when carried across state lines, of interstate commerce; or unless the power to regulate interstate commerce includes the absolute and exclusive power to prohibit the transportation of anything or anybody from one state to another. . . .

Is the carriage of lottery tickets from one state to another commercial intercourse? [The dissent concluded that it is not, leaning heavily on the fact that state laws prohibited the sale of these lottery tickets both in their state of origin and in the states to which they were sent.] So lottery tickets forbidden to be issued or dealt in by the laws of Texas, the *terminus a quo*, and by the laws of California or Utah, the *terminus ad quem*, were not vendible; and for this reason, also, not articles of commerce. . . . An invitation to dine, or to take a drive, or a note of introduction, all become articles of commerce under the ruling in this case, by being deposited with an express company for transportation. This in effect breaks down all the differences between that which is, and that which is not, an article of commerce, and the necessary consequence is to take from the states all jurisdiction over the subject so far as interstate communication is concerned. It is a long step in the direction of wiping out all traces of state lines, and the creation of a centralized government. . . .

It will not do to say—a suggestion which has heretofore been made in this case—that state laws have been found to be ineffective for the suppression of lotteries, and therefore Congress should interfere. The scope of the commerce clause of the Constitution cannot be enlarged because of present views of public interest. In countries whose fundamental law is flexible it may be that the homely maxim, "to ease the shoe where it pinches," may be applied, but under the Constitution of the United States it cannot be availed of to justify action by Congress or by the courts. The Constitution gives no countenance to the theory that Congress is vested with the full powers of the British Parliament, and that, although subject to constitutional limitations, it is the sole judge of their extent and application; and the decisions of this court from the beginning have been to the contrary. . . .

The power to prohibit the transportation of diseased animals and infected goods over railroads or on steamboats is an entirely different thing, for they would be in themselves injurious to the transaction of interstate commerce, and, moreover, are essentially commercial in their nature. And the exclusion of diseased persons rests on different ground, for nobody would pretend that persons could be kept off the trains because they were going from one state to another to engage in the lottery business. However enticing that business may be, we do not understand these pieces of paper themselves can communicate bad principles by contact. . . .

FOR DISCUSSION

If you were Justice Harlan, how might you respond to the last paragraph of the dissent?

Fifteen years later, the Court refused to extend the principles of *Champion* to a federal prohibition on shipping goods manufactured under conditions that Congress thought unacceptable.

Hammer v. Dagenhart

Supreme Court of the United States, 1918.
247 U.S. 251.

Mr. Justice Day delivered the opinion of the Court.

A bill was filed in the United States District Court for the Western District of North Carolina by a father in his own behalf and as next friend of his two minor sons, one under the age of fourteen years and the other between the ages of fourteen and sixteen years, employees in a cotton mill at Charlotte, North Carolina, to enjoin the enforcement of the act of Congress intended to prevent interstate commerce in the products of child labor. Act Sept. 1, 1916.

The District Court held the act unconstitutional and entered a decree enjoining its enforcement. This appeal brings the case here. The first section of the act provides:

> That no producer, manufacturer, or dealer shall ship or deliver for shipment in interstate or foreign commerce . . . the product of any mill, cannery, workshop, factory, or manufacturing establishment, situated in the United States, in which within thirty days prior to the removal of such product therefrom [either:]
>
> > children under the age of fourteen years have been employed or permitted to work, or
> >
> > children between the ages of fourteen years and sixteen years have been employed or permitted to work more than eight hours in any day, or more than six days in any week, or [outside the hours of 6am–7pm].

. . . . The power essential to the passage of this act, the Government contends, is found in the commerce clause of the Constitution which authorizes Congress to regulate commerce with foreign nations and among the States.

In *Gibbons v. Ogden*, Chief Justice Marshall, speaking for this court, and defining the extent and nature of the commerce power, said, "It is the power to regulate; that is, to prescribe the rule by which commerce is to be governed." In other words, the power is one to control the means by which commerce is carried on, which is directly the contrary of the assumed right to forbid commerce from moving and thus destroying it as to particular commodities.

But it is insisted that adjudged cases in this court establish the doctrine that the power to regulate given to Congress incidentally includes the authority to prohibit the movement of ordinary commodities and therefore that the subject is not open for discussion. The cases demonstrate the contrary. They rest upon the character of the particular subjects dealt with and the fact that the scope of governmental authority, state or national, possessed over them is such that the authority to prohibit is as to them but the exertion of the power to regulate.

The first of these cases is *Champion v. Ames*, the so-called Lottery Case, in which it was held that Congress might pass a law having the effect to keep the channels of commerce free from use in the transportation of tickets used in the promotion of lottery schemes. In *Hipolite Egg Co. v. United States* (1911), this court sustained the power of Congress to [prohibit] the introduction into the States by means of interstate commerce of impure foods and drugs. In *Hoke v. United States* (1913), this court sustained the constitutionality of the so-called "White Slave Traffic Act" (Act June 25, 1910), whereby the transportation of a woman in interstate commerce for the purpose of prostitution was forbidden. In that case we said, having reference to the authority of Congress, under the regulatory power, to protect the channels of interstate commerce:

> If the facility of interstate transportation can be taken away from the demoralization of lotteries, the debasement of obscene literature, the contagion of diseased cattle or persons, the impurity of food and drugs, the like facility can be taken away from the systematic enticement to, and the enslavement in prostitution and debauchery of women, and, more insistently, of girls. . . .

In each of these instances the use of interstate transportation was necessary to the accomplishment of harmful results. In other words, although the power over interstate transportation was to regulate, that could only be accomplished by prohibiting the use of the facilities of interstate commerce to effect the evil intended.

This element is wanting in the present case. The thing intended to be accomplished by this statute is the denial of the facilities of interstate commerce to those manufacturers in the states who employ children within the prohibited ages. The act in its effect does not regulate transportation among the States, but aims to standardize the ages at which children may be employed in mining and manufacturing within the States. The goods shipped are of themselves harmless. The act permits them to be freely shipped after thirty days from the time of their removal from the factory. When offered for shipment, and before transportation begins, the labor of their production is over, and the mere fact that they were intended for interstate commerce transportation does not make their production subject to federal control under the commerce power. . . .

Over interstate transportation, or its incidents, the regulatory power of Congress is ample, but the production of articles, intended for interstate commerce, is a matter of local regulation. "When the commerce begins is determined, not by the character of the commodity, nor by the intention of the owner to transfer it to another state for sale, nor by his preparation of it for transportation, but by its actual delivery to a common carrier for transportation, or the actual commencement of its transfer to another state." Mr. Justice Jackson in *Re Greene*. This principle has been recognized often in this court. . . . If it were otherwise, all manufacture intended for interstate shipment would be brought under federal control to the practical exclusion of the authority of the States, a result certainly not contemplated by the framers of the Constitution when they vested in Congress the authority to regulate commerce among the States. *Kidd v. Pearson* (1888).

It is further contended that the authority of Congress may be exerted to control interstate commerce in the shipment of childmade goods because of the effect of the circulation of such goods in other states where the evil of this class of labor has been recognized by local legislation, and the right to thus employ child labor has been more rigorously restrained than in the State of production. In other words, that the unfair competition, thus engendered, may be controlled by closing the channels of interstate commerce to manufacturers in those States where the local laws do not meet what Congress deems to be the more just standard of other States.

There is no power vested in Congress to require the States to exercise their police power so as to prevent possible unfair competition. Many causes may co-operate to give one State, by reason of local laws or conditions, an economic advantage over others. The Commerce Clause was not intended to give to Congress a general authority to equalize such conditions. In some of the States laws have been passed fixing minimum wages for women, in others the local law regulates the hours of labor of women in various employments. Business done in such States may be at an economic disadvantage when compared with States which have no such regulations; surely, this fact does not give Congress the power to deny transportation in interstate commerce to those who carry on business where the hours of labor and the rate of compensation for women have not been fixed by a standard in use in other States and approved by Congress. . . .

That there should be limitations upon the right to employ children in mines and factories in the interest of their own and the public welfare, all will admit. That such employment is generally deemed to require regulation is shown by the fact that the brief of counsel states that every State in the Union has a law upon the subject, limiting the right to thus employ children. In North Carolina, the State wherein is located the factory in which the employment was had in the present case, no child under twelve years of age is permitted to work.

It may be desirable that such laws be uniform, but our Federal Government is one of enumerated powers. *McCulloch v. Maryland*.

A statute must be judged by its natural and reasonable effect. . . . The control by Congress over interstate commerce cannot authorize the exercise of authority not entrusted to it by the Constitution. The maintenance of the authority of the States over matters purely local is as essential to the preservation of our institutions as is the conservation of the supremacy of the federal power in all matters entrusted to the Nation by the federal Constitution.

In interpreting the Constitution it must never be forgotten that the Nation is made up of States to which are entrusted the powers of local government. And to them and to the people the powers not expressly delegated to the National Government are reserved. The power of the States to regulate their purely internal affairs by such laws as seem wise to the local authority is inherent and has never been surrendered to the general government. To sustain this statute would not be in our judgment a recognition of the lawful exertion of congressional authority over interstate commerce, but would sanction an invasion by the federal power of the control of a matter purely local in its character, and over which no authority has been delegated to Congress in conferring the power to regulate commerce among the States.

We have neither authority nor disposition to question the motives of Congress in enacting this legislation. . . . [But in] our view the necessary effect of this act is, by means of a prohibition against the movement in interstate commerce of ordinary commercial commodities to regulate the hours of labor of children in factories and mines within the States, a purely state authority. Thus the act in a two-fold sense is repugnant to the Constitution. It not only transcends the authority delegated to Congress over commerce but also exerts a power as to a purely local matter to which the federal authority does not extend. The far reaching result of upholding the act cannot be more plainly indicated than by pointing out that if Congress can thus regulate matters entrusted to local authority by prohibition of the movement of commodities in interstate commerce, all freedom of commerce will be at an end, and the power of the states over local matters may be eliminated, and thus our system of government be practically destroyed.

For these reasons we hold that this law exceeds the constitutional authority of Congress.

Mr. Justice Holmes, [joined by Justices McKenna, Brandeis, and Clarke,] dissenting.

The single question in this case is whether Congress has power to prohibit the shipment in interstate or foreign commerce of any product of a cotton mill situated in the United States, in which [certain kinds of child labor have been employed]. The objection urged against the power is that the States have exclusive control over their methods of production and that Congress cannot meddle with them, and taking the proposition in the sense of direct intermeddling I agree to it and suppose that no one denies it.

But if an act is within the powers specifically conferred upon Congress, it seems to me that it is not made any less constitutional because of the indirect effects that it may have, however obvious it may be that it will have those effects, and that we are not at liberty upon such grounds to hold it void.

The first step in my argument is to make plain what no one is likely to dispute—that the statute in question is within the power expressly given to Congress if considered only as to its immediate effects and that if invalid it is so only upon some collateral ground. The statute confines itself to prohibiting the carriage of certain goods in interstate or foreign commerce. Congress is given power to regulate such commerce in unqualified terms. It would not be argued today that the power to regulate does not include the power to prohibit. Regulation means the prohibition of something, and when interstate commerce is the matter to be regulated I cannot doubt that the regulation may prohibit any part of such commerce that Congress sees fit to forbid. At all events it is established by the *Lottery Case* and others that have followed it that a law is not beyond the regulative power of Congress merely because it prohibits certain transportation out and out. *Champion v. Ames.* So I repeat that this statute in its immediate operation is clearly within the Congress's constitutional power.

The question then is narrowed to whether the exercise of its otherwise constitutional power by Congress can be pronounced unconstitutional because of its possible reaction upon the conduct of the States in a matter upon which I have admitted that they are free from direct control. I should have thought that that matter had been disposed of so fully as to leave no room for doubt. I should have thought that the most conspicuous decisions of this Court had made it clear that the power to regulate commerce and other constitutional powers could not be cut down or qualified by the fact that it might interfere with the carrying out of the domestic policy of any State. . . .

The notion that prohibition is any less prohibition when applied to things now thought evil I do not understand. But if there is any matter upon which civilized countries have agreed—far more unanimously than they have with regard to intoxicants and some other matters over which this country is now emotionally aroused—it is the evil of premature and excessive child labor. I should have thought that if we were to introduce our own moral conceptions where in my opinion they do not belong, this was preeminently a case for upholding the exercise of all its powers by the United States.

But I had thought that the propriety of the exercise of a power admitted to exist in some cases was for the consideration of Congress alone and that this Court always had disavowed the right to intrude its judgment upon questions of policy or morals. It is not for this Court to pronounce when prohibition is necessary to regulation if it ever may be necessary—to say that it is permissible as against strong drink but not as against the product of ruined lives.

The Act does not meddle with anything belonging to the States. They may regulate their internal affairs and their domestic commerce as they like. But when they seek to send their products across the State line they are no longer within their rights. . . .

Questions

Is *Hammer* consistent with *Champion v. Ames*? Suppose Congress prohibited shipment of any product made in a factory that did not require its employees to pass a federally prescribed Latin test. Should that be constitutional?

---

b.   Commerce Clause—the New Deal Transformation

The Great Depression—traditionally dated from the collapse of the stock market on October 29, 1929 ("Black Tuesday")—was a catastrophic implosion of the United States economy, leading to what Justice Brandeis termed in 1932 "an emergency more serious than war." From 1929 to 1933, the gross domestic product fell by almost 50%, and unemployment rose as high as 25%. Many observers believed the crisis posed an existential threat to the American economic and political system. The nation was desperate to find a way out.

With the election of Franklin Delano Roosevelt, popular demands for large-scale government intervention as a solution to the government crisis found their outlet in one of the most active administrations in U.S. history. Roosevelt became President in March 1933, when the economy was at a nadir and the banking system on the edge of destruction. In his Inaugural Address, Roosevelt proclaimed, "This Nation is asking for action, and action now." The New Deal, as Roosevelt called his program for national recovery, aggressively used the powers of the federal government, sometimes in novel and unprecedented ways.

This all put enormous pressure on the existing constitutional framework. The Supreme Court did countenance some dramatic governmental actions at both the state and federal levels. *See Nebbia v. New York* (1934), pp. 206–213, *Home Building & Loan Ass'n v. Blaisdell* (1934), pp. 195–206, and *The Gold Clause Cases* (1935), pp. 216–217. But the Court was quite hostile to other Roosevelt reforms, invalidating some of the New Deal's core elements in cases like *A.L.A. Schechter Poultry v. United States* (1935) and *Carter v. Carter Coal Co.* (1936).

A.L.A. Schechter Poultry Corporation v. United States

Supreme Court of the United States, 1935.
295 U.S. 495.

Mr. Chief Justice Hughes delivered the opinion of the Court.

Petitioners . . . were convicted in the District Court of the United States for the Eastern District of New York on eighteen counts of an indictment charging violations of what is known as the "Live Poultry Code," and on an additional count for conspiracy to commit such violations. By demurrer to the indictment and appropriate motions on the trial, the defendants contended . . . that the Code . . . attempted to regulate intrastate transactions which lay outside the authority of Congress. . . .

New York City is the largest live poultry market in the United States. Ninety-six per cent. of the live poultry there marketed comes from other States. Three-fourths of this amount arrives by rail and is consigned to commission men or receivers. Most of these freight shipments (about 75 per cent.) come in at the Manhattan Terminal of the New York Central Railroad, and the remainder at one of the four terminals in New Jersey serving New York City. The commission men transact by far the greater part of the business on a commission basis, representing the shippers as agents, and remitting to them the proceeds of sale, less commissions, freight, and handling charges. Otherwise, they buy for their own account. They sell to slaughterhouse operators who are also called marketmen.

The defendants are slaughterhouse operators of the latter class. A.L.A. Schechter Poultry Corporation and Schechter Live Poultry Market are corporations conducting wholesale poultry slaughterhouse markets in Brooklyn, New York City. Joseph Schechter operated the latter corporation and also guaranteed the credits of the former corporation, which was operated by Martin, Alex, and Aaron Schechter. Defendants ordinarily purchase their live poultry from commission men at the West Washington Market in New York City or at the railroad terminals serving the city, but occasionally they purchase from commission men in Philadelphia. They buy the poultry for slaughter and resale. After the poultry is trucked to their slaughterhouse markets in Brooklyn, it is there sold, usually within twenty-four hours, to retail poultry dealers and butchers who sell directly to consumers. The poultry purchased from defendants is immediately slaughtered, prior to delivery, by shochtim in defendants' employ. Defendants do not sell poultry in interstate commerce.

The "Live Poultry Code" was promulgated under § 3 of the National Industrial Recovery Act[, which] authorizes the President to approve "codes of fair competition." . . . The "Live Poultry Code" was approved by the President on April 13, 1934 . . . as "a code for fair competition for the live poultry industry of the metropolitan area in and about the City of New York." That area is described as embracing the five boroughs of New York City, the counties of Rockland, Westchester, Nassau, and Suffolk in the State of New York, the counties of Hudson and Bergen in the State of New Jersey, and the county of Fairfield in the State of Connecticut. . . .

The Code fixes the number of hours for workdays. It provides that no employee, with certain exceptions, shall be permitted to work in excess of forty hours in any one week, and that no employees, save as stated, "shall be paid in any pay period less than at the rate of fifty (50) cents per hour." The article containing "general labor provisions" prohibits the employment of any person under 16 years of age, and declares that employees shall have the right of "collective bargaining" and freedom of choice with respect to labor organizations.

The minimum number of employees, who shall be employed by slaughterhouse operators, is fixed; the number being graduated according to the average volume of weekly sales.

. . . . The Administrator for Industrial Recovery stated in his report that the Code had been sponsored by trade associations representing about 350 wholesale firms, 150 retail shops, and 21 commission agencies; that these associations represented about 90 per cent. of the live poultry industry by numbers and volume of business; and that the industry as defined in the Code supplied the consuming public with practically all the live poultry coming into the metropolitan area from forty-one states and transacted an aggregate annual business of approximately $90,000,000. He further said that about 1,610 employees were engaged in the industry; that it had suffered severely on account of the prevailing economic conditions and because of unfair methods of competition and the abuses that had developed as a result of the "uncontrolled methods of doing business"; and that these conditions had reduced the number of employees by approximately 40 per cent. He added that the report of the Research and Planning Division indicated that the Code would bring about an increase in wages of about 20 per cent. in this industry and an increase in employment of 19.2 per cent.

[Defendants were convicted of a range of Code violations, including failure to comply with its minimum wage and maximum hour provisions, the sale of "unfit" chickens, the sale of chickens that had not been inspected by the relevant authorities, the sale of chickens to unlicensed slaughterers, and the filing of false reports about at least some of the above practices.]

Two preliminary points are stressed by the government with respect to the appropriate approach to the important questions presented. We are told that the provision of the statute authorizing the adoption of codes must be viewed in the light of the grave national crisis with which Congress was confronted. Undoubtedly, the conditions to which power is addressed are always to be considered when the exercise of power is challenged. Extraordinary conditions may call for extraordinary remedies. But the argument necessarily stops short of an attempt to justify action which lies outside the sphere of constitutional authority. Extraordinary conditions do not create or enlarge constitutional power. *Home Building & Loan Association v. Blaisdel* (1934). The Constitution established a national government with powers deemed to be adequate, as they have proved to be both in war and peace, but these powers of the national government are limited by the constitutional grants. Those who act under these grants are not at liberty to transcend the imposed limits because they believe that more or different power is necessary. Such assertions of extraconstitutional authority were anticipated and precluded by the explicit terms of the Tenth Amendment—"The powers not delegated to the United States by the Constitution, nor prohibited by it to the States, are reserved to the States respectively, or to the people."

The further point is urged that the national crisis demanded a broad and intensive co-operative effort by those engaged in trade and industry, and that this necessary co-operation was sought to be fostered by permitting them to initiate the adoption of codes. But the statutory plan is not simply one for voluntary effort. It does not seek merely to endow voluntary trade or industrial associations or groups with privileges or immunities. It involves the coercive exercise of the lawmaking power. The codes of fair competition which the statute attempts to authorize are codes of laws. If valid, they place all persons within their reach under the obligation of positive law, binding equally those who assent and those who do not assent. Violations of the provisions of the codes are punishable as crimes. . . .

This aspect of the case presents the question whether the particular provisions of the Live Poultry Code, which the defendants were convicted for violating and for having conspired to violate, were within the regulating power of Congress. These provisions relate to the hours and wages of those employed by defendants in their slaughterhouses in Brooklyn and to the sales there made to retail dealers and butchers.

Were these transactions "in" interstate commerce? Much is made of the fact that almost all the poultry coming to New York is sent there from other States. But the code provisions, as here applied, do not concern the transportation of the poultry from other States to New York, or the transactions of the commission men or others to whom it is consigned, or the sales made by such consignees to defendants. When defendants had made their purchases, whether at the West Washington Market in New York City or at the railroad terminals serving the city, or elsewhere, the poultry was trucked to their slaughterhouses in Brooklyn for local disposition. The interstate transactions in relation to that poultry then ended. Defendants held the poultry at their slaughterhouse markets for slaughter and local sale to retail dealers and butchers who in turn sold directly to consumers. Neither the slaughtering nor the sales by defendants were transactions in interstate commerce.

The undisputed facts thus afford no warrant for the argument that the poultry handled by defendants at their slaughterhouse markets was in a "*current*" or "*flow*" of interstate commerce, and was thus subject to congressional regulation. The mere fact that there may be a constant flow of commodities into a State does not mean that the flow continues after the property has arrived and has become commingled with the mass of property within the State and is there held solely for local disposition and use. So far as the poultry here in question is concerned, the flow in interstate commerce had ceased. The poultry had come to a permanent rest within the state. It was not held, used, or sold by defendants in relation to any further transactions in interstate commerce and was not destined for transportation to other States. Hence decisions which deal with a stream of interstate commerce—where goods come to rest within a State temporarily and are later to go forward in interstate commerce—and with the regulations of transactions involved in that practical continuity of movement, are not applicable here. See [*e.g.*] *Stafford v. Wallace* (1922).

Did the defendants' transactions directly "*affect*" interstate commerce so as to be subject to federal regulation? The power of Congress extends, not only to the regulation of transactions which are part of interstate commerce, but to the protection of that commerce from injury. It matters not that the injury may be due to the conduct of those engaged in intrastate operations. . . .

In determining how far the federal government may go in controlling intrastate transactions upon the ground that they "affect" interstate commerce, there is a necessary and well-established distinction between direct and indirect effects. The precise line can be drawn only as individual cases arise, but the distinction is clear in principle. Direct effects are illustrated by the railroad cases we have cited, as, *e.g.,* the effect of failure to use prescribed safety appliances on railroads which are the highways of both interstate and intrastate commerce, injury to an employee engaged in interstate transportation by the negligence of an employee engaged in an intrastate movement, the fixing of rates for intrastate transportation which unjustly discriminate against interstate commerce.

But where the effect of intrastate transactions upon interstate commerce is merely indirect, such transactions remain within the domain of state power. If the commerce clause were construed to reach all enterprises and transactions which could be said to have an indirect effect upon interstate commerce, the federal authority would embrace practically all the activities of the people, and the authority of the State over its domestic concerns would exist only by sufferance of the federal government. . . .

The question of chief importance relates to the provisions of the Code as to the hours and wages of those employed in defendants' slaughterhouse markets. It is plain that these requirements are imposed in order to govern the details of defendants' management of their local business. The persons employed in slaughtering and selling in local trade are not employed in interstate commerce. Their hours and wages have no direct relation to interstate commerce. The question of how many hours these employees should work and what they should be paid differs in no essential respect from similar questions in other local businesses which handle commodities brought into a State and there dealt in as a part of its internal commerce. . . .

[T]he government argues that hours and wages affect prices; that slaughterhouse men sell at a small margin above operating costs; that labor represents 50 to 60 per cent. of these costs; that a slaughterhouse operator paying lower wages or reducing his cost by exacting long hours of work translates his saving into lower prices; that this results in demands for a cheaper grade of goods: and that the cutting of prices brings about a demoralization of the price structure. Similar conditions may be adduced in relation to other businesses.

The argument of the government proves too much. If the federal government may determine the wages and hours of employees in the internal commerce of a State, because of their relation to cost and prices and their indirect effect upon interstate commerce, it would seem that a similar control might be exerted over other elements of cost, also affecting prices, such as the number of employees, rents, advertising, methods of doing business, etc. All the processes of production and distribution that enter into cost could likewise be controlled. If the cost of doing an intrastate business is in itself the permitted object of federal control, the extent of the regulation of cost would be a question of discretion and not of power. . . . It is not the province of the Court to consider the economic advantages or disadvantages of such a centralized system. It is sufficient to say that the Federal Constitution does not provide for it. . . .

We are of the opinion that the attempt through the provisions of the Code to fix the hours and wages of employees of defendants in their intrastate business was not a valid exercise of federal power. [W]e hold the code provisions here in question to be invalid and that the judgment of conviction must be reversed.

MR. JUSTICE CARDOZO (concurring).

. . . I find no authority in [the Commerce Clause] for the regulation of wages and hours of labor in the intrastate transactions that make up the defendants' business. As to this feature of the case, little can be added to the opinion of the court.

There is a view of causation that would obliterate the distinction between what is national and what is local in the activities of commerce. Motion at the outer rim is communicated perceptibly, though minutely, to recording instruments at the center. A society such as ours "is an elastic medium which transmits all tremors throughout its territory; the only question is of their size." Per Learned Hand, J., in the court below. The law is not indifferent to considerations of degree. Activities local in their immediacy do not become interstate and national because of distant repercussions. What is near and what is distant may at times be uncertain. There is no penumbra of uncertainty obscuring judgment here. To find immediacy or directness here is to find it almost everywhere. If centripetal forces are to be isolated to the exclusion of the forces that oppose and counteract them, there will be an end to our federal system. . . .

I am authorized to state that Mr. Justice Stone joins in this opinion.

Schechter Poultry was a unanimous decision. The following year, by contrast, in *Carter v. Carter Coal Co.* (1936), a 5–4 majority of the Court held unconstitutional the Bituminous Coal Conservation Act of 1935. An oddity of the case is that, for the most part, the justices in the majority and in the minority discussed different issues.

The Act, intended to correct overproduction in the nation's bituminous coal mines, contained a legislative finding that "all production of bituminous coal and distribution by the producers thereof bear upon and directly affect its interstate commerce." It imposed a heavy sales tax on bituminous coal, but rebated 90% of the exaction for any operator who accepted and operated according to a code to be formulated by the National Bituminous Coal Commission. The codes were to contain two basic sets of provisions, one governing labor conditions at the mines and the other the marketing of the coal. Among the code's labor provisions were to be guarantees of the right to organize and bargain collectively. Part III(g) provided that if a specified percentage of the operators and miners negotiated consistent wage and hour standards, those standards would be binding on anyone who had agreed to operate pursuant to the code.

The majority, per Sutherland, held that the labor provisions were unconstitutional as a regulation of mining, which as a form of production had long been held to be a local activity rather than part of interstate commerce. Here are excerpts from the majority's discussion of the Commerce Clause issues:

> The proposition, often advanced and as often discredited, that the power of the federal government inherently extends to purposes affecting the Nation as a whole with which the states severally cannot deal or cannot adequately deal, and the related notion that Congress, entirely apart from those powers delegated by the Constitution, may enact laws to promote the general welfare, have never been accepted but always definitely rejected by this court. . . . In the Framers Convention, the proposal to confer a general power akin to that just discussed was [considered, in the form of a resolution recognizing Congress's power] "to legislate in all cases to which the separate States are incompetent, or in which the harmony of the United States may be interrupted by the exercise of individual Legislation." The convention, however, declined to confer upon Congress power in such general terms; instead of which it carefully limited the powers which it thought wise to intrust to Congress by specifying them, thereby denying all others not granted expressly or by necessary implication. It made no grant of authority to Congress to legislate substantively for the general welfare; and no such authority exists, save as the general welfare may be promoted by the exercise of the powers which are granted. . . .
>
> The general rule with regard to the respective powers of the national and the state governments under the Constitution is not in doubt. The states were before the Constitution; and, consequently, their legislative powers antedated the Constitution. Those who framed and those who adopted that instrument meant to carve from the general mass of legislative powers, then possessed by the states, only such portions as it was thought wise to confer upon the federal government; and in order that there should be no uncertainty in respect of what was taken and what was left, the national powers of legislation were not aggregated but enumerated—with the result that

what was not embraced by the enumeration remained vested in the states without change or impairment. . . .

Every journey to a forbidden end begins with the first step; and the danger of such a step by the federal government in the direction of taking over the powers of the states is that the end of the journey may find the states so despoiled of their powers, or—what may amount to the same thing—so relieved of the responsibilities which possession of the powers necessarily enjoins, as to reduce them to little more than geographical subdivisions of the national domain. It is safe to say that if, when the Constitution was under consideration, it had been thought that any such danger lurked behind its plain words, it would never have been ratified.

[W]e shall find no grant of power which authorizes Congress to legislate in respect of [the] general purposes [of the Act] unless it be found in the commerce clause—and this we now consider. . . .

[Under the] commerce clause, [the] function to be exercised is that of regulation. The thing to be regulated is the commerce described. In exercising the authority conferred by this clause of the Constitution, Congress is powerless to regulate anything which is not commerce, as it is powerless to do anything about commerce which is not regulation.

The distinction between manufacture and commerce was discussed in *Kidd v. Pearson* (1888), and it was said:

> No distinction is more popular to the common mind, or more clearly expressed in economic and political literature, than that between manufactures and commerce. Manufacture is transformation—the fashioning of raw materials into a change of form for use. The functions of commerce are different. . . . If it be held that the term includes the regulation of all such manufactures as are intended to be the subject of commercial transactions in the future, it is impossible to deny that it would also include all productive industries that contemplate the same thing.

The result would be that congress would be invested, to the exclusion of the states, with the power to regulate, not only manufacture, but also agriculture, horticulture, stock-raising, domestic fisheries, mining—in short, every branch of human industry. For is there one of them that does not contemplate, more or less clearly, an interstate or foreign market? . . .

That commodities produced or manufactured within a state are intended to be sold or transported outside the state does not render their production or manufacture subject to federal regulation under the commerce clause. . . .

We have seen that the word "commerce" is the equivalent of the phrase "intercourse for the purposes of trade." Plainly, the incidents leading up to and culminating in the mining of coal do not constitute such intercourse. The employment of men, the fixing of their wages, hours of labor, and working conditions, the bargaining in respect of these things—whether carried on separately or collectively—each and all constitute intercourse for the purposes of production, not of trade. The latter is a thing apart from the relation of employer and employee, which in all producing occupations is purely local in character. Extraction of coal from the mine is the aim and the completed result of local activities. . . . Mining brings the subject-matter of commerce into existence. Commerce disposes of it. . . .

. . . Everything which moves in interstate commerce has had a local origin. Without local production somewhere, interstate commerce, as now carried on, would practically disappear. Nevertheless, the local character of mining, of manufacturing, and of crop growing is a fact, and remains a fact, whatever may be done with the products. . . .

That the production of every commodity intended for interstate sale and transportation has some effect upon interstate commerce may be, if it has not already been, freely granted; and we are brought to the final and decisive inquiry, whether here that effect is direct, as the "Preamble" recites, or indirect. The distinction is not formal, but substantial in the highest degree, as we pointed out in the *Schechter Case*. "If the commerce clause were construed," we there said, "to reach all enterprises and transactions which could be said to have an indirect effect upon interstate commerce, the federal authority would embrace practically all the activities of the people, and the authority of the state over its domestic concerns would exist only by sufferance of the federal government. . . .”

Whether the effect of a given activity or condition is direct or indirect is not always easy to determine. The word “direct” implies that the activity or condition invoked or blamed shall operate proximately—not mediately, remotely, or collaterally—to produce the effect. It connotes the absence of an efficient intervening agency or condition. And the extent of the effect bears no logical relation to its character.

The distinction between a direct and an indirect effect turns, not upon the magnitude of either the cause or the effect, but entirely upon the manner in which the effect has been brought about. If the production by one man of a single ton of coal intended for interstate sale and shipment, and actually so sold and shipped, affects interstate commerce indirectly, the effect does not become direct by multiplying the tonnage, or increasing the number of men employed, or adding to the expense or complexities of the business, or by all combined. It is quite true that rules of law are sometimes qualified by considerations of degree, as the government argues. But the matter of degree has no bearing upon the question here, since that question is not—What is the extent of the local activity or condition, or the extent of the effect produced upon interstate commerce? but—What is the relation between the activity or condition and the effect?

Much stress is put upon the evils which come from the struggle between employers and employees over the matter of wages, working conditions, the right of collective bargaining, etc., and the resulting strikes, curtailment, and irregularity of production and effect on prices; and it is insisted that interstate commerce is greatly affected thereby. But, in addition to what has just been said, the conclusive answer is that the evils are all local evils over which the federal government has no legislative control. . . . Such effect as they may have upon commerce, however extensive it may be, is secondary and indirect. An increase in the greatness of the effect adds to its importance. It does not alter its character.

> The government's contentions in defense of the labor provisions are really disposed of adversely by our decision in the *Schechter Case*. The only perceptible difference between that case and this is that in the *Schechter Case* the federal power was asserted with respect to commodities which had come to rest after their interstate transportation; while here, the case deals with commodities at rest before interstate commerce has begun. That difference is without significance. The federal regulatory power ceases when interstate commercial intercourse ends; and, correlatively, the power does not attach until interstate commercial intercourse begins . . . .

And so the majority invalidated the labor provisions of the code. But what of the marketing provisions, which set minimum and maximum prices at which coal could be sold? The majority never reached the issue. When a court holds one portion of a statute unconstitutional but another is, or may be valid, the court confronts the question of whether the invalid portion may be *severed* from the rest, leaving the remainder standing. In some cases, the answer is affirmative: The legislature would rather have half a loaf than none. In other cases, the answer is negative: The parts of the statute may have been so mutually dependent that the legislature might have thought that the surviving half loaf was worse than nothing at all. In this case, the Act actually contained a severability clause, providing that if any portion of it were held invalid, the remainder "shall not be affected thereby." But Sutherland wrote that this provision merely reversed a presumption of inseverability, and he held that the marketing provisions were not severable from the labor provisions; hence, the entire statute was unenforceable.

Justice Cardozo, in a dissent joined by the other liberals on the Court, Brandeis and Stone, said that the majority opinion "begins at the wrong end": He believed that the marketing provisions were clearly valid, and were sufficient to require the coal companies "to come in under the code" or pay the price for refusal—so he did not need to address the constitutionality of the labor provisions. He thought the conclusion with respect to interstate sales was easy, because they "constitute interstate commerce, and do not merely 'affect' it." Beyond that, he tried, as in *Schechter*, to soften the traditional direct-indirect demarcation applied by the majority:

[T]he question remains whether [regulation of prices] comes within [the commerce] power as applied to intrastate sales where interstate prices are directly or intimately affected. . . . The relation may be tenuous or the opposite according to the facts. Always the setting of the facts is to be viewed if one would know the closeness of the tie. Perhaps, if one group of adjectives is to be chosen in preference to another, "intimate" and "remote" will be found to be as good as any. At all events, "direct" and "indirect," even if accepted as sufficient, must not be read too narrowly. A survey of the cases shows that the words have been interpreted with suppleness of adaptation and flexibility of meaning. The power is as broad as the need that evokes it. . . .

Hughes also dissented, but somewhat more equivocally. He thought Part III(g) was "legislative delegation in its most obnoxious form," as well as a denial of due process in that it permitted a group of producers and miners to make rules for others who were not parties to the agreement. As for the commerce power, Hughes agreed with the traditional view that the power is not one "to regulate industry within the state"; in one conclusory sentence he asserted that Part III(g) "goes beyond any proper measure of protection of interstate commerce, and attempts a broad regulation of industry within the State." He did not express a view on the other labor provisions. But he believed "the provisions for marketing in interstate commerce" were plainly constitutional, severable from the labor provisions, and sufficient to sustain the code.

Schechter Poultry and especially *Carter Coal* seemed to augur poorly for the watershed National Labor Relations Act. Enacted in 1935, that statute regulated labor relations in industries that affected interstate commerce—regardless of whether any particular industry was engaged in "production" or "commerce" as defined by the Court. By the time the statute reached the Supreme Court for review, however, three important developments had occurred. First, Roosevelt won re-election by a landslide in 1936, losing only Maine and Vermont. Second, emboldened by his victory, Roosevelt in February 1937 began an ultimately unsuccessful campaign to pack the Court by adding seats so that he could appoint additional justices more receptive to governmental regulation. Finally, a flurry of sit-down strikes spread across the nation throughout late 1936 and early 1937, affecting perhaps one million workers.

Historians disagree about the impact that these developments had on the Court—and in particular on Hughes and Roberts, the two justices in the ideological middle. Whatever their reasons, however, the justices' decision in the next case reflected a substantial, and historically crucial, broadening of Congress's commerce power. As you read *NLRB v. Jones & Laughlin*, try to decide whether you think it represents a reasonable application of existing doctrine, a harbinger of a new era in Commerce Clause doctrine—or perhaps both.

WORTH NOTING

For an argument that Hughes's views were unaffected by these developments, and that Roberts's views may have been affected by the labor unrest, but were probably not affected by the election or the Court-packing plan, see Richard D. Friedman, *Switching Time and Other Thought Experiments: The Hughes Court and Constitutional Transformation*, 142 U. Pa. L. Rev. 1891 (1994). See also, *e.g.*, G. Edward White, The Constitution and the New Deal (2000); Barry Cushman, Rethinking the New Deal Court: The Structure of a Constitutional Revolution (1998); William E. Leuchtenburg, The Supreme Court Reborn: The Constitutional Revolution in the Age of Roosevelt (1996).

National Labor Relations Board v. Jones & Laughlin Steel Corp.

Supreme Court of the United States, 1937.
301 U.S. 1.

MR. CHIEF JUSTICE HUGHES delivered the opinion of the Court.

In a proceeding under the National Labor Relations Act of 1935, the National Labor Relations Board found that the respondent, Jones & Laughlin Steel Corporation, had violated the Act by engaging in unfair labor practices affecting commerce. [A union instituted the proceeding, contending that the company fired some employees in an attempt to interfere with the employees' self-organization. The Board ordered the company to reinstate ten employees, with back pay.]

The scheme of the National Labor Relations Act—which is too long to be quoted in full—may be briefly stated. The first section sets forth findings with respect to the injury to commerce resulting from the denial by employers of the right of employees to organize and from the refusal of employers to accept the procedure of collective bargaining. There follows a declaration that it is the policy of the United States to eliminate these causes of obstruction to the free flow of commerce. The Act then . . . creates the National Labor Relations Board and prescribes its organization. §§ 3–6. It sets forth the right of employees to self-organization and to bargain collectively through representatives of their own choosing. § 7. It defines "unfair labor practices." § 8. It lays down rules as to the representation of employees for the purpose of collective bargaining. § 9. The Board is empowered to prevent the described unfair labor practices affecting commerce and the Act prescribes the procedure to that end. . . .

Contesting the ruling of the Board, the respondent argues (1) that the Act is in reality a regulation of labor relations and not of interstate commerce; [and] (2) that the act can have no application to the respondent's relations with its production employees because they are not subject to regulation by the federal government. . . .

The Labor Board has found: The corporation is organized under the laws of Pennsylvania and has its principal office at Pittsburgh. It is engaged in the business of manufacturing iron and steel in plants situated in Pittsburgh and nearby Aliquippa, Pa. It manufactures and distributes a widely diversified line of steel and pig iron, being the fourth largest producer of steel in the United States. With its subsidiaries—nineteen in number—it is a completely integrated enterprise, owning and operating ore, coal and limestone properties, lake and river transportation facilities and terminal railroads located at its manufacturing plants.

It owns or controls mines in Michigan and Minnesota. It operates four ore steamships on the Great Lakes, used in the transportation of ore to its factories. It owns coal mines in Pennsylvania. It operates towboats and steam barges used in carrying coal to its factories. It owns limestone properties in various places in Pennsylvania and West Virginia. It owns the Monongahela connecting railroad which connects the plants of the Pittsburgh works and forms an interconnection with the Pennsylvania, New York Central and Baltimore & Ohio Railroad systems. It owns the Aliquippa & Southern Railroad Company, which connects the Aliquippa works with the Pittsburgh & Lake Erie, part of the New York Central system. Much of its product is shipped to its warehouses in Chicago, Detroit, Cincinnati and Memphis—to the last two places by means of its own barges and transportation equipment. In Long Island City, New York, and in New Orleans it operates structural steel fabricating shops in connection with the warehousing of semifinished materials sent from its works. Through one of its wholly-owned subsidiaries it owns, leases, and operates stores, warehouses,

and yards for the distribution of equipment and supplies for drilling and operating oil and gas wells and for pipe lines, refineries and pumping stations.
It has sales offices in twenty cities in the United States and a wholly-owned
subsidiary which is devoted exclusively to distributing its product in Canada.
Approximately 75 per cent. of its product is shipped out of Pennsylvania.

Summarizing these operations, the Labor Board concluded that the works
in Pittsburgh and Aliquippa

> might be likened to the heart of a self-contained, highly integrated
> body. They draw in the raw materials from Michigan, Minnesota,
> West Virginia, Pennsylvania in part through arteries and by means
> controlled by the respondent; they transform the materials and then
> pump them out to all parts of the nation through the vast mechanism
> which the respondent has elaborated.

To carry on the activities of the entire steel industry, 33,000 men mine ore,
44,000 men mine coal, 4,000 men quarry limestone, 16,000 men manufacture
coke, 343,000 men manufacture steel, and 83,000 men transport its product.
Respondent has about 10,000 employees in its Aliquippa plant, which is located
in a community of about 30,000 persons. . . .

The Act is challenged in its entirety as an attempt to regulate all industry, thus invading the reserved powers of the States over their local concerns.
It is asserted that . . . the Act is not a true regulation of such commerce or of
matters which directly affect it, but on the contrary has the fundamental object of placing under the compulsory supervision of the federal government all
industrial labor relations within the nation. . . .

The grant of authority to the Board does not purport to extend to the relationship between all industrial employees and employers. Its terms do not
impose collective bargaining upon all industry regardless of effects upon interstate or foreign commerce. It purports to reach only what may be deemed to
burden or obstruct that commerce and, thus qualified, it must be construed as
contemplating the exercise of control within constitutional bounds.

It is a familiar principle that acts which directly burden or obstruct
interstate or foreign commerce, or its free flow, are within the reach of the congressional power. Acts having that effect are not rendered immune because they
grow out of labor disputes. It is the effect upon commerce, not the source of
the injury, which is the criterion. Whether or not particular action does affect

commerce in such a close and intimate fashion as to be subject to federal control, and hence to lie within the authority conferred upon the Board, is left by the statute to be determined as individual cases arise. We are thus to inquire whether in the instant case the constitutional boundary has been passed. . . .

Respondent says that, whatever may be said of employees engaged in interstate commerce, the industrial relations and activities in the manufacturing department of respondent's enterprise are not subject to federal regulation. The argument rests upon the proposition that manufacturing in itself is not commerce. *Coronado Coal Co. v. United Mine Workers* (1925); *Schechter Corporation v. United States* (1935); *Carter v. Carter Coal Co* (1936).

The government distinguishes these cases. The various parts of respondent's enterprise are described as interdependent and as thus involving "a great movement of iron ore, coal and limestone along well-defined paths to the steel mills, thence through them, and thence in the form of steel products into the consuming centers of the country—a definite and well-understood course of business." It is urged that these activities constitute a "stream" or "flow" of commerce, of which the Aliquippa manufacturing plant is the focal point, and that industrial strife at that point would cripple the entire movement. Reference is made to . . . *Stafford v. Wallace* (1922). The Court found [in that case] that the stockyards were but a "throat" through which the current of commerce flowed and the transactions which there occurred could not be separated from that movement. . . .

Respondent contends that the instant case presents material distinctions. Respondent says that the Aliquippa plant is extensive in size and represents a large investment in buildings, machinery and equipment. The raw materials which are brought to the plant are delayed for long periods and, after being subjected to manufacturing processes "are changed substantially as to character, utility and value." The finished products which emerge "are to a large extent manufactured without reference to pre-existing orders and contracts and are entirely different from the raw materials which enter at the other end." Hence respondent argues that, "If importation and exportation in interstate commerce do not singly transfer purely local activities into the field of congressional regulation, it should follow that their combination would not alter the local situation."

We do not find it necessary to determine whether these features of defendant's business dispose of the asserted analogy to the "stream of commerce" cases. The instances in which that metaphor has been used are but particular, and not exclusive, illustrations of the protective power which the government invokes in support of the present act.

The congressional authority to protect interstate commerce from burdens and obstructions is not limited to transactions which can be deemed to be an essential part of a "flow" of interstate or foreign commerce. Burdens and obstructions may be due to injurious action springing from other sources. . . . Although activities may be intrastate in character when separately considered, if they have such a close and substantial relation to interstate commerce that their control is essential or appropriate to protect that commerce from burdens and obstructions, Congress cannot be denied the power to exercise that control. *Schechter Corporation v. United States.*

Undoubtedly the scope of this power must be considered in the light of our dual system of government and may not be extended so as to embrace effects upon interstate commerce so indirect and remote that to embrace them, in view of our complex society, would effectually obliterate the distinction between what is national and what is local and create a completely centralized government. The question is necessarily one of degree. . . .

That intrastate activities, by reason of close and intimate relation to interstate commerce, may fall within federal control is demonstrated in the case of carriers who are engaged in both interstate and intrastate transportation. There federal control has been found essential to secure the freedom of interstate traffic from interference or unjust discrimination and to promote the efficiency of the interstate service. *The Shreveport Case* (1914) . . . . The close and intimate effect which brings the subject within the reach of federal power may be due to activities in relation to productive industry although the industry when separately viewed is local.

It is thus apparent that the fact that the employees here concerned were engaged in production is not determinative. The question remains as to the effect upon interstate commerce of the labor practice involved. In the *Schechter Case*, we found that the effect there was so remote as to be beyond the federal power. To find "immediacy or directness" there was to find it "almost everywhere," a result inconsistent with the maintenance of our federal system. In the *Carter [Coal] Case*, the Court was of the opinion that the provisions of the statute relating to production were invalid upon several grounds, [including not only exceeding the reach of the commerce power, but also delegation and due process limitations]. These cases are not controlling here. . . .

Giving full weight to respondent's contention with respect to a break in the complete continuity of the "stream of commerce" by reason of respondent's manufacturing operations, the fact remains that the stoppage of those operations by industrial strife would have a most serious effect upon interstate commerce. In view of respondent's far-flung activities, it is idle to say that the effect would be indirect or remote. It is obvious that it would be immediate and might be catastrophic.

We are asked to shut our eyes to the plainest facts of our national life and to deal with the question of direct and indirect effects in an intellectual vacuum. Because there may be but indirect and remote effects upon interstate commerce in connection with a host of local enterprises throughout the country, it does not follow that other industrial activities do not have such a close and intimate relation to interstate commerce as to make the presence of industrial strife a matter of the most urgent national concern. When industries organize themselves on a national scale, making their relation to interstate commerce the dominant factor in their activities, how can it be maintained that their industrial labor relations constitute a forbidden field into which Congress may not enter when it is necessary to protect interstate commerce from the paralyzing consequences of industrial war? We have often said that interstate commerce itself is a practical conception. It is equally true that interferences with that commerce must be appraised by a judgment that does not ignore actual experience. . . .

The steel industry is one of the great basic industries of the United States, with ramifying activities affecting interstate commerce at every point. The Government aptly refers to the steel strike of 1919–1920 with its far-reaching consequences. . . . It is not necessary again to detail the facts as to respondent's enterprise. Instead of being beyond the pale, we think that it presents in a most striking way the close and intimate relation which a manufacturing industry may have to interstate commerce and we have no doubt that Congress had constitutional authority to safeguard the right of respondent's employees to self-organization and freedom in the choice of representatives for collective bargaining.

Reversed and remanded.

Jones & Laughlin was decided along with two companion cases. In *NLRB v. Fruehauf Trailer Co.* (1937), the sanctioned company had the largest share of the truck trailer market; indeed, Fruehauf remains a major force in the industry to this day. With only 900 employees, one plant, and $3 million in annual sales, however, it was not an industrial giant. The company in *NLRB v. Friedman-Harry Marks Clothing Co.* (1937) was even less significant, with 800 employees, one plant, and a negligible share of its market. But the Court did not linger over fine distinctions; it held tersely that the principles stated in *Jones & Laughlin* applied to the companion cases as well.

Justice McReynolds wrote a dissent that applied to all three cases. Joined by Justices Van Devanter, Sutherland, and Butler, his objections focused on Friedman-Harry Marks, which he called a "relatively small concern." This meant, he argued, that "[a]ny effect on interstate commerce by the discharge of employees shown here would be indirect and remote in the highest degree." He posed a series of problems he thought would certainly arise from the majority decision: Could Congress prescribe employment conditions on a ranch if the cattle were delivered into interstate commerce, or prevent a mill owner from shutting down, or make arson of a factory a federal offense? "Whatever effect any cause of [worker] discontent may ultimately have upon commerce," he contended, "is far too indirect to justify congressional regulation. Almost anything—marriage, birth, death—may in some fashion affect commerce."

For Discussion

(1) Was the *Jones & Laughlin* decision revolutionary? Was it consistent with *Schechter Poultry*? (If not, what accounts for the switch of five Justices?) Was it consistent with *Carter Coal*? (If not, what accounts for the switch of Hughes and Roberts?) How, if at all, did it alter prior law? Was it rightly decided?

(2) Why do you suppose Hughes wrote a long opinion in *Jones & Laughlin* and very brief ones in the other two? Was this proper?

Whatever the doctrinal particulars, many observers thought the implication of *Jones & Laughlin* and its companion cases was unmistakable: the Supreme Court's efforts to police the commerce power had been dramatically relaxed. The extent of that relaxation became clear in the next two cases, both of which were unanimously decided. (Justice McReynolds, the last of the "Four Horsemen," retired two days before *United States v. Darby* was issued.)

United States v. Darby

Supreme Court of the United States, 1941.
312 U.S. 100.

MR. JUSTICE STONE delivered the opinion of the Court.

The two principal questions raised by the record in this case are, *first*, whether Congress has constitutional power to prohibit the shipment in interstate commerce of lumber manufactured by employees whose wages are less than a prescribed minimum or whose weekly hours of labor at that wage are greater than a prescribed maximum, and, *second*, whether it has power to prohibit the employment of workmen in the production of goods "for interstate commerce" at other than prescribed wages and hours. . . .

SUMMARY OF THE FACTS

Federal prosecutors indicted a Georgia lumber mill and its owner for violating the Fair Labor Standards Act of 1938. The mill had produced and shipped lumber without complying with §§ 6 and 7 of the Act, which imposed minimum wage and maximum hour standard on productive industries. According to the indictment, "a large proportion" of the mill's lumber output was shipped to out-of-state customers.

The demurrer, so far as now relevant to the appeal, challenged the validity of the Fair Labor Standards Act under the Commerce Clause and the . . . Tenth Amendment[ ]. The district court quashed the indictment in its entirety upon the broad grounds that the Act, which it interpreted as a regulation of manufacture within the states, is unconstitutional. It declared that manufacture is not interstate commerce and that the regulation by the Fair Labor Standards Act of wages and hours of employment of those engaged in the manufacture of goods . . . is not within the congressional power to regulate interstate commerce. . . .

The prohibition of shipment of the proscribed goods in interstate commerce.

Section 15(a)(1) prohibits, and the indictment charges, the shipment in interstate commerce, of goods produced for interstate commerce by employees whose wages and hours of employment do not conform to the requirements of the Act. Since this section is not violated unless the commodity shipped has been produced under labor conditions prohibited by § 6 and § 7 [of the Act], the only question arising under the commerce clause with respect to such shipments is whether Congress has the constitutional power to prohibit them.

While manufacture is not of itself interstate commerce[,] the shipment of manufactured goods interstate is such commerce and the prohibition of such shipment by Congress is indubitably a regulation of the commerce. The power to regulate commerce is the power "to prescribe the rule by which commerce is to be governed." *Gibbons v. Ogden* (1824). It extends not only to those regulations which aid, foster and protect the commerce, but embraces those which prohibit it. *Lottery Case (Champion v. Ames)* (1903). It is conceded that the power of Congress to prohibit transportation in interstate commerce includes noxious articles, *Lottery Case*; *Hipolite Egg Co. v. United States* (1911). . . .

But it is said that the present prohibition falls within the scope of none of these categories; that while the prohibition is nominally a regulation of the commerce[,] its motive or purpose is regulation of wages and hours of persons engaged in manufacture, the control of which has been reserved to the states and upon which Georgia and some of the states of destination have placed no restriction; that the effect of the present statute is not to exclude the prescribed articles from interstate commerce in aid of state regulation . . . , but instead, under the guise of a regulation of interstate commerce, it undertakes to regulate wages and hours within the state contrary to the policy of the state which has elected to leave them unregulated.

The power of Congress over interstate commerce "is complete in itself, may be exercised to its utmost extent, and acknowledges no limitations, other than are prescribed by the Constitution." *Gibbons v. Ogden*. That power can neither be enlarged nor diminished by the exercise or non-exercise of state power. Congress, following its own conception of public policy concerning the restrictions which may appropriately be imposed on interstate commerce, is free to exclude from the commerce articles whose use in the states for which they are destined it may conceive to be injurious to the public health, morals or welfare, even though the state has not sought to regulate their use. . . .

Such regulation is not a forbidden invasion of state power merely because either its motive or its consequence is to restrict the use of articles of commerce within the states of destination . . . . It is no objection to the assertion of the power to regulate interstate commerce that its exercise is attended by the same incidents which attend the exercise of the police power of the states. . . .

The motive and purpose of the present regulation are plainly to make effective the Congressional conception of public policy that interstate commerce should not be made the instrument of competition in the distribution of goods produced under substandard labor conditions, which competition is injurious to the commerce and to the states from and to which the commerce flows. The motive and purpose of a regulation of interstate commerce are matters for the legislative judgment upon the exercise of which the Constitution places no restriction and over which the courts are given no control. . . . Whatever their motive and purpose, regulations of commerce which do not infringe some constitutional prohibition are within the plenary power conferred on Congress by the Commerce Clause. . . .

[T]here would be little occasion for repeating [these principles] now were it not for the decision of this Court twenty-two years ago in *Hammer v. Dagenhart*. . . . The distinction on which the decision was rested[—]that Congressional power to prohibit interstate commerce is limited to articles which in themselves have some harmful or deleterious property— . . . was novel when made and unsupported by any provision of the Constitution. The thesis of the opinion that the motive of the prohibition or its effect to control in some measure the use or production within the states of the article thus excluded from the commerce can operate to deprive the regulation of its constitutional authority has long since ceased to have force. [As] we have declared, "[t]he authority of the Federal Government over interstate commerce does not differ in extent or character from that retained by the states over intrastate commerce." *United States v. Rock Royal Co-Operative, Inc* (1939). The conclusion is inescapable that *Hammer v. Dagenhart* was a departure from the principles which have prevailed in the interpretation of the Commerce Clause both before and since the decision. . . . It should be and now is overruled.

Validity of the wage and hour requirements.

Section 15(a)(2) and §§ 6 and 7 require employers to conform to the wage and hour provisions with respect to all employees engaged in the production of goods for interstate commerce. . . .

The obvious purpose of the Act was not only to prevent the interstate transportation of the proscribed product, but to stop the initial step toward transportation, production with the purpose of so transporting it. Congress was not unaware that most manufacturing businesses shipping their product in interstate commerce make it in their shops without reference to its ultimate destination and then after manufacture select some of it for shipment interstate and some intrastate according to the daily demands of their business, and that it would be practically impossible, without disrupting manufacturing businesses, to restrict the prohibited kind of production to the particular pieces of lumber, cloth, furniture or the like which later move in interstate rather than intrastate commerce. . . .

There remains the question whether such restriction on the production of goods for commerce is a permissible exercise of the commerce power.

The power of Congress over interstate commerce is not confined to the regulation of commerce among the states. It extends to those activities intrastate which so affect interstate commerce or the exercise of the power of Congress over it as to make regulation of them appropriate means to the attainment of a legitimate end[:] the exercise of the granted power of Congress to regulate interstate commerce. *McCulloch v. Maryland*; *NLRB v. Jones & Laughlin Steel Corp.*; *Coronado Coal Co. v. United Mine Workers*; *Shreveport Rate Cases.* . . .

In such legislation Congress has sometimes left it to the courts to determine whether the intrastate activities have the prohibited effect on the commerce, as in the Sherman Act. It has sometimes left it to an administrative board or agency to determine whether the activities sought to be regulated or prohibited have such effect, as in the case of the Interstate Commerce Act and the National Labor Relations Act . . . . And sometimes Congress itself has said that a particular activity affects the commerce as it did in the present act, the Safety Appliance Act, and the Railway Labor Act. In passing on the validity of legislation of the class last mentioned the only function of courts is to determine whether the particular activity regulated or prohibited is within the reach of the federal power.

Congress, having by the present Act adopted the policy of excluding from interstate commerce all goods produced for the commerce which do not conform to the specified labor standards, it may choose the means reasonably adapted to the attainment of the permitted end, even though they involve control of intrastate activities. Such legislation has often been sustained with respect to powers, other than the commerce power granted to the national government, when the means chosen, although not themselves within the granted power, were nevertheless deemed appropriate aids to the accomplishment of some purpose within an admitted power of the national government. . . . A familiar like exercise of power is the regulation of intrastate transactions which are so commingled with or related to interstate commerce that all must be regulated if the interstate commerce is to be effectively controlled. *Shreveport Case.* . . .

We think also that § 15(a)(2), now under consideration, is sustainable independently of § 15(a)(1), which prohibits shipment or transportation of the proscribed goods. As we have said the evils aimed at by the Act are the spread of substandard labor conditions through the use of the facilities of interstate commerce for competition by the goods so produced with those produced under the prescribed or better labor conditions; and the consequent dislocation of the commerce itself caused by the impairment or destruction of local businesses by competition made effective through interstate commerce. . . .

Congress, to attain its objective in the suppression of nationwide competition in interstate commerce by goods produced under substandard labor conditions, has made no distinction as to the volume or amount of shipments in the commerce or of production for commerce by any particular shipper or producer. It recognized that in present day industry, competition by a small part may affect the whole and that the total effect of the competition of many small producers may be great. See H. Rept. No. 2182, 75th Cong. 1st Sess. The legislation aimed at a whole embraces all its parts. . . .

Our conclusion is unaffected by the Tenth Amendment which provides: "The powers not delegated to the United States by the Constitution, nor prohibited by it to the States, are reserved to the States respectively, or to the people." The amendment states but a truism that all is retained which has not been surrendered. There is nothing in the history of its adoption to suggest that it was more than declaratory of the relationship between the national and state governments as it had been established by the Constitution before the amendment or that its purpose was other than to allay fears that the new national government might seek to exercise powers not granted, and that the states might not be able to exercise fully their reserved powers. See *e.g.*, Elliot's *Debates*; Annals of Congress; Story, *Commentaries on the Constitution.* . . .

Reversed.

Wickard v. Filburn

Supreme Court of the United States, 1942.
317 U.S. 111.

MR. JUSTICE JACKSON delivered the opinion of the Court.

The appellee filed his complaint against[, inter alia,] the Secretary of Agriculture of the United States. He sought . . . a declaratory judgment that the wheat marketing quota provisions of the [Agricultural Adjustment Act of 1938] as amended and applicable to him were unconstitutional because not sustainable under the Commerce Clause . . . .

The appellee for many years past has owned and operated a small farm in Montgomery County, Ohio, maintaining a herd of dairy cattle, selling milk, raising poultry, and selling poultry and eggs. It has been his practice to raise a small acreage of winter wheat, sown in the Fall and harvested in the following July; to sell a portion of the crop; to feed part to poultry and livestock on the farm, some of which is sold; to use some in making flour for home consumption; and to keep the rest for the following seeding. The intended disposition of the crop here involved has not been expressly stated.

In July of 1940, pursuant to the Agricultural Adjustment Act of 1938, as then amended, [the Secretary of Agriculture] established for the appellee's 1941 crop a wheat acreage allotment of 11.1 acres and a normal yield of 20.1 bushels of wheat an acre. [Filburn] was given notice of such allotment in July of 1940 before the Fall planting of his 1941 crop of wheat, and again in July of 1941, before it was harvested. He sowed, however, 23 acres, and harvested from his 11.9 acres of excess acreage 239 bushels, which under the terms of the Act as amended on May 26, 1941, constituted farm marketing excess, subject to a penalty of 49 cents a bushel, or $117.11 in all. The appellee has not paid the penalty and he has not postponed or avoided it by storing the excess under regulations of the Secretary of Agriculture, or by delivering it up to the Secretary. . . .

The general scheme of the Agricultural Adjustment Act of 1938 as related to wheat is to control the volume moving in interstate and foreign commerce in order to avoid surpluses and shortages and the consequent abnormally low or high wheat prices and obstructions to commerce. . . . The Act provides . . . that [in the event of a wheat oversupply of 35% or more relative to demand,] a compulsory national marketing quota shall be in effect with respect to the marketing of wheat. . . . [The statute required a referendum of farmers subject to the quota before it went into effect; the overwhelming majority approved.]

It is urged that under the Commerce Clause of the Constitution, Article I, § 8, clause 3, Congress does not possess the power it has in this instance sought to exercise. The question would merit little consideration since our decision in *United States v. Darby* (1941), sustaining the federal power to regulate production of goods for commerce, except for the fact that this Act extends federal regulation to production not intended in any part for commerce but wholly for consumption on the farm. . . . Hence, [the Act's] marketing quotas not only embrace all that may be sold without penalty but also what may be consumed on the premises. . . .

Appellee says that this is a regulation of production and consumption of wheat. Such activities are, he urges, beyond the reach of Congressional power under the Commerce Clause, since they are local in character, and their effects upon interstate commerce are at most "indirect." In answer the Government argues that the statute regulates neither production nor consumption, but only marketing. . . .

The Government's concern lest the Act be held to be a regulation of production or consumption rather than of marketing is attributable to a few dicta and decisions of this Court which might be understood to lay it down that activities such as "production," "manufacturing," and "mining" are strictly "local" and, except in special circumstances which are not present here, cannot be regulated under the commerce power because their effects upon interstate commerce are, as matter of law, only "indirect." . . . We believe that a review of the course of decision under the Commerce Clause will make plain, however, that questions of the power of Congress are not to be decided by reference to any formula which would give controlling force to nomenclature such as "production" and "indirect" and foreclose consideration of the actual effects of the activity in question upon interstate commerce. . . .

At the beginning Chief Justice Marshall described the Federal commerce power with a breadth never yet exceeded. *Gibbons v. Ogden* (1824). He made emphatic the embracing and penetrating nature of this power by warning that effective restraints on its exercise must proceed from political rather than from judicial processes.

For nearly a century, however, decisions of this Court under the Commerce Clause dealt rarely with questions of what Congress might do in the exercise of its granted power under the Clause . . . . It was not until 1887 with the enactment of the Interstate Commerce Act that the interstate commerce power began to exert positive influence in American law and life. This first important federal resort to the commerce power was followed in 1890 by the Sherman Anti-Trust Act and, thereafter, mainly after 1903, by many others. These statutes ushered in new phases of adjudication, which required the Court to approach the interpretation of the Commerce Clause in the light of an actual exercise by Congress of its power thereunder.

When it first dealt with this new legislation, the Court adhered to its earlier pronouncements, and allowed but little scope to the power of Congress. *United States v. E. C. Knight Co.* (1895). . . . The Court's recognition of the relevance of the economic effects in the application of the Commerce Clause[, however,] has made the mechanical application of legal formulas no longer feasible. Once an economic measure of the reach of the power granted to Congress in the Commerce Clause is accepted, questions of federal power cannot be decided simply by finding the activity in question to be "production" nor can consideration of its economic effects be foreclosed by calling them "indirect."

Whether the subject of the regulation in question was "production," "consumption," or "marketing" is, therefore, not material for purposes of deciding the question of federal power before us. That an activity is of local character may help in a doubtful case to determine whether Congress intended to reach it. . . . But even if appellee's activity be local and though it may not be regarded as commerce, it may still, whatever its nature, be reached by Congress if it exerts a substantial economic effect on interstate commerce and this irrespective of whether such effect is what might at some earlier time have been defined as "direct" or "indirect."

The parties have stipulated a summary of the economics of the wheat industry. . . . The wheat industry has been a problem industry for some years. Largely as a result of increased foreign production and import restrictions, annual exports of wheat and flour from the United States during the ten-year period ending in 1940 averaged less than 10 per cent of total production, while during the 1920's they averaged more than 25 per cent. The decline in the export trade has left a large surplus in production which in connection with an abnormally large supply of wheat and other grains in recent years caused congestion in a number of markets; tied up railroad cars; and caused elevators in some instances to turn away grains, and railroads to institute embargoes to prevent further congestion.

Many countries, both importing and exporting, have sought to modify the impact of the world market conditions on their own economy. . . . The four large exporting countries of Argentina, Australia, Canada, and the United States have all undertaken various programs for the relief of growers. . . .

The effect of consumption of homegrown wheat on interstate commerce is due to the fact that it constitutes the most variable factor in the disappearance of the wheat crop. Consumption on the farm where grown appears to vary in an amount greater than 20 per cent of average production. . . .

The maintenance by government regulation of a price for wheat undoubtedly can be accomplished as effectively by sustaining or increasing the demand as by limiting the supply. The effect of the statute before us is to restrict the amount which may be produced for market and the extent as well to which one may forestall resort to the market by producing to meet his own needs. That appellee's own contribution to the demand for wheat may be trivial by itself is not enough to remove him from the scope of federal regulation where, as here, his contribution, taken together with that of many others similarly situated, is far from trivial.

It is well established by decisions of this Court that the power to regulate commerce includes the power to regulate the prices at which commodities in that commerce are dealt in and practices affecting such prices. One of the primary purposes of the Act in question was to increase the market price of wheat and to that end to limit the volume thereof that could affect the market. It can hardly be denied that a factor of such volume and variability as home-consumed wheat would have a substantial influence on price and market conditions. This may arise because being in marketable condition such wheat overhangs the market and if induced by rising prices tends to flow into the market and check price increases. But . . . if we assume that it is never marketed, it supplies a need of the man who grew it which would otherwise be reflected by purchases in the open market. Home-grown wheat in this sense competes with wheat in commerce. The stimulation of commerce is a use of the regulatory function quite as definitely as prohibitions or restrictions thereon.

This record leaves us in no doubt that Congress may properly have considered that wheat consumed on the farm where grown if wholly outside the scheme of regulation would have a substantial effect in defeating and obstructing its purpose to stimulate trade therein at increased prices.

It is said, however, that this Act, forcing some farmers into the market to buy what they could provide for themselves, is an unfair promotion of the markets and prices of specializing wheat growers. It is of the essence of regulation that it lays a restraining hand on the self-interest of the regulated and that advantages from the regulation commonly fall to others. The conflicts of economic interest between the regulated and those who advantage by it are wisely left under our system to resolution by the Congress under its more flexible and responsible legislative process. Such conflicts rarely lend themselves to judicial determination. And with the wisdom, workability, or fairness, of the plan of regulation we have nothing to do. [The Court also rejected Due Process objections to the quota.]

Reversed.

c.   Commerce Clause—Aftermath of the Transformation

In the aftermath of the great transformation wrought by the New Deal cases, some observers came to believe that judicially enforceable limits on congressional commerce authority had effectively disappeared. They pointed to a string of cases—including *Wickard* and those that follow below—as imposing no meaningful check on Congress's ability to determine that *any* human activity taken in the aggregate substantially affects commerce. As you read these cases, see if you agree.

Did the mid-twentieth-century Court simply abandon the project of meaningful Commerce Clause review?

Heart of Atlanta Motel and *Katzenbach v. McClung* were companion cases addressing Congress's reliance on the Commerce Clause as one basis for the 1964 Civil Rights Act.

Heart of Atlanta Motel, Inc. v. United States

Supreme Court of the United States, 1964.
379 U.S. 241.

Mr. Justice Clark delivered the opinion of the Court.

This is a declaratory judgment action attacking the constitutionality of Title II of the Civil Rights Act of 1964 . . . .

1.   The Factual Background and Contentions of the Parties.

The case comes here on admissions and stipulated facts. Appellant owns and operates the Heart of Atlanta Motel which has 216 rooms available to transient guests. The motel is located on Courtland Street, two blocks from downtown Peachtree Street. It is readily accessible to interstate highways 75 and 85 and state highways 23 and 41. Appellant solicits patronage from outside the State of Georgia through various national advertising media, including magazines of national circulation; it maintains over 50 billboards and highway signs within the State, soliciting patronage for the motel; it accepts convention trade from outside Georgia and approximately 75% of its registered guests are from out of State.

Prior to passage of the Act the motel had followed a practice of refusing to rent rooms to Negroes, and it alleged that it intended to continue to do so. In an effort to perpetuate that policy this suit was filed. The appellant contends that Congress in passing this Act exceeded its power to regulate commerce . . . [and] that by requiring appellant to rent available rooms to Negroes against its will, Congress is subjecting it to involuntary servitude in contravention of the Thirteenth Amendment. . . .

3.   Title II of the [Civil Rights] Act.

This Title is divided into seven sections beginning with § 201(a) which provides that:

> All persons shall be entitled to the full and equal enjoyment of the goods, services, facilities, privileges, advantages, and accommodations of any place of public accommodation, as defined in this section, without discrimination or segregation on the ground of race, color, religion, or national origin.

. . . Section 203 prohibits the withholding or denial, etc., of any right or privilege secured by § 201 . . . .

4.   Application of Title II to Heart of Atlanta Motel.

It is admitted that the operation of the motel brings it within the provisions of § 201(a) of the Act and that appellant refused to provide lodging for transient Negroes because of their race or color and that it intends to continue that policy unless restrained.

The sole question posed is, therefore, the constitutionality of the Civil Rights Act of 1964 as applied to these facts. The legislative history of the Act indicates that Congress based the Act on § 5 and the Equal Protection Clause of the Fourteenth Amendment as well as [on] its power to regulate interstate commerce under Art. I, § 8, cl. 3, of the Constitution. . . . Our study of the legislative record, made in the light of prior cases, has brought us to the conclusion that Congress possessed ample power [under the Commerce Clause], and we have therefore not considered the other grounds relied upon. . . .

> **CROSS REFERENCE** Chapter V focuses on the portion of § 1 of the Fourteenth Amendment that provides that no State "shall . . . deny to any person within its jurisdiction the equal protection of the laws." Section 5 of the amendment, which gives Congress the enumerated power to enforce that guarantee ("The Congress shall have power to enforce, by appropriate legislation, the provisions of this article."), is addressed below in subchapter A.9.

6.   The Basis of Congressional Action.

While the Act as adopted carried no congressional findings, the record of its passage through each house is replete with evidence of the burdens that discrimination by race or color places upon interstate commerce.

This testimony included the fact that our people have become increasingly mobile with millions of people of all races traveling from State to State; that Negroes in particular have been the subject of discrimination in transient accommodations, having to travel great distances to secure the same; that often they have been unable to obtain accommodations and have had to call upon friends to put them up overnight; and that these conditions had become so acute as to require the listing of available lodging for Negroes in a special guidebook which was itself "dramatic testimony to the difficulties" Negroes encounter in travel. These exclusionary practices were found to be nationwide, the Under Secretary of Commerce testifying that there is "no question that this discrimination in the North still exists to a large degree" and in the West and Midwest as well.

This testimony indicated a qualitative as well as quantitative effect on interstate travel by Negroes. The former was the obvious impairment of the Negro traveler's pleasure and convenience that resulted when he continually was uncertain of finding lodging. As for the latter, there was evidence that this uncertainty stemming from racial discrimination had the effect of discouraging travel on the part of a substantial portion of the Negro community. This was the conclusion not only of the Under Secretary of Commerce but also of the Administrator of the Federal Aviation Agency who wrote the Chairman of the Senate Commerce Committee that it was his "belief that air commerce is adversely affected by the denial to a substantial segment of the traveling public of adequate and desegregated public accommodations." We shall not burden this opinion with further details since the voluminous testimony presents overwhelming evidence that discrimination by hotels and motels impedes interstate travel.

7.   The Power of Congress Over Interstate Travel.

[T]he determinative test of the exercise of power by the Congress under the Commerce Clause is simply whether the activity sought to be regulated is "commerce which concerns more States than one" and has a real and substantial relation to the national interest. . . . That the "intercourse" of which the Chief Justice spoke [in *Gibbons v. Ogden*] included the movement of persons through more States than one was settled as early as 1849, in the *Passenger Cases (Smith v. Turner)* . . . . Nor does it make any difference whether the transportation is commercial in character. *Id.* . . .

The same interest in protecting interstate commerce which led Congress to deal with segregation in interstate carriers and the white-slave traffic has prompted it to extend the exercise of its power to gambling, *Lottery Case (Champion v Ames)* (1903); to criminal enterprises; to deceptive practices in the sale of products; to fraudulent security transactions; to misbranding of drugs; to wages and hours, *United States v. Darby* (1941); to members of labor unions, *National Labor Relations Board v. Jones & Laughlin Steel Corp.* (1937); [and] to crop control, *Wickard v. Filburn* (1942). . . . That Congress was legislating against moral wrongs in many of these areas rendered its enactments no less valid.

In framing Title II of this Act Congress was also dealing with what it considered a moral problem. But that fact does not detract from the overwhelming evidence of the disruptive effect that racial discrimination has had on commercial intercourse. It was this burden which empowered Congress to enact appropriate legislation, and, given this basis for the exercise of its power, Congress was not restricted by the fact that the particular obstruction to interstate commerce with which it was dealing was also deemed a moral and social wrong.

It is said that the operation of the motel here is of a purely local character. But, assuming this to be true, "[i]f it is interstate commerce that feels the pinch, it does not matter how local the operation which applies the squeeze." *United States v. Women's Sportswear Mfg. Ass'n* (1949). *See National Labor Relations Board v. Jones & Laughlin Steel Corp*[;] *United States v. Darby*. Thus the power of Congress to promote interstate commerce also includes the power to regulate the local incidents thereof, including local activities in both the States of origin and destination, which might have a substantial and harmful effect upon that commerce. One need only examine the evidence which we have discussed above to see that Congress may—as it has—prohibit racial discrimination by motels serving travelers, however "local" their operations may appear. . . .

We find no merit in the remainder of appellant's contentions, including that of "involuntary servitude." . . . We could not say that the requirements of the Act in this regard are in any way "akin to African slavery." *Butler v. Perry* (1916).

We, therefore, conclude that the action of the Congress in the adoption of the Act as applied here to a motel which concededly serves interstate travelers is within the power granted it by the Commerce Clause of the Constitution, as interpreted by this Court for 140 years. . . . Affirmed.

Katzenbach v. McClung

Supreme Court of the United States, 1964.
379 U.S. 294.

MR. JUSTICE CLARK delivered the opinion of the Court.

This case was argued with *Heart of Atlanta Motel v. United States*, decided this date. . . . This complaint for injunctive relief against appellants attacks the constitutionality of the Act as applied to a restaurant. . . .

2.   The Facts.

Ollie's Barbecue is a family-owned restaurant in Birmingham, Alabama, specializing in barbecued meats and homemade pies, with a seating capacity of

220 customers. It is located on a state highway 11 blocks from an interstate one and a somewhat greater distance from railroad and bus stations. The restaurant caters to a family and white-collar trade with a take-out service for Negroes. It employs 36 persons, two-thirds of whom are Negroes.

In the 12 months preceding the passage of the Act, the restaurant purchased locally approximately $150,000 worth of food, $69,683 or 46% of which was meat that it bought from a local supplier who had procured it from outside the State. The District Court expressly found that a substantial portion of the food served in the restaurant had moved in interstate commerce. The restaurant has refused to serve Negroes in its dining accommodations since its original opening in 1927, and since July 2, 1964, it has been operating in violation of the Act. The court below concluded that if it were required to serve Negroes it would lose a substantial amount of business.

The basic holding in *Heart of Atlanta Motel* answers many of the contentions made by the appellees. . . . In this case we consider its application to restaurants which serve food a substantial portion of which has moved in commerce.

3.   The Act As Applied.

Section 201(a) of Title II commands that all persons shall be entitled to the full and equal enjoyment of the goods and services of any place of public accommodation without discrimination or segregation on the ground of race, color, religion, or national origin. . . . Sections 201(b)(2) and (c) place any "restaurant . . . principally engaged in selling food for consumption on the premises" under the Act "if . . . it serves or offers to serve interstate travelers or a substantial portion of the food which it serves . . . has moved in commerce."

Ollie's Barbecue admits that it is covered by these provisions of the Act. The Government makes no contention that the discrimination at the restaurant was supported by the State of Alabama. There is no claim that interstate travelers frequented the restaurant. The sole question, therefore, narrows down to whether Title II, as applied to a restaurant annually receiving about $70,000 worth of food which has moved in commerce, is a valid exercise of the power of Congress.

4.   The Congressional Hearings. . . .

The record is replete with testimony of the burdens placed on interstate commerce by racial discrimination in restaurants. A comparison of per capita spending by Negroes in restaurants, theaters, and like establishments indicated less spending, after discounting income differences, in areas where discrimination is widely practiced. This condition, which was especially aggravated in the South, was attributed in the testimony of the Under Secretary of Commerce to racial segregation. This diminutive spending springing from a refusal to serve Negroes and their total loss as customers has, regardless of the absence of direct evidence, a close connection to interstate commerce. The fewer customers a restaurant enjoys the less food it sells and consequently the less it buys. In addition, the Attorney General testified that this type of discrimination imposed "an artificial restriction on the market" and interfered with the flow of merchandise. In addition, there were many references to discriminatory situations causing wide unrest and having a depressant effect on general business conditions in the respective communities.

Moreover there was an impressive array of testimony that discrimination in restaurants had a direct and highly restrictive effect upon interstate travel by Negroes. This resulted, it was said, because discriminatory practices prevent Negroes from buying prepared food served on the premises while on a trip, except in isolated and unkempt restaurants and under most unsatisfactory and often unpleasant conditions. This obviously discourages travel and obstructs interstate commerce for one can hardly travel without eating. Likewise, it was said, that discrimination deterred professional, as well as skilled, people from moving into areas where such practices occurred and thereby caused industry to be reluctant to establish there.

We believe that this testimony afforded ample basis for the conclusion that established restaurants in such areas sold less interstate goods because of the discrimination, that interstate travel was obstructed directly by it, that business in general suffered and that many new businesses refrained from establishing there as a result of it. . . .

It goes without saying that, viewed in isolation, the volume of food purchased by Ollie's Barbecue from sources supplied from out of state was insignificant when compared with the total foodstuffs moving in commerce. But, as our late Brother Jackson said for the Court in *Wickard v. Filburn*: "That appellee's own contribution to the demand for wheat may be trivial by itself is not enough to remove him from the scope of federal regulation where, as here, his contribution, taken together with that of many others similarly situated, is far from trivial." . . .

450 DOCTRINE AND PRACTICE SERIES: CONSTITUTIONAL LAW

5.   The Power of Congress to Regulate Local Activities.

Article I, § 8, cl. 3, confers upon Congress the power "[t]o regulate Commerce . . . among the several States" and Clause 18 of the same Article grants it the power "[t]o make all Laws which shall be necessary and proper for carrying into Execution the foregoing Powers . . . ."

Much is said about a restaurant business being local but "even if appellee's activity be local and though it may not be regarded as commerce, it may still, whatever its nature, be reached by Congress if it exerts a substantial economic effect on interstate commerce. . . ." *Wickard v. Filburn.* The activities that are beyond the reach of Congress are "those which are completely [within] a particular State, which do not affect other States, and with which it is not necessary to interfere, for the purpose of executing some of the general powers of the government." *Gibbons v. Ogden.* . . . This rule is as good today as it was when Chief Justice Marshall laid it down almost a century and a half ago. . . .

The appellees contend that Congress has arbitrarily created a conclusive presumption that all restaurants meeting the criteria set out in the Act "affect commerce." Stated another way, they object to the omission of a provision for a case-by-case determination—judicial or administrative—that racial discrimination in a particular restaurant affects commerce.

But Congress' action in framing this Act was not unprecedented. . . . Here, as [in *U.S. v Darby*], Congress has determined for itself that refusals of service to Negroes have imposed burdens both upon the interstate flow of food and upon the movement of products generally. Of course, the mere fact that Congress has said when particular activity shall be deemed to affect commerce does not preclude further examination by this Court. But where we find that the legislators, in light of the facts and testimony before them, have a rational basis for finding a chosen regulatory scheme necessary to the protection of commerce, our investigation is at an end. . . .

Confronted as we are with the facts laid before Congress, we must conclude that it had a rational basis for finding that racial discrimination in restaurants had a direct and adverse effect on the free flow of interstate commerce. Insofar as the sections of the Act here relevant are concerned, Congress prohibited discrimination only in those establishments having a close tie to interstate commerce, i.e., those, like the McClungs', serving food that has come from out of the State. [C]ongress acted well within its power to protect and foster commerce in extending the coverage of Title II only to those restaurants offering to serve interstate travelers or serving food, a substantial portion of which has moved in interstate commerce. . . .

The Civil Rights Act of 1964, as here applied, we find to be plainly appropriate in the resolution of what the Congress found to be a national commercial problem of the first magnitude. . . .

The Court was unanimous in both *Heart of Atlanta* and *Katzenbach*. Three justices wrote separate concurrences that were applicable to both cases.

Mr. Justice Black, concurring.

. . . I recognize that every remote, possible, speculative effect on commerce should not be accepted as an adequate constitutional ground to uproot and throw into the discard all our traditional distinctions between what is purely local, and therefore controlled by state laws, and what affects the national interest and is therefore subject to control by federal laws. I recognize too that some isolated and remote lunchroom which sells only to local people and buys almost all its supplies in the locality may possibly be beyond the reach of the power of Congress to regulate commerce, just as such an establishment is not covered by the present Act.

But in deciding the constitutional power of Congress in cases like the two before us we do not consider the effect on interstate commerce of only one isolated, individual, local event, without regard to the fact that this single local event when added to many others of a similar nature may impose a burden on interstate commerce by reducing its volume or distorting its flow. *Wickard v. Filburn*; *United States v. Darby*. . . . Measuring, as this Court has so often held is required, by the aggregate effect of a great number of such acts of discrimination, I am of the opinion that Congress has constitutional power under the Commerce and Necessary and Proper Clauses to protect interstate commerce from the injuries bound to befall it from these discriminatory practices. . . .

Mr. Justice Douglas, concurring.

Though I join the Court's opinions, I am somewhat reluctant here . . . to rest solely on the Commerce Clause. [T]he "right of persons to move freely from State to State . . . occupies a more protected position in our constitutional system than does the movement of cattle, fruit, steel and coal across state lines." *Edwards v. People of State of California* (1941). . . . Hence I would prefer to rest on the assertion of legislative power contained in [the explicit equality protections] of the Fourteenth Amendment.

A decision based on the Fourteenth Amendment would have a more settling effect, making unnecessary litigation over whether a particular restaurant or inn is within the commerce definitions of the Act or whether a particular customer is an interstate traveler. Under my construction, the Act would apply to all customers in all the enumerated places of public accommodation. And that construction would put an end to all obstructionist strategies and finally close one door on a bitter chapter in American history.

MR. JUSTICE GOLDBERG, concurring.

I join in the opinions and judgments of the Court, since I agree "that the action of the Congress in the adoption of the Act as applied here . . . is within the power granted it by the Commerce Clause of the Constitution, as interpreted by this Court for 140 years." The primary purpose of the Civil Rights Act of 1964, however, as the Court recognizes, and as I would underscore, is the vindication of human dignity and not mere economics. . . .

Between 1936 and 1995, the Supreme Court never held a federal statute (or application of a federal statute) invalid on the ground that it exceeded Congress's power under the Commerce Clause. Occasionally there were dissents.

For example, consider *Daniel v. Paul* (1969), which concerned the application of Title II to the Lake Nixon Club, an amusement place located 12 miles from Little Rock, Ark. As summarized in the syllabus to the case, the Club

> has recreation facilities, including swimming, boating, and dancing, and a snack bar serving four food items, at least three of which contain ingredients coming from outside the State. The Club leases 15 paddle boats on a royalty basis from an Oklahoma company (from which it purchased one boat) and operates a juke box which, along with records it plays, is manufactured outside Arkansas. The Club is advertised in a monthly magazine distributed at Little Rock hotels, motels, and restaurants, in a monthly newspaper published at a nearby Air Force base, and over two area radio stations. Approximately 100,000 whites patronize the establishment each season and

are routinely furnished "membership" cards in the "club," on payment of a 25¢ fee. Negroes are denied admission.

The Supreme Court, per Justice Brennan, held the statute applicable to the Club, in part on the basis that "it would be unrealistic to assume that none of the 100,000 patrons actually served by the Club each season was an interstate traveler," and in part because a "substantial portion of the food" served by the Club—hot dogs and hamburgers on buns, soft drinks, and milk—had moved in interstate commerce. The record was spare on this point, but the district court had taken judicial notice that the principal ingredients in the bread were produced and processed out of state, and that some ingredients of the soft drinks were "probably obtained" from out of state, so the Court concluded that "three of the four food items sold at the snack bar contain ingredients originating outside of the State."

Justice Black dissented in *Daniel v. Paul*, objecting to "guesswork" and "assumptions," while affirming that he would support application of the Act had it been based on § 5 of the Fourteenth Amendment. See also *Perez v. United States* (1971), in which Justice Stewart dissented from a decision upholding the constitutionality of a federal prohibition on loansharking. "In order to sustain this law," he wrote, "we would, in my view, have to be able at the least to say that Congress could rationally have concluded that loansharking is an activity with interstate attributes that distinguish it in some substantial respect from other local crime. But it is not enough to say that loansharking is a national problem, for all crime is a national problem. It is not enough to say that some loansharking has interstate characteristics, for any crime may have an interstate setting. And the circumstance that loansharking has an adverse impact on interstate business is not a distinguishing attribute, for interstate business suffers from almost all criminal activity, be it shoplifting or violence in the streets."

d.   Commerce Clause—the Rehnquist "Revolution"

After years of upholding all commerce legislation against constitutional challenge, the Supreme Court startled many observers in 1995 when it struck down a gun control measure as exceeding the scope of Commerce Clause authority. In reaching this outcome, *United States v. Lopez* became a central element in what has sometimes been called "the Rehnquist Revolution." The term refers to a series of cases across a range of formally unrelated doctrinal categories in which the Supreme Court—with Chief Justice Rehnquist in the majority—either restricted or outright rejected exercises of federal power in

As you read *Lopez* and the decisions that followed it, see whether you agree—with the benefit of hindsight—that it was "revolutionary."

ways that seemed at odds with the much more deferential approach that had dominated federalism review since the New Deal.

United States v. Lopez

Supreme Court of the United States, 1995.
514 U.S. 549.

Chief Justice Rehnquist delivered the opinion of the Court.

In the Gun-Free School Zones Act of 1990, Congress made it a federal offense "for any individual knowingly to possess a firearm at a place that the individual knows, or has reasonable cause to believe, is a school zone." 18 U.S.C. § 922(q)(1)(A). The Act neither regulates a commercial activity nor contains a requirement that the possession be connected in any way to interstate commerce. We hold that the Act exceeds the authority of Congress "[t]o regulate Commerce . . . among the several States. . . ."

On March 10, 1992, respondent, who was then a 12th-grade student, arrived at Edison High School in San Antonio, Texas, carrying a concealed .38-caliber handgun and five bullets. Acting upon an anonymous tip, school authorities confronted respondent, who admitted that he was carrying the weapon. He was arrested and charged under Texas law with firearm possession on school premises. The next day, the state charges were dismissed after federal agents charged respondent by complaint with violating the Gun-Free School Zones Act of 1990.[1]

NLRB v. Jones & Laughlin Steel (1937), *United States v. Darby* (1941), and *Wickard v. Filburn* (1942) ushered in an era of Commerce Clause jurisprudence that greatly expanded the previously defined authority of Congress under that Clause. In part, this was a recognition of the great changes that had occurred in the way business was carried on in this country. Enterprises that had once been

---

[1] The term "school zone" is defined as "in, or on the grounds of, a public, parochial or private school" or "within a distance of 1,000 feet from the grounds of a public, parochial or private school."

local or at most regional in nature had become national in scope. But the doctrinal change also reflected a view that earlier Commerce Clause cases artificially had constrained the authority of Congress to regulate interstate commerce. But even these modern-era precedents which have expanded congressional power under the Commerce Clause confirm that this power is subject to outer limits. *Jones & Laughlin Steel* . . . .

Consistent with this structure, we have identified three broad categories of activity that Congress may regulate under its commerce power.

[1] First, Congress may regulate the use of the channels of interstate commerce. *See, e.g., Darby*; *Heart of Atlanta Motel v. United States* (1964) (" '[T]he authority of Congress to keep the channels of interstate commerce free from immoral and injurious uses has been frequently sustained, and is no longer open to question.' ").

[2] Second, Congress is empowered to regulate and protect the instrumentalities of interstate commerce, or persons or things in interstate commerce, even though the threat may come only from intrastate activities. *See, e.g., Shreveport Rate Cases* (1914); . . . *Perez v. United States* (1971) ("[F]or example, the destruction of an aircraft, or . . . thefts from interstate shipments . . .").

[3] Finally, Congress' commerce authority includes the power to regulate those activities having a substantial relation to interstate commerce, *i.e.*, those activities that substantially affect interstate commerce. . . . [T]he proper test requires an analysis of whether the regulated activity "substantially affects" interstate commerce.

We now turn to consider the power of Congress, in the light of this framework, to enact § 922(q). The first two categories of authority may be quickly disposed of: § 922(q) is not a regulation of the use of the channels of interstate commerce, nor is it an attempt to prohibit the interstate transportation of a commodity through the channels of commerce; nor can § 922(q) be justified as a regulation by which Congress has sought to protect an instrumentality of interstate commerce or a thing in interstate commerce. Thus, if § 922(q) is to be sustained, it must be under the third category as a regulation of an activity that substantially affects interstate commerce.

First, we have upheld a wide variety of congressional Acts regulating intrastate economic activity where we have concluded that the activity substantially affected interstate commerce. Examples include the regulation of intrastate coal mining, *Hodel v. Virginia Surface Mining & Reclamation Assn.* (1981); intrastate extortionate credit transactions, *Perez v. United States*; restaurants utilizing substantial interstate supplies, *Katzenbach v. McClung* (1964); inns and hotels catering to interstate guests, *Heart of Atlanta Motel*; and production and consumption of homegrown wheat, *Wickard v. Filburn*. These examples are by no means exhaustive, but the pattern is clear. Where economic activity substantially affects interstate commerce, legislation regulating that activity will be sustained.

Even *Wickard*, which is perhaps the most far reaching example of Commerce Clause authority over intrastate activity, involved economic activity in a way that the possession of a gun in a school zone does not. . . . [As the Court said in that case,] "Home-grown wheat . . . competes with wheat in commerce."

Section 922(q) is a criminal statute that by its terms has nothing to do with "commerce" or any sort of economic enterprise, however broadly one might define those terms. Section 922(q) is not an essential part of a larger regulation of economic activity, in which the regulatory scheme could be undercut unless the intrastate activity were regulated. It cannot, therefore, be sustained under our cases upholding regulations of activities that arise out of or are connected with a commercial transaction, which viewed in the aggregate, substantially affects interstate commerce. . . .

Second, § 922(q) contains no jurisdictional element which would ensure, through case-by-case inquiry, that the firearm possession in question affects interstate commerce. Unlike the statute in [*United States v.*] *Bass*, [which made it a crime for a felon to receive, possess, or transport a firearm "in commerce or affecting commerce,"] § 922(q) has no express jurisdictional element which might limit its reach to a discrete set of firearm possessions that additionally have an explicit connection with or effect on interstate commerce. . . .

[T]he Government concedes that "[n]either the statute nor its legislative history contain[s] express congressional findings regarding the effects upon interstate commerce of gun possession in a school zone." We agree with the Government that Congress normally is not required to make formal findings as to the substantial burdens that an activity has on interstate commerce. But to the extent that congressional findings would enable us to evaluate the legislative judgment that the activity in question substantially affected interstate commerce, even though no such substantial effect was visible to the naked eye, they are lacking here. . . .

The Government's essential contention, *in fine*, is that we may determine here that § 922(q) is valid because possession of a firearm in a local school zone does indeed substantially affect interstate commerce. The Government argues that possession of a firearm in a school zone may result in violent crime and that violent crime can be expected to affect the functioning of the national economy in two ways. First, the costs of violent crime are substantial, and, through the mechanism of insurance, those costs are spread throughout the population. Second, violent crime reduces the willingness of individuals to travel to areas within the country that are perceived to be unsafe. Cf. *Heart of Atlanta Motel*. The Government also argues that the presence of guns in schools poses a substantial threat to the educational process by threatening the learning environment. A handicapped educational process, in turn, will result in a less productive citizenry. That, in turn, would have an adverse effect on the Nation's economic well-being. As a result, the Government argues that Congress could rationally have concluded that § 922(q) substantially affects interstate commerce.

We pause to consider the implications of the Government's arguments. The Government admits, under its "costs of crime" reasoning, that Congress could regulate not only all violent crime, but all activities that might lead to violent crime, regardless of how tenuously they relate to interstate commerce. Similarly, under the Government's "national productivity" reasoning, Congress could regulate any activity that it found was related to the economic productivity of individual citizens: family law (including marriage, divorce, and child custody), for example. Under the theories that the Government presents in support of § 922(q), it is difficult to perceive any limitation on federal power, even in areas such as criminal law enforcement or education where States historically have been sovereign. Thus, if we were to accept the Government's arguments, we are hard pressed to posit any activity by an individual that Congress is without power to regulate.

[The government's] analysis would be equally applicable, if not more so, to subjects such as family law and direct regulation of education. For instance, if Congress can, pursuant to its Commerce Clause power, regulate activities that adversely affect the learning environment, then, *a fortiori*, it also can regulate the educational process directly. Congress could determine that a school's curriculum has a "significant" effect on the extent of classroom learning. As a result, Congress could mandate a federal curriculum for local elementary and secondary schools because what is taught in local schools has a significant "effect on classroom learning," . . . and that, in turn, has a substantial effect on interstate commerce.

Justice Breyer rejects our reading of precedent and argues that "Congress . . . could rationally conclude that schools fall on the commercial side of the line." Again, Justice Breyer's rationale lacks any real limits because, depending on the level of generality, any activity can be looked upon as commercial. Under the dissent's rationale, Congress could just as easily look at child rearing as "fall[ing] on the commercial side of the line" because it provides a "valuable service—namely, to equip [children] with the skills they need to survive in life and, more specifically, in the workplace." *Ibid.* . . .

Admittedly, a determination whether an intrastate activity is commercial or noncommercial may in some cases result in legal uncertainty. But, so long as Congress' authority is limited to those powers enumerated in the Constitution, and so long as those enumerated powers are interpreted as having judicially enforceable outer limits, congressional legislation under the Commerce Clause always will engender "legal uncertainty." As Chief Justice Marshall stated in *McCulloch v. Maryland* (1819), ". . . the question respecting the extent of the powers actually granted, is perpetually arising, and will probably continue to arise, as long as our system shall exist." . . . Any possible benefit from eliminating this "legal uncertainty" would be at the expense of the Constitution's system of enumerated powers.

In *Jones & Laughlin Steel*, we held that the question of congressional power under the Commerce Clause "is necessarily one of degree." . . . These are not precise formulations, and in the nature of things they cannot be. But we think they point the way to a correct decision of this case. The possession of a gun in a local school zone is in no sense an economic activity that might, through repetition elsewhere, substantially affect any sort of interstate commerce. Respondent was a local student at a local school; there is no indication that he had recently moved in interstate commerce, and there is no requirement that his possession of the firearm have any concrete tie to interstate commerce.

To uphold the Government's contentions here, we would have to pile inference upon inference in a manner that would bid fair to convert congressional authority under the Commerce Clause to a general police power of the sort retained by the States. Admittedly, some of our prior cases have taken long steps down that road, giving great deference to congressional action. The broad language in these opinions has suggested the possibility of additional expansion, but we decline here to proceed any further. To do so would require us to conclude that the Constitution's enumeration of powers does not presuppose something not enumerated, cf. *Gibbons v. Ogden* (1824), and that there never will be a distinction between what is truly national and what is truly local, cf. *Jones & Laughlin Steel*. This we are unwilling to do.

For the foregoing reasons the judgment of the Court of Appeals is

Affirmed.

JUSTICE KENNEDY, with whom JUSTICE O'CONNOR joins, concurring.

The history of the judicial struggle to interpret the Commerce Clause during the transition from the economic system the Founders knew to the single, national market still emergent in our own era counsels great restraint before the Court determines that the Clause is insufficient to support an exercise of the national power. That history gives me some pause about today's decision, but I join the Court's opinion with these observations on what I conceive to be its necessary though limited holding. . . .

The progression of our Commerce Clause cases from *Gibbons* to the present was not marked . . . by a coherent or consistent course of interpretation . . . .

One approach the Court used . . . was to draw content-based or subject-matter distinctions, thus defining by semantic or formalistic categories those activities that were commerce and those that were not. [T]hat approach . . . was not at all propitious . . . . This became evident when the Court began to confront federal economic regulation enacted in response to the rapid industrial development in the late 19th century. Thus, it relied upon the manufacture-commerce dichotomy [to strike down federal regulation in] *United States v. E.C. Knight Co.* (1895). . . . In another line of cases, the Court addressed Congress' efforts to impede local activities it considered undesirable by prohibiting the interstate movement of some essential element. [See, *e.g., Lottery Case* (1903); *Hammer v. Dagenhart* (1918).]

Even while it was experiencing difficulties in finding satisfactory principles in these cases, the Court was pursuing a more sustainable and practical approach in other lines of decisions. . . . The case that seems to mark the Court's definitive commitment to the practical conception of the commerce power is *NLRB v. Jones & Laughlin Steel Corp.*, where the Court sustained labor laws that applied to manufacturing facilities, making no real attempt to distinguish *Carter v. Carter Coal* (1936) [(striking down labor laws that applied to mining facilities)] and *Schechter Poultry v. United States* (1935) [(striking down federal regulation of poultry industry)]. The deference given to Congress has since been confirmed. [*United States v. Darby; Wickard v. Filburn; Heart of Atlanta Motel, Inc. v. United States; Katzenbach v. McClung; Perez v. United States.*] These and like authorities are within the fair ambit of the Court's practical conception of commercial regulation and are not called in question by our decision today.

The history of our Commerce Clause decisions contains at least two lessons of relevance to this case. The first, as stated at the outset, is the imprecision of content-based boundaries used without more to define the limits of the Commerce Clause. The second, related to the first but of even greater consequence, is that the Court as an institution and the legal system as a whole have an immense stake in the stability of our Commerce Clause jurisprudence as it has evolved to this point. *Stare decisis* operates with great force in counseling us not to call in question the essential principles now in place respecting the congressional power to regulate transactions of a commercial nature. That fundamental restraint on our power forecloses us from reverting to an understanding of commerce that would serve only an 18th-century economy . . . . Congress can regulate in the commercial sphere on the assumption that we have a single market and a unified purpose to build a stable national economy. . . .

[F]ederalism was the unique contribution of the Framers to political science and political theory. Though on the surface the idea may seem counterintuitive, it was the insight of the Framers that freedom was enhanced by the creation of two governments, not one.

> In the compound republic of America, the power surrendered by the people is first divided between two distinct governments, and then the portion allotted to each subdivided among distinct and separate departments. Hence a double security arises to the rights of the people. The different governments will control each other, at the same time that each will be controlled by itself.

The Federalist No. 51. See also . . . *New York v. United States* ("[T]he Constitution divides authority between federal and state governments for the protection of individuals. State sovereignty is not just an end in itself.") . . . .

To be sure, one conclusion that could be drawn from The Federalist Papers is that the balance between national and state power is entrusted in its entirety to the political process. . . . Whatever the judicial role, it is axiomatic that Congress does have substantial discretion and control over the federal balance. . . . At the same time, the absence of structural mechanisms to require those officials to undertake this principled task, and the momentary political convenience often attendant upon their failure to do so, argue against a complete renunciation of the judicial role. . . .

The statute before us upsets the federal balance to a degree that renders it an unconstitutional assertion of the commerce power, and our intervention is required. . . . The statute makes the simple possession of a gun within 1,000 feet of the grounds of the school a criminal offense. In a sense any conduct in this interdependent world of ours has an ultimate commercial origin or consequence, but we have not yet said the commerce power may reach so far.

If Congress attempts that extension, then at the least we must inquire whether the exercise of national power seeks to intrude upon an area of traditional state concern. An interference of these dimensions occurs here, for it is well established that education is a traditional concern of the States. *Milliken v. Bradley* (1974). The proximity to schools, including of course schools owned and operated by the States or their subdivisions, is the very premise for making the conduct criminal. In these circumstances, we have a particular duty to ensure that the federal-state balance is not destroyed. . . .

The statute now before us forecloses the States from experimenting and exercising their own judgment in an area to which States lay claim by right of history and expertise, and it does so by regulating an activity beyond the realm of commerce in the ordinary and usual sense of that term. . . .

For these reasons, I join in the opinion and judgment of the Court.

JUSTICE THOMAS, concurring.

. . . Although I join the majority, I write separately to observe that our case law has drifted far from the original understanding of the Commerce Clause. In a future case, we ought to temper our Commerce Clause jurisprudence in a manner that both makes sense of our more recent case law and is more faithful to the original understanding of that Clause.

We have said that Congress may regulate not only "Commerce . . . among the several States," but also anything that has a "substantial effect" on such commerce. This test, if taken to its logical extreme, would give Congress a "police power" over all aspects of American life. Unfortunately, we have never come to grips with this implication of our substantial effects formula. . . . [Justice Thomas goes on to suggest that the Court made a "wrong turn" in its "dramatic departure in the 1930s from a century and a half of precedent," and that it should again draw a sharp line between commerce and local activities such as production.]

JUSTICE STEVENS, dissenting.

. . . Guns are both articles of commerce and articles that can be used to restrain commerce. Their possession is the consequence, either directly or indirectly, of commercial activity. In my judgment, Congress' power to regulate commerce in firearms includes the power to prohibit possession of guns at any location because of their potentially harmful use; it necessarily follows that Congress may also prohibit their possession in particular markets. The market for the possession of handguns by school-age children is, distressingly, substantial. Whether or not the national interest in eliminating that market would have justified federal legislation in 1789, it surely does today.

JUSTICE SOUTER, dissenting.

. . . The modern respect for the competence and primacy of Congress in matters affecting commerce developed only after one of this Court's most chastening experiences, when it perforce repudiated an earlier and untenably expansive conception of judicial review in derogation of congressional commerce power. . . .

There is today, however, a backward glance at both the old pitfalls, as the Court treats deference under the rationality rule as subject to gradation according to the commercial or noncommercial nature of the immediate subject of the challenged regulation. The distinction between what is patently commercial and what is not looks much like the old distinction between what directly affects commerce and what touches it only indirectly. . . . Thus, it seems fair to ask whether the step taken by the Court today does anything but portend a return to the untenable jurisprudence from which the Court extricated itself almost 60 years ago. The answer is not reassuring. . . .

Because Justice Breyer's opinion demonstrates beyond any doubt that the Act in question passes the rationality review that the Court continues to espouse, today's decision may be seen as only a misstep, its reasoning and its suggestions not quite in gear with the prevailing standard, but hardly an epochal case. I would not argue otherwise, but I would raise a caveat. Not every epochal case has come in epochal trappings. *Jones & Laughlin* did not reject the direct-indirect standard in so many words; it just said the relation of the regulated subject matter to commerce was direct enough. But we know what happened.

I respectfully dissent.

JUSTICE BREYER, with whom JUSTICE STEVENS, JUSTICE SOUTER, and JUSTICE GINSBURG join, dissenting.

. . . I apply three basic principles of Commerce Clause interpretation. First, the power to "regulate Commerce . . . among the several States," U.S. Const., Art. I, § 8, cl. 3, encompasses the power to regulate local activities insofar as they significantly affect interstate commerce. See, *e.g., Gibbons v. Ogden*. . . .

Second, in determining whether a local activity will likely have a significant effect upon interstate commerce, a court must consider, not the effect of an individual act (a single instance of gun possession), but rather the cumulative effect of all similar instances (i.e., the effect of all guns possessed in or near schools). See, *e.g., Wickard*. . . .

Third, [c]ourts must give Congress a degree of leeway in determining the existence of a significant factual connection between the regulated activity and interstate commerce—both because the Constitution delegates the commerce power directly to Congress and because the determination requires an empirical judgment of a kind that a legislature is more likely than a court to make with accuracy. The traditional words "rational basis" capture this leeway. Thus, the specific question before us, as the Court recognizes, is not whether the "regulated activity sufficiently affected interstate commerce," but, rather, whether Congress could have had "*a rational basis*" for so concluding. *Ante* (emphasis added). . . .

II

Applying these principles to the case at hand, we must ask whether Congress could have had a *rational basis* for finding a significant (or substantial) connection between gun-related school violence and interstate commerce. Or, to put the question in the language of the *explicit* finding that Congress made when it amended this law in 1994: Could Congress rationally have found that "violent crime in school zones," through its effect on the "quality of education," significantly (or substantially) affects "interstate" or "foreign commerce"? As long as one views the commerce connection, not as a "technical legal conception," but as "a practical one," *Swift & Co. v. United States* (1905), the answer to this question must be yes.

> **WORTH NOTING**
>
> Here, Justice Breyer (a former Senate staffer) conducts an extensive discussion of the evidence, supplemented by a lengthy appendix with references to government studies, social science literature, and other sources.

The economic links [between education and productivity] seem fairly obvious. Why then is it not equally obvious, in light of those links, that a widespread, serious, and substantial physical threat to teaching and learning *also* substantially threatens the commerce to which that teaching and learning is inextricably tied? . . .

To hold this statute constitutional is not to "obliterate" the "distinction between what is national and what is local," nor is it to hold that the Commerce Clause permits the Federal Government to "regulate any activity that it found was related to the economic productivity of individual citizens," to regulate "marriage, divorce, and child custody," or to regulate any and all aspects of education. First, this statute is aimed at curbing a particularly acute threat to the educational process—the possession (and use) of life-threatening firearms in, or near, the classroom. The empirical evidence that I have discussed above unmistakably documents the special way in which guns and education are incompatible. This Court has previously recognized the singularly disruptive potential on interstate commerce that acts of violence may have. See *Perez*. Second, the immediacy of the connection between education and the national economic well-being is documented by scholars and accepted by society at large in a way and to a degree that may not hold true for other social institutions. . . .

In sum, a holding that the particular statute before us falls within the commerce power would not expand the scope of that Clause. Rather, it simply would apply preexisting law to changing economic circumstances. It would recognize that, in today's economic world, gun-related violence near the classroom makes a significant difference to our economic, as well as our social, well-being. . . .

III

The majority's holding [is grounded in] . . . its apparent belief that it can reconcile its holding with earlier cases by making a critical distinction between "commercial" and noncommercial "transaction[s]." That is to say, the Court believes the Constitution would distinguish between two local activities, each of which has an identical effect upon interstate commerce, if one, but not the other, is "commercial" in nature.

As a general matter, this approach fails to heed this Court's earlier warning not to turn "questions of the power of Congress" upon "formula[s]" that would give "controlling force to nomenclature such as 'production' and 'indirect' and foreclose consideration of the actual effects of the activity in question upon interstate commerce." *Wickard*. . . . In fact, the *Wickard* Court expressly held that Filburn's consumption of home-grown wheat, "*though it may not be regarded as commerce*," could nevertheless be regulated—"*whatever its nature*"—so long as "it exerts a substantial economic effect on interstate commerce." *Wickard* (emphasis added) . . . .

The majority clearly cannot intend such a distinction to focus narrowly on an act of gun possession standing by itself, for such a reading could not be reconciled with either the civil rights cases (*McClung* and *Daniel v. Paul* (1969)) or *Perez*—in each of those cases the specific transaction (the race-based exclusion, the use of force) was not itself "commercial." And, if the majority instead means to distinguish generally among broad categories of activities, differentiating what is educational from what is commercial, then, as a practical matter, the line becomes almost impossible to draw. Schools that teach reading, writing, mathematics, and related basic skills serve *both* social and commercial purposes, and one cannot easily separate the one from the other. American industry itself has been, and is again, involved in teaching. When, and to what extent, does its involvement make education commercial? Does the number of vocational classes that train students directly for jobs make a difference? Does it matter if the school is public or private, nonprofit or profit seeking? Does it matter if a city or State adopts a voucher plan that pays private firms to run a school? Even if one were to ignore these practical questions, why should there be a theoretical distinction between education, when it significantly benefits commerce, and environmental pollution, when it causes economic harm?

Regardless, if there is a principled distinction that could work both here and in future cases, Congress (even in the absence of vocational classes, industry involvement, and private management) could rationally conclude that schools fall on the commercial side of the line. In 1990, the year Congress enacted the statute before us, primary and secondary schools spent $230 billion—that is, nearly a quarter of a trillion dollars—which accounts for a significant portion of our $5.5 trillion gross domestic product for that year. The business of schooling

requires expenditure of these funds on student transportation, food and custodial services, books, and teachers' salaries. These expenditures enable schools to
provide a valuable service—namely, to equip students with the skills they need
to survive in life and, more specifically, in the workplace. Certainly, Congress
has often analyzed school expenditure as if it were a commercial investment,
closely analyzing whether schools are efficient, whether they justify the significant resources they spend, and whether they can be restructured to achieve
greater returns. . . . Why could Congress, for Commerce Clause purposes, not
consider schools as roughly analogous to commercial investments from which
the Nation derives the benefit of an educated work force?

IV

. . . Upholding this legislation would do no more than simply recognize
that Congress had a "rational basis" for finding a significant connection between
guns in or near schools and (through their effect on education) the interstate
and foreign commerce they threaten. For these reasons, I would reverse the
judgment of the Court of Appeals. Respectfully, I dissent.

In response to *Lopez*, Congress revised the Gun Free School Zones Act
to include a jurisdictional element. The revised statute reads as follows, with
its new language emphasized:

> It shall be unlawful for any individual knowingly to possess a firearm
> *that has moved in or that otherwise affects interstate or foreign commerce*
> at a place that the individual knows, or has reasonable cause to be-
> lieve, is a school zone.

The Circuit Courts reviewing the revised Act have uniformly upheld it. See,
e.g., United States v. Dorsey, 418 F.3d 1038 (9th Cir. 2005) (holding without
much discussion that the amended version "resolves the shortcomings that the
Lopez Court found in the prior version of this statute because it incorporates a
'jurisdictional element which would ensure, through case-by-case inquiry, that
the firearm possession in question affects interstate commerce.' ").

FOR DISCUSSION

Do you believe the addition of the jurisdictional element significantly limited the reach of the statute? If a firearm has not actually moved in interstate commerce (most do), what standard should a court use in determining whether it has affected such commerce?

Any thoughts that *Lopez* was a fluke were dispelled by the Supreme Court's decision in *United States v. Morrison* (2000). The case involved a provision of the Violence Against Women Act of 1994 that gave a private right of action to victims of crimes of violence motivated by gender. Plaintiff Christy Brzonkala sued under this provision, claiming that she had been sexually assaulted by Morrison and another member of the Virginia Tech football team; the United States intervened on her behalf. Chief Justice Rehnquist again wrote an opinion for a 5–4 majority, invalidating the relevant portion of

CROSS REFERENCE Excerpts dealing with Congress's power under § 5 of the Fourteenth Amendment are presented at pp. 630–633.

the statute and holding that Congress may not "regulate noneconomic, violent criminal conduct based solely on that conduct's aggregate effect on interstate commerce." He emphasized that "[t]he regulation and punishment of intrastate violence that is not directed at the instrumentalities, channels, or goods involved in interstate commerce has always been the province of the States," and that "every attenuated effect upon interstate commerce" could not support the exercise of federal power.

Gonzales v. Raich

Supreme Court of the United States, 2005.
545 U.S. 1.

JUSTICE STEVENS delivered the opinion of the Court.

SUMMARY OF THE FACTS

California's Compassionate Use Act of 1996 repealed state-law prohibitions against the medical use of marijuana, but the federal Controlled Substances Act ("CSA"), which contains a general prohibition on marijuana possession, does not make any provision for such use. Respondents Angel Raich and Diane Monson were California residents who suffered from a variety of medical conditions and whose physicians concluded that marijuana was the only drug available that would provide effective treatment. Raich relied on caregivers who provided her with locally grown marijuana at no charge; Monson cultivated her own.

I

. . . On August 15, 2002, county deputy sheriffs and agents from the federal Drug Enforcement Administration (DEA) came to Monson's home. After a thorough investigation, the county officials concluded that her use of marijuana was entirely lawful as a matter of California law. Nevertheless, after a 3-hour standoff, the federal agents seized and destroyed all six of her cannabis plants. Respondents thereafter brought this action against the Attorney General of the United States and the head of the DEA seeking injunctive and declaratory relief prohibiting the enforcement of the federal Controlled Substances Act (CSA) to the extent it prevents them from possessing, obtaining, or manufacturing cannabis for their personal medical use. . . .

The case is made difficult by respondents' strong arguments that they will suffer irreparable harm because, despite a congressional finding to the contrary, marijuana does have valid therapeutic purposes. The question before us, however, is not whether it is wise to enforce the statute in these circumstances; rather, it is whether Congress' power to regulate interstate markets for medicinal substances encompasses the portions of those markets that are supplied with drugs produced and consumed locally. Well-settled law controls our answer. The CSA is a valid exercise of federal power, even as applied to the troubling facts of this case. We accordingly vacate the judgment of the Court of Appeals. . . .

II

The Comprehensive Drug Abuse Prevention and Control Act of 1970 . . . categorizes all controlled substances into five schedules. The drugs are grouped together based on their accepted medical uses, the potential for abuse, and their psychological and physical effects on the body. Each schedule is associated with a distinct set of controls regarding the manufacture, distribution, and use of the substances listed therein. . . . By classifying marijuana as a Schedule I drug, as opposed to listing it on a lesser schedule, the manufacture, distribution, or possession of marijuana became a criminal offense, with the sole exception being use of the drug as part of a Food and Drug Administration preapproved research study. . . .

III

[The modern cases] have identified three general categories of regulation in which Congress is authorized to engage under its commerce power. First, Congress can regulate the channels of interstate commerce. Second, Congress has authority to regulate and protect the instrumentalities of interstate commerce, and persons or things in interstate commerce. Third, Congress has the power to regulate activities that substantially affect interstate commerce. Only the third category is implicated in the case at hand.

Our decision in *Wickard v. Filburn* (1942) is of particular relevance. . . . The similarities between this case and *Wickard* are striking. Like the farmer in *Wickard*, respondents are cultivating, for home consumption, a fungible commodity for which there is an established, albeit illegal, interstate market. Just as the Agricultural Adjustment Act was designed "to control the volume [of wheat] moving in interstate and foreign commerce in order to avoid surpluses . . ." and consequently control the market price, a primary purpose of the CSA is to control the supply and demand of controlled substances in both lawful and unlawful drug markets. In *Wickard*, we had no difficulty concluding that Congress had a rational basis for believing that, when viewed in the aggregate, leaving home-consumed wheat outside the regulatory scheme would have a substantial influence on price and market conditions. Here too, Congress had a rational basis for concluding that leaving home-consumed marijuana outside federal control would similarly affect price and market conditions. . . .

More concretely, one concern prompting inclusion of wheat grown for home consumption in the 1938 Act was that rising market prices could draw such wheat into the interstate market, resulting in lower market prices. *Wickard*. The parallel concern making it appropriate to include marijuana grown for home consumption in the CSA is the likelihood that the high demand in the interstate market will draw such marijuana into that market. While the diversion of homegrown wheat tended to frustrate the federal interest in stabilizing prices by regulating the volume of commercial transactions in the interstate market, the diversion of homegrown marijuana tends to frustrate the federal interest in eliminating commercial transactions in the interstate market in their entirety. In both cases, the regulation is squarely within Congress' commerce power because production of the commodity meant for home consumption, be it wheat or marijuana, has a substantial effect on supply and demand in the national market for that commodity.

To be sure, the wheat market is a lawful market that Congress sought to protect and stabilize, whereas the marijuana market is an unlawful market that Congress sought to eradicate. This difference, however, is of no constitutional import. It has long been settled that Congress' power to regulate commerce includes the power to prohibit commerce in a particular commodity. *United States v. Lopez* (1995); *Wickard*.

Nonetheless, respondents suggest that *Wickard* differs from this case in [that] *Wickard* involved a "quintessential economic activity"—a commercial farm—whereas respondents do not sell marijuana. . . . [E]ven though Filburn was indeed a commercial farmer, [however,] the activity he was engaged in— the cultivation of wheat for home consumption—was not treated by the Court as part of his commercial farming operation. . . .[30]

Given the enforcement difficulties that attend distinguishing between marijuana cultivated locally and marijuana grown elsewhere, and concerns about diversion into illicit channels, we have no difficulty concluding that Congress had a rational basis for believing that failure to regulate the intrastate manufacture and possession of marijuana would leave a gaping hole in the CSA. Thus, as in *Wickard*, [t]hat the regulation ensnares some purely intrastate activity is of no moment. As we have done many times before, we refuse to excise individual components of that larger scheme.

IV

To support their contrary submission, respondents rely heavily on two of our more recent Commerce Clause cases. . . . Those two cases, of course, are *United States v. Lopez* (1996) and *United States v. Morrison* (2000). . . .

At issue in *Lopez*, was the validity of the Gun-Free School Zones Act of 1990, which was a brief, single-subject statute making it a crime for an individual to possess a gun in a school zone. . . .

The statutory scheme that the Government is defending in this litigation is at the opposite end of the regulatory spectrum. As explained above, the CSA . . . was a lengthy and detailed statute creating a comprehensive framework for regulating . . . five classes of "controlled substances." [The CSA] identified 42

---

[30] See *Wickard* (recognizing that Filburn's activity "may not be regarded as commerce").

opiates, 22 opium derivatives, and 17 hallucinogenic substances as Schedule I drugs. Marijuana was listed as the 10th item in the 3d subcategory. That classification, unlike the discrete prohibition established by the Gun-Free School Zones Act of 1990, was merely one of many "essential part[s] of a larger regulation of economic activity, in which the regulatory scheme could be undercut unless the intrastate activity were regulated." *Lopez*. Our opinion in Lopez casts no doubt on the validity of such a program.

Nor does this Court's holding in *United States v. Morrison* [require a different outcome]. The Violence Against Women Act of 1994 created a federal civil remedy for the victims of gender-motivated crimes of violence. . . . Despite congressional findings that such crimes had an adverse impact on interstate commerce, we held the statute unconstitutional because, like the statute in Lopez, it did not regulate economic activity. We concluded: " 'Where economic activity substantially affects interstate commerce, legislation regulating that activity will be sustained.' " . . .

Unlike those at issue in *Lopez* and *Morrison*, the activities regulated by the CSA are quintessentially economic. "Economics" refers to "the production, distribution, and consumption of commodities." *Webster's Third New International Dictionary* (1966). The CSA is a statute that regulates the production, distribution, and consumption of commodities for which there is an established, and lucrative, interstate market. Prohibiting the intrastate possession or manufacture of an article of commerce is a rational (and commonly utilized) means of regulating commerce in that product. Such prohibitions include specific decisions requiring that a drug be withdrawn from the market as a result of the failure to comply with regulatory requirements as well as decisions excluding Schedule I drugs entirely from the market. Because the CSA is a statute that directly regulates economic, commercial activity, our opinion in *Morrison* casts no doubt on its constitutionality. . . .

The case is remanded for further proceedings consistent with this opinion. . . .

JUSTICE SCALIA, concurring in the judgment.

. . . Since *Perez v. United States* (1971), our cases have mechanically recited that the Commerce Clause permits congressional regulation of three categories: (1) the channels of interstate commerce; (2) the instrumentalities of interstate commerce, and persons or things in interstate commerce; and (3) activities that "substantially affect" interstate commerce. . . . The first two categories are self-evident, since they are the ingredients of interstate commerce itself. See *Gibbons v. Ogden* (1824). The third category, however, is different in kind, and its recitation without explanation is misleading and incomplete.

It is *misleading* because, unlike the channels, instrumentalities, and agents of interstate commerce, activities that substantially affect interstate commerce are not themselves part of interstate commerce, and thus the power to regulate them cannot come from the Commerce Clause alone. Rather, . . . Congress's regulatory authority over intrastate activities that are not themselves part of interstate commerce (including activities that have a substantial effect on interstate commerce) derives from the Necessary and Proper Clause. And the category of "activities that substantially affect interstate commerce," *Lopez*, is *incomplete* because the authority to enact laws necessary and proper for the regulation of interstate commerce is not limited to laws governing intrastate activities that substantially affect interstate commerce. Where necessary to make a regulation of interstate commerce effective, Congress may regulate even those intrastate activities that do not themselves substantially affect interstate commerce. . . .

Though the conduct in *Lopez* was not economic, the Court nevertheless recognized that it could be regulated as "an essential part of a larger regulation of economic activity, in which the regulatory scheme could be undercut unless the intrastate activity were regulated." This statement referred to those cases permitting the regulation of intrastate activities "which in a substantial way interfere with or obstruct the exercise of the granted power." . . . The relevant question is simply whether the means chosen are "reasonably adapted" to the attainment of a legitimate end under the commerce power. See *United States v. Darby* (1941).

. . . To dismiss this distinction as "superficial and formalistic," see *post* (O'Connor, J., dissenting), is to misunderstand the nature of the Necessary and Proper Clause, which empowers Congress to enact laws in effectuation of its enumerated powers that are not within its authority to enact in isolation. See *McCulloch v. Maryland* (1819). . . .

The application of these principles to the case before us is straightforward. In the CSA, Congress has undertaken to extinguish the interstate market in Schedule I controlled substances, including marijuana. The Commerce Clause unquestionably permits this. The power to regulate interstate commerce "extends not only to those regulations which aid, foster and protect the commerce, but embraces those which prohibit it." *Darby*; *Lottery Case* (1903). To effectuate its objective, Congress has prohibited almost all intrastate activities related to Schedule I substances—both economic activities (manufacture, distribution, possession with the intent to distribute) and noneconomic activities (simple possession). That simple possession is a noneconomic activity is immaterial to whether it can be prohibited as a necessary part of a larger regulation. Rather, Congress's authority to enact all of these prohibitions of intrastate controlled-substance activities depends only upon whether they are appropriate means of achieving the legitimate end of eradicating Schedule I substances from interstate commerce. . . .

Drugs like marijuana are fungible commodities. As the Court explains, marijuana that is grown at home and possessed for personal use is never more than an instant from the interstate market—and this is so whether or not the possession is for medicinal use or lawful use under the laws of a particular State. Congress need not accept on faith that state law will be effective in maintaining a strict division between a lawful market for "medical" marijuana and the more general marijuana market. . . .

I thus agree with the Court that, however the class of regulated activities is subdivided, Congress could reasonably conclude that its objective of prohibiting marijuana from the interstate market "could be undercut" if those activities were excepted from its general scheme of regulation. That is sufficient to authorize the application of the CSA to respondents.

JUSTICE O'CONNOR, with whom THE CHIEF JUSTICE and JUSTICE THOMAS join as to all but Part III, dissenting.

One of federalism's chief virtues . . . is that it promotes innovation by allowing for the possibility that "a single courageous State may, if its citizens choose, serve as a laboratory; and try novel social and economic experiments without risk to the rest of the country." *New State Ice Co. v. Liebmann* (1932) (Brandeis, J., dissenting). This case exemplifies the role of States as laboratories. . . .

The Court's definition of economic activity is breathtaking. It defines as economic any activity involving the production, distribution, and consumption of commodities. . . . Putting to one side the problem endemic to the Court's opinion—the shift in focus from the activity at issue in this case to the entirety of what the CSA regulates, see *Lopez* ("depending on the level of generality, any activity can be looked upon as commercial")—the Court's definition of economic activity for purposes of Commerce Clause jurisprudence threatens to sweep all of productive human activity into federal regulatory reach.

The Court uses a dictionary definition of economics to skirt the real problem of drawing a meaningful line between "what is national and what is local," *Jones & Laughlin Steel*. It will not do to say that Congress may regulate noncommercial activity simply because it may have an effect on the demand for commercial goods, or because the noncommercial endeavor can, in some sense, substitute for commercial activity. Most commercial goods or services have some sort of privately producible analogue. Home care substitutes for daycare. Charades games substitute for movie tickets. Backyard or windowsill gardening substitutes for going to the supermarket. To draw the line wherever private activity affects the demand for market goods is to draw no line at all, and to declare everything economic. We have already rejected the result that would follow—a federal police power . . . .

Justice Thomas, dissenting.

Respondents Diane Monson and Angel Raich use marijuana that has never been bought or sold, that has never crossed state lines, and that has had no demonstrable effect on the national market for marijuana. If Congress can regulate this under the Commerce Clause, then it can regulate virtually anything—and the Federal Government is no longer one of limited and enumerated powers. . . .

Even the majority does not argue that respondents' conduct is itself "Commerce, among the several States." . . . More difficult, however, is whether the CSA is a valid exercise of Congress' power to enact laws that are "necessary and proper for carrying into Execution" its power to regulate interstate commerce. . . . Even assuming the CSA's ban on locally cultivated and consumed marijuana is "necessary," that does not mean it is also "proper." The means selected by Congress to regulate interstate commerce cannot be "prohibited" by, or inconsistent with the "letter and spirit" of, the Constitution. *McCulloch*. . . .

. . . If the Federal Government can regulate growing a half-dozen cannabis plants for personal consumption (not because it is interstate commerce, but because it is inextricably bound up with interstate commerce), then Congress' Article I powers—as expanded by the Necessary and Proper Clause—have no meaningful limits. . . .

I respectfully dissent.

For Discussion

After *Raich*, may Congress rely on the Commerce Clause to adopt the following regulations?

(1) The No More Con Law Casebooks Act

    (a) The interstate transportation of Con Law casebooks is prohibited.

    (b) The production of new Con Law casebooks is prohibited.

(2) The Social Club Desegregation Act

    No non-profit social club that uses supplies produced in another state may discriminate on the basis of race.

(3) The Equal Access to Travel Facilities Act

    No restaurant that serves people who are traveling between states may discriminate on the basis of race.

(4) The Garment Industry Support Act

    Knitting sweaters is prohibited outside of garment factories that have obtained a license from the federal government.

4. The Taxing Power

Like all governments, the United States needs money to fund its operations. To that end, the first sentence of Article I, § 8, provides:

> The Congress shall have Power To lay and collect Taxes, Duties, Imposts and Excises, to pay the Debts and provide for the common Defence and general Welfare of the United States; but all Duties, Imposts and Excises shall be uniform throughout the United States.

The tax provision obviously empowers the federal government to collect revenue. But might it also create a regulatory tool that the Government can use to affect behavior in the real world? And if so, how can we tell whether a given measure is really a tax, or simply a prohibition enforced by a financial penalty rather than jail? In *McCulloch*, John Marshall had declared that "the power to tax involves the power to destroy." There, he was concerned that a state, though forbidden to regulate a federal instrumentality, might try to achieve much the same end by taxing it instead. The same concern has frequently run in reverse—might Congress try to achieve through taxation what it could not do by regulation?

Luther Martin, a delegate to the Constitutional Convention who opposed ratification, certainly worried that the distinction between regulatory acts and revenue acts was easy to manipulate:

> [E]very regulation of commerce—every law relative to excises—stamps—the post-office—the imposition of taxes, and their collection—the creation of courts and offices;—in fine, every law for the union, if enforced by any pecuniary sanctions, as they would tend to bring money into the continental treasury, might and probably would be considered a revenue act. . . .

Martin wasn't talking about the Tax Clause in this passage. Rather, he was focused on Article I's requirement that "All Bills for raising Revenue shall originate in the House of Representatives." He worried that, by expedients like those described above, the House would abuse its origination authority to label *everything* a revenue bill and thereby render the Senate "almost useless," fit merely "to wait the proceedings of the house of representatives, and afterwards examine and approve, or propose amendments."

FOR DISCUSSION

Martin suggests that it would be easy to label anything a "revenue act." Is he right? How exactly does he think a "regulation of commerce" could be structured in the way he fears? Try drafting a two or three line "revenue act" that would use the taxing power as a way of forcing all employers to pay a minimum wage.

The materials that follow explore the risk that Martin only gestured at. The first two decisions arise from the period right after World War I, when the Supreme Court was still imposing significant limits on Congress's power to regulate local matters under the Commerce Clause. That gave Congress an incentive to achieve through the tax power what it could not do through the commerce power. This in turn created a dilemma for courts charged with reviewing these workarounds. Note how the Court came out on opposite sides of that dilemma in these two cases.

United States v. Doremus

Supreme Court of the United States, 1919.
249 U.S. 86.

Mr. Justice Day delivered the opinion of the Court.

Doremus was indicted for violating § 2 of the so-called Harrison Narcotic Drug Act. . . .

Section 1 of the act requires persons who [distribute opium and other specified drugs] to register with the collector of internal revenue of the district. . . . At the time of such registry every person who [distributes any of the covered drugs] is required to pay to the collector a special tax of $1 per annum. It is made unlawful for any person required to register under the terms of the act to [distribute] any of the said drugs without having registered and paid the special tax provided in the act.

Section 2 provides in part:

It shall be unlawful for any person to [distribute] any of the aforesaid drugs except in pursuance of a written order . . . , on a form to be issued in blank for that purpose by the Commissioner of Internal Revenue. [The records shall be preserved for two years] in such a way as to be readily accessible to inspection by . . . the Treasury Department . . . , and [by] the state, territorial, district, municipal, and insular officials named in section five of this act. . . .

Nothing contained in this section shall apply . . . to the dispensing or distribution of any of the aforesaid drugs to a patient by a physician . . . regularly registered under this act in the course of his professional practice only: Provided, that such physician, dentist, or veterinary surgeon shall keep a record of all such drugs dispensed or distributed, showing the amount dispensed or distributed, the date and the name and address of the patient to whom such drugs are dispensed or distributed. . . .

WORTH NOTING

Under § 5, officials entitled to inspect the records compiled pursuant to § 2 included "such officials of any State or Territory, or of any organized municipality therein . . . as shall be charged with the enforcement of any law or municipal ordinance regulating the sale, prescribing, dispensing, dealing in, or distribution of the . . . drugs" covered by the Harrison Act.

SUMMARY OF THE FACTS

Doremus was a physician who had registered with the IRS as an opium distributor and paid the $1 tax as required by the act. The indictment charged Doremus with giving a patient 500 tablets of heroin—an opium derivative—without filling out the blank IRS form required by § 2 of the Harrison Act. The indictment further specified—apparently in order to rule out § 2's exception for prescriptions issued "in the course of [a physician's] professional practice"—that the patient was a known "dope fiend." Doremus was therefore alleged to have given his patient the pills "not for the treatment of any disease from which [the patient] was suffering," but "for the purpose of gratifying his appetite for the drug as an habitual user thereof."

In striking down the statute below, the District Court stated:

> The national act provides for an annual tax of one dollar for each registered "dealer," and then so restricts and narrows the uses of the drug that no vital or important excess of revenue could reasonably be expected. The tax is nominal, yet the penalty for violating any provision of the act is so disproportionate to the gravamen of the offense as to be further convincing that Congress was more concerned with the moral ends to be subserved than with the revenue to be derived. . . .

WORTH NOTING

In a companion case issued the same day, the Supreme Court held, under a related provision of the Act, that it did not qualify as a " 'prescription' " for "a practicing and registered physician [to] issue[ ] an order for morphine to an habitual user thereof, the order not being issued by him in the course of professional treatment in the attempted cure of the habit, but being issued for the purpose of providing the user with morphine sufficient to keep him comfortable by maintaining his customary use . . . ." *Webb v. U.S.* (1919).

The only limitation upon the power of Congress to levy excise taxes of the character now under consideration is geographical uniformity throughout the United States. This court has often declared it cannot add others. Subject to such limitation Congress may select the subjects of taxation, and may exercise the power conferred at its discretion. Of course Congress may not in the exercise of federal power exert authority wholly reserved to the states. Many decisions of this court have so declared. And [yet] from an early day the court has held that the fact that other motives may impel the exercise of federal taxing power does not authorize the courts to inquire into that subject. If the legislation enacted has some reasonable relation to the exercise of the taxing authority conferred by the Constitution, it cannot be invalidated because of the supposed motives which induced it. . . .

The act may not be declared unconstitutional because its effect may be to accomplish another purpose as well as the raising of revenue. If the legislation is within the taxing authority of Congress—that is sufficient to sustain it. . . . Considering the full power of Congress over excise taxation the decisive question here is: Have the provisions in question any relation to the raising of revenue?

That Congress might levy an excise tax upon such dealers, and others who are named in § 1 of the act, cannot be successfully disputed. The provisions of § 2, to which we have referred, aim to confine sales to registered dealers and to those dispensing the drugs as physicians, and to those who come to dealers with legitimate prescriptions of physicians. Congress, with full power over the subject, short of arbitrary and unreasonable action which is not to be assumed, inserted these provisions in an act specifically providing for the raising of revenue. Considered of themselves, we think they tend to keep the traffic aboveboard and subject to inspection by those authorized to collect the revenue. They tend to diminish the opportunity of unauthorized persons to obtain the drugs and sell them clandestinely without paying the tax imposed by the federal law.

This case well illustrates the possibility which may have induced Congress to insert the provisions limiting sales to registered dealers and requiring patients to obtain these drugs as a medicine from physicians or upon regular prescriptions. [Doremus's patient], being as the indictment charges, an addict may not have used this great number of doses for himself. He might sell some to others without paying the tax, at least Congress may have deemed it wise to prevent such possible dealings because of their effect upon the collection of the revenue.

We cannot agree with the contention that the provisions of § 2, controlling the disposition of these drugs in the ways described, can have nothing to do with facilitating the collection of the revenue, as we should be obliged to do if we were to declare this act beyond the power of Congress acting under its constitutional authority to impose excise taxes. It follows that the judgment of the District Court must be reversed.

Reversed.

THE CHIEF JUSTICE dissents because he is of opinion that the court below correctly held the act of Congress, in so far as it embraced the matters complained of, to be beyond the constitutional power of Congress to enact because to such extent the statute was a mere attempt by Congress to exert a power not delegated, that is, the reserved police power of the states. MR. JUSTICE McKENNA, and MR. JUSTICE VAN DEVANTER and MR. JUSTICE McREYNOLDS concur in this dissent.

Child labor was one of the great social issues of the early 20th century. Congress was motivated to impose what it regarded as suitable labor conditions, but under the doctrine of cases like *United States v. E.C. Knight* (1895), it had no power to regulate production under the Commerce Clause. Congress therefore enacted a statute banning interstate shipment of goods produced in establishments that employed child labor under specified conditions. The Supreme Court invalidated that statute by a 5–4 vote in *Hammer v. Dagenhart* (1918), which is presented in more detail at pp. 407–413. The next year, Congress responded by enacting a rather transparent end run: the Child Labor Tax Law. The new statute imposed a tax of 10% of yearly profits on any establishment permitting the same substandard conditions specified in the statute just struck down by *Dagenhart*.

Bailey v. Drexel Furniture Co. ("Child Labor Tax Case")

Supreme Court of the United States, 1922.
259 U.S. 20.

MR. CHIEF JUSTICE TAFT delivered the opinion of the Court.

This case presents the question of the constitutional validity of the Child Labor Tax Law. The plaintiff below, the Drexel Furniture Company, is engaged in the manufacture of furniture in the Western district of North Carolina. On September 20, 1921, it received a notice from Bailey, United States Collector of Internal Revenue for the District, that it had been assessed $6,312.79 for having during the taxable year 1919 employed and permitted to work in its factory a boy under 14 years of age, thus incurring the tax of 10 per cent. on its net profits for that year. The company paid the tax under protest, and, after rejection of its claim for a refund, brought this suit. . . .

The Child Labor Tax Law . . . , approved February 24, 1919, [provides] as follows:

> That every person . . . operating . . . any mill, cannery, workshop, factory, or manufacturing establishment situated in the United States in which [either]
>
>> children [known to be] under the age of fourteen years have been employed or permitted to work, or
>>
>> children [known to be] between the ages of fourteen and sixteen have been employed or permitted to work more than eight hours in any day or more than six days in any week, or [outside the hours of 6am–7pm]
>
> shall pay for each taxable year, in addition to all other taxes imposed by law, an excise tax equivalent to 10 per centum of the entire net profits received or accrued for such year from the sale or disposition of the product of such mine, quarry, mill, cannery, workship, factory, or manufacturing establishment.

. . . The law is attacked on the ground that it is a regulation of the employment of child labor in the States—an exclusively state function under the federal Constitution and within the reservations of the Tenth Amendment. It

Say it is not a just a tax

is defended on the ground that it is a mere excise tax levied by the Congress of the United States under its broad power of taxation conferred by § 8, Article 1, of the federal Constitution. We must construe the law and interpret the intent, and meaning of Congress from the language of the act. . . .

Does this law impose a tax with only that incidental restraint and regulation which a tax must inevitably involve? Or does it regulate by the use of the so-called tax as a penalty? If a tax, it is clearly an excise. If it were an excise on a commodity or other thing of value, we might not be permitted under previous decisions of this court to infer solely from its heavy burden that the act intends a prohibition instead of a tax.

This does more than tax a commodity

But this act is more. It provides a heavy exaction for a departure from a detailed and specified course of conduct in business. . . . If an employer departs from this prescribed course of business, he is to pay to the Government one-tenth of his entire net income in the business for a full year. The amount is not to be proportioned in any degree to the extent or frequency of the departures, but is to be paid by the employer in full measure whether he employs 500 children for a year, or employs only one for a day. Moreover, if he does not know the child is within the named age limit, he is not to pay; that is to say, it is only where he knowingly departs from the prescribed course that payment is to be exacted. Scienter is associated with penalties, not with taxes. The employer's factory is to be subject to inspection at any time not only by the taxing officers of the Treasury, the Department normally charged with the collection of taxes, but also by the Secretary of Labor and his subordinates, whose normal function is the advancement and protection of the welfare of the workers.

In the light of these features of the act, a court must be blind not to see that the so-called tax is imposed to stop the employment of children within the age limits prescribed. Its prohibitory and regulatory effect and purpose are palpable. All others can see and understand this. How can we properly shut our minds to it? . . . Out of a proper respect for the acts of a co-ordinate branch of the Government, this court has gone far to sustain taxing acts as such, even though there has been ground for suspecting, from the weight of the tax, it was intended to destroy its subject. But in the act before us the presumption of validity cannot prevail, because the proof of the contrary is found on the very face of its provisions.

Grant the validity of this law, and all that Congress would need to do, hereafter, in seeking to take over to its control any one of the great number of

Regulation than tax from (1) big tax from a departure from a specific prescription of business (2) not proportional by degree (3) greater regulatory = "penalty" b/c blame (4) secretary of labor inspects (5) All of this purpose. of the act is to regulate, not tax.

subjects of public interest, jurisdiction of which the states have never parted
with, and which are reserved to them by the Tenth Amendment, would be to
enact a detailed measure of complete regulation of the subject and enforce it by
a so called tax upon departures from it. To give such magic to the word "tax"
would be to break down all constitutional limitation of the powers of Congress
and completely wipe out the sovereignty of the States.

[handwritten margin note: is it down to major + incidental purpose?]

The difference between a tax and a penalty is sometimes difficult to define,
and yet the consequences of the distinction in the required method of their collection often are important. Where the sovereign enacting the law has power
to impose both tax and penalty, the difference between revenue production and
mere regulation may be immaterial, but not so when one sovereign can impose
a tax only, and the power of regulation rests in another.

[handwritten margin note: Dif between tax + penalty:]

Taxes are occasionally imposed in the discretion of the Legislature on
proper subjects with the primary motive of obtaining revenue from them and
with the incidental motive of discouraging them by making their continuance
onerous. They do not lose their character as taxes because of the incidental
motive. But there comes a time in the extension of the penalizing features of
the so-called tax when it loses its character as such and becomes a mere penalty, with the characteristics of regulation and punishment. Such is the case
in the law before us. Although Congress does not invalidate the contract of
employment or expressly declare that the employment within the mentioned
ages is illegal, it does exhibit its intent practically to achieve the latter result by
adopting the criteria of wrongdoing and imposing its principal consequence on
those who transgress its standard. . . .

[handwritten margin note: This distinction is only relevant bc Congress doesn't have to power to reg. this]

In the case at the bar, Congress in the name of a tax which on the face of
the act is [a] penalty seeks to do the same thing [as the statute in *Hammer v.
Dagenhart*], and the effort must be equally futile.

The analogy of the *Dagenhart Case* is clear. The congressional power over
interstate commerce is, within its proper scope, just as complete and unlimited
as the congressional power to tax, and the legislative motive in its exercise is
just as free from judicial suspicion and inquiry. Yet when Congress threatened
to stop interstate commerce in ordinary and necessary commodities, unobjectionable as subjects of transportation, and to deny the same to the people of a
State in order to coerce them into compliance with Congress' regulation of state
concerns, the court said this was not in fact regulation of interstate commerce,
but rather that of State concerns and was invalid. So here the so-called tax is

a penalty to ⟨coerce⟩ people of a State to act as Congress wishes them to act in respect of a matter completely the business of the state government under the Federal Constitution.

This case requires as did the *Dagenhart Case* the application of the principle announced by Chief Justice Marshall in *McCulloch v. Maryland*, in a much-quoted passage:

[handwritten annotation: Requires application of the principle]

> Should Congress, in the execution of its powers, adopt measures which are prohibited by the Constitution; or should Congress, under the pretext of executing its powers, pass laws for the accomplishment of objects not intrusted to the government; it would become the painful duty of this tribunal, should a case requiring such a decision come before it, to say that such an act was not the law of the land.

But it is pressed upon us that this court has gone so far in sustaining taxing measures the effect or tendency of which was to accomplish purposes not directly within congressional power that we are bound by authority to maintain this law. . . . [The Court proceeded to distinguish the cases that the Government cited to support this claim.] [In] *United States v. Doremus* (1919), . . . [t]he validity of a special tax in the nature of an excise tax on the manufacture, importation, and sale of [opioids] was, of course, unquestioned. . . . The court, there, made manifest its view that the provisions of the so-called taxing act must be naturally and reasonably adapted to the collection of the tax and not solely to the achievement of some other purpose plainly within state power.

For the reasons given, we must hold the Child Labor Tax Law invalid and the judgment of the District Court is

Affirmed.

MR. JUSTICE CLARKE dissents.

FOR DISCUSSION   Assuming the validity of *Hammer*, and recognizing that virtually all taxes (except perhaps on death) may discourage the taxed activity, did the Court get this case right? If you think it did, which, if any, of the points made by Chief Justice Taft was crucial to the decision?

Just as the Supreme Court dramatically loosened the limits on Commerce Clause regulation, so too did it appear to retreat from *Bailey v. Drexel Furniture*'s strict approach to Tax Clause analysis. The next case is fairly representative of the hands-off attitude that dominated the Court's assessment of even the most obviously regulatory uses of the taxing power for the remainder of the twentieth century.

United States v. Kahriger

Supreme Court of the United States, 1953.
345 U.S. 22.

MR. JUSTICE REED delivered the opinion of the Court.

The issue raised by this appeal is the constitutionality of the occupational tax provisions of the Revenue Act of 1951, which levy a [10% excise] tax on persons engaged in the business of accepting wagers, and require such persons to register with the Collector of Internal Revenue. . . . [Criminal charges were] filed against appellee alleging that he was in the business of accepting wagers and that he willfully failed to register for and pay the occupational tax in question. . . .

The substance of respondent's position with respect to the Tenth Amendment is that Congress has chosen to tax a specified business which is not within its power to regulate. The precedents are many upholding taxes similar to this wagering tax as a proper exercise of the federal taxing power. . . .

Appellee would have us say that because there is legislative history indicating a congressional motive to suppress wagering,[3] this tax is not a proper exercise of such taxing power. In the *License Tax Cases* (1866), it was admitted that the federal [tax] "discouraged" the activities [of selling liquor and lottery tickets]. The intent to curtail and hinder, as well as tax, was also manifest in

---

[3] There are suggestions in the debates that Congress sought to hinder, if not prevent the type of gambling taxed. See 97 Cong. Rec. 6892:

> Mr. Hoffman of Michigan. Then I will renew my observation that it might if properly construed be considered an additional penalty on the illegal activities.

> Mr. Cooper. Certainly, and we might indulge the hope that the imposition of this type of tax would eliminate that kind of activity.

See also 97 Cong. Rec. 12236:

> If the local official does not want to enforce the law and no one catches him winking at the law, he may keep on winking at it, but when the Federal Government identifies a law violator and the local newspaper gets hold of it and the local church organizations get hold of it and the people who do want the law enforced get hold of it, they say, "Mr. Sheriff, what about it? We understand that there is a place down here licensed to sell liquor." He says, "Is that so? I will put him out of business."

the following cases, and in each of them the tax was upheld: *Veazie Bank v. Fenno* (1869) (tax on paper money issued by state banks); *McCray v. United States* (1904) (tax on colored oleomargarine); *United States v. Doremus* (1919) and *Nigro v. United States* (1928) (tax on narcotics); *Sonzinsky v. United States* (1937) (tax on firearms); *United States v. Sanchez* (1950) (tax on marihuana).

It is conceded that a federal excise tax does not cease to be valid merely because it discourages or deters the activities taxed. Nor is the tax invalid because the revenue obtained is negligible. Appellee, however, argues that the sole purpose of the statute is to penalize only illegal gambling in the states through the guise of a tax measure. As with the above excise taxes which we have held to be valid, the instant tax has a regulatory effect. But regardless of its regulatory effect, the wagering tax produces revenue. As such it surpasses both the narcotics and firearms taxes which we have found valid.

One of the indicia which appellee offers to support his contention that the wagering tax is not a proper revenue measure is that the tax amount collected under it was $4,371,869 as compared with an expected amount of $400,000,000 a year. The figure of $4,371,869, however, is relatively large when it is compared with the $3,501 collected under the tax on adulterated and process or renovated butter and filled cheese, the $914,910 collected under the tax on narcotics, including marihuana and special taxes, and the $28,911 collected under the tax on firearms transfer and occupational taxes.

It is axiomatic that the power of Congress to tax is extensive and sometimes falls with crushing effect on businesses deemed unessential or inimical to the public welfare, or where, as in dealings with narcotics, the collection of the tax also is difficult. . . . The remedy for excessive taxation is in the hands of Congress, not the courts. . . .

Penalty provisions in tax statutes added for breach of a regulation concerning activities in themselves subject only to state regulation have caused this Court to declare the enactments invalid. [Citing *Bailey*, among other cases.] Unless there are provisions, extraneous to any tax need, courts are without authority to limit the exercise of the taxing power.

MR. JUSTICE JACKSON, concurring.

. . . It will be a sad day for the revenues if the good will of the people toward their taxing system is frittered away in efforts to accomplish by taxation moral reforms that cannot be accomplished by direct legislation. But the evil that can come from this statute will probably soon make itself manifest to Congress. The evil of a judicial decision impairing the legitimate taxing power by extreme constitutional interpretations might not be transient. Even though this statute approaches the fair limits of constitutionality, I join the decision of the Court.

MR. JUSTICE FRANKFURTER, dissenting.

. . . Constitutional issues are likely to arise whenever Congress draws on the taxing power not to raise revenue but to regulate conduct. This is so, of course, because of the distribution of legislative power as between the Congress and the State Legislatures in the regulation of conduct.

. . . Two generalizations may . . . safely be drawn from [our precedents]. Congress may make an oblique use of the taxing power in relation to activities with which Congress may deal directly, as for instance, commerce between the States. . . . However, when oblique use is made of the taxing power as to matters which substantively are not within the powers delegated to Congress, the Court cannot shut its eyes to what is obviously, because designedly, an attempt to control conduct which the Constitution left to the responsibility of the States, merely because Congress wrapped the legislation in the verbal cellophane of a revenue measure.

Concededly the constitutional questions presented by such legislation are difficult. . . . Issues of such gravity affecting the balance of powers within our federal system are not susceptible of comprehensive statement by smooth formulas such as that a tax is nonetheless a tax although it discourages the activities taxed, or, that a tax may be imposed although it may effect ulterior ends. No such phrase, however fine and well-worn, enables one to decide the concrete case.

What is relevant to judgment here is that, even if the history of this legislation as it went through Congress did not give one the libretto to the song, the context of the circumstances which brought forth this enactment—sensationally exploited disclosures regarding gambling in big cities and small, the relation of this gambling to corrupt politics, the impatient public response to these disclosures, the feeling of ineptitude or paralysis on the part of local law-enforcing agencies—emphatically supports what was revealed on the floor of Congress, namely, that what was formally a means of raising revenue for the Federal Government was essentially an effort to check if not to stamp out professional gambling. . . .

Mr. Justice Douglas, while not joining in the entire opinion, agrees with the views expressed herein that this tax is an attempt by the Congress to control conduct which the Constitution has left to the responsibility of the States.

MR. JUSTICE BLACK, with whom MR. JUSTICE DOUGLAS concurs, dissenting.

The Fifth Amendment declares that no person "shall be compelled in any criminal case to be a witness against himself". The Court nevertheless here sustains an Act which requires a man to register and confess that he is engaged in the business of gambling[, which is a crime under state law. We] have a Bill of Rights that condemns coerced confessions, however refined or legalistic may be the technique of extortion. I would hold that this Act violates the Fifth Amendment.

For Discussion

(1) Is *Bailey* compatible with *Doremus*? With *Kahriger*?

(2) Under *Wickard v. Filburn*, could Congress have regulated gambling directly under the Commerce Clause? If the answer is yes, then does *Kahriger* really represent a new approach to the Tax Clause? (Also, why didn't Congress just prohibit gambling directly?)

---

5.   The Spending Power

In addition to authorizing taxation, Article I also authorizes the expenditure of funds once collected. This opens up at least two doors for federal policymaking. First, it allows Congress to pursue affirmative projects—say, the construction of roads or the remediation of environmental damage. Such efforts require supplies, institutions, and actors to implement Congress's instructions—all of which costs money. The second way that the spending power can facilitate federal policymaking is more complex. Rather than undertaking some project in its own right, the federal government can also pay someone else to pursue its objectives as an agent or contractor.

As You READ

If you recognize congressional authority to pay third parties to implement federal policy, you have to consider the possibility that Congress could pay states and private parties to comply with policies that it couldn't forcibly require them to obey. Is that a problem? The following cases explore that question.

The Court was forced to confront the regulatory potential of the spending power during the crisis years of the 1930s. In *United States v. Butler* (1936), the Court invalidated key provisions of the Agricultural Adjustment Act of 1933, which remained a popular statute and a cornerstone of the New Deal. Aiming to restore farm prices hard hit by the Depression, the Act operated simply and boldly. The federal Agricultural Adjustment Administration was authorized to boost market prices by renting cultivable land, by purchasing surpluses, and by making straight-out benefit payments to farmers in return for agreements not to produce. The funds to operate this program for any particular commodity were raised by a tax on the processors of that commodity. In court, the Administration did not attempt to justify the Act on the basis of the Commerce Clause. (Recall that agriculture was considered production beyond the reach of the commerce power, so the argument embraced six years later in *Wickard v. Filburn* (1942) would have been an almost sure loser.) Rather, the Administration relied on the taxing and spending powers.

Justice Roberts, writing for the Court in an opinion joined by Chief Justice Hughes and the conservative foursome, rejected this argument. The statute's taxes and appropriations, he held, were "but means to an unconstitutional end." The federal government had no authority to regulate agriculture, and participation in the AAA program could not truly be considered voluntary—the threatened loss of benefits strong-armed farmers into participation. "This is coercion by economic pressure," Roberts wrote:

> [The] regulation is not in fact voluntary. The farmer, of course, may refuse to comply, but the price of such refusal is the loss of benefits. The amount offered is intended to be sufficient to exert pressure on him to agree to the proposed regulation. The power to confer or withhold unlimited benefits is the power to coerce or destroy. If the cotton grower elects not to accept the benefits, he will receive less for his crops; those who receive payments will be able to undersell him. The result may well be financial ruin.

Even if the program of benefits were not coercive, moreover, it would still be unconstitutional: "Congress has no power to enforce its commands on the farmer to the ends sought by the Agricultural Adjustment Act. It must follow that it may not indirectly accomplish those ends by taxing and spending to purchase compliance."

Justice Stone, joined by the other two liberals, wrote a bitter and forceful dissent. He denied that the Act was coercive, asserting that "[t]hreat of loss, not hope of gain, is the essence of economic coercion" and pointing out that a substantial minority of farmers declined to participate in the program. In his view, the Act merely imposed appropriate conditions on a public expenditure:

> The power of Congress to spend is inseparable from persuasion to action over which Congress has no legislative control. Congress may not command that the science of agriculture be taught in state universities. But if it would aid the teaching of that science by grants to state institutions, it is appropriate, if not necessary, that the grant be on the condition . . . that it be used for the intended purpose.

Although *Butler* was an immediate defeat for the exercise of federal power, it laid the seeds for future expansions. The true meaning of the General Welfare Clause had never been definitively resolved. James Madison had contended that Congress could tax and spend only in the exercise of its other enumerated powers; on the other hand, Alexander Hamilton, seconded by the later writings of Joseph Story, had contended that the grant was of a distinct substantive power to spend in service of a much broader conception of "the General Welfare." (A third possibility, which had gotten less attention and seems dubious both textually and historically, was that the Clause gave Congress the power to *act* in any way that would support the general welfare.) In *Butler*, Roberts emphatically endorsed the Hamilton-Story interpretation.

Why, given that the Court held against the particular exercise of power in the case, did Roberts include this statement? The answer is found in the record of a later conversation, scrawled by Felix Frankfurter on the appropriate page in his copy of the United States Reports:

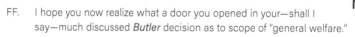
WORTH NOTING

    FF.   I hope you now realize what a door you opened in your—shall I say—much discussed *Butler* decision as to scope of "general welfare."

    OJR.   I do realize, and often wonder why the hell I did it just to please the Chief.

Hughes had advocated the Hamilton-Story view while in private practice and evidently felt strongly about it.

For Discussion

(1)   Which view of the General Welfare Clause do you believe is most persuasive?

(2)   Do you believe that the offer of payments to farmers in return for promises not to produce was coercive? Assuming it was not coercive, should the Act have been held invalid as "purchased regulation"?

In 1937, Roberts's dictum on the General Welfare Clause bore fruit when, in the middle of the Court-packing battle, the Court issued a pair of decisions rejecting challenges to the 1935 Social Security Act. In *Helvering v. Davis* (1937), a 7–2 majority held—with only Justices McReynolds and Butler dissenting—that the payment of old-age pension benefits under the Act was a valid exercise of Congress's power under the General Welfare Clause. Citing *Butler*'s broad conception of the clause, Justice Cardozo's majority opinion noted that "[w]e will not resurrect the contest. It is now settled by decision." As for the contention that the benefit payments were too particular to be in service of the "general welfare," Cardozo concluded such a challenge could succeed only if there was "no reasonable possibility [that] the challenged legislation fall[s] within the wide range of discretion permitted to the Congress":

> The line must still be drawn between one welfare and another, between particular and general. Where this shall be placed cannot be known through a formula in advance of the event. There is a middle ground or certainly a penumbra in which discretion is at large. The discretion, however, is not confided to the courts. The discretion belongs to Congress, unless the choice is clearly wrong, a display of arbitrary power, not an exercise of judgment. . . . Nor is the concept of the general welfare static. Needs that were narrow or parochial a century ago may be interwoven in our day with the well-being of the nation. What is critical or urgent changes with the times.

Under the circumstances presented in *Helvering*, it was clearly permissible for Congress to conclude that the general welfare was at stake:

> The purge of nation-wide calamity that began in 1929 has taught us many lessons. Not the least is the solidarity of interests that may once have seemed to be divided. Unemployment spreads from state to state, the hinterland now settled that in pioneer days gave an avenue

of escape. Spreading from state to state, unemployment is an ill not particular but general, which may be checked, if Congress so determines, by the resources of the nation. . . . But the ill is all one or at least not greatly different whether men are thrown out of work because there is no longer work to do or because the disabilities of age make them incapable of doing it. Rescue becomes necessary irrespective of the cause. The hope behind this statute is to save men and women from the rigors of the poor house as well as from the haunting fear that such a lot awaits them when journey's end is near.

FOR DISCUSSION Are you persuaded that payments to aged individuals for them to use as they see fit is an expenditure in support of the "general welfare" of the nation?

In the second case, the Supreme Court upheld the Social Security Act's more intricate unemployment relief program. *Steward Machine Co. v. Davis* (1937). Title IX of the Act levied a tax on employers but credited up to 90% of it for amounts contributed instead to qualifying state unemployment funds. Such contributions were paid over to a trust fund maintained by the Secretary of Treasury and then withdrawn by the states for unemployment compensation on terms specified in the Social Security Act. The aim of this scheme was to encourage the states to set up their own unemployment programs without fear of placing themselves at a competitive disadvantage against other states that chose to do nothing.

Again writing for the Court, Cardozo rejected the argument that the plan constituted improper coercion of the states. "To draw the line intelligently between duress and inducement," he wrote, "there is need to remind ourselves of facts as to the problem of unemployment that are now matters of common knowledge":

During the years 1929 to 1936, when the country was passing through a cyclical depression, the number of the unemployed mounted to unprecedented heights. Often the average was more than 10 million; at times a peak was attained of 16 million or more. Disaster to the breadwinner meant disaster to dependents. Accordingly the roll of the unemployed, itself formidable enough, was only a partial roll of the destitute or needy. The fact developed quickly that the states were unable to give the requisite relief. The problem had become national in area and dimensions. There was need of help from the nation if the people were not to starve. It is too late today for the argument to be heard with tolerance that in a crisis so extreme the use of the moneys of the nation to relieve the unemployed and their dependents is a use for any purpose narrower than the promotion of the general welfare. Cf. *United States v. Butler*; *Helvering v. Davis*.

Cardozo then refused to conclude that Alabama was acting under duress when it cooperated with the federal plan:

> The assailants of the statute say that its dominant end and aim is to drive the state Legislatures under the whip of economic pressure into the enactment of unemployment compensation laws at the bidding of the central government. . . .

> The difficulty with the petitioner's contention is that it confuses motive with coercion. "Every tax is in some measure regulatory. To some extent it interposes an economic impediment to the activity taxed as compared with others not taxed." *Sonzinsky v. United States* (1937). In like manner every rebate from a tax when conditioned upon conduct is in some measure a temptation. But to hold that motive or temptation is equivalent to coercion is to plunge the law in endless difficulties. The outcome of such a doctrine is the acceptance of a philosophical determinism by which choice becomes impossible. . . .

> Nothing in the case suggests the exertion of a power akin to undue influence, if we assume that such a concept can ever be applied with fitness to the relations between state and nation. Even on that assumption the location of the point at which pressure turns into compulsion . . . would be a question of degree. . . . The point had not been reached when Alabama made her choice. We cannot say that [Alabama] was acting, not of her unfettered will, but under the strain of a persuasion equivalent to undue influence, when she chose to have relief administered under laws of her own making, by agents of her own selection, instead of under federal laws, administered by federal officers, with all the ensuing evils, at least to many minds, of federal patronage and power. . . .

We do not fix the outermost line. Enough for present purposes that wherever the line may be, this statute is within it. Definition more precise must abide the wisdom of the future. . . .

WORTH NOTING

Justices McReynolds and Butler dissented broadly on the ground that the Act exceeded federal power. Justices Sutherland and Van Devanter expressed agreement with most of Cardozo's opinion, but dissented because they believed the statute required the state to abdicate its powers by depositing funds in the Federal Treasury.

South Dakota v. Dole

Supreme Court of the United States, 1987.
483 U.S. 203.

CHIEF JUSTICE REHNQUIST delivered the opinion of the Court.

Petitioner South Dakota permits persons 19 years of age or older to purchase beer containing up to 3.2% alcohol. In 1984 Congress enacted 23 U.S.C. § 158, which directs the Secretary of Transportation to withhold a percentage of federal highway funds otherwise allocable from States "in which the purchase or public possession . . . of any alcoholic beverage by a person who is less than twenty-one years of age is lawful." The State sued in United States District Court seeking a declaratory judgment that § 158 violates the [Constitution].

South Dakota asserts that the setting of minimum drinking ages is clearly within the "core powers" reserved to the States under § 2 of the [Twenty-first] Amendment.[1] Despite the extended treatment of the question by the parties, however, we need not decide in this case whether that Amendment would prohibit an attempt by Congress to legislate directly a national minimum drinking age. Here, Congress has acted indirectly under its spending power to encourage uniformity in the States' drinking ages. As we explain below, we find this legislative effort within constitutional bounds even if Congress may not regulate drinking ages directly.

---

[1]   Section 2 of the Twenty-first Amendment provides: "The transportation or importation into any State, Territory, or possession of the United States for delivery or use therein of intoxicating liquors, in violation of the laws thereof, is hereby prohibited."

The Constitution empowers Congress to "lay and collect Taxes, Duties, Imposts, and Excises, to pay the Debts and provide for the common Defence and general Welfare of the United States." Art. I, § 8, cl. 1. Incident to this power, Congress may attach conditions on the receipt of federal funds, and has repeatedly employed the power "to further broad policy objectives by conditioning receipt of federal moneys upon compliance by the recipient with federal statutory and administrative directives." *Fullilove v. Klutznick* (1980). The breadth of this power was made clear in *United States v. Butler* (1936), where the Court [held that] objectives not thought to be within Article I's "enumerated legislative fields" may nevertheless be attained through the use of the spending power and the conditional grant of federal funds.

The spending power is of course not unlimited, but is instead subject to several general restrictions articulated in our cases. The first of these limitations is derived from the language of the Constitution itself: the exercise of the spending power must be in pursuit of "the general welfare." In considering whether a particular expenditure is intended to serve general public purposes, courts should defer substantially to the judgment of Congress. *Helvering v. Davis* (1937).[2] Second, we have required that if Congress desires to condition the States' receipt of federal funds, it "must do so unambiguously . . . , enabl[ing] the States to exercise their choice knowingly, cognizant of the consequences of their participation." *Pennhurst State School & Hospital v. Halderman* (1981). Third, our cases have suggested (without significant elaboration) that conditions on federal grants might be illegitimate if they are unrelated "to the federal interest in particular national projects or programs." *Massachusetts v. United States* (1978). Finally, we have noted that other constitutional provisions may provide an independent bar to the conditional grant of federal funds. . . .

South Dakota does not seriously claim that § 158 is inconsistent with any of the first three restrictions mentioned above.

[First, we] can readily conclude that the provision is designed to serve the general welfare, especially in light of the fact that "the concept of welfare or the opposite is shaped by Congress. . . ." *Helvering v. Davis*. Congress found that the differing drinking ages in the States created particular incentives for young persons to combine their desire to drink with their ability to drive, and that this interstate problem required a national solution. The means it chose

---

[2]   The level of deference to the congressional decision is such that the Court has more recently questioned whether "general welfare" is a judicially enforceable restriction at all. See *Buckley v. Valeo* (1976).

to address this dangerous situation were reasonably calculated to advance the general welfare.

[Second, the] conditions upon which States receive the funds . . . could not be more clearly stated by Congress.

[Third, we are satisfied with the] germaneness of the condition to federal purposes. . . . Indeed, the condition imposed by Congress is directly related to one of the main purposes for which highway funds are expended—safe interstate travel.[3] This goal of the interstate highway system had been frustrated by varying drinking ages among the States. A Presidential commission appointed to study alcohol-related accidents and fatalities on the Nation's highways concluded that the lack of uniformity in the States' drinking ages created "an incentive to drink and drive" because "young persons commut[e] to border States where the drinking age is lower." Presidential Commission on Drunk Driving, Final Report (1983). By enacting § 158, Congress conditioned the receipt of federal funds in a way reasonably calculated to address this particular impediment to a purpose for which the funds are expended.

The remaining question about the validity of § 158—and the basic point of disagreement between the parties—is whether the Twenty-first Amendment constitutes an "independent constitutional bar" to the conditional grant of federal funds. [Our] cases establish that the "independent constitutional bar" limitation on the spending power is not, as petitioner suggests, a prohibition on the indirect achievement of objectives which Congress is not empowered to achieve directly. Instead, we think that the language in our earlier opinions stands for the unexceptionable proposition that the power may not be used to induce the States to engage in activities that would themselves be unconstitutional. Thus, for example, a grant of federal funds conditioned on invidiously discriminatory state action or the infliction of cruel and unusual punishment would be an illegitimate exercise of the Congress' broad spending power. But no such claim can be or is made here. Were South Dakota to succumb to the blandishments offered by Congress and raise its drinking age to 21, the State's action in so doing would not violate the constitutional rights of anyone.

---

[3]   Our cases have not required that we define the outer bounds of the "germaneness" or "relatedness" limitation on the imposition of conditions under the spending power. *Amici* urge that we take this occasion to establish that a condition on federal funds is legitimate only if it relates directly to the purpose of the expenditure to which it is attached. See Brief for National Conference of State Legislatures et al. as *Amici Curiae*. Because petitioner has not sought such a restriction, and because we find any such limitation on conditional federal grants satisfied in this case in any event, we do not address whether conditions less directly related to the particular purpose of the expenditure might be outside the bounds of the spending power.

Our decisions have recognized that in some circumstances the financial inducement offered by Congress might be so coercive as to pass the point at which "pressure turns into compulsion." *Steward Machine Co. v. Davis* (1937). Here, however, Congress has directed only that a State desiring to establish a minimum drinking age lower than 21 lose a relatively small percentage of certain federal highway funds. Petitioner contends that the coercive nature of this program is evident from the degree of success it has achieved. We cannot conclude, however, that a conditional grant of federal money of this sort is unconstitutional simply by reason of its success in achieving the congressional objective.

When we consider, for a moment, that all South Dakota would lose if she adheres to her chosen course as to a suitable minimum drinking age is 5% of the funds otherwise obtainable under specified highway grant programs, the argument as to coercion is shown to be more rhetoric than fact. . . . Here Congress has offered relatively mild encouragement to the States to enact higher minimum drinking ages than they would otherwise choose. But the enactment of such laws remains the prerogative of the States not merely in theory but in fact. Even if Congress might lack the power to impose a national minimum drinking age directly, we conclude that encouragement to state action found in § 158 is a valid use of the spending power.

JUSTICE BRENNAN, dissenting.

I agree with Justice O'Connor that regulation of the minimum age of purchasers of liquor falls squarely within the ambit of those powers reserved to the States by the Twenty-first Amendment. Since States possess this constitutional power, Congress cannot condition a federal grant in a manner that abridges this right. The Amendment, itself, strikes the proper balance between federal and state authority. I therefore dissent.

JUSTICE O'CONNOR, dissenting.

[Section] 158 is not a condition on spending reasonably related to the expenditure of federal funds and cannot be justified on that ground. Rather, it is an attempt to regulate the sale of liquor, an attempt that lies outside Congress' power to regulate commerce because it falls within the ambit of § 2 of the Twenty-first Amendment.

My disagreement with the Court is relatively narrow on the spending power issue. . . . I agree that there are four separate types of limitations on the spending power: the expenditure must be for the general welfare, the conditions imposed must be unambiguous, they must be reasonably related to the purpose of the expenditure, and the legislation may not violate any independent constitutional prohibition. . . .

WORTH NOTING Justice O'Connor did not challenge the Court's analysis of the first, second, and fourth limitations.

But the Court's application of the requirement that the condition imposed be reasonably related to the purpose for which the funds are expended is cursory and unconvincing. We have repeatedly said that Congress may condition grants under the spending power only in ways reasonably related to the purpose of the federal program. *Steward Machine Co. v. Davis* ("We do not say that a tax is valid, when imposed by act of Congress, if it is laid upon the condition that a state may escape its operation through the adoption of a statute unrelated in subject matter to activities fairly within the scope of national policy and power"). In my view, establishment of a minimum drinking age of 21 is not sufficiently related to interstate highway construction to justify so conditioning funds appropriated for that purpose. . . .

[T]he Court asserts the reasonableness of the relationship between the supposed purpose of the expenditure—"safe interstate travel"—and the drinking age condition. The Court reasons that Congress wishes that the roads it builds may be used safely, that drunken drivers threaten highway safety, and that young people are more likely to drive while under the influence of alcohol under existing law than would be the case if there were a uniform national drinking age of 21. It hardly needs saying, however, that if the purpose of § 158 is to deter drunken driving, it is far too over and under-inclusive. It is over-inclusive because it stops teenagers from drinking even when they are not about to drive on interstate highways. It is under-inclusive because teenagers pose only a small part of the drunken driving problem in this Nation. See, *e.g.*, 130 Cong. Rec. 18648 (1984) (remarks of Sen. Humphrey) ("Eighty-four percent of all highway fatalities involving alcohol occur among those whose ages exceed 21"). . . .

When Congress appropriates money to build a highway, it is entitled to insist that the highway be a safe one. But it is not entitled to insist as a condition of the use of highway funds that the State impose or change regulations in other areas of the State's social and economic life because of an attenuated or tangential relationship to highway use or safety. Indeed, if the rule were otherwise, the Congress could effectively regulate almost any area of a State's social, political, or economic life on the theory that use of the interstate transportation system is somehow enhanced. If, for example, the United States were to condition highway moneys upon moving the state capital, I suppose it might argue that interstate transportation is facilitated by locating local governments in places easily accessible to interstate highways—or, conversely, that highways might become overburdened if they had to carry traffic to and from the state capital. In my mind, such a relationship is hardly more attenuated than the one which the Court finds supports § 158. Cf. Tr. of Oral Arg. (counsel for the United States conceding that to condition a grant upon adoption of a unicameral legislature would violate the "germaneness" requirement).

There is a clear place at which the Court can draw the line between permissible and impermissible conditions on federal grants. It is the line identified in the Brief for the National Conference of State Legislatures et al. as *Amici Curiae*:

> Congress has the power to *spend* for the general welfare, it has the power to *legislate* only for delegated purposes. . . .
>
> The appropriate inquiry, then, is whether the spending requirement or prohibition is a condition on a grant or whether it is regulation. The difference turns on whether the requirement specifies in some way how the money should be spent, so that Congress' intent in making the grant will be effectuated. Congress has no power under the Spending Clause to impose requirements on a grant that go beyond specifying how the money should be spent. A requirement that is not such a specification is not a condition, but a regulation, which is valid only if it falls within one of Congress' delegated regulatory powers.

This approach harks back to *United States v. Butler*, the last case in which this Court struck down an Act of Congress as beyond the authority granted by the Spending Clause. There the Court wrote that "[t]here is an obvious difference between a statute stating the conditions upon which moneys shall be expended and one effective only upon assumption of a contractual obligation to submit to a regulation which otherwise could not be enforced." The *Butler* Court saw the Agricultural Adjustment Act for what it was—an exercise of regulatory, not spending, power. . . .

While *Butler's* authority is questionable insofar as it assumes that Congress has no regulatory power over farm production [under the Commerce Clause], its discussion of the spending power and its description of both the power's breadth and its limitations remain sound. . . . If the spending power is to be limited only by Congress' notion of the general welfare, the reality, given the vast financial resources of the Federal Government, is that the Spending Clause gives "power to the Congress to tear down the barriers, to invade the states' jurisdiction, and to become a parliament of the whole people, subject to no restrictions save such as are self-imposed." *United States v. Butler*. This, of course, as *Butler* held, was not the Framers' plan and it is not the meaning of the Spending Clause. . . .

6. Interlude: The Tenth Amendment as an Independent Limit

The Tenth Amendment provides:

> "The powers not delegated to the United States by the Constitution, nor prohibited by it to the States, are reserved to the States respectively, or to the people."

Recall that in *United States v. Darby* (1941), the Supreme Court said that this language "states but a truism that all is retained which has not been surrendered." Congress may of course preempt state law when regulating private individuals and entities; that much is clear on the face of the Supremacy Clause of Article VI. See pp. 641–642. But what if Congress regulates the activities of the states themselves, or even conscripts states as agents of federal policy? In the last quarter of the twentieth century, questions like these prompted the emergence of the Tenth Amendment as an independent limit on congressional power. At times, the modern Court has interpreted the Amendment to limit the extent to which Congress can directly regulate or restrain state activity. Since 1992 it has crafted a doctrine preventing the federal government from "commandeering" state actors to serve federal purposes.

Some of the most important initial developments concerned the same statute at issue in *Darby*: the Fair Labor Standards Act of 1938. At first, it exempted state employees. But in a series of amendments, Congress whittled away this exemption. So was it permissible for Congress to prescribe the wages that states and municipalities must pay such governmental actors as firefighters and transit workers? The issue led to a remarkable double flipflop by the Supreme Court.

Maryland v. Wirtz (1968) concerned a 1961 amendment that eliminated the state-employee exemption as applied to employees of state hospitals and schools, among other institutions. A 6–2 majority of the Court, per Justice Harlan, had no difficulty concluding that the resulting restrictions were a valid exercise of the commerce power: "If a State is engaging in economic activities that are validly regulated by the Federal Government when engaged in by private persons, the State too may be forced to conform its activities to federal regulation." Justice Douglas, joined by Justice Stewart, dissented. While recognizing that the Court's opinion accurately reflected Commerce Clause doctrine by itself, they thought that, because the provision at issue threatened to "overwhelm state fiscal policy," it was "such a serious invasion of state sovereignty protected by the Tenth Amendment" that it was "not consistent with our constitutional federalism."

Just eight years later, in *National League of Cities v. Usery* (1976), the Court overruled *Wirtz* by a 5–4 vote. The case involved a challenge to the 1974 amendments to the FLSA, which made virtually all employees of states and their subdivisions subject to the Act's wage and hour provisions. The challengers conceded that the provision was within the scope of the commerce power, but they argued that the Tenth Amendment and concepts of intergovernmental immunity imposed an independent affirmative limit on the exercise of that power.

The majority, per Justice Rehnquist, accepted that argument. The Court, he wrote, had "never doubted that there are limits upon the power of Congress to override state sovereignty, even when exercising its otherwise plenary powers . . . conferred by Art. I of the Constitution." Congress could, of course, regulate private businesses and in so doing preempt state laws on the same subjects. But it would be a different matter, he thought, "to uphold a similar exercise of congressional authority directed, not to private citizens, but to the States as States." Indeed, the Court had "repeatedly recognized that there are attributes of sovereignty attaching to every state government which may not be impaired by Congress, not because Congress may lack an affirmative grant of legislative authority to reach the matter, but because the Constitution prohibits it from exercising the authority in that manner."

As an example, Justice Rehnquist cited *Coyle v. Oklahoma* (1911), which had invalidated the statutory condition on Oklahoma's admission to the union that barred the state from changing its capital until 1913. On his account, the *Coyle* decision turned on the fact that a state's powers to choose and to change its own seat of government were "essentially and peculiarly state pow-ers." That same principle, he thought, controlled the result in *National League of Cities*. Here too, Congress had infringed functions essential to the states, by "displac[ing] state policies regarding the manner in which they will struc-ture delivery of those governmental services which their citizens require." In applying this principle, the Court's opinion put special emphasis on tradition: "insofar as the challenged amendments operate to directly displace the States' freedom to structure integral operations in areas of traditional governmental functions," they were not within Congress's delegated powers.

Justice Blackmun, joined the Court's opinion on the hopeful under-standing that it adopted "a balancing approach" and would "not outlaw federal power in areas such as environmental protection, where the federal interest is demonstrably greater and where state facility compliance with imposed federal standards would be essential."

Justice Brennan, joined by Justices White and Marshall, dissented. Dis-mayed that the Court had turned the Tenth Amendment into "a limitation on congressional exercise of powers delegated by the Constitution to Congress," he expressed confidence "that the States' influence in the political process is adequate to safeguard their sovereignty"; he contrasted the situation of relative-ly powerless litigants who had often been left to the political processes. Justice Stevens also dissented, finding the FLSA requirements indistinguishable from the many ways in which the Federal Government may control activities of and concerning a state employed janitor—tax, environmental, and safety regula-tions, for example.

In a case involving federal preemption of state mining regulations, the Supreme Court later observed that the Tenth Amendment limit recog-nized in *National League of Cities* did not apply to congressional ac-tion under the Fourteenth Amendment:

FOR DISCUSSION

> *National League of Cities* expressly left open the question "whether different results might obtain if Congress seeks to affect integral operations of state governments by exercising authority granted it under . . . § 5 of the Fourteenth Amendment [(authorizing Congress to "enforce, by ap-propriate legislation" the individual rights granted by that amendment)].
>
> In *Fitzpatrick v. Bitzer* (1976), the Court upheld Congress' power under § 5 of the Fourteenth Amendment to authorize private damages actions against state governments for discrimination in employment. The Court explained that because the Amendment was adopted with the specific purpose of limiting state autonomy, constitutional principles of federalism do not restrict congressional

power to invade state autonomy when Congress legislates under § 5 of the
Fourteenth Amendment. Similarly, in *City of Rome v. United States* (1980), we
held that the Tenth Amendment places no restrictions on congressional power
"to enforce the Civil War Amendments 'by appropriate legislation.' "

Hodel v. Virginia Surface Mining and Reclamation Association (1981). Does it make
sense that the Tenth Amendment should impose an independent restriction on congressional action under the Commerce Clause, but not on congressional action under
the Fourteenth Amendment's enforcement power? Should it matter for that purpose
that the Fourteenth Amendment was enacted in 1868 after a bitter civil war?

Courts had great difficulty applying the "traditional governmental functions" standard of *National League of Cities* (*NLC*). As the Court noted in
Garcia v. San Antonio Metropolitan Transit Authority (1985), it was "difficult, if
not impossible, to identify an organizing principle" that could account for the
array of results reached by the lower courts:

> [C]ourts have held that regulating ambulance services, licensing au-
> tomobile drivers, operating a municipal airport, performing solid
> waste disposal, and operating a highway authority are functions *pro-
> tected* under *National League of Cities*. At the same time, courts have
> held that issuance of industrial development bonds, regulation of
> intrastate natural gas sales, reg-
> ulation of traffic on public
> roads, regulation of air trans-
> portation, operation of a
> telephone system, leasing and
> sale of natural gas, operation of
> a mental health facility, and
> provision of in-house domestic
> services for the aged and hand-
> icapped are *not* entitled to
> immunity.

WORTH NOTING — In *Transportation Union v. Long Island R. Co.* (1982), relying in part on "the historical reality" that state operation of railroads was not a traditional governmental function, the Court held that a state-owned railroad fell outside the *NLC* doctrine.

In *Garcia*, the Court abandoned the attempt to apply *NLC* and instead
overruled the decision. Thus, within seventeen years the Court did two complete
U-turns, both by 5–4 votes. Justice Blackmun, who had previously advocated
a balancing approach to the problem, wrote the majority opinion, which began by emphasizing the practical challenges of applying the *NLC* standard. A
historical approach simply would not work, he thought; the roles of the states
had changed over time, with some "once-private functions like education" now

being taken on by the states and their subdivisions; even public parks were at one time an innovation. And standards that sought to identify "uniquely" or "necessarily" governmental functions would be no more manageable.

The problem of discerning a manageable standard pointed to a deeper issue, Justice Blackmun thought:

> The essence of our federal system is that within the realm of authority left open to them under the Constitution, the States must be equally free to engage in any activity that their citizens choose for the common weal, no matter how unorthodox or unnecessary anyone else—including the judiciary—deems state involvement to be. Any rule of state immunity that looks to the "traditional," "integral," or "necessary" nature of governmental functions inevitably invites an unelected federal judiciary to make decisions about which state policies it favors and which ones it dislikes.

Thus, while asserting that "undoubtedly" there are "limits on the Federal Government's power to interfere with state functions," Justice Blackmun asserted that "we must look elsewhere" than the courts to find them. Drawing heavily on the writings of Madison, he concluded that

> the Framers chose to rely on a federal system in which special restraints on federal power over the States inhered principally in the workings of the National Government itself, rather than in discrete limitations on the objects of federal authority. State sovereign interests, then, are more properly protected by procedural safeguards inherent in the structure of the federal system than by judicially created limitations on federal power.

He recognized that the Seventeenth Amendment, by providing for the election of the Senate by popular vote rather than by the Legislatures, significantly altered the original framework. Yet he pointed to the success of the states, both in procuring large amounts of federal funding and in securing important exemptions from federal regulations, as a measure of their continuing political effectiveness. And while acknowledging—with a citation to *Coyle v. Oklahoma*, the 1911 case involving placement of the state capital—that constitutional structure might impose some "affirmative limits . . . on federal action affecting the States under the Commerce Clause," he quoted Justice Frankfurter for the proposition that "[t]he process of Constitutional adjudication does not thrive

on conjuring up horrible possibilities that never happen in the real world and devising doctrines sufficiently comprehensive in detail to cover the remotest contingency."

Justice Powell dissented, joined by Chief Justice Burger and Justices Rehnquist and O'Connor. He emphasized that "the Tenth Amendment was adopted specifically to ensure that the important role promised the States by the proponents of the Constitution was realized," and complained that the decision "effectively reduces the Tenth Amendment to meaningless rhetoric when Congress acts pursuant to the Commerce Clause." He found unpersuasive the majority's insistence that the *NLC* doctrine disserved democratic self-governance; a former school board president, he argued that the majority "disregards entirely the far more effective role of democratic self-government at the state and local levels."

Justice O'Connor wrote a separate dissent, joined by Justices Powell and Rehnquist. "With the abandonment of *National League of Cities*," she warned, "all that stands between the remaining essentials of state sovereignty and Congress is the latter's underdeveloped capacity for self-restraint." She thought the acknowledged difficulties of crafting bright lines to implement the *NLC* doctrine were "to be expected whenever constitutional concerns as important as federalism and the effectiveness of the commerce power come into conflict." That the Court appealed to the "essence of federalism" while shunning the task of reconciling the competing concerns could, she thought, "provide scant comfort to those who believe our federal system requires something more than a unitary, centralized government."

Justice Rehnquist, the author of the majority opinion in *NLC*, added a brief dissent of his own, expressing confidence that its principle would "in time again command the support of a majority of this Court."

Despite Justice Rehnquist's prediction, *Garcia* has not (yet) been overruled. But its effect has been confined in two significant respects. The first limitation is the "plain statement" rule adopted by *Gregory v. Ashcroft* (1991). In that case, the Supreme Court considered the impact of the Age Discrimination in Employment Act of 1967 (ADEA) on a provision of the Missouri Constitution providing that "all judges other than municipal judges shall retire at the age of seventy years." With some exceptions, the ADEA made it unlawful for an "employer" to "discharge any individual" who is at least 40 years old "because of such individual's age." And "employer" was specifically defined to include "a State or political subdivision of a State."

Writing for the majority, Justice O'Connor held that "inasmuch as this Court in *Garcia* has left primarily to the political process the protection of the States against intrusive exercises of Congress' Commerce Clause powers, we must be absolutely certain that Congress intended such an exercise." Here, the Act excepted elected officials and certain others, including "an appointee on the policymaking level." Justice O'Connor admitted that, particularly in the context of the exceptions that surrounded it in the statute, this phrasing was "an odd way for Congress to exclude judges." But, imposing a "plain statement" obligation on Congress, she wrote: "We will not read the ADEA to cover state judges unless Congress has made it clear that judges are included."

Justice White, joined by Justice Stevens, thought that the "plain statement" rule could not be reconciled with *Garcia*. Unlike the majority, Justice White did not believe that there would be a serious constitutional problem if the ADEA applied to state judges, and he regarded the political process as an adequate protection of the states. As a matter of "simple statutory construction," however, the Missouri judges fell within the policymaker exception. Justice Blackmun, joined by Justice Marshall, dissented. They agreed with Justice White's rejection of the "plain statement" rule, but they did not believe that the judges fell within the exception.

The second significant limitation on *Garcia* is known as the commandeering doctrine, which emerged from dictum in *Hodel v. Virginia Surface Mining and Reclamation Association* (1981). In that case, a federal statute allowed states to "assume permanent regulatory authority" over coal mining in non-federal lands, but only if the Secretary of the Interior approved the regulatory program proposed by the state legislature. If a state failed "to submit or enforce a satisfactory state program," on the other hand, then the Secretary would continue to directly administer federal regulations "unless and until a 'state program' is approved." The Supreme Court approved the program, reasoning as follows:

> [The Act does not compel] the States . . . to enforce [its] standards, to expend any state funds, or to participate in the federal regulatory program in any manner whatsoever. If a State does not wish to submit a proposed permanent program that complies with the Act and implementing regulations, the full regulatory burden will be borne by

the Federal Government. Thus, there can be no suggestion that the Act commandeers the legislative processes of the States by directly compelling them to enact and enforce a federal regulatory program. Cf. *Maryland v. EPA* (4th Cir. 1975). The most that can be said is that the Surface Mining Act establishes a program of cooperative federalism that allows the States, within limits established by federal minimum standards, to enact and administer their own regulatory programs, structured to meet their own particular needs. . . .

The Fourth Circuit case cited in *Hodel* had involved a challenge to EPA regulations that "require[d] [Maryland to] enact programs calling for retrofit of pollution control devices on certain classes of vehicles," and to " 'establish' an [automobile] inspection and maintenance program . . . and a system of bikeways and parking facilities. . . ." *Maryland v. EPA* (4th Cir. 1975). Relying on the constitutional avoidance canon, the Fourth Circuit held that the EPA had no statutory authority to command State governments to promulgate legislation or regulation:

> [T]hese astonishing regulations[, in] a nutshell, . . . direct[ ] Maryland and her legislature to legislate under pain of civil and criminal penalties. . . . Inviting Maryland to administer the regulations, and compelling her to do . . . are two entirely different propositions. We are thus of the opinion, and so hold, that the EPA was without authority under the statute . . . , to require Maryland to establish the programs and furnish legal authority for the administration thereof.

The groundwork laid by these discussions in *Maryland v. EPA* and *Hodel* came to fruition some ten years after the latter was decided.

In *New York v. United States* (1992), Justice O'Connor wrote for a majority of the Supreme Court in holding that "the Constitution does not confer upon Congress the ability simply to compel the States" to provide for the disposal of the radioactive waste generated within their borders. At issue were provisions of the Low-Level Radioactive Waste Policy Act of 1980. The statute provided that each state "shall be responsible for providing" for the disposal of such waste in accordance with criteria established by the statute. Rather than construing the statute as a mandate to the states to regulate, the Court construed it as setting a series of incentives to regulate. This construction, the Court said, was in accordance with the general principle that a statute ought to be construed to avoid constitutional problems unless doing so is "plainly contrary to the intent of Congress."

The first set of incentives, in which Congress conditioned grants to the states upon the states' attainment of a set of criteria, was held to be within the authority of Congress under the Commerce and Spending Clauses. The second set of incentives, in which Congress authorized states and regional compacts of states that had disposal sites to increase the cost of access to the sites to radioactive waste generated in states that do not meet federal deadlines, was also held valid because it was "within the power of Congress to authorize the States to discriminate against interstate commerce."

CROSS REFERENCE For an explanation of this doctrine, see *Prudential Insurance Co. v. Benjamin* (1946) at pp. 692–694.

The third "incentive," however, was held invalid. This portion of the statute provided that if the state in which radioactive waste was generated was not able to provide adequately for the disposal of the waste by January 1, 1996, the state, "upon request of the generator or owner of the waste, shall take title to the waste, be obligated to take possession of the waste, and shall be liable for all damages directly or indirectly incurred" as a consequence of failure to take possession. The statute thus offered the states the choice between either "accepting ownership of waste" or "regulating according to the instructions of Congress." Reasoning that the Constitution didn't permit Congress to impose either option individually, the Court concluded that requiring the states to choose between them was also unconstitutional:

> On one hand, the Constitution would not permit Congress simply to transfer radioactive waste from generators to state governments. Such a forced transfer, standing alone, would in principle be no different than a congressionally compelled subsidy from state governments to radioactive waste producers. [This] would "commandeer" state governments into the service of federal regulatory purposes, and would for this reason be inconsistent with the Constitution's division of authority between federal and state governments.
>
> On the other hand, the second alternative held out to state governments—regulating pursuant to Congress' direction—would, standing alone, present a simple command to state governments to

implement legislation enacted by Congress. As we have seen, the Constitution does not empower Congress to subject state governments to this type of instruction. . . .

A choice between two unconstitutionally coercive regulatory techniques is no choice at all. Either way, "the Act commandeers the legislative processes of the States by directly compelling them to enact and enforce a federal regulatory program," *Hodel v. Virginia Surface Mining & Reclamation Assn., Inc.* . . .

At the heart of the Court's decision was its holding that Congress may not "commandeer" the legislative processes of the states, directly compelling them to enact a federal regulatory program. The Court grounded its conclusion in historical observations about the Founding:

> Under the Articles of Confederation, Congress lacked the authority in most respects to govern the people directly. In practice, Congress "could not directly tax or legislate upon individuals; it had no explicit 'legislative' or 'governmental' power to make binding 'law' enforceable as such."

> The inadequacy of this governmental structure was responsible in part for the Constitutional Convention. Alexander Hamilton observed: "The great and radical vice in the construction of the existing Confederation is in the principle of LEGISLATION for STATES or GOVERNMENTS, in their CORPORATE or COLLECTIVE CAPACITIES, and as contra-distinguished from the INDIVIDUALS of whom they consist. " The Federalist No. 15. As Hamilton saw it, [t]he new National Government "must carry its agency to the persons of the citizens. It must stand in need of no intermediate legislations. . . . The government of the Union, like that of each State, must be able to address itself immediately to the hopes and fears of individuals." *Id.*, No. 16. . . .

> In the end, the Convention opted for a Constitution in which Congress would exercise its legislative authority directly over individuals rather than over States. . . .

Under the structure that resulted, the Court continued,

States are not mere political subdivisions of the United States. State governments are neither regional offices nor administrative agencies of the Federal Government. The positions occupied by state officials appear nowhere on the Federal Government's most detailed organizational chart. The Constitution instead "leaves to the several States a residuary and inviolable sovereignty," The Federalist No. 39, reserved explicitly to the States by the Tenth Amendment.

Whatever the outer limits of that sovereignty may be, one thing is clear: The Federal Government may not compel the States to enact or administer a federal regulatory program. . . . The Constitution enables the Federal Government to pre-empt state regulation contrary to federal interests, and it permits the Federal Government to hold out incentives to the States as a means of encouraging them to adopt suggested regulatory schemes. It does not, however, authorize Congress simply to direct the States to provide for the disposal of the radioactive waste generated within their borders.

Justices White, Blackmun, and Stevens dissented from most of the decision in *New York*, agreeing only with the portions upholding the first two sets of incentives. Justice White emphasized that the statute "resulted from the efforts of state leaders to achieve a state-based set of remedies to the waste problem. They sought not federal pre-emption or intervention, but rather congressional sanction of interstate compromises they had reached." (The Governor of New York was one of those who had supported the statute.) Thus, he pointed to the "ultimate irony" of the decision, that "in its formalistically rigid obeisance to 'federalism,' the Court gives Congress fewer incentives to defer to the wishes of state officials in achieving local solutions to local problems." Justice White also contended that the Court drew an unsupported distinction "between a federal statute's regulation of States and private parties" and "a regulation solely on the activities of States."

Justice Stevens wrote a separate opinion, contesting the majority's historical account:

Under the Articles of Confederation, the Federal Government had the power to issue commands to the States. *See* Arts. of Confed. VIII, IX. Because that indirect exercise of federal power proved ineffective, the Framers of the Constitution empowered the Federal Government to exercise legislative authority directly over individuals within the States, even though that direct authority constituted a greater intrusion on state sovereignty. Nothing in that history suggests that the Federal Government may not also impose its will upon the several States as it did under the Articles. The Constitution enhanced, rather than diminished, the power of the Federal Government.

Indeed, he argued, the federal government "directs state governments in many realms," regulating the operations of state-operated railroads, school systems, prisons, and elections. Absent the statute, he said, if one state's radioactive waste harmed its neighbors, the Court would have had authority to require the state to take remedial action. "If this Court has such authority," he concluded, "surely Congress has similar authority."

Printz v. United States

Supreme Court of the United States, 1997.
521 U.S. 898.

JUSTICE SCALIA delivered the opinion of the Court.

The question presented in these cases is whether certain interim provisions of the Brady Handgun Violence Prevention Act, commanding state and local law enforcement officers to conduct background checks on prospective handgun purchasers and to perform certain related tasks, violate the Constitution.

I

The Gun Control Act of 1968 (GCA) establishes a detailed federal scheme governing the distribution of firearms. It prohibits firearms dealers from transferring handguns to any person under 21, not resident in the dealer's State, or prohibited by state or local law from purchasing or possessing firearms, § 922(b). It also forbids possession of a firearm by, and transfer of a firearm to, convicted felons, fugitives from justice, unlawful users of controlled substances, persons adjudicated as mentally defective or committed to mental institutions, aliens unlawfully present in the United States, persons dishonorably discharged from the Armed Forces, persons who have renounced their citizenship, and persons who have been subjected to certain restraining orders or been convicted of a misdemeanor offense involving domestic violence.

In 1993, Congress amended the GCA by enacting the Brady Act. The Act requires the Attorney General to establish a national instant background-check system by November 30, 1998 and immediately puts in place certain interim provisions until that system becomes operative. Under the interim provisions, a firearms dealer who proposes to transfer a handgun must first:

(1)   receive from the transferee a statement (the Brady Form) containing the name, address, and date of birth of the proposed transferee along with a sworn statement that the transferee is not among any of the classes of prohibited purchasers [specified in the GCA, *supra*];

(2)   verify the identity of the transferee by examining an identification document; and

(3)   provide the "chief law enforcement officer" (CLEO) of the transferee's residence with notice of the contents (and a copy) of the Brady Form.

With some exceptions, the dealer must then wait five business days before consummating the sale, unless the CLEO earlier notifies the dealer that he has no reason to believe the transfer would be illegal. . . .

In [many circumstances,] CLEOs are required to perform certain duties. When a CLEO receives the required notice of a proposed transfer from the firearms dealer, the CLEO must

make a reasonable effort to ascertain within 5 business days whether receipt or possession would be in violation of the law, including research in whatever State and local recordkeeping systems are available and in a national system designated by the Attorney General.

The Act does not require the CLEO to take any particular action if he determines that a pending transaction would be unlawful; he may notify the firearms dealer to that effect, but is not required to do so. If, however, the CLEO notifies a gun dealer that a prospective purchaser is ineligible to receive a handgun, he must, upon request, provide the would-be purchaser with a written statement of the reasons for that determination. Moreover, if the CLEO does not discover any basis for objecting to the sale, he must destroy any records in his possession relating to the transfer, including his copy of the Brady Form.

Under a separate provision of the GCA, any person who "knowingly violates [the section of the GCA amended by the Brady Act] shall be fined under this title, imprisoned for not more than 1 year, or both." § 924(a)(5).

Petitioners Jay Printz and Richard Mack, the CLEOs for Ravalli County, Montana, and Graham County, Arizona, respectively, filed separate actions challenging the constitutionality of the Brady Act's interim provisions. . . .

II

From the description set forth above, it is apparent that the Brady Act purports to direct state law enforcement officers to participate, albeit only temporarily, in the administration of a federally enacted regulatory scheme. . . . Petitioners here object to being pressed into federal service, and contend that congressional action compelling state officers to execute federal laws is unconstitutional. . . .

A

[T]he Framers rejected the concept of a central government that would act upon and through the States, and instead designed a system in which the State and Federal Governments would exercise concurrent authority over the people[.] We have set forth the historical record in more detail elsewhere, *see New York v. United States*, and need not repeat it here. It suffices to repeat the conclusion: "the Framers explicitly chose a Constitution that confers upon Congress the power to regulate individuals, not States."[10] . . . The power of the Federal Government would be augmented immeasurably if it were able to impress into its service—and at no cost to itself—the police officers of the 50 States.

B

[F]ederal control of state officers . . . would also have an effect upon . . . the separation and equilibration of powers between the three branches of the Federal Government itself. The Constitution does not leave to speculation who is to administer the laws enacted by Congress; the President, it says, "shall take Care that the Laws be faithfully executed," Art. II, § 3, personally and through officers whom he appoints (save for such inferior officers as Congress

---

[10]   The dissent, reiterating Justice Stevens' dissent in *New York*, maintains that the Constitution merely augmented the pre-existing power under the Articles to issue commands to the States with the additional power to make demands directly on individuals. That argument, however, was squarely rejected by the Court in *New York*[.]

may authorize to be appointed by the "Courts of Law" or by "the Heads of Departments" who are themselves Presidential appointees), Art. II, § 2.

The Brady Act effectively transfers this responsibility to thousands of CLEOs in the 50 States, who are left to implement the program without meaningful Presidential control (if indeed meaningful Presidential control is possible without the power to appoint and remove). The insistence of the Framers upon unity in the Federal Executive—to ensure both vigor and accountability—is well known. See *The Federalist* No. 70 (A. Hamilton); see also Calabresi & Prakash, *The President's Power to Execute the Laws*, 104 Yale L.J. 541 (1994). That unity would be shattered, and the power of the President would be subject to reduction, if Congress could act as effectively without the President as with him, by simply requiring state officers to execute its laws.[12]

The dissent of course resorts to the last, best hope of those who defend ultra vires congressional action, the Necessary and Proper Clause. It reasons that the power to regulate the sale of handguns under the Commerce Clause, coupled with the power to "make all Laws which shall be necessary and proper for carrying into Execution the foregoing Powers," Art. I, § 8, conclusively establishes the Brady Act's constitutional validity, because the Tenth Amendment imposes no limitations on the exercise of *delegated* powers but merely prohibits the exercise of powers "*not* delegated to the United States." What destroys the dissent's Necessary and Proper Clause argument, however, is not the Tenth Amendment but the Necessary and Proper Clause itself. When a "La[w] . . . for carrying into Execution" the Commerce Clause violates the principle of state sovereignty reflected in the various constitutional provisions we mentioned earlier, it is not a "La[w] . . . *proper* for carrying into Execution the Commerce Clause," and is thus, in the words of The Federalist, "merely [an] ac[t] of usurpation" which "deserve[s] to be treated as such." *The Federalist* No. 33 (A. Hamilton). . . .

IV

Finally, and most conclusively in the present litigation, we turn to the prior jurisprudence of this Court. . . .

[I]n *New York v. United States* (1992), [w]e concluded that Congress . . . "may not compel the States to enact or administer a federal regulatory

---

[12] The dissent is correct that control by the unitary Federal Executive is also sacrificed when States voluntarily administer federal programs, but the condition of voluntary state participation significantly reduces the ability of Congress to use this device as a means of reducing the power of the Presidency.

program." The Government contends that *New York* is distinguishable on the following ground: Unlike the "take title" provisions invalidated there, the background-check provision of the Brady Act does not require state legislative or executive officials to make policy, but instead issues a final directive to state CLEOs. It is permissible, the Government asserts, for Congress to command state or local officials to assist in the implementation of federal law so long as "Congress itself devises a clear legislative solution that regulates private conduct" and requires state or local officers to provide only "limited, non-policymaking help in enforcing that law." "[T]he constitutional line is crossed only when Congress compels the States to make law in their sovereign capacities." Brief for United States.

The Government's distinction between "making" law and merely "enforcing" it, between "policymaking" and mere "implementation," is an interesting one. It is perhaps not meant to be the same as, but it is surely reminiscent of, the line that separates proper congressional conferral of Executive power from unconstitutional delegation of legislative authority for federal separation-of-powers purposes. See *A.L.A. Schechter Poultry Corp. v. United States* (1935); *Panama Refining Co. v. Ryan* (1935). This Court has not been notably successful in describing the latter line; indeed, some think we have abandoned the effort to do so. We are doubtful that the new line the Government proposes would be any more distinct.

Executive action that has utterly no policymaking component is rare, particularly at an executive level as high as a jurisdiction's chief law enforcement officer. Is it really true that there is no policymaking involved in deciding, for example, what "reasonable efforts" shall be expended to conduct a background check? . . . Is this decision whether to devote maximum "reasonable efforts" or minimum "reasonable efforts" not preeminently a matter of policy? It is quite impossible, in short, to draw the Government's proposed line at "no policymaking," and we would have to fall back upon a line of "not too much policymaking." How much is too much is not likely to be answered precisely; and an imprecise barrier against federal intrusion upon state authority is not likely to be an effective one.

Even assuming, moreover, that the Brady Act leaves no "policymaking" discretion with the States, we fail to see how that improves rather than worsens the intrusion upon state sovereignty. Preservation of the States as independent and autonomous political entities is arguably less undermined by requiring them to make policy in certain fields than (as Judge Sneed aptly described it over two decades ago) by "reduc[ing] [them] to puppets of a ventriloquist Congress." *Brown v. EPA* (9th Cir. 1975). It is an essential attribute of the States' retained sovereignty that they remain independent and autonomous within their proper sphere of authority. It is no more compatible with this independence and autonomy that their officers be "dragooned" (as Judge Fernandez put it in his dissent below) into administering federal law, than it would be compatible with the independence and autonomy of the United States that its officers be impressed into service for the execution of state laws. . . .

The Government also maintains that requiring state officers to perform discrete, ministerial tasks specified by Congress does not violate the principle of *New York* because it does not diminish the accountability of state or federal officials. This argument fails even on its own terms. By forcing state governments to absorb the financial burden of implementing a federal regulatory program, Members of Congress can take credit for "solving" problems without having to ask their constituents to pay for the solutions with higher federal taxes. And even when the States are not forced to absorb the costs of implementing a federal program, they are still put in the position of taking the blame for its burdensomeness and for its defects. Under the present law, for example, it will be the CLEO and not some federal official who stands between the gun purchaser and immediate possession of his gun. And it will likely be the CLEO, not some federal official, who will be blamed for any error (even one in the designated federal database) that causes a purchaser to be mistakenly rejected. . . .

Finally, the Government puts forward a cluster of arguments that can be grouped under the heading: "The Brady Act serves very important purposes, is most efficiently administered by CLEOs during the interim period, and places a minimal and only temporary burden upon state officers." There is considerable disagreement over the extent of the burden, but we need not pause over that detail. [W]here, as here, it is the whole *object* of the law to direct the functioning of the state executive, and hence to compromise the structural framework of dual sovereignty, such a "balancing" analysis is inappropriate. It is the very *principle* of separate state sovereignty that such a law offends, and no comparative assessment of the various interests can overcome that fundamental defect. . . .

* * *

We held in *New York* that Congress cannot compel the States to enact or enforce a federal regulatory program. Today we hold that Congress cannot circumvent that prohibition by conscripting the State's officers directly. The Federal Government may neither issue directives requiring the States to address particular problems, nor command the States' officers, or those of their political subdivisions, to administer or enforce a federal regulatory program. It matters not whether policymaking is involved, and no case-by-case weighing of the burdens or benefits is necessary; such commands are fundamentally incompatible with our constitutional system of dual sovereignty. . . .

JUSTICE O'CONNOR, concurring.

. . . The Brady Act violates the Tenth Amendment to the extent it forces States and local law enforcement officers to perform background checks on prospective handgun owners and to accept Brady Forms from firearms dealers. Our holding, of course, does not spell the end of the objectives of the Brady Act. States and chief law enforcement officers may voluntarily continue to participate in the federal program. . . . Congress is also free to amend the interim program to provide for its continuance on a contractual basis with the States if it wishes, as it does with a number of other federal programs. See, *e.g.,* 23 U.S.C. § 402 (conditioning States' receipt of federal funds for highway safety program on compliance with federal requirements).

In addition, the Court appropriately refrains from deciding whether other purely ministerial reporting requirements imposed by Congress on state and local authorities pursuant to its Commerce Clause powers are similarly invalid. See, *e.g.,* 42 U.S.C. § 5779(a) (requiring state and local law enforcement agencies to report cases of missing children to the Department of Justice). The provisions invalidated here, however, which directly compel state officials to administer a federal regulatory program, utterly fail to adhere to the design and structure of our constitutional scheme.

JUSTICE THOMAS, concurring.

. . . Although I join the Court's opinion in full, I write separately to emphasize that . . . the Commerce Clause . . . does not extend to the regulation of wholly *intra*state, point-of-sale transactions. Absent the underlying authority to regulate the intrastate transfer of firearms, Congress surely lacks the corollary power to impress state law enforcement officers into administering and enforcing such regulations. . . .

JUSTICE STEVENS, with whom JUSTICE SOUTER, JUSTICE GINSBURG, and JUSTICE BREYER join, dissenting.

When Congress exercises the powers delegated to it by the Constitution, it may impose affirmative obligations on executive and judicial officers of state and local governments as well as ordinary citizens. This conclusion is firmly supported by the text of the Constitution, the early history of the Nation, decisions of this Court, and a correct understanding of the basic structure of the Federal Government.

These cases do not implicate the more difficult questions associated with congressional coercion of state legislatures addressed in *New York v. United States* (1992). Nor need we consider the wisdom of relying on local officials rather than federal agents to carry out aspects of a federal program, or even the question whether such officials may be required to perform a federal function on a permanent basis. The question is whether Congress, acting on behalf of the people of the entire Nation, may require local law enforcement officers to perform certain duties during the interim needed for the development of a federal gun control program. It is remarkably similar to the question, heavily debated by the Framers of the Constitution, whether Congress could require state agents to collect federal taxes. Or the question whether Congress could impress state judges into federal service to entertain and decide cases that they would prefer to ignore. . . .

There is not a clause, sentence, or paragraph in the entire text of the Constitution of the United States that supports the proposition that a local police officer can ignore a command contained in a statute enacted by Congress pursuant to an express delegation of power enumerated in Article I. . . .

Under the Articles of Confederation the National Government had the power to issue commands to the several sovereign States, but it had no authority to govern individuals directly. Thus, it raised an army and financed its operations by issuing requisitions to the constituent members of the Confederacy, rather than by creating federal agencies to draft soldiers or to impose taxes.

That method of governing proved to be unacceptable, not because it demeaned the sovereign character of the several States, but rather because it was cumbersome and inefficient. Indeed, a confederation that allows each of its members to determine the ways and means of complying with an overriding requisition is obviously more deferential to state sovereignty concerns than a National Government that uses its own agents to impose its will directly on the citizenry. The basic change in the character of the government that the Framers conceived was designed to enhance the power of the National Government, not to provide some new, unmentioned immunity for state officers. Because indirect control over individual citizens ("the only proper objects of government") was ineffective under the Articles of Confederation, Alexander Hamilton explained that "we must *extend* the authority of the Union to the persons of the citizens." *The Federalist* No. 15 (emphasis added).

Indeed, the historical materials strongly suggest that the founders intended to enhance the capacity of the Federal Government by empowering it—as a part of the new authority to make demands directly on individual citizens—to act through local officials. Hamilton made clear that the new Constitution, "by extending the authority of the federal head to the individual citizens of the several States, will enable the government to employ the ordinary magistracy of each in the execution of its laws." *The Federalist* No. 27. This point is made especially clear in Hamilton's statement that "the legislatures, courts, and magistrates, of the respective members, will be incorporated into the operations of the national government *as far as its just and constitutional authority extends; and will be rendered auxiliary to the enforcement of its laws.*" *Ibid.* (second emphasis added). It is hard to imagine a more unequivocal statement that state judicial and executive branch officials may be required to implement federal law where the National Government acts within the scope of its affirmative powers.

Absent even a modicum of textual foundation for its judicially crafted constitutional rule, there should be a presumption that if the Framers had actually intended such a rule, at least one of them would have mentioned it.[15]

The Court's "structural" arguments are not sufficient to rebut that presumption. The fact that the Framers intended to preserve the sovereignty of the several States simply does not speak to the question whether individual state employees may be required to perform federal obligations, such as registering young adults for the draft, 40 Stat. 80–81, creating state emergency response

---

[15]   Indeed, despite the exhaustive character of the Court's response to this dissent, it has failed to find even an iota of evidence that any of the Framers of the Constitution or any Member of Congress who supported or opposed the statutes discussed in the text ever expressed doubt as to the power of Congress to impose federal responsibilities on local judges or police officers. Even plausible rebuttals of evidence consistently pointing in the other direction are no substitute for affirmative evidence. In short, a neutral historian would have to conclude that the Court's discussion of history does not even begin to establish a prima facie case.

commissions designed to manage the release of hazardous substances, 42 U.S.C. §§ 11001, 11003, collecting and reporting data on underground storage tanks that may pose an environmental hazard, § 6991a, and reporting traffic fatalities, 23 U.S.C. § 402(a), and missing children, 42 U.S.C. § 5779(a), to a federal agency.

As we explained in *Garcia v. San Antonio Metropolitan Transit Authority* (1985): "[T]he principal means chosen by the Framers to ensure the role of the States in the federal system lies in the structure of the Federal Government itself." . . . Given the fact that the Members of Congress are elected by the people of the several States, with each State receiving an equivalent number of Senators in order to ensure that even the smallest States have a powerful voice in the Legislature, it is quite unrealistic to assume that they will ignore the sovereignty concerns of their constituents. It is far more reasonable to presume that their decisions to impose modest burdens on state officials from time to time reflect a considered judgment that the people in each of the States will benefit therefrom. . . .

Perversely, the majority's rule seems more likely to damage than to preserve the safeguards against tyranny provided by the existence of vital state governments. By limiting the ability of the Federal Government to enlist state officials in the implementation of its programs, the Court creates incentives for the National Government to aggrandize itself. In the name of State's rights, the majority would have the Federal Government create vast national bureaucracies to implement its policies. This is exactly the sort of thing that the early Federalists promised would not occur, in part as a result of the National Government's ability to rely on the magistracy of the States. *See, e.g.,* The Federalist No. 36 (A. Hamilton); *id.,* No. 45 (J. Madison).

[Justice Stevens discusses *Testa v. Katt* (1947), in which "the Court unanimously held that state courts of appropriate jurisdiction must occupy themselves adjudicating claims brought by private litigants under the federal Emergency Price Control Act of 1942, regardless of how otherwise crowded their dockets might be with state law matters."]

Accordingly, I respectfully dissent.

JUSTICE SOUTER, dissenting.

. . . In deciding these cases, which I have found closer than I had anticipated, it is *The Federalist* that finally determines my position. . . . I cannot persuade myself that the statements from No. 27 speak of anything less than the authority of the National Government, when exercising an otherwise legitimate power (the commerce power, say), to require state "auxiliaries" to take appropriate action. To be sure, it does not follow that any conceivable requirement may be imposed on any state official. I continue to agree, for example, that Congress may not require a state legislature to enact a regulatory scheme and that *New York v. United States* (1992) was rightly decided. . . .

JUSTICE BREYER, with whom JUSTICE STEVENS joins, dissenting.

[T]he United States is not the only nation that seeks to reconcile the practical need for a central authority with the democratic virtues of more local control. At least some other countries, facing the same basic problem, have found that local control is better maintained through application of a principle that is the direct opposite of the principle the majority derives from the silence of our Constitution. The federal systems of Switzerland, Germany, and the European Union, for example, all provide that constituent states, not federal bureaucracies, will themselves implement many of the laws, rules, regulations, or decrees enacted by the central "federal" body. . . .

Of course, we are interpreting our own Constitution, not those of other nations, and there may be relevant political and structural differences between their systems and our own. But their experience may nonetheless cast an empirical light on the consequences of different solutions to a common legal problem—in this case the problem of reconciling central authority with the need to preserve the liberty-enhancing autonomy of a smaller constituent governmental entity. And that experience here offers empirical confirmation of the implied answer to a question Justice Stevens asks: Why, or how, would what the majority sees as a constitutional alternative—the creation of a new federal gun-law bureaucracy, or the expansion of an existing federal bureaucracy—better promote either state sovereignty or individual liberty? . . .

Reno v. Condon

Supreme Court of the United States, 2000.
528 U.S. 141.

Rehnquist, C.J., delivered the opinion for a unanimous Court.

The Driver's Privacy Protection Act of 1994 (DPPA) regulates the disclosure of personal information contained in the records of state motor vehicle departments (DMVs). We hold that in enacting this statute Congress did not run afoul of the federalism principles enunciated in *New York v. United States* (1992) and *Printz v. United States* (1997).

The DPPA regulates the disclosure and resale of personal information contained in the records of state DMVs. State DMVs require drivers and automobile owners to provide personal information, which may include a person's name, address, telephone number, vehicle description, Social Security number, medical information, and photograph, as a condition of obtaining a driver's license or registering an automobile. Congress found that many States, in turn, sell this personal information to individuals and businesses. These sales generate significant revenues for the States. See *Travis v. Reno* (C.A.7 1998) (noting that the Wisconsin Department of Transportation receives approximately $8 million each year from the sale of motor vehicle information).

. . . The DPPA generally prohibits any state DMV, or officer, employee, or contractor thereof, from "knowingly disclos[ing] or otherwise mak[ing] available to any person or entity personal information about any individual obtained by the department in connection with a motor vehicle record." . . . The DPPA's ban on disclosure of personal information does not apply if drivers have consented to the release of their data. . . .

The DPPA's prohibition of nonconsensual disclosures is also subject to a number of statutory exceptions. For example, the DPPA *requires* disclosure of personal information "for use in connection with matters of motor vehicle or driver safety and theft, motor vehicle emissions, motor vehicle product alterations, recalls, or advisories, performance monitoring of motor vehicles and dealers by motor vehicle manufacturers, and removal of non-owner records from the original owner records of motor vehicle manufacturers to carry out the purposes of [various federal regulatory schemes]." The DPPA *permits* DMVs to disclose personal information from motor vehicle records for a number of [other] purposes. . . .

The DPPA's provisions do not apply solely to States. The Act also regulates the resale and redisclosure of drivers' personal information by private persons who have obtained that information from a state DMV. In general, the Act allows private persons who have obtained drivers' personal information for one of the aforementioned permissible purposes to further disclose that information for any one of those purposes. If a State has obtained drivers' consent to disclose their personal information to private persons generally and a private person has obtained that information, the private person may redisclose the information for any purpose. . . .

The United States asserts that the DPPA is a proper exercise of Congress' authority to regulate interstate commerce under the Commerce Clause. . . . We agree with the United States' contention. The motor vehicle information which the States have historically sold is used by insurers, manufacturers, direct marketers, and others engaged in interstate commerce to contact drivers with customized solicitations. The information is also used in the stream of interstate commerce by various public and private entities for matters related to interstate motoring. Because drivers' information is, in this context, an article of commerce, its sale or release into the interstate stream of business is sufficient to support congressional regulation. We therefore need not address the Government's alternative argument that the States' individual, intrastate activities in gathering, maintaining, and distributing drivers' personal information have a sufficiently substantial impact on interstate commerce to create a constitutional base for federal legislation.

But the fact that drivers' personal information is, in the context of this case, an article in interstate commerce does not conclusively resolve the constitutionality of the DPPA. In *New York* and *Printz,* we held federal statutes invalid, not because Congress lacked legislative authority over the subject matter, but because those statutes violated the principles of federalism contained in the Tenth Amendment. . . .

South Carolina contends that the DPPA violates the Tenth Amendment because it "thrusts upon the States all of the day-to-day responsibility for administering its complex provisions," and thereby makes "state officials the unwilling implementors of federal policy." South Carolina emphasizes that the DPPA requires the State's employees to learn and apply the Act's substantive restrictions, which are summarized above, and notes that these activities will consume the employees' time and thus the State's resources. South Carolina further notes that the DPPA's penalty provisions hang over the States as a potential punishment should they fail to comply with the Act.

We agree with South Carolina's assertion that the DPPA's provisions will require time and effort on the part of state employees, but reject the State's argument that the DPPA violates the principles laid down in either *New York* or *Printz*. We think, instead, that this case is governed by our decision in *South Carolina v. Baker* (1988). In *Baker*, we upheld a statute that prohibited States from issuing unregistered bonds because the law "regulate[d] state activities," rather than "seek[ing] to control or influence the manner in which States regulate private parties." We further noted: "Any federal regulation demands compliance. That a State wishing to engage in certain activity must take administrative and sometimes legislative action to comply with federal standards regulating that activity is a commonplace that presents no constitutional defect."

Like the statute at issue in *Baker*, the DPPA does not require the States in their sovereign capacity to regulate their own citizens. The DPPA regulates the States as the owners of data bases. It does not require the South Carolina Legislature to enact any laws or regulations, and it does not require state officials to assist in the enforcement of federal statutes regulating private individuals. We accordingly conclude that the DPPA is consistent with the constitutional principles enunciated in *New York* and *Printz*.

As a final matter, we turn to South Carolina's argument that the DPPA is unconstitutional because it regulates the States exclusively. The essence of South Carolina's argument is that Congress may only regulate the States by means of "generally applicable" laws, or laws that apply to individuals as well as States. But we need not address the question whether general applicability is a constitutional requirement for federal regulation of the States, because the DPPA is generally applicable. The DPPA regulates the universe of entities that participate as suppliers to the market for motor vehicle information—the States as initial suppliers of the information in interstate commerce and private resellers or redisclosers of that information in commerce.

The judgment of the Court of Appeals is therefore

Reversed.

7.   Bringing Things Together: *NFIB v. Sebelius*

Some constitutional cases are politically important. Some constitutional cases are legally important. Some constitutional cases are great teaching tools. The Court's decision in *National Federation of Independent Business v. Sebelius*, 567 U.S. 519 (2012) is all three. The case involved a set of constitutional challenges to "Obamacare," a statute more formally known as the Patient Protection and Affordable Care Act of 2010. The ACA represented the culmination of a decades-long effort by predominantly (but not exclusively) liberal policymakers to radically extend the scope and availability of health insurance coverage in the United States. For both political and policy reasons, Congress adopted a highly complicated system that involved subsidies to the states, subsidies to individuals, new obligations on insurance companies, and a mandate requiring all persons subject to the Act to purchase a health insurance policy. The challengers trained their fire on two key provisions of the Act. The resulting opinions conduct a sweeping survey of many of the federalism questions we've discussed so far: the Commerce Clause, the Necessary & Proper Clause, the Taxing Power, the Spending Power, and the Tenth Amendment.

In the first paragraph of his opinion, parts of which spoke for the Court, Chief Justice Roberts explained:

> Today we resolve constitutional challenges to two provisions of the Patient Protection and Affordable Care Act of 2010: the individual mandate, which requires individuals to purchase a health insurance policy providing a minimum level of coverage; and the Medicaid expansion, which gives funds to the States on the condition that they provide specified health care to all citizens whose income falls below a certain threshold. We do not consider whether the Act embodies sound policies. That judgment is entrusted to the Nation's elected leaders. We ask only whether Congress has the power under the Constitution to enact the challenged provisions.

Ultimately, five members of the Court—the Chief Justice and the four more conservative justices (Scalia, Kennedy, Thomas, and Alito)—held that the individual mandate could not be upheld as an exercise of Congress's commerce power. But another five-member majority—the Chief and the four more liberal justices (Ginsburg, Breyer, Sotomayor, and Kagan)—held that it could be upheld under Congress's taxing power. Seven justices (all but Ginsburg and

Sotomayor) concluded that the Medicaid expansion violated the Constitution by threatening states with the loss of their Medicaid funding under previously enacted statutes if they declined to comply with the expansion. But five justices (the same group that upheld the mandate) concluded that the threatened loss of Medicaid funds was severable from the rest of the statute.

WORTH NOTING

We speak of the Court holding that the Medicaid expansion was unconstitutional, because that is the way the justices spoke of the issue. But it is important to understand that what the Court held unconstitutional was not the expansion of Medicaid in itself but the condition that if a state did not accept the expansion it would lose funds under previously legislated Medicaid programs. To date, 39 states (including the District of Columbia) have accepted the expansion.

Part I of the Chief Justice's opinion laid out the terms of the Act; Part II discussed whether the Anti-Injunction Act barred a challenge to the mandate. Part III-A addressed the Commerce Clause, Parts III-B and C addressed the taxing power, and Part III-D defended inclusion of the portion on the commerce power. Part IV addressed the Medicaid expansion, including the severability issue. All four liberals joined Parts I, II, and III-C of the Chief's opinion. Justice Scalia wrote a dissent, joined by Justices Kennedy, Thomas, and Alito. While the dissenters did not join any part of the Chief Justice's opinion, they agreed with his bottom-line conclusion about the Commerce Clause and Spending Power—which meant that he was able to form a majority on those issues. Justice Thomas also wrote a brief opinion on the commerce issue.

You can get a sense of the complexity of the Court's decision from the beginning of the report of the Chief Justice's opinion:

WORTH NOTING

Chief Justice Roberts announced the judgment of the Court and delivered the opinion of the Court with respect to Parts I, II, and III-C, an opinion with respect to Part IV, in which Justice Breyer and Justice Kagan join, and an opinion with respect to Parts III-A, III-B, and III-D.

As You READ These long and complex opinions are presented here as follows. Section (a) lays out the background of the case with excerpts from the opinions by the Chief Justice and Justice Ginsburg. Section (b) presents a general discussion of federalism offered by the Chief Justice at the outset of his opinion. Sections (c) and (d) then present excerpts from the opinions dealing with the Commerce Clause and Tax Power issues, respectively. Section (e) presents excerpts from the opinions on the spending issue, and Section (f) presents excerpts on severability. To avoid confusion, in presenting this case our own text will be left- and right-indented and set off by divider lines, while the justices' opinions will span the full width of the page.

a. **Background of the Litigation**

The Court's four more liberal members joined this portion of the Chief Justice's opinion, which thus speaks for a five-member majority.

CHIEF JUSTICE ROBERTS . . . :

In 2010, Congress enacted the Patient Protection and Affordable Care Act. The Act aims to increase the number of Americans covered by health insurance and decrease the cost of health care. The Act's 10 titles stretch over 900 pages and contain hundreds of provisions. This case concerns constitutional challenges to two key provisions, commonly referred to as the individual mandate and the Medicaid expansion.

The individual mandate requires most Americans to maintain "minimum essential" health insurance coverage. 26 U.S.C. § 5000A. The mandate does not apply to some individuals, such as prisoners and undocumented aliens. Many individuals will receive the required coverage through their employer, or from a government program such as Medicaid or Medicare. But for individuals who are not exempt and do not receive health insurance through a third party, the means of satisfying the requirement is to purchase insurance from a private company.

Beginning in 2014, those who do not comply with the mandate must make a "[s]hared responsibility payment" to the Federal Government. § 5000A(b)(1). That payment, which the Act describes as a "penalty," is calculated as a percentage of household income, subject to a floor based on a specified dollar amount and a ceiling based on the average annual premium the individual would have to pay for qualifying private health insurance. In 2016, for example, the penalty will be 2.5 percent of an individual's household income, but no less than $695 and no more than the average yearly premium for insurance that covers 60 percent of the cost of 10 specified services (*e.g.*, prescription drugs and hospitalization). The Act provides that the penalty will be paid to the Internal Revenue Service with an individual's taxes, and "shall be assessed and collected in the same manner" as tax penalties, such as the penalty for claiming too large an income tax refund. The Act, however, bars the IRS from using several of its normal enforcement tools, such as criminal prosecutions and levies. And some individuals who are subject to the mandate are nonetheless exempt from the penalty—for example, those with income below a certain threshold and members of Indian tribes.

On the day the President signed the Act into law, Florida and 12 other States filed a complaint in the Federal District Court for the Northern District of Florida. Those plaintiffs . . . were subsequently joined by 13 more States, several individuals, and the National Federation of Independent Business. The plaintiffs alleged, among other things, that the individual mandate provisions of the Act exceeded Congress's powers under Article I of the Constitution. . . .

JUSTICE GINSBURG, with whom JUSTICE SOTOMAYOR[,] JUSTICE BREYER[,] and JUSTICE KAGAN join as to [this part], concurring in part, concurring in the judgment in part, and dissenting in part.

[I.]A

In enacting the Patient Protection and Affordable Care Act (ACA), Congress comprehensively reformed the national market for health-care products and services. By any measure, that market is immense. Collectively, Americans spent $2.5 trillion on health care in 2009, accounting for 17.6% of our Nation's economy. Within the next decade, it is anticipated, spending on health care will nearly double.

The health-care market's size is not its only distinctive feature. Unlike the market for almost any other product or service, the market for medical care is one in which all individuals inevitably participate. Virtually every person residing in the United States, sooner or later, will visit a doctor or other health-care professional. See Dept. of Health and Human Services, *Summary Health Statistics for U.S. Adults* (Over 99.5% of adults above 65 have visited a health-care professional.). Most people will do so repeatedly. See *id.* (In 2009 alone, 64% of adults made two or more visits to a doctor's office.) . . .

When individuals make those visits, they face another reality of the current market for medical care: its high cost. In 2010, on average, an individual in the United States incurred over $7,000 in health-care expenses. . . . When a person requires nonroutine care, the cost will generally exceed what he or she can afford to pay. [And although] every U.S. domiciliary will incur significant medical expenses during his or her lifetime, the time when care will be needed is often unpredictable. An accident, a heart attack, or a cancer diagnosis commonly occurs without warning. Inescapably, we are all at peril of needing medical care without a moment's notice.

To manage the risks associated with medical care—its high cost, its unpredictability, and its inevitability—most people in the United States obtain health insurance. . . . Not all U.S. residents, however, have health insurance. In 2009, approximately 50 million people were uninsured, either by choice or, more likely, because they could not afford private insurance and did not qualify for government aid. As a group, uninsured individuals annually consume more than $100 billion in healthcare services, nearly 5% of the Nation's total. Over 60% of those without insurance visit a doctor's office or emergency room in a given year.

B

The large number of individuals without health insurance, Congress found, heavily burdens the national health-care market. As just noted, the cost of emergency care or treatment for a serious illness generally exceeds what an individual can afford to pay on her own. Unlike markets for most products, however, the inability to pay for care does not mean that an uninsured individual will receive no care. Federal and state law, as well as professional obligations and embedded social norms, require hospitals and physicians to provide care when it is most needed, regardless of the patient's ability to pay. As a consequence, medical-care providers deliver significant amounts of care to the uninsured for which the providers receive no payment. . . .

Health-care providers do not absorb these bad debts. Instead, they raise their prices, passing along the cost of uncompensated care to those who do pay reliably: the government and private insurance companies. In response, private insurers increase their premiums, shifting the cost of the elevated bills from providers onto those who carry insurance. The net result: Those with health insurance subsidize the medical care of those without it. As economists would describe what happens, the uninsured "free ride" on those who pay for health insurance. The size of this subsidy is considerable. Congress found that the cost-shifting just described "increases family [insurance] premiums by on average over $1,000 a year." Higher premiums, in turn, render health insurance less affordable, forcing more people to go without insurance and leading to further cost-shifting. . . .

The failure of individuals to acquire insurance has other deleterious effects on the health-care market. Because those without insurance generally lack access to preventative care, they do not receive treatment for conditions—like hypertension and diabetes—that can be successfully and affordably treated if diagnosed early on. When sickness finally drives the uninsured to seek care, once treatable conditions have escalated into grave health problems, requiring more costly and extensive intervention. . . .

C

States cannot resolve the problem of the uninsured on their own. Like Social Security benefits, a universal health-care system, if adopted by an individual State, would be "bait to the needy and dependent elsewhere, encouraging them to migrate and seek a haven of repose." *Helvering v. Davis* (1937). An influx of unhealthy individuals into a State with universal health care would result in increased spending on medical services. To cover the increased costs, a State would have to raise taxes, and private health-insurance companies would have to increase premiums. Higher taxes and increased insurance costs would, in turn, encourage businesses and healthy individuals to leave the State.

States that undertake health-care reforms on their own thus risk "placing themselves in a position of economic disadvantage as compared with neighbors or competitors." . . . Facing that risk, individual States are unlikely to take the initiative in addressing the problem of the uninsured, even though solving that problem is in all States' best interests. Congress' intervention was needed to overcome this collective-action impasse.

D

Aware that a national solution was required, Congress could have taken over the health-insurance market by establishing a tax-and-spend federal program like Social Security. Such a program, commonly referred to as a single-payer system (where the sole payer is the Federal Government), would have left little, if any, room for private enterprise or the States. Instead of going this route, Congress enacted the ACA, a solution that retains a robust role for private insurers and state governments. . . .

Of particular concern to Congress were people who, though desperately in need of insurance, often cannot acquire it: persons who suffer from preexisting medical conditions. Before the ACA's enactment, private insurance companies took an applicant's medical history into account when setting insurance rates or deciding whether to insure an individual. Because individuals with preexisting medical conditions cost insurance companies significantly more than those without such conditions, insurers routinely refused to insure these individuals, charged them substantially higher premiums, or offered only limited coverage that did not include the preexisting illness.

To ensure that individuals with medical histories have access to affordable insurance, Congress devised a three-part solution. First, Congress imposed a "guaranteed issue" requirement, which bars insurers from denying coverage to any person on account of that person's medical condition or history. Second, Congress required insurers to use "community rating" to price their insurance policies. Community rating, in effect, bars insurance companies from charging higher premiums to those with preexisting conditions.

But these two provisions, Congress comprehended, could not work effectively unless individuals were given a powerful incentive to obtain insurance.

In the 1990's, several States—including New York, New Jersey, Washington, Kentucky, Maine, New Hampshire, and Vermont—enacted guaranteed-issue and community-rating laws without requiring universal acquisition of insurance coverage. The results were disastrous. "All seven states suffered from skyrocketing insurance premium costs, reductions in individuals with coverage, and reductions in insurance products and providers." Brief for American Association of People with Disabilities as *Amicus Curiae*. See also Brief for Governor of Washington Christine Gregoire as *Amicus Curiae* (describing the "death spiral" in the insurance market Washington experienced when the State passed a law requiring coverage for preexisting conditions).

Congress comprehended that guaranteed-issue and community-rating laws alone will not work. When insurance companies are required to insure the sick at affordable prices, individuals can wait until they become ill to buy insurance. Pretty soon, those in need of immediate medical care—*i.e.*, those who cost insurers the most—become the insurance companies' main customers. This "adverse selection" problem leaves insurers with two choices: They can either raise premiums dramatically to cover their ever-increasing costs or they can exit the market. In the seven States that tried guaranteed-issue and community-rating requirements without a minimum coverage provision, that is precisely what insurance companies did. [Citing evidence that Maine, New York, and Kentucky suffered a "dramatic exodus" of insurers and a "doubl[ing of] premiums."]

Massachusetts, Congress was told, cracked the adverse selection problem. By requiring most residents to obtain insurance, see Mass. Gen. Laws, ch. 111M, § 2, the Commonwealth ensured that insurers would not be left with only the sick as customers. As a result, federal lawmakers observed, Massachusetts succeeded where other States had failed. See Brief for Commonwealth of Massachusetts as *Amicus Curiae* (noting that the Commonwealth's reforms reduced the number of uninsured residents to less than 2%, the lowest rate in the Nation, and cut the amount of uncompensated care by a third). In coupling the minimum coverage provision with guaranteed-issue and community-rating prescriptions, Congress followed Massachusetts' lead.

In sum, Congress passed the minimum coverage provision as a key component of the ACA to address an economic and social problem that has plagued the Nation for decades: the large number of U.S. residents who are unable or unwilling to obtain health insurance. . . .

---

b.　An Essay on Federalism

After the first paragraph of his opinion, the Chief Justice turned to an extensive discussion on federalism. It is not clear that any other justice joined this discussion, because it comes before Part I; the reporter's comment indicating who joined portions of the opinion makes no mention of this discussion.

In our federal system, the National Government possesses only limited powers; the States and the people retain the remainder. Nearly two centuries ago, Chief Justice Marshall observed that "the question respecting the extent of the powers actually granted" to the Federal Government "is perpetually arising, and will probably continue to arise, as long as our system shall exist." *McCulloch v. Maryland* (1819). In this case we must again determine whether the Constitution grants Congress powers it now asserts, but which many States and individuals believe it does not possess. Resolving this controversy requires us to examine both the limits of the Government's power, and our own limited role in policing those boundaries.

The Federal Government "is acknowledged by all to be one of enumerated powers." *Ibid.* That is, rather than granting general authority to perform all the conceivable functions of government, the Constitution lists, or enumerates, the Federal Government's powers. Congress may, for example, "coin Money," "establish Post Offices," and "raise and support Armies." Art. I, § 8. The enumeration of powers is also a limitation of powers, because "[t]he enumeration presupposes something not enumerated." *Gibbons v. Ogden* (1824). The Constitution's express conferral of some powers makes clear that it does not grant others. And the Federal Government "can exercise only the powers granted to it." *McCulloch.*

Today, the restrictions on government power foremost in many Americans' minds are likely to be affirmative prohibitions, such as contained in the Bill of Rights. These affirmative prohibitions come into play, however, only where the Government possesses authority to act in the first place. If no enumerated power authorizes Congress to pass a certain law, that law may not be enacted, even if it would not violate any of the express prohibitions in the Bill of Rights or elsewhere in the Constitution.

Indeed, the Constitution did not initially include a Bill of Rights at least partly because the Framers felt the enumeration of powers sufficed to restrain the Government. As Alexander Hamilton put it, "the Constitution is itself, in every rational sense, and to every useful purpose, a bill of rights." The Federalist No. 84. And when the Bill of Rights was ratified, it made express what the enumeration of powers necessarily implied: "The powers not delegated to the United States by the Constitution . . . are reserved to the States respectively, or to the people." Amdt. 10. The Federal Government has expanded dramatically over the past two centuries, but it still must show that a constitutional grant of power authorizes each of its actions. See, *e.g., United States v. Comstock* (2010).

The same does not apply to the States, because the Constitution is not the source of their power. The Constitution may restrict state governments—as it does, for example, by forbidding them to deny any person the equal protection of the laws. But where such prohibitions do not apply, state governments do not need constitutional authorization to act. The States thus can and do perform many of the vital functions of modern government—punishing street crime, running public schools, and zoning property for development, to name but a few—even though the Constitution's text does not authorize any government to do so. Our cases refer to this general power of governing, possessed by the States but not by the Federal Government, as the "police power." See, *e.g.*, *United States v. Morrison* (2000). . . .

This case concerns two powers that the Constitution does grant the Federal Government, but which must be read carefully to avoid creating a general federal authority akin to the police power. The Constitution authorizes Congress to "regulate Commerce with foreign Nations, and among the several States, and with the Indian Tribes." Art. I, § 8. Our precedents read that to mean that Congress may regulate "the channels of interstate commerce," "persons or things in interstate commerce," and "those activities that substantially affect interstate commerce." The power over activities that substantially affect interstate commerce can be expansive. That power has been held to authorize federal regulation of such seemingly local matters as a farmer's decision to grow wheat for himself and his livestock, and a loan shark's extortionate collections from a neighborhood butcher shop. See *Wickard v. Filburn* (1942); *Perez v. United States* (1971).

Congress may also "lay and collect Taxes, Duties, Imposts and Excises, to pay the Debts and provide for the common Defence and general Welfare of the United States." U.S. Const., Art. I, § 8. Put simply, Congress may tax and spend. This grant gives the Federal Government considerable influence even in areas where it cannot directly regulate. The Federal Government may enact a tax on an activity that it cannot authorize, forbid, or otherwise control. See, *e.g.*, *License Tax Cases* (1867). And in exercising its spending power, Congress may offer funds to the States, and may condition those offers on compliance with specified conditions. See, *e.g.*, *College Savings Bank v. Florida Prepaid Postsecondary Ed. Expense Bd.* (1999). These offers may well induce the States to adopt policies that the Federal Government itself could not impose. See, *e.g.*, *South Dakota v. Dole* (1987) (conditioning federal highway funds on States raising their drinking age to 21).

The reach of the Federal Government's enumerated powers is broader still because the Constitution authorizes Congress to "make all Laws which shall be necessary and proper for carrying into Execution the foregoing Powers." Art.

I, § 8. We have long read this provision to give Congress great latitude in exercising its powers: "Let the end be legitimate, let it be within the scope of the constitution, and all means which are appropriate, which are plainly adapted to that end, which are not prohibited, but consist with the letter and spirit of the constitution, are constitutional." *McCulloch*.

Our permissive reading of these powers is explained in part by a general reticence to invalidate the acts of the Nation's elected leaders. "Proper respect for a coordinate branch of the government" requires that we strike down an Act of Congress only if "the lack of constitutional authority to pass [the] act in question is clearly demonstrated." *United States v. Harris* (1883). Members of this Court are vested with the authority to interpret the law; we possess neither the expertise nor the prerogative to make policy judgments. Those decisions are entrusted to our Nation's elected leaders, who can be thrown out of office if the people disagree with them. It is not our job to protect the people from the consequences of their political choices.

Our deference in matters of policy cannot, however, become abdication in matters of law. "The powers of the legislature are defined and limited; and that those limits may not be mistaken, or forgotten, the constitution is written." *Marbury v. Madison* (1803). . . . And there can be no question that it is the responsibility of this Court to enforce the limits on federal power by striking down acts of Congress that transgress those limits. *Marbury*.

The questions before us must be considered against the background of these basic principles.

---

c.   **Commerce Clause**

This portion of the Chief Justice's opinion spoke only for himself, though the four conservative justices agreed with its substance.

CHIEF JUSTICE ROBERTS . . . :

III

The Government advances two theories for the proposition that Congress had constitutional authority to enact the individual mandate. . . .

A

The Government's first argument is that the individual mandate is a valid exercise of Congress's power under the Commerce Clause and the Necessary and Proper Clause. . . .

In the Affordable Care Act, Congress addressed the problem of those who cannot obtain insurance coverage because of preexisting conditions or other health issues. It did so through the Act's "guaranteed-issue" and "community-rating" provisions. These provisions together prohibit insurance companies from denying coverage to those with such conditions or charging unhealthy individuals higher premiums than healthy individuals.

The guaranteed-issue and community-rating reforms do not, however, address the issue of healthy individuals who choose not to purchase insurance to cover potential health care needs. In fact, the reforms sharply exacerbate that problem, by providing an incentive for individuals to delay purchasing health insurance until they become sick, relying on the promise of guaranteed and affordable coverage. The reforms also threaten to impose massive new costs on insurers, who are required to accept unhealthy individuals but prohibited from charging them rates necessary to pay for their coverage. This will lead insurers to significantly increase premiums on everyone.

The individual mandate was Congress's solution to these problems. By requiring that individuals purchase health insurance, the mandate prevents cost shifting by those who would otherwise go without it. In addition, the mandate forces into the insurance risk pool more healthy individuals, whose premiums on average will be higher than their health care expenses. This allows insurers to subsidize the costs of covering the unhealthy individuals the reforms require them to accept. The Government claims that Congress has power under the Commerce and Necessary and Proper Clauses to enact this solution.

1

The Government contends that the individual mandate is within Congress's power because the failure to purchase insurance "has a substantial and deleterious effect on interstate commerce" by creating the cost-shifting problem. The path of our Commerce Clause decisions has not always run smooth, see *United States v. Lopez* (1995), but it is now well established that Congress has broad authority under the Clause. We have recognized, for example, that "[t]he power of Congress over interstate commerce is not confined to the regulation of commerce among the states," but extends to activities that "have a substantial effect on interstate commerce." *United States v. Darby* (1941). Congress's power, moreover, is not limited to regulation of an activity that by itself substantially affects interstate commerce, but also extends to activities that do so only when aggregated with similar activities of others. See *Wickard*.

Given its expansive scope, it is no surprise that Congress has employed the commerce power in a wide variety of ways to address the pressing needs of the time. But Congress has never attempted to rely on that power to compel individuals not engaged in commerce to purchase an unwanted product.[3] Legislative novelty is not necessarily fatal; there is a first time for everything. . . . At the very least, we should "pause to consider the implications of the Government's arguments" when confronted with such new conceptions of federal power. *Lopez*.

The Constitution grants Congress the power to "*regulate* Commerce." Art. I, § 8 (emphasis added). The power to *regulate* commerce presupposes the existence of commercial activity to be regulated. If the power to "regulate" something included the power to create it, many of the provisions in the Constitution would be superfluous. For example, the Constitution gives Congress the power to "coin Money," in addition to the power to "regulate the Value thereof." *Id*. And it gives Congress the power to "raise and support Armies" and to "provide and maintain a Navy," in addition to the power to "make Rules for the Government and Regulation of the land and naval Forces." *Id*. If the power to regulate the Armed Forces or the value of money included the power to bring the subject of the regulation into existence, the specific grant of such powers would have been unnecessary. The language of the Constitution reflects the natural understanding that the power to regulate assumes there is already something to be regulated.[4]

---

[3]   The examples of other congressional mandates cited by Justice Ginsburg . . . are not to the contrary. Each of those mandates—to report for jury duty, to register for the draft, to purchase firearms in anticipation of militia service, to exchange gold currency for paper currency, and to file a tax return—are based on constitutional provisions other than the Commerce Clause. See Art. I, § 8, cl. 9 (to "constitute Tribunals inferior to the supreme Court"); *id.*, cl. 12 (to "raise and support Armies"); *id.*, cl. 16 (to "provide for organizing, arming, and disciplining, the Militia"); *id.*, cl. 5 (to "coin Money"); *id.*, cl. 1 (to "lay and collect Taxes").

[4]   Justice Ginsburg suggests that "at the time the Constitution was framed, to 'regulate' meant, among other things, to require action." But to reach this conclusion, the case cited by Justice Ginsburg relied on a dictionary in which "[t]o order; to command" was the fifth-alternative definition of "to direct," which was itself the second-alternative definition of "to regulate." *Post* (citing S. Johnson, *Dictionary of the English Language* (1773)). It is unlikely that the Framers had such an obscure meaning in mind when they used the word "regulate." Far more commonly, "[t]o regulate" meant "[t]o adjust by rule or method," which presupposes something to adjust. See also *Gibbons* (defining the commerce power as the power "to prescribe the rule by which commerce is to be governed").

Our precedent also reflects this understanding. As expansive as our cases construing the scope of the commerce power have been, they all have one thing in common: They uniformly describe the power as reaching "activity." It is nearly impossible to avoid the word when quoting them. *See, e.g., Lopez* ("Where economic activity substantially affects interstate commerce, legislation regulating that activity will be sustained"); *Perez* ("Where the *class of activities* is regulated and that *class* is within the reach of federal power, the courts have no power to excise, as trivial, individual instances of the class" (emphasis in original)); *Wickard* ("[E]ven if appellee's activity be local and though it may not be regarded as commerce, it may still, whatever its nature, be reached by Congress if it exerts a substantial economic effect on interstate commerce"); *NLRB v. Jones & Laughlin Steel Corp.* (1937) [(recognizing congressional power over "activities [that] have such a close and substantial relation to interstate commerce that their control is essential or appropriate to protect that commerce")].[5]

The individual mandate, however, does not regulate existing commercial activity. It instead compels individuals to *become* active in commerce by purchasing a product, on the ground that their failure to do so affects interstate commerce. Construing the Commerce Clause to permit Congress to regulate individuals precisely *because* they are doing nothing would open a new and potentially vast domain to congressional authority. Every day individuals do not do an infinite number of things. In some cases they decide not to do something; in others they simply fail to do it. Allowing Congress to justify federal regulation by pointing to the effect of inaction on commerce would bring countless decisions an individual could *potentially* make within the scope of federal regulation, and—under the Government's theory—empower Congress to make those decisions for him.

Applying the Government's logic to the familiar case of *Wickard v. Filburn* shows how far that logic would carry us from the notion of a government of limited powers. . . . *Wickard* has long been regarded as "perhaps the most far reaching example of Commerce Clause authority over intrastate activity," *Lopez*, but the Government's theory in this case would go much further. . . . The farmer in *Wickard* was at least actively engaged in the production of wheat, and

---

[5]   Justice Ginsburg cites two eminent domain cases from the 1890s to support the proposition that our case law does not "toe the activity versus inactivity line." *Post* (citing *Monongahela Nav. Co. v. United States* (1893), and *Cherokee Nation v. Southern Kansas R. Co.* (1890)). The fact that the Fifth Amendment requires the payment of just compensation when the Government exercises its power of eminent domain does not turn the taking into a commercial transaction between the landowner and the Government, let alone a government-compelled transaction between the landowner and a third party.

the Government could regulate that activity because of its effect on commerce. The Government's theory here would effectively override that limitation, by establishing that individuals may be regulated under the Commerce Clause whenever enough of them are not doing something the Government would have them do.

Indeed, the Government's logic would justify a mandatory purchase to solve almost any problem. To consider a different example in the health care market, many Americans do not eat a balanced diet. That group makes up a larger percentage of the total population than those without health insurance. The failure of that group to have a healthy diet increases health care costs to a greater extent than the failure of the uninsured to purchase insurance. Those increased costs are borne in part by other Americans who must pay more, just as the uninsured shift costs to the insured. Congress addressed the insurance problem by ordering everyone to buy insurance. Under the Government's theory, Congress could address the diet problem by ordering everyone to buy vegetables.

People, for reasons of their own, often fail to do things that would be good for them or good for society. Those failures—joined with the similar failures of others—can readily have a substantial effect on interstate commerce. Under the Government's logic, that authorizes Congress to use its commerce power to compel citizens to act as the Government would have them act.

 WORTH NOTING Hypothetical federal mandates to buy vegetables—particularly broccoli—featured prominently throughout the litigation, leading Justice Ginsburg to coin a new term, "the broccoli horrible." In another portion of the opinion, the Chief Justice dismissed the Government's argument that health insurance is not bought for its own sake but as a means to an end; broccoli, he said, is bought "to cover the need for . . . food."

That is not the country the Framers of our Constitution envisioned. . . . Congress already enjoys vast power to regulate much of what we do. Accepting the Government's theory would give Congress the same license to regulate what we do not do, fundamentally changing the relation between the citizen and the Federal Government.[6]

---

[6]   In an attempt to recast the individual mandate as a regulation of commercial activity, Justice Ginsburg suggests that "[a]n individual who opts not to purchase insurance from a private insurer can be seen as actively selecting another form of insurance: self-insurance." But "self-insurance" is, in this context, nothing more than

To an economist, perhaps, there is no difference between activity and inactivity; both have measurable economic effects on commerce. But the distinction between doing something and doing nothing would not have been lost on the Framers, who were "practical statesmen," not metaphysical philosophers. As we have explained, "the framers of the Constitution were not mere visionaries, toying with speculations or theories, but practical men, dealing with the facts of political life as they understood them, putting into form the government they were creating, and prescribing in language clear and intelligible the powers that government was to take." *South Carolina v. United States* (1905). The Framers gave Congress the power to *regulate* commerce, not to *compel* it, and for over 200 years both our decisions and Congress's actions have reflected this understanding. There is no reason to depart from that understanding now.

The Government sees things differently. It argues that because sickness and injury are unpredictable but unavoidable, "the uninsured as a class are active in the market for health care, which they regularly seek and obtain." The individual mandate "merely regulates how individuals finance and pay for that active participation—requiring that they do so through insurance, rather than through attempted self-insurance with the back-stop of shifting costs to others."

The Government repeats the phrase "active in the market for health care" throughout its brief, but that concept has no constitutional significance. An individual who bought a car two years ago and may buy another in the future is not "active in the car market" in any pertinent sense. The phrase "active in the market" cannot obscure the fact that most of those regulated by the individual mandate are not currently engaged in any commercial activity involving health care, and that fact is fatal to the Government's effort to "regulate the uninsured as a class." Our precedents recognize Congress's power to regulate "class[es] of *activities*," *Gonzales v. Raich* (2005) (emphasis added), not classes of *individuals*, apart from any activity in which they are engaged. . . .

The Government, however, claims that this does not matter. The Government regards it as sufficient to trigger Congress's authority that almost all those who are uninsured will, at some unknown point in the future, engage in a health care transaction. Asserting that "[t]here is no temporal limitation in the Commerce Clause," the Government argues that because "[e]veryone

---

a description of the failure to purchase insurance. Individuals are no more "activ[e] in the self-insurance market" when they fail to purchase insurance than they are active in the "rest" market when doing nothing.

subject to this regulation is in or will be in the health care market," they can be "regulated in advance."

The proposition that Congress may dictate the conduct of an individual today because of prophesied future activity finds no support in our precedent. We have said that Congress can anticipate the *effects* on commerce of an economic activity. But we have never permitted Congress to anticipate that activity itself in order to regulate individuals not currently engaged in commerce. Each one of our cases, including those cited by Justice Ginsburg, involved preexisting economic activity. See, *e.g.*, *Wickard* (producing wheat); *Raich* (growing marijuana). . . .

[F]or most of those targeted by the mandate, significant health care needs will be years, or even decades, away. The proximity and degree of connection between the mandate and the subsequent commercial activity is too lacking to justify an exception of the sort urged by the Government. The individual mandate forces individuals into commerce precisely because they elected to refrain from commercial activity. Such a law cannot be sustained under a clause authorizing Congress to "regulate Commerce."

2

The Government next contends that Congress has the power under the Necessary and Proper Clause to enact the individual mandate because the mandate is an "integral part of a comprehensive scheme of economic regulation"—the guaranteed-issue and community-rating insurance reforms. Under this argument, it is not necessary to consider the effect that an individual's inactivity may have on interstate commerce; it is enough that Congress regulate commercial activity in a way that requires regulation of inactivity to be effective.

The power to "make all Laws which shall be necessary and proper for carrying into Execution" the powers enumerated in the Constitution vests Congress with authority to enact provisions "incidental to the [enumerated] power, and conducive to its beneficial exercise," *McCulloch*. Although the Clause gives Congress authority to "legislate on that vast mass of incidental powers which must be involved in the constitution," it does not license the exercise of any "great substantive and independent power[s]" beyond those specifically enumerated. *Id.* Instead, the Clause is " 'merely a declaration, for the removal of all uncertainty, that the means of carrying into execution those [powers] otherwise granted are included in the grant.' " *Kinsella v. United States ex rel. Singleton* (1960) (quoting James Madison).

As our jurisprudence under the Necessary and Proper Clause has developed, we have been very deferential to Congress's determination that a regulation is "necessary." We have thus upheld laws that are " 'convenient, or useful' or 'conducive' to the authority's 'beneficial exercise.' " *United States v. Comstock* (2010) (quoting *McCulloch*). But we have also carried out our responsibility to declare unconstitutional those laws that undermine the structure of government established by the Constitution. Such laws, which are not "consist[ent] with the letter and spirit of the constitution," *McCulloch*, are not "*proper* [means] for carrying into Execution" Congress's enumerated powers. Rather, they are, "in the words of The Federalist, 'merely acts of usurpation' which 'deserve to be treated as such.' " *Printz v. United States* (1997) (quoting *The Federalist* No. 33 (A. Hamilton)).

Applying these principles, the individual mandate cannot be sustained under the Necessary and Proper Clause as an essential component of the insurance reforms. Each of our prior cases upholding laws under that Clause involved exercises of authority derivative of, and in service to, a granted power. For example, we have upheld provisions permitting continued confinement of those *already in federal custody* when they could not be safely released, *Comstock*; criminalizing bribes involving organizations *receiving federal funds*, *Sabri v. United States* (2004); and tolling state statutes of limitations while cases are *pending in federal court*, *Jinks v. Richland County* (2003). The individual mandate, by contrast, vests Congress with the extraordinary ability to create the necessary predicate to the exercise of an enumerated power.

This is in no way an authority that is "narrow in scope," *Comstock*, or "incidental" to the exercise of the commerce power, *McCulloch*. Rather, such a conception of the Necessary and Proper Clause would work a substantial expansion of federal authority. No longer would Congress be limited to regulating under the Commerce Clause those who by some preexisting activity bring themselves within the sphere of federal regulation. Instead, Congress could reach beyond the natural limit of its authority and draw within its regulatory scope those who otherwise would be outside of it. Even if the individual mandate is "necessary" to the Act's insurance reforms, such an expansion of federal power is not a "proper" means for making those reforms effective.

The Government relies primarily on our decision in *Gonzales v. Raich*. In *Raich*, . . . Congress's attempt to regulate the interstate market for marijuana would . . . have been substantially undercut if it could not also regulate intrastate possession and consumption. Accordingly, we recognized that "Congress was acting well within its authority" under the Necessary and Proper Clause even though its "regulation ensnare[d] some purely intrastate activity." *Raich* thus did not involve the exercise of any "great substantive and independent power," *McCulloch*, of the sort at issue here. Instead, it concerned only the constitutionality of "individual *applications* of a concededly valid statutory scheme." *Raich* (emphasis added).

Just as the individual mandate cannot be sustained as a law regulating the substantial effects of the failure to purchase health insurance, neither can it be upheld as a "necessary and proper" component of the insurance reforms. The commerce power thus does not authorize the mandate.

JUSTICE SCALIA, JUSTICE KENNEDY, JUSTICE THOMAS, and JUSTICE ALITO, dissenting.

. . . Whatever may be the conceptual limits upon the Commerce Clause and upon the power to tax and spend, they cannot be such as will enable the Federal Government to regulate all private conduct and to compel the States to function as administrators of federal programs.

That clear principle carries the day here. The striking case of *Wickard v. Filburn* (1942), which held that the economic activity of growing wheat, even for one's own consumption, affected commerce sufficiently that it could be regulated, always has been regarded as the ne plus ultra of expansive Commerce Clause jurisprudence. To go beyond that, and to say the failure to grow wheat (which is not an economic activity, or any activity at all) nonetheless affects commerce and therefore can be

WORTH NOTING

Justices Scalia, Kennedy, Thomas, and Alito agreed with Chief Justice Roberts that the individual mandate could not be justified under the Commerce and Necessary & Proper Clauses. Like the separate opinion of Justice Thomas, however, this opinion is styled as a dissent because they disagreed with the ultimate decision: They would have struck down the statute, but the Chief Justice (for reasons stated below) agreed with the four liberals that it should be upheld.

federally regulated, is to make mere breathing in and out the basis for federal prescription and to extend federal power to virtually all human activity. . . . If Congress can reach out and command even those furthest removed from an interstate market to participate in the market, then the Commerce Clause becomes a font of unlimited power. . . .

Gonzales v. Raich (2005) is no precedent for what Congress has done here. That case's prohibition of growing (cf. *Wickard*), and of possession (cf. innumerable federal statutes) did not represent the expansion of the federal power to direct into a broad new field. The mandating of economic activity does, and since it is a field so limitless that it converts the Commerce Clause into a general authority to direct the economy, that mandating is not "consist[ent] with the letter and spirit of the constitution." *McCulloch.* Moreover, [t]he Court's opinion in *Raich* pointed out that the growing and possession prohibitions were the only practicable way of enabling the prohibition of interstate traffic in marijuana to be effectively enforced. See also *Shreveport Rate Cases* (1914) (Necessary and Proper Clause allows regulations of intrastate transactions if necessary to the regulation of an interstate market). . . .

With the present statute, by contrast, there are many ways other than this unprecedented Individual Mandate by which the regulatory scheme's goals of reducing insurance premiums and ensuring the profitability of insurers could be achieved. For instance, those who did not purchase insurance could be subjected to a surcharge when they do enter the health insurance system. Or they could be denied a full income tax credit given to those who do purchase the insurance.

The Government was invited, at oral argument, to suggest what federal controls over private conduct (other than those explicitly prohibited by the Bill of Rights or other constitutional controls) could *not* be justified as necessary and proper for the carrying out of a general regulatory scheme. It was unable to name any. As we said at the outset, whereas the precise scope of the Commerce Clause and the Necessary and Proper Clause is uncertain, the proposition that the Federal Government cannot do everything is a fundamental precept. . . .

[Justice Ginsburg's] exposition of the wonderful things the Federal Government has achieved through exercise of its assigned powers, such as "the provision of old-age and survivors' benefits" in the Social Security Act, is quite beside the point. The issue here is whether the Federal Government can impose the Individual Mandate through the Commerce Clause. And the relevant history is not that Congress has achieved wide and wonderful results through the proper exercise of its assigned powers in the past, but that it has never before used the Commerce Clause to compel entry into commerce. . . .[3]

---

[3]   In its effort to show the contrary, Justice Ginsburg's dissent comes up with nothing more than two condemnation cases, which it says demonstrate "Congress' authority under the commerce power to compel an 'inactive' landholder to submit to an unwanted sale." Wrong on both scores. As its name suggests, the condemnation power does not "compel" anyone to do anything. It acts in rem, against the property that is condemned, and is effective

JUSTICE THOMAS, dissenting.

. . . I adhere to my view that "the very notion of a 'substantial effects' test under the Commerce Clause is inconsistent with the original understanding of Congress' powers and with this Court's early Commerce Clause cases." *United States v. Morrison* (2000) (Thomas, J., concurring). As I have explained, the Court's continued use of that test "has encouraged the Federal Government to persist in its view that the Commerce Clause has virtually no limits." *Morrison.* The Government's unprecedented claim in this suit that it may regulate not only economic activity but also inactivity that substantially affects interstate commerce is a case in point.

JUSTICE GINSBURG, with whom JUSTICE SOTOMAYOR[,] JUSTICE BREYER[,] and JUSTICE KAGAN join as to [this part], concurring in part, concurring in the judgment in part, and dissenting in part.

. . . The provision of health care is today a concern of national dimension, just as the provision of old-age and survivors' benefits was in the 1930's. In the Social Security Act, Congress installed a federal system to provide monthly benefits to retired wage earners and, eventually, to their survivors. Beyond question, Congress could have adopted a similar scheme for health care. Congress chose, instead, to preserve a central role for private insurers and state governments. According to The Chief Justice, the Commerce Clause does not permit that preservation. This rigid reading of the Clause makes scant sense and is stunningly retrogressive.

Since 1937, our precedent has recognized Congress' large authority to set the Nation's course in the economic and social welfare realm. *See NLRB v. Jones & Laughlin Steel Corp.* (1937) ("[The commerce] power is plenary and may be exerted to protect interstate commerce no matter what the source of the dangers which threaten it" (internal quotation marks omitted)). The Chief Justice's crabbed reading of the Commerce Clause harks back to the era in which the Court routinely thwarted Congress' efforts to regulate the national economy in the interest of those who labor to sustain it. *See, e.g., Railroad Retirement Bd. v. Alton R. Co.* (1935) (invalidating compulsory retirement and pension plan for employees [as] related essentially "to the social welfare of the worker, and

---

with or without a transfer of title from the former owner. More important, the power to condemn for public use is a separate sovereign power, explicitly acknowledged in the Fifth Amendment, which provides that "private property [shall not] be taken for public use, without just compensation."

therefore remote from any regulation of commerce as such"). It is a reading that should not have staying power. . . .

II

A

The Commerce Clause, it is widely acknowledged, "was the Framers' response to the central problem that gave rise to the Constitution itself." *EEOC v. Wyoming* (1983) (Stevens, J., concurring). Under the Articles of Confederation, the Constitution's precursor, the regulation of commerce was left to the States. This scheme proved unworkable, because the individual States, understandably focused on their own economic interests, often failed to take actions critical to the success of the Nation as a whole. See James Madison, Vices of the Political System of the United States.

What was needed was a "national Government . . . armed with a positive & compleat authority in all cases where uniform measures are necessary." See Letter from James Madison to Edmund Randolph (Apr. 8, 1787). The Framers' solution was the Commerce Clause, which, as they perceived it, granted Congress the authority to enact economic legislation "in all Cases for the general Interests of the Union, and also in those Cases to which the States are separately incompetent." Records of the Federal Convention of 1787. . . .

The Framers understood that the "general Interests of the Union" would change over time, in ways they could not anticipate. Accordingly, they recognized that the Constitution was of necessity a "great outlin[e]," not a detailed blueprint, see *McCulloch v. Maryland* (1819). . . . Alexander Hamilton emphasized, ". . . [t]here ought to be a CAPACITY to provide for future contingencies[,] as they may happen; and as these are illimitable in their nature, it is impossible safely to limit that capacity." *The Federalist* No. 34.

B

Consistent with the Framers' intent, we have repeatedly emphasized that Congress' authority under the Commerce Clause is dependent upon "practical" considerations, including "actual experience." *Jones & Laughlin Steel Corp.*; see *Wickard v. Filburn* (1942); *United States v. Lopez* (1995) (Kennedy, J., concurring) (emphasizing "the Court's definitive commitment to the practical conception of the commerce power"). . . .

Until today, this Court's pragmatic approach to judging whether Congress validly exercised its commerce power was guided by two familiar principles. First, Congress has the power to regulate economic activities "that substantially affect interstate commerce." *Gonzales v. Raich* (2005). This capacious power extends even to local activities that, viewed in the aggregate, have a substantial impact on interstate commerce. See also *Wickard* ("[E]ven if appellee's activity be local and though it may not be regarded as commerce, it may still, *whatever its nature,* be reached by Congress if it exerts a substantial economic effect on interstate commerce." (emphasis added)).

Second, we owe a large measure of respect to Congress when it frames and enacts economic and social legislation. [W]e presume the statute under review is constitutional and may strike it down only on a "plain showing" that Congress acted irrationally. *United States v. Morrison* (2000).

C

Straightforward application of these principles would require the Court to hold that the minimum coverage provision is proper Commerce Clause legislation. Beyond dispute, Congress had a rational basis for concluding that the uninsured, as a class, substantially affect interstate commerce. Those without insurance consume billions of dollars of health-care products and services each year. Those goods are produced, sold, and delivered largely by national and regional companies who routinely transact business across state lines. The uninsured also cross state lines to receive care. Some have medical emergencies while away from home. Others, when sick, go to a neighboring State that provides better care for those who have not prepaid for care.

Not only do those without insurance consume a large amount of health care each year; critically, as earlier explained, their inability to pay for a significant portion of that consumption drives up market prices, foists costs on other consumers, and reduces market efficiency and stability. Given these far-reaching effects on interstate commerce, the decision to forgo insurance is hardly inconsequential or equivalent to "doing nothing," *ante*; it is, instead, an economic decision Congress has the authority to address under the Commerce Clause. See also *Wickard* ("It is well established by decisions of this Court that the power to regulate commerce includes the power to regulate the prices at which commodities in that commerce are dealt in and *practices affecting such prices.*" (emphasis added)).

The minimum coverage provision, furthermore, bears a "reasonable connection" to Congress' goal of protecting the health-care market from the disruption caused by individuals who fail to obtain insurance. By requiring those who do not carry insurance to pay a toll, the minimum coverage provision gives individuals a strong incentive to insure. This incentive, Congress had good reason to believe, would reduce the number of uninsured and, correspondingly, mitigate the adverse impact the uninsured have on the national health-care market.

Congress also acted reasonably in requiring uninsured individuals, whether sick or healthy, either to obtain insurance or to pay the specified penalty. As earlier observed, because every person is at risk of needing care at any moment, all those who lack insurance, regardless of their current health status, adversely affect the price of health care and health insurance. Moreover, an insurance-purchase requirement limited to those in need of immediate care simply could not work. Insurance companies would either charge these individuals prohibitively expensive premiums, or, if community-rating regulations were in place, close up shop. . . .

D

Rather than evaluating the constitutionality of the minimum coverage provision in the manner established by our precedents, the Chief Justice relies on a newly minted constitutional doctrine. The commerce power does not, the Chief Justice announces, permit Congress to "compe[l] individuals to become active in commerce by purchasing a product." *Ante* (emphasis deleted).

1

a

The Chief Justice's novel constraint on Congress' commerce power gains no force from our precedent and for that reason alone warrants disapprobation. But even assuming, for the moment, that Congress lacks authority under the Commerce Clause to "compel individuals not engaged in commerce to purchase an unwanted product," such a limitation would be inapplicable here. Everyone will, at some point, consume health-care products and services. Thus, if the Chief Justice is correct that an insurance-purchase requirement can be applied only to those who "actively" consume health care, the minimum coverage provision fits the bill.

The Chief Justice does not dispute that all U.S. residents participate in the market for health services over the course of their lives. But, the Chief Justice insists, the uninsured cannot be considered active in the market for health care, because "[t]he proximity and degree of connection between the [uninsured today] and [their] subsequent commercial activity is too lacking." *Ante.*

This argument has multiple flaws.

First, more than 60% of those without insurance visit a hospital or doctor's office each year. Nearly 90% will within five years. An uninsured's consumption of health care is thus quite proximate: It is virtually certain to occur in the next five years and more likely than not to occur this year. Equally evident, Congress has no way of separating those uninsured individuals who will need emergency medical care today (surely their consumption of medical care is sufficiently imminent) from those who will not need medical services for years to come. No one knows when an emergency will occur, yet emergencies involving the uninsured arise daily. To capture individuals who unexpectedly will obtain medical care in the very near future, then, Congress needed to include individuals who will not go to a doctor anytime soon. Congress, our decisions instruct, has authority to cast its net that wide. See *Perez v. United States* (1971) ("[W]hen it is necessary in order to prevent an evil to make the law embrace more than the precise thing to be prevented it may do so.").

Second, it is Congress' role, not the Court's, to delineate the boundaries of the market the Legislature seeks to regulate. The Chief Justice defines the health-care market as including only those transactions that will occur either in the next instant or within some (unspecified) proximity to the next instant. But Congress could reasonably have viewed the market from a long-term perspective, encompassing all transactions virtually certain to occur over the next decade, not just those occurring here and now.

Third, contrary to the Chief Justice's contention, our precedent does indeed support "[t]he proposition that Congress may dictate the conduct of an individual today because of prophesied future activity." . . . [*Raich,* for example,] upheld Congress' authority to regulate marijuana grown for personal use. Homegrown marijuana substantially affects the interstate market for marijuana, we observed, for "the high demand in the interstate market will [likely] draw such marijuana into that market."

Our decisions thus acknowledge Congress' authority, under the Commerce Clause, to direct the conduct of an individual today (the farmer in *Wickard,* stopped from growing excess wheat; the plaintiff in *Raich,* ordered to cease cultivating marijuana) because of a prophesied future transaction (the eventual sale of that wheat or marijuana in the interstate market). Congress' actions are even more rational here, where the future activity (the consumption of medical care) is certain to occur, the sole uncertainty being the time the activity will take place.

Maintaining that the uninsured are not active in the health-care market, the Chief Justice draws an analogy to the car market. An individual "is not 'active in the car market,' " the Chief Justice observes, simply because he or she may someday buy a car. The analogy is inapt. The inevitable yet unpredictable need for medical care and the guarantee that emergency care will be provided when required are conditions nonexistent in other markets. That is so of the market for cars, and of the market for broccoli as well. Although an individual *might* buy a car or a crown of broccoli one day, there is no certainty she will ever do so. And if she eventually wants a car or has a craving for broccoli, she will be obliged to pay at the counter before receiving the vehicle or nourishment. She will get no free ride or food, at the expense of another consumer forced to pay an inflated price. See *Thomas More Law Center v. Obama* (6th Cir. 2011) (Sutton, J., concurring in part) ("Regulating how citizens pay for what they already receive (health care), never quite know when they will need, and in the case of severe illnesses or emergencies generally will not be able to afford, has few (if any) parallels in modern life."). Upholding the minimum coverage provision on the ground that all are participants or will be participants in the health-care market would therefore carry no implication that Congress may justify under the Commerce Clause a mandate to buy other products and services.

Nor is it accurate to say that the minimum coverage provision "compel[s] individuals . . . to purchase an unwanted product". . . . Health insurance is a means of paying for [health] care, nothing more. In requiring individuals to obtain insurance, Congress is therefore not mandating the purchase of a discrete, unwanted product. Rather, Congress is merely defining the terms on which individuals pay for an interstate good they consume: Persons subject to the mandate must now pay for medical care in advance (instead of at the point of service) and through insurance (instead of out of pocket). Establishing payment terms for goods in or affecting interstate commerce is quintessential economic regulation well within Congress' domain.

      . . .

b

. . . Nothing in [the Commerce Clause's] language implies that Congress' commerce power is limited to regulating those actively engaged in commercial transactions. Indeed, as the D.C. Circuit observed, "[a]t the time the Constitution was [framed], to 'regulate' meant," among other things, "to require action." See *Seven-Sky v. Holder* (D.C. Cir. 2011). . . .

[T]he Chief Justice asserts, [nonetheless, that] "[t]he language of the Constitution reflects the natural understanding that the power to regulate assumes there is already something to be regulated." This argument is difficult to fathom. Requiring individuals to obtain insurance unquestionably regulates the interstate health-insurance and health-care markets, both of them in existence well before the enactment of the ACA. See *Wickard* ("The stimulation of commerce is a use of the regulatory function quite as definitely as prohibitions or restrictions thereon."). Thus, the "something to be regulated" was surely there when Congress created the minimum coverage provision.

Nor does our case law toe the activity versus inactivity line. In *Wickard*, for example, we upheld the penalty imposed on a farmer who grew too much wheat, even though the regulation had the effect of compelling farmers to purchase wheat in the open market. "[F]orcing some farmers into the market to buy what they could provide for themselves" was, the Court held, a valid means of regulating commerce. *Id.* In another context, this Court similarly upheld Congress' authority under the commerce power to compel an "inactive" landholder to submit to an unwanted sale. See *Monongahela Nav. Co. v. United States* (1893) ("[U]pon *the [great] power to regulate commerce*[,]" Congress has the authority to mandate the sale of real property to the Government, where the sale is essential to the improvement of a navigable waterway (emphasis added)); *Cherokee Nation v. Southern Kansas R. Co.* (1890) (similar reliance on the commerce power regarding mandated sale of private property for railroad construction).

In concluding that the Commerce Clause does not permit Congress to regulate commercial "inactivity," and therefore does not allow Congress to adopt the practical solution it devised for the health-care problem, the Chief Justice views the Clause as a "technical legal conception," precisely what our case law tells us not to do. *Wickard* (internal quotation marks omitted). This Court's former endeavors to impose categorical limits on the commerce power have not fared well. In several pre-New Deal cases, the Court attempted to cabin Congress' Commerce Clause authority by distinguishing "commerce" from activity once conceived to be noncommercial, notably, "production," "mining," and "manufacturing." The Court also sought to distinguish activities having a "direct" effect on interstate commerce, and for that reason, subject to federal regulation, from those having only an "indirect" effect, and therefore not amenable to federal control.

These line-drawing exercises were untenable, and the Court long ago abandoned them. "[Q]uestions of the power of Congress [under the Commerce Clause]," we held in *Wickard*, "are not to be decided by reference to any formula which would give controlling force to nomenclature such as 'production' and 'indirect' and foreclose consideration of the actual effects of the activity in question upon interstate commerce." . . .

It is not hard to show the difficulty courts (and Congress) would encounter in distinguishing statutes that regulate "activity" from those that regulate "inactivity." As Judge Easterbrook noted, "it is possible to restate most actions as corresponding inactions with the same effect." *Archie v. Racine* (7th Cir. 1988) (en banc). Take the instant litigation as an example. An individual who opts not to purchase insurance from a private insurer can be seen as actively selecting another form of insurance: self-insurance. . . . *Wickard* is another example. Did the statute there at issue target activity (the growing of too much wheat) or inactivity (the farmer's failure to purchase wheat in the marketplace)? If anything, the Court's analysis suggested the latter.

At bottom, the Chief Justice's and the joint dissenters' "view that an individual cannot be subject to Commerce Clause regulation absent voluntary, affirmative acts that enter him or her into, or affect, the interstate market expresses a concern for individual liberty that [is] more redolent of Due Process Clause arguments." *Seven-Sky* (D.C. Cir. 2011). . . . Plaintiffs have abandoned any argument pinned to substantive due process, however, and now concede that the provisions here at issue do not offend the Due Process Clause.

2

Underlying the Chief Justice's view that the Commerce Clause must be confined to the regulation of active participants in a commercial market is a fear that the commerce power would otherwise know no limits. . . . The joint dissenters express a similar apprehension. . . . This concern is unfounded.

First, the Chief Justice could certainly uphold the individual mandate without giving Congress *carte blanche* to enact any and all purchase mandates.

As several times noted, the unique attributes of the health-care market render everyone active in that market and give rise to a significant free-riding problem that does not occur in other markets. . . .

Other provisions of the Constitution also check congressional overreaching. A mandate to purchase a particular product would be unconstitutional if, for example, the edict impermissibly abridged the freedom of speech, interfered with the free exercise of religion, or infringed on a liberty interest protected by the Due Process Clause.

Supplementing these legal restraints is a formidable check on congressional power: the democratic process. See *Raich*; *Wickard* (repeating Chief Justice Marshall's "warning [from *Gibbons*] that effective restraints on [the commerce power's] exercise must proceed from political rather than judicial processes"). . . .

When contemplated in its extreme, almost any power looks dangerous. The commerce power, hypothetically, would enable Congress to prohibit the purchase and home production of all meat, fish, and dairy goods, effectively compelling Americans to eat only vegetables. Cf. *Raich*; *Wickard*. Yet no one would offer the "hypothetical and unreal possibilit[y]," *Pullman Co. v. Knott* (1914), of a vegetarian state as a credible reason to deny Congress the authority ever to ban the possession and sale of goods. The Chief Justice accepts just such specious logic when he cites the broccoli horrible as a reason to deny Congress the power to pass the individual mandate. Cf. R. Bork, The Tempting of America 169 (1990) ("Judges and lawyers live on the slippery slope of analogies; they are not supposed to ski it to the bottom.").

3

To bolster his argument that the minimum coverage provision is not valid Commerce Clause legislation, the Chief Justice emphasizes the provision's novelty. While an insurance-purchase mandate may be novel, the Chief Justice's argument certainly is not. "[I]n almost every instance of the exercise of the [commerce] power differences are asserted from previous exercises of it and made a ground of attack." *Hoke v. United States* (1913). . . . For decades, the Court has declined to override legislation because of its novelty, and for good reason. As our national economy grows and changes, we have recognized, Congress must adapt to the changing "economic and financial realities." Hindering Congress' ability to do so is shortsighted; if history is any guide, today's constriction of the Commerce Clause will not endure.

III

A

. . . When viewed as a component of the entire ACA, the provision's constitutionality becomes even plainer.

The Necessary and Proper Clause "empowers Congress to enact laws in effectuation of its [commerce] powe[r] that are not within its authority to enact in isolation." *Raich* (Scalia, J., concurring in judgment). . . . "It is enough that the challenged provisions are an integral part of the regulatory program and that the regulatory scheme when considered as a whole satisfies this test." *Hodel v. Indiana* (1981). . . .

Recall that one of Congress' goals in enacting the ACA was to eliminate the insurance industry's practice of charging higher prices or denying coverage to individuals with preexisting medical conditions. . . . Without the individual mandate, Congress learned, guaranteed-issue and community-rating requirements would trigger an adverse-selection death spiral in the health-insurance market: Insurance premiums would skyrocket, the number of uninsured would increase, and insurance companies would exit the market. When complemented by an insurance mandate, on the other hand, guaranteed issue and community rating would work as intended, increasing access to insurance and reducing uncompensated care.

The minimum coverage provision is thus an "essential par[t] of a larger regulation of economic activity"; without the provision, "the regulatory scheme [w]ould be undercut." *Raich* (internal quotation marks omitted). . . .

B

Asserting that the Necessary and Proper Clause does not authorize the minimum coverage provision, the Chief Justice focuses on the word "proper." A mandate to purchase health insurance is not "proper" legislation, the Chief Justice urges, because the command "undermine[s] the structure of government established by the Constitution." If long on rhetoric, the Chief Justice's argument is short on substance.

The Chief Justice cites only two cases in which this Court concluded that a federal statute impermissibly transgressed the Constitution's boundary between state and federal authority: *Printz v. United States* (1997), and *New York v. United States* (1992). The statutes at issue in both cases, however, compelled *state officials* to act on the Federal Government's behalf. . . . *Printz; New York.* The minimum coverage provision, in contrast, acts "directly upon individuals, without employing the States as intermediaries." *New York.* The provision is thus entirely consistent with the Constitution's design. See *Printz* ("[T]he Framers explicitly chose a Constitution that confers upon Congress the power to regulate individuals, not States."). . . .[10]

In failing to explain why the individual mandate threatens our constitutional order, the Chief Justice disserves future courts. How is a judge to decide, when ruling on the constitutionality of a federal statute, whether Congress employed an "independent power" or merely a "derivative" one[?] Whether the power used is "substantive" or just "incidental"? The instruction the Chief Justice, in effect, provides lower courts: You will know it when you see it.

It is more than exaggeration to suggest that the minimum coverage provision improperly intrudes on "essential attributes of state sovereignty." First, the ACA does not operate "in [an] are[a] such as criminal law enforcement or education where States historically have been sovereign." *Lopez.* As evidenced by Medicare, Medicaid, the Employee Retirement Income Security Act of 1974, and the Health Insurance Portability and Accountability Act of 1996, the Federal Government plays a lead role in the health-care sector, both as a direct payer and as a regulator.

Second, and perhaps most important, the minimum coverage provision, along with other provisions of the ACA, addresses the very sort of interstate problem that made the commerce power essential in our federal system. The crisis created by the large number of U.S. residents who lack health insurance is one of national dimension that States are "separately incompetent" to handle. Far from trampling on States' sovereignty, the ACA attempts a federal solution for the very reason that the States, acting separately, cannot meet the need. Notably, the ACA serves the general welfare of the people of the United States while retaining a prominent role for the States. See Maryland Brief. . . .

In a separate argument, the joint dissenters contend that the minimum coverage provision is not necessary and proper because it was not the "only . . . way" Congress could have made the guaranteed-issue and community-rating

---

[10]   Indeed, Congress regularly and uncontroversially requires individuals who are "doing nothing" to take action. Examples include federal requirements to report for jury duty, 28 U.S.C. § 1866(g); to register for selective service, 50 U.S.C. App. § 453; to purchase firearms and gear in anticipation of service in the Militia, 1 Stat. 271 (Uniform Militia Act of 1792); to turn gold currency over to the Federal Government in exchange for paper currency, see *Nortz v. United States* (1935); and to file a tax return, 26 U.S.C. § 6012.

reforms work. [E]ven assuming there were "practicable" alternatives to the minimum coverage provision, "we long ago rejected the view that the Necessary and Proper Clause demands that an Act of Congress be '*absolutely* necessary' to the exercise of an enumerated power." *Jinks v. Richland County* (2003) (quoting *McCulloch v. Maryland* (1819)). Rather, the statutory provision at issue need only be "conducive" and "[reasonably] adapted" to the goal Congress seeks to achieve. The minimum coverage provision meets this requirement.

IV

In the early 20th century, this Court regularly struck down economic regulation enacted by the peoples' representatives in both the States and the Federal Government. *See, e.g., Carter Coal Co.*; *Dagenhart*; *Lochner v. New York* (1905). The Chief Justice's Commerce Clause opinion, and even more so the joint dissenters' reasoning, bear a disquieting resemblance to those long-overruled decisions.

For Discussion

(1) It is long-established law that the commerce power "may be exerted to protect interstate commerce no matter what the source of the dangers which threaten it." Should that have been enough to uphold the mandate?

(2) As Justice Ginsburg notes, p. 545, Congress could have imposed a tax-and-spend program that would have provided every American with a single-payer health-care plan. Should Congress be able instead to require people to buy their own plans, meeting prescribed criteria?

---

d. The Taxing Power

As we have learned, Congress can sometimes use the taxing power to encourage behavior that it's not allowed simply to require. Having rejected the government's arguments under the Commerce and Necessary & Proper Clauses, Chief Justice Roberts therefore turned to the government's claim that the mandate was really just a tax on disfavored behavior. Our excerpt of Chief Justice Roberts's discussion of the tax issues begins with Part II of his opinion, which spoke for a majority in dismissing a statutory limitation that might have prevented the Court from hearing the case at all.

CHIEF JUSTICE ROBERTS . . . :

II

Before turning to the merits, we need to be sure we have the authority to do so. The Anti-Injunction Act provides that "no suit for the purpose of restraining the assessment or collection of any tax shall be maintained in any court by any person, whether or not such person is the person against whom such tax was assessed." This statute protects the Government's ability to collect a consistent stream

 WORTH NOTING Because the parties to the litigation were eager to have the matter adjudicated, the Court appointed an *amicus* (friend of the Court) to argue that it had no jurisdiction.

of revenue, by barring litigation to enjoin or otherwise obstruct the collection of taxes. Because of the Anti-Injunction Act, taxes can ordinarily be challenged only after they are paid, by suing for a refund.

The penalty for not complying with the Affordable Care Act's individual mandate first becomes enforceable in 2014. The present challenge to the mandate thus seeks to restrain the penalty's future collection. *Amicus* contends that the Internal Revenue Code treats the penalty as a tax, and that the Anti-Injunction Act therefore bars this suit.

The text of the pertinent statutes suggests otherwise. The Anti-Injunction Act applies to suits "for the purpose of restraining the assessment or collection of any *tax*." § 7421(a) (emphasis added). Congress, however, chose to describe the "[s]hared responsibility payment" imposed on those who forgo health insurance not as a "tax," but as a "penalty." §§ 5000A(b), (g)(2). There is no immediate reason to think that a statute applying to "any tax" would apply to a "penalty." Congress's decision to label this exaction a "penalty" rather than a "tax" is significant because the Affordable Care Act describes many other exactions it creates as "taxes." Where Congress uses certain language in one part of a statute and different language in another, it is generally presumed that Congress acts intentionally.

Amicus argues that even though Congress did not label the shared responsibility payment a tax, we should treat it as such under the Anti-Injunction Act because it functions like a tax. It is true that Congress cannot change whether an exaction is a tax or a penalty for *constitutional* purposes simply by describing

it as one or the other. Congress may not, for example, expand its power under the Taxing Clause, or escape the Double Jeopardy Clause's constraint on
criminal sanctions, by labeling a severe financial punishment a "tax." See *Child
Labor Tax Case (Bailey v. Drexel Furniture Co.)* (1922); *Department of Revenue
of Mont. v. Kurth Ranch* (1994).

The Anti-Injunction Act and the Affordable Care Act, however, are
creatures of Congress's own creation. How they relate to each other is up to
Congress, and the best evidence of Congress's intent is the statutory text. We
have thus applied the Anti-Injunction Act to statutorily described "taxes" even
where that label was inaccurate. See *Bailey v. George* (1922) (Anti-Injunction
Act applies to "Child Labor Tax" struck down as exceeding Congress's taxing
power in *Drexel Furniture*). . . .

[After discussing the statutory provisions at length, the Chief Justice concluded as follows:] The Affordable Care Act does not require that the penalty
for failing to comply with the individual mandate be treated as a tax for purposes of the Anti-Injunction Act. The Anti-Injunction Act therefore does not
apply to this suit, and we may proceed to the merits.

All the justices agreed that the Anti-Injunction Act did not apply; the four liberals joined that part of the Chief Justice's opinion,
making it to that extent an opinion of the Court.

We turn now to the other tax issue in the case: whether the
individual mandate could be upheld as an exercise of the congressional *taxing* power. In Part III.B, Roberts wrote for himself alone; the
four more liberal justices joined him in Part III.C, which therefore
spoke for the Court.

CHIEF JUSTICE ROBERTS . . . :

III

B

. . . Because the Commerce Clause does not support the individual mandate, it is necessary to turn to the Government's second argument: that the

mandate may be upheld as within Congress's enumerated power to "lay and collect Taxes."

The Government's tax power argument asks us to view the statute differently than we did in considering its commerce power theory. In making its Commerce Clause argument, the Government defended the mandate as a regulation requiring individuals to purchase health insurance. The Government does not claim that the taxing power allows Congress to issue such a command. Instead, the Government asks us to read the mandate not as ordering individuals to buy insurance, but rather as imposing a tax on those who do not buy that product.

[I]t is well established that if a statute has two possible meanings, one of which violates the Constitution, courts should adopt the meaning that does not do so. "[T]he rule is settled that as between two possible interpretations of a statute, by one of which it would be unconstitutional and by the other valid, our plain duty is to adopt that which will save the Act." *Blodgett v. Holden* (1927) (Holmes, J., concurring).

The most straightforward reading of the mandate is that it commands individuals to purchase insurance. After all, it states that individuals "shall" maintain health insurance. 26 U.S.C. § 5000A(a). Congress thought it could enact such a command under the Commerce Clause, and the Government primarily defended the law on that basis. But, for the reasons explained above, the Commerce Clause does not give Congress that power. Under our precedent, it is therefore necessary to ask whether the Government's alternative reading of the statute—that it only imposes a tax on those without insurance—is a reasonable one.

Under the mandate, if an individual does not maintain health insurance, the only consequence is that he must make an additional payment to the IRS when he pays his taxes. See § 5000A(b). That, according to the Government, means the mandate can be regarded as establishing a condition—not owning health insurance—that triggers a tax—the required payment to the IRS. Under that theory, the mandate is not a legal command to buy insurance. Rather, it makes going without insurance just another thing the Government taxes, like buying gasoline or earning income. And if the mandate is in effect just a tax hike on certain taxpayers who do not have health insurance, it may be within Congress's constitutional power to tax.

The question is not whether that is the most natural interpretation of the mandate, but only whether it is a "fairly possible" one. *Crowell v. Benson* (1932). As we have explained, "every reasonable construction must be resorted to, in order to save a statute from unconstitutionality." *Hooper v. California* (1895). The Government asks us to interpret the mandate as imposing a tax, if it would otherwise violate the Constitution. Granting the Act the full measure of deference owed to federal statutes, it can be so read, for the reasons set forth below.

C

The exaction the Affordable Care Act imposes on those without health insurance looks like a tax in many respects. The "[s]hared responsibility payment," as the statute entitles it, is paid into the Treasury by "taxpayer[s]" when they file their tax returns. 26 U.S.C. § 5000A(b). It does not apply to individuals who do not pay federal income taxes because their household income is less than the filing threshold in the Internal Revenue Code. For taxpayers who do owe the payment, its amount is determined by such familiar factors as taxable income, number of dependents, and joint filing status. The requirement to pay is found in the Internal Revenue Code and enforced by the IRS, which—as we previously explained—must assess and collect it "in the same manner as taxes." This process yields the essential feature of any tax: It produces at least some revenue for the Government. *United States v. Kahriger* (1953). Indeed, the payment is expected to raise about $4 billion per year by 2017. Congressional Budget Office, *Payments of Penalties for Being Uninsured Under the Patient Protection and Affordable Care Act* (2010).

It is of course true that the Act describes the payment as a "penalty," not a "tax." But while that label is fatal to the application of the Anti-Injunction Act, it does not determine whether the payment may be viewed as an exercise of Congress's taxing power. It is up to Congress whether to apply the Anti-Injunction Act to any particular statute, so it makes sense to be guided by Congress's choice of label on that question. That choice does not, however, control whether an exaction is within Congress's constitutional power to tax.

Our precedent reflects this: In 1922, we decided two challenges to the "Child Labor Tax" on the same day. In the first, we held that a suit to enjoin collection of the so-called tax was barred by the Anti-Injunction Act. Congress knew that suits to obstruct taxes had to await payment under the Anti-Injunction Act; Congress called the child labor tax a tax; Congress therefore intended the Anti-Injunction Act to apply. In the second case, however, we held that the same exaction, although labeled a tax, was not in fact authorized by Congress's taxing power. *Drexel Furniture*. That constitutional question was not controlled by Congress's choice of label. We have similarly held that exactions not labeled taxes nonetheless were authorized by Congress's power to tax. In the *License Tax Cases*, for example, we held that federal licenses to sell liquor and lottery tickets—for which the licensee had to pay a fee—could be sustained as exercises of the taxing power. . . .

We thus ask whether the shared responsibility payment falls within Congress's taxing power, "[d]isregarding the designation of the exaction, and viewing its substance and application." *United States v. Constantine* (1935); cf. *Quill Corp. v. North Dakota* (1992) ("[M]agic words or labels" should not "disable an otherwise constitutional levy"); *United States v. Sotelo* (1978) ("That the funds due are referred to as a 'penalty' . . . does not alter their essential character as taxes"). . . .

Our cases confirm this functional approach. For example, in *Drexel Furniture,* we focused on three practical characteristics of the so-called tax on employing child laborers that convinced us the "tax" was actually a penalty. First, the tax imposed an exceedingly heavy burden—10 percent of a company's net income—on those who employed children, no matter how small their infraction. Second, it imposed that exaction only on those who knowingly employed underage laborers. Such scienter requirements are typical of punitive statutes, because Congress often wishes to punish only those who intentionally break the law. Third, this "tax" was enforced in part by the Department of Labor, an agency responsible for punishing violations of labor laws, not collecting revenue. . . .

The same analysis here suggests that the shared responsibility payment may for constitutional purposes be considered a tax, not a penalty: First, for most Americans the amount due will be far less than the price of insurance, and, by statute, it can never be more.[8] It may often be a reasonable financial decision to make the payment rather than purchase insurance, unlike the "prohibitory" financial punishment in *Drexel Furniture*. Second, the individual mandate contains no scienter requirement. Third, the payment is collected solely by the IRS through the normal means of taxation—except that the Service is *not* allowed to use those means most suggestive of a punitive sanction, such as criminal

---

[8]   In 2016, for example, individuals making $35,000 a year are expected to owe the IRS about $60 for any month in which they do not have health insurance. Someone with an annual income of $100,000 a year would likely owe about $200. The price of a qualifying insurance policy is projected to be around $400 per month.

prosecution. See § 5000A(g)(2). The reasons the Court in *Drexel Furniture* held that what was called a "tax" there was a penalty support the conclusion that what is called a "penalty" here may be viewed as a tax.[9]

None of this is to say that the payment is not intended to affect individual conduct. Although the payment will raise considerable revenue, it is plainly designed to expand health insurance coverage. But taxes that seek to influence conduct are nothing new. Some of our earliest federal taxes sought to deter the purchase of imported manufactured goods in order to foster the growth of domestic industry. Cf. J. Story, *Commentaries on the Constitution of the United States* (1833) ("the taxing power is often, very often, applied for other purposes than revenue"). . . . Today, federal and state taxes can compose more than half the retail price of cigarettes, not just to raise more money, but to encourage people to quit smoking. And we have upheld such obviously regulatory measures as taxes on selling marijuana and sawed-off shotguns. [See] *Sonzinsky v. United States* (1937). Indeed, "[e]very tax is in some measure regulatory. To some extent it interposes an economic impediment to the activity taxed as compared with others not taxed." *Ibid.* . . .

In distinguishing penalties from taxes, this Court has explained that "if the concept of penalty means anything, it means punishment for an unlawful act or omission." *United States v. Reorganized CF & I Fabricators of Utah, Inc.* (1996). While the individual mandate clearly aims to induce the purchase of health insurance, it need not be read to declare that failing to do so is unlawful. Neither the Act nor any other law attaches negative legal consequences to not buying health insurance, beyond requiring a payment to the IRS. The Government agrees with that reading, confirming that if someone chooses to pay rather than obtain health insurance, they have fully complied with the law.

Indeed, it is estimated that four million people each year will choose to pay the IRS rather than buy insurance. See Congressional Budget Office, *Payments of Penalties*. We would expect Congress to be troubled by that prospect if such conduct were unlawful. That Congress apparently regards such extensive failure to comply with the mandate as tolerable suggests that Congress did not think it was creating four million outlaws. It suggests instead that the shared

---

[9]　We do not suggest that any exaction lacking a scienter requirement and enforced by the IRS is within the taxing power. Congress could not, for example, expand its authority to impose criminal fines by creating strict liability offenses enforced by the IRS rather than the FBI. But the fact the exaction here is paid like a tax, to the agency that collects taxes—rather than, for example, exacted by Department of Labor inspectors after ferreting out willful malfeasance—suggests that this exaction may be viewed as a tax.

responsibility payment merely imposes a tax citizens may lawfully choose to pay in lieu of buying health insurance. . . .

There may, however, be a more fundamental objection to a tax on those who lack health insurance. Even if only a tax, the payment under § 5000A(b) remains a burden that the Federal Government imposes for an omission, not an act. If it is troubling to interpret the Commerce Clause as authorizing Congress to regulate those who abstain from commerce, perhaps it should be similarly troubling to permit Congress to impose a tax for not doing something.

WORTH NOTING

The Chief Justice also rejected an argument that, if the individual mandate did constitute a tax, it was a direct tax that had to be apportioned among the states according to population pursuant to Art. I, § 9, cl. 4. In doing so, he emphasized the narrow categories of taxes to which this provision has applied.

Three considerations allay this concern. First, and most importantly, it is abundantly clear the Constitution does not guarantee that individuals may avoid taxation through inactivity. A capitation, after all, is a tax that everyone must pay simply for existing, and capitations are expressly contemplated by the Constitution. [More generally,] Congress's use of the Taxing Clause to encourage buying something is . . . not new. Tax incentives already promote, for example, purchasing homes and professional educations. Sustaining the mandate as a tax depends only on whether Congress *has* properly exercised its taxing power to encourage purchasing health insurance, not whether it *can*. . . .

Second, Congress's ability to use its taxing power to influence conduct is not without limits. A few of our cases policed these limits aggressively, invalidating punitive exactions obviously designed to regulate behavior otherwise regarded at the time as beyond federal authority. *See, e.g., United States v. Butler* (1936); *Drexel Furniture*. More often and more recently we have declined to closely examine the regulatory motive or effect of revenue-raising measures. See *Kahriger* (collecting cases). We have nonetheless maintained that " 'there comes a time in the extension of the penalizing features of the so-called tax when it loses its character as such and becomes a mere penalty with the characteristics of regulation and punishment.' " *Kurth Ranch*.

We have already explained that the shared responsibility payment's practical characteristics pass muster as a tax under our narrowest interpretations of the taxing power. Because the tax at hand is within even those strict limits, we need not here decide the precise point at which an exaction becomes so punitive that the taxing power does not authorize it. It remains true, however, that the " 'power to tax is not the power to destroy while this Court sits.' " *Oklahoma Tax Comm'n v. Texas Co.* (1949).

Third, although the breadth of Congress's power to tax is greater than its power to regulate commerce, the taxing power does not give Congress the same degree of control over individual behavior. Once we recognize that Congress may regulate a particular decision under the Commerce Clause, the Federal Government can bring its full weight to bear. Congress may simply command individuals to do as it directs. An individual who disobeys may be subjected to criminal sanctions. . . .

By contrast, Congress's authority under the taxing power is limited to requiring an individual to pay money into the Federal Treasury, no more. If a tax is properly paid, the Government has no power to compel or punish individuals subject to it. We do not make light of the severe burden that taxation—especially taxation motivated by a regulatory purpose—can impose. But imposition of a tax nonetheless leaves an individual with a lawful choice to do or not do a certain act, so long as he is willing to pay a tax levied on that choice.

The Affordable Care Act's requirement that certain individuals pay a financial penalty for not obtaining health insurance may reasonably be characterized as a tax. Because the Constitution permits such a tax, it is not our role to forbid it, or to pass upon its wisdom or fairness. . . .

. . . The individual mandate cannot be upheld as an exercise of Congress's power under the Commerce Clause. That Clause authorizes Congress to regulate interstate commerce, not to order individuals to engage in it. In this case, however, it is reasonable to construe what Congress has done as increasing taxes on those who have a certain amount of income, but choose to go without health insurance. Such legislation is within Congress's power to tax. . . .

FOR DISCUSSION
Seems like pretty fancy footwork on the part of the Chief—it's not a tax for purposes of the procedural statute, but it is a tax for purposes of the Constitution. Are you persuaded by both legs of this argument? If not, what do you think motivated the Chief?

JUSTICE SCALIA, JUSTICE KENNEDY, JUSTICE THOMAS, and JUSTICE ALITO, dissenting.

Congress has attempted to regulate beyond the scope of its Commerce Clause authority, and [the individual mandate created by] § 5000A is therefore invalid. The Government contends, however, [that the Individual Mandate is] a creature never hitherto seen in the United States Reports: a penalty for constitutional purposes that is *also* a tax for constitutional purposes. In all our cases the two are mutually exclusive. The provision challenged under the Constitution is either a penalty or else a tax. . . .[5] The issue is not whether Congress had the *power* to frame the minimum-coverage provision as a tax, but whether it *did* so. . . .

Our cases establish a clear line between a tax and a penalty: " '[A] tax is an enforced contribution to provide for the support of government; a penalty . . . is an exaction imposed by statute as punishment for an unlawful act.' " *United States v. Reorganized CF & I Fabricators of Utah, Inc.* (1996). In a few cases, this Court has held that a "tax" imposed upon private conduct was so onerous as to be in effect a penalty. But we have never held—*never*—that a penalty imposed for violation of the law was so trivial as to be in effect a tax. We have never held that *any* exaction imposed for violation of the law is an exercise of Congress' taxing power—even when the statute *calls* it a tax, much less when (as here) the statute repeatedly calls it a penalty. When an Act "adopt[s] the criteria of wrongdoing" and then imposes a monetary penalty as the "principal consequence on those who transgress its standard," it creates a regulatory penalty, not a tax. *Child Labor Tax Case* (1922).

So the question is, quite simply, whether the exaction here is imposed for violation of the law. It unquestionably is. The minimum-coverage provision is found in 26 U.S.C. § 5000A, entitled "*Requirement* to maintain minimum essential coverage." (Emphasis added.) It commands that every "applicable individual *shall* . . . ensure that the individual . . . is covered under minimum essential coverage." (emphasis added). And the immediately following provision states that, "[i]f . . . an applicable individual . . . fails to meet the *requirement* of subsection (a) . . . there is hereby imposed . . . a *penalty*." § 5000A(b) (emphasis added). . . .

---

[5]   Of course it can be both for statutory purposes, since Congress can define "tax" and "penalty" in its enactments any way it wishes.

Quite separately, the fact that Congress (in its own words) "imposed . . . a penalty," 26 U.S.C. § 5000A(b)(1), for failure to buy insurance is alone sufficient to render that failure unlawful. It is one of the canons of interpretation that a statute that penalizes an act makes it unlawful: . . . "If a statute inflicts a penalty for doing an act, the penalty implies a prohibition, and the thing is unlawful, though there be no prohibitory words in the statute." J. Kent, *Commentaries on American Law* (1826). . . . Eighteen times in § 5000A itself and elsewhere throughout the Act, Congress called the exaction in § 5000A(b) a "penalty." [Justice Scalia points out that some people, such as those who earn too little to have to file an income tax return, are exempt from the penalty though they are not usually exempt from the mandate.]

Against the mountain of evidence that the minimum coverage requirement is what the statute calls it—a requirement—and that the penalty for its violation is what the statute calls it—a penalty—the Government brings forward the flimsiest of indications to the contrary. It notes that "[t]he minimum coverage provision amends the Internal Revenue Code. . ." and that "[t]he [Internal Revenue Service (IRS)] will assess and collect the penalty in the same manner as assessable penalties under the Internal Revenue Code." The manner of collection could perhaps suggest a tax if IRS penalty-collection were unheard-of or rare. It is not. See, *e.g.*, 26 U.S.C. § 527(j) (IRS-collectible penalty for failure to make campaign-finance disclosures); § 5761(c) (IRS-collectible penalty for domestic sales of tobacco products labeled for export); § 9707 (IRS-collectible penalty for failure to make required health-insurance premium payments on behalf of mining employees). In *Reorganized CF & I Fabricators of Utah, Inc.* (1996), we held that an exaction not only *enforced* by the Commissioner of Internal Revenue but even *called* a "tax" was in fact a penalty. "[I]f the concept of penalty means anything," we said, "it means punishment for an unlawful act or omission." . . .

The Government points out that "[t]he amount of the penalty will be calculated as a percentage of household income for federal income tax purposes, subject to a floor and [a] ca[p]," and that individuals who earn so little money that they "are not required to file income tax returns for the taxable year are not subject to the penalty" (though they are, as we discussed earlier, subject to the mandate). But varying a penalty according to ability to pay is an utterly familiar practice. See, *e.g.*, 33 U.S.C. § 1319(d) ("In determining the amount of a civil penalty the court shall consider . . . the economic impact of the penalty on the violator"). . . .

The last of the feeble arguments in favor of petitioners that we will address is the contention that what this statute repeatedly calls a penalty is in fact a tax because it contains no scienter requirement. The *presence* of such a requirement suggests a penalty—though one can imagine a tax imposed only on willful action; but the *absence* of such a requirement does not suggest a tax. Penalties for absolute-liability offenses are commonplace. And where a statute is silent as to scienter, we traditionally presume a *mens rea* requirement if the statute imposes a "severe penalty." *Staples v. United States* (1994). Since we have an entire jurisprudence addressing when it is that a scienter requirement should be inferred from a penalty, it is quite illogical to suggest that a penalty is not a penalty for want of an express scienter requirement.

And the nail in the coffin is that the mandate and penalty are located in Title I of the Act, its operative core, rather than where a tax would be found—in Title IX, containing the Act's "Revenue Provisions." In sum, "the terms of [the] act rende[r] it unavoidable," *Parsons v. Bedford* (1830), that Congress imposed a regulatory penalty, not a tax.

For all these reasons, to say that the Individual Mandate merely imposes a tax is not to interpret the statute but to rewrite it. Judicial tax-writing is particularly troubling. Taxes have never been popular, see, *e.g.*, Stamp Act of 1765, and in part for that reason, the Constitution requires tax increases to originate in the House of Representatives. See Art. I, § 7, cl. 1. That is to say, they must originate in the legislative body most accountable to the people . We have no doubt that Congress knew precisely what it was doing when it rejected an earlier version of this legislation that imposed a tax instead of a requirement-with-penalty. . . .

Justice Ginsburg agreed with Chief Justice Roberts that the mandate could be upheld as a tax. But she disagreed with his conclusion that the mandate could not be justified under the Commerce Clause—and suggested that his conclusion should be read as dictum because it was irrelevant to his resolution of the case:

FOR DISCUSSION

Ultimately, the Court upholds the individual mandate as a proper exercise of Congress' power to tax and spend "for the . . . general Welfare of the United States." Art. I, § 8, cl. 1. I concur in that determination, which makes the Chief Justice's Commerce Clause essay all the more puzzling. Why should the Chief Justice strive so mightily to hem in Congress' capacity to meet the new problems arising constantly in our ever-developing modern economy? I find no satisfying response to that question in his opinion.

In his opinion, Chief Justice Roberts responded as follows:

> Justice Ginsburg questions the necessity of rejecting the Government's commerce power argument, given that § 5000A can be upheld under the taxing power. But the statute reads more naturally as a command to buy insurance than as a tax, and I would uphold it as a command if the Constitution allowed it. It is only because the Commerce Clause does not authorize such a command that it is necessary to reach the taxing power question. And it is only because we have a duty to construe a statute to save it, if fairly possible, that § 5000A can be interpreted as a tax. Without deciding the Commerce Clause question, I would find no basis to adopt such a saving construction.
>
> The Federal Government does not have the power to order people to buy health insurance. Section 5000A would therefore be unconstitutional if read as a command. The Federal Government does have the power to impose a tax on those without health insurance. Section 5000A is therefore constitutional, because it can reasonably be read as a tax.

Justice Ginsburg dropped a footnote in reply:

> The Chief Justice states that he must evaluate the constitutionality of the minimum coverage provision under the Commerce Clause because the provision "reads more naturally as a command to buy insurance than as a tax." The Chief Justice ultimately concludes, however, that interpreting the provision as a tax is a "fairly possible" construction. That being so, I see no reason to undertake a Commerce Clause analysis that is not outcome determinative.

Should Chief Justice Roberts's discussion of the Commerce Clause be considered part of the holding of his opinion (which would make him the fifth vote against the government's Commerce and Necessary & Proper Clause arguments), or should it be considered dictum (which would leave the Court deadlocked on those questions)? Should it matter whether he thinks the commerce discussion is necessary to the result?

---

e.   Medicaid Expansion and the Spending Power

In addition to mandating the private purchase of health insurance, the Affordable Care Act also dramatically expanded the federal Medicaid program, which provides medical care to low-income Americans and is administered by the states. This expansion had two components. First, Congress massively increased the amount of federal funds offered through the program. Second, Congress required states to expand the categories of beneficiaries eligible for Medicaid support. If states didn't agree to expand the categories of beneficiary to include those specified in the Affordable Care Act, they forfeited all federal Medicaid funds for all categories of beneficiaries. To track the Court's resolution of the challenge to these new requirements, we again begin with the Chief Justice's opinion—joined here by Justices Breyer and Kagan.

Chief Justice Roberts . . . :

The second provision of the Affordable Care Act directly challenged here is the Medicaid expansion. Enacted in 1965, Medicaid offers federal funding to States to assist pregnant women, children, needy families, the blind, the elderly, and the disabled in obtaining medical care. In order to receive that funding, States must comply with federal criteria governing matters such as who receives care and what services are provided at what cost. By 1982 every State had chosen to participate in Medicaid. Federal funds received through the Medicaid program have become a substantial part of state budgets, now constituting over 10 percent of most States' total revenue.

The Affordable Care Act expands the scope of the Medicaid program and increases the number of individuals the States must cover. For example, the Act requires state programs to provide Medicaid coverage to adults with incomes up to 133 percent of the federal poverty level, whereas many States now cover adults with children only if their income is considerably lower, and do not cover childless adults at all. The Act increases federal funding to cover the States' costs in expanding Medicaid coverage, although States will bear a portion of the costs on their own. If a State does not comply with the Act's new coverage requirements, it may lose not only the federal funding for those requirements, but all of its federal Medicaid funds. . . .

IV

A

The States . . . contend that the Medicaid expansion exceeds Congress's authority under the Spending Clause. They claim that Congress is coercing the States to adopt the changes it wants by threatening to withhold all of a State's Medicaid grants, unless the State accepts the new expanded funding and complies with the conditions that come with it. This, they argue, violates the basic principle that the "Federal Government may not compel the States to enact or administer a federal regulatory program." *New York v. United States* (1992).

There is no doubt that the Act dramatically increases state obligations under Medicaid. The current Medicaid program requires States to cover only certain discrete categories of needy individuals—pregnant women, children, needy families, the blind, the elderly, and the disabled. There is no mandatory coverage for most childless adults, and the States typically do not offer any such coverage. The States also enjoy considerable flexibility with respect to the coverage levels for parents of needy families. On average States cover only those unemployed parents who make less than 37 percent of the federal poverty level, and only those employed parents who make less than 63 percent of the poverty line.

The Medicaid provisions of the Affordable Care Act, in contrast, require States to expand their Medicaid programs by 2014 to cover *all* individuals under the age of 65 with incomes below 133 percent of the federal poverty line. The Act also establishes a new "[e]ssential health benefits" package, which States must provide to all new Medicaid recipients—a level sufficient to satisfy a recipient's obligations under the individual mandate. The Affordable Care Act provides that the Federal Government will pay 100 percent of the costs of covering these newly eligible individuals through 2016. In the following years, the federal payment level gradually decreases, to a minimum of 90 percent. In light of the expansion in coverage mandated by the Act, the Federal Government estimates that its Medicaid spending will increase by approximately $100 billion per year, nearly 40 percent above current levels. . . .

. . . We have long recognized that Congress may use [the spending] power to grant federal funds to the States, and may condition such a grant upon the States' "taking certain actions that Congress could not require them to take." *College Savings Bank.* . . .

At the same time, our cases have recognized limits on Congress's power under the Spending Clause to secure state compliance with federal objectives. "We have repeatedly characterized . . . Spending Clause legislation as 'much in the nature of a *contract.*'" *Barnes v. Gorman* (2002). The legitimacy of Congress's exercise of the spending power "thus rests on whether the State voluntarily and knowingly accepts the terms of the 'contract.'" Respecting this limitation is critical to ensuring that Spending Clause legislation does not undermine the status of the States as independent sovereigns in our federal system. . . .

That insight has . . . led us to scrutinize Spending Clause legislation to ensure that Congress is not using financial inducements to exert a "power akin to undue influence." *Steward Machine Co. v. Davis* (1937). Congress may use its spending power to create incentives for States to act in accordance with federal policies. But when "pressure turns into compulsion," the legislation runs contrary to our system of federalism. "[T]he Constitution simply does not give Congress the authority to require the States to regulate." *New York*. That is true whether Congress directly commands a State to regulate or indirectly coerces a State to adopt a federal regulatory system as its own. . . .

Permitting the Federal Government to force the States to implement a federal program would threaten the political accountability key to our federal system. . . . Spending Clause programs do not pose this danger when a State has a legitimate choice whether to accept the federal conditions in exchange for federal funds. In such a situation, state officials can fairly be held politically accountable for choosing to accept or refuse the federal offer. But when the State has no choice, the Federal Government can achieve its objectives without accountability. . . . Indeed, this danger is heightened when Congress acts under the Spending Clause, because Congress can use that power to implement federal policy it could not impose directly under its enumerated powers. . . .

As our decision in *Steward Machine* confirms, Congress may attach appropriate conditions to federal taxing and spending programs to preserve its control over the use of federal funds. In the typical case we look to the States to defend their prerogatives by adopting "the simple expedient of not yielding" to federal blandishments when they do not want to embrace the federal policies as their own. *Massachusetts v. Mellon* (1923). The States are separate and independent sovereigns. Sometimes they have to act like it.

The States, however, argue that the Medicaid expansion is far from the typical case. They object that Congress has "crossed the line distinguishing encouragement from coercion," *New York*, in the way it has structured the funding: Instead of simply refusing to grant the new funds to States that will not accept the new conditions, Congress has also threatened to withhold those States' existing Medicaid funds. The States claim that this threat serves no purpose other than to force unwilling States to sign up for the dramatic expansion in health care coverage effected by the Act.

Given the nature of the threat and the programs at issue here, we must agree. We have upheld Congress's authority to condition the receipt of funds on the States' complying with restrictions on the use of those funds, because that is the means by which Congress ensures that the funds are spent according to its view of the "general Welfare." Conditions that do not here govern the use of the funds, however, cannot be justified on that basis. When, for example, such conditions take the form of threats to terminate other significant independent grants, the conditions are properly viewed as a means of pressuring the States to accept policy changes.

In *South Dakota v. Dole*, we considered a challenge to a federal law that threatened to withhold five percent of a State's federal highway funds if the State did not raise its drinking age to 21. The Court found that the condition was "directly related to one of the main purposes for which highway funds are expended—safe interstate travel." At the same time, the condition was not a restriction on how the highway funds—set aside for specific highway improvement and maintenance efforts—were to be used.

We accordingly asked whether "the financial inducement offered by Congress" was "so coercive as to pass the point at which 'pressure turns into compulsion.'" By "financial inducement" the Court meant the threat of losing five percent of highway funds; no new money was offered to the States to raise their drinking ages. We found that the inducement was not impermissibly coercive, because Congress was offering only "relatively mild encouragement to the States." We observed that "all South Dakota would lose if she adheres to her chosen course as to a suitable minimum drinking age is 5%" of her highway funds. In fact, the federal funds at stake constituted less than half of one percent of South Dakota's budget at the time. In consequence, "we conclude[d] that [the] encouragement to state action [was] a valid use of the spending power." Whether to accept the drinking age change "remain[ed] the prerogative of the States not merely in theory but in fact."

In this case, the financial "inducement" Congress has chosen is much more than "relatively mild encouragement"—it is a gun to the head. Section 1396c of the Medicaid Act provides that if a State's Medicaid plan does not comply with the Act's requirements, the Secretary of Health and Human Services may declare that "further payments will not be made to the State." A State that opts out of the Affordable Care Act's expansion in health care coverage thus stands to lose not merely "a relatively small percentage" of its existing Medicaid funding, but *all* of it. Medicaid spending accounts for over 20 percent of the average State's total budget, with federal funds covering 50 to 83 percent of those costs. The Federal Government estimates that it will pay out approximately $3.3 trillion between 2010 and 2019 in order to cover the costs of *pre*-expansion Medicaid. In addition, the States have developed intricate statutory and administrative regimes over the course of many decades to implement their objectives under existing Medicaid. It is easy to see how the *Dole* Court could conclude that the threatened loss of less than half of one percent of South Dakota's budget left that State with a "prerogative" to reject Congress's desired policy, "not merely in theory but in fact." The threatened loss of over 10 percent of a State's overall budget, in contrast, is economic dragooning that leaves the States with no real option but to acquiesce in the Medicaid expansion.

Justice Ginsburg claims that *Dole* is distinguishable because here "Congress has not threatened to withhold funds earmarked for any other program." But that begs the question: The States contend that the expansion is in reality a new program and that Congress is forcing them to accept it by threatening the funds for the existing Medicaid program. We cannot agree that existing Medicaid and the expansion dictated by the Affordable Care Act are all one program simply because "Congress styled" them as such. *Post.* If the expansion is not properly viewed as a modification of the existing Medicaid program, Congress's decision to so title it is irrelevant.

Here, the Government claims that the Medicaid expansion is properly viewed merely as a modification of the existing program because the States agreed that Congress could change the terms of Medicaid when they signed on in the first place. The Government observes that the Social Security Act, which includes the original Medicaid provisions, contains a clause expressly reserving "[t]he right to alter, amend, or repeal any provision" of that statute. So it does. But "if Congress intends to impose a condition on the grant of federal moneys, it must do so unambiguously." *Pennhurst State School and Hospital v. Halderman* (1981). A State confronted with statutory language reserving the right to "alter" or "amend" the pertinent provisions of the Social Security Act might reasonably assume that Congress was entitled to make adjustments to the Medicaid program as it developed. Congress has in fact done so, sometimes conditioning only the new funding, other times both old and new. *See, e.g.,* Social Security Amendments of 1972 (extending Medicaid eligibility, but partly conditioning only the new funding); Omnibus Budget Reconciliation Act of 1990 (extending eligibility, and conditioning old and new funds).

The Medicaid expansion, however, accomplishes a shift in kind, not merely degree. The original program was designed to cover medical services for four particular categories of the needy: the disabled, the blind, the elderly, and needy families with dependent children. Previous amendments to Medicaid eligibility merely altered and expanded the boundaries of these categories. Under the Affordable Care Act, Medicaid is transformed into a program to meet the health care needs of the entire nonelderly population with income below 133 percent of the poverty level. It is no longer a program to care for the neediest among us, but rather an element of a comprehensive national plan to provide universal health insurance coverage.[14]

. . . As we have explained, "[t]hough Congress' power to legislate under the spending power is broad, it does not include surprising participating States with post-acceptance or 'retroactive' conditions." *Pennhurst*. A State could hardly anticipate that Congress's reservation of the right to "alter" or "amend" the Medicaid program included the power to transform it so dramatically.

Justice Ginsburg claims that in fact this expansion is no different from the previous changes to Medicaid, such that "a State would be hard put to complain that it lacked fair notice." But the prior change she discusses—presumably the most dramatic alteration she could find—does not come close to working the transformation the expansion accomplishes. She highlights an amendment requiring States to cover pregnant women and increasing the number of eligible children. But this modification can hardly be described as a major change in a program that—from its inception—provided health care for "families with dependent children." Previous Medicaid amendments simply do not fall into the same category as the one at stake here.

The Court in *Steward Machine* did not attempt to "fix the outermost line" where persuasion gives way to coercion. The Court found it "[e]nough for present purposes that wherever the line may be, this statute is within it." We have no need to fix a line either. It is enough for today that wherever that line may be, this statute is surely beyond it. Congress may not simply "conscript state [agencies] into the national bureaucratic army," *FERC v. Mississippi* (1982) (O'Connor, J., concurring in judgment in part and dissenting in part), and that is what it is attempting to do with the Medicaid expansion. . . .

JUSTICE SCALIA, JUSTICE KENNEDY, JUSTICE THOMAS, and JUSTICE ALITO, dissenting.

---

[14] Justice Ginsburg suggests that the States can have no objection to the Medicaid expansion, because "Congress could have repealed Medicaid [and,] [t]hereafter, . . . could have enacted Medicaid II, a new program combining the pre-2010 coverage with the expanded coverage required by the ACA." But it would certainly not be that easy. Practical constraints would plainly inhibit, if not preclude, the Federal Government from repealing the existing program and putting every feature of Medicaid on the table for political reconsideration. Such a massive undertaking would hardly be "ritualistic." The same is true of Justice Ginsburg's suggestion that Congress could establish Medicaid as an exclusively federal program.

. . .

IV

. . . The ACA does not legally compel the States to participate in the expanded Medicaid program, but the Act authorizes a severe sanction for any State that refuses to go along: termination of all the State's Medicaid funding. For the average State, the annual federal Medicaid subsidy is equal to more than one-fifth of the State's expenditures.[7] . . .

B

One way in which Congress may spend to promote the general welfare is by making grants to the States. Monetary grants, so-called grants-in-aid, became more frequent during the 1930s, and by 1950 they had reached $20 billion or 11.6% of state and local government expenditures from their own sources. By 1970 this number had grown to $123.7 billion or 29.1% of state and local government expenditures from their own sources. As of 2010, federal outlays to state and local governments came to over $608 billion or 37.5% of state and local government expenditures.

When Congress makes grants to the States, it customarily attaches conditions, and this Court has long held that the Constitution generally permits Congress to do this. See *South Dakota v. Dole* (1987); *Steward Machine.* . . . [While] Congress may seek to induce States to accept conditional grants, Congress may not cross the "point at which pressure turns into compulsion, and ceases to be inducement." *Steward Machine.* Accord *Dole.* . . .

Once it is recognized that spending-power legislation cannot coerce state participation, two questions remain: (1) What is the meaning of coercion in this context? (2) Is the ACA's expanded Medicaid coverage coercive? We now turn to those questions.

D

1

The answer to the first of these questions—the meaning of coercion in the present context—is straightforward. [I]f States really have no choice other than to accept the package, the offer is coercive, and the conditions cannot be

---

[7]   "State expenditures" is used here to mean annual expenditures from the States' own funding sources, and it excludes federal grants unless otherwise noted.

sustained under the spending power. And as our decision in *South Dakota v. Dole* makes clear, theoretical voluntariness is not enough. . . .

2

The Federal Government's argument in this case at best pays lip service to the anticoercion principle. The Federal Government suggests that it is sufficient if States are "free, *as a matter of law*, to turn down" federal funds. Brief for Respondents (emphasis added). According to the Federal Government, neither the amount of the offered federal funds nor the amount of the federal taxes extracted from the taxpayers of a State to pay for the program in question is relevant in determining whether there is impermissible coercion.

This argument ignores reality. When a heavy federal tax is levied to support a federal program that offers large grants to the States, States may, as a practical matter, be unable to refuse to participate in the federal program and to substitute a state alternative. Even if a State believes that the federal program is ineffective and inefficient, withdrawal would likely force the State to impose a huge tax increase on its residents, and this new state tax would come on top of the federal taxes already paid by residents to support subsidies to participating States.[13]

Acceptance of the Federal Government's interpretation of the anticoercion rule would permit Congress to dictate policy in areas traditionally governed primarily at the state or local level. Suppose, for example, that Congress enacted legislation offering each State a grant equal to the State's entire annual expenditures for primary and secondary education. Suppose also that this funding came with conditions governing such things as school curriculum, the hiring and tenure of teachers, the drawing of school districts, the length and hours of the school day, the school calendar, a dress code for students, and rules for student discipline. *As a matter of law,* a State could turn down that offer, but if it did so, its residents would not only be required to pay the federal taxes needed to support this expensive new program, but they would also be forced to pay an equivalent amount in state taxes. And if the State gave in to the federal law, the State and its subdivisions would surrender their traditional authority in the field of education. Asked at oral argument whether such a law would

---

[13] Justice Ginsburg argues that "[a] State . . . has no claim on the money its residents pay in federal taxes." This is true as a formal matter. . . . But unless Justice Ginsburg thinks that there is no limit to the amount of money that can be squeezed out of taxpayers, heavy federal taxation diminishes the practical ability of States to collect their own taxes.

be allowed under the spending power, the Solicitor General responded that it would. Tr. of Oral Arg. (Mar. 28, 2012). . . .

The Medicaid Expansion therefore exceeds Congress' spending power. . . .

JUSTICE GINSBURG, with whom JUSTICE SOTOMAYOR joins . . . , dissenting in part:

V

Through Medicaid, Congress has offered the States an opportunity to furnish health care to the poor with the aid of federal financing. To receive federal Medicaid funds, States must provide health benefits to specified categories of needy persons, including pregnant women, children, parents, and adults with disabilities. Guaranteed eligibility varies by category: for some it is tied to the federal poverty level . . . ; for others it depends on criteria such as eligibility for designated state or federal assistance programs. The ACA enlarges the population of needy people States must cover to include adults under age 65 with incomes up to 133% of the federal poverty level.

The spending power conferred by the Constitution, the Court has never doubted, permits Congress to define the contours of programs financed with federal funds. And to expand coverage, Congress could have recalled the existing legislation, and replaced it with a new law making Medicaid as embracive of the poor as Congress chose.

The question posed by the 2010 Medicaid expansion, then, is essentially this: To cover a notably larger population, must Congress take the repeal/reenact route, or may it achieve the same result by amending existing law? The answer should be that Congress may expand by amendment the classes of needy persons entitled to Medicaid benefits. A ritualistic requirement that Congress repeal and reenact spending legislation in order to enlarge the population served by a federally funded program would advance no constitutional principle and would scarcely serve the interests of federalism. To the contrary, such a requirement would rigidify Congress' efforts to empower States by partnering with them in the implementation of federal programs.

Medicaid is a prototypical example of federal-state cooperation in serving the Nation's general welfare. Rather than authorizing a federal agency to administer a uniform national health-care system for the poor, Congress offered States the opportunity to tailor Medicaid grants to their particular needs, so long as they remain within bounds set by federal law. In shaping Medicaid,

Congress did not endeavor to fix permanently the terms participating States must meet; instead, Congress reserved the "right to alter, amend, or repeal" any provision of the Medicaid Act. 42 U.S.C. § 1304. States, for their part, agreed to amend their own Medicaid plans consistent with changes from time to time made in the federal law. See 42 CFR § 430.12(c)(i) (2011). And from 1965 to the present, States have regularly conformed to Congress' alterations of the Medicaid Act.

The Chief Justice acknowledges that Congress may "condition the receipt of [federal] funds on the States' complying with restrictions on the use of those funds," but nevertheless concludes that the 2010 expansion is unduly coercive. His conclusion rests on three premises, each of them essential to his theory. First, the Medicaid expansion is, in the Chief Justice's view, a new grant program, not an addition to the Medicaid program existing before the ACA's enactment. Congress, the Chief Justice maintains, has threatened States with the loss of funds from an old program in an effort to get them to adopt a new one. Second, the expansion was unforeseeable by the States when they first signed on to Medicaid. Third, the threatened loss of funding is so large that the States have no real choice but to participate in the Medicaid expansion.

The Chief Justice therefore—*for the first time ever*—finds an exercise of Congress' spending power unconstitutionally coercive.

> **CROSS REFERENCE** Is it really the first time ever? Recall *United States v. Butler* (1936), presented at pp. 489–490.

Medicaid, as amended by the ACA, however, is not two spending programs; it is a single program with a constant aim—to enable poor persons to receive basic health care when they need it. Given past expansions, plus express statutory warning that Congress may change the requirements participating States must meet, there can be no tenable claim that the ACA fails for lack of notice. Moreover, States have no entitlement to receive any Medicaid funds; they enjoy only the opportunity to accept funds on Congress' terms. Future Congresses are not bound by their predecessors' dispositions; they have authority to spend federal revenue as they see fit. The Federal Government, therefore, is not, as the Chief Justice charges, threatening States with the loss of "existing" funds from one spending program in order to induce them to opt into another program. Congress is simply requiring States to do what States have long been required to do to receive Medicaid funding: comply with the conditions Congress prescribes for participation.

A

Expansion has been characteristic of the Medicaid program. Akin to the ACA in 2010, the Medicaid Act as passed in 1965 augmented existing federal grant programs jointly administered with the States. States were not required to participate in Medicaid. But if they did, the Federal Government paid at least half the costs. To qualify for these grants, States had to offer a minimum level of health coverage to beneficiaries of four federally funded, state-administered welfare programs: Aid to Families with Dependent Children; Old Age Assistance; Aid to the Blind; and Aid to the Permanently and Totally Disabled. At their option, States could enroll additional "medically needy" individuals; these costs, too, were partially borne by the Federal Government at the same, at least 50%, rate.

Since 1965, Congress has amended the Medicaid program on more than 50 occasions, sometimes quite sizably. Most relevant here, between 1988 and 1990, Congress required participating States to include among their beneficiaries pregnant women with family incomes up to 133% of the federal poverty level, children up to age 6 at the same income levels, and children ages 6 to 18 with family incomes up to 100% of the poverty level. . . . These amendments added millions to the Medicaid-eligible population. . . .

Compared to past alterations, the ACA is notable for the extent to which the Federal Government will pick up the tab. Medicaid's 2010 expansion is financed largely by federal outlays. In 2014, federal funds will cover 100% of the costs for newly eligible beneficiaries; that rate will gradually decrease before settling at 90% in 2020. By comparison, federal contributions toward the care of beneficiaries eligible pre-ACA range from 50% to 83%, and averaged 57% between 2005 and 2008. Nor will the expansion exorbitantly increase state Medicaid spending. The Congressional Budget Office (CBO) projects that States will spend 0.8% more than they would have, absent the ACA. But see *ante* (Roberts, C.J.) ("[T]he Act dramatically increases state obligations under Medicaid."). Whatever the increase in state obligations after the ACA, it will pale in comparison to the increase in federal funding.

Finally, any fair appraisal of Medicaid would require acknowledgment of the considerable autonomy States enjoy under the Act. Far from "conscript[ing] state agencies into the national bureaucratic army," *ante*, Medicaid "is designed to advance cooperative federalism." Subject to its basic requirements, the Medicaid Act empowers States to "select dramatically different levels of funding and coverage, alter and experiment with different financing and delivery modes, and opt to cover (or not to cover) a range of particular procedures and therapies. States have leveraged this policy discretion to generate a myriad of dramatically different Medicaid programs over the past several decades." Ruger, *Of Icebergs and Glaciers*, 75 Law & Contemp. Prob. 215 (2012). The ACA does not jettison this approach. States, as first-line administrators, will continue to guide the distribution of substantial resources among their needy populations.

The alternative to conditional federal spending, it bears emphasis, is not state autonomy but state marginalization. In 1965, Congress elected to nationalize health coverage for seniors through Medicare. It could similarly have established Medicaid as an exclusively federal program. Instead, Congress gave the States the opportunity to partner in the program's administration and development. Absent from the nationalized model, of course, is the state-level policy discretion and experimentation that is Medicaid's hallmark; undoubtedly the interests of federalism are better served when States retain a meaningful role in the implementation of a program of such importance. See Caminker, *State Sovereignty and Subordinacy*, 95 Colum. L. Rev. 1001 (1995).[17]...

B

... Congress' authority to condition the use of federal funds is not confined to spending programs as first launched. The Legislature may, and often does, amend the law, imposing new conditions grant recipients henceforth must meet in order to continue receiving funds. See *infra* (describing [enforcement of] restriction added five years after adoption of educational program).

Yes, there are federalism-based limits on the use of Congress' conditional spending power. In the leading decision in this area, *South Dakota v. Dole* (1987), the Court identified four criteria. The conditions placed on federal grants to States must (1) promote the "general welfare," (2) "unambiguously" inform States what is demanded of them, (3) be germane "to the federal interest in particular national projects or programs," and (4) not "induce the States to engage in activities that would themselves be unconstitutional."

The Court in *Dole* mentioned, but did not adopt, a further limitation, one hypothetically raised a half-century earlier: In "some circumstances," Congress

---

[17] The Chief Justice and the joint dissenters perceive in cooperative federalism a "threa[t]" to "political accountability." By that, they mean voter confusion: Citizens upset by unpopular government action, they posit, may ascribe to state officials blame more appropriately laid at Congress' door. But no such confusion is apparent in this case: Medicaid's status as a federally funded, state-administered program is hardly hidden from view.

might be prohibited from offering a "financial inducement . . . so coercive as to pass the point at which 'pressure turns into compulsion.' " *Id.* (quoting *Steward Machine Co. v. Davis* (1937)). Prior to today's decision, however, the Court has never ruled that the terms of any grant crossed the indistinct line between temptation and coercion. . . .

This litigation does not present the concerns that led the Court in *Dole* even to consider the prospect of coercion. In *Dole*, the condition—set 21 as the minimum drinking age—did not tell the States how to use funds Congress provided for highway construction. Further, in view of the Twenty-First Amendment, it was an open question whether Congress could directly impose a national minimum drinking age.

The ACA, in contrast, relates solely to the federally funded Medicaid program; if States choose not to comply, Congress has not threatened to withhold funds earmarked for any other program. Nor does the ACA use Medicaid funding to induce States to take action Congress itself could not undertake. The Federal Government undoubtedly could operate its own health-care program for poor persons, just as it operates Medicare for seniors' health care.

That is what makes this such a simple case, and the Court's decision so unsettling. Congress, aiming to assist the needy, has appropriated federal money to subsidize state health-insurance programs that meet federal standards. The principal standard the ACA sets is that the state program cover adults earning no more than 133% of the federal poverty line. Enforcing that prescription ensures that federal funds will be spent on health care for the poor in furtherance of Congress' present perception of the general welfare.

C

The Chief Justice asserts that . . . Congress' threat to withhold "old" Medicaid funds based on a State's refusal to participate in the "new" program is a "threa[t] to terminate [an]other . . . independent gran[t]." And because the threat to withhold a large amount of funds from one program "leaves the States with no real option but to acquiesce [in a newly created program]," the Chief Justice concludes, the Medicaid expansion is unconstitutionally coercive.

1

The starting premise on which the Chief Justice's coercion analysis rests is that the ACA did not really "extend" Medicaid; instead, Congress created an entirely new program to coexist with the old. The Chief Justice calls the

ACA new, but in truth, it simply reaches more of America's poor than Congress originally covered.

Medicaid was created to enable States to provide medical assistance to "needy persons." See S. Rep. No. 404, 89th Cong., 1st Sess. (1965). By bringing health care within the reach of a larger population of Americans unable to afford it, the Medicaid expansion is an extension of that basic aim.

The Medicaid Act contains hundreds of provisions governing operation of the program, setting conditions ranging from "Limitation on payments to States for expenditures attributable to taxes," to "Medical assistance to aliens not lawfully admitted for permanent residence." The Medicaid expansion leaves unchanged the vast majority of these provisions; it adds beneficiaries to the existing program and specifies the rate at which States will be reimbursed for services provided to the added beneficiaries. The ACA does not describe operational aspects of the program for these newly eligible persons; for that information, one must read the existing Medicaid Act.

Congress styled and clearly viewed the Medicaid expansion as an amendment to the Medicaid Act, not as a "new" health-care program. To the four categories of beneficiaries for whom coverage became mandatory in 1965, and the three mandatory classes added in the late 1980s, the ACA adds an eighth: individuals under 65 with incomes not exceeding 133% of the federal poverty level. The expansion is effectuated by § 2001 of the ACA, aptly titled: "Medicaid Coverage for the Lowest Income Populations." That section amends . . . the Medicaid Act, [which] filled some 278 pages in 2006. Section 2001 of the ACA would add approximately three pages. . . .

Endeavoring to show that Congress created a new program, the Chief Justice . . . asserts that, in covering those earning no more than 133% of the federal poverty line, the Medicaid expansion, unlike pre-ACA Medicaid, does not "care for the neediest among us." What makes that so? Single adults earning no more than $14,856 per year—133% of the current federal poverty level—surely rank among the Nation's poor. . . .

Consider also that Congress could have repealed Medicaid. Thereafter, Congress could have enacted Medicaid II, a new program combining the pre-2010 coverage with the expanded coverage required by the ACA. By what right does a court stop Congress from building up without first tearing down?

2

The Chief Justice finds the Medicaid expansion vulnerable because it took participating States by surprise. . . .

The Chief Justice appears to find in *Pennhurst State School and Hospital v. Halderman* (1984) a requirement that, when spending legislation is first passed, or when States first enlist in the federal program, Congress must provide clear notice of conditions it might later impose. If I understand his point correctly, it was incumbent on Congress, in 1965, to warn the States clearly of the size and shape potential changes to Medicaid might take. And absent such notice, sizable changes could not be made mandatory. Our decisions do not support such a requirement. *Pennhurst*'s rule demands that conditions on federal funds be unambiguously clear at the time a State receives and uses the money—not at the time, perhaps years earlier, when Congress passed the law establishing the program. See also *Dole* (finding *Pennhurst* satisfied based on the clarity of the Federal Aid Highway Act as amended in 1984, without looking back to 1956, the year of the Act's adoption).

In any event, from the start, the Medicaid Act put States on notice that the program could be changed: "The right to alter, amend, or repeal any provision of [Medicaid]," the statute has read since 1965, "is hereby reserved to the Congress." 42 U.S.C. § 1304. The "effect of these few simple words" has long been settled. By reserving the right to "alter, amend, [or] repeal" a spending program, Congress "has given special notice of its intention to retain . . . full and complete power to make such alterations and amendments . . . as come within the just scope of legislative power." *National Railroad Passenger Corporation v. Atchison, T. & S.F.R. Co.* (1985). . . .

The Chief Justice nevertheless would rewrite § 1304 to countenance only the "right to alter *somewhat*," or "amend, *but not too much*." Congress, however, did not so qualify § 1304. Indeed, Congress retained discretion to "repeal" Medicaid, wiping it out entirely. Cf. *Delta Air Lines, Inc. v. August* (1981) (Rehnquist, J., dissenting) (invoking "the common-sense maxim that the greater includes the lesser"). [N]o State could reasonably have read § 1304 as reserving to Congress authority to make adjustments only if modestly sized.

The Chief Justice insists that the most recent expansion, in contrast to its predecessors, "accomplishes a shift in kind, not merely degree." But why was Medicaid altered only in degree, not in kind, when Congress required States to cover millions of children and pregnant women? In short, given § 1304 and the enlargement of Medicaid in the years since 1965,[23] a State would be hard put to complain that it lacked fair notice when, in 2010, Congress altered Medicaid to embrace a larger portion of the Nation's poor.

3

The Chief Justice ultimately asks whether "the financial inducement offered by Congress . . . pass[ed] the point at which pressure turns into compulsion." The financial inducement Congress employed here, he concludes, crosses that threshold: The threatened withholding of "existing Medicaid funds" is "a gun to the head" that forces States to acquiesce.[24]

The Chief Justice sees no need to "fix the outermost line," *Steward Machine,* "where persuasion gives way to coercion." Neither do the joint dissenters. Notably, the decision on which they rely, *Steward Machine,* found the statute at issue inside the line, "wherever the line may be."

When future Spending Clause challenges arrive, as they likely will in the wake of today's decision, how will litigants and judges assess whether "a State has a legitimate choice whether to accept the federal conditions in exchange for federal funds"? Are courts to measure the number of dollars the Federal Government might withhold for noncompliance? The portion of the State's budget at stake? And which State's—or States'—budget is determinative: the lead plaintiff, all challenging States (26 in this case, many with quite different fiscal situations), or some national median? Does it matter that Florida, unlike most States, imposes no state income tax, and therefore might be able to replace foregone federal funds with new state revenue?[26] Or that the coercion state officials in fact fear is punishment at the ballot box for turning down a politically popular federal grant?

The coercion inquiry, therefore, appears to involve political judgments that defy judicial calculation. See *Baker v. Carr* (1962). Even commentators

---

[23]   Note, in this regard, the extension of Social Security, which began in 1935 as an old-age pension program, then expanded to include survivor benefits in 1939 and disability benefits in 1956. See Social Security Act; Social Security Act Amendments of 1939; Social Security Amendments of 1956.

[24]   The joint dissenters, for their part, would make this the entire inquiry. . . . For [them], all that matters, it appears, is whether States can resist the temptation of a given federal grant. On this logic, any federal spending program, sufficiently large and well-funded, would be unconstitutional. . . . But how is a court to judge whether "only 6.6% of all state expenditures" is an amount States could or would do without? . . .

[26]   Federal taxation of a State's citizens, according to the joint dissenters, may diminish a State's ability to raise new revenue. [But w]hen the United States Government taxes United States citizens, it taxes them "in their individual capacities" as "the people of America"—not as residents of a particular State. . . . A State therefore has no claim on the money its residents pay in federal taxes, and federal "spending programs need not help people in all states in the same measure." . . .

sympathetic to robust enforcement of *Dole*'s limitations have concluded that conceptions of "impermissible coercion" premised on States' perceived inability to decline federal funds "are just too amorphous to be judicially administrable." Baker & Berman, *Getting off the* Dole, 78 Ind. L.J. 459 (2003) (citing, *e.g.*, Scalia, *The Rule of Law as a Law of Rules*, 56 U. Chi. L. Rev. 1175 (1989)).

At bottom, my colleagues' position is that the States' reliance on federal funds limits Congress' authority to alter its spending programs. This gets things backwards: Congress, not the States, is tasked with spending federal money in service of the general welfare. And each successive Congress is empowered to appropriate funds as it sees fit. When the 110th Congress reached a conclusion about Medicaid funds that differed from its predecessors' view, it abridged no State's right to "existing," or "pre-existing," funds. For, in fact, there are no such funds. There is only money States *anticipate* receiving from future Congresses. . . .

I would uphold the Eleventh Circuit's decision that the Medicaid expansion is within Congress' spending power.

FOR DISCUSSION

Theoretically, as Justice Ginsburg suggests, Congress could shut down the entire Medicaid program—and soon after create a much larger program, making participation of any state dependent on its compliance with a more extensive set of conditions. Does this possibility bear on whether the actual Medicaid expansion was valid?

f.   Severability

Having decided that the mandate was constitutional but that the Medicaid expansion was not, Chief Justice Roberts's controlling opinion had to decide whether the unconstitutionality of the latter infected the entire statute to a degree that it all had to fall. In discussing that question he was joined once again by Justices Breyer and Kagan.

CHIEF JUSTICE ROBERTS . . . :

. . . In light of the Court's holding, the Secretary cannot apply § 1396c to withdraw existing Medicaid funds for failure to comply with the requirements set out in the expansion.

That fully remedies the constitutional violation we have identified. The chapter of the United States Code that contains § 1396c includes a severability clause confirming that we need go no further. That clause specifies[:]

> If any provision of this chapter, or the application thereof to any person or circumstance, is held invalid, the remainder of the chapter, and the application of such provision to other persons or circumstances shall not be affected thereby.

§ 1303. Today's holding does not affect the continued application of § 1396c to the existing Medicaid program. Nor does it affect the Secretary's ability to withdraw funds provided under the Affordable Care Act if a State that has chosen to participate in the expansion fails to comply with the requirements of that Act.

This is not to say, as the joint dissent suggests, that we are "rewriting the Medicaid Expansion." Instead, we determine, first, that § 1396c is unconstitutional when applied to withdraw existing Medicaid funds from States that decline to comply with the expansion. We then follow Congress's explicit textual instruction to leave unaffected "the remainder of the chapter, and the application of [the challenged] provision to other persons or circumstances." § 1303. When we invalidate an application of a statute because that application is unconstitutional, we are not "rewriting" the statute; we are merely enforcing the Constitution.

The question remains whether today's holding affects other provisions of the Affordable Care Act. In considering that question, "[w]e seek to determine what Congress would have intended in light of the Court's constitutional holding." *United States v. Booker* (2005). . . . The question here is whether Congress would have wanted the rest of the Act to stand, had it known that States would have a genuine choice whether to participate in the new Medicaid expansion. Unless it is "evident" that the answer is no, we must leave the rest of the Act intact. *Champlin Refining Co. v. Corporation Comm'n of Okla.* (1932).

We are confident that Congress would have wanted to preserve the rest of the Act. . . . We have no way of knowing how many States will accept the terms of the expansion, but we do not believe Congress would have wanted the whole Act to fall, simply because some may choose not to participate. The other reforms Congress enacted, after all, will remain "fully operative as a law,"

Champlin, and will still function in a way "consistent with Congress' basic objectives in enacting the statute," *Booker.* Confident that Congress would not have intended anything different, we conclude that the rest of the Act need not fall in light of our constitutional holding. . . .

Justice Ginsburg, with whom Justice Sotomayor joins . . . :

[I]n view of the Chief Justice's disposition, I agree with him that the Medicaid Act's severability clause [§ 1303] determines the appropriate remedy. . . . Even absent § 1303's command, we would have no warrant to invalidate the Medicaid expansion, not to mention the entire ACA. For when a court confronts an unconstitutional statute, its endeavor must be to conserve, not destroy, the legislature's dominant objective. See, *e.g., Ayotte v. Planned Parenthood of Northern New Eng.* (2006). . . . I therefore concur in the judgment with respect to [the portion of] the Chief Justice's opinion [relating to severability].

Justice Scalia, Justice Kennedy, Justice Thomas, and Justice Alito, dissenting in part. . . .

The Court has applied a two-part guide as the framework for severability analysis. . . . First, if the Court holds a statutory provision unconstitutional, it then determines whether the now truncated statute will operate in the manner Congress intended. If not, the remaining provisions must be invalidated. . . . Second, even if the remaining provisions can operate as Congress designed them to operate, the Court must determine if Congress would have enacted them standing alone and without the unconstitutional portion. If Congress would not, those provisions, too, must be invalidated. . . .

Without the Individual Mandate and Medicaid Expansion, the Affordable Care Act's insurance regulations and insurance taxes impose risks on insurance companies and their customers that this Court cannot measure. Those risks would undermine Congress' scheme of "shared responsibility." . . .

The actual cost of the regulations and taxes may be more or less than predicted. What is known, however, is that severing other provisions from the Individual Mandate and Medicaid Expansion necessarily would impose significant risks and real uncertainties on insurance companies, their customers, all other major actors in the system, and the government treasury. And what also is known is this: Unnecessary risks and avoidable uncertainties are hostile to economic progress and fiscal stability and thus to the safety and welfare of the Nation and the Nation's freedom. If those risks and uncertainties are to be imposed, it must not be by the Judiciary. . . .

The Court today decides to save a statute Congress did not write. It rules that what the statute declares to be a requirement with a penalty is instead an option subject to a tax. And it changes the intentionally coercive sanction of a total cut-off of Medicaid funds to a supposedly noncoercive cut-off of only the incremental funds that the Act makes available. . . .

FOR DISCUSSION

Suppose the Court had invalidated the individual mandate as well as the Medicaid funds cutoff. The surviving statutory system would then be very different from the one that Congress had created. Different enough that the Court should have thrown out the whole statute?

8. The Treaty Power

When it comes to international agreements, the Constitution provides that the President

> "shall have Power, by and with the Advice and Consent of the Senate, to make Treaties, provided two thirds of the Senators present concur."
>
> Art II, Sec. 2.

For our purposes, perhaps the most significant thing about Article II treaties is that, under the Article VI Supremacy Clause, "all Treaties made . . . under the Authority of the United States" automatically become part of "the supreme Law of the Land." To what extent does the adoption of a treaty actually expand Congress's power, by enabling it to take actions that it could not otherwise justify? Moreover, if an Article II treaty is written to have immediate domestic effect without the need for implementing legislation, the treaty supersedes any existing congressional statute with which it conflicts!

Given that the Treaty Clause is not explicitly limited to an enumerated list of subject matters, should it be understood to authorize effectively legislative action (either in its own right or in combination with the Necessary & Proper Clause) that goes beyond Congress's other enumerated powers? The following readings explore the question of whether there are any subject matter limits on what such "Treaties" can contain, require, or authorize.

WORTH NOTING

Article II treaties aren't the only way for the United States to enter international agreements—"congressional-presidential agreements," for example, are made through a bicameral legislative process and "sole executive agreements" are made by the President alone. But the Treaty Clause is an especially important way for the U.S. to do foreign policy, partly because of the possibility that the other two are constitutionally limited to specific subject matters, and partly because of deeply embedded traditions that neither the State Department nor Congress seem interested in upsetting. For an argument that the U.S. not only can but should stop using the Article II Treaty Clause almost entirely, see Oona Hathaway, *Treaties' End: The Past, Present, and Future of International Lawmaking in the United States*, 117 Yale L. J. 1236 ("By gradually replacing most Article II treaties with ex post congressional-executive agreements, policymakers can make America's domestic engagement with international law more sensible, effective, and democratic.").

The Founding Generation and the Treaty Power

During the Virginia Ratifying Convention, the antifederalist Patrick Henry—one of the great orators of his age—rose to attack the Treaty Power:

> Mr. *Henry,*—Mr. Chairman.—Gentlemen say, that the King of Great-Britain has the same right of making treaties that our President has here. I will have no objection to this, if you make your President a King. . . .

> I say again, that if you consent to this power, you depend on the justice and equity of those in power. . . . Sure I am if treaties are made, infringing our liberties, it will be too late to say that our constitutional rights are violated. . . . Suppose you be arraigned as offenders and violators of a treaty made by this Government. Will you have that fair trial which offenders are entitled to in your own Government? Will you plead a right to the trial by jury? You will have no right to appeal to your own Constitution. You must appeal to your Continental Constitution. A treaty may be made giving away your rights and inflicting unusual punishments on its violators.

It is contended, that if the King of Great-Britain makes a treaty within the line of his prerogative, it is the law of the land. I agree that this is proper, and if I could see the same checks in that paper which I see in the British Government, I would consent to it. Can the English Monarch make a treaty which shall subvert the common law of England, and the Constitution? Dare he make a treaty that shall violate Magna Charta, or the Bill of Rights? Dare he do any thing derogatory to the honor, or subversive of the great privileges of his people? No, Sir. If he did it would be nugatory, and the attempt would endanger his existence.

The next day, the Federalist George Nicholas responded to Henry's charges. Do you think he accepted their substance, denied it, or tried to identify some middle ground?

Mr. *George Nicholas* again drew a parellel between the power of the King of Great-Britain, and that of Congress with respect to making treaties.—He contended, they were on the same foundation, and that every possible security which existed in the one instance, was to be found in the other.—To prove that there was no constitutional limits to the King's power of making treaties, and that treaties when once by him made, were the supreme law of the land, he quoted the following lines in *Blackstone's Commentaries*,

It is also the King's prerogative to make treaties, leagues, and alliances, with foreign States and Princes.—For it is, by the law of nations, essential to the goodness of a league, that it be made by the sovereign power; and then it is binding upon the whole community:—And in England the sovereign power, *quoad hoc*, is vested in the person of the King.—Whatever contracts therefore he engages in, no other power in the kingdom can legally delay, resist, or annul.

. . . How does this apply to this Constitution?—The President and Senate have the same power of making treaties; and when made they are to have the same force and validity. They are to be the supreme law of the land here—This book shews us they are so in England. Have we not seen in America that treaties were violated [by states during the pre-constitutional period], though they are in all countries considered as the supreme law of the land?—Was it not therefore necessary to declare in explicit terms, that they should be so here?—How then is this Constitution on a different footing with the Government of Britain?

The worthy Member [Patrick Henry] says, they can make a treaty relinquishing our rights, and inflicting punishments; because all treaties are declared paramount to the Constitutions and laws of the States.—An attentive consideration of this, will shew the Committee, that they can do no such thing. The provision of the sixth article, is, that this Constitution and the laws of the United States, which shall be made in *pursuance* thereof, and all treaties made, or which shall be made, *under the authority of the United States*, shall be the supreme law of the land.—They can by this make no treaty which shall be repugnant to the spirit of the Constitution, or inconsistent with the delegated powers. . . . It is sufficiently secured, because it only declares, that in *pursuance* of the powers given they shall be the supreme law of the land, notwithstanding any thing in the Constitution or laws of particular States. . . .

Missouri v. Holland

Supreme Court of the United States, 1920.
252 U.S. 416.

MR. JUSTICE HOLMES delivered the opinion of the Court.

This is a bill in equity brought by the State of Missouri to prevent a game warden of the United States from attempting to enforce the Migratory Bird Treaty Act of July 3, 1918, and the regulations made by the Secretary of Agriculture in pursuance of the same. . . .

On December 8, 1916, a treaty between the United States and Great Britain was proclaimed by the President. It recited that many species of birds in their annual migrations traversed many parts of the United States and of Canada, that they were of great value as a source of food and in destroying insects injurious to vegetation, but were in danger of extermination through lack of adequate protection. It therefore provided for specified closed seasons and protection in other forms, and agreed that the two powers would take or propose to their lawmaking bodies the necessary measures for carrying the treaty out.

The above mentioned act of July 3, 1918, entitled an act to give effect to the convention, prohibited the killing, capturing or selling any of the migratory birds included in the terms of the treaty except as permitted by regulations compatible with those terms, to be made by the Secretary of Agriculture. . . .

[B]y Article 2, § 2, the power to make treaties is delegated expressly, and by Article 6 treaties made under the authority of the United States, along with the Constitution and laws of the United States made in pursuance thereof, are declared the supreme law of the land. If the treaty is valid there can be no dispute about the validity of the statute under Article 1, § 8, as a necessary and proper means to execute the powers of the Government. The language of the Constitution as to the supremacy of treaties being general, the question before us is narrowed to an inquiry into the ground upon which the present supposed exception is placed.

It is said that a treaty cannot be valid if it infringes the Constitution, that there are limits, therefore, to the treaty-making power, and that one such limit is that what an act of Congress could not do unaided, in derogation of the powers reserved to the States, a treaty cannot do. An earlier act of Congress that attempted by itself and not in pursuance of a treaty to regulate the killing of migratory birds within the States had been held bad in the District Court. *United States v. Shauver* (E.D. Ark. 1914); *United States v. McCullagh* (D. Kan. 1915) Those decisions were supported by arguments that migratory birds were owned by the States in their sovereign capacity for the benefit of their people, and that . . . this control was one that Congress had no power to displace. The same argument is supposed to apply now with equal force.

Whether the two cases cited were decided rightly or not they cannot be accepted as a test of the treaty power. Acts of Congress are the supreme law of the land only when made in pursuance of the Constitution, while treaties are declared to be so when made under the authority of the United States. It is open to question whether the authority of the United States means more than the formal acts prescribed to make the convention. We do not mean to imply that there are no qualifications to the treaty-making power; but they must be ascertained in a different way. It is obvious that there may be matters of the sharpest exigency for the national well being that an act of Congress could not deal with but that a treaty followed by such an act could, and it is not lightly to be assumed that, in matters requiring national action, "a power which must belong to and somewhere reside in every civilized government" is not to be found. *Andrews v. Andrews* (1903) [(holding that each individual state must have the power to set its own divorce regime, since "it is certain that the Constitution . . . confers no power whatever upon the [federal] government")]. What was said in that case with regard to the powers of the States applies with equal force to the powers of the nation in cases where the States individually are incompetent to act. . . .

The treaty in question does not contravene any prohibitory words to be found in the Constitution. The only question is whether it is forbidden by some invisible radiation from the general terms of the Tenth Amendment. We must consider what this country has become in deciding what that amendment has reserved.

The State as we have intimated founds its claim of exclusive authority upon an assertion of title to migratory birds, an assertion that is embodied in statute. No doubt it is true that as between a State and its inhabitants the State may regulate the killing and sale of such birds, but it does not follow that its authority is exclusive of paramount powers. To put the claim of the State upon title is to lean upon a slender reed. Wild birds are not in the possession of anyone; and possession is the beginning of ownership. The whole foundation of the State's rights is the presence within their jurisdiction of birds that yesterday had not arrived, tomorrow may be in another State and in a week a thousand miles away. . . .

Valid treaties of course "are as binding within the territorial limits of the States as they are elsewhere throughout the dominion of the United States." *Baldwin v. Franks* (1887). No doubt the great body of private relations usually fall within the control of the State, but a treaty may override its power. We do not have to invoke the later developments of constitutional law for this proposition; it was recognized as early as *Hopkirk v. Bell* (1806) [(holding that Virginia's statute of limitations was overriden by the peace treaty between United States and Great Britain)] with regard to statutes of limitation, and even earlier, as to confiscation, in *Ware v. Hylton* (1796) [(holding that Virginia's confiscation of debts to British subjects was voided by the same peace treaty)]. . . . So as to a limited jurisdiction of foreign consuls within a State. *Wildenhus' Case* (1887) [(holding that New Jersey's criminal jurisdiction over a murder was displaced by a treaty giving Belgian consul "exclusive charge of the internal order of the merchant vessels of their nation")]. Further illustration seems unnecessary, and it only remains to consider the application of established rules to the present case.

Here a national interest of very nearly the first magnitude is involved. It can be protected only by national action in concert with that of another power. The subject matter is only transitorily within the State and has no permanent habitat therein. But for the treaty and the statute there soon might be no birds for any powers to deal with. We see nothing in the Constitution that compels the Government to sit by while a food supply is cut off and the protectors of our forests and our crops are destroyed. It is not sufficient to rely upon the States. The reliance is vain, and were it otherwise, the question is whether the United States is forbidden to act. We are of opinion that the treaty and statute must be upheld. . . .

Decree affirmed.

Mr. Justice Van Devanter and Mr. Justice Pitney dissent [without opinion].

The next case involves a more complicated version of the question presented in *Missouri v. Holland*. It too deals with the domestic application of an Article II treaty pursuant to the Supremacy Clause, but embeds that question in a larger transnational scheme of the interrelationship between judicial systems.

Medellín v. Texas

Supreme Court of the United States, 2008.
552 U.S. 491.

Chief Justice Roberts delivered the opinion of the Court.

The International Court of Justice (ICJ), located in the Hague, is a tribunal established pursuant to the United Nations Charter to adjudicate disputes between member states. *In the Case Concerning Avena and Other Mexican Nationals* (*Mex. v. U.S.*), that tribunal considered a claim brought by Mexico against the United States. The ICJ held that, based on violations of the Vienna Convention, 51 named Mexican nationals were entitled to review and reconsideration of their state-court convictions and sentences in the United States. This was so regardless of any forfeiture of the right to raise Vienna Convention claims because of a failure to comply with generally applicable state rules governing challenges to criminal convictions. . . .

Petitioner José Ernesto Medellín, who had been convicted and sentenced in Texas state court for murder, is one of the 51 Mexican nationals named in the *Avena* decision. Relying on the ICJ's decision and the President's Memorandum, Medellín filed an application for a writ of habeas corpus in state court. The Texas Court of Criminal Appeals dismissed Medellín's application as an abuse of the writ under state law, given Medellín's failure to raise his Vienna Convention claim in a timely manner under state law.

We granted certiorari to decide [whether] the ICJ's judgment in *Avena* [is] directly enforceable as domestic law in a state court in the United States. . . . We conclude that . . . *Avena* [does not] constitute[ ] directly enforceable federal law that pre-empts state limitations on the filing of successive habeas petitions. . . .

I

A

In 1969, the United States, upon the advice and consent of the Senate, ratified the Vienna Convention on Consular Relations, and [its] Optional Protocol Concerning the Compulsory Settlement of Disputes. [The Vienna Convention] provides that if a person detained by a foreign country "so requests, the competent authorities of the receiving State shall, without delay, inform the consular post of the sending State" of such detention, and "inform the [detainee] of his righ[t]" to request assistance from the consul of his own state. Art. 36(1)(b).

The Optional Protocol provides a venue for the resolution of disputes arising out of the interpretation or application of the Vienna Convention[, including the obligation allegedly violated during Texas's prosecution of Medellin]. Under the Protocol, such disputes "shall lie within the compulsory jurisdiction of the International Court of Justice" and "may accordingly be brought before the [ICJ] . . . by any party to the dispute being a Party to the present Protocol." The ICJ . . . was established in 1945 pursuant to the United Nations Charter. . . . Under Article 94(1) of the U.N. Charter, "[e]ach Member of the United Nations undertakes to comply with the decision of the [ICJ] in any case to which it is a party." . . .

II

. . . No one disputes that the *Avena* decision—a decision that flows from the treaties through which the United States submitted to ICJ jurisdiction with respect to Vienna Convention disputes—constitutes an *international* law obligation on the part of the United States. But not all international law obligations automatically constitute binding federal law enforceable in United States courts. The question we confront here is whether the *Avena* judgment has automatic *domestic* legal effect such that the judgment of its own force applies in state and federal courts. . . .

As a signatory to the Optional Protocol, the United States agreed to submit disputes arising out of the Vienna Convention to the ICJ. . . . The Protocol says nothing about the effect of an ICJ decision and does not itself commit signatories to comply with an ICJ judgment. The Protocol is similarly silent as to any enforcement mechanism.

The obligation on the part of signatory nations to comply with ICJ judgments derives not from the Optional Protocol, but rather from Article 94 of the United Nations Charter—the provision that specifically addresses the effect of ICJ decisions. Article 94(1) provides that "[e]ach Member of the United Nations *undertakes to comply* with the decision of the [ICJ] in any case to which it is a party." (emphasis added). The Executive Branch contends that the phrase "undertakes to comply" is not "an acknowledgement that an ICJ decision will have immediate legal effect in the courts of U.N. members," but rather "a *commitment* on the part of U.N. Members to take *future* action through their political branches to comply with an ICJ decision."

We agree with this construction of Article 94. The Article is not a directive to domestic courts. It does not provide that the United States "shall" or "must" comply with an ICJ decision, nor indicate that the Senate that ratified the U.N. Charter intended to vest ICJ decisions with immediate legal effect in domestic courts. Instead, "[t]he words of Article 94 . . . call upon governments to take certain action." . . .

The remainder of Article 94 confirms that the U.N. Charter does not contemplate the automatic enforceability of ICJ decisions in domestic courts. Article 94(2)—the enforcement provision—provides the sole remedy for noncompliance: referral to the United Nations Security Council by an aggrieved state.[6] The U.N. Charter's provision of an express diplomatic—that is, non-judicial—remedy is itself evidence that ICJ judgments were not meant to be enforceable in domestic courts. . . .

We do not suggest that treaties can never afford binding domestic effect to international tribunal judgments—only that the U.N. Charter, the Optional Protocol, and the ICJ Statute do not do so. . . . In sum, while the ICJ's judgment in *Avena* creates an international law obligation on the part of the United States, it does not of its own force constitute binding federal law. . . .

WORTH NOTING

Justice Stevens concurred in the judgment, rejecting what he called the majority's "presumption against self-execution," but concluding that "[i]n the end, . . . I am persuaded that the relevant treaties do not authorize this Court to enforce the judgment of the International Court of Justice." Justice Breyer dissented, in an opinion joined by Justices Souter and Ginsburg. He argued that under a proper analysis of international law, "the treaty obligations, and hence the [ICJ] judgment, . . . bind the courts no less than would "an act of the [federal] legislature.' *Foster v. Neilson* (1829)."

Our final excerpt on the Article II treaty power returns to the implications of *Missouri v. Holland*. Can any treaty on any subject be converted into domestic law by the Senate-approved stroke of the presidential pen? And what is the proper relationship between the Treaty Power and the Necessary and Proper Clause?"

---

6   Article 94(2) provides in full: "If any party to a case fails to perform the obligations incumbent upon it under a judgment rendered by the Court, the other party may have recourse to the Security Council, which may, if it deems necessary, make recommendations or decide upon measures to be taken to give effect to the judgment."

Bond v. United States

Supreme Court of the United States, 2014.
572 U.S. 844.

Chief Justice Roberts delivered the opinion of the Court.

I

A

. . . In 1997, the President of the United States, upon the advice and consent of the Senate, ratified the Convention on the Prohibition of the Development, Production, Stockpiling, and Use of Chemical Weapons and on Their Destruction [("Convention")]. The nations that ratified the Convention (State Parties) had bold aspirations for it: "general and complete disarmament under strict and effective international control, including the prohibition and elimination of all types of weapons of mass destruction." Convention Preamble. This purpose traces its origin to World War I, when "[o]ver a million casualties, up to 100,000 of them fatal, are estimated to have been caused by chemicals . . . , a large part following the introduction of mustard gas in 1917." . . . The Convention aimed to achieve [its objectives] by prohibiting the development, stockpiling, or use of chemical weapons by any State Party or person within a State Party's jurisdiction. . . .

[Article I of the] Convention provides:

(1) Each State Party to this Convention undertakes never under any circumstances:

    (a) To develop, produce, otherwise acquire, stockpile or retain chemical weapons, or transfer, directly or indirectly, chemical weapons to anyone;

    (b) To use chemical weapons;

    (c) To engage in any military preparations to use chemical weapons;

    (d) To assist, encourage or induce, in any way, anyone to engage in any activity prohibited to a State Party under this Convention.

"Chemical Weapons" are defined in relevant part as "[t]oxic chemicals and their precursors, except where intended for purposes not prohibited under this Convention, as long as the types and quantities are consistent with such purposes." Art. II(1)(a). "Toxic Chemical," in turn, is defined as "Any chemical which through its chemical action on life processes can cause death, temporary incapacitation or permanent harm to humans or animals. This includes all such chemicals, regardless of their origin or of their method of production, and regardless of whether they are produced in facilities, in munitions or elsewhere." Art. II(2). "Purposes Not Prohibited Under this Convention" means "[i]ndustrial, agricultural, research, medical, pharmaceutical or other peaceful purposes," Art. II(9)(a), and other specific purposes not at issue here, Arts. II(9)(b)–(d).

[The Convention also provides that] each State Party shall "[p]rohibit natural and legal persons anywhere . . . under its jurisdiction . . . from undertaking any activity prohibited to a State Party under this Convention, including enacting penal legislation with respect to such activity." Art. VII(1)(a).

Congress gave the Convention domestic effect in 1998 when it passed the Chemical Weapons Convention Implementation Act. The Act closely tracks the text of the treaty: It forbids any person knowingly "to develop, produce, otherwise acquire, transfer directly or indirectly, receive, stockpile, retain, own,

WORTH NOTING

Notwithstanding the Supremacy Clause, the Supreme Court has held that some treaties do not have immediate domestic effect. The doctrine is both complicated and contested, but in essence, the idea is that some treaties on their own terms create only *international* obligations rather than immediately enforceable domestic ones. Treaties that have direct domestic effect are called "self-executing." Treaties that create only international obligations are called "non-self-executing."

possess, or use, or threaten to use, any chemical weapon." 18 U.S.C. § 229(a)(1). It defines "chemical weapon" in relevant part as "[a] toxic chemical and its precursors, except where intended for a purpose not prohibited under this chapter as long as the type and quantity is consistent with such a purpose." § 229F(1)(A). "Toxic chemical," in turn, is defined in general as "any chemical which through its chemical action on life processes can cause death, temporary incapacitation or permanent harm to humans or animals. The term includes all such chemicals, regardless of their origin or of their method of production, and regardless of whether they are produced in facilities, in munitions or elsewhere." § 229F(8)(A). Finally, "purposes not prohibited by this chapter" is defined as "[a]ny peaceful purpose related to an industrial, agricultural, research, medical, or pharmaceutical activity or other activity," and other specific purposes. § 229F(7). A person who violates § 229 may be subject to severe punishment: imprisonment "for any term of years," or if a victim's death results, the death penalty or imprisonment "for life." § 229A(a).

B

Petitioner Carol Anne Bond is a microbiologist from Lansdale, Pennsylvania. In 2006, Bond's closest friend, Myrlinda Haynes, announced that she was pregnant. When Bond discovered that her husband was the child's father, she sought revenge against Haynes. Bond stole a quantity of 10-chloro-10H-phenoxarsine (an arsenic-based compound) from her employer, a chemical manufacturer. She also ordered a vial of potassium dichromate (a chemical commonly used in printing photographs or cleaning laboratory equipment) on Amazon.com. Both chemicals are toxic to humans and, in high enough doses, potentially lethal. It is undisputed, however, that Bond did not intend to kill Haynes. She instead hoped that Haynes would touch the chemicals and develop an uncomfortable rash.

Between November 2006 and June 2007, Bond went to Haynes's home on at least 24 occasions and spread the chemicals on her car door, mailbox, and door knob. These attempted assaults were almost entirely unsuccessful. The chemicals that Bond used are easy to see, and Haynes was able to avoid them all but once. On that occasion, Haynes suffered a minor chemical burn on her thumb, which she treated by rinsing with water. Haynes repeatedly called the local police to report the suspicious substances, but they took no action. When Haynes found powder on her mailbox, she called the police again, who told her to call the post office. Haynes did so, and postal inspectors placed surveillance cameras around her home. The cameras caught Bond opening Haynes's mailbox, stealing an envelope, and stuffing potassium dichromate inside the muffler of Haynes's car.

Federal prosecutors naturally charged Bond with two counts of mail theft. . . . More surprising, they also charged her with two counts of possessing and using a chemical weapon, in violation of § 229(a). Bond entered a conditional guilty plea that reserved her right to appeal. The District Court sentenced Bond to six years in federal prison plus five years of supervised release, and ordered her to pay a $2,000 fine and $9,902.79 in restitution.

Bond appealed, . . . argu[ing] that § 229 does not reach her conduct because the statute's exception for the use of chemicals for "peaceful purposes" should be understood in contradistinction to the "warlike" activities that the Convention was primarily designed to prohibit. Bond argued that her conduct, though reprehensible, was not at all "warlike." The Court of Appeals rejected this argument. . . . The Third Circuit also rejected Bond's constitutional challenge to her conviction, holding that § 229 was "necessary and proper to carry the Convention into effect." The Court of Appeals relied on this Court's opinion in *Missouri v. Holland* (1920), which stated that "[i]f the treaty is valid there can be no dispute about the validity of the statute" that implements it "as a necessary and proper means to execute the powers of the Government." We again granted certiorari.

II

[The Government explicitly disavowed reliance on the commerce power.] As a result, in this Court the parties have devoted significant effort to arguing whether § 229, as applied to Bond's offense, is a necessary and proper means of executing the National Government's power to make treaties. U.S. Const., Art. II, § 2, cl. 2.

Bond argues that the lower court's reading of *Missouri v. Holland* would remove all limits on federal authority, so long as the Federal Government ratifies a treaty first. She insists that to effectively afford the Government a police power whenever it implements a treaty would be contrary to the Framers' careful decision to divide power between the States and the National Government as a means of preserving liberty. To the extent that *Holland* authorizes such usurpation of traditional state authority, Bond says, it must be either limited or overruled.

The Government replies that this Court has never held that a statute implementing a valid treaty exceeds Congress's enumerated powers. To do so here, the Government says, would contravene another deliberate choice of the Framers: to avoid placing subject matter limitations on the National Government's power to make treaties. And it might also undermine confidence in the United States as an international treaty partner.

Notwithstanding this debate, it is "a well-established principle governing the prudent exercise of this Court's jurisdiction that normally the Court will not decide a constitutional question if there is some other ground upon which to dispose of the case." *Escambia County v. McMillan* (1984) (*per curiam*); see also *Ashwander v. TVA* (1936) (Brandeis, J., concurring) [(synthesizing the interpretive canon of constitutional avoidance)]. Bond argues that § 229 does not cover her conduct. So we consider that argument first.

III

Section 229 exists to implement the Convention, so we begin with that international agreement. As explained, the Convention's drafters intended for it to be a comprehensive ban on chemical weapons. But even with its broadly worded definitions, we have doubts that a treaty about *chemical weapons* has anything to do with Bond's conduct. The Convention, a product of years of worldwide study, analysis, and multinational negotiation, arose in response to war crimes and acts of terrorism. There is no reason to think the sovereign nations that ratified the Convention were interested in anything like Bond's common law assault. . . .

Fortunately, we have no need to interpret the scope of the Convention in this case. Bond was prosecuted under § 229, and the statute—unlike the Convention—must be read consistent with principles of federalism inherent in our constitutional structure.

In the Government's view, the conclusion that Bond "knowingly" "use[d]" a "chemical weapon" in violation of § 229(a) is simple: The chemicals that Bond placed on Haynes's home and car are "toxic chemical[s]" as defined by the statute, and Bond's attempt to assault Haynes was not a "peaceful purpose." §§ 229F(1), (8), (7). The problem with this interpretation is that it would "dramatically intrude[ ] upon traditional state criminal jurisdiction," and we avoid reading statutes to have such reach in the absence of a clear indication that they do. *United States v. Bass* (1971) [("[W]e will not be quick to assume that Congress has meant to effect a significant change in the sensitive relation between federal and state criminal jurisdiction.")] . . . .

[*Bass*, in part to avoid federalizing a type of criminal conduct traditionally treated as local, concluded that a statute prohibiting any convicted felon from "receiv[ing], possess[ing], or transport[ing] in commerce or affecting commerce . . . any firearm" should be interpreted to require proof of a connection to interstate commerce in every case. For similar reasons, *Jones v. United States* (2000) interpreted the federal arson statute—which prohibited burning " 'any . . . property used in interstate or foreign commerce or in any activity affecting interstate or foreign commerce' "—to reach only buildings used in "active employment for commercial purposes," thereby excluding an owner-occupied private residence. "[A]rson," the Court observed, "is a paradigmatic common-law state crime."]

These precedents make clear that it is appropriate to refer to basic principles of federalism embodied in the Constitution to resolve ambiguity in a federal statute. In this case, the ambiguity derives from the improbably broad reach of the key statutory definition given the term—"chemical weapon"—being defined; the deeply serious consequences of adopting such a boundless reading; and the lack of any apparent need to do so in light of the context from which the statute arose—a treaty about chemical warfare and terrorism. We conclude that, in this curious case, we can insist on a clear indication that Congress meant to reach purely local crimes, before interpreting the statute's expansive language in a way that intrudes on the police power of the States.

We do not find any such clear indication in § 229. . . .

The Government would have us brush aside the ordinary meaning and adopt a reading of § 229 that would sweep in everything from the detergent under the kitchen sink to the stain remover in the laundry room. . . . Any parent would be guilty of a serious federal offense—possession of a chemical weapon—when, exasperated by the children's repeated failure to clean the goldfish tank, he considers poisoning the fish with a few drops of vinegar. We are reluctant to ignore the ordinary meaning of "chemical weapon" when doing so would transform a statute passed to implement the international Convention on Chemical Weapons into one that also makes it a federal offense to poison goldfish. . . .

The Government's reading of § 229 would " 'alter sensitive federal-state relationships,' " convert an astonishing amount of "traditionally local criminal conduct" into "a matter for federal enforcement," and "involve a substantial extension of federal police resources." *Bass*. It would transform the statute from one whose core concerns are acts of war, assassination, and terrorism into a massive federal anti-poisoning regime that reaches the simplest of assaults. . . .

This case is unusual, and our analysis is appropriately limited. Our disagreement with our colleagues reduces to whether § 229 is "utterly clear." *Post* (Scalia, J., concurring in judgment). We think it is not, given that the definition of "chemical weapon" in a particular case can reach beyond any normal notion of such a weapon, that the context from which the statute arose demonstrates a much more limited prohibition was intended, and that the most sweeping reading of the statute would fundamentally upset the Constitution's balance between national and local power. . . .

Justice Scalia, with whom Justice Thomas joins, and with whom Justice Alito joins as to Part I, concurring in the judgment.

. . . As sweeping and unsettling as the Chemical Weapons Convention Implementation Act of 1998 may be, it is clear beyond doubt that it covers what Bond did; and we have no authority to amend it. So we are forced to decide—there is no way around it—whether the Act's application to what Bond did was constitutional. I would hold that it was not, and for that reason would reverse the judgment of the Court of Appeals for the Third Circuit.

I. The Statutory Question

. . . The meaning of the Act is plain. . . . Applying [its] provisions to this case is hardly complicated. Bond possessed and used "chemical[s] which through [their] chemical action on life processes can cause death, temporary incapacitation or permanent harm." Thus, she possessed "toxic chemicals." And, because they were not possessed or used only for a "purpose not prohibited," § 229F(1)(A), they were "chemical weapons." Ergo, Bond violated the Act. End of statutory analysis.

II. The Constitutional Question

Since the Act is clear, the *real* question this case presents is whether the Act is constitutional as applied to petitioner. An unreasoned and citation-less sentence from our opinion in *Missouri v. Holland* (1920), purported to furnish the answer: "If the treaty is valid"—and no one argues that the Convention is not—"there can be no dispute about the validity of the statute under Article I, § 8, as a necessary and proper means to execute the powers of the Government." Petitioner and her *amici* press us to consider whether there is anything to this *ipse dixit*. The Constitution's text and structure show that there is not. . . .

A. Text

. . . Read together, the [Necessary and Proper Clause of Article I, § 8, cl. 18, and the Treaty Clause of Article II, § 2, cl. 2,] empower Congress to pass laws "necessary and proper for carrying into Execution . . . [the] Power . . . to make Treaties."

It is obvious what the Clauses, read together, do *not* say. They do not authorize Congress to enact laws for carrying into execution "Treaties," even treaties that do not execute themselves, such as the Chemical Weapons Convention. Surely it makes sense, the Government contends, that Congress would have the power to carry out the obligations to which the President and the Senate have committed the Nation. The power to "carry into Execution" the "Power . . . to make Treaties," it insists, *has to* mean the power to execute the treaties themselves.

That argument, which makes no pretense of resting on text, unsurprisingly misconstrues it. Start with the phrase "to make Treaties." A treaty is a contract with a foreign nation *made*, the Constitution states, by the President with the concurrence of "two thirds of the Senators present." . . . Upon the President's agreement and the Senate's ratification, a treaty—no matter what kind—has been *made* and is not susceptible of any more making.

How might Congress have helped "carr[y]" the power to make the treaty—here, the Chemical Weapons Convention—"into Execution"? In any number of ways. It could have appropriated money for hiring treaty negotiators, empowered the Department of State to appoint those negotiators, formed a commission to study the benefits and risks of entering into the agreement, or paid for a bevy of spies to monitor the treaty-related deliberations of other potential signatories. The Necessary and Proper Clause interacts similarly with other Article II powers: "[W]ith respect to the executive branch, the Clause would allow Congress to institute an agency to help the President wisely employ his pardoning power. . . .

But a power to help the President *make* treaties is not a power to *implement* treaties already made. Once a treaty has been made, Congress's power to do what is "necessary and proper" to assist the making of treaties drops out of the picture. To legislate compliance with the United States' treaty obligations, Congress must rely upon its independent (though quite robust) Article I, § 8, powers.

B. Structure

[I]n *Holland*, the proponents of unlimited congressional power found a loophole: "By negotiating a treaty and obtaining the requisite consent of the Senate, the President . . . may endow Congress with a source of legislative authority independent of the powers enumerated in Article I." Tribe, *American Constitutional Law* (2000). Though *Holland*'s change to the Constitution's text appears minor (the power to carry into execution the *power to make treaties* becomes the power to carry into execution *treaties*), the change to its structure is seismic.

To see why vast expansion of congressional power is not just a remote possibility, consider two features of the modern practice of treaty making. In our Nation's early history, and extending through the time when *Holland* was written, treaties were typically bilateral, and addressed only a small range of topics relating to the obligations of each state to the other, and to citizens of the other—military neutrality, for example, or military alliance, or guarantee of most-favored-nation trade treatment. See Bradley, *The Treaty Power and American Federalism*, 97 Mich. L. Rev. 390 (1998). But beginning in the last half of the last century, many treaties were "detailed multilateral instruments negotiated and drafted at international conferences," *ibid.*, and they sought to regulate states' treatment of their own citizens, or even "the activities of individuals and private entities," A. Chayes & A. Chayes, *The New Sovereignty: Compliance with International Regulatory Agreements* (1995). "[O]ften vague and open-ended," such treaties "touch on almost every aspect of domestic civil, political, and cultural life." Bradley & Goldsmith, *Treaties, Human Rights, and Conditional Consent*, 149 U. Pa. L. Rev. 399 (2000).

Consider also that, at least according to some scholars, the Treaty Clause comes with no implied subject-matter limitations. On this view, "[t]he Tenth Amendment . . . does not limit the power to make treaties or other agreements," Restatement (Third) of Foreign Relations Law of the United States, and the treaty power can be used to regulate matters of strictly domestic concern.

If that is true, then the possibilities of what the Federal Government may accomplish, with the right treaty in hand, are endless and hardly farfetched. It could begin, as some scholars have suggested, with abrogation of this Court's constitutional rulings. For example, the holding that a statute prohibiting the carrying of firearms near schools went beyond Congress's enumerated powers, *United States v. Lopez* (1995), could be reversed by negotiating a treaty with Latvia providing that neither sovereign would permit the carrying of guns near schools. Similarly, Congress could reenact the invalidated part of the Violence Against Women Act of 1994 that provided a civil remedy for victims of gender-motivated violence, just so long as there were a treaty on point—and some authors think there already is, see MacKinnon, *The Supreme Court, 1999 Term*, 114 Harv. L. Rev. 135 (2000). . . .

* * *

We have here [left] in place an ill-considered *ipse dixit* that enables the fundamental constitutional principle of limited federal powers to be set aside by the President and Senate's exercise of the treaty power. We should not have shirked our duty and distorted the law to preserve that assertion; we should have welcomed and eagerly grasped the opportunity—nay, the obligation—to consider and repudiate it.

JUSTICE THOMAS, with whom JUSTICE SCALIA joins, . . . concurring in the judgment.

. . . The Constitution does not . . . comprehensively define the proper bounds of the Treaty Power, and this Court has not yet had occasion to do so. As a result, some have suggested that the Treaty Power is boundless— that it can reach any subject matter, even those that are of strictly domestic concern. See, *e.g.*, Restatement

WORTH NOTING

Justice Alito also joined portions of this opinion not presented here.

(Third) of Foreign Relations Law of the United States (1986). A number of recent treaties reflect that suggestion by regulating what appear to be purely domestic affairs.

Yet to interpret the Treaty Power as extending to every conceivable domestic subject matter—even matters without any nexus to foreign relations—would destroy the basic constitutional distinction between domestic and foreign powers. It would also lodge in the Federal Government the potential for "a 'police power' over all aspects of American life." . . . And a treaty-based police power would pose an even greater threat when exercised through a self-executing treaty because it would circumvent the role of the House of Representatives in the legislative process. I doubt the Treaty Power creates such a gaping loophole in our constitutional structure. . . .

JUSTICE ALITO, concurring in the judgment.

. . . I believe that the treaty power is limited to agreements that address matters of legitimate international concern. . . . The control of true chemical weapons, as that term is customarily understood, is a matter of great international concern, and therefore the heart of the Convention clearly represents a valid exercise of the treaty power. But insofar as the Convention may be read to obligate the United States to enact domestic legislation criminalizing conduct of the sort at issue in this case, which typically is the sort of conduct regulated by the States, the Convention exceeds the scope of the treaty power. . . .

9.   The Power to Enforce the Reconstruction Amendments

After the Civil War, a series of three constitutional amendments known as the Reconstruction Amendments were drafted, proposed, and ratified by the Republican coalition that dominated the national government. U.S. Const., amdts. 13, 14, 15. (See pp. 156–158, 166–183 for more detail on the historical context of their enactment.) The Reconstruction Amendments were enacted on a background of Republican skepticism about the courts, especially in the wake of decisions like *Scott v. Sandford* (1857), which had declared that slavery was constitutionally protected. So while the Reconstruction Congress clearly expected the judiciary to help enforce new individual rights like the Equal Protection Clause and the Due Process Clause, the drafters of these amendments also made sure to include express provision for *congressional* enforcement of those guarantees. That is to say, they enacted new sources of enumerated legislative authority, the extent of which was dependent at least in part on the boundaries of the rights that Congress was charged with protecting. We will focus on the congressional enforcement provision created by § 5 of the Fourteenth Amendment, which provides: "The Congress shall have power to enforce, by appropriate legislation, the provisions of this article."

"The Civil Rights Cases"

Supreme Court of the United States, 1883.
109 U.S. 3.

BRADLEY, J. [for the Court.]

These cases are all founded on the first and second sections of the act of Congress known as the "Civil Rights Act," passed March 1, 1875, entitled "An Act to protect all citizens in their civil and legal rights." Two of the cases [are] indictments for denying to persons of color the accommodations and privileges of an inn or hotel; two of them [are] for denying to individuals the privileges and accommodations of a theater, [one at] Maguire's theater in San Francisco [and the other at] the Grand Opera House in New York. [Another case was based on] the refusal by the conductor of the railroad company to allow the wife to ride in the ladies' car, for the reason . . . that she was a person of African descent. . . .

It is obvious that the primary and important question in all the cases is the constitutionality of the law: for if the law is unconstitutional none of the prosecutions can stand.

The sections of the law referred to provide as follows:

> Sec. 1. That all persons within the jurisdiction of the United States shall be entitled to the full and equal enjoyment of the accomodations, advantages, facilities, and privileges of inns, public conveyances on land or water, theaters, and other places of public amusement; subject only to the conditions and limitations established by law, and applicable alike to citizens of every race and color, regardless of any previous condition of servitude.

> Sec. 2. That any person who shall violate the foregoing section . . . shall . . . pay the sum of $500 to the person aggrieved thereby . . . and shall, also, for every such offense, be deemed guilty of a misdemeanor. . . .

. . . Has Congress constitutional power to make such a law? Of course, no one will contend that the power to pass it was contained in the Constitution before the adoption of the last three amendments. The power is sought, first, in the Fourteenth Amendment, and the views and arguments of distinguished Senators, advanced while the law was under consideration, claiming authority to pass it by virtue of that amendment, are the principal arguments adduced in favor of the power. . . .

The first section of the Fourteenth Amendment . . . is prohibitory in its character, and prohibitory upon the States. . . . It is State action of a particular character that is prohibited. Individual invasion of individual rights is not the subject-matter of the amendment. It has a deeper and broader scope. It nullifies and makes void all State legislation, and State action of every kind, which impairs the privileges and immunities of citizens of the United States, or which injures them in life, liberty, or property without due process of law, or which denies to any of them the equal protection of the laws.

[In] order that the national will, thus declared, may not be a mere *brutum fulmen*, the last section of the amendment invests Congress with power to enforce it by appropriate legislation. To enforce what? To enforce the prohibition. To adopt appropriate legislation for correcting the effects of such prohibited

State law and State acts, and thus to render them effectually null, void, and innocuous. This is the legislative power conferred upon Congress, and this is the whole of it. . . .

And so in the present case, until some State law has been passed, or some State action through its officers or agents has been taken, adverse to the rights of citizens sought to be protected by the Fourteenth Amendment, no legislation of the United States under said amendment, nor any proceeding under such legislation, can be called into activity, for the prohibitions of the amendment are against State laws and acts done under State authority. . . . Such legislation cannot properly cover the whole domain of rights appertaining to life, liberty, and property, defining them and providing for their vindication. That would be to establish a code of municipal law regulative of all private rights between man and man in society. It would be to make Congress take the place of the State legislatures and to supersede them. . . .

We have not overlooked the fact that the fourth section of the act now under consideration[, prohibiting racial discrimination in jury selection,] has been held by this court to be constitutional. . . . But a moment's attention to its terms will show that the section is entirely corrective in its character. Disqualifications for service on juries are only created by the law, and the first part of the section is aimed at certain disqualifying laws, namely, those which make mere race or color a disqualification; and the second clause is directed against those who, assuming to use the authority of the State government, carry into effect such a rule of disqualification. . . .

In this connection it is proper to state that civil rights, such as are guarantied by the Constitution against State aggression, cannot be impaired by the wrongful acts of individuals, unsupported by State authority in the shape of laws, customs, or judicial or executive proceedings. The wrongful act of an individual, unsupported by any such authority, is simply a private wrong, or a crime of that individual; an invasion of the rights of the injured party, it is true, whether they affect his person, his property, or his reputation; but if not sanctioned in some way by the State, or not done under State authority, his rights remain in full force, and may presumably be vindicated by resort to the laws of the State for redress. . . .

Of course, these remarks do not apply to those cases in which congress is clothed with direct and plenary powers of legislation over the whole subject, accompanied with an express or implied denial of such power to the states, as in the regulation of commerce with foreign nations, among the several states, and with the Indian tribes. . . . In these cases congress has power to pass laws for regulating the subjects specified, in every detail, and the conduct and transactions of individuals in respect thereof.

On the whole, we are of opinion that no countenance of authority for the passage of the law in question can be found [and] it must necessarily be declared void, at least so far as its operation in the several States is concerned. . . .

HARLAN, J., dissenting.

The opinion in these cases proceeds, as it seems to me, upon grounds entirely too narrow and artificial. The substance and spirit of the recent amendments of the Constitution have been sacrificed by a subtle and ingenious verbal criticism. . . . Constitutional provisions, adopted in the interest of liberty, and for the purpose of securing, through national legislation, if need be, rights inhering in a state of freedom, and belonging to American citizenship, have been so construed as to defeat the ends the people desired to accomplish, which they attempted to accomplish, and which they supposed they had accomplished by changes in their fundamental law. . . .

Before considering the particular language and scope of these amendments it will be proper to recall the relations which, prior to their adoption, subsisted between the national government and the institution of slavery. . . .

Before the adoption of the recent amendments it had become, as we have seen, the established doctrine of this court that negroes, whose ancestors had been imported and sold as slaves, could not become citizens of a State, or even of the United States, with the rights and privileges guarantied to citizens by the national Constitution. . . . Still further, between the adoption of the Thirteenth Amendment and the proposal by Congress of the Fourteenth Amendment, on June 16, 1866, the statute books of several of the states, as we have seen, had become loaded down with enactments which, under the guise of Apprentice, Vagrant, and Contract regulations, sought to keep the colored race in a condition, practically, of servitude [despite their formal emancipation by the Thirteenth Amendment]. . . . To meet this new peril to the black race, that the purposes of the nation might not be doubted or defeated, and by way of further enlargement of the power of Congress, the Fourteenth Amendment was proposed for adoption. . . .

The assumption that this amendment consists wholly of prohibitions upon State laws and State proceedings in hostility to its provisions, is unauthorized by its language. The first clause of the first section . . . is of a distinctly affirmative character. In its application to the colored race, previously liberated, it created and granted, as well citizenship of the United States, as citizenship of the State in which they respectively resided. It introduced all of that race, whose ancestors had been imported and sold as slaves, at once, into the political community known as the "People of the United States." They became, instantly, citizens of the United States, and of their respective states. . . .

The citizenship thus acquired by that race, in virtue of an affirmative grant by the nation, may be protected, not alone by the judicial branch of the government, but by Congressional legislation of a primary direct character [under § 5 of the Fourteenth Amendment.] It is, therefore, an essential inquiry what, if any, right, privilege, or immunity was given by the nation to colored persons when they were made citizens of the State in which they reside? . . .

There is one, if there be no others—exemption from race discrimination in respect of any civil right belonging to citizens of the white race in the same State. That, surely, is their constitutional privilege when within the jurisdiction of other States. And such must be their constitutional right, in their own State, unless the recent amendments be "splendid baubles," thrown out to delude those who deserved fair and generous treatment at the hands of the nation. Citizenship in this country necessarily imports equality of civil rights among citizens of every race in the same State. . . . If, then, exemption from discrimination in respect of civil rights is a new constitutional right, secured by the grant of State citizenship to colored citizens of the United States—and I do not see how this can now be questioned—why may not the nation, by means of its own legislation of a primary direct character, guard, protect, and enforce that right? It is a right and privilege which the nation conferred. It did not come from the States in which those colored citizens reside. . . .

My brethren say, that when a man has emerged from slavery, and by the aid of beneficent legislation has shaken off the inseparable concomitants of that state, there must be some stage in the progress of his elevation when he takes the rank of a mere citizen, and ceases to be the special favorite of the laws, and when his rights as a citizen, or a man, are to be protected in the ordinary modes by which other men's rights are protected. It is, I submit, scarcely just to say that the colored race has been the special favorite of the laws. . . .

The Civil Rights Act of 1964 was enacted in response to the broad social mobilization for racial justice commonly known as the civil rights movement. In part, the Act provides that "[a]ll persons shall be entitled to the full and equal enjoyment of the goods, services, [and] facilities . . . of any place of public accommodation . . . without discrimination or segregation on the ground of race, color, religion, or national origin." In *Heart of Atlanta Motel v. United States* (1964), the Supreme Court rejected a constitutional challenge to the Civil Rights Act as applied to a private commercial facility that refused to serve African-Americans. Among

 CROSS REFERENCE *Heart of Atlanta* is presented at pp. 444–452.

other arguments, the motel relied on *The Civil Rights Cases* to claim that Congress had no power to enact public accommodations statutes under § 5 of the Fourteenth Amendment. The Supreme Court sidestepped that argument, explaining that the Commerce Clause provided an independent basis for the 1964 Civil Rights Act:

> Unlike [the Civil Rights Act], the 1875 Act [did not limit] the categories of affected businesses to those impinging upon interstate commerce. In contrast, the applicability of Title II is carefully limited to enterprises having a direct and substantial relation to the interstate flow of goods and people, except where state action is involved. . . .

The Court therefore "conclude[d] that the Civil Rights Cases have no relevance to the basis of decision here where the Act explicitly relies upon the commerce power," and proceeded to hold that the Civil Rights Act of 1964 was a valid exercise of the federal Commerce Clause authority.

In other cases during the 1960s, the Court could not so easily rely on the Commerce Clause as a basis for federal civil rights legislation. For reasons discussed in the materials on commandeering, pp. 506–524, and state sovereign immunity, see Online Supplement, this was particularly true where the target of a civil rights obligation was a state actor. In 1966, one such case led the Supreme Court to tackle the § 5 question head on.

Katzenbach v. Morgan

Supreme Court of the United States, 1966.
384 U.S. 641.

MR. JUSTICE BRENNAN delivered the opinion of the Court.

These cases concern the constitutionality of § 4(e) of the Voting Rights Act of 1965. That law, in the respects pertinent in these cases, provides that no person who has successfully completed the sixth primary grade in a public school in, or a private school accredited by, the Commonwealth of Puerto Rico in which the language of instruction was other than English shall be denied the right to vote in any election because of his inability to read or write English.

Appellees, registered voters in New York City, brought this suit to challenge the constitutionality of § 4(e) insofar as it . . . prohibits the enforcement of the election laws of New York requiring an ability to read and write English as a condition of voting. Under these laws many of the several hundred thousand New York City residents who have migrated there from the Commonwealth of Puerto Rico had previously been denied the right to vote, and appellees attack § 4(e) insofar as it would enable many of these citizens to vote. . . .[3]

We hold that, in the application challenged in these cases, § 4(e) is a proper exercise of the powers granted to Congress by § 5 of the Fourteenth Amendment and that by force of the Supremacy Clause, Article VI, the New York English literacy requirement cannot be enforced to the extent that it is inconsistent with § 4(e). . . .

The Attorney General of the State of New York argues that an exercise of congressional power under § 5 of the Fourteenth Amendment that prohibits the enforcement of a state law can only be sustained if the judicial branch determines that the state law is prohibited by the provisions of the Amendment that Congress sought to enforce. More specifically, he urges that § 4(e) cannot be sustained as appropriate legislation to enforce the Equal Protection Clause unless the judiciary decides—even with the guidance of a congressional

---

[3] [Section 4(e)] was sponsored in the Senate . . . for the explicit purpose of dealing with the disenfranchisement of large segments of the Puerto Rican population in New York. Throughout the congressional debate it was repeatedly acknowledged that s 4(e) had particular reference to the Puerto Rican population in New York. . . . The Solicitor General . . . advises us that, aside from the schools in the Commonwealth of Puerto Rico, there are no public or parochial schools in the territorial limits of the United States in which the predominant language of instruction is other than English and which would have generally been attended by persons who are otherwise qualified to vote save for their lack of literacy in English.

judgment—that the application of the English literacy requirement prohibited by § 4(e) is forbidden by the Equal Protection Clause itself.

We disagree. Neither the language nor history of § 5 supports such a construction. As was said with regard to § 5 in *Ex parte Com. of Virginia* (1879), "It is the power of Congress which has been enlarged. . . ." A construction of § 5 that would require a judicial determination that the enforcement of the state law precluded by Congress violated the Amendment, as a condition of sustaining the congressional enactment, would depreciate both congressional resourcefulness and congressional responsibility for implementing the Amendment. It would confine the legislative power in this context to the insignificant role of abrogating only those state laws that the judicial branch was prepared to adjudge unconstitutional, or of merely informing the judgment of the judiciary by particularizing the "majestic generalities" of § 1 of the Amendment.

Thus our task in this case is not to determine whether the New York English literacy requirement as applied to deny the right to vote to a person who successfully completed the sixth grade in a Puerto Rican school violates the Equal Protection Clause. Accordingly, our decision in *Lassiter v. Northampton County Bd. of Election* (1959), sustaining the North Carolina English literacy requirement as not in all circumstances prohibited by the first sections of the Fourteenth and Fifteenth Amendments, is inapposite. *Lassiter* did not present the question before us here: Without regard to whether the judiciary would find that the Equal Protection Clause itself nullifies New York's English literacy requirement as so applied, could Congress prohibit the enforcement of the state law by legislating under

WORTH NOTING

In *Lassiter*, the Supreme Court held that facially neutral literacy requirements for voter registration did not violate the Fourteenth Amendment. *Lassiter* left open the possibility that such requirements would be unconstitutional if challengers could show either (i) a racially discriminatory motive for their enactment, or (ii) that the requirements were applied by state officials in a racially discriminatory fashion.

§ 5 of the Fourteenth Amendment? In answering this question, our task is limited to determining whether such legislation is, as required by § 5, appropriate legislation to enforce the Equal Protection Clause.

By including § 5 the draftsmen sought to grant to Congress, by a specific provision applicable to the Fourteenth Amendment, the same broad powers expressed in the Necessary and Proper Clause.[9] The classic formulation of the reach of those powers was established by Chief Justice Marshall in *McCulloch v. Maryland*:

> Let the end be legitimate, let it be within the scope of the constitution, and all means which are appropriate, which are plainly adapted to that end, which are not prohibited, but consist with the letter and spirit of the constitution, are constitutional.

Ex parte Com. of Virginia, decided 12 years after the adoption of the Fourteenth Amendment, held that congressional power under § 5 had this same broad scope:

> Whatever legislation is appropriate, that is, adapted to carry out the objects the amendments have in view, whatever tends to enforce submission to the prohibitions they contain, and to secure to all persons the enjoyment of perfect equality of civil rights and the equal protection of the laws against State denial or invasion, if not prohibited, is brought within the domain of congressional power.

Thus the *McCulloch v. Maryland* standard is the measure of what constitutes "appropriate legislation" under § 5 of the Fourteenth Amendment. Correctly viewed, § 5 is a positive grant of legislative power authorizing Congress to exercise its discretion in determining whether and what legislation is needed to secure the guarantees of the Fourteenth Amendment.

We therefore proceed to the consideration whether § 4(e) is "appropriate legislation" to enforce the Equal Protection Clause, that is, under the *McCulloch v. Maryland* standard, whether § 4(e) may be regarded as an enactment to enforce the Equal Protection Clause, whether it is "plainly adapted to that end" and whether it is not prohibited by but is consistent with "the letter and spirit of the constitution."

There can be no doubt that § 4(e) may be regarded as an enactment to enforce the Equal Protection Clause. Congress explicitly declared that it enacted § 4(e) "to secure the rights under the fourteenth amendment of persons educated in American-flag schools in which the predominant classroom language was other than English." The persons referred to include those who have migrated

---

[9]   In fact, earlier drafts of the proposed Amendment employed the "necessary and proper" terminology to describe the scope of congressional power under the Amendment. See tenBroek, *The Antislavery Origins of the Fourteenth Amendment* (1951). The substitution of the "appropriate legislation" formula was never thought to have the effect of diminishing the scope of this congressional power. See, *e.g.*, Cong. Globe, 42d Cong., 1st Sess. (Representative Bingham, a principal draftsman of the Amendment and the earlier proposals).

from the Commonwealth of Puerto Rico to New York and who have been denied the right to vote because of their inability to read and write English, and the Fourteenth Amendment rights referred to include those emanating from the Equal Protection Clause. More specifically, § 4(e) may be viewed as a measure to secure for the Puerto Rican community residing in New York nondiscriminatory treatment by government—both in the imposition of voting qualifications and the provision or administration of governmental services, such as public schools, public housing and law enforcement.

Section 4(e) may be readily seen as "plainly adapted" to furthering these aims of the Equal Protection Clause. The practical effect of § 4(e) is to prohibit New York from denying the right to vote to large segments of its Puerto Rican community. Congress has thus prohibited the State from denying to that community the right that is "preservative of all rights." This enhanced political power will be helpful in gaining nondiscriminatory treatment in public services for the entire Puerto Rican community. Section 4(e) thereby enables the Puerto Rican minority better to obtain "perfect equality of civil rights and the equal protection of the laws." It was well within congressional authority to say that this need of the Puerto Rican minority for the vote warranted federal intrusion upon any state interests served by the English literacy requirement.

It was for Congress, as the branch that made this judgment, to assess and weigh the various conflicting considerations—the risk or pervasiveness of the discrimination in governmental services, the effectiveness of eliminating the state restriction on the right to vote as a means of dealing with the evil, the adequacy or availability of alternative remedies, and the nature and significance of the state interests that would be affected by the nullification of the English literacy requirement as applied to residents who have successfully completed the sixth grade in a Puerto Rican school. It is not for us to review the congressional resolution of these factors. It is enough that we be able to perceive a basis upon which the Congress might resolve the conflict as it did. There plainly was such a basis to support § 4(e) in the application in question in this case. Any contrary conclusion would require us to be blind to the realities familiar to the legislators.

The result is no different if we confine our inquiry to the question whether § 4(e) was merely legislation aimed at the elimination of an invidious discrimination in establishing voter qualifications. We are told that New York's English literacy requirement originated in the desire to provide an incentive for non-English speaking immigrants to learn the English language and in order to assure the intelligent exercise of the franchise. Yet Congress might well have questioned, in light of the many exemptions provided,[13] and some evidence suggesting that prejudice played a prominent role in the enactment of the requirement,[14] whether these were actually the interests being served. Congress might have also questioned whether denial of a right deemed so precious and fundamental in our society was a necessary or appropriate means of encouraging persons to learn English, or of furthering the goal of an intelligent exercise of the franchise. Finally, Congress might well have concluded that as a means of furthering the intelligent exercise of the franchise, an ability to read or understand Spanish is as effective as ability to read English for those to whom Spanish-language newspapers and Spanish-language radio and television programs are available to inform them of election issues and governmental affairs.[16]

Since Congress undertook to legislate so as to preclude the enforcement of the state law, and did so in the context of a general appraisal of literacy requirements for voting, to which it brought a specially informed legislative competence, it was Congress' prerogative to weigh these competing considerations. Here again, it is enough that we perceive a basis upon which Congress might predicate a judgment that the application of New York's English literacy requirement to deny the right to vote to a person with a sixth grade education in Puerto Rican schools in which the language of instruction was other than English constituted an invidious discrimination in violation of the Equal Protection Clause. . . .

We therefore conclude that § 4(e), in the application challenged in this case, is appropriate legislation to enforce the Equal Protection Clause and that the judgment of the District Court must be and hereby is reversed.

Reversed.

---

[13]   The principal exemption complained of is that for persons who had been eligible to vote before January 1, 1922.

[14]   This evidence consists in part of statements made in the Constitutional Convention first considering the English literacy requirement, such as the following made by the sponsor of the measure:

> More precious even than the forms of government are the mental qualities of our race. While those stand unimpaired, all is safe. They are exposed to a single danger, and that is that by constantly changing our voting citizenship through the wholesale, but valuable and necessary infusion of Southern and Eastern European races . . . . The danger has begun. . . . We should check it.

New York State Constitutional Convention (1916). . . .

[16]   The record in this case includes affidavits describing the nature of New York's two major Spanish-language newspapers, one daily and one weekly, and its three full-time Spanish-language radio stations and affidavits from those who have campaigned in Spanish-speaking areas.

Justice Douglas concurred in the Court's opinion, except for a portion holding that § 4(e) was not rendered unconstitutional by the fact that it only applied to persons educated in schools in the territorial jurisdiction of the United States. He would have reserved judgment on that question.

MR. JUSTICE HARLAN, whom MR. JUSTICE STEWART joins, dissenting.

[F]or me, applying the basic equal protection standard, the issue in this case is whether New York has shown that its English-language literacy test is reasonably designed to serve a legitimate state interest. I think that it has. In 1959, in *Lassiter v. Northampton Election Bd.* (1959), [w]e held that there was "wide scope" for State qualifications of this sort. . . . I believe the same interests recounted in *Lassiter* indubitably point toward upholding the rationality of the New York voting test. . . . Although to be sure there is a difference between a totally illiterate person and one who is literate in a foreign tongue, I do not believe that this added factor vitiates the constitutionality of the New York statute. . . .

The pivotal question in this instance is what effect the added factor of a congressional enactment has on the straight equal protection argument dealt with above. . . .

When recognized state violations of federal constitutional standards have occurred, Congress is of course empowered by § 5 to take appropriate remedial measures to redress and prevent the wrongs. But it is a judicial question whether the condition with which Congress has thus sought to deal is in truth an infringement of the Constitution, something that is the necessary prerequisite to bringing the § 5 power into play at all. Thus, in *Ex parte Virginia* (1879), involving a federal statute making it a federal crime to disqualify anyone from jury service because of race, the Court first held as a matter of constitutional law that "the Fourteenth Amendment secures . . . an impartial jury trial, by jurors . . . chosen without discrimination against such jurors because of their color." Only then did the Court hold that to enforce this prohibition upon state discrimination, Congress could enact a criminal statute of the type under consideration. . . .

Section 4(e), however, presents a significantly different type of congressional enactment. The question here is not whether the statute is appropriate remedial legislation to cure an established violation of a constitutional command, but whether there has in fact been an infringement of that constitutional command, that is, whether a particular state practice or, as here, a statute is so arbitrary or irrational as to offend the command of the Equal Protection Clause of the Fourteenth Amendment. That question is one for the judicial branch ultimately to determine. . . .

In effect the Court reads § 5 of the Fourteenth Amendment as giving Congress the power to define the *substantive* scope of the Amendment. If that indeed be the true reach of § 5, then I do not see why Congress should not be able as well to exercise its § 5 "discretion" by enacting statutes so as in effect to dilute equal protection and due process decisions of this Court. In all such cases there is room for reasonable men to differ as to whether or not a denial of equal protection or due process has occurred, and the final decision is one of judgment. Until today this judgment has always been one for the judiciary to resolve.

I do not mean to suggest in what has been said that a legislative judgment of the type incorporated in § 4(e) is without any force whatsoever. Decisions on questions of equal protection and due process are based not on abstract logic, but on empirical foundations. To the extent "legislative facts" are relevant to a judicial determination, Congress is well equipped to investigate them, and such determinations are of course entitled to due respect. But no such factual data provide a legislative record supporting § 4(e) by way of showing that Spanish-speaking citizens are fully as capable of making informed decisions in a New York election as are English-speaking citizens. Nor was there any showing whatever to support the Court's alternative argument that § 4(e) should be viewed as but a remedial measure designed to cure or assure against unconstitutional discrimination of other varieties, *e.g.*, in "public schools, public housing and law enforcement," to which Puerto Rican minorities might be subject in such communities as New York. There is simply no legislative record supporting such hypothesized discrimination of the sort we have hitherto insisted upon when congressional power is brought to bear on constitutionally reserved state concerns. . . .

Thus, we have here not a matter of giving deference to a congressional estimate, based on its determination of legislative facts, bearing upon the validity *vel non* of a statute, but rather what can at most be called a legislative announcement that Congress believes a state law to entail an unconstitutional deprivation of equal protection. . . .

In *Employment Division, Dept. of Human Resources of Oregon v. Smith* (1990), the Supreme Court considered a claim brought by members of a Native American church under the Free Exercise Clause of the First Amendment. After having been fired from their jobs with a drug rehabilitation program because of their use of peyote, the petitioners were denied unemployment benefits on the ground that they had been discharged for work-related misconduct. They contended that because they used peyote for sacramental purposes, they should be exempted from a generally applicable state law criminalizing its use. In the course of rejecting their claim, the Court declined to apply *Sherbert v. Verner* (1963), under which state laws substantially burdening a religious practice must be justified by a compelling government interest.

In response to *Smith*, Congress passed the Religious Freedom Restoration Act (RFRA), with the stated purpose of restoring the rule of *Sherbert*. RFRA prohibited government agencies from "substantially burden[ing]" a person's exercise of religion even if the burden results from a rule of general applicability unless the government can demonstrate the burden "(1) is in furtherance of a compelling governmental interest; and (2) is the least restrictive means of furthering that compelling governmental interest." The next case arose when the city, on historical preservation grounds, denied the application of the local Catholic archbishop, for a building permit to expand a church, which he said the congregation had outgrown.

 CROSS REFERENCE Much of the *Boerne* majority's historical discussion of the Fourteenth Amendment is presented at pp. 179–180.

City of Boerne v. Flores

Supreme Court of the United States, 1997.

521 U.S. 507.

JUSTICE KENNEDY delivered the opinion of the Court.

A decision by local zoning authorities to deny a church a building permit was challenged under the Religious Freedom Restoration Act of 1993 (RFRA or Act). The case calls into question the authority of Congress to enact RFRA. We conclude the statute exceeds Congress' power.

I

Situated on a hill in the city of Boerne, Texas, some 28 miles northwest of San Antonio, is St. Peter Catholic Church. Built in 1923, the church's structure replicates the mission style of the region's earlier history. The church seats about 230 worshippers, a number too small for its growing parish. Some 40 to 60 parishioners cannot be accommodated at some Sunday masses. In order to meet the needs of the congregation the Archbishop of San Antonio gave permission to the parish to plan alterations to enlarge the building.

A few months later, the Boerne City Council passed an ordinance authorizing the city's Historic Landmark Commission to prepare a preservation plan with proposed historic landmarks and districts. Under the ordinance, the commission must preapprove construction affecting historic landmarks or buildings in a historic district. Soon afterwards, the Archbishop applied for a building permit so construction to enlarge the church could proceed. City authorities, relying on the ordinance and the designation of a historic district (which, they argued, included the church), denied the application. The Archbishop brought this suit challenging the permit denial. . . .

The complaint contained various claims, but to this point the litigation has centered on RFRA and the question of its constitutionality. The Archbishop relied upon RFRA as one basis for relief from the refusal to issue the permit. [T]he Fifth Circuit [found] RFRA to be constitutional. We granted certiorari, and now reverse.

II

. . . The Act's stated purposes are:

(1)   to restore the compelling interest test as set forth in *Sherbert v. Verner* (1963) . . . and to guarantee its application in all cases where free exercise of religion is substantially burdened; and

(2)   to provide a claim or defense to persons whose religious exercise is substantially burdened by government.

RFRA prohibits "[g]overnment" from "substantially burden[ing]" a person's exercise of religion even if the burden results from a rule of general applicability unless the government can demonstrate the burden "(1) is in furtherance of a compelling governmental interest; and (2) is the least restrictive means of furthering that compelling governmental interest." The Act's mandate applies to any "branch, department, agency, instrumentality, and official (or other person acting under color of law) of the United States," as well as to any "State, or . . . subdivision of a State." . . .

III

A

. . . Congress relied on its Fourteenth Amendment enforcement power in enacting the most far-reaching and substantial of RFRA's provisions, those which impose its requirements on the States. . . . The parties disagree over whether RFRA is a proper exercise of Congress' § 5 power "to enforce" by "appropriate legislation". . . one of the liberties guaranteed by the Fourteenth Amendment's Due Process Clause, the free exercise of religion. . . .

WORTH NOTING

The substance of the First Amendment's Free Exercise Clause (which applies only to the federal government) has been applied to the states through the Fourteenth Amendment Due Process Clause through a process called the "incorporation" of the Bill of Rights. See *McDonald v. City of Chicago*, presented at pp. 1314–1330, for a summary of the doctrinal moves that produce this result. For present purposes, you need know only (1) that the City of Boerne is bound by a constitutional obligation not to interfere with the free exercise of religion, (2) Congress enacted RFRA to "enforce" that constitutional obligation under § 5 of the Fourteenth Amendment, and (3) Congress's conception of that obligation was broader than the one enunciated by the Supreme Court in *Employment Division v. Smith*.

All must acknowledge that § 5 is "a positive grant of legislative power" to Congress, *Katzenbach v. Morgan* (1966). . . . Legislation which deters or remedies constitutional violations can fall within the sweep of Congress' enforcement power even if in the process it prohibits conduct which is not itself unconstitutional and intrudes into "legislative spheres of autonomy previously reserved to the States." For example, the Court upheld a suspension of literacy tests and similar voting requirements under Congress' parallel power to enforce the provisions of the Fifteenth Amendment as a measure to combat racial discrimination in voting, *South Carolina v. Katzenbach* (1966), despite the facial constitutionality of the tests under *Lassiter v. Northampton County Bd. of Elections* (1959). We have also concluded that other measures protecting voting rights are within Congress' power to enforce the Fourteenth and Fifteenth Amendments, despite the burdens those measures placed on the States. *South Carolina v. Katzenbach* (upholding several provisions of the Voting Rights Act of 1965); *Katzenbach v. Morgan* (upholding ban on literacy tests that prohibited certain people schooled in Puerto Rico from voting); *Oregon v. Mitchell* (1970) (upholding 5-year nationwide ban on literacy tests and similar voting requirements for registering to vote). . . .

It is also true, however, that "[a]s broad as the congressional enforcement power is, it is not unlimited." In assessing the breadth of § 5's enforcement power, we begin with its text. Congress has been given the power "to enforce" the "provisions of this article." We agree with respondent, of course, that Congress can enact legislation under § 5 enforcing the constitutional right to the free exercise of religion. The "provisions of this article," to which § 5 refers, include the Due Process Clause of the Fourteenth Amendment. Congress' power to enforce the Free Exercise Clause follows from our holding in *Cantwell v. Connecticut* (1940), that the "fundamental concept of liberty embodied in [the Fourteenth Amendment's Due Process Clause] embraces the liberties guaranteed by the First Amendment." . . .

Congress' power under § 5, however, extends only to "enforc[ing]" the provisions of the Fourteenth Amendment. The Court has described this power as "remedial," *South Carolina v. Katzenbach*. The design of the Amendment and the text of § 5 are inconsistent with the suggestion that Congress has the power to decree the substance of the Fourteenth Amendment's restrictions on the States. Legislation which alters the meaning of the Free Exercise Clause cannot be said to be enforcing the Clause. Congress does not enforce a constitutional right by changing what the right is. It has been given the power "to enforce," not the power to determine what constitutes a constitutional violation. Were it not so, what Congress would be enforcing would no longer be, in any meaningful sense, the "provisions of [the Fourteenth Amendment]."

While the line between measures that remedy or prevent unconstitutional actions and measures that make a substantive change in the governing law is not easy to discern, and Congress must have wide latitude in determining where it lies, the distinction exists and must be observed. There must be a congruence and proportionality between the injury to be prevented or remedied and the means adopted to that end. Lacking such a connection, legislation may become substantive in operation and effect. . . .

The remedial and preventive nature of Congress' enforcement power, and the limitation inherent in the power, [have been] confirmed in [our] cases, [which] revolve around the question whether § 5 legislation can be considered remedial. [T]he Court [has] continued to acknowledge the necessity of using strong remedial and preventive measures to respond to the widespread and persisting deprivation of constitutional rights resulting from this country's history of racial discrimination. See *Oregon v. Mitchell* ("In enacting the literacy test ban . . . Congress had before it a long history of the discriminatory use of literacy tests to disfranchise voters on account of their race") (opinion of Black, J.); . . . *Katzenbach v. Morgan* (Congress had a factual basis to conclude that New York's literacy requirement "constituted an invidious discrimination in violation of the Equal Protection Clause"). . . .

There is language in our opinion in *Katzenbach v. Morgan* (1966) which could be interpreted as acknowledging a power in Congress to enact legislation that expands the rights contained in § 1 of the Fourteenth Amendment. This is not a necessary interpretation, however, or even the best one. . . . Both [of the Court's] rationales for upholding [the Voting Rights Act provision which prohibited New York's literacy test] rested on unconstitutional discrimination by New York and Congress' reasonable attempt to combat it. As Justice Stewart explained in *Oregon v. Mitchell*, interpreting *Morgan* to give Congress the power to interpret the Constitution "would require an enormous extension of that decision's rationale." If Congress could define its own powers by altering the Fourteenth Amendment's meaning, no longer would the Constitution be "superior paramount law, unchangeable by ordinary means." It would be "on a level with ordinary legislative acts, and, like other acts, . . . alterable when the legislature shall please to alter it." *Marbury v. Madison*. Under this approach, it is difficult to conceive of a principle that would limit congressional power. . . . Shifting legislative majorities could change the Constitution and effectively circumvent the difficult and detailed amendment process contained in Article V.

We now turn to consider whether RFRA can be considered enforcement legislation under § 5 of the Fourteenth Amendment.

B

Respondent contends that RFRA is a proper exercise of Congress' remedial or preventive power. The Act, it is said, is a reasonable means of protecting the free exercise of religion as defined by *Smith*. It prevents and remedies laws which are enacted with the unconstitutional object of targeting religious beliefs and practices. See *Church of Lukumi Babalu Aye, Inc. v. Hialeah* (1993) ("[A] law targeting religious beliefs as such is never permissible"). To avoid the difficulty of proving such violations, it is said, Congress can simply invalidate any law which imposes a substantial burden on a religious practice unless it is justified by a compelling interest and is the least restrictive means of accomplishing that interest. If Congress can prohibit laws with discriminatory effects in order to prevent racial discrimination in violation of the Equal Protection Clause, see [Title VII of the Civil Rights Act], then it can do the same, respondent argues, to promote religious liberty.

WORTH NOTING Title VII of the Civil Rights Act prohibits some employment practices that have disparate impact on protected classes, even if those practices are not motivated by discriminatory intent. As interpreted by the Supreme Court in *Washington v. Davis* (1976), pp. 1036–1043, the Fourteenth Amendment contains no such proscription.

While preventive rules are sometimes appropriate remedial measures, there must be a congruence between the means used and the ends to be achieved. The appropriateness of remedial measures must be considered in light of the evil presented. Strong measures appropriate to address one harm may be an unwarranted response to another, lesser one.

A comparison between RFRA and the Voting Rights Act is instructive. In contrast to the record which confronted Congress and the Judiciary in the voting rights cases, RFRA's legislative record lacks examples of modern instances of generally applicable laws passed because of religious bigotry. The history of persecution in this country detailed in the hearings mentions no episodes occurring in the past 40 years. . . . The absence of more recent episodes stems from the fact that, as one witness testified, "deliberate persecution is not the usual problem in this country." Rather, the emphasis of the hearings was on laws of general applicability which place incidental burdens on religion. Much of the discussion centered upon anecdotal evidence of autopsies performed on Jewish individuals and Hmong immigrants in violation of their religious beliefs, and on zoning regulations and historic preservation laws (like the one at issue here), which, as an incident of their normal operation, have adverse effects on churches and synagogues. It is difficult to maintain that they are examples of legislation enacted or enforced due to animus or hostility to the burdened religious practices or that they indicate some widespread pattern of religious discrimination in this country. Congress' concern was with the incidental burdens imposed, not the object or purpose of the legislation.

This lack of support in the legislative record, however, is not RFRA's most serious shortcoming. . . . Regardless of the state of the legislative record, RFRA cannot be considered remedial, preventive legislation, if those terms are to have any meaning. RFRA is so out of proportion to a supposed remedial or preventive object that it cannot be understood as responsive to, or designed to prevent, unconstitutional behavior. It appears, instead, to attempt a substantive change in constitutional protections. Preventive measures prohibiting certain types of laws may be appropriate when there is reason to believe that many of the laws affected by the congressional enactment have a significant likelihood of being unconstitutional. See *City of Rome* (since "jurisdictions with a demonstrable history of intentional racial discrimination . . . create the risk of purposeful discrimination," Congress could "prohibit changes that have a discriminatory impact" in those jurisdictions). Remedial legislation under § 5 "should be adapted to the mischief and wrong which the [Fourteenth] [A]mendment was intended to provide against." *Civil Rights Cases.*

RFRA is not so confined. Sweeping coverage ensures its intrusion at every level of government, displacing laws and prohibiting official actions of almost every description and regardless of subject matter. RFRA's restrictions apply to every agency and official of the Federal, State, and local Governments. RFRA applies to all federal and state law, statutory or otherwise, whether adopted before or after its enactment. RFRA has no termination date or termination mechanism. Any law is subject to challenge at any time by any individual who alleges a substantial burden on his or her free exercise of religion.

The reach and scope of RFRA distinguish it from other measures passed under Congress' enforcement power, even in the area of voting rights. In *South Carolina v. Katzenbach,* the challenged provisions were confined to those regions of the country where voting discrimination had been most flagrant, and affected a discrete class of state laws, *i.e.,* state voting laws. Furthermore, to ensure that the reach of the Voting Rights Act was limited to those cases in which constitutional violations were most likely (in order to reduce the possibility of overbreadth), the coverage under the Act would terminate "at the behest of States and political subdivisions in which the danger of substantial voting discrimination has not materialized during the preceding five years." The provisions restricting and banning literacy tests, upheld in *Katzenbach v. Morgan* (1966), and *Oregon v. Mitchell,* attacked a particular type of voting qualification, one with a long history as a "notorious means to deny and abridge voting rights on racial grounds." . . .

This is not to say, of course, that § 5 legislation requires termination dates, geographic restrictions, or egregious predicates. Where, however, a congressional enactment pervasively prohibits constitutional state action in an effort to remedy or to prevent unconstitutional state action, limitations of this kind tend to ensure Congress' means are proportionate to ends legitimate under § 5. . . .

The stringent test RFRA demands of state laws reflects a lack of proportionality or congruence between the means adopted and the legitimate end to be achieved. If an objector can show a substantial burden on his free exercise, the State must demonstrate a compelling governmental interest and show that the law is the least restrictive means of furthering its interest. Claims that a law substantially burdens someone's exercise of religion will often be difficult to contest. Requiring a State to demonstrate a compelling interest and show that it has adopted the least restrictive means of achieving that interest is the most demanding test known to constitutional law. Laws valid under *Smith* would fall under RFRA without regard to whether they had the object of stifling or punishing free exercise. . . . This is a considerable congressional intrusion into the States' traditional prerogatives and general authority to regulate for the health and welfare of their citizens.

The substantial costs RFRA exacts, both in practical terms of imposing a heavy litigation burden on the States and in terms of curtailing their traditional general regulatory power, far exceed any pattern or practice of unconstitutional conduct under the Free Exercise Clause as interpreted in *Smith*. Simply put, RFRA is not designed to identify and counteract state laws likely to be unconstitutional because of their treatment of religion. In most cases, the state laws to which RFRA applies are not ones which will have been motivated by religious bigotry. If a state law disproportionately burdened a particular class of religious observers, this circumstance might be evidence of an impermissible legislative motive. Cf. *Washington v. Davis* (1976). RFRA's substantial-burden test, however, is not even a discriminatory effects or disparate-impact test. It is a reality of the modern regulatory state that numerous state laws, such as the zoning regulations at issue here, impose a substantial burden on a large class of individuals. . . .

* * *

It is for Congress in the first instance to "determin[e] whether and what legislation is needed to secure the guarantees of the Fourteenth Amendment," and its conclusions are entitled to much deference. *Katzenbach v. Morgan*.

Congress' discretion is not unlimited, however, and the courts retain the power, as they have since *Marbury v. Madison,* to determine if Congress has exceeded its authority under the Constitution. Broad as the power of Congress is under the Enforcement Clause of the Fourteenth Amendment, RFRA contradicts vital principles necessary to maintain separation of powers and the federal balance. The judgment of the Court of Appeals sustaining the Act's constitutionality is reversed.

It is so ordered.

WORTH NOTING

Chief Justice Rehnquist and Justices Stevens, Thomas, and Ginsburg joined Justice Kennedy's opinion in full. Justice Scalia joined all but the discussion of the history of the Fourteenth Amendment, presented at pp. 179–180. Justice Stevens concurred on the ground that, in his view, RFRA was a "law respecting an establishment of religion" in violation of the First Amendment to the Constitution. Justice Scalia wrote a brief opinion, joined by Justice Stevens, responding to Justice O'Connor's contention that historical materials support a result contrary to that of *Smith.* And Justice Souter would have dismissed the writ as improvidently granted, because he did not believe the issue decided by the *Smith* case was properly presented.

Justice O'Connor dissented because she continued to believe that *Smith* was wrongly decided, and she would have used *Boerne* to re-examine the holding of that case. Justice Breyer joined all of Justice O'Connor's opinion except for the following paragraph:

> I agree with much of the reasoning set forth in Part III-A of the Court's opinion. Indeed, if I agreed with the Court's standard in *Smith,* I would join the opinion. As the Court's careful and thorough historical analysis shows, Congress lacks the "power to decree the *substance* of the Fourteenth Amendment's restrictions on the States." (emphasis added). Rather, its power under § 5 of the Fourteenth Amendment extends only to *enforcing* the Amendment's provisions. In short, Congress lacks the ability independently to define or expand the scope of constitutional rights by statute. Accordingly, whether Congress has exceeded its § 5 powers turns on whether there is a "congruence and proportionality between the injury to be prevented or remedied and the means adopted to that end." . . . But when it enacts legislation in furtherance of its delegated powers, Congress must make its judgments consistent with this Court's exposition of

the Constitution and with the limits placed on its legislative authority by provisions such as the Fourteenth Amendment.

In *U.S. v. Morrison*, a student at Virginia Tech accused two members of the Virginia Tech football team of sexual assault. She brought suit against them under 42 U.S.C. § 13981, a provision of the Violence Against Women Act of 1994 that created a private right of action for crimes of violence "committed because of gender or on the basis of gender, and due, at least in part, to an animus based on the victim's gender." The Supreme Court held that the Violence Against Women Act was not a valid exercise of congressional power. In addition to rejecting the government's Commerce Clause argument, see p. 467, the Court held that the statute could not be justified under § 5 of the Fourteenth Amendment.

United States v. Morrison

Supreme Court of the United States, 2000.
529 U.S. 598.

Chief Justice Rehnquist delivered the opinion of the Court.

. . . Petitioners' § 5 argument is founded on an assertion that there is pervasive bias in various state justice systems against victims of gender-motivated violence. This assertion is supported by a voluminous congressional record. Specifically, Congress received evidence that many participants in state justice systems are perpetuating an array of erroneous stereotypes and assumptions. Congress concluded that these discriminatory stereotypes often result in insufficient investigation and prosecution of gender-motivated crime, inappropriate focus on the behavior and credibility of the victims of that crime, and unacceptably lenient punishments for those who are actually convicted of gender-motivated violence. Petitioners contend that this bias denies victims of gender-motivated violence the equal protection of the laws and that Congress therefore acted appropriately in enacting a private civil remedy against the perpetrators of gender-motivated violence to both remedy the States' bias and deter future instances of discrimination in the state courts. . . .

[T]he language and purpose of the Fourteenth Amendment place certain limitations on the manner in which Congress may attack discriminatory conduct. . . . Foremost among these limitations is the time-honored principle that the Fourteenth Amendment, by its very terms, prohibits only state action. . . . "That Amendment erects no shield against merely private conduct, however discriminatory or wrongful." *Shelley v. Kraemer* (1948). . . .

In [the *Civil Rights Cases*], we held that the public accommodation provisions of the Civil Rights Act of 1875, which applied to purely private conduct, were beyond the scope of the § 5 enforcement power. The force of the doctrine of *stare decisis* behind [this] decision[ ] stems not only from the length of time [it has] been on the books, but also from the insight attributable to the Members of the Court at that time. Every Member had been appointed by President Lincoln, Grant, Hayes, Garfield, or Arthur and each of their judicial appointees obviously had intimate knowledge and familiarity with the events surrounding the adoption of the Fourteenth Amendment. We believe that the description of the § 5 power contained in the *Civil Rights Cases* is correct: . . . "any legislation by Congress in the matter must necessarily be corrective in its character, adapted to counteract and redress the operation of such prohibited state laws or proceedings of [s]tate officers."

Petitioners alternatively argue that, unlike the situation in the *Civil Rights Cases*, here there has been gender-based disparate treatment by state authorities, whereas in those cases there was no indication of such state action. There is abundant evidence, however, to show that the Congresses that enacted the Civil Rights Acts of 1871 and 1875 had a purpose similar to that of Congress in enacting § 13981: There were state laws on the books bespeaking equality of treatment, but in the administration of these laws there was discrimination against newly freed slaves. . . .

But even if that distinction were valid, we do not believe it would save § 13981's civil remedy. For the remedy is simply not "corrective in its character, adapted to counteract and redress the operation of such prohibited [s]tate laws or proceedings of [s]tate officers." *Civil Rights Cases*. Or, as we have phrased it in more recent cases, prophylactic legislation under § 5 must have a "congruence and proportionality between the injury to be prevented or remedied and the means adopted to that end." *City of Boerne v. Flores*. Section 13981 is not aimed at proscribing discrimination by officials which the Fourteenth Amendment might not itself proscribe; it is directed not at any State or state actor, but at individuals who have committed criminal acts motivated by gender bias.

In the present cases, for example, § 13981 visits no consequence whatever on any Virginia public official involved in investigating or prosecuting Brzonkala's assault. The section is, therefore, unlike any of the § 5 remedies that we have previously upheld. For example, in *Katzenbach v. Morgan* (1966), [the] law . . . was directed at New York officials who administered the State's election law and prohibited them from using a provision of that law. In *South Carolina v. Katzenbach* (1966), Congress imposed voting rights requirements on States that, Congress found, had a history of discriminating against blacks in voting. The remedy was also directed at state officials in those States. Similarly, in *Ex parte Virginia* (1879), Congress criminally punished state officials who intentionally discriminated in jury selection; again, the remedy was directed to the culpable state official.

Section 13981 is also different from these previously upheld remedies in that it applies uniformly throughout the Nation. Congress' findings indicate that the problem of discrimination against the victims of gender-motivated crimes does not exist in all States, or even most States. By contrast, the § 5 remedy upheld in *Katzenbach v. Morgan* was directed only to the State where the evil found by Congress existed, and in *South Carolina v. Katzenbach* the remedy was directed only to those States in which Congress found that there had been discrimination.

For these reasons, we conclude that Congress' power under § 5 does not extend to the enactment of § 13981.

Justice Breyer, dissenting.

. . . Given my conclusion [that] the Commerce Clause [authorizes this statute], I need not consider Congress' authority under § 5 of the Fourteenth Amendment. Nonetheless, I doubt the Court's reasoning rejecting that source of authority. The Court points out that in . . . the *Civil Rights Cases* the Court held that § 5 does not authorize Congress to use the Fourteenth Amendment as a source of power to remedy the conduct of *private persons*. That is certainly so. The Federal Government's argument, however, is that Congress used § 5 to remedy the actions of *state actors*, namely, those States which, through discriminatory design or the discriminatory conduct of their officials, failed to provide adequate (or any) state remedies for women injured by gender-motivated violence—a failure that the States, and Congress, documented in depth. . . .

The Court responds directly to the relevant "state actor" claim by finding that the present law lacks " 'congruence and proportionality' " to the state discrimination that it purports to remedy. See *City of Boerne v. Flores*. That is because the law . . . is not "directed . . . at any State or state actor." But why can Congress not provide a remedy against private actors? Those private actors, of course, did not themselves violate the Constitution. But this Court has held that Congress at least sometimes can enact remedial "[l]egislation . . . [that] prohibits conduct which is not itself unconstitutional." *Flores*. The statutory remedy does not in any sense purport to "determine what constitutes a constitutional violation." *Flores*. It intrudes little upon either States or private parties. It may lead state actors to improve their own remedial systems, primarily through example. It restricts private actors only by imposing liability for private conduct that is, in the main, already forbidden by state law. Why is the remedy "disproportionate"? And given the relation between remedy and violation—the creation of a federal remedy to substitute for constitutionally inadequate state remedies—where is the lack of "congruence"? . . .

Despite my doubts about the majority's § 5 reasoning, I need not, and do not, answer the § 5 question, which I would leave for more thorough analysis if necessary on another occasion.

———————————

To fully appreciate the stakes of the judicial battles over the scope of the § 5 power, it is important to have a basic understanding of state sovereign immunity. The Eleventh Amendment expressly prohibits some suits against states in federal court. The Supreme Court has interpreted the Amendment to reflect a much broader concept of sovereign immunity already implicit in the Constitution that goes well beyond the text of the amendment itself. *Alden v. Maine* (1999) (applying sovereign immunity principle to a claim under federal law brought in state-court lawsuit). State sovereign immunity does not prohibit suits against individual state officers, *Ex Parte Young* (1908), though in some circumstances such "officer suits" are limited by other legal barriers. But where Eleventh Amendment immunity applies, Congress cannot authorize a cause of action against the states unless it is acting pursuant to constitutional authority that conveys the power to eliminate—or "abrogate"—that immunity.

Not all congressional enumerations have been interpreted to convey this power of abrogation. On one hand, the Court has held that Congress may not abrogate state sovereign immunity if it is acting under the Commerce Clause.

Seminole Tribe of Florida v. Florida (1996). On the other hand, Congress may abrogate sovereign immunity if it is acting under § 5 of the Fourteenth Amendment, which "sanctioned intrusions by Congress . . . into the . . . spheres of autonomy previously reserved to the States. . . ." *Fitzpatrick v. Bitzer* (1976). That means that a federal civil rights statute's validity under the Commerce Clause is not independently sufficient to support a private right of action if the alleged violator is a state. Rather, insofar as the statute is said to authorize judicial action against the states, courts must determine whether it can be justified as an exercise of § 5 authority. For two important cases further exploring the scope of that authority, see *Kimel v. Florida Board of Regents* (2000) and *Nevada Department of Human Resources v. Hibbs* (2003), both of which are in the online supplement.

Note—the Thinnest Possible View of the Enforcement Power

In *Tennessee v. Lane* (2004), a paraplegic criminal defendant sued the State of Tennessee for violating Title II of the Americans with Disabilities Act of 1990 (which forbids public entities to discriminate against disabled persons in the provision of services) by failing to make the county courthouse wheelchair-accessible. Tennessee objected that Title II was not a valid exercise of § 5 authority. The Supreme Court disagreed, holding that the statutory requirement was

> congruent and proportional to [Congress's] object of enforcing the right of access to the courts. The unequal treatment of disabled persons in the administration of judicial services has a long history, and has persisted despite several legislative efforts to remedy the problem of disability discrimination. Faced with considerable evidence of the shortcomings of previous legislative responses, Congress was justified in concluding that this "difficult and intractable proble[m]" warranted "added prophylactic measures in response."

Justice Scalia dissented. He did not challenge the majority's application of the "congruence and proportionality" test. Rather, he suggested that the test should be abandoned in its entirety:

. . . I joined the Court's opinion in *Boerne* with some misgiving. I have generally rejected tests based on such malleable standards as "proportionality," because they have a way of turning into vehicles for the implementation of individual judges' policy preferences. . . .

I [now] yield to the lessons of experience. The "congruence and proportionality" standard, like all such flabby tests, is a standing invitation to judicial arbitrariness and policy-driven decisionmaking. Worse still, it casts this Court in the role of Congress's taskmaster. Under it, the courts (and ultimately this Court) must regularly check Congress's homework to make sure that it has identified sufficient constitutional violations to make its remedy congruent and proportional. [W]hen conflict is unavoidable, we should not come to do battle with the United States Congress armed only with a test ("congruence and proportionality") that has no demonstrable basis in the text of the Constitution and cannot objectively be shown to have been met or failed. . . .

I would replace "congruence and proportionality" with another test—one that provides a clear, enforceable limitation supported by the text of § 5. Section 5 grants Congress the power "to *enforce*, by appropriate legislation," the other provisions of the Fourteenth Amendment. *Morgan* notwithstanding, one does not, within any normal meaning of the term, "enforce" a prohibition by issuing a still broader prohibition directed to the same end. One does not, for example, "enforce" a 55-mile-per-hour speed limit by imposing a 45-mile-per-hour speed limit—even though that is indeed directed to the same end of automotive safety and will undoubtedly result in many fewer violations of the 55-mile-per-hour limit. And one does not "enforce" the right of access to the courts at issue in this case by requiring that disabled persons be provided access to *all* of the "services, programs, or activities" furnished or conducted by the State. That is simply not what the power to enforce means—or ever meant. . . .

Nothing in § 5 allows Congress to go *beyond* the provisions of the Fourteenth Amendment to proscribe, prevent, or "remedy" conduct that does not *itself* violate any provision of the Fourteenth Amendment. So-called "prophylactic legislation" is reinforcement rather than enforcement. . . .

Is Justice Scalia treating § 5 as surplusage? What would count as "enforcement" of an individual right, on his view? Consider in this respect that the Supreme Court has held that the Constitution does not itself always authorize courts to award damages for its violation. See, *e.g.*, *Schweiker v. Chilicky* (1988) ("The absence of statutory relief for a constitutional violation . . . does not by any means necessarily imply that courts should award money damages against the officers responsible for the violation."). Also bear in mind that Congress can, if it chooses, provide for governmental enforcement actions of the substantive provisions of the Fourteenth Amendment.

A Note on the Voting Rights Act

In response to various state actions that effectively limited voting by African-Americans in much of the South, Congress passed the Voting Rights Act of 1965 (VRA). Section 2, as subsequently amended, forbids any "standard, practice, or procedure" that "results in a denial or abridgement of the right of any citizen of the United States to vote on account of race or color"; a violation may be shown if members of a racial group "have less opportunity than other members of the electorate to participate in the political process and to elect representatives of their choice." This section applies nationwide, and it is permanent. Notice that this provision, by creating a "results" test, goes beyond the prohibition that the Fourteenth and Fifteenth Amendments create of their own force. The Supreme Court has not definitively resolved the constitutionality of this provision, but courts have consistently assumed that it is a valid exercise of Congress's enforcement powers.

Section 5 of the VRA applied only to certain jurisdictions listed in § 4—six southern states plus 39 counties in North Carolina and one in Arizona—that had maintained a "test or device" as a prerequisite to voting as of November 1, 1964, and had less than 50% voter registration or turnout in the 1964 presidential election. Section 5 provided that these jurisdictions could not change their voting procedures unless "precleared" by authorities in Washington (either the Attorney General or a special three-judge federal court); a jurisdiction could only gain preclearance by showing that the change had neither "the purpose [nor] the effect of denying or abridging the right to vote on account of race or color." This section was meant to prevent "retrogression"—that is, changes that would put a minority group in a worse position than it was before the change. A jurisdiction with a clean record for five years could "bail out" of coverage. Sections 4 and 5 were initially set to expire after five years. The Supreme Court upheld the provisions against constitutional challenge in *South Carolina v. Katzenbach* (1966), ruling that despite their "uncommon" nature they were justified by "exceptional" and "unique" conditions.

In 1970, Congress reauthorized these provisions for five years, and in 1975 for another seven. Both of these extensions updated the coverage formula; the 1975 formula extended coverage to jurisdictions that had a voting test and less than 50 percent voter registration or turnout as of 1972. These changes brought some non-southern states and counties within the coverage of § 5 of the VRA. In 1982, Congress reauthorized the provisions for 25 years. This time, it did not alter the coverage formula, but it did tighten up on the bail-out provisions; for example, bail-out would not be available if a jurisdiction had failed to gain pre-clearance on a proposed change within the previous ten years. The Supreme Court upheld each of these extensions. *E.g., City of Rome v. United States* (1980).

In 2006, Congress again extended these provisions for 25 years, again without altering the coverage formula. Congress did, however, expand the scope of § 5 of the VRA, so that it forbade voting changes with "any discriminatory purpose" as well as voting changes that diminish the ability of citizens, on account of race, color, or language minority status, "to elect their preferred candidates of choice." This time, the Supreme Court refused to allow implementation of the extension. *Shelby County, Alabama v. Holder* (2013).

Shelby County was a 5–4 decision, with Chief Justice Roberts writing for the majority, joined by Justices Scalia, Kennedy, Thomas, and Alito. Justice Thomas added a brief concurrence. Justice Ginsburg dissented, joined by Justices Breyer, Sotomayor, and Kagan. The majority insisted that its decision did not bear on § 5 itself, but only on the continued use of the 1975 coverage formula in § 4. (Justice Thomas's concurrence contended that the reasoning of the majority opinion warranted going further and holding § 5 unconstitutional.)

The Chief Justice argued that there was a "tradition of equal sovereignty" of the states, which on his account had two parts: (1) "Outside the strictures of the Supremacy Clause, States retain broad autonomy in structuring their governments and pursuing legislative objectives"; and (2) the Court has long spoken of the Nation as "a union of States, equal in power, dignity and authority."

(quoting *Coyle v. Smith* (1911) (holding unconstitutional a federal statute requiring Oklahoma to locate the state capital in Briscoe as a condition of admission to the Union). The "blight of racial discrimination in voting" had previously justified the extraordinary departure from this tradition provided by § 5 of the VRA. But if the departure were to continue—that is, if some jurisdictions, but not others, would continue to be required to submit changes in their electoral systems for pre-clearance—the covered jurisdictions would have "to be singled out on a basis that makes sense in light of current conditions."

The Court was not persuaded that continued use of the 1975 formula was so justified. It presented a chart that was before Congress during consideration of the 2006 re-authorization, showing percentages of eligible citizens registered in 1965 and 2004 in the six states originally covered by the VRA:

	1965			2004		
	White	Black	Gap	White	Black	Gap
Alabama	69.2	19.3	49.9	73.8	72.9	0.9
Georgia	62.[6]	27.4	35.2	63.5	64.2	-0.7
Louisiana	80.5	31.6	48.9	75.1	71.1	4.0
Mississippi	69.9	6.7	63.2	72.3	76.1	-3.8
South Carolina	75.7	37.3	38.4	74.4	71.1	3.3
Virginia	61.1	38.3	22.8	68.2	57.4	10.8

In response, Justice Ginsburg's dissent emphasized another aspect of the evidence before Congress at the time of the 2006 re-authorization—an extensive record showing continued attempts to enact discriminatory legislation, and hundreds of DOJ decisions blocking proposed changes on the grounds that they were discriminatory. In combination with other evidence, the dissent concluded, this was ample support for a congressional conclusion that continued operation of § 5 was appropriate to "facilitate completion of the impressive gains thus far made" and to "guard against backsliding."

The majority responded:

Congress did not use the record it compiled to shape a coverage formula grounded in current conditions. It instead reenacted a formula based on 40-year-old facts having no logical relation to the present day. . . . We cannot pretend that we are reviewing an updated statute, or try our hand at updating the statute ourselves, based on the new record compiled by Congress. Contrary to the dissent's contention, we are not ignoring the record; we are simply recognizing that it played no role in shaping the statutory formula before us today.

The very day that *Shelby County* was decided, Texas put into operation a statute, which had previously been held up because it had not yet been pre-cleared, requiring voters to show officially issued photo identification. (Apparently hundreds of thousands of Texas voters do not have such IDs.) The Fifth Circuit upheld a determination that the law violated § 2 of the VRA and remanded a determination that the law was intentionally discriminatory in violation of the Fourteenth Amendment. *Veasey v. Abbott* (5th Cir. 2016), *cert. denied* (2017). Ultimately, Texas passed a statute that allows voters to show alternative forms of identification such as original utility bills, bank statements and paychecks. A district court issued an injunction against this statute, but the Fifth Circuit reversed. *Veasey v. Abbott* (5th Cir. 2018).

Meanwhile, in North Carolina—which had recently emerged as a swing state in national elections as African American voting swelled under the pre-clearance regime—the day after *Shelby County* the chair of the Senate Rules Committee, a Republican, announced plans to bring forward an omnibus voting law. That statute passed promptly. It imposed photo-identification requirements for voters, reduced the number of early voting days, eliminated same-day registration, and prohibited counting of out-of-precinct provisional ballots. Ultimately, the Fourth Circuit enjoined these provisions under both the Fourteenth Amendment and § 2 of the VRA. *North Carolina State Conference of NAACP v. McCrory* (4th Cir. 2016), *cert. denied* (2017) ("In many ways, the challenged provisions . . . constitute solutions in search of a problem. The only clear factor linking these various "reforms" is their impact on African American voters.").

B. Federalism Constraints on the States

1.   The Supremacy Principle

The Supremacy Clause provides that

> "[t]his Constitution, and the laws of the United States which shall be made in pursuance thereof . . . shall be the supreme law of the land; and the judges in every state shall be bound thereby, anything in the Constitution or laws of any State to the contrary notwithstanding."

This supremacy principle prompted significant criticism during the ratification process. Consider what one Federalist had to say in defense of it.

A Rhode-Island Man

Newport Mercury (Feb. 25, 1788)

Now let us consider the objections that are laid against [the Constitution], it is said to be a consolidation, [and] if by consolidation is meant the union of several [smaller] societies into one supreme council for the sake of uniformity, efficiency, and dispatch,—it is confessed the constitution is and was meant to be so far a consolidation of the powers of the United States. The supremacy of the General Assembly of the State of Rhode-Island over the several towns and town meetings [is] just such a consolidation of the various towns, as the new constitution is of the United States,—and there is no argument against a union of States, but what is equally forcible against a union of towns in our General Assembly, for our Assembly has a sovereign unlimited power;

[B]ut let us suppose for a moment this doctrine was put in practice by dissolving our Assembly and restoring sovereignty and independence to the towns, their power of refusing state taxes would soon be sanctified by pretended reason, and each town would prove, by endless arguments that they had been ever over taxed, and least they should pay too much, would take care to pay nothing, town taxes would soon be thought inconvenient and tyrannical, and therefore abolished, we should soon enjoy the blessed freedom of savages, we should be free from the fees of sheriffs and judges, every man would judge his own cause and execute his own judgment, if my neighbor kills my pigeons, I kill one of his children, I fall next, and retaliation goes on until each family is extinct. . . .

[That would be] the happy [tendency] of cautiously keeping our power in our own [hands], but Judge Blackstone says, that to suppose a government without a supreme controling power some where lodged, is the highth of political absurdity—[why] may not supreme power be as secure from abuse in Congress, as in a General Assembly of Massachusetts, Rhode-Island, or any other State.

One implication of the Supremacy Clause is that when the federal government makes constitutionally valid "laws"—including not only statutes enacted pursuant to bicameralism and presentment, but also regulations promulgated under valid authority—they override any state provision to the contrary. (Recall in this respect that *McCulloch v. Maryland* (1819) invalidated a state tax on the ground that it could burden operation of a federal instrumentality, and that *Gibbons v. Ogden* (1824) struck down a state ferry monopoly that was said to conflict with a federal licensing regime.)

So if the federal government prohibits driving faster than 60 mph on interstate highways and says no state may pass a law on the subject, then any state speed limits would be preempted. Even without such an explicit prohibition on state legislation, the federal law would preempt a state law requiring drivers to drive at least 65 mph on the highway. What if the state enacts a 55 mph minimum? Then the constitutional outcome turns on a question of statutory interpretation: did Congress only mean to set an absolute upper limit, leaving states free to enact more restrictive laws, or did it mean to create a consistent standard binding through the nation? And what if states put up speed bumps on the highways? There is no logical conflict with federal law, but a court might well hold that the state has obstructed—in this case, quite literally—a federal policy, to allow fast travel on the highway.

Ultimately, this kind of preemption by statute (or regulation) is a matter of statutory construction; so long as there is a valid source of enumerated authority, Congress can decide the extent to which it wishes to preempt state law. This process of interpretation, however, is conducted in the shadow of the Constitution: The closer Congress is deemed to be verging to the limits of its constitutional power, the more the courts are likely to demand that it be clear in stating an attempt to preempt. See, *e.g.*, *Gregory v. Ashcroft* (1991), pp. 505–506.

But what if a state regulation allegedly interferes with some federal interest to which Congress has not squarely spoken? In some cases, a different kind of preemption arises pursuant to the Constitution itself. In these cases, states are constrained by the mere existence of a federal power—even if that power has not actually been exercised, but has instead lain *dormant*. The remainder of this chapter deals with two areas where this question can arise: dormant foreign affairs preemption and the Dormant Commerce Clause.

2.   The Dormant Foreign Affairs Power

Under the doctrine of "dormant foreign affairs preemption," the Constitution directly preempts certain kinds of state interference with foreign policy, even if the federal government has not staked out a contrary position on the question at issue.

Zschernig v. Miller

Supreme Court of the United States, 1968.
389 U.S. 429.

MR. JUSTICE DOUGLAS delivered the opinion of the Court.

This case concerns the disposition of the estate of a resident of Oregon who died there intestate in 1962. Appellants are decedent's sole heirs and they are residents of East Germany. Appellees include members of the State Land Board that petitioned the Oregon probate court for the escheat of the net proceeds of the estate under the provisions of Ore. Rev. Stat. § 111.070, which provides for escheat in cases where a nonresident alien claims real or personal property unless three requirements are satisfied:

(1)   the existence of a reciprocal right of a United States citizen to take property on the same terms as a citizen or inhabitant of the foreign country;

(2)   the right of United States citizens to receive payment here of funds from estates in the foreign country; and

(3)   the right of the foreign heirs to receive the proceeds of Oregon
      estates "without confiscation."

We conclude that the history and operation of this Oregon statute make
clear that § 111.070 is an intrusion by the State into the field of foreign affairs
which the Constitution entrusts to the President and the Congress. See *Hines
v. Davidowitz* (1941).

As already noted, one of the conditions of inheritance under the Oregon
statute requires "proof that such foreign heirs, distributees, devisees or legatees may receive the benefit, use or control of money or property from estates
of persons dying in this state without confiscation, in whole or in part, by the
governments of such foreign countries," the burden being on the nonresident
alien to establish that fact. This provision came into Oregon's law in 1951. Pri-
or to that time the rights of aliens under the Oregon statute were defined in
general terms of reciprocity, similar to the California Act which we had before
us in *Clark v. Allen* (1947).

We held in *Clark v. Allen* that a general reciprocity clause did not on its
face intrude on the federal domain. We noted that the California statute, then
a recent enactment, would have only "some incidental or indirect effect in foreign countries." . . . It now appears[, however,] that in this reciprocity area
under inheritance statutes, the probate courts of various States have launched
inquiries into the type of governments that obtain in particular foreign nations—whether aliens under their law have enforceable rights, whether the
so-called "rights" are merely dispensations turning upon the whim or caprice
of government officials, whether the representation of consuls, ambassadors,
and other representatives of foreign nations is credible or made in good faith,
whether there is in the actual administration in the particular foreign system
of law any element of confiscation.

In a California case, involving a reciprocity provision, the United States
made the following representation:

> the operation and effect of the statute is inextricably enmeshed in in-
> ternational affairs and matters of foreign policy. The statute does not
> work disinheritance of, or affect ownership of property in California
> by, any group or class, but on the contrary operates in fields exclusively
> for, and preempted by, the United States; namely, the control of the
> international transmission of property, funds, and credits, and the

capture of enemy property. The statute is not an inheritance statute, but a statute of confiscation and retaliation.

In re Bevilacqua's Estate (Dist. Ct. App. Cal. 1945). In its brief *amicus curiae* [in the present case], the Department of Justice states that: "The government does not . . . contend that the application of the Oregon escheat statute in the circumstances of this case unduly interferes with the United States' conduct of foreign relations."

The Government's acquiescence in the ruling of *Clark v. Allen* certainly does not justify extending the principle of that case, as we would be required to do here to uphold the Oregon statute as applied; for it has more than "some incidental or indirect effect in foreign countries," and its great potential for disruption or embarrassment makes us hesitate to place it in the category of a diplomatic bagatelle.

As we read the [state court] decisions [on inheritance reciprocity] that followed in the wake of *Clark v. Allen*, we find that they radiate some of the attitudes of the "cold war," where the search is for the "democracy quotient" of a foreign regime as opposed to the Marxist theory.[6] The Oregon statute introduces the concept of "confiscation," which is of course opposed to the Just Compensation Clause of the Fifth Amendment. And this has led into minute inquiries concerning the actual administration of foreign law, into the credibility of foreign diplomatic statements, and into speculation whether the fact that some received delivery of funds should "not preclude wonderment as to how many may have been denied 'the right to receive' . . . ." *See State Land Board v. Kolovrat*, 220 Or. 448 (1961).

That kind of state involvement in foreign affairs and international relations—matters which the Constitution entrusts solely to the Federal Government—is not sanctioned by *Clark v. Allen*. Yet such forbidden state activity

---

[6] See *Estate of Gogabashvele* (Cal. Apps. 1961), disapproved in *Estate of Larkin* (Cal. 1966), and *Estate of Chichernea* (Cal. 1967). One commentator has described the *Gogabashvele* decision in the following manner:

> The court analyzed the general nature of rights in the Soviet system instead of examining whether Russian inheritance rights were granted equally to aliens and residents. The court found Russia had no separation of powers, too much control in the hands of the Communist Party, no independent judiciary, confused legislation, unpublished statutes, and unrepealed obsolete statutes. Before stating its holding of no reciprocity, the court also noted Stalin's crimes, the Beria trial, the doctrine of crime by analogy, Soviet xenophobia, and demonstrations at the American Embassy in Moscow unhindered by the police. The court concluded that a leading Soviet jurist's construction of article 8 of the law enacting the R.S.F.S.R. Civil Code seemed modeled after Humpty Dumpty, who said, "When I use a word. . . , it means just what I choose it to mean—neither more nor less."

Note, 55 Calif. L. Rev. 592 (1967).

has infected each of the three provisions of § 111.070, as applied by Oregon. [The Court reviewed several Oregon decisions, including one that prompted a complaint from the government of Bulgaria to the U.S. State Department that Bulgarians were having a hard time securing the transfer of property probated in Oregon courts.]

As one reads the Oregon decisions, it seems that foreign policy attitudes, the freezing or thawing of the "cold war," and the like are the real desiderata.[8] Yet they of course are matters for the Federal Government, not for local probate courts.

[In one Oregon case, the court] held that not only must the foreign law give inheritance rights to Americans, but the political body making the law must have "membership in the family of nations," because the purpose of the Oregon provision was to serve as "an inducement to foreign nations to so frame the inheritance laws of their respective countries in a manner which would insure to Oregonians the same opportunities to inherit and take personal property abroad that they enjoy in the state of Oregon."

[Another Oregon case held that although] certain provisions of the written law of Nazi Germany appeared to permit Americans to inherit, they created no "right," since Hitler had absolute dictatorial powers and could prescribe to German courts rules and procedures at variance with the general law. Bequests "grossly opposed to sound sentiment of the people" would not be given effect.

In short, it would seem that Oregon judges in construing § 111.070 seek to ascertain whether "rights" protected by foreign law are the same "rights" that

---

[8] Such attitudes are not confined to the Oregon courts. . . . In Pennsylvania, a judge stated at the trial of a case involving a Soviet claimant that "If you want to say that I'm prejudiced, you can, because when it comes to Communism I'm a bigoted anti-Communist." . . . A California judge, upon being asked if he would hear argument on the law, replied, "No, I won't send any money to Russia." The judge took "judicial notice that Russia kicks the United States in the teeth all the time," and told counsel for the Soviet claimant that "I would think your firm would feel it honor bound to withdraw as representing the Russian government. No American can make it too strong." Berman, *Soviet Heirs in American Courts*, 62 Colum. L. Rev. 257 (1962).

A particularly pointed attack was made by Judge Musmanno of the Pennsylvania Supreme Court, where he stated with respect to the Pennsylvania Act that:

All the known facts of a Sovietized state lead to the irresistible conclusion that sending American money to a person within the borders of an Iron Curtain country is like sending a basket of food to Little Red Ridinghood in care of her "grandmother." It could be that the greedy, gluttonous grasp of the government collector in Yugoslavia does not clutch as rapaciously as his brother confiscators in Russia, but it is abundantly clear that there is no assurance upon which an American court can depend that a named Yugoslavian individual beneficiary of American dollars with have anything left to shelter, clothe and feed himself once he has paid financial involuntary tribute to the tyranny of a totalitarian regime.

Belemecich's Estate, 411 Pa. 506 (1963).

citizens of Oregon enjoy. If . . . the alleged foreign "right" may be vindicated only through Communist-controlled state agencies, then there is no "right" of the type § 111.070 requires. The same seems to be true if enforcement may require approval of a Fascist dictator. . . . The statute as construed seems to make unavoidable judicial criticism of nations established on a more authoritarian basis than our own.

It seems inescapable that the type of probate law that Oregon enforces affects international relations in a persistent and subtle way. The practice of state courts in withholding remittances to legatees residing in Communist countries or in preventing them from assigning them is notorious.

The several States, of course, have traditionally regulated the descent and distribution of estates. But those regulations must give way if they impair the effective exercise of the Nation's foreign policy. Where those laws conflict with a treaty, they must bow to the superior federal policy. See *Kolovrat v. Oregon.* Yet, even in absence of a treaty, a State's policy may disturb foreign relations. As we stated in *Hines v. Davidowitz,* "Experience has shown that international controversies of the gravest moment, sometimes even leading to war, may arise from real or imagined wrongs to another's subjects inflicted, or permitted, by a government." Certainly a State could not deny admission to a traveler from East Germany nor bar its citizens from going there. If there are to be such restraints, they must be provided by the Federal Government. The present Oregon law is not as gross an intrusion in the federal domain as those others might be. Yet, as we have said, it has a direct impact upon foreign relations and may well adversely affect the power of the central government to deal with those problems.

The Oregon law does, indeed, illustrate the dangers which are involved if each State, speaking through its probate courts, is permitted to establish its own foreign policy.

Reversed.

Mr. Justice Marshall took no part in the consideration or decision of this case.

Mr. Justice Stewart, with whom Mr. Justice Brennan joins, concurring.

. . . The Solicitor General, as *amicus curiae,* says that the Government does not "contend that the application of the Oregon escheat statute in the circumstances of this case unduly interferes with the United States' conduct of foreign relations." But that is not the point. We deal here with the basic allocation of power between the States and the Nation. Resolution of so fundamental a constitutional issue cannot vary from day to day with the shifting winds at the State Department. Today, we are told, Oregon's statute does not conflict with the national interest. Tomorrow it may. But, however that may be, the fact remains that the conduct of our foreign affairs is entrusted under the Constitution to the National Government, not to the probate courts of the several States. To the extent that *Clark v. Allen*, is inconsistent with these views, I would overrule that decision.

MR. JUSTICE HARLAN, concurring in the result.

. . . Article IV of the 1923 Treaty of Friendship, Commerce and Consular Rights with Germany . . . should be construed as guaranteeing to citizens of the contracting parties the rights to inherit personal property from a decedent who dies in his own country. . . . Properly construed, the 1923 treaty, which [as an Article II treaty] of course takes precedence over the Oregon statute under the Supremacy Clause, entitles the appellants in this case to succeed to the personal as well as the real property of the decedent despite the state statute. [Justice Harlan analyzes the treaty with Germany at length.]

Upon my view of this case, it would be unnecessary to reach the issue whether Oregon's statute governing inheritance by aliens amounts to an unconstitutional infringement upon the foreign relations power of the Federal Government. However, since this is the basis upon which the Court has chosen to rest its decision, I feel that I should indicate briefly why I believe the decision to be wrong on that score. . . .

Prior decisions have established that in the absence of a conflicting federal policy or violation of the express mandates of the Constitution the States may legislate in areas of their traditional competence even though their statutes may have an incidental effect on foreign relations. Application of this rule to the case before us compels the conclusion that the Oregon statute is constitutional. Oregon has so legislated in the course of regulating the descent and distribution of estates of Oregon decedents, a matter traditionally within the power of a State. Apart from the 1923 treaty, which the Court finds it unnecessary to consider, there is no specific interest of the Federal Government which might be interfered with by this statute. The appellants concede that Oregon might deny inheritance rights to all nonresident aliens. Assuming that this is so, the statutory exception permitting inheritance by aliens whose countries permit Americans to inherit would seem to be a measure wisely designed to avoid any offense to foreign governments and thus any conflict with general federal interests: a foreign government can hardly object to the denial of rights which it does not itself accord to the citizens of other countries.

[The majority's] notion appears to be that application of the parts of the statute which require that reciprocity actually exist and that the alien heir actually be able to enjoy his inheritance will inevitably involve the state courts in evaluations of foreign laws and governmental policies, and that this is likely to result in offense to foreign governments. There are several defects in this rationale.

The most glaring is that it is based almost entirely on speculation. My Brother Douglas does cite a few unfortunate remarks made by state court judges in applying statutes resembling the one before us. However, the Court does not mention, nor does the record reveal, any instance in which such an occurrence has been the occasion for a diplomatic protest, or, indeed, has had any foreign relations consequence whatsoever.[27] The United States says in its brief as *amicus curiae* that it "does not . . . contend that the application of the Oregon escheat statute in the circumstances of this case unduly interferes with the United States' conduct of foreign relations." At an earlier stage in this case, the Solicitor General told this Court: "The Department of State has advised us . . . that State reciprocity laws, including that of Oregon, have had little effect on the foreign relations and policy of this country. . . ."

Essentially, the Court's basis for decision appears to be that alien inheritance laws afford state court judges an opportunity to criticize in dictum the policies of foreign governments, and that these dicta may adversely affect our foreign relations. In addition to finding no evidence of adverse effect in the record, I believe this rationale to be untenable because logically it would apply to many other types of litigation which come before the state courts. It is true that, in addition to the many state court judges who have applied alien inheritance statutes with proper judicial decorum, some judges have seized the opportunity to make derogatory remarks about foreign governments. However, judges have been known to utter dicta critical of foreign governmental policies even in purely domestic cases, so that the mere possibility of offensive utterances can hardly be the test.

---

[27]   The communication from the Bulgarian Government mentioned in the majority opinion . . . apparently refers not to intemperate comments by state-court judges but to the very existence of state statutes which result in the denial of inheritance rights to Bulgarians.

If the flaw in the statute is said to be that it requires state courts to inquire into the administration of foreign law, I would suggest that that characteristic is shared by other legal rules which I cannot believe the Court wishes to invalidate. For example, the Uniform Foreign Money-Judgments Recognition Act provides that a foreign-country money judgment shall not be recognized if it "was rendered under a system which does not provide impartial tribunals or procedures compatible with the requirements of due process of law." When there is a dispute as to the content of foreign law, the court is required under the common law to treat the question as one of fact and to consider any evidence presented as to the actual administration of the foreign legal system. And in the field of choice of law there is a nonstatutory rule that the tort law of a foreign country will not be applied if that country is shown to be "uncivilized." Surely, all of these rules possess the same "defect" as the statute now before us. Yet I assume that the Court would not find them unconstitutional.

I therefore concur in the judgment of the Court upon the sole ground that the application of the Oregon statute in this case conflicts with the 1923 Treaty of Friendship, Commerce and Consular Rights with Germany.

MR. JUSTICE WHITE, dissenting.

I would affirm the judgment below. Generally for the reasons stated by Mr. Justice Harlan in . . . his separate opinion, I do not consider the Oregon statute to be an impermissible interference with foreign affairs. . . .

FOR DISCUSSION

More than half the states have adopted versions of the Uniform Foreign-Country Money Judgments Recognition Act, which (like the earlier Uniform Act mentioned by Justice Harlan) prohibits the enforcement of any foreign judgment for money damages that "was rendered under a judicial system that does not provide impartial tribunals or procedures compatible with the requirements of due process of law." Have these states all violated the constitutional rule of *Zschernig*? What more, if anything, would you need to know to decide the answer to that question?

3.   The Dormant Commerce Clause

In *Zschernig v. Miller*, state power was constrained by a limit that doesn't actually appear in the text of the Constitution, but rather is implied by the existence of federal power over foreign affairs. A similar phenomenon frequently arises under the so-called "Dormant Commerce Clause," which represents the *negative* implications of the textual Commerce Clause's *affirmative* grant of congressional power to "regulate commerce among the several states." Where the doctrine applies, the courts will strike down certain kinds of state regulations that interfere with commerce—even when Congress has not affirmatively legislated to preempt them. The doctrine is complicated, internally contradictory, controversial, and extremely important.

To get a sense for how it emerged, bear in mind that economic competition, conflict, and obstructionism among the states had created a crisis under the Articles of Confederation. Looking back in 1835, James Madison had this to say about the "rival, conflicting, and angry [state] regulations" that plagued the young nation during the critical period leading up to the constitutional convention:

> [T]he States having ports for foreign commerce, taxed & irritated the adjoining states, trading thro' them. . . . Some of the States, as Connecticut, taxed imports as from Massts, higher than imports even from G.B. of wch Massts complained to Virga and doubtless to other States. . . . In sundry instances [t]he navigation laws treated the Citizens of other states as aliens.

Concurring in *Gibbons v. Ogden* (1824), Justice Johnson put the point strongly:

> The strong sympathies, rather than the feeble government, which bound the States together during a common war [with Great Britain], dissolved on the return of peace; and the very principles which gave rise to the war of the revolution, began to threaten the confederacy with anarchy and ruin. . . .

> [T]hat selfish principle which, well controlled, is so salutary, and which, unrestricted, is so unjust and tyrannical, guided by inexperience and jealousy, began to show itself in iniquitous laws and impolitic measures, from which grew up a conflict of commercial regulations, destructive to the harmony of the States, and fatal to their commercial interests abroad. This was the immediate cause, that led to the forming of a convention. . . .

Destructive trade wars and opportunistic tariff policy were thus a central concern to many Founders.

Given the salience of the problem, the lack of clear language providing a comprehensive solution in the Constitution is perhaps surprising. Art. I, § 10 prohibited the states from imposing import and export taxes, but at most that provided a very partial solution. (In *Woodruff v. Parham* (1869), the Supreme Court held that this clause applied only to foreign trade, although that understanding has been challenged. See *Camps Newfound/Owatonna, Inc. v. Town of Harrison* (1997) (Thomas, J., dissenting)). Instead, the principal constitutional solution was the creation of what Madison in *The Federalist* No. 42 called "a superintending authority over the reciprocal trade of confederated States": the Commerce Clause.

The Clause clearly serves as an affirmative authorization for *Congress* to intervene and—using its supremacy within interstate commerce jurisdiction—to put a stop to state interference with the flow of goods. In the earliest years of the Republic, however, it was impractical for Congress to monitor all state legislation and other lawmaking. And so the question quickly arose whether the Commerce Clause *of its own force* prohibited certain kinds of protectionist or isolationist regulations by the states.

The strongest version of such a theory is that the commerce power is exclusive, so that the grant to Congress precludes the states from enacting any laws that might be deemed to be a regulation of interstate commerce. In the closing stages of the Philadelphia drafting convention, Madison gestured toward something like this idea:

> Whether the States are now restrained from laying tonnage duties depends on the extent of the power 'to regulate commerce.' These terms are vague but seem to exclude this power of the States. . . . He was more & more convinced that the regulation of Commerce was in its nature indivisible and ought to be wholly under one authority.

In *Gibbons v. Ogden* (1824), Chief Justice Marshall lent further force to the exclusivity theory:

> It has been contended by the counsel for the appellant, that, as the word "to regulate" implies in its nature, full power over the thing to be regulated, it excludes, necessarily, the action of all others that would perform the same operation on the same thing. That regulation is designed for the entire result, applying to those parts which remain as they were, as well as to those which are altered. It produces

a uniform whole, which is as much disturbed and deranged by changing what the regulating power designs to leave untouched, as that
on which it has operated. There is great force in this argument, and
the Court is not satisfied that it has been refuted.

This passage was *dictum*, because the Court decided the case on the basis that
a federal statute governed. Justice Johnson's concurrence, however, was based
on the exclusivity theory; he wrote that "the grant of this power carries with it
the whole subject, leaving nothing for the State to act upon."

Over the succeeding decades, numerous decisions proceeded on the assumption that Congress's power over interstate commerce was exclusive. But
what did that mean for state legislation that regulated internal matters but also
had some impact on interstate commerce? There was often great pressure on
the courts not to characterize such legislation as regulating commerce in the
constitutional sense; Marshall's opinion in *Willson v. Black Bird Creek Marsh
Company* (1829), presented at pp. 89–90, holding that Delaware had validly authorized the construction of a dam across a navigable stream, may be
considered an example. The exclusivity theory was also thought to require a
binary view of regulatory jurisdiction: in any given circumstance, either the
federal government could impose regulation or the states could—but not both.
Thus, the Supreme Court held that so long as an article shipped in interstate or
foreign commerce remained in the hands of its importer in its original package, it remained subject to federal law only, but that once these conditions no
longer held it was no longer part of interstate or foreign commerce and could
be regulated and taxed by the states. Drawing such dividing lines constituted
much of the constitutional law of the 19th century.

The exclusivity thesis remained a matter of intense debate. In *The License
Cases* (1847), presented at pp. 91–93, Chief Justice Taney appeared to take
the opposite view, concluding that the Commerce Clause of its own force did
not invalidate any state laws:

[I]t appears to me to be very clear, that the mere grant of power to
the general government cannot, upon any just principles of construction, be construed to be an absolute prohibition to the exercise of
any power over the same subject by the States. The controlling and
supreme power over commerce with foreign nations and the several
States is undoubtedly conferred upon Congress. Yet, in my judgment,

the State may nevertheless, for the safety or convenience of trade, or for the protection of the health of its citizens, make regulations of commerce for its own ports and harbours, and for its own territory; and such regulations are valid unless they come in conflict with a law of Congress.

In *Cooley v. Board of Wardens* (1852), available in the online supplement, the Court articulated an intermediate view:

[W]hen the nature of a power like this is spoken of, when it is said that the nature of the power requires that it should be exercised exclusively by Congress, it must be intended to refer to the subjects of that power, and to say they are of such a nature as to require exclusive legislation by Congress. Now the power to regulate commerce, embraces a vast field, containing not only many, but exceedingly various subjects, quite unlike in their nature; some imperatively demanding a single uniform rule, operating equally on the commerce of the United States in every port; and some . . . as imperatively demanding that diversity, which alone can meet the local necessities of navigation.

For more than a century and a half since then, the Dormant Commerce Clause has remained a matter of judicial push-and-pull. Most justices have accepted the existence of some form of the doctrine as a given. Dissenting from a decision striking down Maryland's income tax as "discriminat[ion] in favor of intrastate over interstate economic activity," however, Justice Scalia once called for a root-and-branch elimination of the entire doctrine:

The Court holds unconstitutional Maryland's refusal to give its residents full credits against income taxes paid to other States. It does this by invoking the negative Commerce Clause, a judge-invented rule under which judges may set aside state laws that they think impose too much of a burden upon interstate commerce. The fundamental problem with our negative Commerce Clause cases is that the Constitution does not contain a negative Commerce Clause. It contains only a Commerce Clause. Unlike the negative Commerce Clause adopted by the judges, the real Commerce Clause adopted by the People merely empowers Congress to "regulate Commerce with foreign Nations, and among the several States, and with the Indian Tribes." The Clause says nothing about prohibiting state laws that burden commerce. The Court's efforts to justify this judicial economic veto come to naught. The Court claims that the doctrine "has deep roots." So it does, like many weeds. But age alone does not make up for brazen invention.

Comptroller of the Treasury of Maryland v. Wynne (2015) (Scalia, J., dissenting) (joined by Thomas, J.).

WORTH NOTING

For an academic argument leading to the same conclusion about the Dormant Commerce Clause, see Richard D. Friedman, *Putting the Dormancy Doctrine Out of Its Misery*, 12 Cardozo L. Rev. 1745 (1991).

Whatever the right answer as a matter of history and sound constitutional construction, the Dormant Commerce Clause is unlikely to disappear in the foreseeable future. So our project in this unit will be to explore its scope, its exceptions, and the rationales for each.

a.   Dormant Commerce Clause—the Basic Framework

As you read the following, bear in mind that one of the core cases of a Dormant Commerce Clause violation would be a prohibition of movement among the states. See, *e.g.*, *Northwest Airlines, Inc. v. County of Kent* (1994) (airport tolls permitted so long as they are roughly keyed to cost of operations); *Evansville-Vanderburgh Airport Authority Dist. v. Delta Airlines, Inc.* (1972) (similar); *Willson v. Black-Bird Creek Marsh Co.* (1829) ("We do not think that the [state] act empowering the Black Bird Creek Marsh Company to place a dam across the creek, can, under all the circumstances of the case, be considered as repugnant to the power to regulate commerce in its dormant state. . . ."). *Cf. Pennsylvania v. Wheeling and Belmont Bridge Co. I* (1850) (construction of bridge prohibited where it would interfere with travel on Ohio River). How are the state regulations in the following cases similar to that kind of direct barrier to travel? How are they different?

City of Philadelphia v. New Jersey

Supreme Court of the United States, 1978.
437 U.S. 617.

MR. JUSTICE STEWART delivered the opinion of the Court.

A New Jersey law prohibits the importation of most "solid or liquid waste which originated or was collected outside the territorial limits of the State . . . ." In this case we are required to decide whether this statutory prohibition violates the Commerce Clause of the United States Constitution.

I

The statutory provision in question is ch. 363 of 1973 N.J. Laws, which took effect in early 1974. In pertinent part it provides:

> No person shall bring into this State any solid or liquid waste which originated or was collected outside the territorial limits of the State, except garbage to be fed to swine in the State of New Jersey, until the commissioner [of the State Department of Environmental Protection] shall determine that such action can be permitted without endangering the public health, safety and welfare and has promulgated regulations permitting and regulating the treatment and disposal of such waste in this State.

As authorized by ch. 363, the Commissioner promulgated regulations permitting four categories of waste to enter the State. Apart from these narrow exceptions, however, New Jersey closed its borders to all waste from other States.

Immediately affected by these developments were the operators of private landfills in New Jersey, and several cities in other States that had agreements with these operators for waste disposal. They brought suit against New Jersey and its Department of Environmental Protection in state court, attacking the statute and

WORTH NOTING

The exceptions were for garbage to be fed to swine in New Jersey; clean materials intended for recycling facilities; municipal solid waste "separated or processed into usable secondary materials"; and certain materials headed for registered solid waste disposal facilities.

regulations on a number of state and federal grounds. [The New Jersey Supreme Court upheld the statute and regulations.]

II

. . . The state court found that ch. 363 as narrowed by the state regulations . . . banned only "those wastes which can[not] be put to effective use," and therefore those wastes were not commerce at all, unless "the mere transportation and disposal of valueless waste between states constitutes interstate commerce within the meaning of the constitutional provision."

We think the state court misread our cases. . . . All objects of interstate trade merit Commerce Clause protection; none is excluded by definition at the outset. In *Bowman v. Chicago & Northwestern R. Co.* (1888) and similar cases, the Court held simply that because the articles' worth in interstate commerce was far outweighed by the dangers inhering in their very movement, States could prohibit their transportation across state lines. Hence, we reject the state court's suggestion that the banning of "valueless" out-of-state wastes by ch. 363 implicates no constitutional protection. Just as Congress has power to regulate the interstate movement of these wastes, States are not free from constitutional scrutiny when they restrict that movement.

III

A

Although the Constitution gives Congress the power to regulate commerce among the States, many subjects of potential federal regulation under that power inevitably escape congressional attention. . . . In the absence of federal legislation, these subjects are open to control by the States so long as they act within the restraints imposed by the Commerce Clause itself. The bounds of these restraints appear nowhere in the words of the Commerce Clause, but have emerged gradually in the decisions of this Court giving effect to its basic purpose.

That broad purpose was well expressed by Mr. Justice Jackson in his opinion for the Court in *H. P. Hood & Sons, Inc. v. Du Mond* (1949):

> This principle that our economic unit is the Nation, which alone has the gamut of powers necessary to control of the economy, including the vital power of erecting customs barriers against foreign competition, has as its corollary that the states are not separable economic

units. As the Court said in *Baldwin v. Seelig*, "what is ultimate is the principle that one state in its dealings with another may not place itself in a position of economic isolation."

The opinions of the Court through the years have reflected an alertness to the evils of "economic isolation" and protectionism, while at the same time recognizing that incidental burdens on interstate commerce may be unavoidable when a State legislates to safeguard the health and safety of its people.

Thus, where simple economic protectionism is effected by state legislation, a virtually *per se* rule of invalidity has been erected. See, *e.g.*, *H. P. Hood & Sons, Inc. v. Du Mond* [(ruling unconstitutional a state's refusal to approve a milk receiving depot on the grounds that the milk collected there would then be shipped out of state)]; *Toomer v. Witsell* (1948) [(striking down requirement that shrimp be unloaded, packed, and stamped at in-state port before being shipped out of state)]; *Baldwin v. G. A. F. Seelig, Inc.* (1935) [(striking down law prohibiting sale of out-of-state milk that had been purchased for less than the minimum price set for purchases within the state)]; *Buck v. Kuykendall* (1925) [(declaring unconstitutional Washington's refusal to permit an auto stage line between Portland and Seattle)]. The clearest example of such legislation is a law that overtly blocks the flow of interstate commerce at a State's borders. Cf. *Welton v. Missouri* (1875) [(striking down license requirement for "peddler[s]" selling goods manufactured out of state)].

But where other legislative objectives are credibly advanced and there is no patent discrimination against interstate trade, the Court has adopted a much more flexible approach, the general contours of which were outlined in *Pike v. Bruce Church, Inc.* (1970):

> Where the statute regulates evenhandedly to effectuate a legitimate local public interest, and its effects on interstate commerce are only incidental, it will be upheld unless the burden imposed on such commerce is clearly excessive in relation to the putative local benefits. . . . If a legitimate local purpose is found, then the question becomes one of degree. And the extent of the burden that will be tolerated will of course depend on the nature of the local interest involved, and on whether it could be promoted as well with a lesser impact on interstate activities. . . .

The crucial inquiry, therefore, must be directed to determining whether ch. 363 is basically a protectionist measure, or whether it can fairly be viewed as a law directed to legitimate local concerns, with effects upon interstate commerce that are only incidental. . . .

B

. . . The appellants strenuously contend that ch. 363, "while outwardly cloaked 'in the currently fashionable garb of environmental protection,' . . . is actually no more than a legislative effort to suppress competition and stabilize the cost of solid waste disposal for New Jersey residents" . . .

This dispute about ultimate legislative purpose need not be resolved, because its resolution would not be relevant to the constitutional issue to be decided in this case. Contrary to the evident assumption of the state court and the parties, the evil of protectionism can reside in legislative means as well as legislative ends. Thus, it does not matter whether the ultimate aim of ch. 363 is to reduce the waste disposal costs of New Jersey residents or to save remaining open lands from pollution, for we assume New Jersey has every right to protect its residents' pocketbooks as well as their environment. And it may be assumed as well that New Jersey may pursue those ends by slowing the flow of *all* waste into the State's remaining landfills, even though interstate commerce may incidentally be affected. But whatever New Jersey's ultimate purpose, it may not be accomplished by discriminating against articles of commerce coming from outside the State unless there is some reason, apart from their origin, to treat them differently. Both on its face and in its plain effect, ch. 363 violates this principle of nondiscrimination.

The Court has consistently found parochial legislation of this kind to be constitutionally invalid, whether the ultimate aim of the legislation was to assure a steady supply of milk by erecting barriers to allegedly ruinous outside competition, *Baldwin v. G. A. F. Seelig, Inc.*; or to create jobs by keeping industry within the State, *Toomer v. Witsell*; or to preserve the State's financial resources from depletion by fencing out indigent immigrants, *Edwards v. California* (1941) [(striking down statute criminalizing the act of "bringing into the State any indigent person who is not a resident of the State")]. In each of these cases, a presumably legitimate goal was sought to be achieved by the illegitimate means of isolating the State from the national economy.

Also relevant here are the Court's decisions holding that a State may not accord its own inhabitants a preferred right of access over consumers in other States to natural resources located within its borders. *West, Attorney General of Oklahoma v. Kansas Natural Gas Co.* (1911); *Pennsylvania v. West Virginia*

(1923). These cases stand for the basic principle that a "State is without power to prevent privately owned articles of trade from being shipped and sold in interstate commerce on the ground that they are required to satisfy local demands or because they are needed by the people of the State."[6] *Foster-Fountain Packing Co. v. Haydel.*

. . . It is true that in our previous cases the scarce natural resource was itself the article of commerce, whereas here the scarce resource and the article of commerce are distinct. But that difference is without consequence. In both instances, the State has overtly moved to slow or freeze the flow of commerce for protectionist reasons. It does not matter that the State has shut the article of commerce inside the State in one case and outside the State in the other. What is crucial is the attempt by one State to isolate itself from a problem common to many by erecting a barrier against the movement of interstate trade.

The appellees argue that not all laws which facially discriminate against out-of-state commerce are forbidden protectionist regulations. In particular, they point to quarantine laws, which this Court has repeatedly upheld even though they appear to single out interstate commerce for special treatment. See *Bowman v. Chicago & Northwestern R. Co.* (1888). In the appellees' view, ch. 363 is analogous to such health-protective measures, since it reduces the exposure of New Jersey residents to the allegedly harmful effects of landfill sites.

It is true that certain quarantine laws have not been considered forbidden protectionist measures, even though they were directed against out-of-state commerce. See *Asbell v. Kansas* (1908); *Reid v. Colorado* (1902); *Bowman v. Chicago & Northwestern R. Co.* But those quarantine laws banned the importation of articles such as diseased livestock that required destruction as soon as possible because their very movement risked contagion and other evils. Those laws thus did not discriminate against interstate commerce as such, but simply prevented traffic in noxious articles, whatever their origin.

The New Jersey statute is not such a quarantine law. There has been no claim here that the very movement of waste into or through New Jersey endangers health, or that waste must be disposed of as soon and as close to its point of generation as possible. The harms caused by waste are said to arise after its

_____

[6] We express no opinion about New Jersey's power, consistent with the Commerce Clause, to restrict to state residents access to state-owned resources, compare *Douglas v. Seacoast Products, Inc.* (1977) with *Toomer v. Witsell* (1948), or New Jersey's power to spend state funds solely on behalf of state residents and businesses, compare *Hughes v. Alexandria Scrap Corp.* (1976) (Stevens, J., concurring) with *id.* (Brennan, J., dissenting). . . .

disposal in landfill sites, and at that point, as New Jersey concedes, <u>there is no basis to distinguish out-of-state waste from domestic waste</u>. If one is inherently harmful, so is the other. Yet New Jersey has banned the former while leaving its landfill sites open to the latter. . . .

Today, cities in Pennsylvania and New York find it expedient or necessary to send their waste into New Jersey for disposal, and New Jersey claims the right to close its borders to such traffic. Tomorrow, cities in New Jersey may find it expedient or necessary to send their waste into Pennsylvania or New York for disposal, and those States might then claim the right to close their borders. The Commerce Clause will protect New Jersey in the future, just as it protects her neighbors now, <u>from efforts by one State to isolate itself in the stream of interstate commerce from a problem shared by all.</u> The judgment is

Reversed.

Mr. Justice Rehnquist, with whom The Chief Justice joins, dissenting.

[T]he State of New Jersey legislatively recognized the unfortunate fact that landfills . . . present extremely serious health and safety problems. . . . Landfills [also], "needless to say, do not help New Jersey's aesthetic appearance nor New Jersey's noise or water or air pollution problems."

. . . Other, hopefully safer, methods of disposing of solid wastes are still in the development stage and cannot presently be used. But appellees obviously cannot completely stop the tide of solid waste that its citizens will produce in the interim. For the moment, therefore, appellees must continue to use sanitary landfills to dispose of New Jersey's own solid waste despite the critical environmental problems thereby created.

[According to the Court,] New Jersey must either prohibit *all* landfill operations, leaving itself to cast about for a presently nonexistent solution to the serious problem of disposing of the waste generated within its own borders, or it must accept waste from every portion of the United States, thereby multiplying the health and safety problems which would result if it dealt only with such wastes generated within the State. Because past precedents establish that the Commerce Clause does not present appellees with such a Hobson's choice, I dissent. . . .

In my opinion, [the quarantine] cases are dispositive of the present one. Under them, New Jersey may require germ-infected rags or diseased meat to be disposed of as best as possible within the State, but at the same time prohibit the *importation* of such items for disposal at the facilities that are set up within New Jersey for disposal of such material generated *within* the State. . . . I simply see no way to distinguish solid waste, on the record of this case, from germ-infected rags, diseased meat, and other noxious items.

. . . According to the Court, the New Jersey law is distinguishable from these other laws, and invalid, because the concern of New Jersey is not with the *movement* of solid waste but with the present inability to safely *dispose* of it once it reaches its destination. But I think it far from clear that the State's law has as limited a focus as the Court imputes to it: Solid waste which is a health hazard when it reaches its destination may in all likelihood be an equally great health hazard in transit. . . .

Second, the Court implies that the challenged laws must be invalidated because New Jersey has left its landfills open to domestic waste. But, as the Court notes, this Court has repeatedly upheld quarantine laws "even though they appear to single out interstate commerce for special treatment." The fact that New Jersey has left its landfill sites open for domestic waste does not, of course, mean that solid waste is not innately harmful. Nor does it mean that New Jersey prohibits importation of solid waste for reasons other than the health and safety of its population. New Jersey must out of sheer necessity treat and dispose of its solid waste in some fashion, just as it must treat New Jersey cattle suffering from hoof-and-mouth disease. It does not follow that New Jersey must, under the Commerce Clause, accept solid waste or diseased cattle from outside its borders and thereby exacerbate its problems.

The Supreme Court of New Jersey expressly found that ch. 363 was passed "to preserve the health of New Jersey residents by keeping their exposure to solid waste and landfill areas to a minimum." The Court points to absolutely no evidence that would contradict this finding by the New Jersey Supreme Court. Because I find no basis for distinguishing the laws under challenge here from our past cases upholding state laws that prohibit the importation of items that could endanger the population of the State, I dissent.

Kassel v. Consolidated Freightways Corp.

Supreme Court of the United States, 1981.
450 U.S. 662.

Justice Powell announced the judgment of the Court and delivered an opinion, in which Justice White, Justice Blackmun, and Justice Stevens joined.

The question is whether an Iowa statute that prohibits the use of certain large trucks within the State unconstitutionally burdens interstate commerce.

I

Appellee Consolidated Freightways Corporation of Delaware (Consolidated) is one of the largest common carriers in the country. It offers service in 48 States under a certificate of public convenience and necessity issued by the Interstate Commerce Commission. Among other routes, Consolidated carries commodities through Iowa on Interstate 80, the principal east-west route linking New York, Chicago, and the west coast, and on Interstate 35, a major north-south route.

Consolidated mainly uses two kinds of trucks. One consists of a three-axle tractor pulling a 40-foot two-axle trailer. This unit, commonly called a single, or "semi," is 55 feet in length overall. Such trucks have long been used on the Nation's highways. Consolidated also uses a two-axle tractor pulling a single-axle trailer which, in turn, pulls a single-axle dolly and a second single-axle trailer. This combination, known as a double, or twin, is 65 feet long overall. Many trucking companies, including Consolidated, increasingly prefer to use doubles to ship certain kinds of commodities. Doubles have larger capacities, and the trailers can be detached and routed separately if necessary. Consolidated would like to use 65-foot doubles on many of its trips through Iowa.

The State of Iowa, however, by statute restricts the length of vehicles that may use its highways. Unlike all other States in the West and Midwest, Iowa generally prohibits the use of 65-foot doubles within its borders. Instead, most truck combinations are restricted to 55 feet in length. Doubles . . . are permitted to be as long as 60 feet. [The statute provided exemptions, some of which are discussed below.][7]

---

[7]   The parochial restrictions [allowing movement of oversized mobile homes so long as they were going from a point within Iowa or delivered for an Iowa resident] were enacted after Governor Ray vetoed a bill that would have permitted the interstate shipment of all mobile homes through Iowa. Governor Ray commented, in his veto

[After a 14-day trial, the District Court found that the "evidence clearly establishes that the twin is as safe as the semi." It therefore concluded that the Iowa state law impermissibly burdened interstate commerce. The Court of Appeals for the Eighth Circuit affirmed.]

II

. . . The [Commerce] Clause permits Congress to legislate when it perceives that the national welfare is not furthered by the independent actions of the States. It is now well established, also, that the Clause itself is "a limitation upon state power even without congressional implementation." *Hunt v. Washington Apple Advertising Comm'n* (1977). The Clause requires that some aspects of trade generally must remain free from interference by the States. When a State ventures excessively into the regulation of these aspects of commerce, it "trespasses upon national interests," *Great A & P Tea Co. v. Cottrell* (1976), and the courts will hold the state regulation invalid under the Clause alone.

The Commerce Clause does not, of course, invalidate all state restrictions on commerce. It has long been recognized that, "in the absence of conflicting legislation by Congress, there is a residuum of power in the state to make laws governing matters of local concern which nevertheless in some measure affect interstate commerce or even, to some extent, regulate it." *Southern Pacific Co. v. Arizona* (1945). The extent of permissible state regulation is not always easy to measure. It may be said with confidence, however, that a State's power to regulate commerce is never greater than in matters traditionally of local concern. *Washington Apple Advertising Comm'n.* For example, regulations that touch upon safety—especially highway safety—are those that "the Court has been most reluctant to invalidate." *Raymond Motor Transportation, Inc. v. Rice* (1978). . . . Those who would challenge such bona fide safety regulations must overcome a "strong presumption of validity." *Bibb v. Navajo Freight Lines, Inc.* (1959).

But the incantation of a purpose to promote the public health or safety does not insulate a state law from Commerce Clause attack. Regulations designed for that salutary purpose nevertheless may further the purpose so marginally, and interfere with commerce so substantially, as to be invalid under the Commerce Clause. In the Court's recent unanimous decision in *Raymond*, we declined to "accept the State's contention that the inquiry under the

message: "This bill . . . would make Iowa a bridge state as these oversized units are moved into Iowa after being manufactured in another state and sold in a third. None of this activity would be of particular economic benefit to Iowa."

Commerce Clause is ended without a weighing of the asserted safety purpose against the degree of interference with interstate commerce." This "weighing" by a court requires—and indeed the constitutionality of the state regulation depends on—"a sensitive consideration of the weight and nature of the state regulatory concern in light of the extent of the burden imposed on the course of interstate commerce." *Id.; accord Pike v. Bruce Church, Inc.* (1970). . . .

WORTH NOTING

Raymond Motor Transportation held invalid Wisconsin regulations that prohibited driving on the state's highways in any truck that was longer than 55 feet or pulled more than one other vehicle. The decision left open the possibility, however, that it might be possible to present evidence sufficient to support similar limitations in future cases.

III

Applying these general principles, we conclude that the Iowa truck-length limitations unconstitutionally burden interstate commerce.

[T]he State failed to present any persuasive evidence that 65-foot doubles are less safe than 55-foot singles. Moreover, Iowa's law is now out of step with the laws of all other Midwestern and Western States. Iowa thus substantially burdens the interstate flow of goods by truck. In the absence of congressional action to set uniform standards,[11] some burdens associated with state safety regulations must be tolerated. But where, as here, the State's safety interest has been found to be illusory, and its regulations impair significantly the federal interest in efficient and safe interstate transportation, the state law cannot be harmonized with the Commerce Clause.[12]

A

Iowa made a . . . serious effort to support the safety rationale of its law . . . , but its effort was no[t] persuasive. . . .

The trial focused on a comparison of the performance of the two kinds of trucks in various safety categories. The evidence showed, and the District Court found, that the 65-foot double was at least the equal of the 55-foot single in the ability to brake, turn, and maneuver. The double, because of its axle

---

[11]   The Senate last year passed a bill that would have pre-empted the field of truck lengths by setting a national limit of 65 feet. See S. 1390, 96th Cong., 2d Sess. (1980). The House took no action before adjournment.

[12]   It is highly relevant that . . . the state statute contains exemptions that weaken the deference traditionally accorded to a state safety regulation. See § IV, infra.

placement, produces less splash and spray in wet weather. And, because of its articulation in the middle, the double is less susceptible to dangerous "off-track-ing,"[14] and to wind.

None of these findings is seriously disputed by Iowa. Indeed, the State points to only three ways in which the 55-foot single is even arguably superior: singles take less time to be passed and to clear intersections; they may back up for longer distances; and they are somewhat less likely to jackknife.

The first two of these characteristics are of limited relevance on modern interstate highways. As the District Court found, the negligible difference in the time required to pass, and to cross intersections, is insignificant on 4-lane divided highways because passing does not require crossing into oncoming traffic lanes, and interstates have few, if any, intersections. The concern over backing capability also is insignificant because it seldom is necessary to back up on an interstate.[15]

Statistical studies supported the view that 65-foot doubles are at least as safe overall as 55-foot singles and 60-foot doubles. One such study, which the District Court credited, reviewed Consolidated's comparative accident experience in 1978 with its own singles and doubles. Each kind of truck was driven 56 million miles on identical routes. The singles were involved in 100 accidents resulting in 27 injuries and one fatality. The 65-foot doubles were involved in 106 accidents resulting in 17 injuries and one fatality. Iowa's expert statistician admitted that this study provided "moderately strong evidence" that singles have a higher injury rate than doubles. Another study, prepared by the Iowa Department of Transportation at the request of the state legislature, concluded that "[s]ixty-five foot twin trailer combinations have *not* been shown by experiences in other states to be less safe than 60 foot twin trailer combinations *or* conventional tractor-semitrailers" (emphasis in original). Numerous insurance company executives, and transportation officials from the Federal Government and various States, testified that 65-foot doubles were at least as safe as 55-foot singles.

Iowa concedes that it can produce no study that establishes a statistically significant difference in safety between the 65-foot double and the kinds of vehicles the State permits. Nor, as the District Court noted, did Iowa present

---

14   "Off-tracking" refers to the extent to which the rear wheels of a truck deviate from the path of the front wheels while turning.

15   Evidence at trial did show that doubles could back up far enough to move around an accident.

a single witness who testified that 65-foot doubles were more dangerous overall than the vehicles permitted under Iowa law.[16]

B

Consolidated, meanwhile, demonstrated that Iowa's law substantially burdens interstate commerce. Trucking companies that wish to continue to use 65-foot doubles must route them around Iowa or detach the trailers of the doubles and ship them through separately. Alternatively, trucking companies must use the smaller 55-foot singles or 60-foot doubles permitted under Iowa law. Each of these options engenders inefficiency and added expense. . . .

In addition[, f]ifty-five foot singles carry less freight than 65-foot doubles. Either more small trucks must be used to carry the same quantity of goods through Iowa, or the same number of larger trucks must drive longer distances to bypass Iowa. In either case, as the District Court noted, the restriction requires more highway miles to be driven to transport the same quantity of goods. Other things being equal, accidents are proportional to distance traveled. Thus, if 65-foot doubles are as safe as 55-foot singles, Iowa's law tends to *increase* the number of accidents, and to shift the incidence of them from Iowa to other States.[18]

IV

. . . The Court normally [accords] "special deference" to state highway safety regulations. *Raymond.* . . . Less deference to the legislative judgment is due, however, where the local regulation bears disproportionately on out-of-state residents and businesses. Such a disproportionate burden is apparent here. Iowa's scheme, although generally banning large doubles from the State, nevertheless has several exemptions that secure to Iowans many of the benefits of large trucks while shunting to neighboring States many of the costs associated with their use.

---

[16] In suggesting that Iowa's law actually promotes safety, the dissenting opinion ignores the findings of the courts below and relies on largely discredited statistical evidence. The dissent implies that a statistical study identified doubles as more dangerous than singles. At trial, however, the author of that study—Iowa's own statistician—conceded that his calculations were statistically biased, and therefore "not very meaningful."

[18] The District Court, in denying a stay pending appeal, noted that Iowa's law causes "more accidents, more injuries, more fatalities and more fuel consumption." Appellant Kassel conceded as much at trial. Kassel explained, however, that most of these additional accidents occur in States other than Iowa because truck traffic is deflected around the State. He noted: "Our primary concern is the citizens of Iowa and our own highway system we operate in this state."

At the time of trial there were two particularly significant exemptions. First, singles hauling livestock or farm vehicles were permitted to be as long as 60 feet. As the Court of Appeals noted, this provision undoubtedly was helpful to local interests. Second, cities abutting other States were permitted to en- act local ordinances adopting the larger length limitation of the neighboring State. This exemption offered the benefits of longer trucks to individuals and businesses in important border cities[20] without burdening Iowa's highways with interstate through traffic.

The origin of the "border cities exemption" also suggests that Iowa's statute may not have been designed to ban dangerous trucks, but rather to discourage interstate truck traffic. In 1974, the legislature passed a bill that would have permitted 65-foot doubles in the State. Governor Ray vetoed the bill. He said:

> [T]his bill . . . would benefit only a few Iowa-based companies while providing a great advantage for out-of-state trucking firms and com- petitors at the expense of our Iowa citizens.[23]

After the veto, the "border cities exemption" was immediately enacted and signed by the Governor.

It is thus far from clear that Iowa was motivated primarily by a judgment that 65-foot doubles are less safe than 55-foot singles. Rather, Iowa seems to have hoped to limit the use of its highways by deflecting some through traffic. In the District Court and Court of Appeals, the State explicitly attempted to justify the law by its claimed interest in keeping trucks out of Iowa. The Court of Appeals correctly concluded that a State cannot constitutionally promote its own parochial interests by requiring safe vehicles to detour around it.

V

In sum, the statutory exemptions, their history, and the arguments Iowa has advanced in support of its law in this litigation, all suggest that the def- erence traditionally accorded a State's safety judgment is not warranted. . . . Because Iowa has imposed this burden without any significant countervailing

---

[20]   Five of Iowa's ten largest cities—Davenport, Sioux City, Dubuque, Council Bluffs, and Clinton—are by their location entitled to use the "border cities exemption."

[23]   Governor Ray further commented that "if we have thousands more trucks crossing our state, there will be millions of additional miles driven in Iowa and that does create a genuine concern for safety."

safety interest,[26] its statute violates the Commerce Clause. The judgment of the Court of Appeals is affirmed.

It is so ordered.

JUSTICE BRENNAN, with whom JUSTICE MARSHALL joins, concurring in the judgment.

. . .

II

My Brothers Powell and Rehnquist make the mistake of disregarding the intention of Iowa's lawmakers and assuming that resolution of the case must hinge upon the argument offered by Iowa's attorneys: that 65-foot doubles are more dangerous than shorter trucks. They then canvass the factual record and findings of the courts below and reach opposite conclusions as to whether the evidence adequately supports that empirical judgment.

[M]y Brothers Powell and Rehnquist have asked and answered the wrong question. For although Iowa's lawyers in this litigation have defended the truck-length regulation on the basis of the safety advantages of 55-foot singles and 60-foot doubles over 65-foot doubles, Iowa's actual rationale for maintaining the regulation had nothing to do with these purported differences. Rather, Iowa sought to discourage interstate truck traffic on Iowa's highways.[2] Thus, the safety advantages and disadvantages of the types and lengths of trucks involved in this case are irrelevant to the decision. . . .

III

Though my Brother Powell recognizes that the State's actual purpose in maintaining the truck-length regulation was "to limit the use of its highways by deflecting some through traffic," he fails to recognize that this purpose, being *protectionist* in nature, is *impermissible* under the Commerce Clause. The Governor admitted that he blocked legislative efforts to raise the length of trucks because the change "would benefit only a few Iowa-based companies while

---

[26]   As noted above, the District Court and the Court of Appeals held that the Iowa statutory scheme unconstitutionally burdened interstate commerce. The District Court, however, found that the statute did not discriminate against such commerce. Because the record fully supports the decision below with respect to the burden on interstate commerce, we need not consider whether the statute also operated to discriminate against that commerce. The latter theory was neither briefed nor argued in this Court.

[2]   In the District Court and the Court of Appeals, Iowa's attorneys forthrightly defended the regulation in part on the basis of the State's interest in discouraging interstate truck traffic through Iowa.

providing a great advantage for out-of-state trucking firms and competitors at the expense of our Iowa citizens." Appellant Raymond Kassel, Director of the Iowa Department of Transportation, while admitting that the greater 65-foot length standard would be *safer* overall, defended the more restrictive regulations because of their benefits *within Iowa*:

> Q: Overall, there would be fewer miles of operation, fewer accidents and fewer fatalities?
>
> A: Yes, on the national scene.
>
> Q: Does it not concern the Iowa Department of Transportation that banning 65-foot twins causes more accidents, more injuries and more fatalities?
>
> A: Do you mean outside of our state border?
>
> Q: Overall.
>
> A: Our primary concern is the citizens of Iowa and our own highway system we operate in this state.

Iowa may not shunt off its fair share of the burden of maintaining interstate truck routes, nor may it create increased hazards on the highways of neighboring States in order to decrease the hazards on Iowa highways. Such an attempt has all the hallmarks of the "simple . . . protectionism" this Court has condemned in the economic area. *Philadelphia v. New Jersey* (1978). . . . Iowa's attempt to deflect interstate truck traffic has been found to make the Nation's highways as a whole more hazardous. That attempt should therefore be subject to "a virtually *per se* rule of invalidity." *Ibid.* . . .

JUSTICE REHNQUIST, with whom THE CHIEF JUSTICE and JUSTICE STEWART join, dissenting.

. . . Iowa's action in limiting the length of trucks which may travel on its highways is in no sense unusual. Every State in the Union regulates the length of vehicles permitted to use the public roads. Nor is Iowa a renegade in having length limits which operate to exclude the 65-foot doubles favored by Consolidated. These trucks are prohibited in other areas of the country as well, some 17 States and the District of Columbia, including all of New England and most of the Southeast. [T]he plurality neglects to note that both Pennsylvania and New Jersey, through which Interstate 80 runs before reaching New York, also ban 65-foot doubles. In short, the persistent effort in the plurality opinion to paint Iowa as an oddity standing alone to block commerce carried in 65-foot doubles is simply not supported by the facts. . . .

. . . There can be no doubt that the challenged statute is a valid highway safety regulation and thus entitled to the strongest presumption of validity against Commerce Clause challenges. . . . There can also be no question that the particular limit chosen by Iowa—60 feet—is rationally related to Iowa's safety objective. Most truck limits are between 55 and 65 feet, and Iowa's choice is thus well within the widely accepted range.

Iowa adduced evidence supporting the relation between vehicle length and highway safety. The evidence indicated that longer vehicles take greater time to be passed, thereby increasing the risks of accidents, particularly during the inclement weather not uncommon in Iowa. The 65-foot vehicle exposes a passing driver to visibility-impairing splash and spray during bad weather for a longer period than do the shorter trucks permitted in Iowa. Longer trucks are more likely to clog intersections, and although there are no intersections on the Interstate Highways, the order below went beyond the highways them-selves and the concerns about greater length at intersections would arise "[a]t every trip origin, every trip destination, every intermediate stop for picking up trailers, reconfiguring loads, change of drivers, eating, refueling—every intermediate stop would generate this type of situation." The Chief of the Di-vision of Patrol in the Iowa Department of Public Safety testified that longer vehicles pose greater problems at the scene of an accident. For example, trucks involved in accidents often must be unloaded at the scene, which would take longer the bigger the load.

In rebuttal of Consolidated's evidence on the relative safety of 65-foot doubles to trucks permitted on Iowa's highways, Iowa introduced evidence that doubles are more likely than singles to jackknife or upset. The District Court concluded that this was so and that singles are more stable than doubles. . . .[7] In addition Iowa elicited evidence undermining the probative value of Con-solidated's evidence. For example, Iowa established that the more experienced drivers tended to drive doubles, because they have seniority and driving doubles is a higher paying job than driving singles. Since the leading cause of accidents was driver error, Consolidated's evidence of the relative safety record of doubles

---

[7]   Although the District Court noted that doubles are more maneuverable, it certainly is reasonable for a leg-islature to conclude that stability is a more critical factor than maneuverability on the straight expanses of the Interstates.

may have been based in large part not on the relative safety of the vehicles themselves but on the experience of the drivers. . . .

The District Court approached the case as if the question were whether Consolidated's 65-foot trucks were as safe as others permitted on Iowa highways, and the Court of Appeals as if its task were to determine if the District Court's factual findings in this regard were "clearly erroneous." The question, however, is whether the Iowa Legislature has acted rationally in regulating vehicle lengths and whether the safety benefits from this regulation are more than slight or problematical. . . .

The answering of the relevant question is not appreciably advanced by comparing trucks slightly over the length limit with those at the length limit. It is emphatically not our task to balance any incremental safety benefits from prohibiting 65-foot doubles as opposed to 60-foot doubles against the burden on interstate commerce. Lines drawn for safety purposes will rarely pass muster if the question is whether a slight increment can be permitted without sacrificing safety. As Justice Holmes put it:

> When a legal distinction is determined, as no one doubts that it may be, between night and day, childhood and maturity, or any other extremes, a point has to be fixed or a line has to be drawn, or gradually picked out by successive decisions, to mark where the change takes place. Looked at by itself without regard to the necessity behind it the line or point seems arbitrary. It might as well or nearly as well be a little more to one side or the other. But when it is seen that a line or point there must be, and that there is no mathematical or logical way of fixing it precisely, the decision of the legislature must be accepted unless we can say that it is very wide of any reasonable mark.

Louisville Gas & Electric Co. v. Coleman (1928) (dissenting opinion).

. . . Any direct balancing of marginal safety benefits against burdens on commerce would make the burdens on commerce the sole significant factor, and make likely the odd result that similar state laws enacted for identical safety reasons might violate the Commerce Clause in one part of the country but not another. For example, Mississippi and Georgia prohibit trucks over 55 feet. Since doubles are not operated in the Southeast, the demonstrable burden on commerce may not be sufficient to strike down these laws, while Consolidated maintains that it is in this case, even though the doubles here are given an additional five feet. . . .

Striking down Iowa's law because Consolidated has made a voluntary business decision to employ 65-foot doubles, a decision based on the actions of other state legislatures, would essentially be compelling Iowa to yield to the policy choices of neighboring States. Under our constitutional scheme, however, there is only one legislative body which can pre-empt the rational policy determination of the Iowa Legislature and that is Congress. Forcing Iowa to yield to the policy choices of neighboring States perverts the primary purpose of the Commerce Clause, that of vesting power to regulate interstate commerce in Congress, where all the States are represented.

Both the plurality and the concurrence attach great significance to the Governor's [1974] veto of a bill passed by the Iowa Legislature permitting 65-foot doubles. Whatever views one may have about the significance of legislative motives, it must be emphasized that the law which the Court strikes down today was not passed to achieve the protectionist goals the plurality and the concurrence ascribe to the Governor. Iowa's 60-foot length limit was established in 1963, at a time when very few States permitted 65-foot doubles. Striking down legislation on the basis of asserted legislative motives is dubious enough, but the plurality and concurrence strike down the legislation involved in this case because of asserted impermissible motives for *not* enacting *other* legislation, motives which could not possibly have been present when the legislation under challenge here was considered and passed. . . .

Perhaps, after all is said and done, the Court today neither says nor does very much at all. We know only that Iowa's law is invalid and that the jurisprudence of the "negative side" of the Commerce Clause remains hopelessly confused.

Maine v. Taylor

Supreme Court of the United States, 1986.
477 U.S. 131.

JUSTICE BLACKMUN delivered the opinion of the Court.

Once again, a little fish has caused a commotion. See *Hughes v. Oklahoma* (1979); *TVA v. Hill* (1978); *Cappaert v. United States* (1976). The fish in this case is the golden shiner, a species of minnow commonly used as live bait in sport fishing.

Appellee Robert J. Taylor operates a bait business in Maine. Despite a Maine statute prohibiting the importation of live baitfish, he arranged to have 158,000 live golden shiners delivered to him from outside the State. The shipment was intercepted, and [Taylor was indicted under the federal Lacey Act, which] makes it a federal crime "to import, export, transport, sell, receive, acquire, or purchase in interstate or foreign commerce . . . any fish or wildlife taken, possessed, transported, or sold in violation of any law or regulation of any State or in violation of any foreign law."

Taylor moved to dismiss the indictment on the ground that Maine's import ban unconstitutionally burdens interstate commerce and therefore may not form the basis for a federal prosecution under the Lacey Act. Maine intervened to defend the validity of its statute, arguing that the ban legitimately protects the State's fisheries from parasites and nonnative species that might be included in shipments of live baitfish. . . .

II

. . . "Although the [Commerce] Clause . . . speaks in terms of powers bestowed upon Congress, the Court long has recognized that it also limits the power of the States to erect barriers against interstate trade." *Lewis v. BT Investment Managers, Inc.* (1980).

Maine's statute restricts interstate trade in the most direct manner possible, blocking all inward shipments of live baitfish at the State's border. Still, as both the District Court and the Court of Appeals recognized, this fact alone does not render the law unconstitutional. . . .

In determining whether a State has overstepped its role in regulating interstate commerce, this Court has distinguished between state statutes that burden interstate transactions only incidentally, and those that affirmatively discriminate against such transactions. While statutes in the first group violate the Commerce Clause only if the burdens they impose on interstate trade are "clearly excessive in relation to the putative local benefits," *Pike v. Bruce Church, Inc.* (1970), statutes in the second group are subject to more demanding scrutiny. The Court explained in *Hughes v. Oklahoma* that once a state law is shown to discriminate against interstate commerce "either on its face or in practical effect," the burden falls on the State to demonstrate both that the statute "serves a legitimate local purpose," and that this purpose could not be served as well by available nondiscriminatory means. . . .

[S]ince Maine's import ban discriminates on its face against interstate trade, it should be subject to the strict requirements of *Hughes v. Oklahoma* . . . .

III

. . .

A

The evidentiary hearing on which the District Court based its conclusions was one before a Magistrate. Three scientific experts testified for the prosecution and one for the defense. The prosecution experts testified that live baitfish imported into the State posed two significant threats to Maine's unique and fragile fisheries.[8] First, Maine's population of wild fish—including its own indigenous golden shiners—would be placed at risk by three types of parasites prevalent in out-of-state baitfish, but not common to wild fish in Maine. Second, nonnative species inadvertently included in shipments of live baitfish could disturb Maine's aquatic ecology to an unpredictable extent by competing with native fish for food or habitat, by preying on native species, or by disrupting the environment in more subtle ways.

The prosecution experts further testified that there was no satisfactory way to inspect shipments of live baitfish for parasites or commingled species. According to their testimony, the small size of baitfish and the large quantities in which they are shipped made inspection for commingled species "a physical impossibility."[12] Parasite inspection posed a separate set of difficulties because the examination procedure required destruction of the fish. Although statistical sampling and inspection techniques had been developed for salmonids (*i.e.,* salmon and trout), so that a shipment could be certified parasite-free based on a standardized examination of only some of the fish, no scientifically accepted procedures of this sort were available for baitfish.[13]

---

[8]   One prosecution witness testified that Maine's lakes contain unusually clean water and originally supported "a rather delicate community of just a few species of fish." Another stressed that "no other state . . . has any real landlocked salmon fishing. You come to Maine for that or you live in Maine for that."

[12]   The shipment intercepted in this case contained approximately 158,000 fish, with about 70 specimens to the pound. [It also contained at least two of the three parasites said to be prevalent in baitfish outside Maine.]

[13]   According to the prosecution testimony, the design of sampling and inspection techniques must take into account the particular parasites of concern, and baitfish parasites differ from salmonid parasites. [Defendant's] expert agreed. There was also testimony that the physical layout of bait farms makes inspection at the source of shipment particularly difficult, and that border inspections are not feasible because the fish would die in the time it takes to complete the tests.

Appellee's expert denied that any scientific justification supported Maine's total ban on the importation of baitfish. He testified that none of the three parasites discussed by the prosecution witnesses posed any significant threat to fish in the wild[.][14]. . .

B

Although the proffered justification for any local discrimination against interstate commerce must be subjected to "the strictest scrutiny," *Hughes v. Oklahoma*, the empirical component of that scrutiny, like any other form of factfinding, " 'is the basic responsibility of district courts, rather than appellate courts,' " *Pullman-Standard v. Swint* (1982). . . .

No matter how one describes the abstract issue whether "alternative means could promote this local purpose as well without discriminating against interstate commerce," *Hughes v. Oklahoma*, the more specific question whether scientifically accepted techniques exist for the sampling and inspection of live baitfish is one of fact, and the District Court's finding that such techniques have not been devised cannot be characterized as clearly erroneous. . . . .

More importantly, we agree with the District Court that the "abstract possibility," of developing acceptable testing procedures, particularly when there is no assurance as to their effectiveness, does not make those procedures an "[a]vailabl[e] . . . nondiscriminatory alternativ[e]," *Hunt v. Washington Apple Advertising Comm'n* (1977), for purposes of the Commerce Clause. A State must make reasonable efforts to avoid restraining the free flow of commerce across its borders, but it is not required to develop new and unproven means of protection at an uncertain cost. . . .

C

. . . Shielding in-state industries from out-of-state competition is almost never a legitimate local purpose, and state laws that amount to "simple economic protectionism" consequently have been subject to a "virtually *per se* rule of invalidity." *Philadelphia v. New Jersey* (1978). But there is little reason in this case to believe that the legitimate justifications the State has put forward for its statute are merely a sham or a "*post hoc* rationalization." . . . *Hughes.*

---

[14] For several reasons, the District Court discounted the testimony of appellee's expert that baitfish parasites did not pose so serious a threat as disease organisms found in salmonids. The court noted that "considerable scientific debate" surrounded even the threat posed by salmonid diseases, that appellee's expert testified largely about the effects that baitfish parasites had in commercial hatcheries rather than in the wild, and that he was unfamiliar with northeast fisheries.

In suggesting to the contrary, the Court of Appeals relied heavily on a 3-sentence passage near the end of a 2,000-word statement submitted in 1981 by the Maine Department of Inland Fisheries and Wildlife in opposition to appellee's proposed repeal of the State's ban on the importation of live baitfish:

> [W]e can't help asking why we should spend our money [on baitfish raised] in Arkansas when it is far better spent at home? It is very clear that much more can be done here in Maine to provide our sportsmen with safe, home-grown bait. There is also the possibility that such an industry could develop a lucrative export market in neighboring states.

Baitfish Importation: The Position of the Maine Department of Inland Fisheries and Wildlife. We fully agree with the Magistrate that "[t]hese three sentences do not convert the Maine statute into an economic protectionism measure." As the Magistrate pointed out, the context of the statements cited by appellee "reveals [they] are advanced not in direct support of the statute, but to counter the argument that inadequate bait supplies in Maine require acceptance of the environmental risks of imports. Instead, the Department argues, Maine's own bait supplies can be increased." Furthermore, the comments were made by a state administrative agency long after the statute's enactment, and thus constitute weak evidence of legislative intent in any event.

. . . Finally, it is of little relevance that fish can swim directly into Maine from New Hampshire. As the Magistrate explained: "The impediments to complete success . . . cannot be a ground for preventing a state from using its best efforts to limit [an environmental] risk."

IV

The Commerce Clause significantly limits the ability of States and localities to regulate or otherwise burden the flow of interstate commerce, but it does not elevate free trade above all other values. As long as a State does not needlessly obstruct interstate trade or attempt to "place itself in a position of economic isolation," *Baldwin v. G.A.F. Seelig, Inc.* (1935), it retains broad regulatory authority to protect the health and safety of its citizens and the integrity of its natural resources.

The evidence in this case amply supports the District Court's findings that Maine's ban on the importation of live baitfish serves legitimate local purposes that could not adequately be served by available nondiscriminatory alternatives. This is not a case of arbitrary discrimination against interstate commerce; the

from them, we held that it] did not involve "the kind of action with which the Commerce Clause is concerned." Unlike prior cases voiding state laws inhibiting interstate trade, "Maryland has not sought to prohibit the flow of hulks, or to regulate the conditions under which it may occur. Instead, it has entered into the market itself to bid up their price," "as a purchaser, in effect, of a potential article of interstate commerce," and has restricted "its trade to its own citizens or businesses within the State." Having characterized Maryland as a market participant, rather than as a market regulator, the Court found no reason to "believe the Commerce Clause was intended to require independent justification for [the State's] action." The Court couched its holding in unmistakably broad terms. "Nothing in the purposes animating the Commerce Clause prohibits a State, in the absence of congressional action, from participating in the market and exercising the right to favor its own citizens over others."

The basic distinction drawn in *Alexandria Scrap* between States as market participants and States as market regulators makes good sense and sound law. As that case explains, the Commerce Clause responds principally to state taxes and regulatory measures impeding free private trade in the national marketplace. [See] *H. P. Hood & Sons v. DuMond* (1949) (referring to "home embargoes," "customs duties," and "regulations" excluding imports). There is no indication of a constitutional plan to limit the ability of the States themselves to operate freely in the free market. The precedents comport with this distinction. Restraint in this area is also counseled by considerations of state sovereignty, the role of each State " 'as guardian and trustee for its people,' " and "the long recognized right of trader or manufacturer, engaged in an entirely private business, freely to exercise his own independent discretion as to parties with whom he will deal." . . . Given these factors, *Alexandria Scrap* wisely recognizes that, as a rule, the adjustment of interests in this context is a task better suited for Congress than this Court.

South Dakota, as a seller of cement, unquestionably fits the "market participant" label more comfortably than a State acting to subsidize local scrap processors. Thus, the general rule of *Alexandria Scrap* plainly applies here. Petitioner argues, however, that the exemption for marketplace participation necessarily admits of exceptions. While conceding that possibility, we perceive in this case no sufficient reason to depart from the general rule. . . .

First, petitioner protests that South Dakota's preference for its residents responds solely to the "non-governmental objectiv[e]" of protectionism. Therefore, petitioner argues, the policy is *per se* invalid. See *Philadelphia v. New Jersey* (1978). We find the label "protectionism" of little help in this context. The State's refusal to sell to buyers other than South Dakotans is "protectionist" only in the sense that it limits benefits generated by a state program to those who fund the state treasury and whom the State was created to serve. Petitioner's argument apparently also would characterize as "protectionist" rules restricting to state residents the enjoyment of state educational institutions, energy generated by a state-run plant, police and fire protection, and agricultural improvement and business development programs. Such policies, while perhaps "protectionist" in a loose sense, reflect the essential and patently unobjectionable purpose of state government—to serve the citizens of the State.

Second, petitioner echoes the District Court's warning:

> If a state in this union, were allowed to hoard its commodities or resources for the use of their own residents only, a drastic situation might evolve. For example, Pennsylvania or Wyoming might keep their coal, the northwest its timber, and the mining states their minerals. The result being that embargo may be retaliated by embargo and commerce would be halted at state lines."

This argument, although rooted in the core purpose of the Commerce Clause, does not fit the present facts. Cement is not a natural resource, like coal, timber, wild game, or minerals. Cf. *Hughes v. Oklahoma* (1979) (minnows); *Philadelphia v. New Jersey* (landfill sites); *Pennsylvania v. West Virginia* (1923) (natural gas). It is the end product of a complex process whereby a costly physical plant and human labor act on raw materials. South Dakota has not sought to limit access to the State's limestone or other materials used to make cement. Nor has it restricted the ability of private firms or sister States to set up plants within its borders. Moreover, petitioner has not suggested that South Dakota possesses unique access to the materials needed to produce cement. Whatever limits might exist on a State's ability to invoke the *Alexandria Scrap* exemption to hoard resources which by happenstance are found there, those limits do not apply here. . . .

We conclude, then, that the arguments for invalidating South Dakota's resident-preference program are weak at best. Whatever residual force inheres in them is more than offset by countervailing considerations of policy and fairness. Reversal would discourage similar state projects, even though this project demonstrably has served the needs of state residents and has helped the entire region for more than a half century. Reversal also would rob South Dakota of the intended benefit of its foresight, risk, and industry. Under these circumstances, there is no reason to depart from the general rule of *Alexandria Scrap*. . . .

MR. JUSTICE POWELL, with whom MR. JUSTICE BRENNAN, MR. JUSTICE WHITE, and MR. JUSTICE STEVENS join, dissenting.

The South Dakota Cement Commission has ordered that in times of shortage the state cement plant must turn away out-of-state customers until all orders from South Dakotans are filled. This policy represents precisely the kind of economic protectionism that the Commerce Clause was intended to prevent. . . .[1] I agree with the Court that the State of South Dakota may provide cement for its public needs without violating the Commerce Clause. But I cannot agree that South Dakota may withhold its cement from interstate commerce in order to benefit private citizens and businesses within the State. . . .

The application of the Commerce Clause to this case should turn on the nature of the governmental activity involved. If a public enterprise undertakes an "integral operatio[n] in areas of traditional governmental functions," *National League of Cities v. Usery* (1976), the Commerce Clause is not directly relevant. If, however, the State enters the private market and operates a commercial enterprise for the advantage of its private citizens, it may not evade the constitutional policy against economic Balkanization. This distinction derives from the power of governments to supply their own needs, and from the purpose of the Commerce Clause itself, which is designed to protect "the natural functioning of the interstate market." In procuring goods and services for the operation of government, a State may act without regard to the private marketplace and remove itself from the reach of the Commerce Clause. But when a State itself becomes a participant in the private market for other purposes, the Constitution forbids actions that would impede the flow of interstate commerce.

I share the Court's desire to preserve state sovereignty. But the Commerce Clause long has been recognized as a limitation on that sovereignty, consciously designed to maintain a national market and defeat economic provincialism. The Court today approves protectionist state policies. In the absence of contrary

---

[1] By "protectionism," I refer to state policies designed to protect private economic interests within the State from the forces of the interstate market. I would exclude from this term policies relating to traditional governmental functions, such as education, and subsidy programs like the one at issue in *Hughes v. Alexandria Scrap Corp.*

congressional action, those policies now can be implemented as long as the State itself directly participates in the market. . . .[6]

White v. Massachusetts Council of Construction Employers, Inc.

Supreme Court of the United States, 1983.
460 U.S. 204.

Justice Rehnquist delivered the opinion of the Court.

In 1979 the mayor of Boston, Massachusetts, issued an executive order[1] which required that all construction projects funded in whole or in part by city funds, or funds which the city had the authority to administer, should be performed by a work force consisting of at least half *bona fide* residents of Boston. The Supreme Judicial Court of Massachusetts decided that the order was unconstitutional, observing that the Commerce Clause "presents a clear obstacle to the city's order." We granted certiorari to decide whether the Commerce Clause . . . prevents the city from giving effect to the mayor's order. We now conclude that it does not and reverse. . . .

The Supreme Judicial Court of Massachusetts expressed reservations as to the application of the "market participation" principle to the city here, reasoning that "the implementation of the mayor's order will have a significant impact on those firms which engage in specialized areas of construction and employ permanent works crews composed of out-of-State residents." Even if this conclusion is factually correct, it is not relevant to the inquiry of whether the city is participating in the marketplace when it provides city funds for building construction.

---

[6]   Since the Court's decision contains no limiting principles, a State will be able to manufacture any commercial product and withhold it from citizens of other States. This prerogative could extend, for example, to pharmaceutical goods, food products, or even synthetic or processed energy sources.

[1]   The executive order provides [in part]:

On any construction project funded in whole or in part by City funds . . . shall be performed . . . as follows:

    a. at least 50% by bona fide Boston residents;

    b. at least 25% by minorities;

    c. at least 10% by women.

Only the residency requirement is being challenged.

If the city is a market participant, then the Commerce Clause establishes no barrier to conditions such as these which the city demands for its participation. Impact on out-of-state residents figures in the equation only after it is decided that the city is regulating the market rather than participating in it, for only in the former case need it be determined whether any burden on interstate commerce is permitted by the Commerce Clause. The same may be said of the Massachusetts court's finding that the executive order sweeps too broadly, creating more burden than is necessary to accomplish its stated objectives. While relevant if the Commerce Clause imposes restraints on the city's activity, this characterization is of no help in deciding whether those restraints apply. . . .

We hold that on the record before us the application of the Mayor's executive order to the contracts in question did not violate the Commerce Clause of the United States Constitution. . . .

JUSTICE BLACKMUN, with whom JUSTICE WHITE joins, concurring in part and dissenting in part.

. . . Neither [*Hughes v. Alexandria Scrap Corp.* (1976) nor *Reeves, Inc. v. Stake* (1980)] went beyond ensuring that the States enjoy " 'the long recognized right of trader or manufacturer, engaged in an entirely private business, freely to exercise his own independent discretion as to parties with whom he will deal.' " *Reeves.*

Boston's executive order goes much further. The city has not attempted merely to choose the "parties with whom [it] will deal." Instead, it has imposed as a condition of obtaining a public construction contract the requirement that *private firms* hire only Boston residents for 50% of specified jobs. Thus, the order directly restricts the ability of private employers to hire nonresidents, and thereby curtails nonresidents' access to jobs with private employers. I had thought it well established that, under the Commerce Clause, States and localities cannot impose restrictions granting their own residents either the exclusive right, or a priority, to private sector economic opportunities. See *H.P. Hood & Sons v. Du Mond* (1949). . . .

The legitimacy of a claim to the market participant exemption . . . should turn primarily on whether a particular state action more closely resembles an attempt to impede trade among private parties, or an attempt, analogous to the accustomed right of merchants in the private sector, to govern the State's own economic conduct and to determine the parties with whom it will deal. . . . As the Court recognizes, the order constitutes "parochial favoritism" of Boston residents over nonresidents of Boston and Massachusetts for access to private sector jobs. Thus, the order is a "protectionist measure" subject to the rule of virtually *per se* invalidity established by many of this Court's cases. See, e.g. *Philadelphia v. New Jersey* (1978). . . .

ii.   Subsidies

If a state imposed a tariff on milk—a tax on all milk produced out-of-state but sold in-state—that would plainly violate the Dormant Commerce Clause. On the other hand, if the state decided to promote milk production in the state by granting subsidies to in-state producers, the usual view has been that such a program would be valid; promoting its own commerce is, after all, something we expect states to do. Now suppose a state imposes a nominally non-discriminatory tax but then uses the revenue to subsidize the in-state industry. Depending on the particulars, such a program might achieve in two steps the equivalent of what the state could not do in one: a discriminatory tax on out-of-staters. The next case engages a borderline example presenting this kind of issue, offering a comprehensive overview of the subsidy exception more generally.

West Lynn Creamery, Inc. v. Healey

Supreme Court of the United States, 1994.
512 U.S. 186.

Justice Stevens delivered the opinion of the Court.

A Massachusetts pricing order imposes an assessment on all fluid milk sold by dealers to Massachusetts retailers. About two-thirds of that milk is produced out of State. The entire assessment, however, is distributed to Massachusetts dairy farmers. The question presented is whether the pricing order unconstitutionally discriminates against interstate commerce. We hold that it does.

. . . In the 1980's and early 1990's, Massachusetts dairy farmers began to lose market share to lower cost producers in neighboring States. In response, the Governor of Massachusetts appointed a Special Commission to study the dairy industry. The commission found that many producers had sold their dairy farms during the past decade and that if prices paid to farmers for their milk were not significantly increased, a majority of the remaining farmers in Massachusetts would be "forced out of business within the year."

[R]elying on the commission's report, the Commissioner of the Massachusetts Department of Food and Agriculture . . . declared a State of Emergency. . . . Promptly after his declaration of emergency, [he] issued the pricing order that is challenged in this proceeding. The order requires every "dealer" in Massachusetts to make a monthly "premium payment" into the "Massachusetts Dairy Equalization Fund." . . . Each month the fund is distributed to Massachusetts producers. Each Massachusetts producer receives a share of the total fund equal to his proportionate contribution to the State's total production of raw milk. . . .

The Commerce Clause . . . limits the power of the Commonwealth of Massachusetts to adopt regulations that discriminate against interstate commerce. . . . The paradigmatic example of a law discriminating against interstate commerce is the protective tariff or customs duty, which taxes goods imported from other States, but does not tax similar products produced in State. A tariff is an attractive measure because it simultaneously raises revenue and benefits local producers by burdening their out-of-state competitors. Nevertheless, it violates the principle of the unitary national market by handicapping out-of-state competitors, thus artificially encouraging in-state production even when the same goods could be produced at lower cost in other States.

Because of their distorting effects on the geography of production, tariffs have long been recognized as violative of the Commerce Clause. In fact, tariffs against the products of other States are so patently unconstitutional that our cases reveal not a single attempt by any State to enact one. Instead, the cases are filled with state laws that aspire to reap some of the benefits of tariffs by other means. In *Baldwin v. G.A.F. Seelig, Inc.* (1935), the State of New York attempted to protect its dairy farmers from the adverse effects of Vermont competition by establishing a single minimum price for all milk, whether produced in New York or elsewhere. This Court did not hesitate, however, to strike it down. Writing for a unanimous Court, Justice Cardozo reasoned:

> Neither the power to tax nor the police power may be used by the state of destination with the aim and effect of establishing an economic barrier against competition with the products of another state or the labor of its residents. Restrictions so contrived are an unreasonable clog upon the mobility of commerce. They set up what is equivalent to a rampart of customs duties designed to neutralize advantages belonging to the place of origin.

Thus, because the minimum price regulation had the same effect as a tariff or customs duty—neutralizing the advantage possessed by lower cost out-of-state producers—it was held unconstitutional. . . . Other cases of this kind are legion.

Under these cases, Massachusetts' pricing order is clearly unconstitutional. Its avowed purpose and its undisputed effect are to enable higher cost Massachusetts dairy farmers to compete with lower cost dairy farmers in other States. The "premium payments" are effectively a tax which makes milk produced out of State more expensive. Although the tax also applies to milk produced in Massachusetts, its effect on Massachusetts producers is entirely (indeed more than) offset by the subsidy provided exclusively to Massachusetts dairy farmers. Like an ordinary tariff, the tax is thus effectively imposed only on out-of-state products. The pricing order thus allows Massachusetts dairy farmers who produce at higher cost to sell at or below the price charged by lower cost out-of-state producers. . . . This effect renders the program unconstitutional, because it, like a tariff, "neutraliz[es] advantages belonging to the place of origin."

* * *

Respondent's principal argument is that, because "the milk order achieves its goals through lawful means," the order as a whole is constitutional. He argues that the payments to Massachusetts dairy farmers from the Dairy Equalization Fund are valid, because subsidies are constitutional exercises of state power, and that the order premium which provides money for the fund is valid, because it is a nondiscriminatory tax. Therefore the pricing order is constitutional, because it is merely the combination of two independently lawful regulations. In effect, respondent argues, if the State may impose a valid tax on dealers, it is free to use the proceeds of the tax as it chooses; and if it may independently subsidize its farmers, it is free to finance the subsidy by means of any legitimate tax.

Even granting respondent's assertion that both components of the pricing order would be constitutional standing alone,[15] the pricing order nevertheless must fall. A pure subsidy funded out of general revenue ordinarily imposes no burden on interstate commerce, but merely assists local business. The pricing order in this case, however, is funded principally from taxes on the sale of milk

---

[15]   We have never squarely confronted the constitutionality of subsidies, and we need not do so now. We have, however, noted that "[d]irect subsidization of domestic industry does not ordinarily run afoul" of the negative Commerce Clause. *New Energy Co. of Ind. v. Limbach* (1988). In addition, it is undisputed that States may try to attract business by creating an environment conducive to economic activity, as by maintaining good roads, sound public education, or low taxes.

produced in other States.[16] By so funding the subsidy, respondent not only assists local farmers, but burdens interstate commerce. The pricing order thus violates the cardinal principle that a State may not "benefit in-state economic interests by burdening out-of-state competitors." . . .

More fundamentally, respondent errs in assuming that the constitutionality of the pricing order follows logically from the constitutionality of its component parts. By conjoining a tax and a subsidy, Massachusetts has created a program more dangerous to interstate commerce than either part alone. Nondiscriminatory measures, like the evenhanded tax at issue here, are generally upheld, in spite of any adverse effects on interstate commerce, in part because "[t]he existence of major in-state interests adversely affected . . . is a powerful safeguard against legislative abuse." *Minnesota v. Clover Leaf Creamery Co.* (1981). However, when a nondiscriminatory tax is coupled with a subsidy to one of the groups hurt by the tax, a State's political processes can no longer be relied upon to prevent legislative abuse, because one of the in-state interests which would otherwise lobby against the tax has been mollified by the subsidy. . . . [B]ecause the tax was coupled with a subsidy, one of the most powerful of these groups, Massachusetts dairy farmers, instead of exerting their influence against the tax, were in fact its primary supporters. . . .

Our Commerce Clause jurisprudence is not so rigid as to be controlled by the form by which a State erects barriers to commerce. Rather our cases have eschewed formalism for a sensitive, case-by-case analysis of purposes and effects. As the Court declared over 50 years ago: "The commerce clause forbids discrimination, whether forthright or ingenious. . . ." *Best & Co. v. Maxwell* (1940). . . .

[R]espondent [also] argues that any incidental burden on interstate commerce "is outweighed by the 'local benefits' of preserving the Massachusetts dairy industry." In a closely related argument, respondent urges that "the purpose of the order, to save an industry from collapse, is not protectionist." . . . With his characteristic eloquence, Justice Cardozo responded to an argument that respondent echoes today:

---

[16]   It is undisputed that an overwhelming majority of the milk sold in Massachusetts is produced elsewhere. Thus, even though the tax is applied even-handedly to milk produced in State and out of State, most of the tax collected comes from taxes on milk from other States. In addition, the tax on in-state milk, unlike that imposed on out-of-state milk, does not impose any burden on in-state producers, because in-state dairy farmers can be confident that the taxes paid on their milk will be returned to them via the Dairy Equalization Fund.

. . . Let such an exception be admitted, and all that a state will have to do in times of stress and strain is to say that its farmers and merchants and workmen must be protected against competition from without, lest they go upon the poor relief lists or perish altogether. To give entrance to that excuse would be to invite a speedy end of our national solidarity. The Constitution was framed under the dominion of a political philosophy less parochial in range. It was framed upon the theory that the peoples of the several states must sink or swim together, and that in the long run prosperity and salvation are in union and not division.

Baldwin v. G.A.F. Seelig, Inc. (1935). In a later case, also involving the welfare of Massachusetts dairy farmers, Justice Jackson described the same overriding interest in the free flow of commerce across state lines:

Our system, fostered by the Commerce Clause, is that every farmer and every craftsman shall be encouraged to produce by the certainty that he will have free access to every market in the Nation, that no home embargoes will withhold his exports, and no foreign state will by customs duties or regulations exclude them. Likewise, every consumer may look to the free competition from every producing area in the Nation to protect him from exploitation by any. Such was the vision of the Founders; such has been the doctrine of this Court which has given it reality.

H.P. Hood & Sons, Inc. v. Du Mond (1949).

The judgment of the Supreme Judicial Court of Massachusetts is reversed.

Justice Scalia, with whom Justice Thomas joins, concurring in the judgment.

. . . The purpose of the negative Commerce Clause, we have often said, is to create a national market. It does not follow from that, however, and we have never held, that every state law which obstructs a national market violates the Commerce Clause. Yet that is what the Court says today. It seems to have canvassed the entire corpus of negative-Commerce-Clause opinions, culled out every free-market snippet of reasoning, and melded them into the sweeping principle that the Constitution is violated by any state law or regulation that "artificially encourag[es] in-state production even when the same goods could be produced at lower cost in other States." . . . .

As the Court seems to appreciate by its eagerness expressly to reserve the question of the constitutionality of subsidies for in-state industry, this expansive view of the Commerce Clause calls into question a wide variety of state laws that have hitherto been thought permissible. It seems to me that a state subsidy would *clearly* be invalid under any formulation of the Court's guiding principle identified above. [E]ven where the funding does not come in any part from taxes on out-of-state goods, "merely assist[ing]" in-State businesses, unquestionably neutralizes advantages possessed by out-of-state enterprises. Such subsidies, particularly where they are in the form of cash or (what comes to the same thing) tax forgiveness, are often admitted to have as their purpose—*indeed, are nationally advertised as having as their purpose*—making it more profitable to conduct business in-state than elsewhere, *i.e.,* distorting normal market incentives. . . .

These results would greatly extend the negative Commerce Clause beyond its current scope. If the Court does not intend these consequences, and does not want to foster needless litigation concerning them, it should not have adopted its expansive rationale. Another basis for deciding the case is available, which I proceed to discuss. . . .

There are at least four possible devices that would enable a State to produce the economic effect that Massachusetts has produced here:

(1)   a discriminatory tax upon the industry, imposing a higher liability on out-of-state members than on their in-state competitors;

(2)   a tax upon the industry that is nondiscriminatory in its assessment, but that has an "exemption" or "credit" for in-state members;

(3)   a nondiscriminatory tax upon the industry, the revenues from which are placed into a segregated fund, which fund is disbursed as "rebates" or "subsidies" to in-state members of the industry (the situation at issue in this case); and

(4)   with or without nondiscriminatory taxation of the industry, a subsidy for the in-state members of the industry, funded from the State's general revenues.

It is long settled that the first of these methodologies is unconstitutional under the negative Commerce Clause. The second of them, "exemption" from or "credit" against a "neutral" tax, is no different in principle from the first, and has likewise been held invalid. The fourth methodology, application of a state subsidy from general revenues, is so far removed from what we have hitherto held to be unconstitutional, that prohibiting it must be regarded as an extension of our negative-Commerce-Clause jurisprudence and therefore, to me, unacceptable. . . .

The issue before us in the present case is whether the third of these methodologies must fall. Although the question is close, I conclude it would not be a principled point at which to disembark from the negative-Commerce-Clause train. The only difference between methodology (2) (discriminatory "exemption" from nondiscriminatory tax) and methodology (3) (discriminatory refund of nondiscriminatory tax) is that the money is taken and returned rather than simply left with the favored in-state taxpayer in the first place. The difference between (3) and (4), on the other hand, is the difference between assisting in-state industry through discriminatory taxation and assisting in-state industry by other means. I would therefore allow a State to subsidize its domestic industry so long as it does so from nondiscriminatory taxes that go into the State's general revenue fund. . . .

Chief Justice Rehnquist, with whom Justice Blackmun joins, dissenting.

. . . Massachusetts has dealt with [the threat to its dairy industry] by providing a subsidy to aid its beleaguered dairy farmers. In case after case, we have approved the validity under the Commerce Clause of such enactments. "No one disputes that a State may enact laws pursuant to its police powers that have the purpose and effect of encouraging domestic industry." *Bacchus Imports, Ltd. v. Dias* (1984). "Direct subsidization of domestic industry does not ordinarily run afoul of [the dormant Commerce Clause]; discriminatory taxation of out-of-state manufacturers does." *New Energy Co. of Ind. v. Limbach* (1988). But today the Court relegates these well-established principles to a footnote and, at the same time, gratuitously casts doubt on the validity of state subsidies, observing that "[w]e have never squarely confronted" their constitutionality. . . .

No decided case supports the Court's conclusion that the negative Commerce Clause prohibits the State from using money that it has lawfully obtained through a neutral tax on milk dealers and distributing it as a subsidy to dairy farmers. Indeed, the case which comes closest to supporting the result the Court reaches is the ill-starred opinion in *United States v. Butler* (1936), in which the Court held unconstitutional what would have been an otherwise valid tax on the processing of agricultural products because of the use to which the revenue raised by the tax was put. . . .

The wisdom of a messianic insistence on a grim sink-or-swim policy of laissez-faire economics would be debatable had Congress chosen to enact it; but Congress has done nothing of the kind. It is the Court which has imposed the policy under the dormant Commerce Clause, a policy which bodes ill for the values of federalism which have long animated our constitutional jurisprudence.

c.   Dormant Commerce Clause—Congressional Authorization

As a negative limitation on the states, Dormant Commerce Clause doctrine is grounded in the implications of the Constitution's positive grant of commerce authority to Congress. Given this conceptual grounding, what happens if Congress decides that it is perfectly comfortable with state restrictions that the Court has found (or would find) to be unconstitutional interference with commerce?

The following case, *Prudential Insurance Co. v. Benjamin* (1946), answers that question. But first, some background. For decades, the Supreme Court had deemed insurance to be outside of interstate commerce, leaving it to be governed by state regulation. See *Paul v. Virginia* (1868). In *United States v. South-Eastern Underwriters Ass'n* (1944), the Supreme Court effectively overruled *Paul* on this point, holding that an insurance company doing substantial business across state lines was engaged in interstate commerce. This raised doubts about the continued viability of the longstanding system of state regulation of insurance, and Congress promptly responded with the McCarran-Ferguson Act of 1945. Section 1 of the Act states:

> The Congress hereby declares that the continued regulation and taxation by the several States of the business of insurance is in the public interest, and that silence on the part of the Congress shall not be construed to impose any barrier to the regulation or taxation of such business by the several States.

As the Supreme Court explained in *Prudential Insurance*, "The McCarran Act is, in effect, a determination by Congress that the business of insurance, though done in interstate commerce, is not of such a character as to require uniformity of treatment within the distinction taken in the doctrine of [the Dormant

Commerce Clause].” But would the Court conclude that the statute could and did effectively authorize legislation that plainly discriminated against interstate commerce?

Prudential Insurance Co. v. Benjamin

Supreme Court of the United States, 1946.
328 U.S. 408.

MR. JUSTICE RUTLEDGE delivered the opinion of the Court.

[Prudential Insurance Company challenges South Carolina's right to] collect taxes from Prudential, a New Jersey corporation, which for years prior to 1945 the state had levied and the company had paid. The tax is laid on foreign insurance companies and must be paid annually as a condition of receiving a certificate of authority to carry on the business of insurance within the state. The exaction amounts to three per cent of the aggregate of premiums received from business done in South Carolina, without reference to its interstate or local character. No similar tax is required of South Carolina corporations.

Prudential insists that the tax discriminates against interstate commerce and in favor of local business. . . . Accordingly it says the tax cannot stand consistently with many decisions of this Court outlawing state taxes which discriminate against interstate commerce. South Carolina . . . maintains that the tax is valid, more particularly in view of the McCarran Act, by which it is claimed Congress has consented to continuance of this form of taxation and thus has removed any possible constitutional objection which otherwise might exist. . . .

We are not required however to consider whether . . . the [Dormant Commerce Clause] authorities on which Prudential chiefly relies would require invalidation of South Carolina's tax. For they are not in point. As has been stated, they are the cases which . . . have outlawed state taxes found to discriminate against interstate commerce. No one of them involved a situation like that now here. In each the question of validity of the state taxing statute arose when Congress' power lay dormant. In none had Congress acted or purported to act, either by way of consenting to the state's tax or otherwise. Those cases therefore presented no question of the validity of such a tax where Congress had taken affirmative action consenting to it or purporting to give it validity. . . .

[T]he cases most important for the decision in this cause . . . are the ones involving situations where the silence of Congress or the dormancy of its power has been taken judicially, on one view or another of its constitutional effects, as forbidding state action, only to have Congress later disclaim the prohibition or undertake to nullify it. Not yet has this Court held such a disclaimer invalid or that state action supported by it could not stand. On the contrary in each instance it has given effect to the Congressional judgment contradicting its own previous one. . . .[29] None of the decisions conceded, because none involved any question of, the power of Congress to make conclusive its own mandate concerning what is commerce. But apart from that function of defining the outer boundary of its power, whenever Congress' judgment has been uttered affirmatively to contradict the Court's previously expressed view that specific action taken by the states in Congress' silence was forbidden by the commerce clause, this body has accommodated its previous judgment to Congress' expressed approval. . . .

The power of Congress over commerce . . . is not restricted, except as the Constitution expressly provides, by any limitation which forbids it to discriminate against interstate commerce and in favor of local trade. Its plenary scope enables Congress not only to promote but also to prohibit interstate commerce, as it has done frequently and for a great variety of reasons. That power does not run down a one-way street or one of narrowly fixed dimensions. Congress may keep the way open, confine it broadly or closely, or close it entirely, subject only to the restrictions placed upon its authority by other constitutional provisions and the requirement that it shall not invade the domains of action reserved exclusively for the states.

This broad authority Congress may exercise alone, subject to those limitations, or in conjunction with coordinated action by the states, in which case limitations imposed for the preservation of their powers become inoperative and only those designed to forbid action altogether by any power or combination of powers in our governmental system remain effective. Here both Congress and South Carolina have acted, and in complete coordination, to sustain the tax. It is therefore reinforced by the exercise of all the power of government residing

---

[29] *Pennsylvania v. Wheeling and Belmont Bridge Co. II* (1855) [(permitting bridge over river in light of congressional act approving it)], with which compare *Pennsylvania v. Wheeling and Belmont Bridge Co. I* (1850) [(enjoining construction of bridge prior to congressional act)]; . . . *Leisy & Co. v. Hardin* (1890) [(prohibiting state regulation of liquor shipments)], with which compare *In re Rahrer* (1891) [(permitting state regulation of liquor shipments)]. . . .

in our scheme. Clear and gross must be the evil which would nullify such an exertion, one which could arise only by exceeding beyond cavil some explicit and compelling limitation imposed by a constitutional provision or provisions designed and intended to outlaw the action taken entirely from our constitutional framework. . . .

The judgment accordingly is affirmed.

Mr. Justice Black concurs in the result.

Mr. Justice Jackson, took no part in the consideration or decision of this case.

For Discussion

(1) Congress could not validly authorize South Carolina to discriminate against African-Americans. Why should it be allowed to authorize South Carolina to discriminate against out-of state corporations?

(2) The Privileges and Immunities Clause of Art. IV has been interpreted to operate as a sort of equal protection clause in favor of citizens of other states. The focus of this clause is on the individual citizen rather than on commerce. There is no market participant exception to it, and Congress cannot abrogate the right. Not all discriminations against citizens of other states implicate the right; discrimination in granting licenses to hunt elk, for example, does not. *Baldwin v. Montana Fish and Game Comm'n*, 436 U.S. 371 (1978). Notwithstanding *White v. Massachusetts Council of Construction Employers, Inc.*, presented at pp. 682–684, on the other hand, discrimination in public employment does implicate the right—though there may be room for the state to justify the discrimination. *United Building & Construction Trades Council v. Mayor and Council of Camden* (1984). Does this suggest that objections to the Dormant Commerce Clause might fade if its doctrine were "relocated" to the Article IV Privileges and Immunities Clause? Cf. *McDonald v. Chicago* (2010) (refusing to transplant substantive due process doctrine to the Privileges *or* Immunities Clause of the Fourteenth Amendment). Or does the Privileges and Immunities Clause of Art. IV express a constitutional value that stakes a greater claim to judicial protection than does the doctrine of the Dormant Commerce Clause?

 TEST YOUR KNOWLEDGE: To assess your understanding of the material in this chapter, **click here** to take a quiz.

CHAPTER IV

The "Separation" of Powers: Distribution of Authority Within the National Government

A. Presidential Power—a Conceptual Framework

As a matter of the original understanding, the presidential power provisions of Article II were structured around the same enumeration principle that permeates the Constitution as a whole. As Edmund Randolph explained at the Virginia ratifying convention in 1788:

> There is not a word said in the State Government of the powers given to it, be[c]ause they are general. But in the general Constitution, its powers are enumerated. Is it not then fairly deducible, that it has no power but what is expressly given it?

So what enumerated powers can the President call on? Compared to the constitutional grants of congressional power, there are surprisingly few specific provisions on presidential authority. Take a look at Sections 1, 2, and 3 of Article II, in particular the Executive Power Clause, the Commander-in-Chief Clause, the Opinions Clause, the Pardon Power, the Treaty Clause, the Appointments Clause, the Receive Ambassadors Clause, and the Take Care Clause.

We will have occasion to discuss a number of these powers. But it makes sense to start with the first words of Article II:

> The executive Power shall be vested in a President of the United States of America.

This sentence presents one of the most important questions in constitutional law: what does "the executive power" entail? Broadly speaking, there are three possibilities. First, the clause might have no standalone content; the scope of executive power might be defined entirely by the more specific powers listed later in Article II. Second, the clause might authorize the President to supervise the execution of the laws, including both their restrictive prohibitions and the affirmative projects they assign. Third, the clause might grant a more amorphous suite of powers likely to be useful for an executive magistrate to possess—perhaps including war powers, foreign affairs powers, or even emergency powers in some shape or form.

As a matter of original understanding, it's pretty clear that the Founders understood the clause to vest the authority to execute law, and nothing more. See Mortenson, *Article II Vests the Executive Power, Not the Royal Prerogative,* 119 Colum. L. Rev. 1169 (2019) and Mortenson, *The Executive Power Clause,* 168 U. Pa. L. Rev. 1269 (2020). For a contrary view, see Michael McConnell, *The President Who Would Not Be King* (2020); Prakash & Ramsey, *The Executive Power Over Foreign Affairs,* 111 Yale L.J. 231 (2001). That doesn't settle the legal question, however, because most interpreters don't claim to limit themselves to the original understanding—and fewer still actually do so in reality.

As You READ

In the cases that follow, see if you can identify the precise source of legal authority that is said to justify the challenged executive action. It's also worth considering whether the Justices' various opinions seem to share the same commitment to the enumeration principle.

So you'll want to pay close attention to how the majority, concurring, and dissenting opinions in this section deploy the Article II Vesting Clause, whether in conjunction with the other enumerated powers or perhaps even as a standalone source of authority.

In re Neagle

Supreme Court of the United States, 1890.

135 U.S. 1.

Opinion of MILLER, J. [for the court.]

SUMMARY OF THE FACTS

Stephen J. Field, a justice of the Supreme Court from California, made enemies easily. One of them was David S. Terry, who had preceded Field as chief justice of the California Supreme Court (before leaving the state after killing a U.S. Senator in a duel). Sitting as a circuit justice, Field ruled against Terry's wife in a forged-will case and sent him to jail for contempt after a courtroom altercation. In response to threats made by Terry, the U.S. Attorney for the Northern District of California recommended, and the Attorney General authorized, the hiring of Deputy Marshals to accompany and protect Field, both when he was in court and in transit; David Neagle was assigned the job. Sure enough, as Field was traveling between sittings in Los Angeles and San Francisco, Terry assaulted the justice one morning while he and Neagle were at breakfast. Neagle killed Terry instantly with two revolver shots, for which he was charged with murder by state authorities and imprisoned by the sheriff of San Joaquin County. Neagle then brought a petition for habeas corpus in federal court.

WORTH NOTING

The facts in *Neagle* are the stuff of pulp fiction. Forged marriage licenses! Courtroom fisticuffs! Hair pulling! Revolvers in handbags! Gunplay over breakfast in the dining car on the Los Angeles Special! See the online supplement if you're in the mood for a fun read.

Section 753 of the Revised [U.S.] Statutes reads as follows: "The writ of *habeas corpus* shall in no case extend to a prisoner in jail, unless where he is . . . in custody for an act done or omitted in pursuance of a law of the United States . . . or is in custody in violation of the constitution, or of a law or treaty of the United States. . . ." This, of course, means that if he is held in custody in violation of the constitution or a law of the United States, or for an act done or omitted in pursuance of a law of the United States, he must be discharged. . . .

It is not supposed that any special act of Congress exists which authorizes the marshals or deputy-marshals of the United States, in express terms, to accompany the judges of the Supreme Court through their circuits, and act as a bodyguard to them, to defend them against malicious assaults against their persons. But . . . we are satisfied that, if it was [nonetheless] the duty of Neagle, under the circumstances—a duty which could only arise under the laws of the United States—to defend Mr. Justice Field from a murderous attack upon him, he brings himself within the meaning of the section we have recited. . . .

In the view we take of the Constitution of the United states, any obligation fairly and properly inferable from that instrument, or any duty of the marshal to be derived from the general scope of his duties under the laws of the United States, is a "law," within the meaning of this phrase. . . .

It would be a great reproach to the system of government of the United States, declared to be within its sphere sovereign and supreme, if there is to be found within the domain of its powers no means of protecting the judges, in the conscientious and faithful discharge of their duties, from the malice and hatred of those upon whom their judgments may operate unfavorably. . . . If a person in the situation of Judge Field could have no other guaranty of his personal safety while engaged in the conscientious discharge of a disagreeable duty than the fact that, if he was murdered, his murderer would be subject to the laws of a state, and by those laws could be punished, the security would be very insufficient. . . .

Where, then, are we to look for the protection which we have shown Judge Field was entitled to when engaged in the discharge of his official duties?

Not to the courts of the United States, because, as has been more than once said in this court, in the division of the powers of government between the three great departments, executive, legislative, and judicial, the judicial is the weakest for the purposes of self-protection, and for the enforcement of the powers which it exercises. The ministerial officers through whom its commands must be executed are marshals of the United States, and belong emphatically to the executive department of the government. They are appointed by the President, with the advice and consent of the Senate. They are removable from office at his pleasure. They are subjected by act of Congress to the supervision and control of the Department of Justice, in the hands of one of the cabinet officers of the president, and their compensation is provided by acts of Congress. The same may be said of the district attorneys of the United States who prosecute and defend the claims of the government in the courts.

The legislative branch of the government can only protect the judicial officers by the enactment of laws for that purpose, and the argument we are now combating assumes that no such law has been passed by Congress.

If we turn to the executive department of the government, we find a very different condition of affairs. The Constitution, § 3, art. 2, declares that the President "shall take care that the laws be faithfully executed;" and he is provided with the means of fulfilling this obligation by his authority to commission all the officers of the United States, and, by and with the advice and consent of the Senate, to appoint the most important of them, and to fill vacancies. He is declared to be the commander in chief of the army and navy of the United States.

The duties which are thus imposed upon him he is further enabled to perform by the recognition in the constitution, and the creation by acts of Congress, of executive departments, which have varied in number from four or five to seven or eight, who are familiarly called "cabinet ministers." These aid him in the performance of the great duties of his office, and represent him in a thousand acts to which it can hardly be supposed his personal attention is called; and thus he is enabled to fulfill the duty of his great department, expressed in the phrase that "he shall take care that the laws be faithfully executed." Is this duty limited to the enforcement of acts of Congress or of treaties of the United States according to their express terms; or does it include the rights, duties, and obligations growing out of the Constitution itself, our international relations, and all the protection implied by the nature of the government under the constitution? . . .

We cannot doubt the power of the President to take measures for the protection of a judge of one of the courts of the United States who, while in the discharge of the duties of his office, is threatened with a personal attack which may probably result in his death; and we think it clear that where this protection is to

WORTH NOTING

The opinion reproduces an exchange of letters among the U.S. Marshall, the local U.S. Attorney, and the Attorney General. The U.S. Attorney eventually recommended that "in view of the direful threats made against Justice Field . . . I would therefore suggest that [the U.S. Marshall] be authorized, in his discretion, to retain one or more deputies, at such times as he may deem necessary, for the purposes suggested." The Attorney General responded by authorizing funding for the requested deputies.

be afforded through the civil power, the Department of Justice is the proper one to set in motion the necessary means of protection. The correspondence [which resulted in Neagle's assignment to protect Justice Field], although prescribing no very specific mode of affording this protection by the Attorney General, is sufficient, we think, to warrant the marshal in taking the steps which he did take, in making the provisions which he did make, for the protection and defense of Mr. Justice Field.

But there is positive law investing the marshals and their deputies with powers which not only justify what Marshal Neagle did in this matter, but which imposed it upon him as a duty. [The Court here turns to examine Rev. Stat. § 788, which gives federal marshals in any state "the same powers in executing the laws of the United States as the sheriffs and their deputies in such state may have, by law, in executing the laws thereof." Because a separate California statute authorized state sheriffs to "preserve the peace," the Court concluded that—under the circumstances—§ 788 authorized Neagle to protect Field by killing Terry.]

. . . We therefore affirm the judgment of the Circuit Court authorizing his discharge from the custody of the sheriff of San Joaquin county.

FIELD, J., did not sit at the hearing of this case, and took no part in its decision.

 Hmm. Perhaps he was too busy?

LAMAR, J., (dissenting[, and joined by FULLER, C.J.])

The chief justice and myself . . . agree, taking the facts of the case as they are shown by the record, that the personal protection of Mr. Justice Field as a private citizen, even to the death of Terry, was not only the right, but was also the duty, of Neagle, and of any other by-stander; and we maintain that for the exercise of that right or duty he is answerable to the courts of the State of California, and to them alone. But we deny that, upon the facts of this record, he, as deputy-marshal Neagle, or as private citizen Neagle, had any duty imposed on him by the laws of the United States growing out of the official character of Judge Field as a Circuit Justice. . . .

We must . . . call attention again to the formal and deliberate admission that it is not pretended that there is any *single*, specific statute making it, in so many words, Neagle's duty to protect the justice. . . . We recognize that the powers of the government, "within its sphere," . . . extend to the protection of itself and all of its agencies, as well as to the preservation and the perpetuation of its usefulness; and that these powers may be found not only in the express authorities conferred by the Constitution, but also in necessary and proper implications. . . .

[The Necessary and Proper Clause of Art. I, § 8] is that which contains the germ of all the implication of powers under the Constitution. . . . And that clause alone conclusively refutes the assertion of the Attorney General that it was "the duty of the executive department of the United States to guard and protect at any hazard the life of Mr. Justice Field in the discharge of his duty, because such protection is essential to the existence of the government." Waiving the question of the essentiality of any such protection to the existence of the government, the manifest answer is that the protection needed and to be given must proceed not from the President, but primarily from Congress.

Again, while it is the President's duty to take care that the laws be faithfully executed, it is not his duty to make laws or a law of the United States. The laws he is to see executed are manifestly those contained in the Constitution and those enacted by Congress. . . . That body was perfectly able to pass such laws as it should deem expedient in reference to [carrying into execution the powers of federal courts]. Indeed, it has passed such laws in reference to elections, expressly directing the United States Marshals to attend places of election, to act as peace-officers, to arrest with and without process, and to protect the supervisors of election in the discharge of their duties; and there was not the slightest legal necessity out of which to imply any such power in the President. For these reasons the letters of the Attorney General to Marshal Franks, granting that they did import what is claimed, and granting that the Attorney General was to all intents and purposes, *pro hac vice*, the President, invested Neagle with no special powers whatever. . . .

As before stated, if the killing of Terry was done "in pursuance of a law of the United States," that law had somewhere an origin. There are, under the general government, only two possible sources of law. . . . The legislative power possessed by the United States must be found, either exercised in the Constitution as fundamental law, or by some body or person to whom it was delegated by the Constitution. It has already been pointed out that the Constitution does not itself create any such law as that contended for, and that it could not have been created by any executive or judicial action or status is made manifest . . . , by sec. 1, Art. 1, [which] provides that "*all* legislative power herein granted shall be vested in a Congress of the United States. . . ." Thus we are driven to look for the source of this asserted law to some legislation of Congress. . . .

It is claimed that the law needed for appellee's case can be found in section 788 of the Revised Statutes. . . . This line of argument seems to us wholly untenable. . . . That section gives to the officers named the same measure of powers when in the discharge of their duties as those possessed by the sheriffs, it is true; but it does not alter the duties themselves. . . . They are still, by the very terms of the statute itself, limited to the execution of "the laws of the United States," and are not in any way, by adoption, mediate or immediate, from the Code or the common law, authorized to execute the laws of California. The statute, therefore, leaves the matter just where it found it. . . .

For these reasons, as briefly stated as possible, we think the judgment of the court below should be reversed, and the prisoner remanded to the custody of the sheriff of San Joaquin County, California; and we are the less reluctant to express this conclusion because we cannot permit ourselves to doubt that the authorities of the State of California are competent and willing to do justice, and that, even if the appellee had been indicted and had gone to trial upon this record, God and his country would have given him a good deliverance.

Youngstown Sheet & Tube Co. v. Sawyer

Supreme Court of the United States, 1952.
343 U.S. 579.

MR. JUSTICE BLACK delivered the opinion of the Court.

We are asked to decide whether the President was acting within his constitutional power when he issued an order directing the Secretary of Commerce to take possession of and operate most of the Nation's steel mills. . . .

In the latter part of 1951, a dispute arose between the steel companies and their employees over terms and conditions that should be included in new collective bargaining agreements. Long-continued conferences failed to resolve the dispute[, and on] April 4, 1952, the Union gave notice of a nation-wide strike called to begin at 12:01 a.m. April 9. The indispensability of steel as a component of substantially all weapons and other war materials led the President to believe that the proposed work stoppage would immediately jeopardize our national defense and that governmental seizure of the steel mills was necessary in order to assure the continued availability of steel.

Reciting these considerations for his action, the President, a few hours before the strike was to begin, issued Executive Order 10340. The order directed the Secretary of Commerce to take possession of most of the steel mills and keep them running. The Secretary immediately issued his own possessory orders, calling upon the presidents of the various seized companies to serve as operating managers for the United States. They were directed to carry on their activities in accordance with regulations

WORTH NOTING

Of particular relevance to the labor dispute, Section 3 of the Executive Order provided that the Secretary "shall determine and prescribe terms and conditions of employment under which the plants, facilities, and other properties possession of which is taken pursuant to this order shall be operated."

and directions of the Secretary. The next morning the President sent a message to Congress reporting his action. Twelve days later he sent a second message. Congress has taken no action.

Obeying the Secretary's orders under protest, the companies brought proceedings against him in the District Court. Their complaints charged that the seizure was not authorized by an act of Congress or by any constitutional provisions. . .

II.

The President's power, if any, to issue the order must stem either from an act of Congress or from the Constitution itself. There is no statute that expressly authorizes the President to take possession of property as he did here. Nor is there any act of Congress to which our attention has been directed from which such a power can fairly be implied. Indeed, we do not understand the Government to rely on statutory authorization for this seizure. [The Selective Service Act of 1948 and the Defense Production Act of 1950] do authorize the President to take both personal and real property under certain conditions. However, the Government admits that these conditions were not met and that the President's order was not rooted in either of the statutes. The Government refers to the seizure provisions of [the Defense Production Act] . . . as "much too cumbersome, involved, and time-consuming for the crisis which was at hand."

Moreover, the use of the seizure technique to solve labor disputes in order to prevent work stoppages was not only unauthorized by any congressional enactment; prior to this controversy, Congress had refused to adopt that method of settling labor disputes. When the Taft-Hartley Act was under consideration in 1947, Congress rejected an amendment which would have authorized such governmental seizures in cases of emergency. Apparently it was thought that the technique of seizure, like that of compulsory arbitration, would interfere with the process of collective bargaining. Consequently, the plan Congress adopted in that Act did not provide for seizure under any circumstances. Instead, the plan sought to bring about settlements by use of the customary devices of mediation, conciliation, investigation by boards of inquiry, and public reports. . . .

It is clear that if the President had authority to issue the order he did, it must be found in some provisions of the Constitution. And it is not claimed that express constitutional language grants this power to the President. The contention is that presidential power should be implied from the aggregate of his powers under the Constitution. Particular reliance is placed on provisions in Article II which say that "the executive Power shall be vested in a President"; that "he shall take Care that the Laws be faithfully executed"; and that he "shall be Commander in Chief of the Army and Navy of the United States."

The order cannot properly be sustained as an exercise of the President's military power as Commander in Chief of the Armed Forces. The Government attempts to do so by citing a number of cases upholding broad powers in military commanders engaged in day-to-day fighting in a theater of war. Such cases need not concern us here. Even though "theater of war" be an expanding concept, we cannot with faithfulness to our constitutional system hold that the Commander in Chief of the Armed Forces has the ultimate power as such to take possession of private property in order to keep labor disputes from stopping production. This is a job for the Nation's lawmakers, not for its military authorities.

Nor can the seizure order be sustained because of the several constitutional provisions that grant executive power to the President. In the framework of our Constitution, the President's power to see that the laws are faithfully executed refutes the idea that he is to be a lawmaker. The Constitution limits his functions in the lawmaking process to the recommending of laws he thinks wise and the vetoing of laws he thinks bad. And the Constitution is neither silent nor equivocal about who shall make laws which the President is to execute. The first section of the first article says that "All legislative Powers herein granted shall be vested in a Congress of the United States." After granting many powers to the Congress, Article I goes on to provide that Congress may "make all Laws which shall be necessary and proper for carrying into Execution the foregoing

Powers and all other Powers vested by this Constitution in the Government of the United States, or in any Department or Officer thereof."

The President's order does not direct that a congressional policy be executed in a manner prescribed by Congress—it directs that a presidential policy be executed in a manner prescribed by the President. The preamble of the order itself, like that of many statutes, sets out reasons why the President believes certain policies should be adopted, proclaims these policies as rules of conduct to be followed, and again, like a statute, authorizes a government official to promulgate additional rules and regulations consistent with the policy proclaimed and needed to carry that policy into execution. The power of Congress to adopt such public policies as those proclaimed by the order is beyond question. . . . The Constitution did not subject this law-making power of Congress to presidential or military supervision or control.

It is said that other Presidents without congressional authority have taken possession of private business enterprises in order to settle labor disputes. But even if this be true, Congress has not thereby lost its exclusive constitutional authority to make laws necessary and proper to carry out the powers vested by the Constitution "in the Government of the United States, or in any Department or Officer thereof."

The Founders of this Nation entrusted the law making power to the Congress alone in both good and bad times. It would do no good to recall the historical events, the fears of power and the hopes for freedom that lay behind their choice. Such a review would but confirm our holding that this seizure order cannot stand.

The judgment of the District Court [enjoining the Secretary from "continuing the seizure and possession of the plant"] is affirmed.

MR. JUSTICE JACKSON, concurring in the judgment and opinion of the Court.

That comprehensive and undefined presidential powers hold both practical advantages and grave dangers for the country will impress anyone who has served as legal adviser to a President in time of transition

WORTH NOTING

Justice Jackson, who had served as Solicitor General and then as Attorney General in the Roosevelt administration, had been responsible for some of the executive branch memos that the Truman administration relied on to support its position in *Youngstown*.

[handwritten margin note: there actually isn't much guidance on this issue]

and public anxiety. . . . But as we approach the question of presidential power, we half overcome mental hazards by recognizing them. . . .

A judge, like an executive adviser, may be surprised at the poverty of really useful and unambiguous authority applicable to concrete problems of executive power as they actually present themselves. Just what our forefathers did envision, or would have envisioned had they foreseen modern conditions, must be divined from materials almost as enigmatic as the dreams Joseph was called upon to interpret for Pharaoh. A century and a half of partisan debate and scholarly speculation yields no net result but only supplies more or less apt quotations from respected sources on each side of any question. They largely cancel each other.[1] And court decisions are indecisive because of the judicial practice of dealing with the largest questions in the most narrow way.

The actual art of governing under our Constitution does not and cannot conform to judicial definitions of the power of any of its branches based on iso-lated clauses or even single Articles torn from context. While the Constitution diffuses power the better to secure liberty, it also contemplates that practice will integrate the dispersed powers into a workable government. It enjoins upon its branches separateness but interdependence, autonomy but reciprocity. Presidential powers are not fixed but fluctuate depending upon their disjunc-tion or conjunction with those of Congress. We may well begin by a somewhat over-simplified grouping of practical situations in which a President may doubt, or others may challenge, his powers, and by distinguishing roughly the legal consequences of this factor of relativity.

1.   When the President acts pursuant to an express or implied au-thorization of Congress, his authority is at its maximum, for it includes all that he possesses in his own right plus all that Congress can delegate.[2] In these circumstances, and in these only, may he be said (for what it may be worth), to personify the federal sovereignty. If his act is held unconstitutional under these

---

[1]   A Hamilton may be matched against a Madison. [Cites to debate over Washington's Neutrality Proclama-tion are omitted.] Professor Taft is counterbalanced by Theodore Roosevelt. Taft, *Our Chief Magistrate and His Powers*; Theodore Roosevelt, *Autobiography*. It even seems that President Taft cancels out Professor Taft. Com-pare his "Temporary Petroleum Withdrawal No. 5" of 1909 with his appraisal of executive power in *Our Chief Magistrate and His Powers*.

[2]   It is in this class of cases that we find the broadest recent statements of presidential power, including those relied on here. *United States v. Curtiss-Wright Export Corp.* involved, not the question of the President's power to act without congressional authority, but the question of his right to act under and in accord with an Act of Congress. . . . That case does not solve the present controversy.

circumstances, it usually means that the Federal Government as an undivided whole lacks power. A seizure executed by the President pursuant to an Act of Congress would be supported by the strongest of presumptions and the widest latitude of judicial interpretation, and the burden of persuasion would rest heavily upon any who might attack it.

2. When the President acts in absence of either a congressional grant or denial of authority, he can only rely upon his own independent powers, but there is a zone of twilight in which he and Congress may have concurrent authority, or in which its distribution is uncertain. Therefore, congressional inertia, indifference or quiescence may sometimes, at least as a practical matter, enable, if not invite, measures on independent presidential responsibility. In this area, any actual test of power is likely to depend on the imperatives of events and contemporary imponderables rather than on abstract theories of law.[3]

    [handwritten margin note: Sometimes it is ambiguous so it would depend on the situation]

3. When the President takes measures incompatible with the expressed or implied will of Congress, his power is at its lowest ebb, for then he can rely only upon his own constitutional powers minus any constitutional powers of Congress over the matter. Courts can sustain exclusive Presidential control in such a case only by disabling the Congress from acting upon the subject. Presidential claim to a power at once so conclusive and preclusive must be scrutinized with caution, for what is at stake is the equilibrium established by our constitutional system.

Into which of these classifications does this executive seizure of the steel industry fit? It is eliminated from the first by admission, for it is conceded that no congressional authorization exists for this seizure. That takes away also the support of the many precedents and declarations which were made in relation, and must be confined, to this category.[5]

---

[3]   Since the Constitution implies that the writ of habeas corpus may be suspended in certain circumstances but does not say by whom, President Lincoln asserted and maintained it as an executive function in the face of judicial challenge and doubt. *Ex parte Merryman*; *Ex parte Milligan*; see *Ex parte Bollman*. Congress eventually ratified his action. Habeas Corpus Act of March 3, 1863. . . .

[5]   The oft-cited Louisiana Purchase had nothing to do with the separation of powers as between the President and Congress, but only with state and federal power. The Louisiana Purchase was subject to rather academic criticism, not upon the ground that Mr. Jefferson acted without authority from Congress, but that neither had express authority to expand the boundaries of the United States by purchase or annexation. Mr. Jefferson himself [wrote:]

Can it then be defended under flexible tests available to the second category? It seems clearly eliminated from that class because Congress has not left seizure of private property an open field but has covered it by three statutory policies inconsistent with this seizure. In cases where the purpose is to supply needs of the Government itself, two courses are provided: one, seizure of a plant which fails to comply with obligatory orders placed by the Government [under the Selective Service Act of 1948]; another, condemnation of facilities, including temporary use under the power of eminent domain [under the Defense Production Act of 1950]. The third is applicable [under the Taft-Hartley Act] where it is the general economy of the country that is to be protected rather than exclusive governmental interests. None of these were invoked. In choosing a different and inconsistent way of his own, the President cannot claim that it is necessitated or invited by failure of Congress to legislate upon the occasions, grounds and methods for seizure of industrial properties.

This leaves the current seizure to be justified only by the severe tests under the third grouping, where it can be supported only by any remainder of executive power after subtraction of such powers as Congress may have over the subject. In short, we can sustain the President only by holding that seizure of such strike-bound industries is within his domain and beyond control by Congress. Thus, this Court's first review of such seizures occurs under circumstances which leave Presidential power most vulnerable to attack and in the least favorable of possible constitutional postures.

I did not suppose, and I am not persuaded, that history leaves it open to question, at least in the courts, that the executive branch, like the Federal Government as a whole, possesses only delegated powers. The purpose of the Constitution was not only to grant power, but to keep it from getting out of hand. However, because the President does not enjoy unmentioned powers does not mean that the mentioned ones should be [unduly] narrowed. . . . I have heretofore, and do now, give to the enumerated powers the scope and elasticity afforded by what seem to be reasonable, practical implications instead of the rigidity dictated by a doctrinaire textualism.

The Constitution has made no provision for our holding foreign territory, still less for incorporating foreign nations into our Union. The executive in seizing the fugitive occurrence which so much advances the good of their country, have done an act beyond the Constitution. The Legislature is casting behind them metaphysical subtleties, and risking themselves like faithful servants, must ratify and pay for it, and throw themselves on their country for doing for them unauthorized, what we know they would have done for themselves had they been in a situation to do it.

The Solicitor General seeks the power of seizure in three clauses of the Executive Article, the first reading, "The executive Power shall be vested in a President of the United States of America." Lest I be thought to exaggerate, I quote the interpretation which his brief puts upon it: "In our view, this clause constitutes a grant of all the executive powers of which the Government is capable." If that be true, it is difficult to see why the forefathers bothered to add several specific items, including some trifling ones.[9]

The example of such unlimited executive power that must have most impressed the forefathers was the prerogative exercised by George III, and the description of its evils in the Declaration of Independence leads me to doubt that they were creating their new Executive in his image. Continental European examples were no more appealing. And if we seek instruction from our own times, we can match it only from the executive powers in those governments we disparagingly describe as totalitarian. I cannot accept the view that this clause is a grant in bulk of all conceivable executive power but regard it as an allocation to the presidential office of the generic powers thereafter stated.

The clause on which the Government next relies is that "The President shall be Commander in Chief of the Army and Navy of the United States." These cryptic words have given rise to some of the most persistent controversies in our constitutional history. Of course, they imply something more than an empty title. But just what authority goes with the name has plagued Presidential advisers who would not waive or narrow it by nonassertion yet cannot say where it begins or ends. It undoubtedly puts the Nation's armed forces under Presidential command. Hence, this loose appellation is sometimes advanced as support for any Presidential action, internal or external, involving use of force, the idea being that it vests power to do anything, anywhere, that can be done with an army or navy.

That seems to be the logic of an argument tendered at our bar—that the President having, on his own responsibility, sent American troops abroad [as part of the Korean War] derives from that act "affirmative power" to seize the means of producing a supply of steel for them. . . . Thus, it is said he has invested himself with "war powers."

---

9   "[H]e may require the Opinion, in writing, of the principal Officer in each of the executive Departments, upon any Subject relating to the Duties of their respective Offices." He "shall Commission all the Officers of the United States." Matters such as those would seem to be inherent in the Executive if anything is.

I cannot foresee all that it might entail if the Court should indorse this argument. Nothing in our Constitution is plainer than that declaration of a war is entrusted only to Congress. Of course, a state of war may in fact exist without a formal declaration. But no doctrine that the Court could promulgate would seem to me more sinister and alarming than that a President whose conduct of foreign affairs is so largely uncontrolled, and often even is unknown, can vastly enlarge his mastery over the internal affairs of the country by his own commitment of the Nation's armed forces to some foreign venture. I do not, however, find it necessary or appropriate to consider the legal status of the Korean enterprise to discountenance argument based on it.

Assuming that we are in a war *de facto*, whether it is or is not a war *de jure*, does that empower the Commander in Chief to seize industries he thinks necessary to supply our army? The Constitution expressly places in Congress power "to raise and *support* Armies" and "to *provide* and *maintain* a Navy." (Emphasis supplied.) This certainly lays upon Congress primary responsibility for supplying the armed forces. Congress alone controls the raising of revenues and their appropriation and may determine in what manner and by what means they shall be spent for military and naval procurement. I suppose no one would doubt that Congress can take over war supply as a Government enterprise. On the other hand, if Congress sees fit to rely on free private enterprise collectively bargaining with free labor for support and maintenance of our armed forces, can the Executive because of lawful disagreements incidental to that process, seize the facility for operation upon Government-imposed terms?

There are indications that the Constitution did not contemplate that the title Commander in Chief of the Army and Navy will constitute him also Commander in Chief of the country, its industries and its inhabitants. He has no monopoly of "war powers," whatever they are. While Congress cannot deprive the President of the command of the army and navy, only Congress can provide him an army or navy to command. It is also empowered to make rules for the "Government and Regulation of land and naval forces," by which it may to some unknown extent impinge upon even command functions.

That military powers of the Commander in Chief were not to supersede representative government of internal affairs seems obvious from the Constitution and from elementary American history. Time out of mind, and even now in many parts of the world, a military commander can seize private housing to shelter his troops. Not so, however, in the United States, for the Third

Amendment says, "No Soldier shall, in time of peace be quartered in any house, without the consent of the Owner, nor in time of war, but in a manner to be prescribed by law." Thus, even in war time, his seizure of needed military housing must be authorized by Congress. It also was expressly left to Congress to "provide for calling forth the Militia to execute the Laws of the Union, suppress Insurrections and repel Invasions." [Art I., § 8, Cl. 15.] Such a limitation on the command power, written at a time when the militia rather than a standing army was contemplated as the military weapon of the Republic, underscores the Constitution's policy that Congress, not the Executive, should control utilization of the war power as an instrument of domestic policy. . . .

While broad claims under this rubric often have been made, advice to the President in specific matters usually has carried overtones that powers, even under this head, are measured by the command functions usual to the topmost officer of the army and navy. Even then, heed has been taken of any efforts of Congress to negative his authority.[14]

. . . The purpose of lodging dual titles in one man was to insure that the civilian would control the military, not to enable the military to subordinate the presidential office. No penance would ever expiate the sin against free government of holding that a President can escape control of executive powers by law through assuming his military role. What the power of command may include I do not try to envision, but I think it is not a military prerogative, without support of law, to seize persons or property because they are important or even essential for the military and naval establishment.

The third clause in which the Solicitor General finds seizure powers is that "he shall take Care that the Laws be faithfully executed." [Art. II, § 3.] That authority must be matched against words of the Fifth Amendment that "No person shall be . . . deprived of life, liberty, or property, without due process of law. . . ." One gives a governmental authority that reaches so far as there is law, the other gives a private right that authority shall go no farther. These signify about all there is of the principle that ours is a government of laws, not of men, and that we submit ourselves to rulers only if under rules.

---

[14]   In 1940, President Roosevelt proposed to transfer to Great Britain certain overage destroyers and small patrol boats then under construction. He did not presume to rely upon any claim of constitutional power as Commander in Chief. On the contrary, he was advised that such destroyers . . . could be "transferred, exchanged, sold, or otherwise disposed of," because Congress had so authorized him. Accordingly, the destroyers were exchanged for air bases. In the same opinion, he was advised that Congress had prohibited the release or transfer of the so-called "mosquito boats" then under construction, so those boats were not transferred. [Citing two Opinions of the Attorney General, both authored by Jackson].

The Solicitor General lastly grounds support of the seizure upon nebulous, inherent powers never expressly granted but said to have accrued to the office from the customs and claims of preceding administrations. The plea is for a resulting power to deal with a crisis or an emergency according to the necessities of the case, the unarticulated assumption being that necessity knows no law.

Loose and irresponsible use of adjectives colors all non-legal and much legal discussion of presidential powers. "Inherent" powers, "implied" powers, "incidental" powers, "plenary" powers, "war" powers and "emergency" powers are used, often interchangeably and without fixed or ascertainable meanings. . . . But prudence [by the executive branch] has counseled that actual reliance on such nebulous claims stop short of provoking a judicial test. . . .[16]

The appeal, however, that we declare the existence of inherent powers *ex necessitate* to meet an emergency asks us to do what many think would be wise, although it is something the forefathers omitted. They knew what emergencies were, knew the pressures they engender for authoritative action, knew, too, how they afford a ready pretext for usurpation. We may also suspect that they suspected that emergency powers would tend to kindle emergencies. Aside from suspension of the privilege of the writ of habeas corpus in time of rebellion or invasion, when the public safety may require it, Art. I, § 9, Cl. 2, they made no express provision for exercise of extraordinary authority because of a crisis. . . .[19]

In the practical working of our Government we already have evolved a technique within the framework of the Constitution by which normal executive powers may be considerably expanded to meet an emergency. Congress may

---

[16]   President Wilson, just before our entrance into World War I, went before the Congress and asked its approval of his decision to authorize merchant ships to carry defensive weapons. He said:

> No doubt I already possess that authority without special warrant of law, by the plain implication of my constitutional duties and powers; but I prefer in the present circumstances not to act upon general implication. I wish to feel that the authority and the power of the Congress are behind me in whatever it may become necessary for me to do. . . .

When our Government was itself in need of shipping whilst ships flying the flags of nations overrun by Hitler, as well as belligerent merchantmen, were immobilized in American harbors where they had taken refuge, President Roosevelt did not assume that it was in his power to seize such foreign vessels to make up our own deficit. He informed Congress: "I am satisfied, after consultation with the heads of the interested departments and agencies, that we should have statutory authority to take over such vessels as our needs require. . . ." The necessary statutory authority was shortly forthcoming. . . .

It is interesting to note Holdsworth's comment on the powers of legislation by proclamation when in the hands of the Tudors. "The extent to which they could be legally used was never finally settled in this century, because the Tudors made so tactful a use of their powers that no demand for the settlement of this question was raised." Holdsworth, *History of English Law*.

[19]   I exclude, as in a very limited category by itself, the establishment of martial law. Cf. *Ex parte Milligan* (1966); *Duncan v. Kahanamoku* (1946).

and has granted extraordinary authorities which lie dormant in normal times but may be called into play by the Executive in war or upon proclamation of a national emergency. In 1939, upon congressional request, the Attorney General listed ninety-nine such separate statutory grants by Congress of emergency or war-time executive powers. They were invoked from time to time as need appeared. Under this procedure we retain Government by law—special, temporary law, perhaps, but law nonetheless. . . .

In view of the ease, expedition and safety with which Congress can grant and has granted large emergency powers, certainly ample to embrace this crisis, I am quite unimpressed with the argument that we should affirm possession of them without statute. Such power either has no beginning or it has no end. If it exists, it need submit to no legal restraint. I am not alarmed that it would plunge us straightway into dictatorship, but it is at least a step in that wrong direction.

As to whether there is imperative necessity for such powers, it is relevant to note the gap that exists between the President's paper powers and his real powers. . . . Executive power has the advantage of concentration in a single head in whose choice the whole Nation has a part, making him the focus of public hopes and expectations. In drama, magnitude and finality his decisions so far overshadow any others that almost alone he fills the public eye and ear. No other personality in public life can begin to compete with him in access to the public mind through modern methods of communications. . . .

Moreover, rise of the party system has made a significant extraconstitutional supplement to real executive power. No appraisal of his necessities is realistic which overlooks that he heads a political system as well as a legal system. Party loyalties and interests, sometimes more binding than law, extend his effective control into branches of government other than his own and he often may win, as a political leader, what he cannot command under the Constitution. . . . I cannot be brought to believe that this country will suffer if the Court refuses further to aggrandize the presidential office, already so potent and so relatively immune from judicial review, at the expense of Congress.

But I have no illusion that any decision by this Court can keep power in the hands of Congress if it is not wise and timely in meeting its problems. A crisis that challenges the President equally, or perhaps primarily, challenges Congress. . . . We may say that power to legislate for emergencies belongs in the hands of Congress, but only Congress itself can prevent power from slipping through its fingers. . . .

The executive action we have here originates in the individual will of the President and represents an exercise of authority without law. . . . With all its defects, delays and inconveniences, men have discovered no technique for long preserving free government except that the Executive be under the law, and that the law be made by parliamentary deliberations. Such institutions may be destined to pass away. But it is the duty of the Court to be last, not first, to give them up.

MR. JUSTICE BURTON, concurring in both the opinion and judgment of the Court.

. . . The present situation is not comparable to that of an imminent invasion or threatened attack. We do not face the issue of what might be the President's constitutional power to meet such catastrophic situations. Nor is it claimed that the current seizure is in the nature of a military command addressed by the President, as Commander-in-Chief, to a mobilized nation waging, or imminently threatened with, total war.

The controlling fact here is that Congress, within its constitutionally delegated power, has prescribed for the President specific procedures, exclusive of seizure, for his use in meeting the present type of emergency. Congress has reserved to itself the right to determine where and when to authorize the seizure of property in meeting such an emergency. Under these circumstances, the President's order of April 8 invaded the jurisdiction of Congress. . . .

MR. JUSTICE CLARK, concurring in the judgment of the Court.

One of this Court's first pronouncements upon the powers of the President under the Constitution was made by Chief Justice John Marshall some one hundred and fifty years ago. In *Little v. Barreme* (1804), he used this characteristically clear language in discussing the power of the President to instruct the seizure of the "Flying-Fish," a vessel bound *from* a French port:

> [W]hen it is observed that [an act of Congress] gives a special authority to seize on the high seas, and limits that authority to the seizure of vessels bound or sailing to a French port, the legislature seem to have prescribed that the manner in which this law shall be carried into execution, was to exclude a seizure of any vessel *not* bound *to* a French port.

Accordingly, a unanimous Court held that the President's instructions had been issued without authority and that they could not "legalize an act which without those instructions would have been a plain trespass." . . .

I conclude that where Congress has laid down specific procedures to deal with the type of crisis confronting the President, he must follow those procedures in meeting the crisis; but that in the absence of such action by Congress, the President's independent power to act depends upon the gravity of the situation confronting the nation. I cannot sustain the seizure in question because here, as in *Little v. Barreme,* Congress had prescribed methods to be followed by the President in meeting the emergency at hand. . . .

For these reasons I concur in the judgment of the Court. . . .

MR. JUSTICE DOUGLAS, concurring.

. . . The Congress, as well as the President, is trustee of the national welfare. . . . Legislative action may indeed often be cumbersome, time-consuming, and apparently inefficient. But as Mr. Justice Brandeis stated in his dissent in *Myers v. United States,* "The doctrine of the separation of powers was adopted by the Convention of 1787 not to promote efficiency but to preclude the exercise of arbitrary power. The purpose was not to avoid friction, but, by means of the inevitable friction incident to the distribution of the governmental powers among three departments, to save the people from autocracy." . . .

Today a kindly President uses the seizure power to effect a wage increase and to keep the steel furnaces in production. Yet tomorrow another President might use the same power to prevent a wage increase, to curb trade unionists, to regiment labor as oppressively as industry thinks it has been regimented by this seizure.

MR. JUSTICE FRANKFURTER, concurring.

. . . It is absurd to see a dictator in a representative product of the sturdy democratic traditions of the Mississippi Valley. The accretion of dangerous power does not come in a day. It does come, however slowly, from the generative force of unchecked disregard of the restrictions that fence in even the most disinterested assertion of authority. . . .

The Framers, however, did not make the judiciary the overseer of our government. . . . The attitude with which this Court must approach its duty when confronted with such issues is precisely the opposite of that normally manifested by the general public. So-called constitutional questions seem to exercise a mesmeric influence over the popular mind. This eagerness to settle—preferably forever—a specific problem on the basis of the broadest possible constitutional pronouncements may not unfairly be called one of our minor national traits. An English observer of our scene has acutely described it:

> At the first sound of a new argument over the United States Constitution and its interpretation the hearts of Americans leap with a fearful joy. The blood stirs powerfully in their veins and a new lustre brightens their eyes. Like King Harry's men before Harfleur, they stand like greyhounds in the slips, straining upon the start.

The Economist, May 10, 1952. The path of duty for this Court, it bears repetition, lies in the opposite direction. . . . The issue before us can be met, and therefore should be, without attempting to define the President's powers comprehensively. . . .

The question before the Court comes in this setting. Congress has frequently—at least 16 times since 1916—specifically provided for executive seizure of production, transportation, communications, or storage facilities. In every case it has qualified this grant of power with limitations and safeguards. This body of enactments—summarized in tabular form in [a long appendix to Justice Frankfurter's opinion]—demonstrates that Congress deemed seizure so drastic a power as to require that it be carefully circumscribed whenever the President was vested with this extraordinary authority. The power to seize has uniformly been given only for a limited period or for a defined emergency, or has been repealed after a short period. Its exercise has been restricted to particular circumstances such as "time of war or when war is imminent," the needs of "public safety" or of "national security or defense," or "urgent and impending need." The period of governmental operation has been limited, as, for instance, to "sixty days after the restoration of productive efficiency." Seizure statutes usually make executive action dependent on detailed conditions: for example, (a) failure or refusal of the owner of a plant to meet governmental supply needs or (b) failure of voluntary negotiations with the owner for the use of a plant necessary for great public ends. . . .

Congress in 1947 was again called upon to consider whether governmental seizure should be used to avoid serious industrial shutdowns. . . . Under the urgency of telephone and coal strikes in the winter of 1946, Congress addressed itself to the problems raised by 'national emergency' strikes and lockouts. . . .

Authorization for seizure as an available remedy for potential dangers was un-equivocally put aside. The Senate Labor Committee, through its Chairman, explicitly reported to the Senate that a general grant of seizure powers had been considered and rejected in favor of reliance on *ad hoc* legislation, as a particular emergency might call for it. An amendment presented in the House providing that where necessary "to preserve and protect the public health and security" the President might seize any industry in which there is an impending cur-tailment of production, was voted down after debate, by a vote of more than three to one. . . .

It cannot be contended that the President would have had power to issue this order had Congress explicitly negated such authority in formal legislation. Congress has expressed its will to withhold this power from the President as though it had said so in so many words. The authoritatively expressed purpose of Congress to disallow such power to the President . . . could not be more de-cisive if it had been written into [the Taft-Hartley Act]. . . . Congress said to the President, "You may not seize. Please report to us and ask for seizure power if you think it is needed in a specific situation." . . .

To be sure, the content of the three authorities of government is not to be derived from an abstract analysis. The areas are partly interacting, not wholly disjointed. The Constitution is a framework for government. Therefore the way the framework has consistently operated fairly establishes that it has operated according to its true nature. Deeply embedded traditional ways of conduct-ing government cannot supplant the Constitution or legislation, but they give meaning to the words of a text or supply them. It is an inadmissibly narrow conception of American constitutional law to confine it to the words of the Constitution and to disregard the gloss which life has written upon them.

In short, a systematic, unbroken, executive practice, long pursued to the knowledge of the Congress and never before questioned, engaged in by Presi-dents who have also sworn to uphold the Constitution, making as it were such exercise of power part of the structure of our government, may be treated as a gloss on "executive Power" vested in the President by § 1 of Art. II. . . .

No remotely comparable practice can be vouched for executive seizure of property at a time when this country was not at war, in the only constitution-al way in which it can be at war. It would pursue the irrelevant to reopen the controversy over the constitutionality of some acts of Lincoln during the Civil War. Suffice it to say that he seized railroads in territory where armed hostilities had already interrupted the movement of troops to the beleaguered Capitol, and his order was ratified by the Congress. The only other instances of seizures are those during the periods of the first and second World Wars. In his eleven seizures of industrial facilities, President Wilson acted, or at least purported to act, under authority granted by Congress. Thus his seizures cannot be adduced as interpretations by a President of his own powers in the absence of statute.

Down to the World War II period, then, the record is barren of instances comparable to the one before us. Of twelve seizures by President Roosevelt prior to the enactment of the War Labor Disputes Act in June, 1943, three were sanctioned by existing law, and six others were effected after Congress, on December 8, 1941, had declared the existence of a state of war. In this case, reliance on the powers that flow from declared war has been commendably disclaimed by the Solicitor General. Thus the list of executive assertions of the power of seizure in circumstances comparable to the present reduces to three in the six-month period from June to December of 1941. We need not split hairs in comparing those actions to the one before us, though much might be said by way of differentiation. Without passing on their validity, as we are not called upon to do, it suffices to say that these three isolated instances do not add up, either in number, scope, duration or contemporaneous legal justification, to the kind of executive construction of the Constitution [that might make a difference here]. Nor do they come to us sanctioned by long-continued acquiescence of Congress giving decisive weight to a construction by the Executive of its powers.

A scheme of government like ours no doubt at times feels the lack of power to act with complete, all-embracing, swiftly moving authority. No doubt a government with distributed authority, subject to be challenged in the courts of law, at least long enough to consider and adjudicate the challenge, labors under restrictions from which other governments are free. It has not been our tradition to envy such governments. . . .

Mr. Chief Justice Vinson, with whom Mr. Justice Reed and Mr. Justice Minton join, dissenting.

. . . Those who suggest that this is a case involving extraordinary powers should be mindful that these are extraordinary times. A world not yet recovered from the devastation of World War II has been forced to face the threat of another and more terrifying global conflict. . . . For almost two full years, our armed forces have been fighting in Korea, suffering casualties of over 108,000 men. Hostilities have not abated. The "determination of the United Nations to continue its action in Korea to meet the aggression" has been reaffirmed. Congressional support of the action in Korea has been manifested by provisions for increased military manpower and equipment and for economic stabilization, as hereinafter described. . . .

We . . . assume without deciding that the courts may go behind a President's finding of fact that an emergency exists. But there is not the slightest basis for suggesting that the President's finding in this case can be undermined. . . . Defendant . . . fil[ed] uncontroverted affidavits of Government officials describing the facts underlying the President's order. The Secretary of Defense stated that: "We are holding the line [in Korea] with ammunition and not with the lives of our troops." . . . The affidavits emphasize the critical need for steel in our defense program, the absence of appreciable inventories of steel, and the drastic results of any interruption in steel production.

One is not here called upon even to consider the possibility of executive seizure of a farm, a corner grocery store or even a single industrial plant. Such considerations arise only when one ignores the central fact of this case—that the Nation's entire basic steel production would have shut down completely if there had been no Government seizure. Even ignoring for the moment whatever confidential information the President may possess as "the Nation's organ for foreign affairs," the uncontroverted affidavits in this record amply support the finding that "a work stoppage would immediately jeopardize and imperil our national defense." . . .

Accordingly, if the President has any power under the Constitution to meet a critical situation in the absence of express statutory authorization, there is no basis whatever for criticizing the exercise of such power in this case. . . .

The steel mills were seized for a public use. The power of eminent domain, invoked in that case, is an essential attribute of sovereignty and has long been recognized as a power of the Federal Government. . . . Admitting that the Government could seize the mills, plaintiffs claim that the implied power of eminent domain can be exercised only under an

WORTH NOTING

Chief Justice Vinson argued that the Fifth Amendment's takings clause "is no bar to this seizure for, if the taking is not otherwise unlawful, plaintiffs are assured of receiving the required just compensation." See U.S. Const., Amdt. V ("nor shall private property be taken for public use without just compensation").

Act of Congress; under no circumstances, they say, can that power be exercised by the President unless he can point to an express provision in enabling legislation.

[Under this view,] the President's only course in the face of an emergency is to present the matter to Congress and await the final passage of legislation which will enable the Government to cope with threatened disaster. Under this view, the President is left powerless at the very moment when the need for action may be most pressing and when no one, other than he, is immediately capable of action. Under this view, he is left powerless because a power not expressly given to Congress is nevertheless found to rest exclusively with Congress. . . .

The whole of the "executive Power" is vested in the President. Before entering office, the President swears that he "will faithfully execute the Office of President of the United States, and will to the best of [his] Ability, preserve, protect and defend the Constitution of the United States." Art. II, § 1.

This comprehensive grant of the executive power to a single person was bestowed soon after the country had thrown the yoke of monarchy. Only by instilling initiative and vigor in all of the three departments of Government, declared Madison, could tyranny in any form be avoided. Hamilton added:

> Energy in the Executive is a leading character in the definition of good government. It is essential to the protection of the community against foreign attacks; it is not less essential to the steady administration of the laws; to the protection of property against those irregular and high-handed combinations which sometimes interrupt the ordinary course of justice; to the security of liberty against the enterprises and assaults of ambition, of faction, and of anarchy.

The Federalist No. 70. It is thus apparent that the Presidency was deliberately fashioned as an office of power and independence. Of course, the Framers created no autocrat capable of arrogating any power unto himself at any time. But neither did they create an automaton impotent to exercise the powers of Government at a time when the survival of the Republic itself may be at stake. . . .

A review of executive action demonstrates that our Presidents have on many occasions exhibited the leadership contemplated by the Framers when they made the President Commander in Chief, and imposed upon him the trust to "take Care that the Laws be faithfully executed." . . .

In an action furnishing a most apt precedent for this case, President Lincoln without statutory authority directed the seizure of rail and telegraph lines leading to Washington. Many months later, Congress recognized and confirmed the power of the President to seize railroads and telegraph lines and provided criminal penalties for interference with Government operation. This Act did not confer on the President any additional powers of seizure. Congress plainly rejected the view that the President's acts had been without legal sanction until ratified by the legislature. Sponsors of the bill declared that its purpose was only to confirm the power which the President already possessed. Opponents insisted a statute authorizing seizure was unnecessary and might even be construed as limiting existing Presidential powers.

WORTH NOTING

Vinson reviews numerous historical precedents of Presidential initiative, including Washington's response to the Whiskey Rebellion; Jefferson's Louisiana Purchase; Jackson's removal of Government deposits from the Second Bank of the United States; Lincoln's mustering troops; his imposition of a naval blockade, tested in *The Prize Cases*, see pp. 845–849; and his Emancipation Proclamation.

Focusing now on the situation confronting the President on the night of April 8, 1952, we cannot but conclude that the President was performing his duty under the Constitution to "take Care that the Laws be faithfully executed" . . . .

Unlike an administrative commission confined to the enforcement of the statute under which it was created, or the head to a department when administering a particular statute, the President is a constitutional officer charged with taking care that a "mass of legislation" be executed. Flexibility as to mode of execution to meet critical situations is a matter of practical necessity. This practical construction of the "Take Care" clause . . . was adopted by this Court in *In re Neagle*. . . .

Whatever the extent of Presidential power on more tranquil occasions . . . , the single Presidential purpose disclosed on this record is to faithfully execute the laws by acting in an emergency to maintain the status quo, thereby preventing collapse of the legislative programs until Congress could act. The President's action served the same purposes as a judicial stay entered to maintain the status quo in order to preserve the jurisdiction of a court. In his Message to Congress immediately following the seizure, the President explained the necessity of his action in executing the military procurement and anti-inflation legislative programs and expressed his desire to cooperate with any legislative proposals approving, regulating or rejecting the seizure of the steel mills. Consequently, there is no evidence whatever of any Presidential purpose to defy Congress or act in any way inconsistent with the legislative will. . . . Certainly there is no basis for fear of dictatorship when the Executive acts, as he did in this case, only to save the situation until Congress could act. . . .

The broad executive power granted by Article II to an officer on duty 365 days a year cannot, it is said, be invoked to avert disaster. Instead, the President must confine himself to sending a message to Congress recommending action. Under this messenger-boy concept of the Office, the President cannot even act to preserve legislative programs from destruction so that Congress will have something left to act upon. . . .

For Discussion

(1)   The three-part rubric laid out by Jackson's concurrence—subsequently adopted as controlling authority in *Dames & Moore v. Regan* (1981)—is one of the most celebrated analytical frameworks in constitutional law. Jackson put the Youngstown Sheet & Tube seizure in the third category, or "zone," of this rubric. Was he right to do so? Does it make sense to accord significance to Congress's consideration of provisions that it did not adopt?

(2)   Suppose Congress had never considered seizure at all. Would that strengthen or weaken the constitutional case for President Truman's seizure?

(3)   The United States never declared war in Korea. The Truman administration justified America's entry into the conflict under a U.N. Security Council resolution, and then justified the continuation of hostilities on the basis of the congressional appropriations that funded them. Would or should it have made a difference in *Youngstown* if Congress had formally declared war in Korea?

(4)   Suppose that after the Korean conflict began Congress passed a joint resolution declaring that "the President is authorized to use all necessary and appropriate force" to prevail in the conflict. Cf. Authorization for the Use of Military Force, Sept. 18, 2001, p. 851. Which of Jackson's categories would the case be in then? What should the outcome be? Suppose the word "force" were replaced by "means"—what then?

(5) Can you state a situation, real or imagined, that is clearly within Jackson's third category but in which the President's power prevails?

(6) Can you state a situation, real or imagined, that is clearly within Jackson's first category but in which the President's power does not prevail?

B. Powers of the President

1. The President as Regulator-in-Chief

a. The Administrative State

Under the civics class paradigm of regulatory governance, the legislature enacts rules and the executive branch enforces them. In the United States, things have long since ceased to be so simple. Like advanced industrial democracies around the world, U.S. governance responded to the explosion of regulatory needs in an increasingly diverse economy and society by delegating rulemaking authority to executive agencies. Those agencies then use that authority to develop specific rules governing all manner of social economic activity.

With the *Youngstown* analytical framework in mind, this next part offers a survey of some of the President's principal substantive powers. As you read, pay close attention to the sources of authority asserted by the executive branch. Are they constitutional, or statutory? And within either framework, are they express or implied?

The administrative law judge's decision in *Secretary of Labor v. 21st Century Roofing Systems, Inc.* (2011) offers a typical—and rather mundane—example of how this architecture works in practice. The Occupational Safety and Health Administration ("OSHA") is an agency within the Department of Labor. In December 2009, OSHA conducted an inspection of a job site in Taunton, Massachusetts run by 21st Century Roofing Systems, Inc., a roofing contractor. As a result of the inspection, OSHA issued a pair of citations to the contractor: a "serious" citation, for failure to create a warning line at least 6 feet from the roof edge; and a "repeat" citation, for failure to protect employees engaged in roofing activities on a low-sloped roof from falls.

No statute required the warning line or specifically required affirmative protection against falls. Rather, the obligations violated by 21st Century

Roofing were ultimately grounded in § 5(a) of the Occupational Safety and Health Act of 1970. That provision requires "[e]ach employer" with a specified nexus to interstate commerce

(1) [to] furnish to each of his employees employment and a place of employment which are free from recognized hazards that are causing or are likely to cause death or serious physical harm to his employees; [and also]

(2) [to] comply with occupational safety and health standards promulgated under this chapter.

The standards referred to by § 5(a)(2) are promulgated by the Secretary of Labor under § 6 of the Act, which provides that

the Secretary [of Labor] shall, as soon as practicable . . . by rule promulgate as an occupational safety or health standard any national consensus standard, and any established Federal standard, unless he determines that the promulgation of such a standard would not result in improved safety or health for specifically designated employees.

If there is a conflict among such standards, the statute requires the Secretary to "promulgate the standard which assures the greatest protection of the safety or health of the affected employees." Section 8 of Act authorizes the Secretary to inspect workplaces, and § 9 of the Act authorizes the Secretary to issue citations for violations of rules. An employer who "willfully or repeatedly violates" the requirements of § 5 or of a rule is subject to substantial civil penalties.

The Secretary implemented the Act by creating OSHA and charging it with the implementation of the Secretary's principal responsibilities under the Act. Secretary's Order No. 12–71, 36 FR 8754, May 12, 1971. And OSHA has, as Congress intended, promulgated rules under the Act—lots of them. Title 29 of the CFR consists of regulations related to labor, and Part 1926 contains a very long set of regulations of safety and health in construction.

WORTH NOTING

FR stands for "Federal Register." This is a journal of the federal government, published every weekday except for holidays, that contains agency rules, proposed rules, and public notices. Final agency rules are organized by topic and codified in the Code of Federal Regulations (CFR), which is updated annually.

Among the Title 29 regulations are the pair of requirements that 21st Century was charged with violating. The first provision reads as follows:

29 C.F.R. § 1926.501(b)(10)

Roofing work on Low-slope roofs. Except as otherwise provided in paragraph (b) of this section, each employee engaged in roofing activities on low-slope roofs, with unprotected sides and edges 6 feet (1.8 m) or more above lower levels shall be protected from falling by guardrail systems, safety net systems, personal fall arrest systems, or a combination of warning line system and guardrail system, warning ling system and safety net system, or warning line system and personal fall arrest system, or warning line system and safety monitoring system. . . .

The second provision elaborates on the requirements for a satisfactory warning line:

29 C.F.R. § 1926.502(f)(1)

(f) *Warning line systems.* Warning line systems [See § 1926.501(b)(10)] and their use shall comply with the following provisions:

(1) The warning line shall be erected around all sides of the roof work area.

(i) When mechanical equipment is not being used, the warning line shall be erected not less than 6 feet (1.8 m) from the roof edge. . . .

In July 2011, the matter was presented for a formal hearing in Providence, Rhode Island, in front of an Administrative Law Judge (ALJ). ALJs are not Article III judges, appointed by the President with the advice and consent of the Senate. Rather, they are executive officials. The ALJ who heard this case was appointed by the chair of the Occupational Health and Safety Review Commission (an entity created by § 12 of the Act and headed by members appointed by the President with the advice and consent of the Senate). The Secretary was represented by a Labor Department lawyer out of Boston; 21st Century did not appear. (Its president later claimed he had not received notice of the hearing, but the ALJ did not find that credible.) After taking testimony and receiving evidence at the hearing, the ALJ issued an opinion in October 2011 ruling that 21st Century had indeed violated the agency regulations. The ALJ increased the penalties sought by the Secretary, imposing a fine of $2,500 for the "serious" citation and $14,000 for the "repeat" citation. These fines became final when the Commission did not review them within 30 days.

The administrative actions in *21st Century Roofing* were uncontroversially authorized by statute. And if the defendant roofing company was dissatisfied with the result, it was entitled to challenge the agency ruling through a limited though serious form of judicial review in federal court under the Administrative Procedure Act. (The details of that regime occupy weeks of class time in courses like administrative law or legislation and regulation.) But were the agency's actions *constitutional*? And, even if constitutional, did they threaten liberty and the process by which we purport to be a self-governing people? In thinking about that question, consider the following excerpts.

The Federalist No. 47 (James Madison)

February 1, 1788

To the People of the State of New York:

One of the principal objections inculcated by the more respectable adversaries to the Constitution, is its supposed violation of the political maxim, that the legislative, executive, and judiciary departments ought to be separate and distinct. In the structure of the federal government, no regard, it is said, seems to have been paid to this essential precaution in favor of liberty. The several departments of power are distributed and blended in such a manner as at once to destroy all symmetry and beauty of form. . . .

No political truth is certainly of greater intrinsic value, or is stamped with the authority of more enlightened patrons of liberty, than that on which the objection is founded. The accumulation of all powers, legislative, executive, and judiciary, in the same hands, whether of one, a few, or many, and whether hereditary, self appointed, or elective, may justly be pronounced the very definition of tyranny. . . .

The oracle who is always consulted and cited on this subject is the celebrated Montesquieu. . . . The British Constitution was to Montesquieu what Homer has been to the didactic writers on epic poetry. . . . [Madison reviews aspects of the British Constitution, and points out that "the legislative, executive, and judiciary departments are by no means totally separate and distinct from each other" in Great Britain. For example, the Crown formed "an integral part of the legislative authority," made treaties that could have "the force of legislative acts," and appointed judges. And the House of Lords served as the court of impeachment and the supreme appellate court.]

From these facts, . . . it may clearly be inferred that, in saying "There can be no liberty where the legislative and executive powers are united in the same person, or body of magistrates[." Montesquieu] did not mean that these departments ought to have no partial agency in, or no control over, the acts of each other. His meaning, as his own words import, and still more conclusively as illustrated by the example in his eye, can amount to no more than this, that where the whole power of one department is exercised by the same hands which possess the whole power of another department, the fundamental principles of a free constitution are subverted. This would have been the case in the constitution examined by him, if the king, who is the sole executive magistrate, had possessed also the complete legislative power, or the supreme administration of justice; or if the entire legislative body had possessed the supreme judiciary, or the supreme executive authority. This, however, is not among the vices of that constitution. . . .

The reasons on which Montesquieu grounds his maxim are a further demonstration of his meaning. "When the legislative and executive powers are united in the same person or body," says he, "there can be no liberty, because apprehensions may arise lest the same monarch or senate should enact tyrannical laws to execute them in a tyrannical manner." Again: "Were the power of judging joined with the legislative, the life and liberty of the subject would be exposed to arbitrary control, for the judge would then be the legislator. Were it joined to the executive power, the judge might behave with all the violence of an oppressor." Some of these reasons are more fully explained in other passages;

but briefly stated as they are here, they sufficiently establish the meaning which we have put on this celebrated maxim of this celebrated author. . . .

The Federalist No. 37 (James Madison)

January 11, 1788

The boundaries between the great kingdom of nature, and, still more, between the various provinces, and lesser portions, into which they are subdivided, afford another illustration of the same important truth. The most sagacious and laborious naturalists have never yet succeeded in tracing with certainty the line which separates the district of vegetable life from the neighboring region of unorganized matter, or which marks the [t]ermination of the former and the commencement of the animal empire. A still greater obscurity lies in the distinctive characters by which the objects in each of these great departments of nature have been arranged and assorted.

When we pass from the works of nature, in which all the delineations are perfectly accurate, and appear to be otherwise only from the imperfection of the eye which surveys them, to the institutions of man, in which the obscurity arises as well from the object itself as from the organ by which it is contemplated, we must perceive the necessity of moderating still further our expectations and hopes from the efforts of human sagacity. Experience has instructed us that no skill in the science of government has yet been able to discriminate and define, with sufficient certainty, its three great provinces the legislative, executive, and judiciary; or even the privileges and powers of the different legislative branches. Questions daily occur in the course of practice, which prove the obscurity which reins in these subjects, and which puzzle the greatest adepts in political science.

David Dyzenhaus, The Constitution of Law: Legality in a Time of Emergency

2006

[A] grey hole is a legal space in which there are some legal constraints on executive action—it is not a lawless void—but the constraints are so insubstantial that they pretty well permit government to do as it pleases. In addition, since such grey holes permit government to have its cake and eat it too, to seem to be governing not only by law but in accordance with the rule of law, they and their endorsement by judges and academics might be even more dangerous [for] the rule of law than true black holes.

Nicholas Bagley, The Procedure Fetish

118 Mich. L. Rev. 345 (2019)

Here's the standard story: Agencies house executive, legislative, and judicial functions under one roof, in apparent contravention of the lawmaking process described in the Constitution. They thus evade the checks and balances that are supposed to channel federal power. Agencies are also said to labor under an acute democratic deficit: they lack the populist pedigree of either the legislature or the president, yet they wield immense government power. . . .

It's almost impossible to overstate how entrenched this perspective has become. To judge from the casebooks, students are barely introduced to the administrative state before they are told of its enduring "tension" with the constitutional separation of powers. Endless law review pages have been devoted to defending the view that separation-of-powers principles inspire or even compel various aspects of administrative law. The warnings in the case law are dark: Chief Justice Roberts, in deploring the rise of federal agencies, is apt to quote James Madison for the view that the "accumulation of all powers, legislative, executive, and judiciary, in the same hands . . . may justly be pronounced the very definition of tyranny." The lesson is clear: the modern administrative state is a regrettable symptom of constitutional decay. . . .

It is long past time to retire this line of reasoning. James Freedman noted almost a half-century ago that anxiety about "the place and function of the administrative process in American government" has been with us from the outset, yielding an "enduring sense of crisis historically associated with the administrative agencies." But a crisis that endures is not a crisis; it is the steady state. Agencies have wielded legislative, executive, and judicial powers from the beginning of the Republic. Their proliferation was essential to the prosecution of two world wars, to the rise of the post-New Deal welfare state, and to the regulation of novel risks ranging from automobile safety to industrial pollution. Measured against any theory of constitutional interpretation to which liberals claim fealty—whether that's common law constitutionalism, settlement through historical practice, or the liquidation of constitutional principles—the administrative state's undiminished persistence stands as a convincing refutation of the view that it's somehow constitutionally suspect. There must be an expiration date for worrying about the fundamental consistency of the administrative state with our constitutional structure. Surely that date has passed. . . .

b.   Delegation Doctrine and Its Consequences

As the bureaucratization of American governance accelerated in the early twentieth century, political anxiety about consolidated power increased as well. The cases and excerpts that follow explore the conceptual and pragmatic concerns that motivated the Supreme Court to announce judicially enforceable limits on administrative delegations of rulemaking power—and then to back off from those limits almost entirely.

As late as 1933, the Court appeared to take a relatively tolerant approach to delegation of legislative authority. See, *e.g., J.W. Hampton, Jr. & Co. v. United States* (1928) (upholding a provision of the Tariff Act of 1922 that allowed the President to vary tariff rates, because the statute articulated "an intelligible principle" to which he had to conform); *Federal Radio Commission v. Nelson Brothers Bond & Mortgage Co.* (1933) (holding that Commission's authority to allocate radio licenses "as public convenience, interest, or necessity requires" was sufficiently specific to pass constitutional scrutiny). But that year marked the beginning of the New Deal, and with it a dramatic expansion not only of the exercise of federal power but also of delegation of authority to the executive. One of the keystones of the New Deal was the 1933 National Industrial Recovery Act (NIRA). Two years after its enactment, the NIRA prompted a pair of Supreme Court decisions on legislative delegation to regulatory agencies.

The first of these was *Panama Refining Co. v. Ryan* (1935), which involved a narrow provision of the NIRA, § 9(c), authorizing the President to ban the shipment in interstate or foreign commerce of "hot oil" (essentially, petroleum that was produced or withdrawn from storage in excess of state quotas intended to prevent oversupply). Writing for all the members of the Court besides Cardozo, Chief Justice Hughes held that this was an improper delegation of legislative authority:

The President was not required to ascertain and proclaim the conditions prevailing in the industry which made the prohibition necessary. The Congress left the matter to the President without standard or rule, to be dealt with as he pleased. [However construed, the Act] permits such a breadth of authorized action as essentially to commit to the President the functions of a Legislature, rather than those of an executive or administrative officer executing a declared legislative policy.

Cardozo, dissenting, thought this was mildly hysterical. In his view, § 9(c) was a narrow grant of authority to take only one specific action: the prohibition of hot oil. And the express statutory policies—"to eliminate unfair competitive practices," "to conserve natural resources," to "promote the fullest possible utilization of the present productive capacity of industries," and to "avoid undue restriction of production" except as "temporarily required"—provided sufficient guidance to the President in exercising his authority. "Discretion is not unconfined and vagrant," Cardozo wrote. "It is canalized within banks that keep it from overflowing."

The second case, *A.L.A. Schechter Poultry Corp. v. United States* (1935), was very different. Recall that § 3 of the NIRA authorized the President, either on his own initiative or on application by a trade group, to promulgate a "code of fair competition" for a particular industry that would immediately have the force of law.

 CROSS REFERENCE We have seen the *Schechter* case already in Chapter III, pp. 414–420.

These codes could specify unfair trade practices; prescribe wages, hours, and other employment conditions for the industry; and require collective bargaining. The President used this authority to promulgate extremely detailed codes governing many industries; the famous Blue Eagle of the National Recovery Administration became one of the enduring symbols of the New Deal. In the portion of the case presented in Chapter III, the Supreme Court held that § 3 exceeded Congress's power under the Commerce Clause. The portion presented here analyzes whether, in promulgating a Live Poultry Code under § 3, the President exercised rule-making authority that could not be constitutionally delegated to him. *Schechter* is often referred to as "the sick chicken case" because one of the code violations charged was that the Schechter brothers had sold a diseased chicken.

A.L.A. Schechter Poultry Corporation v. United States

Supreme Court of the United States, 1935.
295 U.S. 495.

MR. CHIEF JUSTICE HUGHES delivered the opinion of the Court.

Petitioners . . . were convicted in the District Court of the United States for the Eastern District of New York on eighteen counts of an indictment charging violations of what is known as the "Live Poultry Code," and on an additional count for conspiracy to commit such violations. . . . The "Live Poultry Code" was promulgated under section 3 of the [1933] National Industrial Recovery Act. That section . . . authorizes the President to approve "codes of fair competition."

Such a code may be approved for a trade or industry, upon application by one or more trade or industrial associations or groups, if the President finds (1) that such associations or groups "impose no inequitable restrictions on admission to membership therein and are truly representative," and (2) that such codes are not designed "to promote monopolies or to eliminate or oppress small enterprises and will not operate to discriminate against them, and will tend to effectuate the policy" of Title 1 of the Act. Such codes "shall not permit monopolies or monopolistic practices." As a condition of his approval, the President may "impose such conditions (including requirements for the making of reports and the keeping of accounts) for the protection of consumers, competitors, employees, and others, and in furtherance of the public interest, and may provide such exceptions to and exemptions from the provisions of such code as the President in his discretion deems necessary to effectuate the policy herein declared."

Where such a code has not been approved, the President may prescribe one, either on his own motion or on complaint. Violation of any provision of a code (so approved or prescribed) "in any transaction in or affecting interstate or foreign commerce" is made a misdemeanor punishable by a fine of not more than $500 for each offense, and each day the violation continues is to be deemed a separate offense.

The "Live Poultry Code" was approved by the President on April 13, 1934. Its divisions indicate its nature and scope. The Code has eight articles entitled (1) purposes, (2) definitions, (3) hours, (4) wages, (5) general labor provisions, (6) administration, (7) trade practice provisions, and (8) general. . . . The Code fixes the number of hours for workdays. It provides that no employee, with certain exceptions, shall be permitted to work in excess of forty hours in any one week, and that no employees, save as stated, "shall be paid in any pay period less than at the rate of fifty (50) cents per hour." The article containing "general labor provisions" prohibits the employment of any person under 16 years of age, and declares that employees shall have the right of "collective bargaining" and freedom of choice with respect to labor organizations. . . . The minimum number of employees, who shall be employed by slaughterhouse operators, is fixed; the number being graduated according to the average volume of weekly sales.

The President approved the Code by an executive order. . . .

The Question of the Delegation of Legislative Power.—

We recently had occasion to review the pertinent decisions and the general principles which govern the determination of this question. *Panama Refining Company v. Ryan* (1935). The Constitution provides that "All legislative powers herein granted shall be vested in a Congress of the United States, which shall consist of a Senate and House of Representatives." Article 1, § 1. And the Congress is authorized "To make all Laws which shall be necessary and proper for carrying into execution" its general powers. Article 1, § 8, par. 18.

The Congress is not permitted to abdicate or to transfer to others the essential legislative functions with which it is thus vested. We have repeatedly recognized the necessity of adapting legislation to complex conditions involving a host of details with which the national Legislature cannot deal directly. We pointed out in the *Panama Refining Company Case* that the Constitution has never been regarded as denying to Congress the necessary resources of flexibility and practicality, which will enable it to perform its function in laying down policies and establishing standards, while leaving to selected instrumentalities the making of subordinate rules within prescribed limits and the determination of facts to which the policy as declared by the Legislature is to apply. But we said that the constant recognition of the necessity and validity of such provisions, and the wide range of administrative authority which has been developed by means of them, cannot be allowed to obscure the limitations of the authority to delegate, if our constitutional system is to be maintained.

Accordingly, we look to the statute to see whether Congress has overstepped these limitations—whether Congress in authorizing "codes of fair competition" has itself established the standards of legal obligation, thus performing its essential legislative function, or, by the failure to enact such standards, has attempted to transfer that function to others. . . .

What is meant by "fair competition" as the term is used in the Act? Does it refer to a category established in the law, and is the authority to make codes limited accordingly? Or is it used as a convenient designation for whatever set of laws the formulators of a code for a particular trade or industry may propose and the President may approve (subject to certain restrictions), or the President may himself prescribe, as being wise and beneficient provisions for the government of the trade or industry in order to accomplish the broad purposes of rehabilitation, correction, and expansion which are stated in the first section of Title 1?

The Act does not define "fair competition." . . . Unfairness in competition has been predicated of acts which lie outside the ordinary course of business and are tainted by fraud or coercion or conduct otherwise prohibited by law. But it is evident that in its widest range, "unfair competition," as it has been understood in the law, does not reach the objectives of the codes which are authorized by the National Industrial Recovery Act. The codes may, indeed, cover conduct which existing law condemns, but they are not limited to conduct of that sort. The Government does not contend that the act contemplates such a limitation. It would be opposed both to the declared purposes of the Act and to its administrative construction.

The Federal Trade Commission Act introduced the expression "unfair methods of competition," which were declared to be unlawful. That was an expression new in the law. . . . We have said that the substituted phrase has a broader meaning, that it does not admit of precise definition; its scope being left to judicial determination as controversies arise. *Federal Trade Commission v. Raladam Co.* (1931). What are "unfair methods of competition" are thus to be determined in particular instances, upon evidence, in the light of particular competitive conditions and of what is found to be a specific and substantial public interest. To make this possible, Congress set up a special procedure. A commission, a quasi judicial body, was created. Provision was made for formal complaint, for notice and hearing, for appropriate findings of fact supported by adequate evidence, and for judicial review to give assurance that the action of the commission is taken within its statutory authority.

In providing for codes, the National Industrial Recovery Act dispenses with this administrative procedure and with any administrative procedure of an analogous character. But the difference between the code plan of the Recovery

Act and the scheme of the Federal Trade Commission Act lies not only in procedure but in subject-matter. . . . The "fair competition" of the codes has a much broader range and a new significance. . . .

For a statement of the authorized objectives and content of the "codes of fair competition," we are referred repeatedly to the "Declaration of Policy" in section one of Title 1 of the Recovery Act. . . . It is there declared to be "the policy of Congress"—

> to remove obstructions to the free flow of interstate and foreign commerce which tend to diminish the amount thereof; and to provide for the general welfare by promoting the organization of industry for the purpose of cooperative action among trade groups, to induce and maintain united action of labor and management under adequate governmental sanctions and supervision, to eliminate unfair competitive practices, to promote the fullest possible utilization of the present productive capacity of industries, to avoid undue restriction of production (except as may be temporarily required), to increase the consumption of industrial and agricultural products by increasing purchasing power, to reduce and relieve unemployment, to improve standards of labor, and otherwise to rehabilitate industry and to conserve natural resources.

Under § 3, whatever "may tend to effectuate" these general purposes may be included in the "codes of fair competition."

We think the conclusion is inescapable that the authority sought to be conferred by § 3 was not merely to deal with "unfair competitive practices" which offend against existing law, and could be the subject of judicial condemnation without further legislation, or to create administrative machinery for the application of established principles of law to particular instances of violation. Rather, the purpose is clearly disclosed to authorize new and controlling prohibitions through codes of laws which would embrace what the formulators would propose, and what the President would approve or prescribe, as wise and beneficient measures for the government of trades and industries in order to bring about their rehabilitation, correction, and development, according to the general declaration of policy in section one. Codes of laws of this sort are styled "codes of fair competition."

The Government urges that the codes will "consist of rules of competition deemed fair for each industry by representative members of that industry— by the persons most vitally concerned and most familiar with its problems." Instances are cited in which Congress has availed itself of such assistance; as, e.g., in the exercise of its authority over the public domain, with respect to the recognition of local customs or rules of miners as to mining claims, Act of July 26, 1866, or, in matters of a more or less technical nature, as in designating the standard height of drawbars. Act of March 2, 1893. But would it be seriously contended that Congress could delegate its legislative authority to trade or industrial associations or groups so as to empower them to enact the laws they deem to be wise and beneficent for the rehabilitation and expansion of their trade or industries? Could trade or industrial associations or groups be constituted legislative bodies for that purpose because such associations or groups are familiar with the problems of their enterprises? And could an effort of that sort be made valid by such a preface of generalities as to permissible aims as we find in section 1 of title I? The answer is obvious. Such a delegation of legislative power is unknown to our law, and is utterly inconsistent with the constitutional prerogatives and duties of Congress.

The question, then, turns upon the authority which § 3 of the Recovery Act vests in the President to approve or prescribe. If the codes have standing as penal statutes, this must be due to the effect of the executive action. But Congress cannot delegate legislative power to the President to exercise an unfettered discretion to make whatever laws he thinks may be needed or advisable for the rehabilitation and expansion of trade or industry. See *Panama Refining Company v. Ryan* and cases there reviewed.

Accordingly we turn to the Recovery Act to ascertain what limits have been set to the exercise of the President's discretion: *First*, the President, as a condition of approval, is required to find that the trade or industrial associations or groups which propose a code "impose no inequitable restrictions on admission to membership" and are "truly representative." That condition, however, relates only to the status of the initiators of the new laws and not to the permissible scope of such laws. *Second*, the President is required to find that the code is not "designed to promote monopolies or to eliminate or oppress small enterprises and will not operate to discriminate against them." And to this is added a proviso that the code "shall not permit monopolies or monopolistic practices." But these restrictions leave virtually untouched the field of policy envisaged by section one, and, in that wide field of legislative possibilities, the proponents of a code, refraining from monopolistic designs, may roam at will, and the President may approve or disapprove their proposals as he may see fit. That is the precise effect of the further finding that the President is to make—that the code "will tend to effectuate the policy of this title." While this is called a finding, it is really but a statement of an opinion as to the general effect upon the promotion of trade or industry of a scheme of laws. . . .

Nor is the breadth of the President's discretion left to the necessary implications of this limited requirement as to his findings. As already noted, the President in approving a code may impose his own conditions, adding to or taking from what is proposed, as "in his discretion" he thinks necessary "to effectuate the policy" declared by the act. Of course, he has no less liberty when he prescribes a code on his own motion or on complaint, and he is free to prescribe one if a code has not been approved. . . . And this authority relates to a host of different trades and industries, thus extending the President's discretion to all the varieties of laws which he may deem to be beneficial in dealing with the vast array of commercial and industrial activities throughout the country.

Such a sweeping delegation of legislative power finds no support in the decisions upon which the government especially relies. [W]e have held that the Radio Act of 1927 established standards to govern radio communications, and, in view of the limited number of available broadcasting frequencies, Congress authorized allocation and licenses. The Federal Radio Commission was created as the licensing authority, in order to secure a reasonable equality of opportunity in radio transmission and reception. The authority of the Commission to grant licenses "as public convenience, interest or necessity requires" was limited by the nature of radio communications, and by the scope, character, and quality of the services to be rendered and the relative advantages to be derived through distribution of facilities. These standards established by Congress were to be enforced upon hearing and evidence by an administrative body acting under statutory restrictions adapted to the particular activity. *Federal Radio Commission v. Nelson Brothers Bond & Mtg. Co.* (1933). . . .

To summarize and conclude upon this point: Section 3 of the Recovery Act is without precedent. It supplies no standards for any trade, industry, or activity. It does not undertake to prescribe rules of conduct to be applied to particular states of fact determined by appropriate administrative procedure. Instead of prescribing rules of conduct, it authorizes the making of codes to prescribe them. For that legislative undertaking, § 3 sets up no standards, aside from the statement of the general aims of rehabilitation, correction, and expansion described in section one. In view of the scope of that broad declaration and of the nature of the few restrictions that are imposed, the discretion of the President in approving or prescribing codes, and thus enacting laws for the government of trade and industry throughout the country, is virtually unfettered. We think that the code-making authority thus conferred is an unconstitutional delegation of legislative power. . . .

[W]e hold the code provisions here in question to be invalid and that the judgment of conviction must be reversed.

MR. JUSTICE CARDOZO, concurring.

The delegated power of legislation which has found expression in this code is not canalized within banks that keep it from overflowing. It is unconfined and vagrant, if I may borrow my own words in an earlier opinion. *Panama Refining Co. v. Ryan.* . . . Here, in the case before us, is an attempted delegation not confined to any single act nor to any class or group of acts identified or described by reference to a standard. Here in effect is a roving commission to inquire into evils and upon discovery correct them.

I have said that there is no standard, definite or even approximate, to which legislation must conform. Let me make my meaning more precise. If codes of fair competition are codes eliminating "unfair" methods of competition ascertained upon inquiry to prevail in one industry or another, there is no unlawful delegation of legislative functions when the President is directed to inquire into such practices and denounce them when discovered. For many years a like power has been committed to the Federal Trade Commission with the approval of this court in a long series of decisions. Delegation in such circumstances is born of the necessities of the occasion. The industries of the country are too many and diverse to make it possible for Congress, in respect of matters such as these, to legislate directly with adequate appreciation of varying conditions. Nor is the substance of the power changed because the President may act at the instance of trade or industrial associations having special knowledge of the facts. Their function is strictly advisory; it is the *imprimatur* of the President that begets the quality of law. When the task that is set before one is that of cleaning house, it is prudent as well as usual to take counsel of the dwellers.

But there is another conception of codes of fair competition, their significance and function, which leads to very different consequences. . . . By this other conception a code is not to be restricted to the elimination of business practices that would be characterized by general acceptance as oppressive or unfair. It is to include whatever ordinances may be desirable or helpful for the well-being or prosperity of the industry affected. In that view, the function of its adoption is not merely negative, but positive; the planning of improvements as well as the extirpation of abuses. What is fair, as thus conceived, is not something to be contrasted with what is unfair or fraudulent or tricky. The extension becomes as wide as the field of industrial regulation. If that conception shall prevail, anything that Congress may do within the limits of the commerce clause for the betterment of business may be done by the President upon the recommendation of a trade association by calling it a code. This is delegation running riot. No such plenitude of power is susceptible of transfer. The statute, however, aims at nothing less, as one can learn both from its terms and from the administrative practice under it. Nothing less is aimed at by the code now submitted to our scrutiny. . . .

One of the new rules, the source of ten counts in the indictment, is aimed at an established practice, not unethical or oppressive, the practice of selective buying. Many others could be instanced as open to the same objection if the sections of the code were to be examined one by one. . . . What is excessive is not sporadic or superficial. It is deep-seated and pervasive. The licit and illicit sections are so combined and welded as to be incapable of severance without destructive mutilation. . . .

I am authorized to state that Mr. Justice Stone joins in this opinion.

As the next case shows, the Supreme Court quickly abandoned what turned out to be its brief New Deal experiment with the serious application of a non-delegation doctrine.

Whitman v. American Trucking Associations, Inc.

Supreme Court of the United States, 2001.
531 U.S. 457.

Justice Scalia delivered the opinion of the Court.

[The Clean Air Act] requires the Administrator of the [Environmental Protection Agency (EPA)] to promulgate [national ambient air quality standards ("NAAQS")] for each air pollutant for which "air quality criteria" have been issued [by the agency.]

[O]n July 18, 1997, the Administrator revised the NAAQS for particulate matter and ozone. American Trucking Associations, Inc. and its co-respondents . . . challenged the new standards in the Court of Appeals for the District of Columbia Circuit. The District of Columbia Circuit [held that the Clean Air Act] delegated legislative power to the Administrator in contravention of the United States Constitution, Art. I, § 1, because it found that the EPA had interpreted the statute to provide no "intelligible principle" to guide the agency's exercise of authority. . . .

Section 109(b)(1) of the CAA instructs the EPA to set "ambient air quality standards the attainment and maintenance of which in the judgment of the Administrator, based on [EPA research] and allowing an adequate margin of safety, are requisite to protect the public health." The Court of Appeals held that this section as interpreted by the Administrator did not provide an "intelligible principle" to guide the EPA's exercise of authority in setting NAAQS. "[The] EPA," it said, "lack[ed] any determinate criteria for drawing lines. It has failed to state intelligibly how much is too much." The court hence found that the EPA's interpretation (but not the statute itself) violated the nondelegation doctrine. We disagree.

In a delegation challenge, the constitutional question is whether the statute has delegated legislative power to the agency. Article I, § 1, of the Constitution vests "[a]ll legislative Powers herein granted . . . in a Congress of the United States." This text permits no delegation of those powers, and so we repeatedly have said that when Congress confers decisionmaking authority upon agencies *Congress* must "lay down by legislative act an intelligible principle to which the person or body authorized to [act] is directed to conform." *J.W. Hampton, Jr., & Co. v. United States* (1928). We have never suggested that an agency can cure an unlawful delegation of legislative power by adopting in its discretion a limiting

construction of the statute. . . . The idea that an agency can cure an unconstitutionally standardless delegation of power by declining to exercise some of that
power seems to us internally contradictory. The very choice of which portion
of the power to exercise—that is to say, the prescription of the standard that
Congress had omitted—would *itself* be an exercise of the forbidden legislative
authority. Whether the statute delegates legislative power is a question for the
courts, and an agency's voluntary self-denial has no bearing upon the answer.

We agree with the Solicitor General that the text of § 109(b)(1) of the
CAA at a minimum requires that "[f]or a discrete set of pollutants and based
on published air quality criteria that reflect the latest scientific knowledge, [the]
EPA must establish uniform national standards at a level that is requisite to
protect public health from the adverse effects of the pollutant in the ambient
air." Requisite, in turn, "mean[s] sufficient, but not more than necessary." These
limits on the EPA's discretion are strikingly similar to the ones we approved in
Touby v. United States (1991), which permitted the Attorney General to designate a drug as a controlled substance for purposes of criminal drug enforcement
if doing so was " 'necessary to avoid an imminent hazard to the public safety.' "
They also resemble the Occupational Safety and Health Act of 1970 provision
requiring the agency to " 'set the standard which most adequately assures, to
the extent feasible, on the basis of the best available evidence, that no employee
will suffer any impairment of health' "—which the Court upheld in *Industrial
Union Dept., AFL-CIO v. American Petroleum Institute* (1980), and which even
then-Justice Rehnquist, who alone in that case thought the statute violated the
nondelegation doctrine, would have upheld if, like the statute here, it did not
permit economic costs to be considered.

The scope of discretion § 109(b)(1) allows is in fact well within the outer
limits of our nondelegation precedents. In the history of the Court we have
found the requisite "intelligible principle" lacking in only two statutes, one of
which provided literally no guidance for the exercise of discretion, and the other
of which conferred authority to regulate the entire economy on the basis of no
more precise a standard than stimulating the economy by assuring "fair competition." See *Panama Refining Co.* v. *Ryan* (1935); *A.L.A. Schechter Poultry Corp.
v. United States* (1935). We have, on the other hand, upheld the validity of the
Public Utility Holding Company Act of 1935, which gave the Securities and
Exchange Commission authority to modify the structure of holding company
systems so as to ensure that they are not "unduly or unnecessarily complicate[d]"
and do not "unfairly or inequitably distribute voting power among security

holders." *American Power & Light Co. v. SEC* (1946). We have approved the wartime conferral of agency power to fix the prices of commodities at a level that " 'will be generally fair and equitable and will effectuate the [in some respects conflicting] purposes of th[e] Act.' " *Yakus v. United States* (1944). And we have found an "intelligible principle" in various statutes authorizing regulation in the "public interest." See, *e.g.*, *National Broadcasting Co. v. United States* (1943) (Federal Communications Commission's power to regulate airwaves); *New York Central Securities Corp. v. United States* (1932) (Interstate Commerce Commission's power to approve railroad consolidations). In short, we have "almost never felt qualified to second-guess Congress regarding the permissible degree of policy judgment that can be left to those executing or applying the law." *Mistretta v. United States* (1989) (Scalia, J., dissenting).

WORTH NOTING The Court did not mention *Carter v. Carter Coal Co.* (1936), see pp. 420–426, which held invalid a portion of the Bituminous Coal Conservation Act of 1935 in part on the ground that it was an improper delegation of legislative authority. The *Carter* Court held that the provision in question was legislative delegation "in its most obnoxious form" because it was "not even delegation to an official or an official body, presumptively disinterested, but to private persons whose interests may be and often are adverse to the interests of others in the same business."

It is true enough that the degree of agency discretion that is acceptable varies according to the scope of the power congressionally conferred. While Congress need not provide any direction to the EPA regarding the manner in which it is to define "country elevators," which are to be exempt from new-stationary-source regulations governing grain elevators, it must provide substantial guidance on setting air standards that affect the entire national economy. But even in sweeping regulatory schemes we have never demanded, as the Court of Appeals did here, that statutes provide a "determinate criterion" for saying "how much [of the regulated harm] is too much." In *Touby*, for example, we did not require the statute to decree how "imminent" was too imminent, or how "necessary" was necessary enough, or even—most relevant here—how "hazardous" was too hazardous. Similarly, the statute at issue in *Lichter* authorized agencies to recoup "excess profits" paid under wartime Government contracts, yet we did not insist that Congress specify how much profit was too much. . . . Section 109(b)(1) of the CAA, which to repeat we interpret as requiring the EPA to set air quality standards at the level that is "requisite"—that is, not lower or higher than is necessary—to protect the public health with an adequate margin of safety, fits comfortably within the scope of discretion permitted by our precedent.

We therefore reverse the judgment of the Court of Appeals remanding for reinterpretation that would avoid a supposed delegation of legislative power. . . .

JUSTICE THOMAS, concurring.

I agree with the majority that § 109's directive to the agency is no less an "intelligible principle" than a host of other directives that we have approved. . . . I write separately, however, to express my concern that there may nevertheless be a genuine constitutional problem with § 109, a problem which the parties did not address.

Although this Court since 1928 has treated the "intelligible principle" requirement as the only constitutional limit on congressional grants of power to administrative agencies, the Constitution does not speak of "intelligible principles." Rather, it speaks in much simpler terms: "*All* legislative Powers herein granted shall be vested in a Congress." U.S. Const., Art. 1, § 1 (emphasis added). I am not convinced that the intelligible principle doctrine serves to prevent all cessions of legislative power. I believe that there are cases in which the principle is intelligible and yet the significance of the delegated decision is simply too great for the decision to be called anything other than "legislative."

As it is, none of the parties to these cases has examined the text of the Constitution or asked us to reconsider our precedents on cessions of legislative power. On a future day, however, I would be willing to address the question whether our delegation jurisprudence has strayed too far from our Founders' understanding of separation of powers.

JUSTICE STEVENS, with whom JUSTICE SOUTER joins, concurring in part and concurring in the judgment.

Section 109(b)(1) delegates to the Administrator of the Environmental Protection Agency (EPA) the authority to promulgate national ambient air quality standards (NAAQS). . . . I wholeheartedly endorse the Court's result and endorse its explanation of its reasons, albeit with the following caveat.

WORTH NOTING

Justice Breyer also wrote a separate opinion, concurring in part and concurring in the judgment. He joined the portion of the Court's opinion addressing delegation, but disagreed with the rationale of another portion of the opinion.

The Court has two choices. We could choose to articulate our ultimate disposition of this issue by frankly acknowledging that the power delegated to the EPA is "legislative" but nevertheless conclude that the delegation is constitutional because adequately limited by the terms of the authorizing statute. Alternatively, we could pretend, as the Court does, that the authority delegated to the EPA is somehow not "legislative power." Despite the fact that there is language in our opinions that supports the Court's articulation of our holding, I am persuaded that it would be both wiser and more faithful to what we have actually done in delegation cases to admit that agency rulemaking authority is "legislative power."

The proper characterization of governmental power should generally depend on the nature of the power, not on the identity of the person exercising it. See Black's Law Dictionary (1990) (defining "legislation" as, *inter alia*, "[f]ormulation of rule[s] for the future"); K. Davis & R. Pierce, *Administrative Law Treatise* (1994) ("If legislative power means the power to make rules of conduct that bind everyone based on resolution of major policy issues, scores of agencies exercise legislative power routinely by promulgating what are candidly called 'legislative rules' "). If the NAAQS that the EPA promulgated had been prescribed by Congress, everyone would agree that those rules would be the product of an exercise of "legislative power." The same characterization is appropriate when an agency exercises rulemaking authority pursuant to a permissible delegation from Congress.

My view is not only more faithful to normal English usage, but is also fully consistent with the text of the Constitution. In Article I, the Framers vested "All legislative Powers" in the Congress, just as in Article II they vested the "executive Power" in the President. Those provisions do not purport to limit the authority of either recipient of power to delegate authority to others. . . . Surely the authority granted to members of the Cabinet and federal law enforcement agents is properly characterized as "Executive" even though not exercised by the President. Cf. *Morrison v. Olson* (1988) (Scalia, J., dissenting) (arguing that the independent counsel exercised "executive power" unconstrained by the President).

It seems clear that an executive agency's exercise of rulemaking authority pursuant to a valid delegation from Congress is "legislative." As long as the delegation provides a sufficiently intelligible principle, there is nothing inherently unconstitutional about it. Accordingly, while I . . . agree with almost everything said [by the Court], I would hold that when Congress enacted § 109, it effected a constitutional delegation of legislative power to the EPA.

Suppose Congress passed a statute providing as follows:

> The President is authorized to promulgate any regulation that would be within the power of Congress to enact as a statute, and will, in the judgment of the President, advance the public health, safety, and welfare. Any regulation so promulgated shall have the same force as if were enacted by statute.

FOR DISCUSSION

Would that statute be constitutional?

All nine justices in *Whitman v. American Trucking* voted to uphold the statute. The unanimity of opinion was so striking that many observers thought the case had effectively put paid to nondelegation doctrine for once and for all. Eighteen years later, however, *Gundy v. United States* (2019) indicated that changes in the Court's membership might make it possible to revisit the question. The case considered a provision of the Sex Offender Registration and Notification Act (SORNA) providing that "[t]he Attorney General shall have the authority to specify the applicability" of the statute's registration requirements to persons who had committed sex offenses before SORNA's enactment.

A four-justice plurality relied heavily on *Whitman* in rejecting the constitutional challenge:

> The nondelegation doctrine bars Congress from transferring its legislative power to another branch of Government. This case requires us to decide whether . . . the Sex Offender Registration and Notification Act (SORNA), violates that doctrine. We hold it does not. Under § 20913(d), the Attorney General must apply SORNA's registration requirements as soon as feasible to offenders convicted before the statute's enactment. That delegation easily passes constitutional muster.

Justice Alito concurred in the judgment, conceding that current doctrine supported the majority's holding. He concluded, however, that "if a majority of this Court were willing to reconsider the approach we have taken for the past 84 years, I would support that effort."

Justices Gorsuch, joined by Chief Justice Roberts and Justice Thomas, dissented:

If Congress could pass off its legislative power to the executive branch, the "[v]esting [c]lauses, and indeed the entire structure of the Constitution," would "make no sense." Gary Lawson, *Delegation and Original Meaning*, 88 Va. L. Rev. 327 (2002). . . . [L]egislation would risk becoming nothing more than the will of the current President. And if laws could be simply declared by a single person, they would not be few in number, the product of widespread social consensus, likely to protect minority interests, or apt to provide stability and fair notice. Accountability would suffer too. . . .

The framers warned us against permitting consequences like these. As Madison explained, " '[t]here can be no liberty where the legislative and executive powers are united in the same person, or body of magistrates.' " *Federalist* 47. . . . Accepting, then, that we have an obligation to decide whether Congress has unconstitutionally divested itself of its legislative responsibilities, the question follows: What's the test? . . .

First, we know that as long as Congress makes the policy decisions when regulating private conduct, it may authorize another branch to "fill up the details." . . . Through all these cases, small or large, runs the theme that Congress must set forth standards "sufficiently definite and precise to enable Congress, the courts, and the public to ascertain" whether Congress's guidance has been followed. *Yakus v. United States* (1944).

Second, once Congress prescribes the rule governing private conduct, it may make the application of that rule depend on executive fact-finding. . . .

Third, Congress may assign the executive and judicial branches certain non-legislative responsibilities. While the Constitution vests all federal legislative power in Congress alone, Congress's legislative authority sometimes overlaps with authority the Constitution separately vests in another branch. So, for example, when a congressional statute confers wide discretion to the executive, no separation-of-powers problem may arise if "the discretion is to be exercised over matters already within the scope of executive power. . . .

Returning to SORNA with this understanding of our charge in hand, problems quickly emerge. . . . If allowing the President to draft a "cod[e] of fair competition" for slaughterhouses was "delegation running riot," then . . . [surely] Congress cannot give the executive branch a blank check to write a code of conduct governing private conduct for a half-million people. . . .

This 4–1–3 alignment was a long way from the 9–0 unanimity in *Whitman v. American Trucking*. And so the plurality expressed concern about the implications of Gorsuch's argument:

> Indeed, if SORNA's delegation is unconstitutional, then most of Government is unconstitutional—dependent as Congress is on the need to give discretion to executive officials to implement its programs. Consider again this Court's longtime recognition: "Congress simply cannot do its job absent an ability to delegate power under broad general directives." *Mistretta v. United States* (1989). . . .
>
> It is wisdom and humility alike that this Court has always upheld such "necessities of government." *Mistretta* (Scalia, J., dissenting); see *ibid*. ("Since Congress is no less endowed with common sense than we are, and better equipped to inform itself of the 'necessities' of government; and since the factors bearing upon those necessities are both multifarious and (in the nonpartisan sense) highly political . . . it is small wonder that we have almost never felt qualified to second-guess Congress regarding the permissible degree of policy judgment that can be left to those executing or applying the law").

FOR DISCUSSION Justice Gorsuch's historical claims about administrative delegations at the Founding have been sharply challenged. For more on the historical debate, compare Julian Davis Mortenson & Nicholas Bagley, *Delegation at the Founding,* 120 Colum. L. Rev. 277 (2021) with, *e.g.* Gary Lawson & Guy Seidman, *A Great Power of Attorney: Understanding the Fiduciary Constitution* (2017), and Philip Hamburger, *Is Administrative Law Unlawful?* (2014). Should the historical understanding matter for purpose of running a modern government?

Even in an era of minimal restrictions on legislative delegations, the Court did find one kind of legislative delegation unconstitutional. In 1998, in *Clinton v. City of New York*, it struck down the Line Item Veto Act (LIVA), which in some circumstances authorized the President to "cancel in whole" three types of provisions within five days (Sunday excluded) after they had become law: "(1) any dollar amount of discretionary budget authority; (2) any item of new direct spending; or (3) any limited tax benefit." To effectuate a cancellation, the President had to determine that it would "(i) reduce the Federal budget deficit; (ii) not impair any essential Government functions; and (iii) not harm the national interest." He then would send a special cancellation message to Congress, which could pass a disapproval bill under an expedited procedure—but subject to Presidential veto. President Clinton made three cancellations, none of which were disapproved, before the Court struck the law down.

The majority, per Justice Stevens, began with the premise that "repeal of statutes, no less than enactment, must conform with Art. I." *INS v. Chadha* (1983). And because cancellation prevented a provision of a previously enacted law "from having legal force or effect," the Court concluded that it was equivalent to repeal of that provision—but without having gone through the procedures required by Art. I, passage by both Houses and presentment to the President.

 Chadha, which held that the so-called legislative veto was unconstitutional, is presented at pp. 881–897.

The dissenters—an unusual combination of Justices O'Connor, Scalia, and Breyer—did not regard cancellations as a repeal, or tantamount to a repeal, given that they were authorized by statute; to them, the situation was the same as if the legislation containing the provision in issue had itself prescribed that the provision would not go into effect if the President made the requisite findings. Thus, Justice Scalia said that the title of the LIVA was a misnomer, presumably adopted for political purposes, and had "succeeded in faking out the Supreme Court." The dissenters did recognize that there might be other reasons, particularly the doctrine on delegation, why the Act could be considered unconstitutional. But they concluded that the standards for cancellation prescribed by the Act fell within the broad bounds within which delegations had been held acceptable. Indeed, Justice Scalia asserted that "there is not a dime's worth of difference between Congress's authorizing the President to *cancel* a spending item, and Congress's authorizing money to be spent on a particular item at the President's discretion. And the latter has been done since the founding of the Nation."

The majority was unpersuaded. Part of the debate concerned *Field v. Clark* (1892), which had upheld a provision of the Tariff Act of 1890 that directed the President, on making prescribed findings, to suspend certain tariff exemptions. The majority said this provision was distinguishable on three grounds. First, the suspension power under the 1890 Act was contingent on conditions that did not exist when the Act was passed, "the imposition of 'reciprocally unequal and unreasonable' import duties by other countries," but President Clinton's cancellations were "necessarily . . . based on the same conditions that Congress evaluated" in enacting the canceled provisions. Second, the Tariff Act imposed a duty to suspend, but under the LIVA the President retained discretion not to cancel. Finally, in suspending an exemption under the Tariff Act, the President "was executing the policy that Congress had embodied in the statute," but in making a cancellation under the LIVA the President was "rejecting the policy judgment made by Congress and relying on his own policy judgment."

Justice Breyer's dissent pointed out that the case did not require the Court to "referee a dispute among the other two branches" and concluded that the LIVA did not "threaten the liberties of individual citizens." This struck a raw nerve with Justice Kennedy, who wrote a concurrence to emphasize that "[l]iberty is always at stake when one or more of the branches seek to transgress the separation of powers." That "Congress surrendered its authority by its own hand" did not matter: "Abdication of responsibility is not part of the constitutional design."

---

c.   The Obligation of Faithful Execution

The Constitution not only *authorizes* the President to execute statutes, it also *obligates* the President to do so—at least to some extent. See U.S. Const., Art. II, § 3 ("[H]e shall take Care that the Laws be faithfully executed"). The following memorandum asks: what does the Take Care Clause require when the president believes a statute is unconstitutional?

 Bear in mind that the memo was written to the White House Counsel by a high-ranking member of the Clinton Justice Department, and thus represents a potentially one-sided view from within the executive branch. As you read it, ask yourself whether a lawyer for Congress would agree with the analysis, and how she might reply.

Walter Dellinger, Presidential Authority to Decline to Execute Unconstitutional Statutes

Assistant Attorney General, Office of
Legal Counsel, U. S. Department of Justice
November 2, 1994

I have reflected further on the difficult questions surrounding a President's decision to decline to execute statutory provisions that the President believes are unconstitutional, and I have a few thoughts to share with you. Let me start with a general proposition that I believe to be uncontroversial: there are circumstances in which the President may appropriately decline to enforce a statute that he views as unconstitutional.

First, there is significant judicial approval of this proposition. Most notable is the Court's decision in *Myers v. United States* (1926). There the Court sustained the President's view that the statute at issue was unconstitutional without any member of the Court suggesting that the President had acted improperly in refusing to abide by the statute. [See] *Youngstown Sheet & Tube Co. v. Sawyer* (1952) (Jackson, J., concurring) (recognizing existence of President's authority to act contrary to a statutory command).

Another part of the opinion quotes this passage from a 1980 opinion by Attorney General Benjamin Civiletti:

> ... *Myers* holds that the President's constitutional duty does not require him to execute unconstitutional statutes; nor does it require him to execute them provisionally, against the day that they are declared unconstitutional by the courts. He cannot be required by statute to retain postmasters against his will unless and until a court says that he may lawfully let them go. If the statute is unconstitutional, it is unconstitutional from the start. . . .

WORTH NOTING

Second, consistent and substantial executive practice also confirms this general proposition. [Internal executive branch opinions] dating to at least 1860 assert the President's authority to decline to effectuate enactments that the President views as unconstitutional. See, *e.g.*, *Memorial of Captain Meigs*, 9 Op. Att'y Gen. 462 (1860) (asserting that the President need not enforce a statute purporting to appoint an officer). Moreover, as we discuss more fully below, numerous Presidents have provided advance notice of their intention not to enforce specific statutory requirements that they have viewed as unconstitutional, and the Supreme Court has implicitly endorsed this practice. See *INS v. Chadha* (1983) (noting that Presidents often sign legislation containing constitutionally objectionable provisions and indicate that they will not comply with those provisions).

While the general proposition that in some situations the President may decline to enforce unconstitutional statutes is unassailable, it does not offer sufficient guidance as to the appropriate course in specific circumstances. To continue our conversation about these complex issues, I offer the following propositions for your consideration.

1.   The President's office and authority are created and bounded by the Constitution; he is required to act within its terms. Put somewhat differently, in serving as the executive created by the Constitution, the President is required to act in accordance with the laws—including the Constitution, which takes precedence over other forms of law. This obligation is reflected in the Take Care Clause and in the President's oath of office.

2.   When bills are under consideration by Congress, the executive branch should promptly identify unconstitutional provisions and communicate its concerns to Congress so that the provisions can be corrected. . . .

3.   The President should presume that enactments are constitutional. There will be some occasions, however, when a statute appears to conflict with the Constitution. In such cases, the President can and should exercise his independent judgment to determine whether the statute is constitutional. In reaching a conclusion, the President should give great deference to the fact that Congress passed the statute and that Congress believed it was upholding its obligation to enact constitutional legislation. Where possible, the President should construe provisions to avoid constitutional problems.

4.   The Supreme Court plays a special role in resolving disputes about the constitutionality of enactments. As a general matter, if the President believes that the Court would sustain a particular provision as constitutional, the President should execute the statute, notwithstanding his own beliefs about the constitutional issue. If, however, the President, exercising his independent judgment, determines both that a provision would violate the Constitution and that it is probable that the Court would agree with him, the President has the authority to decline to execute the statute.

5.   Where the President's independent constitutional judgment and his determination of the Court's probable decision converge on a conclusion of

unconstitutionality, the President must make a decision about whether or not to comply with the provision. That decision is necessarily specific to context, and it should be reached after careful weighing of the effect of compliance with the provision on the constitutional rights of affected individuals and on the executive branch's constitutional authority. Also relevant is the likelihood that compliance or non-compliance will permit judicial resolution of the issue. That is, the President may base his decision to comply (or decline to comply) in part on a desire to afford the Supreme Court an opportunity to review the constitutional judgment of the legislative branch.

6.   The President has enhanced responsibility to resist unconstitutional provisions that encroach upon the constitutional powers of the Presidency. Where the President believes that an enactment unconstitutionally limits his powers, he has the authority to defend his office and decline to abide by it, unless he is convinced that the Court would disagree with his assessment. If the President does not challenge such provisions (*i.e.,* by refusing to execute them), there often will be no occasion for judicial consideration of their constitutionality; a policy of consistent Presidential enforcement of statutes limiting his power thus would deny the Supreme Court the opportunity to review the limitations and thereby would allow for unconstitutional restrictions on the President's authority.

Some legislative encroachments on executive authority, however, will not be justiciable or are for other reasons unlikely to be resolved in court. If resolution in the courts is unlikely and the President cannot look to a judicial determination, he must shoulder the responsibility of protecting the constitutional role of the presidency. This is usually true, for example, of provisions limiting the President's authority as Commander in Chief. Where it is not possible to construe such provisions constitutionally, the President has the authority to act on his understanding of the Constitution. . . .

We recognize that these issues are difficult ones. When the President's obligation to act in accord with the Constitution appears to be in tension with his duty to execute laws enacted by Congress, questions are raised that go to the heart of our constitutional structure. In these circumstances, a President should proceed with caution and with respect for the obligation that each of the branches shares for the maintenance of constitutional government.

2.   The President as Personnel Manager

The President's ability to influence and control the federal bureaucracy is of great significance in the modern regulatory state, in which—as we have seen—an enormous amount of discretionary regulatory power is delegated to administrative agencies. But the importance of controlling executive personnel has been obvious from the beginning. Where the implementation of diplomacy is supervised by a Secretary of State, the implementation of financial policy by a Secretary of the Treasury, and the implementation of military affairs by a Secretary of War or Defense, the competition to influence the people who fill these positions has always been high stakes.

The reference here to "influence" rather than "command" is chosen advisedly. During the run-up to the presidential inauguration of former General Dwight Eisenhower, the incumbent President Harry Truman offered the following prediction—perhaps a little too cheerfully:

> He'll sit here, and he'll say, 'Do this! Do that!' And nothing will happen. Poor Ike—it won't be a bit like the Army. He'll find it very frustrating.

As a descriptive matter, there's a great deal of truth to Truman's observation. This section will be devoted to exploring the formal legal authorities that facilitate the President's efforts to influence the administrative state.

a.   The President's Power of Appointing Executive Branch Personnel

During the drafting of the Constitution in Philadelphia, the delegates hotly debated how best to provide for the appointments of federal personnel. James Wilson explained the stakes: "Good laws are of no effect without a good Executive; and there can be no good Executive without a responsible appointment of officers to execute." The hard question was how to implement "responsibility." On one hand, possessing "the executive power" might be meaningless without assistants whose discretion and good will the President could trust. From that perspective, it seemed like control over the appointment process ought to be vested in the President. On the other hand, the broad statutory powers vested in executive officers led many at the Convention to insist that the legislature play a role in assessing the qualifications and character of those placed in important jobs.

After lengthy discussion of how to structure the constitutional appointments process, the Philadelphia delegates settled on the following language:

> [The President] shall nominate, and by and with the Advice and Consent of the Senate, shall appoint Ambassadors, other public Ministers and Consuls, Judges of the supreme Court, and all other Officers of the United States, whose Appointments are not herein otherwise provided for, and which shall be established by Law:

> but the Congress may by Law vest the Appointment of such inferior Officers, as they think proper, in the President alone, in the Courts of Law, or in the Heads of Departments

The following cases explore how this text has come to be understood and applied.

Buckley v. Valeo

Supreme Court of the United States, 1976.
424 U.S. 1.

Per Curiam.

These appeals present constitutional challenges to the key provisions of the Federal Election Campaign Act of 1971 (Act), and related provisions of the Internal Revenue Code of 1954, all as amended in 1974.

The Court of Appeals, in sustaining the legislation in large part against various constitutional challenges, viewed it as "by far the most comprehensive reform legislation [ever] passed by Congress concerning the election of the President, Vice-President, and members of Congress." [The legislation limited individual political contributions and campaign spending; required disclosure of contributions and expenditures above certain thresholds; created a system for public funding of Presidential campaign activities, and established a Federal Election Commission. Numerous plaintiffs challenged the constitutionality of the legislation on various grounds; the excerpts presented here focus only on the constitution of the Commission.]

IV. The Federal Election Commission

The 1974 amendments to the Act create an eight-member Federal Election Commission (Commission), and vest in it primary and substantial responsibility for administering and enforcing the Act. The question that we address in this portion of the opinion is whether, in view of the manner in which a majority of its members are appointed, the Commission may under the Constitution exercise the powers conferred upon it. . . .

[The Act] makes the Commission the principal repository of the numerous reports and statements which are required by that chapter to be filed by those engaging in the regulated political activities. Its duties . . . with respect to these reports and statements include filing and indexing, making them available for public inspection, preservation, and auditing and field investigations. It is directed to "serve as a national clearinghouse for information in respect to the administration of elections."

Beyond these recordkeeping, disclosure, and investigative functions, however, the Commission is given extensive rulemaking and adjudicative powers. [The Commission is authorized] "to prescribe suitable rules and regulations to carry out [various] provisions of [the Act] . . . . ," [to] "formulate general policy with respect to the administration of this act," [and] to render advisory opinions with respect to activities possibly violating the Act . . . , the effect of which is that

> [n]otwithstanding any other provision of law, any person with respect to whom an advisory opinion is rendered . . . who acts in good faith in accordance with the provisions and findings [thereof] shall be presumed to be in compliance with the [statutory provision] with respect to which such advisory opinion is rendered.

In the course of administering the provisions for Presidential campaign financing, the Commission may authorize convention expenditures which exceed the statutory limits.

The Commission's enforcement power is both direct and wide ranging. It may institute a civil action for [injunctive or other relief to implement the Act.] If after the Commission's post-disbursement audit of candidates receiving payments under [various statutory provisions] it finds an overpayment, it is empowered to seek repayment of all funds due the Secretary of the Treasury. In no respect do the foregoing civil actions require the concurrence of or participation by the Attorney General. . . .

Finally, as "[a]dditional enforcement authority," [the Act] authorizes the Commission, after notice and opportunity for hearing, to make "a finding that a person . . . while a candidate for Federal office, failed to file" a required report of contributions or expenditures. If that finding is made within the applicable limitations period for prosecutions, the candidate is thereby "disqualified from becoming a candidate in any future election for Federal office for a period of time beginning on the date of such finding and ending one year after the expiration of the term of the Federal office for which such person was a candidate."

The body in which this authority is reposed consists of eight members. The Secretary of the Senate and the Clerk of the House of Representatives are *ex officio* members of the Commission without the right to vote. Two members are appointed by the President *pro tempore* of the Senate "upon the recommendations of the majority leader of the Senate and the minority leader of the Senate." Two more are to be appointed by the Speaker of the House of Representatives, likewise upon the recommendations of its respective majority and minority leaders. The remaining two members are appointed by the President. Each of the six voting members of the Commission must be confirmed by the majority of both Houses of Congress, and each of the three appointing authorities is forbidden to choose both of their appointees from the same political party. . . .

Appellants urge that since Congress has given the Commission wide-ranging rulemaking and enforcement powers with respect to the substantive provisions of the Act, Congress is precluded under the principle of separation of powers from vesting in itself the authority to appoint those who will exercise such authority. Their argument is based on the language of Art. II, § 2, cl. 2, of the Constitution, which provides in pertinent part as follows:

> [The President] shall nominate, and by and with the Advice and Consent of the Senate, shall appoint . . . all other Officers of the United States, whose Appointments are not herein otherwise provided for, and which shall be established by Law: but the Congress may by Law vest the Appointment of such inferior Officers, as they think proper, in the President alone, in the Courts of Law, or in the Heads of Departments.

Appellants' argument is that this provision is the exclusive method by which those charged with executing the laws of the United States may be chosen. Congress, they assert, cannot have it both ways. If the Legislature wishes the Commission to exercise all of the conferred powers, then its members are in fact "Officers of the United States" and must be appointed under the Appointments Clause. But if Congress insists upon retaining the power to appoint, then the members of the Commission may not discharge those many functions of the Commission which can be performed only by "Officers of the United States," as that term must be construed within the doctrine of separation of powers. . . .

The principle of separation of powers was not simply an abstract general-ization in the minds of the Framers: it was woven into the document that they drafted in Philadelphia in the summer of 1787. [The court cites the Vesting Clauses of Articles I, II, and III.] The further concern of the Framers of the Constitution with maintenance of the separation of powers is found in the so-called "Ineligibility" and "Incompatibility" Clauses contained in Art. I, § 6:

> No Senator or Representative shall, during the Time for which he was elected, be appointed to any civil Office under the Authority of the United States, which shall have been created, or the Emoluments whereof shall have been increased during such time; and no Person holding any Office under the United States, shall be a Member of either House during his Continuance in Office.

It is in the context of these cognate provisions of the document that we must examine the language of Art. II, § 2, cl. 2, which appellants contend provides the only authorization for appointment of those to whom substantial executive or administrative authority is given by statute. . . .

We think that the term "Officers of the United States" as used in Art. II, defined to include "all persons who can be said to hold an office under the government" in *United States v. Germaine* (1879), is a term intended to have substantive meaning. We think its fair import is that any appointee exercising significant authority pursuant to the laws of the United States is an "Officer of the United States," and must, therefore, be appointed in the manner prescribed by § 2, cl. 2, of that Article.

If "all persons who can be said to hold an office under the government about to be established under the Constitution were intended to be included within one or the other of these modes of appointment," *Germaine,* it is difficult to see how the members of the Commission may escape inclusion. If a postmaster first class, *Myers v. United States* (1926), and the clerk of a district court, *Ex parte Hennen* (1839), are inferior officers of the United States within the meaning of the Appointments Clause, as they are, surely the Commissioners before us are at the very least such "inferior Officers" within the meaning of that Clause.[162]

---

[162] "Officers of the United States" does not include all employees of the United States, but there is no claim made that the Commissioners are employees of the United States rather than officers. Employees are lesser function-aries subordinate to officers of the United States, whereas the Commissioners, appointed for a statutory term, are not subject to the control or direction of any other executive, judicial, or legislative authority.

Although two members of the Commission are initially selected by the President, his nominations are subject to confirmation not merely by the Senate, but by the House of Representatives as well. The remaining four voting members of the Commission are appointed by the President *pro tempore* of the Senate and by the Speaker of the House. While the second part of the Clause authorizes Congress to vest the appointment of the officers described in that part in "the Courts of Law, or in the Heads of Departments," neither the Speaker of the House nor the President pro tempore of the Senate comes within this language.

The phrase "Heads of Departments," used as it is in conjunction with the phrase "Courts of Law," suggests that the Departments referred to are themselves in the Executive Branch or at least have some connection with that branch. While the Clause expressly authorizes Congress to vest the appointment of certain officers in the "Courts of Law," the absence of similar language to include Congress must mean that neither Congress nor its officers were included within the language "Heads of Departments" in this part of cl. 2.

Thus with respect to four of the six voting members of the Commission, neither the President, the head of any department, nor the Judiciary has any voice in their selection.

The Appointments Clause specifies the method of appointment only for "Officers of the United States" whose appointment is not "otherwise provided for" in the Constitution. But there is no provision of the Constitution remotely providing any alternative means for the selection of the members of the Commission or for anybody like them. Appellee Commission has argued, and the Court of Appeals agreed, that the Appointments Clause of Art. II should not be read to exclude the "inherent power of Congress" to appoint its own officers to perform functions necessary to that body as an institution. . . . [N]othing in our holding with respect to Art. II, § 2, cl. 2, will deny to Congress "all power to appoint its own inferior officers to carry out appropriate legislative functions." . . .

[T]he debates of the Constitutional Convention, and the Federalist Papers, are replete with expressions of fear that the Legislative Branch of the National Government will aggrandize itself at the expense of the other two branches. The debates during the Convention, and the evolution of the draft version of the Constitution, seem to us to lend considerable support to our reading of the language of the Appointments Clause itself. An interim version of the draft Constitution had vested in the Senate the authority to appoint Ambassadors, public Ministers, and Judges of the Supreme Court, and the language of Art. II as finally adopted is a distinct change in this regard. We believe that it was a deliberate change made by the Framers with the intent to deny Congress any authority itself to appoint those who were "Officers of the United States." . . .

We are also told by appellees and *amici* that Congress had good reason for not vesting in a Commission composed wholly of Presidential appointees the authority to administer the Act, since the administration of the Act would undoubtedly have a bearing on any incumbent President's campaign for re-election. . . . But such fears, however rational, do not by themselves warrant a distortion of the Framers' work. . . .

3.   The Commission's Powers

Thus, on the assumption that all of the powers granted in the statute may be exercised by an agency whose members *have been* appointed in accordance with the Appointments Clause, the ultimate question is which, if any, of those powers may be exercised by the present voting Commissioners, none of whom *was* appointed as provided by that Clause. Our previous description of the statutory provisions disclosed that the Commission's powers fall generally into three categories: functions relating to the flow of necessary information—receipt, dissemination, and investigation; functions with respect to the Commission's task of fleshing out the statute—rulemaking and advisory opinions; and functions necessary to ensure compliance with the statute and rules—informal procedures, administrative determinations and hearings, and civil suits.

Insofar as the powers confided in the Commission are essentially of an investigative and informative nature, falling in the same general category as those powers which Congress might delegate to one of its own committees, there can be no question that the Commission as presently constituted may exercise them. As this Court stated in *McGrain*:

> A legislative body cannot legislate wisely or effectively in the absence of information respecting the conditions which the legislation is intended to affect or change; and where the legislative body does not itself possess the requisite information which not infrequently is true recourse must be had to others who do possess it. Experience has taught that mere requests for such information often are unavailing, and also that information which is volunteered is not always accurate or complete; so some means of compulsion are essential to obtain what is needed. All this was true before and when the Constitution

was framed and adopted. In that period the power of inquiry, with enforcing process, was regarded and employed as a necessary and appropriate attribute of the power to legislate, indeed, was treated as inhering in it.

But when we go beyond this type of authority to the more substantial powers exercised by the Commission, we reach a different result. The Commission's enforcement power, exemplified by its discretionary power to seek judicial relief, is authority that cannot possibly be regarded as merely in aid of the legislative function of Congress. A lawsuit is the ultimate remedy for a breach of the law, and it is to the President, and not to the Congress, that the Constitution entrusts the responsibility to "take Care that the Laws be faithfully executed." Art. II, § 3. . . .

This Court observed . . . in *Springer v. Philippine Islands* [that]:

. . . Not having the power of appointment, unless expressly granted or incidental to its powers, the legislature cannot ingraft executive duties upon a legislative office, since that would be to usurp the power of appointment by indirection, though the case might be different if the additional duties were devolved upon an appointee of the executive.

We hold that these provisions of the Act, vesting in the Commission primary responsibility for conducting civil litigation in the courts of the United States for vindicating public rights, violate Art. II, § 2, cl. 2, of the Constitution. Such functions may be discharged only by persons who are "Officers of the United States" within the language of that section.

All aspects of the Act are brought within the Commission's broad administrative powers: rulemaking, advisory opinions, and determinations of eligibility for funds and even for federal elective office itself. These functions, exercised free from day-to-day supervision of either Congress or the Executive Branch, are more legislative and judicial in nature than are the Commission's enforcement powers, and are of kinds usually performed by independent regulatory agencies or by some department in the Executive Branch under the direction of an Act of Congress. Congress viewed these broad powers as essential to effective and impartial administration of the entire substantive framework of the Act. Yet each of these functions also represents the performance of a significant governmental duty exercised pursuant to a public law. While the President may not insist that such functions be delegated to an appointee of his removable at will, *Humphrey's Executor v. United States* (1935), none of them operates merely in aid of congressional authority to legislate or is sufficiently removed from the administration and enforcement of public law to allow it to be performed by the present Commission. These administrative functions may therefore be exercised only by persons who are "Officers of the United States."

It is also our view that the Commission's inability to exercise certain powers because of the method by which its members have been selected should not affect the validity of the Commission's administrative actions and determinations to this date. . . . The past acts of the Commission are therefore accorded *de facto* validity, just as we have recognized should be the case with respect to legislative acts performed by legislators held to have been elected in accordance with an unconstitutional apportionment plan.

We also . . . stay, for a period not to exceed 30 days, the Court's judgment insofar as it affects the authority of the Commission to exercise the duties and powers granted it under the Act. This limited stay will afford Congress an opportunity to reconstitute the Commission by law or to adopt other valid enforcement mechanisms without interrupting enforcement of the provisions the Court sustains, allowing the present Commission in the interim to function *de facto* in accordance with the substantive provisions of the Act. . . .

So ordered.

MR. JUSTICE STEVENS took no part in the consideration or decision of these cases.

JUSTICE WHITE, concurring in [relevant] part. . . .

. . . There is no doubt that the development of the administrative agency in response to modern legislative and administrative need has placed severe strain on the separation-of-powers principle in its pristine formulation. Any notion that the Constitution bans any admixture of powers that might be deemed legislative, executive, and judicial has had to give way. The independent agency has survived attacks from various directions: that it exercises invalidly delegated legislative power; that it invalidly exercises judicial power; and that its functions are so executive in nature that its members must be subject to Presidential control.

Until now, however, it has not been insisted that the commands of the Appointments Clause must also yield to permit congressional appointments of members of a major agency. With the Court, I am not convinced that we should create a broad exception to the requirements of that Clause that all officers of the United States be appointed in accordance with its terms. The provision applies to all officers, however their duties may be classified[,] and even if some of the FEC's functions, such as rulemaking, are purely legislative. . . .

WORTH NOTING   Chief Justice Burger and Justices Marshall, Blackmun, and Rehnquist each wrote separate opinions dissenting with respect to other issues in the case. All four of them concurred in Part IV of the majority opinion.

Morrison v. Olson

Supreme Court of the United States, 1988.
487 U.S. 654.

CHIEF JUSTICE REHNQUIST delivered the opinion of the Court.

This case presents us with a challenge to the independent counsel provisions of the Ethics in Government Act of 1978. We hold today that these provisions of the Act do not violate the Appointments Clause of the Constitution, Art. II, § 2, cl. 2, or the limitations of Article III. . . .

I

Briefly stated, Title VI of the Ethics in Government Act allows for the appointment of an "independent counsel" to investigate and, if appropriate, prosecute certain high-ranking Government officials for violations of federal criminal laws.[2]

The Act requires the Attorney General, upon receipt of information that he determines is "sufficient to constitute grounds to investigate whether any person [covered by the Act] may have violated any Federal criminal law," to conduct a preliminary investigation of the matter. When the Attorney General has completed this investigation, or 90 days has elapsed, he is required to report to a special court (the Special Division) created by the Act "for the purpose of

---

[2]   The Act was first enacted by Congress in 1978. . . . The current version of the statute states that, with certain exceptions, it shall "cease to be effective five years after the date of the enactment of the Independent Counsel Reauthorization Act of 1987."

appointing independent counsels."[3] If the Attorney General determines that "there are no reasonable grounds to believe that further investigation is warranted," then he must notify the Special Division of this result. In such a case, "the division of the court shall have no power to appoint an independent counsel." If, however, the Attorney General has determined that there are "reasonable grounds to believe that further investigation or prosecution is warranted," then he "shall apply to the division of the court for the appointment of an independent counsel." . . . Upon receiving this application, the Special Division "shall appoint an appropriate independent counsel and shall define that independent counsel's prosecutorial jurisdiction." Upon request of the Attorney General, in lieu of appointing an independent counsel the Special Division may "expand the prosecutorial jurisdiction of an [existing] independent counsel."

With respect to all matters within the independent counsel's jurisdiction, the Act grants the counsel "full power and independent authority to exercise all investigative and prosecutorial functions and powers of the Department of Justice, the Attorney General, and any other officer or employee of the Department of Justice." The functions of the independent counsel include conducting grand jury proceedings and other investigations, participating in civil and criminal court proceedings and litigation, and appealing any decision in any case in which the counsel participates in an official capacity. . . . [T]he counsel's powers also include "initiating and conducting prosecutions in any court of competent jurisdiction, framing and signing indictments, filing informations, and handling all aspects of any case, in the name of the United States." The counsel may appoint employees, may request and obtain assistance from the Department of Justice, and may accept referral of matters from the Attorney General if the matter falls within the counsel's jurisdiction as defined by the Special Division. The Act also states that an independent counsel "shall, except where not possible, comply with the written or other established policies of the Department of Justice respecting enforcement of the criminal laws." In addition, whenever a matter has been referred to an independent counsel under the Act, the Attorney General and the Justice Department are required to suspend all investigations and proceedings regarding the matter. . . .

---

[3]   The Special Division is a division of the United States Court of Appeals for the District of Columbia Circuit. 28 U.S.C. § 49. The court consists of three circuit court judges or justices appointed by the Chief Justice of the United States. . . .

Two statutory provisions govern the length of an independent counsel's tenure in office. The first defines the procedure for removing an independent counsel. Section 596(a)(1) provides:

> An independent counsel appointed under this chapter may be removed from office, other than by impeachment and conviction, only by the personal action of the Attorney General and only for good cause, physical disability, mental incapacity, or any other condition that substantially impairs the performance of such independent counsel's duties.

If an independent counsel is removed pursuant to this section, the Attorney General is required to submit a report to both the Special Division and the Judiciary Committees of the Senate and the House "specifying the facts found and the ultimate grounds for such removal." Under the current version of the Act, an independent counsel can obtain judicial review of the Attorney General's action by filing a civil action in the United States District Court for the District of Columbia. . . . The reviewing court is authorized to grant reinstatement or "other appropriate relief."

The other provision governing the tenure of the independent counsel defines the procedures for "terminating" the counsel's office. Under § 596(b)(1), the office of an independent counsel terminates when he or she notifies the Attorney General that he or she has completed or substantially completed any investigations or prosecutions undertaken pursuant to the Act. In addition, the Special Division, acting either on its own or on the suggestion of the Attorney General, may terminate the office of an independent counsel at any time if it finds that "the investigation of all matters within the prosecutorial jurisdiction of such independent counsel . . . [and any resulting prosecutions] have been completed or so substantially completed that it would be appropriate for the Department of Justice to complete such investigations and prosecutions."

Finally, the Act provides for congressional oversight of the activities of independent counsel. An independent counsel may from time to time send Congress statements or reports on his or her activities. The "appropriate committees of the Congress" are given oversight jurisdiction in regard to the official conduct of an independent counsel, and the counsel is required by the Act to cooperate with Congress in the exercise of this jurisdiction. The counsel is required to inform the House of Representatives of "substantial and credible information which [the counsel] receives . . . that may constitute grounds for an impeachment." . . .

The proceedings in this case provide an example of how the Act works in practice. [In 1983, the House Judiciary Committee began an investigation into the Justice Department's role in a dispute over documents that two Subcommittees of the House had sought to secure from the Environmental Protection Agency the previous year. In 1985, the majority members of the Judiciary Committee published a report suggesting that appellees Olson, Schmults, and Dinkins—all high-ranking officials of the Justice Department—had committed misconduct during the investigation, Olson by giving false testimony and the others by wrongfully withholding documents.] The Chairman of the Judiciary Committee forwarded a copy of the report to the Attorney General with a request . . . that he seek the appointment of an independent counsel to investigate the allegations against Olson, Schmults, and Dinkins.

[After a preliminary investigation by the Public Integrity Section of the Criminal Division of the Justice Department, the Attorney General decided to seek appointment of an independent counsel solely with respect to the charges against Olson. The Special Division first appointed James C. McKay and then (after he later resigned) appellant Alexia Morrison. Morrison asked the Attorney General to refer the accusations against Schmults and Dinkins for her investigation, but he refused. The Special Division ruled that the Attorney General's decision was unreviewable, but also] that its original grant of jurisdiction to appellant was broad enough to permit inquiry into whether Olson may have conspired with others, including Schmults and Dinkins, to obstruct the Committee's investigation.

Following this ruling, in May and June 1987, appellant caused a grand jury to issue and serve subpoenas *ad testificandum* and *duces tecum* on appellees. All three appellees moved to quash the subpoenas, claiming, among other things, that the independent counsel provisions of the Act were unconstitutional and that appellant accordingly had no authority to proceed. On July 20, 1987, the District Court upheld the constitutionality of the Act and denied the motions to quash. The court subsequently ordered that appellees be held in contempt . . . for continuing to refuse to comply with the subpoenas. The court stayed the effect of its contempt orders pending expedited appeal. A divided Court of Appeals reversed. . . . Appellant then sought review by this Court, and we noted probable jurisdiction. We now reverse. . . .

III

As we stated in *Buckley v. Valeo* (1976): "[P]rincipal officers are selected by the President with the advice and consent of the Senate. Inferior officers Congress may allow to be appointed by the President alone, by the heads of departments, or by the Judiciary." The initial question is, accordingly, whether appellant is an "inferior" or a "principal" officer.[12] If she is the latter, as the Court of Appeals concluded, then the Act is in violation of the Appointments Clause.

The line between "inferior" and "principal" officers is one that is far from clear, and the Framers provided little guidance into where it should be drawn. See, *e.g.*, J. Story, *Commentaries on the Constitution* (1858) ("In the practical course of the government there does not seem to have been any exact line drawn, who are and who are not to be deemed *inferior* officers, in the sense of the constitution, whose appointment does not necessarily require the concurrence of the senate").

We need not attempt here to decide exactly where the line falls between the two types of officers, because in our view appellant clearly falls on the "inferior officer" side of that line. Several factors lead to this conclusion.

First, appellant is subject to removal by a higher Executive Branch official. Although appellant may not be "subordinate" to the Attorney General (and the President) insofar as she possesses a degree of independent discretion to exercise the powers delegated to her under the Act, the fact that she can be removed by the Attorney General indicates that she is to some degree "inferior" in rank and authority.

Second, appellant is empowered by the Act to perform only certain, limited duties. An independent counsel's role is restricted primarily to investigation and, if appropriate, prosecution for certain federal crimes. Admittedly, the Act delegates to appellant "full power and independent authority to exercise all investigative and prosecutorial functions and powers of the Department of Justice," but this grant of authority does not include any authority to formulate policy for the Government or the Executive Branch, nor does it give appellant any administrative duties outside of those necessary to operate her office. The

---

[12]   It is clear that appellant is an "officer" of the United States, not an "employee." See *Buckley*.

Act specifically provides that in policy matters appellant is to comply to the extent possible with the policies of the Department.

Third, appellant's office is limited in jurisdiction. Not only is the Act itself restricted in applicability to certain federal officials suspected of certain serious federal crimes, but an independent counsel can only act within the scope of the jurisdiction that has been granted by the Special Division pursuant to a request by the Attorney General.

Finally, appellant's office is limited in tenure. There is concededly no time limit on the appointment of a particular counsel. Nonetheless, the office of independent counsel is "temporary" in the sense that an independent counsel is appointed essentially to accomplish a single task, and when that task is over the office is terminated, either by the counsel herself or by action of the Special Division. Unlike other prosecutors, appellant has no ongoing responsibilities that extend beyond the accomplishment of the mission that she was appointed for and authorized by the Special Division to undertake.

In our view, these factors relating to the "ideas of tenure, duration . . . and duties" of the independent counsel, *United States v. Germaine* (1879), are sufficient to establish that appellant is an "inferior" officer in the constitutional sense.

This conclusion is consistent with our few previous decisions that considered the question whether a particular government official is a "principal" or an "inferior" officer. In *United States v. Eaton* (1898), for example, we approved Department of State regulations that allowed executive officials to appoint a "vice-consul" during the temporary absence of the consul, terming the "vice-consul" a "subordinate officer" notwithstanding the Appointment Clause's specific reference to "Consuls" as principal officers. As we stated: "Because the subordinate officer is charged with the performance of the duty of the superior for a limited time and under special and temporary conditions he is not thereby transformed into the superior and permanent official." In *Ex parte Siebold* (1880), the Court found that federal "supervisor[s] of elections," who were charged with various duties involving oversight of local congressional elections, were inferior officers for purposes of the Clause. In *Go-Bart Importing Co. v. United States* (1931), we held that "United States commissioners are inferior officers." These commissioners had various judicial and prosecutorial powers, including the power to arrest and imprison for trial, to issue warrants, and to institute prosecutions under "laws relating to the elective franchise and civil rights." All of this is consistent with our reference in *United States v. Nixon* (1974) to the office of Watergate Special Prosecutor—whose authority was similar to that of appellant—as a "subordinate officer."

This does not, however, end our inquiry under the Appointments Clause. Appellees argue that even if appellant is an "inferior" officer, the Clause does not empower Congress to place the power to appoint such an officer outside the Executive Branch. They contend that the Clause does not contemplate congressional authorization of "interbranch appointments," in which an officer of one branch is appointed by officers of another branch.

The relevant language of the Appointments Clause is worth repeating. It reads: ". . . but the Congress may by Law vest the Appointment of such inferior Officers, as they think proper, in the President alone, in the courts of Law, or in the Heads of Departments." On its face, the language of this "excepting clause" admits of no limitation on interbranch appointments. Indeed, the inclusion of "as they think proper" seems clearly to give Congress significant discretion to determine whether it is "proper" to vest the appointment of, for example, executive officials in the "courts of Law." We recognized as much in one of our few decisions in this area, *Ex parte Siebold*, where we stated:

> It is no doubt usual and proper to vest the appointment of inferior officers in that department of the government, executive or judicial, or in that particular executive department to which the duties of such officers appertain. But there is no absolute requirement to this effect in the Constitution; and, if there were, it would be difficult in many cases to determine to which department an office properly belonged. . . . [A]s the Constitution stands, the selection of the appointing power, as between the functionaries named, is a matter resting in the discretion of Congress. . . .

[W]e see no reason now to depart from the holding of *Siebold* that such appointments are not proscribed by the excepting clause.

We also note that the history of the Clause provides no support for appellees' position. Throughout most of the process of drafting the Constitution, the Convention concentrated on the problem of who should have the authority to appoint judges. . . . [T]here was little or no debate on the question whether the Clause empowers Congress to provide for interbranch appointments, and there is nothing to suggest that the Framers intended to prevent Congress from having that power.

We do not mean to say that Congress' power to provide for interbranch appointments of "inferior officers" is unlimited. In addition to separation-of-powers concerns, which would arise if such provisions for appointment had the potential to impair the constitutional functions assigned to one of the branches, *Siebold* itself suggested that Congress' decision to vest the appointment power in the courts would be improper if there was some "incongruity" between the functions normally performed by the courts and the performance of their duty to appoint.

In this case, however, we do not think it impermissible for Congress to vest the power to appoint independent counsel in a specially created federal court. We thus disagree with the Court of Appeals' conclusion that there is an inherent incongruity about a court having the power to appoint prosecutorial officers.[13] We have recognized that courts may appoint private attorneys to act as prosecutor for judicial contempt judgments. *Young v. United States ex rel. Vuitton et Fils S.A.* (1987). In *Go-Bart Importing Co. v. United States* (1931), we approved court appointment of United States commissioners, who exercised certain limited prosecutorial powers. In *Siebold*, as well, we indicated that judicial appointment of federal marshals, who are "executive officer[s]," would not be inappropriate. Lower courts have also upheld interim judicial appointments of United States Attorneys, see *United States v. Solomon* (S.D.N.Y. 1963), and Congress itself has vested the power to make these interim appointments in the district courts, see 28 U.S.C. § 546(d).

Congress, of course, was concerned when it created the office of independent counsel with the conflicts of interest that could arise in situations when the Executive Branch is called upon to investigate its own high-ranking officers. If it were to remove the appointing authority from the Executive Branch, the most logical place to put it was in the Judicial Branch. In the light of the Act's provision making the judges of the Special Division ineligible to participate in any

WORTH NOTING

After a hiatus, the Independent Counsel statute was renewed for five years in 1994 with the approval of President Clinton—who later had cause to regret the move. The statute was then allowed to lapse in 1999.

---

[13] Indeed, in light of judicial experience with prosecutors in criminal cases, it could be said that courts are especially well qualified to appoint prosecutors. This is not a case in which judges are given power to appoint an officer in an area in which they have no special knowledge or expertise, as in, for example, a statute authorizing the courts to appoint officials in the Department of Agriculture or the Federal Energy Regulatory Commission.

matters relating to an independent counsel they have appointed, we do not think that appointment of the independent counsel by the court runs afoul of the constitutional limitation on "incongruous" interbranch appointments. . . .

In sum, we conclude today that it does not violate the Appointments Clause for Congress to vest the appointment of independent counsel in the Special Division. . . .

JUSTICE SCALIA, dissenting.

[T]he Court does not attempt to "decide exactly" what establishes the line between principal and "inferior" officers, but is confident that, whatever the line may be, appellant "clearly falls on the 'inferior officer' side" of it. The Court gives three reasons: *First*, she "is subject to removal by a higher Executive Branch official," namely, the Attorney General. *Second*, she is "empowered by the Act to perform only certain, limited duties." *Third*, her office is "limited in jurisdiction" and "limited in tenure."

The first of these lends no support to the view that appellant is an inferior officer. Appellant is removable only for "good cause" or physical or mental incapacity. . . . And I do not see how it could possibly make any difference to her superior or inferior status that the President's limited power to remove her must be exercised through the Attorney General. If she were removable at will by the Attorney General, then she would be subordinate to him and thus properly designated as inferior; but the Court essentially admits that she is not subordinate. If it were common usage to refer to someone as "inferior" who is subject to removal for cause by another, then one would say that the President is "inferior" to Congress.

The second reason offered by the Court—that appellant performs only certain, limited duties—may be relevant to whether she is an inferior officer, but it mischaracterizes the extent of her powers. As the Court states: "Admittedly, the Act delegates to appellant [the] '*full power and independent authority to exercise all investigative and prosecutorial functions and powers of the Department of Justice.*'" Moreover, in addition to this general grant of power she is given a broad range of specifically enumerated powers, including a power not even the Attorney General possesses: to "contes[t] in court . . . any claim of privilege or attempt to withhold evidence on grounds of national security." Once all of this is "admitted," it seems to me impossible to maintain that appellant's authority is so "limited" as to render her an inferior officer. The Court seeks to brush this away by asserting that the independent counsel's power does not include any authority to "formulate policy for the Government or the Executive Branch." But the same could be said for all officers of the Government, with the single exception of the President. All of them only formulate policy within their respective spheres of responsibility—as does the independent counsel, who must comply with the policies of the Department of Justice only to the extent possible. § 594(f).

The final set of reasons given by the Court for why the independent counsel clearly is an inferior officer emphasizes the limited nature of her jurisdiction and tenure. Taking the latter first, I find nothing unusually limited about the independent counsel's tenure. To the contrary, unlike most high-ranking Executive Branch officials, she continues to serve until she (or the Special Division) decides that her work is substantially completed. This particular independent prosecutor has already served more than two years, which is at least as long as many Cabinet officials. As to the scope of her jurisdiction, there can be no doubt that is small (though far from unimportant). But within it she exercises more than the full power of the Attorney General. The Ambassador to Luxembourg is not anything less than a principal officer, simply because Luxembourg is small. And the federal judge who sits in a small district is not for that reason "inferior in rank and authority." If the mere fragmentation of executive responsibilities into small compartments suffices to render the heads of each of those compartments inferior officers, then Congress could deprive the President of the right to appoint his chief law enforcement officer by dividing up the Attorney General's responsibilities among a number of "lesser" functionaries. . . .

[T]he text of the Constitution and the division of power that it establishes . . . demonstrate, I think, that the independent counsel is not an inferior officer because she is not *subordinate* to any officer in the Executive Branch (indeed, not even to the President). Dictionaries in use at the time of the Constitutional Convention gave the word "inferiour" two meanings which it still bears today: (1) "[l]ower in place, . . . station, . . . rank of life, . . . value or excellency," and (2) "[s]ubordinate." S. Johnson, Dictionary of the English Language (1785). In a document dealing with the structure (the constitution) of a government, one would naturally expect the word to bear the latter meaning—indeed, in such a context it would be unpardonably careless to use the word *unless* a relationship of subordination was intended. If what was meant was merely "lower in station or rank," one would use instead a term such as "lesser officers." . . .

To be sure, it is not a *sufficient* condition for "inferior" officer status that one be subordinate to a principal officer. Even an officer who is subordinate to a department head can be a principal officer. . . . But it is surely a *necessary* condition for inferior officer status that the officer be subordinate to another officer.

The independent counsel is not even subordinate to the President. The Court essentially admits as much, noting that "appellant may not be 'subordinate' to the Attorney General (and the President) insofar as she possesses a degree of independent discretion to exercise the powers delegated to her under the Act." In fact, there is no doubt about it. As noted earlier, the Act specifically grants her the "*full* power and *independent* authority to exercise *all* investigative and prosecutorial functions of the Department of Justice," and makes her removable only for "good cause," a limitation specifically intended to ensure that she be *independent* of, not *subordinate* to, the President and the Attorney General.

 CROSS REFERENCE The portions of the opinions addressing the Act's "good cause" restrictions on removal of the independent counsel are presented at pp. 780–789.

Because appellant is not subordinate to another officer, she is not an "inferior" officer and her appointment other than by the President with the advice and consent of the Senate is unconstitutional. . . .

Morrison deals with the distinction between principal and inferior officers. But the Appointments Clause has also been interpreted to give rise to a second distinction: between officers, who "exercis[e] significant authority pursuant to the laws of the United States," and employees, who "are lesser functionaries subordinate to officers of the United States." *Buckley v. Valeo* (1976). While the Appointments Clause provides the exclusive mechanism for appointing officers, employees don't trigger its requirements in any way: "the Appointments Clause cares not a whit about who named them." *Lucia v. Securities and Exchange Commission* (2018). Drawing the line between officials with "significant" authority and "lesser functionaries" can therefore be a high-stakes question.

In *United States v. Germaine* (1879), for example, the Supreme Court held that the "civil surgeons" hired to perform various physical exams were employees because their duties were "occasional or temporary" rather than "continuing and permanent." In *Freytag v. Commissioner* (1991), on the other hand, the Court held that the "special trial judges" assigned to preside over some United States Tax Court hearings were officers. Even though the special trial judges could only "prepare proposed findings and an opinion" in major matters for potential adoption by a regular Tax Court judge, the *Freytag* Court emphasized that the special trial judges also exercised "significant discretion" in conducting hearings and enforcing compliance with discovery orders.

Lucia v. Securities and Exchange Commission (2018) reached the same conclusion about administrative law judges (ALJs) of the Securities and Exchange Commission (SEC), who exercise procedural authority comparable to that of a judge conducting a bench trial. In her opinion for the *Lucia* majority, Justice Kagan found the case even easier than *Freytag* because the SEC could "opt[ ] against" reviewing the ALJ's decision at all, in which case the ALJ decision would simply become final. Because the ALJs were therefore officers for purposes of the Appointment Clause, that meant they should have been appointed by the SEC itself rather than by its staff members. Justice Thomas, joined by Justice Gorsuch, would have held more broadly that any civil official "with responsibility for an ongoing statutory duty" is an officer of the United States subject to the Appointments Clause; Justice Breyer would have decided the case without reaching the constitutional issue; and Justice Sotomayor, joined by Justice Ginsburg, dissented on the ground that the ALJs did not have "the ability to make final, binding decisions on behalf of the Government."

b. The President's Power of Removal

The flip side of appointments is removal. If the power of appointment allows you to fill an office with someone you've screened for policy preferences, loyalty, and other desirable characteristics, the power of removal allows you to fire someone who's either incompetent or simply not doing what you want. Unlike appointments, the Constitution doesn't speak directly to the ordinary removal process—a silence that has prompted strong disagreement since 1789. The following materials trace how modern removal doctrine has evolved.

The Tenure of Office Act of March 2, 1867, passed over President Johnson's veto, provided that any civil officer suspended by the President when the Senate was not in session had to be reinstated when the Senate reconvened— unless the suspension was ratified by the Senate. Johnson's resistance to this law led to his impeachment. The law was modified after he left office and repealed exactly 20 years after it was passed. But other laws passed during this era involved the Senate in the removal process. For example, the Act of July 25, 1868, passed with the approval of President Johnson, established Wyoming as a territory and allowed the President to remove the governor and certain other officers, but subject to the consent of the Senate. Another statute, enacted July 12, 1876, provided:

> Postmasters of the first, second and third classes shall be appointed and may be removed by the President by and with the advice and consent of the Senate and shall hold their offices for four years unless sooner removed or suspended according to law.

In that era, the great majority of civilian appointees by President were postmasters of these classes.

In February 1920, President Wilson directed the removal of Myers, a postmaster of the first class in Portland, Oregon. The Senate did not consent. But the Supreme Court held that the 1876 Act's limitation on the President's removal power was unconstitutional, and it strongly implied that the 1867 Act had been invalid as well. *Myers v. United States* (1926).

Chief Justice Taft, himself a former President, wrote for the majority. He drew a sharp distinction between the role of the Senate in appointment and in removal:

> When a nomination is made, it may be presumed that the Senate is, or may become, as well advised as to the fitness of the nominee as the President, but in the nature of things the defects in ability or intelligence or loyalty in the administration of the laws of one who has served as an officer under the President are facts as to which the President, or his trusted subordinates, must be better informed than the Senate, and the power to remove him may, therefore, be regarded as confined, for very sound and practical reasons, to the governmental authority which has administrative control. The power of removal is incident to the power of appointment, not to the power of advising and consenting to appointment . . . .
>
> Finding [officers in his administrative control] to be negligent and inefficient, the President should have the power to remove them.

Taft did not believe this holding interfered with Civil Service protections. Recall that under the Appointments Clause inferior officers need not be appointed by the President, and he asserted that "Congress, in committing the appointment of such inferior officers to the heads of departments, may prescribe incidental regulations controlling and restricting the latter in the exercise of the power of removal." But, even in the case of an inferior officer, if Congress decided to give the appointment to the President, then "the power of removal must remain where the Constitution places it, with the President, as part of the executive power . . . ."

Justices Holmes, McReynolds, and Brandeis dissented. (You might ask yourself: Which of those is not like the others?) Holmes applied a simple greater-includes-the-lesser logic. Because the postmastership was "an office that owes its existence to Congress and that Congress may abolish to-morrow," he did not see a problem with Congress requiring Senate consent for removal. McReynolds emphasized the lack of an explicit presidential removal power in the text of the Constitution:

> Nothing short of language clear beyond serious disputation should be held to clothe the President with authority wholly beyond congressional control arbitrarily to dismiss every officer whom he appoints except a few judges. There are no such words in the Constitution . . . .

Brandeis, in addition to emphasizing the "persistent" nature of the legislative practice at issue, combined the perspectives of both Holmes and McReynolds:

> [T]he ability to remove a subordinate executive officer . . . is not a power inherent in a chief executive. The President's power of removal from statutory civil inferior offices, like the power of appointment to them, comes immediately from Congress. It is true that . . . when the Senate grants or withholds consent to a removal by the President, it participates in an executive act. But the Constitution has confessedly granted to Congress the legislative power to create offices, and to prescribe the tenure thereof; and it has not in terms denied to Congress the power to control removals. To prescribe the tenure involves prescribing the conditions under which incumbency shall cease.

Nor did he believe that the President's responsibility to "take Care that the Laws be faithfully executed" provided any constraint: "The end to which the President's efforts are to be directed is not the most efficient civil service conceivable, but the faithful execution of the laws consistent with the provisions therefor made by Congress."

In 1933, President Roosevelt removed William E. Humphrey from his position as Commissioner of the Federal Trade Commission (FTC). Roosevelt's termination correspondence made clear that the removal was prompted by policy differences with Humphrey, who had been appointed by his predecessor, Herbert Hoover. Given the result in *Myers*, Roosevelt may have felt that his removal stood on solid legal ground despite the facts that Humphrey had a seven-year term and the governing statute allowed removal only "for inefficiency, neglect of duty, or malfeasance in office." But to his chagrin, in *Humphrey's Executor v. United States* (1935), the Supreme Court held unanimously that the statutory provision was valid and the removal was not. Justice Sutherland, a former Senator, delivered the Court's opinion; Justice McReynolds added a brief nyah-nyah statement that simply pointed to his *Myers* dissent.

WORTH NOTING *Humphrey's Executor* was issued the same day (sometimes referred to as Black Monday) as the *Schechter Poultry* case and another that invalidated a significant piece of New Deal legislation. All three were unanimous.

In distinguishing *Myers*, Sutherland began by emphasizing that the two removal provisions were actually quite different. In *Myers*, "the narrow point actually decided was only that the President had power to remove a postmaster of the first class, without the advice and consent of the Senate as required by act of Congress." But most of his discussion focused on the differences in the offices involved.

The FTC is a five-member commission directed to prevent the use of unfair methods of competition in commerce. In this role, it typically begins by stating a complaint against a person or entity accused of violating the statute, and then holds a hearing at which the respondent may appear. If the FTC finds a statutory violation, it makes a written report and issues a cease-and-desist order; if necessary, the Commission can apply to the appropriate court of appeals for enforcement. While describing these functions, Justice Sutherland emphasized comments in the legislative history of the FTC Act indicating that

Congress believed the independence of the Commission was crucial; one, for example, asserted that the Commission should be "separate and apart from any existing department of the government—not subject to the orders of the President."

The FTC was created in 1914, during the Progressive Era, a period of great confidence in the value of scientific, nonpolitical expertise.

Under the Act, Justice Sutherland wrote,

> [the] commission is to be nonpartisan; and it must, from the very nature of its duties, act with entire impartiality. It is charged with the enforcement of no policy except the policy of the law. Its duties are neither political nor executive, but predominantly quasi judicial and quasi legislative. Like the Interstate Commerce Commission, its members are called upon to exercise the trained judgment of a body of experts "appointed by law and informed by experience."
>
> Such a body cannot in any proper sense be characterized as an arm or an eye of the executive. Its duties are performed without executive leave and, in the contemplation of the statute, must be free from executive control. In administering the provisions of the statute in respect of "unfair methods of competition," that is to say, in filling in and administering the details embodied by that general standard, the commission acts in part quasi legislatively and in part quasi judicially. In making investigations and reports thereon for the information of Congress under § 6, in aid of the legislative power, it acts as a legislative agency. Under § 7, which authorizes the commission to act as a master in chancery under rules prescribed by the court, it acts as an agency of the judiciary. To the extent that it exercises any executive function, as distinguished from executive power in the constitutional sense, it does so in the discharge and effectuation of its quasi legislative or quasi judicial powers, or as an agency of the legislative or judicial departments of the government.

Sutherland was disturbed by the prospect that striking down the removal restriction in this case would mean that the President had "illimitable" power for all civil officers other than the judiciary. He responded by moving far in the other direction. Characterizing a postmaster as a "subordinate and aid" to the President, "an executive officer restricted to the performance of executive functions[,] charged with no duty at all related to either the legislative or judicial power," his opinion held that "the necessary reach" of *Myers* went "far enough to include all purely executive officers" and "no farther." And he explicitly disapproved all statements in dicta in *Myers* that were "out of harmony with the views here set forth."

Sutherland claimed that the result of the decision was in keeping with "[t]he fundamental necessity of maintaining each of the three general departments of government entirely free from the control or coercive influence, direct or indirect, of either of the others"; the removal power claimed here "threatens the independence of a commission, which is not only wholly disconnected from the executive department, but which . . . was created by Congress as a means of carrying into operation legislative and judicial powers, and as an agency of the legislative and judicial departments."

At the close of the opinion, recognizing that the other cases might fall into "a field of doubt" between the *Myers* and *Humphrey's* situations, Sutherland said, "[W]e leave such cases as may fall within it for future consideration and determination as they may arise." And, over time, arise they did.

In *Bowsher v. Synar* (1986), the U.S. Supreme Court revisited *Myers* as part of its review of the deficit reduction scheme known as the Gramm-Rudman-Hollings Act. The Act authorized the Comptroller General of the United States to impose spending cuts across the entire federal budget on a program-by-program basis. The only way to remove the Comptroller General from office was by a joint congressional resolution, a form of legislative action that is subject to presidential veto in the same way as a statute. Before Congress could vote to remove the Comptroller General, however, it had to find one of the following causes: "(i) permanent disability; (ii) inefficiency; (iii) neglect of duty; (iv) malfeasance; or (v) a felony or conduct involving moral turpitude."

The Court held this portion of the Act unconstitutional. Most importantly, it held that the Comptroller General was an executive officer:

> Appellants suggest that the duties assigned to the Comptroller General in the Act are essentially ministerial and mechanical so that their performance does not constitute "execution of the law" in a meaningful sense. On the contrary, we view these functions as plainly entailing execution of the law in constitutional terms. Interpreting

a law enacted by Congress to implement the legislative mandate is the very essence of "execution" of the law.

This rendered the statutory scheme unconstitutional. Citing *Myers* as authoritative precedent on the point, the Court held that

> Congress cannot reserve for itself the power of removal of an officer charged with the execution of the laws except by impeachment. To permit the execution of the laws to be vested in an officer answerable only to Congress would, in practical terms, reserve in Congress control over the execution of the laws. . . . The structure of the Constitution does not permit Congress to execute the laws; it follows that Congress cannot grant to an officer under its control what it does not possess. . . .

Justice Stevens, joined by Justice Marshall, concurred in the judgment, but disagreed with the Court's separation-of-powers reasoning. In his view, the Court's analysis rested on "the unstated and unsound premise that there is a definite line that distinguishes executive power from legislative power." To the contrary, he argued,

> "[t]he great ordinances of the Constitution do not establish and divide fields of black and white." *Springer v. Philippine Islands* (1928) (Holmes, J., dissenting). . . . One reason that the exercise of legislative, executive, and judicial powers cannot be categorically distributed among three mutually exclusive branches of Government is that governmental power cannot always be readily characterized with only one of those three labels. On the contrary, as our cases demonstrate, a particular function, like a chameleon, will often take on the aspect of the office to which it is assigned.

Indeed, he argued, "[t]he powers delegated to the Comptroller General by § 251 of the Act before us today have a similar chameleon-like quality." If budgetary decisions enacted through bicameralism and presentment would be viewed as legislative, then

> Under the . . . analysis adopted by the majority today, it would . . . appear that the function at issue is "executive" if performed by the Comptroller General but "legislative" if performed by the Congress. . . . Thus, I do not agree that the Comptroller General's

responsibilities under the Gramm-Rudman-Hollings Act must be termed "executive powers," or even that our inquiry is much advanced by using that term. . . .

Justices White and Blackmun dissented. While Justice White had "no quarrel with the proposition that the powers exercised by the Comptroller under the Act may be characterized as 'executive' in that they involve the interpretation and carrying out of the Act's mandate," he observed that the "practical result of the removal provision is not to render the Comptroller unduly dependent upon or subservient to Congress, but to render him one of the most independent officers in the entire federal establishment."

Recall that *Morrison v. Olson* (1988) held that an independent counsel under the Ethics in Government Act of 1978 was an inferior officer who could be appointed by a federal court. See pp. 762–772. The following excerpt from *Morrison* confronts the same statute's substantive "good cause" restriction on removing an independent counsel.

Morrison v. Olson

Supreme Court of the United States, 1988.
487 U.S. 654.

CHIEF JUSTICE REHNQUIST delivered the opinion of the Court.

. . . Briefly stated, Title VI of the Ethics in Government Act allows for the appointment of an "independent counsel" to investigate and, if appropriate, prosecute certain high-ranking Government officials for violations of federal criminal laws.

[T]he procedure for removing an independent counsel . . . provides:

An independent counsel appointed under this chapter may be removed from office, other than by impeachment and conviction, only by the personal action of the Attorney General and only for good cause, physical disability, mental incapacity, or any other condition that substantially impairs the performance of such independent counsel's duties.

[A]n independent counsel can obtain judicial review of the Attorney General's action by filing a civil action in the United States District Court for the District of Columbia. . . .

V

We now turn to consider whether the Act is invalid under the constitutional principle of separation of powers. Two related issues must be addressed: The first is whether the provision of the Act restricting the Attorney General's power to remove the independent counsel to only those instances in which he can show "good cause," taken by itself, impermissibly interferes with the President's exercise of his constitutionally appointed functions. The second is whether, taken as a whole, the Act violates the separation of powers by reducing the President's ability to control the prosecutorial powers wielded by the independent counsel.

A

. . . Unlike both *Bowsher v. Synar* (1986) and *Myers v. United States* (1926), this case does not involve an attempt by Congress itself to gain a role in the removal of executive officials other than its established powers of impeachment and conviction. The Act instead puts the removal power squarely in the hands of the Executive Branch; an independent counsel may be removed from office, "only by the personal action of the Attorney General, and only for good cause."[23] There is no requirement of congressional approval of the Attorney General's removal decision, though the decision is subject to judicial review. In our view, the removal provisions of the Act make this case more analogous to *Humphrey's Executor v. United States* (1935) . . . than to *Myers* or *Bowsher*. . . .

Appellees contend that *Humphrey's Executor* [is] distinguishable from this case because [it] did not involve officials who performed a "core executive function." They argue that our decision in *Humphrey's Executor* rests on a distinction between "purely executive" officials and officials who exercise "quasi-legislative" and "quasi-judicial" powers. In their view, when a "purely executive" official is involved, the governing precedent is *Myers*, not *Humphrey's Executor*. And, under *Myers*, the President must have absolute discretion to discharge "purely" executive officials at will.

---

[23] As noted, an independent counsel may also be removed through impeachment and conviction. In addition, the Attorney General may remove a counsel for "physical disability, mental incapacity, or any other condition that substantially impairs the performance" of his or her duties.

We undoubtedly did rely on the terms "quasi-legislative" and "quasi-ju-dicial" to distinguish the official[ ] involved in *Humphrey's Executor* . . . from those in *Myers*, but our present considered view is that the determination of whether the Constitution allows Congress to impose a "good cause"-type re-striction on the President's power to remove an official cannot be made to turn on whether or not that official is classified as "purely executive." The analysis contained in our removal cases is designed not to define rigid categories of those officials who may or may not be removed at will by the President,[28] but to ensure that Congress does not interfere with the President's exercise of the "executive power" and his constitutionally appointed duty to "take care that the laws be faithfully executed" under Article II. . . .[29] [T]he characterization of the agencies in *Humphrey's Executor* . . . as "quasi-legislative" or "quasi-judicial" in large part reflected our judgment that it was not essential to the President's proper execution of his Article II powers that these agencies be headed up by individuals who were removable at will.[30]

We do not mean to suggest that an analysis of the functions served by the officials at issue is irrelevant. But the real question is whether the remov-al restrictions are of such a nature that they impede the President's ability to perform his constitutional duty, and the functions of the officials in question must be analyzed in that light.

Considering for the moment the "good cause" removal provision in isola-tion from the other parts of the Act at issue in this case, we cannot say that the imposition of a "good cause" standard for removal by itself unduly trammels on executive authority. There is no real dispute that the functions performed by the independent counsel are "executive" in the sense that they are law enforce-ment functions that typically have been undertaken by officials within the Executive Branch. As we noted above, however, the independent counsel is an

---

[28]   The difficulty of defining such categories of "executive" or "quasi-legislative" officials is illustrated by a com-parison of our decisions in cases such as *Humphrey's Executor*, *Buckley v. Valeo*, and *Bowsher v. Synar*.

[29]   The dissent says that the language of Article II vesting the executive power of the United States in the Pres-ident requires that every officer of the United States exercising any part of that power must serve at the pleasure of the President and be removable by him at will. This rigid demarcation—a demarcation incapable of being altered by law in the slightest degree, and applicable to tens of thousands of holders of offices neither known nor foreseen by the Framers—depends upon an extrapolation from general constitutional language which we think is more than the text will bear. . . .

[30]   The terms also may be used to describe the circumstances in which Congress might be more inclined to find that a degree of independence from the Executive, such as that afforded by a "good cause" removal standard, is necessary to the proper functioning of the agency or official. It is not difficult to imagine situations in which Congress might desire that an official performing "quasi-judicial" functions, for example, would be free of ex-ecutive or political control.

inferior officer under the Appointments Clause, with limited jurisdiction and tenure and lacking policymaking or significant administrative authority. Although the counsel exercises no small amount of discretion and judgment in deciding how to carry out his or her duties under the Act, we simply do not see how the President's need to control the exercise of that discretion is so central to the func-

 CROSS REFERENCE For more detail on the independent counsel's responsibilities, see *Morrison*'s appointments discussion, presented at pp. 762–772.

tioning of the Executive Branch as to require as a matter of constitutional law that the counsel be terminable at will by the President.[31]

Nor do we think that the "good cause" removal provision at issue here impermissibly burdens the President's power to control or supervise the independent counsel, as an executive official, in the execution of his or her duties under the Act. This is not a case in which the power to remove an executive official has been completely stripped from the President, thus providing no means for the President to ensure the "faithful execution" of the laws. Rather, because the independent counsel may be terminated for "good cause," the Executive, through the Attorney General, retains ample authority to assure that the counsel is competently performing his or her statutory responsibilities in a manner that comports with the provisions of the Act.

Although we need not decide in this case exactly what is encompassed within the term "good cause" under the Act, the legislative history of the removal provision also makes clear that the Attorney General may remove an independent counsel for "misconduct." See H.R. Conf. Rep. No. 100–452 (1987). Here, as with the provision of the Act conferring the appointment authority of the independent counsel on the special court, the congressional determination to limit the removal power of the Attorney General was essential, in the view of Congress, to establish the necessary independence of the office. We do not think that this limitation as it presently stands sufficiently deprives the President of control over the independent counsel to interfere impermissibly with his constitutional obligation to ensure the faithful execution of the laws.

---

[31] We note by way of comparison that various federal agencies whose officers are covered by "good cause" removal restrictions exercise civil enforcement powers that are analogous to the prosecutorial powers wielded by an independent counsel. See, *e.g.*, 15 U.S.C. § 45(m) (giving the FTC the authority to bring civil actions to recover civil penalties for the violations of rules respecting unfair competition); 15 U.S.C. §§ 2061, 2071, 2076(b)(7)(A) (giving the Consumer Product Safety Commission the authority to obtain injunctions and apply for seizure of hazardous products).

B

The final question to be addressed is whether the Act, taken as a whole, violates the principle of separation of powers by unduly interfering with the role of the Executive Branch. Time and again we have reaffirmed the importance in our constitutional scheme of the separation of governmental powers into the three coordinate branches. . . . We have not hesitated to invalidate provisions of law which violate this principle. On the other hand, we have never held that the Constitution requires that the three branches of Government "operate with absolute independence." . . .

We observe first that this case does not involve an attempt by Congress to increase its own powers at the expense of the Executive Branch. Unlike some of our previous cases, most recently *Bowsher v. Synar*, this case simply does not pose a "dange[r] of congressional usurpation of Executive Branch functions." Indeed, with the exception of the power of impeachment—which applies to all officers of the United States—Congress retained for itself no powers of control or supervision over an independent counsel. The Act does empower certain Members of Congress to request the Attorney General to apply for the appointment of an independent counsel, but the Attorney General has no duty to comply with the request. . . .

Similarly, we do not think that the Act works any *judicial* usurpation of properly executive functions. As should be apparent from our discussion of the Appointments Clause above, the power to appoint inferior officers such as independent counsel is not in itself an "executive" function in the constitutional sense, at least when Congress has exercised its power to vest the appointment of an inferior office in the "courts of Law." . . . The Act does give a federal court the power to review the Attorney General's decision to remove an independent counsel, but in our view this is a function that is well within the traditional power of the Judiciary.

Finally, we do not think that the Act "impermissibly undermine[s]" the powers of the Executive Branch, *CFTC v. Schor* (1986), or "disrupts the proper balance between the coordinate branches [thus] preventing the Executive Branch from accomplishing its constitutionally assigned functions," *Nixon v. Administrator of General Services* (1977). It is undeniable that the Act reduces the amount of control or supervision that the Attorney General and, through him, the President exercises over the investigation and prosecution of a certain class of alleged criminal activity. The Attorney General is not allowed to appoint the individual of his choice; he does not determine the counsel's jurisdiction; and his power to remove a counsel is limited.[34] Nonetheless, the Act does give the Attorney General several means of supervising or controlling the prosecutorial powers that may be wielded by an independent counsel. Most importantly, the Attorney General retains the power to remove the counsel for "good cause," a power that we have already concluded provides the Executive with substantial ability to ensure that the laws are "faithfully executed" by an independent counsel. No independent counsel may be appointed without a specific request by the Attorney General, and the Attorney General's decision not to request appointment if he finds "no reasonable grounds to believe that further investigation is warranted" is committed to his unreviewable discretion. The Act thus gives the Executive a degree of control over the power to initiate an investigation by the independent counsel. In addition, the jurisdiction of the independent counsel is defined with reference to the facts submitted by the Attorney General, and once a counsel is appointed, the Act requires that the counsel abide by Justice Department policy unless it is not "possible" to do so.

Notwithstanding the fact that the counsel is to some degree "independent" and free from executive supervision to a greater extent than other federal prosecutors, in our view these features of the Act give the Executive Branch sufficient control over the independent counsel to ensure that the President is able to perform his constitutionally assigned duties.

VI

In sum, we conclude today that . . . the Act does not violate the separation-of-powers principle by impermissibly interfering with the functions of the Executive Branch. The decision of the Court of Appeals is therefore

Reversed.

Justice Kennedy took no part in the consideration or decision of this case.

Justice Scalia, dissenting.

[T]he Founders conspicuously and very consciously declined to sap the Executive's strength in the same way they had weakened the Legislature: by dividing the executive power. Proposals to have multiple executives, or a council

---

[34]   With these provisions, the degree of control exercised by the Executive Branch over an independent counsel is clearly diminished in relation to that exercised over other prosecutors, such as the United States Attorneys, who are appointed by the President and subject to termination at will.

of advisers with separate authority were rejected. Thus, while "[a]ll legislative Powers herein granted shall be vested in a Congress of the United States, which shall consist of a Senate *and* House of Representatives," U.S. Const., Art. I, § 1 (emphasis added), "[t]he executive Power shall be vested in *a President of the United States,*" Art. II, § 1, cl. 1 (emphasis added).

That is what this suit is about. Power. The allocation of power among Congress, the President, and the courts in such fashion as to preserve the equilibrium the Constitution sought to establish—so that "a gradual concentration of the several powers in the same department," Federalist No. 51 (J. Madison), can effectively be resisted. Frequently an issue of this sort will come before the Court clad, so to speak, in sheep's clothing: the potential of the asserted principle to effect important change in the equilibrium of power is not immediately evident, and must be discerned by a careful and perceptive analysis. But this wolf comes as a wolf.

I

The present case began when [Congress sent the Attorney General a formal request that he appoint an independent counsel to investigate Mr. Olson and others.] As a practical matter, it would be surprising if the Attorney General had any choice (assuming this statute is constitutional) but to seek appointment of an independent counsel to pursue the charges. . . . Merely the political consequences (to him and the President) of seeming to break the law by refusing to do so would have been substantial. How could it not be, the public would ask, that a 3,000-page indictment drawn by our representatives over 2 ½ years does not even establish "reasonable grounds to believe" that further investigation or prosecution is warranted with respect to at least the principal alleged culprit?

But the Act establishes more than just practical compulsion. Although the Court's opinion asserts that the Attorney General had "no duty to comply with the [congressional] request," that is not entirely accurate. He *had* a duty to comply unless he could conclude that there were "*no reasonable grounds to believe,*" not that prosecution was warranted, but merely that "*further investigation*" was warranted, after a 90-day investigation in which he was prohibited from using such routine investigative techniques as grand juries, plea bargaining, grants of immunity, or even subpoenas. . . .

Thus, by the application of this statute in the present case, Congress has effectively compelled a criminal investigation of a high-level appointee of the President in connection with his actions arising out of a bitter power dispute between the President and the Legislative Branch. . . . The decisions regarding the scope of that further investigation, its duration, and, finally, whether or not prosecution should ensue, are likewise beyond the control of the President and his subordinates.

II

. . . It is rare in a case dealing, as this one does, with the constitutionality of a statute passed by the Congress of the United States, not to find anywhere in the Court's opinion the usual, almost formulary caution that we owe great deference to Congress' view that what it has done is constitutional, and that we will decline to apply the statute only if the presumption of constitutionality can be overcome. That caution is not recited by the Court in the present case *because it does not apply*. Where a private citizen challenges action of the Government on grounds unrelated to separation of powers, harmonious functioning of the system demands that we ordinarily give some deference, or a presumption of validity, to the actions of the political branches in what is agreed, between themselves at least, to be within their respective spheres. But where the issue pertains to separation of powers, and the political branches are (as here) in disagreement, neither can be presumed correct. . . . The playing field for the present case, in other words, is a level one. As one of the interested and coordinate parties to the underlying constitutional dispute, Congress, no more than the President, is entitled to the benefit of the doubt.

To repeat, Article II, § 1, cl. 1, of the Constitution provides: "The executive Power shall be vested in a President of the United States." As I described at the outset of this opinion, this does not mean *some of* the executive power, but *all of* the executive power.

It seems to me, therefore, that the decision of the Court of Appeals invalidating the present statute must be upheld on fundamental separation-of-powers principles if the following two questions are answered affirmatively:

(1) Is the conduct of a criminal prosecution (and of an investigation to decide whether to prosecute) the exercise of purely executive power?

(2) Does the statute deprive the President of the United States of exclusive control over the exercise of that power?

Surprising to say, the Court appears to concede an affirmative answer to both questions, but seeks to avoid the inevitable conclusion that since the statute vests some purely executive power in a person who is not the President of the United States it is void.

The Court concedes that "[t]here is no real dispute that the functions performed by the independent counsel are 'executive'," though it qualifies that concession by adding "in the sense that they are law enforcement functions that typically have been undertaken by officials within the Executive Branch." The qualifier adds nothing but atmosphere. In what *other* sense can one identify "the executive Power" that is supposed to be vested in the President (unless it includes everything the Executive Branch is given to do) *except* by reference to what has always and everywhere—if conducted by government at all—been conducted never by the legislature, never by the courts, and always by the executive. There is no possible doubt that the independent counsel's functions fit this description. . . . Governmental investigation and prosecution of crimes is a quintessentially executive function. See *Buckley v. Valeo* (1976); *United States v. Nixon* (1974).

As for the second question, whether the statute before us deprives the President of exclusive control over that quintessentially executive activity: The Court does not, and could not possibly, assert that it does not. . . . Instead, the Court points out that the President, through his Attorney General, has at least *some* control. . . .

As I have said, however, it is ultimately irrelevant *how much* the statute reduces Presidential control. . . . It effects a revolution in our constitutional jurisprudence for the Court, once it has determined that (1) purely executive functions are at issue here, and (2) those functions have been given to a person whose actions are not fully within the supervision and control of the President, nonetheless to proceed further to [ask questions of degree]. It is not for us to determine, and we have never presumed to determine, how much of the purely executive powers of government must be within the full control of the President. The Constitution prescribes that they *all* are. . . .

Is it unthinkable that the President should have such exclusive power, even when alleged crimes by him or his close associates are at issue? . . . A system of separate and coordinate powers necessarily involves an acceptance of exclusive power that can theoretically be abused. . . . The checks against any branch's abuse of its exclusive powers are twofold: First, retaliation by one of the other branch's use of *its* exclusive powers: Congress, for example, can impeach the executive who willfully fails to enforce the laws; the executive can decline to prosecute under unconstitutional statutes; and the courts can dismiss malicious prosecutions. Second, and ultimately, there is the political check that the people will replace those in the political branches . . . who are guilty of abuse. Political pressures produced special prosecutors—for Teapot Dome and for Watergate, for example—long before this statute created the independent counsel.

The Court has, nonetheless, replaced the clear constitutional prescription that the executive power belongs to the President with a "balancing test." What are the standards to determine how the balance is to be struck, that is, how much removal of Presidential power is too much? . . . The most amazing feature of the Court's opinion is that it does not even purport to give an answer. It simply *announces*, with no analysis, that the ability to control the decision whether to investigate and prosecute the President's closest advisers, and indeed the President himself, is not "so central to the functioning of the Executive Branch" as to be constitutionally required to be within the President's control. . . . Evidently, the governing standard is to be what might be called the unfettered wisdom of a majority of this Court, revealed to an obedient people on a case-by-case basis. This is not only not the government of laws that the Constitution established; it is not a government of laws at all. . . .

"[O]ur present considered view" is simply that *any* executive officer's removal can be restricted, so long as the President remains "able to accomplish his constitutional role." There are now no lines. If the removal of a prosecutor, the virtual embodiment of the power to "take care that the laws be faithfully executed," can be restricted, what officer's removal cannot? This is an open invitation for Congress to experiment. . . .

For Discussion

(1) What is the *Morrison* majority's test for whether a removal restriction is unconstitutional? On that test, which of the following officers could be insulated from at-will removal by a for-cause statutory requirement?

> The Secretary of State, whose portfolio includes international diplomacy, the negotiation of treaties, and the administration of the State Department's worldwide network of embassies and consulates.

> The Attorney General, who runs the Department of Justice and is ultimately responsible for most litigation conducted on behalf of the United States, including both civil and criminal controversies.

> The Secretary of Defense, who is in charge of the Army, Navy, Marine Corps, and Air Force and in that capacity is primarily concerned with securing the national security of the United States.

> The seven-member Board of Governors of the Federal Reserve System, which is the central bank of the United States and in that capacity conducts the official U.S. monetary policy (which has important effects on employment and inflation) and supervises the private financial system. Its members are appointed on a staggered basis every two years for a seven-year term.

If the answers to these questions aren't clear, how might their resolution be achieved? How satisfying are the possible options for doing so?

(2) Justice Scalia frames his opinion around the attractively simple claim that Article II vested "all" the executive power in the President. This assertion would have nonplussed the Founders. Alexander Hamilton described the conventional understanding as follows:

> Is there any one branch in which the whole legislative and executive powers are lodged? No. The legislative authority is lodged in three distinct branches properly balanced: The executive authority is divided between two branches and the judicial is still reserved for an independent body, who hold their office during good behaviour.

Alexander Hamilton, New York Convention Debates and Proceedings (June 26, 1788). See also Mortenson, *The Executive Power Clause,* 168 U. Pa. L. Rev. 1269 (2020). If Hamilton and Mortenson are correct, does this mistake in the linchpin of Justice Scalia's argument affect the persuasiveness of his opinion? Does the answer depend on whether you are an originalist?

(3) People tend (understandably) to read Justice Scalia to claim that the logical consequences of vesting "the" executive power in the President require that he have unfettered removal authority over those who wield it in his stead. As it turns out, that reading is incorrect. Elsewhere in his opinion, Scalia drops the following footnote:

> The Court misunderstands my opinion to say that "every officer of the United States exercising any part of [the executive] power must serve at the pleasure of the President and be removable by him at will." Of course, as my discussion here demonstrates, that has never been the law and I do not assert otherwise. What I do assert—and what the Constitution seems plainly to prescribe—is

that the President must have control over all exercises of the executive power. That requires that he have plenary power to remove
principal officers such as the independent counsel, but it does
not require that he have plenary power to remove inferior officers.
Since the latter are, as I have described, subordinate to, i.e., subject
to the supervision of, principal officers who (being removable at
will) have the President's complete confidence, it is enough—at
least if they have been appointed by the President or by a principal
officer—that they be removable for cause, which would include,
of course, the failure to accept supervision. Thus, *United States v.
Perkins* (1886) [(upholding for-cause standard on the removal of
inferior officers)] is in no way inconsistent with my views.

Does Scalia's position on inferior officers surprise you, given his criticism
of the majority's test as mushy and standardless? Can you reconcile his
claim that "the purely executive powers of government must be within the
full control of the President" with his concession that lower-level executive
officials can be protected by a good-cause standard? Can you explain what
is "enough" supervision on Scalia's approach without resorting to what he
elsewhere calls "ad hoc, standardless judgment"? If the answers to these
questions aren't clear, how might their resolution be achieved? How satisfying are the possible options for doing so?

The Court applied the *Morrison* removal test in *Free Enterprise Fund v.
Public Company Accounting Oversight Board* (2010). The Board, typically short-
handed as PCAOB and pronounced "peekaboo," was created as part of the
Sarbanes-Oxley Act of 2002, in an effort to tighten regulation of the accounting
industry. Its five members were appointed by the Security and Exchange Commission (itself an independent agency whose Commissioners were understood
to be protected by a good-cause standard). While the PCAOB Board could not
issue rules or impose sanctions without the SEC's approval, they could only
be removed by the SEC "for good cause shown," a standard understood to be
similar to that applicable to the FTC Commissioners in *Humphrey's Executor*.

The Supreme Court, per Chief Justice Roberts, held that this structure was
unconstitutional even as applied to inferior officers, because "the *dual* for-cause
limitations on the removal of Board members contravene the Constitution's
separation of powers" (emphasis added). It explained:

[W]e have previously upheld limited restrictions on the President's
removal power. In those cases, however, only one level of protected

tenure separated the President from an officer exercising executive power. It was the President—or a subordinate he could remove at will—who decided whether the officer's conduct merited removal under the good-cause standard. The Act before us does something quite different. It not only protects Board members from removal except for good cause, but withdraws from the President any decision on whether that good cause exists. That decision is vested instead in other tenured officers—the Commissioners—none of whom is subject to the President's direct control. The result is a Board that is not accountable to the President, and a President who is not responsible for the Board. The added layer of tenure protection makes a difference. . . .

This novel structure does not merely add to the Board's independence, but transforms it. Neither the President, nor anyone directly responsible to him, nor even an officer whose conduct he may review only for good cause, has full control over the Board. The President is stripped of the power our precedents have preserved, and his ability to execute the laws—by holding his subordinates accountable for their conduct—is impaired. That arrangement is contrary to Article II's vesting of the executive power in the President. Without the ability to oversee the Board, or to attribute the Board's failings to those whom he *can* oversee, the President is no longer the judge of the Board's conduct. He is not the one who decides whether Board members are abusing their offices or neglecting their duties. He can neither ensure that the laws are faithfully executed, nor be held responsible for a Board member's breach of faith. . . .

Indeed, if allowed to stand, this dispersion of responsibility could be multiplied. If Congress can shelter the bureaucracy behind two layers of good-cause tenure, why not a third? At oral argument, the Government was unwilling to concede that even *five* layers between the President and the Board would be too many. The officers of such an agency—safely encased within a Matryoshka doll of tenure protections—would be immune from Presidential oversight, even as they exercised power in the people's name. . . .

In an opinion authored by Justice Breyer, four dissenting justices worried that the Court's decision threatened the widespread use of tenure protections for line-level civil servants and administrative law judges in independent agencies. The majority suggested that this might not be true:

> [M]any civil servants within independent agencies would not qualify as "Officers of the United States," who "exercis[e] significant authority pursuant to the laws of the United States." *Buckley v. Valeo* (1976).[9] The parties here concede that Board members are executive "Officers," as that term is used in the Constitution. We do not decide the status of other Government employees, nor do we decide whether "lesser functionaries subordinate to officers of the United States" must be subject to the same sort of control as those who exercise "significant authority pursuant to the laws." *Buckley.* Nor do the employees referenced by the dissent enjoy the same significant and unusual protections from Presidential oversight as members of the Board. . . . Nothing in our opinion, therefore, should be read to cast doubt on the use of what is colloquially known as the civil service system within independent agencies. . . .

The majority likewise suggested that the independence of administrative law judges might not necessarily be affected by its decision in *PCAOB*:

> For similar reasons, our holding also does not address that subset of independent agency employees who serve as administrative law judges. See, e.g., 5 U.S.C. §§ 556(c), 3105. Whether administrative law judges are necessarily "Officers of the United States" is disputed. And unlike members of the Board, many administrative law judges of course perform adjudicative rather than enforcement or policymaking functions, or possess purely recommendatory powers. The Government below refused to identify either "civil service tenure-protected employees in independent agencies" or administrative law judges as "precedent for the PCAOB."

FOR DISCUSSION

Are you convinced by the Court's efforts to distinguish the PCAOB Board from administrative law judges?

---

[9]   One "may be an agent or employee working for the government and paid by it, as nine-tenths of the persons rendering service to the government undoubtedly are, without thereby becoming its office[r]." *United States v. Germaine* (1879). The applicable proportion has of course increased dramatically since 1879.

The Court's most recent removal case was prompted by Congress's creation, during the Obama Administration, of a new regulatory agency called the Consumer Financial Protection Bureau. The agency—which was funded directly by the Federal Reserve rather than through the congressional appropriations process—was headed by a single Director, who could only be removed from office for good cause.

As you read the majority opinion and dissent in *Seila Law v. CFPB*, consider which opinion better characterizes the state of the law prior to this decision. Does the case simply consolidate existing precedent, or does it shift removal doctrine in a new direction?

Seila Law v. Consumer Financial Protection Bureau

Supreme Court of the United States, 2020.
140 S.Ct. 2183.

CHIEF JUSTICE ROBERTS delivered the opinion of the Court with respect to Parts I, II, and III.

In the wake of the 2008 financial crisis, Congress established the Consumer Financial Protection Bureau (CFPB), an independent regulatory agency tasked with ensuring that consumer debt products are safe and transparent. In organizing the CFPB, Congress deviated from the structure of nearly every other independent administrative agency in our history. Instead of placing the agency under the leadership of a board with multiple members, Congress provided that the CFPB would be led by a single Director, who serves for a longer term than the President and cannot be removed by the President except for inefficiency, neglect, or malfeasance. The CFPB Director has no boss, peers, or voters to report to. Yet the Director wields vast rulemaking, enforcement, and adjudicatory authority over a significant portion of the U. S. economy. The question before us is whether this arrangement violates the Constitution's separation of powers. . . .

I

A

In the summer of 2007, then-Professor Elizabeth Warren called for the creation of a new, independent federal agency focused on regulating consumer financial products. Warren, *Unsafe at Any Rate,* Democracy (2007). Professor Warren believed the financial products marketed to ordinary American households—credit cards, student loans, mortgages, and the like—had grown increasingly unsafe due to a "regulatory jumble" that paid too much attention to banks and too little to consumers. [Within months of Warren's writing, the subprime mortgage market collapsed, precipitating a devastating financial crisis. The incoming Obama administration adopted her recommendation for a new agency.] Like Professor Warren, the administration envisioned a traditional independent agency, run by a multimember board with a "diverse set of viewpoints and experiences."

In 2010, Congress acted on these proposals and created the Consumer Financial Protection Bureau (CFPB) as an independent financial regulator within the Federal Reserve System. Congress tasked the CFPB with "implement[ing]" and "enforc[ing]" a large body of financial consumer protection laws to "ensur[e] that all consumers have access to markets for consumer financial products and services and that markets for consumer financial products and services are fair, transparent, and competitive." Congress transferred the administration of 18 existing federal statutes to the CFPB, including the Fair Credit Reporting Act, the Fair Debt Collection Practices Act, and the Truth in Lending Act. In addition, Congress enacted a new prohibition on "any unfair, deceptive, or abusive act or practice" by certain participants in the consumer-finance sector. Congress authorized the CFPB to implement that broad standard (and the 18 pre-existing statutes placed under the agency's purview) through binding regulations.

Congress also vested the CFPB with potent enforcement powers. The agency has the authority to conduct investigations, issue subpoenas and civil investigative demands, initiate administrative adjudications, and prosecute civil actions in federal court. To remedy violations of federal consumer financial law, the CFPB may seek restitution, disgorgement, and injunctive relief, as well as civil penalties of up to $1,000,000 (inflation adjusted) for each day that a violation occurs. Since its inception, the CFPB has obtained over $11 billion in relief for over 25 million consumers, including a $1 billion penalty against a single bank in 2018.

The CFPB's rulemaking and enforcement powers are coupled with extensive adjudicatory authority. The agency may conduct administrative proceedings to "ensure or enforce compliance with" the statutes and regulations it administers. When the CFPB acts as an adjudicator, it has "jurisdiction to grant any appropriate legal or equitable relief." The "hearing officer" who presides over the proceedings may issue subpoenas, order depositions, and resolve any motions filed by the parties. At the close of the proceedings, the hearing officer issues a "recommended decision," and the CFPB Director considers that recommendation and "issue[s] a final decision and order."

Congress's design for the CFPB differed from the proposals of Professor Warren and the Obama administration in one critical respect. Rather than create a traditional independent agency headed by a multimember board or commission, Congress elected to place the CFPB under the leadership of a single Director. The CFPB Director is appointed by the President with the advice and consent of the Senate. The Director serves for a term of five years, during which the President may remove the Director from office only for "inefficiency, neglect of duty, or malfeasance in office."

Unlike most other agencies, the CFPB does not rely on the annual appropriations process for funding. Instead, the CFPB receives funding directly from the Federal Reserve, which is itself funded outside the appropriations process through bank assessments. Each year, the CFPB requests an amount that the Director deems "reasonably necessary to carry out" the agency's duties, and the Federal Reserve grants that request so long as it does not exceed 12% of the total operating expenses of the Federal Reserve (inflation adjusted). In recent years, the CFPB's annual budget has exceeded half a billion dollars.

B

Seila Law LLC is a California-based law firm that provides debt-related legal services to clients. In 2017, the CFPB issued a civil investigative demand to Seila Law to determine whether the firm had "engag[ed] in unlawful acts or practices in the advertising, marketing, or sale of debt relief services." The demand (essentially a subpoena) directed Seila Law to produce information and documents related to its business practices. . . .

When Seila Law refused [to comply], the CFPB filed a petition to enforce the demand in the District Court. . . . We granted certiorari to address the constitutionality of the CFPB's structure. . . .

III

We hold that the CFPB's leadership by a single individual removable only for inefficiency, neglect, or malfeasance violates the separation of powers.

A

Article II provides that "[t]he executive Power shall be vested in a President," who must "take Care that the Laws be faithfully executed." Art. II, § 1, cl. 1; *id.*, § 3. The entire "executive Power" belongs to the President alone. But because it would be "impossib[le]" for "one man" to "perform all the great business of the State," the Constitution assumes that lesser executive officers will "assist the supreme Magistrate in discharging the duties of his trust." *Writings of George Washington.*

These lesser officers must remain accountable to the President, whose authority they wield. As Madison explained, "[I]f any power whatsoever is in its nature Executive, it is the power of appointing, overseeing, and controlling those who execute the laws." Annals of Cong. (1789). That power, in turn, generally includes the ability to remove executive officials, for it is "only the authority that can remove" such officials that they "must fear and, in the performance of [their] functions, obey." *Bowsher v. Synar* (1986).

The President's removal power has long been confirmed by history and precedent. It "was discussed extensively in Congress when the first executive departments were created" in 1789. *Free Enterprise Fund v. Public Company Accounting Oversight Bd.* (2010). "The view that 'prevailed, as most consonant to the text of the Constitution' and 'to the requisite responsibility and harmony in the Executive Department,' was that the executive power included a power to oversee executive officers through removal." *Id.* (quoting Letter from James Madison to Thomas Jefferson (June 30, 1789)). . . .

The Court recognized the President's prerogative to remove executive officials in *Myers v. United States* (1926). . . . We recently reiterated the President's general removal power in *Free Enterprise Fund.* . . .

Free Enterprise Fund left in place two exceptions to the President's unrestricted removal power.

First, in *Humphrey's Executor v. United States* (1935) . . . the Court upheld a statute that protected the Commissioners of the FTC from removal except for "inefficiency, neglect of duty, or malfeasance in office." In reaching that conclusion, the Court stressed that Congress's ability to impose such removal restrictions "will depend upon the character of the office."

[T]he contours of the *Humphrey's Executor* exception [therefore] depend upon the characteristics of the agency before the Court. Rightly or wrongly, the Court viewed the FTC (as it existed in 1935) as exercising "no part of the executive power." Instead, it was "an administrative body" that performed "specified duties as a legislative or as a judicial aid." It acted "as a legislative agency" in "making investigations and reports" to Congress and "as an agency of the judiciary" in making recommendations to courts as a master in chancery. . . .[2]

The Court identified several organizational features that helped explain its characterization of the FTC as non-executive. Composed of five members—no more than three from the same political party—the Board was designed to be "non-partisan" and to "act with entire impartiality." The FTC's duties were "neither political nor executive," but instead called for "the trained judgment of a body of experts" "informed by experience." And the Commissioners' staggered, seven-year terms enabled the agency to accumulate technical expertise and avoid a "complete change" in leadership "at any one time."

In short, *Humphrey's Executor* permitted Congress to give for-cause removal protections to a multimember body of experts, balanced along partisan lines, that performed legislative and judicial functions and was said not to exercise any executive power. . . . *Humphrey's Executor* [also] reaffirmed the core holding of *Myers* that the President has "unrestrictable power . . . to remove purely executive officers." *Humphrey's Executor.* . . .

We have recognized a second exception for *inferior* officers in two cases, *United States v. Perkins* (1886) and *Morrison v. Olson* (1988). In *Perkins*, we upheld tenure protections for a naval cadet-engineer. And, in *Morrison*, we upheld a provision granting good-cause tenure protection to an independent counsel appointed to investigate and prosecute particular alleged crimes by high-ranking Government officials. Backing away from the reliance in *Humphrey's Executor* on the concepts of "quasi-legislative" and "quasi-judicial" power, we viewed the ultimate question as whether a removal restriction is of "such a nature that [it] impede[s] the President's ability to perform his constitutional duty." . . .

---

[2]   The Court's conclusion that the FTC did not exercise executive power has not withstood the test of time. As we observed in *Morrison v. Olson* (1988), "[I]t is hard to dispute that the powers of the FTC at the time of *Humphrey's Executor* would at the present time be considered 'executive,' at least to some degree."

These two exceptions—one for multimember expert agencies that do not wield substantial executive power, and one for inferior officers with limited duties and no policymaking or administrative authority—"represent what up to now have been the outermost constitutional limits of permissible congressional restrictions on the President's removal power." *PHH Corp. v. CFPB* (D.C. Cir. 2018) (Kavanaugh, J., dissenting).

B

Neither *Humphrey's Executor* nor *Morrison* resolves whether the CFPB Director's insulation from removal is constitutional. Start with *Humphrey's Executor*. Unlike the New Deal-era FTC upheld there, the CFPB is led by a single Director who cannot be described as a "body of experts" and cannot be considered "non-partisan" in the same sense as a group of officials drawn from both sides of the aisle. Moreover, while the staggered terms of the FTC Commissioners prevented complete turnovers in agency leadership and guaranteed that there would always be some Commissioners who had accrued significant expertise, the CFPB's single-Director structure and five-year term guarantee abrupt shifts in agency leadership and with it the loss of accumulated expertise.

In addition, the CFPB Director is hardly a mere legislative or judicial aid. Instead of making reports and recommendations to Congress, as the 1935 FTC did, the Director possesses the authority to promulgate binding rules fleshing out 19 federal statutes, including a broad prohibition on unfair and deceptive practices in a major segment of the U. S. economy. And instead of submitting recommended dispositions to an Article III court, the Director may unilaterally issue final decisions awarding legal and equitable relief in administrative adjudications. Finally, the Director's enforcement authority includes the power to seek daunting monetary penalties against private parties on behalf of the United States in federal court—a quintessentially executive power not considered in *Humphrey's Executor*.

The logic of *Morrison* also does not apply. Everyone agrees the CFPB Director is not an inferior officer, and her duties are far from limited. [T]he CFPB Director has the authority to bring the coercive power of the state to bear on millions of private citizens and businesses, imposing even billion-dollar penalties through administrative adjudications and civil actions.

In light of these differences, the constitutionality of the CFPB Director's insulation from removal cannot be settled by *Humphrey's Executor* or *Morrison* alone.

C

The question instead is whether to extend those precedents to the "new situation" before us, namely an independent agency led by a single Director and vested with significant executive power. *Free Enterprise Fund.* We decline to do so. Such an agency has no basis in history and no place in our constitutional structure.

1

"Perhaps the most telling indication of [a] severe constitutional problem" with an executive entity "is [a] lack of historical precedent" to support it. *Id.* An agency with a structure like that of the CFPB is almost wholly unprecedented. After years of litigating the agency's constitutionality, the Courts of Appeals, parties, and *amici* have identified "only a handful of isolated" incidents in which Congress has provided good-cause tenure to principal officers who wield power alone rather than as members of a board or commission. [The court discusses the Social Security Administration, the Federal Housing Finance Agency, and the Office of the Special Counsel, as well as the Comptroller of the Currency, which existed for one year during the Civil War.] With the exception of the one-year blip for the Comptroller of the Currency, these isolated examples are modern and contested. And they do not involve regulatory or enforcement authority remotely comparable to that exercised by the CFPB. . . .

2

In addition to being a historical anomaly, the CFPB's single-Director configuration is incompatible with our constitutional structure. Aside from the sole exception of the Presidency, that structure scrupulously avoids concentrating power in the hands of any single individual. . . . The Executive Branch is a stark departure from all this division. . . . The Framers . . . gave the Executive the "[d]ecision, activity, secrecy, and dispatch" that "characterise the proceedings of one man." [*The Federalist* No. 70 (Hamilton)]. The resulting constitutional strategy is straightforward: divide power everywhere except for the Presidency, and render the President directly accountable to the people through regular elections. In that scheme, individual executive officials will still wield significant authority, but that authority remains subject to the ongoing supervision and control of the elected President. . . .

The CFPB's single-Director structure contravenes this carefully calibrated system by vesting significant governmental power in the hands of a single individual accountable to no one. The Director is neither elected by the people nor meaningfully controlled (through the threat of removal) by someone who is. . . . Yet the Director may *unilaterally*, without meaningful supervision, issue final regulations, oversee adjudications, set enforcement priorities, initiate prosecutions, and determine what penalties to impose on private parties. . . .

The CFPB Director's insulation from removal by an accountable President is enough to render the agency's structure unconstitutional. But several other features of the CFPB combine to make the Director's removal protection even more problematic. . . . Because the CFPB is headed by a single Director with a five-year term, some Presidents may not have any opportunity to shape its leadership and thereby influence its activities. . . . That means an unlucky President might get elected on a consumer-protection platform and enter office only to find herself saddled with a holdover Director from a competing political party who is dead set *against* that agenda. . . .

The CFPB's receipt of funds outside the appropriations process further aggravates the agency's threat to Presidential control. The President normally has the opportunity to [propose,] recommend[,] or veto spending bills that affect the operation of administrative agencies. . . . Presidents frequently use these budgetary tools "to influence the policies of independent agencies." *PHH Corp. v. CFPB* (D.C. Cir. 2018) (Henderson, J., dissenting) (citing Pasachoff, *The President's Budget as a Source of Agency Policy Control*, 125 Yale L. J. 2182 (2016)). But no similar opportunity exists for the President to influence the CFPB Director. . . . This financial freedom makes it even more likely that the agency will "slip from the Executive's control, and thus from that of the people." *Free Enterprise Fund*.

3

Amicus . . . questions the textual basis for the removal power. . . . But those concerns are misplaced. It is true that "there is no 'removal clause' in the Constitution," but neither is there a "separation of powers clause" or a "federalism clause." These foundational doctrines are instead evident from the Constitution's vesting of certain powers in certain bodies. As we have explained many times before, the President's removal power stems from Article II's vesting of the "executive Power" in the President. [T]ext, first principles, the First Congress's decision in 1789, *Myers*, and *Free Enterprise Fund* all establish that the President's removal power is the rule, not the exception. . . .[11]. . .

IV

Having concluded that the CFPB's leadership by a single independent Director violates the separation of powers, we now turn to the appropriate remedy.

[Writing here only for a plurality of the court, Chief Justice Roberts found that the removal provision could be severed from the remainder of the Act—in part because the statute included an express severability provision. The Court therefore remanded the case to the lower courts to consider whether the civil investigative demand,] "though initially issued by a Director unconstitutionally insulated from removal, [could] still be enforced . . . because [after personnel turnover] it has since been ratified by an Acting Director accountable to the President." . . .

JUSTICE THOMAS, with whom JUSTICE GORSUCH joins, concurring in part and dissenting in part.

Because the Court takes a step in the right direction by limiting *Humphrey's Executor* to "multimember expert agencies that *do not wield substantial executive power*," I join Parts I, II, and III of its opinion. [I]n the future, we should reconsider *Humphrey's Executor in toto.* . . .

While I think that the Court correctly resolves the merits of the constitutional question, I do not agree with its decision to sever the removal restriction. . . . As the Court recognizes, the enforcement of a civil investigative demand by an official with unconstitutional removal protection injures Seila. Presented with an enforcement request from an unconstitutionally insulated Director, I would simply deny the CFPB's petition for an order of enforcement. This approach would resolve the dispute before us without addressing the issue of severability. . . .

JUSTICE KAGAN, with whom JUSTICE GINSBURG, JUSTICE BREYER, and JUSTICE SOTOMAYOR join, concurring in the judgment with respect to severability and

---

[11]   . . . The "clearest" (and only) "example" the dissent can muster for what may be prohibited is a for-cause removal restriction placed on the President's "close military or diplomatic advisers." . . . The dissent claims to see a constitutional distinction between the President's "own constitutional duties in foreign relations and war" and his duty to execute laws passed by Congress. But the same Article that establishes the President's foreign relations and war duties expressly entrusts him to take care that the laws be faithfully executed. . . .

dissenting in part.

Throughout the Nation's history, this Court has left most decisions about how to structure the Executive Branch to Congress and the President, acting through legislation they both agree to. In particular, the Court has commonly allowed those two branches to create zones of administrative independence by limiting the President's power to remove agency heads. The Federal Reserve Board. The Federal Trade Commission (FTC). The National Labor Relations Board. Statute after statute establishing such entities instructs the President that he may not discharge their directors except for cause—most often phrased as inefficiency, neglect of duty, or malfeasance in office. Those statutes, whose language the Court has repeatedly approved, provide the model for the removal restriction before us today. If precedent were any guide, that provision would have survived its encounter with this Court—and so would the intended independence of the Consumer Financial Protection Bureau (CFPB).

Our Constitution and history demand that result. The text of the Constitution allows these common for-cause removal limits. Nothing in it speaks of removal. And it grants Congress authority to organize all the institutions of American governance, provided only that those arrangements allow the President to perform his own constitutionally assigned duties. Still more, the Framers' choice to give the political branches wide discretion over administrative offices has played out through American history in ways that have settled the constitutional meaning. From the first, Congress debated and enacted measures to create spheres of administration—especially of financial affairs—detached from direct presidential control. As the years passed, and governance became ever more complicated, Congress continued to adopt and adapt such measures—confident it had latitude to do so under a Constitution meant to "endure for ages to come." *McCulloch v. Maryland* (1819) (approving the Second Bank of the United States).

Not every innovation in governance—not every experiment in administrative independence—has proved successful. And debates about the prudence of limiting the President's control over regulatory agencies, including through his removal power, have never abated. But the Constitution—both as originally drafted and as practiced—mostly leaves disagreements about administrative structure to Congress and the President, who have the knowledge and experience needed to address them. Within broad bounds, it keeps the courts—who do not—out of the picture.

The Court today fails to respect its proper role. It recognizes that this Court has approved limits on the President's removal power over heads of agencies much like the CFPB. Agencies possessing similar powers, agencies charged with similar missions, agencies created for similar reasons. The majority's explanation is that the heads of those agencies fall within an "exception"—one for multimember bodies and another for inferior officers—to a "general rule" of unrestricted presidential removal power. And the majority says the CFPB Director does not.

That account, though, is wrong in every respect. The majority's general rule does not exist. Its exceptions, likewise, are made up for the occasion—gerrymandered so the CFPB falls outside them. And the distinction doing most of the majority's work—between multimember bodies and single directors—does not respond to the constitutional values at stake. If a removal provision violates the separation of powers, it is because the measure so deprives the President of control over an official as to impede his own constitutional functions. But with or without a for-cause removal provision, the President has at least as much control over an individual as over a commission—and possibly more. That means the constitutional concern is, if anything, ameliorated when the agency has a single head. . . .

I

The text of the Constitution, the history of the country, the precedents of this Court, and the need for sound and adaptable governance—all stand against the majority's opinion. They point not to the majority's "general rule" of "unrestricted removal power" with two grudgingly applied "exceptions." Rather, they bestow discretion on the legislature to structure administrative institutions as the times demand, so long as the President retains the ability to carry out his constitutional duties. And most relevant here, they give Congress wide leeway to limit the President's removal power in the interest of enhancing independence from politics in regulatory bodies like the CFPB.

A

[T]he Constitution . . . giv[es] Congress broad authority to establish and organize the Executive Branch. Article II presumes the existence of "Officer[s]" in "executive Departments." But it does not, as you might think from reading the majority opinion, give the President authority to decide what kinds of officers—in what departments, with what responsibilities—the Executive Branch requires. See *ante* ("The entire 'executive Power' belongs to the President alone"). Instead, Article I's Necessary and Proper Clause puts those decisions in the legislature's hands. Congress has the power "[t]o make all Laws which shall be necessary and proper for carrying into Execution" not just its own enumerated powers but also "all other Powers vested by this Constitution in the Government of the United States, or in any Department or Officer thereof."[3]

The majority relies for its contrary vision on Article II's Vesting Clause, but the provision can't carry all that weight. Or as Chief Justice Rehnquist wrote of a similar claim in *Morrison v. Olson*, "extrapolat[ing]" an unrestricted removal power from such "general constitutional language"—which says only that "[t]he executive Power shall be vested in a President"—is "more than the text will bear." Dean John Manning has well explained [that the] Necessary and Proper Clause . . . makes it impossible to "establish a constitutional violation simply by showing that Congress has constrained the way '[t]he executive Power' is implemented"; that is exactly what the Clause gives Congress the power to do. *Separation of Powers as Ordinary Interpretation*, 124 Harv. L. Rev. 1939 (2011). Only "a *specific* historical understanding" can bar Congress from enacting a given constraint. *Ibid.* And nothing of that sort broadly prevents Congress from limiting the President's removal power. . . .

Nor can the Take Care Clause come to the majority's rescue. That Clause cannot properly serve as a "placeholder for broad judicial judgments" about presidential control. Goldsmith & Manning, *The Protean Take Care Clause*, 164 U. Pa. L. Rev. 1835 (2016); but see *ante* (using it that way). To begin with, the provision—"he shall take Care that the Laws be faithfully executed"—speaks of duty, not power. . . . And yet more important, the text of the Take Care Clause requires only enough authority to make sure "the laws [are] faithfully executed"—meaning with fidelity to the law itself, not to every presidential policy preference. As this Court has held, a President can ensure " 'faithful execution' of the laws"—thereby satisfying his "take care" obligation—with a removal provision like the one here. *Morrison*. . . .

---

[3]   Article II's Opinions Clause also demonstrates the possibility of limits on the President's control over the Executive Branch. Under that Clause, the President "may require the Opinion, in writing, of the principal Officer in each of the executive Departments, upon any Subject relating to the Duties of their respective Offices." For those in the majority's camp, that Clause presents a puzzle: If the President must always have the direct supervisory control they posit, including by threat of removal, why would he ever need a constitutional warrant to demand agency heads' opinions? The Clause becomes at least redundant—though really, inexplicable—under the majority's idea of executive power.

Finally, recall the Constitution's telltale silence: Nowhere does the text say anything about the President's power to remove subordinate officials at will. The majority professes unconcern. After all, it says, "neither is there a 'separation of powers clause' or a 'federalism clause.'" But those concepts are carved into the Constitution's text—the former in its first three articles separating powers, the latter in its enumeration of federal powers and its reservation of all else to the States. And anyway, at-will removal is hardly such a "foundational doctrine[ ]": You won't find it on a civics class syllabus. That's because removal is a *tool*—one means among many, even if sometimes an important one, for a President to control executive officials. To find that authority hidden in the Constitution as a "general rule" is to discover what is nowhere there. . . .

B

History no better serves the majority's cause. . . . The early history—including the fabled Decision of 1789—shows mostly debate and division about removal authority. And when a "settle[ment of] meaning" at last occurred, it was not on the majority's terms. Instead, it supports wide latitude for Congress to create spheres of administrative independence.

1

Begin with evidence from the Constitution's ratification. And note that this moment is indeed the beginning: Delegates to the Constitutional Convention never discussed whether or to what extent the President would have power to remove executive officials. As a result, the Framers advocating ratification had no single view of the matter. In Federalist No. 77, Hamilton presumed that under the new Constitution "[t]he consent of [the Senate] would be necessary to displace as well as to appoint" officers of the United States. . . . By contrast, Madison thought the Constitution allowed Congress to decide how any executive official could be removed. He explained in Federalist No. 39: "The tenure of the ministerial offices generally will be a subject of legal regulation, conformably to the reason of the case, and the example of the State Constitutions." Neither view, of course, at all supports the majority's story.

The second chapter is the Decision of 1789, when Congress addressed the removal power while considering the bill creating the Department of Foreign Affairs. Speaking through Chief Justice Taft—a judicial presidentialist if ever there was one—this Court in *Myers v. United States* (1926), read that debate as expressing Congress's judgment that the Constitution gave the President illimitable power to remove executive officials. The majority rests its own historical claim on that analysis (though somehow also finding room for its two exceptions). But Taft's historical research has held up even worse than *Myers'* holding (which was mostly reversed). . . .

The best view is that the First Congress was "deeply divided" on the President's removal power, and "never squarely addressed" the central issue here. Manning, *supra*; Prakash, *New Light on the Decision of 1789*, 91 Cornell L. Rev. 1021 (2006). The congressional debates revealed three main positions. Some shared Hamilton's Federalist No. 77 view: The Constitution required Senate consent for removal. At the opposite extreme, others claimed that the Constitution gave absolute removal power to the President. And a third faction maintained that the Constitution placed Congress in the driver's seat: The legislature could regulate, if it so chose, the President's authority to remove. In the end, Congress passed a bill saying nothing about removal, leaving the President free to fire the Secretary of Foreign Affairs at will. But the only one of the three views definitively rejected was Hamilton's theory of necessary Senate consent. As even strong proponents of executive power have shown, Congress never "endorse[d] the view that [it] lacked authority to modify" the President's removal authority when it wished to. Prakash, *supra*; see Manning, *supra*. The summer of 1789 thus ended without resolution of the critical question. . . .

At the same time, the First Congress gave officials handling financial affairs—as compared to diplomatic and military ones—some independence from the President. . . . Congress left the organization of the Departments of Foreign Affairs and War skeletal, enabling the President to decide how he wanted to staff them. By contrast, Congress listed each of the offices within the Treasury Department, along with their functions. . . . And perhaps most notable, Congress soon deemed the Comptroller of the Treasury's settlements of public accounts "final and conclusive." That decision, preventing presidential overrides, marked the Comptroller as exercising independent judgment. True enough, no statute shielded the Comptroller from discharge. But even James Madison, who at this point opposed most removal limits, told Congress that "there may be strong reasons why an officer of this kind should not hold his office at the pleasure" of the Secretary or President. Annals of Cong. . . .

Contrary to the majority's view, then, the founding era closed without any agreement that Congress lacked the power to curb the President's removal authority. And as it kept that question open, Congress took the first steps—which would launch a tradition—of distinguishing financial regulators from diplomatic and military officers. The latter mainly helped the President carry out his own constitutional duties in foreign relations and war. The former chiefly carried out statutory duties, fulfilling functions Congress had assigned to their offices. In addressing the new Nation's finances, Congress had begun to use its powers under the Necessary and Proper Clause to design effective administrative institutions. And that included taking steps to insulate certain officers from political influence.

2

As the decades and centuries passed, those efforts picked up steam. Confronting new economic, technological, and social conditions, Congress—and often the President—saw new needs for pockets of independence within the federal bureaucracy. And that was especially so, again, when it came to financial regulation. [Justice Kagan here canvasses "just a few highlights," including the Second Bank of the United States, the Comptroller of the Currency, the Interstate Commerce Commission, the Federal Reserve Board, the Federal Trade Commission, the Federal Deposit Insurance Corporation, and the Securities and Exchange Committee.] By one count, across all subject matter areas, 48 agencies have heads (and below them hundreds more inferior officials) removable only for cause. So year by year by year, the broad sweep of history has spoken to the constitutional question before us: Independent agencies are everywhere.

C

What is more, the Court's precedents before today have accepted the role of independent agencies in our governmental system. To be sure, the line of our decisions has not run altogether straight. But we have repeatedly upheld provisions that prevent the President from firing regulatory officials except for such matters as neglect or malfeasance. In those decisions, we sounded a caution, insisting that Congress could not impede through removal restrictions the President's performance of his own constitutional duties. (So, to take the clearest example, Congress could not curb the President's power to remove his close military or diplomatic advisers.) But within that broad limit, this Court held, Congress could protect from at-will removal the officials it deemed to need some independence from political pressures. Nowhere do those precedents suggest what the majority announces today: that the President has an "unrestricted removal power" subject to two bounded exceptions.

The majority grounds its new approach in *Myers*, ignoring the way this Court has cabined that decision. *Myers*, the majority tells us, found an unrestrained removal power "essential to the [President's] execution of the laws." What the majority does not say is that within a decade the Court abandoned that view (much as later scholars rejected Taft's one-sided history). In *Humphrey's Executor v. United States* (1935), the Court unceremoniously—and unanimously—confined *Myers* to its facts. . . . (Indeed . . . everything in *Myers* "out of harmony" with *Humphrey's* was expressly "disapproved.") Half a century later, the Court was more generous. Two decisions read *Myers* as standing for the principle that Congress's own "participation in the removal of executive officers is unconstitutional." *Bowsher*; *Morrison*. . . .

The majority's description of *Morrison* is not true to the decision. (Mostly, it seems, the majority just wishes the case would go away.) First, *Morrison* is no "exception" to a broader rule from *Myers*. *Morrison* echoed all of *Humphrey's* criticism of the by-then infamous *Myers* "dicta." [Indeed, *Morrison*] yet further confined *Myers*' reach, making clear that Congress could restrict the President's removal of officials carrying out even the most traditional executive functions. And the decision, with care, set out the governing rule—again, that removal restrictions are permissible so long as they do not impede the President's performance of his own constitutionally assigned duties. Second, as all that suggests, *Morrison* is not limited to inferior officers. In the eight pages addressing the removal issue, the Court constantly spoke of "officers" and "officials" in general. By contrast, the Court there used the word "inferior" in just one sentence (which of course the majority quotes), when applying its general standard to the case's facts. Indeed, Justice Scalia's dissent emphasized that the counsel's inferior-office status played no role in the Court's decision. . . .

So caselaw joins text and history in establishing the general permissibility of for-cause provisions giving some independence to agencies. Contrary to the majority's view, those laws do not represent a suspicious departure from illimitable presidential control over administration. . . .

D

The deferential approach this Court has taken gives Congress the flexibility it needs to craft administrative agencies. Diverse problems of government demand diverse solutions. They call for varied measures and mixtures of democratic accountability and technical expertise, energy and efficiency. Sometimes, the arguments push toward tight presidential control of agencies. The President's engagement, some people say, can disrupt bureaucratic stagnation, counter in-dustry capture, and make agencies more responsive to public interests. See, well, Kagan, *Presidential Administration*, 114 Harv. L. Rev. 2245 (2001) [(making a policy case for more presidential control over agencies and charting various administrative mechanisms for implementing that control)]. At other times, the arguments favor greater independence from presidential involvement. . . . (Consider, for example, how the Federal Reserve's independence stops a Presi-dent trying to win a second term from manipulating interest rates.) Of course, the right balance between presidential control and independence is often uncer-tain, contested, and value-laden. No mathematical formula governs institutional design; trade-offs are endemic to the enterprise. But that is precisely why . . . . courts should stay (mostly) out of the way. Rather than impose rigid rules like the majority's, they should let Congress and the President figure out what blend of independence and political control will best enable an agency to perform its intended functions.

Judicial intrusion into this field usually reveals only how little courts know about governance. . . . A given agency's independence (or lack of it) depends on a wealth of features, relating not just to removal standards, but also to ap-pointments practices, procedural rules, internal organization, oversight regimes, historical traditions, cultural norms, and (inevitably) personal relationships. . . . In that light, even the judicial opinions' perennial focus on removal standards is a bit of a puzzle. Removal is only the most obvious, not necessarily the most potent, means of control. That is because informal restraints can prevent Pres-idents from firing at-will officers—and because other devices can keep officers with for-cause protection under control. . . . [T]hat is yet more reason for courts to defer to the branches charged with fashioning administrative structures, and to hesitate before ruling out agency design specs like for-cause removal standards. . . .

II

. . . The question here, which by now you're well equipped to answer, is whether including [a] for-cause standard in the statute creating the CFPB vi-olates the Constitution. . . .

Applying our longstanding precedent, the answer is clear: It does not. This Court, as the majority acknowledges, has sustained the constitutionality of the FTC and similar independent agencies. The for-cause protections for the heads of those agencies, the Court has found, do not impede the President's ability to perform his own constitutional duties, and so do not breach the separation of powers. There is nothing different here. The CFPB wields the same kind of power as the FTC and similar agencies. And all of their heads receive the same kind of removal protection. No less than those other entities—by now part of the fabric of government—the CFPB is thus a permissible exercise of Congress's power under the Necessary and Proper Clause to structure administration.

First, the CFPB's powers are nothing unusual in the universe of independent agencies. The CFPB, as the majority notes, can issue regulations, conduct its own adjudications, and bring civil enforcement actions in court—all backed by the threat of penalties. But then again, so too can (among others) the FTC and SEC, two agencies whose regulatory missions parallel the CFPB's. Just for a comparison, the CFPB now has 19 enforcement actions pending, while the SEC brought 862 such actions last year alone. . . . Congress, to be sure, gave the CFPB new authority over "unfair, deceptive, or abusive act[s] or practice[s]" in transactions involving a "consumer financial product or service." But again, the FTC has power to go after "unfair or deceptive acts or practices in or affecting commerce"—a portfolio spanning a far wider swath of the economy. And if influence on economic life is the measure, consider the Federal Reserve, whose every act has global consequence. The CFPB, gauged by that comparison, is a piker.

Second, the removal protection given the CFPB's Director is standard fare. The removal power rests with the President alone; Congress has no role to play, as it did in the laws struck down in *Myers* and *Bowsher*. The statute provides only one layer of protection, unlike the law in *Free Enterprise Fund*. And the clincher, which you have heard before: The for-cause standard used for the CFPB is identical to the one the Court upheld in *Humphrey's*. Both enable the President to fire an agency head for "inefficiency, neglect of duty, or malfeasance in office." . . .

The analysis is as simple as simple can be. The CFPB Director exercises the same powers, and receives the same removal protections, as the heads of other, constitutionally permissible independent agencies. How could it be that this opinion is a dissent? . . .

The majority focuses on one (it says sufficient) reason: The CFPB Director is singular, not plural. . . . And a solo CFPB Director does not fit within either of the majority's supposed exceptions. He is not an inferior officer, so (the majority says) *Morrison* does not apply; and he is not a multimember board, so (the majority says) neither does *Humphrey's*. . . . I'm tempted at this point just to say: No. All I've explained about constitutional text, history, and precedent invalidates the majority's thesis. But I'll set out here some more targeted points, taking step by step the majority's reasoning. [Among other points, Justice Kagan emphasizes that *Humphrey's* and subsequent cases had not put any weight on the "groupiness" of the agencies there involved, that "the CFPB's single-director structure has a fair bit of precedent behind it," and that, to the extent generalization is possible, "individuals are easier than groups to supervise."]

III

Recall again how this dispute got started. In the midst of the Great Recession, Congress and the President came together to create an agency [that] would protect consumers from the reckless financial practices that had caused the then-ongoing economic collapse. . . .

And now consider how the dispute ends—with five unelected judges rejecting the result of that democratic process. . . . Nothing in the Constitution requires that outcome; to the contrary. . . . The Framers took pains to craft a document that would allow the structures of governance to change, as times and needs change. The Constitution says only a few words about administration. As Chief Justice Marshall wrote: Rather than prescribing "immutable rules," it enables Congress to choose "the means by which government should, in all future time, execute its powers." *McCulloch.* It authorizes Congress to meet new exigencies with new devices. So Article II does not generally prohibit independent agencies. Nor do any supposed structural principles. Nor do any odors wafting from the document. Save for when those agencies impede the President's performance of his own constitutional duties, the matter is left up to Congress. . . .

3. The President's Powers over Foreign Affairs

Article II enumerates a number of presidential powers that specifically relate to foreign affairs and foreign policy, including the following:

- "The President shall be Commander in Chief of the Army and Navy of the United States, and of the Militia of the several States, when called into the actual Service of the United States." Art. II, § 2, cl. 1.

- "He shall have Power, by and with the Advice and Consent of the Senate, to make Treaties, provided two thirds of the Senators present concur." Art. II, § 2, cl. 2.
- "[H]e shall nominate, and by and with the Advice and Consent of the Senate, shall appoint Ambassadors, other public Ministers and Consuls." Art. II, § 2, cl. 2.
- "[H]e shall receive Ambassadors and other public Ministers." Art. II, § 3.

The Constitution also gives Congress a number of specific powers over foreign affairs and foreign policy, including the following:

- "To regulate Commerce with foreign Nations," Art. I, § 8, cl. 3.
- "To establish an uniform Rule of Naturalization," Art. I, § 8, cl. 4.
- "To . . . regulate the Value . . . of foreign Coin," Art. I, § 8, cl. 5.
- "To define and punish Piracies and Felonies committed on the high Seas, and Offences against the Law of Nations," Art. I, § 8, cl. 10.
- "To declare War, grant Letters of Marque and Reprisal, and make Rules concerning Captures on Land and Water," Art. I, § 8, cl. 11.
- "To raise and support Armies" and to "provide and maintain a Navy" Art. I, § 8, cl. 12–13.
- "To make Rules for the Government and Regulation of the land and naval Forces," Art. I, § 8, cl. 14.
- "To provide for calling forth the Militia to repel Invasions," Art. I, § 8, cl. 15.

For Discussion

(1)   What do you notice about these two lists of powers?

(2)   Do the enumerated powers specifically authorize all possible actions that might be necessary during the course of conducting relations with foreign nations? What solutions might exist for covering any gaps in the constitutional text?

(3)   Are the two lists of authorities they mutually exclusive, or do they overlap to some extent? If they overlap, what should happen if Congress and the President disagree about what to do? Whose preference wins out?

The following cases explore questions like these.

Dames & Moore v. Regan

Supreme Court of the United States, 1981.
453 U.S. 654.

Jᴜsᴛɪᴄᴇ RᴇʜɴQᴜɪsᴛ delivered the opinion of the Court.

. . . As [nearly two centuries of] writings reveal[,] it is doubtless both futile and perhaps dangerous to find any epigrammatical explanation of how this country has been governed. [T]he decisions of the Court in this area have been rare, episodic, and afford little precedential value for subsequent cases. . . .

As we now turn to the factual and legal issues in this case, we freely confess that we are obviously deciding only one more episode in the never-ending tension between the President exercising the executive authority in a world that presents each day some new challenge with which he must deal and the Constitution under which we all live and which no one disputes embodies some sort of system of checks and balances.

I

On November 4, 1979, the American Embassy in Tehran was seized and our diplomatic personnel were captured and held hostage.

In response to that crisis, President Carter, acting pursuant to the International Emergency Economic Powers Act (hereinafter IEEPA), declared a national emergency on November 14, 1979,[1] and blocked the removal or transfer of "all property and interests in property of the Government of Iran, its instrumentalities and controlled entities and the Central Bank of Iran which are or become subject to the jurisdiction of the United States. . . ." Exec. Order No. 12170. President Carter authorized the Secretary of the Treasury to promulgate regulations carrying out the blocking order.

On November 15, 1979, the Treasury Department's Office of Foreign Assets Control issued a regulation providing that "[u]nless licensed or authorized . . . any attachment, judgment, decree, lien, execution, garnishment, or other judicial process is null and void with respect to any property in which on or since [November 14, 1979,] there existed an interest of Iran." The regulations also made clear that any licenses or authorizations granted could be "amended, modified, or revoked at any time." On November 26, 1979, the President granted a general license authorizing certain judicial proceedings against Iran. [Three weeks later, the Administration clarified that the general license also authorized pre-judgment attachments.]

On December 19, 1979, petitioner Dames & Moore filed suit . . . against the Government of Iran . . . claiming that it was owed $3,436,694.30 plus interest for services performed under [a contract with the Atomic Energy Organization to conduct site studies for a proposed nuclear power plant]. The District Court issued orders of attachment directed against property of the defendants, and the property of certain Iranian banks was then attached to secure any judgment that might be entered against them.

On January 20, 1981, the Americans held hostage were released by Iran pursuant to an Agreement entered into the day before and embodied in [the Algiers Accords]. The Agreement stated that "[i]t is the purpose of [the United States and Iran] to terminate all litigation as between the Government of each party and the nationals of the other, and to bring about the settlement and termination of all such claims through binding arbitration." In furtherance of this goal, the Agreement called for the establishment of an Iran-United States Claims Tribunal which would arbitrate any claims not settled within six months.

---

[1]   Section 1701(a) [of IEEPA] states that the President's authority under the Act "may be exercised to deal with any unusual and extraordinary threat, which has its source in whole or substantial part outside the United States, to the national security, foreign policy, or economy of the United States, if the President declares a national emergency with respect to such threat." Petitioner does not challenge President Carter's declaration of a national emergency.

Awards of the Claims Tribunal are to be "final and binding" and "enforceable . . . in the courts of any nation in accordance with its laws."

Under the Agreement, the United States is obligated

> to terminate all legal proceedings in United States courts involving claims of United States persons and institutions against Iran and its state enterprises, to nullify all attachments and judgments obtained therein, to prohibit all further litigation based on such claims, and to bring about the termination of such claims through binding arbitration.

In addition, the United States must "act to bring about the transfer" by July 19, 1981, of all Iranian assets held in this country by American banks. One billion dollars of these assets will be deposited in a security account in the Bank of England, to the account of the Algerian Central Bank, and used to satisfy awards rendered against Iran by the Claims Tribunal.

On [his last full day in office], President Carter issued a series of Executive Orders implementing the terms of the agreement. These Orders revoked all licenses permitting the exercise of "any right, power, or privilege" with regard to Iranian funds, securities, or deposits; "nullified" all non-Iranian interests in such assets acquired subsequent to the blocking order of November 14, 1979; and required those banks holding Iranian assets to transfer them "to the Federal Reserve Bank of New York, to be held or transferred as directed by the Secretary of the Treasury." . . .

On February 24, 1981, President Reagan issued . . . Executive Order [No. 12294,] in which he "ratified" the January 19th Executive Orders. Moreover, he "suspended" all "claims which may be presented to the . . . Tribunal" and provided that such claims "shall have no legal effect in any action now pending in any court of the United States." The suspension of any particular claim terminates if the Claims Tribunal determines that it has no jurisdiction over that claim; claims are discharged for all purposes when the Claims Tribunal either awards some recovery and that amount is paid, or determines that no recovery is due.

Meanwhile, [Dames & Moore won summary judgment in its original action against the Government of Iran and the Atomic Energy Organization.] However . . . the District Court stayed execution of its judgment pending appeal by [defendants]. The District Court also ordered that all prejudgment attachments obtained against the Iranian defendants be vacated and that further proceedings against the bank defendants be stayed in light of the Executive Orders discussed above.

On April 28, 1981, petitioner filed this action in the District Court for declaratory and injunctive relief against the United States and the Secretary of the Treasury, seeking to prevent enforcement of the Executive Orders and Treasury Department regulations implementing the Agreement with Iran. In its complaint, petitioner alleged that the actions of the President and the Secretary of the Treasury implementing the Agreement with Iran were beyond their statutory and constitutional powers. . . .

II

The parties and the lower courts, confronted with the instant questions, have all agreed that much relevant analysis is contained in *Youngstown Sheet & Tube Co. v. Sawyer*. Justice Black's opinion for the Court in that case, involving the validity of President Truman's effort to seize the country's steel mills in the wake of a nationwide strike, recognized that "[t]he President's power, if any, to issue the order must stem either from an act of Congress or from the Constitution itself."

Justice Jackson's concurring opinion elaborated in a general way the consequences of different types of interaction between the two democratic branches in assessing Presidential authority to act in any given case. . . . Although we have in the past found and do today find Justice Jackson's classification of executive actions into three general categories analytically useful, we should be mindful [that] Justice Jackson himself recognized that his three categories represented "a somewhat over-simplified grouping," and it is doubtless the case that executive action in any particular instance falls, not neatly in one of three pigeonholes, but rather at some point along a spectrum running from explicit congressional authorization to explicit congressional prohibition. This is particularly true as respects cases such as the one before us, involving responses to international crises the nature of which Congress can hardly have been expected to anticipate in any detail.

III

In nullifying post-November 14, 1979, attachments and directing those persons holding blocked Iranian funds and securities to transfer them to the Federal Reserve Bank of New York for ultimate transfer to Iran, President

Carter cited five sources of express or inherent power. The Government, how-ever, has principally relied on § 203 of the IEEPA, [which gives the President broad authority to address "an unusual and extraordinary threat" to national security that arises in substantial part outside the United States. Among these are the powers to "regulate, direct and compel, nullify . . . or prohibit, any ac-quisition, holding, withholding, use, transfer, . . . or dealing in, or exercising any right . . . with respect to, or transactions involving, any property in which any foreign country or a national thereof has any interest."]

The Government contends that the acts of "nullifying" the attachments and ordering the "transfer" of the frozen assets are specifically authorized by the plain language of the above statute. [Dames & Moore] contends that we should ignore the plain language of this statute because an examination of its legislative history . We do not agree and refuse to read out of § 1702 all meaning to the words "transfer," "compel," or "nullify." Although Congress intended [IEEPA] to limit the President's emergency power in peacetime, we do not think the changes brought about by the enactment of the IEEPA in any way affected the authority of the President to take the specific actions taken here.

This Court has previously recognized that the congressional purpose in authorizing blocking orders is "to put control of foreign assets in the hands of the President. . . ." Such orders permit the President to maintain the foreign assets at his disposal for use in negotiating the resolution of a declared nation-al emergency. The frozen assets serve as a "bargaining chip" to be used by the President when dealing with a hostile country. Accordingly, it is difficult to accept petitioner's argument because the practical effect of it is to allow indi-vidual claimants throughout the country to minimize or wholly eliminate this "bargaining chip" through attachments, garnishments, or similar encumbrances on property. Neither the purpose the statute was enacted to serve nor its plain language supports such a result.

Because the President's action in nullifying the attachments and ordering the transfer of the assets was taken pursuant to specific congressional authori-zation, it is "supported by the strongest of presumptions and the widest latitude of judicial interpretation, and the burden of persuasion would rest heavily upon any who might attack it." *Youngstown* (Jackson, J., concurring). Under the circumstances of this case, we cannot say that petitioner has sustained that heavy burden. A contrary ruling would mean that the Federal Government as a whole lacked the power exercised by the President, see *id.*, and that we are not prepared to say.

IV

Although we have concluded that the IEEPA constitutes specific congressional authorization to the President to nullify the attachments and order the transfer of Iranian assets, there remains the question of the President's authority to suspend claims pending in American courts. Such claims have, of course, an existence apart from the attachments which accompanied them. In terminating these claims through Executive Order No. 12294 the President purported to act under authority of the IEEPA and the so-called "Hostage Act."

We conclude that although the IEEPA authorized the nullification of the attachments, it cannot be read to authorize the suspension of the claims. The claims of American citizens against Iran are not in themselves transactions involving Iranian property or efforts to exercise any rights with respect to such property. An *in personam* lawsuit, although it might eventually be reduced to judgment and that judgment might be executed upon, is an effort to establish liability and fix damages and does not focus on any particular property within the jurisdiction. The terms of the IEEPA therefore do not authorize the President to suspend claims in American courts. This is the view of all the courts which have considered the question.

The Hostage Act, passed in 1868, provides:

> Whenever it is made known to the President that any citizen of the United States has been unjustly deprived of his liberty by . . . any foreign government, it shall be the duty of the President forthwith to demand of that government the reasons of such imprisonment;
>
> and if it appears to be wrongful and in violation of the rights of American citizenship, the President shall forthwith demand the release of such citizen;
>
> and if the release so demanded is unreasonably delayed or refused, the President shall use such means, not amounting to acts of war, as he may think necessary and proper to obtain or effectuate the release. . . .

We are reluctant to conclude that this provision constitutes specific authorization to the President to suspend claims in American courts. Although the broad language of the Hostage Act suggests it may cover this case, there are several difficulties with such a view. The legislative history indicates that the Act was passed in response to a situation unlike the recent Iranian crisis. Congress in 1868 was concerned with the activity of certain countries refusing to recognize the citizenship of naturalized Americans traveling abroad, and repatriating such citizens against their will. . . . The legislative history is also somewhat ambiguous on the question whether Congress contemplated Presidential action such as that involved here or rather simply reprisals directed against the offending foreign country and *its* citizens.

Concluding that neither the IEEPA nor the Hostage Act constitutes specific authorization of the President's action suspending claims, however, is not to say that these statutory provisions are entirely irrelevant to the question of the validity of the President's action. We think both statutes highly relevant in the looser sense of indicating congressional acceptance of a broad scope for executive action in circumstances such as those presented in this case.

As noted in Part III, the IEEPA delegates broad authority to the President to act in times of national emergency with respect to property of a foreign country. The Hostage Act similarly indicates congressional willingness that the President have broad discretion when responding to the hostile acts of foreign sovereigns. . . .

Proponents of the bill recognized that it placed a "loose discretion" in the President's hands, (Sen. Stewart), but argued that "[s]omething must be intrusted to the Executive" and that "[t]he President ought to have the power to do what the exigencies of the case require to rescue [a] citizen from imprisonment." (Sen. Williams). . . .

Although we have declined to conclude that the IEEPA or the Hostage Act directly authorizes the President's suspension of claims for the reasons noted, we cannot ignore the general tenor of Congress' legislation in this area in trying to determine whether the President is acting alone or at least with the acceptance of Congress. As we have noted, Congress cannot anticipate and legislate with regard to every possible action the President may find it necessary to take or every possible situation in which he might act. Such failure of Congress specifically to delegate authority does not, "especially . . . in the areas of foreign policy and national security," imply "congressional disapproval" of action taken by the Executive. *Haig v. Agee* (1981). On the contrary, the enactment of legislation closely related to the question of the President's authority in a particular case which evinces legislative intent to accord the President broad discretion may be considered to "invite" "measures on independent presidential responsibility," *Youngstown* (Jackson, J., concurring). At least this is so where there is no contrary indication of legislative intent and when, as here, there is a history of congressional acquiescence in conduct of the sort engaged in by the President. It is to that history which we now turn.

Not infrequently in affairs between nations, outstanding claims by nationals of one country against the government of another country are "sources of friction" between the two sovereigns. *United States v. Pink* (1942). To resolve these difficulties, nations have often entered into agreements settling the claims of their respective nationals. . . . Consistent with that principle, the United States has repeatedly exercised its sovereign authority to settle the claims of its nationals against foreign countries.

Though those settlements have sometimes been made by treaty, there has also been a longstanding practice of settling such claims by executive agreement without the advice and consent of the Senate. Under such agreements, the President has agreed to renounce or extinguish claims of United States nationals against foreign governments in return for lump-sum payments or the establishment of arbitration procedures. . . . It is clear that the practice of settling claims continues today. Since 1952, the President has entered into at least 10 binding settlements with foreign nations, including an $80 million settlement with the People's Republic of China.

Crucial to our decision today is the conclusion that Congress has implicitly approved the practice of claim settlement by executive agreement. This is best demonstrated by Congress' enactment of the International Claims Settlement Act of 1949. The Act had two purposes: (1) to allocate to United States nationals funds received in the course of an executive claims settlement with Yugoslavia, and (2) to provide a procedure whereby funds resulting from future settlements could be distributed. To achieve these ends Congress created . . . the Foreign Claims Settlement Commission, and gave it jurisdiction to make final and binding decisions with respect to claims by United States nationals against settlement funds. By creating a procedure to implement future settlement agreements, Congress placed its stamp of approval on such agreements. . . .

Over the years Congress has frequently amended the International Claims Settlement Act to provide for particular problems arising out of settlement agreements, thus demonstrating Congress' continuing acceptance of the President's claim settlement authority. . . .

Finally, the legislative history of the IEEPA further reveals that Congress has accepted the authority of the Executive to enter into settlement agreements. Though the IEEPA was enacted to provide for some limitation on the President's emergency powers, Congress stressed that "[n]othing in this act is intended . . . to interfere with the authority of the President to [block assets], or to impede the settlement of claims of U. S. citizens against foreign countries." S.Rep. No. 95–466 (1977). . . .[10]

In light of all of the foregoing—the inferences to be drawn from the character of the legislation Congress has enacted in the area, such as the IEEPA and the Hostage Act, and from the history of acquiescence in executive claims settlement—we conclude that the President was authorized to suspend pending claims pursuant to Executive Order No. 12294. As Justice Frankfurter pointed out in *Youngstown*, "a systematic, unbroken, executive practice, long pursued to the knowledge of the Congress and never before questioned . . . may be treated as a gloss on 'Executive Power' vested in the President by § 1 of Art. II." [Justice Rehnquist asserts that this conclusion is buttressed by creation of the Claims Tribunal. He notes that claims before it are relieved of jurisdictional and other procedural impediments, and so, even while expressing skepticism about the chances of American claimants, he says that it offers a forum "before which they may well recover something on their claims."]

Just as importantly, Congress has not disapproved of the action taken here. Though Congress has held hearings on the Iranian Agreement itself, Congress has not enacted legislation, or even passed a resolution, indicating its displeasure with the Agreement. Quite the contrary, the relevant Senate Committee has stated that the establishment of the Tribunal is "of vital importance to the United States." S. Rep. No. 97–71 (1981).[13] We are thus clearly not confronted

---

[10]   Indeed, Congress has consistently failed to object to this longstanding practice of claim settlement by executive agreement, even when it has had an opportunity to do so. In 1972, Congress entertained legislation relating to congressional oversight of such agreements. But Congress took only limited action, requiring that the text of significant executive agreements be transmitted to Congress. 1 U.S.C. § 112b. . . .

[13]   Contrast congressional reaction to the Iranian Agreements with congressional reaction to a 1973 Executive Agreement with Czechoslovakia. There the President sought to settle over $105 million in claims against Czechoslovakia for $20.5 million. Congress quickly demonstrated its displeasure by enacting legislation requiring that the Agreement be renegotiated. Though Congress has shown itself capable of objecting to executive agreements, it has rarely done so and has not done so in this case.

with a situation in which Congress has in some way resisted the exercise of Presidential authority.

Finally, we re-emphasize the narrowness of our decision. We do not decide that the President possesses plenary power to settle claims, even as against foreign governmental entities. . . . But where, as here, the settlement of claims has been determined to be a necessary incident to the resolution of a major foreign policy dispute between our country and another, and where, as here, we can conclude that Congress acquiesced in the President's action, we are not prepared to say that the President lacks the power to settle such claims. . . .

V

We do not think it appropriate at the present time to address petitioner's contention that the suspension of claims, if authorized, would constitute a taking of property in violation of the Fifth Amendment to the United States Constitution in the absence of just compensation. Both petitioner and the Government concede that the question whether the suspension of the claims constitutes a taking is not ripe for review. . . . [T]o the extent petitioner believes it has suffered an unconstitutional taking by the suspension of the claims, we see no jurisdictional obstacle to an appropriate action in the United States Court of Claims. . . .

WORTH NOTING

In an omitted section of the opinion, the Court held that the nullification of the attachments was not an unconstitutional taking. The Court noted that the Treasury regulations—issued before attachments were granted pursuant to a general license authorized by those regulations—"specifically provided that any attachment is null and void 'unless licensed,' and [that] all licenses may be revoked at any time." The Court therefore concluded that, because of the conditional and revocable nature of the authorization, "petitioner did not acquire any 'property' interest in its attachments of the sort that would support a constitutional claim for compensation.

JUSTICE STEVENS, concurring in part.

In my judgment the possibility that requiring this petitioner to prosecute its claim in another forum will constitute an unconstitutional "taking" is so remote that I would not address the jurisdictional question considered in Part V of the Court's opinion. However, I join the remainder of the opinion.

Justice Powell, concurring and dissenting in part.

I [dissent from] the Court's . . . decision that the nullification of the attachments did not effect a taking of property interests giving rise to claims for just compensation. . . .

I agree[, however,] with the Court's opinion with respect to the suspension and settlement of claims against Iran and its instrumentalities. The opinion makes clear that some claims may not be adjudicated by the Claims Tribunal and that others may not be paid in full. The Court holds that parties whose valid claims are not adjudicated or not fully paid may bring a "taking" claim against the United States in the Court of Claims, the jurisdiction of which this Court acknowledges. The Government must pay just compensation when it furthers the Nation's foreign policy goals by using as "bargaining chips" claims lawfully held by a relatively few persons and subject to the jurisdiction of our courts. . . .

The next case returns to a President's effort to leverage an international agreement as a basis for domestic action.

SUMMARY OF THE FACTS

José Ernesto Medellín, a Mexican national, was convicted of murder in a Texas state court. The International Court of Justice subsequently held that his conviction violated the Vienna Convention on Consular Rights. *In the Case Concerning Avena and Other Mexican Nationals* (*Mex. v. U.S.*). After the *Avena* decision, President George W. Bush "determined" that the United States would "discharge its international obligations" under *Avena* "by having State courts give effect to the decision." Memorandum to the Attorney General (Feb. 28, 2005). Medellín sought habeas corpus in state court based on the Convention violation, but the Texas courts rejected it on procedural grounds.

Portions of the *Medellín* opinion dealing with the treaty power are presented at pp. 594–597.

Medellín v. Texas

Supreme Court of the United States, 2008.
552 U.S. 491.

CHIEF JUSTICE ROBERTS delivered the opinion of the Court.

We granted certiorari to decide [whether] the President's Memorandum . . . require[s] the States to provide review and reconsideration of the claims of the 51 Mexican nationals named in *Avena* without regard to state procedural default rules[.] We conclude that . . . the President's Memorandum [does not] constitute[ ] directly enforceable federal law that pre-empts state limitations on the filing of successive habeas petitions. . . .

> **CROSS REFERENCE** The Court began by holding that the *Avena* decision constituted an international obligation of the United States under the United Nations Charter and could be enforced through the Security Council, but that the decision did not have "automatic *domestic* legal effect such that the judgment of its own force applies in state and federal courts." This part of the opinion is presented at p. 596.

III

Medellín . . . argues that the ICJ's judgment in *Avena* is binding on state courts by virtue of the President's February 28, 2005 Memorandum. The United States contends that while the *Avena* judgment does not of its own force require domestic courts to set aside ordinary rules of procedural default, that judgment became the law of the land with precisely that effect pursuant to the President's Memorandum and his power "to establish binding rules of decision that preempt contrary state law. Accordingly, we must decide whether the President's declaration alters our conclusion that the *Avena* judgment is not a rule of domestic law binding in state and federal courts.[13]

---

[13]   The dissent refrains from deciding the issue, but finds it "difficult to believe that in the exercise of his Article II powers pursuant to a ratified treaty, the President can *never* take action that would result in setting aside state law." We agree. The questions here are the far more limited ones of whether he may unilaterally create federal law by giving effect to the judgment of this international tribunal pursuant to this non-self-executing treaty, and, if not, whether he may rely on other authority under the Constitution to support the action taken in this particular case. Those are the only questions we decide.

A

... The President's authority to act, as with the exercise of any governmental power, "must stem either from an act of Congress or from the Constitution itself." *Youngstown; Dames & Moore v. Regan* (1981). Justice Jackson's familiar tripartite scheme provides the accepted framework for evaluating executive action in this area. ...

B

The United States marshals two principal arguments in favor of the President's authority "to establish binding rules of decision that preempt contrary state law." The Solicitor General first argues that the relevant treaties give the President the authority to implement the *Avena* judgment and that Congress has acquiesced in the exercise of such authority. The United States also relies upon an "independent" international dispute-resolution power wholly apart from the asserted authority based on the pertinent treaties. Medellín adds the additional argument that the President's Memorandum is a valid exercise of his power to take care that the laws be faithfully executed.

1

The United States maintains that the President's Memorandum is authorized by . . . the relevant treaties[, which] "create an obligation to comply with *Avena*," [and therefore] "*implicitly* give the President authority to implement that treaty-based obligation." As a result, the President's Memorandum is well grounded in the first category of the *Youngstown* framework.

We disagree. . . . Once a treaty is ratified without provisions clearly according it domestic effect . . . whether the treaty will ever have such effect is governed by the fundamental constitutional principle that " '[t]he power to make the necessary laws is in Congress; the power to execute in the President.' " *Hamdan v. Rumsfeld* (2006). [T]he terms of a non-self-executing treaty can become domestic law only in the same way as any other law—through passage of legislation by both Houses of Congress, combined with either the President's signature or a congressional

WORTH NOTING

A non-self-executing treaty cannot be directly enforced by domestic courts in its own right. In order for such treaties to have domestic effect, the legislature must enact an enabling statute that implements their terms as a matter of domestic law.

override of a Presidential veto. See Art. I, § 7. Indeed, "the President's power to see that the laws are faithfully executed refutes the idea that he is to be a lawmaker." *Youngstown*.

A non-self-executing treaty, by definition, is one that was ratified with the understanding that it is not to have domestic effect of its own force. That understanding precludes the assertion that Congress has implicitly authorized the President—acting on his own—to achieve precisely the same result. We therefore conclude, given the absence of congressional legislation, that the non-self-executing treaties at issue here did not "express[ly] or implied[ly]" vest the President with the unilateral authority to make them self-executing. *Youngstown* (Jackson, J., concurring). Accordingly, the President's Memorandum does not fall within the first category of the *Youngstown* framework.

Indeed, the preceding discussion should make clear that the non-self-executing character of the relevant treaties not only refutes the notion that the ratifying parties vested the President with the authority to unilaterally make treaty obligations binding on domestic courts, but also implicitly prohibits him from doing so. When the President asserts the power to "enforce" a non-self-executing treaty by unilaterally creating domestic law, he acts in conflict with the implicit understanding of the ratifying Senate. His assertion of authority, insofar as it is based on the pertinent non-self-executing treaties, is therefore within Justice Jackson's third category, not the first or even the second.

The United States nonetheless maintains that the President's Memorandum should be given effect as domestic law because "this case involves a valid Presidential action in the context of Congressional 'acquiescence.' ". . .

The United States first locates congressional acquiescence in Congress's failure to act following the President's resolution of prior ICJ controversies. A review of the Executive's actions in those prior cases, however, cannot support the claim that Congress acquiesced in this particular exercise of Presidential authority, for none of them remotely involved transforming an international obligation into domestic law and thereby displacing state law. [Details omitted.]

The United States also directs us to the President's "related" statutory responsibilities and to his "established role" in litigating foreign policy concerns as support for the President's asserted authority to give the ICJ's decision in *Avena* the force of domestic law. Congress has indeed authorized the President to represent the United States before the United Nations, the ICJ, and the Security Council, but the authority of the President to represent the United States before such bodies speaks to the President's *international* responsibilities, not any unilateral authority to create domestic law. The authority expressly conferred by Congress in the international realm cannot be said to "invite" the Presidential action at issue here. See *Youngstown* (Jackson, J., concurring).

At bottom, none of the sources of authority identified by the United States supports the President's claim that Congress has acquiesced in his asserted power to establish on his own federal law or to override state law. . . . The President may comply with the treaty's obligations by some other means, so long as they are consistent with the Constitution. But he may not rely upon a non-self-executing treaty to "establish binding rules of decision that preempt contrary state law."

2

We thus turn to the United States' claim that—independent of the United States' treaty obligations—the Memorandum is a valid exercise of the President's foreign affairs authority to resolve claims disputes with foreign nations. The United States relies on a series of cases in which this Court has upheld the authority of the President to settle foreign claims pursuant to an executive agreement. See *Am. Ins. Ass'n v. Garamendi* (2003); *Dames & Moore*; *United States v. Pink* (1942); *United States v. Belmont* (1937). In these cases this Court has explained that, if pervasive enough, a history of congressional acquiescence can be treated as a "gloss on 'Executive Power' vested in the President by § 1 of Art. II." *Dames & Moore*.

This argument is of a different nature than the one rejected above. Rather than relying on the United States' treaty obligations, the President relies on an independent source of authority in ordering Texas to put aside its procedural bar to successive habeas petitions. Nevertheless, we find that our claims-settlement cases do not support the authority that the President asserts in this case.

The claims-settlement cases involve a narrow set of circumstances: the making of executive agreements to settle civil claims between American citizens and foreign governments or foreign nationals. They are based on the view that "a systematic, unbroken, executive practice, long pursued to the knowledge of the Congress and never before questioned," can "raise a presumption that the [action] had been [taken] in pursuance of its consent." *Dames & Moore*. As this Court explained in *Garamendi*: "Making executive agreements to settle claims of American nationals against foreign governments is a particularly longstanding practice[.]" . . . Even still, the limitations on this source of executive power are clearly set forth and the Court has been careful to note that "[p]ast practice does not, by itself, create power." *Dames & Moore.*

The President's Memorandum is not supported by a "particularly long-standing practice" of congressional acquiescence, see *Garamendi*. . . . Indeed, the Government has not identified a single instance in which the President has attempted (or Congress has acquiesced in) a Presidential directive issued to state courts, much less one that reaches deep into the heart of the State's police powers and compels state courts to reopen final criminal judgments and set aside neutrally applicable state laws. The Executive's narrow and strictly limited authority to settle international claims disputes pursuant to an executive agreement cannot stretch so far as to support the current Presidential Memorandum.

3

Medellín argues that the President's Memorandum is a valid exercise of his "Take Care" power. The United States, however, does not rely upon the President's responsibility to "take Care that the Laws be faithfully executed." U.S. Const., Art. II, § 3. We think this a wise concession. This authority allows the President to execute the laws, not make them. For the reasons we have stated, the *Avena* judgment is not domestic law; accordingly, the President cannot rely on his Take Care powers here. . . .

JUSTICE STEVENS, concurring in the judgment.

In the end, . . . I am persuaded that the relevant treaties do not authorize this Court to enforce the judgment of the International Court of Justice in *Case Concerning Avena and Other Mexican Nationals (Mex. v. U.S.)*. . . .

Even though the ICJ's judgment in *Avena* is not "the supreme Law of the Land," U.S. Const., Art. VI, cl. 2, no one disputes that it constitutes an international law obligation on the part of the United States. By issuing a memorandum declaring that state courts should give effect to the judgment in *Avena*, the President made a commendable attempt to induce the States to discharge the Nation's obligation. I agree with the Texas judges and the majority of this Court that the President's memorandum is not binding law. Nonetheless, the fact that the President cannot legislate unilaterally does not absolve the United States from its promise to take action necessary to comply with the ICJ's judgment. . . .

One consequence of our form of government is that sometimes States must shoulder the primary responsibility for protecting the honor and integrity of the Nation. Texas' duty in this respect is all the greater since it was Texas that—by failing to provide consular notice in accordance with the Vienna Convention—ensnared the United States in the current controversy. Having already put the Nation in breach of one treaty, it is now up to Texas to prevent the breach of another. . . .

JUSTICE BREYER, with whom JUSTICE SOUTER and JUSTICE GINSBURG join, dissenting.

. . . I would find that the United States' treaty obligation to comply with the ICJ judgment in *Avena* is enforceable in court in this case without further congressional action beyond Senate ratification of the relevant treaties. . . .

III

Because the majority concludes that the Nation's international legal obligation to enforce the ICJ's decision is not automatically a domestic legal obligation, it must then determine whether the President has the constitutional authority to enforce it. And the majority finds that he does not. . . .

It is difficult to believe that in the exercise of his Article II powers pursuant to a ratified treaty, the President can *never* take action that would result in setting aside state law. Cf. *United States v. Pink* ("No State can rewrite our foreign policy to conform to its own domestic policies"). Suppose that the President believes it necessary that he implement a treaty provision requiring a prisoner exchange involving someone in state custody in order to avoid a proven military threat. Or suppose he believes it necessary to secure a foreign consul's treaty-based rights to move freely or to contact an arrested foreign national. Does the Constitution require the President in each and every such instance to obtain a special statute authorizing his action? On the other hand, the Constitution must impose significant restrictions upon the President's ability, by invoking Article II treaty-implementation authority, to circumvent ordinary legislative processes and to pre-empt state law as he does so. . . .

Given the Court's comparative lack of expertise in foreign affairs; given the importance of the Nation's foreign relations; given the difficulty of finding the proper constitutional balance among state and federal, executive and legislative, powers in such matters; and given the likely future importance of this Court's efforts to do so, I would very much hesitate before concluding that the Constitution implicitly sets forth broad prohibitions (or permissions) in this area.

I would thus be content to leave the matter in the constitutional shade from which it has emerged. Given my view of this case, I need not answer the question. And I shall not try to do so. That silence, however, cannot be taken as agreement with the majority's Part III conclusion.

Zivotofsky v. Kerry

Supreme Court of the United States, 2015.
576 U.S. 1.

JUSTICE KENNEDY delivered the opinion of the Court.

. . . The Court addresses two questions to resolve the interbranch dispute now before it. First, it must determine whether the President has the exclusive power to grant formal recognition to a foreign sovereign. Second, if he has that power, the Court must determine whether Congress can command the President and his Secretary of State to issue a formal statement that contradicts the earlier recognition. The statement in question here is a congressional mandate that allows a United States citizen born in Jerusalem to direct the President and Secretary of State, when issuing his passport, to state that his place of birth is "Israel."

I

Jerusalem's political standing has long been, and remains, one of the most sensitive issues in American foreign policy, and indeed it is one of the most delicate issues in current international affairs. [I]n contrast to a consistent policy of formal recognition of Israel, neither President Truman nor any later United States President has issued an official statement or declaration acknowledging any country's sovereignty over Jerusalem. Instead, the Executive Branch has maintained that " 'the status of Jerusalem . . . should be decided not unilaterally but in consultation with all concerned.' " . . .

The President's position on Jerusalem is reflected in State Department policy regarding passports and consular reports of birth abroad. Understanding that passports will be construed as reflections of American policy, the State Department's Foreign Affairs Manual instructs its employees, in general, to record the place of birth on a passport as the "country [having] present sovereignty over the actual area of birth." If a citizen objects to the country listed as sovereign by the State Department, he or she may list the city or town of birth rather than the country. The FAM, however, does not allow citizens to list a sovereign that conflicts with Executive Branch policy. Because the United States does not recognize any country as having sovereignty over Jerusalem, the FAM instructs employees to record the place of birth for citizens born there as "Jerusalem."

In 2002, Congress passed the Act at issue here, the Foreign Relations Authorization Act, Fiscal Year 2003. Section 214 of the Act is titled "United States Policy with Respect to Jerusalem as the Capital of Israel." The subsection that lies at the heart of this case, § 214(d), addresses passports. That subsection seeks to override the FAM by allowing citizens born in Jerusalem to list their place of birth as "Israel." Titled "Record of Place of Birth as Israel for Passport Purposes," § 214(d) states[:]

> For purposes of the registration of birth, certification of nationality, or issuance of a passport of a United States citizen born in the city of Jerusalem, the Secretary shall, upon the request of the citizen or the citizen's legal guardian, record the place of birth as Israel.

When he signed the Act into law, President George W. Bush issued a statement declaring his position that § 214 would, "if construed as mandatory rather than advisory, impermissibly interfere with the President's constitutional authority to formulate the position of the United States, speak for the Nation in international affairs, and determine the terms on which recognition is given to foreign states." The President concluded, "U.S. policy regarding Jerusalem has not changed."

In 2002, petitioner Menachem Binyamin Zivotofsky was born to United States citizens living in Jerusalem. In December 2002, Zivotofsky's mother visited the American Embassy in Tel Aviv to request both a passport and a consular report of birth abroad for her son. Pursuant to § 214(d), Zivotofsky claims the right to have "Israel" recorded as his place of birth in his passport. . . .

II

In considering claims of Presidential power this Court refers to Justice Jackson's familiar tripartite framework from *Youngstown Sheet & Tube Co. v. Sawyer* (1952) (concurring opinion). . . .

In this case the Secretary contends that § 214(d) infringes on the President's exclusive recognition power by "requiring the President to contradict his recognition position regarding Jerusalem in official communications with foreign sovereigns." In so doing the Secretary acknowledges the President's power is "at its lowest ebb." *Youngstown*. Because the President's refusal to implement § 214(d) falls into Justice Jackson's third category, his claim must be "scrutinized with caution," and he may rely solely on powers the Constitution grants to him alone. . . .

A

Recognition is a "formal acknowledgement" that a particular "entity possesses the qualifications for statehood" or "that a particular regime is the effective government of a state." Restatement (Third) of Foreign Relations Law of the United States § 203 (1986). . . . Despite the importance of the recognition power in foreign relations, the Constitution does not use the term "recognition," either in Article II or elsewhere.

The Secretary asserts that the President exercises the recognition power based on the Reception Clause, which directs that the President "shall receive Ambassadors and other public Ministers." Art. II, § 3. As Zivotofsky notes, the Reception Clause received little attention at the Constitutional Convention. In fact, during the ratification debates, Alexander Hamilton claimed that the power to receive ambassadors was "more a matter of dignity than of authority," a ministerial duty largely "without consequence." The Federalist No. 69.

At the time of the founding, however, prominent international scholars suggested that receiving an ambassador was tantamount to recognizing the sovereignty of the sending state. See E. de Vattel, *The Law of Nations* (1758); see also C. van Bynkershoek, *On Questions of Public Law* (1737); H. Grotius, *On the Law of War and Peace* (1625). It is a logical and proper inference, then, that a Clause directing the President alone to receive ambassadors would be understood to acknowledge his power to recognize other nations.

This in fact occurred early in the Nation's history when President Washington recognized the French Revolutionary Government by receiving its ambassador. After this incident the import of the Reception Clause became clear—causing Hamilton to change his earlier view. He wrote that the Reception Clause "includes th[e power] of judging, in the case of a revolution of government in a foreign country, whether the new rulers are competent organs of the national will, and ought to be recognised, or not." . . . As a result, the Reception Clause provides support, although not the sole authority, for the President's power to recognize other nations.

The inference that the President exercises the recognition power is further supported by his additional Article II powers. It is for the President, "by and with the Advice and Consent of the Senate," to "make Treaties, provided two thirds of the Senators present concur." Art. II, § 2, cl. 2. In addition, "he shall nominate, and by and with the Advice and Consent of the Senate, shall appoint Ambassadors" as well as "other public Ministers and Consuls."

As a matter of constitutional structure, these additional powers give the President control over recognition decisions. At international law, recognition may be effected by different means, but each means is dependent upon Presidential power. In addition to receiving an ambassador, recognition may occur on "the conclusion of a bilateral treaty," or the "formal initiation of diplomatic relations," including the dispatch of an ambassador. The President has the sole power to negotiate treaties, see *United States v. Curtiss-Wright Export Corp.* (1936), and the Senate may not conclude or ratify a treaty without Presidential action. The President, too, nominates the Nation's ambassadors and dispatches other diplomatic agents. . . . The Constitution thus assigns the President means to effect recognition on his own initiative. Congress, by contrast, has no constitutional power that would enable it to initiate diplomatic relations with a foreign nation.

Because these specific Clauses confer the recognition power on the President, the Court need not consider whether or to what extent the Vesting Clause, which provides that the "executive Power" shall be vested in the President, provides further support for the President's action here.

The text and structure of the Constitution grant the President the power to recognize foreign nations and governments. The question then becomes whether that power is exclusive. The various ways in which the President may unilaterally effect recognition—and the lack of any similar power vested in Congress—suggest that it is. So, too, do functional considerations. Put simply, the Nation must have a single policy regarding which governments are legitimate in the eyes of the United States and which are not. Foreign countries need to know, before entering into diplomatic relations or commerce with the United States, whether their ambassadors will be received; whether their officials will be immune from suit in federal court; and whether they may initiate lawsuits here to vindicate their rights. These assurances cannot be equivocal. Recognition is a topic on which the Nation must " 'speak . . . with one voice.' " *American Ins. Assn. v. Garamendi* (2003). That voice must be the President's. . . .

It remains true, of course, that many decisions affecting foreign relations—including decisions that may determine the course of our relations with recognized countries—require congressional action. Congress may "regulate Commerce with foreign Nations," "establish an uniform Rule of Naturalization," "define and punish Piracies and Felonies committed on the high Seas, and Offences against the Law of Nations," "declare War," "grant Letters of Marque and Reprisal," and "make Rules for the Government and Regulation of the land and naval Forces." U.S. Const., Art. I, § 8. In addition, the President cannot make a treaty or appoint an ambassador without the approval of the Senate. Art. II, § 2, cl. 2. The President, furthermore, could not build an American Embassy abroad without congressional appropriation of the necessary funds. Art. I, § 8, cl. 1. Under basic separation-of-powers principles, it is for the Congress to enact the laws, including "all Laws which shall be necessary and proper for carrying into Execution" the powers of the Federal Government. § 8, cl. 18.

In foreign affairs, as in the domestic realm, the Constitution "enjoins upon its branches separateness but interdependence, autonomy but reciprocity." *Youngstown* (Jackson, J., concurring). Although the President alone effects the formal act of recognition, Congress' powers, and its central role in making laws, give it substantial authority regarding many of the policy determinations that precede and follow the act of recognition itself. If Congress disagrees with the President's recognition policy, there may be consequences. Formal recognition may seem a hollow act if it is not accompanied by the dispatch of an ambassador, the easing of trade restrictions, and the conclusion of treaties. And those decisions require action by the Senate or the whole Congress. . . .

C

Having examined the Constitution's text and this Court's precedent, it is appropriate to turn to accepted understandings and practice. . . . Here, history is not all on one side, but on balance it provides strong support for the conclusion that the recognition power is the President's alone. . . . [E]ven a brief survey of the major historical examples, with an emphasis on those said to favor Zivotofsky, establishes no more than that some Presidents have chosen to cooperate with Congress, not that Congress itself has exercised the recognition power. . . .

The first debate over the recognition power arose in 1793, after France had been torn by revolution. See Prakash & Ramsey, *The Executive Power over Foreign Affairs*, 111 Yale L.J. 231 (2001). Once the Revolutionary Government was established, Secretary of State Jefferson and President Washington, without consulting Congress, authorized the American Ambassador to resume relations with the new regime. Soon thereafter, the new French Government proposed to send an ambassador, Citizen Genet, to the United States. Members of the President's Cabinet agreed that receiving Genet would be a binding and public act of recognition. They decided, however, both that Genet should be received and that consultation with Congress was not necessary. See Cabinet Opinion on Washington's Questions on Neutrality and the Alliance with France (Apr. 19, 1793). Congress expressed no disagreement with this position, and Genet's reception marked the Nation's first act of recognition—one made by the President alone.

[Justice Kennedy discusses other examples. Some Presidents sought concurrence of Congress in recognition decisions, and President Jackson explicitly expressed doubt where the power lay. But according to Justice Kennedy, when President Carter de-recognized the Taiwanese government as the proper government of China, Congress appeared to regard the President's power as exclusive.]

This history confirms the Court's conclusion in the instant case that the power to recognize or decline to recognize a foreign state and its territorial bounds resides in the President alone. For the most part, Congress has respected the Executive's policies and positions as to formal recognition. At times, Congress itself has defended the President's constitutional prerogative. Over the last 100 years, there has been scarcely any debate over the President's power to recognize foreign states. In this respect the Legislature, in the narrow context of recognition, on balance has acknowledged the importance of speaking "with one voice." The weight of historical evidence indicates Congress has accepted that the power to recognize foreign states and governments and their territorial bounds is exclusive to the Presidency.

III

As the power to recognize foreign states resides in the President alone, the question becomes whether § 214(d) infringes on the Executive's consistent decision to withhold recognition with respect to Jerusalem.

Section 214(d) requires that, in a passport or consular report of birth abroad, "the Secretary shall, upon the request of the citizen or the citizen's legal guardian, record the place of birth as Israel" for a "United States citizen born in the city of Jerusalem." That is, § 214(d) requires the President, through the Secretary, to identify citizens born in Jerusalem who so request as being born in Israel. . . .

If the power over recognition is to mean anything, it must mean that the President not only makes the initial, formal recognition determination but also that he may maintain that determination in his and his agent's statements. This conclusion is a matter of both common sense and necessity. If Congress could command the President to state a recognition position inconsistent with his own, Congress could override the President's recognition determination. Under international law, recognition may be effected by "written or oral declaration of the recognizing state." J. Moore, *Digest of International Law.* In addition an act of recognition must "leave no doubt as to the intention to grant it." Oppenheim's International Law. Thus, if Congress could alter the President's statements on matters of recognition or force him to contradict them, Congress in effect would exercise the recognition power. . . .

It is true, as Zivotofsky notes, that Congress has substantial authority over passports. . . . The problem with § 214(d), however, lies in how Congress exercised its authority over passports. . . . To allow Congress to control the President's communication in the context of a formal recognition determination is to allow Congress to exercise that exclusive power itself. As a result, the statute is unconstitutional.

* * *

In holding § 214(d) invalid the Court does not question the substantial powers of Congress over foreign affairs in general or passports in particular. This case is confined solely to the exclusive power of the President to control recognition determinations, including formal statements by the Executive Branch acknowledging the legitimacy of a state or government and its territorial bounds. . . .

WORTH NOTING Justice Breyer wrote a very brief concurrence; he joined the Court's opinion, but would have held that the case presented a non-justiciable political question had the Court not previously held otherwise in *Zivotofsky v. Clinton* (2012), which is presented on pp. 290–303.

JUSTICE THOMAS, concurring in the judgment in part and dissenting in part.

Our Constitution allocates the powers of the Federal Government over foreign affairs in two ways. First, it expressly identifies certain foreign affairs powers and vests them in particular branches, either individually or jointly. Second, it vests the residual foreign affairs powers of the Federal Government—i.e., those not specifically enumerated in the Constitution—in the President by way of Article II's Vesting Clause.

Section 214(d) of the Foreign Relations Authorization Act, Fiscal Year 2003, ignores that constitutional allocation of power insofar as it directs the President, contrary to his wishes, to list "Israel" as the place of birth of Jerusalem-born citizens on their passports. The President has long regulated passports under his residual foreign affairs power, and this portion of § 214(d) does not fall within any of Congress' enumerated powers. [Justice Thomas argued that the provision fell outside of congressional power to make rules for naturalization, because a passport is merely a travel document. A consular report, by contrast, was meant to effectuate the naturalization process. He did not believe the statute had recognition implications.]

I concur . . . in the portion of the Court's judgment holding § 214(d) unconstitutional as applied to passports. . . .

CHIEF JUSTICE ROBERTS, with whom JUSTICE ALITO joins, dissenting.

Today's decision is a first: Never before has this Court accepted a President's direct defiance of an Act of Congress in the field of foreign affairs. We have instead stressed that the President's power reaches "its lowest ebb" when he contravenes the express will of Congress, "for what is at stake is the equilibrium established by our constitutional system." *Youngstown Sheet & Tube Co. v. Sawyer* (1952) (Jackson, J., concurring). Justice Scalia's principal dissent, which I join in full, refutes the majority's unprecedented holding in detail. I write separately to underscore the stark nature of the Court's error on a basic question of separation of powers. . . .

The majority places great weight on the Reception Clause, which directs that the Executive "shall receive Ambassadors and other public Ministers." Art. II, § 3. But that provision, framed as an obligation rather than an authorization, appears alongside the *duties* imposed on the President by Article II, Section 3, not the *powers* granted to him by Article II, Section 2. Indeed, the People ratified the Constitution with Alexander Hamilton's assurance that executive reception of ambassadors "is more a matter of dignity than of authority" and "will be without consequence in the administration of the government." The Federalist No. 69. . . .

The majority's other asserted textual bases are even more tenuous. The President does have power to make treaties and appoint ambassadors. Art. II,

§ 2. But those authorities are *shared* with Congress, *ibid.*, so they hardly support an inference that the recognition power is *exclusive*. . . .

As for history, the majority admits that it too points in both directions. Some Presidents have claimed an exclusive recognition power, but others have expressed uncertainty about whether such preclusive authority exists. Those in the skeptical camp include Andrew Jackson and Abraham Lincoln, leaders not generally known for their cramped conceptions of Presidential power. Congress has also asserted its authority over recognition determinations at numerous points in history. The majority therefore falls short of demonstrating that "Congress has accepted" the President's exclusive recognition power. In any event, we have held that congressional acquiescence is only "pertinent" when the President acts in the absence of express congressional authorization, not when he asserts power to disregard a statute, as the Executive does here. *Medellín*; see *Dames & Moore*.

In sum, although the President has authority over recognition, I am not convinced that the Constitution provides the "conclusive and preclusive" power required to justify defiance of an express legislative mandate. *Youngstown* (Jackson, J., concurring).

But even if the President does have exclusive recognition power, he still cannot prevail in this case, because the statute at issue *does not implicate recognition*. The relevant provision, § 214(d), simply gives an American citizen born in Jerusalem the option to designate his place of birth as Israel "[f]or purposes of" passports and other documents. . . . And the annals of diplomatic history record no examples of official recognition accomplished via optional passport designation. . . .

JUSTICE SCALIA, with whom THE CHIEF JUSTICE and JUSTICE ALITO join, dissenting.

. . . The People . . . adopted a Constitution that divides responsibility for the Nation's foreign concerns between the legislative and executive departments. . . . "Fully eleven of the powers that Article I, § 8 grants Congress deal in some way with foreign affairs." L. Tribe, *American Constitutional Law*. . . .

Before turning to Presidential power under Article II, I think it well to establish the statute's basis in congressional power under Article I. Congress's power to "establish an uniform Rule of Naturalization," Art. I, § 8, cl. 4, enables it to grant American citizenship to someone born abroad. The naturalization power also enables Congress to furnish the people it makes citizens with papers verifying their citizenship—say a consular report of birth abroad (which certifies citizenship of an American born outside the United States) or a passport (which certifies citizenship for purposes of international travel). As the Necessary and Proper Clause confirms, every congressional power "carries with it all those incidental powers which are necessary to its complete and effectual execution." *Cohens v. Virginia* (1821). Even on a miserly understanding of Congress's incidental authority, Congress may make grants of citizenship "effectual" by providing for the issuance of certificates authenticating them.

One would think that if Congress may grant Zivotofsky a passport and a birth report, it may also require these papers to record his birthplace as "Israel." The birthplace specification promotes the document's citizenship-authenticating function by identifying the bearer, distinguishing people with similar names but different birthplaces from each other, helping authorities uncover identity fraud, and facilitating retrieval of the Government's citizenship records. To be sure, recording Zivotofsky's birthplace as "Jerusalem" rather than "Israel" would fulfill these objectives, but when faced with alternative ways to carry its powers into execution, Congress has the "discretion" to choose the one it deems "most beneficial to the people." *McCulloch v. Maryland* (1819). It thus has the right to decide that recording birthplaces as "Israel" makes for better foreign policy. Or that regardless of international politics, a passport or birth report should respect its bearer's conscientious belief that Jerusalem belongs to Israel. . . .

II

. . . The Court holds that the Constitution makes the President alone responsible for recognition and that § 214(d) invades this exclusive power. I agree that the Constitution *empowers* the President to extend recognition on behalf of the United States, but I find it a much harder question whether it makes that power exclusive. The Court tells us that "the weight of historical evidence" supports exclusive executive authority over "the formal determination of recognition." But even with its attention confined to formal recognition, the Court is forced to admit that "history is not all on one side." . . . Neither text nor history nor precedent yields a clear answer to these questions. Fortunately, I have no need to confront these matters today—nor does the Court—because § 214(d) plainly does not concern recognition. . . .

Section 214(d) does not require the Secretary to make a formal declaration about Israel's sovereignty over Jerusalem. And nobody suggests that international custom infers acceptance of sovereignty from the birthplace designation on a passport or birth report, as it does from bilateral treaties or exchanges of ambassadors. . . . That would be true even if the statute required *all* passports to list "Israel." But in fact it requires only those passports to list "Israel" for which the citizen (or his guardian) *requests* "Israel"; all the rest, under the Secretary's policy, list "Jerusalem." It is utterly impossible for this deference to private requests to constitute an act that unequivocally manifests an intention to grant recognition. . . .

V

Justice Thomas's concurrence deems § 214(d) unconstitutional to the extent it regulates passports. Whereas the Court's analysis threatens congressional power over foreign affairs with gradual erosion, the concurrence's approach shatters it in one stroke[,] produc[ing] a presidency more reminiscent of George III than George Washington. . . . That is not the chief magistrate under which the American People agreed to live when they adopted the national charter.

I dissent.

For Discussion

(1) What do you think was the effect of President Bush's statement about § 214(d) at the time he signed the Act into law?

(2) Should the President be deemed to have exclusive power to recognize foreign governments? Assuming the President does have such exclusive power, does § 214(d) interfere with it?

(3) Does Congress have power to provide a comprehensive set of rules governing the issuance of passports? Of consular reports?

(4) Suppose you are the Solicitor General arguing this case on behalf of the Government. A justice asks, "So far as the Constitution is concerned, can Congress, in setting a system of tariffs, provide that goods produced in Jerusalem shall be deemed to have been produced in Israel?" Your response?

Zivotofsky cast a sharply negative light on one of the best-known discussions of the roles of President and Congress in foreign affairs, in *United States v. Curtiss-Wright Export Corp.* (1936). A congressional resolution authorized the President to prohibit arms sales to Bolivia and Paraguay (which were at war with each other) if, after prescribed consultation, he determined that doing so "may contribute to the establishment of peace between those countries." The same day, President Roosevelt issued such a prohibition, closely tracking the language of the resolution. Curtiss-Wright was charged criminally with having sold arms to Bolivia, and defended itself by arguing that the resolution was an unconstitutional delegation to the President. The Supreme Court rejected this contention by a 7–1 vote. Justice Sutherland's opinion for the majority included this famous passage:

> It is important to bear in mind that we are here dealing not alone with an authority vested in the President by an exertion of legislative power, but with such an authority plus the very delicate, plenary and exclusive power of the President as the sole organ of the federal government in the field of international relations—a power which does not require as a basis for its exercise an act of Congress, but which, of course, like every other governmental power, must be exercised in subordination to the applicable provisions of the Constitution. It is quite apparent that if, in the maintenance of our international relations, embarrassment—perhaps serious embarrassment—is to be avoided and success for our aims achieved, congressional legislation which is to be made effective through negotiation and inquiry within the international field must often accord to the President a degree of discretion and freedom from statutory restriction which would not be admissible were domestic affairs alone involved. Moreover, he, not Congress, has the better opportunity of knowing the conditions which prevail in foreign countries, and especially is this true in time of war. He has his confidential sources of information. He has his agents in the form of diplomatic, consular and other officials. Secrecy in respect of information gathered by them may be highly necessary,

WORTH NOTING

This language traced to an 1800 speech by John Marshall, during his brief tenure in the House of Representatives, defending President Adams's decision to extradite to England an American citizen accused of murder. Marshall said: "The President is the sole organ of the nation in its external relations, and its sole representative with foreign nations." See, *e.g.*, Louis Fisher, *Presidential Inherent Power: The "Sole Organ" Doctrine*, 37 PRES'L STUDS. Q. 139 (2007).

and the premature disclosure of it productive of harmful results. . . .

In *Zivotofsky*, the Court refused to let this passage support the Solicitor General's argument for what it called "unbounded power" over foreign affairs:

> This description of the President's exclusive power was not nec-essary to the holding of *Curtiss-Wright*—which, after all, dealt with congressionally authorized action, not a unilateral Presidential de-termination. Indeed, *Curtiss-Wright* did not hold that the President is free from Congress' lawmaking power in the field of international relations. The President does have a unique role in communicating with foreign governments, as then-Congressman John Marshall ac-knowledged. But whether the realm is foreign or domestic, it is still the Legislative Branch, not the Executive Branch, that makes the law.

4.   The President's War Powers

a.   War Powers—the Framework

The Constitution makes the President the Commander-in-Chief, but it gives Congress the power to declare war. The following materials will explore how this division of responsibilities plays out with respect to the President's use of military force. (See pp. 812–842 for a comparison of the two branches' other foreign affairs authorities, a category typical-ly read to include the Constitution's provisions for national security and war powers.)

An early draft of the Constitution gave Congress the power "to make war." During one colloquy, the delegates to the 1787 Philadelphia Convention dis-cussed this wording before agreeing to revise it to "declare war." Do you think their discussion and the resulting revision tells us anything about the original understanding of presidential war powers?

James Madison's Notes of the Federal Convention

August 17, 1787

"To make war"

Mr Pinkney opposed the vesting this power in the Legislature. Its proceedings were too slow. It wd. meet but once a year. The Hs. of Reps. would be too numerous for such deliberations. The Senate would be the best depositary, being more acquainted with foreign affairs, and most capable of proper resolutions. If the States are equally represented in Senate, so as to give no advantage to large States, the power will notwithstanding be safe, as the small have their all at stake in such cases as well as the large States. It would be singular for one authority to make war, and another peace.

Mr Butler. The Objections agst the Legislature lie in a great degree agst the Senate. He was for vesting the power in the President, who will have all the requisite qualities, and will not make war but when the Nation will support it.

Mr. M(adison) and Mr Gerry moved to insert "*declare*," striking out "*make*" war; leaving to the Executive the power to repel sudden attacks.

Mr Sharman thought it stood very well. The Executive shd. be able to repel and not to commence war. "Make" better than "declare" the latter narrowing the power too much.

Mr Gerry never expected to hear in a republic a motion to empower the Executive alone to declare war.

Mr. Elseworth. there is a material difference between the cases of making *war*, and making *peace*. It shd. be more easy to get out of war, than into it. War also is a simple and overt declaration. peace attended with intricate & secret negociations.

Mr. Mason was agst giving the power of war to the Executive, because not <safely> to be trusted with it; or to the Senate, because not so constructed as to be entitled to it. He was for clogging rather than facilitating war; but for facilitating peace. He preferred "*declare*" to "*make*".

On the Motion to insert declare—in place of Make, <it was agreed to.>

N. H. no. Mas. abst. Cont. no.* Pa ay. Del. ay. Md. ay. Va. ay. N. C. ay. S. C. ay. Geo—ay. [Ayes—7; noes—2; absent—1.]

Mr. Pinkney's motion to strike out whole clause, disagd. to without call of States.

Mr Butler moved to give the Legislature power of peace, as they were to have that of war.

Mr Gerry 2ds. him. 8 Senators may possibly exercise the power if vested in that body, and 14 if all should be present; and May consequently give up part of the U. States. The Senate are more liable to be corrupted by an Enemy than the whole Legislature.

On the motion for adding "and peace" after "war"

N. H. no. Mas. no. Ct. no. Pa. no. Del. no. Md. no. Va. no. N. C. <no> S. C no. Geo. no. [Ayes—0; noes—10.]

Adjourned.

The Supreme Court offered an extensive discussion of presidential war powers in *The Prize Cases* (1863), which involved property confiscated from ships that were caught running a federal blockade of southern ports during the Civil War.

 For more on the larger context of the national government's efforts during the Civil War, see p. 139.

President Lincoln ordered the blockade on April 19, 1861—a week after the Civil War began with South Carolina's bombardment of Fort Sumter. Congress was then out of session; on April 15, Lincoln had called for it to meet in an extraordinary session, although not until July 4. The legality of the seizures came down in part to the question of whether the President's announcement of the blockade was a valid exercise of authority. By a 5–4 vote, the Court concluded the blockade was valid. Justice Grier wrote for the majority, which included the three Lincoln appointees then on the Court:

> That a blockade *de facto* actually existed, and was formally declared and notified by the President on the 27th and 30th of April,

---

*   On the remark by Mr. King that "make" war might be understood to "conduct" it which was an Executive function, Mr. Elseworth gave up his objection (and the vote of Cont was changed to—ay.)

1861, is an admitted fact in these cases. That the President, as the Executive Chief of the Government and Commander-in-chief of the Army and Navy, was the proper person to make such notification, has not been, and cannot be disputed. . . . Let us enquire whether, at the time this blockade was instituted, a state of war existed which would justify a resort to these means of subduing the hostile force.

War has been well defined to be, "That state in which a nation prosecutes its right by force." The parties belligerent in a public war are independent nations. But it is not necessary to constitute war, that both parties should be acknowledged as independent nations or sovereign States. A war may exist where one of the belligerents, claims sovereign rights as against the other.

Insurrection against a government may or may not culminate in an organized rebellion, but a civil war always begins by insurrection against the lawful authority of the Government. A civil war is never solemnly declared; it becomes such by its accidents—the number, power, and organization of the persons who originate and carry it on. When the party in rebellion occupy and hold in a hostile manner a certain portion of territory; have declared their independence; have cast off their allegiance; have organized armies; have commenced hostilities against their former sovereign, the world acknowledges them as belligerents, and the contest a *war*. *They* claim to be in arms to establish their liberty and independence, in order to become a sovereign State, while the sovereign party treats them as insurgents and rebels who owe allegiance, and who should be punished with death for their treason. . . .

As a civil war is never publicly proclaimed, *eo nomine* [by that name], against insurgents, its actual existence is a fact in our domestic history which the Court is bound to notice and to know. . . .

By the Constitution, Congress alone has the power to declare a national or foreign war. It cannot declare war against a State, or any number of States, by virtue of any clause in the Constitution. The Constitution confers on the President the whole Executive power. He is bound to take care that the laws be faithfully executed. He is Commander-in-chief of the Army and Navy of the United States, and of the militia of the several States when called into the actual service of the United States. He has no power to initiate or declare a war either against a foreign nation or a domestic State. But by the Acts of Congress of February 28th, 1795, and 3d of March, 1807, he is authorized to called out the militia and use the military and naval forces of the United States in case of invasion by foreign nations, and to suppress insurrection against the government of a State or of the United States.

If a war be made by invasion of a foreign nation, the President is not only authorized but bound to resist force by force. He does not initiate the war, but is bound to accept the challenge without waiting for any special legislative authority. And whether the hostile party be a foreign invader, or States organized in rebellion, it is none the less a war, although the declaration of it be "*unilateral.*" Lord Stowell observes, "It is not the less a war on *that account,* for war may exist without a declaration on either side. It is so laid down by the best writers on the law of nations. A declaration of war by one country only, is not a mere challenge to be accepted or refused at pleasure by the other." . . .

This greatest of civil wars was not gradually developed by popular commotion, tumultuous assemblies, or local unorganized insurrections. However long may have been its previous conception, it nevertheless sprung forth suddenly from the parent brain, a Minerva in the full panoply of *war.* The President was bound to meet it in the shape it presented itself, without waiting for Congress to baptize it with a name; and no name given to it by him or them could change the fact. . . .

Whether the President in fulfilling his duties, as Commander-in-chief, in suppressing an insurrection, has met with such armed hostile resistance, and a civil war of such alarming proportions as will compel him to accord to them the character of belligerents, is a question to be decided *by him,* and this Court must be governed by the decisions and acts of the political department of the Government to which this power was entrusted. "He must determine what degree of force the crisis demands." The proclamation of blockade is itself official and conclusive evidence to the Court that a state of war existed which demanded and authorized a recourse to such a measure, under the circumstances peculiar to the case. . . .

If it were necessary to the technical existence of a war, that it should have a legislative sanction, we find it in almost every act passed at the extraordinary session of the Legislature of 1861, which was wholly employed in enacting laws to enable the Government to prosecute the war with vigor and efficiency. And finally, in 1861, we find Congress "*ex majore cautela*" [out of an abundance of caution] and in anticipation of such astute objections, passing an act "approving, legalizing, and making valid all the acts, proclamations, and orders of the President, &c., as if they had been *issued and done under the previous express authority* and direction of the Congress of the United States."

WORTH NOTING The quoted language does not exactly track that of the statute, though the italicized passage does. The ratification extended to all Presidential acts, etc., after March 4, 1861 "respecting the army and navy of the United States, and calling out or relating to the militia or volunteers from the States." Act of Aug. 6, 1861, § 3.

Without admitting that such an act was necessary under the circumstances, it is plain that if the President had in any manner assumed powers which it was necessary should have the authority or sanction of Congress, that on the well known principle of law, "*omnis ratihabitio retrotrahitur et mandato equiparatur*" [ratification is equivalent to prior authority], this ratification has operated to perfectly cure the defect. . . . The objection made to this act of ratification, that it is *ex post facto*, and therefore unconstitutional and void, might possibly have some weight on the trial of an indictment in a criminal Court. But precedents from that source cannot be received as authoritative in a tribunal administering public and international law. . . .

[T]herefore we are of the opinion that the President had a right, *jure belli* [by the law of war], to institute a blockade of ports in possession of the States in rebellion, which neutrals are bound to regard. . . .

Justice Nelson wrote for the dissenters. He contended that the President had ample powers to suppress an insurrection under the Constitution and Acts of Feb. 28, 1795 and March 3, 1807. The 1795 Act authorized use of the militia, he argued, and the 1807 Act (the Insurrection Act) authorized use of the nation's armed forces. On Justice Nelson's view, however, these statutes only authorized action against those actually in rebellion. He thought any state of war justifying a blockade would have to be declared by Congress, which in his view could have been assembled at any time on thirty days' notice.

Question

On the Court's explanation, what legal authority justified the President's decision to impose a blockade, which requires the existence of a state of war? Was it the Constitution, a statute, or something else?

b. The President's Use of Authorized Force

The following materials present a case study in the President's use of force under modern circumstances: al Qaeda's September 11, 2001 terrorist strikes on the United States, which killed almost 3,000 people, and the ensuing American invasion of Afghanistan. Where the principal legal question in *The Prize Cases* was the consequence of "war status" for seized property, the legal question that drives the materials below focuses on people: could allegedly hostile individuals captured in Afghanistan be detained indefinitely as what amounted to prisoners of war?

Two historical precedents are important to keep in mind. The first is *Ex parte Milligan* (1866), presented at pp. 141–149. Lambdin Milligan was arrested at his Indiana home in October 1864 on suspicion of supporting rebellion. He was tried by a military commission on several charges and sentenced to be hanged. But the Supreme Court, which was considering the case after the war was over, held that the commission had no power to try Milligan. Justice Davis wrote for the majority:

> This court has judicial knowledge that in Indiana the Federal authority was always unopposed, and its courts always open to hear criminal accusations and redress grievances; and no usage of war could sanction a military trial there for any offence whatever of a citizen in civil life, in nowise connected with the military service. Congress could

grant no such power; and to the honor of our national legislature be it said, it has never been provoked by the state of the country even to attempt its exercise. One of the plainest constitutional provisions was, therefore, infringed when Milligan was tried by a court not ordained and established by Congress, and not composed of judges appointed during good behavior.

Four justices, per Chief Justice Chase, concurred in the result; they believed that Congress did have the constitutional authority to authorize such military commissions, but had not actually done so.

The second precedent is *Ex parte Quirin* (1942), decided in the early days of World War II. Eight Nazi saboteurs came ashore on Long Island in June 1942 and were quickly arrested and tried before a military commission. Before the commission had completed its work, the Supreme Court heard argument on a habeas corpus petition filed on behalf of the eight defendants. The day after arguments concluded, the Court issued a brief *per curiam* deciding that the commission could proceed. The Court did not issue an explanatory opinion until October, after six of the men—including a United States citizen named Herbert Haupt—had been executed. In an opinion written by Chief Justice Stone, the Court held that the men were

> plainly within the ultimate boundaries of the jurisdiction of military tribunals, and were held in good faith for trial by military commission, charged with being enemies who, with the purpose of destroying war materials and utilities, entered or after entry remained in our territory without uniform—an offense against the law of war. Those particular acts constitute an offense against the law of war which the Constitution authorizes to be tried by military commission.

As you read the materials relating to the United States's conflict with al Qaeda, note how the assumptions of cases dealing with conflicts like the Civil War and World War II come under strain in the face of modern reality.

Joint Resolution to authorize the use of United States Armed Forces against those responsible for the recent attacks launched against the United States.

15 Stat. 224, Sept. 18, 2001.

Whereas, on September 11, 2001, acts of treacherous violence were committed against the United States and its citizens; and

Whereas, such acts render it both necessary and appropriate that the United States exercise its rights to self-defense and to protect United States citizens both at home and abroad; and

Whereas, in light of the threat to the national security and foreign policy of the United States posed by these grave acts of violence; and

Whereas, such acts continue to pose an unusual and extraordinary threat to the national security and foreign policy of the United States; and

Whereas, the President has authority under the Constitution to take action to deter and prevent acts of international terrorism against the United States: Now, therefore, be it

Resolved by the Senate and House of Representatives of the United States of America in Congress assembled . . . ,

SECTION 2—AUTHORIZATION FOR USE OF UNITED STATES ARMED FORCES

(a)   IN GENERAL—That the President is authorized to use all necessary and appropriate force against those nations, organizations, or persons he determines planned, authorized, committed, or aided the terrorist attacks that occurred on September 11, 2001, or harbored such organizations or persons, in order to prevent any future acts of international terrorism against the United States by such nations, organizations or persons. . . .

Relying on this Authorization for the Use of Military Force (AUMF), the United States sent armed forces into Afghanistan. Their mission was to confront, engage, and destroy a non-state actor called al Qaeda, the terrorist group that had conducted and claimed responsibility for the September 11 attacks.

They were also charged with taking action as necessary against the Taliban, the group that then dominated most of Afghanistan and claimed governmental authority over the state, because it had sheltered al Qaeda operatives. During the initial months of that conflict, the U.S. military captured and detained many suspected militants. One of them, named Yaser Esam Hamdi, turned out to be an American citizen. Hamdi's father brought a petition for habeas corpus on his behalf, seeking the release of his son.

This challenge to Hamdi's detention eventually reached the Supreme Court, where it produced a splintered decision that did two things. First, a majority of the Court accepted that the executive branch had authority to detain at least some suspected members of terrorist organizations as enemy combatants. Second, a different majority ordered the trial court to conduct a serious inquiry into the facts of Hamdi's case. The excerpts below focus on the first issue; the remainder of the Court's discussion implicates the Due Process Clause, and so it is reproduced in Chapter VI, see pp. 1297–1305.

As you read the following opinions, consider what constitutional significance each would give to the fact of congressional authorization under the AUMF.

Hamdi v. Rumsfeld

Supreme Court of the United States, 2004.
542 U.S. 507.

Justice O'Connor announced the judgment of the Court and delivered an opinion, in which The Chief Justice, Justice Kennedy, and Justice Breyer join.

At this difficult time in our Nation's history, we are called upon to consider the legality of the Government's detention of a United States citizen on United States soil as an "enemy combatant" and to address the process that is constitutionally owed to one who seeks to challenge his classification as such. . . . We hold that although Congress authorized the detention of combatants in the narrow circumstances alleged here, due process demands that a citizen held in the United States as an enemy combatant be given a meaningful opportunity to contest the factual basis for that detention before a neutral decisionmaker.

I

. . . This case arises out of the detention of a man whom the Government alleges took up arms with the Taliban during [the conflict in Afghanistan]. His name is Yaser Esam Hamdi. Born in Louisiana in 1980, Hamdi moved with his family to Saudi Arabia as a child. By 2001, the parties agree, he resided in Afghanistan. At some point that year, he was seized by members of the Northern Alliance, a coalition of military groups opposed to the Taliban government, and eventually was turned over to the United States military. The Government asserts that it initially detained and interrogated Hamdi in Afghanistan before transferring him to the United States Naval Base in Guantanamo Bay in January 2002. In April 2002, upon learning that Hamdi is an American citizen, authorities transferred him to a naval brig in Norfolk, Virginia, where he remained until a recent transfer to a brig in Charleston, South Carolina. The Government contends that Hamdi is an "enemy combatant," and that this status justifies holding him in the United States indefinitely—without formal charges or proceedings—unless and until it makes the determination that access to counsel or further process is warranted. . . .

In June 2002, Hamdi's father, Esam Fouad Hamdi, filed the present petition for a writ of habeas corpus under 28 U.S.C. § 2241 in the Eastern District of Virginia, naming as petitioners his son and himself as next friend. Hamdi's father has asserted . . . that his son went to Afghanistan to do "relief work," and that he had been in that country less than two months before September 11, 2001, and could not have received military training. The 20-year-old was traveling on his own for the first time, his father says, and "[b]ecause of his lack of experience, he was trapped in Afghanistan once the military campaign began."

[T]he Government filed a response and a motion to dismiss the petition. It attached to its response a declaration from one Michael Mobbs (hereinafter Mobbs Declaration), who identified himself as Special Advisor to the Under Secretary of Defense for Policy. Mobbs indicated that in this position, he has been "substantially involved with matters related to the detention of enemy combatants in the current war against the al Qaeda terrorists and those who support and harbor them (including the Taliban)." He expressed his "familiar[ity]" with Department of Defense and United States military policies and procedures applicable to the detention, control, and transfer of al Qaeda and

Taliban personnel, and declared that "[b]ased upon my review of relevant records and reports, I am also familiar with the facts and circumstances related to the capture of . . . Hamdi and his detention by U.S. military forces."

Mobbs then set forth what remains the sole evidentiary support that the Government has provided to the courts for Hamdi's detention. The declaration states that Hamdi "traveled to Afghanistan" in July or August 2001, and that he thereafter "affiliated with a Taliban military unit and received weapons training." It asserts that Hamdi "remained with his Taliban unit following the attacks of September 11" and that, during the time when Northern Alliance forces were "engaged in battle with the Taliban," "Hamdi's Taliban unit surrendered" to those forces, after which he "surrender[ed] his Kalishnikov assault rifle" to them. The Mobbs Declaration also states that, because al Qaeda and the Taliban "were and are hostile forces engaged in armed conflict with the armed forces of the United States," "individuals associated with" those groups "were and continue to be enemy combatants." Mobbs states that Hamdi was labeled an enemy combatant "[b]ased upon his interviews and in light of his association with the Taliban." According to the declaration, a series of "U.S. military screening team[s]" determined that Hamdi met "the criteria for enemy combatants," and "[a] subsequent interview of Hamdi has confirmed the fact that he surrendered and gave his firearm to Northern Alliance forces, which supports his classification as an enemy combatant." . . .

The District Court found that the Mobbs Declaration fell "far short" of supporting Hamdi's detention. It criticized the generic and hearsay nature of the affidavit, calling it "little more than the government's 'say-so.'" It ordered the Government to turn over numerous materials for *in camera* review, including copies of all of Hamdi's statements and the notes taken from interviews with him that related to his reasons for going to Afghanistan and his activities therein; a list of all interrogators who had questioned Hamdi and their names and addresses; statements by members of the Northern Alliance regarding Hamdi's surrender and capture; a list of the dates and locations of his capture and subsequent detentions; and the names and titles of the United States Government officials who made the determinations that Hamdi was an enemy combatant and that he should be moved to a naval brig. The court indicated that all of these materials were necessary for "meaningful judicial review" of whether Hamdi's detention was legally authorized and whether Hamdi had received sufficient process to satisfy the Due Process Clause of the Constitution and relevant treaties or military regulations.

The Government sought to appeal the production order, and the District Court certified the question of whether the Mobbs Declaration, " 'standing alone, is sufficient as a matter of law to allow a meaningful judicial review of [Hamdi's] classification as an enemy combatant.' " The Fourth Circuit reversed[, rehearing en banc was denied,] and we granted certiorari. We now vacate the judgment below and remand.

II

The threshold question before us is whether the Executive has the authority to detain citizens who qualify as "enemy combatants." There is some debate as to the proper scope of this term. . . . [F]or purposes of this case, the "enemy combatant" that it is seeking to detain is an individual who, it alleges, was " 'part of or supporting forces hostile to the United States or coalition partners' " in Afghanistan and who " 'engaged in an armed conflict against the United States' " there. We therefore answer only the narrow question before us: whether the detention of citizens falling within that definition is authorized.

The Government maintains that no explicit congressional authorization is required, because the Executive possesses plenary authority to detain pursuant to Article II of the Constitution. We do not reach the question whether Article II provides such authority, however, because we agree with the Government's alternative position, that Congress has in fact authorized Hamdi's detention, through the AUMF. Our analysis on that point, set forth below, substantially overlaps with our analysis of Hamdi's principal argument for the illegality of his detention. He posits that his detention is forbidden by 18 U.S.C. § 4001(a) [, a 1971 enactment providing] that "[n]o citizen shall be imprisoned or otherwise detained by the United States except pursuant to an Act of Congress." . . .

[F]or the reasons that follow, we conclude that the AUMF is explicit congressional authorization for the detention of individuals in the narrow category we describe. . . .

The AUMF authorizes the President to use "all necessary and appropriate force" against "nations, organizations, or persons" associated with the September 11, 2001, terrorist attacks. There can be no doubt that individuals who fought against the United States in Afghanistan as part of the Taliban, an organization known to have supported the al Qaeda terrorist network responsible for those attacks, are individuals Congress sought to target in passing the AUMF. We conclude that detention of individuals falling into the limited category we are considering, for the duration of the particular conflict in which they were captured, is so fundamental and accepted an incident to war as to be an exercise of the "necessary and appropriate force" Congress has authorized the President to use.

The capture and detention of lawful combatants and the capture, detention, and trial of unlawful combatants, by "universal agreement and practice," are "important incident[s] of war." *Ex parte Quirin* (1942). The purpose of detention is to prevent captured individuals from returning to the field of battle and taking up arms once again. . . .

There is no bar to this Nation's holding one of its own citizens as an enemy combatant. In *Quirin*, one of the detainees, Haupt, alleged that he was a naturalized United States citizen. We held that "[c]itizens who associate themselves with the military arm of the enemy government, and with its aid, guidance and direction enter this country bent on hostile acts, are enemy belligerents within the meaning of . . . the law of war." . . . See also *Lieber Code, Instructions for the Government of Armies of the United States in the Field* (1863) (contemplating, in code binding the Union Army during the Civil War, that "captured rebels" would be treated "as prisoners of war"). Nor can we see any reason for drawing such a line here. A citizen, no less than an alien, can be "part of or supporting forces hostile to the United States or coalition partners" and "engaged in an armed conflict against the United States"; such a citizen, if released, would pose the same threat of returning to the front during the ongoing conflict.

In light of these principles, it is of no moment that the AUMF does not use specific language of detention. Because detention to prevent a combatant's return to the battlefield is a fundamental incident of waging war, in permitting the use of "necessary and appropriate force," Congress has clearly and unmistakably authorized detention in the narrow circumstances considered here.

Hamdi objects, nevertheless, that Congress has not authorized the *indefinite* detention to which he is now subject. The Government responds that "the detention of enemy combatants during World War II was just as 'indefinite' while that war was being fought." We take Hamdi's objection to be not to the lack of certainty regarding the date on which the conflict will end, but to the substantial prospect of perpetual detention. We recognize that the national security underpinnings of the "war on terror," although crucially important, are broad and malleable. As the Government concedes, "given its unconventional nature, the current conflict is unlikely to end with a formal cease-fire agreement." The prospect Hamdi raises is therefore not farfetched. If the Government does not consider this unconventional war won for two generations, and if it maintains during that time that Hamdi might, if released, rejoin forces fighting against the United States, then the position it has taken throughout the litigation of this case suggests that Hamdi's detention could last for the rest of his life.

It is a clearly established principle of the law of war that detention may last no longer than active hostilities. [Citations omitted.] Hamdi contends that the AUMF does not authorize indefinite or perpetual detention. Certainly, we agree that indefinite detention for the purpose of interrogation is not authorized. Further, we understand Congress' grant of authority for the use of "necessary and appropriate force" to include the authority to detain for the duration of the relevant conflict, and our understanding is based on longstanding law-of-war principles.

If the practical circumstances of a given conflict are entirely unlike those of the conflicts that informed the development of the law of war, that understanding may unravel. But that is not the situation we face as of this date. Active combat operations against Taliban fighters apparently are ongoing in Afghanistan. The United States may detain, for the duration of these hostilities, individuals legitimately determined to be Taliban combatants who "engaged in an armed conflict against the United States." If the record establishes that United States troops are still involved in active combat in Afghanistan, those detentions are part of the exercise of "necessary and appropriate force," and therefore are authorized by the AUMF. . . .[1]

WORTH NOTING

Having held that Hamdi could be detained as an enemy combatant if the allegations against him were true, the plurality went on to discuss the process by which he could challenge those allegations on remand. It concluded that "a citizen-detainee seeking to challenge his classification as an enemy combatant must receive notice of the factual basis for his classification, and a fair opportunity to rebut the Government's factual assertions before a neutral decisionmaker." It noted that "[h]earsay . . . may need to be accepted as the most reliable available evidence from the Government in such a proceeding" and stated that "the Constitution would not be offended by a presumption in favor of the Government's evidence, so long as that presumption remained a rebuttable one and fair opportunity for rebuttal were provided." For a detailed excerpt of the plurality's analysis of these procedural issues, as well as the responses from the other opinions, see pp. 1297–1305.

---

[1]   Here the basis asserted for detention by the military is that Hamdi was carrying a weapon against American troops on a foreign battlefield; that is, that he was an enemy combatant. The legal category of enemy combatant has not been elaborated upon in great detail. The permissible bounds of the category will be defined by the lower courts as subsequent cases are presented to them.

JUSTICE SOUTER, with whom JUSTICE GINSBURG joins, concurring in part, dissenting in part, and concurring in the judgment.

. . . The plurality . . . accept[s] the Government's position that if Hamdi's designation as an enemy combatant is correct, his detention (at least as to some period) is authorized by . . . the Authorization for Use of Military Force. Here, I disagree and respectfully dissent. . . .

II

The threshold issue is how broadly or narrowly to read the Non-Detention Act, the tone of which is severe: "No citizen shall be imprisoned or otherwise detained by the United States except pursuant to an Act of Congress." 18 U.S.C. § 4001(a). Should the severity of the Act be relieved when the Government's stated factual justification for incommunicado detention is a war on terrorism, so that the Government may be said to act "pursuant" to congressional terms that fall short of explicit authority to imprison individuals? With one possible though important qualification, [see Part III.D, infra] the answer has to be no. For a number of reasons, the prohibition within § 4001(a) has to be read broadly to accord the statute a long reach and to impose a burden of justification on the Government.

[Justice Souter pointed out that the provision was enacted in wake of the 1971 repeal of the Emergency Detention Act of 1950, "which had authorized the Attorney General, in time of emergency, to detain anyone reasonably thought likely to engage in espionage or sabotage." The repeal was meant to preclude an incident akin to the internments of Japanese Americans in World War II, which, Souter emphasized, "were accomplished by Executive action." Accordingly, § 4001(a) was "intended to preclude reliance on vague congressional authority . . . for detention or imprisonment at the discretion of the Executive." And so Souter concluded that "[i]n requiring that any Executive detention be 'pursuant to an Act of Congress,' . . . Congress necessarily meant to require a congressional enactment that clearly authorized detention or imprisonment."]

The defining character of American constitutional government is its constant tension between security and liberty, serving both by partial helpings of each. . . . Hence the need for an assessment by Congress before citizens are subject to lockup, and likewise the need for a clearly expressed congressional resolution of the competing claims.

III

Under this principle of reading § 4001(a) robustly to require a clear statement of authorization to detain, none of the Government's arguments suffices to justify Hamdi's detention. . . .

. . . Since the [AUMF] was adopted one week after the attacks of September 11, 2001, it naturally speaks with some generality, but its focus is clear, and that is on the use of military power. It is fairly read to authorize the use of armies and weapons, whether against other armies or individual terrorists. But . . . it never so much as uses the word detention, and there is no reason to think Congress might have perceived any need to augment Executive power to deal with dangerous citizens within the United States, given the well-stocked statutory arsenal of defined criminal offenses covering the gamut of actions that a citizen sympathetic to terrorists might commit. [Justice Souter here cited a series of federal crimes.]

Even so, there is one argument for treating the Force Resolution as sufficiently clear to authorize detention of a citizen consistently with § 4001(a). . . . Because the Force Resolution authorizes the use of military force in acts of war by the United States, the argument goes, it is reasonably clear that the military and its Commander in Chief are authorized to deal with enemy belligerents according to the treaties and customs known collectively as the laws of war. . . .

There is no need, however, to address the merits of such an argument in all possible circumstances. For now it is enough to recognize that . . . [b]y holding him incommunicado, . . . the Government obviously has not been treating him [in accordance with the international law requirements for the treatment of] prisoner[s] of war, and in fact the Government claims that no Taliban detainee is entitled to prisoner of war status. This treatment appears to be a violation of the Geneva Convention provision that even in cases of doubt, captives are entitled to be treated as prisoners of war "until such time as their status has been determined by a competent tribunal." . . .

[T]he Government has not made out its claim that in detaining Hamdi in the manner described, it is acting in accord with the laws of war authorized to be applied against citizens by the Force Resolution. I conclude accordingly that the Government has failed to support the position that the Force Resolution authorizes the described detention of Hamdi for purposes of § 4001(a) .

D

Since the Government has given no reason either to deflect the application of § 4001(a) or to hold it to be satisfied, I need to go no further; the Government hints of a constitutional challenge to the statute, but it presents none here. I will, however, . . . recall Justice Jackson's observation that the President is not Commander in Chief of the country, only of the military.

There may be room for one qualification to Justice Jackson's statement, however: in a moment of genuine emergency, when the Government must act with no time for deliberation, the Executive may be able to detain a citizen if there is reason to fear he is an imminent threat to the safety of the Nation and its people (though I doubt there is any want of statutory authority, see *supra*). This case, however, does not present that question, because an emergency power of necessity must at least be limited by the emergency; Hamdi has been locked up for over two years. *Cf. Ex parte Milligan* (1866) (martial law justified only by "actual and present" necessity as in a genuine invasion that closes civilian courts). . . .

WORTH NOTING

Justice Souter agreed with the plurality that the Fourth Circuit's opinion should be reversed. But he was in dissent on the question of authorization: five Justices (including Justice Thomas, whose separate opinion appears infra) agreed that the AUMF authorized Hamdi's detention. Justice Souter therefore needed to address the question of what process should be available for Hamdi to challenge the charges against him on remand. He agreed with the plurality that "someone in Hamdi's position is entitled at a minimum to notice of the Government's claimed factual basis for holding him, and to a fair chance to rebut it before a neutral decisionmaker" as well as "right to counsel." Souter believed the Constitution required more than that, but joined the plurality's judgment because it "order[ed] remand on terms closest to those I would impose." A longer excerpt of that discussion is presented at pp. 1303–1305.

Justice Scalia, with whom Justice Stevens joins, dissenting.

. . . Where the Government accuses a citizen of waging war against it, our constitutional tradition has been to prosecute him in federal court for treason or some other crime. Where the exigencies of war prevent that, the Constitution's Suspension Clause, Art. I, § 9, cl. 2, allows Congress to relax the usual protections temporarily. Absent suspension, however, the Executive's assertion of military exigency has not been thought sufficient to permit detention without charge. No one contends that the congressional Authorization for Use of

Military Force, on which the Government relies to justify its actions here, is an implementation of the Suspension Clause. Accordingly, I would reverse the judgment below.

I

. . . The gist of the Due Process Clause, as understood at the founding and since, was to force the Government to follow those common-law procedures traditionally deemed necessary before depriving a person of life, liberty, or property. When a citizen was deprived of liberty because of alleged criminal conduct, those procedures typically required committal by a magistrate followed by indictment and trial. . . . The Due Process Clause "in effect affirms the right of trial according to the process and proceedings of the common law." J. Story, Commentaries on the Constitution of the United States (1833). To be sure, certain types of permissible *non*criminal detention—that is, those not dependent upon the contention that the citizen had committed a criminal act—did not require the protections of criminal procedure. However, these fell into a limited number of well-recognized exceptions—civil commitment of the mentally ill, for example, and temporary detention in quarantine of the infectious. . . .

These due process rights have historically been vindicated by the writ of habeas corpus. . . . The writ of habeas corpus was preserved in the Constitution—the only common-law writ to be explicitly mentioned. See Art. I, § 9, cl. 2. Hamilton lauded "the establishment of the writ of *habeas corpus*" in his Federalist defense as a means to protect against "the practice of arbitrary imprisonments . . . in all ages, [one of] the favourite and most formidable instruments of tyranny." The Federalist No. 84. . . .

II

The allegations here, of course, are no ordinary accusations of criminal activity. Yaser Esam Hamdi has been imprisoned because the Government believes he participated in the waging of war against the United States. . . .

Justice O'Connor, writing for a plurality of this Court, asserts that captured enemy combatants (other than those suspected of war crimes) have traditionally been detained until the cessation of hostilities and then released. That is probably an accurate description of wartime practice with respect to enemy *aliens*. The tradition with respect to American citizens, however, has been quite different. Citizens aiding the enemy have been treated as traitors subject to the criminal process. [Justice Scalia gives examples dating back to 1350.]

There are times when military exigency renders resort to the traditional criminal process impracticable. English law accommodated such exigencies by allowing legislative suspension of the writ of habeas corpus for brief periods. . . . Our Federal Constitution contains a [comparable] provision explicitly permitting suspension, but limiting the situations in which it may be invoked: "The Privilege of the Writ of Habeas Corpus shall not be suspended, unless when in Cases of Rebellion or Invasion the public Safety may require it." Art. I, § 9, cl. 2. Although this provision does not state that suspension must be effected by, or authorized by, a legislative act, it has been so understood, consistent with English practice and the Clause's placement in Article I. See *Ex parte Bollman* (1807); *Ex parte Merryman* (C.D. Md. 1861) (Taney, C.J., rejecting Lincoln's unauthorized suspension); Story, Commentaries on the Constitution. . . .

The Government . . . places primary reliance upon *Ex parte Quirin* (1942). . . . The case was not this Court's finest hour. . . . The Court eventually explained its reasoning in a written opinion issued several months [after six of the saboteurs had been executed]. Only three paragraphs of the Court's lengthy opinion dealt with the particular circumstances of Haupt's case. . . . [In any event, as a legal matter,] it was uncontested that the petitioners were members of enemy forces. They were "*admitted* enemy invaders" (emphasis added), and it was "undisputed" that they had landed in the United States in service of German forces. The specific holding of the Court was only that, "upon the *conceded* facts," the petitioners were "plainly within [the] boundaries" of military jurisdiction (emphasis added). But where those jurisdictional facts are *not* conceded—where the petitioner insists that he is *not* a belligerent—*Quirin* left the pre-existing law in place: Absent suspension of the writ, a citizen held where the courts are open is entitled either to criminal trial or to a judicial decree requiring his release.

V

It follows from what I have said that Hamdi is entitled to a habeas decree requiring his release unless (1) criminal proceedings are promptly brought, or (2) Congress has suspended the writ of habeas corpus. A suspension of the writ could, of course, lay down conditions for continued detention, similar to those that today's opinion prescribes under the Due Process Clause. Cf. Act of Mar. 3, 1863. But there is a world of difference between the people's representatives' determining the need for that suspension (and prescribing the conditions for it), and this Court's doing so. . . .

There is a certain harmony of approach in the plurality's making up for Congress's failure to invoke the Suspension Clause and its making up for the Executive's failure to apply what it says are needed procedures—an approach that reflects what might be called a Mr. Fix-it Mentality. . . . The problem with this approach is not only that it steps out of the courts' modest and limited role in a democratic society; but that by repeatedly doing what it thinks the political branches ought to do it encourages their lassitude and saps the vitality of government by the people.

VI

Several limitations give my views in this matter a relatively narrow compass. They apply only to citizens, accused of being enemy combatants, who are detained within the territorial jurisdiction of a federal court. This is not likely to be a numerous group; currently we know of only two, Hamdi and Jose Padilla. Where the citizen is captured outside and held outside the United States, the constitutional requirements may be different. Moreover, even within the United States, the accused citizen-enemy combatant may lawfully be detained once prosecution is in progress or in contemplation. The Government has been notably successful in securing conviction, and hence long-term custody or execution, of those who have waged war against the state.

I frankly do not know whether these tools are sufficient to meet the Government's security needs, including the need to obtain intelligence through interrogation. It is far beyond my competence, or the Court's competence, to determine that. But it is not beyond Congress's. If the situation demands it, the Executive can ask Congress to authorize suspension of the writ—which can be made subject to whatever conditions Congress deems appropriate, including even the procedural novelties invented by the plurality today. To be sure, suspension is limited by the Constitution to cases of rebellion or invasion. But whether the attacks of September 11, 2001, constitute an "invasion," and whether those attacks still justify suspension several years later, are questions for Congress rather than this Court. See Story, *Commentaries on the Constitution*.[6] . . .

---

[6]   Justice Thomas worries that the constitutional conditions for suspension of the writ will not exist "during many . . . emergencies during which . . . detention authority might be necessary." It is difficult to imagine situations in which security is so seriously threatened as to justify indefinite imprisonment without trial, and yet the constitutional conditions of rebellion or invasion are not met.

Justice Thomas, dissenting.

. . . The Founders intended that the President have primary responsibility—along with the necessary power—to protect the national security and to conduct the Nation's foreign relations. They did so principally because the structural advantages of a unitary Executive are essential in these domains. To this end, the Constitution vests in the President "[t]he executive Power," Art. II, § 1, provides that he "shall be Commander in Chief of the" Armed Forces, § 2, and places in him the power to recognize foreign governments, § 3.

This Court has long recognized these features and has accordingly held that the President has *constitutional* authority to protect the national security and that this authority carries with it broad discretion.

> If a war be made by invasion of a foreign nation, the President is not only authorized but bound to resist force by force. He does not initiate the war, but is bound to accept the challenge without waiting for any special legislative authority. . . . Whether the President in fulfilling his duties, as Commander in-chief, in suppressing an insurrection, has met with such armed hostile resistance . . . is a question to be decided *by him.*

Prize Cases (1863). . . .

Although the President very well may have inherent authority to detain those arrayed against our troops, I agree with the plurality that we need not decide that question because Congress has authorized the President to do so. The Authorization for Use of Military Force authorizes the President to "use all necessary and appropriate force against those nations, organizations, or persons he determines planned, authorized, committed, or aided the terrorist attacks" of September 11, 2001. . . .

Accordingly, the President's action here is "supported by the strongest of presumptions and the widest latitude of judicial interpretation." *Dames & Moore v. Regan* (1981). The question becomes whether the Federal Government (rather than the President acting alone) has power to detain Hamdi as an enemy combatant. More precisely, we must determine whether the Government may detain Hamdi given the procedures that were used. . . .

I agree with the plurality that the Federal Government has power to detain those that the Executive Branch determines to be enemy combatants. But I do not think that the plurality has adequately explained the breadth of the

President's authority to detain enemy combatants, an authority that includes making virtually conclusive factual findings. In my view, the structural considerations discussed above, as recognized in our precedent, demonstrate that we lack the capacity and responsibility to second-guess this determination. . . .

Accordingly, I conclude that the Government's detention of Hamdi as an enemy combatant does not violate the Constitution. By detaining Hamdi, the President, in the prosecution of a war and authorized by Congress, has acted well within his authority. Hamdi thereby received all the process to which he was due under the circumstances. . . .

Legal historian Mary L. Dudziak writes:

> Once war has begun, time is thought to proceed on a different plane. There are two important consequences of this shift: first, we have entered a time that calls for extraordinary action, and second, we share a belief that this moment will end decisively, so that this shift is temporary. Because of this, built into the idea of wartime is a conception of the future. . . . In wartime thinking, the future is a place beyond war, a time when exceptional measures can be put to rest, and regular life resumed. The future is, in essence, the return to a time that war had suspended.

FOR DISCUSSION

Mary L. Dudziak, *War Time: An Idea, Its History, Its Consequences* (2012) (critiquing this frame). What work does this kind of thinking—whether as model or as debating foil—do in the various *Hamdi* opinions?

WORTH NOTING

About three and a half months after the Supreme Court ordered a close review of the factual basis for Hamdi's detention, he was transferred by military aircraft to Saudi Arabia, with the cooperation of that kingdom. The Defense Department said that "considerations of United States national security did not require his continued detention," but declined to provide further details "because of operational and security considerations." Jerry Markon, *Hamdi Returned to Saudi Arabia*, Washington Post, Oct. 12, 2004.

---

c. The President's Use of Unauthorized Force

In *Hamdi*, a majority of the Supreme Court concluded that Congress had authorized the detention of combatants as part of the conflict with al Qaeda and the Taliban. Not all uses of force by the President, however, have been so plainly authorized as the invasion of Afghanistan. How should we think about the use of force in circumstances where Congress has not authorized it—or perhaps even expressly forbidden it? The following materials explore that question.

In November 1973, Congress enacted the following joint resolution over the veto of President Richard Nixon. As a joint resolution, it has the same legal force as a statute.

Joint Resolution Concerning the War Powers of Congress and the President

87 Stat. 555, Nov. 7, 1973.

Resolved by the Senate and House of Representatives of the United States of America in Congress assembled,

SHORT TITLE

Section 1. This joint resolution may be cited as the "War Powers Resolution".

PURPOSE AND POLICY

Section 2.

(a) It is the purpose of this joint resolution to fulfill the intent of the framers of the Constitution of the United States and insure that the collective judgment of both the Congress and the President will apply to the introduction of United States Armed Forces into hostilities, or into situations where imminent involvement in hostilities is clearly indicated by the circumstances, and to the continued use of such forces in hostilities or in such situations. . . .

(c) The constitutional powers of the President as Commander-in-Chief to introduce United States Armed Forces into hostilities, or into situations where imminent involvement in hostilities is clearly indicated by the circumstances, are exercised only pursuant to (1) a declaration of war, (2) specific statutory authorization, or (3) a national emergency created by attack upon the United States, its territories or possessions, or its armed forces.

CONSULTATION

Section 3. The President in every possible instance shall consult with Congress before introducing United States Armed Forces into hostilities or into situations where imminent involvement in hostilities is clearly indicated by the circumstances, and after every such introduction shall consult regularly with the Congress until United States Armed Forces are no longer engaged in hostilities or have been removed from such situations.

REPORTING

Section 4.

(a) In the absence of a declaration of war, in any case in which United States Armed Forces are introduced

(1) into hostilities or into situations where imminent involvement in hostilities is clearly indicated by the circumstances;

(2) into the territory, airspace of waters of a foreign nation, while equipped for combat, except for deployments which relate solely to supply, replacement, repair, or training of such forces; or

(3) in numbers which substantially enlarge United States Armed Forces equipped for combat already located in a foreign nation;

the President shall submit within 48 hours to the Speaker of the House of Representatives and to the President pro tempore of the Senate a report, in writing, setting forth

(A) the circumstances necessitating the introduction of United States Armed Forces;

(B) the constitutional and legislative authority under which such introduction took place; and

(C) the estimated scope and duration of the hostilities or involvement.

(b) The President shall provide such other information as the Congress may request in the fulfillment of its constitutional responsibilities with respect to committing the Nation to war and to the use of United States Armed Forces abroad.

(c)   Whenever United States Armed Forces are introduced into hostilities or into any situation described in subsection (a) of this section, the President shall, so long as such armed forces continue to be engaged in such hostilities or situation, report to the Congress periodically on the status of such hostilities or situation as well as on the scope and duration of such hostilities or situation, but in no event shall he report to the Congress less often than once every six months.

CONGRESSIONAL ACTION

Section 5.

* * *

(b)   Within sixty calendar days after a report is submitted or is required to be submitted pursuant to section 4(a)(1), whichever is earlier, the President shall terminate any use of United States Armed Forces with respect to which such report was submitted (or required to be submitted), unless the Congress

(1)   has declared war or has enacted a specific authorization for such use of United States Armed Forces,

(2)   has extended by law such sixty-day period, or

(3)   is physically unable to meet as a result of an armed attack upon the United States.

Such sixty-day period shall be extended for not more than an additional thirty days if the President determines and certifies to the Congress in writing that unavoidable military necessity respecting the safety of United States Armed Forces requires the continued use of such armed forces in the course of bringing about a prompt removal of such forces.

(c)   Notwithstanding subsection (b), at any time that United States Armed Forces are engaged in hostilities outside the territory of the United States, its possessions and territories without a declaration of war or specific statutory authorization, such forces shall be removed by the President if the Congress so directs by concurrent resolution. . . .

INTERPRETATION OF JOINT RESOLUTION

Section 8.

(a) Authority to introduce United States Armed Forces into hostilities or into situations wherein involvement in hostilities is clearly indicated by the circumstances shall not be inferred

(1) from any provision of law (whether or not in effect before the date of the enactment of this joint resolution), including any provision contained in any appropriation Act, unless such provision specifically authorizes the introduction of United States Armed Forces into hostilities or into such situations and states that it is intended to constitute specific statutory authorization within the meaning of this joint resolution; or

(2) from any treaty heretofore or hereafter ratified unless such treaty is implemented by legislation specifically authorizing the introduction of United States Armed Forces into hostilities or into such situations and stating that it is intended to constitute specific statutory authorization within the meaning of this joint resolution. . . .

(d) Nothing in this joint resolution—

(1) is intended to alter the constitutional authority of the Congress or of the President, or the provisions of existing treaties; or

(2) shall be construed as granting any authority to the President with respect to the introduction of United States Armed Forces into hostilities or into situations wherein involvement in hostilities is clearly indicated by the circumstances which authority he would not have had in the absence of this joint resolution. . . .

FOR DISCUSSION

Are the reporting provisions in section 4 constitutional? The provision for automatic removal of forces in section 5(b)? The provision in section 5(c) for removal of forces pursuant to a concurrent resolution of Congress, which does not require presentment to the President? See *Immigration and Naturalization Service v. Chadha* (1983), pp. 881–897.

The following memo was written by the Justice Department's Office of Legal Counsel to explain the legal basis for the Obama administration's use of armed force against Libya in 2011. As you read the memo, consider how its analytical framework maps onto the framework asserted by the War Powers Resolution.

Authority to Use Military Force in Libya

Memorandum Opinion for the Attorney General,
Department of Justice, Office of Legal Counsel
April 1, 2011

This memorandum memorializes advice this Office provided to you, prior to the commencement of recent United States military operations in Libya, regarding the President's legal authority to conduct such operations. For the reasons explained below, we concluded that the President had the constitutional authority to direct the use of force in Libya because he could reasonably determine that such use of force was in the national interest. We also advised that prior congressional approval was not constitutionally required to use military force in the limited operations under consideration.

I.

In mid-February 2011, amid widespread popular demonstrations seeking governmental reform in the neighboring countries of Tunisia and Egypt, as well as elsewhere in the Middle East and North Africa, protests began in Libya against the autocratic government of Colonel Muammar Qadhafi, who has ruled Libya since taking power in a 1969 coup. Qadhafi moved swiftly in an attempt to end the protests using military force. Some Libyan government officials and elements of the Libyan military left the Qadhafi regime, and by early March, Qadhafi had lost control over much of the eastern part of the country, including the city of Benghazi. The Libyan government's operations against its opponents reportedly included strafing of protesters and shelling, bombing, and other violence deliberately targeting civilians. Many refugees fled to Egypt and other neighboring countries to escape the violence, creating a serious crisis in the region. . . .

By March 17, 2011, Qadhafi's forces were preparing to retake the city of Benghazi. Pledging that his forces would begin an assault on the city that night and show "no mercy and no pity" to those who would not give up resistance, Qadhafi stated in a radio address: "We will come house by house, room by room. It's over. The issue has been decided." Qadhafi, President Obama later noted, "compared [his people] to rats, and threatened to go door to door to inflict punishment. . . . We knew that if we . . . waited one more day, Benghazi, a city nearly the size of Charlotte, could suffer a massacre that would have reverberated across the region and stained the conscience of the world."

Later the same day, the United Nations Security Council (UNSC) addressed the situation in Libya . . . by adopting, by a vote of 10–0 (with five members abstaining), Resolution 1973, which imposed a no-fly zone and authorized the use of military force to protect civilians. . . . Resolution 1973 authorized member states, acting individually or through regional organizations, "to take all necessary measures . . . to protect civilians and civilian populated areas under threat of attack in [Libya], including Benghazi, while excluding a foreign occupation force of any form on any part of Libyan territory." . . . The resolution also specifically authorized member states to enforce "a ban on all [unauthorized] flights in the airspace of [Libya] in order to help protect civilians." . . .

In remarks on March 18, 2011, President Obama stated that, to avoid military intervention to enforce Resolution 1973, Qadhafi needed to implement an immediate ceasefire. . . . Despite a statement from Libya's Foreign Minister that Libya would honor the requested ceasefire, the Libyan government continued to conduct offensive operations, including attacks on civilians and civilian-populated areas. In response, on March 19, 2011, the United States, with the support of a number of its coalition partners, launched airstrikes against Libyan targets to enforce Resolution 1973.

Consistent with the reporting provisions of the War Powers Resolution, President Obama provided a report to Congress less than forty-eight hours later, on March 21, 2011. The President explained:

> . . . U.S. military forces commenced operations to assist an international effort[,] authorized by the United Nations (U.N.) Security

Council and undertaken with the support of European allies and Arab partners, to prevent a humanitarian catastrophe and address the threat posed to international peace and security by the crisis in Libya. As part of the multilateral response authorized under U.N. Security Council Resolution 1973, U.S. military forces . . . began a series of strikes against air defense systems and military airfields for the purposes of preparing a no-fly zone. These strikes will be limited in their nature, duration, and scope. Their purpose is to support an international coalition as it takes all necessary measures to enforce the terms of U.N. Security Council Resolution 1973. These limited U.S. actions will set the stage for further action by other coalition partners.

Obama March 21, 2011 Report to Congress. The report then described the background to the strikes, including UNSC Resolution 1973, the demand for a ceasefire, and Qadhafi's continued attacks.

. . . As authority for the military operations in Libya, President Obama invoked his "constitutional authority to conduct U.S. foreign relations" and his authority "as Commander in Chief and Chief Executive." . . .

II.

The President explained in his March 21, 2011 report to Congress that the use of military force in Libya serves important U.S. interests in preventing instability in the Middle East and preserving the credibility and effectiveness of the United Nations Security Council. The President also stated that he intended the anticipated United States military operations in Libya to be limited in nature, scope, and duration. The goal of action by the United States was to "set the stage" for further action by coalition partners in implementing UNSC Resolution 1973, particularly through destruction of Libyan military assets that could either threaten coalition aircraft policing the UNSC-declared no-fly zone or engage in attacks on civilians and civilian-populated areas. In addition, no U.S. ground forces would be deployed, except possibly for any search and rescue missions, and the risk of substantial casualties for U.S. forces would be low. As we advised you prior to the commencement of military operations, we believe that, under these circumstances, the President had constitutional authority, as Commander in Chief and Chief Executive and pursuant to his foreign affairs powers, to direct such limited military operations abroad, even without prior specific congressional approval.

A.

Earlier opinions of this Office and other historical precedents establish the framework for our analysis. As we explained in 1992, Attorneys General and this Office "have concluded that the President has the power to commit United States troops abroad," as well as to "take military action," "for the purpose of protecting important national interests," even without specific prior authorization from Congress. *Authority to Use United States Military Forces in Somalia*, 16 Op. O.L.C. 6 (1992) ("*Military Forces in Somalia*"). This independent authority of the President, which exists at least insofar as Congress has not specifically restricted it, *see Deployment of United States Armed Forces into Haiti*, 18 Op. O.L.C. 173 (1994) ("*Haiti Deployment*"), derives from the President's "unique responsibility," as Commander in Chief and Chief Executive, for "foreign and military affairs," as well as national security. *Sale v. Haitian Centers Council, Inc.* (1993); U.S. Const. art. II, § 1, cl. 1; § 2, cl. 2. . . .

"Our history," this Office observed in 1980, "is replete with instances of presidential uses of military force abroad in the absence of prior congressional approval." See generally Richard F. Grimmett, Cong. Research Serv., *Instances of Use of United States Armed Forces Abroad, 1798–2010* (2011). Since then, instances of such presidential initiative have only multiplied, with Presidents ordering, to give just a few examples, bombing in Libya (1986), an intervention in Panama (1989), troop deployments to Somalia (1992), Bosnia (1995), and Haiti (twice, 1994 and 2004), air patrols and airstrikes in Bosnia (1993–1995), and a bombing campaign in Yugoslavia (1999), without specific prior authorizing legislation. This historical practice is an important indication of constitutional meaning, because it reflects the two political branches' practical understanding, developed since the founding of the Republic, of their respective roles and responsibilities with respect to national defense. . . .

Indeed, Congress itself has implicitly recognized this presidential authority. The War Powers Resolution ("WPR") . . . provides that, in the absence of a declaration of war, the President must report to Congress within 48 hours of taking certain actions, including introduction of U.S. forces "into hostilities or into situations where imminent involvement in hostilities is clearly indicated by the circumstances." *Id.* § 1543(a). The Resolution further provides that the President generally must terminate such use of force within 60 days (or 90 days for military necessity) unless Congress extends this deadline, declares war, or "enact[s] a specific authorization." *Id.* § 1544(b). As this Office has explained, although the WPR does not itself provide affirmative statutory authority for military operations, *see id.* § 1547(d)(2), the Resolution's "structure . . . recognizes and presupposes the existence of unilateral presidential authority to deploy armed forces" into hostilities or circumstances presenting an imminent risk of hostilities. *Haiti Deployment*. That structure—requiring a report within 48 hours after the start of hostilities and their termination within 60 days after that—"makes sense only if the President may introduce troops into hostilities or potential hostilities without prior authorization by the Congress." *Haiti Deployment.*

We have acknowledged one possible constitutionally-based limit on this presidential authority to employ military force in defense of important national interests—a planned military engagement that constitutes a "war" within the meaning of the Declaration of War Clause may require prior congressional authorization. See *Proposed Bosnia Deployment*, 19 Op. O.L.C. at 331. But the historical practice of presidential military action without congressional approval precludes any suggestion that Congress's authority to declare war covers every military engagement, however limited, that the President initiates. In our view, determining whether a particular planned engagement constitutes a "war" for constitutional purposes instead requires a fact-specific assessment of the "anticipated nature, scope, and duration" of the planned military operations. *Haiti Deployment.* This standard generally will be satisfied only by prolonged and substantial military engagements, typically involving exposure of U.S. military personnel to significant risk over a substantial period. Again, Congress's own key enactment on the subject reflects this understanding. By allowing United States involvement in hostilities to continue for 60 or 90 days, Congress signaled in the WPR that it considers congressional authorization most critical for "major, prolonged conflicts such as the wars in Vietnam and Korea," not more limited engagements. *Haiti Deployment.* . . .

B.

Under the framework of these precedents, the President's legal authority to direct military force in Libya turns on two questions: first, whether United States operations in Libya would serve sufficiently important national interests to permit the President's action as Commander in Chief and Chief Executive and pursuant to his authority to conduct U.S. foreign relations; and second, whether the military operations that the President anticipated ordering would be sufficiently extensive in "nature, scope, and duration" to constitute a "war" requiring prior specific congressional approval under the Declaration of War Clause. . . .

In our view, the combination of at least two national interests that the President reasonably determined were at stake here—preserving regional stability and supporting the UNSC's credibility and effectiveness—provided a sufficient basis for the President's exercise of his constitutional authority to order the use of military force.[3]

First, the United States has a strong national security and foreign policy interest in security and stability in the Middle East that was threatened by Qadhafi's actions in Libya. As noted, we recognized similar regional stability interests as justifications for presidential military actions in Haiti and Bosnia. . . In addition, in another important precedent, President Clinton justified extensive airstrikes in the Federal Republic of Yugoslavia ("FRY") in 1999—military action later ratified by Congress but initially conducted without specific authorization, see *Authorization for Continuing Hostilities in Kosovo*, 24 Op. O.L.C. 327 (2000)—based on concerns about the threat to regional security created by that government's repressive treatment of the ethnic Albanian population in Kosovo. "The FRY government's violence," President Clinton explained, "creates a conflict with no natural boundaries, pushing refugees across borders and potentially drawing in neighboring countries. The Kosovo region is a tinderbox that could ignite a wider European war with dangerous consequences to the United States."

As his statements make clear, President Obama determined in this case that the Libyan government's actions posed similar risks to regional peace and security. Much as violence in Bosnia and Kosovo in the 1990s risked creating large refugee movements, destabilizing neighboring countries, and inviting wider conflict, here the Libyan government's "illegitimate use of force . . . [was] forcing many [civilians] to flee to neighboring countries, thereby destabilizing the peace and security of the region." . . .

The second important national interest implicated here, which reinforces the first, is the longstanding U.S. commitment to maintaining the credibility

---

[3]   Although President Obama has expressed opposition to Qadhafi's continued leadership of Libya, we understand that regime change is not an objective of the coalition's military operations. See Obama, March 28, 2011 Address ("Of course, there is no question that Libya—and the world—would be better off with Qaddafi out of power. I . . . will actively pursue [that goal] through non-military means. But broadening our military mission to include regime change would be a mistake."). We therefore do not consider any national interests relating to regime change in assessing the President's legal authority to order military operations in Libya.

of the United Nations Security Council and the effectiveness of its actions to promote international peace and security. Since at least the Korean War, the United States government has recognized that " '[t]he continued existence of the United Nations as an effective international organization is a paramount United States interest.' " *Military Forces in Somalia* (quoting *Authority of the President to Repel the Attack in Korea*, 23 Dep't St. Bull. 173 (1950)). Accordingly, although of course the President is not required to direct the use of military force simply because the UNSC has authorized it, this Office has recognized that " 'maintaining the credibility of United Nations Security Council decisions, protecting the security of United Nations and related relief efforts, and ensuring the effectiveness of United Nations peacekeeping operations can be considered a vital national interest' " on which the President may rely in determining that U.S. interests justify the use of military force. *Proposed Bosnia Deployment.*

Here, the UNSC's credibility and effectiveness as an instrument of global peace and stability were at stake in Libya once the UNSC took action to impose a no-fly zone and ensure the safety of civilians—particularly after Qadhafi's forces ignored the UNSC's call for a cease fire and for the cessation of attacks on civilians. . . . We think the President could legitimately find that military action by the United States to assist the international coalition in giving effect to UNSC Resolution 1973 was needed to secure "a substantial national foreign policy objective." *Military Forces in Somalia.*

We conclude, therefore, that the use of military force in Libya was supported by sufficiently important national interests to fall within the President's constitutional power. . . .

[T]urning to the second element of the analysis, we do not believe that anticipated United States operations in Libya amounted to a "war" in the constitutional sense necessitating congressional approval under the Declaration of War Clause. This inquiry, as noted, is highly fact-specific and turns on no single factor. . . .

As in the case of the no-fly zone patrols and periodic airstrikes in Bosnia before the deployment of ground troops in 1995 and the NATO bombing campaign in connection with the Kosovo conflict in 1999—two military campaigns initiated without a prior declaration of war or other specific congressional authorization—President Obama determined that the use of force in Libya by the United States would be limited to airstrikes and associated support missions; the President made clear that "[t]he United States is not going to deploy ground troops in Libya." The planned operations thus avoided the difficulties of withdrawal and risks of escalation that may attend commitment of ground forces—two factors that this Office has identified as "arguably" indicating "a greater need for approval [from Congress] at the outset," to avoid creating a situation in which "Congress may be confronted with circumstances in which the exercise of its power to declare war is effectively foreclosed." *Proposed Bosnia Deployment.*

Furthermore, also as in prior operations conducted without a declaration of war or other specific authorizing legislation, the anticipated operations here served a "limited mission" and did not "aim at the conquest or occupation of territory." . . . [We therefore] do not think the "anticipated nature, scope, and duration" of the use of force by the United States in Libya rose to the level of a "war" in the constitutional sense, requiring the President to seek a declaration of war or other prior authorization from Congress. . . .

Accordingly, we conclude that President Obama could rely on his constitutional power to safeguard the national interest by directing the anticipated military operations in Libya—which were limited in their nature, scope, and duration—without prior congressional authorization.

CAROLINE D. KRASS
Principal Deputy Assistant Attorney General

Recall that (with extremely limited exceptions) the War Powers Resolution requires the president to "terminate any use of United States Armed Forces" within sixty days after "a report is submitted or is required to be submitted pursuant to section 4(a)(1)," unless Congress has "enacted a specific authorization" in the interim. War Powers Resolution, Section 5(b). Recall also that the OLC memo describes President Obama as "provid[ing] a report to Congress less than forty-eight hours" after the commencement of the conflict in Libya, "[c]onsistent with the reporting provisions of the War Powers Resolution." Despite failing to secure congressional authorization for the action at any point during the next sixty days, however, the Obama administration did not terminate the use of force when the deadline hit. The State Department's Legal Advisor, Harold Koh, testified to Congress that such notice was not required.

Harold Koh, Testimony to the Senate
Foreign Relations Committee

June 28, 2011

... We do not believe that the War Powers Resolution's 60-day automatic pullout provision applies to the limited Libya mission. As Senator Kerry quoted, absent express congressional authorization, the resolution directs the President to remove U.S. Armed Forces within 60 days from the date that hostilities or situations where imminent involvement in hostilities is clearly indicated. But as everyone recognizes, the legal trigger for the automatic pullout clock, "hostilities" is an ambiguous term of art that is defined nowhere in the statute. ...

As my testimony recounts and as Senator Kerry has himself noted, there are various leaders of this Congress who have indicated that they do not believe that the United States military operations in Libya amount to the kind of hostilities envisioned by the 60-day pullout provision. We believe that view is correct and confirmed by historical practice. And the historical practice, which I summarize in my testimony, suggests that when U.S. forces engage in a limited military mission that involves limited exposure for U.S. troops and limited risk of serious escalation and employs limited military means, we are not in hostilities of the kind envisioned by the War Powers Resolution that was intended to trigger an automatic 60-day pullout.

Let me say just a word about each of these four limitations. First, the nature of the mission is unusually limited. By Presidential design, U.S. forces are playing a constrained and supporting role in a NATO-led, multinational civilian protection mission charged with enforcing a Security Council resolution. This circumstance is virtually unique, not found in any of the recent historic situations in which the hostilities questions has been debated from the Iranian hostages crisis to El Salvador, to Lebanon, to Grenada, to the fighting with Iran in the Persian Gulf, or to the use of ground troops in Somalia.

Second, the exposure of our Armed Forces is limited. From the transition date of March 31 forward, there have been no U.S. casualties, no threat of significant U.S. casualties, no active exchanges of fire with hostile forces, no significant armed confrontation or sustained confrontation of any kind with hostile forces. And as my testimony describes on page 9, past administrations have not found the 60-day rule to apply even in a situation where far more significant fighting plainly did occur such as in Lebanon and Grenada in 1983 and Somalia in 1993.

Third, the risk of escalation here is limited. In contrast to the U.N.-authorized Desert Storm operation, which presented over 400,000 troops, the same order of magnitude as Vietnam at its peak, Libya has not involved any significant chance of escalation into a full-fledged conflict characterized by a large U.S. ground presence, major casualties, sustained active combat, or an expanding geographic scope. In this respect, Libya contrasts with other recent cases, Lebanon, Central America, Somalia, the Persian Gulf tanker controversy . . . where past administrations declined to find hostilities under the War Powers Resolution, even though United States Armed Forces were repeatedly engaged by other sides' forces and sustained significant casualties.

And fourth and finally, Senators, we are using limited military means, not the kind of full military engagements with which the War Powers Resolution is primarily concerned. . . . The violence U.S. Armed Forces are directly inflicting or facilitating after the handoff to NATO has been modest in terms of its frequency, intensity, and severity. The air-to-ground strikes conducted by the United States are a far cry from the extensive aerial strike operations led by United States Armed Forces in Kosovo in 1999 or the NATO operations in the Balkans in the 1990s, to which the United States forces contributed the vast majority of aircraft and airstrike sorties. To be specific, the bulk of U.S. contributions has been providing intelligence capabilities and refueling assets to the NATO effort. . . . American strikes have been limited on an as-needed basis to the suppression of enemy air defenses to enforce the no-fly zone and limited strikes by Predator unmanned aerial vehicles against discrete targets to support the civilian protection mission. By our best estimate, Senators, since the handoff to NATO, the total number of United States munitions dropped in Libya has been less than 1 percent of those dropped in Kosovo.

Now, we acknowledge that had any of these elements been absent in Libya or present in different degrees, you could draw a different legal conclusion, but it was this unusual confluence of these four limitations, an operation that is limited in mission, limited in exposure, limited in risk of escalation, and limited in choice of military means, that led the President to conclude that the Libya operation did not fall under the automatic 60-day pullout rule. . . .

[F]inally, Senators, we fully recognize reasonable minds may read the resolution differently. And we acknowledge that there were perhaps steps we should have taken or could have taken to foster better communication on these very difficult legal questions. But none of us believes that the best way forward now is for Qadhafi to prevail and to resume his attacks on his own people. Were the United States now to drop out of this collective civilian protection mission [that would permit] Qadhafi to return to brutal attacks on the very civilians whom our intervention has protected. However we may construe the War Powers Resolution, we can all agree it would only serve Qadhafi's interests for the United States to withdraw from this NATO operation before it is finished. . . .

FOR DISCUSSION

Is Koh's legal argument persuasive? What do you make of the last paragraph? Given the circumstances described in the Justice Department memo, what would you have advised the President to do when the sixty-day clock had run?

C.   Checking the President

In the modern regulatory state, the President has enormous powers—certainly in the foreign affairs and national security realms, but domestically as well. Keenly aware of this reality, Congress has tried a variety of means to check executive action and to supervise the President's use of statutory and constitutional authority. The following materials explore some of the more important issues that have arisen from these efforts.

1.   Legislative Veto

Congress delegates a broad array of powers to the executive branch, ranging from the authority to promulgate generally applicable regulations to the authority to adjudicate the implementation of statutes in a particular case. What happens if Congress doesn't like how the executive branch uses those powers? Over a period of decades, Congress frequently constrained delegated power by reserving a so-called *legislative veto*, which enabled Congress itself (or sometimes a single House or even a given committee) to nullify the executive action, without passage of a statute for that purpose. But was it constitutional? The next case addressed that question.

Immigration and Naturalization Service v. Chadha

Supreme Court of the United States, 1983.
462 U.S. 919.

CHIEF JUSTICE BURGER delivered the opinion of the Court.

[This case] presents a challenge to the constitutionality of the provision in § 244(c)(2) of the Immigration and Nationality Act, authorizing one House of Congress, by resolution, to invalidate the decision of the Executive Branch, pursuant to authority delegated by Congress to the Attorney General of the United States, to allow a particular deportable alien to remain in the United States.

I

Chadha is an East Indian who was born in Kenya and holds a British passport. He was lawfully admitted to the United States in 1966 on a nonimmigrant student visa. His visa expired on June 30, 1972. On October 11, 1973, the District Director of the Immigration and Naturalization Service ordered Chadha to show cause why he should not be deported for having "remained in the United States for a longer time than permitted." Pursuant to § 242(b) of the Immigration and Nationality Act (Act), a deportation hearing was held before an Immigration Judge on January 11, 1974. Chadha conceded that he was deportable for overstaying his visa, and the hearing was adjourned to enable him to file an application for suspension of deportation under § 244(a)(1) of the Act. . . .

After Chadha submitted his application . . . , the deportation hearing was resumed on February 7, 1974. On the basis of evidence adduced at the hearing, affidavits submitted with the application, and the results of a character investigation conducted by the INS, the Immigration Judge, on June 25, 1974, ordered that Chadha's deportation be suspended. The Immigration Judge found that Chadha met the requirements of § 244(a)(1): he had resided continuously in the United States for over seven years, was of good moral character, and would suffer "extreme hardship" if deported.

Pursuant to § 244(c)(1) of the Act, the Immigration Judge suspended Chadha's deportation and a report of the suspension was transmitted to Congress. . . . Once the Attorney General's recommendation for suspension of Chadha's deportation was conveyed to Congress, Congress had the power under § 244(c)(2) of the Act, to veto[2] the Attorney General's determination that Chadha should not be deported. Section 244(c)(2) provides:

> (2) In the case of an alien specified in paragraph (1) of subsection (a) of this subsection—if during the session of the Congress at which a case is reported, or prior to the close of the session of the Congress next following the session at which a case is reported, either the Senate or the House of Representatives passes a resolution stating in substance that it does not favor the suspension of such deportation, the Attorney General shall thereupon deport such alien or authorize the alien's voluntary departure at his own expense under the order of deportation in the manner provided by law. . . .

. . . On December 12, 1975, Representative Eilberg, Chairman of the Judiciary Subcommittee on Immigration, Citizenship, and International Law, introduced a resolution opposing "the granting of permanent residence in the United States to [six] aliens", including Chadha. The resolution was passed without debate or recorded vote. Since the House action was pursuant to § 244(c)(2), the resolution was not treated as an Article I legislative act; it was not submitted to the Senate or presented to the President for his action.

After the House veto of the Attorney General's decision to allow Chadha to remain in the United States, the Immigration Judge reopened the deportation proceedings to implement the House order deporting Chadha. . . . On November 8, 1976, Chadha was ordered deported pursuant to the House action. . . .

Pursuant to § 106(a) of the Act, Chadha filed a petition for review of the deportation order in the United States Court of Appeals for the Ninth Circuit. The Immigration and Naturalization Service agreed with Chadha's position before the Court of Appeals and joined him in arguing that § 244(c)(2) is unconstitutional. In light of the importance of the question, the Court of Appeals invited both the Senate and the House of Representatives to file briefs *amici curiae*. After full briefing and oral argument, the Court of Appeals held that the House was without constitutional authority to order Chadha's deportation. . . .

---

[2]   In constitutional terms, "veto" is used to describe the President's power under Art. I, § 7, of the Constitution. It appears, however, that Congressional devices of the type authorized by § 244(c)(2) have come to be commonly referred to as a "veto." We refer to the Congressional "resolution" authorized by § 244(c)(2) as a "one-House veto" of the Attorney General's decision to allow a particular deportable alien to remain in the United States.

The essence of its holding was that § 244(c)(2) violates the constitutional doctrine of separation of powers.

We granted certiorari . . . and we now affirm. . . .

III

A

[T]he fact that a given law or procedure is efficient, convenient, and useful in facilitating functions of government, standing alone, will not save it if it is contrary to the Constitution. Convenience and efficiency are not the primary objectives—or the hallmarks—of democratic government and our inquiry is sharpened rather than blunted by the fact that Congressional veto provisions are appearing with increasing frequency in statutes which delegate authority to executive and independent agencies. . . .

Explicit and unambiguous provisions of the Constitution prescribe and define the respective functions of the Congress and of the Executive in the legislative process. Since the precise terms of those familiar provisions are critical to the resolution of this case, we set them out verbatim. Art. I provides:

> "All legislative Powers herein granted shall be vested in a Congress of the United States, which shall consist of a Senate *and* a House of Representatives." Art. I, § 1 (emphasis added).

> "Every Bill which shall have passed the House of Representatives *and* the Senate, *shall*, before it becomes a Law, be presented to the President of the United States; . . ." Art. I, § 7, cl. 2 (emphasis added).

> "*Every* Order, Resolution, or Vote to which the Concurrence of the Senate and House of Representatives may be necessary (except on a question of Adjournment) *shall be* presented to the President of the United States; and before the Same shall take Effect, *shall be* approved by him, or being disapproved by him, *shall be* repassed by two thirds of the Senate and House of Representatives, according to the Rules and Limitations prescribed in the Case of a Bill." Art. I, § 7, cl. 3 (emphasis added).

These provisions of Art. I are integral parts of the constitutional design for the separation of powers. . . .

B

The Presentment Clauses

The records of the Constitutional Convention reveal that the requirement that all legislation be presented to the President before becoming law was uniformly accepted by the Framers. Presentment to the President and the Presidential veto were considered so imperative that the draftsmen took special pains to assure that these requirements could not be circumvented. During the final debate on Art. I, § 7, cl. 2, James Madison expressed concern that it might easily be evaded by the simple expedient of calling a proposed law a "resolution" or "vote" rather than a "bill." M. Farrand, The Records of the Federal Convention of 1787. As a consequence, Art. I, § 7, cl. 3, was added.

The decision to provide the President with a limited and qualified power to nullify proposed legislation by veto was based on the profound conviction of the Framers that the powers conferred on Congress were the powers to be most carefully circumscribed. It is beyond doubt that lawmaking was a power to be shared by both Houses and the President. In The Federalist No. 73, Hamilton focused on the President's role in making laws: ". . . the [Executive] ought not to be left to the mercy of the [legislative body], but ought to possess a constitutional and effectual power of self-defense." See also J. Story, Commentaries on the Constitution of the United States (1858).

The President's role in the lawmaking process also reflects the Framers' careful efforts to check whatever propensity a particular Congress might have to enact oppressive, improvident, or ill-considered measures. The President's veto role in the legislative process was described later during public debate on ratification:

> It establishes a salutary check upon the legislative body, calculated to guard the community against the effects of faction, precipitancy, or of any impulse unfriendly to the public good which may happen to influence a majority of that body. . . . The primary inducement to conferring the power in question upon the Executive is to enable him to defend himself; the secondary one is to increase the chances in favor of the community against the passing of bad laws through haste, inadvertence, or design. The Federalist No. 73 (A. Hamilton).

The Court also has observed that the Presentment Clauses serve the important purpose of assuring that a "national" perspective is grafted on the legislative process:

> The President is a representative of the people just as the members of the Senate and of the House are, and it may be, at some times, on some subjects, that the President elected by all the people is rather more representative of them all than are the members of either body of the Legislature whose constituencies are local and not countrywide. . . .

Myers v. United States (1926).

C

Bicameralism

The bicameral requirement of Art. I, §§ 1, 7, was of scarcely less concern to the Framers than was the Presidential veto and indeed the two concepts are interdependent. By providing that no law could take effect without the concurrence of the prescribed majority of the Members of both Houses, the Framers reemphasized their belief, already remarked upon in connection with the Presentment Clauses, that legislation should not be enacted unless it has been carefully and fully considered by the Nation's elected officials. In the Constitutional Convention debates on the need for a bicameral legislature, James Wilson, later to become a Justice of this Court, commented:

> Despotism comes on mankind in different shapes. Sometimes in an Executive, sometimes in a military, one. Is there danger of a Legislative despotism? Theory & practice both proclaim it. If the Legislative authority be not restrained, there can be neither liberty nor stability; and it can only be restrained by dividing it within itself, into distinct and independent branches. In a single house there is no check, but the inadequate one, of the virtue & good sense of those who compose it.

. . . These observations are consistent with what many of the Framers expressed, none more cogently than Madison in pointing up the need to divide and disperse power in order to protect liberty:

> In republican government, the legislative authority necessarily predominates. The remedy for this inconveniency is to divide the legislature into different branches; and to render them, by different

modes of election and different principles of action, as little connected with each other as the nature of their common functions and their common dependence on the society will admit.

The Federalist No. 51. See also The Federalist No. 62. . . .

We see therefore that the Framers were acutely conscious that the bicameral requirement and the Presentment Clauses would serve essential constitutional functions. The President's participation in the legislative process was to protect the Executive Branch from Congress and to protect the whole people from improvident laws. The division of the Congress into two distinctive bodies assures that the legislative power would be exercised only after opportunity for full study and debate in separate settings. The President's unilateral veto power, in turn, was limited by the power of two thirds of both Houses of Congress to overrule a veto thereby precluding final arbitrary action of one person. It emerges clearly that the prescription for legislative action in Art. I, §§ 1, 7, represents the Framers' decision that the legislative power of the Federal government be exercised in accord with a single, finely wrought and exhaustively considered, procedure.

IV

The Constitution sought to divide the delegated powers of the new Federal Government into three defined categories, Legislative, Executive and Judicial, to assure, as nearly as possible, that each Branch of government would confine itself to its assigned responsibility. The hydraulic pressure inherent within each of the separate Branches to exceed the outer limits of its power, even to accomplish desirable objectives, must be resisted.

Although not "hermetically" sealed from one another, *Buckley v. Valeo*, the powers delegated to the three Branches are functionally identifiable. When any Branch acts, it is presumptively exercising the power the Constitution has delegated to it. When the Executive acts, it presumptively acts in an executive or administrative capacity as defined in Art. II. And when, as here, one House of Congress purports to act, it is presumptively acting within its assigned sphere.

Beginning with this presumption, we must nevertheless establish that the challenged action under § 244(c)(2) is of the kind to which the procedural requirements of Art. I, § 7, apply. Not every action taken by either House is subject to the bicameralism and presentment requirements of Art. I. Whether actions taken by either House are, in law and fact, an exercise of legislative power depends not on their form but upon "whether they contain matter which is properly to be regarded as legislative in its character and effect." S.Rep. No. 1335, 54th Cong., 2d Sess., 8 (1897).

Examination of the action taken here by one House pursuant to § 244(c)(2) reveals that it was essentially legislative in purpose and effect. In purporting to exercise power defined in Art. I, § 8, cl. 4, to "establish an uniform Rule of Naturalization," the House took action that had the purpose and effect of altering the legal rights, duties and relations of persons, including the Attorney General, Executive Branch officials and Chadha, all outside the Legislative Branch. . . . The one-House veto operated in this case to overrule the Attorney General and mandate Chadha's deportation; absent the House action, Chadha would remain in the United States. Congress has *acted* and its action has altered Chadha's status.

The legislative character of the one-House veto in this case is confirmed by the character of the Congressional action it supplants. Neither the House of Representatives nor the Senate contends that, absent the veto provision in § 244(c)(2), either of them, or both of them acting together, could effectively require the Attorney General to deport an alien once the Attorney General, in the exercise of legislatively delegated authority,[16] had determined the alien should remain in the United States. Without the challenged provision in § 244(c)(2), this could have been achieved, if at all, only by legislation requiring

---

[16]   Congress protests that affirming the Court of Appeals in this case will sanction "lawmaking by the Attorney General. . . . Why is the Attorney General exempt from submitting his proposed changes in the law to the full bicameral process?" Brief of the United States House of Representatives.

To be sure, some administrative agency action—rule making, for example—may resemble "lawmaking." See [the Administrative Procedure Act], which defines an agency's "rule" as "the whole or part of an agency statement of general or particular applicability and future effect designed to implement, interpret, or prescribe law or policy. . . ." This Court has referred to agency activity as being "quasi-legislative" in character. *Humphrey's Executor v. United States* (1935). Clearly, however, "[i]n the framework of our Constitution, the President's power to see that the laws are faithfully executed refutes the idea that he is to be a lawmaker." *Youngstown Sheet & Tube Co. v. Sawyer.* When the Attorney General performs his duties pursuant to § 244, he does not exercise "legislative" power. See *Ernst & Ernst v. Hochfelder* (1976). . . .

It is clear, therefore, that the Attorney General acts in his presumptively Art. II capacity when he administers the Immigration and Nationality Act. Executive action under legislatively delegated authority that might resemble "legislative" action in some respects is not subject to the approval of both Houses of Congress and the President for the reason that the Constitution does not so require. That kind of Executive action is always subject to check by the terms of the legislation that authorized it; and if that authority is exceeded it is open to judicial review as well as the power of Congress to modify or revoke the authority entirely.

A one-House veto is clearly legislative in both character and effect and is not so checked; the need for the check provided by Art. I, §§ 1, 7, is therefore clear. Congress' authority to delegate portions of its power to administrative agencies provides no support for the argument that Congress can constitutionally control administration of the laws by way of a Congressional veto.

deportation.[17] Similarly, a veto by one House of Congress under § 244(c)(2) cannot be justified as an attempt at amending the standards set out in § 244(a)(1), or as a repeal of § 244 as applied to Chadha. Amendment and repeal of statutes, no less than enactment, must conform with Art. I.

The nature of the decision implemented by the one-House veto in this case further manifests its legislative character. After long experience with the clumsy, time consuming private bill procedure, Congress made a deliberate choice to delegate to the Executive Branch, and specifically to the Attorney General, the authority to allow deportable aliens to remain in this country in certain specified circumstances. It is not disputed that this choice to delegate authority is precisely the kind of decision that can be implemented only in accordance with the procedures set out in Art. I. Disagreement with the Attorney General's decision on Chadha's deportation—that is, Congress' decision to deport Chadha—no less than Congress' original choice to delegate to the Attorney General the authority to make that decision, involves determinations of policy that Congress can implement in only one way; bicameral passage followed by presentment to the President. Congress must abide by its delegation of authority until that delegation is legislatively altered or revoked.

Finally, we see that when the Framers intended to authorize either House of Congress to act alone and outside of its prescribed bicameral legislative role, they narrowly and precisely defined the procedure for such action. There are but four provisions in the Constitution, explicit and unambiguous, by which one House may act alone with the unreviewable force of law, not subject to the President's veto:

(a)   The House of Representatives alone was given the power to initiate impeachments. Art. I, § 2, cl. 5;

(b)   The Senate alone was given the power to conduct trials following impeachment on charges initiated by the House and to convict following trial. Art. I, § 3, cl. 6;

---

[17]   We express no opinion as to whether such legislation would violate any constitutional provision. [The Court here cross-references an earlier footnote, which read as follows:] Without the provision for one-House veto, Congress would presumably retain the power, during the time allotted in § 244(c)(2), to enact a law, in accordance with the requirements of Article I of the Constitution, mandating a particular alien's deportation, unless, of course, other constitutional principles place substantive limitations on such action. Cf. Attorney General Jackson's attack on H.R. 9766, 76th Cong., 3d Sess. (1940), a bill to require the Attorney General to deport an individual alien. The Attorney General called the bill "an historical departure from an unbroken American practice and tradition. It would be the first time that an act of Congress singled out a named individual for deportation."

(c)   The Senate alone was given final unreviewable power to approve or to disapprove presidential appointments. Art. II, § 2, cl. 2;

(d)   The Senate alone was given unreviewable power to ratify treaties negotiated by the President. Art. II, § 2, cl. 2.

Clearly, when the Draftsmen sought to confer special powers on one House, independent of the other House, or of the President, they did so in explicit, unambiguous terms. These carefully defined exceptions from presentment and bicameralism underscore the difference between the legislative functions of Congress and other unilateral but important and binding one-House acts provided for in the Constitution. These exceptions are narrow, explicit, and separately justified; none of them authorize the action challenged here. . . .

Since it is clear that the action by the House under § 244(c)(2) was not within any of the express constitutional exceptions authorizing one House to act alone, and equally clear that it was an exercise of legislative power, that action was subject to the standards prescribed in Article I. [Those standards] were intended to erect enduring checks on each Branch and to protect the people from the improvident exercise of power by mandating certain prescribed steps. . . . To accomplish what has been attempted by one House of Congress in this case requires action in conformity with the express procedures of the Constitution's prescription for legislative action: passage by a majority of both Houses and presentment to the President.

The veto authorized by § 244(c)(2) doubtless has been in many respects a convenient shortcut; the "sharing" with the Executive by Congress of its authority over aliens in this manner is, on its face, an appealing compromise. In purely practical terms, it is obviously easier for action to be taken by one House without submission to the President; but it is crystal clear from the records of the Convention, contemporaneous writings and debates, that the Framers ranked other values higher than efficiency. . . .

The choices we discern as having been made in the Constitutional Convention impose burdens on governmental processes that often seem clumsy, inefficient, even unworkable, but those hard choices were consciously made by men who had lived under a form of government that permitted arbitrary governmental acts to go unchecked. . . . With all the obvious flaws of delay, untidiness, and potential for abuse, we have not yet found a better way to preserve freedom than by making the exercise of power subject to the carefully crafted restraints spelled out in the Constitution.

V

We hold that the Congressional veto provision in § 244(c)(2) is unconstitutional. Accordingly, the judgment of the Court of Appeals is

Affirmed.

JUSTICE POWELL, concurring in the judgment.

The Court's decision, based on the Presentment Clauses, Art. I, § 7, cls. 2 and 3, apparently will invalidate every use of the legislative veto. The breadth of this holding gives one pause. Congress has included the veto in literally hundreds of statutes, dating back to the 1930s. Congress clearly views this procedure as essential to controlling the delegation of power to administrative agencies. One reasonably may disagree with Congress' assessment of the veto's utility, but the respect due its judgment as a coordinate branch of Government cautions that our holding should be no more extensive than necessary to decide this case.

In my view, the case may be decided on a narrower ground. When Congress finds that a particular person does not satisfy the statutory criteria for permanent residence in this country it has assumed a judicial function in violation of the principle of separation of powers. Accordingly, I concur only in the judgment. . . .

Before considering whether Congress impermissibly assumed a judicial function, it is helpful to recount briefly Congress' actions. . . . In addition to the report on Chadha, Congress had before it the names of 339 other persons whose deportations also had been suspended by the Service. The House Committee on the Judiciary decided that six of these persons, including Chadha, should not be allowed to remain in this country. Accordingly, it submitted a resolution to the House, which stated simply that "the House of Representatives does not approve the granting of permanent residence in the United States to the aliens hereinafter named." The resolution was not distributed prior to the vote,[6] but the Chairman of the Judiciary Committee explained to the House:

> It was the feeling of the committee, after reviewing 340 cases, that
> the aliens contained in the resolution did not meet [the] statutory

---

[6]   Normally the House would have distributed the resolution before acting on it, but the statute providing for the legislative veto limits the time in which Congress may veto the Service's determination that deportation should be suspended. In this case Congress had Chadha's report before it for approximately a year and a half, but failed to act on it until three days before the end of the limitations period. Accordingly, it was required to abandon its normal procedures for considering resolutions, thereby increasing the danger of arbitrary and ill-considered action.

requirements, particularly as it relates to hardship; and it is the opinion of the committee that their deportation should not be suspended.

Without further explanation and without a recorded vote, the House rejected the Service's determination that these six people met the statutory criteria.

On its face, the House's action appears clearly adjudicatory. The House did not enact a general rule; rather it made its own determination that six specific persons did not comply with certain statutory criteria. It thus undertook the type of decision that traditionally has been left to other branches. . . .

The impropriety of the House's assumption of this function is confirmed by the fact that its action raises the very danger the Framers sought to avoid—the exercise of unchecked power. In deciding whether Chadha deserves to be deported, Congress is not subject to any internal constraints that prevent it from arbitrarily depriving him of the right to remain in this country. Unlike the judiciary or an administrative agency, Congress is not bound by established substantive rules. Nor is it subject to the procedural safeguards, such as the right to counsel and a hearing before an impartial tribunal, that are present when a court or an agency adjudicates individual rights. The only effective constraint on Congress' power is political, but Congress is most accountable politically when it prescribes rules of general applicability. When it decides rights of specific persons, those rights are subject to "the tyranny of a shifting majority."

Chief Justice Marshall observed: "It is the peculiar province of the legislature to prescribe general rules for the government of society; the application of those rules would seem to be the duty of other departments." *Fletcher v. Peck* (1810). In my view, when Congress undertook to apply its rules to Chadha, it exceeded the scope of its constitutionally prescribed authority. I would not reach the broader question whether legislative vetoes are invalid under the Presentment Clauses.

JUSTICE WHITE, dissenting.

Today the Court not only invalidates § 244(c)(2) of the Immigration and Nationality Act, but also sounds the death knell for nearly 200 other statutory provisions in which Congress has reserved a "legislative veto." For this reason, the Court's decision is of surpassing importance. And it is for this reason that the Court would have been well-advised to decide the case, if possible, on the narrower grounds of separation of powers, leaving for full consideration the constitutionality of other congressional review statutes operating on such varied matters as war powers and agency rulemaking, some of which concern the independent regulatory agencies.

The prominence of the legislative veto mechanism in our contemporary political system and its importance to Congress can hardly be overstated. It has become a central means by which Congress secures the accountability of executive and independent agencies. Without the legislative veto, Congress is faced with a Hobson's choice: either to refrain from delegating the necessary authority, leaving itself with a hopeless task of writing laws with the requisite specificity to cover endless special circumstances across the entire policy landscape, or in the alternative, to abdicate its law-making function to the Executive Branch and independent agencies. To choose the former leaves major national problems unresolved; to opt for the latter risks unaccountable policymaking by those not elected to fill that role. Accordingly, over the past five decades, the legislative veto has been placed in nearly 200 statutes. [Justice White's opinion was followed by an appendix with a "selected list and brief description of these provisions."] The device is known in every field of governmental concern: reorganization, budgets, foreign affairs, war powers, and regulation of trade, safety, energy, the environment and the economy.

                                    I

The legislative veto developed initially in response to the problems of reorganizing the sprawling government structure created in response to the Depression. The Reorganization Acts established the chief model for the legislative veto. When President Hoover requested authority to reorganize the government in 1929, he coupled his request that the "Congress be willing to delegate its authority over the problem (subject to defined principles) to the Executive" with a proposal for legislative review. He proposed that the Executive "should act upon approval of a joint committee of Congress or with the reservation of power of revision by Congress within some limited period adequate for its consideration." Congress followed President Hoover's suggestion and authorized reorganization subject to legislative review. Although the reorganization authority reenacted in 1933 did not contain a legislative veto provision, the provision returned during the Roosevelt Administration and has since been renewed numerous times. Over the years, the provision was used extensively. Presidents submitted 115 reorganization plans to Congress of which 23 were disapproved by Congress pursuant to legislative veto provisions.

Shortly after adoption of the Reorganization Act of 1939, Congress and the President applied the legislative veto procedure to resolve the delegation problem for national security and foreign affairs. World War II occasioned the need to transfer greater authority to the President in these areas. The legislative veto offered the means by which Congress could confer additional authority while preserving its own constitutional role. During World War II, Congress enacted over thirty statutes conferring powers on the Executive with legislative veto provisions. President Roosevelt accepted the veto as the necessary price for obtaining exceptional authority.[4]

Over the quarter century following World War II, Presidents continued to accept legislative vetoes by one or both Houses as constitutional, while regularly denouncing provisions by which Congressional committees reviewed Executive activity. The legislative veto balanced delegations of statutory authority in new areas of governmental involvement: the space program, international agreements on nuclear energy, tariff arrangements, and adjustment of federal pay rates.

During the 1970's the legislative veto was important in resolving a series of major constitutional disputes between the President and Congress over claims of the President to broad impoundment, war, and national emergency powers. The key provision of the War Powers Resolution authorizes the termination by concurrent resolution of the use of armed forces in hostilities. . . . These statutes were followed by others resolving similar problems: the National Emergencies Act, resolving the longstanding problems with unchecked Executive emergency power; the Arms Export Control Act, resolving the problem of foreign arms sales; and the Nuclear Non-Proliferation Act of 1978, resolving the problem of exports of nuclear technology. . . .

Even this brief review suffices to demonstrate that the legislative veto is more than "efficient, convenient, and useful." It is an important if not indispensable political invention that allows the President and Congress to resolve major constitutional and policy differences, assures the accountability of independent regulatory agencies, and preserves Congress' control over lawmaking. Perhaps there are other means of accommodation and accountability, but the increasing reliance of Congress upon the legislative veto suggests that the alternatives to which Congress must now turn are not entirely satisfactory.

---

[4]   The Roosevelt Administration submitted proposed legislation containing veto provisions and defended their constitutionality. See, *e.g.*, General Counsel to the Office of Price Administration, "Statement on Constitutionality of Concurrent Resolution Provision of Proposed Price Control Bill (H.R.5479)" (1941).

The history of the legislative veto also makes clear that it has not been a sword with which Congress has struck out to aggrandize itself at the expense of the other branches—the concerns of Madison and Hamilton. Rather, the veto has been a means of defense, a reservation of ultimate authority necessary if Congress is to fulfill its designated role under Article I as the nation's lawmaker. While the President has often objected to particular legislative vetoes, generally those left in the hands of congressional committees, the Executive has more often agreed to legislative review as the price for a broad delegation of authority. To be sure, the President may have preferred unrestricted power, but that could be precisely why Congress thought it essential to retain a check on the exercise of delegated authority.

II

. . . The reality of the situation is that the constitutional question posed today is one of immense difficulty over which the Executive and Legislative Branches—as well as scholars and judges—have understandably disagreed. That disagreement stems from the silence of the Constitution on the precise question: The Constitution does not directly authorize or prohibit the legislative veto. Thus, our task should be to determine whether the legislative veto is consistent with the purposes of Art. I and the principles of Separation of Powers which are reflected in that Article and throughout the Constitution.

We should not find the lack of a specific constitutional authorization for the legislative veto surprising, and I would not infer disapproval of the mechanism from its absence. From the summer of 1787 to the present the Government of the United States has become an endeavor far beyond the contemplation of the Framers. Only within the last half century has the complexity and size of the Federal Government's responsibilities grown so greatly that the Congress must rely on the legislative veto as the most effective if not the only means to insure their role as the nation's lawmakers. But the wisdom of the Framers was to anticipate that the nation would grow and new problems of governance would require different solutions. Accordingly, our Federal Government was intentionally chartered with the flexibility to respond to contemporary needs without losing sight of fundamental democratic principles. . . . In my view, neither Article I of the Constitution nor the doctrine of separation of powers is violated by this mechanism by which our elected representatives preserve their voice in the governance of the nation.

III

. . . The power to exercise a legislative veto is not the power to write new law without bicameral approval or Presidential consideration. The veto must be authorized by statute and may only negative what an Executive department or independent agency has proposed. On its face, the legislative veto no more allows one House of Congress to make law than does the Presidential veto confer such power upon the President. Accordingly, the Court properly recognizes that it "must . . . establish that the challenged action under § 244(c)(2) is of the kind to which the procedural requirements of Art. I, § 7, apply" and admits that "not every action taken by either House is subject to the bicameralism and presentation requirements of Art. I."

A

The terms of the Presentment Clauses suggest only that bills and their equivalent are subject to the requirements of bicameral passage and presentment to the President. . . . There is no record that the Convention contemplated, let alone intended, that these Article I requirements would someday be invoked to restrain the scope of Congressional authority pursuant to duly-enacted law. . . .[18]

When the Convention did turn its attention to the scope of Congress' lawmaking power, the Framers were expansive. The Necessary and Proper Clause, Art. I, § 8, cl. 18, vests Congress with the power "to make all laws which shall be necessary and proper for carrying into Execution the foregoing Powers [the enumerated powers of § 8], and all other Powers vested by this

---

[18]   [T]he practices of the first Congresses demonstrate that the constraints of Article I were not envisioned as a constitutional straightjacket. . . . [T]he Northwest Territories Ordinance of 1787 . . . initially drafted under the Articles of Confederation on July 13, 1787, was the document which governed the territory of the United States northwest of the Ohio River. The ordinance authorized the territories to adopt laws, subject to disapproval in Congress.

The governor and judges, or a majority of them, shall adopt and publish in the district, such laws of the original states, criminal and civil, as may be necessary and best suited to the circumstances of the district, and report them to Congress, from time to time; which laws shall be in force in the district until the organization of the general assembly therein, unless disapproved of by Congress; but afterwards the legislature shall have authority to alter them as they shall think fit.

After the Constitution was enacted, the ordinance was reenacted to conform to the requirements of the Constitution. Act of Aug. 7, 1789. Certain provisions, such as one relating to appointment of officials by Congress, were changed because of constitutional concerns, but the language allowing disapproval by Congress was retained. Subsequent provisions for territorial laws contained similar language. . . .

The histories of the territories, the correspondence of the era, and the Congressional reports contain no indication that such resolutions disapproving of territorial laws were to be presented to the President or that the authorization for such a "congressional veto" in the Act of August 7, 1789 was of doubtful constitutionality. . . . It is surely significant that this body, largely composed of the same men who authored Article I and secured ratification of the Constitution, did not view the Constitution as forbidding a precursor of the modern-day legislative veto.

Constitution in the government of the United States, or in any Department or Officer thereof." It is long-settled that Congress may "exercise its best judgment in the selection of measures, to carry into execution the constitutional powers of the government," and "avail itself of experience, to exercise its reason, and to accommodate its legislation to circumstances." *McCulloch v. Maryland* (1819).

B

The Court heeded this counsel in approving the modern administrative state. The Court's holding today that all legislative-type action must be enacted through the lawmaking process ignores that legislative authority is routinely delegated to the Executive branch, to the independent regulatory agencies, and to private individuals and groups. . . . This Court's decisions sanctioning such delegations make clear that Article I does not require all action with the effect of legislation to be passed as a law.

. . . [F]or present purposes, these cases establish that by virtue of congressional delegation, legislative power can be exercised by independent agencies and Executive departments without the passage of new legislation. For some time, the sheer amount of law—the substantive rules that regulate private conduct and direct the operation of government—made by the agencies has far outnumbered the lawmaking engaged in by Congress through the traditional process. There is no question but that agency rulemaking is lawmaking in any functional or realistic sense of the term. . . . These regulations bind courts and officers of the federal government, may pre-empt state law, and grant rights to and impose obligations on the public. In sum, they have the force of law.

If Congress may delegate lawmaking power to independent and Executive agencies, it is most difficult to understand Article I as forbidding Congress from also reserving a check on legislative power for itself. Absent the veto, the agencies receiving delegations of legislative or quasi-legislative power may issue regulations having the force of law without bicameral approval and without the President's signature. It is thus not apparent why the reservation of a veto over the exercise of that legislative power must be subject to a more exacting test. In both cases, it is enough that the initial statutory authorizations comply with the Article I requirements. . . .

C

The Court also takes no account of perhaps the most relevant consideration: However resolutions of disapproval under § 244(c)(2) are formally characterized, in reality, a departure from the status quo occurs only upon the concurrence of opinion among the House, Senate, and President. . . .

The central concern of the presentation and bicameralism requirements of Article I is that when a departure from the legal status quo is undertaken, it is done with the approval of the President and both Houses of Congress—or, in the event of a Presidential veto, a two-thirds majority in both Houses. This interest is fully satisfied by the operation of § 244(c)(2). The President's approval is found in the Attorney General's action in recommending to Congress that the deportation order for a given alien be suspended. The House and the Senate indicate their approval of the Executive's action by not passing a resolution of disapproval within the statutory period. Thus, a change in the legal status quo—the deportability of the alien—is consummated only with the approval of each of the three relevant actors. The disagreement of any one of the three maintains the alien's pre-existing status: the Executive may choose not to recommend suspension; the House and Senate may each veto the recommendation. The effect on the rights and obligations of the affected individuals and upon the legislative system is precisely the same as if a private bill were introduced but failed to receive the necessary approval. . . .

I do not suggest that all legislative vetoes are necessarily consistent with separation of powers principles. A legislative check on an inherently executive function, for example that of initiating prosecutions, poses an entirely different question. But the legislative veto device here—and in many other settings—is far from an instance of legislative tyranny over the Executive. It is a necessary check on the unavoidably expanding power of the agencies, both Executive and independent, as they engage in exercising authority delegated by Congress. . . .

WORTH NOTING

Justice Rehnquist wrote a separate dissent, joined by Justice White. Notwithstanding a severability clause in the statute, he did not believe that the one-House veto provision was severable from the provision authorizing suspension of deportations. He wrote that "Congress' continuing insistence on retaining control of the suspension process indicates that it has never been disposed to give the Executive Branch a free hand."

---

2. Suing the President

Under the British law familiar to the American founders, it was said that
"the king can do no wrong." This principle had a complicated symbolic background, but one of its practical implications was quite straightforward: the
monarch could not be prosecuted or sued. Perhaps in part because of the obvious risks for liberty presented by royal immunity, British law had developed a
workaround for challenging government action. The eighteenth-century treatise
writer William Blackstone explained:

> Are then, it may be asked, the subjects of England totally destitute
> of remedy, in case the crown should invade their rights [by] public
> oppressions? To this we may answer, that the law has provided a rem-
> edy. . . . For, as a king cannot misuse his power, without the advice
> of evil counsellors, and the assistance of wicked ministers, these men
> may be examined and punished. The constitution has therefore pro-
> vided, by means of indictments, and parliamentary impeachments,
> that no man shall dare to assist the crown in contradiction to the
> laws of the land.

So perhaps the king could do no wrong. But his ministers certainly could—and
they were emphatically subject to judicial process of the sort that could serve as
a bulwark against tyranny. In the cases that follow, see if you can identify how
the U.S. constitutional system has approached similar questions of presidential
privilege and immunity.

During Reconstruction, the principles of executive branch immunity were
put to the test when the state of Mississippi filed suit directly against President
Andrew Johnson, "perpetually to enjoin and restrain" him "from executing, or
in any manner carrying out" the first Reconstruction Act. The Supreme Court
denied Mississippi's claim on jurisdictional grounds, holding that "we are fully
satisfied that this court has no jurisdiction of a bill to enjoin the President in
the performance of his official du-
ties." *Mississippi v. Johnson* (1867).
And as a matter of Supreme Court
doctrine, that's basically where things
stood for many years.

 The *Mississippi* case is presented at pp. 160–163.

Then came the presidency of Richard Nixon. Because of its aggressive, par-
anoid, and sometimes illegal conduct, his Administration generated important

decisions on the liability of the President and his senior aides to various judicial processes. We begin with the most important of these cases, in both legal and historical terms.

SUMMARY OF THE FACTS

Hoping to find political dirt, some of Nixon's political aides ordered a break-in of the Democratic National Committee headquarters, located in the Watergate complex in Washington, D.C. The burglars were discovered, and members of the Administration—including the President—actively participated in a cover-up. The ensuing investigation engulfed Nixon's Presidency. When it came to light that the President made a practice of recording conversations in the Oval Office, the Special Prosecutor appointed to investigate the affair issued a subpoena to secure some of the tapes. Perhaps understanding that disclosure of the tapes would end his Presidency, see p. 935, Nixon resisted. The dispute soon reached the Supreme Court.

United States v. Nixon

Supreme Court of the United States, 1974.
418 U.S. 683.

MR. CHIEF JUSTICE BURGER delivered the opinion of the Court.

This litigation presents for review the denial of a motion, filed in the District Court on behalf of the President of the United States, in the case of *United States v. Mitchell et al.*, to quash a third-party subpoena *duces tecum* issued by the United States District Court for the District of Columbia, pursuant to Fed. Rule Crim. Proc. 17(c). The subpoena directed the President to produce certain tape recordings and documents relating to his conversations with aides and advisers. . . .

On March 1, 1974, a grand jury of the United States District Court for the District of Columbia returned an indictment charging seven named individuals with various offenses, including conspiracy to defraud the United States and to obstruct justice. [Four of the defendants eventually either pleaded guilty or were convicted.] Although he was not designated as such in the indictment, the grand jury named the President, among others, as an unindicted coconspirator.

On April 18, 1974, upon motion of the Special Prosecutor, a subpoena *duces tecum* was issued pursuant to Rule 17(c) to the President by the United States District Court and made returnable on May 2, 1974. This subpoena required the production, in advance of the September 9 trial date, of certain tapes, memoranda, papers, transcripts or other writings relating to certain precisely identified meetings between the President and others. The Special Prosecutor was able to fix the time, place, and persons present at these discussions because the White House daily logs and appointment records had been delivered to him. On April 30, the President publicly released edited transcripts of 43 conversations; portions of 20 conversations subject to subpoena in the present case were included. On May 1, 1974, the President's counsel filed a "special appearance" and a motion to quash the subpoena under Rule 17(c). . . .

On May 20, 1974, the District Court denied the motion to quash and [ordered production of all the subpoenaed items.]

II

Justiciability

In the District Court, the President's counsel argued that the court lacked jurisdiction to issue the subpoena because the matter was an intra-branch dispute between a subordinate and superior officer of the Executive Branch and hence not subject to judicial resolution. That argument has been renewed in this Court with emphasis on the contention that the dispute does not present a "case" or "controversy" which can be adjudicated in the federal courts.

The President's counsel argues that the federal courts should not intrude into areas committed to the other branches of Government. He views the present dispute as essentially a "jurisdictional" dispute within the Executive Branch which he analogizes to a dispute between two congressional committees. Since the Executive Branch has exclusive authority and absolute discretion to decide whether to prosecute a case, it is contended that a President's decision is final in determining what evidence is to be used in a given criminal case. Although his counsel concedes that the President has delegated certain specific powers to the Special Prosecutor, he has not "waived nor delegated to the Special Prosecutor the President's duty to claim privilege as to all materials . . . which fall within the President's inherent authority to refuse to disclose to any executive officer." The Special Prosecutor's demand for the items therefore presents, in the view of the President's counsel, a political question under *Baker v. Carr* (1962), since it involves a "textually demonstrable" grant of power under Art. II. . . .

Our starting point is the nature of the proceeding for which the evidence is sought—here, a pending criminal prosecution. It is a judicial proceeding in a federal court alleging violation of federal laws and is brought in the name of the United States as sovereign. Under the authority of Art. II, § 2, Congress has vested in the Attorney General the power to conduct the criminal litigation of the United States Government. 28 U.S.C. § 516. It has also vested in him the power to appoint subordinate officers to assist him in the discharge of his duties. 28 U.S.C. §§ 509, 510, 515, 533. Acting pursuant to those statutes, the Attorney General has delegated the authority to represent the United States in these particular matters to a Special Prosecutor with unique authority and tenure.[8] The regulation gives the Special Prosecutor explicit power to contest the invocation of executive privilege in the process of seeking evidence deemed relevant to the performance of these specially delegated duties. . . .

This setting assures there is "that concrete adverseness which sharpens the presentation of issues upon which the court so largely depends for illumination of difficult constitutional questions." *Baker v. Carr* (1962). . . . In light of the uniqueness of the setting in which the conflict arises, the fact that both parties are officers of the Executive Branch cannot be viewed as a barrier to justiciability. It would be inconsistent with the applicable law and regulation, and the unique facts of this case, to conclude other than that the Special Prosecutor has standing to bring this action and that a justiciable controversy is presented for decision.

III

Rule 17(c)

The subpoena *duces tecum* is challenged on the ground that the Special Prosecutor failed to satisfy the requirements of Fed. Rule Crim. Proc. 17(c),

---

[8]   The regulation, issued by the Attorney General pursuant to his statutory authority, vests in the Special Prosecutor plenary authority to control the course of investigations and litigation related to "all offenses arising out of the 1972 Presidential Election for which the Special Prosecutor deems it necessary and appropriate to assume responsibility, allegations involving the President, members of the White House staff, or Presidential appointees, and any other matters which he consents to have assigned to him by the Attorney General." 38 Fed. Reg. 30739. . . .

   The regulations then go on to provide [that] . . . "the Special Prosecutor will not be removed from his duties except for extraordinary improprieties on his part and without the President's first consulting the Majority and the Minority Leaders and Chairmen and ranking Minority Members of the Judiciary Committees of the Senate and House of Representatives and ascertaining that their consensus is in accord with his proposed action."

which governs the issuance of subpoenas *duces tecum* in federal criminal proceedings. . . . A subpoena for documents may be quashed if their production would be "unreasonable or oppressive," but not otherwise. . . .

From our examination of the materials submitted by the Special Prosecutor . . . , we are persuaded that . . . the Special Prosecutor has made a sufficient showing to justify a subpoena for production *before* trial. The subpoenaed materials are not available from any other source, and their examination and processing should not await trial in the circumstances shown.

IV

The Claim of Privilege

A

[W]e turn to the claim that the subpoena should be quashed because it demands "confidential conversations between a President and his close advisors that it would be inconsistent with the public interest to produce." . . .

In the performance of assigned constitutional duties each branch of the Government must initially interpret the Constitution, and the interpretation of its powers by any branch is due great respect from the others. . . .

B

In support of his claim of absolute privilege, the President's counsel urges two grounds, one of which is common to all governments and one of which is peculiar to our system of separation of powers. The first ground is the valid need for protection of communications between high Government officials and those who advise and assist them in the performance of their manifold duties; the importance of this confidentiality is too plain to require further discussion. Human experience teaches that those who expect public dissemination of their remarks may well temper candor with a concern for appearances and for their own interests to the detriment of the decisionmaking process. Whatever the nature of the privilege of confidentiality of Presidential communications in the exercise of Art. II powers, the privilege can be said to derive from the supremacy of each branch within its own assigned area of constitutional duties. Certain powers and privileges flow from the nature of enumerated powers;[16]

---

[16] The Special Prosecutor argues that there is no provision in the Constitution for a Presidential privilege as to the President's communications corresponding to the privilege of Members of Congress under the Speech or Debate Clause. But the silence of the Constitution on this score is not dispositive. . . .

the protection of the confidentiality of Presidential communications has similar constitutional underpinnings.

The second ground asserted by the President's counsel in support of the claim of absolute privilege rests on the doctrine of separation of powers. Here it is argued that the independence of the Executive Branch within its own sphere . . . insulates a President from a judicial subpoena in an ongoing criminal prosecution, and thereby protects confidential Presidential communications.

However, neither the doctrine of separation of powers, nor the need for confidentiality of high-level communications, without more, can sustain an absolute, unqualified Presidential privilege of immunity from judicial process under all circumstances. The President's need for complete candor and objectivity from advisers calls for great deference from the courts. However, when the privilege depends solely on the broad, undifferentiated claim of public interest in the confidentiality of such conversations, a confrontation with other values arises. Absent a claim of need to protect military, diplomatic, or sensitive national security secrets, we find it difficult to accept the argument that even the very important interest in confidentiality of Presidential communications is significantly diminished by production of such material for *in camera* inspection with all the protection that a district court will be obliged to provide.

The impediment that an absolute, unqualified privilege would place in the way of the primary constitutional duty of the Judicial Branch to do justice in criminal prosecutions would plainly conflict with the function of the courts under Art. III. . . . To read the Art. II powers of the President as providing an absolute privilege as against a subpoena essential to enforcement of criminal statutes on no more than a generalized claim of the public interest in confidentiality of nonmilitary and nondiplomatic discussions would upset the constitutional balance of "a workable government" and gravely impair the role of the courts under Art. III.

C

Since we conclude that the legitimate needs of the judicial process may outweigh Presidential privilege, it is necessary to resolve those competing interests in a manner that preserves the essential functions of each branch. The right and indeed the duty to resolve that question does not free the Judiciary from according high respect to the representations made on behalf of the President.

The expectation of a President to the confidentiality of his conversations and correspondence, like the claim of confidentiality of judicial deliberations, for example, has all the values to which we accord deference for the privacy of all citizens[. A]dded to those values . . . is the necessity for protection of the public interest in candid, objective, and even blunt or harsh opinions in Presidential decisionmaking. A President and those who assist him must be free to explore alternatives in the process of shaping policies and making decisions and to do so in a way many would be unwilling to express except privately. These are the considerations justifying a presumptive privilege for Presidential communications. The privilege is fundamental to the operation of Government and inextricably rooted in the separation of powers under the Constitution. . . . We agree with Mr. Chief Justice Marshall's observation, therefore, that "[I]n no case of this kind would a court be required to proceed against the president as against an ordinary individual." *United States v. Burr* (C.C. Va. 1807).

But this presumptive privilege must be considered in light of our historic commitment to the rule of law. This is nowhere more profoundly manifest than in our view that "the twofold aim [of criminal justice] is that guilt shall not escape or innocence suffer." . . . The very integrity of the judicial system and public confidence in the system depend on full disclosure of all the facts, within the framework of the rules of evidence. To ensure that justice is done, it is imperative to the function of courts that compulsory process be available for the production of evidence needed either by the prosecution or by the defense.

Only recently the Court restated the ancient proposition of law, albeit in the context of a grand jury inquiry rather than a trial, "that 'the public . . . has a right to every man's evidence,' except for those persons protected by a constitutional, common-law, or statutory privilege." *Branzburg v. Hayes* (1972).

The privileges referred to by the Court are designed to protect weighty and legitimate competing interests. Thus, the Fifth Amendment to the Constitution provides that no man "shall be compelled in any criminal case to be a witness against himself." And, generally, an attorney or a priest may not be required to disclose what has been revealed in professional confidence. These and other interests are recognized in law by privileges against forced disclosure, established in the Constitution, by statute, or at common law. Whatever their origins, these exceptions to the demand for every man's evidence are not lightly created nor expansively construed, for they are in derogation of the search for truth.

In this case the President challenges a subpoena served on him as a third party requiring the production of materials for use in a criminal prosecution; he does so on the claim that he has a privilege against disclosure of confidential communications. He does not place his claim of privilege on the ground they are military or diplomatic secrets. As to these areas of Art. II duties the courts have traditionally shown the utmost deference to Presidential responsibilities. In *C. & S. Air Lines v. Waterman S.S. Corp.* (1948), dealing with Presidential authority involving foreign policy considerations, the Court said:

> The President, both as Commander-in-Chief and as the Nation's organ for foreign affairs, has available intelligence services whose reports are not and ought not to be published to the world. It would be intolerable that courts, without the relevant information, should review and perhaps nullify actions of the Executive taken on information properly held secret.

In *United States v. Reynolds* (1953), dealing with a claimant's demand for evidence in a Tort Claims Act case against the Government, the Court said:

> It may be possible to satisfy the court, from all the circumstances of the case, that there is a reasonable danger that compulsion of the evidence will expose military matters which, in the interest of national security, should not be divulged. When this is the case, the occasion for the privilege is appropriate, and the court should not jeopardize the security which the privilege is meant to protect by insisting upon an examination of the evidence, even by the judge alone, in chambers.

No case of the Court, however, has extended this high degree of deference to a President's generalized interest in confidentiality. . . .

In this case we must weigh the importance of the general privilege of confidentiality of Presidential communications in performance of the President's responsibilities against the inroads of such a privilege on the fair administration of criminal justice.[19] The interest in preserving confidentiality is weighty indeed and entitled to great respect. However, we cannot conclude that advisers will be moved to temper the candor of their remarks by the infrequent occasions of

---

[19]   We are not here concerned with the balance between the President's generalized interest in confidentiality and the need for relevant evidence in civil litigation, nor with that between the confidentiality interest and congressional demands for information, nor with the President's interest in preserving state secrets. We address only the conflict between the President's assertion of a generalized privilege of confidentiality and the constitutional need for relevant evidence in criminal trials.

disclosure because of the possibility that such conversations will be called for in the context of a criminal prosecution. . . .

A President's acknowledged need for confidentiality in the communications of his office is general in nature, whereas the constitutional need for production of relevant evidence in a criminal proceeding is specific and central to the fair adjudication of a particular criminal case in the administration of justice. Without access to specific facts a criminal prosecution may be totally frustrated. The President's broad interest in confidentiality of communications will not be vitiated by disclosure of a limited number of conversations preliminarily shown to have some bearing on the pending criminal cases.

We conclude that when the ground for asserting privilege as to subpoenaed materials sought for use in a criminal trial is based only on the generalized interest in confidentiality, it cannot prevail over the fundamental demands of due process of law in the fair administration of criminal justice. The generalized assertion of privilege must yield to the demonstrated, specific need for evidence in a pending criminal trial.

D

We have earlier determined that the District Court did not err in authorizing the issuance of the subpoena. If a President concludes that compliance with a subpoena would be injurious to the public interest he may properly, as was done here, invoke a claim of privilege on the return of the subpoena. Upon receiving a claim of privilege from the Chief Executive, it became the further duty of the District Court to treat the subpoenaed material as presumptively privileged and to require the Special Prosecutor to demonstrate that the Presidential material was "essential to the justice of the [pending criminal] case." *United States v. Burr.*

Here the District Court treated the material as presumptively privileged, proceeded to find that the Special Prosecutor had made a sufficient showing to rebut the presumption, and ordered an *in camera* examination of the subpoenaed material. On the basis of our examination of the record we are unable to conclude that the District Court erred in ordering the inspection. Accordingly we affirm the order of the District Court that subpoenaed materials be transmitted to that court.

E

We now turn to the important question of the District Court's responsibilities in conducting the *in camera* examination of Presidential materials or communications delivered under the compulsion of the subpoena *duces tecum*. . . .

Statements that meet the test of admissibility and relevance must be isolated; all other material must be excised. . . . It is elementary that *in camera* inspection of evidence is always a procedure calling for scrupulous protection against any release or publication of material not found by the court, at that stage, probably admissible in evidence and relevant to the issues of the trial for which it is sought. That being true of an ordinary situation, it is obvious that the District Court has a very heavy responsibility to see to it that Presidential conversations, which are either not relevant or not admissible, are accorded that high degree of respect due the President of the United States. . . .

[A] President's communications and activities encompass a vastly wider range of sensitive material than would be true of any "ordinary individual." It is therefore necessary[21] in the public interest to afford Presidential confidentiality the greatest protection consistent with the fair administration of justice. The need for confidentiality even as to idle conversations with associates in which casual reference might be made concerning political leaders within the country or foreign statesmen is too obvious to call for further treatment. We have no doubt that the District Judge will . . . discharge his responsibility to see to it that until released to the Special Prosecutor no *in camera* material is revealed to anyone. This burden applies with even greater force to excised material; once the decision is made to excise, the material is restored to its privileged status and should be returned under seal to its lawful custodian.

Affirmed.

Mr. Justice Rehnquist took no part in the consideration or decision of these cases.

Four years after the Watergate subpoena case, the Supreme Court turned from the problem of specific evidentiary privileges to the larger question of

---

[21]   When the subpoenaed material is delivered to the District Judge *in camera*, questions may arise as to the excising of parts, and it lies within the discretion of that court to seek the aid of the Special Prosecutor and the President's counsel for *in camera* consideration of the validity of particular excisions, whether the basis of excision is relevancy or admissibility or under such cases as *United States v. Reynolds* (1953) [(military secrets privilege)], or *C. & S. Air Lines v. Waterman S.S. Corp.* (1948) [(foreign affairs secrets privilege)].

categorical immunity from suit. The occasion came in a pair of decisions prompt-ed by a lawsuit brought against Nixon and two of his aides by A. Ernest Fitzgerald, a former official who alleged unlawful retaliation for his truthful testimony before Congress. (Though Fitzgerald had testified during the last weeks of the previous Administration, it appears that the Nixon Administration regarded his testimony as a demonstration of intolerable disloyalty to superiors.) The first decision resolved Nixon's assertion of categorical im-munity for suit based on actions during his time as President; the sec-ond involved analogous claims by his aides.

Do you think the next two cases are consis-tent in their treatment of the tradeoff be-tween institutional pre-rogative and legal accountability?

Nixon v. Fitzgerald

Supreme Court of the United States, 1982.
457 U.S. 731.

Justice Powell delivered the opinion of the Court.

The plaintiff in this lawsuit seeks relief in civil damages from a former President of the United States. The claim rests on actions allegedly taken in the former President's official capacity during his tenure in office. The issue before us is the scope of the immunity possessed by the President of the United States.

I

In January 1970 the respondent A. Ernest Fitzgerald lost his job as a management analyst with the Department of the Air Force. Fitzgerald's dis-missal occurred in the context of a departmental reorganization and reduction in force, in which his job was eliminated. In announcing the reorganization, the Air Force characterized the action as taken to promote economy and effi-ciency in the Armed Forces.

Respondent's discharge attracted unusual attention in Congress and in the press. Fitzgerald had attained national prominence approximately one year earlier, during the waning months of the Presidency of Lyndon B. Johnson. On November 13, 1968, Fitzgerald appeared before the Subcommittee on Econ-omy in Government of the Joint Economic Committee of the United States

Congress. To the evident embarrassment of his superiors in the Department of Defense, Fitzgerald testified that cost-overruns on the C-5A transport plane could approximate $2 billion. He also revealed that unexpected technical difficulties had arisen during the development of the aircraft. . . .

In a letter of January 20, 1970, [Fitzgerald] alleged that his separation represented unlawful retaliation for his truthful testimony before a congressional Committee. . . . At a news conference on January 31, 1973, the President . . . assume[d] personal responsibility for Fitzgerald's dismissal. . . . A day later, however, the White House press office issued a retraction of the President's statement. According to a press spokesman, the President had confused Fitzgerald with another former executive employee. On behalf of the President, the spokesman asserted that Mr. Nixon had not had "put before him the decision regarding Mr. Fitzgerald." . . .

Fitzgerald filed a suit for damages in the United States District Court [against defendants who eventually included former president Richard Nixon and two of his White House aides, Bryce Harlow and Alexander Butterfield. Among other counts, Fitzgerald claimed defendants had conspired to deprive him of his job. He invoked two statutes prohibiting interference with Congressional testimony: one provided generally that "the right of employees . . . to . . . furnish information to either House of Congress . . . may not be interfered with or denied," and the other made it a crime to obstruct congressional testimony.]

Denying a motion for summary judgment, the District Court ruled . . . that [former President Nixon] was not entitled to claim absolute Presidential immunity. . . . As this Court has not ruled on the scope of immunity available to a President of the United States, we granted certiorari to decide this important issue. . . .

IV

Here a former President asserts his immunity from civil damages claims of two kinds. He stands named as a defendant in a direct action under the Constitution and in two statutory actions under federal laws of general applicability. In neither case has Congress taken express legislative action to subject the President to civil liability for his official acts. . . .[27]

---

[27]   In the present case we therefore are presented only with "implied" causes of action, and we need not address directly the immunity question as it would arise if Congress expressly had created a damages action against the President of the United States.

Applying the principles of our cases to claims of this kind, we hold that petitioner, as a former President of the United States, is entitled to absolute immunity from damages liability predicated on his official acts. We consider this immunity a functionally mandated incident of the President's unique office, rooted in the constitutional tradition of the separation of powers and supported by our history. . . .

A

. . . The President's unique status under the Constitution distinguishes him from other executive officials.

Because of the singular importance of the President's duties, diversion of his energies by concern with private lawsuits would raise unique risks to the effective functioning of government. As is the case with prosecutors and judges—for whom absolute immunity now is established—a President must concern himself with matters likely to "arouse the most intense feelings." Yet, as our decisions have recognized, it is in precisely such cases that there exists the greatest public interest in providing an official "the maximum ability to deal fearlessly and impartially with" the duties of his office. This concern is compelling where the officeholder must make the most sensitive and far-reaching decisions entrusted to any official under our constitutional system. Nor can the sheer prominence of the President's office be ignored. In view of the visibility of his office and the effect of his actions on countless people, the President would be an easily identifiable target for suits for civil damages. Cognizance of this personal vulnerability frequently could distract a President from his public duties, to the detriment of not only the President and his office but also the Nation that the Presidency was designed to serve.

B

Courts traditionally have recognized the President's constitutional responsibilities and status as factors counseling judicial deference and restraint. For example, while courts generally have looked to the common law to determine the scope of an official's evidentiary privilege, we have recognized that the Presidential privilege is "rooted in the separation of powers under the Constitution." *United States v. Nixon.*

WORTH NOTING

The Court here cited *Mississippi v. Johnson* (1867) for the proposition that "[t]his tradition can be traced far back into our constitutional history." In that case, which is presented pp. 160–163, the Court refused to consider the merits of Mississippi's challenge to President Andrew Johnson's enforcement of two Reconstruction statutes. In terms drawn from *Marbury v. Madison,* the Court held that "[t]he duty . . . imposed on the President [by the Reconstruction statutes] is in no sense just ministerial. It is purely executive and political."

It is settled law that the separation-of-powers doctrine does not bar every exercise of jurisdiction over the President of the United States. See, *e.g., United States v. Nixon* (1974); *United States v. Burr* (C.C. Va. 1807); cf. *Youngstown Sheet & Tube Co. v. Sawyer* (1952).[36] But our cases also have established that a court, before exercising jurisdiction, must balance the constitutional weight of the interest to be served against the dangers of intrusion on the authority and functions of the Executive Branch. See *United States v. Nixon.* When judicial action is needed to serve broad public interests—as when the Court acts, not in derogation of the separation of powers, but to maintain their proper balance, *cf. Youngstown Sheet & Tube Co. v. Sawyer, supra,* or to vindicate the public interest in an ongoing criminal prosecution, see *United States v. Nixon, supra*—the exercise of jurisdiction has been held warranted. In the case of this merely private suit for damages based on a President's official acts, we hold it is not. . . .

V

A rule of absolute immunity for the President will not leave the Nation without sufficient protection against misconduct on the part of the Chief Executive. There remains the constitutional remedy of impeachment.[39] In addition, there are formal and informal checks on Presidential action that do not apply with equal force to other executive officials. The President is subjected to constant scrutiny by the press. Vigilant oversight by Congress also may serve to deter Presidential abuses of office, as well as to make credible the threat of impeachment.[40] Other incentives to avoid misconduct may include a desire to

---

[36]   Although the President was not a party [in *Youngstown*], the Court enjoined the Secretary of Commerce from executing a direct Presidential order.

[39]   The same remedy plays a central role with respect to the misconduct of federal judges, who also possess absolute immunity. Congressmen may be removed from office by a vote of their colleagues. U.S. Const., Art. I, § 5, cl. 2.

[40]   Prior to petitioner Nixon's resignation from office, the House Judiciary Committee had convened impeachment hearings.

earn reelection, the need to maintain prestige as an element of Presidential influence, and a President's traditional concern for his historical stature.

The existence of alternative remedies and deterrents establishes that absolute immunity will not place the President "above the law." For the President, as for judges and prosecutors, absolute immunity merely precludes a particular private remedy for alleged misconduct in order to advance compelling public ends. . . .

CHIEF JUSTICE BURGER, concurring.

I join the Court's opinion, but I write separately to underscore that the Presidential immunity derives from and is mandated by the constitutional doctrine of separation of powers. . . .

It strains the meaning of the words used to say this places a President "above the law." *United States v. Nixon* (1974). The dissents are wide of the mark to the extent that they imply that the Court today recognizes sweeping immunity for a President for all acts. The Court does no such thing. The immunity is limited to civil damages claims. Moreover, a President, like Members of Congress, judges, prosecutors, or congressional aides—all having absolute immunity—are not immune for acts outside official duties. Even the broad immunity of the Speech and Debate Clause has its limits. . . .[3]

JUSTICE WHITE, with whom JUSTICE BRENNAN, JUSTICE MARSHALL, and JUSTICE BLACKMUN join, dissenting.

. . . A President, acting within the outer boundaries of what Presidents normally do, may [now], without liability, deliberately cause serious injury to any number of citizens even though he knows his conduct violates a statute or tramples on the constitutional rights of those who are injured. Even if the President in this case ordered Fitzgerald fired by means of a trumped-up reduction in force, knowing that such a discharge was contrary to the civil service laws, he would be absolutely immune from suit. By the same token, if a President, without following the statutory procedures which he knows apply to himself as well as to other federal officials, orders his subordinates to wiretap or break into a home for the purpose of installing a listening device, and the officers comply with his request, the President would be absolutely immune from suit.

---

[3] In *United States v. Brewster* (1972), we held that the Speech and Debate Clause does not prohibit prosecution of a Senator for accepting a bribe designed to influence his legislative acts.

He would be immune regardless of the damage he inflicts, regardless of how violative of the statute and of the Constitution he knew his conduct to be, and regardless of his purpose. . . .

I find this approach completely unacceptable. I do not agree that if the Office of President is to operate effectively, the holder of that Office must be permitted, without fear of liability and regardless of the function he is performing, deliberately to inflict injury on others by conduct that he knows violates the law. . . .

WORTH NOTING

Justice Blackmun, joined by Justices Brennan and Marshall, also filed a separate dissent. He thought that the Court was inconsistent in holding that absolute immunity was compelled by separation of powers concerns and yet leaving open the possibility that the President could be subject to congressionally created forms of liability.

Harlow v. Fitzgerald

Supreme Court of the United States, 1982.
457 U.S. 800.

JUSTICE POWELL delivered the opinion of the Court.

. . . In this suit for civil damages petitioners Bryce Harlow and Alexander Butterfield are alleged to have participated in a conspiracy to violate the constitutional and statutory rights of the respondent A. Ernest Fitzgerald. Respondent avers that petitioners entered the conspiracy in their capacities as senior White House aides to former President Richard M. Nixon. As the alleged conspiracy is the same as that involved in *Nixon v. Fitzgerald*, the facts need not be repeated in detail. . . .

II

. . . Our decisions have recognized immunity defenses of two kinds. For officials whose special functions or constitutional status requires complete protection from suit, we have recognized the defense of "absolute immunity." The absolute immunity of legislators, in their legislative functions, and of judges, in their judicial functions, now is well settled. Our decisions also have extended absolute immunity to certain officials of the Executive Branch. These include prosecutors and similar officials, executive officers engaged in adjudicative functions, and the President of the United States, see *Nixon v. Fitzgerald*. For executive officials in general, however, our cases make plain that qualified immunity represents the norm. . . .

Petitioners argue that they are entitled to a blanket protection of absolute immunity as an incident of their offices as Presidential aides. In deciding this claim we do not write on an empty page. In *Butz v. Economou* (1974), the Secretary of Agriculture—a Cabinet official directly accountable to the President—asserted a defense of absolute official immunity from suit for civil damages. We rejected his claim. In so doing we did not question the power or the importance of the Secretary's office. Nor did we doubt the importance to the President of loyal and efficient subordinates in executing his duties of office. Yet we found these factors, alone, to be insufficient to justify absolute immunity. "[T]he greater power of [high] officials," we reasoned, "affords a greater potential for a regime of lawless conduct." Damages actions against high officials were therefore "an important means of vindicating constitutional guarantees."

Having decided in *Butz* that Members of the Cabinet ordinarily enjoy only qualified immunity from suit, we conclude today that it would be equally untenable to hold absolute immunity an incident of the office of every Presidential subordinate based in the White House. Members of the Cabinet are direct subordinates of the President, frequently with greater responsibilities, both to the President and to the Nation, than White House staff. The considerations that supported our decision in *Butz* apply with equal force to this case. It is no disparagement of the offices held by petitioners to hold that Presidential aides, like Members of the Cabinet, generally are entitled only to a qualified immunity[, as described in Part IV.]

IV

Even if they cannot establish that their official functions require absolute immunity, petitioners assert that public policy at least mandates an application of the qualified immunity standard that would permit the defeat of insubstantial claims without resort to trial. We agree. . . .

The resolution of immunity questions inherently requires a balance between the evils inevitable in any available alternative. In situations of abuse of office, an action for damages may offer the only realistic avenue for vindication of constitutional guarantees. It is this recognition that has required the denial of absolute immunity to most public officers. At the same time, however, it cannot be disputed seriously that claims frequently run against the innocent as well as the guilty—at a cost not only to the defendant officials, but to society as a whole. These social costs include the expenses of litigation, the diversion of official energy from pressing public issues, and the deterrence of able citizens from acceptance of public office. Finally, there is the danger that fear of being sued will "dampen the ardor of all but the most resolute, or the most irresponsible [public officials], in the unflinching discharge of their duties." . . .

Qualified or "good faith" immunity is an affirmative defense that must be pleaded by a defendant official. [Q]ualified immunity would be defeated if an official "*knew or reasonably should have known* that the action he took within his sphere of official responsibility would violate the constitutional rights of the [plaintiff], *or* if he took the action *with the malicious intention* to cause a deprivation of constitutional rights or other injury. . . ." *Wood v. Strickland* (1975).

By defining the limits of qualified immunity essentially in objective terms, we provide no license to lawless conduct. The public interest in deterrence of unlawful conduct and in compensation of victims remains protected by a test that focuses on the objective legal reasonableness of an official's acts. Where an official could be expected to know that certain conduct would violate statutory or constitutional rights, he should be made to hesitate; and a person who suffers injury caused by such conduct may have a cause of action. But where an official's duties legitimately require action in which clearly established rights are not implicated, the public interest may be better served by action taken "with independence and without fear of consequences." . . .

The Court remanded so that the trial court could reconsider the issue in light of the Court's opinion. Every member of the Court but Chief Justice Burger joined the opinion. The four *Nixon v. Fitzgerald* dissenters filed a one-sentence concurring statement disassociating themselves from any implication that *Nixon* was correctly decided. Justice Brennan, joined by Justices Marshall and Blackmun, wrote a brief concurrence noting that discovery might sometimes be necessary to determine what an official knew at the time of the relevant actions. Justice Rehnquist also wrote a brief concurrence; he agreed that *Butz* controlled, but said that he would "with alacrity" re-examine that case's holding. The Chief Justice dissented:

The Court today decides in *Nixon v. Fitzgerald*, what has been taken for granted for 190 years, that it is implicit in the Constitution that a President of the United States has absolute immunity from civil suits arising out of official acts as Chief Executive. . . . In this case[, however,] the Court decides that senior aides of the President do not have derivative immunity from the President. . . . How can we conceivably hold that a President of the United States . . . should not have "alter egos" with comparable immunity? To perform the constitutional duties assigned to the Executive would be "literally impossible, in view of the complexities of the modern [Executive] process, . . . without the help of aides and assistants." . . .

Nixon v. Fitzgerald involved a suit against a former President for his official conduct in office; plainly, a sitting President would have the same immunity against a suit arising out of official conduct. But what about a civil suit against a sitting President arising out of conduct that has nothing to do with the office? A few such suits were litigated in the 20th century, but only one, *Clinton v. Jones* (1997), yielded a decision of constitutional significance.

WORTH NOTING

Complaints against Theodore Roosevelt and Harry Truman were dismissed before they took office, and the dismissals were affirmed after they took office. *People ex rel. Hurley v. Roosevelt* (N.Y. 1904); *DeVault v. Truman* (Mo. 1946). John F. Kennedy argued after inauguration that he had a statutory right to a stay of actions brought against him that rose out of a campaign traffic accident; he lost the motion and settled the matter.

Clinton arose out of an alleged act of sexual harassment committed in 1991 by Bill Clinton when he was Governor of Arkansas. The plaintiff, Paula Jones, who had been a state employee, sued him in 1994, when he was President. The trial judge denied Clinton's motion to dismiss on immunity grounds and ruled that discovery could proceed, but she ordered that any trial would be held after Clinton's Presidency ended. The case ultimately reached the Supreme Court during Clinton's second term. The Court denied Clinton's contention that "in all but the most exceptional cases" he had immunity during his tenure from civil damages litigation arising from events that occurred before he took office. It also held that the trial judge had abused her discretion by delaying trial, because a lengthy and categorical stay took "no account whatever of [Jones's] interest in bringing the case to trial."

Justice Stevens wrote for the Court, concluding that the "principal rationale" for according immunity—to ensure that officials perform their functions without fear of personal liability—simply did not apply to unofficial conduct. He relegated to a footnote discussion of the assertion in *Nixon v. Fitzgerald* that "diversion of [the President's] energies by concern with private lawsuits would raise unique risks to the effective functioning of government"; the *Nixon* Court's "dominant concern," he claimed, "was with the diversion of the President's attention during the decisionmaking process caused by needless worry as to the possibility of damages actions stemming from any particular official decision."

The Court also rejected Clinton's argument that, because the President needs to devote undivided time and attention to the office, separation-of-powers principles prevent the federal judiciary from entertaining civil damages actions against him. Justice Stevens acknowledged the burdens imposed by the Presidency, but given the paucity of previous civil actions against Presidents, the possibility of pretrial judgment as a matter of law in appropriate cases, and the availability of sanctions in frivolous ones, he thought it "unlikely that a deluge of such litigation will ever engulf the Presidency." With proper management of the *Jones* case, he believed it would be "highly unlikely to occupy any substantial amount of [Clinton's] time." For example, the President's testimony, both for discovery and trial, could be taken at the White House at a time convenient for him—with due deference to his responsibilities, especially in matters related to national security—and he would not need to attend a trial in person.

Justice Stevens noted both that, as in *Youngstown*, "the Judiciary may severely burden the Executive Branch by reviewing the legality of the President's official conduct," and that it is "settled that the President is subject to judicial process in appropriate circumstances." (This issue is canvassed in some detail in *Trump v. Vance*, which is presented at pp. 918–927.) Accordingly, he concluded that "it must follow that the federal courts have power to determine the legality of [the President's] unofficial conduct.

There were no dissents, but Justice Breyer wrote separately, concurring in the judgment. He believed the majority was too sanguine about the burden on the President. Given "Article II's vesting of the entire 'executive Power' in a single individual," he thought that if the President set forth "a reasoned explanation" of the need for a postponement of trial, then a federal judge could not "interfere with the President's discharge of his public duties." But absent such an explanation, he agreed that the postponement of a trial was premature.

WORTH NOTING

Jones's lawsuit never did go to trial; the district judge granted summary judgment against her because she had not presented sufficient evidence of adverse consequences of "her refusal to submit to the Governor's alleged advances." But Clinton's false denial during a deposition of having had "sexual relations" with a White House intern led to his impeachment; he was acquitted and remained in office.

The presidency of Donald Trump brought questions of presidential privilege and immunity back into the spotlight, with Congress, state officials, and private litigants all seeking information relating to alleged misconduct by the executive branch, the White House, and the President himself. The following two cases, decided the same day, address two different settings in which Trump's lawyers asserted privilege: a state criminal proceeding and a congressional investigation. Which seems more likely to trigger special constitutional concern?

Trump v. Vance

Supreme Court of the United States, 2020.
140 S. Ct. 2412.

Chief Justice Roberts delivered the opinion of the Court.

In our judicial system, "the public has a right to every man's evidence." Since the earliest days of the Republic, "every man" has included the President of the United States. Beginning with Jefferson and carrying on through Clinton, Presidents have uniformly testified or produced documents in criminal proceedings when called upon by federal courts. This case involves—so far as we and the parties can tell—the first *state* criminal subpoena directed to a President. . . .

I

In the summer of 2018, the New York County District Attorney's Office opened an investigation into what it opaquely describes as "business transactions involving multiple individuals whose conduct may have violated state law." A year later, the office—acting on behalf of a grand jury—served a subpoena *duces tecum* (essentially a request to produce evidence) on Mazars USA, LLP, the personal accounting firm of President Donald J. Trump. The subpoena directed Mazars to produce financial records relating to the President and business organizations affiliated with him, including "[t]ax returns and related schedules," from "2011 to the present." The President, acting in his personal capacity, sued the district attorney and Mazars in Federal District Court to enjoin enforcement of the subpoena. . . .

II

[In the 1807 treason trial of Aaron Burr, the defendant] moved for a subpoena *duces tecum* directed at [President Thomas] Jefferson. The draft subpoena required the President to produce an October 21, 1806 letter from [Burr's co-conspirator and accuser James] Wilkinson and accompanying documents, which Jefferson had referenced in [a] message to Congress. The prosecution opposed the request, arguing that a President could not be subjected to such a subpoena and that the letter might contain state secrets. Following four days of argument, Marshall announced his ruling to a packed chamber.

The President, Marshall declared, does not "stand exempt from the general provisions of the constitution" or, in particular, the Sixth Amendment's guarantee that those accused have compulsory process for obtaining witnesses for their defense. *United States v. Burr* (C.C. Va. 1807). At common law the "single reservation" to the duty to testify in response to a subpoena was "the case of the king," whose "dignity" was seen as "incompatible" with appearing "under the process of the court." But, as Marshall explained, a king is born to power and can "do no wrong." The President, by contrast, is "of the people" and subject to the law. According to Marshall, the sole argument for exempting the President from testimonial obligations was that his "duties as chief magistrate demand his whole time for national objects." But, in Marshall's assessment, those demands were "not unremitting." And should the President's duties preclude his attendance at a particular time and place, a court could work that out upon return of the subpoena.

Marshall also rejected the prosecution's argument that the President was immune from a subpoena *duces tecum* because executive papers might contain state secrets. "A subpoena duces tecum," he said, "may issue to any person to whom an ordinary subpoena may issue." . . . As for "the propriety of introducing any papers," that would "depend on the character of the paper, not on the character of the person who holds it." Marshall acknowledged that the papers sought by Burr could contain information "the disclosure of which would endanger the public safety," but stated that, again, such concerns would have "due consideration" upon the return of the subpoena.

While the arguments unfolded, Jefferson, who had received word of the motion, wrote to the prosecutor indicating that he would—subject to the prerogative to decide which executive communications should be withheld—"furnish on all occasions, whatever the purposes of justice may require." His "personal attendance," however, was out of the question, for it "would leave the nation without" the "sole branch which the constitution requires to be always in function." Letter from T. Jefferson to G. Hay (June 17, 1807).

Before Burr received the subpoenaed documents, Marshall rejected the prosecution's core legal theory for treason and Burr was accordingly acquitted. Jefferson, however, was not done. Committed to salvaging a conviction, he directed the prosecutors to proceed with a misdemeanor (yes, misdemeanor) charge for inciting war against Spain. Burr then renewed his request for Wilkinson's October 21 letter, which he later received a copy of, and subpoenaed a second letter, dated November 12, 1806, which the prosecutor claimed was privileged. Acknowledging that the President may withhold information to protect public safety, Marshall instructed that Jefferson should "state the particular reasons" for withholding the letter. *United States v. Burr* (C.C. Va. 1807). The court, paying "all proper respect" to those reasons, would then decide whether to compel disclosure. But that decision was averted when the misdemeanor trial was cut short after it became clear that the prosecution lacked the evidence to convict.

In the two centuries since the Burr trial, successive Presidents have accepted Marshall's ruling that the Chief Executive is subject to subpoena. In 1818, President Monroe received a subpoena to testify in a court-martial against one of his appointees. His Attorney General, William Wirt—who had served as a prosecutor during Burr's trial—advised Monroe that, per Marshall's ruling, a subpoena to testify may "be properly awarded to the President." Monroe offered to sit for a deposition and ultimately submitted answers to written interrogatories.

Following Monroe's lead, his successors have uniformly agreed to testify when called in criminal proceedings, provided they could do so at a time and place of their choosing. In 1875, President Grant submitted to a three-hour deposition in the criminal prosecution of a political appointee embroiled in a network of tax-evading whiskey distillers. A century later, President Ford's attempted assassin subpoenaed him to testify in her defense. *See United States v. Fromme* (E.D. Cal. 1975). Ford obliged—from a safe distance—in the first videotaped deposition of a President. President Carter testified via the same means in the trial of two local officials who, while Carter was Governor of Georgia, had offered to contribute to his campaign in exchange for advance warning of any state gambling raids. Two years later, Carter gave videotaped testimony to a federal grand jury investigating whether a fugitive financier had entreated the White House to quash his extradition proceedings. President Clinton testified three times, twice via deposition pursuant to subpoenas in federal criminal trials of associates implicated during the Whitewater investigation, and once by video for a grand jury investigating possible perjury.

The bookend to Marshall's ruling came in 1974 when the question he never had to decide—whether to compel the disclosure of official communications over the objection of the President—came to a head. [Here, the Chief Justice describes *United States v. Nixon*, presented at pp. 899–907, and notes that two weeks after the decision, "President Nixon dutifully released the tapes."]

III

The history surveyed above all involved *federal* criminal proceedings. Here we are confronted for the first time with a subpoena issued to the President by a local grand jury operating under the supervision of a *state* court.[5]

In the President's view, that distinction makes all the difference. He argues that the Supremacy Clause gives a sitting President absolute immunity from state criminal subpoenas because compliance with those subpoenas would categorically impair a President's performance of his Article II functions. The Solicitor General, [on the other hand,] urges us to resolve this case by holding

---

[5]   While the subpoena was directed to the President's accounting firm, the parties agree that the papers at issue belong to the President and that Mazars is merely the custodian. Thus, for purposes of immunity, it is functionally a subpoena issued to the President.

that a state grand jury subpoena for a sitting President's personal records must, at the very least, "satisfy a heightened standard of need," which the Solicitor General contends was not met here.

A

We begin with the question of absolute immunity. . . . To be clear, the President does not contend here that *this* subpoena, in particular, is impermissibly burdensome. Instead he makes a *categorical* argument about the burdens generally associated with state criminal subpoenas, focusing on three: diversion, stigma, and harassment. We address each in turn.

1

The President's primary contention, which the Solicitor General supports, is that complying with state criminal subpoenas would necessarily divert the Chief Executive from his duties. . . . But *Nixon v. Fitzgerald* did not hold that distraction was sufficient to confer absolute immunity. . . . Indeed, we expressly rejected immunity based on distraction alone 15 years later in *Clinton v. Jones*. . . . The Court recognized that Presidents constantly face myriad demands on their attention, "some private, some political, and some as a result of official duty." But, the Court concluded, "[w]hile such distractions may be vexing to those subjected to them, they do not ordinarily implicate constitutional . . . concerns." *Clinton v. Jones*.

The same is true of criminal subpoenas. . . . If anything, we expect that in the mine run of cases, where a President is subpoenaed during a proceeding targeting someone else, as Jefferson was, the burden on a President will ordinarily be lighter than the burden of defending against a civil suit.

The President, however, believes the district attorney is investigating him and his businesses. In such a situation, he contends, the "toll that criminal process . . . exacts from the President is even heavier" than the distraction at issue in *Fitzgerald* and *Clinton*, because "criminal litigation" poses unique burdens on the President's time and will generate a "considerable if not overwhelming degree of mental preoccupation." But the President is not seeking immunity from the diversion occasioned by the prospect of future criminal *liability*. Instead he concedes—consistent with the position of the Department of Justice—that state grand juries are free to investigate a sitting President with an eye toward charging him after the completion of his term. The President's objection therefore must be limited to the *additional* distraction caused by the subpoena itself.

But that argument runs up against the 200 years of precedent establishing that Presidents, and their official communications, are subject to judicial process, even when the President is under investigation.

2

The President next claims that the stigma of being subpoenaed will undermine his leadership at home and abroad. Notably, the Solicitor General does not endorse this argument, perhaps because we have twice denied absolute immunity claims by Presidents in cases involving allegations of serious misconduct. *See Clinton*; *Nixon*.

But even if a tarnished reputation were a cognizable impairment, there is nothing inherently stigmatizing about a President performing "the citizen's normal duty of . . . furnishing information relevant" to a criminal investigation. *Branzburg v. Hayes* (1972). . . .

3

Finally, the President and the Solicitor General warn that subjecting Presidents to state criminal subpoenas will make them "easily identifiable target[s]" for harassment. *Fitzgerald*. . . .

We recognize, as does the district attorney, that harassing subpoenas could, under certain circumstances, threaten the independence or effectiveness of the Executive. Even so, in *Clinton* we found that the risk of harassment was not "serious" because federal courts have the tools to deter and, where necessary, dismiss vexatious civil suits. And, while we cannot ignore the possibility that state prosecutors may have political motivations, here again the law already seeks to protect against the predicted abuse.

First, grand juries are prohibited from engaging in "arbitrary fishing expeditions" and initiating investigations "out of malice or an intent to harass." *United States v. R. Enterprises, Inc.* (1991). . . . And, in the event of such harassment, a President would be entitled to the protection of federal courts. The policy against federal interference in state criminal proceedings, while strong, allows "intervention in those cases where the District Court properly finds that the state proceeding is motivated by a desire to harass or is conducted in bad faith." *Huffman v. Pursue, Ltd.* (1975). . . . Second, . . . [a]ny effort to manipulate a President's policy decisions or to "retaliate" against a President for official acts through issuance of a subpoena [would] be an unconstitutional attempt to "influence" a superior sovereign "exempt" from such obstacles, *see McCulloch v. Maryland* (1819). . . .

Given these safeguards and the Court's precedents, we cannot conclude that absolute immunity is necessary or appropriate under Article II or the Supremacy Clause. Our dissenting colleagues agree. . . . On that point the Court is unanimous.

B

We next consider whether a state grand jury subpoena seeking a President's private papers must satisfy a heightened need standard. The Solicitor General would require a threshold showing that the evidence sought is "critical" for "specific charging decisions" and that the subpoena is a "last resort," meaning the evidence is "not available from any other source" and is needed "now, rather than at the end of the President's term." . . .

We disagree, for [two] reasons. First, such a heightened standard would extend protection designed for official documents to the President's private papers. . . . [T]he relevant passage from *Burr* [is]: "If there be a paper in the possession of the executive, which is *not of an official nature*, he must stand, as respects that paper, in nearly the same situation with any other individual" (emphasis added). And it is only "nearly"—and not "entirely"—because the President retains the right to assert privilege over documents that, while ostensibly private, "partake of the character of an official paper." . . .

[Second, given the trial protections discussed in Part III.A.3], the public interest in fair and effective law enforcement cuts in favor of comprehensive access to evidence. Requiring a state grand jury to meet a heightened standard of need would hobble the grand jury's ability to acquire "all information that might possibly bear on its investigation." *R. Enterprises, Inc.* And, even assuming the evidence withheld under that standard were preserved until the conclusion of a President's term, in the interim the State would be deprived of investigative leads that the evidence might yield, allowing memories to fade and documents to disappear. . . .

Rejecting a heightened need standard does not leave Presidents with "no real protection." *Post* (opinion of Alito, J.). To start, a President may avail himself of the same protections available to every other citizen. These include the right to challenge the subpoena on any grounds permitted by state law, which usually include bad faith and undue burden or breadth. . . . Furthermore, . . .

[a] President can raise subpoena-specific constitutional challenges, in either a state or federal forum. As previously noted, he can [also] challenge the subpoena as an attempt to influence the performance of his official duties, in violation of the Supremacy Clause. . . . In addition, the Executive can . . . argue that compliance with a particular subpoena would impede his constitutional duties. . . .

* * *

Two hundred years ago, a great jurist of our Court established that no citizen, not even the President, is categorically above the common duty to produce evidence when called upon in a criminal proceeding. We reaffirm that principle today. . . . The "guard[ ] furnished to this high officer" lies where it always has—in "the conduct of a court" applying established legal and constitutional principles to individual subpoenas in a manner that preserves both the independence of the Executive and the integrity of the criminal justice system. *Burr.*

. . . We affirm the judgment of the Court of Appeals and remand the case for further proceedings consistent with this opinion. . . .

JUSTICE KAVANAUGH, with whom JUSTICE GORSUCH joins, concurring in the judgment.

The question here . . . is how to balance the State's interests and the Article II interests. The longstanding precedent that has applied to federal criminal subpoenas for official, privileged Executive Branch information is *United States v. Nixon* (1974). That landmark case requires that a prosecutor establish a "demonstrated, specific need" for the President's information. Cf. *Senate Select Committee on Presidential Campaign Activities v. Nixon* (CADC 1974) (en banc) (similar standard for congressional subpoenas to the Executive Branch). . . . Because this case again entails a clash between the interests of the criminal process and the Article II interests of the Presidency, I would apply the longstanding *Nixon* "demonstrated, specific need" standard to this case. . . .

In any event, in my view, lower courts in cases of this sort involving a President will almost invariably have to begin by delving into why the State wants the information; why and how much the State needs the information, including whether the State could obtain the information elsewhere; and whether compliance with the subpoena would unduly burden or interfere with a President's official duties. . . .

I agree that the case should be remanded to the District Court for further proceedings, where the President may raise constitutional and legal objections to the state grand jury subpoena as appropriate.

Justice Thomas, dissenting.

. . . The President argues that he is absolutely immune from the issuance of any subpoena, but that if the Court disagrees, we should remand so that the District Court can develop a record about this particular subpoena. I agree with the majority that the President is not entitled to absolute immunity from *issuance* of the subpoena. But he [is] entitled to relief against its *enforcement* [if he] can show that "his duties as chief magistrate demand his whole time for national objects," *United States v. Burr* (C.C. Va. 1807). . . . I would vacate and remand to allow the District Court to [make that determination]. Accordingly, I respectfully dissent.

Justice Alito, dissenting.

. . . If a sitting President were charged in New York County, would he be arrested and fingerprinted? He would presumably be required to appear for arraignment in criminal court, where the judge would set the conditions for his release. Could he be sent to Rikers Island or be required to post bail? Could the judge impose restrictions on his travel? If the President were scheduled to travel abroad—perhaps to attend a G-7 meeting—would he have to get judicial approval? If the President were charged with a complicated offense requiring a long trial, would he have to put his Presidential responsibilities aside for weeks on end while sitting in a Manhattan courtroom? While the trial was in progress, would aides be able to approach him and whisper in his ear about pressing matters? Would he be able to obtain a recess whenever he needed to speak with an aide at greater length or attend to an urgent matter, such as speaking with a foreign leader? Could he effectively carry out all his essential Presidential responsibilities after the trial day ended and at the same time adequately confer with his trial attorneys regarding his defense? Or should he be expected to give up the right to attend his own trial and be tried in absentia? And if he were convicted, could he be imprisoned? Would aides be installed in a nearby cell?

This entire imagined scene is farcical. . . . It is not enough to recite sayings like "no man is above the law" and "the public has a right to every man's evidence." These sayings are true—and important—but they beg the question. The law applies equally to all persons, including a person who happens for a period of time to occupy the Presidency. But there is no question that the nature of the office demands in some instances that the application of laws be adjusted at least until the person's term in office ends. . . .

I agree with the Court that not all such subpoenas should be barred. There may be situations in which there is an urgent and critical need for the subpoenaed information. The situation in the Burr trial, where the documents at issue were sought by a criminal defendant to defend against a charge of treason, is a good example. But in a case like the one at hand, a subpoena should not be allowed unless a heightened standard is met. [Justice Alito earlier describes that standard as "taking into account the need to prevent interference with a President's discharge of the responsibilities of the office."] Respect for the structure of Government created by the Constitution demands greater protection for an institution that is vital to the Nation's safety and well-being. I therefore respectfully dissent.

Trump v. Mazars USA

Supreme Court of the United States, 2020.
140 S. Ct. 2019.

CHIEF JUSTICE ROBERTS delivered the opinion of the Court.

Over the course of five days in April 2019, three committees of the U. S. House of Representatives issued four subpoenas seeking information about the finances of President Donald J. Trump, his children, and affiliated businesses. We have held that the House has authority under the Constitution to issue subpoenas to assist it in carrying out its legislative responsibilities. The House asserts that the financial information sought here—encompassing a decade's worth of transactions by the President and his family—will help guide legislative reform in areas ranging from money laundering and terrorism to foreign involvement in U.S. elections. The President contends that the House lacked a valid legislative aim and instead sought these records to harass him, expose personal matters, and conduct law enforcement activities beyond its authority. The question presented is whether the subpoenas exceed the authority of the House under the Constitution.

We have never addressed a congressional subpoena for the President's information. . . . Here the President's information is sought not by prosecutors or private parties in connection with a particular judicial proceeding, but by committees of Congress that have set forth broad legislative objectives. . . .

A

Each of the three committees sought overlapping sets of financial documents, but each supplied different justifications for the requests. . . .

SUMMARY OF THE FACTS

The House Committee on Financial Services served subpoenas on two banks, seeking Trump's financial records since at least 2010 as part of an effort to "close loopholes that allow corruption, terrorism, and money laundering to infiltrate our country's financial system," and to "examine the implementation, effectiveness, and enforcement" of laws designed to prevent money laundering and the financing of terrorism. The Permanent Select Committee on Intelligence issued an identical subpoena to one of the banks as part of an investigation into alleged attempts by Russia to influence the 2016 election and in connection with "legislation and policy reforms to . . . counter future efforts to undermine our political process and national security." The House Committee on Oversight and Reform issued a subpoena to the President's personal accounting firm for Trump's financial records since at least 2011 as part of an investigation of whether the President "engaged in illegal conduct before and during his tenure in office," "has undisclosed conflicts of interest," "is complying with the Emoluments Clauses of the Constitution," and "has accurately reported his finances to the Office of Government Ethics."

II

A

The question presented is whether the subpoenas exceed the authority of the House under the Constitution. Historically, disputes over congressional demands for presidential documents have not ended up in court. Instead, they have been hashed out in the "hurly-burly, the give-and-take of the political process between the legislative and the executive."

That practice began with George Washington and the early Congress. [In response to a House Committee request for documents relating to a military defeat in a campaign against Native American tribes in the Northwest Territory in 1792, the Cabinet concluded that the House had authority to "call for papers" but that the President could "exercise a discretion" over disclosures.] President Washington then dispatched Jefferson to speak to individual congressmen and "bring them by persuasion into the right channel." The discussions were apparently fruitful, as the House later narrowed its request and the documents were supplied without recourse to the courts. . . . Ever since, congressional demands for the President's information have been resolved by the political branches without involving this Court. . . .

Congress and the President maintained this tradition of negotiation and compromise—without the involvement of this Court—until the present dispute. Indeed, from President Washington until now, we have never considered a dispute over a congressional subpoena for the President's records. And, according to the parties, the appellate courts have addressed such a subpoena only once, when a Senate committee subpoenaed President Nixon during the Watergate scandal. In that case, the court refused to enforce the subpoena, and the Senate did not seek review by this Court.

This dispute therefore represents a significant departure from historical practice. . . . With that in mind, we turn to the question presented.

B

Congress has no enumerated constitutional power to conduct investigations or issue subpoenas, but we have held that each House has power "to secure needed information" in order to legislate. *McGrain v. Daugherty* (1927). This "power of inquiry—with process to enforce it—is an essential and appropriate auxiliary to the legislative function." Without information, Congress would be shooting in the dark, unable to legislate "wisely or effectively." The congressional power to obtain information is "broad" and "indispensable." *Watkins v. United States* (1957). It encompasses inquiries into the administration of existing laws, studies of proposed laws, and "surveys of defects in our social, economic or political system for the purpose of enabling the Congress to remedy them."

Because this power is "justified solely as an adjunct to the legislative process," it is subject to several limitations. *Watkins v. United States* (1957). Most importantly, a congressional subpoena is valid only if it is "related to, and in furtherance of, a legitimate task of the Congress." *Id.* The subpoena must serve a "valid legislative purpose," *Quinn v. United States* (1955); it must "concern[ ] a subject on which legislation 'could be had,' " *Eastland v. United States Servicemen's Fund* (1975).

Furthermore, Congress may not issue a subpoena for the purpose of "law enforcement," because "those powers are assigned under our Constitution to the Executive and the Judiciary." *Quinn.* Thus Congress may not use subpoenas to "try" someone "before [a] committee for any crime or wrongdoing." *McGrain.* Congress has no " 'general' power to inquire into private affairs and compel disclosures," and "there is no congressional power to expose for the sake of exposure," *Watkins.* "Investigations conducted solely for the personal aggrandizement of the investigators or to 'punish' those investigated are indefensible."

Finally, recipients of legislative subpoenas retain their constitutional rights throughout the course of an investigation. And recipients have long been understood to retain common law and constitutional privileges with respect to certain materials, such as attorney-client communications and governmental communications protected by executive privilege.

C

The President contends, as does the Solicitor General appearing on behalf of the United States, that the usual rules for congressional subpoenas do not govern here because the President's papers are at issue. They argue for a more demanding standard based in large part on cases involving the Nixon tapes . . . *See United States v. Nixon* (1974) and *Senate Select Committee on Presidential Campaign Activities v. Nixon* (D.C. Cir. 1974).

Those cases, the President and the Solicitor General now contend, establish the standard that should govern the House subpoenas here. Quoting *Nixon,* the President asserts that the House must establish a "demonstrated, specific need" for the financial information, just as the Watergate special prosecutor was required to do in order to obtain the tapes. And drawing on *Senate Select Committee*—the D. C. Circuit case refusing to enforce the Senate subpoena for the tapes—the President and the Solicitor General argue that the House must show that the financial information is "demonstrably critical" to its legislative purpose.

We disagree that these demanding standards apply here. Unlike the cases before us, *Nixon* and *Senate Select Committee* involved Oval Office communications over which the President asserted executive privilege. That privilege safeguards the public interest in candid, confidential deliberations within the Executive Branch; it is "fundamental to the operation of Government." *Nixon.* As a result, information subject to executive privilege deserves "the greatest protection consistent with the fair administration of justice." *Id.* We decline to transplant that protection root and branch to cases involving nonprivileged, private information, which by definition does not implicate sensitive Executive Branch deliberations.

The standards proposed by the President and the Solicitor General—if applied outside the context of privileged information—would risk seriously impeding Congress in carrying out its responsibilities. . . .

> It is the proper duty of a representative body to look diligently into every affair of government and to talk much about what it sees. It is meant to be the eyes and the voice, and to embody the wisdom and will of its constituents. Unless Congress have and use every means of acquainting itself with the acts and the disposition of the administrative agents of the government, the country must be helpless to learn how it is being served.

United States v. Rumely (1953). . . . Legislative inquiries might involve the President in appropriate cases; as noted, Congress's responsibilities extend to "every affair of government." *Rumely.* Because the President's approach does not take adequate account of these significant congressional interests, we do not adopt it.

D

The House meanwhile would have us ignore that these suits involve the President. Invoking our precedents concerning investigations that did not target the President's papers, the House urges us to uphold its subpoenas because they "relate[ ] to a valid legislative purpose" or "concern[ ] a subject on which legislation could be had." That approach is appropriate, the House argues, because the cases before us are not "momentous separation-of-powers disputes." . . .

The House's approach fails to take adequate account of the significant separation of powers issues raised by congressional subpoenas for the President's information. Congress and the President have an ongoing institutional relationship as the "opposite and rival" political branches established by the Constitution. *The Federalist* No. 51. As a result, congressional subpoenas directed at the President differ markedly from congressional subpoenas we have previously reviewed, *e.g., Eastland,* and they bear little resemblance to criminal subpoenas issued to the President in the course of a specific investigation, see *Vance; Nixon.* Unlike those subpoenas, congressional subpoenas for the President's information unavoidably pit the political branches against one another.

Far from accounting for separation of powers concerns, the House's approach aggravates them by leaving essentially no limits on the congressional power to subpoena the President's personal records. Any personal paper possessed by a President could potentially "relate to" a conceivable subject of legislation, for Congress has broad legislative powers that touch a vast number of subjects. The President's financial records could relate to economic reform, medical records to health reform, school transcripts to education reform, and so on. Indeed, at argument, the House was unable to identify *any* type of information that lacks some relation to potential legislation.

Without limits on its subpoena powers, Congress could "exert an imperious controul" over the Executive Branch and aggrandize itself at the President's expense, just as the Framers feared. *Bowsher v. Synar* (1986). And a limitless subpoena power would transform the "established practice" of the political branches. *NLRB v. Noel Canning* (2014). Instead of negotiating over information requests, Congress could simply walk away from the bargaining table and compel compliance in court. . . .

The interbranch conflict here does not vanish simply because the subpoenas seek personal papers or because the President sued in his personal capacity. The President is the only person who alone composes a branch of government. As a result, there is not always a clear line between his personal and official affairs. . . . In fact, a subpoena for personal papers may pose a heightened risk of such impermissible purposes, precisely because of the documents' personal nature and their less evident connection to a legislative task. No one can say that the controversy here is less significant to the relationship between the branches simply because it involves personal papers. Quite the opposite. That appears to be what makes the matter of such great consequence to the President and Congress.

In addition, separation of powers concerns are no less palpable here simply because the subpoenas were issued to third parties. Congressional demands for the President's information present an interbranch conflict no matter where the information is held—it is, after all, the President's information. Were it otherwise, Congress could sidestep constitutional requirements any time a President's information is entrusted to a third party—as occurs with rapidly increasing frequency. Indeed, Congress could declare open season on the President's information held by schools, archives, internet service providers, e-mail clients, and financial institutions. The Constitution does not tolerate such ready evasion. . . .

E

. . . A balanced approach is necessary, one that takes a "considerable impression" from "the practice of the government," *McCulloch v. Maryland* (1819), and "resist[s]" the "pressure inherent within each of the separate Branches to exceed the outer limits of its power," *INS v. Chadha* (1983). We therefore conclude that, in assessing whether a subpoena directed at the President's personal information is "related to, and in furtherance of, a legitimate task of the Congress," *Watkins*, courts must perform a careful analysis that takes adequate account of the separation of powers principles at stake, including both the significant legislative interests of Congress and the "unique position" of the President, *Clinton*. Several special considerations inform this analysis.

First, courts should carefully assess whether the asserted legislative purpose warrants the significant step of involving the President and his papers. . . . Congress may not rely on the President's information if other sources could reasonably provide Congress the information it needs in light of its particular legislative objective. The President's unique constitutional position means that Congress may not look to him as a "case study" for general legislation. Unlike in criminal proceedings, where "[t]he very integrity of the judicial system" would be undermined without "full disclosure of all the facts," *Nixon*, efforts to craft legislation involve predictive policy judgments that are "not hamper[ed] . . . in quite the same way" when every scrap of potentially relevant evidence is not available, *Cheney v. U.S. District Court* (2004). . . .

Second, to narrow the scope of possible conflict between the branches, courts should insist on a subpoena no broader than reasonably necessary to support Congress's legislative objective. The specificity of the subpoena's request "serves as an important safeguard against unnecessary intrusion into the operation of the Office of the President." *Cheney*.

Third, courts should be attentive to the nature of the evidence offered by Congress to establish that a subpoena advances a valid legislative purpose. The more detailed and substantial the evidence of Congress's legislative purpose, the better. . . . That is particularly true when Congress contemplates legislation that raises sensitive constitutional issues, such as legislation concerning the Presidency. In such cases, it is "impossible" to conclude that a subpoena is designed to advance a valid legislative purpose unless Congress adequately identifies its aims and explains why the President's information will advance its consideration of the possible legislation. *Watkins*.

Fourth, courts should be careful to assess the burdens imposed on the President by a subpoena. We have held that burdens on the President's time and attention stemming from judicial process and litigation, without more, generally do not cross constitutional lines. See *Vance*; *Clinton*. But burdens imposed by a congressional subpoena should be carefully scrutinized, for they stem from a rival political branch that has an ongoing relationship with the President and incentives to use subpoenas for institutional advantage.

Other considerations may be pertinent as well; one case every two centuries does not afford enough experience for an exhaustive list.

When Congress seeks information "needed for intelligent legislative action," it "unquestionably" remains "the duty of *all* citizens to cooperate." *Watkins* (emphasis added). Congressional subpoenas for information from the President, however, implicate special concerns regarding the separation of powers. The courts below did not take adequate account of those concerns. The judgments of the Courts of Appeals for the D. C. Circuit and the Second Circuit are vacated, and the cases are remanded for further proceedings consistent with this opinion.

It is so ordered.

Justice Thomas, dissenting.

. . . I would hold that Congress has no power to issue a legislative subpoena for private, nonofficial documents—whether they belong to the President or not. . . . At the time of the founding, the power to subpoena private, nonofficial documents was not included by necessary implication in any of Congress' legislative powers. . . .

If the Committees wish to investigate alleged wrongdoing by the President and obtain documents from him, the Constitution provides Congress with a special mechanism for doing so: impeachment. . . . I express no view today on the boundaries of the power to demand documents in connection with impeachment proceedings. But the power of impeachment provides the House with authority to investigate and hold accountable Presidents who commit high crimes or misdemeanors. That is the proper path by which the Committees should pursue their demands. . . .

Justice Alito, dissenting.

. . . I agree that the lower courts erred and that these cases must be remanded, but I do not think that the considerations outlined by the Court can be properly satisfied unless the House is required to show more than it has put forward to date.

Specifically, the House should provide a description of the type of legislation being considered, and while great specificity is not necessary, the description should be sufficient to permit a court to assess whether the particular records sought are of any special importance. The House should also spell out its constitutional authority to enact the type of legislation that it is contemplating, and it should justify the scope of the subpoenas in relation to the articulated legislative needs. In addition, it should explain why the subpoenaed information, as opposed to information available from other sources, is needed. Unless the House is required to make a showing along these lines, I would hold that enforcement of the subpoenas cannot be ordered. Because I find the terms of the Court's remand inadequate, I must respectfully dissent.

---

3.   Impeaching the President

The ultimate constitutional remedy for presidential misbehavior is the impeachment process, which can result in the President's removal from office. Removing the President by this mechanism is extremely hard to do. First, a majority of the House must vote in favor of impeachment; then, after the Senate "trial" that is triggered by the House's vote, two-thirds of the Senate must vote to remove. Three Presidents have been impeached: Andrew Johnson, Bill Clinton, and Donald Trump (twice). None of them were removed (the second Trump impeachment trial was held after his term expired), and only the vote on Johnson came close to the requisite supermajority. The impeachment process did, however, result in Richard Nixon's departure from office. He resigned shortly after the House Judiciary Committee approved three articles of impeachment against him; his ultimate decision was prompted by the public reaction to the tapes released because of the decision in *United States v. Nixon*.

Not just the President, but all "civil officers of the United States," are subject to the impeachment process, which Hamilton labeled "a method of NATIONAL INQUEST into the conduct of public men." *The Federalist*, No. 65. In fact, impeachment has most often been invoked against federal judges.

As You READ The following materials begin with the relevant constitutional text and a famous statement by then-Representative Gerald Ford on the differences between impeachment of judges and of other officers. We will then turn to the impeachment of Richard Nixon in 1974 as a case study. Try to decide how you would have voted on each count against Nixon if you were in the House or the Senate—and whether your partisan affiliation and other policy goals would have been legally or ethically appropriate considerations in your decision.

U.S. Constitution

Art. II, § 4	The President, Vice President and all civil officers of the United States, shall be removed from office on impeachment for, and conviction of, treason, bribery, or other high crimes and misdemeanors.
Art. III, § 1	The Judges, both of the supreme and inferior Courts, shall hold their Offices during good Behaviour. . . .
Art. I, § 2, cl. 5	The House of Representatives shall chuse their Speaker and other Officers; and shall have the sole Power of Impeachment.
Art. I, § 3, cl. 6–7	The Senate shall have the sole Power to try all Impeachments. When sitting for that Purpose, they shall be on Oath or Affirmation. When the President of the United States is tried the Chief Justice shall preside; And no Person shall be convicted without the Concurrence of two thirds of the Members present.
	Judgement in Cases of Impeachment shall not extend further than to removal from Office, and disqualification to hold and enjoy any Office of honor, Trust or Profit under the United States: but the Party convicted shall nevertheless be liable and subject to Indictment, Trial, Judgement and Punishment, according to Law.

Rep. Gerald Ford, Speech on Proposed Impeachment of Justice William Douglas

April 15, 1970
116 Cong. Rec. 11,912–14

[I] endeavor[ ] to correct two common misconceptions: first, that Federal judges are appointed for life and, second, that they can be removed only by being convicted, with all ordinary protections and presumptions of innocence to which an accused is entitled, of violating the law. This is not the case. Federal judges can be and have been impeached for improper personal habits such as chronic intoxication on the bench, and one of the charges brought against President Andrew Johnson was that he delivered "intemperate, inflammatory and scandalous harangues."

I have studied the principal impeachment actions that have been initiated over the years and frankly, there are too few cases to make very good law. About the only thing the authorities can agree upon in recent history, though it was [previously] hotly argued up to President Johnson's impeachment and the trial of Judge Swayne, is that an offense need not be indictable to be impeachable. In other words, something less than a criminal act or criminal dereliction of duty may nevertheless be sufficient grounds for impeachment and removal from public office.

What, then, is an impeachable offense? The only honest answer is that an impeachable offense is whatever a majority of the House of Representatives considers to be at a given moment in history; conviction results from whatever offense or offenses two-thirds of the other body considers to be sufficiently serious to require removal of the accused from office.

Again, the historical context and political climate are important; there are few fixed principles among the handful of precedents. I think it is fair to come to one conclusion, however, from our history of impeachments: a higher standard is expected of Federal judges than of any other "civil officers" of the United States. The President and Vice President, and all persons holding office at the pleasure of the President, can be thrown out of office by the voters at least every 4 years. To remove them in midterm—it has been tried only twice and never done—would indeed require crimes of the magnitude of treason and bribery. Other elective officials such as Members of the Congress, are so vulnerable to public displeasure that their removal by the complicated impeachment route has not even been tried since 1798. But nine Federal judges, including one Associate Justice of the Supreme Court, have been impeached by this House and tried by the Senate; four were acquitted; four convicted and removed from office; and one resigned during trial and the impeachment was dismissed.

WORTH NOTING Justice Douglas was not impeached, but five more federal judges have been since Ford's speech. Four were convicted and removed, and one resigned during the trial.

Staff Report, House Judiciary Committee, Constitutional Grounds for Presidential Impeachment

Report by the staff of the Impeachment Inquiry,
House Judiciary Committee
February 1974

. . . II. The Historical Origins of Impeachment

. . . B. The Intention of the Framers

. . . 2. Adoption of "High Crimes and Misdemeanors"

Briefly, and late in the convention, the framers addressed the question how to describe the grounds for impeachment consistent with its intended function. They did so only after the mode of the President's election was settled in a way that did not make him (in the words of James Wilson) "the Minion of the Senate."

The draft of the Constitution then before the Convention provided for his removal upon impeachment and conviction for "treason or bribery." George Mason objected that these grounds were too limited. . . . Mason then moved to add the word "maladministration" to the other two grounds. Maladministration was a term in use in six of the thirteen state constitutions as a ground for impeachment, including Mason's home state of Virginia. When James Madison objected that "so vague a term will be equivalent to a tenure during pleasure of the Senate," Mason withdrew "maladministration" and substituted "high crimes and misdemeanors agst. the State," which was adopted eight states to three, apparently with no further debate.

That the framers were familiar with English parliamentary impeachment proceedings is clear. The impeachment of Warren Hastings, Governor-General of India, for high crimes and misdemeanors was voted just a few weeks before the beginning of the Constitutional Convention and George Mason referred to it in the debates. Hamilton, in the Federalist No. 65, referred to Great Britain as "the model from which [impeachment] has been borrowed." . . .

The Convention had earlier demonstrated its familiarity with the term "high misdeameanor." A draft constitution had used "high misdeameanor" in its provision for the extradition of offenders from one state to another. The Convention, apparently unanimously[,] struck "high misdemeanor" and inserted "other crime," "in order to comprehend all proper cases: it being doubtful whether 'high misdemeanor' had not a technical meaning too limited."

The "technical meaning" referred to is the parliamentary use of the term "high misdemeanor." Blackstone's *Commentaries on the Laws of England* . . . included "high misdemeanors" as one term for positive offenses "against the king and government." The "first and principal" high misdemeanor, according to Blackstone, was "mal-administration of such high officers, as are in public trust and employment," usually punished by the method of parliamentary impeachment. . . .

3. Grounds for Impeachment

Mason's suggestion to add "maladministration," Madison's objection to it as "vague," and Mason's substitution of "high crimes and misdemeanors against the State" are the only comments in the Philadelphia convention specifically directed to the constitutional language describing the grounds for impeachment of the President. Mason's objection to limiting the grounds to treason and bribery was that treason would "not reach many great and dangerous offences" including "[a]ttempts to subvert the Constitution." His willingness to substitute "high Crimes and Misdemeanors," especially given his apparent familiarity with the English use of the term as evidenced by his reference to the Warren Hastings impeachment, suggests that he believed "high Crimes and Misdemeanors" would cover the offenses about which he was concerned.

Contemporaneous comments on the scope of impeachment are persuasive as to the intention of the framers. In Federalist No. 65, Alexander Hamilton described the subject of impeachment as

> those offences which proceed from the misconduct of public men, or, in other words, from the abuse or violation of some public trust. They are of a nature which may with peculiar propriety be denominated

POLITICAL, as they relate chiefly to injuries done immediately to the society itself.

Comments in the state ratifying conventions also suggest that those who adopted the Constitution viewed impeachment as a remedy for usurpation or abuse of power or serious breach of trust. Thus, Charles Cotesworth Pinckney of South Carolina stated that the impeachment power of the House reaches "those who behave amiss, or betray their public trust." . . .

In short, the framers who discussed impeachment in the state ratifying conventions, as well as other delegates who favored the Constitution, implied that it reached offenses against the government, and especially abuses of constitutional duties. The opponents did not argue that the grounds for impeachment had been limited to criminal offenses.

An extensive discussion of the scope of the impeachment power occurred in the House of Representatives in the First Session of the First Congress. . . . Madison argued during [a debate over the power of the President to remove executive officers] that the President would be subject to impeachment for "the wanton removal of meritorious officers." He also contended that the power of the President unilaterally to remove subordinates was "absolutely necessary" because "it will make him in a peculiar manner, responsible for [the] conduct" of executive officers. It would, Madison said,

> subject him to impeachment himself, if he suffers them to perpetrate with impunity high crimes or misdemeanors against the United States, or neglects to superintend their conduct, so as to check their excesses.

Elbridge Gerry of Massachusetts, who had also been a framer though he had opposed the ratification of the Constitution, disagreed with Madison's contentions about the impeachability of the President. He could not be impeached for dismissing a good officer, Gerry said, because he would be "doing an act which the Legislature has submitted to his discretion." And he should not be held responsible for the acts of subordinate officers, who were themselves subject to impeachment and should bear their own responsibility.

Another framer, Abraham Baldwin of Georgia, . . . spoke of the President's impeachability for failure to perform the duties of the Executive. If, said Baldwin, the President "in a fit of passion" removed "all the good officers of the Government" and the Senate were unable to choose qualified successors, the consequence would be that the President "would be obliged to do the duties himself; or, if he did not, we would impeach him, and turn him out of office, as he had done others."

Elias Boudinot of New Jersey . . . suggested that disability resulting from sickness or accident "would not furnish any good ground for impeachment; it could not be laid as treason or bribery, nor perhaps as a high crime or misdemeanor." Fisher Ames of Massachusetts argued for the President's removal power because "mere intention [to do a mischief] would not be cause of impeachment" and "there may be numerous causes for removal which do not amount to a crime." Later in the same speech Ames suggested that impeachment was available if an officer "misbehaves" and for "mal-conduct." . . .

From the comments of the framers and their contemporaries, the remarks of the delegates to the state ratifying conventions, and the removal power debate in the First Congress, it is apparent that the scope of impeachment was not viewed narrowly. It was intended to provide a check on the President through impeachment, but not to make him dependent on the unbridled will of the Congress.

Impeachment, as Justice Joseph Story wrote in his *Commentaries on the Constitution* in 1833, applies to offenses of "a political character":

> Not but that crimes of a strictly legal character fall within the scope of the power . . . ; but that it has a more enlarged operation, and reaches, what are aptly termed political offenses, growing out of personal misconduct or gross neglect, or usurpation, or habitual disregard of the public interests, in the discharge of the duties of public office. These are so various in their character, and so indefinable in their actual involutions, that it is almost impossible to provide systematically for them by positive law. . . .

Minority Report, House Judiciary Committee, Impeachment of Richard M. Nixon, President of the United States

Report of the House Judiciary Committee, H.R. Rep. No. 93–1305
Minority Views of Ten Committee Members
Aug. 1974

. . . B. Meaning of "Treason, Bribery or other high Crimes and Misdemeanors"

. . . We do not believe that a President or any other civil officer of the United States government may constitutionally be impeached and convicted for errors in the administration of his office.

1. ADOPTION OF "TREASON, BRIBERY, OR OTHER HIGH CRIMES AND MISDEMEANORS" AT CONSTITUTIONAL CONVENTION

. . . A review of [the debate of July 20, 1787] hardly leaves the impression that the Framers intended the grounds for impeachment to be left to the discretion, even the "sound" discretion, of the legislature. On a fair reading, Madison's notes reveal the Framers' fear that the impeachment power would render the executive dependent on the legislature. The concrete examples used in the debate all refer not only to crimes, but to extremely grave crimes. . . . Edmund Randolph mentioned the great opportunities for abuse of the executive power, "particularly in time of war when the military force, and in some respects the public money will be in his hands." He cautioned against "tumults & insurrections." Gouverneur Morris similarly contemplated that the executive might corrupt his own electors or "be bribed by a greater interest to betray his trust"—just as the King of England had been bribed by Louis XIV—and felt he should therefore be impeachable for "treachery."

 WORTH NOTING — Nixon resigned before this Report was issued.

After the July 20 vote to retain the impeachment clause, the resolution containing it was referred to the Committee on Detail, which substituted "treason, bribery or corruption" for "mal-practice or neglect of duty." No surviving records explain the reasons for the change, but they are not difficult to understand, in light of the floor discussion just summarized. The change fairly captured the sense of the July 20 debate, in which the grounds for impeachment seem to have been such acts as would either cause danger to the very existence of the

United States, or involve the purchase and sale of the "Chief of Magistracy," which would tend to the same result. It is *not* a fair summary of this debate—which is the only surviving discussion of any length by the Framers as to the grounds for impeachment—to say that the Framers were principally concerned with reaching a course of conduct, whether or not criminal, generally inconsistent with the proper and effective exercise of the office of the presidency. They . . . steadfastly reiterated the importance of putting a check on the legislature's use of power and refused to expand the narrow definition they had given to treason in the Constitution. They saw punishment as a significant purpose of impeachment. . . .

[After elimination of the reference to corruption, the] revised clause, containing the grounds "treason and bribery," came before the full body again on September 8, late in the Convention. George Mason moved to add to the enumerated grounds for impeachment. Madison's Journal reflects the following exchange:

> Col. Mason. Why is the provision restrained to Treason & bribery only? Treason as defined in the Constitution will not reach many great and dangerous offenses. Hastings is not guilty of Treason. Attempts to subvert the Constitution may not be Treason as above defined—as bills of attainder which have saved the British Constitution are forbidden, it is the more necessary to extend: the power of impeachments. He movd. to add after "bribery" "or maladministration." Mr. Gerry seconded him—
>
> Mr. Madison. So vague a term will be equivalent to a tenure during pleasure of the Senate.
>
> Mr. Govr. Morris., it will not be put in force & can do no harm—An election of every four years will prevent maladministration.
>
> Col. Mason withdrew "maladministration" & substitutes "other high crimes and misdemeanors" agst. the State.
>
> On the question thus altered, the motion of Colonel Mason passed by a vote of eight states to three.

Madison's notes reveal no debate as to the meaning of the phrase "other high Crimes and Misdemeanors." All that appears is that Mason was concerned with the narrowness of the definition of treason; that his purpose in proposing "maladministration" was to reach *great* and *dangerous* offenses; and that Madison felt that "maladministration," which was included as a ground for impeachment of public officials in the constitutions of six states, including his own, would be too "vague" and would imperil the independence of the President.

It is our judgment, based upon this constitutional history, that the Framers of the United States Constitution intended that the President should be removable by the legislative branch only for serious misconduct dangerous to the system of government established by the Constitution. . . . We have never had a British parliamentary system in this country, and we have never adopted the device of a parliamentary vote of no-confidence in the chief executive. If it is thought desirable to adopt such a system of government, the proper way to do so is by amending our written Constitution—not by removing the President.

2. ARE "HIGH CRIMES AND MISDEMEANORS" NON-CRIMINAL?

a.   *Language of the Constitution*

The language of the Constitution indicates that impeachment can lie only for serious criminal offenses.

First, of course, treason and bribery were indictable offenses in 1787, as they are now. The words "crime" and "misdemeanor," as well, both had an accepted meaning in the English law of the day, and referred to criminal acts. . . .

c.   *American impeachment practice*

The impeachment of President Andrew Johnson is the most important precedent for a consideration of what constitutes grounds for impeachment of a President, even if it has been historically regarded (and probably fairly so) as an excessively partisan exercise of the impeachment power.

The Johnson impeachment was the product of a fundamental and bitter split between the President and the Congress as to Reconstruction policy in the Southern states following the Civil War. Johnson's vetoes of legislation, his use of pardons, and his choice of appointees in the South all made it impossible for the Reconstruction Acts to be enforced in the manner which Congress not only desired, but thought urgently necessary.

[A first attempt to impeach Johnson in 1867 was beaten decisively.] Earlier in 1867, the Congress had passed the Tenure-of-Office Act, which took away the President's authority to remove members of his own Cabinet, and provided that violation of the Act should be punishable by imprisonment of up to five

years and a fine of up to ten thousand dollars and "shall be deemed a high misdemeanor"—fair notice that Congress would consider violation of the statute
an impeachable, as well as a criminal, offense. . . .

Two and a half months later, however, Johnson removed Stanton from
office, in apparent disregard of the Tenure-of-Office Act. The response of Congress was immediate: Johnson was impeached three days later, on February 24,
1868, by a vote of 128 to 47—an even greater margin than that by which the
first impeachment vote had failed.

The reversal is a dramatic demonstration that the House of Representatives
believed it had to find the President guilty of a crime before impeaching him. . . .

Rep. Barbara Jordan, Speech on the Impeachment of President Richard Nixon

House Judiciary Committee, 1974

We know the nature of impeachment. We have been talking about it
awhile now. It is chiefly designed for the President and his high ministers to
somehow be called into account. It is designed to "bridle" the Executive if he
engages in excesses. It is designed as a method of national inquest into the
conduct of public men. The framers confined in the Congress the power, if
need be, to remove the President in order to strike a delicate balance between
a President swollen with power and grown tyrannical and preservation of the
independence of the Executive.

The nature of impeachment is a narrowly channeled exception to the separation of powers maxim; the federal convention of 1787 said that. It limited
impeachment to high crimes and misdemeanors and discounted and opposed
the term, "maladministration." "It is to be used only for great misdemeanors,"
so it was said in the North Carolina ratification convention. . . . The drawing of
political lines goes to the motivation behind impeachment; but impeachment
must proceed within the confines of the constitutional term, "high crime and
misdemeanors." Of the impeachment process, it was Woodrow Wilson who
said that "nothing short of the grossest offenses against the plain law of the
land will suffice to give them speed and effectiveness. Indignation so great as
to overgrow party interest may secure a conviction; but nothing else can." . . .

Beginning shortly after the Watergate break-in and continuing to the present time, the President has engaged in a series of public statements and actions designed to thwart the lawful investigation by government prosecutors. Moreover, the President has made public announcements and assertions bearing on the Watergate case which the evidence will show he knew to be false. These assertions, false assertions; impeachable, those who misbehave. Those who "behave amiss or betray their public trust." . . .

James Madison, again at the constitutional convention: "A President is impeachable if he attempts to subvert the Constitution." The Constitution charges the President with the task of taking care that the laws be faithfully executed, and yet the President has counseled his aides to commit perjury, willfully disregarded the secrecy of grand jury proceedings, concealed surreptitious entry, attempted to compromise a federal judge while publicly displaying his cooperation with the process of criminal justice. "A President is impeachable if he attempts to subvert the Constitution."

Has the President committed offenses and planned and directed and acquiesced in a course of conduct which the Constitution will not tolerate? This is the question. We know that. We know the question. We should now forthwith proceed to answer the question.

The charges referred to by Representative Jordan were laid out in detail in the following Articles of Impeachment. While approved by the House Judiciary Committee, the Articles never made it to the Senate; Nixon resigned before the House could vote on which (if any) of the charges to approve for Senate trial.

Articles of Impeachment Exhibited by the House of Representatives of the United States of America in the Name of Itself and of All of the People of the United States of America, Against Richard M. Nixon, President of the United States of America, in Maintenance and Support of Its Impeachment Against Him for High Crimes and Misdemeanours

Article 1

In his conduct of the office of President of the United States, Richard M. Nixon, in violation of his constitutional oath faithfully to execute the office of President of the United States and, to the best of his ability, preserve, protect, and defend the Constitution of the United States, and in violation of his constitutional duty to take care that the laws be faithfully executed, has prevented, obstructed, and impeded the administration of justice, in that:

On June 17, 1972, and prior thereto, agents of the Committee for the Re-election of the President committed unlawful entry of the headquarters of the Democratic National Committee in Washington, District of Columbia, for the purpose of securing political intelligence. Subsequent thereto, Richard M. Nixon, using the powers of his high office, engaged personally and through his close subordinates and agents, in a course of conduct or plan designed to delay, impede, and obstruct the investigation of such illegal entry; to cover up, conceal and protect those responsible; and to conceal the existence and scope of other unlawful covert activities.

The means used to implement this course of conduct or plan included one or more of the following:

1.   making false or misleading statements to lawfully authorized investigative officers and employees of the United States;

2.   withholding relevant and material evidence or information from lawfully authorized investigative officers and employees of the United States;

3.   approving, condoning, acquiescing in, and counselling witnesses with respect to the giving of false or misleading statements to lawfully authorized investigative officers and employees of the United States and false or misleading testimony in duly instituted judicial and congressional proceedings;

4.   interfering or endeavouring to interfere with the conduct of investigations by the Department of Justice of the United States, the Federal Bureau of Investigation, the office of Watergate Special Prosecution Force, and Congressional Committees;

5.   approving, condoning, and acquiescing in, the surreptitious payment of substantial sums of money for the purpose of obtaining the silence or influencing the testimony of witnesses, potential witnesses or individuals who participated in such unlawful entry and other illegal activities;

6.   endeavouring to misuse the Central Intelligence Agency, an agency of the United States;

7.   disseminating information received from officers of the Department of Justice of the United States to subjects of investigations conducted by lawfully authorized investigative officers and employees of the United States, for the purpose of aiding and assisting such subjects in their attempts to avoid criminal liability;

8.   making or causing to be made false or misleading public statements for the purpose of deceiving the people of the United States into believing that a thorough and complete investigation had been conducted with respect to allegations of misconduct on the part of personnel of the executive branch of the United States and personnel of the Committee for the Re-election of the President, and that there was no involvement of such personnel in such misconduct; or

9.   endeavouring to cause prospective defendants, and individuals duly tried and convicted, to expect favoured treatment and consideration in return for their silence or false testimony, or rewarding individuals for their silence or false testimony.

In all of this, Richard M. Nixon has acted in a manner contrary to his trust as President and subversive of constitutional government, to the great prejudice of the cause of law and justice and to the manifest injury of the people of the United States.

Wherefore Richard M. Nixon, by such conduct, warrants impeachment and trial, and removal from office.

Adopted 27–11 by the Committee on the Judiciary of the House of Representatives, at 7:07pm on Saturday, 27th July, 1974, in Room 2141 of the Rayburn Office Building, Washington D.C.

Article 2

Using the powers of the office of President of the United States, Richard M. Nixon, in violation of his constitutional oath faithfully to execute the office of President of the United States and, to the best of his ability, preserve, protect, and defend the Constitution of the United States, and in disregard of his constitutional duty to take care that the laws be faithfully executed, has repeatedly engaged in conduct violating the constitutional rights of citizens, impairing the due and proper administration of justice and the conduct of lawful inquiries, or contravening the laws governing agencies of the executive branch and the purposes of these agencies.

This conduct has included one or more of the following:

1.   He has, acting personally and through his subordinates and agents, endeavoured to obtain from the Internal Revenue Service, in violation of the constitutional rights of citizens, confidential information contained in income tax returns for purposes not authorized by law, and to cause, in violation of the constitutional rights of citizens, income tax audits or other income tax investigations to be intitiated or conducted in a discriminatory manner.

2.   He misused the Federal Bureau of Investigation, the Secret Service, and other executive personnel, in violation or disregard of the constitutional rights of citizens, by directing or authorizing such agencies or personnel to conduct or continue electronic surveillance or other investigations for purposes unrelated to national security, the enforcement of laws, or any other lawful function of his office; he did direct, authorize, or permit the use of information obtained thereby for purposes unrelated to national security, the enforcement of laws, or any other lawful function of his office; and he did direct the concealment of certain records made by the Federal Bureau of Investigation of electronic surveillance.

3.   He has, acting personally and through his subordinates and agents, in violation or disregard of the constitutional rights of citizens, authorized and permitted to be maintained a secret investigative unit within the office of the President, financed in part with money derived from campaign contributions, which unlawfully utilized the resources of the Central Intelligence Agency, engaged in covert and unlawful activities, and attempted to prejudice the constitutional right of an accused to a fair trial.

4.   He has failed to take care that the laws were faithfully executed by failing to act when he knew or had reason to know that his close subordinates

endeavoured to impede and frustrate lawful inquiries by duly constituted executive, judicial and legislative entities concerning the unlawful entry into the headquarters of the Democratic National Committee, and the cover-up thereof, and concerning other unlawful activities including those relating to the confirmation of Richard Kleindienst as Attorney General of the United States, the electronic surveillance of private citizens, the break-in into the offices of Dr. Lewis Fielding, and the campaign financing practices of the Committee to Re-elect the President.

5.   In disregard of the rule of law, he knowingly misused the executive power by interfering with agencies of the executive branch, including the Federal Bureau of Investigation, the Criminal Division, and the Office of Watergate Special Prosecution Force, of the Department of Justice, and the Central Intelligence Agency, in violation of his duty to take care that the laws be faithfully executed.

In all of this, Richard M. Nixon has acted in a manner contrary to his trust as President and subversive of constitutional government, to the great prejudice of the cause of law and justice and to the manifest injury of the people of the United States.

Wherefore Richard M. Nixon, by such conduct, warrants impeachment and trial, and removal from office.

Adopted 28–10 by the Committee on the Judiciary of the House of Representatives.

Article 3

In his conduct of the office of President of the United States, Richard M. Nixon, contrary to his oath faithfully to execute the office of President of the United States and, to the best of his ability, preserve, protect, and defend the Constitution of the United States, and in violation of his constitutional duty to take care that the laws be faithfully executed, has failed without lawful cause or excuse to produce papers and things as directed by duly authorized subpoenas issued by the Committee on the Judiciary of the House of Representatives on April 11, 1974, May 15, 1974, May 30, 1974, and June 24, 1974, and willfully disobeyed such subpoenas.

The subpoenaed papers and things were deemed necessary by the Committee in order to resolve by direct evidence fundamental, factual questions relating to Presidential direction, knowledge or approval of actions demonstrated by other evidence to be substantial grounds for impeachment of the President. In refusing to produce these papers and things Richard M. Nixon, substituting his judgment as to what materials were necessary for the inquiry, interposed the powers of the Presidency against the lawful subpoenas of the House of Representatives, thereby assuming to himself functions and judgments necessary to the exercise of the sole power of impeachment vested by the Constitution in the House of Representatives.

In all of this, Richard M. Nixon has acted in a manner contrary to his trust as President and subversive of constitutional government, to the great prejudice of the cause of law and justice, and to the manifest injury of the people of the United States.

Wherefore, Richard M. Nixon, by such conduct, warrants impeachment and trial, and removal from office.

Adopted 21–17 by the Committee on the Judiciary of the House of Representatives.

 TEST YOUR KNOWLEDGE: To assess your understanding of the material in this chapter, **click here** to take a quiz.

CHAPTER V

Equal Protection

The Equal Protection Clause is part of the first section of the Fourteenth Amendment. The full sentence containing the clause reads as follows, with the relevant language italicized:

> No state shall make or enforce any law which shall abridge the privileges or immunities of citizens of the United States; *nor shall any state* deprive any person of life, liberty, or property, without due process of law; nor *deny to any person within its jurisdiction the equal protection of the laws.*

Note at the outset that, as part of the Fourteenth Amendment, the Clause does not itself apply against the federal government. But the Supreme Court has invoked the Due Process Clause of the Fifth Amendment to apply substantially identical constraints of equal treatment when federal action is involved.

The materials in this chapter will explore what "equal protection" requires, and why the answer to that question is both immensely complicated and hugely important.

A. Rational Basis Review—Discriminating Between Paper and Plastic

Life is filled with choices. Take a simple example. It's lunchtime. What do you want to do? Are you hungry enough to eat yet? Suppose you decide to buy a deli sandwich. Do you want to go to the one on the corner, or walk two blocks to the place you have a coupon for? Do you want meat or veggies? Do you want it in a paper bag or a plastic sack? And these choices just multiply. For most of the choices we make in any given day—and we make lots—we don't feel the need, or have the opportunity, to study the options extensively or articulate our reasoning, either about *what* we choose to accomplish or *how* we go about doing it. We're content to go by guess and by golly. Otherwise we'd just freeze.

The government faces similar problems at a vastly more complicated level. Should the city hire extra workers to finish that bridge construction, or hire more investigators for the civilian policing review board? If we decide to bolster the construction crew, what kinds of qualifications should applicants be required to have? And do we really need to keep the bridge clear of all vehicles while it's under construction? Maybe we could just prohibit all traffic going eastbound, but permit westbound bikes, pedestrians, and sedans to cross the bridge in a single dedicated lane? The challenge of these choices is magnified by how many more people they affect than the typical person's individual choice about which values to prioritize and which method to use.

How does this relate to equal protection? Well, start with the fact that virtually no law applies until some triggering criteria is satisfied. This means that just about any law can be described as "discriminatory"—either against somebody who *does* satisfy the criteria (if the law imposes a penalty or a restriction on behavior) or against someone who *doesn't* satisfy the criteria (if the law confers a privilege or benefit). That means that if discrimination were categorically intolerable under the Equal Protection Clause, we would run into big problems very quickly. Does banning plastic bags deny "equal protection of the laws" to their manufacturers because cloth-based competitors are left alone? Does extending welfare benefits only to people below 125% of the poverty line deny "equal protection of the laws" to people whose income is at the 126% mark? And how would we know?

The result is that, inevitably, the Equal Protection Clause is understood to tolerate most of the mundane distinctions made by the political organs of government. Government classifications are still subject to scrutiny under the clause, but only under the tolerant standard of "rational basis review." Before exploring the question of how to apply rational basis review in particular cases, we present a classic statement of some of its general principles, from Justice Thomas's opinion for the Court in *Federal Communications Commission v. Beach Communications, Inc.* (1993):

> Whether embodied in the Fourteenth Amendment [as applied to the states] or inferred from the Fifth [as applied to the federal government], equal protection is not a license for courts to judge the

wisdom, fairness, or logic of legislative choices. In areas of social and economic policy, a statutory classification that neither proceeds along suspect lines nor infringes fundamental constitutional rights must be upheld against equal protection challenge if there is any reasonably conceivable state of facts that could provide a rational basis for the classification. Where there are "plausible reasons" for Congress' action, "our inquiry is at an end." This standard of review is a paradigm of judicial restraint. "The Constitution presumes that, absent some reason to infer antipathy, even improvident decisions will eventually be rectified by the democratic process and that judicial intervention is generally unwarranted no matter how unwisely we may think a political branch has acted."

On rational-basis review, a classification in a [challenged] statute . . . comes to us bearing a strong presumption of validity, and those attacking the rationality of the legislative classification have the burden "to negative every conceivable basis which might support it." Moreover, because we never require a legislature to articulate its reasons for enacting a statute, it is entirely irrelevant for constitutional purposes whether the conceived reason for the challenged distinction actually motivated the legislature. Thus, the absence of " 'legislative facts' " explaining the distinction "[o]n the record," [as the opinion below had required], has no significance in rational-basis analysis. In other words, a legislative choice is not subject to courtroom fact-finding and may be based on rational speculation unsupported by evidence or empirical data. See also *Minnesota v. Clover Leaf Creamery Co.* (1981). . . .

These restraints on judicial review have added force "where the legislature must necessarily engage in a process of line-drawing." Defining the class of persons subject to a regulatory requirement—much like classifying governmental beneficiaries—"inevitably requires that some persons who have an almost equally strong claim to favored treatment be placed on different sides of the line, and the fact [that] the line might have been drawn differently at some points is a matter for legislative, rather than judicial, consideration." *United States Railroad Retirement Bd. v. Fritz* (1980).

The following material focuses on application of the rational basis standard to various regulatory classifications; some of the cases involve federal action and so are decided under the Due Process Clause of the Fifth Amendment rather than the Equal Protection Clause, but the substance of the legal standard is the same.

CROSS REFERENCE   The process by which the Fifth Amendment Due Process Clause came to be read as including an equal protection requirement is known as "reverse incorporation." For more on this development and the logic of its delightfully wonky name, see p. 1331–1332.

---

1.   Rational Basis: Commercial Regulations

United States v. Carolene Products Co.

Supreme Court of the United States, 1938.
304 U.S. 144.

MR. JUSTICE STONE delivered the opinion of the Court.

The question for decision is whether the "Filled Milk Act" of 1923, which prohibits the shipment in interstate commerce of skimmed milk compounded with any fat or oil other than milk fat, so as to resemble milk or cream . . . infringes the Fifth Amendment.

Appellee was indicted in the District Court for Southern Illinois for violation of the Act by the shipment in interstate commerce of certain packages of "Milnut," a compound of condensed skimmed milk and coconut oil made in imitation or semblance of condensed milk or cream. . . . [Carolene Products] complains that the statute denies to it equal protection of the laws, and in violation of the Fifth Amendment, deprives it of its property without due process of law, particularly in that the statute purports to make binding and conclusive upon appellee the legislative declaration that appellee's product "is an adulterated article of food, injurious to the public health, and its sale constitutes a fraud on the public."

The prohibition of shipment of appellee's product in interstate commerce does not infringe the Fifth Amendment. [E]vidence has steadily accumulated of the danger to the public health from the general consumption of foods which have been stripped of elements essential to the maintenance of health. The Filled Milk Act was adopted by Congress after committee hearings, in the course of which eminent scientists and health experts testified. . . . [Committees in both chambers of Congress] concluded, as the statute itself declares, that the use of filled milk as a substitute for pure milk is generally injurious to health and facilitates fraud on the public.

WORTH NOTING In a footnote, the Court summarized Congress's basis for this conclusion, including its finding that "use of filled milk as a dietary substitute for pure milk results, especially in the case of children, in undernourishment, and induces diseases which attend malnutrition."

Appellee raises no valid objection to the present statute by arguing that its prohibition has not been extended to oleomargarine or other butter substitutes in which vegetable fats or oils are substituted for butter fat. The Fifth Amendment has no equal protection clause, and even that of the Fourteenth, applicable only to the states, does not compel their Legislatures to prohibit all like evils, or none. A Legislature may hit at an abuse which it has found, even though it has failed to strike at another. . . .

We may assume for present purposes that no pronouncement of a Legislature can forestall attack upon the constitutionality of the prohibition which it enacts by applying opprobrious epithets to the prohibited act, and that a statute would deny due process which precluded the disproof in judicial proceedings of all facts which would show or tend to show that a statute depriving the suitor of life, liberty, or property had a rational basis.

But such we think is not the purpose or construction of the statutory characterization of filled milk as injurious to health and as a fraud upon the public. There is no need to consider it here as more than a declaration of the legislative findings deemed to support and justify the action taken as a constitutional exertion of the legislative power, aiding informed judicial review, as do the reports of legislative committees, by revealing the rationale of the legislation. Even in the absence of such aids, the existence of facts supporting the legislative judgment is to be presumed, for regulatory legislation affecting ordinary commercial transactions is not to be pronounced unconstitutional unless in the light of the facts made known or generally assumed it is of such a character as to preclude the assumption that it rests upon some rational basis within the knowledge and experience of the legislators. . . .

CROSS REFERENCE
Here the Court drops the famous *"Carolene* Footnote 4," which lays the groundwork for a more skeptical review of at least some statutes that go beyond merely "affecting ordinary commercial transactions." The full text of that footnote is reproduced at p. 1179–1180; see also p. 225.

Where the existence of a rational basis for legislation whose constitutionality is attacked depends upon facts beyond the sphere of judicial notice, such facts may properly be made the subject of judicial inquiry, and the constitutionality of a statute predicated upon the existence of a particular state of facts may be challenged by showing to the court that those facts have ceased to exist. Similarly we recognize that the constitutionality of a statute, valid on its face, may be assailed by proof of facts tending to show that the statute as applied to a particular article is without support in reason because the article, although within the prohibited class, is so different from others of the class as to be without the reason for the prohibition, though the effect of such proof depends on the relevant circumstances of each case, as for example the administrative difficulty of excluding the article from the regulated class. . . .

But by their very nature such inquiries, where the legislative judgment is drawn in question, must be restricted to the issue whether any state of facts either known or which could reasonably be assumed affords support for it. Here . . . it is evident from all the considerations presented to Congress, and those of which we may take judicial notice, that the question is at least debatable whether commerce in filled milk should be left unregulated, or in some measure restricted, or wholly prohibited. As that decision was for Congress, neither the finding of a court arrived at by weighing the evidence, nor the verdict of a jury can be substituted for it.

WORTH NOTING
Justice Black concurred in the result and in most of the opinion, but not in the portion including the last four paragraphs presented of this excerpt. Justice McReynolds stated without opinion that the judgment below, which held the statute unconstitutional, should be affirmed. Neither Justice Cardozo, who was mortally ill, nor Justice Reed, who had recently served as Solicitor General, participated in the case.

The prohibition of shipment in interstate commerce of appellee's product, as described in the indictment, is a constitutional exercise of the power to regulate interstate commerce. As the statute is not unconstitutional on its face, the demurrer should have been overruled and the judgment will be reversed. . . .

FOR DISCUSSION Suppose you were a member of the Supreme Court and you were persuaded that, as has been seriously contended, filled milk was in fact "a healthful, nutritious, and low-cost food," and that the prohibition resulted from the superior political power of the dairy industry, which regarded filled milk as a threat and benefited from "encouraging the use as baby food of a sweetened condensed milk product that was 42% sugar." See Geoffrey P. Miller, *The True Story of* Carolene Products, 1987 Sup. Ct. Rev. 397. Should that change the outcome? In 1972, in a case involving the successor company to Carolene Products, a district court concluded that, because competitive conditions had changed, it could consider a new challenge to the statute, which it held unconstitutional. *Milnot Company v. Richardson,* 350 F. Supp. 221 (S.D. Ill. 1972). Milnot evaporated filled milk is still readily available for purchase.

Railway Express Agency v. New York

Supreme Court of the United States, 1949.
336 U.S. 106.

MR. JUSTICE DOUGLAS delivered the opinion of the Court.

Section 124 of the Traffic Regulations of the City of New York promulgated by the Police Commissioner provides:

> No person shall operate, or cause to be operated, in or upon any street an advertising vehicle; provided that nothing herein contained shall prevent the putting of business notices upon business delivery vehicles, so long as such vehicles are engaged in the usual business or regular work of the owner and not used merely or mainly for advertising.

Appellant is engaged in a nation-wide express business. It operates about 1,900 trucks in New York City and sells the space on the exterior sides of these trucks for advertising. That advertising is for the most part unconnected with its own business. It was convicted in the magistrates court and fined. . . .

The question of equal protection of the laws is pressed . . . strenuously. It is pointed out that the regulation draws the line between advertisements of products sold by the owner of the truck and general advertisements. It is argued that unequal treatment on the basis of such a distinction is not justified by the aim and purpose of the regulation. It is said, for example, that one of appellant's trucks carrying the advertisement of a commercial house would not cause any greater distraction of pedestrians and vehicle drivers than if the commercial house carried the same advertisement on its own truck. Yet the regulation allows the latter to do what the former is forbidden from doing. It is therefore contended that the classification which the regulation makes has no relation to the traffic problem since a violation turns not on what kind of advertisements are carried on trucks but on whose trucks they are carried.

That, however, is a superficial way of analyzing the problem, even if we assume that it is premised on the correct construction of the regulation. The local authorities may well have concluded that those who advertised their own wares on their trucks do not present the same traffic problem in view of the nature or extent of the advertising which they use. It would take a degree of omniscience which we lack to say that such is not the case. If that judgment is correct, the advertising displays that are exempt have less incidence on traffic than those of appellants.

We cannot say that that judgment is not an allowable one. [And] if it is [thus allowable], the classification has relation to the purpose for which it is made and does not contain the kind of discrimination against which the Equal Protection Clause affords protection. It is by such practical considerations based on experience rather than by theoretical inconsistencies that the question of equal protection is to be answered. . . . And the fact that New York City sees fit to eliminate from traffic this kind of distraction but does not touch what may be even greater ones in a different category, such as the vivid displays on Times Square, is immaterial. It is no requirement of equal protection that all evils of the same genus be eradicated or none at all.

Affirmed.

MR. JUSTICE RUTLEDGE acquiesces in the Court's opinion and judgment, *dubitante* on the question of equal protection of the laws.

MR. JUSTICE JACKSON, concurring.

. . . I regard it as a salutary doctrine that cities, states and the Federal Government must exercise their powers so as not to discriminate between their inhabitants except upon some reasonable differentiation fairly related to the object of regulation.

This equality is not merely abstract justice. The framers of the Constitution knew, and we should not forget today, that there is no more effective practical guaranty against arbitrary and unreasonable government than to require that the principles of law which officials would impose upon a minority must be imposed generally. Conversely, nothing opens the door to arbitrary action so effectively as to allow those officials to pick and choose only a few to whom they will apply legislation and thus to escape the political retribution that might be visited upon them if larger numbers were affected. Courts can take no better measure to assure that laws will be just than to require that laws be equal in operation. . . .

The question in my mind comes to this. Where [trucks with advertising on them] contribute to an evil or danger in the same way and to the same degree, may those who do so for hire be prohibited, while those who do so for their own commercial ends but not for hire be allowed to continue? I think the answer has to be that the hireling may be put in a class by himself and may be dealt with differently than those who act on their own. [T]here is a real difference between doing in self-interest and doing for hire. [I]t is not difficult to see that, in a day of extravagant advertising more or less subsidized by tax deduction, the rental of truck space could become an obnoxious enterprise.

While I do not think highly of this type of regulation, that is not my business. [I]n view of the control I would concede to cities to protect citizens in quiet and orderly use for their proper purposes of the highways and public places, I think the judgment below must be affirmed.

Williamson v. Lee Optical of Oklahoma, Inc.

Supreme Court of the United States, 1955.
348 U.S. 483.

MR. JUSTICE DOUGLAS delivered the opinion of the Court.

This suit [challenges an Oklahoma statute that makes] it unlawful for any person not a licensed optometrist or ophthalmologist to fit lenses to a face or to duplicate or replace into frames lenses or other optical appliances, except upon written prescriptive authority of an Oklahoma licensed ophthalmologist or optometrist. An ophthalmologist is a duly licensed physician who special-izes in the care of the eyes. An optometrist examines eyes for refractive error, recognizes (but does not treat) diseases of the eye, and fills prescriptions for eyeglasses. The optician is an artisan qualified to grind lenses, fill prescriptions, and fit frames.

The effect of [the statute] is to forbid the optician from fitting or dupli-cating lenses without a prescription from an ophthalmologist or optometrist. In practical effect, it means that no optician can fit old glasses into new frames or supply a lens, whether it be a new lens or one to duplicate a lost or broken lens, without a prescription.

The District Court conceded that it was in the competence of the police power of a State to regulate the examination of the eyes. But it rebelled at the notion that a State could require a prescription from an optometrist or oph-thalmologist "to take old lenses and place them in new frames and then fit the completed spectacles to the face of the eyeglass wearer." It held that such a re-quirement was not "reasonably and rationally related to the health and welfare of the people." The court found that through mechanical devices and ordinary skills the optician could take a broken lens or a fragment thereof, measure its power, and reduce it to prescriptive terms. The court held that "Although on this precise issue of duplication, the legislature in the instant regulation was dealing with a matter of public interest, the particular means chosen are neither rea-sonably necessary nor reasonably related to the end sought to be achieved." . . .

The Oklahoma law may exact a needless, wasteful requirement in many cases. But it is for the legislature, not the courts, to balance the advantages and disadvantages of the new requirement.

It appears that in many cases the optician can easily supply the new frames or new lenses without reference to the old written prescription. It also appears that many written prescriptions contain no directive data in regard to fitting spectacles to the face. But in some cases the directions contained in the pre-scription are essential, if the glasses are to be fitted so as to correct the particular defects of vision or alleviate the eye condition. The legislature might have con-cluded that the frequency of occasions when a prescription is necessary was sufficient to justify this regulation of the fitting of eyeglasses. Likewise, when it is necessary to duplicate a lens, a written prescription may or may not be necessary. But the legislature might have concluded that one was needed often enough to require one in every case.

Or the legislature may have concluded that eye examinations were so critical, not only for correction of vision but also for detection of latent ailments or diseases, that every change in frames and every duplication of a lens should be accompanied by a prescription from a medical expert. To be sure, the present law does not require a new examination of the eyes every time the frames are changed or the lenses duplicated. For if the old prescription is on file with the optician, he can go ahead and make the new fitting or duplicate the lenses. But the law need not be in every respect logically consistent with its aims to be constitutional. It is enough that there is an evil at hand for correction, and that it might be thought that the particular legislative measure was a rational way to correct it. . . .

The problem of legislative classification is a perennial one, admitting of no doctrinaire definition. Evils in the same field may be of different dimensions and proportions, requiring different remedies. Or so the legislature may think. Or the reform may take one step at a time, addressing itself to the phase of the problem which seems most acute to the legislative mind. The legislature may select one phase of one field and apply a remedy there, neglecting the others. The prohibition of the Equal Protection Clause goes no further than the invidious discrimination. We cannot say that that point has been reached here. For all this record shows, the ready-to-wear branch of this business may not loom large in Oklahoma or may present problems of regulation distinct from the other branch. . . .

MR. JUSTICE HARLAN took no part in the consideration or decision of this case.

FOR DISCUSSION

Consider *Minnesota v. Clover Leaf Creamery Company* (1981). The state banned the sake of milk in nonreturnable, nonrefillable containers made of plastic, but permitted its sale in those made of paperboard. The resins used in plastic containers were made exclusively outside the state, but the pulp used in making paperboard was a major Minnesota product. Who might want to challenge this statute? If you were representing them, what story would you like to tell about how the statute came to be enacted? If you were representing the state, what justifications would you hope to offer in support of the statute? If you were a judge inclined to believe that the statute was principally a product of raw political power, how would you be inclined to rule on an Equal Protection challenge?

---

2. Rational Basis: Harder Cases

Rational basis review is at its most straightforward as applied to government decisions that don't seem to discriminate against vulnerable or otherwise socially disadvantaged groups of individuals. Even if you think that the *Carolene Products* ban on filled milk was just a grubby political win for the dairy industry, for example, you might still be skeptical of judicial intervention to protect Milnut from its competitors' superior lobbying prowess—not least because in the mine run of cases, it might be hard to tell which laws are solely the result of self-interested lobbying, and which laws are grounded in at least some measure of good faith analysis by the government. Reactions can become more complicated, however, when the exaggerated deference given to ordinary commercial regulations is applied to circumstances that arguably call for more skepticism.

Consider, for example, whether the use of rational basis review in *New York City Transit Authority v. Beazer* (1979) comports with your own intuitions about fairness and equal protection. In *Beazer*, the Transit Authority (TA) had a flat rule against employing anybody who was using narcotic drugs—a category of substances that included methadone, which is used to treat heroin addiction. (Methadone eases the severe difficulties of heroin withdrawal without giving the user any pleasurable effects of heroin; indeed, it prevents heroin from having those effects on the user.) The employment exclusion apparently applied for five years after a heroin user had successfully completed a methadone program.

The district court held that the blanket exclusion was unconstitutional, because some methadone users were capable of performing some TA jobs, and because (as the Supreme Court later explained) "normal personnel-screening procedures—at least if augmented by some method of obtaining information from the staffs of methadone programs—would enable TA to identify the unqualified applicants on an individual basis." Under the resulting injunction, which was upheld by the appeals court, the TA could exclude all methadone users from certain safety-sensitive functions, but all methadone users with at least one year of satisfactory participation in a treatment program had to be considered fully eligible for the remaining jobs.

In an opinion written by Justice Stevens, the Supreme Court reversed, concluding that the TA policy was a rational means of improving public safety and administrative efficiency. The Court's opinion began by emphasizing that the TA "employs about 47,000 persons, of whom many—perhaps most—are employed in positions that involve danger to themselves or to the public. For example, some 12,300 are subway motormen, towermen, conductors, or bus operators." The majority then noted that "even among participants with more than 12 months' tenure in methadone maintenance programs, the incidence of drug and alcohol abuse may often approach and even exceed 25%." Since there was no bright line marking the point during treatment at which the risk of regression ends, that meant that "the 'no drugs' policy now enforced by [the] TA" was "supported by the legitimate inference that as long as a treatment program (or other drug use) continues, a degree of uncertainty persists." Justice Powell concurred to the extent that the policy applied to current methadone users, but agreed with the lower courts that there was no rational basis for an absolute bar on anyone who had used methadone in the past five years.

Justice White, joined by Justice Marshall and in part by Justice Brennan, dissented. "The evidence," he observed, "indicates that poor risks will shake out of a methadone maintenance program within six months," such that those who had successfully completed a year (itself a readily ascertainable criterion) were "no more likely than the average applicant to turn out to be poor employees." Justice White thought it particularly irrational for the TA to single out "successfully maintained" methadone users for a blanket exclusion when no such rule applied to other groups suffering a disability or other condition presumptively related to employability—"ex-offenders, former alcoholics and mental patients, diabetics, epileptics, and those currently using tranquilizers, for example," all of whom would be assessed for employability on a case by case basis.

The real question was what level of scrutiny to apply. The majority acknowledged that "between 62% and 65% of all methadone-maintained persons in New York City are black or Hispanic," but emphasized the trial court "expressly found that the policy was not adopted with a discriminatory purpose." To the contrary, the TA's policy was "[q]uite plainly" motivated by its "interest in operating a safe and efficient transportation system, rather than by any special animus against a specific group of persons." Accordingly, there was nothing to warrant a presumption of illegality or to warrant the Court's "especially 'attentive judgment.'" For the majority, this meant the case was governed by ordinary rational basis review, which made its legal conclusion easy:

> At its simplest, the District Court's conclusion was that TA's rule is broader than necessary to exclude those methadone users who are not actually qualified to work for TA. We may assume not only that

this conclusion is correct but also that it is probably unwise for a large employer like TA to rely on a general rule instead of individualized consideration of every job applicant. But these assumptions concern matters of personnel policy that do not implicate the principle safeguarded by the Equal Protection Clause. . . . No matter how unwise it may be for TA to refuse employment to individual car cleaners, track repairmen, or bus drivers simply because they are receiving methadone treatment, the Constitution does not authorize a federal court to interfere in that policy decision.

Although Justice White's dissent likewise analyzed the case under the rational-basis standard, he devoted a long footnote to challenging the majority's conclusion that the TA's classification presented no special risk of unfair treatment:

> Heroin addiction is a special problem of the poor, and the addict population is composed largely of racial minorities that the Court has previously recognized as politically powerless and historical subjects of majoritarian neglect. Persons on methadone maintenance have few interests in common with members of the majority, and thus are unlikely to have their interests protected, or even considered, in governmental decisionmaking. Indeed, petitioners stipulated that "[o]ne of the reasons for the . . . drug policy is the fact that [petitioners] fee[l] an adverse public reaction would result if it were generally known that [petitioners] employed persons with a prior history of drug abuse, including persons participating in methadone maintenance programs." . . .

> On the other hand, the afflictions to which petitioners are more sympathetic, such as alcoholism and mental illness, are shared by both white and black, rich and poor. Some weight should also be given to the history of the rule. Petitioners admit that it was not the result of a reasoned policy decision and stipulated that they had never studied the ability of those on methadone maintenance to perform petitioners' jobs. . . .

> These factors together strongly point to a conclusion of invidious discrimination. The Court, however, refuses to view this rule as one "circumscrib[ing] a class of persons characterized by some unpopular

trait or affiliation," because it is admittedly justified as applied to many current and former heroin addicts. [A]ll that shows, however, is that the characteristic in question is a legitimate basis of distinction in some circumstances. . . . But sometimes antipathy extends beyond the facts that may have given rise to it, and when that happens the "stereotyped reaction may have no rational relationship—other than pure prejudicial discrimination—to the stated purpose for which the classification is being made." That is the case here.

FOR DISCUSSION

How would you have voted in *Beazer*? Would your answer change if the ban on employment were permanent rather than expiring five years after the applicant's most recent use of methadone? What if the challengers had been denied a job because they were still using hero-in? What if their last use of heroin was two years ago? Three? Four? Ten?

B. Strict Scrutiny—Discriminating Among Racial Groups

As we have seen, the default rule is that the government may classify between groups without being careful, accurate, or even particularly thoughtful. But not all discrimination is treated with the same deference as the classification between paper and plastic. For the most "suspect classifications," as the doctrine calls them, courts apply what is called "strict scrutiny," demanding both a compelling interest that justifies the measure and also an extremely good explanation for why the adopted classification is basically the only way that interest can be protected.

The archetypal case for strict scrutiny involves discrimination on the basis of race—which Bill Clinton called "America's constant curse." Racial subjugation in the extreme form of slavery led to the Civil War; slavery, the war, and emancipation provided the backdrop for the adoption of the Fourteenth Amendment. Central to the drafters' thinking was the protection of African Americans in the Reconstruction South, on the background of emancipation and a radical reworking of the southern social and economic structure that the governing political coalition initially had in mind. That starting point has guided discussion of the Equal Protection Clause ever since.

1.   The Core Case: Racial Subjugation

The core concern motivating the drafters of the Equal Protection Clause was laws that classified by race, with the purpose and effect of contributing to the racial subjugation of African Americans. But racial classifications may also contribute to subjugation in more subtle ways, by reinforcing a social system of racial hierarchy. So it is important to think about what makes a classification racially subjugating—and why exactly we are likely to be skeptical of any racial classification. Is it that we are concerned about hostile efforts to oppress whole groups, and that we recognize racial classifications as the quintessential basis for such efforts in our national history? Or do we think it is so rare for racial distinctions to be genuinely relevant rather than indifferently stereotypical that we simply don't trust them even when they're not intended to produce apartheid? Or does some combination of these perspectives—perhaps along with others—underlie the exceptionally rigorous standard of review applicable to racial classifications, known as "strict scrutiny"? In the cases that follow, see if you can trace the varying theories for this special concern about racial classifications.

Strauder v. West Virginia

Supreme Court of the United States, 1880.
100 U.S. 303.

MR. JUSTICE STRONG delivered the opinion of the court.

The plaintiff in error, a colored man, was indicted for murder in the Circuit Court of Ohio County, in West Virginia, on the 20th of October, 1874, and upon trial was convicted and sentenced. . . .

[Defendant showed] that "by virtue of the laws of the State of West Virginia no colored man was eligible to be a member of the grand jury or to serve on a petit jury in the State; that white men are so eligible, and that by reason of his being a colored man and having been a slave . . . he [therefore] had less chance of enforcing in the courts of the State his rights . . . than if he was a white man." . . . The [statute] was enacted on the 12th of March, 1873, and it is as follows:

> All white male persons who are twenty-one years of age and who are citizens of this State shall be liable to serve as jurors, except as herein provided.

The persons excepted are State officials. . . .

[T]he controlling question [is] whether, by the Constitution and laws of the United States, every citizen of the United States has a right to a trial of an indictment against him by a jury selected and impanelled without discrimination against his race or color, because of race or color . . . . [The issue] is not whether a colored man, when an indictment has been preferred against him, has a right to a grand or a petit jury composed in whole or in part of persons of his own race or color. It is whether, in the composition or selection of jurors by whom he is to be indicted or tried, all persons of his race or color may be excluded by law, solely because of their race or color, so that by no possibility can any colored man sit upon the jury. . . .

The Fourteenth Amendment . . . . is one of a series of constitutional provisions having a common purpose; namely, securing to a race recently emancipated, a race that through many generations had been held in slavery, all the civil rights that the superior race enjoy. The true spirit and meaning of the amendments, as we said in the *Slaughter-House Cases*, cannot be understood without keeping in view the history of the times when they were adopted, and the general objects they plainly sought to accomplish. At the time when they were incorporated into the Constitution, it required little knowledge of human nature to anticipate that those who had long been regarded as an inferior and subject race would, when suddenly raised to the rank of citizenship, be looked upon with jealousy and positive dislike, and that State laws might be enacted or enforced to perpetuate the distinctions that had before existed. Discriminations against them had been habitual. It was well known that in some States laws making such discriminations then existed, and others might well be expected.

See pp. 167–172 for the *Slaughter-House Cases*.

The colored race, as a race, was abject and ignorant, and in that condition was unfitted to command the respect of those who had superior intelligence. Their training had left them mere children, and as such they needed the protection which a wise government extends to those who are unable to protect themselves. They especially needed protection against unfriendly action in the States where they were resident.

It was in view of these considerations the Fourteenth Amendment was framed and adopted. It was designed to assure to the colored race the enjoyment of all the civil rights that under the law are enjoyed by white persons, and to give to that race the protection of the general government, in that enjoyment, whenever it should be denied by the States. . . . To quote the language used by us in the *Slaughter-House Cases,*

> No one can fail to be impressed with the one pervading purpose found in all the amendments, lying at the foundation of each, and without which none of them would have been suggested—we mean the freedom of the slave race, the security and firm establishment of that freedom, and the protection of the newly made freeman and citizen from the oppressions of those who had formerly exercised unlimited dominion over them. . . .

> The existence of laws in the States where the newly emancipated negroes resided, which discriminated with gross injustice and hardship against them as a class, was the evil to be remedied, and by [the Fourteenth Amendment] such laws were forbidden. . . . We doubt very much whether any action of a State, not directed by way of discrimination against the negroes, as a class, will ever be held to come within the purview of this provision.

If this is the spirit and meaning of the amendment, whether it means more or not, it is to be construed liberally, to carry out the purposes of its framers. . . . It ordains that no State shall . . . deny to any person within its jurisdiction the equal protection of the laws. What is this but declaring that the law in the States shall be the same for the black as for the white; that all persons, whether colored or white, shall stand equal before the laws of the States, and, in regard to the colored race, for whose protection the amendment was primarily designed, that no discrimination shall be made against them by law because of their color? The words of the amendment, it is true, are prohibitory, but they contain a necessary implication of a positive immunity, or right, most valuable to the colored race—the right to exemption from unfriendly legislation against them distinctively as colored—exemption from legal discriminations, implying inferiority in civil society, lessening the security of their enjoyment of the rights which others enjoy, and discriminations which are steps towards reducing them to the condition of a subject race.

That the West Virginia statute respecting juries—the statute that controlled the selection of the grand and petit jury in the case of the plaintiff in error—is such a discrimination ought not to be doubted. Nor would it be if the persons excluded by it were white men. If in those States where the colored people constitute a majority of the entire population a law should be enacted excluding all white men from jury service, thus denying to them the privilege of participating equally with the blacks in the administration of justice, we apprehend no one would be heard to claim that it would not be a denial to white men of the equal protection of the laws. Nor if a law should be passed excluding all naturalized Celtic Irishmen, would there be any doubt of its inconsistency with the spirit of the amendment. The very fact that colored people are singled out and expressly denied by a statute all right to participate in the administration of the law, as jurors, because of their color, though they are citizens, and may be in other respects fully qualified, is practically a brand upon them, affixed by the law, an assertion of their inferiority, and a stimulant to that race prejudice which is an impediment to securing to individuals of the race that equal justice which the law aims to secure to all others. . . .

The very idea of a jury is a body of men composed of the peers or equals of the person whose rights it is selected or summoned to determine; that is, of his neighbors, fellows, associates, persons having the same legal status in society as that which he holds. Blackstone, in his *Commentaries*, says, "The right of trial by jury, or the country, is a trial by the peers of every Englishman, and is the grand bulwark of his liberties, and is secured to him by the [Magna Charta]." It is also guarded by statutory enactments intended to make impossible what Mr. Bentham called "packing juries." It is well known that prejudices often exist against particular classes in the community, which sway the judgment of jurors, and which, therefore, operate in some cases to deny to persons of those classes the full enjoyment of that protection which others enjoy. . . .

In view of these considerations, it is hard to see why the statute of West Virginia should not be regarded as discriminating against a colored man when he is put upon trial for an alleged criminal offence against the State. It is not easy to comprehend how it can be said that while every white man is entitled to a trial by a jury selected from persons of his own race or color, or, rather, selected without discrimination against his color, and a negro is not, the latter is equally protected by the law with the former. Is not protection of life and liberty against race or color prejudice, a right, a legal right, under the constitutional amendment? And how can it be maintained that compelling a colored man to submit to a trial for his life by a jury drawn from a panel from which the State has expressly excluded every man of his race, because of color alone, however well qualified in other respects, is not a denial to him of equal legal protection?

We do not say that within the limits from which it is not excluded by the amendment a State may not prescribe the qualifications of its jurors, and in so doing make discriminations. It may confine the selection to males, to freeholders, to citizens, to persons within certain ages, or to persons having educational qualifications. We do not believe the Fourteenth Amendment was ever intended to prohibit this. Looking at its history, it is clear it had no such purpose. Its aim was against discrimination because of race or color. As we have said more than once, its design was to protect an emancipated race, and to strike down all possible legal discriminations against those who belong to it. . . . We are not now called upon to affirm or deny that it had other purposes. . . .

[We conclude], therefore, that the statute of West Virginia, discriminating in the selection of jurors, as it does, against negroes because of their color, amounts to a denial of the equal protection of the laws to a colored man when he is put upon trial for an alleged offence against the State. . . . There was error, therefore, in proceeding to the trial of the indictment against him after his petition was filed, as also in overruling his challenge to the array of the jury, and in refusing to quash the panel. . . .

So ordered.

MR. JUSTICE FIELD, dissenting.

I dissent from the judgment of the court in this case, on the grounds stated in my opinion in *Ex parte Virginia* (1878). [In that case, Justice Field had written: "All persons within the jurisdiction of the State, whether permanent residents or temporary sojourners, whether old or young, male or female, are to be equally protected [by the Equal Protection Clause]. Yet no one will contend that equal protection to women, to children, to the aged, to aliens, can only be secured by allowing persons of the class to which they belong to act as jurors in cases affecting their interests. The equality of protection intended does not require that all persons shall be permitted to participate in the government of the State and the administration of its laws, to hold its offices, or be clothed with any public trusts."]

Mr. Justice Clifford concurs with me.

FOR DISCUSSION

Does the conclusion that West Virginia's law violated Strauder's right to equal protection depend on the perception that an African American juror would be more likely to vote to acquit than a white juror would? If Strauder were white, would he have had standing to complain about the West Virginia law?

Plessy v. Ferguson

Supreme Court of the United States, 1896.
163 U.S. 537.

MR. JUSTICE BROWN . . . delivered the opinion of the court.

This case turns upon the constitutionality of an act of the General Assembly of the State of Louisiana, passed in 1890, providing for separate railway carriages for the white and colored races.

The first section of the statute enacts

> that all railway companies carrying passengers in their coaches in this State, shall provide equal but separate accommodations for the white, and colored races, by providing two or more passenger coaches for each passenger train, or by dividing the passenger coaches by a partition so as to secure separate accommodations: provided, that this section shall not be construed to apply to street railroads. No person or persons shall be admitted to occupy seats in coaches, other than the ones assigned to them, on account of the race they belong to. . . .

The third section provides penalties for the refusal or neglect of the officers, directors, conductors, and employés of railway companies to comply with the act, with a proviso that "nothing in this act shall be construed as applying to nurses attending children of the other race." . . .

The information filed in the criminal district court charged, in substance, that Plessy, being a passenger between two stations within the State of Louisiana, was assigned by officers of the company to the coach used for the race to which he belonged, but he insisted upon going into a coach used by the race to which he did not belong. . . .

The petition for the writ of prohibition averred that petitioner was seven-eighths Caucasian and one-eighth African blood; that the mixture of colored blood was not discernible in him; and that he was entitled to every right, privilege, and immunity secured to citizens of the United States of the white race; and that, upon such theory, he took possession of a vacant seat in a coach where passengers of the white race were accommodated, and was ordered by the conductor to vacate said coach, and take a seat in another, assigned to persons of the colored race, and, having refused to comply with such demand, he was forcibly ejected, with the aid of a police officer, and imprisoned in the parish jail to answer a charge of having violated the above act.

The constitutionality of this act is attacked upon the ground that it conflicts both with the Thirteenth Amendment of the Constitution, abolishing slavery, and the Fourteenth Amendment, which prohibits certain restrictive legislation on the part of the States.

1.   That it does not conflict with the Thirteenth Amendment, which abolished slavery and involuntary servitude, except as a punishment for crime, is too clear for argument. Slavery implies involuntary servitude—a state of bondage; the ownership of mankind as a chattel, or, at least, the control of the labor and services of one man for the benefit of another, and the absence of a legal right to the disposal of his own person, property, and services. This amendment was . . . intended primarily to abolish slavery, as it had been previously known in this country, and . . . it equally forbade Mexican peonage or the Chinese coolie trade, when they amounted to slavery or involuntary servitude[;] the use of the word "servitude" was intended to prohibit the use of all forms of involuntary slavery, of whatever class or name. . . .

[T]his amendment was regarded by the statesmen of that day as insufficient to protect the colored race from certain laws which had been enacted in the Southern States, imposing upon the colored race onerous disabilities and burdens, and curtailing their rights in the pursuit of life, liberty, and property to such an extent that their freedom was of little value; and . . . the Fourteenth Amendment was devised to meet this exigency. . . .

A statute which implies merely a legal distinction between the white and colored races—a distinction which is founded in the color of the two races, and which must always exist so long as white men are distinguished from the other race by color—has no tendency to destroy the legal equality of the two races, or re-establish a state of involuntary servitude. Indeed, we do not understand that the Thirteenth Amendment is strenuously relied upon by the plaintiff in error in this connection.

2.   . . . The proper construction of [the Fourteenth Amendment] was first called to the attention of this court in the *Slaughter-House Cases*. . . . The case did not call for any expression of opinion as to the exact rights it was intended to secure to the colored race, but it was said generally that its main purpose was to establish the citizenship of the negro, to give definitions of citizenship of the United States and of the States, and to protect from the hostile legislation of the states the privileges and immunities of citizens of the United States, as distinguished from those of citizens of the States.

The object of the amendment was undoubtedly to enforce the absolute equality of the two races before the law, but, in the nature of things, it could not have been intended to abolish distinctions based upon color, or to enforce social, as distinguished from political equality, or a commingling of the two races upon terms unsatisfactory to either. Laws permitting, and even requiring, their separation, in places where they are liable to be brought into contact, do not necessarily imply the inferiority of either race to the other, and have been generally, if not universally, recognized as within the competency of the state legislatures in the exercise of their police power. The most common instance of this is connected with the establishment of separate schools for white and colored children, which have been held to be a valid exercise of the legislative power even by courts of states where the political rights of the colored race have been longest and most earnestly enforced.

One of the earliest of these cases is that of *Roberts v. City of Boston* (Mass. 1950), in which the Supreme Judicial Court of Massachusetts held that the general school committee of Boston had power to make provision for the instruction of colored children in separate schools established exclusively for them, and to prohibit their attendance upon the other schools[:]

> [W]hen [the] great principle [of equality before the laws] comes to be applied to the actual and various conditions of persons in society, it will not warrant the assertion that men and women are legally clothed with the same civil and political powers . . . , and that children and adults are legally to have the same functions and be subject to the same treatment; but only that the rights of all . . . are equally

entitled to the paternal consideration and protection of the law for their maintenance and security. . . .

Similar laws have been enacted by Congress under its general power of legislation over the District of Columbia, as well as by the legislatures of many of the states, and have been generally, if not uniformly, sustained by the courts. [The Court cites state cases from Ohio, Missouri, California, Louisiana, New York, Indiana, and Kentucky.]

Laws forbidding the intermarriage of the two races may be said in a technical sense to interfere with the freedom of contract, and yet have been universally recognized as within the police power of the state. *State v. Gibson* (Indiana 1871).

The distinction between laws interfering with the political equality of the negro and those requiring the separation of the two races in schools, theaters, and railway carriages has been frequently drawn by this court. Thus, in *Strauder v. West Virginia*, it was held that a law of West Virginia limiting to white male persons 21 years of age, and citizens of the state, the right to sit upon juries, was a discrimination which implied a legal inferiority in civil society, which lessened the security of the right of the colored race, and was a step towards reducing them to a condition of servility. . . .

In this connection, it is . . . suggested by the learned counsel for the plaintiff in error that the same argument that will justify the state legislature in requiring railways to provide separate accommodations for the two races will also authorize them to require separate cars to be provided for people whose hair is of a certain color, or who are aliens, or who belong to certain nationalities, or to enact laws requiring colored people to walk upon one side of the street, and white people upon the other, or requiring white men's houses to be painted white, and colored men's black, or their vehicles or business signs to be of different colors, upon the theory that one side of the street is as good as the other, or that a house or vehicle of one color is as good as one of another color. The reply to all this is that every exercise of the police power must be reasonable, and extend only to such laws as are enacted in good faith for the promotion of the public good, and not for the annoyance or oppression of a particular class. Thus, in *Yick Wo v. Hopkins* (1886), it was held by this court that a municipal ordinance of the city of San Francisco, to regulate the carrying on of public

CROSS REFERENCE   *Yick Wo* is presented below at pp. 1051–1054.

laundries . . . was . . . a covert attempt on the part of the municipality to make an arbitrary and unjust discrimination against the Chinese race. . . .

So far, then, as a conflict with the fourteenth amendment is concerned, the case reduces itself to the question whether the statute of Louisiana is a reasonable regulation, and with respect to this there must necessarily be a large discretion on the part of the legislature. In determining the question of reasonableness, it is at liberty to act with reference to the established usages, customs, and traditions of the people, and with a view to the promotion of their comfort, and the preservation of the public peace and good order. Gauged by this standard, we cannot say that a law which authorizes or even requires the separation of the two races in public conveyances is unreasonable, or more obnoxious to the fourteenth amendment than the acts of congress requiring separate schools for colored children in the District of Columbia, the constitutionality of which does not seem to have been questioned, or the corresponding acts of state legislatures.

We consider the underlying fallacy of the plaintiff's argument to consist in the assumption that the enforced separation of the two races stamps the colored race with a badge of inferiority. If this be so, it is not by reason of anything found in the act, but solely because the colored race chooses to put that construction upon it. The argument necessarily assumes that if, as has been more than once the case, and is not unlikely to be so again, the colored race should become the dominant power in the state legislature, and should enact a law in precisely similar terms, it would thereby relegate the white race to an inferior position. We imagine that the white race, at least, would not acquiesce in this assumption.

The argument also assumes that social prejudices may be overcome by legislation, and that equal rights cannot be secured to the negro except by an enforced commingling of the two races. We cannot accept this proposition. If the two races are to meet upon terms of social equality, it must be the result of natural affinities, a mutual appreciation of each other's merits, and a voluntary consent of individuals. . . . Legislation is powerless to eradicate racial instincts, or to abolish distinctions based upon physical differences, and the attempt to do so can only result in accentuating the difficulties of the present situation. If the civil and political rights of both races be equal, one cannot be inferior to the other civilly or politically. If one race be inferior to the other socially, the constitution of the United States cannot put them upon the same plane.

It is true that the question of the proportion of colored blood necessary to constitute a colored person, as distinguished from a white person, is one upon which there is a difference of opinion in the different states; some holding that any visible admixture of black blood stamps the person as belonging to the colored race, *State v. Chavers* (North Carolina 1857); others, that it depends upon the preponderance of blood, *Gray v. State* (Ohio 1829); and still others, that the predominance of white blood must only be in the proportion of three-fourths, *People v. Dean* (Michigan 1866); *Jones v. Commonwealth* (Virginia 1885). But these are questions to be determined under the laws of each state, and are not properly put in issue in this case. Under the allegations of his petition, it may undoubtedly become a question of importance whether, under the laws of Louisiana, the petitioner belongs to the white or colored race.

The judgment of the court below is therefore affirmed.

MR. JUSTICE BREWER did not hear the argument or participate in the decision of this case.

MR. JUSTICE HARLAN dissenting.

. . . While there may be in Louisiana persons of different races who are not citizens of the United States, the words in the act "white and colored races" necessarily include all citizens of the United States of both races residing in that state. So that we have before us a state enactment that compels, under penalties, the separation of the two races in railroad passenger coaches, and makes it a crime for a citizen of either race to enter a coach that has been assigned to citizens of the other race.

Thus, the state regulates the use of a public highway by citizens of the United States solely upon the basis of race. However apparent the injustice of such legislation may be, we have only to consider whether it is consistent with the Constitution of the United States. . . .

In respect of civil rights, common to all citizens, the Constitution of the United States does not, I think, permit any public authority to know the race of those entitled to be protected in the enjoyment of such rights. Every true man has pride of race, and under appropriate circumstances, when the rights of others, his equals before the law, are not to be affected, it is his privilege to express such pride and to take such action based upon it as to him seems proper. But I deny that any legislative body or judicial tribunal may have regard to the race of citizens when the civil rights of those citizens are involved. Indeed, such legislation as that here in question is inconsistent not only with that equality of rights which pertains to citizenship, national and state, but with the personal liberty enjoyed by every one within the United States.

[The 13th, 14th, and 15th Amendments were] notable additions to the fundamental law [and] welcomed by the friends of liberty throughout the world. They removed the race line from our governmental systems. They had, as this court has said, a common purpose, namely, to secure "to a race recently emancipated . . . . the right to exemption from unfriendly legislation against them distinctively as colored; exemption from legal discriminations, implying inferiority in civil society, lessening the security of their enjoyment of the rights which others enjoy; and discriminations which are steps towards reducing them to the condition of a subject race." *Strauder v. West Virginia* (1880). . . .

It was said in argument that the statute of Louisiana does not discriminate against either race, but prescribes a rule applicable alike to white and colored citizens. But this argument does not meet the difficulty. Every one knows that the statute in question had its origin in the purpose, not so much to exclude white persons from railroad cars occupied by blacks, as to exclude colored people from coaches occupied by or assigned to white persons. Railroad corporations of Louisiana did not make discrimination among whites in the matter of accommodation for travellers. The thing to accomplish was, under the guise of giving equal accommodation for whites and blacks, to compel the latter to keep to themselves while traveling in railroad passenger coaches. No one would be so wanting in candor as to assert the contrary. . . .

It is one thing for railroad carriers to furnish, or to be required by law to furnish, equal accommodations for all whom they are under a legal duty to carry. It is quite another thing for government to forbid citizens of the white and black races from traveling in the same public conveyance, and to punish officers of railroad companies for permitting persons of the two races to occupy the same passenger coach. If a state can prescribe, as a rule of civil conduct, that whites and blacks shall not travel as passengers in the same railroad coach, why may it not so regulate the use of the streets of its cities and towns as to compel white citizens to keep on one side of a street, and black citizens to keep on the other? Why may it not, upon like grounds, punish whites and blacks who ride together in street cars or in open vehicles on a public road or street? Why may it not require sheriffs to assign whites to one side of a court room, and blacks to the other? And why may it not also prohibit the commingling of the two races in the galleries of legislative halls or in public assemblages convened for the consideration of the political questions of the day? Further, if this statute of Louisiana is consistent with the personal liberty of citizens, why may not the state require the separation in railroad coaches of native and naturalized citizens of the United States, or of Protestants and Roman Catholics?

The answer given at the argument to these questions was that regulations of the kind they suggest would be unreasonable, and could not, therefore, stand before the law. Is it meant that the determination of questions of legislative power depends upon the inquiry whether the statute whose validity is questioned is, in the judgment of the courts, a reasonable one, taking all the circumstances into consideration? A statute may be unreasonable merely because a sound public policy forbade its enactment. But I do not understand that the courts have anything to do with the policy or expediency of legislation. A statute may be valid, and yet, upon grounds of public policy, may well be characterized as unreasonable. Mr. Sedgwick correctly states the rule when he says that, the legislative intention being clearly ascertained, "the courts have no other duty to perform than to execute the legislative will, without any regard to their views as to the wisdom or justice of the particular enactment." St. & Const. Constr. (1874). . . .

The white race deems itself to be the dominant race in this country. And so it is, in prestige, in achievements, in education, in wealth, and in power. So, I doubt not, it will continue to be for all time, if it remains true to its great heritage, and holds fast to the principles of constitutional liberty. But in view of the constitution, in the eye of the law, there is in this country no superior, dominant, ruling class of citizens. There is no caste here. Our constitution is color-blind, and neither knows nor tolerates classes among citizens. In respect of civil rights, all citizens are equal before the law. The humblest is the peer of the most powerful. The law regards man as man, and takes no account of his surroundings or of his color when his civil rights as guaranteed by the supreme law of the land are involved. It is therefore to be regretted that this high tribunal, the final expositor of the fundamental law of the land, has reached the conclusion that it is competent for a state to regulate the enjoyment by citizens of their civil rights solely upon the basis of race.

In my opinion, the judgment this day rendered will, in time, prove to be quite as pernicious as the decision made by this tribunal in the *Dred Scott Case* (1857). . . . The recent amendments of the constitution, it was supposed, had eradicated [the] principles [of that case] from our institutions. But it seems that we have yet, in some of the states, a dominant race—a superior class of citizens—which assumes to regulate the enjoyment of civil rights, common to all citizens, upon the basis of race. The present decision, it may well be apprehended, will not only stimulate aggressions, more or less brutal and irritating, upon the admitted rights of colored citizens, but will encourage the belief that it is possible, by means of state enactments, to defeat the beneficent purposes which the people of the United States had in view when they adopted the recent amendments of the constitution, by one of which the blacks of this country were made citizens of the United States and of the states in which they respectively reside, and whose privileges and immunities, as citizens, the states are forbidden to abridge.

Sixty millions of whites are in no danger from the presence here of eight millions of blacks. The destinies of the two races, in this country, are indissolubly linked together, and the interests of both require that the common government of all shall not permit the seeds of race hate to be planted under the sanction of law. What can more certainly arouse race hate, what more certainly create and perpetuate a feeling of distrust between these races, than state enactments which, in fact, proceed on the ground that colored citizens are so inferior and degraded that they cannot be allowed to sit in public coaches occupied by white citizens? That, as all will admit, is the real meaning of such legislation as was enacted in Louisiana. . . .

State enactments regulating the enjoyment of civil rights upon the basis of race, and cunningly devised to defeat legitimate results of the war, under the pretense of recognizing equality of rights, can have no other result than to render permanent peace impossible, and to keep alive a conflict of races, the continuance of which must do harm to all concerned. This question is not met by the suggestion that social equality cannot exist between the white and black races in this country. That argument, if it can be properly regarded as one, is scarcely worthy of consideration; for social equality no more exists between two races when traveling in a passenger coach or a public highway than when members of the same races sit by each other in a street car or in the jury box, or stand or sit with each other in a political assembly, or when they use in common the streets of a city or town, or when they are in the same room for the purpose of having their names placed on the registry of voters, or when they approach the ballot box in order to exercise the high privilege of voting.

There is a race so different from our own that we do not permit those belonging to it to become citizens of the United States. Persons belonging to it are, with few exceptions, absolutely excluded from our country. I allude to the

Chinese race. But, by the statute in question, a Chinaman can ride in the same passenger coach with white citizens of the United States, while citizens of the black race in Louisiana, many of whom, perhaps, risked their lives for the preservation of the Union, who are entitled, by law, to participate in the political control of the state and nation, who are not excluded, by law or by reason of their race, from public stations of any kind, and who have all the legal rights that belong to white citizens, are yet declared to be criminals, liable to imprisonment, if they ride in a public coach occupied by citizens of the white race. It is scarcely just to say that a colored citizen should not object to occupying a public coach assigned to his own race. He does not object, nor, perhaps, would he object to separate coaches for his race if his rights under the law were recognized. But he objects, and ought never to cease objecting . . . , that citizens of the white and black races can be adjudged criminals because they sit, or claim the right to sit, in the same public coach on a public highway. . . .

We boast of the freedom enjoyed by our people above all other peoples. But it is difficult to reconcile that boast with a state of the law which, practically, puts the brand of servitude and degradation upon a large class of our fellow citizens—our equals before the law. The thin disguise of "equal" accommodations for passengers in railroad coaches will not mislead any one, nor atone for the wrong this day done. . . .

Korematsu v. United States

Supreme Court of the United States, 1944.
323 U.S. 214.

MR. JUSTICE BLACK delivered the opinion of the Court.

The petitioner, an American citizen of Japanese descent, was convicted in a federal district court for remaining in San Leandro, California, a "Military Area," contrary to Civilian Exclusion Order No. 34 of the Commanding General of the Western Command, U.S. Army, which directed that after May 9, 1942, all persons of Japanese ancestry should be excluded from that area. No question was raised as to petitioner's loyalty to the United States. . . .

It should be noted, to begin with, that all legal restrictions which curtail the civil rights of a single racial group are immediately suspect. That is not to say that all such restrictions are unconstitutional. It is to say that courts must subject them to the most rigid scrutiny. Pressing public necessity may sometimes justify the existence of such restrictions; racial antagonism never can.

In the instant case prosecution of the petitioner was begun by information charging violation of an Act of Congress, of March 21, 1942, which [made it a criminal violation for any person to "enter, remain in, leave, or commit any act in any military area . . . contrary to the restrictions applicable to any such area" as announced by the Secretary of War or his designee, if the defendant "knew or should have known of the existence and extent of the restrictions."] Exclusion Order No. 34, which the petitioner knowingly and admittedly violated, was one of a number of military orders and proclamations, all of which were substantially based upon Executive Order No. 9066. That order, issued after we were at war with Japan, declared that "the successful prosecution of the war requires every possible protection against espionage and against sabotage to national-defense material, national-defense premises, and national-defense utilities. . . ."

One of the series of orders and proclamations, a curfew order, which like the exclusion order here was promulgated pursuant to Executive Order 9066, subjected all persons of Japanese ancestry in prescribed West Coast military areas to remain in their residences from 8 p.m. to 6 a.m. As is the case with the exclusion order here, that prior curfew order was designed as a "protection against espionage and against sabotage." In *Hirabayashi v. United States* (1943), we sustained a conviction obtained for violation of the curfew order. The *Hirabayashi* conviction and this one thus rest on the same 1942 Congressional Act and the same basic executive and military orders, all of which orders were aimed at the twin dangers of espionage and sabotage. . . .

In the light of the principles we announced in the *Hirabayashi* case, we are unable to conclude that it was beyond the war power of Congress and the Executive to exclude those of Japanese ancestry from the West Coast war area at the time they did. True, exclusion from the area in which one's home is located is a far greater deprivation than constant confinement to the home from 8 p.m. to 6 a.m. Nothing short of apprehension by the proper military authorities of the gravest imminent danger to the public safety can constitutionally justify either. But exclusion from a threatened area, no less than curfew, has a definite and close relationship to the prevention of espionage and sabotage. The military authorities, charged with the primary responsibility of defending our shores, concluded that curfew provided inadequate protection and ordered exclusion. They did so, as pointed out in our *Hirabayashi* opinion, in accordance with Congressional authority to the military to say who should, and who should not, remain in the threatened areas.

In this case the petitioner challenges the assumptions upon which we rested our conclusions in the *Hirabayashi* case. He also urges that by May 1942, when Order No. 34 was promulgated, all danger of Japanese invasion of the West Coast had disappeared. After careful consideration of these contentions we are compelled to reject them.

Here, as in the *Hirabayashi* case,

[W]e cannot reject as unfounded the judgment of the military authorities and of Congress that there were disloyal members of that population, whose number and strength could not be precisely and quickly ascertained. We cannot say that the war-making branches of the Government did not have ground for believing that in a critical hour such persons could not readily be isolated and separately dealt with, and constituted a menace to the national defense and safety, which demanded that prompt and adequate measures be taken to guard against it.

Like curfew, exclusion of those of Japanese origin was deemed necessary because of the presence of an unascertained number of disloyal members of the group, most of whom we have no doubt were loyal to this country. It was because we could not reject the finding of the military authorities that it was impossible to bring about an immediate segregation of the disloyal from the loyal that we sustained the validity of the curfew order as applying to the whole group. In the instant case, temporary exclusion of the entire group was rested by the military on the same ground. The judgment that exclusion of the whole group was for the same reason a military imperative answers the contention that the exclusion was in the nature of group punishment based on antagonism to those of Japanese origin. That there were members of the group who retained loyalties to Japan has been confirmed by investigations made subsequent to the exclusion. Approximately five thousand American citizens of Japanese ancestry refused to swear unqualified allegiance to the United States and to renounce allegiance to the Japanese Emperor, and several thousand evacuees requested repatriation to Japan [citing congressional hearings and General John L. De-Witt's *Final Report, Japanese Evacuation from the West Coast* (1942)].

We uphold the exclusion order as of the time it was made and when the petitioner violated it. In doing so, we are not unmindful of the hardships imposed by it upon a large group of American citizens. But hardships are part of war, and war is an aggregation of hardships. All citizens alike, both in and out of uniform, feel the impact of war in greater or lesser measure. Citizenship has its responsibilities as well as its privileges, and in time of war the burden is always heavier. Compulsory exclusion of large groups of citizens from their homes, except under circumstances of direst emergency and peril, is inconsistent with our basic governmental institutions. But when under conditions of modern warfare our shores are threatened by hostile forces, the power to protect must be commensurate with the threatened danger. . . .

. . . It is now argued that the validity of the exclusion order cannot be considered apart from the orders requiring him, after departure from the area, to report and to remain in an assembly or relocation center. The contention is that we must treat these separate orders as one and inseparable; that, for this reason, if detention in the assembly or relocation center would have illegally deprived the petitioner of his liberty, the exclusion order and his conviction under it cannot stand.

We are thus being asked to pass at this time upon the whole subsequent detention program in both assembly and relocation centers, although the only issues framed at the trial related to petitioner's remaining in the prohibited area in violation of the exclusion order. Had petitioner here left the prohibited area and gone to an assembly center we cannot say either as a matter of fact or law, that his presence in that center would have resulted in his detention in a relocation center. Some who did report to the assembly center were not sent to relocation centers, but were released upon condition that they remain outside the prohibited zone until the military orders were modified or lifted. This illustrates that they pose different problems and may be governed by different principles. The lawfulness of one does not necessarily determine the lawfulness of the others. . . . The *Endo* case graphically illustrates the difference between the

WORTH NOTING

Ex parte Endo was decided the same day as *Korematsu*. In *Endo*, the Supreme Court unanimously ordered the release of a concededly loyal citizen of Japanese descent from the internment camp where she was being held against her will. Citing the canon of constitutional avoidance, the Supreme Court held that neither Executive Order 9066 nor the congressional act effectively ratifying it could be interpreted as authorizing ongoing detention of someone in petitioner's circumstances. Endo was therefore "entitled to an unconditional release by the War Relocation Authority."

validity of an order to exclude and the validity of a detention order after exclusion has been effected.

Since the petitioner has not been convicted of failing to report or to remain in an assembly or relocation center, we cannot in this case determine the validity of those separate provisions of the order. It is sufficient here for us to pass upon the order which petitioner violated. . . .

It is said that we are dealing here with the case of imprisonment of a citizen in a concentration camp solely because of his ancestry, without evidence or inquiry concerning his loyalty and good disposition towards the United States. Our task would be simple, our duty clear, were this a case involving the imprisonment of a loyal citizen in a concentration camp because of racial prejudice. Regardless of the true nature of the assembly and relocation centers—and we deem it unjustifiable to call them concentration camps with all the ugly connotations that term implies—we are dealing specifically with nothing but an exclusion order. To cast this case into outlines of racial prejudice, without reference to the real military dangers which were presented, merely confuses the issue.

Korematsu was not excluded from the Military Area because of hostility to him or his race. He was excluded because we are at war with the Japanese Empire, because the properly constituted military authorities feared an invasion of our West Coast and felt constrained to take proper security measures, because they decided that the military urgency of the situation demanded that all citizens of Japanese ancestry be segregated from the West Coast temporarily, and finally, because Congress, reposing its confidence in this time of war in our military leaders—as inevitably it must—determined that they should have the power to do just this. There was evidence of disloyalty on the part of some, the military authorities considered that the need for action was great, and time was short. We cannot—by availing ourselves of the calm perspective of hindsight—now say that at that time these actions were unjustified.

Affirmed.

From 1943 to 1944, the Supreme Court reviewed several features of the racially discriminatory regime that was created by Executive Order No. 9066 and the congressional act ratifying it. The Court reached different results on different aspects of the regime: nightly curfew (*Hirabayashi*) and exclusion from the West Coast (*Korematsu*) on the basis of race were upheld, but detention in an internment camp (*Endo*) was not.

FOR DISCUSSION

Notably, although *Endo* was a statutory case, the Court's interpretation of the statute relied on what is known as constitutional avoidance—that is, the Court construed the statute not to authorize the detention of Mitsuye Endo precisely to avoid what it perceived as a serious question whether a statute that *did* authorize detention would be constitutional. Given the outcomes in *Hirabayashi* and *Korematsu*, why might the Supreme Court have been in doubt about the constitutionality of racial discrimination when it came to internment? How might you articulate your answer in terms of the constitutional test articulated in *Korematsu*?

MR. JUSTICE FRANKFURTER, concurring.

. . . The provisions of the Constitution which confer on the Congress and the President powers to enable this country to wage war are as much part of the Constitution as provisions looking to a nation at peace. And we have had recent occasion to quote approvingly the statement of former Chief Justice Hughes that the war power of the Government is "the power to wage war successfully." *Hirabayashi v. United States*. Therefore, the validity of action under the war power must be judged wholly in the context of war. That action is not to be stigmatized as lawless because like action in times of peace would be lawless. . . .

To find that the Constitution does not forbid the military measures now complained of does not carry with it approval of that which Congress and the Executive did. That is their business, not ours.

MR. JUSTICE ROBERTS, dissenting.

I dissent, because I think the indisputable facts exhibit a clear violation of Constitutional rights.

This is not a case of keeping people off the streets at night as was *Hirabayashi v. United States*, nor a case of temporary exclusion of a citizen from an area for his own safety or that of the community, nor a case of offering him an opportunity to go temporarily out of an area where his presence might cause danger to himself or to his fellows. On the contrary, it is the case of convicting a citizen as a punishment for not submitting to imprisonment in a concentration camp, based on his ancestry, and solely because of his ancestry, without evidence or inquiry concerning his loyalty and good disposition towards the United States. . . .

The Government's argument, and the opinion of the court, in my judgment, erroneously divide that which is single and indivisible and thus make the case appear as if the petitioner violated a Military Order, sanctioned by Act of Congress, which excluded him from his home, by refusing voluntarily to leave and, so, knowingly and intentionally, defying the order and the Act of Congress. . . .

[T]he petitioner's supposed offense did not, in truth, consist in his refusal voluntarily to leave the area which included his home in obedience to the order excluding him therefrom. . . . [Rather, the] predicament in which the petitioner thus found himself was this: He was forbidden, by Military Order, to leave the zone in which he lived; he was forbidden, by Military Order, after a date fixed, to be found within that zone unless he were in an Assembly Center located in that zone. . . . In the dilemma that he dare not remain in his home, or voluntarily leave the area, without incurring criminal penalties, and that the only way he could avoid punishment was to go to an Assembly Center and submit himself to military imprisonment, the petitioner did nothing. . . .

[T]he petitioner was tried under a plea of not guilty and convicted. Sentence was suspended and he was placed on probation for five years. We know, however . . . , that . . . the petitioner has [since that time] been confined either in an Assembly Center, within the zone in which he had lived or [in] a Relocation Center [located elsewhere]. . . .

[The Court's decision], I think, is a substitution of an hypothetical case for the case actually before the court. I might agree with the court's disposition of the hypothetical case.[8] The liberty of every American citizen freely to come and to go must frequently, in the face of sudden danger, be temporarily limited or suspended. The civil authorities must often resort to the expedient of excluding citizens temporarily from a locality. The drawing of fire lines in the case of a conflagration, the removal of persons from the area where a pestilence has broken out, are familiar examples. If the exclusion worked by Exclusion Order No. 34 were of that nature the *Hirabayashi* case would be authority for sustaining it. But the facts . . . show that the exclusion was but a part of an

---

[8]   My agreement would depend on the definition and application of the terms "temporary" and "emergency." No pronouncement of the commanding officer can, in my view, preclude judicial inquiry and determination whether an emergency ever existed and whether, if so, it remained, at the date of the restraint out of which the litigation arose.

over-all plan for forceable detention. This case cannot, therefore, be decided on any such narrow ground as the possible validity of a Temporary Exclusion Order under which the residents of an area are given an opportunity to leave and go elsewhere in their native land outside the boundaries of a military area. To make the case turn on any such assumption is to shut our eyes to reality. . . .

[Korematsu was subject to] two conflicting orders, one which commanded him to stay and the other which commanded him to go, [and together these] were nothing but a cleverly devised trap to accomplish the real purpose of the military authority, which was to lock him up in a concentration camp. The only course by which the petitioner could avoid arrest and prosecution was to go to that camp according to instructions to be given him when he reported at a Civil Control Center. We know that is the fact. Why should we set up a figmentary and artificial situation instead of addressing ourselves to the actualities of the case? . . .

I would reverse the judgment of conviction.

MR. JUSTICE MURPHY, dissenting.

This exclusion of "all persons of Japanese ancestry, both alien and non-alien," from the Pacific Coast area on a plea of military necessity in the absence of martial law ought not to be approved. Such exclusion goes over "the very brink of constitutional power" and falls into the ugly abyss of racism.

In dealing with matters relating to the prosecution and progress of a war, we must accord great respect and consideration to the judgments of the military authorities who are on the scene and who have full knowledge of the military facts. . . . At the same time, however, it is essential that there be definite limits to military discretion, especially where martial law has not been declared. Individuals must not be left impoverished of their constitutional rights on a plea of military necessity that has neither substance nor support. . . . "What are the allowable limits of military discretion, and whether or not they have been overstepped in a particular case, are judicial questions." *Sterling v. Constantin* (1932).

The judicial test of whether the Government, on a plea of military necessity, can validly deprive an individual of any of his constitutional rights is whether the deprivation is reasonably related to a public danger that is so "immediate, imminent, and impending" as not to admit of delay and not to permit the intervention of ordinary constitutional processes to alleviate the danger. Civilian Exclusion Order No. 34, banishing from a prescribed area of the Pacific Coast "all persons of Japanese ancestry, both alien and non-alien," clearly does not meet that test. Being an obvious racial discrimination, the order deprives all those within its scope of the equal protection of the laws as guaranteed by the Fifth Amendment. . . . Yet no reasonable relation to an "immediate, imminent, and impending" public danger is evident to support this racial restriction which is one of the most sweeping and complete deprivations of constitutional rights in the history of this nation in the absence of martial law.

It must be conceded that the military and naval situation in the spring of 1942 was such as to generate a very real fear of invasion of the Pacific Coast, accompanied by fears of sabotage and espionage in that area. The military command was therefore justified in adopting all reasonable means necessary to combat these dangers. In adjudging the military action taken in light of the then apparent dangers, we must not erect too high or too meticulous standards; it is necessary only that the action have some reasonable relation to the removal of the dangers of invasion, sabotage and espionage. But the exclusion, either temporarily or permanently, of all persons with Japanese blood in their veins has no such reasonable relation. And that relation is lacking because the exclusion order necessarily must rely for its reasonableness upon the assumption that all persons of Japanese ancestry may have a dangerous tendency to commit sabotage and espionage and to aid our Japanese enemy in other ways. It is difficult to believe that reason, logic or experience could be marshalled in support of such an assumption.

That this forced exclusion was the result in good measure of this erroneous assumption of racial guilt rather than bona fide military necessity is evidenced by the Commanding General's Final Report on the evacuation from the Pacific Coast area. In it he refers to all individuals of Japanese descent as 'subversive,' as belonging to "an enemy race" whose "racial strains are undiluted," and as constituting "over 112,000 potential enemies . . . at large today" along the Pacific Coast.[2] In support of this blanket condemnation of all persons of Japanese

---

[2]   Further evidence of the Commanding General's attitude toward individuals of Japanese ancestry is revealed in his voluntary testimony on April 13, 1943, in San Francisco before the House Naval Affairs Subcommittee to Investigate Congested Areas:

I don't want any of them [persons of Japanese ancestry] here. They are a dangerous element. There is no way to determine their loyalty. The west coast contains too many vital installations essential to the defense of the country to allow any Japanese on this coast. . . . The danger of the Japanese was, and is now—if they are permitted to come back—espionage and sabotage. It makes no difference whether he is an American citizen, he is still a Japanese. American citizenship does not necessarily determine loyalty. . . . But we must worry about the Japanese all the time until he is wiped off the map. Sabotage and espionage will make problems as long as he is allowed in this area. . . .

descent, however, no reliable evidence is cited to show that such individuals were generally disloyal,[3] or had generally so conducted themselves in this area as to constitute a special menace to defense installations or war industries, or had otherwise by their behavior furnished reasonable ground for their exclusion as a group.

Justification for the exclusion is sought, instead, mainly upon questionable racial and sociological grounds not ordinarily within the realm of expert military judgment, supplemented by certain semi-military conclusions drawn from an unwarranted use of circumstantial evidence. Individuals of Japanese ancestry are condemned because they are said to be "a large, unassimilated, tightly knit racial group, bound to an enemy nation by strong ties of race, culture, custom and religion."[4] They are claimed to be given to "emperor worshipping ceremonies" and to "dual citizenship." Japanese language schools and allegedly pro-Japanese organizations are cited as evidence of possible group disloyalty,[7] together with facts as to certain persons being educated and residing at length in Japan. It is intimated that many of these individuals deliberately resided "adjacent to strategic points," thus enabling them "to carry into execution a tremendous program of sabotage on a mass scale should any considerable number of them have been inclined to do so."[9] The need for protective custody is also asserted. The report refers without identity to "numerous incidents of violence" as well as to other admittedly unverified or cumulative incidents. From this, plus certain other events not shown to have been connected with the Japanese Americans, it is concluded that the "situation was fraught with danger to the Japanese population itself" and that the general public "was ready to take matters into its own

---

[3]   The Final Report casts a cloud of suspicion over the entire group by saying that "while it was *believed* that *some* were loyal, it was known that many were not." (Italics added.)

[4]   To the extent that assimilation is a problem, it is largely the result of certain social customs and laws of the American general public. Studies demonstrate that persons of Japanese descent are readily susceptible to integration in our society if given the opportunity. . . . The failure to accomplish an ideal status of assimilation, therefore, cannot be charged to the refusal of these persons to become Americanized or to their loyalty to Japan. And the retention by some persons of certain customs and religious practices of their ancestors is no criterion of their loyalty to the United States.

[7]   We have had various foreign language schools in this country for generations without considering their existence as ground for racial discrimination. No subversive activities or teachings have been shown in connection with the Japanese schools.

[9]   This insinuation, based purely upon speculation and circumstantial evidence, completely overlooks the fact that the main geographic pattern of Japanese population was fixed many years ago with reference to economic, social and soil conditions. Limited occupational outlets and social pressures encouraged their concentration near their initial points of entry on the Pacific Coast. That these points may now be near certain strategic military and industrial areas is no proof of a diabolical purpose on the part of Japanese Americans.

hands."[10] Finally, it is intimated, though not directly charged or proved, that persons of Japanese ancestry were responsible for three minor isolated shellings and bombings of the Pacific Coast area, as well as for unidentified radio transmissions and night signalling.

The main reasons relied upon by those responsible for the forced evacuation, therefore, do not prove a reasonable relation between the group characteristics of Japanese Americans and the dangers of invasion, sabotage and espionage. The reasons appear, instead, to be largely an accumulation of much of the misinformation, half-truths and insinuations that for years have been directed against Japanese Americans by people with racial and economic prejudices—the same people who have been among the foremost advocates of the evacuation.[12] A military judgment based upon such racial and sociological considerations is not entitled to the great weight ordinarily given the judgments based upon strictly military considerations. Especially is this so when every charge relative to race, religion, culture, geographical location, and legal and economic status has been substantially discredited by independent studies made by experts in these matters.

The military necessity which is essential to the validity of the evacuation order thus resolves itself into a few intimations that certain individuals actively aided the enemy, from which it is inferred that the entire group of Japanese Americans could not be trusted to be or remain loyal to the United States. No one denies, of course, that there were some disloyal persons of Japanese descent on the Pacific Coast who did all in their power to aid their ancestral land. Similar disloyal activities have been engaged in by many persons of German, Italian and even more pioneer stock in our country. But to infer that examples of individual disloyalty prove group disloyalty and justify discriminatory action against the entire group is to deny that under our system of law individual guilt is the sole basis for deprivation of rights. Moreover, this inference, which is at the very heart of the evacuation orders, has been used in support of the

---

[10]   This dangerous doctrine of protective custody, as proved by recent European history, should have absolutely no standing as an excuse for the deprivation of the rights of minority groups.

[12]   Special interest groups were extremely active in applying pressure for mass evacuation. . . . Mr. Austin E. Anson, managing secretary of the Salinas Vegetable Grower-Shipper Association, has frankly admitted that "We're charged with wanting to get rid of the Japs for selfish reasons. We do. It's a question of whether the white man lives on the Pacific Coast or the brown men. They came into this valley to work, and they stayed to take over. . . . They undersell the white man in the markets. . . . They work their women and children while the white farmer has to pay wages for his help. If all the Japs were removed tomorrow, we'd never miss them in two weeks, because the white farmers can take over and produce everything the Jap grows. And we don't want them back when the war ends, either." Quoted [in] *The People Nobody Wants*, Sat. Eve. Post (May 9, 1942).

abhorrent and despicable treatment of minority groups by the dictatorial tyrannies which this nation is now pledged to destroy. . . .

No adequate reason is given for the failure to treat these Japanese Americans on an individual basis by holding investigations and hearings to separate the loyal from the disloyal, as was done in the case of persons of German and Italian ancestry. . . . It is asserted merely that the loyalties of this group "were unknown and time was of the essence." Yet nearly four months elapsed after Pearl Harbor before the first exclusion order was issued; nearly eight months went by until the last order was issued; and the last of these "subversive" persons was not actually removed until almost eleven months had elapsed. Leisure and deliberation seem to have been more of the essence than speed. And the fact that conditions were not such as to warrant a declaration of martial law adds strength to the belief that the factors of time and military necessity were not as urgent as they have been represented to be.

Moreover, there was no adequate proof that the Federal Bureau of Investigation and the military and naval intelligence services did not have the espionage and sabotage situation well in hand during this long period. Nor is there any denial of the fact that not one person of Japanese ancestry was accused or convicted of espionage or sabotage after Pearl Harbor while they were still free,[15] a fact which is some evidence of the loyalty of the vast majority of these individuals and of the effectiveness of the established methods of combatting these evils. It seems incredible that under these circumstances it would have been impossible to hold loyalty hearings for the mere 112,000 persons involved—or at least for the 70,000 American citizens—especially when a large part of this number represented children and elderly men and women.[16] Any inconvenience that may have accompanied an attempt to conform to procedural due process cannot be said to justify violations of constitutional rights of individuals.

I dissent, therefore, from this legalization of racism. Racial discrimination in any form and in any degree has no justifiable part whatever in our democratic

---

[15] The Final Report makes the amazing statement that as of February 14, 1942, "The very fact that no sabotage has taken place to date is a disturbing and confirming indication that such action will be taken." Apparently, in the minds of the military leaders, there was no way that the Japanese Americans could escape the suspicion of sabotage.

[16] During a period of six months, the 112 alien tribunals or hearing boards set up by the British Government shortly after the outbreak of the present war summoned and examined approximately 74,000 German and Austrian aliens. These tribunals determined whether each individual enemy alien was a real enemy of the Allies or only a 'friendly enemy.' About 64,000 were freed from internment and from any special restrictions, and only 2,000 were interned. . . .

way of life. It is unattractive in any setting but it is utterly revolting among a free people who have embraced the principles set forth in the Constitution of the United States. All residents of this nation are kin in some way by blood or culture to a foreign land. Yet they are primarily and necessarily a part of the new and distinct civilization of the United States. They must accordingly be treated at all times as the heirs of the American experiment and as entitled to all the rights and freedoms guaranteed by the Constitution.

As the Department of Justice prepared its legal defense of the exclusion order, it relied principally on a lengthy factual report from the War Department. One DOJ lawyer, however, came to the conclusion that the report was riddled with "wilful historical inaccuracies" and "intentional falsehoods," including for example a range of "assertions concerning radio transmissions and ship-to-shore signaling [that are] directly contradicted by a memorandum from the FBI" and by "a letter from the Federal Communications Commission." In a letter alerting Associate Attorney-General Herbert Wechsler to these problems, the DOJ lawyer also observed that "[t]he general tenor of the report is . . . to the effect that overt acts of treason were being committed," which "is not so," and emphasized that the "War Department . . . contrived to publish this report without the knowledge of this Department by the use of falsehood and evasion."

FOR DISCUSSION

In its brief to the Supreme Court, the Department of Justice included only the following caveat:

> The Final Report of General DeWitt . . . is relied on in this brief for statistics and other details concerning the actual evacuation and the events that took place subsequent thereto. We have specifically recited in this brief the facts relating to the justification for the evacuation, of which we ask the Court to take judicial notice, and we rely upon the Final Report only to the extent that it relates to such facts.

Assuming that the DOJ lawyer's warnings about the War Department report were accurate, was this response to the problem sufficient? If not, should that affect how we think about the Court's decision in *Korematsu*—either as a statement of legal principle or as an example of its application?

MR. JUSTICE JACKSON, dissenting.

Korematsu was born on our soil, of parents born in Japan. The Constitution makes him a citizen of the United States by nativity and a citizen of California by residence. No claim is made that he is not loyal to this country. There is no suggestion that apart from the matter involved here he is not law-abiding and well disposed. Korematsu, however, has been convicted of an act not commonly a crime. It consists merely of being present in the state whereof he is a citizen, near the place where he was born, and where all his life he has lived.

Even more unusual is the series of military orders which made this conduct a crime. They forbid such a one to remain, and they also forbid him to leave. They were so drawn that the only way Korematsu could avoid violation was to give himself up to the military authority. This meant submission to custody, examination, and transportation out of the territory, to be followed by indeterminate confinement in detention camps.

A citizen's presence in the locality, however, was made a crime only if his parents were of Japanese birth. Had Korematsu been one of four—the others being, say, a German alien enemy, an Italian alien enemy, and a citizen of American-born ancestors, convicted of treason but out on parole—only Korematsu's presence would have violated the order. The difference between their innocence and his crime would result, not from anything he did, said, or thought, different than they, but only in that he was born of different racial stock.

Now, if any fundamental assumption underlies our system, it is that guilt is personal and not inheritable. . . .

[T]he "law" which this prisoner is convicted of disregarding is not found in an act of Congress, but in a military order. [T]he Act of Congress . . . would [not alone] afford a basis for this conviction. It rests on the orders of General DeWitt. And it is said that if the military commander had reasonable military grounds for promulgating the orders, they are constitutional and become law, and the Court is required to enforce them. There are several reasons why I cannot subscribe to this doctrine.

It would be impracticable and dangerous idealism to expect or insist that each specific military command in an area of probable operations will conform to conventional tests of constitutionality. When an area is so beset that it must be put under military control at all, the paramount consideration is that its measures be successful, rather than legal. The armed services must protect a society, not merely its Constitution. The very essence of the military job is to marshal physical force, to remove every obstacle to its effectiveness, to give it every strategic advantage. Defense measures will not, and often should not, be held within the limits that bind civil authority in peace. No court can require such a commander in such circumstances to act as a reasonable man; he may be unreasonably cautious and exacting. Perhaps he should be. But a commander in temporarily focusing the life of a community on defense is carrying out a military program; he is not making law in the sense the courts know the term. He issues orders, and they may have a certain authority as military commands, although they may be very bad as constitutional law.

But if we cannot confine military expedients by the Constitution, neither would I distort the Constitution to approve all that the military may deem expedient. That is what the Court appears to be doing, whether consciously or not. I cannot say, from any evidence before me, that the orders of General DeWitt were not reasonably expedient military precautions, nor could I say that they were. But even if they were permissible military procedures, I deny that it follows that they are constitutional. If, as the Court holds, it does follow, then we may as well say that any military order will be constitutional and have done with it.

The limitation under which courts always will labor in examining the necessity for a military order are illustrated by this case. How does the Court know that these orders have a reasonable basis in necessity? No evidence whatever on that subject has been taken by this or any other court. There is sharp controversy as to the credibility of the DeWitt report. So the Court, having no real evidence before it, has no choice but to accept General DeWitt's own unsworn, self-serving statement, untested by any cross-examination, that what he did was reasonable. And thus it will always be when courts try to look into the reasonableness of a military order. . . .

Much is said of the danger to liberty from the Army program for deporting and detaining these citizens of Japanese extraction. But a judicial construction of the due process clause that will sustain this order is a far more subtle blow to liberty than the promulgation of the order itself. A military order, however unconstitutional, is not apt to last longer than the military emergency. Even during that period a succeeding commander may revoke it all. But once a judicial opinion rationalizes such an order to show that it conforms to the Constitution, or rather rationalizes the Constitution to show that the Constitution sanctions such an order, the Court for all time has validated the principle of racial discrimination in criminal procedure and of transplanting American citizens. The principle then lies about like a loaded weapon ready for the hand of any authority that can bring forward a plausible claim of an urgent need. Every repetition imbeds that principle more deeply in our law and thinking and expands it to new purposes. All who observe the work of courts are familiar with what Judge Cardozo described as "the tendency of a principle to expand itself to the limit of its logic." A military commander may overstep the bounds of constitutionality, and it is an incident. But if we review and approve, that passing incident becomes the doctrine of the Constitution. There it has a generative power of its own. . . .

I should hold that a civil court cannot be made to enforce an order which violates constitutional limitations even if it is a reasonable exercise of military authority. The courts can exercise only the judicial power, can apply only law, and must abide by the Constitution, or they cease to be civil courts and become instruments of military policy.

Of course the existence of a military power resting on force, so vagrant, so centralized, so necessarily heedless of the individual, is an inherent threat to liberty. But I would not lead people to rely on this Court for a review that seems to me wholly delusive. The military reasonableness of these orders can only be determined by military superiors. If the people ever let command of the war power fall into irresponsible and unscrupulous hands, the courts wield no power equal to its restraint. The chief restraint upon those who command the physical forces of the country, in the future as in the past, must be their responsibility to the political judgments of their contemporaries and to the moral judgments of history.

My duties as a justice as I see them do not require me to make a military judgment as to whether General DeWitt's evacuation and detention program was a reasonable military necessity. I do not suggest that the courts should have attempted to interfere with the Army in carrying out its task. But I do not think they may be asked to execute a military expedient that has no place in law under the Constitution. I would reverse the judgment and discharge the prisoner.

In 1980, Congress established the Commission on Wartime Relocation and Internment of Civilians, which in 1983 issued a report, *Personal Justice Denied*, condemning the internment and recommending reparations payments to surviving internees. Ultimately, President Reagan signed the Civil Liberties Act of 1988, which asserted that the internment had been based on "race prejudice, war hysteria, and a failure of political leadership" rather than legitimate security needs. Pursuant to the Act, redress payments of about $20,000 each were made to each of more than 82,000 former internees. Meanwhile, in 1983, Korematsu (who had been 23 when he decided not to obey the relocation order) filed in the U.S. District Court for the Northern District of California, in which he had been convicted, a petition for a writ of *coram nobis*; this is a writ by which a court can correct its original judgment on discovery of a fundamental error that did not appear in the original record. The court granted the motion in 1984, on the basis that the Government had withheld information tending to contradict its assertion that it had a reasonable basis for the internment order. *Korematsu v. United States* (N.D. Cal. 1984). (The Government, without admitting prosecutorial error, did not oppose vacating Korematsu's conviction.)

The district court could not, of course, overrule the doctrinal content of the Supreme Court's *Korematsu* decision. While *Korematsu* was long understood to be "anti-canon," in the sense of a case that cannot have been rightly decided, it remained good law as a formal matter for more than thirty years after Fred Korematsu's conviction was vacated. Courts even occasionally cited its "most rigid scrutiny" language when evaluating (and striking down) racial discrimination.

Korematsu did eventually get overruled, although in somewhat counterintuitive circumstances. In 2017, President Trump adopted a series of immigration orders that drastically restricted entry into the United States by citizens of a number of majority Muslim countries. A series of legal challenges claimed that these orders were implementing the President's explicitly discriminatory campaign promise to institute a "Muslim Ban." The Supreme Court dealt a blow to these challenges in *Trump v. Hawaii* (2018), which vacated a lower court's preliminary injunction on the ground that the challengers' complaints did not allege sufficient evidence of animus to justify preliminary relief. The dissenters charged that the Supreme Court was—once again—closing its eyes to the ugly reality of unconstitutional prejudice. The majority responded as follows:

> [T]he dissent invokes *Korematsu v. United States* (1944). Whatever rhetorical advantage the dissent may see in doing so, *Korematsu* has nothing to do with this case. The forcible relocation of U. S. citizens to concentration camps, solely and explicitly on the basis of race, is objectively unlawful and outside the scope of Presidential authority. But it is wholly inapt to liken that morally repugnant order to a facially neutral policy denying certain foreign nationals the privilege of admission. The entry suspension is an act that is well within executive authority and could have been taken by any other President—the

only question is evaluating the actions of this particular President in promulgating an otherwise valid Proclamation.

The dissent's reference to *Korematsu*, however, affords this Court the opportunity to make express what is already obvious: *Korematsu* was gravely wrong the day it was decided, has been overruled in the court of history, and—to be clear—"has no place in law under the Constitution." 323 U. S., at 248 (Jackson, J., dissenting).

This has generally been understood as a full formal overruling of *Korematsu* as affirmative precedent.

The Road to *Brown v. Board of Education*

In the realm of domestic politics, the Supreme Court's early-twentieth-century race jurisprudence hewed to the line established by *Plessy v. Ferguson* (1896) (permitting segregated railway cars as "separate but equal"). Under that principle, racially segregated facilities were permitted so long as the state could plausibly—and often not-so-plausibly—claim that they were equal. Cases striking down discriminatory legislation typically involved inequality that was hard to ignore.

In *McCabe v. Atchison Topeka & Santa Fe R.R.* (1914), for example, an Oklahoma statute required railways to provide "separate" but "equal" coaches—consistent with the requirement of *Plessy*. The Oklahoma law created an exception for "sleeping cars, dining or chair cars," however, permitting them to be provided for only one race without making comparable accommodations for others. The state justified the exception by arguing that these special cars were luxuries, sought by too few African-American passengers to warrant separate accommodations. Although the Court ultimately denied relief because it determined that the case was not yet ripe, its decision squarely rejected the state's substantive defense:

> It makes the constitutional right depend upon the number of persons who may be discriminated against, whereas the essence of the constitutional right is that it is a personal one. Whether or not particular facilities shall be provided may doubtless be conditioned upon there being a reasonable demand therefor; but, if facilities are provided,

substantial equality of treatment of persons traveling under like conditions cannot be refused.

Also noteworthy is *Buchanan v. Warley* (1917), in which the Court unanimously struck down a Louisville ordinance that prohibited anyone from "mov[ing] into and occupy[ing]" a residence on any block that was primarily occupied by members of the other race. (Like many such statutes, this one spoke as though there were only two races.) The Court did not decide the case as a matter of equal protection, but rather as an infringement on "the civil right of a white man to dispose of his property if he saw fit to do so to a person of color and of a colored person to make such disposition to a white person."

A variety of developments allowed such narrow decisions to serve as the thin end of a wedge that resulted in *Brown v. Board of Education*'s termination of formal racial segregation. One factor was certainly the change in racial attitudes as a result of World War II—the war was fought in large part against a violently racist regime, and with the participation of Americans of all races. In April 1947, major league baseball—an institution of great visibility and cultural resonance—began to integrate when Jackie Robinson played his first game for the Brooklyn Dodgers. The next year, President Truman began the process of integrating the armed forces. As these social developments emerged, social movements and especially their litigation wings took increasing aim at Jim Crow segregation. Famously, the NAACP Legal Defense Fund adopted a strategy that its 1934 Annual Report described as "carefully planned . . . to secure decisions, rulings, and public opinion on the broad principle [of equality] instead of being devoted to merely miscellaneous cases." One early fruit of this effort was *Missouri ex rel. Gaines v. Canada* (1938), which held that the state violated Equal Protection by maintaining a law school for whites but not one for blacks; the court rejected Missouri's argument that any constitutional violation was cured by the state's offer to pay for any black applicant's legal education out of state.

On this background, *Sweatt v. Painter* (1950) took the *Gaines* principle a considerable step further. In response to *Gaines*, Texas had set up a separate law school for black students. The Supreme Court held that this was inadequate: the University of Texas Law School had to admit Sweatt.

> In terms of number of the faculty, variety of courses and opportunity for specialization, size of the student body, scope of the library,

availability of law review and similar activities, the University of Texas Law School is superior. What is more important, the University of Texas Law School possesses to a far greater degree those qualities which are incapable of objective measurement but which make for greatness in a law school. Such qualities, to name but a few, include reputation of the faculty, experience of the administration, position and influence of the alumni, standing in the community, traditions and prestige. It is difficult to believe that one who had a free choice between these law schools would consider the question close.

Moreover, although the law is a highly learned profession, we are well aware that it is an intensely practical one. The law school, the proving ground for legal learning and practice, cannot be effective in isolation from the individuals and institutions with which the law interacts. Few students and no one who has practiced law would choose to study in an academic vacuum, removed from the interplay of ideas and the exchange of views with which the law is concerned. The law school to which Texas is willing to admit petitioner excludes from its student body members of the racial groups which number 85% of the population of the State and include most of the lawyers, witnesses, jurors, judges and other officials with whom petitioner will inevitably be dealing when he becomes a member of the Texas Bar. With such a substantial and significant segment of society excluded, we cannot conclude that the education offered petitioner is substantially equal to that which he would receive if admitted to the University of Texas Law School.

The stage was set for more fundamental change.

Brown v. Board of Education of Topeka

Supreme Court of the United States, 1954.
347 U.S. 483.

Mr. Chief Justice Warren delivered the opinion of the Court.

These cases come to us from the States of Kansas, South Carolina, Virginia, and Delaware. They are premised on different facts and different local conditions, but a common legal question justifies their consideration together in this consolidated opinion. . . .

In each of the cases, minors of the Negro race, through their legal representatives, seek the aid of the courts in obtaining admission to the public schools of their community on a nonsegregated basis. In each instance, they have been denied admission to schools attended by white children under laws requiring or permitting segregation according to race. This segregation was alleged to deprive the plaintiffs of the equal protection of the laws under the Fourteenth Amendment. In each of the cases other than the Delaware case, a three-judge federal district court denied relief to the plaintiffs on the so-called "separate but equal" doctrine announced by this Court in *Plessy v. Ferguson* (1896). Under that doctrine, equality of treatment is accorded when the races are provided substantially equal facilities, even though these facilities be separate. In the Delaware case, the Supreme Court of Delaware adhered to that doctrine, but ordered that the plaintiffs be admitted to the white schools because of their superiority to the Negro schools.

The plaintiffs contend that segregated public schools are not "equal" and cannot be made "equal," and that hence they are deprived of the equal protection of the laws. Because of the obvious importance of the question presented, the Court took jurisdiction. Argument was heard in the 1952 Term, and reargument was heard this Term on certain questions propounded by the Court.

Reargument was largely devoted to the circumstances surrounding the adoption of the Fourteenth Amendment in 1868. It covered exhaustively consideration of the Amendment in Congress, ratification by the states, then existing practices in racial segregation, and the views of proponents and opponents of the Amendment. This discussion and our own investigation convince us that, although these sources cast some light, it is not enough to resolve the problem with which we are faced. At best, they are inconclusive. The most avid proponents of the post-War Amendments undoubtedly intended them to remove all legal distinctions among "all persons born or naturalized in the United States." Their opponents, just as certainly, were antagonistic to both the letter and the spirit of the Amendments and wished them to have the most limited effect. What others in Congress and the state legislatures had in mind cannot be determined with any degree of certainty.

An additional reason for the inconclusive nature of the Amendment's history, with respect to segregated schools, is the status of public education at

that time. In the South, the movement toward free common schools, supported by general taxation, had not yet taken hold. Education of white children
was largely in the hands of private groups. Education of Negroes was almost
nonexistent, and practically all of the race were illiterate. In fact, any education of Negroes was forbidden by law in some states. Today, in contrast, many
Negroes have achieved outstanding success in the arts and sciences as well as
in the business and professional world. It is true that public school education at
the time of the Amendment had advanced further in the North, but the effect
of the Amendment on Northern States was generally ignored in the congressional debates. Even in the North, the conditions of public education did not
approximate those existing today. The curriculum was usually rudimentary;
ungraded schools were common in rural areas; the school term was but three
months a year in many states; and compulsory school attendance was virtually
unknown. As a consequence, it is not surprising that there should be so little
in the history of the Fourteenth Amendment relating to its intended effect on
public education.

In the first cases in this Court construing the Fourteenth Amendment,
decided shortly after its adoption, the Court interpreted it as proscribing all
state-imposed discriminations against the Negro race. *In re Slaughter-House
Cases* (1873); *Strauder v. West Virginia* (1880). The doctrine of "separate but
equal" did not make its appearance in this court until 1896 in the case of *Plessy
v. Ferguson*, involving not education but transportation. American courts have
since labored with the doctrine for over half a century. In this Court, there have
been six cases involving the "separate but equal" doctrine in the field of public
education. In more recent cases, all on the graduate school level, inequality was
found in that specific benefits enjoyed by white students were denied to Negro
students of the same educational qualifications. *State of Missouri ex rel. Gaines
v. Canada* (1938); *Sipuel v. Board of Regents of University of Oklahoma* (1948);
Sweatt v. Painter (1950); *McLaurin v. Oklahoma State Regents* (1950). In none
of these cases was it necessary to re-examine the doctrine to grant relief to the
Negro plaintiff. And in *Sweatt v. Painter*, the Court expressly reserved decision on the question whether *Plessy v. Ferguson* should be held inapplicable to
public education.

In the instant cases, that question is directly presented. Here, unlike
Sweatt v. Painter, there are findings below that the Negro and white schools
involved have been equalized, or are being equalized, with respect to buildings,

curricula, qualifications and salaries of teachers, and other "tangible" factors.[9] Our decision, therefore, cannot turn on merely a comparison of these tangible factors in the Negro and white schools involved in each of the cases. We must look instead to the effect of segregation itself on public education.

In approaching this problem, we cannot turn the clock back to 1868 when the Amendment was adopted, or even to 1896 when *Plessy v. Ferguson* was written. We must consider public education in the light of its full development and its present place in American life throughout the Nation. Only in this way can it be determined if segregation in public schools deprives these plaintiffs of the equal protection of the laws.

Today, education is perhaps the most important function of state and local governments. Compulsory school attendance laws and the great expenditures for education both demonstrate our recognition of the importance of education to our democratic society. It is required in the performance of our most basic public responsibilities, even service in the armed forces. It is the very foundation of good citizenship. Today it is a principal instrument in awakening the child to cultural values, in preparing him for later professional training, and in helping him to adjust normally to his environment. In these days, it is doubtful that any child may reasonably be expected to succeed in life if he is denied the opportunity of an education. Such an opportunity, where the state has undertaken to provide it, is a right which must be made available to all on equal terms.

We come then to the question presented: Does segregation of children in public schools solely on the basis of race, even though the physical facilities and other "tangible" factors may be equal, deprive the children of the minority group of equal educational opportunities? We believe that it does.

In *Sweatt v. Painter*, a segregated law school for Negroes could not provide them equal educational opportunities, this Court relied in large part on "those qualities which are incapable of objective measurement but which make for greatness in a law school." In *McLaurin v. Oklahoma State Regents*, the Court, in requiring that a Negro admitted to a white graduate school be treated like all other students, again resorted to intangible considerations: ". . . his ability

---

[9]   In the Kansas case, the court below found substantial equality as to all such factors. In the South Carolina case, the court below found that the defendants were proceeding "promptly and in good faith to comply with the court's decree." In the Virginia case, the court below noted that the equalization program was already "afoot and progressing"; since then, we have been advised, in the Virginia Attorney General's brief on reargument, that the program has now been completed. In the Delaware case, the court below similarly noted that the state's equalization program was well under way.

to study, to engage in discussions and exchange views with other students, and, in general, to learn his profession."

Such considerations apply with added force to children in grade and high schools. To separate them from others of similar age and qualifications solely because of their race generates a feeling of inferiority as to their status in the community that may affect their hearts and minds in a way unlikely ever to be undone. The effect of this separation on their educational opportunities was well stated by a finding in the Kansas case by a court which nevertheless felt compelled to rule against the Negro plaintiffs:

> Segregation of white and colored children in public schools has a detrimental effect upon the colored children. The impact is greater when it has the sanction of the law; for the policy of separating the races is usually interpreted as denoting the inferiority of the negro group. A sense of inferiority affects the motivation of a child to learn. Segregation with the sanction of law, therefore, has a tendency to [retard] the educational and mental development of Negro children and to deprive them of some of the benefits they would receive in a racial[ly] integrated school system.[10]

Whatever may have been the extent of psychological knowledge at the time of *Plessy v. Ferguson*, this finding is amply supported by modern authority.[11] Any language in *Plessy v. Ferguson* contrary to this finding is rejected.

We conclude that in the field of public education the doctrine of "separate but equal" has no place. Separate educational facilities are inherently unequal. Therefore, we hold that the plaintiffs and others similarly situated for whom the actions have been brought are, by reason of the segregation complained of, deprived of the equal protection of the laws guaranteed by the Fourteenth Amendment. . . .

---

[10]   A similar finding was made [by the trial court] in the Delaware case: "I conclude from the testimony that in our Delaware society, State-imposed segregation in education itself results in the Negro children, as a class, receiving educational opportunities which are substantially inferior to those available to white children otherwise similarly situated."

[11]   K. B. Clark, *Effect of Prejudice and Discrimination on Personality Development* (1950); Witmer and Kotinsky, *Personality in the Making* (1952), c. VI; Deutscher and Chein, *The Psychological Effects of Enforced Segregation: A Survey of Social Science Opinion*, 26 J. Psychol. 259 (1948); Chein, *What are the Psychological Effects of Segregation Under Conditions of Equal Facilities?*, 3 Int. J. Opinion and Attitude Res. 229 (1949); Brameld, *Educational Costs, in Discrimination and National Welfare* (MacIver, ed., 1949); Frazier, *The Negro in the United States* (1949). And see generally Myrdal, *An American Dilemma* (1944).

Because these are class actions, because of the wide applicability of this decision, and because of the great variety of local conditions, the formulation of decrees in these cases presents problems of considerable complexity. On reargument, the consideration of appropriate relief was necessarily subordinated to the primary question—the constitutionality of segregation in public education. We have now announced that such segregation is a denial of the equal protection of the laws. In order that we may have the full assistance of the parties in formulating decrees, the cases will be restored to the docket, and the parties are requested to present further argument on [the question of appropriate relief].

It is so ordered.

For Discussion

(1) What is the inequality found in *Brown*?

(2) Suppose that parents and children in a public school district not involved in the *Brown* litigation bring suit challenging their district's mandatory policy of racial segregation. The trial judge makes the following factual finding: "Whatever the situation may be in Kansas and Delaware, the evidence is compelling that in this district both black and white children do better in segregated schools." How should the court rule under *Brown*?

(3) What do you think explains the Supreme Court's repudiation of separate-but-equal doctrine in *Brown*? Consider in this respect Derrick Bell's "interest convergence" thesis, which suggests that the result in *Brown* "cannot be understood without some consideration of the decision's value to whites, not simply those concerned about the immorality of racial inequality, but also those whites in policymaking positions able to see the economic and political advances at home and abroad that would follow abandonment of segregation." Derrick Bell, Brown v. Board of Education *and the Interest-Convergence Dilemma*, 93 Harv. L. Rev. 518 (1980). He then goes on to list some of the benefits such policymakers could expect from *Brown*:

> First, the decision helped to provide immediate credibility to America's struggle with Communist countries to win the hearts and minds of emerging third world peoples. At least this argument was advanced by lawyers for both the NAACP and the federal government. . . . Second, *Brown* [responded to a concern] poignantly expressed by the black actor, Paul Robeson, who in 1949 declared: "It is unthinkable . . . that American Negroes would go to war on behalf of those who have oppressed us for generations . . . against a country [the Soviet Union]

> which in one generation has raised our people to the full human digni-
> ty of mankind." Finally, there were whites who realized that the South
> could make the transition from a rural, plantation society to the sunbelt
> with all its potential and profit only when it ended its struggle to remain
> divided by state-sponsored segregation. Thus, segregation was viewed
> as a barrier to further industrialization in the South.
>
> Bell's argument makes a point of emphasizing that motivations are com-
> plex and varying: "Here, as in the abolition of slavery, there were whites for
> whom recognition of the racial equality principle was sufficient motivation.
> But, as with abolition, the number who would act on morality alone was
> insufficient to bring about the desired racial reform." Do you think the inter-
> est-convergence thesis is plausible? Right? Wrong? Incomplete?

What exactly was the principle announced in *Brown v. Board of Education*, and just how far did it extend? At least rhetorically, the court's analysis seemed to focus heavily on the foundational importance of schooling for citizenship. Consider how that argument applies to segregation in other publicly maintained facilities, and then consider how the *Brown* Court decided a series of challenges to such facilities over the course of the next several years.

In *Mayor and City Council of Baltimore City v. Dawson* (1955), for example, the Supreme Court affirmed a decision of the Fourth Circuit that Baltimore's segregated public beaches violated the Constitution. Its opinion was an 11-word *per curiam*: "The motion to affirm is granted and the judgment is affirmed." In a companion case decided the same day, the Supreme Court vacated a Fifth Circuit decision that would essentially have permitted Atlanta's municipal Bobby Jones Golf Course to remain segregated; the Court ordered the District Court "to enter a decree for petitioners in conformity with *Mayor & City Council of Baltimore City v. Dawson*." *Holmes v. City of Atlanta* (1955). And the following year the Court was similarly terse in affirming a decision invalidating enforced segregation of buses in Montgomery, Alabama. *Gayle v. Browder, Owen v. Browder* (1956).

The lower courts were not always quite so conclusory in considering the impact of *Brown* outside the realm of education. In the Baltimore case, for example, the Fourth Circuit said:

> It is now obvious . . . that segregation cannot be justified as
> a means to preserve the public peace merely because the tangible

facilities furnished to one race are equal to those furnished to the other. The Supreme Court expressed the opinion in *Brown v. Board of Education of Topeka* that it must consider public education in the light of its full development and its present place in American life, and therefore could not turn the clock back to 1896 when *Plessy v. Ferguson* was written, or base its decision on the tangible factors only of a given situation, but must also take into account the psychological factors recognized at this time, including the feeling of inferiority generated in the hearts and minds of Negro children, when separated solely because of their race from those of similar age and qualification.

With this in mind, it is obvious that racial segregation in recreational activities can no longer be sustained as a proper exercise of the police power of the State; for if that power cannot be invoked to sustain racial segregation in the schools, where attendance is compulsory and racial friction may be apprehended from the enforced commingling of the races, it cannot be sustained with respect to public beach and bathhouse facilities, the use of which is entirely optional. . . .

The implications of *Brown v. Board of Education* continued to reverberate across a range of contexts throughout segregated areas of the United States. In the next two cases, the state defendants argued that the challenged policies were genuinely even-handed in both conception and application. Do you think their outcomes can be reconciled with one another? Can they be reconciled with *Brown*?

Loving v. Virginia

Supreme Court of the United States, 1967.
388 U.S. 1.

Mr. Chief Justice Warren delivered the opinion of the Court.

This case presents a constitutional question never addressed by this Court: whether a statutory scheme adopted by the State of Virginia to prevent marriages between persons solely on the basis of racial classifications violates the

Equal Protection and Due Process Clauses of the Fourteenth Amendment. For reasons which seem to us to reflect the central meaning of those constitutional commands, we conclude that these statutes cannot stand consistently with the Fourteenth Amendment.

 CROSS REFERENCE The Court held that the statute violated both the Equal Protection Clause and also the Due Process Clause. Only the separate equal protection analysis is included here. See p. 1371 for an excerpt of the Court's due process analysis.

In June 1958, two residents of Virginia, Mildred Jeter, a Negro woman, and Richard Loving, a white man, were married in the District of Columbia pursuant to its laws. [After their return to Virginia, they were prosecuted for violating Virginia's ban on interracial marriages and sentenced to one year in jail.] [T]he trial judge suspended the sentence . . . on the condition that the Lovings leave the State and not return to Virginia together for 25 years. He stated in an opinion that:

> Almighty God created the races white, black, yellow, malay and red, and he placed them on separate continents. And but for the interference with his arrangement there would be no cause for such marriages. The fact that he separated the races shows that he did not intend for the races to mix. . . .

The Supreme Court of Appeals upheld the constitutionality of the antimiscegenation statutes. . . .

[Virginia state law] provides [that] "If any white person intermarry with a colored person, or any colored person intermarry with a white person, he shall be guilty of a felony and shall be punished by confinement in the penitentiary for not less than one nor more than five years." . . . Other central provisions in the Virginia statutory scheme . . . automatically void[ ] all marriages between "a white person and a colored person" without any judicial proceeding,[3] and define "white persons" and "colored persons and Indians" for purposes of the statutory prohibitions.[4] The Lovings have never disputed in the course of this

---

3   "Marriages void without decree.—All marriages between a white person and a colored person shall be absolutely void without any decree of divorce or other legal process." Va. Code Ann. § 20–57.

4   Section 20–54 of the Virginia Code provides:

Intermarriage prohibited; meaning of term "white persons."—It shall hereafter be unlawful for any white person in this State to marry any save a white person, or a person with no other admixture of blood than white and American Indian. For the purpose of this chapter, the term "white person" shall apply only to such person as has no trace whatever of any blood other than Caucasian; but persons who

litigation that Mrs. Loving is a "colored person" or that Mr. Loving is a "white person" within the meanings given those terms by the Virginia statutes.

Virginia is now one of 16 States which prohibit and punish marriages on the basis of racial classifications. Penalties for miscegenation arose as an incident to slavery and have been common in Virginia since the colonial period. The present statutory scheme dates from the adoption of the Racial Integrity Act of 1924, passed during the period of extreme nativism which followed the end of the First World War. The central features of this Act, and current Virginia law, are the absolute prohibition of a "white person" marrying other than another "white person," a prohibition against issuing marriage licenses until the issuing official is satisfied that the applicants' statements as to their race are correct, certificates of "racial composition" to be kept by both local and state registrars, and the carrying forward of earlier prohibitions against racial intermarriage. . . .

In upholding the constitutionality of these provisions in the decision below, the Supreme Court of Appeals of Virginia referred to its 1955 decision in *Naim v. Naim*, 197 Va. 80, as stating the reasons supporting the validity of these laws. In *Naim*, the state court concluded that the State's legitimate purposes were "to preserve the racial integrity of its citizens," and to prevent "the corruption of blood," "a mongrel breed of citizens," and "the obliteration of racial pride," obviously an endorsement of the doctrine of White Supremacy. . . .

[T]he State argues that the meaning of the Equal Protection Clause . . . is only that state penal laws . . . must apply equally to whites and Negroes in the sense that members of each race are punished to the same degree. Thus, the State contends that, because its miscegenation statutes punish equally both the white and the Negro participants in an interracial marriage, these statutes, despite their reliance on racial classifications do not constitute an invidious discrimination based upon race. The second argument advanced by the State assumes the validity of its equal application theory. The argument is that, if the Equal Protection Clause does not outlaw miscegenation statutes because of

---

have one-sixteenth or less of the blood of the American Indian and have no other non-Caucasic blood shall be deemed to be white persons. . . .

Section 1–14 of the Virginia Code provides:

Colored persons and Indians defined.—Every person in whom there is ascertainable any Negro blood shall be deemed and taken to be a colored person, and every person not a colored person having one fourth or more of American Indian blood shall be deemed an American Indian; except that members of Indian tribes existing in this Commonwealth having one fourth or more of Indian blood and less than one sixteenth of Negro blood shall be deemed tribal Indians.

their reliance on racial classifications, the question of constitutionality would thus become whether there was any rational basis for a State to treat interracial marriages differently from other marriages. On this question, the State argues, the scientific evidence is substantially in doubt and, consequently, this Court should defer to the wisdom of the state legislature in adopting its policy of discouraging interracial marriages. . . .

Because we reject the notion that the mere "equal application" of a statute containing racial classifications is enough to remove the classifications from the Fourteenth Amendment's proscription of all invidious racial discriminations, we do not accept the State's contention that these statutes should be upheld if there is any possible basis for concluding that they serve a rational purpose. . . .

The clear and central purpose of the Fourteenth Amendment was to eliminate all official state sources of invidious racial discrimination in the States. *Slaughter-House Cases* (1873); *Strauder v. State of West Virginia* (1880); *Shelley v. Kraemer* (1948). There can be no question but that Virginia's miscegenation statutes rest solely upon distinctions drawn according to race. The statutes proscribe generally accepted conduct if engaged in by members of different races. Over the years, this Court has consistently repudiated "[d]istinctions between citizens solely because of their ancestry" as being "odious to a free people whose institutions are founded upon the doctrine of equality." *Hirabayashi v. United States* (1943). At the very least, the Equal Protection Clause demands that racial classifications, especially suspect in criminal statutes, be subjected to the "most rigid scrutiny," *Korematsu v. United States* (1944), and, if they are ever to be upheld, they must be shown to be necessary to the accomplishment of some permissible state objective, independent of the racial discrimination which it was the object of the Fourteenth Amendment to eliminate. . . .

There is patently no legitimate overriding purpose independent of invidious racial discrimination which justifies this classification. The fact that Virginia prohibits only interracial marriages involving white persons demonstrates that the racial classifications must stand on their own justification, as measures designed to maintain White Supremacy.[11] We have consistently denied the constitutionality of measures which restrict the rights of citizens on

---

[11]   Appellants point out that the State's concern in these statutes, as expressed in the words of the 1924 Act's title, "An Act to Preserve Racial Integrity," extends only to the integrity of the white race. While Virginia prohibits whites from marrying any nonwhite (subject to the exception for the descendants of Pocahontas), Negroes, Orientals, and any other racial class may intermarry without statutory interference. Appellants contend that this distinction renders Virginia's miscegenation statutes arbitrary and unreasonable even assuming the constitutional validity of an official purpose to preserve "racial integrity." We need not reach this contention because we find the

account of race. There can be no doubt that restricting the freedom to marry solely because of racial classifications violates the central meaning of the Equal Protection Clause. . . .

MR. JUSTICE STEWART, concurring.

I have previously expressed the belief that "it is simply not possible for a state law to be valid under our Constitution which makes the criminality of an act depend upon the race of the actor." *McLaughlin v. Florida* (1964) (concurring opinion). Because I adhere to that belief, I concur in the judgment of the Court.

WORTH NOTING

In *McLaughlin*, the Court struck down a state statute that prohibited cohabitation by unmarried white and Negro persons of the opposite sex.

In a segregated society structured around systematic racial subjugation in all sectors of public life, decisions like *Brown* and *Loving* prompted not cooperation but what quickly became known as "massive resistance." As discussed further at pp. 1087–1088, the segregated states quickly implemented a range of tactics for opposing the full implications of *Brown*'s equality principle.

In the following case, the city of Jackson, Mississippi, discontinued a nonessential city service—an action that ordinarily would raise no constitutional problem. Under the circumstances, was it plausible that the city's decision was motivated by non-discriminatory aims? And if not, what should the consequences be?

---

racial classifications in these statutes repugnant to the Fourteenth Amendment, even assuming an even-handed state purpose to protect the "integrity" of all races.

Palmer v. Thompson

Supreme Court of the United States, 1971.
403 U.S. 217.

MR. JUSTICE BLACK delivered the opinion of the Court.

In 1962 the city of Jackson, Mississippi, was maintaining five public parks along with swimming pools, golf links, and other facilities for use by the public on a racially segregated basis. Four of the swimming pools were used by whites only and one by Negroes only. Plaintiffs brought an action [challenging] this state-enforced segregation of the races[, and] the District Court entered a judgment declaring that enforced segregation denied equal protection of the laws. . . . The city proceeded to desegregate its public parks, auditoriums, golf courses, and the city zoo. However, the city council decided not to try to operate the public swimming pools on a desegregated basis. Acting in its legislative capacity, the council surrendered its lease on one pool and closed four which the city owned. A number of Negro citizens of Jackson then filed this suit to force the city to reopen the pools and operate them on a desegregated basis. . . .

I

. . . It should be noted first that neither the Fourteenth Amendment nor any Act of Congress purports to impose an affirmative duty on a State to begin to operate or to continue to operate swimming pools. Furthermore, this is not a case where whites are permitted to use public facilities while blacks are denied access. It is not a case where a city is maintaining different sets of facilities for blacks and whites and forcing the races to remain separate in recreational or educational activities. See, *e.g.*, *Brown v. Board of Education* (1954). Unless, therefore, . . . closing the pools to all denied equal protection to Negroes, we must agree with the courts below and affirm.

II

. . . *Griffin v. County School Board of Prince Edward County* (1964) [does not] lead[ ] us to reverse the judgment here. . . .

In *Griffin* the public schools of Prince Edward County, Virginia, were closed under authority of state and county law, and so-called "private schools" were set up in their place to avoid a court desegregation order. At the same time, public schools in other counties in Virginia remained open. In Prince Edward

County the "private schools" were open to whites only and these schools were in fact run by a practical partnership between State and county, designed to preserve segregated education. We pointed out in *Griffin* the many facets of state involvement in the running of the "private schools." The State General Assembly had made available grants of $150 per child to make the program possible. This was supplemented by a county grant program of $100 per child and county property tax credits for citizens contributing to the "private schools." Under those circumstances we held that the closing of public schools in just one county while the State helped finance "private schools" was a scheme to perpetuate segregation in education which constituted a denial of equal protection of the laws. Thus the *Griffin* case simply treated the school program for what it was—an operation of Prince Edward County schools under a thinly disguised "private" school system actually planned and carried out by the State and the county to maintain segregated education with public funds.

That case can give no comfort to petitioners here. This record supports no intimation that Jackson has not completely and finally ceased running swimming pools for all time. Unlike Prince Edward County, Jackson has not pretended to close public pools only to run them under a "private" label. It is true that the Leavell Woods pool, previously leased by the city from the YMCA, is now run by that organization and appears to be open only to whites. And according to oral argument, another pool owned by the city before 1963 is now owned and operated by Jackson State College, a predominantly black institution, for college students and their guests. But unlike the "private schools" in Prince Edward County there is nothing here to show the city is directly or indirectly involved in the funding or operation of either pool. If the time ever comes when Jackson attempts to run segregated public pools either directly or indirectly, or participates in a subterfuge whereby pools are nominally run by "private parties" but actually by the city, relief will be available in the federal courts. . . .

III

Petitioners have also argued that respondents' action violates the Equal Protection Clause because the decision to close the pools was motivated by a desire to avoid integration of the races. But no case in this Court has held that a legislative act may violate equal protection solely because of the motivations of the men who voted for it. . . .

[Previous opinions have] explained well the hazards of declaring a law unconstitutional because of the motivations of its sponsors. First, it is extremely difficult for a court to ascertain the motivation, or collection of different motivations, that lie behind a legislative enactment. Here, for example, petitioners have argued that the Jackson pools were closed because of ideological opposition to racial integration in swimming pools. Some evidence in the record appears to support this argument. On the other hand, the courts below found that the pools were closed because the city council felt they could not be operated safely and economically on an integrated basis. There is substantial evidence in the record to support this conclusion. It is difficult or impossible for any court to determine the "sole" or "dominant" motivation behind the choices of a group of legislators. . . .

It is true there is language in some of our cases interpreting the Fourteenth and Fifteenth Amendments which may suggest that the motive or purpose behind a law is relevant to its constitutionality. *Griffin*; *Gomillion v. Lightfoot* (1960). But the focus in those cases was on the actual effect of the enactments, not upon the motivation which led the States to behave as they did. In *Griffin*, as discussed supra, the State was in fact perpetuating a segregated public school system by financing segregated "private" academies. And in *Gomillion* the Alabama Legislature's gerrymander of the boundaries of Tuskegee excluded virtually all Negroes from voting in town elections.

 CROSS REFERENCE *Griffin* is further discussed at pp. 1087–1088 and *Gomillion* is presented at pp. 1055–1057.

Here the record indicates only that Jackson once ran segregated public swimming pools and that no public pools are now maintained by the city. Moreover, there is no evidence in this record to show that the city is now covertly aiding the maintenance and operation of pools which are private in name only. It shows no state action affecting blacks differently from whites. . . .

Should citizens of Jackson or any other city be able to establish in court that public, tax-supported swimming pools are being denied to one group because of color and supplied to another, they will be entitled to relief. But that is not the case here. The judgment is affirmed.

 WORTH NOTING Chief Justice Burger joined the majority opinion, but he wrote separately to assert that to hold "that every public facility or service, once opened, constitutionally 'locks in' the public sponsor so that it may not be dropped . . . would plainly discourage the expansion and enlargement of needed services in the long run."

Mr. Justice Blackmun, concurring.

. . . Cases such as this are "hard" cases for there is much to be said on each side. . . . The dissent of Mr. Justice White rests on a conviction that the closing of the Jackson pools was racially motivated, at least in part, and that municipal action so motivated is not to be tolerated. . . . Mr. Justice Black's opinion stresses, on the other hand, the facially equal effect upon all citizens of the decision to discontinue the pools. . . .

I remain impressed with the following factors:

(1)   No other municipal recreational facility in the city of Jackson has been discontinued. Indeed, every other service—parks, auditoriums, golf courses, zoo—that once was segregated, has been continued and operates on a nonsegregated basis. One must concede that this was effectuated initially under pressure of the 1962 declaratory judgment of the federal court.

(2)   The pools are not part of the city's educational system. They are a general municipal service of the nice-to-have but not essential variety, and they are a service, perhaps a luxury, not enjoyed by many communities.

(3)   The pools had operated at a deficit. It was the judgment of the city officials that these deficits would increase.

(4)   I cannot read into the closing of the pools an official expression of inferiority toward black citizens, . . . and certainly on this record I cannot perceive this to be a "fact" or anything other than speculation. . . .

(5)   The [affirmative] response of petitioners' counsel at oral argument to my inquiry whether the city was to be "locked in" with its pools for an indefinite time in the future, despite financial loss of whatever amount, just because at one time the pools of Jackson had been segregated, is disturbing. . . .

On balance, in the light of the factors I have listed above, my judgment is that this is neither the time nor the occasion to be punitive toward Jackson for its past constitutional sins of segregation. On the record as presented to us in this case, I therefore vote to affirm.

Justice Douglas dissented on the ground that, "though a State may discontinue any of its municipal services[,] . . . it may not do so for the purpose of perpetuating or installing apartheid or because it finds life in a multi-racial community difficult or unpleasant."

MR. JUSTICE WHITE, with whom MR. JUSTICE BRENNAN and MR. JUSTICE MARSHALL join, dissenting.

. . . Jackson, Mississippi, closed its swimming pools when a district judge struck down the city's tradition of segregation in municipal services and made clear his expectation that public facilities would be integrated. The circumstances surrounding this action and the absence of other credible reasons for the closings leave little doubt that shutting down the pools was nothing more or less than a most effective expression of official policy that Negroes and whites must not be permitted to mingle together when using the services provided by the city. . . . With all due respect, I am quite unable to agree with the majority's assertion, that there is "substantial evidence in the record" to support the conclusion of the lower courts that the pools could not be operated safely and economically on an integrated basis. . . . [T]he only evidence in this record is the conclusions of the officials themselves, unsupported by even a scintilla of added proof. . . .

I thus arrive at the question of whether closing public facilities to citizens of both races, whatever the reasons for such action, is a special kind of state action somehow insulated from scrutiny under the Fourteenth Amendment. . . . *Griffin v. County School Board of Prince Edward County* (1964) is perhaps distinguishable, but only if one ignores its basic rationale and the purpose and direction of this Court's decisions since *Brown*. First, and most importantly, *Griffin* stands for the proposition that the reasons underlying certain official acts are highly relevant in assessing the constitutional validity of those acts. . . . [I]f effect was all that the Court considered relevant in *Griffin*, there was no need [for that case] to mention underlying purpose and to stress the delay that took place in Virginia in implementing *Brown*.

[Moreover, as] Judge Wisdom said in dissent below, the argument that the closing of the pools operated equally on Negroes and whites "is a tired contention, one that has been overworked in civil rights cases." . . . [T]he reality is that the impact of the city's act falls on the minority. Quite apart from the question whether the white citizens of Jackson have a better chance to swim than do their Negro neighbors absent city pools, there are deep and troubling effects on the racial minority that should give us all pause.

As stated at the outset of this opinion, by closing the pools solely because of the order to desegregate, the city is expressing its official view that Negroes are so inferior that they are unfit to share with whites this particular type of public facility. . . . [But] in *Brown* itself . . . we quoted with approval the finding of a district judge that:

> Segregation of white and colored children in public schools has a detrimental effect upon the colored children. The impact is greater when it has the sanction of the law; for the policy of separating the races is usually interpreted as denoting the inferiority of the negro group."

These considerations were not abandoned as *Brown* was applied in other contexts, and it is untenable to suggest that the closing of the swimming pools—a pronouncement that Negroes are somehow unfit to swim with whites—operates equally on Negroes and whites. Whites feel nothing but disappointment and perhaps anger at the loss of the facilities. Negroes feel that and more. They are stigmatized by official implementation of a policy that the Fourteenth Amendment condemns as illegal. And the closed pools stand as mute reminders to the community of the official view of Negro inferiority.

Moreover, this Court has carefully guarded the rights of Negroes to attack state-sanctioned segregation through the peaceful channels of the judicial process. . . . It is evident that closing a public facility after a court has ordered its desegregation has an unfortunate impact on the minority considering initiation of further suits or filing complaints with the Attorney General. As Judge Wisdom said [in dissent below],

> [T]he price of protest is high. Negroes . . . now know that they risk losing even segregated public facilities if they dare to protest . . . segregated public parks, segregated public libraries, or other segregated facilities. They must first decide whether they wish to risk living without the facility altogether. . .

It is difficult to measure the extent of this impact, but it is surely present and surely we should not ignore it. The action of the city in this case interposes a major deterrent to seeking judicial or executive help in eliminating racial restrictions on the use of public facilities. . . .

The city has only opposition to desegregation to offer as a justification for closing the pools, and this opposition operates both to demean the Negroes of Jackson and to deter them from exercising their constitutional and statutory rights. . . . I would reverse the judgment of the Court of Appeals and remand the cause for further proceedings.

MR. JUSTICE MARSHALL, with whom MR. JUSTICE BRENNAN and MR. JUSTICE WHITE join, dissenting.

. . . I cannot conceive why the writers of the concurring opinions believe that the city is "locked in" and must operate the pools no matter what the economic consequences. Certainly, I am not bound by any admission of an attorney at oral argument as to his version of the law. Equity courts have always had continuing supervisory powers over their decrees; and if a proper basis for closing the facilities—other than a conclusory statement about the projected human and thus economic consequences of desegregation—could be shown, swimming pools, as I imagine schools or even golf courses, could be closed.

I dissent.

"What *Is* Race/Nationality/Ethnicity?"

"Race" is of course an essentially contested concept—and it isn't the only category that prompts strict scrutiny. Courts often speak more or less interchangeably of race, ethnicity, and nationality as equivalently suspect classifications. The following materials begin to engage the question of understanding what we mean by such categories, and what normative significance they have for equal protection analysis.

Michael James and Adam Burgos, Race

Stanford Encyclopedia of Philosophy (rev. 2020)

The concept of race has historically signified the division of humanity into a small number of groups based upon five criteria: (1) Races reflect some type of biological foundation, be it Aristotelian essences or modern genes; (2) This biological foundation generates discrete racial groupings, such that all and only all members of one race share a set of biological characteristics that are not shared by members of other races; (3) This biological foundation is inherited from generation to generation, allowing observers to identify an individual's race through her ancestry or genealogy; (4) Genealogical investigation should identify each race's geographic origin, typically in Africa, Europe, Asia, or North and South America; and (5) This inherited racial biological foundation manifests itself primarily in physical phenotypes, such as skin color, eye shape, hair texture, and bone structure, and perhaps also behavioral phenotypes, such as intelligence or delinquency.

This historical concept of race has faced substantial scientific and philosophical challenge, with some important thinkers denying both the logical coherence of the concept and the very existence of races. Others defend the concept of race, albeit with substantial changes to the foundations of racial identity, which they depict as either socially constructed or, if biologically grounded, neither discrete nor essentialist, as the historical concept would have it.

Both in the past and today, determining the boundaries of discrete races has proven to be most vexing and has led to great variations in the number of human races believed to be in existence. Thus, some thinkers categorized humans into only four distinct races (typically white or Caucasian, Black or African, yellow or Asian, and red or Native American), and downplayed any biological or phenotypical distinctions within racial groups (such as those between Scandinavians and Spaniards within the white or Caucasian race). Other thinkers classified humans into many more racial categories, for instance arguing that those humans "indigenous" to Europe could be distinguished into discrete Nordic, Alpine, and Mediterranean races.

The ambiguities and confusion associated with determining the boundaries of racial categories have provoked a widespread scholarly consensus that discrete or essentialist races are socially constructed, not biologically real. However, significant scholarly debate persists regarding whether reproductive isolation, either during human evolution or through modern practices barring miscegenation, may have generated sufficient genetic isolation as to justify using the term race to signify the existence of non-discrete human groups that share not only physical phenotypes but also clusters of genetic material. In addition, scholarly debate exists concerning the formation and character of socially constructed, discrete racial categories. For instance, some scholars suggest that race is inconceivable without racialized social hierarchies, while others argue that egalitarian race relations are possible. Finally, substantial controversy surrounds the moral status of racial identity and solidarity and the justice and legitimacy of policies or institutions aimed at undermining racial inequality. . . .

David A. Hollinger, The One Drop Rule and the One Hate Rule

Daedalus, Winter 2005

Two portentous practices within the public discussion of "race" in the United States since the late 1960s are rarely analyzed together. One is the method by which we decide which individuals are "black." The other is our habit of conflating the mistreatment of blacks with that of nonblack minorities. Both practices compress a great range of phenomena into ostensibly manageable containers. Both function to keep the concept of race current amid mounting pressures that threaten to render it anachronistic. Both invite reassessment at the start of the twenty-first century.

The prevailing criterion for deciding who is black is of course the principle of hypodescent. This "one drop rule" has meant that anyone with a visually discernable trace of African . . . ancestry is, simply, black. Comparativists have long noted the peculiar ordinance this mixture-denying principle has exercised over the history of the United States. Although it no longer has the legal status it held in many states during the Jim Crow era, this principle was reinforced in the civil rights era as a basis for antidiscrimination remedies. Today it remains in place as a formidable convention in many settings and dominates debates about the categories appropriate for the federal census. The movement for recognition of "mixed race" identity has made some headway, including for people with a fraction of African ancestry, but most governments, private agencies, educational institutions, and advocacy organizations that classify and count people by ethnoracial categories at all continue to perpetuate hypodescent racialization when they talk about African Americans.

The second portentous practice is the treating of all victims of white racism alike, regardless of how differently this racism has affected African Americans, Latinos, Indians, and Asian Americans, to say nothing of the subdivisions within each of these communities of descent. When federal agencies developed affirmative action programs in the late 1960s, they identified Asian Americans, Hispanics, and Indians along with African Americans as eligible groups. . . . [E]ntitlements for nonblack groups were predicated on the assumption that such groups were like blacks in their social experience. Other disadvantaged groups, including women, impoverished Anglo whites, impoverished European ethnics, and gays and lesbians, were less successful in gaining entitlements during the so-called minority rights revolution because they were not perceived as victims of white racism.

The notion that all descent groups whose ancestry could be located outside Europe were like blacks, however, had not been prominent previously in the proclaimed self-conception of these nonblack minority groups, nor in much of what public discussion there was of their history and circumstances. The histories of each of these communities were almost always presented to their own members as well as to the society at large in terms that took their differences into account, including the specific ways in which whites had abused them. These histories, moreover, were usually about particular descent groups, such as Chinese Americans or Mexican Americans, rather than about what came to be called "panethnic" groups, such as Asian Americans and Latinos. . . .

[In] the late 1960s[, however,] political alliances were forged between black advocacy organizations and organizations speaking for other descent groups. The idea that Asian Americans, Latinos, and Indians were indeed like blacks gained ground and was marked vividly with a designation especially popular in the 1980s: "people of color." The downplaying of the differences between nonblack minorities and blacks was practiced first by officials and then by activists who came to understand that by applying "the black model" to their own group they had a better chance of getting the sympathetic attention of officials and courts. White racism thus ironically came to be assigned the same capacity traditionally assigned to one drop of black blood: the capacity to define equally whatever it touched, no matter how the affected entity was constituted and what its life circumstances might have been. We have been living by a principle of white racist hypovictimization: we can call it the one hate rule. . . .

The most unabashedly explicit judicial investigations of litigants' "real" classifications belong mostly to the past, when systematic racial subjugation was the legal order of the day. Courts facing freedom suits by enslaved persons sometimes had little choice but to engage in the crudest forms of racial sorting.

In the 1806 Virginia case of *Hudgins v. Wrights*, for example, the three plaintiffs claimed a right to emancipation from slavery "as having been descended, in the maternal line, from a free Indian woman." The lower court judge, "perceiving from his own view, that the youngest of the appellees was perfectly white, and that there were gradual shades of difference in colour between the grand-mother, mother, and grand-daughter (all of whom were before the Court), and considering the evidence in the cause, determined that the appellees were entitled to their freedom." The Virginia Supreme Court affirmed. One judge reasoned as follows:

> The distinguishing characteristics of the different species of the human race are so visibly marked, that those species may be readily discriminated from each other by mere inspection only. This, at least, is emphatically true in relation to the negroes, to the Indians of North America, and the European white people.

> When, however, these races become intermingled, it is difficult, if not impossible, to say from inspection only, which race predominates in the offspring, and certainly impossible to determine whether the descent from a given race has been through the paternal or maternal line. . . . [W]here an intermixture has taken place in relation to the person in question, . . . testimony must be resorted to for the purpose of shewing through what line a descent from a given stock has been deduced; and also to ascertain, perhaps, whether the colouring of the complexion has been derived from a negro or an Indian ancestor.

> In the case of a person visibly appearing to be a negro, the presumption is, in this country, that he is a slave, and it is incumbent on him to make out his right to freedom: but in the case of a person visibly appearing to be a white man, or an Indian, the presumption is that he is free, and it is necessary for his adversary to shew that he is a slave.

> In the present case it is not and cannot be denied that the appellees have entirely the appearance of white people: and how does the appellant attempt to deprive them of the blessing of liberty to which all such persons are entitled? He brings no testimony to shew that any ancestor in the female line was a negro slave or even an Indian rightfully held in slavery. . . .

For most constitutional purposes, the question of what "counts" as race (as opposed to ethnicity, nationality, or some other form of categorization based at least in part on familial descent) is not significant. That's because the application of strict scrutiny does not ordinarily depend on a classification being considered racial as such; the courts have often referred to national origin and religion as suspect classifications just like race, and it appears that the term would be applied to any ethnic classification. Thus, we may readily expect courts to apply strict scrutiny to governmental action that treats persons of Arabic, Romani, or Jewish ancestry, or persons with Hispanic surnames, differently from others, without much worry as to whether the classification should be considered racial. Cf. *Saint Francis College v. Al-Khazraji* (1987) (holding that in 42 U.S.C. § 1981 "Congress intended to protect from discrimination identifiable classes of persons who are subjected to intentional discrimination solely because of their ancestry or ethnic characteristics . . . whether or not [such discrimination] would be classified as racial in terms of modern scientific theory"); *Walker v. Secretary of the Treasury*, 713 F. Supp. 403 (N.D. Ga. 1989) (holding that discrimination by a dark-skinned black supervisor against a light-skinned black employee is proscribed by Title VII of the 1964 Civil Rights Act).

But in one constitutional setting, such boundaries may make a difference. *Batson v. Kentucky* (1986) held that a prosecutor may not exercise peremptory challenges to excuse potential jurors "solely on account of their race." It seems clear that *Batson* applies to Hispanic and Latino jurors, see, *e.g., Hernandez v. New York* (1991) (speaking both of race and ethnicity), but courts have been reluctant to apply it to Italian-Americans, see, *e.g., Rico v. Leftridge-Byrd*, 340 F.3d 178 (3d Cir. 2003) (asserting that the Supreme Court has "not extended *Batson* to any European-American ethnicity or to national origin"). And the Supreme Court has declined the opportunity to decide whether *Batson* precludes use of peremptories on grounds of religion. *Davis v. Minnesota* (1994) (denying certiorari in *State v. Davis*, 504 N.W. 2d 767 (Minn. 1993), over the dissent of Thomas, J., joined by Scalia, J., who asserted that "no principled reason immediately appears for declining to apply *Batson* to any strike based on a classification that is accorded heightened scrutiny under the Equal Protection Clause"). One could imagine a prosecutor responding to a *Batson* challenge by arguing that

CROSS REFERENCE   *Batson* is further discussed at p. 1065, and *Hernandez* is presented at pp. 1065–1072; see also p. 340.

she is not discriminating because of personal racial animus, but merely responding to the objective reality of racism among private individuals—some of whom will be on the jury. *Batson* gave no force to that kind of objection, which had been recently rejected in a different context in *Palmore v. Sidoti* (1984) ("Private biases may be outside the reach of the law, but the law cannot, directly or indirectly, give them effect").

 CROSS REFERENCE *Palmore* is presented below at pp. 1186–1188.

2. Potentially Non-Subjugating Racial Classifications

It's essentially impossible to defend the subordinating, subjugating racial classifications in cases like *Brown*, *Loving*, and *Korematsu* as public-minded efforts to promote the general good. But might there be some cases where it seems like the government is actually trying to use racial categories in genuinely equal-spirited good faith? It's easier to recognize the cases where that possibility seems plausible than it is to articulate a hard-edged description of the category they represent.

 As You READ
The next two cases review a pair of racial classifications in the prison context where—given the unique safety concerns in play—the underlying rule could at least plausibly be understood to have been adopted for genuinely public-spirited ends. Assuming that's right, should it make a difference to the Court's constitutional review?

Lee v. Washington

Supreme Court of the United States, 1968.
390 U.S. 333.

PER CURIAM.

This appeal challenges a decree of a three-judge District Court declaring that certain Alabama statutes violate the Fourteenth Amendment to the extent that they require segregation of the races in prisons and jails, and establishing a schedule for desegregation of these institutions.

The State's contention[ ] that the challenged statutes are not unconstitutional [is] without merit. The remaining contention of the State is that the specific orders directing desegregation of prisons and jails make no allowance for the necessities of prison security and discipline, but we do not so read the "Order, Judgment and Decree" of the District Court, which when read as a whole we find unexceptionable.

The judgment is affirmed.

MR. JUSTICE BLACK, MR. JUSTICE HARLAN, and MR. JUSTICE STEWART, concurring.

In joining the opinion of the Court, we wish to make explicit something that is left to be gathered only by implication from the Court's opinion. This is that prison authorities have the right, acting in good faith and in particularized circumstances, to take into account racial tensions in maintaining security, discipline, and good order in prisons and jails. We are unwilling to assume that state or local prison authorities might mistakenly regard such an explicit pronouncement as evincing any dilution of this Court's firm commitment to the Fourteenth Amendment's prohibition of racial discrimination.

Johnson v. California

Supreme Court of the United States, 2005.
543 U.S. 499.

JUSTICE O'CONNOR delivered the opinion of the Court.

The California Department of Corrections (CDC) has an unwritten policy of racially segregating prisoners in double cells in reception centers for up to 60 days each time they enter a new correctional facility. We consider whether strict scrutiny is the proper standard of review for an equal protection challenge to that policy.

I

CDC institutions house all new male inmates and all male inmates transferred from other state facilities in reception centers for up to 60 days upon their arrival. During that time, prison officials evaluate the inmates to determine their ultimate placement. Double-cell assignments in the reception centers are based on a number of factors, predominantly race. In fact, the CDC has admitted that the chances of an inmate being assigned a cellmate of another race are " '[p]retty close' " to zero percent. The CDC further subdivides prisoners within each racial group. Thus, Japanese-Americans are housed separately from Chinese-Americans, and northern California Hispanics are separated from southern California Hispanics.

The CDC's asserted rationale for this practice is that it is necessary to prevent violence caused by racial gangs. It cites numerous incidents of racial violence in CDC facilities and identifies five major prison gangs in the State: Mexican Mafia, Nuestra Familia, Black Guerilla Family, Aryan Brotherhood, and Nazi Low Riders. The CDC also notes that prison-gang culture is violent and murderous. An associate warden testified that if race were not considered in making initial housing assignments, she is certain there would be racial conflict in the cells and in the yard. Other prison officials also expressed their belief that violence and conflict would result if prisoners were not segregated. The CDC claims that it must therefore segregate all inmates while it determines whether they pose a danger to others.

With the exception of the double cells in reception areas, the rest of the state prison facilities—dining areas, yards, and cells—are fully integrated. After the initial 60-day period, prisoners are allowed to choose their own cellmates. The CDC usually grants inmate requests to be housed together, unless there are security reasons for denying them. . . .

II

A

We have held that "*all* racial classifications [imposed by government] . . . must be analyzed by a reviewing court under strict scrutiny." *Adarand Constructors, Inc. v. Peña* (1995) (emphasis added). Under strict scrutiny, the government has the burden of proving that racial classifications "are narrowly tailored measures that further compelling governmental interests." . . .

The reasons for strict scrutiny are familiar. Racial classifications raise special fears that they are motivated by an invidious purpose. Thus, we have admonished time and again that, "[a]bsent searching judicial inquiry into the justification for such race-based measures, there is simply no way of determining . . . what classifications are in fact motivated by illegitimate notions of racial inferiority or simple racial politics." *Richmond v. J.A. Croson Co.* (1989) (plurality opinion). We therefore apply strict scrutiny to *all* racial classifications to " 'smoke out' illegitimate uses of race by assuring that [government] is pursuing a goal important enough to warrant use of a highly suspect tool."

The CDC claims that its policy should be exempt from our categorical rule because it is "neutral"—that is, it "neither benefits nor burdens one group or individual more than any other group or individual." Brief for Respondents. In other words, strict scrutiny should not apply because all prisoners are "equally" segregated. The CDC's argument ignores our repeated command that "racial classifications receive close scrutiny even when they may be said to burden or benefit the races equally." Indeed, we rejected the notion that separate can ever be equal—or "neutral"—50 years ago in *Brown v. Board of Education* (1954), and we refuse to resurrect it today. See also *Powers v. Ohio* (1991) (rejecting the argument that race-based peremptory challenges were permissible because they [could be] applied equally to white and black jurors and holding that "[i]t is axiomatic that racial classifications do not become legitimate on the assumption that all persons suffer them in equal degree").

We have previously applied a heightened standard of review in evaluating racial segregation in prisons. [*Lee v. Washington* (1968).] The need for strict scrutiny is no less important here, where prison officials cite racial violence as the reason for their policy. As we have recognized in the past, racial classifications "threaten to stigmatize individuals by reason of their membership in a racial group and to *incite racial hostility*." Indeed, by insisting that inmates be housed only with other inmates of the same race, it is possible that prison officials will breed further hostility among prisoners and reinforce racial and ethnic divisions. By perpetuating the notion that race matters most, racial segregation of inmates "may exacerbate the very patterns of [violence that it is] said to counteract." See also Trulson & Marquart, *The Caged Melting Pot: Toward an Understanding of the Consequences of Desegregation in Prisons* (2002) (in a study of prison desegregation, finding that "over [10 years] the rate of violence between inmates segregated by race in double cells surpassed the rate among those racially integrated"). See also Brief for Former State Corrections Officials as *Amici Curiae* (opinion of former corrections officials from six States that "racial integration of cells tends to diffuse racial tensions and thus diminish interracial violence" and that "a blanket policy of racial segregation of inmates is contrary to sound prison management").

The CDC's policy is unwritten. . . . Virtually all other States and the Federal Government manage their prison systems without reliance on racial segregation. Federal regulations governing the Federal Bureau of Prisons (BOP) expressly prohibit racial segregation. ("[BOP] staff shall not discriminate against inmates on the basis of race, religion, national origin, sex, disability, or political belief. This includes the making of administrative decisions and providing access to work, housing and programs."). The United States contends that racial integration actually "leads to less violence in BOP's institutions and better prepares inmates for re-entry into society." Indeed, the United States argues, based on its experience with the BOP, that it is possible to address "concerns of prison security through individualized consideration without the use of racial segregation, unless warranted as a necessary and temporary response to a race riot or other serious threat of race-related violence." As to transferees, in particular, whom the CDC has already evaluated at least once, it is not clear why more individualized determinations are not possible.

Because the CDC's policy is an express racial classification, it is "immediately suspect." We therefore hold that the Court of Appeals erred when it failed to apply strict scrutiny to the CDC's policy and to require the CDC to demonstrate that its policy is narrowly tailored to serve a compelling state interest.

B

The CDC invites us to make an exception to the rule that strict scrutiny applies to all racial classifications, and instead to apply [a] deferential standard of review . . . because its segregation policy applies only in the prison context. We decline the invitation. . . . In the prison context, when the government's power is at its apex, we think that searching judicial review of racial classifications is necessary to guard against invidious discrimination. . . .

The CDC argues that "[d]eference to the particular expertise of prison officials in the difficult task of managing daily prison operations" requires a more relaxed standard of review for its segregation policy. But we have refused to defer to state officials' judgments on race in other areas where those officials traditionally exercise substantial discretion. . . . We did not relax the standard of review for racial classifications in prison in *Lee*, and we refuse to do so today. Rather, we explicitly reaffirm what we implicitly held in *Lee*: The "necessities of prison security and discipline" are a compelling government interest justifying only those uses of race that are narrowly tailored to address those necessities. See *J. A. Croson Co.* (1989) (Scalia, J., concurring in judgment) (citing *Lee* for the proposition that "only a social emergency rising to the level of imminent danger to life and limb—for example, a prison race riot, requiring temporary segregation of inmates—can justify an exception to the [color-blindness] principle").

Justice Thomas would subject race-based policies in prisons to [a] deferential standard of review. . . . [U]nder Justice Thomas' view, there is no obvious limit to permissible segregation in prisons. It is not readily apparent why, if segregation in reception centers is justified, segregation in the dining halls, yards, and general housing areas is not also permissible. Any of these areas could be the potential site of racial violence. If Justice Thomas' approach were to carry the day, even the blanket segregation policy struck down in *Lee* might stand a chance of survival if prison officials simply asserted that it was necessary to prison management. We therefore reject [a deferential] standard for racial classifications in prisons because it would make rank discrimination too easy to defend.

The CDC protests that strict scrutiny will handcuff prison administrators and render them unable to address legitimate problems of race-based violence in prisons. Not so. Strict scrutiny is not " 'strict in theory, but fatal in fact.' " *Adarand* [(denying that this common description of strict scrutiny is accurate)]; *Grutter v. Bollinger* (2003) ("Although all governmental uses of race are subject to strict scrutiny, not all are invalidated by it."). Strict scrutiny does not preclude the ability of prison officials to address the compelling interest in prison safety. Prison administrators, however, will have to demonstrate that any race-based policies are narrowly tailored to that end. . . .

On remand, the CDC will have the burden of demonstrating that its policy is narrowly tailored with regard to new inmates as well as transferees. Prisons are dangerous places, and the special circumstances they present may justify racial classifications in some contexts. Such circumstances can be considered in applying strict scrutiny, which is designed to take relevant differences into account. . . . The judgment of the Court of Appeals is reversed, and the case is remanded for further proceedings consistent with this opinion.

It is so ordered.

The Chief Justice took no part in the decision of this case.

Justice Ginsburg, with whom Justice Souter and Justice Breyer join, concurring.

The Court today resoundingly reaffirms the principle that state-imposed racial segregation is highly suspect and cannot be justified on the ground that " 'all persons suffer [the separation] in equal degree.' " . . . Experience in other States and in federal prisons . . . strongly suggests that CDC's race-based assignment of new inmates and transferees, administratively convenient as it may be, is not necessary to the safe management of a penal institution. . . .

JUSTICE STEVENS, dissenting.

In my judgment a state policy of segregating prisoners by race during the first 60 days of their incarceration, as well as the first 60 days after their transfer from one facility to another, violates the Equal Protection Clause of the Fourteenth Amendment. The California Department of Corrections (CDC) has had an ample opportunity to justify its policy during the course of this litigation, but has utterly failed to do so whether judged under strict scrutiny or [a] more deferential standard. . . . The CDC [has not] made any offer of proof to suggest that a remand for further factual development would serve any purpose other than to postpone the inevitable. I therefore agree with the submission of the United States as *amicus curiae* that the Court should hold the policy unconstitutional on the current record.

The CDC's segregation policy is based on a conclusive presumption that housing inmates of different races together creates an unacceptable risk of racial violence. Under the policy's logic, an inmate's race is a proxy for gang membership, and gang membership is a proxy for violence. The CDC, however, has offered scant empirical evidence or expert opinion to justify this use of race under even a minimal level of constitutional scrutiny. The presumption underlying the policy is undoubtedly overbroad. The CDC has made no effort to prove what fraction of new or transferred inmates are members of race-based gangs, nor has it shown more generally that interracial violence is disproportionately greater than intraracial violence in its prisons. Proclivity toward racial violence unquestionably varies from inmate to inmate, yet the CDC applies its blunderbuss policy to *all* new and transferred inmates housed in double cells regardless of their criminal histories or records of previous incarceration. Under the CDC's policy, for example, two car thieves of different races—neither of whom has any history of gang involvement, or of violence, for that matter— would be barred from being housed together during their first two months of prison. This result derives from the CDC's inflexible judgment that such integrated living conditions are simply too dangerous. This Court has never countenanced such racial prophylaxis. . . .

To establish a link between integrated cells and violence, the CDC relies on the views of two state corrections officials. They attested to their belief that double-celling members of different races would lead to violence and that this violence would spill out into the prison yards. One of these officials, an associate warden, testified as follows:

> [W]ith the Asian population, the control sergeants have to be more careful than they do with Blacks, Whites, and Hispanics because, for example, you cannot house a Japanese inmate with a Chinese inmate. You cannot. They will kill each other. They won't even tell you about it. They will just do it. The same with Laotians, Vietnamese, Cambodians, Filipinos. You have to be very careful about housing other Asians with other Asians. It's very culturally heavy.

Such musings inspire little confidence. Indeed, this comment supports the suspicion that the policy is based on racial stereotypes and outmoded fears about the dangers of racial integration. This Court should give no credence to such cynical, reflexive conclusions about race. . . .

The very real risk that prejudice (whether conscious or not) partly underlies the CDC's policy counsels in favor of relaxing the usual deference we pay to corrections officials in these matters. We should instead insist on hard evidence, especially given that California's policy is an outlier when compared to nationwide practice. . . . Tellingly, the CDC can only point to two other States, Texas and Oklahoma, that use racial status in assigning inmates in prison reception areas. . . .

Given the inherent indignity of segregation and its shameful historical connotations, one might assume that the CDC came to its policy only as a last resort. Distressingly, this is not so: There is no evidence that the CDC has ever experimented with, or even carefully considered, race-neutral methods of achieving its goals. That the policy is unwritten reflects, I think, the evident lack of deliberation that preceded its creation.

Specifically, the CDC has failed to explain why it could not, as an alternative to automatic segregation, rely on an individualized assessment of each inmate's risk of violence when assigning him to a cell in a reception center. The Federal Bureau of Prisons and other state systems do so without any apparent difficulty. For inmates who are being transferred from one facility to another—who represent approximately 85% of those subject to the segregation policy—the CDC can simply examine their prison records to determine if they have any known gang affiliations or if they have ever engaged in or threatened racial violence. For example, the CDC has had an opportunity to observe petitioner for almost 20 years; surely the CDC could have determined his placement without subjecting him to a period of segregation. For new inmates, assignments can be based on their presentence reports, which contain information about offense conduct, criminal record, and personal history—including any available information about gang affiliations. In fact, state law requires the county probation officer to transmit a presentence report to the CDC along with an inmate's commitment papers.

Despite the rich information available in these records, the CDC considers these records only rarely in assigning inmates to cells in the reception centers. The CDC's primary explanation for this is administrative inefficiency—the records, it says, simply do not arrive in time. The CDC's counsel conceded at oral argument that presentence reports "have a fair amount of information," but she stated that ". . . [i]t follows some period of time [after the inmate arrives]." . . . Similarly, with regard to transferees, counsel stated that their prison records do not arrive at the reception centers in time to make cell assignments. Even if such inefficiencies might explain a temporary expedient in some cases, they surely do not justify a systemwide policy. When the State's interest in administrative convenience is pitted against the Fourteenth Amendment's ban on racial segregation, the latter must prevail. . . . In fact, the CDC's failure to demand timely presentence reports and prison records undercuts the sincerity of its concern for inmate security during the reception process. Race is an unreliable and necessarily underinclusive predictor of violence. Without the inmate-specific information found in the records, there is a risk that corrections officials will, for example, house together inmates of the same race who are nevertheless members of rival gangs, such as the Bloods and Crips.

Accordingly . . . I respectfully dissent from the Court's refusal to decide, on the basis of the record before us, that the CDC's policy is unconstitutional.

Justice Thomas, with whom Justice Scalia joins, dissenting.

. . . The Constitution has always demanded less within the prison walls. Time and again, even when faced with constitutional rights no less "fundamental" than the right to be free from state-sponsored racial discrimination, we have deferred to the reasonable judgments of officials experienced in running this Nation's prisons. There is good reason for such deference in this case. California oversees roughly 160,000 inmates in prisons that have been a breeding ground for some of the most violent prison gangs in America—all of them organized along racial lines. In that atmosphere, California racially segregates a portion of its inmates, in a part of its prisons, for brief periods of up to 60 days, until the State can arrange permanent housing. The majority is concerned with sparing inmates the indignity and stigma of racial discrimination. California is concerned with their safety and saving their lives. I respectfully dissent. . . .

According to the State, housing inmates in double cells without regard to race threatens not only prison discipline, but also the physical safety of inmates and staff. That is because double cells are especially dangerous. The risk of racial violence in public areas of prisons is high, and the tightly confined, private conditions of cells hazard even more violence. Prison staff cannot see into the cells without going up to them, and inmates can cover the windows to prevent the staff from seeing inside the cells. The risk of violence caused by this privacy is grave, for inmates are confined to their cells for much of the day.

Nevertheless, while race is the predominant factor in pairing cellmates, it is hardly the only one. After dividing this subset of inmates based on race, the CDC further divides them based on geographic or national origin. As an example, Hispanics from northern and southern California are not housed together in reception centers because they often belong to rival gangs—La Nuestra Familia and the Mexican Mafia, respectively. Likewise, Chinese and Japanese inmates are not housed together, nor are Cambodians, Filipinos, Laotians, or Vietnamese. In addition to geographic and national origin, prison officials consider a host of other factors, including inmates' age, mental health, medical needs, criminal history, and gang affiliation. For instance, when Johnson was admitted in 1987, he was a member of the Crips, a black street gang. He was therefore ineligible to be housed with nonblack inmates. . . .

* * *

Petitioner Garrison Johnson challenges not permanent, but temporary, segregation of only a portion of California's prisons. Of the 17 years Johnson has been incarcerated, California has assigned him a cellmate of the same race for no more than a year (and probably more like four months); Johnson has had black cellmates during the other 16 years, but by his own choice. Nothing in the record demonstrates that if Johnson (or any other prisoner) requested to be housed with a person of a different race, it would be denied (though Johnson's gang affiliation with the Crips might stand in his way). Moreover, Johnson concedes that California's prisons are racially violent places, and that he lives in fear of being attacked because of his race. Perhaps on remand the CDC's policy will survive strict scrutiny, but in the event that it does not, Johnson may well have won a Pyrrhic victory.

A POSTSCRIPT

Following the Supreme Court's decision, the parties signed an elaborate settlement agreement, which included the following commitment:

> As a direct result of Plaintiff's claims and the opinion of the Supreme Court of the United States in *Johnson v. California*, [the California Department of Corrections (CDC)] has begun formulating and implementing a plan
>
>> by which inmates shall be housed at [CDC] reception centers without using race as the determinative housing criterion, while minimizing any potential impact upon inmates' safety and that of institutions, [CDC] personnel, and the public,
>>
>> and by which prisoners housed in [CDC] facilities shall be racially integrated upon implementation of adequate safety measures, except in instances where to do so would compromise the safety and security of inmates, staff, facilities or the public[.][a]

3.   Facial Neutrality

In any equal protection challenge, perhaps the most important question is what level of scrutiny to apply. If the court finds that a given classification is suspicious and prompts some form of heightened review, that's generally bad news for the government. If the court finds that a given classification prompts only rational basis review, that's generally bad news for the challenger. This slotting question is often outcome determinative; in Gerald Gunther's famous formulation, the highest level of scrutiny is often "strict in theory, but fatal in fact."

So far, we have been dealing with governmental actions that explicitly classified by race. When that occurs, it is clear that strict scrutiny applies, and the governmental action will almost always be held invalid. But some of the most important problems in the realm of race and equal protection arise with respect to governmental actions that do not explicitly classify on the basis of race—but nevertheless have racially disparate impacts. What then?

If only as a practical matter, it cannot be that any disparate impact always renders a governmental action unconstitutional. If that were the rule, then, for example, a city would often be precluded from raising its transit fares; racial groups that are poorer on average will tend to be harmed by the raise more than others, both because they will find any additional cost harder to bear and

---

[a]   Source: Margo Schlanger, Civil Rights Clearinghouse, *at* https://www.clearinghouse.net/chDocs/public/PC-CA-0041-0001.pdf.

because they are likely more dependent on public transit. On the other hand, facial neutrality cannot by itself be a ticket to a clean bill of health for the governmental action, not least because discriminatory purpose can often easily be hidden behind a neutral veneer. Even assuming that such a purpose is necessary to render the action invalid, the disproportion of the impact on racial groups may sometimes be so great as to support a conclusion that the purpose must have been discriminatory. In other cases, a government action uses a classification that is so closely correlated with race that one might argue it should be treated as tantamount to a racial classification. And in all these cases, the government actor might contend that its action was supported by valid reasons having nothing to do with race and so calling for light judicial scrutiny.

These cases thus present hard evidentiary questions about what's really going on behind the scenes in the government decision-making process. And all of them force us to confront what "equal protection of the laws" even means in the first place.

a. Facial Neutrality—Disparate Impact

The next case is one of the most important equal protection decisions ever handed down by the Supreme Court. Does that seem like a strong characterization? See if you can articulate how constitutional equality litigation might look different if *Washington v. Davis* had come out the other way.

Washington v. Davis

Supreme Court of the United States, 1976.
426 U.S. 229.

MR. JUSTICE WHITE delivered the opinion of the Court.

This case involves the validity of a qualifying test administered to applicants for positions as police officers in the District of Columbia Metropolitan Police Department. The test was sustained by the District Court but invalidated by the Court of Appeals. We are in agreement with the District Court and hence reverse the judgment of the Court of Appeals.

I

. . . According to the findings and conclusions of the District Court, to be accepted by the Department and to enter an intensive 17-week training program, the police recruit was required to satisfy certain physical and character standards, to be a high school graduate or its equivalent, and to receive a grade of at least 40 out of 80 on "Test 21," which is "an examination that is used generally throughout the federal service," which "was developed by the [federal government's] Civil Service Commission, not the [District of Columbia] Police Department," and which was "designed to test verbal ability, vocabulary, reading and comprehension."

The validity of Test 21 was the sole issue before the court on the motions for summary judgment. The District Court noted that there was no claim of "an intentional discrimination or purposeful discriminatory acts" but only a claim that Test 21 bore no relationship to job performance and "has a highly discriminatory impact in screening out black candidates." Respondents' evidence, the District Court said, warranted three conclusions:

(a) The number of black police officers, while substantial, is not proportionate to the population mix of the city.

(b) A higher percentage of blacks fail the Test than whites.

(c) The Test has not been validated to establish its reliability for measuring subsequent job performance.

This showing was deemed sufficient to shift the burden of proof to the defendants in the action, petitioners here; but the court nevertheless concluded that on the undisputed facts respondents were not entitled to relief.

The District Court relied on several factors. Since August 1969, 44% of new police force recruits had been black; that figure also represented the proportion of blacks on the total force and was roughly equivalent to [that of] 20- to 29-year-old blacks in the 50-mile radius in which the recruiting efforts of the Police Department had been concentrated. It was undisputed that the Department had systematically and affirmatively sought to enroll black officers many of whom passed the test but failed to report for duty. The District Court rejected the assertion that Test 21 was culturally slanted to favor whites and was "satisfied that the undisputable facts prove the test to be reasonably and directly related to the requirements of the police recruit training program and that it is neither so designed nor operates [sic] to discriminate against otherwise qualified blacks." . . .

The Court of Appeals, addressing that issue, announced that it would be guided by *Griggs v. Duke Power Co.* (1971), a case involving the interpretation and application of Title VII of the Civil Rights Act of 1964, and held that the statutory standards . . . were to govern the due process question tendered in this one. The court went on to declare that lack of discriminatory intent in designing and administering Test 21 was irrelevant; the critical fact was rather that a far greater proportion of blacks—four times as many—failed the test than did whites. This disproportionate impact, standing alone and without regard to whether it indicated a discriminatory purpose, was held sufficient to establish a constitutional violation, absent proof by petitioners that the test was an adequate measure of job performance in addition to being an indicator of probable success in the training program, a burden which the court ruled petitioners had failed to discharge. . . .

WORTH NOTING

Title VII prohibits discrimination in employment "because of . . . race, color, religion, sex, or national origin."

II

Because the Court of Appeals erroneously applied the legal standards applicable to Title VII cases in resolving the constitutional issue before it, we reverse its judgment in respondents' favor. . . .

As the Court of Appeals understood Title VII, employees or applicants proceeding under it need not concern themselves with the employer's possibly discriminatory purpose but instead may focus solely on the racially differential impact of the challenged hiring or promotion practices. This is not the constitutional rule. We have never held that the constitutional standard for adjudicating claims of invidious racial discrimination is identical to the standards applicable under Title VII, and we decline to do so today.

The central purpose of the Equal Protection Clause of the Fourteenth Amendment is the prevention of official conduct discriminating on the basis of race. It is also true that the Due Process Clause of the Fifth Amendment contains an equal protection component prohibiting the United States from invidiously discriminating between individuals or groups. *Bolling v. Sharpe* (1954). But our cases have not embraced the proposition that a law or other official act, without regard to whether it reflects a racially discriminatory purpose, is unconstitutional solely because it has a racially disproportionate impact.

Almost 100 years ago, *Strauder v. West Virginia* (1880) established that the exclusion of Negroes from grand and petit juries in criminal proceedings violated the Equal Protection Clause, but the fact that a particular jury or a series of juries does not statistically reflect the racial composition of the community does not in itself make out an invidious discrimination forbidden by the Clause. "A purpose to discriminate must be present which may be proven by systematic exclusion of eligible jurymen of the proscribed race or by unequal application of the law to such an extent as to show intentional discrimination." *Akins v. Texas* (1945). . . .

The school desegregation cases have also adhered to the basic equal protection principle that the invidious quality of a law claimed to be racially discriminatory must ultimately be traced to a racially discriminatory purpose. That there are both predominantly black and predominantly white schools in a community is not alone violative of the Equal Protection Clause. The essential element of de jure segregation is "a current condition of segregation resulting from intentional state action. The differentiating factor between *de jure* segregation and so-called *de facto* segregation . . . is *purpose* or *intent* to segregate." *Keyes v. School Dist. No. 1* (1973). . . .

This is not to say that the necessary discriminatory racial purpose must be express or appear on the face of the statute, or that a law's disproportionate impact is irrelevant in cases involving Constitution-based claims of racial discrimination. A statute, otherwise neutral on its face, must not be applied so as invidiously to discriminate on the basis of race. *Yick Wo v. Hopkins* (1886). It is also clear from the cases dealing with racial discrimination in the selection of juries that . . . [a] prima facie case of discriminatory purpose may be proved as well by the absence of Negroes on a particular jury combined with the failure of the jury commissioners to be informed of eligible Negro jurors in a community, *Hill v. Texas* (1942). . . . With a prima facie case made out, "the burden of proof shifts to the State to rebut the presumption of unconstitutional action by showing that permissible racially neutral selection criteria and procedures have produced the monochromatic result."

Necessarily, an invidious discriminatory purpose may often be inferred from the totality of the relevant facts, including the fact, if it is true, that the law bears more heavily on one race than another. It is also not infrequently true that the discriminatory impact—in the jury cases, for example, the total or seriously disproportionate exclusion of Negroes from jury venires—may for all practical purposes demonstrate unconstitutionality because in various circumstances the discrimination is very difficult to explain on nonracial grounds. Nevertheless, we have not held that a law, neutral on its face and serving ends otherwise within the power of government to pursue, is invalid under the Equal Protection Clause simply because it may affect a greater proportion of one race than of another. Disproportionate impact is not irrelevant, but it is not the sole touchstone of an invidious racial discrimination forbidden by the Constitution. Standing alone, it does not trigger the rule that racial classifications are to be subjected to the strictest scrutiny and are justifiable only by the weightiest of considerations. . . .

[V]arious Courts of Appeals have held in several contexts, including public employment, that the substantially disproportionate racial impact of a statute or official practice standing alone and without regard to discriminatory purpose, suffices to prove racial discrimination violating the Equal Protection Clause absent some justification going substantially beyond what would be necessary to validate most other legislative classifications. The cases impressively demonstrate that there is another side to the issue; but, with all due respect, to the extent that those cases rested on or expressed the view that proof of discriminatory racial purpose is unnecessary in making out an equal protection violation, we are in disagreement.

As an initial matter, we have difficulty understanding how a law establishing a racially neutral qualification for employment is nevertheless racially discriminatory and denies "any person . . . equal protection of the laws" simply because a greater proportion of Negroes fail to qualify than members of other racial or ethnic groups. Had respondents, along with all others who had failed Test 21, whether white or black, brought an action claiming that the test denied each of them equal protection of the laws as compared with those who had passed with high enough scores to qualify them as police recruits, it is most unlikely that their challenge would have been sustained. Test 21, which is administered generally to prospective Government employees, concededly seeks to ascertain whether those who take it have acquired a particular level of verbal skill; and it is untenable that the Constitution prevents the Government from seeking modestly to upgrade the communicative abilities of its employees rather than to be satisfied with some lower level of competence, particularly where the job requires special ability to communicate orally and in writing. Respondents, as Negroes, could no more successfully claim that the test denied them equal protection than could white applicants who also failed. The conclusion would not be different in the face of proof that more Negroes than whites had been disqualified by Test 21. That other Negroes also failed to score well would, alone, not demonstrate that respondents individually were being denied equal protection of the laws. . . .

Nor on the facts of the case before us would the disproportionate impact of Test 21 warrant the conclusion that it is a purposeful device to discriminate against Negroes and hence an infringement of the constitutional rights of respondents as well as other black applicants. As we have said, the test is neutral on its face and rationally may be said to serve a purpose the Government is constitutionally empowered to pursue. Even agreeing with the District Court that the differential racial effect of Test 21 called for further inquiry, we think the District Court correctly held that the affirmative efforts of the Metropolitan Police Department to recruit black officers, the changing racial composition of the recruit classes and of the force in general, and the relationship of the test to the training program negated any inference that the Department discriminated on the basis of race or that "a police officer qualifies on the color of his skin rather than ability." . . .

A rule that a statute designed to serve neutral ends is nevertheless invalid, absent compelling justification, if in practice it benefits or burdens one race more than another would be far-reaching and would raise serious questions about, and perhaps invalidate, a whole range of tax, welfare, public service, regulatory, and licensing statutes that may be more burdensome to the poor and to the average black than to the more affluent white.[14] Given that rule, such consequences would perhaps be likely to follow. However, in our view, extension of the rule beyond those areas where it is already applicable by reason of statute, such as in the field of public employment, should await legislative prescription. . . .

III

We also hold that . . . Respondents were [not] entitled to relief on . . . statutory grounds. . . .

---

[14] Goodman, *De Facto School Segregation: A Constitutional and Empirical Analysis*, 60 Calif. L. Rev. 275 (1972), suggests that disproportionate-impact analysis might invalidate "tests and qualifications for voting, draft deferment, public employment, jury service, and other government-conferred benefits and opportunities . . . ; (s)ales taxes, bail schedules, utility rates, bridge tolls, license fees, and other state-imposed charges." It has also been argued that minimum wage and usury laws as well as professional licensing requirements would require major modifications in light of the unequal-impact rule. . . .

The judgment of the Court of Appeals accordingly is reversed.

Mr. Justice Stewart joins Parts I and II of the Court's opinion.

Mr. Justice Stevens, concurring.

While I agree with the Court's disposition of this case, I add these comments on the constitutional issue discussed in Part II. . . .

The requirement of purposeful discrimination is a common thread running through the cases summarized in Part II. . . . Frequently the most probative evidence of intent will be objective evidence of what actually happened rather than evidence describing the subjective state of mind of the actor. For normally the actor is presumed to have intended the natural consequences of his deeds. This is particularly true in the case of governmental action which is frequently the product of compromise, of collective decisionmaking, and of mixed motivation. It is unrealistic, on the one hand, to require the victim of alleged discrimination to uncover the actual subjective intent of the decisionmaker or, conversely, to invalidate otherwise legitimate action simply because an improper motive affected the deliberation of a participant in the decisional process. A law conscripting clerics should not be invalidated because an atheist voted for it.

My point in making this observation is to suggest that the line between discriminatory purpose and discriminatory impact is not nearly as bright, and perhaps not quite as critical, as the reader of the Court's opinion might assume. I agree, of course, that a constitutional issue does not arise every time some disproportionate impact is shown. On the other hand, when the disproportion is as dramatic as in *Gomillion v. Lightfoot* (1960) or *Yick Wo v. Hopkins* (1886), it really does not matter whether the standard is phrased in terms of purpose or effect. Therefore, although I accept the statement of the general rule in the Court's opinion, I am not yet prepared to indicate how that standard should be applied in the many cases which have formulated the governing standard in different language. . . .

There are two reasons why I am convinced that the challenge to Test 21 is insufficient. First, the test serves the neutral and legitimate purpose of requiring all applicants to meet a uniform minimum standard of literacy. Reading ability is manifestly relevant to the police function, there is no evidence that the required passing grade was set at an arbitrarily high level, and there is sufficient disparity among high schools and high school graduates to justify the use of a separate uniform test. Second, the same test is used throughout the federal service. The applicants for employment in the District of Columbia Police Department represent such a small fraction of the total number of persons who have taken the test that their experience is of minimal probative value in assessing the neutrality of the test itself. That evidence, without more, is not sufficient to overcome the presumption that a test which is this widely used by the Federal Government is in fact neutral in its effect as well as its "purpose" as that term is used in constitutional adjudication. . . .

WORTH NOTING

Justice Brennan, joined by Justice Marshall, dissented. Given the procedural posture of the case, they would have applied Title VII standards, and affirmed decision of the Court of Appeals, without reaching constitutional issues.

FOR DISCUSSION

Concurring in *Washington v. Davis*, Justice Stevens observes that in many doctrinal areas, an actor "normally . . . is presumed to have intended the natural consequences of his deeds." He suggests that principle should be "particularly true" for government action. Does that seem right? Why or why not?

In *Personnel Administrator of Massachusetts v. Feeney* (1979), the Court returned to the issue of disparate impact. It said:

"Discriminatory purpose" . . . implies more than intent as volition or intent as awareness of consequences. It implies that the decisionmaker, in this case a state legislature, selected or reaffirmed a particular course of action at least in part "because of," not merely "in spite of," its adverse effects upon an identifiable group.

In *Feeney*, an affirmative action program for military veterans "operate[d] overwhelmingly to the advantage of males." Applying the "because of" standard, the Supreme Court upheld the statute:

[While] it cannot seriously be argued that the Legislature of Massachusetts could have been unaware that most veterans are men . . . , nothing in the record demonstrates that this preference for veterans was originally devised or subsequently re-enacted because it would accomplish the collateral goal of keeping women in a stereotypic and predefined place in the Massachusetts Civil Service.

For more context, see the longer *Feeney* excerpt at pp. 1241–1248.

b. Facial Neutrality—Demonstrable Racial Purpose

Under *Washington v. Davis*, all facially neutral laws get rational basis review unless they were motivated by a desire to discriminate on the basis of race—and regardless of the disparate racial impact they may produce. The *Davis* Court cautioned, however, that "[t]his is not to say that the necessary discriminatory racial purpose must be express or appear on the face of the statute." In the following cases, plaintiffs attempted to introduce direct evidence of invidious intent by the government actors who adopted the challenged classifications.

Hunter v. Underwood

Supreme Court of the United States, 1985.
471 U.S. 222.

Justice Rehnquist delivered the opinion of the Court.

We are required in this case to decide the constitutionality of Art. VIII, § 182, of the Alabama Constitution of 1901, which provides for the disenfranchisement of persons convicted of, among other offenses, "any crime . . . involving moral turpitude." Appellees Carmen Edwards, a black, and Victor Underwood, a white, have been blocked from the voter rolls pursuant to § 182 . . . because they each have been convicted of presenting a worthless check. In determining that the misdemeanor of presenting a worthless check is a crime involving moral turpitude, the Registrars relied on opinions of the Alabama Attorney General.

Edwards and Underwood sued the Montgomery and Jefferson Boards of Registrars . . . for a declaration invalidating § 182 as applied to persons convicted of . . . misdemeanors. . . .

The predecessor to § 182 was Art. VIII, § 3, of the Alabama Constitution of 1875, which denied persons "convicted of treason, embezzlement of public funds, malfeasance in office, larceny, bribery, or other crime punishable by imprisonment in the penitentiary" the right to register, vote or hold public office. These offenses were largely, if not entirely, felonies. The drafters of § 182, which was adopted by the 1901 convention, expanded the list of enumerated crimes substantially to include the following:

> treason, murder, arson, embezzlement, malfeasance in office, larceny, receiving stolen property, obtaining property or money under false pretenses, perjury, subornation of perjury, robbery, assault with intent to rob, burglary, forgery, bribery, assault and battery on the wife, bigamy, living in adultery, sodomy, incest, rape, miscegenation, [and] crime against nature.

The drafters retained the general felony provision—"any crime punishable by imprisonment in the penitentiary"—but also added a new catchall provision covering "any . . . crime involving moral turpitude." This latter phrase is not defined, but it was subsequently interpreted by the Alabama Supreme Court to mean an act that is " 'immoral in itself, regardless of the fact whether it is punishable by law. The doing of the act itself, and not its prohibition by statute, fixes the moral turpitude.' " *Pippin v. State*, 197 Ala. 613 (1916).

The enumerated crimes contain within them many misdemeanors. If a specific crime does not fall within one of the enumerated offenses, the Alabama Boards of Registrars consult Alabama case law or, in absence of a court precedent, opinions of the Alabama Attorney General to determine whether it is covered by § 182. Various minor nonfelony offenses such as presenting a worthless check and petty larceny fall within the sweep of § 182, while more serious nonfelony offenses such as second-degree manslaughter, assault on a police officer, mailing pornography, and aiding the escape of a misdemeanant do not because they are neither enumerated in § 182 nor considered crimes involving moral turpitude. It is alleged, and the Court of Appeals found, that the crimes selected for inclusion in § 182 were believed by the [constitutional convention] delegates to be more frequently committed by blacks.

Section 182 on its face is racially neutral, applying equally to anyone convicted of one of the enumerated crimes or a crime falling within one of the catchall provisions. Appellee Edwards nonetheless claims that the provision has had a racially discriminatory impact. The District Court made no finding on this claim, but the Court of Appeals implicitly found the evidence of discriminatory impact indisputable:

> The registrars' expert estimated that by January 1903 section 182 had disfranchised approximately ten times as many blacks as whites. This disparate effect persists today. In Jefferson and Montgomery Counties blacks are by even the most modest estimates at least 1.7 times as likely as whites to suffer disfranchisement under section 182 for the commission of nonprison offenses.

. . . Presented with a neutral state law that produces disproportionate effects along racial lines, the Court of Appeals was correct in applying the approach of *Arlington Heights v. Metropolitan Housing Development Corp.* (1977) to determine whether the law violates the Equal Protection Clause of the Fourteenth Amendment:

> [O]fficial action will not be held unconstitutional solely because it
> results in a racially disproportionate impact. . . . Proof of racially dis-
> criminatory intent or purpose is required to show a violation of the
> Equal Protection Clause.

See *Washington v. Davis* (1976). Once racial discrimination is shown to have
been a "substantial" or "motivating" factor behind enactment of the law, the
burden shifts to the law's defenders to demonstrate that the law would have
been enacted without this factor. See *Mt. Healthy v. Doyle* (1977).

Proving the motivation behind official action is often a problematic undertaking. When we move from an examination of a board of county commissioners
. . . to a body the size of the Alabama Constitutional Convention of 1901, the
difficulties in determining the actual motivations of the various legislators that
produced a given decision increase. With respect to Congress, the Court said
in *United States v. O'Brien* (1968):

> Inquiries into congressional motives or purposes are a hazardous
> matter. When the issue is simply the interpretation of legislation,
> the Court will look to statements by legislators for guidance as to
> the purpose of the legislature, because the benefit to sound deci-
> sion-making in this circumstance is thought sufficient to risk the
> possibility of misreading Congress' purpose. It is entirely a different
> matter when we are asked to void a statute that is, under well-settled
> criteria, constitutional on its face, on the basis of what fewer than a
> handful of Congressmen said about it. What motivates one legislator
> to make a speech about a statute is not necessarily what motivates
> scores of others to enact it, and the stakes are sufficiently high for us
> to eschew guesswork.

But the sort of difficulties of which the Court spoke in *O'Brien* do not
obtain in this case. Although understandably no "eyewitnesses" to the 1901 proceedings testified, testimony and opinions of historians were offered and received
without objection. These showed that the Alabama Constitutional Convention
of 1901 was part of a movement that swept the post-Reconstruction South to
disenfranchise blacks. See S. Hackney, *Populism to Progressivism in Alabama*
(1969); C. Vann Woodward, *Origins of the New South, 1877–1913* (1971). The
delegates to the all-white convention were not secretive about their purpose.
John B. Knox, president of the convention, stated in his opening address:

And what is it that we want to do? Why it is within the limits imposed by the Federal Constitution, to establish white supremacy in this State.

Indeed, neither the District Court nor appellants seriously dispute the claim that this zeal for white supremacy ran rampant at the convention. . . .

[The opinion of the Court of Appeals] presents a thorough analysis of the evidence and demonstrates conclusively that § 182 was enacted with the intent of disenfranchising blacks. We see little purpose in repeating that factual analysis here. At oral argument in this Court appellants' counsel essentially conceded this point, stating: "I would be very blind and naive [to] try to come up and stand before this Court and say that race was not a factor in the enactment of Section 182; that race did not play a part in the decisions of those people who were at the constitutional convention of 1901 and I won't do that."

In their brief to this Court, appellants maintain on the basis of their expert's testimony that the real purpose behind § 182 was to disenfranchise poor whites as well as blacks. The Southern Democrats, in their view, sought in this way to stem the resurgence of Populism which threatened their power. . . . Even were we to accept this explanation as correct, it hardly saves § 182 from invalidity. The explanation concedes both that discrimination against blacks, as well as against poor whites, was a motivating factor for the provision and that § 182 certainly would not have been adopted by the convention or ratified by the electorate in the absence of the racially discriminatory motivation. . . . Whether or not intentional disenfranchisement of poor whites would qualify as a "permissible motive" . . . , an additional purpose to discriminate against poor whites would not render nugatory the purpose to discriminate against all blacks, and it is beyond peradventure that the latter was a "but-for" motivation for the enactment of § 182.

Appellants contend that the State has a legitimate interest in denying the franchise to those convicted of crimes involving moral turpitude, and that § 182 should be sustained on that ground. The Court of Appeals convincingly demonstrated that such a purpose simply was not a motivating factor of the 1901 convention. In addition to the general catchall phrase "crimes involving moral turpitude" the suffrage committee selected such crimes as vagrancy, living in adultery, and wife beating that were thought to be more commonly committed by blacks:

Most of the proposals disqualified persons committing any one of a long list of petty as well as serious crimes which the Negro, and to a lesser extent the poor whites, most often committed. . . . Most of the crimes contained in the report of the suffrage committee came from an ordinance by John Fielding Burns, a Black Belt planter. The crimes he listed were those he had taken cognizance of for years in his justice of the peace court in the Burnsville district, where nearly all his cases involved Negroes.

M. McMillan, *Constitutional Development in Alabama, 1798–1901* (1955).

. . . Without deciding whether § 182 would be valid if enacted today without any impermissible motivation, we simply observe that its original enactment was motivated by a desire to discriminate against blacks on account of race and the section continues to this day to have that effect. As such, it violates equal protection. . . .

The judgment of the Court of Appeals is affirmed.

Justice Powell took no part in the consideration or decision of this case.

Now consider *Trump v. Hawaii* (2018), reviewing a claim that an immigration restriction was motivated by the purpose of discriminating on the basis of religion. The case involved a challenge to a Proclamation issued by President Trump that severely restricted entry into the United States from seven nations (initially eight), all but two of which were majority-Muslim. The case did not involve race as such, and the doctrinal hook for the challenge was the Establishment of Religion Clause of the First Amendment. But the essential claim was that the Proclamation was motivated by the purpose of discriminating on the basis of religion, and so the basic mode of analysis tracked the question asked in *Washington v. Davis*.

 CROSS REFERENCE Recall that *Trump* was the case in which the Supreme Court formally declared that *Korematsu* was no longer good law; see pp. 998–999.

The challengers drew on statements Trump had made during his Presidential campaign. For example, he had published a "Statement on Preventing Muslim Immigration" that called for a "total and complete shutdown of

Muslims entering the United States until our country's representatives can fig-ure out what is going on." He also asserted that "Islam hates us" and that the United States was "having problems with Muslims coming into the country."

After his inauguration, Trump indicated that he still intended to "ban Muslim immigration," and quickly issued an Executive Order suspending entry by foreign nationals from seven majority-Muslim nations. As the majority acknowledged,

WORTH NOTING

What might explain why a majority of the Court rejected plain-tiffs' challenge: the ev-idence, the legal con-text, or the actors involved?

> one of the President's campaign advisers explained that when the President "first announced it, he said, 'Muslim ban.' He called me up. He said, 'Put a commission together. Show me the right way to do it legally.' " The adviser said he assembled a group of Members of Congress and lawyers that "focused on, instead of religion, danger. . . . [The order] is based on places where there [is] substantial evidence that people are sending terrorists into our country."

When implementation of the first order was preliminarily enjoined, Trump replaced it with a somewhat narrower order applicable to six of the countries, and ultimately by the Proclamation at issue—justified on the basis of the cov-ered countries' failure to share adequate information for an informed entry determination, or otherwise by the substantial security risks they allegedly presented. Before issuing the Proclamation, Trump asserted that the "travel ban . . . should be far larger, tougher, and more specific," but observed that that would "stupidly . . . not be politically correct."

Justice Sotomayor, joined by Justice Ginsburg, thought that "the unrebutted evidence shows . . . that a reasonable observer would conclude, quite easily, that the primary purpose and function of the Proclamation is to disfavor Islam by banning Muslims from entering our country." (In prior Establishment Clause cases, the Court had asked whether a reasonable observer would view gov-ernment action as enacted for the purpose of favoring or disfavoring religion.) Justice Breyer, joined by Justice Kagan, reached a similar conclusion, empha-sizing the manner in which the Administration granted waivers. Accordingly, those four justices voted to uphold a preliminary injunction against the Proclamation—but they were in the minority.

Chief Justice Roberts wrote for the majority. He emphasized that the Proclamation was "neutral on its face," with a text that "says nothing about religion," and that it was "expressly premised on legitimate purposes: preventing entry of nationals who cannot be adequately vetted and inducing other nations to improve their practices." Because this is "a matter within the core of executive responsibility," the Court would "look behind the face of the Proclamation" only "to the extent of applying rational basis review." (To Justice Sotomayor's assertion that this choice of standard was "perplexing," the Chief Justice retorted that it would be "far more problematic" to assume that in this context the Court should apply the same "reasonable observer" inquiry that it applied in Establishment Clause cases "involving holiday displays and graduation ceremonies.")

Under rational-basis review, the majority concluded, the fact that most of the nations covered by the Proclamation had Muslim-majority populations did not "alone . . . support an inference of religious hostility, given that the policy covers just 8% of the world's Muslim population and is limited to countries that were previously designated by Congress or prior administrations as posing national security risks." The Court also noted that the Proclamation "reflects the results of a worldwide review process undertaken by multiple Cabinet officials and their agencies." The dissenters doubted the seriousness of that review, and also the likely efficacy of the restrictions, which they regarded as overbroad, in protecting national security. But the Court regarded these as matters on which great deference had to be paid to Executive judgment.

c.   Facial Neutrality—Extraordinary Disproportion

The next set of cases present claims by plaintiffs, not that the government has admitted its intent to discriminate, but that the very disproportion of the law cannot be explained by anything else. The first involves a nineteenth-century challenge by a Chinese immigrant to a San Francisco ordinance. On the face of the ordinance it appears clearly to serve a legitimate public interest, and it *could* have been implemented in an even-handed way, without discriminatory purpose or effect. But that is not what happened.

Recall that in addition to permitting plaintiffs to introduce direct evidence of discriminatory intent, *Washington v. Davis* also noted that "an invidious discriminatory purpose may often be inferred from the totality of the relevant facts, including the fact, if it is true, that the law bears more heavily on one race than another." Pay attention to how that principle plays out in the cases in this section.

Yick Wo v. Hopkins

Supreme Court of the United States, 1886.
118 U.S. 356.

OPINION.

. . . The plaintiff in error, Yick Wo, on August 24, 1885, petitioned the supreme court of California for the writ of *habeas corpus*, alleging that he was illegally deprived of his personal liberty by the defendant as sheriff of the city and county of San Francisco.

The ordinances for the violation of which he had been found guilty [provide] as follows: . . .

> Section 1. It shall be unlawful, from and after the passage of this order, for any person or persons to establish, maintain, or carry on a laundry, within the corporate limits of the city and county of San Francisco, without having first obtained the consent of the board of supervisors, except the same be located in a building constructed either of brick or stone.

The following facts are also admitted on the record: [P]etitioner is a native of China, and came to California in 1861, and is still a subject of the Emperor of China[.] [H]e has been engaged in the laundry business in the same premises and building for 22 years last past[, and] had a license from the board of fire-wardens, dated March 3, 1884, [which indicated that the premises had passed inspection.] [T]he petitioner applied to the board of supervisors, June 1, 1885, for consent of said board to maintain and carry on his laundry, but . . . said board, on July 1, 1885, refused said consent. . . .

It is also admitted to be true, as alleged in the petition, that on February 24, 1880, "there were about 320 laundries in the city and county of San Francisco, of which about 240 were owned and conducted by subjects of China, and of the whole number, viz., 320, about 310 were constructed of wood, the same material that constitutes nine-tenths of the houses in the city of San Francisco. . . ." It was alleged in the petition, that "your petitioner, and more than one hundred and fifty of his countrymen, have been arrested upon the charge of carrying on business without having such special consent, while those who are not subjects of China, and who are conducting eighty odd laundries under similar conditions, are left unmolested, and free to enjoy the enhanced trade and profits arising from this hurtful and unfair discrimination. . . ."

It was also admitted "that petitioner and 200 of his countrymen similarly situated petitioned the board of supervisors for permission to continue their business in the various houses which they had been occupying and using for laundries for more than twenty years, and such petitions were denied, and all the petitions of those who were not Chinese, with one exception of Mrs. Mary Meagles, were granted." . . .

In [a related case], the learned Circuit Judge Sawyer . . . [wrote]:

> [T]he uncontradicted petition shows that all Chinese applications are, in fact, denied, and those of Caucasians granted; thus, in fact, making the discriminations in the administration of the ordinance which its terms permit. The fact that the right to give consent is reserved in the ordinance shows that carrying on the laundry business in wooden buildings is not deemed of itself necessarily dangerous. It must be apparent to every well-informed mind that a fire, properly guarded, for laundry purposes, in a wooden building, is just as necessary, and no more dangerous, than a fire for cooking purposes or for warming a house. . . .

> The effect of the execution of this ordinance in the manner indicated in the record would seem to be necessarily to close up the many Chinese laundries now existing, or compel their owners to pull down their present buildings and reconstruct of brick or stone, or to drive them outside the city and county of San Francisco, to the adjoining counties, beyond the convenient reach of customers, either of which results would be little short of absolute confiscation of the

large amount of property shown to be now, and to have been for a long time, invested in these occupations. . . .

If this means prohibition of the occupation, and a destruction of the business and property, of the Chinese laundrymen in San Francisco—as it seems to us this must be the effect of executing the ordinance—and not merely the proper regulation of the business, then there is discrimination, and a violation of other highly important rights secured by the Fourteenth Amendment. . . . That it does mean prohibition, as to the Chinese, it seems to us must be apparent to every citizen of San Francisco who has been here long enough to be familiar with the cause of an active and aggressive branch of public opinion and of public notorious events. Can a court be blind to what must be necessarily known to every intelligent person in the state?

See *Ah Kow v. Nunan* (Cal. Cir. Ct. 1879). . . .

MATTHEWS, J.[, writing for the Court.]

. . . The rights of the petitioners, as affected by the proceedings of which they complain, are not less because they are aliens and subjects of the Emperor of China. . . . The Fourteenth Amendment to the Constitution is not confined to the protection of citizens. It says: "Nor shall any state deprive any person of life, liberty, or property without due process of law; nor deny to any person within its jurisdiction the equal protection of the laws." These provisions are universal in their application, to all persons within the territorial jurisdiction, without regard to any differences of race, of color, or of nationality; and the equal protection of the laws is a pledge of the protection of equal laws. . . .

It is contended on the part of the petitioners, that the ordinances for violations of which they are severally sentenced to imprisonment, are void on their face, as being within the prohibitions of the Fourteenth Amendment, and, in the alternative, if not so, that they are void by reason of their administration, operating unequally, so as to punish in the present petitioners what is permitted to others as lawful, without any distinction of circumstances—an unjust and illegal discrimination, it is claimed, which, though not made expressly by the ordinances, is made possible by them.

When we consider the nature and the theory of our institutions of government, the principles upon which they are supposed to rest, and review the history of their development, we are constrained to conclude that they do not mean to leave room for the play and action of purely personal and arbitrary power. . . .

[But in] the present case[ ], we are not obliged to reason from the probable to the actual, and pass upon the validity of the ordinances complained of, as tried merely by the opportunities which their terms afford, of unequal and unjust discrimination in their administration[. This case presents] the ordinances in actual operation, and the facts shown establish an administration directed so exclusively against a particular class of persons as to warrant and require the conclusion that, whatever may have been the intent of the ordinances as adopted, they are applied by the public authorities charged with their administration . . . with a mind so unequal and oppressive as to amount to a practical denial by the State of that equal protection of the laws. . . .

Though the law itself be fair on its face, and impartial in appearance, yet, if it is applied and administered by public authority with an evil eye and an unequal hand, so as practically to make unjust and illegal discriminations between persons in similar circumstances, material to their rights, the denial of equal justice is still within the prohibition of the Constitution. . . .

The present cases, as shown by the facts disclosed in the record, are within this class. It appears that . . . petitioner [has] complied with every requisite deemed by the law, or by the public officers charged with its administration, necessary for the protection of neighboring property from fire, or as a precaution against injury to the public health. No reason whatever, except the will of the supervisors, is assigned why [he] should not be permitted to carry on, in the accustomed manner, [his] harmless and useful occupation, on which [he] depend[s] for a livelihood; and while this consent of the supervisors is withheld from [him], and from 200 others who have also petitioned, all of whom happen to be Chinese subjects, 80 others, not Chinese subjects, are permitted to carry on the same business under similar conditions. The fact of this discrimination is admitted. No reason for it is shown, and the conclusion cannot be resisted that no reason for it exists except hostility to the race and nationality to which the petitioners belong, and which, in the eye of the law, is not justified.

The discrimination is, therefore, illegal, and the public administration which enforces it is a denial of the equal protection of the laws, and a violation of the Fourteenth Amendment of the Constitution. The imprisonment of the petitioner[ ] is therefore illegal, and [he] must be discharged. . . .

In *Yick Wo*, the ordinance was applied individual by individual. We will now read two cases in which public authorities made a single decision, or at least a simultaneous set of decisions, that affected the entire community as a whole—but in very different ways. In the first of these two, not only is the racially disparate impact entirely obvious, but it would be difficult to believe that the law could have been adopted for any purpose other than to achieve that impact.

Gomillion v. Lightfoot

Supreme Court of the United States, 1960.
364 U.S. 339.

MR. JUSTICE FRANKFURTER delivered the opinion of the Court.

This litigation challenges the validity, under the United States Constitution, of Local Act No. 140, passed by the Legislature of Alabama in 1957, redefining the boundaries of the City of Tuskegee. Petitioners [are] Negro citizens of Alabama who were, at the time of this redistricting measure, residents of the City of Tuskegee. . . . [They claim] that enforcement of the statute, which alters the shape of Tuskegee from a square to an uncouth twenty-eight-sided figure, will constitute a discrimination against them in violation of the . . . Equal Protection Clause[ ] and . . . the Fifteenth Amendment.

The complaint, charging that Act 140 is a device to disenfranchise Negro citizens, alleges the following facts: Prior to Act 140 the City of Tuskegee was square in shape; the Act transformed it into a strangely irregular twenty-eight-sided figure as indicated in the diagram appended to this opinion. The essential inevitable effect of this redefinition of Tuskegee's boundaries is to remove from the city all save four or five of its 400 Negro voters while not removing a single white voter or resident. The result of the Act is to deprive the Negro petitioners discriminatorily of the benefits of residence in Tuskegee, including, *inter alia*, the right to vote in municipal elections.

These allegations, if proven, would abundantly establish that Act 140 was not an ordinary geographic redistricting measure even within familiar abuses of gerrymandering. If these allegations upon a trial remained uncontradicted or unqualified, the conclusion would be irresistible, tantamount for all practical purposes to a mathematical demonstration, that the legislation is solely concerned with segregating white and colored voters by fencing Negro citizens out of town so as to deprive them of their pre-existing municipal vote. . . .

The complaint amply alleges a claim of racial discrimination. Against this claim the respondents have never suggested, either in their brief or in oral argument, any countervailing municipal function which Act 140 is designed to serve. The respondents invoke generalities expressing the State's unrestricted power—unlimited, that is, by the United States Constitution—to establish, destroy, or reorganize by contraction or expansion its political subdivisions, to wit, cities, counties, and other local units. We freely recognize the breadth and importance of this aspect of the State's political power. To exalt this power into an absolute is to misconceive the reach and rule of this Court's decisions. . . . Legislative control of municipalities, no less than other state power, lies within the scope of relevant limitations imposed by the United States Constitution. . . .

The petitioners are entitled to prove their allegations at trial.

WORTH NOTING

The map below was reproduced as an appendix to the Court's decision:

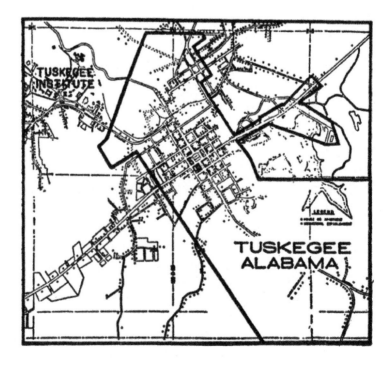

The entire area of the square comprised the City prior to Act 140. The irregular border within the square represents the "uncouth twenty-eight sided figure" that was the post-enactment city. Is this an instance where the thing truly speaks for itself? On remand, the district court struck down the gerrymander and the electoral districts reverted to their previous allocations.

d.   Facial Neutrality—Obvious Proxies

If facially neutral laws get rational basis review, then in at least some cases the courts will have to decide what qualifies as neutrality. What if a law uses terms that seem like a proxy for race? The following cases explore that question—and its analytical overlap with the problem of disparate impact.

Ho Ah Kow v. Nunan

Circuit Court, District of California, 1879.
12 F. Cas. 252.

Before FIELD, CIRCUIT JUSTICE, and SAWYER, CIRCUIT JUDGE.

FIELD, CIRCUIT JUSTICE.

The plaintiff is a subject of the emperor of China, and the present action is brought to recover damages for his alleged maltreatment by the defendant, . . . the sheriff of the city and county of San Francisco. The maltreatment consisted in having wantonly and maliciously cut off the queue of the plaintiff, a queue being worn by all Chinamen, and its deprivation being regarded by them as degrading and as entailing future suffering.

[The plaintiff was convicted of violating an 1876 state law that made it a misdemeanor "within the limits of [an] incorporated cit[y]" to lodge in a room that contained less than five hundred cubic feet of space per inhabitant. He was sentenced to pay a $10 fine, or failing that, to be imprisoned five days in the county jail.] Failing to pay the fine, he was imprisoned. The defendant, as sheriff of the city and county, had charge of the jail, and during the imprisonment of the plaintiff cut off his queue, as alleged.

The complaint avers that it is the custom of Chinamen to shave the hair from the front of the head and to wear the remainder of it braided into a queue; that the deprivation of the queue is regarded by them as a mark of disgrace, and is attended, according to their religious faith, with misfortune and suffering after death; that the defendant knew of this custom and religious faith of the Chinese, and knew also that the plaintiff venerated the custom and held the faith; yet, in disregard of his rights, inflicted the injury complained of; and that the plaintiff has, in consequence of it, suffered great mental anguish, been disgraced in the eyes of his friends and relatives, and ostracised from association with his countrymen; and that hence he has been damaged to the amount of ten thousand dollars.

[The sheriff justified] his conduct under an ordinance of the city and county of San Francisco. . . . The ordinance referred to was passed on the fourteenth of June, 1876, and it declares that every male person imprisoned in the county jail, under the judgment of any court having jurisdiction in criminal cases in the city and county, shall immediately upon his arrival at the jail have the hair of his head "cut or clipped to an uniform length of one inch from the scalp thereof." . . .

The validity of this ordinance is denied by the plaintiff on [the] ground[ ] that it is special legislation imposing a degrading and cruel punishment upon a class of persons who are entitled, alike with all other persons within the jurisdiction of the United States, to the equal protection of the laws. We are of opinion that [this position is] well taken. . . . The claim . . . put forth that the measure was prescribed as one of health is notoriously a mere pretense. . . .

It is special legislation on the part of the supervisors against a class of persons who, under the constitution and laws of the United States, are entitled to the equal protection of the laws. The ordinance was intended only for the Chinese in San Francisco. This was avowed by the supervisors on its passage, and was so understood by every one. The ordinance is known in the community as the "Queue Ordinance," being so designated from its purpose to reach the queues of the Chinese, and it is not enforced against any other persons. The reason advanced for its adoption, and now urged for its continuance, is, that only the dread of the loss of his queue will induce a Chinaman to pay his fine. . . .

The class character of this legislation is none the less manifest because of the general terms in which it is expressed. The statements of supervisors in debate on the passage of the ordinance cannot, it is true, be resorted to for the purpose of explaining the meaning of the terms used; but they can be resorted to for the purpose of ascertaining the general object of the legislation proposed, and the mischiefs sought to be remedied. Besides, we cannot shut our eyes to matters of public notoriety and general cognizance. When we take our seats on the bench we are not struck with blindness, and forbidden to know as judges what we see as men; and where an ordinance, though general in its terms, only operates upon a special race, sect or class, it being universally understood that it is to be enforced only against that race, sect or class, we may justly conclude that it was the intention of the body adopting it that it should only have such operation, and treat it accordingly. We may take notice of the limitation given to the general terms of an ordinance by its practical construction as a fact in its history, as we do in some cases that a law has practically become obsolete. If this were not so, the most important provisions of the constitution, intended for the security of personal rights, would, by the general terms of an enactment, often be evaded and practically annulled. . . .

Many illustrations might be given where ordinances, general in their terms, would operate only upon a special class, or upon a class, with exceptional severity, and thus incur the odium and be subject to the legal objection of intended hostile legislation against them. We have, for instance, in our community a large number of Jews. They are a highly intellectual race, and are generally obedient to the laws of the country. But, as is well known, they have peculiar opinions with respect to the use of certain articles of food, which they cannot be forced to disregard without extreme pain and suffering. They look, for example, upon the eating of pork with loathing. It is an offense against their religion, and is associated in their minds with uncleanness and impurity. Now, if they should in some quarter of the city overcrowd their dwellings and thus become amenable, like the Chinese, to [the prohibition on crowded lodging-houses], an ordinance of the supervisors requiring that all prisoners confined in the county jail should be fed on pork would be seen by every one to be leveled at them; and, notwithstanding its general terms, would be regarded as a special law in its purpose and operation.

During various periods of English history, legislation, general in its character, has often been enacted with the avowed purpose of imposing special burdens and restrictions upon Catholics; but that legislation has since been regarded as not less odious and obnoxious to animadversion than if the persons at whom it was aimed had been particularly designated.

But in our country hostile and discriminating legislation by a state against persons of any class, sect, creed or nation, in whatever form it may be expressed, is forbidden by the fourteenth amendment of the constitution. . . . It is certainly something in which a citizen of the United States may feel a generous pride that the government of his country extends protection to all persons within its jurisdiction; and that every blow aimed at any of them, however humble, come from what quarter it may, is "caught upon the broad shield of our blessed constitution and our equal laws."

We are aware of the general feeling—amounting to positive hostility—prevailing in California against the Chinese, which would prevent their further immigration hither and expel from the state those already here. Their dissimilarity in physical characteristics, in language, manners and religion would seem, from past experience, to prevent the possibility of their assimilation with our people. And thoughtful persons, looking at the millions which crowd the opposite shores of the Pacific, and the possibility at no distant day of their pouring over in vast hordes among us, giving rise to fierce antagonisms of race, hope that some way may be devised to prevent their further immigration.

We feel the force and importance of these considerations; but the remedy for the apprehended evil is to be sought from the general government, where, except in certain special cases, all power over the subject lies. To that government belong[s] exclusively . . . the power to prescribe the conditions of immigration or importation of persons. The state in these particulars, with . . . exceptions [for "paupers and convicts of other countries, persons incurably diseased, and others likely to become a burden upon its resources, " and "perhaps" for "persons whose presence would be dangerous to its established institutions"], is powerless, and nothing is gained by the attempted assertion of a control which can never be admitted. . . . For restrictions necessary or desirable in these matters, the appeal must be made to the general government; and it is not believed that the appeal will ultimately be disregarded.

Be that as it may, nothing can be accomplished in that direction by hostile and spiteful legislation on the part of the state, or of its municipal bodies, like the ordinance in question—legislation which is unworthy of a brave and manly people. Against such legislation it will always be the duty of the judiciary to declare and enforce the paramount law of the nation. . . .

The next case involves a challenge to workplace rules that effectively banned corn rows—a braided hairstyle then primarily associated with African American women. Because the defendant was a private employer, the case did not present a constitutional challenge; rather it was litigated under federal statutory protections that do not require intent to discriminate as a condition of liability. And because the employee in *Rogers* didn't have to claim racial motivation, she effectively conceded that the policy had been "adopted in order to help [the employer] project a conservative and business-like image." Imagine, however, that the plaintiff hadn't conceded the intent issue, and that the employer were a government agency subject to the Constitution. Would the analysis below hold up as an application of equal protection doctrine under *Washington v. Davis* and *Ho Ah Kow*? Why or why not?

Rogers v. American Airlines, Inc.

527 F. Supp. 229 (S.D.N.Y. 1981).

SOFAER, DISTRICT JUDGE.

Plaintiff is a black woman who seeks $10,000 damages, injunctive, and declaratory relief against enforcement of a grooming policy of the defendant American Airlines that prohibits employees in certain employment categories from wearing an all-braided hairstyle.

Plaintiff has been an American Airlines employee for approximately eleven years, and has been an airport operations agent for over one year. Her duties involve extensive passenger contact, including greeting passengers, issuing boarding passes, and checking luggage. She alleges that the policy violates her rights . . . under Title VII of the Civil Rights Act and under 42 U.S.C. § 1981, in that it discriminates against her as a woman, and more specifically as a black woman. . . .

WORTH NOTING

Title VII provides that "[i]t shall be an unlawful employment practice for an employer [to] discriminate against any individual with respect to his . . . terms [or] . . . privileges of employment, because of such individual's race. . . ." Section 1981 provides that "[a]ll persons . . . shall have the same right . . . to make and enforce contracts, . . . and to the full and equal benefit of all laws and proceedings for the security of persons and property as is enjoyed by white citizens. . . ."

[P]laintiff[ ] assert[s] that the "corn row" style has a special significance for black women. She contends that it

> has been, historically, a fashion and style adopted by Black American women, reflective of cultural, historical essence of the Black women in American society. . . . The style was "popularized" so to speak, within the larger society, when Cicely Tyson adopted the same for an appearance on nationally viewed Academy Awards presentation several years ago. . . . It was and is analogous to the public statement by the late Malcolm X regarding the Afro hair style. . . . At the bottom line, the completely braided hair style, sometimes referred to as corn rows, has been and continues to be part of the cultural and historical essence of Black American women. . . .

Plaintiff is entitled to a presumption that her arguments, largely repeated in her affidavit, are true. But the grooming policy applies equally to members of all races, and plaintiff does not allege that an all-braided hair style is worn exclusively or even predominantly by black people. . . .

Plaintiff may be correct that an employer's policy prohibiting the "Afro/bush" style might offend Title VII and section 1981. But if so, this chiefly would be because banning a natural hairstyle would implicate the policies underlying the prohibition of discrimination on the basis of immutable characteristics. But cf. *Smith v. Delta Air Lines* (5th Cir. 1973) (upholding no-mustache, short-side-burn policy despite showing that black males had more difficulty complying due to nature of hair growth).

In any event, an all-braided hairstyle is a different matter. It is not the product of natural hair growth but of artifice. An all-braided hair style is an "easily changed characteristic," and, even if socioculturally associated with a particular race or nationality, is not an impermissible basis for distinctions in the application of employment practices by an employer. The Fifth Circuit recently upheld, without requiring any showing of business purpose, an employer's policy prohibiting the speaking of any language but English in the workplace, despite the importance of Spanish to the ethnic identity of Mexican-Americans. *Garcia v. Gloor* (5th Cir. 1980). The court stated that . . . "a hiring policy . . . such as grooming codes or length of hair . . . is related more closely to the employer's choice of how to run his business than to equality of employment opportunity." . . .

Moreover, the airline did not require plaintiff to restyle her hair. It suggested that she could wear her hair as she liked while off duty, and permitted her to pull her hair into a bun and wrap a hairpiece around the bun during working hours. Plaintiff has done this, but alleges that the hairpiece has caused her severe headaches. A larger hairpiece would seem in order. But even if any hairpiece would cause such discomfort, the policy does not offend a substantial interest. Cf. *EEOC v. Greyhound Lines, Inc.*, 635 F.2d 188 (3d Cir. 1980) (upholding no-beard policy despite showing that some black men had difficulty complying due to racially-linked skin disease).

Plaintiff also asserts in her complaint that the regulation has been applied in an uneven and discriminatory manner. She claims that white women in particular have been permitted to wear pony tails and shag cuts. She goes on to claim, in fact, that some black women are permitted to wear the same hairstyle that she has been prohibited from wearing. These claims seriously undercut her assertion that the policy discriminates against women, and her claim that it discriminates against black women in particular. Conceivably, however, the complaint could be construed as alleging that the policy has been applied in a discriminatory manner against plaintiff because she is black by some representative of the defendant. On its face, this allegation is sufficient, although it might be subject to dismissal on a summary judgment motion if it is not supplemented with some factual claims. . . .

The *Rogers* decision has become the touchstone case on the regulation of African-American hairstyles. As the 11th Circuit wrote in *Equal Employment Opportunity Commission v. Catastrophe Management Solutions*, 852 F.3d 1018 (11th Cir. 2016),

> We recognize that the distinction between immutable and mutable characteristics of race can sometimes be a fine (and difficult) one, but it is a line that courts have drawn. So, for example, discrimination on the basis of black hair texture (an immutable characteristic) is prohibited by Title VII, while adverse action on the basis of black hairstyle (a mutable choice) is not. *Compare, e.g., Jenkins v. Blue Cross Mut. Hosp. Ins., Inc.* (7th Cir. 1976) (en banc) (recognizing a claim for racial discrimination based on the plaintiff's allegation that she was denied a promotion because she wore her hair in a natural Afro),

with, e.g., *Rogers v. Am. Airlines, Inc.* (S.D.N.Y. 1981) (holding that a grooming policy prohibiting an all-braided hairstyle did not constitute racial discrimination, and distinguishing policies that prohibit Afros, because braids are not an immutable characteristic but rather "the product of . . . artifice").

In response to decisions like *Rogers* and *Catastrophe Management*, a nationwide movement has gained sufficient traction to push through to enactment in several states the CROWN Act ("Create a Respectful and Open World for Natural Hair"). California was the first state to adopt a form of the Act, in 2019. The key operative provisions of California's version add to the provisions defining "race" for purposes of anti-discrimination laws the following language:

> "Race" is inclusive of traits historically associated with race, including, but not limited to, hair texture and protective hairstyles.

In turn, the Act defines "protective hairstyles" to include, without limitation, "such hairstyles as braids, locks, and twists." The Act's preamble makes the following legislative findings:

(b) . . . Professionalism was, and still is, closely linked to European features and mannerisms, which entails that those who do not naturally fall into Eurocentric norms must alter their appearances, sometimes drastically and permanently, in order to be deemed professional. . . .

(d) Workplace dress code and grooming policies that prohibit natural hair, including afros, braids, twists, and locks, have a disparate impact on Black individuals as these policies are more likely to deter Black applicants and burden or punish Black employees than any other group.

(e) Federal courts accept that Title VII of the Civil Rights Act of 1964 prohibits discrimination based on race, and therefore protects against discrimination against afros. However, the courts do not understand that afros are not the only natural presentation of Black hair. Black hair can also be naturally presented in braids, twists, and locks.

(f)   In a society in which hair has historically been one of many determining factors of a person's race, and whether they were a second class citizen, hair today remains a proxy for race. Therefore, hair discrimination targeting hairstyles associated with race is racial discrimination. . . .

In trial litigation, parties are typically permitted to exercise a prescribed number of peremptory challenges to strike potential jurors from consideration. The use of a peremptory means that the juror is excused without any need for the challenging party to show that the juror should be excused for cause (such as an inability to act fairly or competently). In *Batson v. Kentucky* (1986), however, the Supreme Court held that a prosecutor may not exercise peremptories on a racially discriminatory basis—a rule that has since been extended to other parties, and to discrimination on the basis of sex. When a *Batson* claim is made, prosecutors must offer some explanation other than race for their exercise of a peremptory strike; as the following case indicates, this can pose a difficult problem for the court when the explanation is arguably a pretext or a proxy for race.

Hernandez v. New York

Supreme Court of the United States, 1991.
500 U.S. 352.

JUSTICE KENNEDY announced the judgment of the Court and delivered an opinion in which THE CHIEF JUSTICE, JUSTICE WHITE and JUSTICE SOUTER join.

Petitioner Dionisio Hernandez asks us to review the New York state courts' rejection of his claim that the prosecutor in his criminal trial exercised peremptory challenges to exclude Latinos from the jury by reason of their ethnicity. If true, the prosecutor's discriminatory use of peremptory strikes would violate the Equal Protection Clause as interpreted by our decision in *Batson v. Kentucky* (1986). We must determine whether the prosecutor offered a race-neutral basis for challenging Latino potential jurors and, if so, whether the state courts' decision to accept the prosecutor's explanation should be sustained.

Petitioner and respondent both use the term "Latino" in their briefs to this
Court. The *amicus* brief employs instead the term "Hispanic," and the parties
referred to the excluded jurors by that term in the trial court. . . . No attempt
has been made at a distinction by the parties and we make no attempt to distinguish the terms in this opinion. We will refer to the excluded venirepersons
as Latinos in deference to the terminology preferred by the parties before the
Court. . . .

I

. . . [Hernandez was convicted] on two counts of attempted murder and
two counts of criminal possession of a weapon. On a Brooklyn street, petitioner
fired several shots at Charlene Calloway and her mother, Ada Saline. Calloway
suffered three gunshot wounds. Petitioner missed Saline and instead hit two
men in a nearby restaurant. The victims survived the incident.

The trial was held in [Brooklyn, New York]. . . . After 63 potential jurors
had been questioned and 9 had been empaneled, defense counsel objected that
the prosecutor had used four peremptory challenges to exclude Latino potential
jurors. Two of the Latino venirepersons challenged by the prosecutor had brothers who had been convicted of crimes, and the brother of one of those potential
jurors was being prosecuted by the same District Attorney's office for a probation violation. Petitioner does not press his *Batson* claim with respect to those
prospective jurors, and we concentrate on the other two excluded individuals.

After petitioner raised his *Batson* objection, the prosecutor . . . . volunteered
his reasons for striking the jurors in question. He explained:

> Your honor, my reason for rejecting the—these two jurors—I'm
> not certain as to whether they're Hispanics. I didn't notice how many
> Hispanics had been called to the panel, but my reason for rejecting
> these two is I feel very uncertain that they would be able to listen
> and follow the interpreter. . . .

> We talked to them for a long time; the Court talked to them,
> I talked to them. I believe that in their heart they will try to follow
> it, but I felt there was a great deal of uncertainty as to whether they
> could accept the interpreter as the final arbiter of what was said by
> each of the witnesses, especially where there were going to be Span-
> ish-speaking witnesses, and I didn't feel, when I asked them whether
> or not they could accept the interpreter's translation of it, I didn't

feel that they could. They each looked away from me and said with some hesitancy that they would try, not that they could, but that they would try to follow the interpreter, and I feel that in a case where the interpreter will be for the main witnesses, they would have an undue impact upon the jury.[1]

Defense counsel moved for a mistrial "based on the conduct of the District Attorney," and the prosecutor requested a chance to call a supervisor to the courtroom before the judge's ruling.

Following a recess, defense counsel renewed his motion, which the trial court denied. Discussion of the objection continued, however, and the prosecutor explained that he would have no motive to exclude Latinos from the jury:

[T]his case, involves four complainants. Each of the complainants is Hispanic. All my witnesses, that is, civilian witnesses, are going to be Hispanic. I have absolutely no reason—there's no reason for me to want to exclude Hispanics because all the parties involved are Hispanic, and I certainly would have no reason to do that.[2]

After further interchange among the judge and attorneys, the trial court again rejected petitioner's claim.

[The New York appeals court] noted that though the ethnicity of one challenged bilingual juror remained uncertain, the prosecutor had challenged the only three prospective jurors with definite Hispanic surnames. . . .

II

. . . Petitioner contends that the reasons given by the prosecutor for challenging the two bilingual jurors were not race neutral. . . . A court addressing this issue must keep in mind the fundamental principle that "official action

---

[1] The prosecutor later gave the same explanation for challenging the bilingual potential jurors:

. . . I felt that from their answers they would be hard pressed to accept what the interpreter said as the final thing on what the record would be. . . . I just felt from the hesitancy in their answers and their lack of eye contact that they would not be able to do it.

[2] The trial judge appears to have accepted the prosecutor's reasoning as to his motivation. In response to a charge by defense counsel that the prosecutor excluded Latino jurors out of fear that they would sympathize with the defendant, the judge stated:

The victims are all Hispanics, he said, and, therefore, they will be testifying for the People, so there could be sympathy for them as well as for the defendant, so he said [it] would not seem logical in this case he would look to throw off Hispanics, because I don't think that his logic is wrong. They might feel sorry for a guy who's had a bullet hole through him, he's Hispanic, so they may relate to him more than they'll relate to the shooter.

will not be held unconstitutional solely because it results in a racially disproportionate impact. . . . Proof of racially discriminatory intent or purpose is
required to show a violation of the Equal Protection Clause." *Arlington Heights
v. Metropolitan Housing Development Corp.* (1977). " 'Discriminatory purpose'
. . . implies more than intent as volition or intent as awareness of consequences.
It implies that the decisionmaker . . . selected . . . a particular course of action
at least in part 'because of,' not merely 'in spite of,' its adverse effects upon an
identifiable group." *Personnel Administrator of Mass. v. Feeney* (1979); see also
McCleskey v. Kemp (1987).

A neutral explanation in the context of our analysis here means an explanation based on something other than the race of the juror. At this step of the
inquiry, the issue is the facial validity of the prosecutor's explanation. Unless
a discriminatory intent is inherent in the prosecutor's explanation, the reason
offered will be deemed race neutral.

Petitioner argues that Spanish-language ability bears a close relation to
ethnicity, and that, as a consequence, it violates the Equal Protection Clause
to exercise a peremptory challenge on the ground that a Latino potential juror
speaks Spanish. He points to the high correlation between Spanish-language
ability and ethnicity in New York, where the case was tried. We need not address that argument here, for the prosecutor did not rely on language ability
without more. . . .

The prosecutor here offered a race-neutral basis for these peremptory
strikes. As explained by the prosecutor, the challenges rested neither on the
intention to exclude Latino or bilingual jurors, nor on stereotypical assumptions about Latinos or bilinguals. The prosecutor's articulated basis for these
challenges divided potential jurors into two classes: those whose conduct during
voir dire would persuade him they might have difficulty in accepting the translator's rendition of Spanish-language testimony and those potential jurors who
gave no such reason for doubt. Each category would include both Latinos and
non-Latinos. While the prosecutor's criterion might well result in the disproportionate removal of prospective Latino jurors, that disproportionate impact
does not turn the prosecutor's actions into a *per se* violation of the Equal Protection Clause. . . .

[D]isparate impact should be given appropriate weight in determining
whether the prosecutor acted with a forbidden intent, but it will not be conclusive in the preliminary race-neutrality step of the *Batson* inquiry. An argument

relating to the impact of a classification does not alone show its purpose. See *Feeney*. Equal protection analysis turns on the intended consequences of government classifications. Unless the government actor adopted a criterion with the intent of causing the impact asserted, that impact itself does not violate the principle of race neutrality. Nothing in the prosecutor's explanation shows that he chose to exclude jurors who hesitated in answering questions about following the interpreter *because* he wanted to prevent bilingual Latinos from serving on the jury. . . .

In the context of this trial, the prosecutor's frank admission that his ground for excusing these jurors related to their ability to speak and understand Spanish raised a plausible, though not a necessary, inference that language might be a pretext for what in fact were race-based peremptory challenges. This was not a case where by some rare coincidence a juror happened to speak the same language as a key witness, in a community where few others spoke that tongue. If it were, the explanation that the juror could have undue influence on jury deliberations might be accepted without concern that a racial generalization had come into play. But this trial took place in a community with a substantial Latino population, and petitioner and other interested parties were members of that ethnic group. It would be common knowledge in the locality that a significant percentage of the Latino population speaks fluent Spanish, and that many consider it their preferred language, the one chosen for personal communication, the one selected for speaking with the most precision and power, the one used to define the self. . . .

The trial judge in this case chose to believe the prosecutor's race-neutral explanation for striking the two jurors in question, rejecting petitioner's assertion that the reasons were pretextual. [And] the trial court's decision on the ultimate question of discriminatory intent represents a finding of fact of the sort accorded great deference on appeal. . . .

Deference to trial court findings on the issue of discriminatory intent makes particular sense in this context because . . . [i]n the typical peremptory challenge inquiry, the decisive question will be whether counsel's race-neutral explanation for a peremptory challenge should be believed[,]and the best evidence often will be the demeanor of the attorney who exercises the challenge. As with the state of mind of a juror, evaluation of the prosecutor's state of mind based on demeanor and credibility lies "peculiarly within a trial judge's province." . . .

In the case before us, we decline to overturn the state trial court's finding on the issue of discriminatory intent unless convinced that its determination was clearly erroneous. . . . Apart from the prosecutor's demeanor, which of course we have no opportunity to review, the court could have relied on the facts that the prosecutor defended his use of peremptory challenges without being asked to do so by the judge, that he did not know which jurors were Latinos, and that the ethnicity of the victims and prosecution witnesses tended to undercut any motive to exclude Latinos from the jury. Any of these factors could be taken as evidence of the prosecutor's sincerity. The trial court, moreover, could rely on the fact that only three challenged jurors can with confidence be identified as Latinos, and that the prosecutor had a verifiable and legitimate explanation for two of those challenges. Given these factors, that the prosecutor also excluded one or two Latino venirepersons on the basis of a subjective criterion having a disproportionate impact on Latinos does not leave us with a "definite and firm conviction that a mistake has been committed." *United States v. United States Gypsum Co* (1948). . . .

Our decision today does not imply that exclusion of bilinguals from jury service is wise, or even that it is constitutional in all cases. . . .

Just as shared language can serve to foster community, language differences can be a source of division. Language elicits a response from others, ranging from admiration and respect, to distance and alienation, to ridicule and scorn. Reactions of the latter type all too often result from or initiate racial hostility. . . . We would face a quite different case if the prosecutor had justified his peremptory challenges with the explanation that he did not want Spanish-speaking jurors. It may well be, for certain ethnic groups and in some communities, that proficiency in a particular language, like skin color, should be treated as a surrogate for race under an equal protection analysis. Cf. *Yu Cong Eng v. Trinidad* (1926) (law prohibiting keeping business records in other than specified languages violated equal protection rights of Chinese businessmen). And, as we make clear, a policy of striking all who speak a given language, without regard to the particular circumstances of the trial or the individual responses of the jurors, may be found by the trial judge to be a pretext for racial discrimination. But that case is not before us. . . .

Affirmed.

JUSTICE O'CONNOR, with whom JUSTICE SCALIA joins, concurring in the judgment.

. . . I believe that the plurality opinion goes further than it needs to in assessing the constitutionality of the prosecutor's asserted justification for his peremptory strikes. . . . In order to demonstrate [a *Batson*] violation, Hernandez must prove that the prosecutor intentionally discriminated against Hispanic jurors on the basis of their race. The trial court found that the prosecutor did not have such intent, and that determination is not clearly erroneous. Hernandez has failed to meet his burden. . . .

JUSTICE STEVENS, with whom JUSTICE MARSHALL joins, dissenting.

A violation of the Equal Protection Clause requires what our cases characterize as proof of "discriminatory purpose." . . . Unless the prosecutor comes forward with an explanation for his peremptories that is sufficient to rebut that prima facie case, no additional evidence of racial animus is required to establish an equal protection violation. . . . An avowed justification that has a significant disproportionate impact will rarely qualify as a legitimate, race-neutral reason sufficient to rebut the prima facie case because disparate impact is itself evidence of discriminatory purpose. See *Arlington Heights v. Metropolitan Housing Development Corp.* (1977); *Washington v. Davis* (1976). . . .

The Court mistakenly believes that it is compelled to reach this result because an equal protection violation requires discriminatory purpose. The Court overlooks, however, the fact that the "discriminatory purpose" which characterizes violations of the Equal Protection Clause can sometimes be established by objective evidence that is consistent with a decisionmaker's honest belief that his motive was entirely benign. "Frequently the most probative evidence of intent will be objective evidence of what actually happened," *Washington v. Davis* (Stevens, J., concurring), including evidence of disparate impact. . . . The line between discriminatory purpose and discriminatory impact is neither as bright nor as critical as the Court appears to believe. . . .

The prosecutor's explanation was insufficient for three reasons. First, the justification would inevitably result in a disproportionate disqualification of Spanish-speaking venirepersons. An explanation that is "race neutral" on its face is nonetheless unacceptable if it is merely a proxy for a discriminatory practice. Second, the prosecutor's concern could easily have been accommodated by less drastic means. As is the practice in many jurisdictions, the jury could have been instructed that the official translation alone is evidence; bilingual jurors could have been instructed to bring to the attention of the judge any disagreements they might have with the translation so that any disputes could be resolved by the court.[2] Third, if the prosecutor's concern was valid and substantiated by the record, it would have supported a challenge for cause. The fact that the prosecutor did not make any such challenge should disqualify him from advancing the concern as a justification for a peremptory challenge.

WORTH NOTING

Justice Blackmun also dissented, "essentially for the reasons" in the last three paragraphs in this excerpt of Justice Stevens's dissent.

Each of these reasons considered alone might not render insufficient the prosecutor's facially neutral explanation. In combination, however, they persuade me that his explanation should have been rejected as a matter of law. Accordingly, I respectfully dissent.

e.   Facial Neutrality—Mixed Motives

Up to now, the cases have largely been framed as though the challenged government action had only one true motive, and as though a straightforward body of evidence existed for assessing it. In truth, of course, there's often more than one reason that "the government" did something—especially where more than one decisionmaker is involved. The following cases are representative of most modern race litigation: complicated people and complicated facts—and courts that seem nervous about intervening except in the most obviously egregious circumstances.

---

[2]   An even more effective solution would be to employ a translator, who is the only person who hears the witness' words and who simultaneously translates them into English, thus permitting the jury to hear only the official translation.

Village of Arlington Heights v. Metropolitan Housing Development Corp.

Supreme Court of the United States, 1977.
429 U.S. 252.

Mr. Justice Powell delivered the opinion of the Court.

In 1971 respondent Metropolitan Housing Development Corporation (MHDC) applied to petitioner, the Village of Arlington Heights, Ill., for the rezoning of a 15-acre parcel from single-family to multiple-family classification. Using federal financial assistance, MHDC planned to build 190 clustered townhouse units for low- and moderate-income tenants. The Village denied the rezoning request. MHDC, joined by other plaintiffs who are also respondents here, . . . alleged that the denial was racially discriminatory and that it violated, *inter alia*, the Fourteenth Amendment. . . .

I

Arlington Heights is a suburb of Chicago, located about 26 miles northwest of the downtown Loop area. Most of the land in Arlington Heights is zoned for detached single-family homes, and this is in fact the prevailing land use. The Village experienced substantial growth during the 1960's, but, like other communities in northwest Cook County, its population of racial minority groups remained quite low. According to the 1970 census, only 27 of the Village's 64,000 residents were black.

The Clerics of St. Viator, a religious order (Order), own an 80-acre parcel just east of the center of Arlington Heights. . . . The Order decided in 1970 to devote some of its land to low- and moderate-income housing. Investigation revealed that the most expeditious way to build such housing was to work through a nonprofit developer experienced in the use of federal housing subsidies. . . . MHDC is such a developer. It was organized in 1968 by several prominent Chicago citizens for the purpose of building low- and moderate-income housing throughout the Chicago area. . . .

After some negotiation, MHDC and the Order entered into a 99-year lease and an accompanying agreement of sale covering a 15-acre site in the southeast corner of the Viatorian property. . . . MHDC engaged an architect and proceeded with the project, to be known as Lincoln Green. The plans called for 20 two-story buildings with a total of 190 units, each unit having its own private entrance from outside. One hundred of the units would have a single bedroom, thought likely to attract elderly citizens. The remainder would have two, three, or four bedrooms. A large portion of the site would remain open, with shrubs and trees to screen the homes abutting the property to the east.

The planned development did not conform to the Village's zoning ordinance and could not be built unless Arlington Heights rezoned the parcel to R-5, its multiple-family housing classification. Accordingly, MHDC filed with the Village Plan Commission a petition for rezoning, accompanied by supporting materials describing the development and specifying that it would be subsidized [by the federal government]. The materials made clear that one requirement [for federal subsidies] is an affirmative marketing plan designed to assure that a subsidized development is racially integrated. . . . To prepare for the hearings before the Plan Commission and to assure compliance with the Village building code, fire regulations, and related requirements, MHDC consulted with the Village staff for preliminary review of the development. The parties have stipulated that every change recommended during such consultations was incorporated into the plans.

During the spring of 1971, the Plan Commission considered the proposal at a series of three public meetings, which drew large crowds. Although many of those attending were quite vocal and demonstrative in opposition to Lincoln Green, a number of individuals and representatives of community groups spoke in support of rezoning. Some of the comments, both from opponents and supporters, addressed what was referred to as the "social issue": the desirability or undesirability of introducing at this location in Arlington Heights low- and moderate-income housing, housing that would probably be racially integrated.

Many of the opponents, however, focused on the zoning aspects of the petition, stressing two arguments. First, the area always had been zoned single-family, and the neighboring citizens had built or purchased there in reliance on that classification. Rezoning threatened to cause a measurable drop in property value for neighboring sites. Second, the Village's apartment policy, adopted by the Village Board in 1962 and amended in 1970, called for R-5 zoning primarily to serve as a buffer between single-family development and land uses thought incompatible, such as commercial or manufacturing districts. Lincoln Green did not meet this requirement, as it adjoined no commercial or manufacturing district.

At the close of the third meeting, the Plan Commission adopted a motion to recommend to the Village's Board of Trustees that it deny the request. The motion stated: "While the need for low and moderate income housing may exist in Arlington Heights or its environs, the Plan Commission would be derelict in recommending it at the proposed location." Two members voted against the motion and submitted a minority report, stressing that in their view the change to accommodate Lincoln Green represented "good zoning." The Village Board met on September 28, 1971, to consider MHDC's request and the recommendation of the Plan Commission. After a public hearing, the Board denied the rezoning by a 6–1 vote. . . .

III

Our decision last Term in *Washington v. Davis* (1976) made it clear that official action will not be held unconstitutional solely because it results in a racially disproportionate impact. "Disproportionate impact is not irrelevant, but it is not the sole touchstone of an invidious racial discrimination." *Id.* Proof of racially discriminatory intent or purpose is required to show a violation of the Equal Protection Clause. . . .

Davis does not require a plaintiff to prove that the challenged action rested solely on racially discriminatory purposes. Rarely can it be said that a legislature or administrative body operating under a broad mandate made a decision motivated solely by a single concern, or even that a particular purpose was the "dominant" or "primary" one. In fact, it is because legislators and administrators are properly concerned with balancing numerous competing considerations that courts refrain from reviewing the merits of their decisions, absent a showing of arbitrariness or irrationality. But racial discrimination is not just another competing consideration. When there is a proof that a discriminatory purpose has been a motivating factor in the decision, this judicial deference is no longer justified.

Determining whether invidious discriminatory purpose was a motivating factor demands a sensitive inquiry into such circumstantial and direct evidence of intent as may be available. The impact of the official action—whether it "bears more heavily on one race than another," *Washington v. Davis*—may provide an important starting point. Sometimes a clear pattern, unexplainable on grounds other than race, emerges from the effect of the state action even when the governing legislation appears neutral on its face. *Yick Wo v. Hopkins* (1886); *Gomillion v. Lightfoot* (1960). The evidentiary inquiry is then relatively easy. But such cases are rare. Absent a pattern as stark as that in *Gomillion* or *Yick Wo*, impact alone is not determinative, and the Court must look to other evidence.[15]

The historical background of the decision is one evidentiary source, particularly if it reveals a series of official actions taken for invidious purposes. The specific sequence of events leading up the challenged decision also may shed some light on the decisionmaker's purposes. For example, if the property involved here always had been zoned R-5 but suddenly was changed to R-3 ["a single-family specification with relatively small minimum lot-size requirements"] when the town learned of MHDC's plans to erect integrated housing, we would have a far different case. Departures from the normal procedural sequence also might afford evidence that improper purposes are playing a role. Substantive departures too may be relevant, particularly if the factors usually considered important by the decisionmaker strongly favor a decision contrary to the one reached.

The legislative or administrative history may be highly relevant, especially where there are contemporary statements by members of the decisionmaking body, minutes of its meetings, or reports. In some extraordinary instances the members might be called to the stand at trial to testify concerning the purpose of the official action, although even then such testimony frequently will be barred by privilege.[18]

The foregoing summary identifies, without purporting to be exhaustive, subjects of proper inquiry in determining whether racially discriminatory intent existed. With these in mind, we now address the case before us.

IV

This case was tried in the District Court and reviewed in the Court of Appeals before our decision in *Washington v. Davis*. The respondents proceeded on the erroneous theory that the Village's refusal to rezone carried a racially discriminatory effect and was, without more, unconstitutional. But both courts below understood that at least part of their function was to examine the purpose underlying the decision. In making its findings on this issue, the District Court noted that some of the opponents of Lincoln Green who spoke at the

---

[15]   In many instances, to recognize the limited probative value of disproportionate impact is merely to acknowledge the "heterogeneity" of the Nation's population.

[18]   This Court has recognized, ever since *Fletcher v. Peck* (1810), that judicial inquiries into legislative or executive motivation represent a substantial intrusion into the workings of other branches of government. Placing a decisionmaker on the stand is therefore "usually to be avoided." *Citizens to Preserve Overton Park v. Volpe* (1971). . . .

various hearings might have been motivated by opposition to minority groups. The court held, however, that the evidence "does not warrant the conclusion that this motivated the defendants." . . .

We also have reviewed the evidence. The impact of the Village's decision does arguably bear more heavily on racial minorities. Minorities constitute 18% of the Chicago area population, and 40% of the income groups said to be eligible for Lincoln Green. But there is little about the sequence of events leading up to the decision that would spark suspicion. The area around the Viatorian property has been zoned R-3 since 1959, the year when Arlington Heights first adopted a zoning map. Single-family homes surround the 80-acre site, and the Village is undeniably committed to single-family homes as its dominant residential land use. The rezoning request progressed according to the usual procedures.[19] The Plan Commission even scheduled two additional hearings, at least in part to accommodate MHDC and permit it to supplement its presentation with answers to questions generated at the first hearing.

The statements by the Plan Commission and Village Board members, as reflected in the official minutes, focused almost exclusively on the zoning aspects of the MHDC petition, and the zoning factors on which they relied are not novel criteria in the Village's rezoning decisions. There is no reason to doubt that there has been reliance by some neighboring property owners on the maintenance of single-family zoning in the vicinity. The Village originally adopted its buffer policy long before MHDC entered the picture and has applied the policy too consistently for us to infer discriminatory purpose from its application in this case. Finally, MHDC called one member of the Village Board to the stand at trial. Nothing in her testimony supports an inference of invidious purpose.

In sum, the evidence does not warrant overturning the concurrent findings of both courts below. Respondents simply failed to carry their burden of proving that discriminatory purpose was a motivating factor in the Village's decision.[21] This conclusion ends the constitutional inquiry. The court of appeals'

---

[19]   Respondents have made much of one apparent procedural departure. The parties stipulated that the Village Planner, the staff member whose primary responsibility covered zoning and planning matters, was never asked for his written or oral opinion of the rezoning request. The omission does seem curious, but respondents failed to prove at trial what role the Planner customarily played in rezoning decisions, or whether his opinion would be relevant to respondents' claims.

[21]   Proof that the decision by the Village was motivated in part by a racially discriminatory purpose would not necessarily have required invalidation of the challenged decision. Such proof would, however, have shifted to the Village the burden of establishing that the same decision would have resulted even had the impermissible purpose not been considered. If this were established, the complaining party in a case of this kind no longer

further finding that the Village's decision carried a discriminatory "ultimate effect" is without independent constitutional significance. . . .

Mr. Justice Stevens took no part in the consideration or decision of this case.

Mr. Justice Marshall, with whom Mr. Justice Brennan joins, concurring in part and dissenting in part.

I concur in Parts I–III of the Court's opinion. However, I believe the proper result would be to remand this entire case to the Court of Appeals for further proceedings consistent with *Washington v. Davis* (1976), and today's opinion. The Court of Appeals is better situated than this Court both to reassess the significance of the evidence developed below in light of the [new] standards we have set forth [since the District Court reached its decision] and to determine whether the interests of justice require further District Court proceedings directed toward those standards.

Mr. Justice White, dissenting.

. . . The Court gives no reason for its failure to follow our usual practice in this situation of vacating the judgment below and remanding in order to permit the lower court to reconsider its ruling in light of our intervening decision. The Court's articulation of a legal standard nowhere mentioned in *Davis* indicates that it feels that the application of *Davis* to these facts calls for substantial analysis. If this is true, we would do better to allow the Court of Appeals to attempt that analysis in the first instance. . . .

The burden shifting scheme described in the last footnote of the majority opinion in *Arlington Heights* was announced in a companion decision announced the same day, *Mt. Healthy v. Doyle* (1977). The *Mt. Healthy* case presented an analogous question of mixed motivations in the First Amendment context: if a public school teacher's employment record was objectively terrible, should that weigh into the court's consideration, given that the school board's decision to fire him seemed motivated at least in part by his (constitutionally protected)

---

fairly could attribute the injury complained of to improper consideration of a discriminatory purpose. In such circumstances, there would be no justification for judicial interference with the challenged decision. But in this case respondents failed to make the required threshold showing. See *Mt. Healthy City School Dist. Bd. of Education v. Doyle* (1977).

criticism of the school board on a local radio show? In approaching that question, the Court explained:

> Clearly the Board legally could have dismissed respondent had the radio station incident never come to its attention. . . .

> [But a] rule of causation which focuses solely on whether protected conduct played a part, "substantial" or otherwise, in a decision not to rehire, could place an employee in a better position as a result of the exercise of constitutionally protected conduct than he would have occupied had he done nothing. The constitutional principle at stake is sufficiently vindicated if such an employee is placed in no worse a position than if he had not engaged in the conduct. A borderline or marginal candidate should not have the employment question resolved against him because of constitutionally protected conduct. But that same candidate ought not to be able, by engaging in such conduct, to prevent his employer from assessing his performance record. . . .

> Initially, in this case, the burden was properly placed upon respondent to show that his conduct was constitutionally protected, and that this conduct was a "substantial factor" or to put it in other words, that it was a "motivating factor" in the Board's decision not to rehire him. Respondent having carried that burden, however, the District Court should have gone on to determine whether the Board had shown by a preponderance of the evidence that it would have reached the same decision as to respondent's reemployment even in the absence of the protected conduct.

> We cannot tell . . . what conclusion [the lower] courts would have reached had they applied this test. The judgment of the Court of Appeals is therefore vacated, and the case remanded for further proceedings consistent with this opinion.

As You READ

The next case involves particularly complex web of motivations. As you read the Fourth Circuit's analysis, consider not only its treatment of the evidence (What's a smoking gun? What's merely circumstantial?) but also the extent to which the court wrestles with the fundamental motivation for the voting restrictions under review.

North Carolina State Conference of the NAACP v. McCrory

United States Court of Appeals for the Fourth Circuit, 2016.
831 F.3d 204.

Diana Gribbon Motz, Circuit Judge, writing for the court . . . :

These consolidated cases challenge provisions of a recently enacted North Carolina election law. . . .

After years of . . . expansion of voting access, by 2013 African American registration and turnout rates had finally reached near-parity with white registration and turnout rates. African Americans were poised to act as a major electoral force. But [in 2013], a leader of the [Republican] party that newly dominated the legislature (and the party that rarely enjoyed African American support) announced an intention to enact what he characterized as an "omnibus" election law. Before enacting that law, the legislature requested data on the use, by race, of a number of voting practices. Upon receipt of the race data, the General Assembly enacted legislation that restricted voting and registration in five different ways, all of which disproportionately affected African Americans. [That legislation was known as SL 2013–381. As explained below, it tightened restrictions on photo ID requirements, limited early voting, and eliminated same-day registration, out-of-precinct voting, and preregistration.]

. . . [The] data [requested by the legislature] showed that African Americans disproportionately lacked the most common kind of photo ID, those issued by the Department of Motor Vehicles (DMV). The [previous voting law] provided that all government-issued IDs, even many that had been expired, would satisfy the requirement as an alternative to DMV-issued photo IDs. [W]ith race data in hand, the legislature amended the bill to exclude many of the alternative photo IDs used by African Americans. As amended, the bill retained only the kinds of IDs that white North Carolinians were more likely to possess. [It allowed drivers licenses and passports, for example, but required that—except for voters over 70—qualifying documents had to be unexpired.]

. . . Early voting . . . increases opportunities to vote for those who have difficulty getting to their polling place on Election Day. The racial data provided to the legislators revealed that African Americans disproportionately used early voting in both 2008 and 2012. ([Trial evidence showed] that 60.36% and 64.01% of African Americans voted early in 2008 and 2012, respectively, compared to 44.47% and 49.39% of whites). In particular, African Americans disproportionately used the first seven days of early voting. After receipt of this racial data, the General Assembly amended the bill to eliminate the first week of early voting, shortening the total early voting period from seventeen to ten days. As a result, SL 2013–381 also eliminated one of two "souls-to-the-polls" Sundays in which African American churches provided transportation to voters.

. . . Prior to SL 2013–381, same-day registration allowed eligible North Carolinians to register in person at an early voting site at the same time as casting their ballots. . . . The legislature's racial data demonstrated that, as the district court found, "it is indisputable that African American voters disproportionately used [same-day registration] when it was available." The district court further found that African American registration applications constituted a disproportionate percentage of the incomplete registration queue. And the court found that African Americans "are more likely to move between counties," and thus "are more likely to need to re-register." As evidenced by the types of errors that placed many African American applications in the incomplete queue, in-person assistance likely would disproportionately benefit African Americans. SL 2013–381 eliminated same-day registration.

Legislators additionally requested a racial breakdown of . . . out-of-precinct voting[, which] required the Board of Elections in each county to count the provisional ballot of an Election Day voter who appeared at the wrong precinct, but in the correct county, for all of the ballot items for which the voter was eligible to vote. This provision assisted those who moved frequently, or who mistook a voting site as being in their correct precinct. The district court found that the racial data revealed that African Americans disproportionately voted provisionally. . . . With SL 2013–381, the General Assembly altogether eliminated out-of-precinct voting.

African Americans also disproportionately used preregistration. Preregistration permitted 16- and 17-year-olds, when obtaining driver's licenses or attending mandatory high school registration drives, to identify themselves and indicate their intent to vote. This allowed County Boards of Elections to verify eligibility and automatically register eligible citizens once they reached eighteen. Although preregistration increased turnout among young adult voters, SL 2013–381 eliminated it. . . .

. . . Because the record evidence is limited regarding Hispanics, we confine our analysis to African Americans. We hold that the challenged provisions of

SL 2013–381 were enacted with racially discriminatory intent in violation of the Equal Protection Clause of the Fourteenth Amendment. . . .

III.

A.

Arlington Heights directs us to consider "[t]he historical background of the decision" challenged as racially discriminatory. . . . [W]hen assessing the intent claim, the [district] court's analysis . . . consisted solely of the finding that "there is little evidence of official discrimination since the 1980s," accompanied by a footnote dismissing examples of more recent official discrimination.

That finding is clearly erroneous. The record is replete with evidence of instances since the 1980s in which the North Carolina legislature has attempted to suppress and dilute the voting rights of African Americans. In some of these instances, the Department of Justice or federal courts have determined that the North Carolina General Assembly acted with discriminatory intent, "reveal[ing] a series of official actions taken for invidious purposes." . . .

The district court failed to take into account these cases and their important takeaway: that state officials continued in their efforts to restrict or dilute African American voting strength well after 1980 and up to the present day. . . . These cases also highlight the manner in which race and party are inexorably linked in North Carolina. This fact constitutes a critical—perhaps the most critical—piece of historical evidence here. The district court failed to recognize this linkage, leading it to accept "politics as usual" as a justification for many of the changes in SL 2013–381. But that cannot be accepted where politics as usual translates into race-based discrimination. . . .

In its results analysis, the court noted that racially polarized voting between African Americans and whites remains prevalent in North Carolina. Indeed, at trial the State admitted as much. As one of the State's experts conceded, "in North Carolina, African-American race is a better predictor for voting Democratic than party registration." For example, in North Carolina, 85% of African American voters voted for John Kerry in 2004, and 95% voted for President Obama in 2008. In comparison, in those elections, only 27% of white North Carolinians voted for John Kerry, and only 35% for President Obama.

Thus, whether the General Assembly knew the exact numbers, it certainly knew that African American voters were highly likely, and that white voters were unlikely, to vote for Democrats. And it knew that . . . much of the recent success of Democratic candidates in North Carolina resulted from African American voters overcoming historical barriers and making their voices heard to a degree unmatched in modern history. . . .

[T]he district court apparently considered SL 2013–381 simply an appropriate means for one party to counter recent success by another party. We recognize that elections have consequences, but winning an election does not empower anyone in any party to engage in purposeful racial discrimination. When a legislature dominated by one party has dismantled barriers to African American access to the franchise, even if done to gain votes, "politics as usual" does not allow a legislature dominated by the other party to re-erect those barriers.

The record evidence is clear that this is exactly what was done here. For example, the State argued before the district court that the General Assembly enacted changes to early voting laws to avoid "political gamesmanship" with respect to the hours and locations of early voting centers. As "evidence of justifications" for the changes to early voting, the State offered purported inconsistencies in voting hours across counties, including the fact that only some counties had decided to offer Sunday voting. The State then elaborated on its justification, explaining that "[c]ounties with Sunday voting in 2014 were disproportionately black" and "disproportionately Democratic." In response, SL 2013–381 did away with one of the two days of Sunday voting. Thus, in what comes as close to a smoking gun as we are likely to see in modern times, the State's very justification for a challenged statute hinges *explicitly* on race—specifically its concern that African Americans, who had overwhelmingly voted for Democrats, had too much access to the franchise. . . .

C.

Arlington Heights also recognizes that the legislative history leading to a challenged provision "may be highly relevant, especially where there are contemporaneous statements by members of the decisionmaking body, minutes of its meetings, or reports." . . .

No minutes of meetings about SL 2013–381 exist. And, as the Supreme Court has recognized, testimony as to the purpose of challenged legislation "frequently will be barred by [legislative] privilege." That is the case here. The district court was correct to note that statements from only a few legislators, or those made by legislators after the fact, are of limited value.[7]

We do find worthy of discussion, however, the General Assembly's requests for and use of race data in connection with SL 2013–381. . . . This data revealed that African Americans disproportionately used early voting, same-day registration, and out-of-precinct voting, and disproportionately lacked DMV-issued ID. Not only that, it also revealed that African Americans did *not* disproportionately use absentee voting; whites did. SL 2013–381 drastically restricted all of these other forms of access to the franchise, but exempted absentee voting from the photo ID requirement. In sum, relying on this racial data, the General Assembly enacted legislation restricting all—and only—practices disproportionately used by African Americans. When juxtaposed against the unpersuasive non-racial explanations the State proffered for the specific choices it made, discussed in more detail below, we cannot ignore the choices the General Assembly made with this data in hand. . . .

IV.

Because Plaintiffs have established race as a factor that motivated enactment of the challenged provisions of SL 2013–381, the burden now "shifts to the law's defenders to demonstrate that the law would have been enacted without this factor." Once the burden shifts, a court must carefully scrutinize a state's non-racial motivations to determine whether they alone can explain enactment of the challenged law. "[J]udicial deference" to the legislature's stated justifications "is no longer justified." . . .

The record evidence plainly establishes race as a "but-for" cause of SL 2013–381.

In enacting the photo ID requirement, the General Assembly stated that it sought to combat voter fraud and promote public confidence in the electoral system.

---

[7]   Some of the statements by those supporting the legislation included a Republican precinct chairman who testified before the House Rules Committee that the photo ID requirement would "disenfranchise some of [Democrats'] special voting blocks [sic]," and that "that within itself is the reason for the photo voter ID, period, end of discussion." Responding to the outcry over the law after its enactment, the same witness later said publicly: "If [SL 2013–381] hurts the whites so be it. If it hurts a bunch of lazy blacks that want the government to give them everything, so be it." Joe Coscarelli, *Don Yelton, GOP Precinct Chair, Delivers Most Baldly Racist Daily Show Interview of All Time*, New York Magazine (Oct. 24, 2013). These statements do not prove that any member of the General Assembly necessarily acted with discriminatory intent. But the sheer outrageousness of these public statements by a party leader does provide some evidence of the racial and partisan political environment in which the General Assembly enacted the law.

The photo ID requirement here is both too restrictive and not restrictive enough to effectively prevent voter fraud. First, the photo ID requirement, which applies only to in-person voting and not to absentee voting, is too narrow to combat fraud. On the one hand, the State has failed to identify even a single individual who has ever been charged with committing in-person voter fraud in North Carolina. On the other, the General Assembly did have evidence of alleged cases of mail-in absentee voter fraud. Notably, the legislature also had evidence that . . . whites disproportionately used absentee voting. The General Assembly then exempted absentee voting from the photo ID requirement. This was so even though . . . the bipartisan State Board of Elections specifically requested that the General Assembly remedy the potential for mail-in absentee voter fraud and expressed no concern about in-person voter fraud.

WORTH NOTING

The court here distinguished *Crawford v. Marion Cty. Election Bd.* (2008), which upheld Indiana's photo ID requirement, principally on the basis that it was supported by the state's interest in preventing voter fraud. The *Crawford* challengers did not allege intentional race discrimination but contended that the requirement was too burdensome on the right to vote generally. The *McCrory* court asserted that the deference shown by *Crawford* to the legislature did not apply here because "the evidence in this case establishes that, at least in part, race motivated the North Carolina legislature."

The photo ID requirement is also too broad, enacting seemingly irrational restrictions unrelated to the goal of combating fraud. This overbreadth is most stark in the General Assembly's decision to exclude as acceptable identification all forms of state-issued ID disproportionately held by African Americans. The State has offered little evidence justifying these exclusions. Review of the record further undermines the contention that the exclusions are tied to concerns of voter fraud. This is so because voters who lack qualifying ID under SL 2013–381 may apply for a free voter card using two of the very same forms of ID excluded by the law. . . . In this way, SL 2013–381 . . . creat[es] hoops through which certain citizens must jump with little discernable gain in deterrence of voter fraud. . . .

[The Court went on to discuss the race-neutral justifications proffered in defense of the other restrictions. It found them similarly wanting.]

In many ways, the challenged provisions in SL 2013–381 constitute solutions in search of a problem. The only clear factor linking these various "reforms" is their impact on African American voters. The record thus makes obvious that the "problem" the majority in the General Assembly sought to remedy was emerging support for the minority party. Identifying and restricting the ways African Americans vote was an easy and effective way to do so. We therefore must conclude that race constituted a but-for cause of SL 2013–381, in violation of the constitutional and statutory prohibitions on intentional discrimination. . . .

4.   Race-Conscious Remedies for Racial Injustice

In general, classifications will not survive constitutional review if they are either expressed in explicitly racial terms or demonstrably motivated by racial intent. The trickiest cases involve situations like *Johnson v. California* (2005), pp. 1026–1035, where at some level we believe that the government could plausibly be making a genuine effort—however ham-handed and ill-advised—to advance a broad-based, non-subjugating vision of the public good. Because strict scrutiny applies to all such classifications, however, even cases like *Johnson* just aren't that hard. In virtually all cases, the extreme demands of strict scrutiny will mean that even the most benignly motivated use of race will fail to pass constitutional muster.

How (if at all) should this framework change when the government uses racial categories as part of an effort to right the wrongs inflicted by prior uses of racial categories to separate, subjugate, and oppress? Consider how the following cases treat such efforts to right racial wrongs—and what significance is attributed to the source of the remedial effort: the judiciary, or the political branches.

a.   Race Conscious Remedies—by the Judicial Branch

In *Brown v. Board of Education* (1954) (*Brown I*), pp. 1001–1006, the Supreme Court held unanimously that "segregation in public education . . . . is a denial of the equal protection of the laws." The question was, what came next.

Recognizing the complexity of crafting a remedial order, the Court ordered reargument—the third round of argument in the case—focused on the question of what relief would be appropriate. The Court then issued the decision known as *Brown II*, again unanimously per Chief Justice Warren. Noting that "[f]ull implementation" of the principles of *Brown I* "may require solution of varied local school problems," the Court held that "[s]chool authorities have the primary responsibility for elucidating, assessing, and solving these problems." *Brown v. Board of Education* (1955). The judiciary would "have to consider whether the action of school authorities constitutes good faith implementation of the governing constitutional principles," a task that was better done in the first instance by local courts.

Under the framework dictated by *Brown II*, courts would be guided by equitable principles, and have the full power and flexibility of courts of equity in fashioning a decree. They should "require that the defendants make a prompt and reasonable start toward full compliance with" the principles of *Brown I*. In formulating decrees, they could

> consider problems related to administration, arising from the physical condition of the school plant, the school transportation system, personnel, revision of school districts and attendance areas into compact units to achieve a system of determining admission to the public schools on a nonracial basis, and revision of local laws and regulations which may be necessary in solving the foregoing problems.

The *Brown II* Court recognized that it might take time to put such plans into operation, but instructed the lower courts to make such orders as necessary "to admit to public schools on a racially nondiscriminatory basis with all deliberate speed the parties to these cases."

That formulation became notorious for its ineffectiveness, as "all deliberate speed" confronted a strategy of "massive resistance" adopted in many places throughout the segregated South. The name comes from Virginia Senator Harry F. Byrd's speech proposing the strategy: "If we can organize the Southern States for massive resistance to this order," he said, "in time, the rest of the country will realize that racial integration is not going to be accepted in the South." In a document known as the Southern Manifesto, 19 Senators and 82 congressional Representatives gave a full throated endorsement of Byrd's plan: "We regard the decision of the Supreme Court in the school cases as a clear abuse of judicial power. . . . We commend the motives of those states which have declared the intention to resist forced integration by any lawful means."

And the resistance came. Virginia's Prince Edward County, for example, simply closed its public schools. In their place, it provided vouchers to pay for private education for all students.

FOR DISCUSSION Should Prince Edward County's decision have been held constitutional? Does it matter that there were no private schools admitting black students in the county? Does the result depend on the purpose for which the schools were closed? Would it matter if in response to *Brown* so many white children had left the public schools that the majority of the voters of the county were no longer willing to finance the public schools? See *Griffin v. County School Board of Prince Edward County* (1964) (holding Prince Edward County's school closure invalid). Should the outcome be different if it were a municipal pool, rather than schools, that was closed? *Palmer v. Thompson* (1971) (refusing by 5–4 vote to find violation in sale of municipal pools, though one remained in private operation for whites only, with another owned by a predominantly black state college); see pp. 1013–1019.

Another technique attempted by some schools in the South was to give students "freedom of choice." Such a plan came before the Supreme Court in *Green v. County School Board of New Kent County* (1968). The county, a rural pocket of Eastern Virginia, was about evenly divided racially. Both black and white families lived throughout the county; there was no systematic residential segregation. The county had only two schools. New Kent on the east side had only white students before *Brown*, and Watkins School on the west side had only black students. Buses transported children of each race from across the county to the school to which they were assigned. After *Brown*, the racial character of the schools was maintained, initially pursuant to a Virginia statute (in force until 1966) that assigned students to the school they had last attended unless they applied for a different school and a state board approved; the board also assigned first-time students. Then, to comply with requirements under the 1964 Civil Rights Act for financial aid, the county adopted a "freedom-of-choice" plan allowing students to choose a school; returning students were presumptively assigned to their prior school.

The Supreme Court, in an opinion by Justice Brennan, characterized this as a "dual system" of the type that must be abolished under *Brown I* and *II*. Justice Brennan recognized that immediately after *Brown II* "[t]he principal focus was on obtaining for those Negro children courageous enough to break with tradition a place in the 'white' schools." But "that immediate goal was only the first step": "The transition to a unitary, nonracial system of public education was and is the ultimate end to be brought about." School boards such as the county's had an "affirmative duty to take whatever steps might be necessary to convert to a unitary system in which racial discrimination would be eliminated root and branch. . . . The burden on a school board today is to come forward with a plan that promises realistically to work, and promises realistically to work now."

The Court expressly declined to hold that a "freedom of choice" plan might be unconstitutional, but it asserted "that in desegregating a dual system a plan utilizing 'freedom of choice' is not an end in itself." The Court noted that not a single white child had chosen to attend Watkins school, and that although some African-American children chose to attend New Kent school, "85% of the Negro children in the system still attend the all-Negro Watkins school."

The Court required the Board to "fashion steps which promise realistically to convert promptly to a system without a 'white' school and a 'Negro' school, but just schools," and it suggested that school zoning might be part of a solution.

FOR DISCUSSION

Green established a requirement of a "unitary" system of public education. What does "unitary" mean in this context?

In *Swann v. Charlotte-Mecklenberg Board of Education* (1971), the Supreme Court followed up on the zoning suggestion, and dug into the details of implementing desegregation in a large metropolitan area in the South. The student body in the district was approximately 71% white and 29% black, but the black population was largely concentrated in the inner city and the white population in the outer areas. The great majority of black students attended schools that were at least 99% black. The district court concluded that the Board had failed to present an adequate plan for desegregation, and imposed one recommended by an expert, requiring not only a dramatic redrawing of district lines but also busing of students between inner and outer areas. In a unanimous opinion by Chief Justice Burger, a Nixon appointee, the Supreme Court upheld the district court's decision.

"Once a right and a violation have been shown," the Chief Justice wrote, "the scope of a district court's equitable powers to remedy past wrongs is broad, for breadth and flexibility are inherent in equitable remedies." Emphasizing the principle that "judicial powers may be exercised only on the basis of a constitutional violation," he noted that courts might find a violation on the basis of a board's decisions about either school locations or district boundaries. Both kinds of decisions, he explained, "may well promote segregated residential patterns" and, "when combined with 'neighborhood zoning,' further lock the school system into the mold of separation of the races."

The district court had directed "that efforts should be made to reach a 71–29 ratio in the various schools so that there will be no basis for contending that one school is racially different from the others." Observing that "[t]he constitutional command to desegregate schools does not mean that every school in every community must always reflect the racial composition of the school system as a whole," the Supreme Court treated this ratio as "no more than a starting point in the process of shaping a remedy, rather than an inflexible requirement." Indeed, the Court noted that "the existence of some small number of one-race, or virtually one-race, schools within a district is not in and of itself the mark of a system that still practices segregation by law."

Focusing on what it called "a frank—and sometimes drastic—gerrymandering of school districts and attendance zones," the Court said:

> The remedy for such segregation may be administratively awkward, inconvenient, and even bizarre in some situations and may impose burdens on some; but all awkwardness and inconvenience cannot be avoided in the interim period when remedial adjustments are being made to eliminate the dual school systems.

The Court declined to articulate guidelines on how far an order could go. But it explicitly approved the district court's use of busing to achieve integration. Busing, it noted, had become an integral part of the nation's public school system for years. In this case, the district court's order required elementary students to be bused an average of seven miles, for trips that it estimated would take 35 minutes at most, and the Court concluded that this requirement was within the district judge's discretion. The Court expressed hope that the district court's order would result in achievement of a unitary system and that "further intervention by a district court should not be necessary."

In *Keyes v. Denver School District No. 1* (1973), the issue of school desegregation moved to a non-southern city that had never had a statutory dual system. Justice Brennan's opinion for the majority noted that the plaintiffs apparently conceded that they "must prove not only that segregated schooling exists but also that it was brought about or maintained by intentional state action." Citywide, the student population was (in the terms used in the litigation) 66% Anglo, 14% Negro, and 20% Hispano. The Court held that plaintiffs were "entitled to have schools with a combined predominance of Negroes and Hispanos included in the category of 'segregated' schools." There was a concentration of segregated schools in two areas, in the core of the city and in Park Hill, in the northeastern portion of the city. The district court found that for a decade following 1960 the school board had adopted a policy designed to isolate black students. The drawing of school zones, the placement and size of new schools, and the assignment of staff on the basis of race were part of this policy. The Court held that unless Park Hill were found to be a separate, identifiable, unrelated unit, the finding that a dual system was operated in Park Hill would mean that the whole city was operated as a dual system; even if Park Hill were found to be separate in that way, the finding of racially segregative intent in Park Hill would create a presumption that the same intent permeated the entire city, contributing to racial segregation, and therefore leading to an obligation to eliminate segregation "root and branch"; the Court emphasized "that the differentiating factor between *de jure* segregation and so-called de *facto* segregation to which we referred in *Swann* is purpose or intent to segregate."

Justice Powell—a Virginian and former president of the Richmond School Board, who had been appointed in fulfilment of a longstanding promise by President Nixon to name a southerner to the Court—wrote an opinion concurring in part and dissenting in part. He noted that in many non-southern cities there was segregation "fully as pervasive as that in southern cities prior to the desegregation decrees of the past decade and a half"—and largely because of the *de facto / de jure* distinction considerably more progress had been made in achieving desegregation in the South. "But," he wrote, "if our national concern is for those who attend such schools, rather than for perpetuating a legalism rooted in history rather than present reality, we must recognize that the evil of operating separate schools is no less in Denver than in Atlanta." He noted a shift after *Brown II*:

> In a series of decisions extending from 1954 to 1971 the concept of state neutrality was transformed into the present constitutional doctrine requiring affirmative state action to desegregate school systems. The keystone case was *Green*, where school boards were declared to have "the affirmative duty to take whatever steps might be necessary to convert to a unitary system in which racial discrimination would be eliminated root and branch." . . .
>
> In imposing on metropolitan southern school districts [in *Swann*] an affirmative duty, entailing large-scale transportation of pupils, to eliminate segregation in the schools, the Court required

these districts to alleviate conditions which in large part did not result from historic, state-imposed *de jure* segregation. Rather, the familiar root cause of segregated schools in all the biracial metropolitan areas of our country is essentially the same: one of segregated residential and migratory patterns the impact of which on the racial composition of the schools was often perpetuated and rarely ameliorated by action of public school authorities. This is a national, not a southern, phenomenon. And it is largely unrelated to whether a particular State had or did not have segregative school laws. . . .

I would not . . . perpetuate the *de jure / de facto* distinction nor would I leave to petitioners the initial tortuous effort of identifying "segregative acts" and deducing "segregative intent." I would hold, quite simply, that where segregated public schools exist within a school district to a substantial degree, there is a *prima facie* case that the duly constituted public authorities . . . are sufficiently responsible to warrant imposing upon them a nationally applicable burden to demonstrate they nevertheless are operating a genuinely integrated school system.

In Justice Powell's view, a system would be integrated in accord with constitutional standards if the responsible authorities had taken appropriate steps to

(i) integrate faculties and administration; (ii) scrupulously assure equality of facilities, instruction, and curriculum opportunities throughout the district; (iii) utilize their authority to draw attendance zones to promote integration; and (iv) locate new schools, close old ones, and determine the size and grade categories with this same objective in mind. Where school authorities decide to undertake the transportation of students, this also must be with integrative opportunities in mind.

FOR DISCUSSION What litigation problem does Justice Powell's approach alleviate? In his view, what constitutes the constitutional violation warranting a remedy?

Justice Douglas concurred separately, indicating agreement with Powell's attempt to do away with the distinction between *de jure* and *de facto* segregation. Chief Justice Burger noted concurrence in the result, without opinion.

Justice White—who was from Denver—did not participate. Justice Rehnquist dissented alone. He wrote:

> Underlying the Court's entire opinion is its apparent thesis that a district judge is at least permitted to find that, if a single attendance zone between two individual schools in the large metropolitan district is found by him to have been "gerrymandered," the school district is guilty of operating a "dual" school system, and is apparently a candidate for what is in practice a federal receivership. . . . It would therefore presumably be open to the District Court to require, *inter alia*, that pupils be transported great distances throughout the district to and from schools whose attendance zones have not been gerrymandered. Yet, unless the Equal Protection Clause of the Fourteenth Amendment now be held to embody a principle of "taint," found in some primitive legal systems but discarded centuries ago in ours, such a result can only be described as the product of judicial fiat. . . .
>
> The drastic extension of *Brown* which *Green* represented was barely, if at all, explicated in the latter opinion. To require that a genuinely "dual" system be disestablished, in the sense that the assignment of a child to a particular school is not made to depend on his race, is one thing. To require that school boards affirmatively undertake to achieve racial mixing in schools where such mixing is not achieved in sufficient degree by neutrally drawn boundary lines is quite obviously something else.
>
> The Court's own language in *Green* makes it unmistakably clear that this significant extension of *Brown*'s prohibition against discrimination, and the conversion of that prohibition into an affirmative duty to integrate, was made in the context of a school system which had for a number of years rigidly excluded Negroes from attending the same schools as were attended by whites. Whatever may be the soundness of that decision in the context of a genuinely "dual" school system, where segregation of the races had once been mandated by law, I can see no constitutional justification for it in a situation such as that which the record shows to have obtained in Denver.

The Court's attention remained on the problem of segregation outside the South with *Milliken v. Bradley* (1974) (*Milliken I*), which involved the

Detroit-area schools. Detroit had experienced a wave of "white flight" in the late 1960s. At the time the suit was brought in 1970, the student population of Detroit was 64% black, but in the metropolitan area as a whole the black population was 19%. The district court found that the Detroit school district had engaged in segregative practices, and it concluded that the only way to make an effective remedy, without encouraging further white flight, was to include some of the suburban districts in a busing plan; the plan was designed to bus students no more than 40 minutes each way.

Chief Justice Burger, writing for the majority, began his opinion by asserting that the Court had granted *certiorari*

> to determine whether a federal court may impose a multi-district, area-wide remedy to a single-district *de jure* segregation problem absent any finding that the other included school districts have failed to operate unitary school systems within their districts, absent any claim or finding that the boundary lines of any affected school district were established with the purpose of fostering racial segregation in public schools, [and] absent any finding that the included districts committed acts which effected segregation within the other districts. . . .

Not surprisingly, his answer was no:

> Before the boundaries of separate and autonomous school districts may be set aside by consolidating the separate units for remedial purposes or by imposing a cross-district remedy, it must first be shown that there has been a constitutional violation within one district that produces a significant segregative effect in another district. Specifically, it must be shown that racially discriminatory acts of the state or local school districts, or of a single school district have been a substantial cause of interdistrict segregation. Thus an interdistrict remedy might be in order where the racially discriminatory acts of one or more school districts caused racial segregation in an adjacent district, or where district lines have been deliberately drawn on the basis of race. In such circumstances an interdistrict remedy would be appropriate to eliminate the interdistrict segregation directly caused by the constitutional violation. Conversely, without an interdistrict violation and interdistrict effect, there is no constitutional wrong calling for an interdistrict remedy.

The record before us, voluminous as it is, contains evidence of *de jure* segregated conditions only in the Detroit schools; indeed, that was the theory on which the litigation was initially based and on which the District Court took evidence. With no showing of significant violation by the 53 outlying school districts and no evidence of any interdistrict violation or effect, the court went beyond the original theory of the case as framed by the pleadings and mandated a metropolitan area remedy. To approve the remedy ordered by the court would impose on the outlying districts, not shown to have committed any constitutional violation, a wholly impermissible remedy based on a standard not hinted at in *Brown I* and *II* or any holding of this Court.

Justices Douglas, Brennan, White, and Marshall dissented. Justice White's dissent noted: "The result is that the State of Michigan, the entity at which the Fourteenth Amendment is directed, has successfully insulated itself from its duty to provide effective desegregation remedies by vesting sufficient power over its public schools in its local school districts." Justice Marshall's dissent called the decision "a giant step backwards." And he said, "To suggest, as does the majority, that a Detroit-only plan somehow remedies the effects of *de jure* segregation of the races is, in my view, to make a solemn mockery of *Brown I*'s holding that separate educational facilities are inherently unequal and of *Swann*'s unequivocal mandate that the answer to *de jure* segregation is the greatest possible degree of actual desegregation."

The *Milliken* case returned to the Court three years later. The district court—not the original judge, who had since died—had entered an order that required various educational programs to remedy the effects of segregation. In *Milliken II*, the Court unanimously approved, Chief Justice Burger writing for the Court:

> The "condition" offending the Constitution is Detroit's *de jure* segregated school system, which was so pervasively and persistently segregated that the District Court found that the need for the educational components flowed directly from constitutional violations by both state and local officials. These specific educational remedies, although normally left to the discretion of the elected school board and professional educators, were deemed necessary to restore the victims of discriminatory conduct to the position they would have

enjoyed in terms of education had these four components been provided in a nondiscriminatory manner in a school system free from pervasive de jure racial segregation.

Milliken v. Bradley (1977). Justice Powell, concurring in the judgment, wrote:

> This protracted litigation commenced in 1970 in this conventional mold. In the intervening years, however, the posture of the litigation has changed so drastically as to leave it largely a friendly suit between the plaintiffs . . . and the original principal defendant, the Detroit School Board. These parties, antagonistic for years, have now joined forces apparently for the purpose of extracting funds from the state treasury. . . . Thus the only complaining party is the State of Michigan (acting through state officials), and its basic complaint concerns money, not desegregation. It has been ordered to pay about $5,800,000 to the Detroit School Board.

Meanwhile, the change of direction signaled by *Milliken I* was confirmed by *Pasadena Board of Education v. Spangler* (1976). The district court, having found a constitutional violation, entered a desegregation order containing a provision that students in the racial minority district-wide should not be in a majority in any school, and it required year-by-year adjustments to achieve this goal. By a 6–2 vote—Justice Rehnquist writing for the majority, Justices Brennan and Marshall dissenting, and Justice Stevens, who was new to the Court, not participating—the Court held that post-order adjustment was improper absent evidence that post-order changes in residential patterns were attributable to "segregative actions chargeable to the defendants."

In *Board of Education of Oklahoma City Public Schools v. Dowell* (1991), the Court, again per Rehnquist, by then Chief Justice, took a significant further step in the same direction. The action had been brought in 1961 and in 1972 had resulted in an order much like the one implemented in Charlotte—indeed, like the one in Charlotte, it was known as the Finger Plan because it was designed by the same expert, John Finger. Five years later, the district court, finding "that substantial compliance with the constitutional requirements has been achieved" and that ending its jurisdiction would not "result in the dismantlement of the Plan or any affirmative action by the defendant to undermine the unitary system so slowly and painfully accomplished over the 16 years during which the cause has been pending before this court," entered an order terminating jurisdiction. The Board continued for several years to follow the Finger Plan. In 1985, however, the Board implemented a Student Reassignment Plan (SRP), in response to demographic changes that had caused students to be bused greater distances; the SRP would end busing of K–4 students. Fearing resegregation, because many of the school zones were single-race, some parents filed a motion to reopen the case. The matter reached the Supreme Court after extensive proceedings in the lower courts.

The Court first held that the parents were not precluded by the 1977 order. Chief Justice Rehnquist wrote:

> The lower courts have been inconsistent in their use of the term "unitary." Some have used it to identify a school district that has completely remedied all vestiges of past discrimination. Under that interpretation of the word, a unitary school district is one that has met the mandate of *Brown II* and *Green*. Other courts, however, have used "unitary" to describe any school district that has currently desegregated student assignments, whether or not that status is solely the result of a court-imposed desegregation plan. In other words, such a school district could be called unitary and nevertheless still contain vestiges of past discrimination. . . .

> We think it is a mistake to treat words such as "dual" and "unitary" as if they were actually found in the Constitution. The constitutional command of the Fourteenth Amendment is that "[n]o State shall . . . deny to any person . . . the equal protection of the laws." Courts have used the terms "dual" to denote a school system which has engaged in intentional segregation of students by race, and "unitary" to describe a school system which has been brought into compliance with the command of the Constitution. We are not sure how useful it is to define these terms more precisely, or to create subclasses within them. . . .

> The District Court's 1977 order is unclear with respect to what it meant by unitary and the necessary result of that finding. We therefore decline to overturn the conclusion of the Court of Appeals that while the 1977 order of the District Court did bind the parties as to the unitary character of the district, it did not finally terminate the Oklahoma City school litigation. In *Pasadena City Bd. of Education*

v. Spangler, we held that a school board is entitled to a rather precise statement of its obligations under a desegregation decree. If such a decree is to be terminated or dissolved, respondents as well as the school board are entitled to a like statement from the court.

On the merits, the Chief Justice emphasized that court intervention was supposed to be limited in time:

> From the very first, federal supervision of local school systems was intended as a temporary measure to remedy past discrimination. *Brown II* considered the "complexities arising from the *transition* to a system of public education freed of racial discrimination" in holding that the implementation of desegregation was to proceed "with all deliberate speed" (emphasis added). *Green* also spoke of the "*transition* to a unitary, nonracial system of public education*" (emphasis added).

> . . . [I]njunctions entered in school desegregation cases . . . are not intended to operate in perpetuity. Local control over the education of children allows citizens to participate in decisionmaking, and allows innovation so that school programs can fit local needs. *Milliken I*. . . . The legal justification for displacement of local authority by an injunctive decree in a school desegregation case is a violation of the Constitution by the local authorities. . . .

> In this case the original finding of *de jure* segregation was entered in 1961, the injunctive decree from which the Board seeks relief was entered in 1972, and the Board complied with the decree in good faith until 1985. Not only do the personnel of school boards change over time, but the same passage of time enables the District Court to observe the good faith of the school board in complying with the decree. The test espoused by the Court of Appeals [under which the desegregation decree would remain in effect until such time as the district could show "grievous wrong evoked by new and unforseen conditions" and "dramatic changes in conditions unforseen at the time of the decree that . . . impose extreme and unexpectedly oppressive hardships on the obligor"] would condemn a school district, once governed by a board which intentionally discriminated, to judicial tutelage for the indefinite future. Neither the principles governing the entry and dissolution of injunctive decrees, nor the commands of

the Equal Protection Clause of the Fourteenth Amendment, require any such Draconian result.

Petitioners urge that we reinstate the decision of the District Court terminating the injunction, but we think that the preferable course is to remand the case to that court so that it may decide, in accordance with this opinion, whether the Board made a sufficient showing of constitutional compliance as of 1985, when the SRP was adopted, to allow the injunction to be dissolved. The District Court should address itself to whether the Board had complied in good faith with the desegregation decree since it was entered, and whether the vestiges of past discrimination had been eliminated to the extent practicable.

In considering whether the vestiges of *de jure* segregation had been eliminated as far as practicable, the District Court should look not only at student assignments, but "to every facet of school operations—faculty, staff, transportation, extra-curricular activities and facilities." *Green*.

After the District Court decides whether the Board was entitled to have the decree terminated, it should proceed to decide respondent's challenge to the SRP. A school district which has been released from an injunction imposing a desegregation plan no longer requires court authorization for the promulgation of policies and rules regulating matters such as assignment of students and the like, but it of course remains subject to the mandate of the Equal Protection Clause of the Fourteenth Amendment. If the Board was entitled to have the decree terminated as of 1985, the District Court should then evaluate the Board's decision to implement the SRP under appropriate equal protection principles.

Justice Marshall, in his last year on the Court, dissented, joined by Justices Stevens and Blackmun. (Justice Brennan had retired, and Justice Souter joined the Court too late to participate.) He believed that a desegregation decree should not be lifted "so long as conditions likely to inflict the stigmatic injury condemned in *Brown I* persist and there remain feasible methods of eliminating such conditions":

In my view, a standard for dissolution of a desegregation decree must take into account the unique harm associated with a system of racially identifiable schools and must expressly demand the elimination of such schools. . . .

The majority suggests a more vague and, I fear, milder standard. Ignoring the harm identified in *Brown I*, the majority asserts that the District Court should find that the purposes of the degree have been achieved so long as "the Oklahoma City School District [is now] being operated in compliance with the commands of the Equal Protection Clause" and "it [is] unlikely that the school board would return to its former ways." Insofar as the majority instructs the District Court, on remand, to "conside[r] whether the vestiges of *de jure* segregation ha[ve] been eliminated as far as practicable," the majority presumably views elimination of vestiges as part of "operat[ing] in compliance with the commands of the Equal Protection Clause." But as to the scope or meaning of "vestiges," the majority says very little.

By focusing heavily on present and future compliance with the Equal Protection Clause, the majority's standard ignores how the stigmatic harm identified in *Brown I* can persist even after the State ceases actively to enforce segregation. It was not enough in *Green*, for example, for the school district to withdraw its own enforcement of segregation, leaving it up to individual children and their families to "choose" which school to attend. For it was clear under the circumstances that these choices would be shaped by and perpetuate the state-created message of racial inferiority associated with the school district's historical involvement in segregation. In sum, our school-desegregation jurisprudence establishes that the effects of past discrimination remain chargeable to the school district regardless of its lack of continued enforcement of segregation, and the remedial decree is required until those effects have been finally eliminated.

In *Freeman v. Pitts* (1992), the Court continued to facilitate the dismantling of lower courts' desegregation decrees. This decision was part of a lawsuit that had yielded a desegregation decree in 1969 against the DeKalb County (Georgia) School System (DCSS). That decree, assigning students to their neighborhood schools, had effectively desegregated the DCSS for a time; indeed, the district court concluded that the DCSS had achieved maximum practical desegregation from 1969–86. But dramatic demographic changes unrelated to any action on the part of the DCSS—primarily black families moving in from Atlanta and white families moving out, so that the African-American percentage of the population rose from 6% in 1969 to 47% in 1986—had led to racial imbalance in many of the schools. Nevertheless, in 1986, the DCSS, claiming that it had achieved unitary status, moved for dissolution of the decree.

The district court in *Freeman* concluded that the DCSS had achieved unitary status in the areas of student assignments (despite the fact that many of the schools were highly segregated), transportation, physical facilities, and extracurricular activities, and decided that it would issue no further orders in these areas. In the areas of faculty assignments and resource allocation, however, the district court concluded that the DCSS had not yet achieved unitary status. The court of appeals held that the DCSS had not yet achieved unitary status because it had not done so in all categories for several years, and therefore the DCSS would have to take further actions to correct the racial imbalance.

In an opinion by Justice Kennedy, the Supreme Court reversed the court of appeals:

> That the term "unitary" does not have fixed meaning or content is not inconsistent with the principles that control the exercise of equitable power. The essence of a court's equity power lies in its inherent capacity to adjust remedies in a feasible and practical way to eliminate the conditions or redress the injuries caused by unlawful action. Equitable remedies must be flexible if these underlying principles are to be enforced with fairness and precision. . . .
>
> Today, we make explicit the rationale that was central in *Spangler*. A federal court in a school desegregation case has the discretion to order an incremental or partial withdrawal of its supervision and control. This discretion derives both from the constitutional authority which justified its intervention in the first instance and its ultimate objectives in formulating the decree. The authority of the court is invoked at the outset to remedy particular constitutional violations. In construing the remedial authority of the district courts, we have been guided by the principles that "judicial powers may be exercised only on the basis of a constitutional violation," and that "the nature of the violation determines the scope of the remedy." *Swann*. A remedy

is justifiable only insofar as it advances the ultimate objective of alleviating the initial constitutional violation. . . .

Partial relinquishment of judicial control, where justified by the facts of the case, can be an important and significant step in fulfilling the district court's duty to return the operations and control of schools to local authorities. In *Dowell*, we emphasized that federal judicial supervision of local school systems was intended as a "temporary measure." Although this temporary measure has lasted decades, the ultimate objective has not changed—to return school districts to the control of local authorities. Just as a court has the obligation at the outset of a desegregation decree to structure a plan so that all available resources of the court are directed to comprehensive supervision of its decree, so too must a court provide an orderly means for withdrawing from control when it is shown that the school district has attained the requisite degree of compliance. A transition phase in which control is relinquished in a gradual way is an appropriate means to this end.

Several of the justices wrote separate opinions concurring or concurring the judgment. Justice Scalia wrote:

At some time, we must acknowledge that it has become absurd to assume, without any further proof, that violations of the Constitution dating from the days when Lyndon Johnson was President, or earlier, continue to have an appreciable effect upon current operation of schools. We are close to that time.

Justice Souter, by contrast, emphasized that the dual system itself might be a cause of the demographic shifts facing a court considering a partial relinquishment of supervision, and that other factors of the type highlighted by *Green* might cause imbalanced student assignment patterns in the future; if these factors left a school racially identifiable, there might be a flight toward identifiable "white" schools. And Justice Blackmun, joined by Justices Stevens and O'Connor, concurred only in the judgment of remand for further proceedings; they would have required the court of appeals to review the district court's finding that DCSS had proven that racially identifiable schools were not a result of past segregative action of the DCSS, either by contributing directly to racial imbalance in the schools or by contributing to the demographic changes.

The Court turned its attention back to higher education in *United States v. Fordice* (1992). Before *Brown*, Mississippi had a system of five universities for whites and three colleges for blacks. The segregated system remained largely intact following *Brown*. Ultimately, private litigants brought suit to force a change, and the United States intervened. Despite efforts to settle, more than 99% of the state's white students were enrolled at one of the historically white institutions, and 71% of the black students were enrolled at one of the historically black colleges. The court of appeals concluded that the state had satisfied its obligation of dismantling the dual system of higher education by adopting race-neutral policies, which included assigning different missions to the various colleges.

The Supreme Court reversed almost unanimously, with Justice Scalia dissenting in part. Justice White's opinion for the court noted broad agreement that higher education institutions stand on a different footing for purposes of desegregation orders than do primary and secondary schools. Traditionally, students are not assigned to local colleges, and institutions vary in their missions. But, he said, "even after a State dismantles its segregative *admissions* policy, there may still be state action that is traceable to the State's prior *de jure* segregation and that continues to foster segregation."

He identified four "suspect" policies that the state would have to justify or abandon. The first was use of ACT cutoff scores for the award of scholarships in the state's three "flagship" universities (Mississippi, Mississippi State, and Southern Mississippi). Originally, he said, the test had been adopted precisely because of its discriminatory effect. Even though the state universities now genuinely relied on the test as a proxy for student preparedness, "[o]bviously, this midpassage justification for perpetuating a policy enacted originally to discriminate against black students does not make the present admissions standards any less constitutionally suspect," at least given that the test continued to have significant discriminatory effect. A second factor that appeared to contribute to continued racial identification of the institutions was duplication by the historically white universities of many of the "nonessential" or "noncore" academic programs maintained by the historically black institutions. Third was mission assignment; the three flagship universities, all historically white, were the three that were designated as "comprehensive" universities. And fourth was maintenance of all eight institutions, which the district court had called "wasteful and irrational."

Concurring, Justice Thomas wrote:

> . . . I agree with the Court that a State does not satisfy its obligation to dismantle a dual system of higher education merely by adopting race-neutral policies for the future administration of that system. Today, we hold that, "[i]f policies traceable to the *de jure* system are still in force and have discriminatory effects, those policies too must be reformed to the extent practicable and consistent with sound educational practices." I agree that this statement defines the appropriate standard to apply in the higher education context. I write separately to emphasize that this standard is far different from the one adopted to govern the grade-school context in *Green* and its progeny. In particular, because it does not compel the elimination of all observed racial imbalance, it portends neither the destruction of historically black colleges nor the severing of those institutions from their distinctive histories and traditions.

By contrast, Justice Scalia wrote:

> With some of what the Court says today, I agree. I agree, of course, that the Constitution compels Mississippi to remove all discriminatory barriers to its state-funded universities. *Brown I.* I agree that the Constitution does not compel Mississippi to remedy funding disparities between its historically black institutions (HBI's) and historically white institutions (HWI's). And I agree that Mississippi's American College Testing Program (ACT) requirements need further review. I reject, however, the effectively unsustainable burden the Court imposes on Mississippi, and all States that formerly operated segregated universities, to demonstrate compliance with *Brown I.* That requirement, which resembles what we prescribed for primary and secondary schools in *Green*, has no proper application in the context of higher education, provides no genuine guidance to States and lower courts, and is as likely to subvert as to promote the interests of those citizens on whose behalf the present suit was brought.

Justice Scalia objected to the Court's purported test, which depended on whether a state policy would "substantially restrict a person's choice of which institution to enter." He believed that when the Court considered the purportedly segregative state practices it effectively transformed the test into one depending on whether the practice "affected" student choice. "Nothing else would explain how . . . Mississippi's mission designations, program duplication, and operation of all eight formerly *de jure* colleges" could fail under this test. "Indeed," he said, "program duplication and continuation of the eight schools have quite the opposite effect [from restricting choice]; they multiply, rather than restrict, limit, or impede the available choices." He then claimed that

> the Court is essentially applying to universities the amorphous standard adopted for primary and secondary schools in *Green*. Like that case, today's decision places upon the State the ordinarily unsustainable burden of proving the negative proposition that it is not responsible for extant racial disparity in enrollment. *Green* requires school boards to prove that racially identifiable schools are not the consequence of past or present discriminatory state action, *Swann*; today's opinion requires state university administrators to prove that racially identifiable schools are not the consequence of any practice or practices (in such impromptu "aggregation" as might strike the fancy of a district judge) held over from the prior *de jure* regime.

On remand, the Fifth Circuit reversed the district court's finding "that the use of ACT cutoff scores as a criterion for the award of scholarships at the HWIs is not traceable to the *de jure* system and does not currently foster segregation." It approved a plan of the district court for requiring uniform admissions standards for all the institutions, and the Supreme Court denied certiorari. *Ayers v. Fordice* (5th Cir. 1997).

Finally, consider *Missouri v. Jenkins* (1995), concerning the Kansas City, Missouri, School District (KCMSD). After extensive litigation, the district court entered a series of orders creating an unusually ambitious educational plan for the KCMSD, with the KCMSD and the state held jointly and severally liable. The court ordered greatly increased funding for the KCMSD schools, on the ground that this would help erase the vestiges of discrimination, and the establishment of an extensive system of magnet schools, which were meant to draw students form outside as well as from within the district. The Supreme Court held 5–4, per Chief Justice Rehnquist, that the order exceeded the district court's discretion. The attempt to improve the "desegregative attractiveness" of the District's schools to lure students into the District was inappropriate given that, as in *Milliken I*, there had not been an inter-district violation. The district court lacked the authority to order an inter-district transfer of students, and it should not be able to accomplish the same goal indirectly through the technique of a magnet school. Justices Stevens, Souter, Ginsburg, and Breyer dissented;

they did not believe *Milliken I* barred a district court from taking into account effects of its order beyond the district where the violation was found.

Justice Thomas wrote a contemplative concurrence. Here are excerpts:

> It never ceases to amaze me that the courts are so willing to assume that anything that is predominantly black must be inferior. Instead of focusing on remedying the harm done to those black schoolchildren injured by segregation, the District Court here sought to convert the KCMSD into a "magnet district" that would reverse the "white flight" caused by desegregation. In this respect, I join the Court's decision concerning the two remedial issues presented for review. . . .

> Two threads in our jurisprudence have produced this unfortunate situation, in which a District Court has taken it upon itself to experiment with the education of the KCMSD's black youth. First, the court has read our cases to support the theory that black students suffer an unspecified psychological harm from segregation that retards their mental and educational development. This approach not only relies upon questionable social science research rather than constitutional principle, but it also rests on an assumption of black inferiority. Second, we have permitted the federal courts to exercise virtually unlimited equitable powers to remedy this alleged constitutional violation. The exercise of this authority has trampled upon principles of federalism and the separation of powers and has freed courts to pursue other agendas unrelated to the narrow purpose of precisely remedying a constitutional harm. . . .

> In order for a "vestige" to supply the ground for an exercise of remedial authority, it must be clearly traceable to the dual school system. The "vestiges of segregation that are the concern of the law in a school case may be subtle and intangible but nonetheless they must be so real that they have a causal link to the *de jure* violation being remedied." *Freeman v. Pitts.* . . .

> Without a basis in any real finding of intentional government action, the District Court's imposition of liability upon the State of Missouri improperly rests upon a theory that racial imbalances are unconstitutional. . . .

It is clear that the District Court misunderstood the meaning of *Brown I*. *Brown I* did not say that "racially isolated" schools were inherently inferior; the harm that it identified was tied purely to *de jure* segregation, not *de facto* segregation. Indeed, *Brown I* itself did not need to rely upon any psychological or social science research in order to announce the simple, yet fundamental truth that the Government cannot discriminate among its citizens on the basis of race. . . .

Segregation was not unconstitutional because it might have caused psychological feelings of inferiority. Public school systems that separated blacks and provided them with superior educational resources—making blacks "feel" superior to whites sent to lesser schools—would violate the Fourteenth Amendment, whether or not the white students felt stigmatized, just as do school systems in which the positions of the races are reversed. Psychological injury or benefit is irrelevant to the question whether state actors have engaged in intentional discrimination—the critical inquiry for ascertaining violations of the Equal Protection Clause. The judiciary is fully competent to make independent determinations concerning the existence of state action without the unnecessary and misleading assistance of the social sciences. . . .

Given that desegregation has not produced the predicted leaps forward in black educational achievement, there is no reason to think that black students cannot learn as well when surrounded by members of their own race as when they are in an integrated environment. Indeed, it may very well be that what has been true for historically black colleges is true for black middle and high schools. Despite their origins in "the shameful history of state enforced segregation," these institutions can be " 'both a source of pride to blacks who have attended them and a source of hope to black families who want the benefits of . . . learning for their children.' " *Fordice* (Thomas, J., concurring). Because of their "distinctive histories and traditions," black schools can function as the center and symbol of black communities, and provide examples of independent black leadership, success, and achievement.

The Upshot: The racial composition of the nation's public schools has changed considerably over the last several decades, as indicated by this chart, taken from Gary Orfield, Erica Frankenberg, et al., *Brown at 60: Great Progress, a Long Retreat and an Uncertain Future* (2014).[b]

Figure 1: *Public School Enrollment from 1968 to 2011*

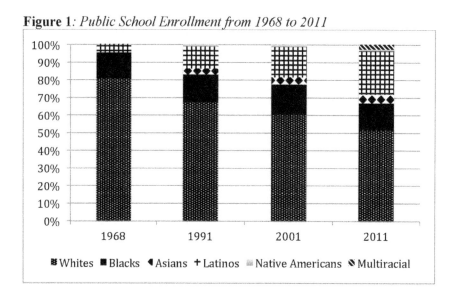

The course of desegregation in the South since the time of *Brown* is indicated by this graph, taken from the same study:

Figure 2: *Southern Desegregation and Resegregation for Black Students, 1954-2011*

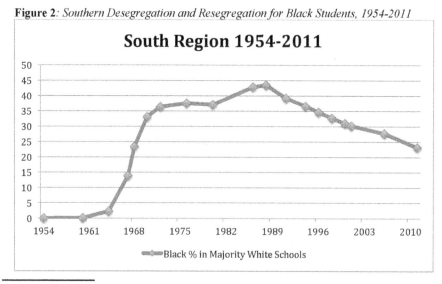

[b]   Los Angeles: UCLA Civil Rights Project, https://www.civilrightsproject.ucla.edu/research/k-12-education/integration-and-diversity/brown-at-60-great-progress-a-long-retreat-and-an-uncertain-future/Brown-at-60-051814.pdf.

And the diagram below shows, for each of five regions, changes over time in the percentage of black students attending schools in which 90% or more of the students are minority members.

Figure 3: *Percentage of Black Students in Intensely Segregated Minority Schools by Region*

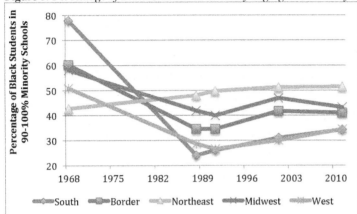

The authors note that, despite substantial resegregation in recent years, the South "is still the least segregated region for black students." Furthermore, they say:

> The growth of segregation has been most dramatic for Latino students, particularly in the West, where there was substantial integration in the 1960s, and segregation has soared. A clear pattern is developing of black and Latino students sharing the same schools. . . .
>
> Segregation is typically segregation by both race and poverty. Black and Latino students tend to be in schools with a substantial majority of poor children, but white and Asian students are typically in middle-class schools.

For Discussion

Consider some possible reactions to these results as a measure of judicial intervention:

(1) That judicial intervention did its job, establishing the implementation of constitutional principles that are not violated by a high percentage of *de facto* segregation?

(2) That somewhere the Supreme Court took a wrong turn? And if the latter, where? In *Brown*? In excessive implementation in the period, say, from *Green* through *Keyes*? In insufficient implementation in the period beginning with *Milliken*?

---

b.   Race Conscious Remedies—by the Political Branches

Now let's turn to efforts by the political branches to remedy the damage done by American apartheid. When the judiciary was doing the desegregating, many critics trained their fire on the courts' comparative political incompetence and lack of democratic legitimacy. The political branches, by contrast, suffer from neither of these comparative disadvantages. Should that affect the constitutionality of racialized categories when used in a good faith effort to rectify historical injustice? Let's start with what might be one example from Reconstruction.

An Act to Establish a Bureau for the Relief of Freedmen and Refugees

March 3, 1865

Be it enacted by the Senate and House of Representatives of the United States of America in Congress assembled, That there is hereby established in the War Department, to continue during the present war of rebellion, and for one year thereafter, a bureau of refugees, freedmen, and abandoned lands, to which shall be committed, as hereinafter provided, the supervision and management of all abandoned lands, and the control of all subjects relating to refugees and freedmen from rebel states, or from any district of country within the territory embraced in the operations of the army, under such rules and regulations as may be prescribed by the head of the bureau and approved by the President. . . .

SEC. 2.   *And be it further enacted,* That the Secretary of War may direct such issues of provisions, clothing, and fuel, as he may deem needful for the immediate and temporary shelter and supply of destitute and suffering refugees and freedmen and their wives and children, under such rules and regulations as he may direct. . . .

SEC. 4. *And be it further enacted,* That the commissioner, under the direction of the President, shall have authority to set apart, for the use of loyal refugees and freedmen, such tracts of land within the insurrectionary states as shall have been abandoned, or to which the United States shall have acquired title by confiscation or sale, or otherwise, and to every male citizen, whether refugee or freedman, as aforesaid, there shall be assigned not more than forty acres of such land, and the person to whom it was so assigned shall be protected in the use and enjoyment of the land for the term of three years at an annual rent not exceeding six per centum upon the value of such land. . . . At the end of said term, or at any time during said term, the occupants of any parcels so assigned may purchase the land and receive such title thereto as the United States can convey, upon paying therefor the value of the land. . . .

APPROVED, March 3, 1865.

Under modern equal protection doctrine, would the Freedmen's Bureau Act be viewed as facially neutral? Does it matter that the benefits of the Act extend to both "freedmen" and "refugees"? How might the analysis differ under cases like *Yick Wo v. Hopkins* (1886), pp. 1051–1054 (overwhelming disproportion), *Ho Ah Kow v. Nunan* (1879) (proxy categories), pp. 1057–1060, and *Personnel Administrator of Massachusetts v. Feeney* (1979) ("despite, not because of" standard), pp. 1241–1248?

FOR DISCUSSION

Consider also the doctrinal implications of the following facts:

> In December of 1865 General [Oliver O.] Howard, the Commissioner of the Freedmen's Bureau, submitted to Congress a report describing the activities of the Bureau under the new statute. The report revealed that in practice most of the Bureau's programs applied only to freedmen. Freedmen were the only beneficiaries of programs such as education, labor regulation, Bureau farms, land distribution, adjustments of real estate disputes, supervision of the civil and criminal justice systems through the freedmen's courts, registration of marriages, and aid to orphans. Both freedmen and refugees received medical assistance, but not in equal numbers: as of October 30, 1865, there were 6,645 freedmen under treatment, but only 238 refugees. Moreover, freedmen received about three quarters of all rations distributed. Only in the area of transportation were the benefits to freedmen and refugees approximately equal, but this represented less than one percent of the Bureau's budget and was a function that Howard's report described as "nearly ceased."

Eric Schnapper, *Affirmative Action and the Legislative History of the Fourteenth Amendment,* 71 Va. L. Rev. 753 (1985). See also, *e.g.,* Act of March 16, 1867 (appropriating funds "for the relief of freedmen or destitute colored people in the District of Columbia"); Act of July 28, 1866 (granting property "for the sole use of schools for colored children in [the] District of Columbia").

The political coalition responsible for enacting the Fourteenth Amendment appears to have been comfortable with using racial categories as part of a good faith effort to ameliorate the damage done by systematic racial oppression. The modern Supreme Court, on the other hand, has been far more skeptical of race-conscious remedial action in such contexts. How much should the original understanding matter here? Should the passage of time since the worst American racial sins change the application of the Constitution's equality guarantee?

A good place to begin discussion of the modern history of what has come to be called affirmative action is President Lyndon Johnson's 1965 commencement address at Howard University (named after the same General Howard who served as Commissioner of the Freedmen's Bureau). After reviewing recent advances in civil and voting rights, Johnson said:

> But freedom is not enough. You do not wipe away the scars of centuries by saying: Now you are free to go where you want, and do as you desire, and choose the leaders you please.
>
> You do not take a person who, for years, has been hobbled by chains and liberate him, bring him up to the starting line of a race and then say, "you are free to compete with all the others," and still justly believe that you have been completely fair. Thus it is not enough just to open the gates of opportunity. All our citizens must have the ability to walk through those gates.
>
> This is the next and the more profound stage of the battle for civil rights. We seek not just freedom but opportunity. We seek not just legal equity but human ability, not just equality as a right and a theory but equality as a fact and equality as a result.

That September, Johnson signed Executive Order 11246, which, building on prior orders, not only imposed on government contractors an obligation to "take affirmative action to ensure that applicants are employed, and that employees are treated during employment, without regard to their race, color, religion, sex or national origin" but also created an effective enforcement mechanism.

In succeeding years, many public institutions, at the federal, state, and local levels, adopted a wide array of race-based remedial programs. Inevitably, these programs were challenged in the courts on equal protection grounds. And so an important question arose. Should a program that gives a preference to members of an historically disadvantaged group—say, setting aside a spot in an institution of higher learning, or creating greater protections against layoffs—be viewed in the same way as racial classifications that had promoted subjugation?

The Supreme Court first considered the substance of such claims in *Regents of the University of California v. Bakke* (1978), involving a program in which the medical school of the University of California at Davis reserved 16 of 100 seats in its entering class for members of designated minority groups. There was no majority opinion. Four members of the Court believed the program satisfied constitutional and statutory requirements. Another four members, without reaching the constitutional question, believed that any consideration of race in admissions by an educational institution receiving federal funds violated Title VI of the 1964 Civil Rights Act. That left Justice Powell with the decisive vote in the middle. He believed that some consideration of race was permissible, but it would have to satisfy the standards of strict scrutiny. Though countering the effects of societal discrimination was a legitimate goal, he did not believe that it could be accomplished at the expense of "innocent individuals." The pedagogical advantages of diversity in the student body was a compelling interest, but the rigid set-aside of Davis's program was not, in his view, sufficiently tailored. Powell suggested that he would accept a more holistic use of race as one "plus factor" among others in university admissions criteria, citing Harvard College's affirmative action program as an example.

For a quarter century, Justice Powell's *Bakke* opinion was the leading judicial authority on affirmative action in higher education. Meanwhile, the Court decided cases presenting an array of affirmative-action issues in government employment and contracting. For example, in *Wygant v. Jackson Board of Education* (1986), the Court considered a school district's contract with a teacher's union that prescribed that in the event of layoffs, despite the usual rule protecting the most senior teacher, there would not be "a greater percentage of minority personnel laid off than the current percentage of minority personnel employed at the time of the layoff." As in *Bakke*, the Court invalidated the program without a majority opinion; this time, however, Justice Powell wrote a four-member plurality opinion that applied strict scrutiny. He declared that the plan was not sufficiently narrowly tailored, in that it imposed severe burdens on innocent parties; in this respect, he indicated that layoffs impose more substantial burdens than hiring goals.

In the following case, a majority of the Court finally adopted strict scrutiny as the standard for reviewing race-conscious remedies.

City of Richmond v. J.A. Croson Co.

Supreme Court of the United States, 1989.
488 U.S. 469.

JUSTICE O'CONNOR announced the judgment of the Court and delivered the opinion of the Court with respect to Parts I, III-B, and IV, an opinion with respect to Part II, in which THE CHIEF JUSTICE and JUSTICE WHITE join, and an opinion with respect to Parts III-A and V, in which THE CHIEF JUSTICE, JUSTICE WHITE, and JUSTICE KENNEDY join.

In this case, we confront once again the tension between the Fourteenth Amendment's guarantee of equal treatment to all citizens, and the use of race-based measures to ameliorate the effects of past discrimination on the opportunities enjoyed by members of minority groups in our society. . . .

I

On April 11, 1983, the Richmond City Council adopted the Minority Business Utilization Plan (the Plan). The Plan required prime contractors to whom the city awarded construction contracts to subcontract at least 30% of the dollar amount of the contract to one or more Minority Business Enterprises (MBE's). The 30% set-aside did not apply to city contracts awarded to minority-owned prime contractors.

The Plan defined an MBE as "[a] business at least fifty-one (51) percent of which is owned and controlled . . . by minority group members." "Minority group members" were defined as "[c]itizens of the United States who are Blacks, Spanish-speaking, Orientals, Indians, Eskimos, or Aleuts." There was no geographic limit to the Plan; an otherwise qualified MBE from anywhere in the United States could avail itself of the 30% set-aside. The Plan declared that it was "remedial" in nature, and enacted "for the purpose of promoting wider participation by minority business enterprises in the construction of public projects." The Plan expired on June 30, 1988, and was in effect for approximately five years. [The Court noted that the expiration of the Plan had not mooted the case, because plaintiff had been injured financially by the city's denial of its bid.]

[The Plan authorized an administrator to grant waivers if a contractor could prove that it was impossible to submit a bid that satisfied Plan requirements; that administrator then promulgated a rule providing that waivers would only be granted "in exceptional circumstances," after "every feasible attempt has been made to comply."]

The Plan was adopted by the Richmond City Council after a public hearing. . . . Proponents of the set-aside provision relied on a study which indicated that, while the general population of Richmond was 50% black, only 0.67% of the city's prime construction contracts had been awarded to minority businesses in the 5-year period from 1978 to 1983. It was also established that a variety of contractors' associations, whose representatives appeared in opposition to the ordinance, had virtually no minority businesses within their membership. . . .

Councilperson Marsh, a proponent of the ordinance, made the following statement:

> There is some information, however, that I want to make sure that we put in the record. I have been practicing law in this community since 1961, and I am familiar with the practices in the construction industry in this area, in the State, and around the nation. And I can say without equivocation, that the general conduct of the construction industry in this area, and the State, and around the nation, is one in which race discrimination and exclusion on the basis of race is widespread.

There was no direct evidence of race discrimination on the part of the city in letting contracts or any evidence that the city's prime contractors had discriminated against minority-owned subcontractors. See Statement of Councilperson Kemp ("[The public witnesses] indicated that the minority contractors were just not available. There wasn't a one that gave any indication that a minority contractor would not have an opportunity, if he were available"). . . .

Representatives of various contractors' associations questioned whether there were enough MBE's in the Richmond area to satisfy the 30% set-aside requirement. Mr. Murphy noted that only 4.7% of all construction firms in the United States were minority owned and that 41% of these were located in California, New York, Illinois, Florida, and Hawaii. He predicted that the ordinance would thus lead to a windfall for the few minority firms in Richmond. Councilperson Gillespie indicated his concern that many local labor jobs, held by both blacks and whites, would be lost because the ordinance put no geographic limit on the MBE's eligible for the 30% set-aside. . . .

[T]he ordinance was enacted by a vote of six to two, with Councilperson Gillespie abstaining.

On September 6, 1983, the city of Richmond issued an invitation to bid on a project for the provision and installation of certain plumbing fixtures at the city jail. On September 30, 1983, . . . J.A. Croson Company (Croson), a mechanical plumbing and heating contractor, received the bid forms. The project involved the installation of stainless steel urinals and water closets in the city jail. . . . [Croson] determined that to meet the 30% set-aside requirement, a minority contractor would have to supply the fixtures. The provision of the fixtures amounted to 75% of the total contract price.

On September 30, [Croson] contacted five or six MBE's that were potential suppliers of the fixtures, after contacting three local and state agencies that maintained lists of MBE's. No MBE expressed interest in the project or tendered a quote.

On October 12, 1983, the day the bids were due, [Croson] again telephoned a group of MBE's. This time, Melvin Brown, president of Continental Metal Hose (Continental), a local MBE, indicated that he wished to participate in the project. Brown subsequently contacted two sources of the specified fixtures . . . in order to obtain a price quotation. One supplier . . . had already made a quotation directly to Croson, and refused to quote the same fixtures to Continental. Brown also contacted . . . one of the two manufacturers of the specified fixtures. The [fixture manufacturer] was not familiar with Brown or Continental, and indicated that a credit check was required which would take at least 30 days to complete.

On October 13, 1983, the sealed bids were opened. Croson turned out to be the only bidder, with a bid of $126,530. Brown and [a Croson manager] met personally at the bid opening, and Brown informed [Croson's manager] that his difficulty in obtaining credit approval had hindered his submission of a bid.

By October 19, 1983, Croson had still not received a bid from Continental. On that date it submitted a request for a waiver of the 30% set-aside. Croson's waiver request indicated that Continental was "unqualified" and that the other MBE's contacted had been unresponsive or unable to quote. . . .

[Continental] subsequently submitted a bid on the fixtures to Croson. Continental's bid was $6,183 higher than the price Croson had included for the fixtures in its bid to the city[,] which constituted a 7% increase over the market price for the fixtures. With added bonding and insurance, using Continental would have raised the cost of the project by $7,663. . . . Brown . . . also called city procurement officials and told them that Continental, an MBE, could supply the fixtures specified in the city jail contract. On November 2, 1983, the city denied Croson's waiver request, indicating that Croson had 10 days to submit an MBE Utilization Commitment Form, and warned that failure to do so could result in its bid being considered unresponsive. . . .

The city [eventually] informed Croson that it had decided to rebid the project. . . . Shortly thereafter Croson brought this action . . . , arguing that the Richmond ordinance was unconstitutional on its face and as applied in this case. . . .

II

The parties and their supporting *amici* fight an initial battle over the scope of the city's power to adopt legislation designed to address the effects of past discrimination. . . . [A]ppellee argues that the city must limit any race-based remedial efforts to eradicating the effects of its own prior discrimination. This is essentially the position taken by the Court of Appeals below. Appellant argues that . . . the city of Richmond enjoys sweeping legislative power to define and attack the effects of prior discrimination in its local construction industry. We find that neither of these two rather stark alternatives can withstand analysis. . . .

As a matter of state law, the city of Richmond has legislative authority over its procurement policies, and can use its spending powers to remedy private discrimination, if it identifies that discrimination with the particularity required by the Fourteenth Amendment. . . . Thus, if the city could show that it had essentially become a "passive participant" in a system of racial exclusion

 WORTH NOTING Here, Justice O'Connor discusses *Fullilove v. Klutznizk* (1980), in which the Court upheld a federal statute that authorized public works grants to state and local governments and required that 10% of each grant presumptively be spent for work done by MBEs. The holding in *Fullilove*, she said, did not apply to the set-aside in *Croson*; unlike state and local governments, Congress "has a specific constitutional mandate to enforce the dictates of the Fourteenth Amendment."

practiced by elements of the local construction industry, we think it clear that the city could take affirmative steps to dismantle such a system. It is beyond dispute that any public entity, state or federal, has a compelling interest in assuring that public dollars, drawn from the tax contributions of all citizens, do not serve to finance the evil of private prejudice.

III

A

. . . As this Court has noted in the past, the "rights created by the first section of the Fourteenth Amendment are, by its terms, guaranteed to the individual. The rights established are personal rights." *Shelley v. Kraemer* (1948). The Richmond Plan denies certain citizens the opportunity to compete for a fixed percentage of public contracts based solely upon their race. To whatever racial group these citizens belong, their "personal rights" to be treated with equal dignity and respect are implicated by a rigid rule erecting race as the sole criterion in an aspect of public decisionmaking.

Absent searching judicial inquiry into the justification for such race-based measures, there is simply no way of determining what classifications are "benign" or "remedial" and what classifications are in fact motivated by illegitimate notions of racial inferiority or simple racial politics. Indeed, the purpose of strict scrutiny is to "smoke out" illegitimate uses of race by assuring that the legislative body is pursuing a goal important enough to warrant use of a highly suspect tool. The test also ensures that the means chosen "fit" this compelling goal so closely that there is little or no possibility that the motive for the classification was illegitimate racial prejudice or stereotype.

Classifications based on race carry a danger of stigmatic harm. Unless they are strictly reserved for remedial settings, they may in fact promote notions of racial inferiority and lead to a politics of racial hostility. See *University of California Regents v. Bakke* (opinion of Powell, J.) ("[P]referential programs may only reinforce common stereotypes holding that certain groups are unable to achieve success without special protection based on a factor having no relation to individual worth"). We thus reaffirm the view expressed by the plurality in *Wygant v. Jackson Board of Education* (1986) that the standard of review under the Equal Protection Clause is not dependent on the race of those burdened or benefited by a particular classification. . . .

Even were we to accept a reading of the guarantee of equal protection under which the level of scrutiny varies according to the ability of different groups to defend their interests in the representative process, heightened scrutiny would still be appropriate in the circumstances of this case. One of the central arguments for applying a less exacting standard to "benign" racial classifications is that such measures essentially involve a choice made by dominant racial groups to disadvantage themselves. If one aspect of the judiciary's role under the Equal Protection Clause is to protect "discrete and insular minorities" from majoritarian prejudice or indifference, see *United States v. Carolene Products Co.* (1938), some maintain that these concerns are not implicated when the "white majority" places burdens upon itself. See J. Ely, *Democracy and Distrust* (1980).

In this case, blacks constitute approximately 50% of the population of the city of Richmond. Five of the nine seats on the city council are held by blacks. The concern that a political majority will more easily act to the disadvantage of a minority based on unwarranted assumptions or incomplete facts would seem to militate for, not against, the application of heightened judicial scrutiny in this case. See Ely, *The Constitutionality of Reverse Racial Discrimination*, 41 U. Chi. L. Rev. 723 (1974) ("Of course it works both ways: a law that favors Blacks over Whites would be suspect if it were enacted by a predominantly Black legislature"). . . .

B

We think it clear that the factual predicate offered in support of the Richmond Plan suffers from [a fatal] defect[.] [A] generalized assertion that there has been past discrimination in an entire industry provides no guidance for a legislative body to determine the precise scope of the injury it seeks to remedy. It "has no logical stopping point." "Relief" for such an ill-defined wrong could extend until the percentage of public contracts awarded to MBE's in Richmond mirrored the percentage of minorities in the population as a whole.

Appellant argues that it is attempting to remedy various forms of past discrimination that are alleged to be responsible for the small number of minority businesses in the local contracting industry. Among these the city cites the exclusion of blacks from skilled construction trade unions and training programs. This past discrimination has prevented them "from following the traditional path from laborer to entrepreneur." The city also lists a host of nonracial factors which would seem to face a member of any racial group attempting to establish a new business enterprise, such as deficiencies in working capital, inability to meet bonding requirements, unfamiliarity with bidding procedures, and disability caused by an inadequate track record.

While there is no doubt that the sorry history of both private and public discrimination in this country has contributed to a lack of opportunities for black entrepreneurs, this observation, standing alone, cannot justify a rigid racial quota in the awarding of public contracts in Richmond, Virginia. Like the claim that discrimination in primary and secondary schooling justifies a rigid racial preference in medical school admissions, an amorphous claim that there has been past discrimination in a particular industry cannot justify the use of an unyielding racial quota.

It is sheer speculation how many minority firms there would be in Richmond absent past societal discrimination, just as it was sheer speculation how many minority medical students would have been admitted to the medical school at Davis absent past discrimination in educational opportunities. Defining these sorts of injuries as "identified discrimination" would give local governments license to create a patchwork of racial preferences based on statistical generalizations about any particular field of endeavor.

These defects are readily apparent in this case. The 30% quota cannot in any realistic sense be tied to any injury suffered by anyone. The District Court relied upon five predicate "facts" in reaching its conclusion that there was an adequate basis for the 30% quota: (1) the ordinance declares itself to be remedial; (2) several proponents of the measure stated their views that there had been past discrimination in the construction industry; (3) minority businesses received 0.67% of prime contracts from the city while minorities constituted 50% of the city's population; (4) there were very few minority contractors in local and state contractors' associations; and (5) in 1977, Congress made a determination that the effects of past discrimination had stifled minority participation in the construction industry nationally.

None of these "findings," singly or together, provide the city of Richmond with a "strong basis in evidence for its conclusion that remedial action was necessary." There is nothing approaching a prima facie case of a constitutional or statutory violation by *anyone* in the Richmond construction industry. . . .

The District Court . . . relied on the highly conclusionary statement of a proponent of the Plan that there was racial discrimination in the construction industry "in this area, and the State, and around the nation." App. 41 (statement of Councilperson Marsh). It also noted that the city manager had related his view that racial discrimination still plagued the construction industry in his home city of Pittsburgh. *Id.*, at 42 (statement of Mr. Deese). . . . But when a legislative body chooses to employ a suspect classification, it cannot rest upon a generalized assertion as to the classification's relevance to its goals. A governmental actor cannot render race a legitimate proxy for a particular condition merely by declaring that the condition exists. . . .

Reliance on the disparity between the number of prime contracts awarded to minority firms and the minority population of the city of Richmond is similarly misplaced. . . . In the employment context, we have recognized that for certain entry level positions or positions requiring minimal training, statistical comparisons of the racial composition of an employer's work force to the racial composition of the relevant population may be probative of a pattern of discrimination. See *Teamsters v. United States* (1977) (statistical comparison between minority truck-drivers and relevant population probative of [purposeful] discriminatory exclusion). But where special qualifications are necessary, the relevant statistical pool for purposes of demonstrating discriminatory exclusion must be the number of minorities qualified to undertake the particular task.

In this case, the city does not even know how many MBE's in the relevant market are qualified to undertake prime or subcontracting work in public construction projects. Nor does the city know what percentage of total city construction dollars minority firms now receive as subcontractors on prime contracts let by the city. . . .

The city and the District Court also relied on evidence that MBE membership in local contractors' associations was extremely low. Again, standing alone this evidence is not probative of any discrimination in the local construction industry. There are numerous explanations for this dearth of minority participation, including past societal discrimination in education and economic opportunities as well as both black and white career and entrepreneurial choices. Blacks may be disproportionately attracted to industries other than construction. . . . For low minority membership in these associations to be relevant, the city would have to link it to the number of local MBE's eligible for membership. If the statistical disparity between eligible MBE's and MBE membership were great enough, an inference of discriminatory exclusion could arise. In such a case, the city would have a compelling interest in preventing its tax dollars from assisting these organizations in maintaining a racially segregated construction market. . . .

The "evidence" relied upon by the dissent, the history of school desegregation in Richmond and numerous congressional reports [about discrimination in the national market], does little to define the scope of any injury to minority contractors in Richmond or the necessary remedy. The factors relied upon by the dissent could justify a preference of any size or duration. Moreover, Justice Marshall's suggestion that findings of discrimination may be "shared" from jurisdiction to jurisdiction in the same manner as information concerning zoning and property values is unprecedented. We have never approved the extrapolation of discrimination in one jurisdiction from the experience of another. See *Milliken v. Bradley* (1974) ("Disparate treatment of white and Negro students occurred within the Detroit school system, and not elsewhere, and on this record the remedy must be limited to that system").

In sum, none of the evidence presented by the city points to any identified discrimination in the Richmond construction industry. We, therefore, hold that the city has failed to demonstrate a compelling interest in apportioning public contracting opportunities on the basis of race. To accept Richmond's claim that past societal discrimination alone can serve as the basis for rigid racial preferences would be to open the door to competing claims for "remedial relief" for every disadvantaged group. The dream of a Nation of equal citizens in a society where race is irrelevant to personal opportunity and achievement would be lost in a mosaic of shifting preferences based on inherently unmeasurable claims of past wrongs. . . . We think such a result would be contrary to both the letter and spirit of a constitutional provision whose central command is equality.

The foregoing analysis applies only to the inclusion of blacks within the Richmond set-aside program. There is *absolutely no evidence* of past discrimination against Spanish-speaking, Oriental, Indian, Eskimo, or Aleut persons in any aspect of the Richmond construction industry. The District Court took judicial notice of the fact that the vast majority of "minority" persons in Richmond were black. It may well be that Richmond has never had an Aleut or Eskimo citizen. The random inclusion of racial groups that, as a practical matter, may never have suffered from discrimination in the construction industry in Richmond suggests that perhaps the city's purpose was not in fact to remedy past discrimination.

If a 30% set-aside was "narrowly tailored" to compensate black contractors for past discrimination, one may legitimately ask why they are forced to share this "remedial relief" with an Aleut citizen who moves to Richmond tomorrow?

The gross overinclusiveness of Richmond's racial preference strongly impugns the city's claim of remedial motivation.

IV

As noted by the court below, it is almost impossible to assess whether the Richmond Plan is narrowly tailored to remedy prior discrimination since it is not linked to identified discrimination in any way. We limit ourselves to two observations in this regard.

First, there does not appear to have been any consideration of the use of race-neutral means to increase minority business participation in city contracting. Many of the barriers to minority participation in the construction industry relied upon by the city to justify a racial classification appear to be race neutral. If MBE's disproportionately lack capital or cannot meet bonding requirements, a race-neutral program of city financing for small firms would, *a fortiori*, lead to greater minority participation. The principal opinion in *Fullilove* found that Congress had carefully examined and rejected race-neutral alternatives before enacting the MBE set-aside. . . . There is no evidence in this record that the Richmond City Council has considered any alternatives to a race-based quota.

Second, the 30% quota cannot be said to be narrowly tailored to any goal, except perhaps outright racial balancing. It rests upon the "completely unrealistic" assumption that minorities will choose a particular trade in lockstep proportion to their representation in the local population. . . .

[T]he Richmond Plan's waiver system focuses solely on the availability of MBE's; there is no inquiry into whether or not the particular MBE seeking a racial preference has suffered from the effects of past discrimination by the city or prime contractors. . . . [T]he city's only interest in maintaining a quota system rather than investigating the need for remedial action in particular cases would seem to be simple administrative convenience. But the interest in avoiding the bureaucratic effort necessary to tailor remedial relief to those who truly have suffered the effects of prior discrimination cannot justify a rigid line drawn on the basis of a suspect classification. Under Richmond's scheme, a successful black, Hispanic, or Oriental entrepreneur from anywhere in the country enjoys an absolute preference over other citizens based solely on their race. We think it obvious that such a program is not narrowly tailored to remedy the effects of prior discrimination.

V

Nothing we say today precludes a state or local entity from taking action to rectify the effects of identified discrimination within its jurisdiction. If the city of Richmond had evidence before it that nonminority contractors were systematically excluding minority businesses from subcontracting opportunities it could take action to end the discriminatory exclusion. Where there is a significant statistical disparity between the number of qualified minority contractors willing and able to perform a particular service and the number of such contractors actually engaged by the locality or the locality's prime contractors, an inference of discriminatory exclusion could arise. Under such circumstances, the city could act to dismantle the closed business system by taking appropriate measures against those who discriminate on the basis of race or other illegitimate criteria. In the extreme case, some form of narrowly tailored racial preference might be necessary to break down patterns of deliberate exclusion. . . .

Even in the absence of evidence of discrimination, the city has at its disposal a whole array of race-neutral devices to increase the accessibility of city contracting opportunities to small entrepreneurs of all races. Simplification of bidding procedures, relaxation of bonding requirements, and training and financial aid for disadvantaged entrepreneurs of all races would open the public contracting market to all those who have suffered the effects of past societal discrimination or neglect. . . . The city may also act to prohibit discrimination in the provision of credit or bonding by local suppliers and banks. Business as usual should not mean business pursuant to the unthinking exclusion of certain members of our society from its rewards.

In the case at hand, the city has not ascertained how many minority enterprises are present in the local construction market nor the level of their participation in city construction projects. The city points to no evidence that qualified minority contractors have been passed over for city contracts or subcontracts, either as a group or in any individual case. Under such circumstances, it is simply impossible to say that the city has demonstrated "a strong basis in evidence for its conclusion that remedial action was necessary." . . .

Because the city of Richmond has failed to identify the need for remedial action in the awarding of its public construction contracts, its treatment of its citizens on a racial basis violates the dictates of the Equal Protection Clause. Accordingly, the judgment of the Court of Appeals for the Fourth Circuit is affirmed.

JUSTICE STEVENS, concurring in part and concurring in the judgment.

I . . . do not agree with the premise that seems to underlie today's decision . . . that a governmental decision that rests on a racial classification is never permissible except as a remedy for a past wrong. I do, however, agree with the Court's explanation of why the Richmond ordinance cannot be justified as a remedy for past discrimination, and therefore join Parts I, III-B, and IV of its opinion. . . .

The justification for the ordinance is the fact that in the past white contractors—and presumably other white citizens in Richmond—have discriminated against black contractors. The class of persons benefited by the ordinance is not, however, limited to victims of such discrimination—it encompasses persons who have never been in business in Richmond. . . .

The ordinance is equally vulnerable because of its failure to identify the characteristics of the disadvantaged class of white contractors that justify the disparate treatment. That class unquestionably includes some white contractors who are guilty of past discrimination against blacks, but it is only habit, rather than evidence or analysis, that makes it seem acceptable to assume that every white contractor covered by the ordinance shares in that guilt. Indeed, even among those who have discriminated in the past, it must be assumed that at least some of them have complied with the city ordinance that has made such discrimination unlawful since 1975. . . . Imposing a common burden on such a disparate class merely because each member of the class is of the same race stems from reliance on a stereotype rather than fact or reason. . . .[9]

JUSTICE KENNEDY, concurring in part and concurring in the judgment.

I join all but Part II of Justice O'Connor's opinion. . . . The nature and scope of the injury that existed; its historical or antecedent causes; the extent to which the city contributed to it, either by intentional acts or by passive complicity in acts of discrimination by the private sector; the necessity for the response adopted, its duration in relation to the wrong, and the precision with which it otherwise bore on whatever injury in fact was addressed, were all matters

---

[9]   There is, of course, another possibility that should not be overlooked. The ordinance might be nothing more than a form of patronage. But racial patronage, like a racial gerrymander, is no more defensible than political patronage or a political gerrymander. . . . A southern State with a long history of discrimination against Republicans in the awarding of public contracts could not rely on such past discrimination as a basis for granting a legislative preference to Republican contractors in the future.

unmeasured, unexplored, and unexplained by the city council. . . . This ordinance is invalid under the Fourteenth Amendment.

Justice Scalia, concurring in the judgment.

I agree with much of the Court's opinion, and, in particular, with Justice O'Connor's conclusion that strict scrutiny must be applied to all governmental classification by race, whether or not its asserted purpose is "remedial" or "benign." I do not agree, however, with Justice O'Connor's dictum suggesting that, despite the Fourteenth Amendment, state and local governments may in some circumstances discriminate on the basis of race in order (in a broad sense) "to ameliorate the effects of past discrimination."

The benign purpose of compensating for social disadvantages, whether they have been acquired by reason of prior discrimination or otherwise, can no more be pursued by the illegitimate means of racial discrimination than can other assertedly benign purposes we have repeatedly rejected. See, *e.g.,* *Wygant v. Jackson Board of Education* (1986) (plurality opinion) (discrimination in teacher assignments to provide "role models" for minority students); *Palmore v. Sidoti* (1984) (awarding custody of child to father, after divorced mother entered an interracial remarriage, in order to spare child social "pressures and stresses"); *Lee v. Washington* (1968) (per curiam) (permanent racial segregation of all prison inmates, presumably to reduce possibility of racial conflict). . . . At least where state or local action is at issue, only a social emergency rising to the level of imminent danger to life and limb—for example, a prison race riot, requiring temporary segregation of inmates, *cf. Lee v. Washington* (1968)—can justify an exception to the principle embodied in the Fourteenth Amendment that "[o]ur Constitution is color-blind, and neither knows nor tolerates classes among citizens." *Plessy v. Ferguson* (1896) (Harlan, J., dissenting).

We have in some contexts approved the use of racial classifications by the Federal Government to remedy the effects of past discrimination. I do not believe that we must or should extend those holdings to the States. . . . [I]t is one thing to permit racially based conduct by the Federal Government—whose legislative powers concerning matters of race were explicitly enhanced by the Fourteenth Amendment, see U.S. Const., Amdt. 14, § 5—and quite another to permit it by the precise entities against whose conduct in matters of race that Amendment was specifically directed, see Amdt. 14, § 1. . . .

A sound distinction between federal and state (or local) action based on race rests not only upon the substance of the Civil War Amendments, but upon social reality and governmental theory. . . . The struggle for racial justice has historically been a struggle by the national society against oppression in the individual States. . . . And the struggle retains that character in modern times. . . .

What the record shows, in other words, is that racial discrimination against any group finds a more ready expression at the state and local than at the federal level. To the children of the Founding Fathers, this should come as no surprise. An acute awareness of the heightened danger of oppression from political factions in small, rather than large, political units dates to the very beginning of our national history. As James Madison observed in support of the proposed Constitution's enhancement of national powers:

> The smaller the society, the fewer probably will be the distinct parties and interests composing it; the fewer the distinct parties and interests, the more frequently will a majority be found of the same party; and the smaller the number of individuals composing a majority, and the smaller the compass within which they are placed, the more easily will they concert and execute their plan of oppression. . . .

The Federalist No. 10. The prophesy of these words came to fruition in Richmond in the enactment of a set-aside clearly and directly beneficial to the dominant political group, which happens also to be the dominant racial group. The same thing has no doubt happened before in other cities (though the racial basis of the preference has rarely been made textually explicit)—and blacks have often been on the receiving end of the injustice. Where injustice is the game, however, turnabout is not fair play.

In my view there is only one circumstance in which the States may act *by race* to "undo the effects of past discrimination": where that is necessary to eliminate their own maintenance of a system of unlawful racial classification. If, for example, a state agency has a discriminatory pay scale compensating black employees in all positions at 20% less than their nonblack counterparts, it may assuredly promulgate an order raising the salaries of "all black employees" to eliminate the differential. This distinction explains our school desegregation cases, in which we have made plain that States and localities sometimes have an obligation to adopt race-conscious remedies. . . . While thus permitting the use of race to *de*classify racially classified students, teachers, and educational resources, however, we have also made it clear that the remedial power extends no further than the scope of the continuing constitutional violation. And it is implicit in our cases that after the dual school system has been completely disestablished, the States may no longer assign students by race. . . .

It is plainly true that in our society blacks have suffered discrimination immeasurably greater than any directed at other racial groups. But those who believe that racial preferences can help to "even the score" display, and reinforce, a manner of thinking by race that was the source of the injustice and that will, if it endures within our society, be the source of more injustice still. The relevant proposition is not that it was blacks, or Jews, or Irish who were discriminated against, but that it was individual men and women, "created equal," who were discriminated against. And the relevant resolve is that that should never happen again. Racial preferences appear to "even the score" (in some small degree) only if one embraces the proposition that our society is appropriately viewed as divided into races, making it right that an injustice rendered in the past to a black man should be compensated for by discriminating against a white. Nothing is worth that embrace. . . .

JUSTICE MARSHALL, with whom JUSTICE BRENNAN and JUSTICE BLACKMUN join, dissenting.

It is a welcome symbol of racial progress when the former capital of the Confederacy acts forthrightly to confront the effects of racial discrimination in its midst. In my view, nothing in the Constitution can be construed to prevent Richmond, Virginia, from allocating a portion of its contracting dollars for businesses owned or controlled by members of minority groups. Indeed, Richmond's set-aside program is indistinguishable in all meaningful respects from—and in fact was patterned upon—the federal set-aside plan which this Court upheld in *Fullilove v. Klutznick* (1980). . . . The essence of the majority's position is that Richmond has failed to catalog adequate findings to prove that past discrimination has impeded minorities from joining or participating fully in Richmond's construction contracting industry.

I find deep irony in second-guessing Richmond's judgment on this point. As much as any municipality in the United States, Richmond knows what racial discrimination is; a century of decisions by this and other federal courts has richly documented the city's disgraceful history of public and private racial discrimination. In any event, the Richmond City Council *has* supported its determination that minorities have been wrongly excluded from local construction contracting. Its proof includes statistics showing that minority-owned businesses have received virtually no city contracting dollars and rarely if ever belonged to area trade associations; testimony by municipal officials that discrimination has been widespread in the local construction industry; and the same exhaustive and widely publicized federal studies relied on in *Fullilove*, studies which showed that pervasive discrimination in the Nation's tight-knit construction industry had operated to exclude minorities from public contracting. . . .

More fundamentally, today's decision marks a deliberate and giant step backward in this Court's affirmative-action jurisprudence. Cynical of one municipality's attempt to redress the effects of past racial discrimination in a particular industry, the majority launches a grapeshot attack on race-conscious remedies in general. . . .

I

As an initial matter, the majority takes an exceedingly myopic view of the factual predicate on which the Richmond City Council relied when it passed the Minority Business Utilization Plan. The majority analyzes Richmond's initiative as if it were based solely upon the facts about local construction and contracting practices adduced during the city council session at which the measure was enacted. In so doing, the majority downplays the fact that the city council had before it a rich trove of evidence[, compiled by Congress for its own legislative purposes,] that discrimination in the Nation's construction industry had seriously impaired the competitive position of businesses owned or controlled by members of minority groups. . . .

[A]s of 1977, there was "abundant evidence" in the public domain "that minority businesses ha[d] been denied effective participation in public contracting opportunities by procurement practices that perpetuated the effects of prior discrimination." Significantly, this evidence demonstrated that discrimination had prevented existing or nascent minority-owned businesses from obtaining not only federal contracting assignments, but state and local ones as well.

The members of the Richmond City Council were well aware of these exhaustive congressional findings, a point the majority, tellingly, elides. The transcript of the session at which the council enacted the local set-aside initiative contains numerous references to the 6-year-old congressional set-aside program, to the evidence of nationwide discrimination barriers described above, and to the *Fullilove* decision itself. . . .

The city council's members also heard . . . testimony from city officials as to the exclusionary history of the local construction industry. As the District

Court noted, not a single person who testified before the city council denied that discrimination in Richmond's construction industry had been widespread. So long as one views Richmond's local evidence of discrimination against the backdrop of systematic nationwide racial discrimination which Congress had so painstakingly identified in this very industry, this case is readily resolved.

II

. . . My view has long been that race-conscious classifications designed to further remedial goals "must serve important governmental objectives and must be substantially related to achievement of those objectives" in order to withstand constitutional scrutiny. *University of California Regents v. Bakke* (1978) (joint opinion of Brennan, White, Marshall, and Blackmun, JJ.) (citations omitted). . . . Analyzed in terms of this two-pronged standard, Richmond's set-aside, like the federal program on which it was modeled, is "plainly constitutional." . . .

A

1

Turning first to the governmental interest inquiry, Richmond has two powerful interests in setting aside a portion of public contracting funds for minority-owned enterprises. The first is the city's interest in eradicating the effects of past racial discrimination. It is far too late in the day to doubt that remedying such discrimination is a compelling, let alone an important, interest. . . . Richmond has a second compelling interest[:] the prospective one of preventing the city's own spending decisions from reinforcing and perpetuating the exclusionary effects of past discrimination. . . .

The majority is wrong to trivialize the continuing impact of government acceptance or use of private institutions or structures once wrought by discrimination. When government channels all its contracting funds to a white-dominated community of established contractors whose racial homogeneity is the product of private discrimination, it does more than place its *imprimatur* on the practices which forged and which continue to define that community. It also provides a measurable boost to those economic entities that have thrived within it, while denying important economic benefits to those entities which, but for prior discrimination, might well be better qualified to receive valuable government contracts. . . .

... Cities like Richmond may not be constitutionally required to adopt set-aside plans. But there can be no doubt that when Richmond acted affirmatively to stem the perpetuation of patterns of discrimination through its own decisionmaking, it served an interest of the highest order. . . .

2

The remaining question with respect to the "governmental interest" prong of equal protection analysis is whether Richmond has proffered satisfactory proof of past racial discrimination to support its twin interests in remediation and in governmental nonperpetuation. . . . The varied body of evidence on which Richmond relied provides a "strong," "firm," and "unquestionably legitimate" basis upon which the city council could determine that the effects of past racial discrimination warranted a remedial and prophylactic governmental response. . . .

. . . The city's local evidence confirmed that Richmond's construction industry did not deviate from [the] pernicious national pattern [of past discrimination producing present inequities in construction contracting]. The fact that just 0.67% of public construction expenditures over the previous five years had gone to minority-owned prime contractors, despite the city's racially mixed population, strongly suggests that construction contracting in the area was rife with "present economic inequities." To the extent this enormous disparity did not itself demonstrate that discrimination had occurred, the descriptive testimony of Richmond's elected and appointed leaders drew the necessary link between the pitifully small presence of minorities in construction contracting and past exclusionary practices. That *no one* who testified challenged this depiction of widespread racial discrimination in area construction contracting lent significant weight to these accounts. . . .

Richmond's reliance on localized, industry-specific findings is a far cry from the reliance on generalized "societal discrimination" which the majority decries as a basis for remedial action. . . .

The majority's perfunctory dismissal of the testimony of Richmond's appointed and elected leaders is also deeply disturbing. These officials—including councilmembers, a former mayor, and the present city manager—asserted that race discrimination in area contracting had been widespread, and that the set-aside ordinance was a sincere and necessary attempt to eradicate the effects of this discrimination. . . .

Had the majority paused for a moment on the facts of the Richmond experience, it would have discovered that the city's leadership is deeply familiar with what racial discrimination is. The members of the Richmond City Council have spent long years witnessing multifarious acts of discrimination, including, but not limited to, the deliberate diminution of black residents' voting rights, resistance to school desegregation, and publicly sanctioned housing discrimination. Numerous decisions of federal courts chronicle this disgraceful recent history. [Justice Marshall here discusses a string of such decisions, quoting judicial descriptions that described, inter alia, "the sordid history of Virginia's, and Richmond's attempts to circumvent, defeat, and nullify the holding of *Brown I*" via "massive resistance" and a variety of "state (also federal) action tending to perpetuate apartheid of the races in ghetto patterns throughout the city."]

. . . It may well be that "the autonomy of a State is an essential component of federalism," *Garcia v. San Antonio Metropolitan Transit Authority* (1985) (O'Connor, J., dissenting), . . . but apparently this is not the case when federal judges, with nothing but their impressions to go on, choose to disbelieve the explanations of these local governments and officials. . . .

B

In my judgment, Richmond's set-aside plan also comports with the second prong of the equal protection inquiry, for it is substantially related to the interests it seeks to serve in remedying past discrimination and in ensuring that municipal contract procurement does not perpetuate that discrimination.

Like the federal provision [upheld in *Fullilove*], Richmond's is limited to five years in duration, and was not renewed when it came up for reconsideration in 1988. Like the federal provision, Richmond's contains a waiver provision freeing from its subcontracting requirements those nonminority firms that demonstrate that they cannot comply with its provisions. Like the federal provision, Richmond's has a minimal impact on innocent third parties. While the measure affects 30% of *public* contracting dollars, that translates to only 3% of overall Richmond area contracting. Finally, like the federal provision, Richmond's does not interfere with any vested right of a contractor to a particular contract; instead it operates entirely prospectively. Richmond's initiative affects only future economic arrangements and imposes only a diffuse burden on nonminority competitors—here, businesses owned or controlled by nonminorities which seek subcontracting work on public construction projects. . . .[11]

III

. . . . Today, for the first time, a majority of this Court has adopted strict scrutiny as its standard of Equal Protection Clause review of race-conscious remedial measures. This is an unwelcome development. . . .

In concluding that remedial classifications warrant no different standard of review under the Constitution than the most brutal and repugnant forms of state-sponsored racism, a majority of this Court signals that it regards racial discrimination as largely a phenomenon of the past, and that government bodies need no longer preoccupy themselves with rectifying racial injustice. I, however, do not believe this Nation is anywhere close to eradicating racial discrimination or its vestiges. In constitutionalizing its wishful thinking, the majority today does a grave disservice not only to those victims of past and present racial discrimination in this Nation whom government has sought to assist, but also to this Court's long tradition of approaching issues of race with the utmost sensitivity. . . .

The battle against pernicious racial discrimination or its effects is nowhere near won. I must dissent.

Justice Blackmun, with whom Justice Brennan joins, dissenting.

. . . I never thought that I would live to see the day when the city of Richmond, Virginia, the cradle of the Old Confederacy, sought on its own, within a narrow confine, to lessen the stark impact of persistent discrimination. But Richmond, to its great credit, acted. Yet this Court, the supposed bastion of equality, strikes down Richmond's efforts as though discrimination had never existed or was not demonstrated in this particular litigation. Justice Marshall convincingly discloses the fallacy and the shallowness of that approach. History is irrefutable, even though one might sympathize with those who—though possibly innocent in themselves—benefit from the wrongs of past decades. . . .

---

[11] The majority also faults Richmond's ordinance for including within its definition of "minority group members" not only black citizens, but also citizens who are "Spanish-speaking, Oriental, Indian, Eskimo, or Aleut persons." This is, of course, precisely the same definition Congress adopted in its set-aside legislation. *Fullilove.* Even accepting the majority's view that Richmond's ordinance is overbroad because it includes groups, such as Eskimos or Aleuts, about whom no evidence of local discrimination has been proffered, it does not necessarily follow that the balance of Richmond's ordinance should be invalidated.

For Discussion

(1) After *Croson*, must a state prove that each individual recipient of affirmative action benefits was *individually* discriminated against on the basis of race? If so, in what sense would such a program be affirmative action on the basis of race rather than a straightforward remediation of a specific and demonstrated injury?

(2) When demonstrating the kind of historical and present discrimination that "counts" for the purpose of justifying a race conscious remedial program, does *Croson* allow states to point to discrimination by private citizens, organizations, and businesses? Or must all such discrimination have been committed by a government actor? And if so, does it need to be the same government actor that is now extending the affirmative action benefits?

A year and a half later, Justice Stevens joined the *Croson* dissenters to form a majority in *Metro Broadcasting, Inc. v. FCC* (1990); relying on *Croson's* distinction of *Fullilove*, their opinion held that "benign race-conscious measures" adopted by the *federal* government were subject only to intermediate scrutiny. The 1991 appointment of Justice Clarence Thomas to replace Justice Marshall, however, yielded a new majority that quickly overruled *Metro Broadcasting* on this question. In *Adarand Constructors Inc. v. Peña* (1995), the plaintiff challenged a federal statute that offered compensation bonuses to government contractors who subcontracted work to small businesses owned by "black, Hispanic, Asian Pacific, Subcontinent Asian, and Native Americans." Justice O'Connor's opinion in *Adarand* held that strict scrutiny would henceforth apply to race based affirmative action by the federal government as well as state and local governments:

> Federal racial classifications, like those of a State, must serve a compelling governmental interest, and must be narrowly tailored to further that interest. . . . We think that requiring strict scrutiny is the best way to ensure that courts will consistently give racial classifications that kind of detailed examination, both as to ends and as to means. . . .
>
> [W]e wish to dispel the notion[, however,] that strict scrutiny is "strict in theory, but fatal in fact." The unhappy persistence of both the practice and the lingering effects of racial discrimination against minority groups in this country is an unfortunate reality, and

government is not disqualified from acting in response to it. . . . When race-based action is necessary to further a compelling interest, such action is within constitutional constraints if it satisfies the "narrow tailoring" test this Court has set out in previous cases.

Justice Scalia—who provided the fifth vote for a majority—submitted a separate opinion, writing:

> I join the opinion of the Court . . . except insofar as it may be inconsistent with the following: In my view, government can never have a "compelling interest" in discriminating on the basis of race in order to "make up" for past racial discrimination in the opposite direction. Individuals who have been wronged by unlawful racial discrimination should be made whole; but under our Constitution there can be no such thing as either a creditor or a debtor race.

Because the lower courts had upheld the federal program under intermediate scrutiny, the Supreme Court remanded the case for reconsideration under the new standard. On remand, the district court held that the program in its original form was both over- and under-inclusive and so failed strict scrutiny. *Adarand Constructors, Inc. v. Peña* (D. Colo. 1997); rev'd on other grounds, *Adarand Constructors, Inc. v. Slater* (10th Cir. 2000).

How might an affirmative action program pass muster under *Croson*? States and municipalities that continue to embrace such policies now typically rely on extensive "disparity studies." To get a sense for the detail and particularity with which such studies are conducted, consider the following description of how the Illinois Department of Transportation (IDOT) tackled the problem:

WORTH NOTING

> [A research firm hired by IDOT] collected information about prime contractors and subcontractors involved with construction, architecture, and engineering contracts awarded [from 2006 to 2008]. The study then determined whether there was a statistically significant under-utilization of DBEs [Disadvantaged Business Enterprises] by calculating the dollars each group would be expected to receive based on availability; calculating the difference between the expected and actual amount of contract dollars received; and ensuring that results were not attributable to chance. The study found that DBEs were significantly under-utilized as prime contractors.

Midwest Fence Corp. v. U.S. Department of Transportation, 840 F.3d 932 (7th Cir. 2016) (holding that IDOT's affirmative action program survived strict scrutiny). New York City conducts periodic studies as part of its Minority- and Women-owned Business Enterprise (M/WBE) program; the city's most recent report clocked in at 231 pages and concluded as follows:

> [T]here is a quantitatively significant disparity between utilization of M/WBEs and their availability in the marketplace. [A]necdotal analysis provide[s] additional corroboration of the barriers that M/WBEs face in participating in the City's procurement process. Furthermore, the evidence from the private sector analysis illustrates the substantial inequities that exist in the City's marketplace, underscoring its compelling interest in continuing to pursue remedies to address these extant gaps.
>
> *City of New York Disparity Study* (2018).

The debates over race-conscious remedial action continued after *Croson* and *Adarand*, perhaps most persistently in the context of higher education. As noted above, the paradigm for such litigation was initially set by Justice Powell's controlling concurrence in *Regents of University of California v. Bakke* (1978). That opinion's touchstone was a willingness to approve the consideration of race where used as just one element of a larger effort to achieve campus diversity. Twenty-five years later, this rationale was put to the test in two companion cases involving affirmative action at the University of Michigan: *Grutter v. Bollinger* (law school admissions) and *Gratz v. Bollinger* (undergraduate college admissions). The two cases came out differently, so reading them together—and trying to understand what constitutional differences the Court saw between them—is instructive.

Grutter v. Bollinger

Supreme Court of the United States, 2003.
539 U.S. 306.

JUSTICE O'CONNOR DELIVERED THE OPINION OF THE COURT.

This case requires us to decide whether the use of race as a factor in student admissions by the University of Michigan Law School (Law School) is unlawful.

I

A

The Law School ranks among the Nation's top law schools. It receives more than 3,500 applications each year for a class of around 350 students. Seeking to "admit a group of students who individually and collectively are among the most capable," the Law School looks for individuals with "substantial promise

for success in law school" and "a strong likelihood of succeeding in the practice of law and contributing in diverse ways to the well-being of others." More
broadly, the Law School seeks "a mix of students with varying backgrounds
and experiences who will respect and learn from each other." In 1992, the dean
of the Law School charged a faculty committee with crafting a written admissions policy to implement these goals. In particular, the Law School sought
to ensure that its efforts to achieve student body diversity complied with this
Court's most recent ruling on the use of race in university admissions. See
Regents of Univ. of Cal. v. Bakke (1978). Upon the unanimous adoption of the
committee's report by the Law School faculty, it became the Law School's official admissions policy.

The hallmark of that policy is its focus on academic ability coupled with
a flexible assessment of applicants' talents, experiences, and potential "to contribute to the learning of those around them." The policy requires admissions
officials to evaluate each applicant based on all the information available in the
file, including a personal statement, letters of recommendation, and an essay
describing the ways in which the applicant will contribute to the life and diversity of the Law School. In reviewing an applicant's file, admissions officials
must consider the applicant's undergraduate grade point average (GPA) and
Law School Admission Test (LSAT) score because they are important (if imperfect) predictors of academic success in law school. The policy stresses that
"no applicant should be admitted unless we expect that applicant to do well
enough to graduate with no serious academic problems."

. . . [T]he policy requires admissions officials to look beyond grades and
test scores to other criteria that are important to the Law School's educational
objectives. So-called " 'soft' variables" such as "the enthusiasm of recommenders,
the quality of the undergraduate institution, the quality of the applicant's essay,
and the areas and difficulty of undergraduate course selection" are all brought
to bear in assessing an "applicant's likely contributions to the intellectual and
social life of the institution."

The policy aspires to "achieve that diversity which has the potential to en-
rich everyone's education and thus make a law school class stronger than the
sum of its parts." The policy does not restrict the types of diversity contributions
eligible for "substantial weight" in the admissions process, but instead recognizes "many possible bases for diversity admissions." The policy does, however,
reaffirm the Law School's longstanding commitment to "one particular type

of diversity," that is, "racial and ethnic diversity with special reference to the inclusion of students from groups which have been historically discriminated against, like African-Americans, Hispanics and Native Americans, who without this commitment might not be represented in our student body in meaningful numbers." By enrolling a " 'critical mass' of [underrepresented] minority students," the Law School seeks to "ensur[e] their ability to make unique contributions to the character of the Law School."

The policy does not define diversity "solely in terms of racial and ethnic status." Nor is the policy "insensitive to the competition among all students for admission to the [L]aw [S]chool." Rather, the policy seeks to guide admissions officers in "producing classes both diverse and academically outstanding, classes made up of students who promise to continue the tradition of outstanding contribution by Michigan Graduates to the legal profession."

B

Petitioner Barbara Grutter is a white Michigan resident who applied to the Law School in 1996 with a 3.8 GPA and 161 LSAT score. The Law School initially placed petitioner on a waiting list, but subsequently rejected her application. . . . Petitioner alleged that respondents discriminated against her on the basis of race in violation of the Fourteenth Amendment. . . .

During the 15-day bench trial, the parties introduced extensive evidence concerning the Law School's use of race in the admissions process. Dennis Shields, Director of Admissions when petitioner applied to the Law School, testified that he did not direct his staff to admit a particular percentage or number of minority students, but rather to consider an applicant's race along with all other factors. Shields testified that at the height of the admissions season, he would frequently consult the so-called "daily reports" that kept track of the racial and ethnic composition of the class (along with other information such as residency status and gender). This was done, Shields testified, to ensure that a critical mass of underrepresented minority students would be reached so as to realize the educational benefits of a diverse student body. Shields stressed, however, that he did not seek to admit any particular number or percentage of underrepresented minority students.

Erica Munzel, who succeeded Shields as Director of Admissions, testified that " 'critical mass' " means " 'meaningful numbers' " or " 'meaningful representation,' " which she understood to mean a number that encourages underrepresented minority students to participate in the classroom and not feel isolated. Munzel stated there is no number, percentage, or range of numbers or percentages that constitute critical mass. . . . The current Dean of the Law School, Jeffrey Lehman, also testified. . . . He indicated that critical mass means numbers such that underrepresented minority students do not feel isolated or like spokespersons for their race. When asked about the extent to which race is considered in admissions, Lehman testified that it varies from one applicant to another. In some cases, according to Lehman's testimony, an applicant's race may play no role, while in others it may be a " 'determinative' " factor.

The District Court heard extensive testimony from Professor Richard Lempert, who chaired the faculty committee that drafted the 1992 policy. Lempert emphasized that the Law School seeks students with diverse interests and backgrounds to enhance classroom discussion and the educational experience both inside and outside the classroom. When asked about the policy's " 'commitment to racial and ethnic diversity with special reference to the inclusion of students from groups which have been historically discriminated against,' " Lempert explained that this language did not purport to remedy past discrimination, but rather to include students who may bring to the Law School a perspective different from that of members of groups which have not been the victims of such discrimination. Lempert acknowledged that other groups, such as Asians and Jews, have experienced discrimination, but explained they were not mentioned in the policy because individuals who are members of those groups were already being admitted to the Law School in significant numbers.

Kent Syverud was the final witness to testify about the Law School's use of race in admissions decisions. Syverud was a professor at the Law School when the 1992 admissions policy was adopted and is now Dean of Vanderbilt Law School. In addition to his testimony at trial, Syverud submitted several expert reports on the educational benefits of diversity. Syverud's testimony indicated that when a critical mass of underrepresented minority students is present, racial stereotypes lose their force because nonminority students learn there is no " 'minority viewpoint' " but rather a variety of viewpoints among minority students. . . .

We granted certiorari to resolve the disagreement among the Courts of Appeals on a question of national importance: Whether diversity is a compelling interest that can justify the narrowly tailored use of race in selecting applicants for admission to public universities.

II

A

We last addressed the use of race in public higher education over 25 years ago. [*Regents of Univ. of Cal. v. Bakke* (1978)]. . . . Since this Court's splintered decision in *Bakke*, Justice Powell's opinion announcing the judgment of the Court has served as the touchstone for constitutional analysis of race-conscious admissions policies. Public and private universities across the Nation have modeled their own admissions programs on Justice Powell's views on permissible race-conscious policies. . . . [F]or the reasons set out below, today we endorse Justice Powell's view that student body diversity is a compelling state interest that can justify the use of race in university admissions.

B

. . . Because the Fourteenth Amendment "protect[s] *persons*, not *groups*," all "governmental action based on race—a *group* classification long recognized as in most circumstances irrelevant and therefore prohibited—should be subjected to detailed judicial inquiry to ensure that the *personal* right to equal protection of the laws has not been infringed." *Adarand Constructors, Inc. v. Peña* (1995). . . .

We have held that all racial classifications imposed by government "must be analyzed by a reviewing court under strict scrutiny." This means that such classifications are constitutional only if they are narrowly tailored to further compelling governmental interests. We apply strict scrutiny to all racial classifications to " 'smoke out' illegitimate uses of race by assuring that [government] is pursuing a goal important enough to warrant use of a highly suspect tool." *Richmond v. J.A. Croson Co.* (1989) (plurality opinion).

Strict scrutiny is not "strict in theory, but fatal in fact." *Adarand Constructors, Inc. v. Peña.* Although all governmental uses of race are subject to strict scrutiny, not all are invalidated by it. . . .

III

A

With these principles in mind, we turn to the question whether the Law School's use of race is justified by a compelling state interest. Before this Court, as they have throughout this litigation, respondents assert only one justification for their use of race in the admissions process: obtaining "the educational benefits that flow from a diverse student body." In other words, the Law School asks us to recognize, in the context of higher education, a compelling state interest in student body diversity. . . .

We first wish to dispel the notion that the Law School's argument has been foreclosed, either expressly or implicitly, by our affirmative-action cases decided since *Bakke.* . . . [W]e have never held that the only governmental use of race that can survive strict scrutiny is remedying past discrimination. Nor, since *Bakke,* have we directly addressed the use of race in the context of public higher education. Today, we hold that the Law School has a compelling interest in attaining a diverse student body.

The Law School's educational judgment that such diversity is essential to its educational mission is one to which we defer. The Law School's assessment that diversity will, in fact, yield educational benefits is substantiated by respondents and their *amici.* Our scrutiny of the interest asserted by the Law School is no less strict for taking into account complex educational judgments in an area that lies primarily within the expertise of the university. Our holding today is in keeping with our tradition of giving a degree of deference to a university's academic decisions, within constitutionally prescribed limits. . . . We have long recognized that, given the important purpose of public education and the expansive freedoms of speech and thought associated with the university environment, universities occupy a special niche in our constitutional tradition. . . . Our conclusion that the Law School has a compelling interest in a diverse student body is informed by our view that attaining a diverse student body is at the heart of the Law School's proper institutional mission, and that "good faith" on the part of a university is "presumed" absent "a showing to the contrary."

As part of its goal of "assembling a class that is both exceptionally academically qualified and broadly diverse," the Law School seeks to "enroll a 'critical mass' of minority students." Brief for Respondent Bollinger et al. The Law School's interest is not simply "to assure within its student body some specified percentage of a particular group merely because of its race or ethnic origin." *Bakke* (opinion of Powell, J.). That would amount to outright racial balancing, which is patently unconstitutional. *Freeman v. Pitts* (1992) ("Racial balance is not to be achieved for its own sake"); *Richmond v. J.A. Croson Co.* Rather, the Law School's concept of critical mass is defined by reference to the educational benefits that diversity is designed to produce.

These benefits are substantial. As the District Court emphasized, the Law School's admissions policy promotes "cross-racial understanding," helps to break down racial stereotypes, and "enables [students] to better understand persons of different races." These benefits are "important and laudable," because "classroom discussion is livelier, more spirited, and simply more enlightening and interesting" when the students have "the greatest possible variety of backgrounds."

The Law School's claim of a compelling interest is further bolstered by its *amici*, who point to the educational benefits that flow from student body diversity. In addition to the expert studies and reports entered into evidence at trial, numerous studies show that student body diversity promotes learning outcomes, and "better prepares students for an increasingly diverse workforce and society, and better prepares them as professionals."

These benefits are not theoretical but real, as major American businesses have made clear that the skills needed in today's increasingly global marketplace can only be developed through exposure to widely diverse people, cultures, ideas, and viewpoints. Brief for 3M et al. as *Amici Curiae*; Brief for General Motors Corp. as *Amicus Curiae*. What is more, high-ranking retired officers and civilian leaders of the United States military assert that, "[b]ased on [their] decades of experience," a "highly qualified, racially diverse officer corps . . . is essential to the military's ability to fulfill its principle mission to provide national security." Brief for Julius W. Becton, Jr., et al. as *Amici Curiae*. The primary sources for the Nation's officer corps are the service academies and the Reserve Officers Training Corps (ROTC), the latter comprising students already admitted to participating colleges and universities. At present, "the military cannot achieve an officer corps that is *both* highly qualified *and* racially diverse unless the service academies and the ROTC used limited race-conscious recruiting and admissions policies." To fulfill its mission, the military "must be selective in admissions for training and education for the officer corps, *and* it must train and educate a highly qualified, racially diverse officer corps in a racially diverse educational setting." We agree that "[i]t requires only a small step from this analysis to conclude that our country's other most selective institutions must remain both diverse and selective." *Ibid.*

We have repeatedly acknowledged the overriding importance of preparing students for work and citizenship, describing education as pivotal to "sustaining our political and cultural heritage" with a fundamental role in maintaining the fabric of society. This Court has long recognized that "education . . . is the very foundation of good citizenship." *Brown v. Board of Education* (1954). For this reason, the diffusion of knowledge and opportunity through public institutions of higher education must be accessible to all individuals regardless of race or ethnicity. . . . And, "[n]owhere is the importance of such openness more acute than in the context of higher education." Effective participation by members of all racial and ethnic groups in the civic life of our Nation is essential if the dream of one Nation, indivisible, is to be realized.

Moreover, universities, and in particular, law schools, represent the training ground for a large number of our Nation's leaders. *Sweatt v. Painter* (1950) (describing law school as a "proving ground for legal learning and practice"). . . . The pattern is even more striking when it comes to highly selective law schools. A handful of these schools accounts for 25 of the 100 United States Senators, 74 United States Courts of Appeals judges, and nearly 200 of the more than 600 United States District Court judges.

In order to cultivate a set of leaders with legitimacy in the eyes of the citizenry, it is necessary that the path to leadership be visibly open to talented and qualified individuals of every race and ethnicity. All members of our heterogeneous society must have confidence in the openness and integrity of the educational institutions that provide this training. As we have recognized, law schools "cannot be effective in isolation from the individuals and institutions with which the law interacts." See *Sweatt v. Painter.* Access to legal education (and thus the legal profession) must be inclusive of talented and qualified individuals of every race and ethnicity, so that all members of our heterogeneous society may participate in the educational institutions that provide the training and education necessary to succeed in America.

The Law School does not premise its need for critical mass on "any belief that minority students always (or even consistently) express some characteristic minority viewpoint on any issue." Brief for Respondent Bollinger. To the contrary, diminishing the force of such stereotypes is both a crucial part of the Law School's mission, and one that it cannot accomplish with only token numbers of minority students. Just as growing up in a particular region or having particular professional experiences is likely to affect an individual's views, so too is one's own, unique experience of being a racial minority in a society, like our own, in which race unfortunately still matters. The Law School has determined, based on its experience and expertise, that a "critical mass" of underrepresented minorities is necessary to further its compelling interest in securing the educational benefits of a diverse student body.

<h2 style="text-align:center">B</h2>

Even in the limited circumstance when drawing racial distinctions is permissible to further a compelling state interest, government is still "constrained in how it may pursue that end: [T]he means chosen to accomplish the [government's] asserted purpose must be specifically and narrowly framed to accomplish that purpose." *Shaw v. Hunt* (1996). The purpose of the narrow tailoring requirement is to ensure that "the means chosen 'fit' th[e] compelling goal so closely that there is little or no possibility that the motive for the classification was illegitimate racial prejudice or stereotype." *Richmond v. J.A. Croson Co.* (plurality opinion). . . .

To be narrowly tailored, a race-conscious admissions program cannot use a quota system—it cannot "insulat[e] each category of applicants with certain desired qualifications from competition with all other applicants." *Bakke* (opinion of Powell, J.). Instead, a university may consider race or ethnicity only as a " 'plus' in a particular applicant's file," without "insulat[ing] the individual from comparison with all other candidates for the available seats." In other words, an admissions program must be "flexible enough to consider all pertinent elements of diversity in light of the particular qualifications of each applicant, and to place them on the same footing for consideration, although not necessarily according them the same weight."

We find that the Law School's admissions program bears the hallmarks of a narrowly tailored plan. As Justice Powell made clear in *Bakke*, truly individualized consideration demands that race be used in a flexible, nonmechanical way. It follows from this mandate that universities cannot establish quotas for members of certain racial groups or put members of those groups on separate admissions tracks. Nor can universities insulate applicants who belong to certain racial or ethnic groups from the competition for admission. Universities can, however, consider race or ethnicity more flexibly as a "plus" factor in the context of individualized consideration of each and every applicant.

We are satisfied that the Law School's admissions program, like the Harvard plan described by Justice Powell, does not operate as a quota. Properly understood, a "quota" is a program in which a certain fixed number or proportion of opportunities are "reserved exclusively for certain minority groups." Quotas " 'impose a fixed number or percentage which must be attained, or which cannot be exceeded,' " and "insulate the individual from comparison with all other candidates for the available seats." In contrast, "a permissible goal . . . require[s] only a good-faith effort . . . to come within a range demarcated by the goal itself," and permits consideration of race as a "plus" factor in any given case while still ensuring that each candidate "compete[s] with all other qualified applicants."

Justice Powell's distinction between the medical school's rigid 16-seat quota [challenged in *Bakke*] and Harvard's flexible use of race as a "plus" factor is instructive. Harvard certainly had minimum *goals* for minority enrollment, even if it had no specific number firmly in mind. What is more, Justice Powell flatly rejected the argument that Harvard's program was "the functional equivalent of a quota" merely because it had some " 'plus' " for race, or gave greater "weight" to race than to some other factors, in order to achieve student body diversity.

The Law School's goal of attaining a critical mass of underrepresented minority students does not transform its program into a quota. As the Harvard plan described by Justice Powell recognized, there is of course "some relationship between numbers and achieving the benefits to be derived from a diverse student body, and between numbers and providing a reasonable environment for those students admitted." "[S]ome attention to numbers," without more, does not transform a flexible admissions system into a rigid quota. . . . [T]he Law School's admissions officers testified without contradiction that they never gave race any more or less weight based on the information contained in [the daily demographic] reports. Moreover, as Justice Kennedy concedes, between 1993 and 1998, the number of African-American, Latino, and Native-American students in each class at the Law School varied from 13.5 to 20.1 percent, a range inconsistent with a quota. . . .

That a race-conscious admissions program does not operate as a quota does not, by itself, satisfy the requirement of individualized consideration. When using race as a "plus" factor in university admissions, a university's admissions program must remain flexible enough to ensure that each applicant is evaluated as an individual and not in a way that makes an applicant's race or ethnicity the defining feature of his or her application. The importance of this individualized consideration in the context of a race-conscious admissions program is paramount.

Here, the Law School engages in a highly individualized, holistic review of each applicant's file, giving serious consideration to all the ways an applicant might contribute to a diverse educational environment. The Law School affords this individualized consideration to applicants of all races. There is no policy, either *de jure* or *de facto*, of automatic acceptance or rejection based on any single "soft" variable. Unlike the program at issue in *Gratz v. Bollinger, infra*, the Law School awards no mechanical, predetermined diversity "bonuses" based on race or ethnicity. See *Gratz* (distinguishing a race-conscious admissions program that automatically awards 20 points based on race from the Harvard plan, which considered race but "did not contemplate that any single characteristic automatically ensured a specific and identifiable contribution to a university's diversity"). . . .

The Law School does not . . . limit in any way the broad range of qualities and experiences that may be considered valuable contributions to student body diversity. To the contrary, the 1992 policy makes clear "[t]here are many possible bases for diversity admissions," and provides examples of admittees who have lived or traveled widely abroad, are fluent in several languages, have overcome personal adversity and family hardship, have exceptional records of extensive community service, and have had successful careers in other fields. The Law School seriously considers each "applicant's promise of making a notable contribution to the class by way of a particular strength, attainment, or characteristic—*e.g.*, an unusual intellectual achievement, employment experience, nonacademic performance, or personal background." All applicants have the opportunity to highlight their own potential diversity contributions through the submission of a personal statement, letters of recommendation, and an essay describing the ways in which the applicant will contribute to the life and diversity of the Law School.

What is more, the Law School actually gives substantial weight to diversity factors besides race. The Law School frequently accepts nonminority applicants with grades and test scores lower than underrepresented minority applicants (and other nonminority applicants) who are rejected. This shows that the Law School seriously weighs many other diversity factors besides race that can make a . . . dispositive difference . . . as well. . . . Justice Kennedy speculates that "race is likely outcome determinative for many members of minority groups" who do not fall within the upper range of LSAT scores and grades. But the same could be said of the Harvard plan discussed approvingly by Justice Powell in *Bakke*, and indeed of any plan that uses race as one of many factors.

Petitioner and the United States argue that the Law School's plan is not narrowly tailored because race-neutral means exist to obtain the educational benefits of student body diversity that the Law School seeks. We disagree. Narrow tailoring does not require exhaustion of every conceivable race-neutral alternative. Nor does it require a university to choose between maintaining a reputation for excellence or fulfilling a commitment to provide educational opportunities to members of all racial groups. See *Wygant v. Jackson Bd. of Ed.* (1986) (alternatives must serve the interest " 'about as well' "). Narrow tailoring does, however, require serious, good faith consideration of workable race-neutral alternatives that will achieve the diversity the university seeks.

We agree with the Court of Appeals that the Law School sufficiently considered workable race-neutral alternatives. The District Court took the Law School to task for failing to consider race-neutral alternatives such as "using a lottery system" or "decreasing the emphasis for all applicants on undergraduate GPA and LSAT scores." But these alternatives would require a dramatic sacrifice of diversity, the academic quality of all admitted students, or both. . . . The United States advocates "percentage plans," recently adopted by public undergraduate institutions in Texas, Florida, and California, to guarantee admission to all students above a certain class-rank threshold in every high school in the State. The United States does not, however, explain how such plans could work for graduate and professional schools. . . .

We are satisfied that the Law School adequately considered race-neutral alternatives currently capable of producing a critical mass without forcing the Law School to abandon the academic selectivity that is the cornerstone of its educational mission. . . .

We are mindful, however, that "[a] core purpose of the Fourteenth Amendment was to do away with all governmentally imposed discrimination based on race." *Palmore v. Sidoti* (1984). Accordingly, race-conscious admissions policies must be limited in time. This requirement reflects that racial classifications, however compelling their goals, are potentially so dangerous that they may be employed no more broadly than the interest demands. . . . In the context of higher education, the durational requirement can be met by sunset provisions in race-conscious admissions policies and periodic reviews to determine whether racial preferences are still necessary to achieve student body diversity. . . .

We take the Law School at its word that it would "like nothing better than to find a race-neutral admissions formula" and will terminate its race-conscious admissions program as soon as practicable. It has been 25 years since Justice Powell first approved the use of race to further an interest in student body diversity in the context of public higher education. Since that time, the number of minority applicants with high grades and test scores has indeed increased. We expect that 25 years from now, the use of racial preferences will no longer be necessary to further the interest approved today.

IV

In summary, the Equal Protection Clause does not prohibit the Law School's narrowly tailored use of race in admissions decisions to further a compelling interest in obtaining the educational benefits that flow from a diverse student body. . . .

Justice Ginsburg, with whom Justice Breyer joins, concurring.

. . . The Court . . . observes that "[i]t has been 25 years since Justice Powell first approved the use of race to further an interest in student body diversity in the context of public higher education." . . . [But] it was only 25 years before *Bakke* that this Court declared public school segregation unconstitutional, a declaration that, after prolonged resistance, yielded an end to a law-enforced racial caste system, itself the legacy of centuries of slavery. See *Brown v. Board of Education* (1954); cf. *Cooper v. Aaron* (1958).

It is well documented that conscious and unconscious race bias, even rank discrimination based on race, remain alive in our land, impeding realization of our highest values and ideals. . . . However strong the public's desire for improved education systems may be, it remains the current reality that many minority students encounter markedly inadequate and unequal educational opportunities.

Despite these inequalities, some minority students are able to meet the high threshold requirements set for admission to the country's finest undergraduate and graduate educational institutions. As lower school education in minority communities improves, an increase in the number of such students may be anticipated. From today's vantage point, one may hope, but not firmly forecast, that over the next generation's span, progress toward nondiscrimination and genuinely equal opportunity will make it safe to sunset affirmative action.

JUSTICE SCALIA, with whom JUSTICE THOMAS joins, concurring in part and dissenting in part.

. . . The "educational benefit" that the University of Michigan seeks to achieve by racial discrimination consists, according to the Court, of " 'cross-racial understanding,' " and " 'better prepar[ation of] students for an increasingly diverse workforce and society,' " all of which is necessary not only for work, but also for good "citizenship." . . . [This] is a lesson of life rather than law—essentially the same lesson taught to . . . people three feet shorter and 20 years younger than the full-grown adults at the University of Michigan Law School, in institutions ranging from Boy Scout troops to public-school kindergartens. If properly considered an "educational benefit" at all, [this] is surely not one that is either uniquely relevant to law school or uniquely "teachable" in a formal educational setting.

And therefore: If it is appropriate for the University of Michigan Law School to use racial discrimination for the purpose of putting together a "critical mass" that will convey generic lessons in socialization and good citizenship, surely it is no less appropriate—indeed, *particularly* appropriate—for the civil service system of the State of Michigan to do so. There, also, those exposed to "critical masses" of certain races will presumably become better Americans, better Michiganders, better civil servants. . . . The nonminority individuals who are deprived of a legal education, a civil service job, or any job at all by reason of their skin color will surely understand.

Unlike a clear constitutional holding that racial preferences in state educational institutions are impermissible, or even a clear anticonstitutional holding that racial preferences in state educational institutions are OK, today's *Grutter-Gratz* split double header seems perversely designed to prolong the controversy and the litigation. Some future lawsuits will presumably focus on whether the discriminatory scheme in question contains enough evaluation of the applicant "as an individual," and sufficiently avoids "separate admissions tracks," to fall under *Grutter* rather than *Gratz*. Some will focus on whether a university has gone beyond the bounds of a " 'good faith effort' " and has so zealously pursued its "critical mass" as to make it an unconstitutional *de facto* quota system, rather than merely " 'a permissible goal.' " Other lawsuits may focus on whether, in the particular setting at issue, any educational benefits flow from racial diversity. . . . Still other suits may challenge the bona fides of the institution's expressed commitment to the educational benefits of diversity that immunize the discriminatory scheme in *Grutter.* (Tempting targets, one would suppose, will be those universities that talk the talk of multiculturalism and racial diversity in the courts but walk the walk of tribalism and racial segregation on their campuses—through minority-only student organizations, separate minority housing opportunities, separate minority student centers, even separate minority-only graduation ceremonies.) And still other suits may claim that the institution's racial preferences have gone below or above the mystical *Grutter*-approved "critical mass." Finally, litigation can be expected on behalf of minority groups intentionally short changed in the institution's composition of its generic minority "critical mass."

I do not look forward to any of these cases. The Constitution proscribes government discrimination on the basis of race, and state-provided education is no exception.

JUSTICE THOMAS, with whom JUSTICE SCALIA joins [in relevant part], concurring in part and dissenting in part.

Frederick Douglass, speaking to a group of abolitionists almost 140 years ago, delivered a message lost on today's majority:

> [I]n regard to the colored people, there is always more that is benevolent, I perceive, than just, manifested towards us. What I ask for the negro is not benevolence, not pity, not sympathy, but simply *justice.* The American people have always been anxious to know what they shall do with us. . . . I have had but one answer from the beginning. Do nothing with us! Your doing with us has already played the mischief with us. Do nothing with us! If the apples will not remain on the tree of their own strength, if they are worm-eaten at the core, if they are early ripe and disposed to fall, let them fall! . . . And if the negro cannot stand on his own legs, let him fall also. All I ask is, give him a chance to stand on his own legs! Let him alone! . . . [Y]our interference is doing him positive injury.

What the Black Man Wants: An Address Delivered in Boston, Massachusetts (January 26, 1865). Like Douglass, I believe blacks can achieve in every avenue of American life without the meddling of university administrators. . . .

The majority upholds the Law School's racial discrimination not by interpreting the people's Constitution, but by responding to a faddish slogan of the cognoscenti. Nevertheless, I concur in part in the Court's opinion. . . . I agree with the Court's holding that racial discrimination in higher education admissions will be illegal in 25 years. I respectfully dissent from the remainder of the Court's opinion and the judgment, however, because I believe that . . . the Constitution means the same thing today as it will in 300 months.

I

The majority agrees that the Law School's racial discrimination should be subjected to strict scrutiny. Before applying that standard to this case, I will briefly revisit the Court's treatment of racial classifications.

. . . A majority of the Court has validated only two circumstances where "pressing public necessity" or a "compelling state interest" can possibly justify racial discrimination by state actors. First, the lesson of *Korematsu* [*v. United States* (1944)] is that national security constitutes a "pressing public necessity," though the government's use of race to advance that objective must be narrowly tailored. Second, the Court has recognized as a compelling state interest a government's effort to remedy past discrimination for which it is responsible. *Richmond v. J.A. Croson Co.* (1989).

The contours of "pressing public necessity" can be further discerned from those interests the Court has rejected as bases for racial discrimination. For example, [consider] the sensitive role of courts in child custody determinations. In *Palmore v. Sidoti* (1984), the Court held that even the best interests of a child did not constitute a compelling state interest that would allow a state court to award custody to the father because the mother was in a mixed-race marriage. (finding the interest "substantial" but holding the custody decision could not be based on the race of the mother's new husband).

Finally, the Court has rejected an interest in remedying general societal discrimination as a justification for race discrimination. See *Croson* (plurality opinion); *id.* (Scalia, J., concurring in judgment). "Societal discrimination, without more, is too amorphous a basis for imposing a racially classified remedy" because a "court could uphold remedies that are ageless in their reach into the past, and timeless in their ability to affect the future."

Where the Court has accepted only national security, and rejected even the best interests of a child, as a justification for racial discrimination, I conclude that only those measures the State must take to provide a bulwark against anarchy, or to prevent violence, will constitute a "pressing public necessity." Cf. *Lee v. Washington* (1968) (per curiam) (Black, J., concurring). . . .

II

Unlike the majority, I seek to define with precision the interest being asserted by the Law School before determining whether that interest is so compelling as to justify racial discrimination. The Law School maintains that it wishes to obtain "educational benefits that flow from student body diversity." This statement must be evaluated carefully, because it implies that both "diversity" and "educational benefits" are components of the Law School's compelling state interest. . . .

Undoubtedly there are other ways to "better" the education of law students aside from ensuring that the student body contains a "critical mass" of under-represented minority students. Attaining "diversity," whatever it means,[3] is the mechanism by which the Law School obtains educational benefits, not an end of itself. The Law School, however, apparently believes that only a racially mixed student body can lead to the educational benefits it seeks. How, then, is the Law School's interest in these allegedly unique educational "benefits" *not* simply the forbidden interest in "racial balancing," that the majority expressly rejects?

A distinction between these two ideas (unique educational benefits based on racial aesthetics and race for its own sake) is purely sophistic—so much so that the majority uses them interchangeably. Compare *ante* ("[T]he Law School has a compelling interest in attaining a diverse student body"), with *ante* (referring to the "compelling interest in securing the *educational benefits* of a diverse student body" (emphasis added)). The Law School's argument, as facile as it is, can only be understood in one way: Classroom aesthetics yields educational benefits, racially discriminatory admissions policies are required to achieve the right racial mix, and therefore the policies are required to achieve the educational benefits. It is the *educational benefits* that are the end, or allegedly compelling state interest, not "diversity."

One must also consider the Law School's refusal to entertain changes to its current admissions system that might produce the same educational benefits. The Law School adamantly disclaims any race-neutral alternative that would reduce "academic selectivity," which would in turn "require the Law School to

---

[3]   "[D]iversity," for all of its devotees, is more a fashionable catchphrase than it is a useful term, especially when something as serious as racial discrimination is at issue. Because the Equal Protection Clause renders the color of one's skin constitutionally irrelevant to the Law School's mission, I refer to the Law School's interest as an "aesthetic." That is, the Law School wants to have a certain appearance, from the shape of the desks and tables in its classrooms to the color of the students sitting at them. I also use the term "aesthetic" because I believe it underlines the ineffectiveness of racially discriminatory admissions in actually helping those who are truly underprivileged . . . , [like] those too poor or uneducated to participate in elite higher education. . . .

become a very different institution, and to sacrifice a core part of its educational mission." Brief for Respondent Bollinger. In other words, the Law School seeks to improve marginally the education it offers without sacrificing too much of its exclusivity and elite status.

The proffered interest that the majority vindicates today, then, is not simply "diversity." Instead the Court upholds the use of racial discrimination as a tool to advance the Law School's interest in offering a marginally superior education while maintaining an elite institution. Unless each constituent part of this state interest is of pressing public necessity, the Law School's use of race is unconstitutional. I find each of them to fall far short of this standard.

III

A close reading of the Court's opinion reveals that all of its legal work is done through one conclusory statement: The Law School has a "compelling interest in securing the educational benefits of a diverse student body." No serious effort is made to explain how these benefits fit with the state interests the Court has recognized (or rejected) as compelling. . . . Today, the Court [thus] insists on radically expanding the range of permissible uses of race to something as trivial (by comparison) as the assembling of a law school class. I can only presume that the majority's failure to justify its decision by reference to any principle arises from the absence of any such principle.

Under the proper standard, there is no pressing public necessity in maintaining a public law school at all and, it follows, certainly not an elite law school. Likewise, marginal improvements in legal education do not qualify as a compelling state interest. . . . While legal education at a public university may be good policy or otherwise laudable, it is obviously not a pressing public necessity when the correct legal standard is applied. . . .

Still, even assuming that a State may, under appropriate circumstances, demonstrate a cognizable interest in having an elite law school, Michigan has failed to do so here. . . . The only cognizable state interests vindicated by operating a public law school are . . . the education of that State's citizens and the training of that State's lawyers. . . . The Law School today, however, does precious little training of those attorneys who will serve the citizens of Michigan. In 2002, graduates of the Law School made up less than 6% of applicants to the Michigan bar, even though the Law School's graduates constitute nearly 30% of all law students graduating in Michigan. Less than 16% of the Law School's graduating class elects to stay in Michigan after law school. Thus, while a mere 27% of the Law School's 2002 entering class is from Michigan, only half of these, it appears, will stay in Michigan. In sum, the Law School trains few Michigan residents and overwhelmingly serves students, who, as lawyers, leave the State of Michigan. . . .

IV

. . . The Court never explicitly holds that the Law School's desire to retain the status quo in "academic selectivity" is itself a compelling state interest, and, as I have demonstrated, it is not. Therefore, the Law School should be forced to choose between its classroom aesthetic and its exclusionary admissions system—it cannot have it both ways. With the adoption of different admissions methods, such as accepting all students who meet minimum qualifications, the Law School could achieve its vision of the racially aesthetic student body without the use of racial discrimination. The Law School concedes this, but the Court holds, implicitly and under the guise of narrow tailoring, that the Law School has a compelling state interest in doing what it wants to do. I cannot agree. . . .

WORTH NOTING

Justice Thomas observed that the Law School could use any of "[a]n infinite variety of admissions methods" not involving racial discrimination. He noted that this included merit-based systems, but—pointing to "legacy" preferences for children of alumni—doubted that "merit admissions are in fact the order of the day at the Nation's universities." And he believed that American universities' fear of " 'too many' Jews" in the early twentieth century meant the system of selective admissions they adopted at that time was driven by "the same desire to select racial winners and losers" that he said was now exhibited by the Law School.

VI

The absence of any articulated legal principle supporting the majority's principal holding suggests another rationale. I believe what lies beneath the Court's decision today are the benighted notions that one can tell when racial discrimination benefits (rather than hurts) minority groups, and that racial discrimination is necessary to remedy general societal ills. . . .

While these students may graduate with law degrees, there is no evidence that they have received a qualitatively better legal education (or become better lawyers) than if they had gone to a less "elite" law school for which they were better prepared. And the aestheticists will never address the real problems facing "underrepresented minorities," instead continuing their social experiments on other people's children. . . . "These programs stamp minorities with a badge of inferiority and may cause them to develop dependencies or to adopt an attitude that they are 'entitled' to preferences." *Adarand* (Thomas, J., concurring in part and concurring in judgment).

. . . When blacks take positions in the highest places of government, industry, or academia, it is an open question today whether their skin color played a part in their advancement. The question itself is the stigma—because either racial discrimination did play a role, in which case the person may be deemed "otherwise unqualified," or it did not, in which case asking the question itself unfairly marks those blacks who would succeed without discrimination. Is this what the Court means by "visibly open"? . . .

* * *

. . . It has been nearly 140 years since Frederick Douglass asked the intellectual ancestors of the Law School to "[d]o nothing with us!" and the Nation adopted the Fourteenth Amendment. Now we must wait another 25 years to see this principle of equality vindicated. I therefore respectfully dissent from the remainder of the Court's opinion and the judgment.

Chief Justice Rehnquist, with whom Justice Scalia, Justice Kennedy, and Justice Thomas join, dissenting.

. . . Before the Court's decision today, we consistently applied the same strict scrutiny analysis regardless of the government's purported reason for using race and regardless of the setting in which race was being used. We rejected calls to use more lenient review in the face of claims that race was being used in "good faith" because " '[m]ore than good motives should be required when government seeks to allocate its resources by way of an explicit racial classification system.' " *Adarand*. . . . Although the Court [today] recites the language of our strict scrutiny analysis, its application of that review is unprecedented in its deference. . . .

In practice, the Law School's program bears little or no relation to its asserted goal of achieving "critical mass." Respondents explain that the Law School seeks to accumulate a "critical mass" of *each* underrepresented minority group. But the record demonstrates that the Law School's admissions practices with respect to these groups differ dramatically and cannot be defended under any consistent use of the term "critical mass."

From 1995 through 2000, the Law School admitted between 1,130 and 1,310 students. Of those, between 13 and 19 were Native American, between

91 and 108 were African-American, and between 47 and 56 were Hispanic. If the Law School is admitting between 91 and 108 African-Americans in order to achieve "critical mass," thereby preventing African-American students from feeling "isolated or like spokespersons for their race," one would think that a number of the same order of magnitude would be necessary to accomplish the same purpose for Hispanics and Native Americans. Similarly, even if all of the Native American applicants admitted in a given year matriculate, which the record demonstrates is not at all the case,* how can this possibly constitute a "critical mass" of Native Americans in a class of over 350 students? . . . Surely strict scrutiny cannot permit these sorts of disparities without at least some explanation. . . .

The Court states that the Law School's goal of attaining a "critical mass" of underrepresented minority students is not an interest in merely " 'assur[ing] within its student body some specified percentage of a particular group merely because of its race or ethnic origin.' " The Court recognizes that such an interest "would amount to outright racial balancing, which is patently unconstitutional." . . . But the correlation between the percentage of the Law School's pool of applicants who are members of the three minority groups and the percentage of the admitted applicants who are members of these same groups is far too precise to be dismissed as merely the result of the school paying "some attention to [the] numbers." . . . [F]rom 1995 through 2000 the percentage of admitted applicants who were members of these minority groups closely tracked the percentage of individuals in the school's applicant pool who were from the same groups.

Table 1						
Year	Number of law school applicants	Number of African-American applicants	% of applicants who were African-American	Number of applicants admitted by the law school	Number of African-American applicants admitted	% of admitted applicants who were African-American
1995	4147	404	9.7%	1130	106	9.4%
1996	3677	342	9.3%	1170	108	9.2%
1997	3429	320	9.3%	1218	101	8.3%
1998	3537	304	8.6%	1310	103	7.9%
1999	3400	247	7.3%	1280	91	7.1%
2000	3432	259	7.5%	1249	91	7.3%

---

* Indeed, during this 5-year time period, enrollment of Native American students dropped to as low as three such students. Any assertion that such a small group constituted a "critical mass" of Native Americans is simply absurd.

Table 2						
Year	Number of law school applicants	Number of Hispanic applicants	% of applicants who were Hispanic	Number of applicants admitted by the law school	Number of Hispanic applicants admitted	% of admitted applicants who were Hispanic
1995	4147	213	*5.1%*	1130	56	*5.0%*
1996	3677	186	*5.1%*	1170	54	*4.6%*
1997	3429	163	*4.8%*	1218	47	*3.9%*
1998	3537	150	*4.2%*	1310	55	*4.2%*
1999	3400	152	*4.5%*	1280	48	*3.8%*
2000	3432	168	*4.9%*	1249	53	*4.2%*

Table 3						
Year	Number of law school applicants	Number of Native American applicants	% of applicants who were Native American	Number of applicants admitted by the law school	Number of Native American applicants admitted	% of admitted applicants who were Native American
1995	4147	45	*1.1%*	1130	14	*1.2%*
1996	3677	31	*0.8%*	1170	13	*1.1%*
1997	3429	37	*1.1%*	1218	19	*1.6%*
1998	3537	40	*1.1%*	1310	18	*1.4%*
1999	3400	25	*0.7%*	1280	13	*1.0%*
2000	3432	35	*1.0%*	1249	14	*1.1%*

. . . The tight correlation between the percentage of applicants and admittees of a given race . . . must result from careful race based planning by the Law School. It suggests a formula for admission based on the aspirational assumption that all applicants are equally qualified academically, and therefore that the proportion of each group admitted should be the same as the proportion of that group in the applicant pool. . . .

JUSTICE KENNEDY, dissenting.

The separate opinion by Justice Powell in *Regents of Univ. of Cal. v. Bakke* (1978) . . . , in my view, states the correct rule for resolving this case. The Court, however, does not apply strict scrutiny. By trying to say otherwise, it undermines both the test and its own controlling precedents. . . .

The Court, in a review that is nothing short of perfunctory, accepts the University of Michigan Law School's assurances that its admissions process meets with constitutional requirements. The majority fails to confront the reality of how the Law School's admissions policy is implemented. . . .

There was little deviation among admitted minority students during the years from 1995 to 1998. The percentage of enrolled minorities fluctuated only by 0.3%, from 13.5% to 13.8%. The number of minority students to whom offers were extended varied by just a slightly greater magnitude of 2.2%, from the high of 15.6% in 1995 to the low of 13.4% in 1998.

The District Court relied on this uncontested fact to draw an inference that the Law School's pursuit of critical mass mutated into the equivalent of a quota. Admittedly, there were greater fluctuations among enrolled minorities in the preceding years, 1987–1994, by as much as 5% or 6%. The percentage of minority offers, however, at no point fell below 12%, historically defined by the Law School as the bottom of its critical mass range. The greater variance during the earlier years, in any event, does not dispel suspicion that the school engaged in racial balancing. The data would be consistent with an inference that the Law School modified its target only twice, in 1991 (from 13% to 19%), and then again in 1995 (back from 20% to 13%). The intervening year, 1993, when the percentage dropped to 14.5%, could be an aberration, caused by the school's miscalculation as to how many applicants with offers would accept or by its redefinition, made in April 1992, of which minority groups were entitled to race-based preference.

Year	Percentage of enrolled minority students
1987	12.3%
1988	13.6%
1989	14.4%
1990	13.4%
1991	19.1%
1992	19.8%
1993	14.5%
1994	20.1%
1995	13.5%
1996	13.8%
1997	13.6%
1998	13.8%

The narrow fluctuation band raises an inference that the Law School subverted individual determination, and strict scrutiny requires the Law School to overcome the inference. Whether the objective of critical mass "is described as a quota or a goal, it is a line drawn on the basis of race and ethnic status," and so risks compromising individual assessment. *Bakke* (opinion of Powell, J.). . . .

The Constitution cannot confer the right to classify on the basis of race even in this special context absent searching judicial review. For these reasons, though I reiterate my approval of giving appropriate consideration to race in this one context, I must dissent in the present case.

Gratz v. Bollinger

Supreme Court of the United States, 2003.
539 U.S. 244.

CHIEF JUSTICE REHNQUIST delivered the opinion of the Court.

We granted certiorari in this case to decide whether "the University of Michigan's use of racial preferences in undergraduate admissions violate[s] the Equal Protection Clause of the Fourteenth Amendment. . . ." Because we find that the manner in which the University considers the race of applicants in its undergraduate admissions guidelines violates these constitutional and statutory provisions, we reverse that portion of the District Court's decision upholding the guidelines.

I

A

Petitioner[ ] Jennifer Gratz . . . applied for admission to the University of Michigan's (University) College of Literature, Science, and the Arts (LSA) as [a] resident[ ] of the State of Michigan. . . . Gratz was notified in April [1996] that the LSA was unable to offer her admission. She enrolled in the University of Michigan at Dearborn, from which she graduated in the spring of 1999. . . .

B

The University has changed its admissions guidelines a number of times during the period relevant to this litigation, and we summarize the most significant of these changes briefly. The University's Office of Undergraduate

Admissions (OUA) .... considers a number of factors in making admissions decisions, including high school grades, standardized test scores, high school quality, curriculum strength, geography, alumni relationships, and leadership. OUA also considers race. During all periods relevant to this litigation, the University has considered African-Americans, Hispanics, and Native Americans to be "underrepresented minorities," and it is undisputed that the University admits "virtually every qualified . . . applicant" from these groups. . . .

[The OUA now relies on a] "selection index," on which an applicant could score a maximum of 150 points. This index was divided linearly into ranges generally calling for admissions dispositions as follows: 100–150 (admit); 95–99 (admit or postpone); 90–94 (postpone or admit); 75–89 (delay or postpone); 74 and below (delay or reject). Each application received points based on high school grade point average, standardized test scores, academic quality of an applicant's high school, strength or weakness of high school curriculum, in-state residency, alumni relationship, personal essay, and personal achievement or leadership. Of particular significance here, under a "miscellaneous" category, an applicant was entitled to 20 points based upon his or her membership in an underrepresented racial or ethnic minority group.

II

. . . To withstand our strict scrutiny analysis, respondents must demonstrate that the University's use of race in its current admissions program employs "narrowly tailored measures that further compelling governmental interests." . . . We find that the University's policy, which automatically distributes 20 points, or one-fifth of the points needed to guarantee admission, to every single "underrepresented minority" applicant solely because of race, is not narrowly tailored to achieve the interest in educational diversity that respondents claim justifies their program. . . .

In *Bakke*, Justice Powell reiterated that "[p]referring members of any one group for no reason other than race or ethnic origin is discrimination for its own sake." He then explained, however, that in his view it would be permissible for a university to employ an admissions program in which "race or ethnic background may be deemed a 'plus' in a particular applicant's file." He explained that such a program might allow for "[t]he file of a particular black applicant [to] be examined for his potential contribution to diversity without the factor of race being decisive when compared, for example, with that of an applicant identified as an Italian-American if the latter is thought to exhibit qualities more likely to promote beneficial educational pluralism." Such a system, in Justice Powell's view, would be "flexible enough to consider all pertinent elements of diversity in light of the particular qualifications of each applicant." . . .

The current LSA policy does not provide such individualized consideration. The LSA's policy automatically distributes 20 points to every single applicant from an "underrepresented minority" group, as defined by the University. The only consideration that accompanies this distribution of points is a factual review of an application to determine whether an individual is a member of one of these minority groups. Moreover, unlike Justice Powell's example, where the race of a "particular black applicant" could be considered without being decisive, the LSA's automatic distribution of 20 points has the effect of making "the factor of race . . . decisive" for virtually every minimally qualified underrepresented minority applicant. . . .

Respondents contend that "[t]he volume of applications and the presentation of applicant information make it impractical for [LSA] to use the . . . admissions system" upheld by the Court today in *Grutter*. But the fact that the implementation of a program capable of providing individualized consideration might present administrative challenges does not render constitutional an otherwise problematic system. See *J.A. Croson Co.* (rejecting " 'administrative convenience' " as a determinant of constitutionality in the face of a suspect classification). . . .

We conclude, therefore, that because the University's use of race in its current freshman admissions policy is not narrowly tailored to achieve respondents' asserted compelling interest in diversity, the admissions policy violates the Equal Protection Clause of the Fourteenth Amendment. . . .

WORTH NOTING Justice O'Connor wrote a concurrence emphasizing the lack of "meaningful individualized review" in the undergraduate admissions program; although there was an Admissions Review Committee, the evidence in the record indicated that it was "a kind of afterthought, rather than an integral component of a system of individualized review." Justice Breyer concurred in the judgment, signing on to all of O'Connor's opinion except the last sentence stating that she joined the Court. He also joined Part I of Justice Ginsburg's dissent. Justice Thomas wrote a concurrence, joining the opinion of the Court but noting that he would hold "that a State's use of racial discrimination in higher education admissions is categorically prohibited by the Equal Protection Clause." Justice Stevens, joined by Justice Souter, dissented on the basis that Gratz and her co-petitioner lacked standing for injunctive relief, because both of them had enrolled at other institutions.

Justice Souter, with whom Justice Ginsburg joins [in relevant part], dissenting.

... The cases now contain two pointers toward the line between the valid and the unconstitutional in race-conscious admissions schemes. *Grutter* reaffirms the permissibility of individualized consideration of race to achieve a diversity of students, at least where race is not assigned a preordained value in all cases. On the other hand, Justice Powell's opinion in *Regents of Univ. of Cal. v. Bakke* (1978), rules out a racial quota or set-aside, in which race is the sole fact of eligibility for certain places in a class. Although the freshman admissions system here is subject to argument on the merits, I think it is closer to what *Grutter* approves than to what *Bakke* condemns, and should not be held unconstitutional on the current record.

The record does not describe a system with a quota like the one struck down in *Bakke*, which "insulate[d]" all nonminority candidates from competition from certain seats. The *Bakke* plan "focused *solely* on ethnic diversity" and effectively told nonminority applicants that "[n]o matter how strong their qualifications, quantitative and extracurricular, including their own potential for contribution to educational diversity, they are never afforded the chance to compete with applicants from the preferred groups for the [set-aside] special admissions seats." *Bakke* (opinion of Powell, J.).

The plan here, in contrast, lets all applicants compete for all places and values an applicant's offering for any place not only on grounds of race, but on grades, test scores, strength of high school, quality of course of study, residence, alumni relationships, leadership, personal character, socioeconomic disadvantage, athletic ability, and quality of a personal essay. A nonminority applicant who scores highly in these other categories can readily garner a selection index exceeding that of a minority applicant who gets the 20-point bonus. . . . In the Court's own words, "each characteristic of a particular applicant [is] considered in assessing the applicant's entire application." . . .

The one qualification to this description of the admissions process is that membership in an underrepresented minority is given a weight of 20 points on the 150-point scale. On the face of things, however, this assignment of specific points does not set race apart from all other weighted considerations. Nonminority students may receive 20 points for athletic ability, socioeconomic disadvantage, attendance at a socioeconomically disadvantaged or predominantly minority high school, or at the Provost's discretion; they may also receive

10 points for being residents of Michigan, 6 for residence in an underrepresented Michigan county, 5 for leadership and service, and so on.

The Court nonetheless finds fault with a scheme that "automatically" distributes 20 points to minority applicants because "[t]he only consideration that accompanies this distribution of points is a factual review of an application to determine whether an individual is a member of one of these minority groups." The objection goes to the use of points to quantify and compare characteristics, or to the number of points awarded due to race, but on either reading the objection is mistaken.

WORTH NOTING

In her separate opinion, Justice O'Connor noted some additional ways for applicants to boost their score: 5 points for personal achievement, 4 points for being the child of a University of Michigan graduate, and 3 points for an outstanding essay.

The very nature of a college's permissible practice of awarding value to racial diversity means that race must be considered in a way that increases some applicants' chances for admission. Since college admission is not left entirely to inarticulate intuition, it is hard to see what is inappropriate in assigning some stated value to a relevant characteristic, whether it be reasoning ability, writing style, running speed, or minority race. Justice Powell's plus factors necessarily are assigned some values. The college simply does by a numbered scale what the law school accomplishes in its "holistic review," *Grutter*; the distinction does not imply that applicants to the undergraduate college are denied individualized consideration or a fair chance to compete on the basis of all the various merits their applications may disclose.

Nor is it possible to say that the 20 points convert race into a decisive factor comparable to reserving minority places as in *Bakke*. Of course we can conceive of a point system in which the "plus" factor given to minority applicants would be so extreme as to guarantee every minority applicant a higher rank than every nonminority applicant in the university's admissions system. But petitioners do not have a convincing argument that the freshman admissions system operates this way. . . . It suffices for me, as it did for the District Court, that there are no *Bakke*-like set-asides and that consideration of an applicant's whole spectrum of ability is no more ruled out by giving 20 points for race than by giving the same points for athletic ability or socioeconomic disadvantage. . . .

Without knowing more about how the Admissions Review Committee actually functions, it seems especially unfair to treat the candor of the admissions plan as an Achilles' heel. In contrast to the college's forthrightness in saying just what plus factor it gives for membership in an underrepresented minority, it is worth considering the character of one alternative thrown up as preferable, because supposedly not based on race. Drawing on admissions systems used at public universities in California, Florida, and Texas, the United States contends that Michigan could get student diversity in satisfaction of its compelling interest by guaranteeing admission to a fixed percentage of the top students from each high school in Michigan.

While there is nothing unconstitutional about such a practice, it nonetheless suffers from a serious disadvantage. It is the disadvantage of deliberate obfuscation. The "percentage plans" are just as race conscious as the point scheme (and fairly so), but they get their racially diverse results without saying directly what they are doing or why they are doing it. In contrast, Michigan states its purpose directly and, if this were a doubtful case for me, I would be tempted to give Michigan an extra point of its own for its frankness. Equal protection cannot become an exercise in which the winners are the ones who hide the ball. . . .

Justice Ginsburg, with whom Justice Souter joins [and Justice Breyer joins except for the last paragraph presented below], dissenting.

. . . Educational institutions, the Court acknowledges, are not barred from any and all consideration of race when making admissions decisions. But the Court once again maintains that the same standard of review controls judicial inspection of all official race classifications. This insistence on "consistency" would be fitting were our Nation free of the vestiges of rank discrimination long reinforced by law. But we are not far distant from an overtly discriminatory past, and the effects of centuries of law-sanctioned inequality remain painfully evident in our communities and schools.

In the wake "of a system of racial caste only recently ended," large disparities endure. Unemployment, poverty, and access to health care vary disproportionately by race. Neighborhoods and schools remain racially divided. African-American and Hispanic children are all too often educated in poverty-stricken and underperforming institutions. Adult African-Americans and Hispanics generally earn less than whites with equivalent levels of education. Equally credentialed job applicants receive different receptions depending on their race. Irrational prejudice is still encountered in real estate markets and consumer transactions. "Bias both conscious and unconscious, reflecting traditional and unexamined habits of thought, keeps up barriers that must come down if equal opportunity and nondiscrimination are ever genuinely to become this country's law and practice." [Justice Ginsburg supports each of these assertions with citations to social science research.]

    . . . In implementing [the] equality instruction [of the Fourteenth Amendment], as I see it, government decisionmakers may properly distinguish between policies of exclusion and inclusion. Actions designed to burden groups long denied full citizenship stature are not sensibly ranked with measures taken to hasten the day when entrenched discrimination and its aftereffects have been extirpated. See Carter, *When Victims Happen To Be Black*, 97 Yale L.J. 420 (1988) ("[T]o say that two centuries of struggle for the most basic of civil rights have been mostly about freedom from racial categorization rather than freedom from racial oppressio[n] is to trivialize the lives and deaths of those who have suffered under racism. To pretend . . . that the issue presented in [*Regents of Univ. of Cal. v. Bakke* (1978)] was the same as the issue in [*Brown v. Board of Education* (1954)] is to pretend that history never happened and that the present doesn't exist.").

    Our jurisprudence ranks race a "suspect" category, "not because [race] is inevitably an impermissible classification, but because it is one which usually, to our national shame, has been drawn for the purpose of maintaining racial inequality." But where race is considered "for the purpose of achieving equality," no automatic proscription is in order. . . . The mere assertion of a laudable governmental purpose, of course, should not immunize a race-conscious measure from careful judicial inspection. Close review is needed "to ferret out classifications in reality malign, but masquerading as benign," and to "ensure that preferences are not so large as to trammel unduly upon the opportunities of others or interfere too harshly with legitimate expectations of persons in once-preferred groups." *Adarand* (Ginsburg, J., dissenting). . . .

    Examining in this light the admissions policy employed by the University of Michigan's College of Literature, Science, and the Arts (College), and for the reasons well stated by Justice Souter, I see no constitutional infirmity. . . .

Epilogue to the *University of Michigan* Cases

Immediately after the Court issued the *Grutter* and *Gratz* decisions, Mary Sue Coleman, the president of the University of Michigan, released the following statement:

> A majority of the Court has firmly endorsed the principle of diversity articulated by Justice Powell in the *Bakke* decision. This is a resounding affirmation that will be heard across the land—from our college classrooms to our corporate boardrooms.

> The Court has provided two important signals. The first is a green light to pursue diversity in the college classroom. The second is a road map to get us there. We will modify our undergraduate system to comply with today's ruling, but make no mistake: We will find the route that continues our commitment to a richly diverse student body.

> I believe these rulings in support of affirmative action will go down in history as among the great landmark decisions of the Supreme Court. And I am proud of the voice the University of Michigan provided in this important debate. We fought for the very principle that defines our country's greatness. Year after year, our student body proves it and now the Court has affirmed it: Our diversity is our strength.

That, however, was not the end of the story. In the 2006 election, Michigan voters voted 58%–42% to adopt the Michigan Civil Rights Initiative ("Proposition 2"), a proposal most visibly supported by an organization whose executive director was Jennifer Gratz. The voters' decision amended the Michigan Constitution's Bill of Rights to include the following new provision:

> The University of Michigan, Michigan State University, Wayne State University, and any other public college or university, community college, or school district shall not discriminate against, or grant preferential treatment to, any individual or group on the basis of race, sex, color, ethnicity, or national origin in the operation of public employment, public education, or public contracting.

Several groups brought a challenge to this provision. Their main claim was that it was an unconstitutional restructuring of the political system: While others seeking a preferential policy in admissions—on the basis, say, of alumni legacies—could secure it by persuading the institution's board of trustees, Proposition 2 required those seeking a policy giving preference on the basis of race to amend the state constitution. The challengers based their argument in large part on *Hunter v. Erickson* (1969) and *Washington v. Seattle School Dist. No. 1* (1982). *Hunter* had held invalid an Akron city charter amendment that prevented the city council from implementing any ordinance dealing with racial, religious, or ancestral discrimination in housing without the approval of a majority of the city's voters. *Seattle* invalidated a state law passed by voters' initiative that effectively prohibited busing (unless court-ordered) for purposes of desegregation.

The challenge to Proposition 2 was rejected by the district court. After the Sixth Circuit reversed, the Supreme Court granted certiorari and ruled 6–2 that Proposition 2 did not violate the federal Constitution. Justice Kennedy wrote the opinion for the majority, and Justices Ginsburg and Sotomayor dissented. Justice Kagan recused herself. *Schuette v. Coalition to Defend Affirmative Action* (2014). To this day, state law prohibits the use of affirmative action by any public educational institution in Michigan.

The *University of Texas* Litigation

For some years, the University of Texas at Austin, in an attempt to increase minority enrollment, considered race in making admissions decisions. In 1996, the Fifth Circuit held this program unconstitutional, and the Supreme Court denied review. See *Hopwood v. Texas* (5th Cir. 1996). In response, the University adopted a plan giving weight to various circumstances, including growing up in a single-family home and speaking a language other than English at home. In addition, the Legislature adopted a Top Ten Percent Law, to which Justices O'Connor, Thomas, Souter and (in a passage not presented above) Ginsburg each referred in opinions in the Michigan litigation. The law granted automatic admission to any public state college, including the University, to all students in the top 10% of their class at high schools in Texas that complied with certain standards. As a result, the percentages of African-Americans and of Hispanics were slightly higher than before the *Hopwood* decision.

After the Supreme Court's decision in *Grutter*, the University resumed consideration of race in admissions, in a manner that it deemed to be consistent with that decision. A challenge was quickly brought, asserting that the new plan could not survive strict scrutiny, because the 10% Plan had achieved sufficient diversity without the use of racial classifications. This time, the University won in the Fifth Circuit, but in *Fisher v. University of Texas at Austin* (2013) ("*Fisher I*"), the Supreme Court reversed and remanded for further consideration. Justice Kennedy wrote for a 7–1 majority, with Justice Kagan recused and only Justice Ginsburg dissenting.

Justice Kennedy wrote that "strict scrutiny . . . require[s] a court to examine with care, and not defer to, a university's 'serious, good faith consideration of workable race-neutral alternatives.' See *Grutter*. . . .

> Strict scrutiny must not be " 'strict in theory, but fatal in fact,' " *Adarand* . . . . But the opposite is also true. Strict scrutiny must not be strict in theory but feeble in fact. In order for judicial review to be meaningful, a university must make a showing that its plan is narrowly tailored to achieve the only interest that this Court has approved in this context: the benefits of a student body diversity that "encompasses a . . . broa[d] array of qualifications and characteristics of which racial or ethnic origin is but a single though important element." *Bakke* (opinion of Powell, J.).

Justice Scalia wrote a brief concurrence, noting that he adhered to the view he had expressed in *Grutter* but that Fisher had not asked the Court to overrule that case. Justice Thomas wrote a longer concurrence; he would have overruled *Grutter*. Justice Ginsburg, by contrast, would simply have affirmed the Fifth Circuit under *Grutter*. She repeated the skepticism she had expressed in *Gratz* about the purported neutrality percentage plans; "only an ostrich," she said, could regard such supposedly neutral alternatives as race unconscious.

On remand, the Fifth Circuit again upheld the plan, and the case bounced back up to the Supreme Court. It was pending when Justice Scalia died, and Justice Kagan was again recused. Accordingly, a seven-member Court decided the case. *Fisher v. University of Texas at Austin* (2013) ("*Fisher II*"). This time, by a 4–3 vote, with Justice Kennedy again writing the majority opinion and

Justices Roberts, Thomas, and Alito in dissent, the Court affirmed. This was the first time Justice Kennedy had voted in favor of an affirmative action program.

Drawing on his opinion in *Fisher I*, he emphasized that "some, but not complete judicial deference" towards an academic decision to pursue the educational benefits of diversity is proper, but that "no deference is owed when determining whether the use of race is narrowly tailored to achieve the university's permissible goals." He also stressed that although a university does not have to "choose between maintaining a reputation for excellence [and] fulfilling a commitment to provide educational opportunities to members of all racial groups," *Grutter*, it does have the burden of demonstrating that sufficient and workable race-neutral alternatives are not available.

Justice Kennedy noted an odd feature of the case: The 10% Plan took up more than 75% of the slots for incoming freshman, but Fisher had not complained about it, and the University could not change it. Thus, the case had been "litigated on a somewhat artificial basis," which could "limit its value for prospective guidance." Indeed, his opinion left open the possibility that a future challenge to the University's plan could succeed. And he appeared to endorse Ginsburg's prior observation about the Plan:

> [Texas's] Top Ten Percent Plan, though facially neutral, cannot be understood apart from its basic purpose, which is to boost minority enrollment. Percentage plans are "adopted with racially segregated neighborhoods and schools front and center stage." *Fisher I* (Ginsburg, dissenting). "It is race consciousness, not blindness to race, that drives such plans." Ibid. Consequently, petitioner cannot assert simply that increasing the University's reliance on a percentage plan would make its admissions policy more race neutral.

But in the actual case, the majority concluded that Fisher had not shown a constitutional violation. Justice Kennedy wrote: "Though a college must continually reassess its need for race-conscious review, here that assessment appears to have been done with care, and a reasonable determination was made that the University had not yet attained its goals." Fisher had failed to show that the University had a workable race-neutral alternative to "attain the benefits of diversity it sought." In response to the suggestion that the University could have expanded its percentage plan, he endorsed the view that Justice Ginsburg had previously asserted; he wrote that "the Top Ten Percent Plan, though facially neutral, cannot be understood apart from its basic purpose, which is to boost minority enrollment." And, he asserted, there were good educational reasons not to place too much emphasis on class rank.

Justice Thomas wrote a brief dissent, once again saying that *Grutter* should be overruled. And he, along with the Chief Justice, joined a long dissent by Justice Alito, which began, "Something strange has happened since our prior decision in this case." The Court, Justice Alito wrote, was "inexplicably" granting a request for deference that it had "emphatically rejected" in *Fisher I*.

The *Parents Involved* Case

The Michigan and Texas cases involved higher education. In *Parents Involved in Community Schools v. Seattle School District No. 1* (2007), the Supreme Court considered race-conscious remedies adopted by the Seattle, Washington, and Jefferson County, Kentucky (Louisville) school districts. According to Chief Justice Roberts, who wrote the lead opinion, both presented the question "whether a public school that had not operated legally segregated schools or has been found to be unitary may choose to classify students by race and rely upon that classification in making school assignments."

In Seattle, some high schools were oversubscribed, and the district used a series of tiebreakers to allocate spots. The first was preference for students with a sibling in the school. The second was race: The district was 41% white overall, with 59% classified as "other." If the racial makeup of the school was not within 10% of this allocation, then the district would choose students whose race "will serve to bring the school into balance." A third tie-breaker was geographical proximity to the school. According to the Chief Justice,

> Seattle has never operated segregated schools—legally separate schools for students of different races—nor has it ever been subject to court-ordered desegregation. It nonetheless employs the racial tiebreaker in an attempt to address the effects of racially identifiable housing patterns on school assignments. Most white students live in the northern part of Seattle, most students of other racial backgrounds in the southern part.

As for Jefferson County, it had operated under a desegregation decree from 1975 to 2000 pursuant to a judicial finding that the Louisville school district operated a public school system segregated by law. In 2000, the District Court dissolved the decree after finding that the district had achieved unitary status by eliminating "[t]o the greatest extent practicable" the vestiges of its prior policy of segregation. The next year, the County adopted the voluntary student assignment plan at issue in this case. Approximately 34 percent of the district's 97,000 students were black; most of the remaining 66 percent were white. The plan required all nonmagnet schools to maintain a minimum black enrollment of 15 percent, and a maximum black enrollment of 50 percent. Elementary schools were grouped into clusters. Parents could indicate a choice of school within their cluster, but if a school had reached the "extremes of the racial guidelines," a student whose race would contribute to the school's racial imbalance would not be assigned there.

By a 5–4 vote, the Supreme Court struck down both plans.

The Chief Justice reiterated that "when the government distributes burdens or benefits on the basis of individual racial classifications, that action is reviewed under strict scrutiny," because "racial classifications are simply too pernicious to permit any but the most exact connection between justification and classification." The Chief Justice noted that the Court cases had recognized two compelling interests for the use of race.

One compelling interest was "remedying the effects of past intentional discrimination." But that did not apply in either case before the Court: the Seattle schools had never been segregated by law, and the Louisville schools had been found by a district court to have achieved "unitary status" after decades under the desegregation decree. The Chief Justice emphasized that "the Constitution is not violated by racial imbalance in the schools, without more." Thus, "[o]nce Jefferson County achieved unitary status, it had remedied the constitutional wrong that allowed race-based assignments. Any continued use of race must be justified on some other basis." Jefferson County argued that it would be incongruous to hold that one day the Louisville school district would be constitutionally required (by the desegregation decree) to make race-based assignments, and that the next day it would be prohibited (by the Equal Protection Clause) from doing so. To this, the Chief Justice responded:

[W]hat was constitutionally required of the district prior to 2000 was the elimination of the vestiges of prior segregation—not racial proportionality in its own right. Once those vestiges were eliminated, Jefferson County was on the same footing as any other school district, and its use of race must be justified on other grounds.

The second compelling interest was "the interest in diversity in higher education." The Court relied on various distinctions, however, to hold that *Grutter* did not provide a good precedent for the practices here: the First Amendment overtones of *Grutter* were not present outside the context of higher education; the school districts' plans did not provide for individualized consideration; and by viewing race exclusively in binary terms, the school districts had approached the question too simplistically.

In a portion of the opinion with which Justice Kennedy did not concur (and which therefore spoke only for a plurality), the Chief Justice rejected an argument based on the "educational and broader socialization benefits [that] flow from a racially diverse learning environment." Whatever those benefit may be, he wrote, "In design and operation, the plans are directed only to racial balance, pure and simple, an objective this Court has repeatedly condemned as illegitimate." The plans were tailored not to achieving the degree of diversity necessary to produce the asserted benefits, but to approximate the respective district's overall demographics, as measured by a binary division:

> This working backward to achieve a particular type of racial balance, rather than working forward from some demonstration of the level of diversity that provides the purported benefits, is a fatal flaw under our existing precedent. We have many times over reaffirmed that "[r]acial balance is not to be achieved for its own sake." *Freeman v. Pitts.* . . .

The Chief Justice also suggested that the relative modesty and amorphousness of the plans—they did not result in many reassignments, and their goals were relatively wide-open—actually counted against them being considered narrowly tailored.

The Chief Justice closed with the following passage:

> The parties and their amici debate which side is more faithful to the heritage of *Brown*, but the position of the plaintiffs in *Brown* was spelled out in their brief and could not have been clearer: "[T]he

Fourteenth Amendment prevents states from according differential treatment to American children on the basis of their color or race." Brief for Appellants in *Brown I*.

What do the racial classifications at issue here do, if not accord differential treatment on the basis of race? . . . Before *Brown*, school-children were told where they could and could not go to school based on the color of their skin. The school districts in these cases have not carried the heavy burden of demonstrating that we should allow this once again—even for very different reasons.

For schools that never segregated on the basis of race, such as Seattle, or that have removed the vestiges of past segregation, such as Jefferson County, the way "to achieve a system of determining admission to the public schools on a nonracial basis," *Brown II*, is to stop assigning students on a racial basis. The way to stop discrimination on the basis of race is to stop discriminating on the basis of race. . . .

Concurring in part and concurring in the judgment, Justice Kennedy wrote a separate opinion to defend school districts' use of race-conscious mechanisms in at least some cases. Rejecting the plurality's claim that " '[t]he way to stop discrimination on the basis of race is to stop discriminating on the basis of race' " as "too dismissive" and "not sufficient to decide these cases," he argued:

A compelling interest exists in avoiding racial isolation, an interest that a school district, in its discretion and expertise, may choose to pursue. Likewise, a district may consider it a compelling interest to achieve a diverse student population. Race may be one component of that diversity, but other demographic factors, plus special talents and needs, should also be considered. . . . [But to] the extent the plurality opinion suggests the Constitution mandates that state and local school authorities must accept the status quo of racial isolation in schools, it is, in my view, profoundly mistaken."

For at least some of the reasons discussed by Chief Justice Roberts, however, Kennedy concluded that the Seattle and Louisville school districts were not actually using race in a narrowly tailored way. He went on to discuss some alternative possibilities for promoting diversity and reducing racial isolation:

School boards may pursue the goal of bringing together students of diverse backgrounds and races through other means, including strategic site selection of new schools; drawing attendance zones with general recognition of the demographics of neighborhoods; allocating resources for special programs; recruiting students and faculty in a targeted fashion; and tracking enrollments, performance, and other statistics by race. These mechanisms are race conscious but do not lead to different treatment based on a classification that tells each student he or she is to be defined by race, so it is unlikely any of them would demand strict scrutiny to be found permissible. . . .

Executive and legislative branches, which for generations now have considered these types of policies and procedures, should be permitted to employ them with candor and with confidence that a constitutional violation does not occur whenever a decisionmaker considers the impact a given approach might have on students of different races. Assigning to each student a personal designation according to a crude system of individual racial classifications is quite a different matter; and the legal analysis changes accordingly.

Justice Breyer, joined by Justices Stevens, Souter, and Ginsburg, dissented at great length. He summarized his views at the outset:

These cases consider the longstanding efforts of two local school boards to integrate their public schools. The school board plans before us resemble many others adopted in the last 50 years by primary and secondary schools throughout the Nation. All of those plans represent local efforts to bring about the kind of racially integrated education that *Brown v. Board of Education* long ago promised—efforts that this Court has repeatedly required, permitted, and encouraged local authorities to undertake. This Court has recognized that the public interests at stake in such cases are "compelling." We have approved of "narrowly tailored" plans that are no less race conscious than the plans before us. And we have understood that the Constitution *permits* local communities to adopt desegregation plans 30 even where it does not *require* them to do so.

Acknowledging the argument that the Court's cases were most fairly read to require "a more lenient standard than 'strict scrutiny' . . . in the present context," Justice Breyer observed that he would "apply the version of strict scrutiny . . . embod[ied]" by "*Grutter* and other precedents." Beginning with the interests at stake, Justice Breyer identified "three essential elements":

> First, there is a historical and remedial element: an interest in setting right the consequences of prior conditions of segregation. . . .

> Second, there is an educational element: an interest in overcoming the adverse educational effects produced by and associated with highly segregated schools. . . .

> Third, there is a democratic element: an interest in producing an educational environment that reflects the "pluralistic society" in which our children will live. It is an interest in helping our children learn to work and play together with children of different racial backgrounds. It is an interest in teaching children to engage in the kind of cooperation among Americans of all races that is necessary to make a land of 300 million people one Nation.

Justice Breyer likewise identified three factors that he believed indicated that the districts' plans were narrowly tailored:

> First, the race-conscious criteria at issue only help set the outer bounds of broad ranges. They constitute but one part of plans that depend primarily upon other, nonracial elements. . . . Choice . . . is the "predominant factor" in these plans. Race is not. Indeed, the race-conscious ranges at issue in these cases often have no effect, either because the particular school is not oversubscribed in the year in question, or because the racial makeup of the school falls within the broad range, or because the student is a transfer applicant or has a sibling at the school. . . .

> Second, broad-range limits on voluntary school choice plans are less burdensome, and hence more narrowly tailored, than other race-conscious restrictions this Court has previously approved. . . . Here, race becomes a factor only in a fraction of students' non-merit-based assignments—not in large numbers of students' merit-based applications. . . .

Third, the manner in which the school boards developed these plans itself reflects "narrow tailoring." Each plan was devised to overcome a history of segregated public schools. Each plan embodies the results of local experience and community consultation.

Justice Breyer closed by joining the battle over the legacy of *Brown*:

> [S]egregation policies did not simply tell schoolchildren "where they could and could not go to school based on the color of their skin"; they perpetuated a caste system rooted in the institutions of slavery and 80 years of legalized subordination. The lesson of history is not that efforts to continue racial segregation are constitutionally indistinguishable from efforts to achieve racial integration. Indeed, it is a cruel distortion of history to compare Topeka, Kansas, in the 1950s to Louisville and Seattle in the modern day—to equate the plight of Linda Brown (who was ordered to attend a Jim Crow school) to the circumstances of Joshua McDonald (whose request to transfer to a school closer to home was initially declined). This is not to deny that there is a cost in applying "a state-mandated racial label." But that cost does not approach, in degree or in kind, the terrible harms of slavery, the resulting caste system, and 80 years of legal racial segregation. . .

The justices in the majority believed that much of Justice Breyer's opinion was irrelevant, because addressed to situations involving *de jure* rather than *de facto* segregation. And Justice Thomas wrote a concurrence addressed largely to the fears raised by Justice Breyer of resegregation: "Racial imbalance is not segregation, and the mere incantation of terms like resegregation and remediation cannot make up the difference." He emphasized social science data indicating that black students can succeed in majority-black institutions, and cautioned, "If our history has taught us anything it has taught us to beware of elites bearing racial theories."

Justice Stevens, while joining Justice Breyer's opinion, added a brief dissent of his own to take issue with the Chief Justice's treatment of *Brown*, which he said reminded him of Anatole France's observation: "[T]he majestic equality of the la[w], . . . forbid[s] rich and poor alike to sleep under the bridges, to beg in the streets, and to steal their bread." The Chief Justice, he said, "fails to note that it was only black schoolchildren who were so ordered; indeed, the history books do not tell stories of white children struggling to attend black schools."

He emphasized that *School Comm. of Boston v. Board of Education* (1968) had dismissed for want of a substantial federal question an appeal from the decision of the Supreme Judicial Court of Massachusetts upholding a state statute mandating racial integration in the Massachusetts school system in circumstances and for purposes that he suggested were directly comparable here. He closed with the following:

> The Court has changed significantly since it decided *School Comm. of Boston* in 1968. It was then more faithful to *Brown* and more respectful of our precedent than it is today. It is my firm conviction that no Member of the Court that I joined in 1975 would have agreed with today's decision.

C. Heightened Scrutiny—Other Suspect Classifications

COURSE THEME So far, we have seen two kinds of equal protection review: rational basis and strict scrutiny. At least in their purest form, they mark the outer ends of the Court's spectrum of skepticism. But the doctrine also recognizes a range of options in between, with the choice among these options triggered by contextual considerations ranging from the class targeted for discrimination to the kinds of substantive interests that are in play.

Here is one summary of the so-called "tiers of scrutiny" that have emerged from modern doctrine:

> In considering whether state legislation violates the Equal Protection Clause of the Fourteenth Amendment, U.S. Const., Amdt. 14, § 1, we apply different levels of scrutiny to different types of classifications.

> At a minimum, a statutory classification must be rationally related to a legitimate governmental purpose. *San Antonio Independent School Dist. v. Rodriguez* (1973); *Cf. Lyng v. Automobile Workers* (1988).

> Classifications based on race or national origin, *e.g., Loving v. Virginia* (1967), and classifications affecting fundamental rights, *e.g., Harper v. Virginia Bd. of Elections* (1966), are given the most exacting scrutiny.

Between these extremes of rational basis review and strict scrutiny lies a level of intermediate scrutiny, which generally has been applied to discriminatory classifications based on sex or illegitimacy. See, *e.g.*, *Mississippi University for Women v. Hogan* (1982); *Mills v. Habluetzel* (1982); *Craig v. Boren* (1976); *Mathews v. Lucas* (1976). To withstand intermediate scrutiny, a statutory classification must be substantially related to an important governmental objective. . . .

Clark v. Jeter (1988). To the list of classifications deemed sufficiently "suspect" to require strict scrutiny, one might add alienage, *Graham v. Richardson* (1971), and religion, *Burlington N. R.R. Co. v. Ford* (1992).

Even this tripartite framework does not capture the full complexity of the situation. Sometimes, as we have seen in the context of affirmative action, the Court has arguably applied strict scrutiny with less rigor than it would in other contexts. In the context of sex discrimination, the Court has sometimes articulated intermediate scrutiny in a way that seems very much like strict scrutiny. And sometimes courts, including the Supreme Court, appear to be applying what has been called "enhanced rational basis" scrutiny, or "rational basis scrutiny with a bite." *E.g.*, *Hooper v. Bernalillo County Assessor* (1985) (veterans' benefits based on duration of in-state residence). Indeed, Justice Thurgood Marshall frequently argued that the Court should frankly adopt a sliding scale of scrutiny. *E.g.*, *Massachusetts Board of Retirement v. Murgia* (1976) (Marshall, J., dissenting). (Justice John Paul Stevens, using different terminology, advocated much the same approach. *E.g.*, *Craig v. Boren* (1976) (Stevens, J., concurring) pp. 1211–1212.) That may describe the reality of how the Court has decided cases, but the Court has not adopted that framework.

Describing the different tiers of scrutiny only begins the analysis. How should a court decide *which* level of scrutiny to apply to any given classification—particularly where existing precedent does not directly answer that question? Here's how one recent district court decision explains the inquiry:

The Supreme Court uses the following four factors to determine whether a "new" classification requires heightened scrutiny:

(1) whether the class has been historically "subjected to discrimination," *Lyng v. Castillo* (1986);

(2) whether the class has a defining characteristic that "frequently bears no relation to ability to perform or contribute
to society," *City of Cleburne v. Cleburne Living Ctr.* (1985);

(3) whether the class exhibits "obvious, immutable, or distinguishing characteristics that define them as a discrete
group," *Lyng*; and

(4) whether the class is "a minority or politically powerless."
Id.

Evancho v. Pine-Richland School District (W.D. Pa. Feb. 27, 2017) (presented
in full below at pp. 1537–1544). The *Evancho* court wasn't freelancing here; it
was building on decades of constitutional thinking about which classifications
should get special attention.

The intellectual foundation for this edifice can plausibly be traced to a
brief footnote from a case involving dairy regulation: *United States v. Carolene
Products Co.* (1938), pp. 956–959. In the course of upholding a commercial
regulation against constitutional challenge, the Court emphasized that courts
should usually defer to the government's explanation for any particular regulation without much skepticism.

> . . . [T]he existence of facts supporting [a] legislative judgment is to
> be presumed, for regulatory legislation affecting ordinary commercial
> transactions is not to be pronounced unconstitutional unless, in the
> light of the facts made known or generally assumed, it is of such a
> character as to preclude the assumption that it rests upon some ratio-
> nal basis within the knowledge and experience of the legislators. . . .

In its famous Footnote 4, however, the court flagged some important exceptions to this general rule:

> There may be narrower scope for operation of the presumption
> of constitutionality when legislation appears on its face to be within
> a specific prohibition of the Constitution, such as those of the first
> ten amendments, which are deemed equally specific when held to be
> embraced within the Fourteenth. See *Stromberg v. California* (1931)
> [(striking down statute banning red flags)]; *Lovell v. Griffin* (1938)
> [(voiding conviction for sales of a religious pamphlet)].

It is unnecessary to consider now whether legislation which restricts those political processes which can ordinarily be expected to bring about repeal of undesirable legislation is to be subjected to more exacting judicial scrutiny under the general prohibitions of the Fourteenth Amendment than are most other types of legislation. On restrictions upon the right to vote, see *Nixon v. Herndon* (1927); *Nixon v. Condon* (1932); on restraints upon the dissemination of information, see *Near v. Minnesota ex rel. Olson* (1931); *Grosjean v. American Press Co.* (1936); *Lovell v. Griffin* (1938); on interferences with political organizations, see *Stromberg v. California* (1931); *Fiske v. Kansas* (1927); *Whitney v. California* (1927); *Herndon v. Lowry* (1937); and see Holmes, J., in *Gitlow v. New York* (1925); as to prohibition of peaceable assembly, see *De Jonge v. Oregon* (1937).

Nor need we enquire whether similar considerations enter into the review of statutes directed at particular religious, *Pierce v. Society of Sisters* (1925), or national, *Meyer v. Nebraska* (1923); *Bartels v. Iowa* (1923); *Farrington v. Tokushige* (1927), or racial minorities, *Nixon v. Herndon* (1927); *Nixon v. Condon* (1932); whether prejudice against discrete and insular minorities may be a special condition, which tends seriously to curtail the operation of those political processes ordinarily to be relied upon to protect minorities, and which may call for a correspondingly more searching judicial inquiry. Compare *McCulloch v. Maryland* (1819); *South Carolina v. Barnwell Bros* (1938), and cases cited.

The first paragraph of Footnote 4 has come to reflect the idea that courts should apply close scrutiny when fundamental rights are at stake. The second paragraph suggests strict scrutiny when government action may distort the political processes. And the third paragraph indicates that strict scrutiny is appropriate when government action disfavors certain numerical minorities— those that are "discrete and insular"—that might be especially vulnerable to exploitation and abuse.

The rest of this chapter explores how the instincts sketched in Footnote 4 have played out in the Court's treatment of classifications outside of the paradigm case of racial discrimination. As you read these materials, consider the following note of skepticism expressed by Justice Rehnquist, dissenting in a pair of cases that struck down state laws disqualifying non-citizens from public employment and from the practice of law. *Sugarman v. Dougall* (1973); *In re Griffiths* (1973). Emphasizing the lack of historical evidence that the Fourteenth Amendment "was intended . . . to protect 'discrete and insular minorities' other than racial minorities," he turned his attention to Footnote 4:

> As Mr. Justice Frankfurter so aptly observed: "A footnote hardly seems to be an appropriate way of announcing a new constitutional doctrine, and the *Carolene* footnote did not purport to announce any new doctrine. . . ." *Kovacs v. Cooper* (1949) (concurring opinion). . . .
>
> The mere recitation of the words "insular and discrete minority" is hardly a constitutional reason for prohibiting state legislative classifications such as are involved here, and is not necessarily consistent with the theory propounded is that footnote. The approach taken in . . . these cases appears to be that whenever the Court feels that a societal group is "discrete and insular," it has the constitutional mandate to prohibit legislation that somehow treats the group differently from some other group.
>
> Our society, consisting of over 200 million individuals of multitudinous origins, customs, tongues, beliefs, and cultures is, to say the least, diverse. It would hardly take extraordinary ingenuity for a lawyer to find "insular and discrete" minorities at every turn in the road. Yet, unless the Court can precisely define and constitutionally justify both the terms and analysis it uses, these decisions today stand for the proposition that the Court can choose a "minority" it "feels" deserves "solicitude" and thereafter prohibit the States from classifying that "minority" differently from the "majority." I cannot find, and the Court does not cite, any constitutional authority for such a "ward of the Court" approach to equal protection.

---

1. Animus, or "Rational Basis Plus"?

In one important line of cases, we can see the Court wavering between identifying key characteristics of protected groups (on one hand) and seeking to ferret out invidious motivation by the government (on the other). The first approach tends to push the Court toward comparing some group's characteristics and circumstances to the paradigm of the African-American experience, and then reasoning toward a standard of review from there. The second approach tends to focus on the subjective animus behind much historic mistreatment of African Americans, and then inquire whether the group in question is likewise the target of comparable animus. As you read the following materials, see which way of thinking makes most sense of these cases for you. Can the two questions be separated?

James Boyd White, Keep Law Alive

(2019)

[One] way . . . our language of "discrimination" misleads is this. In some forms, at least, it assumes that the evil against which it is directed is a kind of stereotyping, that is, a false assumption that a particular individual has a set of social, personal, or physical characteristics in common with the larger group of which he is part. . . . On this view the main vice of discrimination is that people are not judged accurately on their individual merits, but lumped with others with whom they do not belong. As an economist might say, discrimination is bad because it distorts the information flow and leads to defective market judgments in social and commercial relations.

This is indeed a bad thing but it is not the heart of white racism against blacks, which I think is not so much a matter of cognition or perception as of desire. Think of what we call Jim Crow laws, for example, prohibiting blacks from drinking at white water fountains, or sitting in white waiting rooms, or going to white schools. These laws did not rest on a mistaken lumping of the individual with his or her group, but had among their other aims a totally different reward for white people: the pleasure and satisfaction of treating other people like dirt, as less than you, less than human in fact, secure in the knowledge that as beings without rights they presented no legal, economic, or physical threat. This is as base a desire as exists in human nature, but it does exist, potentially in all human beings. . . .

United States Department of Agriculture v. Moreno

Supreme Court of the United States, 1973.
413 U.S. 528.

MR. JUSTICE BRENNAN delivered the opinion of the Court.

This case requires us to consider the constitutionality of § 3(e) of the Food Stamp Act of 1964, as amended in 1971, which, with certain exceptions, excludes from participation in the food stamp program any household containing an individual who is unrelated to any other member of the household. In practical effect, § 3(e) creates two classes of persons for food stamp purposes: one class is composed of those individuals who live in households all of whose members are related to one another, and the other class consists of those individuals who live in households containing one or more members who are unrelated to the rest. The latter class of persons is denied federal food assistance. . . .

I

The federal food stamp program was established in 1964 in an effort to alleviate hunger and malnutrition among the more needy segments of our society. Eligibility for participation in the program is determined on a household rather than an individual basis. An eligible household purchases sufficient food stamps to provide that household with a nutritionally adequate diet. The household pays for the stamps at a reduced rate based upon its size and cumulative income. . . .

As initially enacted, § 3(e) defined a "household" as "a group of *related* or *non-related* individuals, who are not residents of an institution or boarding house, but are living as one economic unit sharing common cooking facilities and for whom food is customarily purchased in common." In January 1971, however, Congress redefined the term "household" [for relevant purposes] so as to include only groups of *related* individuals. Pursuant to this amendment, the Secretary of Agriculture promulgated regulations rendering ineligible for participation in the program any "household" whose members are not "all related to each other."

Appellees in this case consist of several groups of individuals who allege that, although they satisfy the income eligibility requirements for federal food assistance, they have nevertheless been excluded from the program solely because the persons in each group are not "all related to each other." . . . Appellee Sheilah Hejny is married and has three children. Although the Hejnys are indigent, they took in a 20-year-old girl, who is unrelated to them, because "we felt she had emotional problems." The Hejnys receive $144 worth of food stamps each month for $14. If they allow the 20-year-old girl to continue to live with them, they will be denied food stamps by reason of § 3(e). . . . Appellee Victoria Keppler has a daughter with an acute hearing deficiency. The daughter requires special instruction in a school for the deaf. The school is located in an area in which appellee could not ordinarily afford to live. Thus, in order to make the most of her limited resources, appellee agreed to share an apartment near the school with a woman who, like appellee, is on public assistance. Since appellee is not related to the woman, appellee's food stamps have been, and will continue to be, cut off if they continue to live together.

II

Under traditional equal protection analysis, a legislative classification must be sustained, if the classification itself is rationally related to a legitimate governmental interest. The purposes of the Food Stamp Act [as originally enacted] were expressly set forth in the congressional "declaration of policy":

> It is hereby declared to be the policy of Congress . . . to safeguard the health and wellbeing of the Nation's population and raise levels of nutrition among low income households. . . . To alleviate such hunger and malnutrition, a food stamp program is herein authorized. . . .

Regrettably, there is little legislative history to illuminate the purposes of the 1971 amendment of § 3(e). The legislative history that does exist, however, indicates that that amendment was intended to prevent so-called "hippies" and "hippie communes" from participating in the food stamp program. [The Court quotes Sen. Spessard Holland: "[T]he term 'household' was further defined so as to exclude households consisting of unrelated individuals under the age of 60, such as 'hippy' communes, which I think is a good provision in this bill." 116 Cong. Rec. 44439 (1970); see also 116 Cong. Rec. 44431 (1970) (Sen. Ellender) ("Conference Substitute adopts . . . a provision designed to exclude households consisting of unrelated individuals under the age of 60 (such as hippy communes)")].

The challenged classification clearly cannot be sustained by reference to this congressional purpose. For if the constitutional conception of "equal protection of the laws" means anything, it must at the very least mean that a bare congressional desire to harm a politically unpopular group cannot constitute a legitimate governmental interest. As a result, a purpose to discriminate against hippies cannot, in and of itself and without reference to (some independent) considerations in the public interest, justify the 1971 amendment. . . .

The Court went on to hold that the challenged classification was not "rationally related to the clearly legitimate governmental interest in minimizing fraud in the administration of the food stamp program." Justice Douglas joined the majority opinion, but wrote a separate concurrence arguing that when poor people "band[ed] together" by "congregating in households where they can better meet the adversities of poverty," it was a protected exercise of their First Amendment freedom to associate.

Justice Rehnquist dissented, joined by Chief Justice Burger:

> The Court's opinion would make a very persuasive congressional committee report arguing against the adoption of the limitation in question. Undoubtedly, Congress attacked the problem with a rather blunt instrument and, just as undoubtedly, persuasive arguments may be made that what we conceive to be its purpose will not be significantly advanced by the enactment of the limitation. But questions such as this are for Congress, rather than for this Court; our role is limited to the determination of whether there is any rational basis [for the statute.]
>
> I do not think it is unreasonable for Congress to conclude that the basic unit which it was willing to support with federal funding through food stamps is some variation on the family as we know it—a household consisting of related individuals. This unit provides a guarantee which is not provided by households containing unrelated individuals that the household exists for some purpose other than to collect federal food stamps. . . . The fact that the limitation will have unfortunate and perhaps unintended consequences . . . does not make it unconstitutional.

FOR DISCUSSION

What do you think was really going on in *Moreno*? Was this a genuine application of rational basis review?

Palmore v. Sidoti

Supreme Court of the United States, 1984.
466 U.S. 429.

CHIEF JUSTICE BURGER delivered the opinion of the Court.

We granted certiorari to review a judgment of a state court divesting a natural mother of the custody of her infant child because of her remarriage to a person of a different race.

I

When petitioner Linda Sidoti Palmore and respondent Anthony J. Sidoti, both Caucasians, were divorced in May 1980 in Florida, the mother was awarded custody of their 3-year-old daughter.

In September 1981 the father sought custody of the child by filing a petition to modify the prior judgment because of changed conditions. The change was that the child's mother was then cohabiting with a Negro, Clarence Palmore, Jr., whom she married two months later. . . . After hearing testimony from both parties and considering a court counselor's investigative report, the court . . . made a finding that "there is no issue as to either party's devotion to the child, adequacy of housing facilities, or respectability of the new spouse of either parent."

The court then addressed the recommendations of the court counselor, who had made an earlier report "in [another] case coming out of this circuit also involving the social consequences of an interracial marriage." From this vague reference to that earlier case, the court turned to the present case and noted the counselor's recommendation for a change in custody because "[t]he wife [petitioner] has chosen for herself and for her child, a life-style unacceptable to the father and to society. . . . The child . . . is, or at school age will be, subject to environmental pressures not of choice."

The court then concluded that the best interests of the child would be served by awarding custody to the father[:] "*This Court feels that despite the strides that have been made in bettering relations between the races in this country, it is inevitable that Melanie will, if allowed to remain in her present situation and attain[ ] school age and thus more vulnerable to peer pressures, suffer from the social stigmatization that is sure to come.*"

II

. . . The Florida court did not focus directly on the parental qualifications of the natural mother or her present husband, or indeed on the father's qualifications to have custody of the child. The court found that "there is no issue as to either party's devotion to the child, adequacy of housing facilities, or respectability of the new spouse of either parent." This, taken with the absence of any negative finding as to the quality of the care provided by the mother, constitutes a rejection of any claim of petitioner's unfitness to continue the custody of her child.

The court correctly stated that the child's welfare was the controlling factor. But that court was entirely candid and made no effort to place its holding on any ground other than race. Taking the court's findings and rationale at face value, it is clear that the outcome would have been different had petitioner married a Caucasian male of similar respectability.

A core purpose of the Fourteenth Amendment was to do away with all governmentally imposed discrimination based on race. See *Strauder v. West Virginia* (1880). Classifying persons according to their race is more likely to reflect racial prejudice than legitimate public concerns; the race, not the person, dictates the category. Such classifications are subject to the most exacting scrutiny; to pass constitutional muster, they must be justified by a compelling governmental interest and must be "necessary . . . to the accomplishment" of their legitimate purpose. See *Loving v. Virginia* (1967).

The State, of course, has a duty of the highest order to protect the interests of minor children, particularly those of tender years. In common with most states, Florida law mandates that custody determinations be made in the best interests of the children involved. The goal of granting custody based on the best interests of the child is indisputably a substantial governmental interest for purposes of the Equal Protection Clause.

It would ignore reality to suggest that racial and ethnic prejudices do not exist or that all manifestations of those prejudices have been eliminated. There is a risk that a child living with a stepparent of a different race may be subject to a variety of pressures and stresses not present if the child were living with parents of the same racial or ethnic origin. The question, however, is whether the reality of private biases and the possible injury they might inflict are permissible considerations for removal of an infant child from the custody of its natural mother. We have little difficulty concluding that they are not. The

Constitution cannot control such prejudices but neither can it tolerate them. Private biases may be outside the reach of the law, but the law cannot, directly or indirectly, give them effect. "Public officials sworn to uphold the Constitution may not avoid a constitutional duty by bowing to the hypothetical effects of private racial prejudice that they assume to be both widely and deeply held." *Palmer v. Thompson* (1971) (White, J., dissenting).

This is by no means the first time that acknowledged racial prejudice has been invoked to justify racial classifications. In *Buchanan v. Warley* (1917), for example, this Court invalidated a Kentucky law forbidding Negroes to buy homes in white neighborhoods.

> It is urged that this proposed segregation will promote the public peace by preventing race conflicts. Desirable as this is, and important as is the preservation of the public peace, this aim cannot be accomplished by laws or ordinances which deny rights created or protected by the Federal Constitution.

Whatever problems racially mixed households may pose for children in 1984 can no more support a denial of constitutional rights than could the stresses that residential integration was thought to entail in 1917. The effects of racial prejudice, however real, cannot justify a racial classification removing an infant child from the custody of its natural mother found to be an appropriate person to have such custody.

The judgment of the District Court of Appeal is reversed.

Moreno and *Palmore* hold that the government has no constitutionally valid interest in giving legal effect to bare animus against a disfavored group. The next case invoked the same proposition, but to more ambiguous effect. In contrast to the more unguarded admissions made by government actors in *Moreno* and *Palmore*, the defendant in *City of Cleburne* had always defended its regulation by articulating a number of interests other than bare animus. Does the Court's rejection of those alternate explanations as pretextual mean that the case involves the ordinary application of rational basis review to an ordinance that has been found—as a factual matter—to be motivated by animus? Or does the Court's holding necessarily rest on some (unstated) form of heightened scrutiny, given that rational basis review usually grants every factual inference to the government?

City of Cleburne v. Cleburne Living Center

Supreme Court of the United States, 1985.
473 U.S. 432.

JUSTICE WHITE delivered the opinion of the Court.

A Texas city denied a special use permit for the operation of a group home for the mentally retarded, acting pursuant to a municipal zoning ordinance requiring permits for such homes. The Court of Appeals for the Fifth Circuit held that mental retardation is a "quasi-suspect" classification and that the ordinance violated the Equal Protection Clause because it did not substantially further an important governmental purpose. We hold that a lesser standard of scrutiny is appropriate, but conclude that under that standard the ordinance is invalid as applied in this case.

I

In July 1980, respondent Jan Hannah purchased a building at 201 Featherston Street in the city of Cleburne, Texas, with the intention of leasing it to Cleburne Living Center, Inc. (CLC), for the operation of a group home for the mentally retarded. It was anticipated that the home would house 13 retarded men and women, who would be under the constant supervision of CLC staff members. The house had four bedrooms and two baths, with a half bath to be added. CLC planned to comply with all applicable state and federal regulations.

The city informed CLC that a special use permit would be required for the operation of a group home at the site, and CLC accordingly submitted a permit application. In response to a subsequent inquiry from CLC, the city explained that under the zoning regulations applicable to the site, a special use permit, renewable annually, was required for the construction of "[h]ospitals for the insane or feeble-minded, or alcoholic [*sic*] or drug addicts, or penal or correctional institutions." The city had determined that the proposed group home should be classified as a "hospital for the feebleminded." After holding a public hearing on CLC's application, the City Council voted 3 to 1 to deny a special use permit. . . .

II

The Equal Protection Clause of the Fourteenth Amendment . . . is essentially a direction that all persons similarly situated should be treated alike. . . .

The general rule is that legislation is presumed to be valid and will be sustained if the classification drawn by the statute is rationally related to a legitimate state interest. When social or economic legislation is at issue, the Equal Protection Clause allows the States wide latitude, and the Constitution presumes that even improvident decisions will eventually be rectified by the democratic processes.

The general rule gives way, however, when a statute classifies by race, alienage, or national origin. These factors are so seldom relevant to the achievement of any legitimate state interest that laws grounded in such considerations are deemed to reflect prejudice and antipathy—a view that those in the burdened class are not as worthy or deserving as others. For these reasons and because such discrimination is unlikely to be soon rectified by legislative means, these laws are subjected to strict scrutiny and will be sustained only if they are suitably tailored to serve a compelling state interest. . . .

Legislative classifications based on gender also call for a heightened standard of review. That factor generally provides no sensible ground for differential treatment. . . . A gender classification fails unless it is substantially related to a sufficiently important governmental interest.

Because illegitimacy is beyond the individual's control and bears "no relation to the individual's ability to participate in and contribute to society," official discriminations resting on that characteristic are also subject to somewhat heightened review. . . .

We have declined, however, to extend heightened review to differential treatment based on age:

> While the treatment of the aged in this Nation has not been wholly free of discrimination, such persons, unlike, say, those who have been discriminated against on the basis of race or national origin, have not experienced a 'history of purposeful unequal treatment' or been subjected to unique disabilities on the basis of stereotyped characteristics not truly indicative of their abilities.

Massachusetts Board of Retirement v. Murgia (1976) [(upholding a mandatory retirement age of 50 for police officers)]. The lesson of *Murgia* is that where individuals in the group affected by a law have distinguishing characteristics relevant to interests the State has the authority to implement, the courts have been very reluctant, as they should be in our federal system and with our respect for the separation of powers, to closely scrutinize legislative choices as to whether, how, and to what extent those interests should be pursued. In such cases, the Equal Protection Clause requires only a rational means to serve a legitimate end.

III

Against this background, we conclude for several reasons that the Court of Appeals erred in holding mental retardation a quasi-suspect classification calling for a more exacting standard of judicial review than is normally accorded economic and social legislation.

First, it is undeniable, and it is not argued otherwise here, that those who are mentally retarded have a reduced ability to cope with and function in the everyday world. Nor are they all cut from the same pattern: as the testimony in this record indicates, they range from those whose disability is not immediately evident to those who must be constantly cared for. They are thus different, immutably so, in relevant respects, and the States' interest in dealing with and providing for them is plainly a legitimate one. How this large and diversified group is to be treated under the law is a difficult and often a technical matter, very much a task for legislators guided by qualified professionals and not by the perhaps ill-informed opinions of the judiciary. . . .

Second, the distinctive legislative response, both national and state, to the plight of those who are mentally retarded demonstrates not only that they have unique problems, but also that the lawmakers have been addressing their difficulties in a manner that belies a continuing antipathy or prejudice and a corresponding need for more intrusive oversight by the judiciary. Thus, the Federal Government has not only outlawed discrimination against the mentally retarded in federally funded programs, see § 504 of the Rehabilitation Act of 1973, but it has also provided the retarded with the right to receive "appropriate treatment, services, and habilitation" in a setting that is "least restrictive of [their] personal liberty." Developmental Disabilities Assistance and Bill of Rights Act. In addition, the Government has conditioned federal education funds on a State's assurance that retarded children will enjoy an education that, "to the maximum extent appropriate," is integrated with that of nonmentally retarded children. Education of the Handicapped Act. The Government has also facilitated the hiring of the mentally retarded into the federal civil service by exempting them from the requirement of competitive examination. The State of Texas has similarly enacted legislation that acknowledges the special status of the mentally retarded by conferring certain rights upon them, such as "the right to live in the least restrictive setting appropriate to [their] individual needs and abilities," including "the right to live . . . in a group home." Mentally Retarded Persons Act of 1977. . . .

Third, the legislative response, which could hardly have occurred and survived without public support, negates any claim that the mentally retarded are politically powerless in the sense that they have no ability to attract the attention of the lawmakers. Any minority can be said to be powerless to assert direct control over the legislature, but if that were a criterion for higher level scrutiny by the courts, much economic and social legislation would now be suspect.

Fourth, if the large and amorphous class of the mentally retarded were deemed quasi-suspect for the reasons given by the Court of Appeals, it would be difficult to find a principled way to distinguish a variety of other groups who have perhaps immutable disabilities setting them off from others, who cannot themselves mandate the desired legislative responses, and who can claim some degree of prejudice from at least part of the public at large. One need mention in this respect only the aging, the disabled, the mentally ill, and the infirm. We are reluctant to set out on that course, and we decline to do so.

Doubtless, there have been and there will continue to be instances of discrimination against the retarded that are in fact invidious, and that are properly subject to judicial correction under constitutional norms. But the appropriate method of reaching such instances is not to create a new quasi-suspect classification and subject all governmental action based on that classification to more searching evaluation. . . . [W]e will not presume that any given legislative action, even one that disadvantages retarded individuals, is rooted in considerations that the Constitution will not tolerate.

Our refusal to recognize the retarded as a quasi-suspect class does not leave them entirely unprotected from invidious discrimination. To withstand equal protection review, legislation that distinguishes between the mentally retarded and others must be rationally related to a legitimate governmental purpose. This standard, we believe, affords government the latitude necessary both to pursue policies designed to assist the retarded in realizing their full potential, and to freely and efficiently engage in activities that burden the retarded in what is essentially an incidental manner. The State may not rely on a classification whose relationship to an asserted goal is so attenuated as to render the distinction arbitrary or irrational. Furthermore, some objectives—such as "a bare . . .

desire to harm a politically unpopular group," *United States Dept. of Agriculture v. Moreno* (1973)—are not legitimate state interests. . . .

IV

We turn to the issue of . . . whether requiring a special use permit for the Featherston home in the circumstances here deprives respondents of the equal protection of the laws. . . .

The constitutional issue is clearly posed. The city does not require a special use permit in [the relevant] zone for apartment houses, multiple dwellings, boarding and lodging houses, fraternity or sorority houses, dormitories, apartment hotels, hospitals, sanitariums, nursing homes for convalescents or the aged (other than for the insane or feebleminded or alcoholics or drug addicts), private clubs or fraternal orders, and other specified uses. It does, however, insist on a special permit for the Featherston home, and it does so, as the District Court found, because it would be a facility for the mentally retarded. May the city require the permit for this facility when other care and multiple-dwelling facilities are freely permitted?

It is true, as already pointed out, that the mentally retarded as a group are indeed different from others not sharing their misfortune, and in this respect they may be different from those who would occupy other facilities that would be permitted in an R-3 zone without a special permit. But this difference is largely irrelevant unless the Featherston home and those who would occupy it would threaten legitimate interests of the city in a way that other permitted uses such as boarding houses and hospitals would not. Because in our view the record does not reveal any rational basis for believing that the Featherston home would pose any special threat to the city's legitimate interests, we affirm the judgment below insofar as it holds the ordinance invalid as applied in this case.

The District Court found that the City Council's insistence on the permit rested on several factors.

First, the Council was concerned with the negative attitude of the majority of property owners located within 200 feet of the Featherston facility, as well as with the fears of elderly residents of the neighborhood. But mere negative attitudes, or fear, unsubstantiated by factors which are properly cognizable in a zoning proceeding, are not permissible bases for treating a home for the mentally retarded differently from apartment houses, multiple dwellings, and the like. It is plain that the electorate as a whole, whether by referendum or otherwise, could not order city action violative of the Equal Protection Clause, and the City may not avoid the strictures of that Clause by deferring to the wishes or objections of some fraction of the body politic. "Private biases may be outside the reach of the law, but the law cannot, directly or indirectly, give them effect." *Palmore v. Sidoti* (1984).

Second, the Council . . . was concerned that the facility was across the street from a junior high school, and it feared that the students might harass the occupants of the Featherston home. But the school itself is attended by about 30 mentally retarded students, and denying a permit based on such vague, undifferentiated fears is again permitting some portion of the community to validate what would otherwise be an equal protection violation.

[Third, the Council objected] to the home's location [because] it was located on "a five hundred year flood plain."[c] This concern with the possibility of a flood, however, can hardly be based on a distinction between the Featherston home and, for example, nursing homes, homes for convalescents or the aged, or sanitariums or hospitals, any of which could be located on the Featherston site without obtaining a special use permit. The same may be said of another concern of the Council—doubts about the legal responsibility for actions which the mentally retarded might take. If there is no concern about legal responsibility with respect to other uses that would be permitted in the area, such as boarding and fraternity houses, it is difficult to believe that the groups of mildly or moderately mentally retarded individuals who would live at 201 Featherston would present any different or special hazard.

Fourth, the Council was concerned with the size of the home and the number of people that would occupy it. The District Court found, and the Court of Appeals repeated, that "[i]f the potential residents of the Featherston Street home were not mentally retarded, but the home was the same in all other respects, its use would be permitted under the city's zoning ordinance." Given this finding, there would be no restrictions on the number of people who could occupy this home as a boarding house, nursing home, family dwelling, fraternity house, or dormitory. The question is whether it is rational to treat the mentally retarded differently. It is true that they suffer disability not shared by others; but why this difference warrants a density regulation that others need not observe is not at all apparent. . . .

---

[c]   The Federal Emergency Management Agency defines a five-hundred year flood plain as one which has a 1-in-500 (or 0.2%) chance of flooding during any given year.

[Similarly, concerns about concentration of population, congestion of the streets,] fire hazards, the serenity of the neighborhood, and the avoidance of danger to other residents fail rationally to justify singling out a home such as 201 Featherston for the special use permit, yet imposing no such restrictions on the many other uses freely permitted in the neighborhood.

The short of it is that requiring the permit in this case appears to us to rest on an irrational prejudice against the mentally retarded, including those who would occupy the Featherston facility and who would live under the closely supervised and highly regulated conditions expressly provided for by state and federal law.

The judgment of the Court of Appeals is affirmed insofar as it invalidates the zoning ordinance as applied to the Featherston home. The judgment is otherwise vacated, and the case is remanded.

It is so ordered.

Justice Stevens, with whom The Chief Justice joins, concurring.

The Court of Appeals disposed of this case as if a critical question to be decided were which of three clearly defined standards of equal protection review should be applied to a legislative classification discriminating against the mentally retarded. In fact, our cases have not delineated three—or even one or two—such well-defined standards. Rather, our cases reflect a continuum of judgmental responses to differing classifications which have been explained in opinions by terms ranging from "strict scrutiny" at one extreme to "rational basis" at the other. I have never been persuaded that these so-called "standards" adequately explain the decisional process. Cases involving classifications based on alienage, illegal residency, illegitimacy, gender, age, or—as in this case— mental retardation, do not fit well into sharply defined classifications.

"I am inclined to believe that what has become known as the [tiered] analysis of equal protection claims does not describe a completely logical method of deciding cases, but rather is a method the Court has employed to explain decisions that actually apply a single standard in a reasonably consistent fashion." *Craig v. Boren* (1976) (Stevens, J., concurring). In my own approach to these cases, I have always asked myself whether I could find a "rational basis" for the classification at issue. The term "rational," of course, includes a requirement that an impartial lawmaker could logically believe that the classification would serve a legitimate public purpose that transcends the harm to the members of the disadvantaged class. Thus, the word "rational"—for me at least—includes elements of legitimacy and neutrality that must always characterize the performance of the sovereign's duty to govern impartially. . . .

In every equal protection case, we have to ask certain basic questions. What class is harmed by the legislation, and has it been subjected to a "tradition of disfavor" by our laws? What is the public purpose that is being served by the law? What is the characteristic of the disadvantaged class that justifies the disparate treatment? In most cases the answer to these questions will tell us whether the statute has a "rational basis." The answers will result in the virtually automatic invalidation of racial classifications and in the validation of most economic classifications, but they will provide differing results in cases involving classifications based on alienage, gender, or illegitimacy. But that is not because we apply an "intermediate standard of review" in these cases; rather it is because the characteristics of these groups are sometimes relevant and sometimes irrelevant to a valid public purpose, or, more specifically, to the purpose that the challenged laws purportedly intended to serve.

Every law that places the mentally retarded in a special class is not presumptively irrational. The differences between mentally retarded persons and those with greater mental capacity are obviously relevant to certain legislative decisions. . . . Even so, the Court of Appeals correctly observed that through ignorance and prejudice the mentally retarded "have been subjected to a history of unfair and often grotesque mistreatment." . . . The record convinces me that [the] permit [in this case] was required because of the irrational fears of neighboring property owners, rather than for the protection of the mentally retarded persons who would reside in respondent's home. . . .

Accordingly, I join the opinion of the Court.

JUSTICE MARSHALL, with whom JUSTICE BRENNAN and JUSTICE BLACKMUN join, concurring in the judgment in part and dissenting in part.

. . . The Court holds the ordinance invalid on rational-basis grounds and disclaims that anything special, in the form of heightened scrutiny, is taking place. Yet Cleburne's ordinance surely would be valid under the traditional rational-basis test applicable to economic and commercial regulation. . . . [T]he Court's heightened-scrutiny discussion is [particularly] puzzling given that Cleburne's ordinance is invalidated only after being subjected to precisely the sort of probing inquiry associated with heightened scrutiny. To be sure, the

Court does not label its handiwork heightened scrutiny, and perhaps the method employed must hereafter be called "second order" rational-basis review rather than "heightened scrutiny." But however labeled, the rational-basis test invoked today is most assuredly not the rational-basis test of *Williamson v. Lee Optical of Oklahoma, Inc.* (1955). . . .

The Court, for example, concludes that legitimate concerns for fire hazards or the serenity of the neighborhood do not justify singling out respondents to bear the burdens of these concerns, for analogous permitted uses appear to pose similar threats. Yet under the traditional and most minimal version of the rational-basis test, "reform may take one step at a time, addressing itself to the phase of the problem which seems most acute to the legislative mind." *Williamson v. Lee Optical.* The "record" is said not to support the ordinance's classifications, but under the traditional standard we do not sift through the record to determine whether policy

WORTH NOTING

In a portion of his opinion not presented here, Justice Marshall dissented from the Court's decision to strike down the zoning ordinance only "as applied" (which had the limited result of forbidding its application only to Cleburne Living Center's proposed group home on Featherston Street), rather than on its face (which would have forbidden its application in all circumstances).

decisions are squarely supported by a firm factual foundation. *Minnesota v. Clover Leaf Creamery Co.* (1981). Finally, the Court further finds it "difficult to believe" that the retarded present different or special hazards inapplicable to other groups. In normal circumstances, the burden is not on the legislature to convince the Court that the lines it has drawn are sensible; legislation is presumptively constitutional, and a State "is not required to resort to close distinctions or to maintain a precise, scientific uniformity with reference" to its goals.

I share the Court's criticisms of the overly broad lines that Cleburne's zoning ordinance has drawn. But if the ordinance is to be invalidated for its imprecise classifications, it must be pursuant to more powerful scrutiny than the minimal rational-basis test used to review classifications affecting only economic and commercial matters. The same imprecision in a similar ordinance that required opticians but not optometrists to be licensed to practice, see *Williamson v. Lee Optical,* . . . would hardly be fatal to the statutory scheme. . . .

2.   Gender

The paradigmatic equal protection violation is exclusion on the basis of race. As a practical matter, this has meant that the equality jurisprudence for other protected classes has been heavily influenced by forms and considerations that were originally established in the race context. Serena Mayeri, *Reasoning from Race: Feminism, Law, and the Civil Right Revolutions* (2011); John D. Skrentny, *The Minority Rights Revolution* (2002). The process of identifying other suspect categories has thus often involved comparisons to the pathologies of racial thinking. And that has required courts to ask which aspects of "out group" exclusion are most significant: Animus and the risk of exclusion as aggression? Stereotyping and the risk of misperception? Self-dealing, structural indifference, and the risk of political process failures? Or something else?

For much of American history, constitutional law was basically indifferent to sex and gender classifications. A couple of milestones help make the point. While the Fifteenth Amendment prohibited racial discrimination in voting rights in 1870, it wasn't until 1920 that the Nineteenth Amendment prohibited sex-based limitations on the right to vote. *Strauder v. West Virginia* (1880) proclaimed the right of African Americans to serve on juries on an equal basis; sex-based classifications in jury selection, on the other hand, were upheld by the Supreme Court as late as *Hoyt v. Florida* (1961). The story of how constitutional law came to treat sex discrimination seriously is complicated—the result of a sea change in social attitudes, as well as a sophisticated litigation campaign carefully developed by women's rights advocates turning to courts as a vehicle for legal change.

a.   Facial Classification—Gender

In *Bradwell v. Illinois* (1873), the Supreme Court held that the Fourteenth Amendment did not require a state to license a married woman to practice law. Joined by two other justices, Justice Bradley said in concurrence:

. . . [T]he civil law, as well as nature herself, has always recognized a wide difference in the respective spheres and destinies of man and woman. Man is, or should be, woman's protector and defender. The natural and proper timidity and delicacy which belongs to the female sex evidently unfits it for many of the occupations of civil life. The Constitution of the family organization, which is founded in the divine ordinance as well as in the nature of things, indicates the domestic sphere as that which properly belongs to the domain and functions of womanhood. The harmony, not to say identity, of interest and views which belong, or should belong, to the family institution is repugnant to the idea of a woman adopting a distinct and independent career from that of her husband.

So firmly fixed was this sentiment in the founders of the common law that it became a maxim of that system of jurisprudence that a woman had no legal existence separate from her husband, who was regarded as her head and representative in the social state, and, notwithstanding some recent modifications of this civil status, many of the special rules of law flowing from and dependent upon this cardinal principle still exist in full force in most states. One of these is that a married woman is incapable, without her husband's consent, of making contracts which shall be binding on her or him. . . .

It is true that many women are unmarried and not affected by any of the duties, complications, and incapacities arising out of the married state, but these are exceptions to the general rule. The paramount destiny and mission of woman are to fulfill the noble and benign offices of wife and mother. This is the law of the Creator. And the rules of civil society must be adapted to the general constitution of things, and cannot be based upon exceptional cases. . . .

Recall that during the Progressive Era, and into the 1930s, progressive forces generally favored laws providing special protection for women in the workplace. In *Muller v. Oregon* (1908), the Supreme Court unanimously upheld a statute that limited the working hours of women in factories and laundries to ten hours per day. Justice Brewer's opinion asserted:

CROSS REFERENCE   For more extended presentations of *Muller*, see pp. 188–189 and 1352–1354.

History discloses the fact that woman has always been dependent upon man. . . . As minors, though not to the same extent, she has been looked upon in the courts as needing especial care that her rights may be preserved. . . . [E]ven with . . . [the] increase of [women's] capacity for business affairs it is still true that in the struggle for subsistence she is not an equal competitor with her brother. . . . [S]ome legislation to protect her seems necessary to secure a real equality of right . . . , and legislation designed for her protection may be sustained, even when like legislation is not necessary for men, and could not be sustained. . . .

The two sexes differ in structure of body, in the functions to be performed by each, in the amount of physical strength, in the capacity for long continued labor, particularly when done standing, . . . the self-reliance which enables one to assert full rights, and in the capacity to maintain the struggle for subsistence. This difference justifies a difference in legislation, and upholds that which is designed to compensate for some of the burdens which rest upon her. . . .

Although the conservative majority in *Adkins v. Children's Hospital* (1923) cited the recently enacted Nineteenth Amendment as one justification for striking down a law prescribing a minimum wage for women workers, the majority in the climactic case of *West Coast Hotel v. Parrish* (1937) reverted to an expression of special solicitude for women workers as a basis for overruling *Adkins*.

In *Goesaert v. Cleary* (1948), the Supreme Court upheld a Michigan statute that required bartenders to be licensed in all cities having a population of 50,000 or more, but provided that no female could be so licensed unless she were "the wife or daughter of the male owner" of a licensed liquor establishment. Justice Frankfurter wrote for the Court:

Beguiling as the subject is, it need not detain us long. To ask whether or not the Equal Protection of the Laws Clause of the Fourteenth Amendment barred Michigan from making the classification the State has made between wives and daughters of owners of liquor places and wives and daughters of non-owners, is one of those rare instances where to state the question is in effect to answer it.

We are, to be sure, dealing with a historic calling. We meet the alewife, sprightly and ribald, in Shakespeare, but centuries before him she played a role in the social life of England. . . . [Even so, the] Constitution does not require situations "which are different in fact or opinion to be treated in law as though they were the same." *Tigner v. State of Texas* (1940). Since bartending by women may, in the allowable legislative judgment, give rise to moral and social problems against which it may devise preventive measures, the legislature need not go to the full length of prohibition if it believes that as to a defined group of females other factors are operating which either eliminate or reduce the moral and social problems otherwise calling for prohibition. Michigan evidently believes that the oversight assured through ownership of a bar by a barmaid's husband or father minimizes hazards that may confront a barmaid without such protecting oversight. This Court is certainly not in a position to gainsay such belief by the Michigan legislature. . . .

Nor is it unconstitutional for Michigan to withdraw from women the occupation of bartending because it allows women to serve as waitresses where liquor is dispensed. [The legislature may have had sufficient reasons to allow] women to be waitresses in a liquor establishment over which a man's ownership provides control.

Justice Rutledge, joined by Justices Douglas and Murphy, dissented. He regarded the distinction drawn by the statute as "invidious":

The statute arbitrarily discriminates between male and female owners of liquor establishments. A male owner, although he himself is always absent from his bar, may employ his wife and daughter as barmaids. A female owner may neither work as a barmaid herself nor employ her daughter in that position, even if a man is always present in the establishment to keep order. This inevitable result of the classification belies the assumption that the statute was motivated by a legislative solicitude for the moral and physical well-being of women who, but for the law, would be employed as barmaids. Since there could be no other conceivable justification for such discrimination against women owners of liquor establishments, the statute should be held invalid as a denial of equal protection.

The middle of the twentieth century was a period of great social ferment, featuring a profound transformation in attitudes towards the roles and status of women. By the time of the Supreme Court's 1971 decision in *Reed v. Reed*, sex discrimination was already being seen in a different light. The *Reed* case involved a challenge to an Idaho statute requiring that "males must be preferred to females" when probate courts were choosing between otherwise equally situated administrators for a decedent's estate.

The Court struck down the Idaho requirement as an unconstitutional discrimination on the basis of sex:

> In applying [the Equal Protection Clause], this Court has consistently recognized that the Fourteenth Amendment does not deny to States the power to treat different classes of persons in different ways. The Equal Protection Clause of that amendment does, however, deny to States the power to legislate that different treatment be accorded to persons placed by a statute into different classes on the basis of criteria wholly unrelated to the objective of that statute. A classification "must be reasonable, not arbitrary, and must rest upon some ground of difference having a fair and substantial relation to the object of the legislation, so that all persons similarly circumstanced shall be treated alike." *Royster Guano Co. v. Virginia* (1920). The question presented by this case, then, is whether a difference in the sex of competing applicants for letters of administration bears a rational relationship to a state objective that is sought to be advanced by the operation of [this statute]. . . .

> Clearly the objective of reducing the workload on probate courts by [adopting a mandatory rule of thumb] is not without some legitimacy. The crucial question, however, is whether [the statute] advances that objective in a manner consistent with the command of the Equal Protection Clause. We hold that it does not. To give a mandatory preference to members of either sex over members of the other, merely to accomplish the elimination of hearings on the merits, is to make the very kind of arbitrary legislative choice forbidden by the Equal Protection Clause of the Fourteenth Amendment; and whatever may be said as to the positive values of avoiding intrafamily controversy, the choice in this context may not lawfully be mandated solely on the basis of sex.

Although *Reed* purported to apply rational basis scrutiny, it rejected the type of argument that usually suffices to uphold a classification under that level of scrutiny. *Stanley v. Illinois* (1972), though decided as a matter of due process, was to similar effect. Under Illinois law, the children of unwed fathers (but not of unwed mothers) became wards of the state, without any inquiry into the individual's fitness. The Supreme Court was willing to assume "that most unmarried fathers are unsuitable and neglectful parents," and it recognized that "[t]he establishment of prompt efficacious procedures to achieve legitimate state ends is a proper state interest worthy of cognizance in constitutional adjudication," but it held that an individualized determination was constitutionally required.

A year after *Stanley*, the Supreme Court struck down a federal military benefits statute that made it harder for women than for men to claim their spouses as dependents. *Frontiero v. Richardson* (1973). Eight justices agreed that the statute was unconstitutional, but there was no majority opinion on what level of scrutiny to apply. Writing for the four-justice plurality, Justice Brennan said that the discriminatory classification required "close judicial scrutiny":

> Appellant Sharron Frontiero, a lieutenant in the United States Air Force, sought increased quarters allowances, and housing and medical benefits for her husband, appellant Joseph Frontiero, on the ground that he was her "dependent." Although such benefits would automatically have been granted with respect to the wife of a male member of the uniformed services, appellant's application was denied because she failed to demonstrate that her husband was dependent on her for more than one-half of his support. . . .

> There can be no doubt that our Nation has had a long and unfortunate history of sex discrimination. Traditionally, such discrimination was rationalized by an attitude of "romantic paternalism" which, in practical effect, put women, not on a pedestal, but in a cage. . . . [I]t can hardly be doubted that, in part because of the high visibility of the sex characteristic, women still face pervasive, although at times more subtle, discrimination in our educational institutions, in the job market and, perhaps most conspicuously, in the political arena.

> Moreover, since sex, like race and national origin, is an immutable characteristic determined solely by the accident of birth, the

imposition of special disabilities upon the members of a particular sex because of their sex would seem to violate "the basic concept of our system that legal burdens should bear some relationship to individual responsibility. . . ." And what differentiates sex from such non-suspect statuses as intelligence or physical disability, and aligns it with the recognized suspect criteria, is that the sex characteristic frequently bears no relation to ability to perform or contribute to society. As a result, statutory distinctions between the sexes often have the effect of invidiously relegating the entire class of females to inferior legal status without regard to the actual capabilities of its individual members. . . .

With these considerations in mind, we can only conclude that classifications based upon sex, like classifications based upon race, alienage, or national origin, are inherently suspect, and must therefore be subjected to strict judicial scrutiny. Applying the analysis mandated by that stricter standard of review, it is clear that the statutory scheme now before us is constitutionally invalid.

Justice Stewart concurred in the judgment, writing only that he "agree[d] that the statutes before us work an invidious discrimination in violation of the Constitution." Justice Powell concurred in the judgment along with Chief Justice Burger and Justice Blackmun, but he objected that "it is unnecessary for the Court in this case to characterize sex as a suspect classification, with all of the far-reaching implications of such a holding." Justice Rehnquist dissented for the reasons stated in the majority opinion of the district court. Here are excerpts from that opinion:

It seems clear that the reason Congress established a conclusive presumption in favor of married service men was to avoid imposing on the uniformed services a substantial administrative burden of requiring actual proof from some 200,000 male officers and over 1,000,000 enlisted men that their wives were actually dependent upon them. . . .

Such a presumption made to facilitate administration of the law does not violate the equal protection guarantee of the Constitution if it does not unduly burden or oppress one of the classes upon which it operates. . . . The alleged injustice of the distinction lies in the possibility that some married service men are getting "windfall" payments, while married service women are denied them. . . .

[W]e are of the opinion that the incidental bestowal of some undeserved benefits on male members of the uniformed services does not so unreasonably burden female members that the administrative classification should be ruled unconstitutional. . . . The dilemma [a contrary] rule would produce is illustrated dramatically in the instant situation. The Court would be faced with a Hobson-like choice in fashioning a remedy: either strike down the conclusive presumption in favor of married service men, forcing the services to invest the added time and expense necessary to administer the law accurately, or require the presumption to be applied to both male and female married members, thereby abandoning completely the concept of dependency in fact upon which Congress intended to base the extension of benefits.

For Discussion

(1) Who was injured by the legislative classification struck down in *Frontiero*, and in what way?

(2) Assuming that a showing of actual dependency is required, does it constitute sex discrimination to provide benefits to members of the armed services who have dependents? Would your answer depend on any particular data?

(3) Testifying at his confirmation hearings in 1975 for a seat on the Supreme Court, Judge John Paul Stevens said that adoption of the Equal Rights Amendment would be of primarily psychological importance. (The relevant text of that proposal reads: "Equality of rights under the law shall not be denied or abridged . . . on account of sex.") What do you suppose he meant?

For the next several years, the Court continued to decide sex discrimination cases without clearly resolving what level of scrutiny should apply. In *Kahn v. Shevin* (1974), the Court voted 6–3 to uphold a Florida law that gave widows, but not widowers, an annual $500 property tax exemption. "Whether from overt discrimination or from the socialization process of a male-dominated culture," wrote Justice Douglas for the Court, "the job market is inhospitable to the woman seeking any but the lowest paid jobs." The problem was particularly acute for a widow, because "in many cases . . . [she] will find herself suddenly forced into a job market with which she is unfamiliar, and in which, because of her former economic dependency, she will have fewer skills to offer." Thus, the differential had a "fair and substantial relation" to the object of the legislation.

In *Schlesinger v. Ballard* (1975), the Court voted 5–4 to uphold a Navy "up or out" policy under which women had thirteen years to attain promotions necessary to continued service, but men had only nine. In the majority's view, this classification did not reflect "archaic and overbroad generalizations," as in *Reed* and *Frontiero*, but, rather—given then-current "restrictions on women officers' participation in combat and in most sea duty," which had not been challenged in the case—"the demonstrable fact that male and female line officers in the Navy are *not* similarly situated with respect to opportunities for professional service."

Nine weeks later, however, the Court invalidated a provision of the Social Security Act that allowed benefits to mothers of minor children who survive the wage earner, but not to fathers. *Weinberger v. Wiesenfeld* (1975). The unanimous opinion in *Wiesenfeld* was written by Justice Brennan, author of the *Frontiero* plurality opinion. Without stating a formal level of scrutiny, he concluded that the classification rested on an assumption (male workers are more vital to their families' support than female workers) that was "archaic and overbroad," even if "not entirely without empirical support." And the following month, in *Stanton v. Stanton* (1975), the Court invalidated a provision of Utah law that provided post-divorce child support for females to age 18 and for males to age 21. The Court said that it did not need "to decide whether a classification based on sex is inherently suspect," because as in *Reed* this classification imposed "criteria wholly unrelated" to the statute's objective. Only Justice Rehnquist dissented, on the ground that the constitutional issue was not properly presented.

WORTH NOTING

Note that in all of these cases other than *Stanton*, the classification was challenged by a man. Why do you suppose that pattern emerged? It persisted in the next case, in which a majority finally coalesced in support of a form of heightened scrutiny for gender classifications.

Craig v. Boren

Supreme Court of the United States, 1976.
429 U.S. 190.

MR. JUSTICE BRENNAN delivered the opinion of the Court.

The interaction of two sections of an Oklahoma statute . . . prohibits the sale of "nonintoxicating" 3.2% beer to males under the age of 21 and to females under the age of 18. The question to be decided is whether such a gender-based differential constitutes a denial to males 18–20 years of age of the equal protection of the laws in violation of the Fourteenth Amendment.

This action was brought in the District Court for the Western District of Oklahoma on December 20, 1972, by appellant Craig, a male then between 18 and 21 years of age, and by appellant Whitener, a licensed vendor of 3.2% beer. The complaint sought declaratory and injunctive relief against enforcement of the gender-based differential on the ground that it constituted invidious discrimination against males 18–20 years of age. . . .

II

A

Analysis may appropriately begin with the reminder that *Reed v. Reed* (1971) emphasized that statutory classifications that distinguish between males and females are "subject to scrutiny under the Equal Protection Clause." To withstand constitutional challenge, previous cases establish that classifications by gender must serve important governmental objectives and must be substantially related to achievement of those objectives. Thus, in *Reed* the objectives of "reducing the workload on probate courts," and "avoiding intrafamily controversy," were deemed of insufficient importance to sustain use of an overt gender criterion in the appointment of administrators of intestate decedents' estates. Decisions following *Reed* similarly have rejected administrative ease and convenience as sufficiently important objectives to justify gender-based classifications. . . .[6]

---

[6]   *Kahn v. Shevin* (1974) and *Schlesinger v. Ballard* (1975), upholding the use of gender-based classifications, rested upon the Court's perception of the laudatory purposes of those laws as remedying disadvantageous conditions suffered by women in economic and military life. Needless to say, in this case Oklahoma does not suggest that the age-sex differential was enacted to ensure the availability of 3.2% beer for women as compensation for previous deprivations.

Reed v. Reed has also provided the underpinning for decisions that have invalidated statutes employing gender as an inaccurate proxy for other, more germane bases of classification. Hence, "archaic and overbroad" generalizations concerning the financial position of servicewomen and working women could not justify use of a gender line in determining eligibility for certain governmental entitlements. Similarly, increasingly outdated misconceptions concerning the role of females in the home rather than in the "marketplace and world of ideas" were rejected as loose-fitting characterizations incapable of supporting state statutory schemes that were premised upon their accuracy. In light of the weak congruence between gender and the characteristic or trait that gender purported to represent, it was necessary that the legislatures choose either to realign their substantive laws in a gender-neutral fashion, or to adopt procedures for identifying those instances where the sex-centered generalization actually comported with fact. . . .

We turn then to the question whether . . . the difference between males and females with respect to the purchase of 3.2% beer warrants the differential in age drawn by the Oklahoma statute. We conclude that it does not. . . .

C

We accept for purposes of discussion the District Court's identification of the objective underlying [the Oklahoma statute] as the enhancement of traffic safety. Clearly, the protection of public health and safety represents an important function of state and local governments. However, appellees' statistics in our view cannot support the conclusion that the gender-based distinction closely serves to achieve that objective and therefore the distinction cannot under *Reed* withstand equal protection challenge.

The appellees introduced a variety of statistical surveys. First, an analysis of arrest statistics for 1973 demonstrated that 18–20-year-old male arrests for "driving under the influence" and "drunkenness" substantially exceeded female arrests for that same age period. Similarly, youths aged 17–21 were found to be overrepresented among those killed or injured in traffic accidents, with males again numerically exceeding females in this regard. Third, a random roadside survey in Oklahoma City revealed that young males were more inclined to drive and drink beer than were their female counterparts. Fourth, Federal Bureau of Investigation nationwide statistics exhibited a notable increase in arrests for "driving under the influence." Finally, statistical evidence gathered in other jurisdictions, particularly Minnesota and Michigan, was offered to corroborate

Oklahoma's experience by indicating the pervasiveness of youthful participation in motor vehicle accidents following the imbibing of alcohol. Conceding that "the case is not free from doubt," the District Court nonetheless concluded that this statistical showing substantiated "a rational basis for the legislative judgment underlying the challenged classification."

Even were this statistical evidence accepted as accurate, it nevertheless offers only a weak answer to the equal protection question presented here. The most focused and relevant of the statistical surveys, arrests of 18–20-year-olds for alcohol-related driving offenses, exemplifies the ultimate unpersuasiveness of this evidentiary record. Viewed in terms of the correlation between sex and the actual activity that Oklahoma seeks to regulate driving while under the influence of alcohol the statistics broadly establish that .18% of females and 2% of males in that age group were arrested for that offense. While such a disparity is not trivial in a statistical sense, it hardly can form the basis for employment of a gender line as a classifying device. Certainly if maleness is to serve as a proxy for drinking and driving, a correlation of 2% must be considered an unduly tenuous "fit."[12] Indeed, prior cases have consistently rejected the use of sex as a decisionmaking factor even though the statutes in question certainly rested on far more predictive empirical relationships than this.[13]

Moreover, the statistics exhibit a variety of other shortcomings that seriously impugn their value to equal protection analysis. Setting aside the obvious methodological problems,[14] the surveys do not adequately justify the salient features of Oklahoma's gender-based traffic-safety law. None purports to measure the use and dangerousness of 3.2% beer as opposed to alcohol generally, a detail that is of particular importance since, in light of its low alcohol level, Oklahoma apparently considers the 3.2% beverage to be "nonintoxicating."

[12]   Obviously, arrest statistics do not embrace all individuals who drink and drive. But for purposes of analysis, this "underinclusiveness" must be discounted somewhat by the shortcomings inherent in this statistical sample, see n. 14, *infra*. In any event, we decide this case in light of the evidence offered by Oklahoma and know of no way of extrapolating these arrest statistics to take into account the driving and drinking population at large, including those who avoided arrest.

[13]   For example, we can conjecture that in *Reed v. Reed*, Idaho's apparent premise that women lacked experience in formal business matters (particularly compared to men) would have proved to be accurate in substantially more than 2% of all cases. And in both *Frontiero* and *Weinberger v. Wiesenfeld* (1975), we expressly found appellees' empirical defense of mandatory dependency tests for men but not women to be unsatisfactory, even though we recognized that husbands are still far less likely to be dependent on their wives than vice versa.

[14]   The very social stereotypes that find reflection in age-differential laws, are likely substantially to distort the accuracy of these comparative statistics. Hence "reckless" young men who drink and drive are transformed into arrest statistics, whereas their female counterparts are chivalrously escorted home. Moreover, the Oklahoma surveys, gathered under a regime where the age-differential law in question has been in effect, are lacking in controls necessary for appraisal of the actual effectiveness of the male 3.2% beer prohibition. . . .

Okla. Stat., Tit. 37, § 163.1. Moreover, many of the studies, while graphically documenting the unfortunate increase in driving while under the influence of alcohol, make no effort to relate their findings to age-sex differentials as involved here. Indeed, the only survey that explicitly centered its attention upon young drivers and their use of beer albeit apparently not of the diluted 3.2% variety reached results that hardly can be viewed as impressive in justifying either a gender or age classification.[16]

There is no reason to belabor this line of analysis. It is unrealistic to expect either members of the judiciary or state officials to be well versed in the rigors of experimental or statistical technique. But this merely illustrates that proving broad sociological propositions by statistics is a dubious business, and one that inevitably is in tension with the normative philosophy that underlies the Equal Protection Clause. Suffice to say that the showing offered by the appellees does not satisfy us that sex represents a legitimate, accurate proxy for the regulation of drinking and driving. In fact, when it is further recognized that Oklahoma's statute prohibits only the selling of 3.2% beer to young males and not their drinking the beverage once acquired (even after purchase by their 18–20-year-old female companions), the relationship between gender and traffic safety becomes far too tenuous to satisfy *Reed*'s requirement that the gender-based difference be substantially related to achievement of the statutory objective. . . .

In fact, social science studies that have uncovered quantifiable differences in drinking tendencies dividing along both racial and ethnic lines strongly suggest the need for application of the Equal Protection Clause in preventing discriminatory treatment that almost certainly would be perceived as invidious.[22] In sum, the principles embodied in the Equal Protection Clause are not to be rendered inapplicable by statistically measured but loose-fitting generalities concerning the drinking tendencies of aggregate groups. . . .

---

[16]   The random roadside survey of drivers conducted in Oklahoma City during August 1972 found that . . . 16.5% of the men and 11.4% of the women had consumed some alcoholic beverage within two hours of the interview. Finally, a blood alcohol concentration greater than .01% was discovered in 14.6% of the males compared to 11.5% of the females. . . .

[22]   In the past, some States have acted upon their notions of the drinking propensities of entire groups in fashioning their alcohol policies. The most typical recipient of this treatment has been the American Indian; indeed, several States established criminal sanctions for the sale of alcohol to an Indian or "half or quarter breed Indian." [The Court here cites five state statutes that by then had been repealed.] Other statutes and constitutional provisions proscribed the introduction of alcoholic beverages onto Indian reservations. . . . While Indian-oriented provisions were the most common, state alcohol beverage prohibitions also have been directed at other groups, notably German, Italian, and Catholic immigrants. See, *e.g.*, J. Higham, *Strangers in the Land* (1975). The repeal of most of these laws signals society's perception of the unfairness and questionable constitutionality of singling out groups to bear the brunt of alcohol regulation.

We conclude that the gender-based differential contained in Okla. Stat., Tit. 37, § 245 constitutes a denial of the equal protection of the laws to males aged 18–20 and reverse the judgment of the District Court.

It is so ordered.

WORTH NOTING

Justice Powell, concurring, expressed dissatisfaction with a "two-tier" approach to equal protection and reservations about the creation of a third, intermediate tier. But he agreed that gender-based classifications should be subject "to a more critical examination than is normally applied when 'fundamental' constitutional rights and 'suspect classes' are not present." Even if the statistics showed that young men drink, drive, and get into accidents more than young women, Justice Powell did not think these facts supported "a fair and substantial relation" between the object of the legislation and the classification, which he said was "so easily circumvented as to be virtually meaningless."

MR. JUSTICE STEVENS, concurring.

There is only one Equal Protection Clause. It requires every State to govern impartially. It does not direct the courts to apply one standard of review in some cases and a different standard in other cases. Whatever criticism may be leveled at a judicial opinion implying that there are at least three such standards applies with the same force to a double standard.

I am inclined to believe that what has become known as the two-tiered analysis of equal protection claims does not describe a completely logical method of deciding cases, but rather is a method the Court has employed to explain decisions that actually apply a single standard in a reasonably consistent fashion. I also suspect that a careful explanation of the reasons motivating particular decisions may contribute more to an identification of that standard than an attempt to articulate it in all-encompassing terms. It may therefore be appropriate for me to state the principal reasons which persuaded me to join the Court's opinion.

In this case, the classification is not as obnoxious as some the Court has condemned,[1] nor as inoffensive as some the Court has accepted. It is objectionable because it is based on an accident of birth, because it is a mere remnant of the now almost universally rejected tradition of discriminating against males in this age bracket, and because, to the extent it reflects any physical difference

---

[1]   Men as a general class have not been the victims of the kind of historic, pervasive discrimination that has disadvantaged other groups.

between males and females, it is actually perverse.[3] The question then is whether the traffic safety justification put forward by the State is sufficient to make an otherwise offensive classification acceptable.

The classification is not totally irrational. For the evidence does indicate that there are more males than females in this age bracket who drive and also more who drink. Nevertheless, there are several reasons why I regard the justification as unacceptable. It is difficult to believe that the statute was actually intended to cope with the problem of traffic safety, since it has only a minimal effect on access to a not very intoxicating beverage and does not prohibit its consumption. Moreover, the empirical data submitted by the State accentuate the unfairness of treating all 18–20-year-old males as inferior to their female counterparts. The legislation imposes a restraint on 100% of the males in the class allegedly because about 2% of them have probably violated one or more laws relating to the consumption of alcoholic beverages. It is unlikely that this law will have a significant deterrent effect either on that 2% or on the law-abiding 98%. But even assuming some such slight benefit, it does not seem to me that an insult to all of the young men of the State can be justified by visiting the sins of the 2% on the 98%.

WORTH NOTING Justice Blackmun concurred in the majority opinion except for a portion, not presented here, rejecting an argument that the 21st Amendment protected the state law against an equal-protection challenge. While Blackmun agreed with the majority's conclusion on that score, he did not share its reasoning.

Mr. Justice Stewart, concurring in the judgment.

. . . . The disparity created by these Oklahoma statutes amounts to total irrationality. For the statistics upon which the State now relies, whatever their other shortcomings, wholly fail to prove or even suggest that 3.2% beer is somehow more deleterious when it comes into the hands of a male aged 18–20 than of a female of like age. The disparate statutory treatment of the sexes here, without even a colorably valid justification or explanation, thus amounts to invidious discrimination.

---

[3]   Because males are generally heavier than females, they have a greater capacity to consume alcohol without impairing their driving ability than do females.

Mr. Chief Justice Burger, dissenting.

. . . Without an independent constitutional basis supporting the right asserted or disfavoring the classification adopted, I can justify no substantive constitutional protection other than the normal [rational basis] protection afforded by the Equal Protection Clause. The means employed by the Oklahoma Legislature to achieve the objectives sought may not be agreeable to some judges, but since eight Members of the Court think the means not irrational, I see no basis for striking down the statute as violative of the Constitution simply because we find it unwise, unneeded, or possibly even a bit foolish. . . .

Mr. Justice Rehnquist, dissenting.

The Court's disposition of this case is objectionable on two grounds. First is its conclusion that *men* challenging a gender-based statute which treats them less favorably than women may invoke a more stringent standard of judicial review than pertains to most other types of classifications. Second is the Court's enunciation of this standard, without citation to any source, as being that "classifications by gender must serve *important* governmental objectives and must be *substantially* related to achievement of those objectives." *Ante* (emphasis added). The only redeeming feature of the Court's opinion, to my mind, is that it apparently signals a retreat by those who joined the plurality opinion in *Frontiero v. Richardson* (1973) from their view that sex is a "suspect" classification for purposes of equal protection analysis. I think the Oklahoma statute challenged here need pass only the "rational basis" equal protection analysis expounded in cases such as *McGowan v. Maryland* (1961) and *Williamson v. Lee Optical Co.* (1955), and I believe that it is constitutional under that analysis.

I

. . . Subsequent to *Frontiero*, the Court has declined to hold that sex is a suspect class, *Stanton v. Stanton* (1975), and no such holding is imported by the Court's resolution of this case. However, the Court's application here of an elevated or "intermediate" level scrutiny, like that invoked in cases dealing with discrimination against females, raises the question of why the statute here should be treated any differently from countless legislative classifications unrelated to sex which have been upheld under a minimum rationality standard. . . .

Most obviously unavailable to support any kind of special scrutiny in this case, is a history or pattern of past discrimination, such as was relied on by the plurality in *Frontiero* to support its invocation of strict scrutiny. There is no suggestion in the Court's opinion that males in this age group are in any way peculiarly disadvantaged, subject to systematic discriminatory treatment, or otherwise in need of special solicitude from the courts. . . .

[B]efore today, no decision of this Court has applied an elevated level of scrutiny to invalidate a statutory discrimination harmful to males, except where the statute impaired an important personal interest protected by the Constitution. There being no such interest here, and there being no plausible argument that this is a discrimination against females,[1] the Court's reliance on our previous sex-discrimination cases is ill-founded. It treats gender classification as a talisman which—without regard to the rights involved or the persons affected—calls into effect a heavier burden of judicial review.

The Court's conclusion that a law which treats males less favorably than females "must serve important governmental objectives and must be substantially related to achievement of those objectives" apparently comes out of thin air. The Equal Protection Clause contains no such language, and none of our previous cases adopt that standard. I would think we have had enough difficulty with the two standards of review which our cases have recognized—the norm of "rational basis," and the "compelling state interest" required where a "suspect classification" is involved—so as to counsel weightily against the insertion of still another "standard" between those two. How is this Court to divine what objectives are important? How is it to determine whether a particular law is "substantially" related to the achievement of such objective, rather than related in some other way to its achievement? Both of the phrases used are so diaphanous and elastic as to invite subjective judicial preferences or prejudices relating to particular types of legislation, masquerading as judgments whether such legislation is directed at "important" objectives or, whether the relationship to those objectives is "substantial" enough. . . .

[E]ven if we manage to avoid both confusion and the mirroring of our own preferences in the development of this new doctrine, the thousands of judges in other courts who must interpret the Equal Protection Clause may not be so fortunate.

---

[1]   I am not unaware of the argument from time to time advanced, that all discriminations between the sexes ultimately redound to the detriment of females, because they tend to reinforce "old notions" restricting the roles and opportunities of women. As a general proposition applying equally to all sex categorizations, I believe that this argument was implicitly found to carry little weight in our decisions upholding gender-based differences. See *Schlesinger v. Ballard* (1975); *Kahn v. Shevin* (1974). Seeing no assertion that it has special applicability to the situation at hand, I believe it can be dismissed as an insubstantial consideration.

II

[Under t]he applicable rational-basis test . . . , application of the Equal Protection Clause in a context not justifying an elevated level of scrutiny does not demand "mathematical nicety" or the elimination of all inequality. Those cases recognize that the practical problems of government may require rough accommodations of interests, and hold that such accommodations should be respected unless no reasonable basis can be found to support them. Whether the same ends might have been better or more precisely served by a different approach is no part of the judicial inquiry under the traditional minimum rationality approach. . . .

The rationality of a statutory classification for equal protection purposes does not depend upon the statistical "fit" between the class and the trait sought to be singled out. It turns on whether there may be a sufficiently higher incidence of the trait within the included class than in the excluded class to justify different treatment. Therefore the present equal protection challenge to this gender-based discrimination poses only the question whether the incidence of drunk driving among young men is sufficiently greater than among young women to justify differential treatment. Notwithstanding the Court's critique of the statistical evidence, that evidence suggests clear differences between the drinking and driving habits of young men and women. Those differences are grounds enough for the State reasonably to conclude that young males pose by far the greater drunk-driving hazard, both in terms of sheer numbers and in terms of hazard on a per-driver basis. The gender-based difference in treatment in this case is therefore not irrational. . . .

Craig v. Boren adopted a newly-formalized "intermediate scrutiny" standard that required sex classifications to be "substantially related" to the achievement of "important governmental objectives." Some such classifications continued to survive. In *Rostker v. Goldberg* (1981), for example, the Supreme Court held that the Military Selective Service Act does not violate the Constitution by only requiring males to register for the draft. The majority, per Justice Rehnquist, stressed the anticipation that any future draft would be for combat troops, for which women were not then eligible. (That changed incrementally over time, and Secretary of Defense Ashton Carter announced in December 2015 that all combat positions would be open to women, without exceptions. In light of the new draft policy, a district court held that the gender-based draft classification is now unconstitutional, but the Fifth Circuit reversed on the ground that *Rostker* controls and that only the Supreme Court can overrule it. *National Coalition for Men v. Selective Service System* (5th Cir. 2020) (petition for certiorari pending).

The Supreme Court has decided two cases involving single-sex admissions in higher education. The first was *Mississippi University for Women v. Hogan* (1982), involving a state nursing school that offered a 4-year baccalaureate program in nursing open only to women. Joe Hogan—a registered nurse who lived in Columbus, where the university was located—brought suit when his application to the program was rejected solely because of his sex. The Court upheld his claim and ruled the discriminatory admission policy unconstitutional.

Writing for the majority in *Hogan*, Justice O'Connor drew on language from *Personnel Administrator of Massachusetts v. Feeney* (1979) to note that "any state law overtly or covertly designed to prefer males over females in public employment would require an exceedingly persuasive justification to withstand a constitutional challenge." She then repeated what had become the standard formulation: the university could survive constitutional review "only by showing at least that the classification serves 'important governmental objectives and that the discriminatory means employed' are 'substantially related to the achievement of those objectives.' " The Court rejected Mississippi's argument that the school's admissions policy compensated for discrimination against women; there was no showing that women lacked opportunities in nursing when the school opened its doors in 1971. On the contrary, the policy "tends to perpetuate the stereotyped view of nursing as an exclusively woman's job." And given that men were allowed to audit classes or participate in continuing education at the school, there was no showing that the presence of men in classes would undermine the school's educational objective.

WORTH NOTING

There were three dissenting opinions in *Hogan*. Chief Justice Burger contended that, because the majority emphasized traditional female domination of nursing, "a State might well be justified in maintaining, for example, the option of an all women's business school or liberal arts program." Justice Blackmun emphasized that Mississippi offered baccalaureate programs in nursing at two other state universities, in Jackson and Hattiesburg. And Justice Powell, joined by Justice Rehnquist, noting that coeducation was, historically, "a novel educational theory," decried the condemnation of what he termed "an element of diversity that has characterized much of American education and enriched much of American life."

Hogan set the stage for the following case, which has become the canonical statement of the "intermediate scrutiny" standard of review.

United States v. Virginia

Supreme Court of the United States, 1996.
518 U.S. 515.

JUSTICE GINSBURG delivered the opinion of the Court.

Virginia's public institutions of higher learning include an incomparable military college, Virginia Military Institute (VMI). The United States maintains that the Constitution's equal protection guarantee precludes Virginia from reserving exclusively to men the unique educational opportunities VMI affords. We agree. . . .

II

. . . [Established] in 1839 as one of the Nation's first state military colleges, . . . VMI today enrolls about 1,300 men as cadets. Its academic offerings in the liberal arts, sciences, and engineering are also available at other public colleges and universities in Virginia. But VMI's mission is special. It is the mission of the school

> to produce educated and honorable men, prepared for the varied work of civil life, imbued with love of learning, confident in the functions and attitudes of leadership, possessing a high sense of public service, advocates of the American democracy and free enterprise system, and ready as citizen-soldiers to defend their country in time of national peril.

Mission Study Committee of the VMI Board of Visitors, Report, May 16, 1986. In contrast to the federal service academies, institutions maintained "to prepare cadets for career service in the armed forces," VMI's program "is directed at preparation for both military and civilian life"; "[o]nly about 15% of VMI cadets enter career military service." [All remaining quotes in Part II are from the district court opinion.]

VMI produces its "citizen-soldiers" through "an adversative, or doubting, model of education" which features "[p]hysical rigor, mental stress, absolute equality of treatment, absence of privacy, minute regulation of behavior, and indoctrination in desirable values." As one Commandant of Cadets described it, the adversative method " 'dissects the young student,' " and makes him aware of his " 'limits and capabilities,' " so that he knows " 'how far he can go with his anger, . . . how much he can take under stress, . . . exactly what he can do when he is physically exhausted.' "

VMI cadets live in spartan barracks where surveillance is constant and privacy nonexistent; they wear uniforms, eat together in the mess hall, and regularly participate in drills. Entering students are incessantly exposed to the rat line, "an extreme form of the adversative model," comparable in intensity to Marine Corps boot camp. Tormenting and punishing, the rat line bonds new cadets to their fellow sufferers and, when they have completed the 7-month experience, to their former tormentors. VMI's "adversative model" is further characterized by a hierarchical "class system" of privileges and responsibilities, a "dyke system" for assigning a senior class mentor to each entering class "rat," and a stringently enforced "honor code," which prescribes that a cadet " 'does not lie, cheat, steal nor tolerate those who do.' "

VMI attracts some applicants because of its reputation as an extraordinarily challenging military school, and "because its alumni are exceptionally close to the school." "[W]omen have no opportunity anywhere to gain the benefits of [the system of education at VMI]."

In 1990, prompted by a complaint filed with the Attorney General by a female high-school student seeking admission to VMI, the United States sued the Commonwealth of Virginia and VMI, alleging that VMI's exclusively male admission policy violated the Equal Protection Clause of the Fourteenth Amendment. [The Fourth Circuit held the admission policy unconstitutional.] Remanding the case, the appeals court assigned to Virginia, in the first instance, responsibility for selecting a remedial course. The court suggested these options for the Commonwealth: Admit women to VMI; establish parallel institutions or programs; or abandon state support, leaving VMI free to pursue its policies as a private institution. . . .

In response to the Fourth Circuit's ruling, Virginia proposed a parallel program for women: Virginia Women's Institute for Leadership (VWIL). The 4-year, state-sponsored undergraduate program would be located at Mary Baldwin College, a private liberal arts school for women, and would be open, initially, to about 25 to 30 students. Although VWIL would share VMI's mission—to produce "citizen-soldiers"—the VWIL program would differ, as does Mary Baldwin College, from VMI in academic offerings, methods of education, and financial resources.

Virginia returned to the District Court seeking approval of its proposed remedial plan, and the court decided the plan met the requirements of the Equal Protection Clause. . . . A divided Court of Appeals affirmed the District Court's judgment.

CROSS REFERENCE The Court compares the two Virginia programs later in the opinion; see pp. 1226–1228.

III

The cross-petitions in this suit present two ultimate issues. First, does Virginia's exclusion of women from the educational opportunities provided by VMI—extraordinary opportunities for military training and civilian leadership development—deny to women "capable of all of the individual activities required of VMI cadets," the equal protection of the laws guaranteed by the Fourteenth Amendment? Second, if VMI's "unique" situation—as Virginia's sole single-sex public institution of higher education—offends the Constitution's equal protection principle, what is the remedial requirement?

IV

. . . Today's skeptical scrutiny of official action denying rights or opportunities based on sex responds to volumes of history. . . .

Since *Reed v. Reed* (1971), the Court has repeatedly recognized that neither federal nor state government acts compatibly with the equal protection principle when a law or official policy denies to women, simply because they are women, full citizenship stature—equal opportunity to aspire, achieve, participate in and contribute to society based on their individual talents and capacities. See, *e.g.*, *Kirchberg v. Feenstra* (1981) (affirming invalidity of Louisiana law that made husband "head and master" of property jointly owned with his wife, giving him unilateral right to dispose of such property without his wife's consent); *Stanton v. Stanton* (1975) (invalidating Utah requirement that parents support boys until age 21, girls only until age 18).

Without equating gender classifications, for all purposes, to classifications based on race or national origin, the Court, in post-*Reed* decisions, has carefully inspected official action that closes a door or denies opportunity to women (or to men). To summarize the Court's current directions for cases of official classification based on gender: Focusing on the differential treatment or denial of opportunity for which relief is sought, the reviewing court must determine whether the proffered justification is "exceedingly persuasive." The burden of justification is demanding and it rests entirely on the State. The State must show "at least that the [challenged] classification serves 'important governmental objectives and that the discriminatory means employed' are 'substantially related to the achievement of those objectives.'" The justification must be genuine, not hypothesized or invented *post hoc* in response to litigation. And it must not rely on overbroad generalizations about the different talents, capacities, or preferences of males and females.

The heightened review standard our precedent establishes does not make sex a proscribed classification. Supposed "inherent differences" are no longer accepted as a ground for race or national origin classifications. See *Loving v. Virginia* (1967). Physical differences between men and women, however, are enduring: "[T]he two sexes are not fungible; a community made up exclusively of one [sex] is different from a community composed of both." *Ballard v. United States* (1946). "Inherent differences" between men and women, we have come to appreciate, remain cause for celebration, but not for denigration of the members of either sex or for artificial constraints on an individual's opportunity. Sex classifications may be used to compensate women "for particular economic disabilities [they have] suffered," to "promot[e] equal employment opportunity," to advance full development of the talent and capacities of our Nation's people.[7] But such classifications may not be used, as they once were, to create or perpetuate the legal, social, and economic inferiority of women.

Measuring the record in this case against the review standard just described, we conclude that Virginia has shown no "exceedingly persuasive justification" for excluding all women from the citizen-soldier training afforded by VMI. We therefore affirm the Fourth Circuit's initial judgment, which held that Virginia had violated the Fourteenth Amendment's Equal Protection Clause. Because the remedy proffered by Virginia—the Mary Baldwin VWIL

---

7   Several amici have urged that diversity in educational opportunities is an altogether appropriate governmental pursuit and that single-sex schools can contribute importantly to such diversity. Indeed, it is the mission of some single-sex schools "to dissipate, rather than perpetuate, traditional gender classifications." See Brief for Twenty-six Private Women's Colleges as Amici Curiae. We do not question the Commonwealth's prerogative evenhandedly to support diverse educational opportunities. We address specifically and only an educational opportunity recognized by the District Court and the Court of Appeals as "unique," an opportunity available only at Virginia's premier military institute, the Commonwealth's sole single-sex public university or college. Cf. *Mississippi Univ. for Women v. Hogan* (1982) ("Mississippi maintains no other single-sex public university or college. Thus, we are not faced with the question of whether States can provide 'separate but equal' undergraduate institutions for males and females.").

program—does not cure the constitutional violation, *i.e.*, it does not provide equal opportunity, we reverse the Fourth Circuit's final judgment in this case.

V

. . . Virginia . . . asserts two justifications in defense of VMI's exclusion of women. First, the Commonwealth contends, "single-sex education provides important educational benefits," and the option of single-sex education contributes to "diversity in educational approaches." Second, the Commonwealth argues, "the unique VMI method of character development and leadership training," the school's adversative approach, would have to be modified were VMI to admit women. We consider these two justifications in turn.

A

Single-sex education affords pedagogical benefits to at least some students, Virginia emphasizes, and that reality is uncontested in this litigation.[8] Similarly, it is not disputed that diversity among public educational institutions can serve the public good. But Virginia has not shown that VMI was established, or has been maintained, with a view to diversifying, by its categorical exclusion of women, educational opportunities within the Commonwealth. In cases of this genre, our precedent instructs that "benign" justifications proffered in defense of categorical exclusions will not be accepted automatically; a tenable justification must describe actual state purposes, not rationalizations for actions in fact differently grounded. . . .

Neither recent nor distant history bears out Virginia's alleged pursuit of diversity through single-sex educational options. In 1839, when the Commonwealth established VMI, a range of educational opportunities for men and women was scarcely contemplated. Higher education at the time was considered dangerous for women; reflecting widely held views about women's proper place, the Nation's first universities and colleges . . . admitted only men. VMI was not at all novel in this respect. . . .

---

[8]   On this point, the dissent sees fire where there is no flame. "Both men and women can benefit from a single-sex education," the District Court recognized, although "the beneficial effects" of such education, the court added, apparently "are stronger among women than among men." The United States does not challenge that recognition. Cf. C. Jencks & D. Riesman, *The Academic Revolution* (1968): "The pluralistic argument for preserving all-male colleges is uncomfortably similar to the pluralistic argument for preserving all-white colleges. . . . The all-male college would be relatively easy to defend if it emerged from a world in which women were established as fully equal to men. But it does not. It is therefore likely to be a witting or unwitting device for preserving tacit assumptions of male superiority—assumptions for which women must eventually pay."

Our 1982 decision in *Mississippi Univ. for Women* prompted VMI to re-examine its male-only admission policy. Virginia relies on that reexamination as a legitimate basis for maintaining VMI's single-sex character. A Mission Study Committee, appointed by the VMI Board of Visitors, studied the problem from October 1983 until May 1986, and in that month counseled against "change of VMI status as a single-sex college." Whatever internal purpose the Mission Study Committee served—and however well meaning the framers of the report—we can hardly extract from that effort any Commonwealth policy evenhandedly to advance diverse educational options. As the District Court observed, the Committee's analysis "primarily focuse[d] on anticipated difficulties in attracting females to VMI," and the report, overall, supplied "very little indication of how th[e] conclusion was reached."

In sum, we find no persuasive evidence in this record that VMI's male-only admission policy "is in furtherance of a state policy of 'diversity.'" . . . A purpose genuinely to advance an array of educational options, as the Court of Appeals recognized, is not served by VMI's historic and constant plan—a plan to "affor[d] a unique educational benefit only to males." However "liberally" this plan serves the Commonwealth's sons, it makes no provision whatever for her daughters. That is not *equal* protection.

B

Virginia next argues that VMI's adversative method of training provides educational benefits that cannot be made available, unmodified, to women. Alterations to accommodate women would necessarily be "radical," so "drastic," Virginia asserts, as to transform, indeed "destroy," VMI's program. Neither sex would be favored by the transformation, Virginia maintains: Men would be deprived of the unique opportunity currently available to them; women would not gain that opportunity because their participation would "eliminat[e] the very aspects of [the] program that distinguish [VMI] from . . . other institutions of higher education in Virginia."

The District Court forecast from expert witness testimony, and the Court of Appeals accepted, that coeducation would materially affect "at least these three aspects of VMI's program—physical training, the absence of privacy, and the adversative approach." And it is uncontested that women's admission would require accommodations, primarily in arranging housing assignments and physical training programs for female cadets. It is also undisputed, however, that "the VMI methodology could be used to educate women." The District Court even allowed that some women may prefer it to the methodology a women's college might pursue. "[S]ome women, at least, would want to attend [VMI] if they had the opportunity," the District Court recognized, and "some women," the expert testimony established, "are capable of all of the individual activities required of VMI cadets." The parties, furthermore, agree that "*some* women can meet the physical standards [VMI] now impose[s] on men." In sum, as the Court of Appeals stated, "neither the goal of producing citizen soldiers," VMI's *raison d'être*, "nor VMI's implementing methodology is inherently unsuitable to women."

In support of its initial judgment for Virginia, a judgment rejecting all equal protection objections presented by the United States, the District Court made "findings" on "gender-based developmental differences." These "findings" restate the opinions of Virginia's expert witnesses, opinions about typically male or typically female "tendencies." For example, "[m]ales tend to need an atmosphere of adversativeness," while "[f]emales tend to thrive in a cooperative atmosphere." "I'm not saying that some women don't do well under [the] adversative model," VMI's expert on educational institutions testified, "undoubtedly there are some [women] who do"; but educational experiences must be designed "around the rule," this expert maintained, and not "around the exception."

The United States does not challenge any expert witness estimation on average capacities or preferences of men and women. Instead, the United States emphasizes that time and again since this Court's turning point decision in *Reed v. Reed*, we have cautioned reviewing courts to take a "hard look" at generalizations or "tendencies" of the kind pressed by Virginia, and relied upon by the District Court. State actors controlling gates to opportunity, we have instructed, may not exclude qualified individuals based on "fixed notions concerning the roles and abilities of males and females." *Mississippi Univ. for Women*; see *J.E.B.* (equal protection principles, as applied to gender classifications, mean state actors may not rely on "overbroad" generalizations to make "judgments about people that are likely to . . . perpetuate historical patterns of discrimination").

It may be assumed, for purposes of this decision, that most women would not choose VMI's adversative method. As Fourth Circuit Judge Motz observed, however, in her dissent from the Court of Appeals' denial of rehearing en banc, it is also probable that "many men would not want to be educated in such an environment." (On that point, even our dissenting colleague might agree.)

Education, to be sure, is not a "one size fits all" business. The issue, however, is not whether "women—or men—should be forced to attend VMI"; rather, the question is whether the Commonwealth can constitutionally deny to women who have the will and capacity, the training and attendant opportunities that VMI uniquely affords.

The notion that admission of women would downgrade VMI's stature, destroy the adversative system and, with it, even the school, is a judgment hardly proved, a prediction hardly different from other "self-fulfilling prophec[ies]," see *Mississippi Univ. for Women*, once routinely used to deny rights or opportunities. When women first sought admission to the bar and access to legal education, concerns of the same order were expressed. For example, in 1876, the Court of Common Pleas of Hennepin County, Minnesota, explained why women were thought ineligible for the practice of law. Women train and educate the young, the court said, which

> forbids that they shall bestow that time (early and late) and labor, so essential in attaining to the eminence to which the true lawyer should ever aspire. It cannot therefore be said that the opposition of courts to the admission of females to practice . . . is to any extent the outgrowth of . . . "old fogyism[.]" . . . [I]t arises rather from a comprehension of the magnitude of the responsibilities connected with the successful practice of law, and a desire to *grade up* the profession.

In re Application of Martha Angle Dorsett to Be Admitted to Practice as Attorney and Counselor at Law (Minn. C.P. Hennepin Cty., 1876) (emphasis added). . . . Medical faculties similarly resisted men and women as partners in the study of medicine. . . . More recently, women seeking careers in policing encountered resistance based on fears that their presence would "undermine male solidarity"; deprive male partners of adequate assistance; and lead to sexual misconduct. Field studies did not confirm these fears. See F. Heidensohn, *Women in Control?* (1992); P. Bloch & D. Anderson, *Policewomen on Patrol: Final Report* (1974).

Women's successful entry into the federal military academies,[13] and their participation in the Nation's military forces, indicate that Virginia's fears for the future of VMI may not be solidly grounded.[15] The Commonwealth's justification for excluding all women from "citizen-soldier" training for which some

---

[13]   Women cadets have graduated at the top of their class at every federal military academy.

[15]   Inclusion of women in settings where, traditionally, they were not wanted inevitably entails a period of adjustment. As one West Point cadet squad leader recounted: "[T]he classes of '78 and '79 see the women as women,

are qualified, in any event, cannot rank as "exceedingly persuasive," as we have explained and applied that standard.

Virginia and VMI trained their argument on "means" rather than "end," and thus misperceived our precedent. Single-sex education at VMI serves an "important governmental objective," they maintained, and exclusion of women is not only "substantially related," it is essential to that objective. By this notably circular argument, the "straightforward" test *Mississippi Univ. for Women* described was bent and bowed.

The Commonwealth's misunderstanding and, in turn, the District Court's, is apparent from VMI's mission: to produce "citizen-soldiers," individuals

> imbued with love of learning, confident in the functions and attitudes
> of leadership, possessing a high sense of public service, advocates of
> the American democracy and free enterprise system, and ready . . .
> to defend their country in time of national peril.

Mission Study Committee of the VMI Board of Visitors, Report, May 16, 1986. Surely that goal is great enough to accommodate women, who today count as citizens in our American democracy equal in stature to men. Just as surely, the Commonwealth's great goal is not substantially advanced by women's categorical exclusion, in total disregard of their individual merit, from the Commonwealth's premier "citizen-soldier" corps.[16] Virginia, in sum, "has fallen far short of establishing the "exceedingly persuasive justification" that must be the solid base for any gender-defined classification.

VI

In the second phase of the litigation, Virginia presented its remedial plan—maintain VMI as a male-only college and create VWIL as a separate program for women. The plan met District Court approval. The Fourth Circuit, in turn, . . . concluded that Virginia had arranged for men and women opportunities "sufficiently comparable" to survive equal protection evaluation. . . .

---

but the classes of '80 and '81 see them as classmates." U.S. Military Academy, A. Vitters, *Report of Admission of Women* (Project Athena II) (1978).

16   VMI has successfully managed another notable change. The school admitted its first African-American cadets in 1968. See *The VMI Story* (students no longer sing "Dixie" [or] salute the Confederate flag or the tomb of General Robert E. Lee at ceremonies and sports events). As the District Court noted, VMI established a program on "retention of black cadets" designed to offer academic and social-cultural support to "minority members of a dominantly white and tradition-oriented student body." The school maintains a "special recruitment program for blacks" which, the District Court found, "has had little, if any, effect on VMI's method of accomplishing its mission."

A

. . . Virginia chose not to eliminate, but to leave untouched, VMI's exclusionary policy. For women only, however, Virginia proposed a separate program, different in kind from VMI and unequal in tangible and intangible facilities. . . .

VWIL affords women no opportunity to experience the rigorous military training for which VMI is famed. See [District Court opinion] ("No other school in Virginia or in the United States, public or private, offers the same kind of rigorous military training as is available at VMI."). Instead, the VWIL program "deemphasize[s]" military education, and uses a "cooperative method" of education "which reinforces self-esteem." VWIL students participate in ROTC and a "largely ceremonial" Virginia Corps of Cadets, but Virginia deliberately did not make VWIL a military institute. The VWIL House is not a military-style residence and VWIL students need not live together throughout the 4-year program, eat meals together, or wear uniforms during the schoolday. VWIL students thus do not experience the "barracks" life "crucial to the VMI experience," the spartan living arrangements designed to foster an "egalitarian ethic." "[T]he most important aspects of the VMI educational experience occur in the barracks," the District Court found, yet Virginia deemed that core experience nonessential, indeed inappropriate, for training its female citizen-soldiers. . . .

Virginia maintains that these methodological differences are "justified pedagogically," based on "important differences between men and women in learning and developmental needs," "psychological and sociological differences" Virginia describes as "real" and "not stereotypes." The Task Force charged with developing the leadership program for women, drawn from the staff and faculty at Mary Baldwin College, "determined that a military model and, especially VMI's adversative method, would be wholly inappropriate for educating and training *most women*" (emphasis added). . . .

As earlier stated, generalizations about "the way women are," estimates of what is appropriate for *most women*, no longer justify denying opportunity to women whose talent and capacity place them outside the average description. Notably, Virginia never asserted that VMI's method of education suits *most men*. It is also revealing that Virginia accounted for its failure to make the VWIL experience "the entirely militaristic experience of VMI" on the ground that VWIL "is planned for women who do not necessarily expect to pursue military careers." By that reasoning, VMI's "entirely militaristic" program would be inappropriate for men in general or *as a group*, for "[o]nly about 15% of VMI cadets enter career military service."

In contrast to the generalizations about women on which Virginia rests, we note again these dispositive realities: . . . "some women . . . do well under [the] adversative model,"; . . . "some women are capable of all of the individual activities required of VMI cadets," and "can meet the physical standards [VMI] now impose[s] on men." It is on behalf of these women that the United States has instituted this suit, and it is for them that a remedy must be crafted. . . .[19]

B

In myriad respects other than military training, VWIL does not qualify as VMI's equal. VWIL's student body, faculty, course offerings, and facilities hardly match VMI's. Nor can the VWIL graduate anticipate the benefits associated with VMI's 157-year history, the school's prestige, and its influential alumni network. . . .

Virginia, in sum, while maintaining VMI for men only, has failed to provide any "comparable single-gender women's institution." Instead, the Commonwealth has created a VWIL program fairly appraised as a "pale shadow" of VMI in terms of the range of curricular choices and faculty stature, funding, prestige, alumni support and influence.

Virginia's VWIL solution is reminiscent of the remedy Texas proposed 50 years ago, in response to a state trial court's 1946 ruling that, given the equal protection guarantee, African-Americans could not be denied a legal education at a state facility. See *Sweatt v. Painter* (1950). Reluctant to admit African-Americans to its flagship University of Texas Law School, the State set up a separate school for Heman Sweatt and other black law students. . . . More important than the tangible features, the Court emphasized, are "those qualities which are incapable of objective measurement but which make for greatness" in a school, including "reputation of the faculty, experience of the administration, position and influence of the alumni, standing in the community, traditions

---

[19] Admitting women to VMI would undoubtedly require alterations necessary to afford members of each sex privacy from the other sex in living arrangements, and to adjust aspects of the physical training programs. *Cf.* note following 10 U.S.C. § 4342 (academic and other standards for women admitted to the Military, Naval, and Air Force Academies "shall be the same as those required for male individuals, except for those minimum essential adjustments in such standards required because of physiological differences between male and female individuals"). Experience shows such adjustments are manageable. See U.S. Military Academy, A. Vitters, N. Kinzer, & J. Adams, *Report of Admission of Women (Project Athena I–IV)* (1977–1980) (4-year longitudinal study of the admission of women to West Point); Defense Advisory Committee on Women in the Services, *Report on the Integration and Performance of Women at West Point* (1992).

and prestige." Facing the marked differences reported in the *Sweatt* opinion, the Court unanimously ruled that Texas had not shown "substantial equality in the [separate] educational opportunities" the State offered. . . .

In line with *Sweatt*, we rule here that Virginia has not shown substantial equality in the separate educational opportunities the Commonwealth supports at VWIL and VMI. . . .

VII

. . . A prime part of the history of our Constitution, . . . is the story of the extension of constitutional rights and protections to people once ignored or excluded.[21] VMI's story continued as our comprehension of "We the People" expanded. There is no reason to believe that the admission of women capable of all the activities required of VMI cadets would destroy the Institute rather than enhance its capacity to serve the "more perfect Union." . . .

Justice Thomas took no part in the consideration or decision of these cases.

Chief Justice Rehnquist, concurring in the judgment.

. . . While I agree with [the Court's] conclusions, I disagree with [its] analysis and so I write separately. [Justice Rehnquist argued that the Court had departed from the standard of scrutiny articulated in *Craig v. Boren* (1976) ("substantially related" to "important governmental objectives"). He believed that the phrase "exceedingly persuasive justification" was "best confined, as it was first used, as an observation on the difficulty of meeting the applicable test, not as a formulation of the test itself."]

Even if diversity in educational opportunity were the Commonwealth's actual objective, the Commonwealth's position would still be problematic. The difficulty with its position is that the diversity benefited only one sex; there was single-sex public education available for men at VMI, but no corresponding single-sex public education available for women. . . .

---

21   [Consider, for example, the] letter to a friend from Massachusetts patriot (later second President) John Adams, on the subject of qualifications for voting in his home State:

> [I]t is dangerous to open so fruitful a source of controversy and altercation as would be opened by attempting to alter the qualifications of voters; there will be no end of it. New claims will arise; women will demand a vote; lads from twelve to twenty-one will think their rights not enough attended to; and every man who has not a farthing, will demand an equal voice with any other, in all acts of state. It tends to confound and destroy all distinctions, and prostrate all ranks to one common level."

Letter from John Adams to James Sullivan (May 26, 1776).

I do not think, however, that the Commonwealth's options were as limited as the majority may imply. . . . VMI had been in operation for over a century and a half, and had an established, successful, and devoted group of alumni. No legislative wand could instantly call into existence a similar institution for women; and it would be a tremendous loss to scrap VMI's history and tradition. . . . Had Virginia made a genuine effort to devote comparable public resources to a facility for women, and followed through on such a plan, it might well have avoided an equal protection violation. I do not believe the Commonwealth was faced with the stark choice of either admitting women to VMI, on the one hand, or abandoning VMI and starting from scratch for both men and women, on the other. . . .

[Justice Rehnquist expressed agreement with the Court that "maintenance of the adversative method . . . does not serve an important governmental objective": "While considerable evidence shows that a single sex education is pedagogically beneficial for some students, . . . there is no similar evidence in the record that an adversative method is pedagogically beneficial or is any more likely to produce character traits than other methodologies.]

. . . [T]he remedy should not necessarily require either the admission of women to VMI, or the creation of a VMI clone for women. An adequate remedy in my opinion might be a demonstration by Virginia that its interest in educating men in a single sex environment is matched by its interest in educating women in a single sex institution. To demonstrate such, the Commonwealth does not need to create two institutions with the same number of faculty PhD's, similar SAT scores, or comparable athletic fields. Nor would it necessarily require that the women's institution offer the same curriculum as the men's; one could be strong in computer science, the other could be strong in liberal arts. It would be a sufficient remedy, I think, if the two institutions offered the same quality of education and were of the same overall caliber. . . .

JUSTICE SCALIA, dissenting.

Today the Court shuts down an institution that has served the people of the Commonwealth of Virginia with pride and distinction for over a century and a half. . . . Much of the Court's opinion is devoted to deprecating the closed-mindedness of our forebears with regard to women's education, and even with regard to the treatment of women in areas that have nothing to do with education. Closed-minded they were—as every age is, including our own, with regard to matters it cannot guess, because it simply does not consider them debatable. The virtue of a democratic system with a First Amendment is that it readily enables the people, over time, to be persuaded that what they took for granted is not so, and to change their laws accordingly. That system is destroyed if the smug assurances of each age are removed from the democratic process and written into the Constitution.

So to counterbalance the Court's criticism of our ancestors, let me say a word in their praise: They left us free to change. The same cannot be said of this most illiberal Court, which has embarked on a course of inscribing one after another of the current preferences of the society (and in some cases only the counter-majoritarian preferences of the society's law-trained elite) into our Basic Law. Today it enshrines the notion that no substantial educational value is to be served by an all-men's military academy—so that the decision by the people of Virginia to maintain such an institution denies equal protection to women who cannot attend that institution but can attend others. Since it is entirely clear that the Constitution of the United States—the old one—takes no sides in this educational debate, I dissent.

I

I shall devote most of my analysis to evaluating the Court's opinion on the basis of our current equal protection jurisprudence, which regards this Court as free to evaluate everything under the sun by applying one of three tests: "rational basis" scrutiny, intermediate scrutiny, or strict scrutiny. These tests are no more scientific than their names suggest, and a further element of randomness is added by the fact that it is largely up to us which test will be applied in each case. . . .

I have no problem with a system of abstract tests such as rational basis, intermediate, and strict scrutiny (though I think we can do better than applying strict scrutiny and intermediate scrutiny whenever we feel like it). Such formulas are essential to evaluating whether the new restrictions that a changing society constantly imposes upon private conduct comport with that "equal protection" our society has always accorded in the past. But in my view . . . , whatever abstract tests we may choose to devise, they cannot supersede—and indeed ought to be crafted *so as to reflect*—those constant and unbroken national traditions that embody the people's understanding of ambiguous constitutional texts. . . .

The all-male constitution of VMI comes squarely within such a governing tradition. . . . For almost all of VMI's more than a century and a half of existence, its single-sex status reflected the uniform practice for government-supported military colleges. . . . In other words, the tradition of having government-funded military schools for men is as well rooted in the traditions of this country as the tradition of sending only men into military combat. . . .

And the same applies, more broadly, to single-sex education in general, which, as I shall discuss, is threatened by today's decision with the cutoff of all state and federal support. . . . These traditions may of course be changed by the democratic decisions of the people, as they largely have been. . . .

II

To reject the Court's disposition today, however, it is not necessary to accept my view that the Court's made-up tests cannot displace longstanding national traditions as the primary determinant of what the Constitution means. It is only necessary to apply honestly the test the Court has been applying to sex-based classifications for the past two decades. . . . We have denominated this standard "intermediate scrutiny" and under it have inquired whether the statutory classification is "substantially related to an important governmental objective." . . .

Before I proceed to apply this standard to VMI, I must comment upon the manner in which the Court *avoids* doing so. [T]he United States urged us to hold in this litigation "that strict scrutiny is the correct constitutional standard for evaluating classifications that deny opportunities to individuals based on their sex." . . . The Court, while making no reference to the Government's argument, effectively accepts it. . . .

Only the amorphous "exceedingly persuasive justification" phrase, and not the standard elaboration of intermediate scrutiny, can be made to yield this conclusion that VMI's single-sex composition is unconstitutional because there exist several women (or, one would have to conclude under the Court's reasoning, a single woman) willing and able to undertake VMI's program. Intermediate scrutiny has never required a least-restrictive-means analysis, but only a "substantial relation" between the classification and the state interests that it serves. . . .

The Court's intimations are particularly out of place because it is perfectly clear that, if the question of the applicable standard of review for sex-based classifications were to be regarded as an appropriate subject for reconsideration, the stronger argument would be not for elevating the standard to strict scrutiny, but for reducing it to rational-basis review. The latter certainly has a firmer foundation in our past jurisprudence: Whereas no majority of the Court has ever applied strict scrutiny in a case involving sex-based classifications, we routinely applied rational-basis review until the 1970's. And of course normal, rational-basis review of sex-based classifications would be much more in accord with the genesis of heightened standards of judicial review, the famous footnote in *United States v. Carolene Products Co.* (1938)[. Indeed, it] is hard to consider women a "discrete and insular minorit[y]" unable to employ the "political processes ordinarily to be relied upon," when they constitute a majority of the electorate. And the suggestion that they are incapable of exerting that political power smacks of the same paternalism that the Court so roundly condemns. Moreover, a long list of legislation proves the proposition false. See, *e.g.,* Equal Pay Act of 1963; Title VII of the Civil Rights Act of 1964; Title IX of the Education Amendments of 1972; Women's Business Ownership Act of 1988; Violence Against Women Act of 1994.

III

. . . I now proceed to describe how the analysis should have been conducted. . . .

A

It is beyond question that Virginia has an important state interest in providing effective college education for its citizens. That single-sex instruction is an approach substantially related to that interest should be evident enough from the long and continuing history in this country of men's and women's colleges. But beyond that, as the Court of Appeals here stated: "That single-gender education at the college level is beneficial to both sexes is a *fact established in this case*" (emphasis added). The evidence establishing that fact was overwhelming—indeed, "virtually uncontradicted" in the words of the court that received the evidence. As an initial matter, Virginia demonstrated at trial that "[a] substantial body of contemporary scholarship and research supports the proposition that, although males and females have significant areas of developmental overlap, they also have differing developmental needs that are deep seated." . . .

But besides its single-sex constitution, VMI is different from other colleges in another way. It employs a "distinctive educational method," sometimes referred to as the "adversative, or doubting, model of education." . . . [A] State's decision to maintain within its system one school that provides the adversative method is "substantially related" to its goal of good education. Moreover, it was uncontested that "if the state were to establish a women's VMI-type [*i.e.*, adversative] program, the program would attract an insufficient number of participants to make the program work," and it was found by the District Court that if Virginia were to include women in VMI, the school "would eventually find it necessary to drop the adversative system altogether." Thus, Virginia's options were an adversative method that excludes women or no adversative method at all.

[Furthermore, s]ubstantial evidence in the District Court demonstrated that the Commonwealth has long proceeded on the principle that " '[h]igher education resources should be viewed as a whole—public and private' "—because such an approach enhances diversity and because " 'it is academic and economic waste to permit unwarranted duplication' " (quoting 1974 Report of the General Assembly Commission on Higher Education to the General Assembly of Virginia). It is thus significant that, whereas there are "four all-female private [colleges] in Virginia," there is only "one private all-male college," which "indicates that the private sector is providing for th[e] [former] form of education to a much greater extent that it provides for all-male education." In these circumstances, Virginia's election to fund one public all-male institution and one on the adversative model—and to concentrate its resources in a single entity that serves both these interests in diversity—is substantially related to the Commonwealth's important educational interests. . . .

B

. . . The Court focuses on "VMI's mission," which is to produce individuals "imbued with love of learning, confident in the functions and attitudes of leadership, possessing a high sense of public service, advocates of the American democracy and free enterprise system, and ready . . . to defend their country in time of national peril." "Surely," the Court says, "that goal is great enough to accommodate women." . . . The Court's analysis at least has the benefit of producing foreseeable results. Applied generally, it means that whenever a State's ultimate objective is "great enough to accommodate women" (as it always will be), then the State will be held to have violated the Equal Protection Clause if it restricts to men even one means by which it pursues that objective—no matter how few women are interested in pursuing the objective by that means, no matter how much the single-sex program will have to be changed if both sexes are admitted, and no matter how beneficial that program has theretofore been to its participants. . . .

The Court argues that VMI would not have to change very much if it were to admit women. . . . [I]f such a debate were relevant, the Court would certainly be on the losing side. . . . Changes that the District Court's detailed analysis found would be required include new allowances for personal privacy in the barracks, such as locked doors and coverings on windows, which would detract from VMI's approach of regulating minute details of student behavior, "contradict the principle that everyone is constantly subject to scrutiny by everyone else," and impair VMI's "total egalitarian approach" under which every student must be "treated alike"; changes in the physical training program, which would reduce "[t]he intensity and aggressiveness of the current program"; and various modifications in other respects of the adversative training program that permeates student life. . . .

Although there is no precise female-only analogue to VMI, Virginia has created during this litigation the Virginia Women's Institute for Leadership (VWIL), a state-funded all-women's program run by Mary Baldwin College. I have thus far said nothing about VWIL because it is, under our established test, irrelevant, so long as *VMI*'s all-male character is "substantially related" to an important state goal. But VWIL now exists, and the Court's treatment of it shows how far reaching today's decision is.

VWIL was carefully designed by professional educators who have long experience in educating young women. . . . Mary Baldwin College, which runs VWIL, . . . has made the point most succinctly:

> It would have been possible to develop the VWIL program to more closely resemble VMI, with adversative techniques associated with the rat line and barracks-like living quarters. Simply replicating an existing program would have required far less thought, research, and educational expertise. But such a facile approach would have produced a paper program with no real prospect of successful implementation.

Brief for Mary Baldwin College as Amicus Curiae. . . . Even though VWIL was carefully designed by professional educators who have tremendous experience in the area, and survived the test of adversarial litigation, the Court simply declares, with no basis in the evidence, that these professionals acted on " 'overbroad' generalizations."

C

[In response to the Chief Justice's declaration that there was insufficient support in the record that an adversative method of education is pedagogically beneficial, Justice Scalia wrote:] That is simply wrong. See, *e.g.*, 766 F. Supp., at 1426 (factual findings concerning character traits produced by VMI's adversative methodology); *id.*, at 1434 (factual findings concerning benefits for many college-age men of an adversative approach in general). In reality, the pedagogical benefits of VMI's adversative approach were not only proved, but were a *given* in this litigation. . . .

IV

. . . Under the constitutional principles announced and applied today, single-sex public education is unconstitutional. . . . Indeed, the Court indicates that if any program restricted to one sex is "uniqu[e]," it must be opened to members of the opposite sex "who have the will and capacity" to participate in it. I suggest that the single-sex program that will not be capable of being characterized as "unique" is not only unique but nonexistent.[8]

In any event, regardless of whether the Court's rationale leaves some small amount of room for lawyers to argue, it ensures that single-sex public education is functionally dead. The costs of litigating the constitutionality of a single-sex education program, and the risks of ultimately losing that litigation, are simply too high to be embraced by public officials. . . . No state official in his right mind will buy such a high-cost, high-risk lawsuit by commencing a single-sex program. The enemies of single-sex education have won; by persuading only seven Justices (five would have been enough) that their view of the world is enshrined in the Constitution, they have effectively imposed that view on all 50 States.

This is especially regrettable because, as the District Court here determined, educational experts in recent years have increasingly come to "suppor[t] [the] view that substantial educational benefits flow from a single-gender environment, be it male or female, *that cannot be replicated in a coeducational setting.*" . . . Until quite recently, some public officials have attempted to institute new single-sex programs, at least as experiments. In 1991, for example, the Detroit Board of Education announced a program to establish three boys-only

---

8   In this regard, I note that the Court—which I concede is under no obligation to do so—provides no example of a program that *would* pass muster under its reasoning today: not even, for example, a football or wrestling program. On the Court's theory, any woman ready, willing, and physically able to participate in such a program would, *as a constitutional matter*, be entitled to do so.

schools for inner-city youth; it was met with a lawsuit, a preliminary injunction was swiftly entered by a District Court that purported to rely on *Hogan*, and the Detroit Board of Education voted to abandon the litigation and thus abandon the plan. Today's opinion assures that no such experiment will be tried again. . . .

In 2017, The Roanoke Times ran a story by Laurence Hammack, *20 years after their admission, women continue the VMI legacy*, reflecting on the 20-year anniversary of the admission of women to VMI. It read, in part, as follows:

> Sitting in the shade of an elm tree on the parade grounds of Virginia Military Institute, Angela Li savored her last moments of tranquility Saturday afternoon as she prepared to enter the school's infamous rat line. . . .
>
> Other women have done it, too, in numbers that have grown every year since the first coed class was admitted to VMI 20 years ago this weekend. . . . Of the 504 rats—as VMI calls its first-year cadets—that matriculated Saturday, 63 were women. That's more than twice the 30 who made history in 1997 as the first women to enter the rat line, and the second-largest number for a class since then. Women now make up about 11 percent of VMI's corps of cadets, and by most accounts their presence is no longer an issue.
>
> "Everybody is put on a level playing field, " said Patrick Doolin, a first classman and member of the cadre, a group of cadets who will put Li and her fellow rats through boot camp-like training that will last through early next year. "That's the value of VMI," he said. "You put everyone in the same environment and you rise to your own merit." . . .
>
> VMI has made some changes to accommodate women, such as allowing them to keep their hair a little longer than the crew cuts sported by male cadets. The fitness standards have also been tweaked in some cases to acknowledge some physical realities, with males required to do a minimum of five pull-ups and women one. But overall, school officials say their demanding requirements apply to both sexes.

And women have held their own, according to figures provided by the school. The average retention rate for the classes that graduated from 2013 to 2016 was 69 percent for men. Women in those same classes had a retention rate of 66 percent.

For [Gussie Lord, another member of the inaugural female class,] one of her favorite memories from VMI was passing the fitness test. "I had always failed the pull-ups (the minimum was 5), and my last semester I decided to really make an effort to pass," she wrote in an email. "So I worked on it all semester and did 7 pullups—I was very happy and proud about it. Then the woman behind me in line—she was a third classman—jumped up to the bar and did 17! I had to laugh at myself and thought that I should have worked harder, but I was very proud of her."

Since then, 431 women have graduated from VMI.

"Every time a woman matriculates to VMI, she's making history," Sullivan said. "There aren't that many of us, and when I talk to them I say, 'This isn't just about you. This is about continuing to be a part of an amazing group of women who have made history. It's about continuing the legacy of VMI.' "

b.   Facial Neutrality—Gender

Under *Washington v. Davis* (1976), see pp. 1036–1043, facially neutral statutes that produce disparate racial impact are presumptively subject to rational basis review, unless it can be shown that they were motivated by a racial purpose. This doctrine presents some interesting challenges when applied to the gender context. Consider the following cases—the first of which was decided before *Craig v. Boren* adopted intermediate scrutiny for classifications on the basis of sex.

Geduldig v. Aiello

Supreme Court of the United States, 1974.
417 U.S. 484.

Mr. Justice Stewart delivered the opinion of the Court.

SUMMARY OF THE FACTS

California administered a disability insurance system that paid benefits to persons in private employment who were temporarily unable to work because of disability not covered by workmen's compensation. The statute provided that an individual would "be deemed disabled in any day in which, because of his physical or mental condition, he is unable to perform his regular or customary work." But it also provided: "In no case shall the term 'disability' or 'disabled' include any injury or illness caused by or arising in connection with pregnancy up to the termination of such pregnancy and for a period of 28 days thereafter." Aiello and three other women brought a challenge to this exclusion. By the time the Supreme Court decided the case, the challenge had been mooted with respect to three of the women; their claims were paid pursuant to a state court decision that had construed the statute to preclude only the payment of benefits for disability accompanying normal pregnancy.

[T]he issue before the Court on this appeal is whether the California disability insurance program invidiously discriminates against Jaramillo and others similarly situated by not paying insurance benefits for disability that accompanies normal pregnancy and childbirth.

II

. . . We cannot agree that the exclusion of this disability from coverage amounts to invidious discrimination under the Equal Protection Clause. California does not discriminate with respect to the persons or groups which are eligible for disability insurance protection under the program. The classification challenged in this case relates to the asserted underinclusiveness of the set of risks that the State has selected to insure. Although California has created a program to insure most risks of employment disability, it has not chosen to insure all such risks, and this decision is reflected in the level of annual contributions exacted from participating employees.

This Court has held that, consistently with the Equal Protection Clause, a State "may take one step at a time, addressing itself to the phase of the problem which seems most acute to the legislative mind. . . . The legislature may select one phase of one field and apply a remedy there, neglecting the others. . . ." *Williamson v. Lee Optical Co.* (1955). Particularly with respect to social welfare programs, so long as the line drawn by the State is rationally supportable, the courts will not interpose their judgment as to the appropriate stopping point. "[T]he Equal Protection Clause does not require that a State must choose between attacking every aspect of a problem or not attacking the problem at all." *Dandridge v. Williams* (1970).

The District Court suggested that moderate alterations in what it regarded as "variables" of the disability insurance program could be made to accommodate the substantial expense required to include normal pregnancy within the program's protection. The same can be said, however, with respect to the other expensive class of disabilities that are excluded from coverage-short-term disabilities. If the Equal Protection Clause were thought to compel disability payments for normal pregnancy, it is hard to perceive why it would not also compel payments for short-term disabilities suffered by participating employees.

It is evident that a totally comprehensive program would be substantially more costly than the present program and would inevitably require state subsidy, a higher rate of employee contribution, a lower scale of benefits for those suffering insured disabilities, or some combination of these measures. There is nothing in the Constitution, however, that requires the State to subordinate or compromise its legitimate interests solely to create a more comprehensive social insurance program than it already has.

The State has a legitimate interest in maintaining the self-supporting nature of its insurance program. Similarly, it has an interest in distributing the available resources in such a way as to keep benefit payments at an adequate level for disabilities that are covered, rather than to cover all disabilities inadequately. Finally, California has a legitimate concern in maintaining the contribution rate at a level that will not unduly burden participating employees, particularly low-income employees who may be most in need of the disability insurance.

These policies provide an objective and wholly noninvidious basis for the State's decision not to create a more comprehensive insurance program than it has. There is no evidence in the record that the selection of the risks insured by the program worked to discriminate against any definable group or class in terms of the aggregate risk protection derived by that group or class from the program.[20] There is no risk from which men are protected and women are not. Likewise, there is no risk from which women are protected and men are not.[21] . . .

MR. JUSTICE BRENNAN, with whom MR. JUSTICE DOUGLAS and MR. JUSTICE MARSHALL join, dissenting.

. . . In my view, by singling out for less favorable treatment a gender-linked disability peculiar to women, the State has created a double standard for disability compensation: a limitation is imposed upon the disabilities for which women workers may recover, while men receive full compensation for all disabilities suffered, including those that affect only or primarily their sex, such as prostatectomies, circumcision, hemophilia, and gout. In effect, one set of rules is applied to females and another to males. Such dissimilar treatment of men and women, on the basis of physical characteristics inextricably linked to one sex, inevitably constitutes sex discrimination. . . .

In the past, when a legislative classification has turned on gender, the Court has justifiably applied a standard of judicial scrutiny more strict than that generally accorded economic or social welfare programs. *E.g., Reed v. Reed*; *Frontiero v. Richardson.* . . .

The State has clearly failed to meet that burden in the present case. The essence of the State's justification for excluding disabilities caused by a normal pregnancy from its disability compensation scheme is that covering such disabilities would be too costly. To be sure, as presently funded, inclusion of normal pregnancies "would be substantially more costly than the present program."

---

[20]   The dissenting opinion to the contrary, this case is thus a far cry from cases like *Reed v. Reed* (1971), and *Frontiero v. Richardson* (1973), involving discrimination based upon gender as such. The California insurance program does not exclude anyone from benefit eligibility because of gender but merely removes one physical condition—pregnancy—from the list of compensable disabilities. While it is true that only women can become pregnant it does not follow that every legislative classification concerning pregnancy is a sex-based classification like those considered in *Reed* and *Frontiero*. Normal pregnancy is an objectively identifiable physical condition with unique characteristics. Absent a showing that distinctions involving pregnancy are mere pretexts designed to effect an invidious discrimination against the members of one sex or the other, lawmakers are constitutionally free to include or exclude pregnancy from the coverage of legislation such as this on any reasonable basis, just as with respect to any other physical condition.

The lack of identity between the excluded disability and gender as such under this insurance program becomes clear upon the most cursory analysis. The program divides potential recipients into two groups—pregnant women and nonpregnant persons. While the first group is exclusively female, the second includes members of both sexes. The fiscal and actuarial benefits of the program thus accrue to members of both sexes.

[21]   Indeed, the appellant submitted to the District Court data that indicated that both the annual claim rate and the annual claim cost are greater for women than for men. . . .

The present level of benefits for insured disabilities could not be maintained without increasing the employee contribution rate, raising or lifting the yearly contribution ceiling, or securing state subsidies. But whatever role such monetary considerations may play in traditional equal protection analysis, the State's interest in preserving the fiscal integrity of its disability insurance program simply cannot render the State's use of a suspect classification constitutional. For while "a State has a valid interest in preserving the fiscal integrity of its programs[,] . . . a State may not accomplish such a purpose by invidious distinctions between classes of its citizens. . . ." *Shapiro v. Thompson* (1969). Thus, when a statutory classification is subject to strict judicial scrutiny, the State "must do more than show that denying [benefits to the excluded class] saves money." *Memorial Hospital v. Maricopa County* (1974). . . .

Personnel Administrator of Massachusetts v. Feeney

Supreme Court of the United States, 1979.
442 U.S. 256.

MR. JUSTICE STEWART delivered the opinion of the Court.

This case presents a challenge to the constitutionality of the Massachusetts veterans' preference statute. . . . Under [the statute], all veterans who qualify for state civil service positions must be considered for appointment ahead of any qualifying nonveterans. The preference operates overwhelmingly to the advantage of males. . . .

I

The Federal Government and virtually all of the States grant some sort of hiring preference to veterans. The Massachusetts preference, which [dates to 1884 and] is loosely termed an "absolute lifetime" preference, is among the most generous. It applies to all positions in the State's classified civil service, which constitute approximately 60% of the public jobs in the State. It is available to "any person, male or female, including a nurse," who was honorably discharged from the United States Armed Forces after at least 90 days of active service, at least one day of which was during "wartime." . . .

For jobs in the [relevant civil service categories], the preference mechanics are uncomplicated. All applicants for employment must take competitive examinations. . . . Candidates who pass are then ranked in the order of their respective scores on an "eligible list." [The veteran's preference] requires, however, that disabled veterans, veterans, and surviving spouses and surviving parents of veterans be ranked—in the order of their respective scores—above all other candidates. When a public agency has a vacancy, it requisitions a list of "certified eligibles" from the state personnel division. Under formulas prescribed by civil service rules, a small number of candidates from the top of an appropriate list, three if there is only one vacancy, are certified. The appointing agency is then required to choose from among these candidates. Although the veterans' preference thus does not guarantee that a veteran will be appointed, it is obvious that the preference gives to veterans who achieve passing scores a well-nigh absolute advantage. . . .

The veterans' hiring preference in Massachusetts, as in other jurisdictions, has traditionally been justified as a measure designed to reward veterans for the sacrifice of military service, to ease the transition from military to civilian life, to encourage patriotic service, and to attract loyal and well-disciplined people to civil service occupations. . . . Women who have served in official United States military units during wartime . . . have always been entitled to the benefit of the preference. In addition, Massachusetts, through a 1943 amendment to the definition of "wartime service," extended the preference to women who served in unofficial auxiliary women's units. . . .

Notwithstanding the apparent attempts by Massachusetts to include as many military women as possible within the scope of the preference, the statute today benefits an overwhelmingly male class. This is attributable in some measure to the variety of federal statutes, regulations, and policies that have restricted the number of women who could enlist in the United States Armed Forces,[21] and largely to the simple fact that women have never been subjected to a military draft.

When this litigation was commenced, then, over 98% of the veterans in Massachusetts were male; only 1.8% were female. And over one-quarter of the

---

[21]   . . . The authorizations for the women's units during World War II were temporary. The Women's Armed Services Integration Act of 1948 established the women's services on a permanent basis. Under the Act, women were given regular military status. However, quotas were placed on the numbers who could enlist (no more than 2% of total enlisted strength), eligibility requirements were more stringent than those for men, and career opportunities were limited. During the 1950s and 1960s, enlisted women constituted little more than 1% of the total force. In 1967, the 2% quota was lifted, and in the 1970's many restrictive policies concerning women's participation in the military have been eliminated or modified. In 1972, women still constituted less than 2% of the enlisted strength. By 1975, when this litigation was commenced, the percentage had risen to 4.6%.

Massachusetts population were veterans.[d] During the decade between 1963 and 1973 when the appellee was actively participating in the State's merit selection system, 47,005 new permanent appointments were made in the classified official service. Forty-three percent of those hired were women, and 57% were men. Of the women appointed, 1.8% were veterans, while 54% of the men had veteran status. A large unspecified percentage of the female appointees were serving in lower paying positions for which males traditionally had not applied. On each of 50 sample eligible lists that are part of the record in this case, one or more women who would have been certified as eligible for appointment on the basis of test results were displaced by veterans whose test scores were lower.

At the outset of this litigation appellants conceded that for "many of the permanent positions for which males and females have competed" the veterans' preference has "resulted in a substantially greater proportion of female eligibles than male eligibles" not being certified for consideration. The impact of the veterans' preference law upon the public employment opportunities of women has thus been severe. This impact lies at the heart of the appellee's federal constitutional claim.

II

The sole question for decision on this appeal is whether Massachusetts, in granting an absolute lifetime preference to veterans, has discriminated against women in violation of the Equal Protection Clause of the Fourteenth Amendment.

. . . Classifications based upon gender, not unlike those based upon race, have traditionally been the touchstone for pervasive and often subtle discrimination. This Court's recent cases teach that such classifications must bear a close and substantial relationship to important governmental objectives, *Craig v. Boren*, and are in many settings unconstitutional. Although public employment is not a constitutional right, *Massachusetts Bd. of Retirement v. Murgia* (1976), and the States have wide discretion in framing employee qualifications, see, e.g., *New York City Transit Authority v. Beazer* (1979), these precedents dictate that any state law overtly or covertly designed to prefer males over females in public employment would require an exceedingly persuasive justification to withstand a constitutional challenge under the Equal Protection Clause of the Fourteenth Amendment.

---

[d]   The Court appears to be referring to the adult population.

. . . *Washington v. Davis* . . . recognize[s] that when a neutral law has a disparate impact upon a group that has historically been the victim of discrimination, an unconstitutional purpose may still be at work. But [that] case[ ] signaled no departure from the settled rule that the Fourteenth Amendment guarantees equal laws, not equal results. *Davis* upheld a job-related employment test that white people passed in proportionately greater numbers than Negroes, for there had been no showing that racial discrimination entered into the establishment or formulation of the test. . . . Those principles apply with equal force to a case involving alleged gender discrimination.

When a statute gender-neutral on its face is challenged on the ground that its effects upon women are disproportionably adverse, a twofold inquiry is thus appropriate. The first question is whether the statutory classification is indeed neutral in the sense that it is not gender-based. If the classification itself, covert or overt, is not based upon gender, the second question is whether the adverse effect reflects invidious gender-based discrimination. See *Arlington Heights v. Metropolitan Housing Dev. Corp.* (1977). In this second inquiry, impact provides an "important starting point," *id.*, but purposeful discrimination is "the condition that offends the Constitution." *Swann v. Charlotte-Mecklenburg Board of Education* (1971). It is against this background of precedent that we consider the merits of the case before us.

III

The question whether [the veteran's preference] establishes a classification that is overtly or covertly based upon gender must first be considered. The appellee has conceded that [the preference] is neutral on its face. . . . The District Court made two central findings that are relevant here: first, that [the preference] serves legitimate and worthy purposes; second, that the absolute preference was not established for the purpose of discriminating against women. The appellee has thus acknowledged and the District Court has thus found that the distinction between veterans and nonveterans . . . is not a pretext for gender discrimination. The appellee's concession and the District Court's finding are clearly correct.

If the impact of this statute could not be plausibly explained on a neutral ground, impact itself would signal that the real classification made by the law was in fact not neutral. See *Washington v. Davis; Arlington Heights v. Metropolitan Housing Dev. Corp.* But there can be but one answer to the question whether this veteran preference excludes significant numbers of women from preferred state jobs because they are women or because they are nonveterans. Apart from the facts that the definition of "veterans" in the statute has always been neutral as to gender and that Massachusetts has consistently defined veteran status in a way that has been inclusive of women who have served in the military, this is not a law that can plausibly be explained only as a gender-based classification. Indeed, it is not a law that can rationally be explained on that ground. Veteran status is not uniquely male. Although few women benefit from the preference the nonveteran class is not substantially all female. To the contrary, significant numbers of nonveterans are men, and all nonveterans—male as well as female—are placed at a disadvantage. Too many men are affected by [the veteran's preference] to permit the inference that the statute is but a pretext for preferring men over women.

Moreover, as the District Court implicitly found, the purposes of the statute provide the surest explanation for its impact. Just as there are cases in which impact alone can unmask an invidious classification, cf. *Yick Wo v. Hopkins* (1886), there are others, in which—notwithstanding impact—the legitimate noninvidious purposes of a law cannot be missed. This is one. The distinction made by [the veteran's preference], is, as it seems to be, quite simply between veterans and nonveterans, not between men and women.

The dispositive question, then, is whether the appellee has shown that a gender-based discriminatory purpose has, at least in some measure, shaped the Massachusetts veterans' preference legislation. As did the District Court, she points to two basic factors which in her view distinguish [the veterans' hiring preference] from the neutral rule[ ] at issue in . . . *Washington v. Davis*. . . . The first is the nature of the preference, which is said to be demonstrably gender-biased in the sense that it favors a status reserved under federal military policy primarily to men. The second concerns the impact of the absolute lifetime preference upon the employment opportunities of women, an impact claimed to be too inevitable to have been unintended. The appellee contends that these factors, coupled with the fact that the preference itself has little if any relevance to actual job performance, more than suffice to prove the discriminatory intent required to establish a constitutional violation.

The contention that this veterans' preference is "inherently nonneutral" or "gender-biased" presumes that the State, by favoring veterans, intentionally incorporated into its public employment policies the panoply of sex-based and assertedly discriminatory federal laws that have prevented all but a handful of women from becoming veterans. [The most serious difficulty] with this argument [is that] it is wholly at odds with the District Court's central finding that Massachusetts has not offered a preference to veterans for the purpose of discriminating against women. . . . The basic distinction between veterans and nonveterans, having been found not gender-based, [the veteran's preference] must be analyzed as is any other neutral law that casts a greater burden upon women as a group than upon men as a group. The enlistment policies of the Armed Services may well have discriminat[ed] on the basis of sex. But the history of discrimination against women in the military is not on trial in this case.

The appellee's ultimate argument rests upon the presumption, common to the criminal and civil law, that a person intends the natural and foreseeable consequences of his voluntary actions. . . . The decision to grant a preference to veterans was of course "intentional." So, necessarily, did an adverse impact upon nonveterans follow from that decision. And it cannot seriously be argued that the Legislature of Massachusetts could have been unaware that most veterans are men. . . .

"Discriminatory purpose," however, implies more than intent as volition or intent as awareness of consequences.[24] It implies that the decisionmaker, in this case a state legislature, selected or reaffirmed a particular course of action at least in part "because of," not merely "in spite of," its adverse effects upon an identifiable group.[25] Yet, nothing in the record demonstrates that this preference for veterans was originally devised or subsequently re-enacted because it would accomplish the collateral goal of keeping women in a stereotypic and predefined place in the Massachusetts Civil Service.

To the contrary, the statutory history shows that the benefit of the preference was consistently offered to "any person" who was a veteran. That benefit has been extended to women under a very broad statutory definition of the term veteran. The preference formula itself, which is the focal point of this challenge,

---

[24] Proof of discriminatory intent must necessarily usually rely on objective factors, several of which were outlined in *Arlington Heights v. Metropolitan Housing Dev. Corp.* The inquiry is practical. What a legislature or any official entity is "up to" may be plain from the results its actions achieve, or the results they avoid. Often it is made clear from what has been called, in a different context, "the give and take of the situation."

[25] This is not to say that the inevitability or foreseeability of consequences of a neutral rule has no bearing upon the existence of discriminatory intent. Certainly, when the adverse consequences of a law upon an identifiable group are as inevitable as the gender-based consequences of [the veteran's preference], a strong inference that the adverse effects were desired can reasonably be drawn. But in this inquiry—made as it is under the Constitution—an inference is a working tool, not a synonym for proof. When, as here, the impact is essentially an unavoidable consequence of a legislative policy that has in itself always been deemed to be legitimate, and when, as here, the statutory history and all of the available evidence affirmatively demonstrate the opposite, the inference simply fails to ripen into proof.

was first adopted—so it appears from this record—out of a perceived need to help a small group of older Civil War veterans. It has since been reaffirmed and extended only to cover new veterans. When the totality of legislative actions establishing and extending the Massachusetts veterans' preference are considered, see *Washington v. Davis*, the law remains what it purports to be: a preference for veterans of either sex over nonveterans of either sex, not for men over women.

IV

. . . After a war, [veterans' hiring preference] laws have been enacted virtually without opposition. During peacetime, they inevitably have come to be viewed in many quarters as undemocratic and unwise. Absolute and permanent preferences, as the troubled history of this law demonstrates, have always been subject to the objection that they give the veteran more than a square deal. But the Fourteenth Amendment "cannot be made a refuge from ill-advised . . . laws." The substantial edge granted to veterans by [Massachusetts] may reflect unwise policy. The appellee, however, has simply failed to demonstrate that the law in any way reflects a purpose to discriminate on the basis of sex. . . .

MR. JUSTICE MARSHALL, with whom MR. JUSTICE BRENNAN joins, dissenting.

Although acknowledging that in some circumstances, discriminatory intent may be inferred from the inevitable or foreseeable impact of a statute, the Court concludes that no such intent has been established here. I cannot agree. . . .

Individuals in general and lawmakers in particular frequently act for a variety of reasons. . . . Thus, the critical constitutional inquiry is not whether an illicit consideration was the primary or but-for cause of a decision, but rather whether it had an appreciable role in shaping a given legislative enactment. Where there is "proof that a discriminatory purpose has been *a* motivating factor in the decision, . . . judicial deference is no longer justified." *Arlington Heights v. Metropolitan Housing Dev. Corp.* (emphasis added). . . .

WORTH NOTING

Justice Stevens concurred in the Court's opinion, but also wrote separately, in an opinion joined by Justice White. Among other points, he emphasized that the number of men disadvantaged by the veteran's preference (1,867,000) was large and relatively close to the number of women disadvantaged by it (2,954,000).

In the instant case, the impact of the Massachusetts statute on women is undisputed. Any veteran with a passing grade on the civil service exam must be placed ahead of a nonveteran, regardless of their respective scores. The District Court found that, as a practical matter, this preference supplants test results as the determinant of upper level civil service appointments. Because less than 2% of the women in Massachusetts are veterans, the absolute-preference formula has rendered desirable state civil service employment an almost exclusively male prerogative.

As the District Court recognized, this consequence follows foreseeably, indeed inexorably, from the long history of policies severely limiting women's participation in the military. Although neutral in form, the statute is anything but neutral in application. It inescapably reserves a major sector of public employment to "an already established class which, as a matter of historical fact, is 98% male." Where the foreseeable impact of a facially neutral policy is so disproportionate, the burden should rest on the State to establish that sex-based considerations played no part in the choice of the particular legislative scheme.

Clearly, that burden was not sustained here. The legislative history of the statute reflects the Commonwealth's patent appreciation of the impact the preference system would have on women, and an equally evident desire to mitigate that impact only with respect to certain traditionally female occupations. Until 1971, the statute and implementing civil service regulations exempted from operation of the preference any job requisitions "especially calling for women." In practice, this exemption, coupled with the absolute preference for veterans, has created a gender-based civil service hierarchy, with women occupying low-grade clerical and secretarial jobs and men holding more responsible and remunerative positions.

Thus, for over 70 years, the Commonwealth has maintained, as an integral part of its veterans' preference system, an exemption relegating female civil service applicants to occupations traditionally filled by women. Such a statutory scheme both reflects and perpetuates precisely the kind of archaic assumptions about women's roles which we have previously held invalid. . . . The Court's conclusion to the contrary—that "nothing in the record" evinces a "collateral goal of keeping women in a stereotypic and predefined place in the Massachusetts Civil Service"—displays a singularly myopic view of the facts established below.[3] . . .

---

[3] Although it is relevant that the preference statute also disadvantages a substantial group of men, it is equally pertinent that 47% of Massachusetts men over 18 are veterans, as compared to 0.8% of Massachusetts women. Given this disparity, and the indicia of intent noted supra, the absolute number of men denied preference cannot be dispositive, especially since they have not faced the barriers to achieving veteran status confronted by women.

3.   Alienage

As the gender cases suggest, equal protection analysis is hardest when the courts feel suspicious of some classification—perhaps because it has so often been abused to oppress—but also understand that a good-faith government might at least occasionally need to take it into account. Navigating this tension in particular cases can be quite difficult: What does it mean for two people to be similarly situated such that the government must treat them equally? What counts as a valid distinction? The so-called "alienage" cases continue our exploration of this problem by turning to another classification about which the caselaw has obvious ambivalence: discrimination on the basis of citizenship.

Graham v. Richardson

Supreme Court of the United States, 1971.
403 U.S. 365.

MR. JUSTICE BLACKMUN delivered the opinion of the Court.

[The statute involved here creates] two classes of needy persons, indistinguishable except with respect to whether they are or are not citizens of this country. . . . United States citizens living in Pennsylvania, unable to meet the requirements for federally funded benefits, may be eligible for state-supported general assistance, but resident aliens as a class are precluded from that assistance.

. . . [T]he Court's decisions have established that classifications based on alienage, like those based on nationality or race, are inherently suspect and subject to close judicial scrutiny. Aliens as a class are a prime example of a "discrete and insular" minority, see *United States v. Carolene Products Co.* (1938), for whom such heightened judicial solicitude is appropriate. Accordingly, it was said in *Takahashi v. Fish & Game Commission* (1948), that "the power of a state to apply its laws exclusively to its alien inhabitants as a class is confined within narrow limits." . . .

. . . Pennsylvania seek[s] to justify [its] restrictions on the eligibility of aliens for public assistance solely on the basis of a State's "special public interest" in favoring its own citizens over aliens in the distribution of limited resources such as welfare benefits. . . . Whatever may be the contemporary vitality of the special public-interest doctrine in other contexts after *Takahashi*, we conclude that a State's desire to preserve limited welfare benefits for its own citizens is inadequate to justify Pennsylvania's making noncitizens ineligible for public assistance. . . . We agree with the three-judge court [below] that the

> justification of limiting expenses is particularly inappropriate and unreasonable when the discriminated class consists of aliens. Aliens like citizens pay taxes and may be called into the armed forces. Unlike the short-term residents in *Shapiro v. Thompson* (1969), aliens may live within a state for many years, work in the state and contribute to the economic growth of the state.

There can be no "special public interest" in tax revenues to which aliens have contributed on an equal basis with the residents of the State.

Accordingly, we hold that a state statute that denies welfare benefits to resident aliens . . . violate[s] the Equal Protection Clause. . . .

An additional reason why the [Pennsylvania statute does] not withstand constitutional scrutiny emerges from the area of federal-state relations.

The National Government has "broad constitutional powers in determining what aliens shall be admitted to the United States, the period they may remain, regulation of their conduct before naturalization, and the terms and conditions of their naturalization." . . . Congress has not seen fit to impose any burden or restriction on aliens who become indigent after their entry into the United States. Rather, it has broadly declared: "All persons within the jurisdiction of the United States shall have the same right in every State and Territory . . . to the full and equal benefit of all laws and proceedings for the security of persons and property as is enjoyed by white citizens. . . ." 42 U.S.C. § 1981. . . .

WORTH NOTING Justice Harlan concurred in this holding and in the judgment of the Court.

State laws that restrict the eligibility of aliens for welfare benefits merely because of their alienage conflict with these overriding national policies in an area constitutionally entrusted to the Federal Government. . . . Since such laws encroach upon exclusive federal power, they are constitutionally impermissible. . . .

Graham justified its application of strict scrutiny on the ground that non-citizens are a "discrete and insular minority" for whom "heightened judicial solicitude is appropriate." Should that principle vary based on what kind of exclusion the discrimination involves? The next two cases tackle that question.

In re Griffiths

Supreme Court of the United States, 1973.
413 U.S. 717.

Mr. Justice Powell delivered the opinion of the Court.

This case presents a novel question as to the constraints imposed by the Equal Protection Clause of the Fourteenth Amendment on the qualifications which a State may require for admission to the bar. . . .

. . . From its inception, our Nation welcomed and drew strength from the immigration of aliens. Their contributions to the social and economic life of the country were self-evident, especially during the periods when the demand for human resources greatly exceeded the native supply. This demand was by no means limited to the unskilled or the uneducated. . . .

To be sure, the course of decisions protecting the employment rights of resident aliens has not been an unswerving one. In *State of Ohio ex rel. Clarke v. Deckebach* (1927), the Court was faced with a challenge to a city ordinance prohibiting the issuance to aliens of licenses to operate pool and billiard rooms. Characterizing the business as one having "harmful and vicious tendencies," the Court found no constitutional infirmity in the ordinance: "It was competent for the city to make such a choice, not shown to be irrational, by excluding from the conduct of a dubious business an entire class rather than its objectionable members selected by more empirical methods." This easily expandable proposition supported discrimination against resident aliens in a wide range of occupations.

But the doctrinal foundations of *Clarke* were undermined in *Takahashi v. Fish & Game Comm'n* (1948), [which ruled] unconstitutional a California statute barring issuance of fishing licenses to persons "ineligible to citizenship". . . . [See also *Graham v. Richardson* (finding that classifications based on citizenship are "inherently suspect")]. . . .

In order to justify the use of a suspect classification, a State must show that its purpose or interest is both constitutionally permissible and substantial,[9] and that its use of the classification is "necessary . . . to the accomplishment" of its purpose or the safeguarding of its interest.[11] . . .

We hold that the Committee, acting on behalf of the State, has not carried its burden. The State's ultimate interest here implicated is to assure the requisite qualifications of persons licensed to practice law. It is undisputed that a State has a constitutionally permissible and substantial interest in determining whether an applicant possesses "the character and general fitness requisite for an attorney and counselor-at-law." But no question is raised in this case as to appellant's character or general fitness. Rather, the sole basis for disqualification is her status as a resident alien. . . .

In order to establish a link between citizenship and the powers and responsibilities of the lawyer in Connecticut, the Committee contrasts a citizen's undivided allegiance to this country with a resident alien's possible conflict of loyalties. . . .

We find these arguments unconvincing. It is no way denigrates a lawyer's high responsibilities to observe that the powers "to sign writs and subpoenas, take recognizances, [and] administer oaths" hardly involve matters of state policy or acts of such unique responsibility as to entrust them only to citizens. Nor do we think that the practice of law offers meaningful opportunities adversely to affect the interest of the United States. Certainly the Committee has failed to show the relevance of citizenship to any likelihood that a lawyer will fail to protect faithfully the interest of his clients. . . .

Connecticut has wide freedom to gauge on a case-by-case basis the fitness of an applicant to practice law. Connecticut can, and does, require appropriate training and familiarity with Connecticut law. . . . [It also] requires a new lawyer to take both an "attorney's oath" to perform his functions faithfully and

---

[9]   The state interest required has been characterized as "overriding," *McLaughlin v. Florida*, "compelling," *Graham v. Richardson*, "important," *Dunn v. Blumstein*, or "substantial," *ibid*. We attribute no particular significance to these variations in diction.

[11]   We did not decide in *Graham* nor do we decide here whether special circumstances, such as armed hostilities between the United States and the country of which an alien is a citizen, would justify the use of a classification based on alienage.

honestly and a "commissioner's oath" to "support the constitution of the United States, and the constitution of the state of Connecticut[,]" . . . and Connecticut may quite properly conduct a character investigation [prior to admission]. Moreover, once admitted to the bar, lawyers are subject to continuing scrutiny by the organized bar and the courts. In addition to discipline for unprofessional conduct, the range of postadmission sanctions extends from judgments for contempt to criminal prosecutions and disbarment. In sum, the Committee simply has not established that it must exclude all aliens from the practice of law. . . .

We hold that § 8(1) violates the Equal Protection Clause. . . .

WORTH NOTING

Chief Justice Burger dissented, in an opinion joined by Justice Rehnquist. He expressed sympathy "with some aspects of the policy implicit in the Court's holding," but objected to what he saw as a "denigration of the posture and role of a lawyer as an 'officer of the court,' " and argued that the states should be able to rely on that role as a basis for restricting the practice of law to citizens.

MR. JUSTICE REHNQUIST, dissenting.

The Court . . . holds that an alien is not really different from a citizen, and that any legislative classification on the basis of alienage is "inherently suspect." The Fourteenth Amendment, the Equal Protection Clause of which the Court interprets as invalidating the state legislation here involved, contains no language concerning "inherently suspect classifications," or, for that matter, merely "suspect classifications." . . .

The Court . . . fails to mention, let alone rationalize, the fact that the Constitution itself recognizes a basic difference between citizens and aliens. That distinction is constitutionally important in no less than 11 instances in a political document noted for its brevity. Representatives, U.S. Const. Art. I, § 2, cl. 2, and Senators, Art. I, § 3, cl. 3, must be citizens. Congress has the authority "[t]o establish an uniform Rule of Naturalization" by which aliens can become citizen members of our society, Art. I, § 8, cl. 4; the judicial authority of the federal courts extends to suits involving citizens of the United States "and foreign States, Citizens or Subjects," Art. III, § 2, cl. 1, because somehow the parties are "different," a distinction further made by the Eleventh Amendment; the Fifteenth, Nineteenth, Twenty-Fourth, and Twenty-Sixth Amendments are relevant only to "citizens." The President must not only be a citizen but "a natural born Citizen," Art. II, § 1, cl. 5. One might speculate what meaning Art. IV, § 2, cl. 1, has today.

Not only do the numerous classifications on the basis of citizenship that are set forth in the Constitution cut against both the analysis used and the results reached by the Court in these cases; the [first sentence of the] very Amendment which the Court reads to prohibit classifications based on citizenship establishes the very distinction which the Court now condemns as "suspect." . . .

Citizenship meant something, a status in and relationship with a society which is continuing and more basic than mere presence or residence. The language of [the Fourteenth] Amendment carefully distinguishes between "persons" who, whether by birth or naturalization, had achieved a certain status, and "persons" in general. . . . Since that Amendment by its own terms first defined those who had the status as a lesser included class of all "persons," the Court's failure to articulate why such classifications under the same Amendment are now forbidden serves only to illuminate the absence of any constitutional foundation for these instant decisions. . . .

[Besides] a footnote from *United States v. Carolene Products Co.* (1938), a case involving a federal statute prohibiting the interstate shipment of filled milk . . . , [the only] apparent rationale for the invocation of the "suspect classification" approach in these cases is that alienage is a "status". . . . But there is a marked difference between a status or condition such as illegitimacy, national origin, or race, which cannot be altered by an individual and the "status" of the appellant. . . . There is nothing in the record indicating that their status as aliens cannot be changed by their affirmative acts. . . .

In my view, the proper judicial inquiry is whether any rational justification exists for prohibiting aliens from . . . admission to a state bar. . . .

Connecticut's requirement of citizenship reflects its judgment that something more than technical skills are needed to be a lawyer under our system. I do not believe it is irrational for a State that makes that judgment to require that lawyers have an understanding of the American political and social experience, whether gained from growing up in this country, as in the case of a native-born citizen, or from the naturalization process, as in the case of a foreign-born citizen. . . . I suppose the Connecticut Bar Examining Committee could itself administer tests in American history, government, and sociology, but the State did not choose to go this route. Instead, it chose to operate on the assumption that citizens as a class might reasonably be thought to have a significantly greater degree of understanding of our experience than would aliens. Particularly in the case of one such as appellant, who candidly admits that she wants to live and work in the United States but does not want to sever her fundamental social and political relationship with the country of her birth, I do not believe the State's judgment is irrational. . . .

Foley v. Connelie

Supreme Court of the United States, 1978.
435 U.S. 291.

Mr. Chief Justice Burger delivered the opinion of the Court.

SUMMARY OF THE FACTS

Edmund Foley was a citizen of Ireland who was lawfully present in the United States as a permanent resident. He challenged a New York statute that required all members of the state police to be citizens of the United States.

II

. . . Our cases generally reflect a close scrutiny of restraints imposed by States on aliens. But we have never suggested that such legislation is inherently invalid, nor have we held that all limitations on aliens are suspect. Rather, beginning with a case which involved the denial of welfare assistance essential to life itself, the Court has treated certain restrictions on aliens with "heightened judicial solicitude," *Graham v. Richardson* (1971), a treatment deemed necessary since aliens—pending their eligibility for citizenship—have no direct voice in the political processes.[3] Following *Graham*, a series of decisions has resulted requiring state action to meet close scrutiny to exclude aliens as a class from educational benefits, *Nyquist v. Mauclet* (1977), eligibility for a broad range of public employment, *Sugarman v. Dougall* (1973), or the practice of licensed professions, *In re Griffiths* (1973). These exclusions struck at the noncitizens'

---

[3]   The alien's status is, at least for a time, beyond his control since Congress has imposed durational residency requirements for the attainment of citizenship. Federal law generally requires an alien to lawfully reside in this country for five years as a prerequisite to applying for naturalization.

ability to exist in the community, a position seemingly inconsistent with the congressional determination to admit the alien to permanent residence. . . .

It would be inappropriate, however, to require every statutory exclusion of aliens to clear the high hurdle of "strict scrutiny," because to do so would "obliterate all the distinctions between citizens and aliens, and thus depreciate the historic values of citizenship." *Nyquist v. Mauclet* (1977) (Burger, dissenting). The act of becoming a citizen is more than a ritual with no content beyond the fanfare of ceremony. A new citizen has become a member of a Nation, part of a people distinct from others. The individual, at that point, belongs to the polity and is entitled to participate in the processes of democratic decisionmaking. Accordingly, we have recognized "a State's historical power to exclude aliens from participation in its democratic political institutions," as part of the sovereign's obligation " 'to preserve the basic conception of a political community.' " *Sugarman v. Dougall.*

The practical consequence of this theory is that "our scrutiny will not be so demanding where we deal with matters firmly within a State's constitutional prerogatives." The State need only justify its classification by a showing of some rational relationship between the interest sought to be protected and the limiting classification. This is not intended to denigrate the valuable contribution of aliens who benefit from our traditional hospitality. It is no more than recognition of the fact that a democratic society is ruled by its people. Thus, it is clear that a State may deny aliens the right to vote, or to run for elective office, for these lie at the heart of our political institutions. Similar considerations support a legislative determination to exclude aliens from jury service.

Likewise, we have recognized that citizenship may be a relevant qualification for fulfilling those "important nonelective executive, legislative, and judicial positions," held by "officers who participate directly in the formulation, execution, or review of broad public policy." This is not because our society seeks to reserve the better jobs to its members. Rather, it is because this country entrusts many of its most important policy responsibilities to these officers, the discretionary exercise of which can often more immediately affect the lives of citizens than even the ballot of a voter or the choice of a legislator. In sum, then, it represents the choice, and right, of the people to be governed by their citizen peers. To effectuate this result, we must necessarily examine each position in question to determine whether it involves discretionary decisionmaking, or execution of policy, which substantially affects members of the political community.

The essence of our holdings to date is that although we extend to aliens the right to education and public welfare, along with the ability to earn a livelihood and engage in licensed professions, the right to govern is reserved to citizens.

III

A discussion of the police function is essentially a description of one of the basic functions of government, especially in a complex modern society where police presence is pervasive. The police function fulfills a most fundamental obligation of government to its constituency. Police officers in the ranks do not formulate policy, *per se*, but they are clothed with authority to exercise an almost infinite variety of discretionary powers. The execution of the broad powers vested in them affects members of the public significantly and often in the most sensitive areas of daily life. Our Constitution, of course, provides safeguards to persons, homes and possessions, as well as guidance to police officers. And few countries, if any, provide more protection to individuals by limitations on the power and discretion of the police. Nonetheless, police may, in the exercise of their discretion, invade the privacy of an individual in public places. They may under some conditions break down a door to enter a dwelling or other building in the execution of a warrant, or without a formal warrant in very limited circumstances; they may stop vehicles traveling on public highways.

An arrest, the function most commonly associated with the police, is a serious matter for any person even when no prosecution follows or when an acquittal is obtained. Most arrests are without prior judicial authority, as when an officer observes a criminal act in progress or suspects that felonious activity is afoot. Even the routine traffic arrests made by the state trooper—for speeding, weaving, reckless driving, improper license plates, absence of inspection stickers, or dangerous physical condition of a vehicle, to describe only a few of the more obvious common violations—can intrude on the privacy of the individual. In stopping cars, they may, within limits, require a driver or passengers to disembark and even search them for weapons, depending on time, place and circumstances. . . .

Clearly the exercise of police authority calls for a very high degree of judgment and discretion, the abuse or misuse of which can have serious impact on individuals. The office of a policeman is in no sense one of "the common occupations of the community" that the then Mr. Justice Hughes referred to in *Truax v. Raich* (1915) [(state regulatory authority "does not go so far as to make it possible for the State to deny to lawful inhabitants, because of their race or nationality, the ordinary means of earning a livelihood")]. A policeman vested with the plenary discretionary powers we have described is not to be equated with a private person engaged in routine public employment or other "common occupations of the community" who exercises no broad power over people generally. . . .

In short, it would be as anomalous to conclude that citizens may be subjected to the broad discretionary powers of noncitizen police officers as it would be to say that judicial officers and jurors with power to judge citizens can be aliens. It is not surprising, therefore, that most States expressly confine the employment of police officers to citizens, whom the State may reasonably presume to be more familiar with and sympathetic to American traditions. Police officers very clearly fall within the category of "important non-elective . . . officers who participate directly in the . . . *execution* . . . of broad public policy." *Dougall* (emphasis added). In the enforcement and execution of the laws the police function is one where citizenship bears a rational relationship to the special demands of the particular position. A State may, therefore, consonant with the Constitution, confine the performance of this important public responsibility to citizens of the United States. . . .

MR. JUSTICE STEWART, concurring.

The dissenting opinions convincingly demonstrate that it is difficult if not impossible to reconcile the Court's judgment in this case with the full sweep of the reasoning and authority of some of our past decisions. It is only because I have become increasingly doubtful about the validity of those decisions (in at least some of which I concurred) that I join the opinion of the Court in this case.

WORTH NOTING

Justice Blackmun concurred in the result, writing that New York had "vested its state troopers with powers and duties that are basic to the function of state government," and that the state could "rationally conclude that those who are to execute these duties should be limited to persons who can be presumed to share in the values of its political community, as, for example, those who possess citizenship status."

MR. JUSTICE MARSHALL, with whom MR. JUSTICE BRENNAN and MR. JUSTICE STEVENS joins, dissenting.

. . . Today the Court upholds a law excluding aliens from public employment as state troopers. It bases its decision largely on dictum from *Sugarman v. Dougall* to the effect that aliens may be barred from holding "state elective or important nonelective executive, legislative, and judicial positions," because persons in these positions "participate directly in the formulation, execution, or review of broad public policy." I do not agree with the Court that state troopers perform functions placing them within this "narro[w] . . . exception" to our usual rule that discrimination against aliens is presumptively unconstitutional. Accordingly I dissent.

In one sense, of course, it is true that state troopers participate in the execution of public policy. Just as firefighters execute the public policy that fires should be extinguished, and sanitation workers execute the public policy that streets should be kept clean, state troopers execute the public policy that persons believed to have committed crimes should be arrested. But this fact simply demonstrates that the *Sugarman* exception, if read without regard to its context, "would swallow the rule." Although every state employee is charged with the "execution" of public policy, *Sugarman* unambiguously holds that a blanket exclusion of aliens from state jobs is unconstitutional.

Thus the phrase "execution of broad public policy" in *Sugarman* cannot be read to mean simply the carrying out of government programs, but rather must be interpreted to include responsibility for actually setting government policy pursuant to a delegation of substantial authority from the legislature. The head of an executive agency for example, charged with promulgating complex regulations under a statute, executes broad public policy in a sense that file clerks in the agency clearly do not. [A]s *Sugarman* indicates, those "elective or important nonelective" positions that involve broad policymaking responsibilities are the only state jobs from which aliens as a group may constitutionally be excluded. In my view, the job of state trooper is not one of those positions. . . .

The Court places great reliance on the fact that policemen make arrests and perform searches, often "without prior judicial authority." I certainly agree that "[an] arrest is a serious matter," and that we should be concerned about all "intru[sions] on the privacy of the individual." But these concerns do not in any way make it "anomalous" for citizens to be arrested and searched by "noncitizen police officers," at least not in New York State. By statute, New York authorizes "any person" to arrest another who has actually committed a felony or who has committed any other offense in the arresting person's presence. Moreover, a person making an arrest pursuant to this statute is authorized to make a search incident to the arrest. While law enforcement is primarily the responsibility of state troopers, it is nevertheless difficult to understand how the Court can imply that the troopers' arrest and search authority justifies excluding aliens from the police force when the State has given all private persons, including aliens, such authority. . . .

In *Griffiths* we held that the State could not limit the practice of law to citizens, "despite a recognition of the vital public and political role of attorneys." It is similarly not a denigration of the important public role of the state trooper—who, as the Court notes, operates "in the most sensitive areas of daily life"—to find that his law enforcement responsibilities do not "make him a formulator of government policy." *In re Griffiths.* . . .

Mr. Justice Stevens, with whom Mr. Justice Brennan joins, dissenting.

. . . Respect for the law enforcement profession and its essential function, like respect for the military, should not cause us to lose sight of the fact that in our representative democracy neither the constabulary nor the military is vested with broad policymaking responsibility. Instead, each implements the basic policies formulated directly or indirectly by the citizenry. Under the standards announced in *Sugarman*, therefore, a blanket exclusion of aliens from this particular governmental institution is especially inappropriate.

The Court's misapprehension of the role of the institutionalized police function in a democratic society obfuscates the true significance of the distinction between citizenship and alienage. The privilege of participating in the formulation of broad public policy—a privilege largely denied to the institutions exercising the police function in our society—is the essence of individual citizenship. It is this privilege which gives dramatic meaning to the naturalization ceremony. The transition from alienage to citizenship is a fundamental change in the status of a person. This change is qualitatively different from any incremental increase in economic benefits that may accrue to holders of citizenship papers. The new citizen's right to vote and to participate in the democratic decisionmaking process is the honorable prerogative which no alien has a constitutional right to enjoy. . . .

The next case shows another way that the traditional strict scrutiny framework does not map as cleanly onto the Court's alienage jurisprudence as *Graham v. Richardson* seemed to suggest. As it turns out, things look very different when it is the federal government doing the discriminating rather than the states.

Mathews v. Diaz

Supreme Court of the United States, 1976.
426 U.S. 67.

MR. JUSTICE STEVENS delivered the opinion for a unanimous Court.

The question presented by the Secretary's appeal is whether Congress may condition an alien's eligibility for participation in a federal medical insurance program on continuous residence in the United States for a five-year period and admission for permanent residence. [W]e conclude that both conditions are constitutional. . . .

Each of the appellees is a resident alien who was lawfully admitted to the United States less than five years ago. . . . All three are over 65 years old and have been denied enrollment in the Medicare Part B supplemental medical insurance program. . . . They brought this action to challenge the statutory basis for that denial[,] which grants eligibility to resident citizens who are 65 or older but denies eligibility to comparable aliens unless they have been admitted for permanent residence and also have resided in the United States for at least five years. . . .

II

There are literally millions of aliens within the jurisdiction of the United States. The Fifth Amendment, as well as the Fourteenth Amendment, protects every one of these persons from deprivation of life, liberty, or property without due process of law. Even one whose presence in this country is unlawful, involuntary, or transitory is entitled to that constitutional protection. *Wong Yang Sung v. McGrath* (1950).

The fact that all persons, aliens and citizens alike, are protected by the Due Process Clause does not lead to the further conclusion that all aliens are entitled to enjoy all the advantages of citizenship or, indeed, to the conclusion that all aliens must be placed in a single homogeneous legal classification. For a host of constitutional and statutory provisions rest on the premise that a legitimate distinction between citizens and aliens may justify attributes and benefits for one class not accorded to the other;[12] and the class of aliens is itself a heterogeneous multitude of persons with a wide-ranging variety of ties to this country.

---

[12]   The Constitution protects the privileges and immunities only of citizens, Amdt. 14, § 1; see Art. IV, § 2, cl. 1, and the right to vote only of citizens. Amdts. 15, 19, 24, 26. It requires that Representatives have been

In the exercise of its broad power over naturalization and immigration, Congress regularly makes rules that would be unacceptable if applied to citizens. The exclusion of aliens and the reservation of the power to deport have no permissible counterpart in the Federal Government's power to regulate the conduct of its own citizenry. The fact that an Act of Congress treats aliens differently from citizens does not in itself imply that such disparate treatment is "invidious." In particular, the fact that Congress has provided some welfare benefits for citizens does not require it to provide like benefits for all aliens. Neither the overnight visitor, the unfriendly agent of a hostile foreign power, the resident diplomat, nor the illegal entrant, can advance even a colorable constitutional claim to a share in the bounty that a conscientious sovereign makes available to its own citizens and some of its guests. The decision to share that bounty with our guests may take into account the character of the relationship between the alien and this country: Congress may decide that as the alien's tie grows stronger, so does the strength of his claim to an equal share of that munificence. . . .

III.

For reasons long recognized as valid, the responsibility for regulating the relationship between the United States and our alien visitors has been committed to the political branches of the Federal Government. Since decisions in these matters may implicate our relations with foreign powers, and since a wide variety of classifications must be defined in the light of changing political and economic circumstances, such decisions are frequently of a character more appropriate to either the Legislature or the Executive than to the Judiciary. . . . [This] dictate[s] a narrow standard of review of decisions made by the Congress or the President in the area of immigration and naturalization.

Since it is obvious that Congress has no constitutional duty to provide *all aliens* with the welfare benefits provided to citizens, the party challenging

---

citizens for seven years, Art. I, § 2, cl. 2, and Senators citizens for nine, Art. I, § 3, cl. 3, and that the President be a "natural born Citizen." Art. II, § 1, cl. 5. A multitude of federal statutes distinguish between citizens and aliens. The whole of Title 8 of the United States Code, regulating aliens and nationality, is founded on the legitimacy of distinguishing between citizens and aliens. A variety of other federal statutes provide for disparate treatment of aliens and citizens. These include prohibitions and restrictions upon Government employment of aliens, upon private employment of aliens, and upon investments and businesses of aliens; statutes excluding aliens from benefits available to citizens and from protections extended to citizens; and statutes imposing added burdens upon aliens. Several statutes treat certain aliens more favorably than citizens. Other statutes, similar to the one at issue in this case, provide for equal treatment of citizens and aliens lawfully admitted for permanent residence. Still others equate citizens and aliens who have declared their intention to become citizens. Yet others condition equal treatment of an alien upon reciprocal treatment of United States citizens by the alien's own country.

the constitutionality of the particular line Congress has drawn has the burden of advancing principled reasoning that will at once invalidate that line and yet tolerate a different line separating some aliens from others. [If the permanent-residence and five-year requirements in this case] were eliminated, surely Congress would at least require that the alien's entry be lawful; even then, unless mere transients are to be held constitutionally entitled to benefits, some durational requirement would certainly be appropriate. In short, it is unquestionably reasonable for Congress to make an alien's eligibility depend on both the character and the duration of his residence. Since neither requirement is wholly irrational, this case essentially involves nothing more than a claim that it would have been more reasonable for Congress to select somewhat different requirements of the same kind.

We may assume that the five-year line drawn by Congress is longer than necessary to protect the fiscal integrity of the program. We may also assume that unnecessary hardship is incurred by persons just short of qualifying. But it remains true that some line is essential, that any line must produce some harsh and apparently arbitrary consequences, and, of greatest importance, that those who qualify under the test Congress has chosen may reasonably be presumed to have a greater affinity with the United States than those who do not. In short, citizens and those who are most like citizens qualify. Those who are less like citizens do not.

The task of classifying persons for medical benefits, like the task of drawing lines for federal tax purposes, inevitably requires that some persons who have an almost equally strong claim to favored treatment be placed on different sides of the line. When this kind of policy choice must be made, we are especially reluctant to question the exercise of congressional judgment. [Appellees] have, in effect, merely invited us to substitute our judgment for that of Congress in deciding which aliens shall be eligible to participate . . . on the same conditions as citizens. We decline the invitation.

IV

The cases on which appellees rely are consistent with our conclusion that this statutory classification does not deprive them of liberty or property without due process of law.

Graham v. Richardson provides the strongest support for appellees' position. That case holds that state statutes that deny welfare benefits to resident aliens, or to aliens not meeting a requirement of durational residence within the

United States, violate the Equal Protection Clause of the Fourteenth Amendment and encroach upon the exclusive federal power over the entrance and residence of aliens. Of course, the latter ground of decision actually supports our holding today that it is the business of the political branches of the Federal Government, rather than that of either the States or the Federal Judiciary, to regulate the conditions of entry and residence of aliens. The equal protection analysis also involves significantly different considerations because it concerns the relationship between aliens and the States rather than between aliens and the Federal Government.

Insofar as state welfare policy is concerned, there is little, if any, basis for treating persons who are citizens of another State differently from persons who are citizens of another country. Both groups are noncitizens as far as the State's interests in administering its welfare programs are concerned. Thus, a division by a State of the category of persons who are not citizens of that State into subcategories of United States citizens and aliens has no apparent justification, whereas, a comparable classification by the Federal Government is a routine and normally legitimate part of its business. Furthermore, whereas the Constitution inhibits every State's power to restrict travel across its own borders, Congress is explicitly empowered to exercise that type of control over travel across the borders of the United States. . . .

The judgment of the District Court is reversed.

4.   Classifications and Fundamental Rights

If you review the excerpt from *Clark v. Jeter* (1988) in the introduction to Section C of this chapter, you'll note that it describes strict scrutiny as being triggered not only by the use of suspect classifications but also by the use of "classifications affecting fundamental rights." The example given, *Harper v. Virginia Bd. of Elections* (1966), helps illustrate the idea.

In *Harper*, the Supreme Court invalidated Virginia's poll tax, holding that the tax invalidly discriminated against those unable to pay. (The 24th Amendment, adopted in 1964, prohibits poll taxes only with respect to federal elections; the Virginia tax applied to state elections.) But the Court has not deemed wealth a suspect classification; there are numerous government services that carry charges, which the rich are better able to pay than the poor. And the Court did not say that there is a constitutional right to vote for any particular office; a state might organize its government without electing many officials at all. Rather, the Court explained, "once the franchise is granted to the electorate, lines may not be drawn which are inconsistent with the Equal Protection Clause of the Fourteenth Amendment." Given what the Court deemed to be the fundamental nature of the right to vote, it concluded that the effective discrimination against the less affluent was invalid.

There are a couple of oddities here. First, the Court perceives discrimination in allocation of a fundamental right to vote, even though there really is not a right to vote for a given office at all. Perhaps it would be better if the Court spoke of the importance of *interests* that are at stake. Second, if the Court truly believes a fundamental right is violated, then, as we shall see in the next chapter, it can hold that the denial violates due process, without need to consider discrimination. Perhaps these oddities explain why this branch of the equal protection doctrine—strict scrutiny invoked by the fundamental nature of the "right" at stake rather than by the suspect nature of the classification used to allocate it—seems to have passed from favor. But the Supreme Court has never repudiated it, and the nexus between not-quite-suspicious classifications and not-quite-fundamental substantive due process may have re-emerged in the LGBTQ+ cases that we'll see at the end of the book.

For more on all this, see Chapter VI.B.5.

TEST YOUR KNOWLEDGE: To assess your understanding of the material in this chapter, **click here** to take a quiz.

CHAPTER VI

Due Process

The roots of due process as a formal legal guarantee trace back to the English Magna Carta, which was signed by King John in 1215 to resolve a barons' revolt against his rule. Chapter 39 of that instrument provided that "no free man shall be taken or imprisoned or disseized or exiled or in any way destroyed . . . except by the lawful judgment of his peers or by the law of the land." (You will sometimes see modern lawyers use the last phrase in the original Latin: "*per legem terrae.*")

This guarantee that the government will deprive individuals of their interests *only* pursuant to established legal process has been central to the American legal tradition—not just for the Founders, but for many successive generations of lawyers as well. And so the Constitution contains two separate due process guarantees: one in the Fifth Amendment that applies to the federal government, and one in the Fourteenth Amendment that applies to the states. Each provision prohibits the deprivation of "life, liberty, or property, without due process of law." This chapter will trace the application of this guarantee across a variety of contexts.

Begin with the most obvious implications of the textual structure. A series of specific interests—"life, liberty, [and] property"—is protected from government interference. But they are not protected absolutely. That is to say, on its face, the Due Process Clause doesn't say that the government may *never* take someone's life, liberty, or property. Rather, it says that the government may take someone's life, liberty, or property *if and only if* certain conditions are satisfied. As we shall see later, the courts have held in some instances that the Due Process Clauses absolutely prohibit certain kinds of deprivations by the government—or, put another way, that no process could ever be sufficient to justify such deprivations. This latter area of the law, which has come to be known by the curious term *substantive due process*, will occupy our attention for most of this chapter. But first we will begin in Section A by addressing the core procedural requirements of due process—which are themselves known by the equally curious term *procedural due process*.

A. Procedural Due Process

The procedural requirements of due process in any particular case will always depend on the answer to two questions:

- First, the question of what interests are protected. Given that the clauses aren't actually implicated unless a relevant interest has been deprived, courts must begin by deciding whether such an interest is involved. "Life" is straightforward, but what about "liberty" and "property"?

- Second, the question of what process is due. Even if a given interest is covered by the Due Process Clause, that doesn't necessarily mean that it's *absolutely* protected. Rather, the government can usually still deprive the individual of that interest—so long as it's done pursuant to the "due process of law." So the second question asks: what procedural requirements must the government fulfill before we can say that the individual has in fact received all the "process" which is "due"?

The materials that follow explore each of these questions in turn.

1.   PDP: What Interests Are Protected?

Goldberg v. Kelly

Supreme Court of the United States, 1970.
397 U.S. 254.

MR. JUSTICE BRENNAN delivered the opinion of the Court.

The question for decision is whether a State that terminates public assistance payments to a particular recipient without affording him the opportunity for an evidentiary hearing prior to termination denies the recipient proce-dural due process in violation of the Due Process Clause of the Fourteenth Amendment.

This action was brought in the District Court for the Southern District of New York by residents of New York City receiving financial aid under the fed-erally assisted program of Aid to Families with Dependent Children (AFDC) or under New York State's general Home Relief program. Their complaint al-leged that the New York State and New York City officials administering these programs terminated, or were about to terminate, such aid without prior notice and hearing, thereby denying them due process of law.[2] At the time the suits were filed there was no requirement of prior notice or hearing of any kind before termination of financial aid. However, the State and city adopted procedures for notice and hearing after the suits were brought, and the plaintiffs, appel-lees here, then challenged the constitutional adequacy of those procedures. . . .

I

The constitutional issue to be decided . . . is the narrow one whether the Due Process Clause requires that the recipient be afforded an evidentiary hear-ing before the termination of benefits.[7] . . .

Appellant does not contend that procedural due process is not applicable to the termination of welfare benefits. Such benefits are a matter of statutory entitlement for persons qualified to receive them.[8] Their termination involves

---

[2]   . . . For example, Mrs. Altagracia Guzman alleged that she was in danger of losing AFDC payments for failure to cooperate with the City Department of Social Services in suing her estranged husband. She contend-ed that the departmental policy requiring such cooperation was inapplicable to the facts of her case. . . . Home Relief payments to Juan DeJesus were terminated because he refused to accept counseling and rehabilitation for drug addiction. Mr. DeJesus maintains that he does not use drugs. . . .

[7]   Appellant does not question the recipient's due process right to evidentiary review after termination.

[8]   It may be realistic today to regard welfare entitlements as more like "property" than a "gratuity." Much of the existing wealth in this country takes the form of rights that do not fall within traditional common-law concepts of property. It has been aptly noted that

[s]ociety today is built around entitlement. The automobile dealer has his franchise, the doctor and lawyer their professional licenses, the worker his union membership, contract, and pension rights, the executive his contract and stock options; all are devices to aid security and independence. Many of the most important of these entitlements now flow from government: subsidies to farmers and businessmen, routes for airlines and channels for television stations; long term contracts for defense, space, and edu-cation; social security pensions for individuals. Such sources of security, whether private or public, are no longer regarded as luxuries or gratuities; to the recipients they are essentials, fully deserved, and in no sense a form of charity. It is only the poor whose entitlements, although recognized by public policy, have not been effectively enforced.

Reich, *Individual Rights and Social Welfare: The Emerging Legal Issues*, 74 Yale L.J. 1245 (1965). See also Reich, *The New Property*, 73 Yale L.J. 733 (1964).

state action that adjudicates important rights. The constitutional challenge cannot be answered by an argument that public assistance benefits are "a 'privilege' and not a 'right.' " Relevant constitutional restraints apply as much to the withdrawal of public assistance benefits as to disqualification for unemployment compensation, *Sherbert v. Verner* (1963); or to denial of a tax exemption; or to discharge from public employment, *Slochower v. Board of Higher Education* (1956).[9] The extent to which procedural due process must be afforded the recipient is influenced by the extent to which he may be "condemned to suffer grievous loss," and depends upon whether the recipient's interest in avoiding that loss outweighs the governmental interest in summary adjudication. . . . .

It is true, of course, that some governmental benefits may be administratively terminated without affording the recipient a pre-termination evidentiary hearing.[10] But we agree with the District Court that when welfare is discontinued, only a pre-termination evidentiary hearing provides the recipient with procedural due process. Cf. *Sniadach v. Family Finance Corp.* (1969). For qualified recipients, welfare provides the means to obtain essential food, clothing, housing, and medical care. Thus the crucial factor in this context—a factor not present in the case of the blacklisted government contractor, the discharged government employee, the taxpayer denied a tax exemption, or virtually anyone else whose governmental entitlements are ended—is that termination of aid pending resolution of a controversy over eligibility may deprive an eligible recipient of the very means by which to live while he waits. Since he lacks independent resources, his situation becomes immediately desperate. His need to concentrate upon finding the means for daily subsistence, in turn, adversely affects his ability to seek redress from the welfare bureaucracy.

Moreover, important governmental interests are promoted by affording recipients a pre-termination evidentiary hearing. From its founding the Nation's basic commitment has been to foster the dignity and well-being of all persons within its borders. We have come to recognize that forces not within the control of the poor contribute to their poverty. . . . At the same time, welfare guards

---

[9]   See also *Goldsmith v. United States Board of Tax Appeals* (1926) (right of a certified public accountant to practice before the Board of Tax Appeals); *Hornsby v. Allen* (5th Cir. 1964) (right to obtain a retail liquor store license); *Dixon v. Alabama State Board of Education* (5th Cir. 1961) (right to attend a public college).

[10]   One Court of Appeals has stated: "In a wide variety of situations, it has long been recognized that where harm to the public is threatened, and the private interest infringed is reasonably deemed to be of less importance, an official body can take summary action pending a later hearing." *R. A. Holman & Co. v. SEC* (1962) (suspension of exemption from stock registration requirement). See also, for example, *Ewing v. Mytinger & Casselberry, Inc.* (1950) (seizure of mislabeled vitamin product); *North American Cold Storage Co. v. Chicago* (1908) (seizure of food not fit for human use); *Yakus v. United States* (1944) (adoption of wartime price regulations). . . .

against the societal malaise that may flow from a widespread sense of unjustified frustration and insecurity. Public assistance, then, is not mere charity, but a means to "promote the general Welfare, and secure the Blessings of Liberty to ourselves and our Posterity." The same governmental interests that counsel the provision of welfare, counsel as well its uninterrupted provision to those eligible to receive it; pre-termination evidentiary hearings are indispensable to that end.

Appellant does not challenge the force of these considerations but argues that they are outweighed by countervailing governmental interests in conserving fiscal and administrative resources. These interests, the argument goes, justify the delay of any evidentiary hearing until after discontinuance of the grants. Summary adjudication protects the public fisc by stopping payments promptly upon discovery of reason to believe that a recipient is no longer eligible. Since most terminations are accepted without challenge, summary adjudication also conserves both the fisc and administrative time and energy by reducing the number of evidentiary hearings actually held.

We agree with the District Court, however, that these governmental interests are not overriding in the welfare context. The requirement of a prior hearing doubtless involves some greater expense, and the benefits paid to ineligible recipients pending decision at the hearing probably cannot be recouped, since these recipients are likely to be judgment-proof. But the State is not without weapons to minimize these increased costs. Much of the drain on fiscal and administrative resources can be reduced by developing procedures for prompt pre-termination hearings and by skillful use of personnel and facilities. Indeed, the very provision for a post-termination evidentiary hearing in New York's Home Relief program is itself cogent evidence that the State recognizes the primacy of the public interest in correct eligibility determinations and therefore in the provision of procedural safeguards.

Thus, the interest of the eligible recipient in uninterrupted receipt of public assistance, coupled with the State's interest that his payments not be erroneously terminated, clearly outweighs the State's competing concern to prevent any increase in its fiscal and administrative burdens. As the District Court correctly concluded, "[t]he stakes are simply too high for the welfare recipient, and the possibility for honest error or irritable misjudgment too great, to allow termination of aid without giving the recipient a chance, if he so desires, to be fully informed of the case against him so that he may contest its basis and produce evidence in rebuttal."

II

We also agree with the District Court, however, that the pre-termination hearing need not take the form of a judicial or quasi-judicial trial. We bear in mind that the statutory "fair hearing" will provide the recipient with a full administrative review.[14] Accordingly, the pre-termination hearing has one function only: to produce an initial determination of the validity of the welfare department's grounds for discontinuance of payments in order to protect a recipient against an erroneous termination of his benefits. Thus, a complete record and a comprehensive opinion, which would serve primarily to facilitate judicial review and to guide future decisions, need not be provided at the pre-termination stage. We recognize, too, that both welfare authorities and recipients have an interest in relatively speedy resolution of questions of eligibility, that they are used to dealing with one another informally, and that some welfare departments have very burdensome caseloads. These considerations justify the limitation of the pre-termination hearing to minimum procedural safeguards, adapted to the particular characteristics of welfare recipients, and to the limited nature of the controversies to be resolved. We wish to add that we, no less than the dissenters, recognize the importance of not imposing upon the States or the Federal Government in this developing field of law any procedural requirements beyond those demanded by rudimentary due process.

"The fundamental requisite of due process of law is the opportunity to be heard." *Grannis v. Ordean* (1914). The hearing must be "at a meaningful time and in a meaningful manner." *Armstrong v. Manzo* (1965). In the present context these principles require that a recipient have timely and adequate notice detailing the reasons for a proposed termination, and an effective opportunity to defend by confronting any adverse witnesses and by presenting his own arguments and evidence orally. These rights are important in cases such as those before us, where recipients have challenged proposed terminations as resting on incorrect or misleading factual premises or on misapplication of rules or policies to the facts of particular cases.

We are not prepared to say that the seven-day notice currently provided by New York City is constitutionally insufficient *per se,* although there may be cases where fairness would require that a longer time be given. Nor do we see any constitutional deficiency in the content or form of the notice. New York

---

[14]   Due process does not, of course, require two hearings. If, for example, a State simply wishes to continue benefits until after a "fair" hearing there will be no need for a preliminary hearing.

employs both a letter and a personal conference with a caseworker to inform a recipient of the precise questions raised about his continued eligibility. Evidently the recipient is told the legal and factual bases for the Department's doubts. This combination is probably the most effective method of communicating with recipients.

The city's procedures presently do not permit recipients to appear personally with or without counsel before the official who finally determines continued eligibility. Thus a recipient is not permitted to present evidence to that official orally, or to confront or cross-examine adverse witnesses. These omissions are fatal to the constitutional adequacy of the procedures.

The opportunity to be heard must be tailored to the capacities and circumstances of those who are to be heard. It is not enough that a welfare recipient may present his position to the decision maker in writing or second-hand through his caseworker. Written submissions are an unrealistic option for most recipients, who lack the educational attainment necessary to write effectively and who cannot obtain professional assistance. Moreover, written submissions do not afford the flexibility of oral presentations; they do not permit the recipient to mold his argument to the issues the decision maker appears to regard as important. Particularly where credibility and veracity are at issue, as they must be in many termination proceedings, written submissions are a wholly unsatisfactory basis for decision. The second-hand presentation to the decisionmaker by the caseworker has its own deficiencies; since the caseworker usually gathers the facts upon which the charge of ineligibility rests, the presentation of the recipient's side of the controversy cannot safely be left to him. Therefore a recipient must be allowed to state his position orally. Informal procedures will suffice; in this context due process does not require a particular order of proof or mode of offering evidence.

In almost every setting where important decisions turn on questions of fact, due process requires an opportunity to confront and cross-examine adverse witnesses. What we said in *Greene v. McElroy* (1959) is particularly pertinent here: ". . . While this is important in the case of documentary evidence, it is even more important where the evidence consists of the testimony of individuals whose memory might be faulty or who, in fact, might be perjurers." . . .

"The right to be heard would be, in many cases, of little avail if it did not comprehend the right to be heard by counsel." *Powell v. Alabama* (1932). We do not say that counsel must be provided at the pre-termination hearing, but only that the recipient must be allowed to retain an attorney if he so desires. Counsel can help delineate the issues, present the factual contentions in an orderly manner, conduct cross-examination, and generally safeguard the interests of the recipient. We do not anticipate that this assistance will unduly prolong or otherwise encumber the hearing. Evidently HEW has reached the same conclusion. See 45 CFR § 205.10 (1969).

Finally, the decisionmaker's conclusion as to a recipient's eligibility must rest solely on the legal rules and evidence adduced at the hearing. To demonstrate compliance with this elementary requirement, the decision maker should state the reasons for his determination and indicate the evidence he relied on, though his statement need not amount to a full opinion or even formal findings of fact and conclusions of law. And, of course, an impartial decision maker is essential. We agree with the District Court that prior involvement in some aspects of a case will not necessarily bar a welfare official from acting as a decision maker. He should not, however, have participated in making the determination under review.

Affirmed.

MR. JUSTICE BLACK, dissenting.

. . . The more than a million names on the relief rolls in New York, and the more than nine million names on the rolls of all the 50 States . . . are there because state welfare officials believed that those people were eligible for assistance. Probably in the officials' haste to make out the lists many names were put there erroneously in order to alleviate immediate suffering, and undoubtedly some people are drawing relief who are not entitled under the law to do so. Doubtless some draw relief checks from time to time who know they are not eligible, either because they are not actually in need or for some other reason. Many of those who thus draw undeserved gratuities are without sufficient property to enable the government to collect back from them any money they wrongfully receive.

But the Court today holds that it would violate the Due Process Clause of the Fourteenth Amendment to stop paying those people weekly or monthly allowances unless the government first affords them a full "evidentiary hearing" even though welfare officials are persuaded that the recipients are not rightfully entitled to receive a penny under the law. In other words, although some recipients might be on the lists for payment wholly because of deliberate fraud on their part, the Court holds that the government is helpless and must continue, until after an evidentiary hearing, to pay money that it does not owe, never has owed, and never could owe. I do not believe there is any provision in our Constitution that should thus paralyze the government's efforts to protect itself against making payments to people who are not entitled to them. . . .

The Court, however, relies upon the Fourteenth Amendment and in effect says that failure of the government to pay a promised charitable instalment to an individual deprives that individual of his own property, in violation of the Due Process Clause of the Fourteenth Amendment. It somewhat strains credulity to say that the government's promise of charity to an individual is property belonging to that individual when the government denies that the individual is honestly entitled to receive such a payment.

I would have little, if any, objection to the majority's decision in this case if it were written as the report of the House Committee on Education and Labor, but as an opinion ostensibly resting on the language of the Constitution I find it woefully deficient. . . . The majority reaches this result by a process of weighing "the recipient's interest in avoiding" the termination of welfare benefits against "the governmental interest in summary adjudication." Today's balancing act requires a "pre-termination evidentiary hearing," yet there is nothing that indicates what tomorrow's balance will be. Although the majority attempts to bolster its decision with limited quotations from prior cases, it is obvious that today's result doesn't depend on the language of the Constitution itself or the principles of other decisions, but solely on the collective judgment of the majority as to what would be a fair and humane procedure in this case. . . .

The Court apparently feels that this decision will benefit the poor and needy. In my judgment the eventual result will be just the opposite. While today's decision requires only an administrative, evidentiary hearing, the inevitable logic of the approach taken will lead to constitutionally imposed, time-consuming delays of a full adversary process of administrative and judicial review. . . . Since this process will usually entail a delay of several years, the inevitable result of such a constitutionally imposed burden will be that the government will not put a claimant on the rolls initially until it has made an exhaustive investigation to determine his eligibility. While this Court will perhaps have insured that no needy person will be taken off the rolls without a full "due process" proceeding, it will also have insured that many will never get on the rolls, or at least that they will remain destitute during the lengthy proceedings followed to determine initial eligibility.

. . . The operation of a welfare state is a new experiment for our Nation. For this reason, among others, I feel that new experiments in carrying out a welfare program should not be frozen into our constitutional structure. They should be left, as are other legislative determinations, to the Congress and the legislatures that the people elect to make our laws.

Goldberg v. Kelly was a landmark case, recognizing a constitutionally protected interest in at least some government benefits that would traditionally have been classified as "privileges" rather than "rights." Once that principle was announced, the real question was how far it would extend. The next two cases, announced the same day as each other, offer important elaborations on the scope of the interest recognized in *Goldberg*.

The Board of Regents of State Colleges v. Roth

Supreme Court of the United States, 1972.
408 U.S. 564.

Mr. Justice Stewart delivered the opinion of the Court.

In 1968 the respondent, David Roth, was hired for his first teaching job as assistant professor of political science at Wisconsin State University-Oshkosh. He was hired for a fixed term of one academic year. . . . The respondent completed that term. But he was informed that he would not be rehired for the next academic year.

The respondent had no tenure rights to continued employment. Under Wisconsin statutory law a state university teacher can acquire tenure as a "permanent" employee only after four years of year-to-year employment. Having acquired tenure, a teacher is entitled to continued employment "during efficiency and good behavior." A relatively new teacher without tenure, however, is under Wisconsin law entitled to nothing beyond his one-year appointment. There are no statutory or administrative standards defining eligibility for re-employment. . . .

A nontenured teacher . . . is protected to some extent *during* his one-year term. Rules promulgated by the Board of Regents provide that a nontenured teacher "dismissed" before the end of the year may have some opportunity for review of the "dismissal." But the Rules provide no real protection for a non-tenured teacher who simply is not re-employed for the next year. He must be informed by February 1 "concerning retention or non-retention for the ensuing year." But "no reason for non-retention need be given. No review or appeal is provided in such case."

In conformance with these Rules, the President of Wisconsin State University-Oshkosh informed the respondent before February 1, 1969, that he would not be rehired for the 1969–1970 academic year. He gave the respondent no reason for the decision and no opportunity to challenge it at any sort of hearing.

The respondent then brought this action in Federal District Court alleging that the decision not to rehire him for the next year infringed his Fourteenth Amendment rights. He attacked the decision both in substance and procedure. First, he alleged that the true reason for the decision was to punish him for certain statements critical of the University administration, and that it therefore violated his right to freedom of speech. Second, he alleged that the failure of University officials to give him notice of any reason for nonretention and an opportunity for a hearing violated his right to procedural due process of law.

The District Court granted summary judgment for the respondent on the procedural issue, ordering the University officials to provide him with reasons and a hearing. The Court of Appeals, with one judge dissenting, affirmed this partial summary judgment. We granted certiorari. The only question presented to us at this stage in the case is whether the respondent had a constitutional right to a statement of reasons and a hearing on the University's decision not to rehire him for another year. We hold that he did not.

I

The requirements of procedural due process apply only to the deprivation of interests encompassed by the Fourteenth Amendment's protection of liberty and property. When protected interests are implicated, the right to some kind of prior hearing is paramount.[7] But the range of interests protected by procedural due process is not infinite. . . . [T]o determine whether due process requirements apply in the first place, we must look not to the "weight" but to

---

[7]   Before a person is deprived of a protected interest, he must be afforded opportunity for some kind of a hearing, "except for extraordinary situations where some valid governmental interest is at stake that justifies postponing the hearing until after the event." *Boddie v. Connecticut* (1970).

the nature of the interest at stake. We must look to see if the interest is within the Fourteenth Amendment's protection of liberty and property.

"Liberty" and "property" are broad and majestic terms. They are among the "[g]reat [constitutional] concepts . . . purposely left to gather meaning from experience. . . . [T]hey relate to the whole domain of social and economic fact, and the statesmen who founded this Nation knew too well that only a stagnant society remains unchanged." For that reason, the Court has fully and finally rejected the wooden distinction between "rights" and "privileges" that once seemed to govern the applicability of procedural due process rights. The Court has also made clear that the property interests protected by procedural due process extend well beyond actual ownership of real estate, chattels, or money. By the same token, the Court has required due process protection for deprivations of liberty beyond the sort of formal constraints imposed by the criminal process.

Yet, while the Court has eschewed rigid or formalistic limitations on the protection of procedural due process, it has at the same time observed certain boundaries. For the words "liberty" and "property" in the Due Process Clause of the Fourteenth Amendment must be given some meaning.

II

"While this court has not attempted to define with exactness the liberty . . . guaranteed [by the Fourteenth Amendment], the term has received much consideration and some of the included things have been definitely stated. Without doubt, it denotes not merely freedom from bodily restraint but also the right of the individual to contract, to engage in any of the common occupations of life, to acquire useful knowledge, to marry, establish a home and bring up children, to worship God according to the dictates of his own conscience, and generally to enjoy those privileges long recognized . . . as essential to the orderly pursuit of happiness by free men." *Meyer v. Nebraska* (1923). In a Constitution for a free people, there can be no doubt that the meaning of "liberty" must be broad indeed.

There might be cases in which a State refused to re-employ a person under such circumstances that interests in liberty would be implicated. But this is not such a case.

The State, in declining to rehire the respondent, did not make any charge against him that might seriously damage his standing and associations in his community. It did not base the nonrenewal of his contract on a charge, for example, that he had been guilty of dishonesty, or immorality. Had it done so, this would be a different case. For "[w]here a person's good name, reputation, honor, or integrity is at stake because of what the government is doing to him, notice and an opportunity to be heard are essential." In such a case, due process would accord an opportunity to refute the charge before University officials. In the present case, however, there is no suggestion whatever that the respondent's "good name, reputation, honor, or integrity" is at stake.

Similarly, there is no suggestion that the State, in declining to re-employ the respondent, imposed on him a stigma or other disability that foreclosed his freedom to take advantage of other employment opportunities. The State, for example, did not invoke any regulations to bar the respondent from all other public employment in state universities. Had it done so, this, again, would be a different case. For "[t]o be deprived not only of present government employment but of future opportunity for it certainly is no small injury. . . ."

To be sure, the respondent has alleged that the nonrenewal of his contract was based on his exercise of his right to freedom of speech. But this allegation is not now before us. The District Court stayed proceedings on this issue, and the respondent has yet to prove that the decision not to rehire him was, in fact, based on his free speech activities.

Hence, on the record before us, all that clearly appears is that the respondent was not rehired for one year at one university. It stretches the concept too far to suggest that a person is deprived of "liberty" when he simply is not rehired in one job but remains as free as before to seek another.

III

The Fourteenth Amendment's procedural protection of property is a safeguard of the security of interests that a person has already acquired in specific benefits. These interests—property interests—may take many forms. . . .

Certain attributes of "property" interests protected by procedural due process emerge from [our] decisions. To have a property interest in a benefit, a person clearly must have more than an abstract need or desire for it. He must have more than a unilateral expectation of it. He must, instead, have a legitimate claim of entitlement to it. It is a purpose of the ancient institution of property to protect those claims upon which people rely in their daily lives, reliance that must not be arbitrarily undermined. It is a purpose of the constitutional right to a hearing to provide an opportunity for a person to vindicate those claims.

Property interests, of course, are not created by the Constitution. Rather they are created and their dimensions are defined by existing rules or understandings that stem from an independent source such as state law—rules or understandings that secure certain benefits and that support claims of entitlement to those benefits. Thus, the welfare recipients in *Goldberg v. Kelly* had a claim of entitlement to welfare payments that was grounded in the statute defining eligibility for them. The recipients had not yet shown that they were, in fact, within the statutory terms of eligibility. But we held that they had a right to a hearing at which they might attempt to do so.

Just as the welfare recipients' "property" interest in welfare payments was created and defined by statutory terms, so the respondent's "property" interest in employment at Wisconsin State University-Oshkosh was created and defined by the terms of his appointment. Those terms secured his interest in employment up to June 30, 1969. But the important fact in this case is that they specifically provided that the respondent's employment was to terminate on June 30. They did not provide for contract renewal absent "sufficient cause." Indeed, they made no provision for renewal whatsoever.

Thus, the terms of the respondent's appointment secured . . . absolutely no possible claim of entitlement to re-employment. Nor, significantly, was there any state statute or University rule or policy that secured his interest in re-employment or that created any legitimate claim to it.[16] In these circumstances, the respondent surely had an abstract concern in being rehired, but he did not have a property interest sufficient to require the University authorities to give him a hearing when they declined to renew his contract of employment.

IV

. . . The judgment of the Court of Appeals, accordingly, is reversed and the case is remanded for further proceedings consistent with this opinion. . . .

---

[16]   To be sure, the respondent does suggest that most teachers hired on a year-to-year basis by Wisconsin State University-Oshkosh are, in fact, rehired. But the District Court has not found that there is anything approaching a "common law" of re-employment, see *Perry v. Sindermann* (1972), so strong as to require University officials to give the respondent a statement of reasons and a hearing on their decision not to rehire him

MR. JUSTICE POWELL took no part in the decision of this case.

MR. JUSTICE DOUGLAS, dissenting.

Respondent Roth, like Sindermann in the companion case, had no tenure under Wisconsin law and, unlike Sindermann, he had had only one year of teaching at Wisconsin State University-Oshkosh—where during 1968–1969 he had been Assistant Professor of Political Science and International Studies. Though Roth was rated by the faculty as an excellent teacher, he had publicly criticized the administration for suspending an entire group of 94 black students without determining individual guilt. He also criticized the university's regime as being authoritarian and autocratic. He used his classroom to discuss what was being done about the black episode; and one day, instead of meeting his class, he went to the meeting of the Board of Regents. . . .

> **CROSS REFERENCE** Chief Justice Burger wrote a single concurrence in both *Board of Regents v. Roth* and *Perry v. Sindermann*. Justice Brennan, joined by Justice Douglas, also wrote a single opinion that applied to both cases, dissenting in *Roth* and dissenting in part in *Sindermann*. See p. 1286 infra.

I would affirm the judgment of the Court of Appeals.

MR. JUSTICE MARSHALL, dissenting.

. . . While I agree with Part I of the Court's opinion, setting forth the proper framework for consideration of the issue presented, . . . I would go further than the Court does in defining the terms "liberty" and "property." . . . In my view, every citizen who applies for a government job is entitled to it unless the government can establish some reason for denying the employment. This is the "property" right that I believe is protected by the Fourteenth Amendment and that cannot be denied "without due process of law." And it is also liberty—liberty to work—which is the "very essence of the personal freedom and opportunity" secured by the Fourteenth Amendment.

This Court has often had occasion to note that the denial of public employment is a serious blow to any citizen. Thus, when an application for public employment is denied or the contract of a government employee is not renewed, the government must say why, for it is only when the reasons underlying government action are known that citizens feel secure and protected against arbitrary government action. . . .

It may be argued that to provide procedural due process to all public employees or prospective employees would place an intolerable burden on the machinery of government. Cf. *Goldberg v. Kelly*. The short answer to that argument is that it is not burdensome to give reasons when reasons exist. Whenever an application for employment is denied, an employee is discharged, or a decision not to rehire an employee is made, there should be some reason for the decision. It can scarcely be argued that government would be crippled by a requirement that the reason be communicated to the person most directly affected by the government's action. Where there are numerous applicants for jobs, it is likely that few will choose to demand reasons for not being hired. But, if the demand for reasons is exceptionally great, summary procedures can be devised that would provide fair and adequate information to all persons. As long as the government has a good reason for its actions it need not fear disclosure. . . .

It might also be argued that to require a hearing and a statement of reasons is to require a useless act, because a government bent on denying employment to one or more persons will do so regardless of the procedural hurdles that are placed in its path. Perhaps this is so, but a requirement of procedural regularity at least renders arbitrary action more difficult. Moreover, proper procedures will surely eliminate some of the arbitrariness that results, not from malice, but from innocent error. . . . When the government knows it may have to justify its decisions with sound reasons, its conduct is likely to be more cautious, careful, and correct. . . .

Accordingly, I dissent.

Perry v. Sindermann

Supreme Court of the United States, 1972.
408 U.S. 593.

Mr. Justice Stewart delivered the opinion of the Court.

From 1959 to 1969 the respondent, Robert Sindermann, was a teacher in the state college system of the State of Texas. After teaching for two years at the University of Texas and for four years at San Antonio Junior College, he became a professor of Government and Social Science at Odessa Junior College in 1965. He was employed at the college for four successive years, under a series of one-year contracts. He was successful enough to be appointed, for a time, the cochairman of his department.

During the 1968–1969 academic year, however, controversy arose between the respondent and the college administration. The respondent was elected president of the Texas Junior College Teachers Association. In this capacity, he left his teaching duties on several occasions to testify before committees of the Texas Legislature, and he became involved in public disagreements with the policies of the college's Board of Regents. In particular, he aligned himself with a group advocating the elevation of the college to four-year status—a change opposed by the Regents. And, on one occasion, a newspaper advertisement appeared over his name that was highly critical of the Regents.

Finally, in May 1969, the respondent's one-year employment contract terminated and the Board of Regents voted not to offer him a new contract for the next academic year. The Regents issued a press release setting forth allegations of the respondent's insubordination.[1] But they provided him no official statement of the reasons for the nonrenewal of his contract. And they allowed him no opportunity for a hearing to challenge the basis of the nonrenewal.

The respondent then brought this action in Federal District Court. He alleged primarily that the Regents' decision not to rehire him was based on his public criticism of the policies of the college administration and thus infringed his right to freedom of speech. He also alleged that their failure to provide him an opportunity for a hearing violated the Fourteenth Amendment's guarantee of procedural due process. The petitioners—members of the Board of Regents and the president of the college—denied that their decision was made in retaliation for the respondent's public criticism and argued that they had no obligation to provide a hearing. On the basis of these bare pleadings and three brief affidavits filed by the respondent, the District Court granted summary judgment for the petitioners. . . . The Court of Appeals reversed the judgment of the District Court. . . . We granted a writ of certiorari, and we have considered this case along with *Board of Regents v. Roth* (1972). . . .

II

The respondent's lack of formal contractual or tenure security in continued employment at Odessa Junior College, though irrelevant to his free speech

---

[1]   The press release stated, for example, that the respondent had defied his superiors by attending legislative committee meetings when college officials had specifically refused to permit him to leave his classes for that purpose.

claim, is highly relevant to his procedural due process claim. But it may not be entirely dispositive.

. . . As in *Roth*, the mere showing that [Sindermann] was not rehired in one particular job, without more, did not amount to a showing of a loss of liberty. Nor did it amount to a showing of a loss of property.

But the respondent's allegations—which we must construe most favorably to the respondent at this stage of the litigation—do raise a genuine issue as to his interest in continued employment at Odessa Junior College. He alleged that this interest, though not secured by a formal contractual tenure provision, was secured by a no less binding understanding fostered by the college administration. In particular, the respondent alleged that the college had a *de facto* tenure program, and that he had tenure under that program. He claimed that he and others legitimately relied upon an unusual provision that had been in the college's official Faculty Guide for many years:

> Teacher Tenure: Odessa College has no tenure system. The Administration of the College wishes the faculty member to feel that he has permanent tenure as long as his teaching services are satisfactory and as long as he displays a cooperative attitude toward his co-workers and his superiors, and as long as he is happy in his work.

Moreover, the respondent claimed legitimate reliance upon guidelines promulgated by the Coordinating Board of the Texas College and University System that provided that a person, like himself, who had been employed as a teacher in the state college and university system for seven years or more has some form of job tenure.[6] Thus, the respondent offered to prove that a teacher

---

6   The relevant portion of the guidelines, adopted as "Policy Paper 1" by the Coordinating Board on October 16, 1967, reads:

A. Tenure

Tenure means assurance to an experienced faculty member that he may expect to continue in his academic position unless adequate cause for dismissal is demonstrated in a fair hearing, following established procedures of due process.

A specific system of faculty tenure undergirds the integrity of each academic institution. In the Texas public colleges and universities, this tenure system should have these components:

(1) Beginning with appointment to the rank of full-time instructor or a higher rank, the probationary period for a faculty member shall not exceed seven years, including within this period appropriate full-time service in all institutions of higher education. . . .

(3) Adequate cause for dismissal for a faculty member with tenure may be established by demonstrating professional incompetence, moral turpitude, or gross neglect of professional responsibilities.

The respondent alleges that, because he has been employed as a "full-time instructor" or professor within the Texas College and University System for 10 years, he should have "tenure" under these provisions.

with his long period of service at this particular State College had no less a "property" interest in continued employment than a formally tenured teacher at other colleges, and had no less a procedural due process right to a statement of reasons and a hearing before college officials upon their decision not to retain him.

We have made clear in *Roth* that "property" interests subject to procedural due process protection are not limited by a few rigid, technical forms. Rather, "property" denotes a broad range of interests that are secured by "existing rules or understandings." A person's interest in a benefit is a "property" interest for due process purposes if there are such rules or mutually explicit understandings that support his claim of entitlement to the benefit and that he may invoke at a hearing.

[A]bsence of . . . an explicit contractual provision [guaranteeing tenure] may not always foreclose the possibility that a teacher has a "property" interest in reemployment. For example, the law of contracts in most, if not all, jurisdictions long has employed a process by which agreements, though not formalized in writing, may be "implied." Corbin on Contracts (1960). Explicit contractual provisions may be supplemented by other agreements implied from "the promisor's words and conduct in the light of the surrounding circumstances." *Id.* And, "[t]he meaning of [the promisor's] words and acts is found by relating them to the usage of the past." *Ibid.* . . . Just as this Court has found there to be a "common law of a particular industry or of a particular plant" that may supplement a collective-bargaining agreement, *United Steelworkers v. Warrior & Gulf Nav. Co.* (1960), so there may be an unwritten "common law" in a particular university that certain employees shall have the equivalent of tenure. . . .

In this case, the respondent has alleged the existence of rules and understandings, promulgated and fostered by state officials, that may justify his legitimate claim of entitlement to continued employment absent "sufficient cause." We disagree with the Court of Appeals insofar as it held that a mere subjective "expectancy" is protected by procedural due process, but we agree that the respondent must be given an opportunity to prove the legitimacy of his claim of such entitlement in light of "the policies and practices of the institution." Proof of such a property interest would . . . obligate college officials to grant a hearing at his request, where he could be informed of the grounds for his nonretention and challenge their sufficiency.

Therefore, while we do not wholly agree with the opinion of the Court of Appeals, its judgment remanding this case to the District Court is affirmed.

Affirmed.

Mr. Justice Powell took no part in the decision of this case.

Mr. Chief Justice Burger, concurring.

I concur in the Court's judgments and opinions in *Perry* and *Sindermann* but there is one central point in both decisions that I would like to underscore since it may have been obscured in the comprehensive discussion of the cases. That point is that the relationship between a state institution and one of its teachers is essentially a matter of state concern and state law. . . . Thus, whether a particular teacher in a particular context has any right to such administrative hearing hinges on a question of state law. . . .

Mr. Justice Marshall, dissenting in part.

. . . I agree with Part I of the Court's opinion holding that respondent has presented a bona fide First Amendment claim that should be considered fully by the District Court. But, for the reasons stated in my dissenting opinion in *Board of Regents v. Roth*, I would modify the judgment of the Court of Appeals to direct the District Court to enter summary judgment for respondent entitling him to a statement of reasons why his contract was not renewed and a hearing on disputed issues of fact.

WORTH NOTING

Justice Brennan, joined by Justice Douglas, thought that *Roth* should be affirmed and that the judgment in *Sindermann* should be modified as indicated by Justice Marshall. But Brennan agreed with Part I of the Court's decision in *Sindermann*—not reproduced here—which reversed the grant of summary judgment on respondent's First Amendment claim.

---

2. PDP: What Process Is Due?

As explained in the introduction to this chapter, the fact that the government has deprived someone of a constitutionally protected interest does not by itself constitute a violation of the Constitution. To find a constitutional violation requires the court to address a second question: was the deprivation accompanied by sufficient procedural protections to constitute due process of law? The following cases explore the structure of that second inquiry.

Mathews v. Eldridge

Supreme Court of the United States, 1976.
424 U.S. 319.

MR. JUSTICE POWELL delivered the opinion of the Court.

The issue in this case is whether the Due Process Clause of the Fifth Amendment requires that prior to the termination of Social Security disability benefit payments the recipient be afforded an opportunity for an evidentiary hearing.

I

Cash benefits are provided to workers during periods in which they are completely disabled under the disability insurance benefits program created by the 1956 amendments to Title II of the Social Security Act. Respondent Eldridge was first awarded benefits in June 1968. In March 1972, he received a questionnaire from the state agency charged with monitoring his medical condition. Eldridge completed the questionnaire, indicating that his condition had not improved and identifying the medical sources, including physicians, from whom he had received treatment recently. The state agency then obtained reports from his physician and a psychiatric consultant. After considering these reports and other information in his file the agency informed Eldridge by letter that it had made a tentative determination that his disability had ceased in May 1972. The letter included a statement of reasons for the proposed termination of benefits, and advised Eldridge that he might request reasonable time in which to obtain and submit additional information pertaining to his condition.

In his written response, Eldridge disputed one characterization of his medical condition and indicated that the agency already had enough evidence to establish his disability.[2] The state agency then made its final determination

---

[2] Eldridge originally was disabled due to chronic anxiety and back strain. He subsequently was found to have diabetes. The tentative determination letter indicated that aid would be terminated because available medical evidence indicated that his diabetes was under control, that there existed no limitations on his back movements which would impose severe functional restrictions, and that he no longer suffered emotional problems that would preclude him from all work for which he was qualified. In his reply letter he claimed to have arthritis of the spine rather than a strained back.

that he had ceased to be disabled in May 1972. This determination was accepted by the Social Security Administration (SSA), which notified Eldridge in July that his benefits would terminate after that month. The notification also advised him of his right to seek reconsideration by the state agency of this initial determination within six months.

Instead of requesting reconsideration Eldridge commenced this action challenging the constitutional validity of the administrative procedures established by the Secretary of Health, Education, and Welfare for assessing whether there exists a continuing disability. He sought an immediate reinstatement of benefits pending a hearing on the issue of his disability.[3] . . .

[Citing this Court's decision in *Goldberg v. Kelly* (1970),] the District Court held that prior to termination of benefits Eldridge had to be afforded an evidentiary hearing of the type required for welfare beneficiaries under Title IV of the Social Security Act. [T]he Court of Appeals for the Fourth Circuit affirmed. . . . We reverse. . . .

III

A

. . . The dispute centers upon what process is due prior to the initial termination of benefits, pending review.

In recent years this Court increasingly has had occasion to consider the extent to which due process requires an evidentiary hearing prior to the deprivation of some type of property interest even if such a hearing is provided thereafter. In only one case, *Goldberg v. Kelly*, has the Court held that a hearing closely approximating a judicial trial is necessary. In other cases requiring some type of pretermination hearing as a matter of constitutional right the Court has spoken sparingly about the requisite procedures. . . .

These decisions underscore the truism that " '[d]ue process,' unlike some legal rules, is not a technical conception with a fixed content unrelated to time, place and circumstances." "[D]ue process is flexible and calls for such procedural protections as the particular situation demands." Accordingly, resolution of the issue whether the administrative procedures provided here are constitutionally sufficient requires analysis of the governmental and private interests that are affected. More precisely, our prior decisions indicate that identification

---

[3]   The District Court ordered reinstatement of Eldridge's benefits pending its final disposition on the merits.

of the specific dictates of due process generally requires consideration of three distinct factors:

[1]   the private interest that will be affected by the official action;

[2]   the risk of an erroneous deprivation of such interest through the procedures used, and the probable value, if any, of additional or substitute procedural safeguards; and

[3]   the Government's interest, including the function involved and the fiscal and administrative burdens that the additional or substitute procedural requirement would entail.

See, *e.g.*, *Goldberg v. Kelly*. . . .

B

The disability insurance program is administered jointly by state and federal agencies. State agencies make the initial determination whether a disability exists, when it began, and when it ceased. . . .

The continuing-eligibility investigation is made by a state agency acting through a "team" consisting of a physician and a nonmedical person trained in disability evaluation. The agency periodically communicates with the disabled worker, usually by mail in which case he is sent a detailed questionnaire or by telephone, and requests information concerning his present condition, including current medical restrictions and sources of treatment, and any additional information that he considers relevant to his continued entitlement to benefits.

Information regarding the recipient's current condition is also obtained from his sources of medical treatment. . . . [T]he agency may [also] arrange for an examination by an independent consulting physician. Whenever the agency's tentative assessment of the beneficiary's condition differs from his own assessment, the beneficiary is informed that benefits may be terminated, provided a summary of the evidence upon which the proposed determination to terminate is based, and afforded an opportunity to review the medical reports and other evidence in his case file. He also may respond in writing and submit additional evidence.

The state agency then makes its final determination, which is reviewed by an examiner in the SSA Bureau of Disability Insurance. If, as is usually the case, the SSA accepts the agency determination it notifies the recipient in writing, informing him of the reasons for the decision, and of his right to seek de novo reconsideration by the state agency. Upon acceptance by the SSA, benefits are terminated effective two months after the month in which medical recovery is found to have occurred.

If the recipient seeks reconsideration by the state agency and the determination is adverse, the SSA reviews the reconsideration determination and notifies the recipient of the decision. He then has a right to an evidentiary hearing before an SSA administrative law judge. The hearing is nonadversary, and the SSA is not represented by counsel. As at all prior and subsequent stages of the administrative process, however, the claimant may be represented by counsel or other spokesmen. If this hearing results in an adverse decision, the claimant is entitled to request discretionary review by the SSA Appeals Council, and finally may obtain judicial review.[21]

Should it be determined at any point after termination of benefits, that the claimant's disability extended beyond the date of cessation initially established, the worker is entitled to retroactive payments. If, on the other hand, a beneficiary receives any payments to which he is later determined not to be entitled, the statute authorizes the Secretary to attempt to recoup these funds in specified circumstances.

C

Despite the elaborate character of the administrative procedures provided by the Secretary, the courts below held them to be constitutionally inadequate, concluding that due process requires an evidentiary hearing prior to termination. In light of the private and governmental interests at stake here and the nature of the existing procedures, we think this was error.

Since a recipient whose benefits are terminated is awarded full retroactive relief if he ultimately prevails, his sole interest is in the uninterrupted receipt of this source of income pending final administrative decision on his claim. His potential injury is thus similar in nature to that of the welfare recipient in *Goldberg*. . . .

Only in *Goldberg* has the Court held that due process requires an evidentiary hearing prior to a temporary deprivation. It was emphasized there that welfare assistance is given to persons on the very margin of subsistence. . . .

---

[21]   Unlike all prior levels of review, which are de novo, the district court is required to treat findings of fact as conclusive if supported by substantial evidence. 42 U.S.C. § 405(g).

Eligibility for disability benefits, in contrast, is not based upon financial need.[24] Indeed, it is wholly unrelated to the worker's income or support from many other sources, such as earnings of other family members, workmen's compensation awards, tort claims awards, savings, private insurance, public or private pensions, veterans' benefits, food stamps, public assistance, or the "many other important programs, both public and private, which contain provisions for disability payments affecting a substantial portion of the work force. . . ." See Staff of the House Committee on Ways and Means, *Report on the Disability Insurance Program* (1974).

As *Goldberg* illustrates, the degree of potential deprivation that may be created by a particular decision is a factor to be considered in assessing the validity of any administrative decisionmaking process. The potential deprivation here is generally likely to be less than in *Goldberg*, although the degree of difference can be overstated. As the District Court emphasized, to remain eligible for benefits a recipient must be "unable to engage in substantial gainful activity." Thus . . . there is little possibility that the terminated recipient will be able to find even temporary employment to ameliorate the interim loss.

As we recognized last Term in *Fusari v. Steinberg* (1975), "the possible length of wrongful deprivation of . . . benefits [also] is an important factor in assessing the impact of official action on the private interests." The Secretary concedes that . . . the delay between the actual cutoff of benefits and final decision after a hearing exceeds one year.

In view of the torpidity of this administrative review process, and [what the agency's own statistics show to be] the typically modest resources of the family unit of the physically disabled worker, the hardship imposed upon the erroneously terminated disability recipient may be significant. Still, the disabled worker's need is likely to be less than that of a welfare recipient. In addition to the possibility of access to private resources, other forms of [state, local, and federal] government assistance will become available where the termination of disability benefits places a worker or his family below the subsistence level. In view of these potential sources of temporary income, there is less reason here than in *Goldberg* to depart from the ordinary principle, established by our decisions, that something less than an evidentiary hearing is sufficient prior to adverse administrative action.

---

[24] The level of benefits is determined by the worker's average monthly earnings during the period prior to disability, his age, and other factors not directly related to financial need. . . .

D

An additional factor to be considered here is the fairness and reliability of the existing pretermination procedures, and the probable value, if any, of additional procedural safeguards. Central to the evaluation of any administrative process is . . . a medical assessment of the worker's physical or mental condition. . . . This is a more sharply focused and easily documented decision than the typical determination of welfare entitlement. In the latter case, a wide variety of information may be deemed relevant, and issues of witness credibility and veracity often are critical to the decisionmaking process. *Goldberg* noted that in such circumstances "written submissions are a wholly unsatisfactory basis for decision."

By contrast, the decision whether to discontinue disability benefits will turn, in most cases, upon "routine, standard, and unbiased medical reports by physician specialists," *Richardson v. Perales* (1971), concerning a subject whom they have personally examined. . . . [T]here may be "professional disagreement with the medical conclusions". . . , [and] credibility and veracity may be a factor in the ultimate disability assessment in some cases. But procedural due process rules are shaped by the risk of error inherent in the truthfinding process as applied to the generality of cases, not the rare exceptions. The potential value of an evidentiary hearing, or even oral presentation to the decisionmaker, is substantially less in this context than in *Goldberg*.

The decision in *Goldberg* also was based on the Court's conclusion that written submissions were an inadequate substitute for oral presentation because they did not provide an effective means for the recipient to communicate his case to the decisionmaker. Written submissions were viewed as an unrealistic option, for most recipients lacked the "educational attainment necessary to write effectively" and could not afford professional assistance. . . . In the context of the disability-benefits-entitlement assessment the administrative procedures under review here fully answer these objections.

The detailed questionnaire which the state agency periodically sends the recipient identifies with particularity the information relevant to the entitlement decision, and the recipient is invited to obtain assistance from the local SSA office in completing the questionnaire. More important, the information critical to the entitlement decision usually is derived from medical sources, such as the treating physician. Such sources are likely to be able to communicate more effectively through written documents than are welfare recipients or the lay witnesses supporting their cause. The conclusions of physicians often are supported by X-rays and the results of clinical or laboratory tests, information typically more amenable to written than to oral presentation.

A further safeguard against mistake is the policy of allowing the disability recipient's representative full access to all information relied upon by the state agency. In addition, prior to the cutoff of benefits the agency informs the recipient of its tentative assessment, the reasons therefor, and provides a summary of the evidence that it considers most relevant. Opportunity is then afforded the recipient to submit additional evidence or arguments, enabling him to challenge directly the accuracy of information in his file as well as the correctness of the agency's tentative conclusions. These procedures, again as contrasted with those before the Court in *Goldberg*, enable the recipient to "mold" his argument to respond to the precise issues which the decisionmaker regards as crucial.

Despite these carefully structured procedures, *amici* point to the significant reversal rate for appealed cases as clear evidence that the current process is inadequate. Depending upon the base selected and the line of analysis followed, the relevant reversal rates urged by the contending parties vary from a high of 58.6% for appealed reconsideration decisions to an overall reversal rate of only 3.3%.[29] Bare statistics rarely provide a satisfactory measure of the fairness of a decisionmaking process. Their adequacy is especially suspect here since the administrative review system is operated on an open-file basis. A recipient may always submit new evidence, and such submissions may result in additional medical examinations. Such fresh examinations were held in approximately 30% to 40% of the appealed cases, in fiscal 1973, either at the reconsideration or evidentiary hearing stage of the administrative process. In this context, the value of reversal rate statistics as one means of evaluating the adequacy of the pretermination process is diminished. Thus, although we view such information as relevant, it is certainly not controlling in this case.

---

[29] By focusing solely on the reversal rate for appealed reconsideration determinations amici overstate the relevant reversal rate. . . . [I]n order fully to assess the reliability and fairness of a system of procedure, one must also consider the overall rate of error for all denials of benefits. Here that overall rate is 12.2%. Moreover, about 75% of these reversals occur at the reconsideration stage of the administrative process. Since the median period between a request for reconsideration review and decision is only two months, the deprivation is significantly less than that concomitant to the lengthier delay before an evidentiary hearing. Netting out these reconsideration reversals, the overall reversal rate falls to 3.3%.

E

In striking the appropriate due process balance the final factor to be assessed is the public interest. This includes the administrative burden and other societal costs that would be associated with requiring, as a matter of constitutional right, an evidentiary hearing upon demand in all cases prior to the termination of disability benefits. The most visible burden would be the incremental cost resulting from the increased number of hearings and the expense of providing benefits to ineligible recipients pending decision. No one can predict the extent of the increase, but the fact that full benefits would continue until after such hearings would assure the exhaustion in most cases of this attractive option. Nor would the theoretical right of the Secretary to recover undeserved benefits result, as a practical matter, in any substantial offset to the added outlay of public funds. . . .

Financial cost alone is not a controlling weight in determining whether due process requires a particular procedural safeguard prior to some administrative decision. But the Government's interest, and hence that of the public, in conserving scarce fiscal and administrative resources is a factor that must be weighed. At some point the benefit of an additional safeguard to the individual . . . and to society . . . may be outweighed by the cost. Significantly, the cost of protecting those whom the preliminary administrative process has identified as likely to be found undeserving may in the end come out of the pockets of the deserving since resources available for any particular program of social welfare are not unlimited.

But more is implicated in cases of this type than ad hoc weighing of fiscal and administrative burdens against the interests of a particular category of claimants. The ultimate balance involves a determination as to when, under our constitutional system, judicial-type procedures must be imposed upon administrative action to assure fairness. . . . The judicial model of an evidentiary hearing is neither a required, nor even the most effective, method of decision-making in all circumstances. . . . All that is necessary is that the procedures be tailored, in light of the decision to be made, to "the capacities and circumstances of those who are to be heard," *Goldberg v. Kelly*, to insure that they are given a meaningful opportunity to present their case. . . .

We conclude that an evidentiary hearing is not required prior to the termination of disability benefits and that the present administrative procedures fully comport with due process.

The judgment of the Court of Appeals is

Reversed.

MR. JUSTICE STEVENS took no part in the consideration or decision of this case.

MR. JUSTICE BRENNAN, with whom MR. JUSTICE MARSHALL concurs, dissenting.

. . . I agree with the District Court and the Court of Appeals that, prior to termination of benefits, Eldridge must be afforded an evidentiary hearing of the type required for welfare beneficiaries under Title IV of the Social Security Act. See *Goldberg v. Kelly* (1970). I would add that the Court's consideration that a discontinuance of disability benefits may cause the recipient to suffer only a limited deprivation is no argument. It is speculative. Moreover, the very legislative determination to provide disability benefits, without any prerequisite determination of need in fact, presumes a need by the recipient which is not this Court's function to denigrate. Indeed, in the present case, it is indicated that because disability benefits were terminated there was a foreclosure upon the Eldridge home and the family's furniture was repossessed, forcing Eldridge, his wife, and their children to sleep in one bed. Finally, it is also no argument that a worker, who has been placed in the untenable position of having been denied disability benefits, may still seek other forms of public assistance.

Taken together, the companion cases of *Sindermann* and *Roth* give the government substantial control over the scope of property interests protected by the Due Process Clause. See pp. 1276–1286. On the approach defined by those cases, any substantive limits imposed on a benefit when created—like an employment contract expressly precluding tenure—will control the scope of the property right that receives constitutional protection. But what about limitations on procedure? If the government defines the procedures available to protect a benefit at the same time that it creates that benefit, can that pre-deprivation definition control the scope of the process that is due? In *Cleveland Board of Education v. Loudermill* (1985), the Supreme Court said no.

The plaintiff in *Loudermill* was dismissed from his job as a security guard because of making a—plausibly accidental—false statement on his job application. As a "classified civil servant" under Ohio law, he could only be terminated for good cause. In addition to specifying the substantive grounds for termination, though, the statute also "set[ ] out procedures by which termination may take place"—procedures that provided for post-termination administrative review, but not for a pre-termination hearing at which Loudermill could respond to the charges against him. Under these circumstances, the Board of Education argued that "[t]o require additional procedures" under the Due Process Clause "would in effect expand the scope of the property interest itself."

The Supreme Court rejected this argument:

> [We think] the "bitter with the sweet" approach misconceives the constitutional guarantee. If a clearer holding is needed, we provide it today. The point is straightforward: the Due Process Clause provides that certain substantive rights—life, liberty, and property—cannot be deprived except pursuant to constitutionally adequate procedures. . . . "Property" cannot be defined by the procedures provided for its deprivation any more than can life or liberty.

"In short," the Court held, "once it is determined that the Due Process Clause applies, " 'the question remains what process is due.' The answer to that question is not to be found in the Ohio statute," but rather in the doctrine of *Mathews v. Eldredge*. Applying that test, the Court concluded that Loudermill was constitutionally entitled to "some form of pretermination hearing" at which he could respond to the charges before losing his job. The state's failure to give him that opportunity constituted a denial of his due process rights.

FOR DISCUSSION

Is *Loudermill* consistent with *Roth* and *Sindermann*?

We've now seen the Court rely on the same interest-balancing test to define the process that is due before the government can deprive someone of welfare benefits (*Goldberg v. Kelly*) or disability benefits (*Mathews v. Eldredge*). In principle, this same highly contextual approach defines the process due for the deprivation of *any* interest protected by the Due Process Clause—even the deprivation of an accused enemy combatant's liberty.

FOR DISCUSSION

Under a state statute, if a police report asserts that a driver refused to take a breath-analysis test after being arrested for driving under the influence, the driver's license must be suspended for 90 days. After surrendering the license, drivers are entitled to an immediate hearing before the Registrar of Motor Vehicles; if they can then show that the officer did not have reasonable grounds to believe that they were driving under the influence, or that they were not in fact arrested, or that they did not refuse the test, the license is immediately restored. Should a court applying the *Mathews v. Eldredge* test hold this procedure valid? See *Mackey v. Montrym* (1979).

In the 2004 case of *Hamdi v. Rumsfeld*, the habeas petitioner had been captured in Afghanistan, accused of being a member of the Taliban, and detained at a Naval brig in Charleston, S.C. The controlling plurality held that he was entitled to searching review of the charges against him. In reaching that conclusion, the plurality relied on an application of the *Mathews* framework; as you read the following, try to decide whether you think that decision makes sense.

Hamdi v. Rumsfeld

Supreme Court of the United States, 2004.
542 U.S. 507.

Justice O'Connor announced the judgment of the Court and delivered an opinion, in which The Chief Justice, Justice Kennedy, and Justice Breyer join.

CROSS REFERENCE

The plurality began by holding that, if the allegations against Hamdi were true, then his detention was authorized by the 2001 Authorization for the Use of Military Force. Justice Thomas concurred in the judgment on this point, which meant that five justices supported this conclusion. That portion of the opinions is reproduced in Chapter IV, see pp. 852–865

III

Even in cases in which the detention of enemy combatants is legally authorized, there remains the question of what process is constitutionally due to a citizen who disputes his enemy-combatant status. . . . Our resolution of this dispute requires a careful examination both of the writ of habeas corpus, which Hamdi now seeks to employ as a mechanism of judicial review, and of the Due Process Clause, which informs the procedural contours of that mechanism in this instance.

A

[T]he parties . . . agree that, absent suspension, the writ of habeas corpus remains available to every individual detained within the United States. U.S. Const., Art. I, § 9, cl. 2 ("The Privilege of the Writ of Habeas Corpus shall not be suspended, unless when in Cases of Rebellion or Invasion the public Safety may require it"). Only in the rarest of circumstances has Congress seen fit to suspend the writ. See, *e.g.,* Act of Mar. 3, 1863; Act of Apr. 20, 1871. At all other times, it has remained a critical check on the Executive, ensuring that it does not detain individuals except in accordance with law. All agree suspension of the writ has not occurred here. . . .

Further, all agree that 28 U.S.C. § 2241 and its companion provisions provide at least a skeletal outline of the procedures to be afforded a petitioner in federal habeas review. Most notably, . . . § 2246 allows the taking of evidence in habeas proceedings by deposition, affidavit, or interrogatories. The simple outline of § 2241 makes clear both that Congress envisioned that habeas petitioners would have some opportunity to present and rebut facts and that courts in cases like this retain some ability to vary the ways in which they do so as mandated by due process.

The Government recognizes the basic procedural protections required by the habeas statute, but asks us to hold that, given both the flexibility of the habeas mechanism and the circumstances presented in this case, the presentation of the Mobbs Declaration [a two-page affidavit submitted by the Defense Department and containing allegations of Hamdi's affiliation with the Taliban] to the habeas court completed the required factual development. It suggests two separate reasons for its position that no further process is due.

B

First, the Government urges the adoption of the Fourth Circuit's holding below—that because it is "undisputed" that Hamdi's seizure took place in a combat zone, the habeas determination can be made purely as a matter of law, with no further hearing or factfinding necessary. This argument is easily rejected. As the dissenters from the [Fourth Circuit's] denial of rehearing en banc noted, the circumstances surrounding Hamdi's seizure cannot in any way be characterized as "undisputed," as "those circumstances are neither conceded in fact, nor susceptible to concession in law, because Hamdi has not been permitted to speak for himself or even through counsel as to those circumstances." . . .

C

The Government's second argument requires closer consideration. This is the argument that further factual exploration is unwarranted and inappropriate in light of the extraordinary constitutional interests at stake. Under the Government's most extreme rendition of this argument, "[r]espect for separation of powers and the limited institutional capabilities of courts in matters of military decision-making in connection with an ongoing conflict" ought to eliminate entirely any individual process, restricting the courts to investigating only whether legal authorization exists for the broader detention scheme. At most, the Government argues, courts should review its determination that a citizen is an enemy combatant under a very deferential "some evidence" standard. Under this review, a court would assume the accuracy of the Government's articulated basis for Hamdi's detention, as set forth in the Mobbs Declaration, and assess only whether that articulated basis was a legitimate one.

In response, Hamdi emphasizes that this Court consistently has recognized that an individual challenging his detention may not be held at the will of the Executive without recourse to some proceeding before a neutral tribunal to determine whether the Executive's asserted justifications for that detention have basis in fact and warrant in law. . . .

Both of these positions highlight legitimate concerns. And both emphasize the tension that often exists between the autonomy that the Government asserts is necessary in order to pursue effectively a particular goal and the process that a citizen contends he is due before he is deprived of a constitutional right. The ordinary mechanism that we use for balancing such serious competing interests, and for determining the procedures that are necessary to ensure that a citizen is not "deprived of life, liberty, or property, without due process of law," U.S. Const., Amdt. 5, is the test that we articulated in *Mathews v. Eldridge* (1976). . . .

1

It is beyond question that substantial interests lie on both sides of the scale in this case. Hamdi's "private interest . . . affected by the official action" is the most elemental of liberty interests—the interest in being free from physical detention by one's own government.

Nor is the weight on this side of the *Mathews* scale offset by the circumstances of war or the accusation of treasonous behavior, for "[i]t is clear that commitment for *any* purpose constitutes a significant deprivation of liberty that requires due process protection," and at this stage in the *Mathews* calculus, we consider the interest of the *erroneously* detained individual. *Carey v. Piphus* (1978). Indeed, as *amicus* briefs from media and relief organizations emphasize, the risk of erroneous deprivation of a citizen's liberty in the absence of sufficient process here is very real. . . .

2

On the other side of the scale are the weighty and sensitive governmental interests in ensuring that those who have in fact fought with the enemy during a war do not return to battle against the United States. . . . Without doubt, our Constitution recognizes that core strategic matters of warmaking belong in the hands of those who are best positioned and most politically accountable for making them. *Youngstown Sheet & Tube Co. v. Sawyer* (1952) (acknowledging "broad powers in military commanders engaged in day-to-day fighting in a theater of war").

The Government also argues at some length that its interests in reducing the process available to alleged enemy combatants are heightened by the practical difficulties that would accompany a system of trial-like process. In its view, military officers who are engaged in the serious work of waging battle would be unnecessarily and dangerously distracted by litigation half a world away, and discovery into military operations would both intrude on the sensitive secrets of national defense and result in a futile search for evidence buried under the rubble of war. To the extent that these burdens are triggered by heightened procedures, they are properly taken into account in our due process analysis.

3

. . . With due recognition of these competing concerns, we believe that neither the process proposed by the Government nor the process apparently envisioned by the District Court below strikes the proper constitutional balance when a United States citizen is detained in the United States as an enemy combatant. That is, "the risk of an erroneous deprivation" of a detainee's liberty interest is unacceptably high under the Government's proposed rule, while some of the "additional or substitute procedural safeguards" suggested by the

District Court are unwarranted in light of their limited "probable value" and the burdens they may impose on the military in such cases. *Mathews.*

We therefore hold that a citizen-detainee seeking to challenge his classification as an enemy combatant must receive notice of the factual basis for his classification, and a fair opportunity to rebut the Government's factual assertions before a neutral decisionmaker. See *Cleveland Bd. of Ed. v. Loudermill* (1985). "For more than a century the central meaning of procedural due process has been clear: 'Parties whose rights are to be affected are entitled to be heard; and in order that they may enjoy that right they must first be notified.' It is equally fundamental that the right to notice and an opportunity to be heard 'must be granted at a meaningful time and in a meaningful manner.'" *Fuentes v. Shevin* (1972). These essential constitutional promises may not be eroded.

At the same time, the exigencies of the circumstances may demand that, aside from these core elements, enemy-combatant proceedings may be tailored to alleviate their uncommon potential to burden the Executive at a time of ongoing military conflict. Hearsay, for example, may need to be accepted as the most reliable available evidence from the Government in such a proceeding. Likewise, the Constitution would not be offended by a presumption in favor of the Government's evidence, so long as that presumption remained a rebuttable one and fair opportunity for rebuttal were provided. Thus, once the Government puts forth credible evidence that the habeas petitioner meets the enemy-combatant criteria, the onus could shift to the petitioner to rebut that evidence with more persuasive evidence that he falls outside the criteria. A burden-shifting scheme of this sort would meet the goal of ensuring that the errant tourist, embedded journalist, or local aid worker has a chance to prove military error while giving due regard to the Executive once it has put forth meaningful support for its conclusion that the detainee is in fact an enemy combatant. . . .

We think it unlikely that this basic process will have the dire impact on the central functions of warmaking that the Government forecasts. The parties agree that initial captures on the battlefield need not receive the process we have discussed here; that process is due only when the determination is made to *continue* to hold those who have been seized. The Government has made clear in its briefing that documentation regarding battlefield detainees already is kept in the ordinary course of military affairs. Any factfinding imposition created by requiring a knowledgeable affiant to summarize these records to an independent tribunal is a minimal one. . . .

In sum, while the full protections that accompany challenges to detentions in other settings may prove unworkable and inappropriate in the enemy-combatant setting, the threats to military operations posed by a basic system of independent review are not so weighty as to trump a citizen's core rights to challenge meaningfully the Government's case and to be heard by an impartial adjudicator.

D

. . . We have long since made clear that a state of war is not a blank check for the President when it comes to the rights of the Nation's citizens. *Youngstown Sheet & Tube.* . . . Because we conclude that due process demands some system for a citizen-detainee to refute his classification, the proposed "some evidence" standard is inadequate. Any process in which the Executive's factual assertions go wholly unchallenged or are simply presumed correct without any opportunity for the alleged combatant to demonstrate otherwise falls constitutionally short. . . .

Today we are faced only with such a case. Aside from unspecified "screening" processes, Brief for Respondents, and military interrogations in which the Government suggests Hamdi could have contested his classification, Tr. of Oral Arg., Hamdi has received no process. An interrogation by one's captor, however effective an intelligence-gathering tool, hardly constitutes a constitutionally adequate factfinding before a neutral decisionmaker. . . . Plainly, the "process" Hamdi has received is not that to which he is entitled under the Due Process Clause.

WORTH NOTING

During oral argument, the lawyer for the United States suggested that Hamdi received all the process to which he was entitled when "he ha[d] an opportunity to explain it in his own words . . . . during interrogation."

There remains the possibility that the standards we have articulated could be met by an appropriately authorized and properly constituted military tribunal. Indeed, it is notable that military regulations already provide for such process in related instances, dictating that tribunals be made available to determine the status of enemy detainees who assert prisoner-of-war status under the Geneva Convention. In the absence of such process, however, a court that receives a petition for a writ of habeas corpus from an alleged enemy combatant must itself ensure that the minimum requirements of due process are achieved. . . .

As we have discussed, a habeas court in a case such as this may accept affidavit evidence like that contained in the Mobbs Declaration, so long as it also permits the alleged combatant to present his own factual case to rebut the Government's return. We anticipate that a District Court would proceed with the caution that we have indicated is necessary in this setting, engaging in a factfinding process that is both prudent and incremental. We have no reason to doubt that courts faced with these sensitive matters will pay proper heed both to the matters of national security that might arise in an individual case and to the constitutional limitations safeguarding essential liberties that remain vibrant even in times of security concerns.

IV

Hamdi asks us to hold that the Fourth Circuit also erred by denying him immediate access to counsel upon his detention and by disposing of the case without permitting him to meet with an attorney. Since our grant of certiorari in this case, Hamdi has been appointed counsel, . . . with whom he is now being granted unmonitored meetings. He unquestionably has the right to access to counsel in connection with the proceedings on remand. No further consideration of this issue is necessary at this stage of the case.

* * *

The judgment of the United States Court of Appeals for the Fourth Circuit is vacated, and the case is remanded for further proceedings.

JUSTICE SOUTER, with whom JUSTICE GINSBURG joins, concurring in part, dissenting in part, and concurring in the judgment.

. . . [T]he Government contends that Hamdi['s] . . . challenge may go no further than to enquire whether "some evidence" supports [his] designation. . . . Since . . . judicial enquiry so limited would be virtually worthless as a way to contest detention, the Government's concession of jurisdiction to hear Hamdi's habeas claim is more theoretical than practical, leaving the assertion of Executive authority close to unconditional.

The plurality rejects any such limit on the exercise of habeas jurisdiction and so far I agree with its opinion. The plurality does, however, accept the Government's position that if Hamdi's designation as an enemy combatant is correct, his detention (at least as to some period) is authorized by . . . the Authorization for Use of Military Force. Here, I disagree and respectfully dissent. . . .

IV

Because I find Hamdi's detention forbidden by § 4001(a) and unauthorized by the Force Resolution, I would not reach any questions of what process he may be due in litigating disputed issues in a proceeding under the habeas statute or prior to the habeas enquiry itself. [See pp. 852–865.] . . . I would therefore vacate the judgment of the Court of Appeals and remand for proceedings consistent with this view.

Since this disposition does not command a majority of the Court, however, the need to give practical effect to the conclusions of eight Members of the Court rejecting the Government's position calls for me to join with the plurality in ordering remand on terms closest to those I would impose. See *Screws v. United States* (1945) (Rutledge, J., concurring in result). Although I think litigation of Hamdi's status as an enemy combatant is unnecessary, the terms of the plurality's remand will allow Hamdi to offer evidence that he is not an enemy combatant, and he should at the least have the benefit of that opportunity.

It should go without saying that in joining with the plurality to produce a judgment, I do not adopt the plurality's resolution of constitutional issues that I would not reach. It is not that I could disagree with the plurality's determinations (given the plurality's view of the [AUMF]) that someone in Hamdi's position is entitled at a minimum to notice of the Government's claimed factual basis for holding him, and to a fair chance to rebut it before a neutral decisionmaker; nor, of course, could I disagree with the plurality's affirmation of Hamdi's right to counsel. On the other hand, I do not mean to imply agreement that the Government could claim an evidentiary presumption casting the burden of rebuttal on Hamdi, or that an opportunity to litigate before a military tribunal might obviate or truncate enquiry by a court on habeas.

Subject to these qualifications, I join with the plurality in a judgment of the Court vacating the Fourth Circuit's judgment and remanding the case.

JUSTICE SCALIA, with whom JUSTICE STEVENS joins, dissenting.

. . . Where the Government accuses a citizen of waging war against it, our constitutional tradition has been to prosecute him in federal court for treason or some other crime. Where the exigencies of war prevent that, the Constitution's Suspension Clause, Art. I, § 9, cl. 2, allows Congress to relax the usual protections temporarily. Absent suspension, however, the Executive's assertion of military exigency has not been thought sufficient to permit detention without charge. . . . It follows from what I have said that Hamdi is entitled to a habeas decree requiring his release unless (1) criminal proceedings are promptly brought, or (2) Congress has suspended the writ of habeas corpus. . . .

Justice Thomas, dissenting.

. . . By detaining Hamdi, the President, in the prosecution of a war and authorized by Congress, has acted well within his authority. Hamdi thereby received all the process to which he was due under the circumstances. . . .

B. Substantive Due Process

1. "But the Constitution Doesn't Say Anything About . . ."

In many constitutional cases, the plaintiff is asking the Court to protect some right, interest, or activity. Wherever possible, it is then standard operating practice for defendants to respond by demanding—ideally in high dudgeon—"Show me where it says that in the Constitution!" Plaintiffs then typically offer one of the following three responses.

First, the plaintiff may be able to point to one or more specific clauses of the Constitution that arguably do protect the right in question; the First Amendment contains several important examples of clauses that are moderately specific, but still sufficiently general to cover a range of activities not explicitly enunciated. Indeed, sometimes the plaintiff will be able to persuade the courts to give a specific clause a rather creative construction to reach cases to which it might not seem to apply.

Second, the plaintiff might argue that a general clause of the Constitution should be construed to protect the asserted right in question. Despite their apparent procedural focus, the Due Process Clauses of the Fifth and Fourteenth Amendment are the provisions most often invoked successfully for this purpose. And so we are labeling this entire section Substantive Due Process—though occasionally other rubrics will come into play. The courts' use of the Due Process Clauses for this purpose may seem strange given that other clauses of the Constitution might appear better suited for substantive applications. One is the Privileges and Immunities Clause of Art. IV, § 2, which provides:

> The Citizens of each State shall be entitled to all Privileges and Immunities of Citizens in the several States.

A second is the Privileges or Immunities of the Fourteenth Amendment, which provides:

> . . . No State shall make or enforce any law which shall abridge the privileges or immunities of citizens of the United States . . .

And the third is the Ninth Amendment, which provides:

> The enumeration in the Constitution, of certain rights, shall not be construed to deny or disparage others retained by the people.

While these latter three clauses do draw some attention, none of them has become a major fount for the recognition of rights not enumerated elsewhere in the Constitution. The Article IV provision has been understood primarily as a guarantor against certain types of state discrimination against citizens of other states. The Privileges and Immunities Clause of the Fourteenth Amendment has never fully recovered from the demolition job done on it in the *Slaughter-House Cases*, pp. 167–172. And the Ninth Amendment, which was originally focused on the federal government, can plausibly be seen as a reflection of rights generated elsewhere.

And that leads to the third type of response the plaintiff might make: contend that some source other than the text of the Constitution guarantees the right. For a time in the 19th century, jurists sometimes spoke of "general constitutional law." See, *e.g.*, Charles W. McCurdy, *The Problem of General Constitutional Law: Thomas McIntyre Cooley*, Constitutional Limitations, *and the Supreme Court of the United States, 1868–1878*, 18 Geo. J. L. & Pub. Pol'y 1 (2020). Other commentators have suggested that principles of natural law, or those underlying republican government, may provide rights not enumerated in the Constitution.

Calder v. Bull (1798), which involved an inheritance dispute that attracted the attention of the state legislature, is an early discussion of this last type of response. In that case, Bull claimed the right to inherit under the decendent's will, but the Calders won a lower court judgment that the will was invalid. After the period for appeal had expired, the Connecticut Legislature passed an act requiring a new trial in the case. This time, Bull won in the state courts, and the Calders appealed to the U.S. Supreme Court, contending that the statute was an *ex post facto* law prohibited by Art. I, § 10, of the Constitution.

Chief Justice Ellsworth, who was from Connecticut, did not participate, and the other four justices each issued an opinion. They concluded that the act was not in fact an *ex post facto* law; among the reasons given were that the prohibition applies only to criminal cases and that the Connecticut Legislature had a well-established practice of exercising supervisory power over the state's courts. For present purposes, the most significant part of the case is a debate between Justices Chase and Iredell over whether governmental power is constrained by principles found not in the Constitution but in some extra-constitutional source.

Justice Chase wrote:

> I cannot subscribe to the omnipotence of a State Legislature, or that it is absolute and without control; although its authority should not be expressly restrained by the Constitution, or fundamental law, of the State. The people of the United States erected their Constitutions, or forms of government, to establish justice, to promote the general welfare, to secure the blessings of liberty; and to protect their persons and property from violence. The purposes for which men enter into society will determine the nature and terms of the social compact; and as they are the foundation of the legislative power, they will decide what are the proper objects of it: The nature, and ends of legislative power will limit the exercise of it. This fundamental principle flows from the very nature of our free Republican governments, that no man should be compelled to do what the laws do not require; nor to refrain from acts which the laws permit.
>
> There are acts which the Federal, or State, Legislature cannot do, without exceeding their authority. There are certain vital principles in our free Republican governments, which will determine and over-rule an apparent and flagrant abuse of legislative power; as to authorize manifest injustice by positive law; or to take away that security for personal liberty, or private property, for the protection whereof of the government was established. An ACT of the Legislature (for I

cannot call it a law) contrary to the great first principles of the social compact, cannot be considered a rightful exercise of legislative
authority. The obligation of a law in governments established on express compact, and on republican principles, must be determined by
the nature of the power, on which it is founded.

A few instances will suffice to explain what I mean. A law that
punished a citizen for an innocent action, or, in other words, for an
act, which, when done, was in violation of no existing law; a law
that destroys, or impairs, the lawful private contracts of citizens; a
law that makes a man a Judge in his own cause; or a law that takes
property from A and gives it to B: It is against all reason and justice, for a people to entrust a Legislature with SUCH powers; and,
therefore, it cannot be presumed that they have done it. The genius,
the nature, and the spirit, of our State Governments, amount to a
prohibition of such acts of legislation; and the general principles of
law and reason forbid them.

The Legislature may enjoin, permit, forbid, and punish; they
may declare new crimes; and establish rules of conduct for all its citizens in future cases; they may command what is right, and prohibit
what is wrong; but they cannot change innocence into guilt; or punish innocence as a crime; or violate the right of an antecedent lawful
private contract; or the right of private property. To maintain that our
Federal, or State, Legislature possesses such powers, if they had not
been expressly restrained; would, in my opinion, be a political her-
esy, altogether inadmissible in our free republican governments. . . .

By contrast, Justice Iredell wrote:

If . . . a government, composed of Legislative, Executive and
Judicial departments, were established, by a Constitution, which
imposed no limits on the legislative power, the consequence would
inevitably be, that whatever the legislative power chose to enact, would
be lawfully enacted, and the judicial power could never interpose to
pronounce it void. It is true, that some speculative jurists have held,
that a legislative act against natural justice must, in itself, be void;
but I cannot think that, under such a government, any Court of Justice would possess a power to declare it so. Sir William Blackstone,

having put the strong case of an act of Parliament, which should authorise a man to try his own cause, explicitly adds, that even in that case, "there is no court that has power to defeat the intent of the Legislature, when couched in such evident and express words, as leave no doubt whether it was the intent of the Legislature, or no." Blackstone's Commentaries.

In order, therefore, to guard against so great an evil, it has been the policy of all the American states, which have, individually, framed their state constitutions since the revolution, and of the people of the United States, when they framed the Federal Constitution, to define with precision the objects of the legislative power, and to restrain its exercise within marked and settled boundaries.

If any act of Congress, or of the Legislature of a state, violates those constitutional provisions, it is unquestionably void; though, I admit, that as the authority to declare it void is of a delicate and awful nature, the Court will never resort to that authority, but in a clear and urgent case.

If, on the other hand, the Legislature of the Union, or the Legislature of any member of the Union, shall pass a law, within the general scope of their constitutional power, the Court cannot pronounce it to be void, merely because it is, in their judgment, contrary to the principles of natural justice. The ideas of natural justice are regulated by no fixed standard: the ablest and the purest men have differed upon the subject; and all that the Court could properly say, in such an event, would be, that the Legislature (possessed of an equal right of opinion) had passed an act which, in the opinion of the judges, was inconsistent with the abstract principles of natural justice. There are then but two lights, in which the subject can be viewed: 1st. If the Legislature pursue the authority delegated to them, their acts are valid. 2nd. If they transgress the boundaries of that authority, their acts are invalid. In the former case, they exercise the discretion vested in them by the people, to whom alone they are responsible for the faithful discharge of their trust: but in the latter case, they violate a fundamental law, which must be our guide, whenever we are called upon as judges to determine the validity of a legislative act. . . .

It is not sufficient to urge, that [legislative] power may be abused, for, such is the nature of all power, such is the tendency of every human institution: and, it might as fairly be said, that the power of taxation, which is only circumscribed by the discretion of the Body, in which it is vested, ought not to be granted, because the Legislature, disregarding its true objects, might, for visionary and useless projects, impose a tax to the amount of nineteen shillings in the pound. We must be content to limit power where we can, and where we cannot, consistently with its use, we must be content to repose a salutary confidence.

WORTH NOTING

Nineteen shillings per pound would be a 95% tax.

It is our consolation that there never existed a Government, in ancient or modern times, more free from danger in this respect, than the Governments of America.

Now let's fast-forward from the late 18th century to the late 20th, and focus on arguments that purport to have a basis in the constitutional text. If the text of provisions like the Ninth Amendment and the Privileges or Immunities Clause is so abstract as to be capable of virtually any interpretation, then what does it even mean for an argument to be "textual" in the first place? Consider the following perspective on how to think about that question, especially where such provisions are enunciated in an otherwise sparsely-worded founding document.

John Hart Ely, Democracy and Distrust: A Theory of Judicial Review

(1980)

Constitutional provisions exist on a spectrum ranging from the relatively specific to the extremely open-textured. At one extreme—for example the requirement that the President "have attained to the Age of thirty five years"—the language is so clear that a conscious reference to purpose seems unnecessary. . . . Others, such as the First Amendment's prohibition of congressional laws "abridging the freedom of speech," seem to need more. For

one thing, a phrase as terse as the others I have mentioned is here expected
to govern a broader and more important range of problems. For another, and
this may have something to do with the first, we somehow sense that a line of
growth was intended, that the language was not intended to be restricted to
its 1791 meaning. This realization would not faze Justice Black or most other
interpretivists: the job of the person interpreting the provision, they would respond, is to identify the sorts of evils against which the provision was directed
and to move against their contemporary counterparts. Obviously this will be
difficult, but it will remain interpretivism—a determination of "the present
scope and meaning of a decision that the nation, at an earlier time, articulated
and enacted into the constitutional text."

Still other provisions, such as the Eighth Amendment's prohibition of
"cruel and unusual punishments," seem even more insistently to call for a reference to sources beyond the document itself and a "framers' dictionary." It is
possible to construe this prohibition as covering only those punishments that
would have been regarded as "cruel and unusual" in 1791, but that construction
seems untrue to the open-ended quality of the language. The interpretivist can
respond as he did to the First Amendment, that even though it is true that the
clause shouldn't be restricted to its 1791 meaning, it should be restricted to the
general categories of evils at which the provision was aimed. If you pursue this
mode of "interpretation" with regard to the Eighth Amendment, however—and
the First Amendment case will come down to much the same thing—you'll
soon find yourself, at worst, begging a lot of questions or, at best, attributing
to the framers a theory that may be consistent with what they said but is hardly
discoverable in their discussions or their dictionaries. But even admitting this,
the disaster for the interpretivist remains less than complete. The Cruel and
Unusual Punishment Clause does invite the person interpreting it to freelance
to a degree, but the freelancing is bounded. The subject is punishments, not the
entire range of government action, and even in that limited area the delegation
to the interpreter is not entirely unguided: only those punishments that are in
some way serious ("cruel") and susceptible to sporadic imposition ("unusual")
are to be disallowed.

The Eighth Amendment does not mark the end of the spectrum, however.
The Fourteenth Amendment—and I shall argue later that the Ninth Amendment is similar—contains provisions that are difficult to read responsibly as
anything other than quite broad invitations to import into the constitutional

decision process considerations that will not be found in the language of the amendment or the debates that led up to it.

Judge Robert Bork was highly skeptical of the open-ended use of vague constitutional text that Professor Ely's discussion might tend to support. During the hearings on his nomination to the Supreme Court (the Senate ultimately rejected him), Bork testified as follows:

> I do not think you can use the Ninth Amendment unless you know something of what it means. For example, if you had an amendment that says "Congress shall make no" and then there is an inkblot, and you cannot read the rest of it, and that is the only copy you have, I do not think the court can make up what might be under the inkblot if you cannot read it.

Bork elsewhere made a similar point:

> The judge who cannot make out the meaning of a provision is in exactly the same circumstance as a judge who has no Constitution to work with. There being nothing to work with, the judge should refrain from working. A provision whose meaning cannot be ascertained is precisely like a provision that is . . . obliterated past deciphering by an ink blot. No judge is entitled to interpret an ink blot on the ground that there must be something under it.

Robert Bork, *The Tempting of America* (1990). Who has the best of this debate? Are these just academic questions, or do they have real-world stakes?

2.   Incorporation of the Bill of Rights

Justice Iredell's position in *Calder v. Bull* has prevailed: all constitutional claims must be grounded in constitutional text, however broad or vague. So what happens if a plaintiff can't point to any specifically enumerated right in support of her claim? She will very likely turn to the Due Process Clause, invoking what is known to modern constitutional lawyers as "substantive due process."

As a first foray into this area, we will explore what happens when a state is accused of violating one of the provisions of the Bill of Rights—a term we use here to mean the first eight amendments. That might strike you as strange:

We said we were discussing *un*enumerated rights, and the Bill of Rights is the quintessential enumeration of rights. Recall, however, that the Bill of Rights was originally understood as applying only to the federal government—indeed, the First Amendment goes so far as to specifically limit its application to "Congress." And so at least on its face, the Bill of Rights appears to be every bit as "nontextu-

 CROSS REFERENCE See *Barron v. Baltimore* (1833) (holding that the Takings Clause "is intended solely as a limitation on the exercise of power by the government of the United States, and is not applicable to the legislation of the states"), pp. 61–64.

al" a source of judicially enforceable rights *against the states* as the Declaration of Independence, the Articles of Confederation, or a sociological treatise.

Now, Justice Hugo Black denied that this appearance reflected reality. In his view, § 1 of the Fourteenth Amendment "incorporated" the entire Bill of Rights, thereby making the substance of the first eight amendments directly applicable to the states through the textual vehicle of the Due Process and Privileges or Immunities Clauses. The Supreme Court has never adopted Justice Black's claim of "total incorporation." Beginning in the 1920s, however, the Court has engaged in a process of "selective incorporation," holding specific rights, one by one, applicable against the states. In *Gitlow v. New York* (1925), for example, the Court assumed "that the rights of freedom of speech and freedom of the press were among the fundamental personal rights and 'liberties' protected by the due process clause of the Fourteenth Amendment from impairment by the states." In the 1960s, the Court quickly incorporated virtually all the criminal-rights provisions of the Bill of Rights against the states. See also *Penn Central Transportation Co. v. New York City* (1978) (holding that the Takings Clause "of course" is "made applicable to the States" by the Fourteenth Amendment).

As *Gitlow* suggests, selective incorporation took place by the Court declaring one right after another to be fundamental. The process met significant resistance, especially by the second Justice Harlan. Drawing especially on the jurisprudence of Justices Cardozo and Frankfurter, he contended that individual components of the Bill of Rights should not be incorporated "jot-for-jot" against the states; the question was not whether a given clause of the Bill of Rights was "in" or "out," but rather whether the particular aspect of a right asserted was "fundamental to ordered liberty." *Duncan v. Louisiana* (1968) (Harlan, J., dissenting, joined by Stewart, J.).

In the context of the incorporation debate, Justice Black's view plainly gave greater force to the Fourteenth Amendment than did Justice Harlan's. But there was another aspect to the debate. Black believed that, while the Due Process and Privileges or Immunities Clauses of the Fourteenth Amendment incorporated the Bill of Rights totally, that was *all* they did. This comported with his view that judges should not have a free range of power; a judge could not recognize a right without basing it on the language of a specific clause of the Bill of Rights. Justice Harlan, by contrast, believed that § 1 of the Fourteenth Amendment "was meant neither to incorporate, *nor to be limited to*, the specific guarantees of the first eight Amendments." *Duncan* (emphasis added). As we shall see, the expansive component of Justice Harlan's view has prevailed: The Court has concluded that the Due Process Clause protects some rights that are not enumerated in the Bill of Rights, as well as most of those that are.

During the Warren Court era of the 1960s, the impulse for incorporation came largely from the liberal side of the Court. But, as the next case shows, what's sauce for the goose is sauce for the gander.

McDonald v. City of Chicago

Supreme Court of the United States, 2010.
561 U.S. 742.

JUSTICE ALITO announced the judgment of the Court and delivered the opinion of the Court with respect to Parts I, II-A, II-B, II-D, III-A, and III-B, in which THE CHIEF JUSTICE, JUSTICE SCALIA, JUSTICE KENNEDY, and JUSTICE THOMAS join, and an opinion with respect to Parts II-C, IV, and V, in which THE CHIEF JUSTICE, JUSTICE SCALIA, and JUSTICE KENNEDY join.

Two years ago, in *District of Columbia v. Heller* (2008), we held that the Second Amendment protects the right to keep and bear arms for the purpose of self-defense, and we struck down a District of Columbia law that banned the possession of handguns in the home.

The city of Chicago [has] laws that are similar to the District of Columbia's, but Chicago . . . argue[s] that [its] laws are constitutional because the

Second Amendment has no application to the States. We have previously held that most of the provisions of the Bill of Rights apply with full force to both the Federal Government and the States. Applying the standard that is well established in our case law, we hold that the Second Amendment right is fully applicable to the States.

I

Otis McDonald [and the other petitioners] are Chicago residents who would like to keep handguns in their homes for self-defense but are prohibited from doing so by Chicago's firearms laws. A City ordinance provides that "[n]o person shall . . . possess . . . any firearm unless such person is the holder of a valid registration certificate for such firearm." The Code then prohibits registration of most handguns, thus effectively banning handgun possession by almost all private citizens who reside in the City. . . . Otis McDonald, who is in his late seventies, lives in a high-crime neighborhood. He is a community activist involved with alternative policing strategies, and his efforts to improve his neighborhood have subjected him to violent threats from drug dealers. McDonald . . . and the other Chicago petitioners own handguns that they store outside of the city limits, but they would like to keep their handguns in their homes for protection. . . .

II

A

Petitioners argue that the Chicago . . . laws violate the right to keep and bear arms for two reasons. Petitioners' primary submission is that this right is among the "privileges or immunities of citizens of the United States" and that the narrow interpretation of the Privileges or Immunities Clause adopted in the *Slaughter-House Cases* (1873) should now be rejected. As a secondary argument, petitioners contend that the Fourteenth Amendment's Due Process Clause "incorporates" the Second Amendment right. . . .

B

The Bill of Rights, including the Second Amendment, originally applied only to the Federal Government. *Barron ex rel. Tiernan v. Mayor of Baltimore* (1833). . . .

The constitutional Amendments adopted in the aftermath of the Civil War fundamentally altered our country's federal system. The provision at issue in this case, § 1 of the Fourteenth Amendment, provides, among other things, that a State may not abridge "the privileges or immunities of citizens of the United States" or deprive "any person of life, liberty, or property, without due process of law."

Four years after the adoption of the Fourteenth Amendment, this Court was asked to interpret the Amendment's reference to "the privileges or immunities of citizens of the United States." *Slaughter-House Cases* [presented pp. 167–172]. . . . Justice Samuel Miller's opinion for the Court concluded that the Privileges or Immunities Clause protects only those rights "which owe their existence to the Federal government, its National character, its Constitution, or its laws." . . . [T]he Court stated that a [more robust] reading would "radically chang[e] the whole theory of the relations of the State and Federal governments to each other and of both these governments to the people." . . .

Under the Court's narrow reading, the Privileges or Immunities Clause protects such things as the right

> to come to the seat of government to assert any claim [a citizen] may have upon that government, to transact any business he may have with it, to seek its protection, to share its offices, to engage in administering its functions . . . [and to] become a citizen of any State of the Union by a *bonafide* residence therein, with the same rights as other citizens of that State.

Finding no constitutional protection against state intrusion of the kind envisioned by the Louisiana statute, the Court upheld the statute. . . . Today, many legal scholars dispute the correctness of the narrow *Slaughter-House* interpretation. See, *e.g.*, Amar, *Substance and Method in the Year 2000*, 28 Pepperdine L. Rev. 601 (2001) ("Virtually no serious modern scholar—left, right, and center—thinks that this [interpretation] is a plausible reading of the Amendment"). . . .

C

. . . Petitioners argue . . . that we should overrule [this precedent] and hold that the right to keep and bear arms is one of the "privileges or immunities of citizens of the United States." In petitioners' view, the Privileges or Immunities Clause protects all of the rights set out in the Bill of Rights, as well as some others, but petitioners are unable to identify the Clause's full scope. Nor is there any consensus on that question among the scholars who agree that the *Slaughter-House Cases'* interpretation is flawed.

We see no need to reconsider that interpretation here. For many decades, the question of the rights protected by the Fourteenth Amendment against state infringement has been analyzed under the Due Process Clause of that Amendment and not under the Privileges or Immunities Clause. We therefore decline to disturb the *Slaughter-House* holding.

At the same time, however, this Court's decisions . . . do not preclude us from considering whether the Due Process Clause of the Fourteenth Amendment makes the Second Amendment right binding on the States. . . .

D

1

In the late 19th century, the Court began to consider whether the Due Process Clause prohibits the States from infringing rights set out in the Bill of Rights. See *Hurtado v. California* (1884) (due process does not require grand jury indictment); *Chicago, B. & Q.R. Co. v. Chicago* (1897) (due process prohibits States from taking of private property for public use without just compensation). . . . [In a long series of cases,] the Court explained that the only rights protected against state infringement by the Due Process Clause were those rights "of such a nature that they are included in the conception of due process of law." While it was "possible that some of the personal rights safeguarded by the first eight Amendments against National action [might] also be safeguarded against state action," the Court stated, this was "not because those rights are enumerated in the first eight Amendments." *Twining v. New Jersey* (1908).

The Court used different formulations in describing the boundaries of due process. For example, in *Twining*, the Court referred to "immutable principles of justice which inhere in the very idea of free government which no member of the Union may disregard." In *Snyder v. Massachusetts* (1934), the Court spoke of rights that are "so rooted in the traditions and conscience of our people as to be ranked as fundamental." And in *Palko v. Connecticut* (1937), the Court famously said that due process protects those rights that are "the very essence of a scheme of ordered liberty" and essential to "a fair and enlightened system of justice." [I]n some cases decided during this era the Court "can be seen as having asked, when inquiring into whether some particular procedural safeguard was required of a State, if a civilized system could be imagined that would not accord the particular protection." *Duncan v. Louisiana* (1968). . . .

An alternative theory regarding the relationship between the Bill of Rights and § 1 of the Fourteenth Amendment was championed by Justice Black. This theory held that § 1 of the Fourteenth Amendment totally incorporated all of the provisions of the Bill of Rights. See, *e.g., Duncan* (Black, J., concurring). As Justice Black noted, the chief congressional proponents of the Fourteenth Amendment espoused the view that the Amendment made the Bill of Rights applicable to the States and, in so doing, overruled this Court's decision in *Barron.* Nonetheless, the Court never has embraced Justice Black's "total incorporation" theory.

While Justice Black's theory was never adopted, the Court eventually moved in that direction by initiating what has been called a process of "selective incorporation," *i.e.,* the Court began to hold that the Due Process Clause fully incorporates particular rights contained in the first eight Amendments. . . .

Two subsequent decisions bear on the Court's discussion in notes 13 and 14:

WORTH NOTING

(1) In *Timbs v. Indiana* (2019), the Court held that the Eighth Amendment's prohibition of excessive fines does apply to the states.

(2) In *Ramos v. Louisiana* (2020), the Court overruled *Apodaca v. Oregon* (1972) and held that the Sixth Amendment requires unanimity for a criminal conviction in a jury trial.

The Court eventually incorporated almost all of the provisions of the Bill of Rights. Only a handful of the Bill of Rights protections remain unincorporated. . . [13] The Court [has also] held that incorporated Bill of Rights protections "are all to be enforced against the States under the Fourteenth Amendment according to the same standards that protect those personal rights against federal encroachment."[14]. . .

[13] In addition to the right to keep and bear arms (and the Sixth Amendment right to a unanimous jury verdict, see n.14 *infra*), the only rights not fully incorporated are

(1) the Third Amendment's protection against quartering of soldiers;

(2) the Fifth Amendment's grand jury indictment requirement;

(3) the Seventh Amendment right to a jury trial in civil cases; and

(4) the Eighth Amendment's prohibition on excessive fines.

We never have decided whether the Third Amendment or the Eighth Amendment's prohibition of excessive fines applies to the States through the Due Process Clause. Our governing decisions regarding the Grand Jury Clause of the Fifth Amendment and the Seventh Amendment's civil jury requirement long predate the era of selective incorporation.

[14] There is one exception to this general rule. The Court has held that although the Sixth Amendment right to trial by jury requires a unanimous jury verdict in federal criminal trials, it does not require a unanimous jury verdict in state criminal trials. See *Apodaca v. Oregon* (1972). But that ruling was the result of an unusual division among the Justices, not an endorsement of the two-track approach to incorporation.

III

With this framework in mind, we now turn directly to the question whether the Second Amendment right to keep and bear arms is incorporated in the concept of due process. In answering that question, as just explained, we must decide whether the right to keep and bear arms is fundamental to *our* scheme of ordered liberty, or as we have said in a related context, whether this right is "deeply rooted in this Nation's history and tradition," *Washington v. Glucksberg* (1997) [(holding that there is no substantive due process right to physician assisted suicide)].

A

Our decision in *Heller* points unmistakably to the answer. Self-defense is a basic right, recognized by many legal systems from ancient times to the present day, and in *Heller*, we held that individual self-defense is "the *central component*" of the Second Amendment right. . . . *Heller* makes it clear that this right is "deeply rooted in this Nation's history and tradition." *Glucksberg*. . . .

B

. . . In debating the Fourteenth Amendment, the 39th Congress referred to the right to keep and bear arms as a fundamental right deserving of protection. Senator Samuel Pomeroy described three "indispensable" "safeguards of liberty under our form of Government." One of these, he said, was the right to keep and bear arms:

> Every man . . . should have the right to bear arms for the defense of himself and family and his homestead. And if the cabin door of the freedman is broken open and the intruder enters for purposes as vile as were known to slavery, then should a well-loaded musket be in the hand of the occupant to send the polluted wretch to another world, where his wretchedness will forever remain complete.

Even those [like Senator James Nye] who thought the Fourteenth Amendment unnecessary believed that blacks, as citizens, "have equal right to protection, and to keep and bear arms for self-defense."[25] . . .

The right to keep and bear arms was also widely protected by state constitutions at the time when the Fourteenth Amendment was ratified. In 1868,

---

[25] Other Members of the 39th Congress stressed the importance of the right to keep and bear arms in discussing other measures. . . .

22 of the 37 States in the Union had state constitutional provisions explicitly protecting the right to keep and bear arms. Quite a few of these state constitutional guarantees, moreover, explicitly protected the right to keep and bear arms as an individual right to self-defense. What is more, state constitutions adopted during the Reconstruction era by former Confederate States included a right to keep and bear arms. A clear majority of the States in 1868, therefore, recognized the right to keep and bear arms as being among the foundational rights necessary to our system of Government.

In sum, it is clear that the Framers and ratifiers of the Fourteenth Amendment counted the right to keep and bear arms among those fundamental rights necessary to our system of ordered liberty. . . .

IV

Municipal respondents' remaining arguments . . . . in effect, ask us to treat the right recognized in *Heller* as a second-class right, subject to an entirely different body of rules than the other Bill of Rights guarantees that we have held to be incorporated into the Due Process Clause.

Municipal respondents' main argument is [that] if it is possible to imagine *any* civilized legal system that does not recognize a particular right, then the Due Process Clause does not make that right binding on the States. Therefore, the municipal respondents continue, because such countries as England, Canada, Australia, Japan, Denmark, Finland, Luxembourg, and New Zealand either ban or severely limit handgun ownership, it must follow that no right to possess such weapons is protected by the Fourteenth Amendment. This line of argument is, of course, inconsistent with the long-established standard we apply in incorporation cases. See [Part II-B]. And the present-day implications of municipal respondents' argument are stunning. For example, many of the rights that our Bill of Rights provides for persons accused of criminal offenses are virtually unique to this country.[28] If *our* understanding of the right to a jury trial, the right against self-incrimination, and the right to counsel were necessary attributes of *any* civilized country, it would follow that the United States is the only civilized Nation in the world. . . .

We likewise reject municipal respondents' argument that we should depart from our established incorporation methodology on the ground that making the

---

[28]   For example, the United States affords criminal jury trials far more broadly than other countries. . . . Similarly, our rules governing pretrial interrogation differ from those in countries sharing a similar legal heritage. . . .

Second Amendment binding on the States and their subdivisions is inconsistent with principles of federalism and will stifle experimentation. . . .

There is nothing new in the argument that, in order to respect federalism and allow useful state experimentation, a federal constitutional right should not be fully binding on the States. This argument was made repeatedly and eloquently by Members of this Court who rejected the concept of incorporation and urged retention of the two-track approach to incorporation. Throughout the era of "selective incorporation," Justice Harlan in particular, invoking the values of federalism and state experimentation, fought a determined rearguard action to preserve the two-track approach. Time and again, however, those pleas failed. Unless we turn back the clock or adopt a special incorporation test applicable only to the Second Amendment, municipal respondents' argument must be rejected. Under our precedents, if a Bill of Rights guarantee is fundamental from an American perspective, then, unless *stare decisis* counsels otherwise, that guarantee is fully binding on the States. . . .

V

. . . [W]hile there is certainly room for disagreement about *Heller*'s analysis of the history of the right to keep and bear arms, nothing written since *Heller* persuades us to reopen the question there decided. . . .

In *Heller*, we held that the Second Amendment protects the right to possess a handgun in the home for the purpose of self-defense. Unless considerations of *stare decisis* counsel otherwise, a provision of the Bill of Rights that protects a right that is fundamental from an American perspective applies equally to the Federal Government and the States. We therefore hold that the Due Process Clause of the Fourteenth Amendment incorporates the Second Amendment right recognized in *Heller*. . . .

JUSTICE SCALIA, concurring.

I join the Court's opinion. Despite my misgivings about Substantive Due Process as an original matter, I have acquiesced in the Court's incorporation of certain guarantees in the Bill of Rights "because it is both long established and narrowly limited." *Albright v. Oliver* (1994) (Scalia, J., concurring). This case does not require me to reconsider that view, since straightforward application of settled doctrine suffices to decide it. . . .

JUSTICE THOMAS, concurring in part and concurring in the judgment.

I agree with the Court that the Fourteenth Amendment makes the right to keep and bear arms set forth in the Second Amendment "fully applicable to the States." I write separately because I believe there is a more straightforward path to this conclusion, one that is more faithful to the Fourteenth Amendment's text and history. . . . [T]he right to keep and bear arms is a privilege of American citizenship that applies to the States through the Fourteenth Amendment's Privileges or Immunities Clause. . . .

I

. . . In the *Slaughter-House Cases* (1873), decided just five years after the Fourteenth Amendment's adoption, the Court interpreted . . . the Privileges or Immunities Clause for the first time. In a closely divided decision, the Court drew a sharp distinction between the privileges and immunities of state citizenship and those of federal citizenship, and held that the Privileges or Immunities Clause protected only the latter category of rights from state abridgment. The Court defined that category to include only those rights "which owe their existence to the Federal government, its National character, its Constitution, or its laws." This arguably left open the possibility that certain individual rights enumerated in the Constitution could be considered privileges or immunities of federal citizenship. But the Court soon rejected that proposition, interpreting the Privileges or Immunities Clause even more narrowly in its later cases.

Chief among those cases is *United States v. Cruikshank* (1876). [See pp. 175–177.] There, the Court held that members of a white militia who had brutally murdered as many as 165 black Louisianians congregating outside a courthouse had not deprived the victims of their privileges as American citizens to peaceably assemble or to keep and bear arms. *See* L. Keith, *The Colfax Massacre* (2008). According to the Court, the right to peaceably assemble codified in the First Amendment was not a privilege of United States citizenship because "[t]he right . . . existed long *before* the adoption of the Constitution." . . . In the intervening years, the Court has held that the Clause prevents state abridgment of only a handful of rights, such as the right to travel, see *Saenz v. Roe* (1999), that are not readily described as essential to liberty.

As a consequence of this Court's marginalization of the Clause, litigants seeking federal protection of fundamental rights turned to the remainder of § 1 in search of an alternative fount of such rights. They found one in a most curious place—that section's command that every State guarantee "due process" to any person before depriving him of "life, liberty, or property." . . . The Court came to conclude that certain Bill of Rights guarantees *were* sufficiently fundamental to fall within § 1's guarantee of "due process." These included not only procedural protections listed in the first eight Amendments, see, *e.g., Benton v. Maryland* (1969) (protection against double jeopardy), but substantive rights as well, see, *e.g., Gitlow v. New York* (1925) (right to free speech). . . . [O]ur cases continue to adhere to the view that a right is incorporated through the Due Process Clause only if it is sufficiently "fundamental"—a term the Court has long struggled to define. . . .

All of this is a legal fiction. The notion that a constitutional provision that guarantees only "process" before a person is deprived of life, liberty, or property could define the substance of those rights strains credulity for even the most casual user of words. . . .

I acknowledge the volume of precedents that have been built upon the substantive due process framework, and I further acknowledge the importance of *stare decisis* to the stability of our Nation's legal system. But *stare decisis* is only an "adjunct" of our duty as judges to decide by our best lights what the Constitution means. It is not "an inexorable command." . . . I believe this case presents an opportunity to reexamine, and begin the process of restoring, the meaning of the Fourteenth Amendment agreed upon by those who ratified it.

II

[After discussing at length the background to and legislative history of the Fourteenth Amendment, Justice Thomas concludes that] the ratifying public understood the Privileges or Immunities Clause to protect constitutionally enumerated rights, including the right to keep and bear arms. As the Court demonstrates, there can be no doubt that § 1 was understood to enforce the Second Amendment against the States. In my view, this is because the right to keep and bear arms was understood to be a privilege of American citizenship guaranteed by the Privileges or Immunities Clause. . . .

JUSTICE STEVENS, dissenting.

. . . I agree with the plurality's refusal to accept petitioners' primary submission. Their briefs marshal an impressive amount of historical evidence for their argument that the Court interpreted the Privileges or Immunities Clause too narrowly in the *Slaughter-House Cases* (1873). But the original meaning of the Clause is not as clear as they suggest[2]—and not nearly as clear as it would need to be to dislodge 137 years of precedent. The burden is severe for those who seek radical change in such an established body of constitutional doctrine.[3] . . .

I further agree with the plurality that there are weighty arguments supporting petitioners' second submission, [relying on the Due Process Clause,] insofar as it concerns the possession of firearms for lawful self-defense in the home. But these arguments are less compelling than the plurality suggests; they are much less compelling when applied outside the home; and their validity does not depend on the Court's holding in *Heller*. For that holding sheds no light on the meaning of the Due Process Clause of the Fourteenth Amendment. . . . This is a substantive due process case.

I

Section 1 of the Fourteenth Amendment decrees that no State shall "deprive any person of life, liberty, or property, without due process of law." The Court has filled thousands of pages expounding that spare text. As I read the vast corpus of substantive due process opinions, they confirm several important principles that ought to guide our resolution of this case. The principal opinion's lengthy summary of our "incorporation" doctrine, and its implicit (and untenable) effort to wall off that doctrine from the rest of our substantive due process jurisprudence, invite a fresh survey of this old terrain. . . .

The first, and most basic, principle established by our cases is that the rights protected by the Due Process Clause are not merely procedural in nature. At first glance, this proposition might seem surprising, given that the Clause refers to "process." But substance and procedure are often deeply entwined. . . . Procedural guarantees are hollow unless linked to substantive interests; and no amount of process can legitimize some deprivations.

I have yet to see a persuasive argument that the Framers of the Fourteenth Amendment thought otherwise. To the contrary, the historical evidence suggests that, at least by the time of the Civil War if not much earlier, the phrase

---

[2]   . . . Although he urges its elevation in our doctrine, Justice Thomas has acknowledged that, in seeking to ascertain the original meaning of the Privileges or Immunities Clause, "[l]egal scholars agree on little beyond the conclusion that the Clause does not mean what the Court said it meant in 1873." *Saenz v. Roe* (1999) (dissenting opinion); *accord, ante* (plurality opinion).

[3]   It is no secret that the desire to "displace" major "portions of our equal protection and substantive due process jurisprudence" animates some of the passion that attends this interpretive issue. *Saenz* (Thomas, J., dissenting).

"due process of law" had acquired substantive content as a term of art within the legal community. . . .

If text and history are inconclusive on this point, our precedent leaves no doubt: It has been "settled" for well over a century that the Due Process Clause "applies to matters of substantive law as well as to matters of procedure." *Whitney v. California* (1927) (Brandeis, J., concurring). . . . Some of our most enduring precedents, accepted today by virtually everyone, were substantive due process decisions. See, *e.g., Loving v. Virginia* (1967) (recognizing due-process as well as equal-protection-based right to marry person of another race); *Bolling v. Sharpe* (1954) (outlawing racial segregation in District of Columbia public schools). . . .

It follows that the term "incorporation," like the term "unenumerated rights," is something of a misnomer. Whether an asserted substantive due process interest is explicitly named in one of the first eight Amendments to the Constitution or is not mentioned, the underlying inquiry is the same: We must ask whether the interest is "comprised within the term liberty." As the second Justice Harlan has shown, ever since the Court began considering the applicability of the Bill of Rights to the States, "the Court's usual approach has been to ground the prohibitions against state action squarely on due process, without intermediate reliance on any of the first eight Amendments." . . . In his own classic [concurring] opinion in *Griswold v. Connecticut* (1965) [see infra pp. 1401–1402], Justice Harlan memorably distilled these precedents' lesson: "While the relevant inquiry may be aided by resort to one or more of the provisions of the Bill of Rights, it is not dependent on them or any of their radiations. The Due Process Clause of the Fourteenth Amendment stands . . . on its own bottom." Inclusion in the Bill of Rights is neither necessary nor sufficient for an interest to be judicially enforceable under the Fourteenth Amendment. This Court's " 'selective incorporation' " doctrine is not simply "related" to substantive due process, *ante*; it is a subset thereof. . . .

V

While I agree with the Court that our substantive due process cases offer a principled basis for holding that petitioners have a constitutional right to possess a usable firearm in the home, I am ultimately persuaded that a better reading of our case law supports the city of Chicago. I would not foreclose the possibility that a particular plaintiff—say, an elderly widow who lives in a dangerous neighborhood and does not have the strength to operate a long gun—may have a cognizable liberty interest in possessing a handgun. But I cannot accept petitioners' broader submission. A number of factors, taken together, lead me to this conclusion.

First, firearms have a fundamentally ambivalent relationship to liberty. Just as they can help homeowners defend their families and property from intruders, they can help thugs and insurrectionists murder innocent victims. The threat that firearms will be misused is far from hypothetical, for gun crime has devastated many of our communities. *Amici* calculate that approximately 1 million Americans have been wounded or killed by gunfire in the last decade. Urban areas such as Chicago suffer disproportionately from this epidemic of violence. Handguns contribute disproportionately to it. Just as some homeowners may prefer handguns because of their small size, light weight, and ease of operation, some criminals will value them for the same reasons. In recent years, handguns were reportedly used in more than four-fifths of firearm murders and more than half of all murders nationwide.

Hence, in evaluating an asserted right to be free from particular gun-control regulations, liberty is on both sides of the equation. Guns may be useful for self-defense, as well as for hunting and sport, but they also have a unique potential to facilitate death and destruction and thereby to destabilize ordered liberty. . . . It is at least reasonable for a democratically elected legislature to take such concerns into account in considering what sorts of regulations would best serve the public welfare. . . .

Second, the right to possess a firearm of one's choosing is different in kind from the liberty interests we have recognized under the Due Process Clause. Despite the plethora of substantive due process cases that have been decided in the post-*Lochner* century, I have found none that holds, states, or even suggests that the term "liberty" encompasses either the common-law right of self-defense or a right to keep and bear arms. I do not doubt for a moment that many Americans

 The reference is to *Lochner v. New York* (1905), presented at pp. 1334–1346.

feel deeply passionate about firearms, and see them as critical to their way of life as well as to their security. Nevertheless, it does not appear to be the case that the ability to own a handgun, or any particular type of firearm, is critical to leading a life of autonomy, dignity, or political equality: The marketplace offers many tools for self-defense, even if they are imperfect substitutes, and neither petitioners nor their *amici* make such a contention. Petitioners' claim is not the kind of substantive interest, accordingly, on which a uniform, judicially enforced national standard is presumptively appropriate. . . .

Third, the experience of other advanced democracies, including those that share our British heritage, undercuts the notion that an expansive right to keep and bear arms is intrinsic to ordered liberty. Many of these countries place restrictions on the possession, use, and carriage of firearms far more onerous than the restrictions found in this Nation. See Municipal Respondents' Brief (discussing laws of England, Canada, Australia, Japan, Denmark, Finland, Luxembourg, and New Zealand). That the United States is an international outlier in the permissiveness of its approach to guns does not suggest that our laws are bad laws. It does suggest that this Court may not need to assume responsibility for making our laws still more permissive.

Admittedly, these other countries differ from ours in many relevant respects, including their problems with violent crime and the traditional role that firearms have played in their societies. But they are not so different from the United States that we ought to dismiss their experience entirely. . . . While the "American perspective" must always be our focus, *ante*, it is silly—indeed, arrogant—to think we have nothing to learn about liberty from the billions of people beyond our borders. . . .

VII

The fact that the right to keep and bear arms appears in the Constitution should not obscure the novelty of the Court's decision to enforce that right against the States. By its terms, the Second Amendment does not apply to the States; read properly, it does not even apply to individuals outside of the militia context. The Second Amendment was adopted to protect the *States* from federal encroachment. And the Fourteenth Amendment has never been understood by the Court to have "incorporated" the entire Bill of Rights. There was nothing foreordained about today's outcome. . . .

JUSTICE BREYER, with whom JUSTICE GINSBURG and JUSTICE SOTOMAYOR join, dissenting.

In my view, Justice Stevens has demonstrated that the Fourteenth Amendment's guarantee of "substantive due process" does not include a general right to keep and bear firearms for purposes of private self-defense. . . .

The Court . . . asks whether the Second Amendment right to private self-defense is "fundamental" so that it applies to the States through the

Fourteenth Amendment. . . . I can find nothing in the Second Amendment's text, history, or underlying rationale that could warrant characterizing it as "fundamental" insofar as it seeks to protect the keeping and bearing of arms for private self-defense purposes. . . . I therefore conclude that the Fourteenth Amendment does not "incorporate" the Second Amendment's right "to keep and bear Arms." And I consequently dissent.

I

. . . The Court based its conclusions [in *Heller*] almost exclusively upon its reading of history. But the relevant history in *Heller* was far from clear: Four dissenting Justices disagreed with the majority's historical analysis. And subsequent scholarly writing reveals why disputed history provides treacherous ground on which to build decisions written by judges who are not expert at history.

Since *Heller*, historians, scholars, and judges have continued to express the view that the Court's historical account was flawed. [Here, Justice Breyer discusses scholarly criticisms of *Heller*'s analysis.] If history, and history alone, is what matters, why would the Court not now reconsider *Heller* in light of these more recently published historical views? At the least, where *Heller*'s historical foundations are so uncertain, why extend its applicability? . . .

II

[Even] taking *Heller* as a given, the Fourteenth Amendment does not incorporate the Second Amendment right to keep and bear arms for purposes of private self-defense. Under this Court's precedents, to incorporate the private self-defense right the majority must show that the right is, *e.g.*, "fundamental to the American scheme of justice," *Duncan v. Louisiana* (1968). And this it fails to do.

The majority here, like that in *Heller*, relies almost exclusively upon history to make the necessary showing. But to do so for incorporation purposes is both wrong and dangerous. As Justice Stevens points out, our society has historically made mistakes—for example, when considering certain 18th- and 19th-century property rights to be fundamental. And in the incorporation context, as elsewhere, history often is unclear about the answers. . . .

I thus think it proper, above all where history provides no clear answer, to look to other factors in considering whether a right is sufficiently "fundamental" to remove it from the political process in every State. I would include among those factors the nature of the right; any contemporary disagreement about whether the right is fundamental; the extent to which incorporation will further other, perhaps more basic, constitutional aims; and the extent to which incorporation will advance or hinder the Constitution's structural aims, including its division of powers among different governmental institutions (and the people as well). Is incorporation needed, for example, to further the Constitution's effort to ensure that the government treats each individual with equal respect? Will it help maintain the democratic form of government that the Constitution foresees? . . .

How do these considerations apply here? . . . [T]he police power, the superiority of legislative decisionmaking, the need for local decisionmaking, the comparative desirability of democratic decisionmaking, the lack of a manageable judicial standard, and the life-threatening harm that may flow from striking down regulations all argue against incorporation. Where the incorporation of other rights has been at issue, *some* of these problems have arisen. But in this instance *all* these problems are present, *all* at the same time, and *all* are likely to be present in most, perhaps nearly all, of the cases in which the constitutionality of a gun regulation is at issue. At the same time, the important factors that favor incorporation in other instances—*e.g.*, the protection of broader constitutional objectives—are not present here. The upshot is that all factors militate against incorporation—with the possible exception of historical factors.

III

I must, then, return to history. . . . I can find much in the historical record that shows that some Americans in some places at certain times thought it important to keep and bear arms for private self-defense. For instance, the reader will see that many States have constitutional provisions protecting gun possession. But, as far as I can tell, those provisions typically do no more than guarantee that a gun regulation will be a *reasonable* police power regulation. See Winkler, *Scrutinizing the Second Amendment*, 105 Mich. L. Rev. 683 (2007) (the "courts of every state to consider the question apply a deferential 'reasonable regulation' standard"). It is thus altogether unclear whether such provisions would prohibit cities such as Chicago from enacting laws, such as the law before us, banning handguns. . . .

Thus, the specific question before us is not whether there are references to the right to bear arms for self-defense throughout this Nation's history—of course there are—or even whether the Court should incorporate a simple constitutional requirement that firearms regulations not unreasonably burden the right to keep and bear arms, but rather whether there is a consensus that *so substantial* a private self-defense right as the one described in *Heller* applies to the States. . . .

In my view, that record is insufficient to say that the right to bear arms for private self-defense, as explicated by *Heller*, is fundamental in the sense relevant to the incorporation inquiry. As the evidence below shows, States and localities have consistently enacted firearms regulations, including regulations similar to those at issue here, throughout our Nation's history. Courts have repeatedly upheld such regulations. And it is, at the very least, possible, and perhaps likely, that incorporation will impose on every, or nearly every, State a different right to bear arms than they currently recognize—a right that threatens to destabilize settled state legal principles.

I thus . . . . find no more than ambiguity and uncertainty that perhaps even expert historians would find difficult to penetrate. And a historical record that is so ambiguous cannot itself provide an adequate basis for incorporating a private right of self-defense and applying it against the States. [Here Justice Breyer discusses at length state firearms regulation in the eighteenth, nineteenth, and twentieth centuries.]

* * *

In sum . . . nothing in 18th-, 19th-, 20th-, or 21st-century history shows a consensus that the right to private armed self-defense, as described in *Heller*, is "deeply rooted in this Nation's history [or] tradition" or is otherwise "fundamental." Indeed, incorporating the right recognized in *Heller* may change the law in many of the 50 States. Read in the majority's favor, the historical evidence is at most ambiguous. And, in the absence of any other support for its conclusion, ambiguous history cannot show that the Fourteenth Amendment incorporates a private right of self-defense against the States.

With respect, I dissent.

Incorporation and Reverse Incorporation

Although the Supreme Court has never adopted Justice Black's theory of total incorporation, the practical upshot has been quite similar. Putting aside the Third Amendment (not a big generator of litigation), the only provisions of the first eight amendments that have not been incorporated at this point are the Fifth Amendment requirement of grand jury indictment and the Seventh Amendment civil-jury right.

FOR DISCUSSION Why do you suppose the grand jury and civil jury provisions have not been incorporated?

You may not realize it, but we've previously seen a version of the incorporation story—albeit in reverse. In *Brown v. Board of Education*, the Supreme Court held that segregated public schools were a violation of the Equal Protection Clause. No problem with non-textualism there: the Fourteenth Amendment applies explicitly to states, and the consolidated defendants in *Brown* were all state entities. But what about *Bolling v. Sharpe* (1954), which was decided the same day? In that case, the Supreme Court was called on to decide whether public school segregation in the District of Columbia—a *federal* actor—was likewise unconstitutional. To see why this was not a straightforward proposition, recall that the Equal Protection Clause does not mention the federal government; it says instead only that "[n]o *State*" may "deny to any person within its jurisdiction the equal protection of the laws." Did that mean the Constitution had nothing to say about segregation perpetrated by the federal government? The Justices didn't think so. In a move now often called "reverse incorporation," the Supreme Court used the Due Process Clause of the Fifth Amendment as a vehicle to impose on the federal government an equality obligation that, as a matter of text, appeared applicable only to the states. Here's what the *Bolling* Court said, in a unanimous opinion:

> The Fifth Amendment, which is applicable in the District of Columbia, does not contain an equal protection clause as does the Fourteenth Amendment, which applies only to the states. But the concepts of equal protection and due process, both stemming from our American ideal of fairness, are not mutually exclusive. The "equal protection of the laws" is a more explicit safeguard of prohibited unfairness than "due process of law," and, therefore, we do not imply

that the two are always interchangeable phrases. But, as this Court has recognized, discrimination may be so unjustifiable as to be violative of due process.

Classifications based solely upon race must be scrutinized with particular care, since they are contrary to our traditions and hence constitutionally. *Korematsu v. United States* (1944); *Hirabayashi v. United States* (1943). As long ago as 1896, this Court declared the principle "that the Constitution of the United States, in its present form, forbids, so far as civil and political rights are concerned, discrimination by the general government, or by the States, against any citizen because of his race." *Gibson v. Mississippi* (1896). And in *Buchanan v. Warley* (1917), the Court held that a statute which limited the right of a property owner to convey his property to a person of another race was, as an unreasonable discrimination, a denial of due process of law.

Although the Court has not assumed to define "liberty" with any great precision, that term is not confined to mere freedom from bodily restraint. Liberty under law extends to the full range of conduct which the individual is free to pursue, and it cannot be restricted except for a proper governmental objective. Segregation in public education is not reasonably related to any proper governmental objective, and thus it imposes on Negro children of the District of Columbia a burden that constitutes an arbitrary deprivation of their liberty in violation of the Due Process Clause.

In view of our decision that the Constitution prohibits the states from maintaining racially segregated public schools, it would be unthinkable that the same Constitution would impose a lesser duty on the Federal Government. We hold that racial segregation in the public schools of the District of Columbia is a denial of the due process of law guaranteed by the Fifth Amendment to the Constitution.

3. SDP: Economic Liberty

We have seen that Justice Black would have limited the substantive effect of the Due Process and Privileges or Immunities Clauses to incorporation of the Bill of Rights. The Court, however, has long given the Due Process Clauses substantive effect well beyond incorporation. The type of rights to which the Court has given force have varied greatly over time. We'll start with claims sounding in economic liberty; certainly the idea of the right to pursue a calling goes back a long way. In the earliest years of the Fourteenth Amendment, the Court took an abstemious view of its powers to supervise economic legislation under the Due Process Clauses. See *Slaughter-House Cases* (1873). But it soon began to treat certain types of economic liberty—in particular the freedom to enter into contracts in pursuit of what were deemed to be ordinary callings—as constitutionally protected entitlements. By the time Justice Black was appointed in 1937, however, the Court had backed off from doing so more or less entirely. The following cases explore the process by which that happened.

WORTH NOTING

The practice of giving substantive effect to the concept of due process began before the Fourteenth Amendment was even adopted; in *Scott v. Sandford* (1857), see pp. 109–127, the Supreme Court infamously observed that "[a]n act of Congress which deprives a citizen of the United States of his liberty or property, merely because he came himself or brought his property into a particular Territory of the United States, and who had committed no offence against the laws, could hardly be dignified with the name of due process of law."

a.   Economic Liberty—the Era of Significant Supervision

The history of the judicial response to economic regulation between the adoption of the Fourteenth Amendment and the early twentieth century is presented at some length in Chapter I, pp. 184–193. It is important not to caricature this jurisprudence. Although the Supreme Court invalidated many economic regulations, it also upheld many, and many more were never challenged; the area was a battleground, and doctrine was not always consistent.

We begin with the best-known decision from the period, a case that looms so large in historical memory that its name now serves as a shorthand reference for the whole era. This is probably not so much because of any new doctrinal ground broken by *Lochner v. New York* (1905). From the perspective of its contemporaries, the decision was just one among many, some upholding limitations on freedom to contract and some invalidating them. Rather, the historical prominence of the decision is due at least as much to the sparkling dissent it prompted from Justice Holmes as to any distinctive analytical contributions made by the majority. In any event, it is a case that has come to stand for an era.

Lochner v. New York

Supreme Court of the United States, 1905.
198 U.S. 45.

Statement by MR. JUSTICE PECKHAM:

This is a writ of error . . . to review . . . defendant['s conviction] of a misdemeanor on an indictment under a [New York] statute . . . known by its short title as the labor law. [The relevant section provided, with limited exceptions, that no employee of a bakery or similar establishment "shall be required or permitted to work . . . more than sixty hours in any one week, or more than ten hours in any one day." Other provisions of the act regulated drainage, plumbing and ventilation; mandated access to "a proper wash room and water closet" not located "within . . . the bake room"; required bakery owners to arrange furniture, utensils, and storage rooms so that they could be "readily" and "properly" cleaned; and banned "domestic animals, except cats" from both baking and storage areas.]

SUMMARY OF THE FACTS

A Utica bakery owner named Joseph Lochner was convicted of violating the statute by "requir[ing] and permit[ting] an employee . . . to work more than sixty hours in one week." Because this was Lochner's second violation, he was fined $50.

MR. JUSTICE PECKHAM, after making the foregoing statement of the facts, delivered the opinion of the court:

. . . There is no pretense in any of the opinions that the statute was intended to meet a case of involuntary labor in any form. . . . The mandate of the statute [is] an absolute prohibition upon the employer permitting, under any circumstances, more than ten hours' work to be done in his establishment. The employee may desire to earn the extra money which would arise from his working more than the prescribed time, but this statute forbids the employer from permitting the employee to earn it.

The statute necessarily interferes with the right of contract between the employer and employees, concerning the number of hours in which the latter may labor in the bakery of the employer. The general right to make a contract in relation to his business is part of the liberty of the individual protected by the 14th Amendment of the Federal Constitution. *Allgeyer v. Louisiana* (1897). Under that provision no state can deprive any person of life, liberty, or property without due process of law. The right to purchase or to sell labor is part of the liberty protected by this amendment, unless there are circumstances which exclude the right.

There are, however, certain powers, existing in the sovereignty of each state in the Union, somewhat vaguely termed police powers, the exact description and limitation of which have not been attempted by the courts. Those powers, broadly stated, and without, at present, any attempt at a more specific limitation, relate to the safety, health, morals, and general welfare of the public. Both property and liberty are held on such reasonable conditions as may be imposed by the governing power of the state in the exercise of those powers, and with such conditions the 14th Amendment was not designed to interfere.

The state, therefore, has power to prevent the individual from making certain kinds of contracts, and in regard to them the Federal Constitution offers no protection. If the contract be one which the state, in the legitimate exercise of its police power, has the right to prohibit, it is not prevented from prohibiting it by the 14th Amendment. Contracts in violation of a statute, either of the Federal or state government, or a contract to let one's property for immoral purposes, or to do any other unlawful act, could obtain no protection from the Federal Constitution, as coming under the liberty of person or of free contract. . . .

This court has recognized the existence and upheld the exercise of the police powers of the states in many cases which might fairly be considered as border ones, and it has, in the course of its determination of questions regarding the asserted invalidity of such statutes, on the ground of their violation of the rights secured by the Federal Constitution, been guided by rules of a very liberal nature, the application of which has resulted, in numerous instances, in upholding the validity of state statutes thus assailed.

Among the later cases where the state law has been upheld by this court is that of *Holden v. Hardy* (1898). A provision in the act of the legislature of Utah was there under consideration, the act limiting the employment of workmen in all underground mines or workings, to eight hours per day, "except in cases of emergency, where life or property is in imminent danger." It also limited the hours of labor in smelting and other institutions for the reduction or refining of ores or metals to eight hours per day, except in like cases of emergency. The act was held to be a valid exercise of the police powers of the state. A review of many of the cases on the subject, decided by this and other courts, is given in the opinion. It was held that the kind of employment, mining, smelting, etc., and the character of the employees in such kinds of labor, were such as to make it reasonable and proper for the state to interfere to prevent the employees from being constrained by the rules laid down by the proprietors in regard to labor. . . .

It will be observed that, even with regard to that class of labor, the Utah statute provided for cases of emergency wherein the provisions of the statute would not apply. The statute now before this court has no emergency clause in it, and, if the statute is valid, there are no circumstances and no emergencies under which the slightest violation of the provisions of the act would be innocent. There is nothing in *Holden* v. *Hardy* which covers the case now before us. . . . *Knoxville Iron Co. v. Harbison* (1901) is equally far from an authority for this legislation. The employees in that case were held to be at a disadvantage with the employer in matters of wages, they being miners and coal workers, and the act simply provided for the cashing of coal orders when presented by the miner to the employer.

The latest case decided by this court, involving the police power, is that of *Jacobson* v. *Massachusetts* (1905), decided at this term. It related to compulsory vaccination, and the law was held valid as a proper exercise of the police powers with reference to the public health. It was stated in the opinion that it was a case "of an adult who, for aught that appears, was himself in perfect health and a fit subject of vaccination, and yet, while remaining in the community, refused to obey the statute and the regulation, adopted in execution of its provisions, for the protection of the public health and the public safety, confessedly endangered by the presence of a dangerous disease." That case is also far from covering the one now before the court. . . .

It must, of course, be conceded that there is a limit to the valid exercise of the police power by the state. There is no dispute concerning this general proposition. Otherwise the 14th Amendment would have no efficacy and the legislatures of the states would have unbounded power, and it would be enough to say that any piece of legislation was enacted to conserve the morals, the health, or the safety of the people; such legislation would be valid, no matter how absolutely without foundation the claim might be. The claim of the police power would be a mere pretext—become another and delusive name for the supreme sovereignty of the state to be exercised free from constitutional restraint. This is not contended for.

In every case that comes before this court, therefore, where legislation of this character is concerned, and where the protection of the Federal Constitution is sought, the question necessarily arises: Is this a fair, reasonable, and appropriate exercise of the police power of the state, or is it an unreasonable, unnecessary, and arbitrary interference with the right of the individual to his personal liberty, or to enter into those contracts in relation to labor which may seem to him appropriate or necessary for the support of himself and his family? Of course the liberty of contract relating to labor includes both parties to it. The one has as much right to purchase as the other to sell labor.

This is not a question of substituting the judgment of the court for that of the legislature. If the act be within the power of the state it is valid, although the judgment of the court might be totally opposed to the enactment of such a law. But the question would still remain: Is it within the police power of the state? and that question must be answered by the court.

The question whether this act is valid as a labor law, pure and simple, may be dismissed in a few words. There is no reasonable ground for interfering with the liberty of person or the right of free contract, by determining the hours of labor, in the occupation of a baker. There is no contention that bakers as a class are not equal in intelligence and capacity to men in other trades or manual occupations, or that they are not able to assert their rights and care for themselves without the protecting arm of the state, interfering with their independence of judgment and of action. They are in no sense wards of the state. Viewed in the light of a purely labor law, with no reference whatever to the question of health, we think that a law like the one before us involves neither the safety, the morals, nor the welfare, of the public, and that the interest of the public is not in the slightest degree affected by such an act. The law must be upheld, if at all, as a law pertaining to the health of the individual engaged in the occupation of a baker. It does not affect any other portion of the public than those who are engaged in that occupation. Clean and wholesome bread does not depend upon whether the baker works but ten hours per day or only sixty hours a week. The limitation of the hours of labor does not come within the police power on that ground.

It is a question of which of two powers or rights shall prevail—the power of the state to legislate or the right of the individual to liberty of person and freedom of contract. The mere assertion that the subject relates, though but in a remote degree, to the public health, does not necessarily render the enactment valid. The act must have a more direct relation, as a means to an end, and the end itself must be appropriate and legitimate, before an act can be held to be valid which interferes with the general right of an individual to be free in his person and in his power to contract in relation to his own labor. . . .

Although found in what is called a labor law of the state, the court of appeals has upheld the act as one relating to the public health—in other words, as a health law. . . .

We think the limit of the police power has been reached and passed in this case. There is, in our judgment, no reasonable foundation for holding this to be necessary or appropriate as a health law to safeguard the public health, or the health of the individuals who are following the trade of a baker. . . .

We think that there can be no fair doubt that the trade of a baker, in and of itself, is not an unhealthy one to that degree which would authorize the legislature to interfere with the right to labor, and with the right of free contract on the part of the individual, either as employer or employee. In looking through statistics regarding all trades and occupations, it may be true that the trade of a baker does not appear to be as healthy as some other trades, and is also vastly more healthy than still others. To the common understanding the trade of a baker has never been regarded as an unhealthy one. Very likely physicians would not recommend the exercise of that or of any other trade as a remedy for ill health. Some occupations are more healthy than others, but we think there are none which might not come under the power of the legislature to supervise and control the hours of working therein, if the mere fact that the occupation is not absolutely and perfectly healthy is to confer that right upon the legislative department of the government. . . .

It is unfortunately true that labor, even in any department, may possibly carry with it the seeds of unhealthiness. But are we all, on that account, at the mercy of legislative majorities? A printer, a tinsmith, a locksmith, a carpenter, a cabinetmaker, a dry goods clerk, a bank's, a lawyer's, or a physician's clerk, or a clerk in almost any kind of business, would all come under the power of the legislature, on this assumption. No trade, no occupation, no mode of earning one's living, could escape this all-pervading power, and the acts of the legislature in limiting the hours of labor in all employments would be valid, although such limitation might seriously cripple the ability of the laborer to support himself and his family.

In our large cities there are many buildings into which the sun penetrates for but a short time in each day, and these buildings are occupied by people carrying on the business of bankers, brokers, lawyers, real estate, and many other kinds of business, aided by many clerks, messengers, and other employees. Upon the assumption of the validity of this act under review, it is not possible to say that an act, prohibiting lawyers' or bank clerks, or others, from contracting to labor for their employers more than eight hours a day would be invalid. It might be said that it is unhealthy to work more than that number of hours in an apartment lighted by artificial light during the working hours of the day; that the occupation of the bank clerk, the lawyer's clerk, the real estate clerk, or the broker's clerk, in such offices is therefore unhealthy, and the legislature, in its paternal wisdom, must, therefore, have the right to legislate on the subject of, and to limit, the hours for such labor; and, if it exercises that power, and its validity be questioned, it is sufficient to say, it has reference to the public health; it has reference to the health of the employees condemned to labor day after day in buildings where the sun never shines; it is a health law, and therefore it is valid, and cannot be questioned by the courts.

It is also urged, pursuing the same line of argument, that it is to the interest of the state that its population should be strong and robust, and therefore any legislation which may be said to tend to make people healthy must be valid as health laws, enacted under the police power. If this be a valid argument and a justification for this kind of legislation, it follows that the protection of the Federal Constitution from undue interference with liberty of person and freedom of contract is visionary, wherever the law is sought to be justified as a valid exercise of the police power. Scarcely any law but might find shelter under such assumptions, and conduct, properly so called, as well as contract, would come under the restrictive sway of the legislature. Not only the hours of employees, but the hours of employers, could be regulated, and doctors, lawyers, scientists, all professional men, as well as athletes and artisans, could be forbidden to fatigue their brains and bodies by prolonged hours of exercise, lest the fighting strength of the state be impaired.

We mention these extreme cases because the contention is extreme. . . . The act is not, within any fair meaning of the term, a health law, but is an illegal interference with the rights of individuals, both employers and employees, to make contracts regarding labor upon such terms as they may think best, or which they may agree upon with the other parties to such contracts.

Statutes of the nature of that under review, limiting the hours in which grown and intelligent men may labor to earn their living, are mere meddlesome interferences with the rights of the individual, and they are not saved from condemnation by the claim that they are passed in the exercise of the police power and upon the subject of the health of the individual whose rights are interfered with, unless there be some fair ground, reasonable in and of itself, to say that there is material danger to the public health, or to the health of the employees, if the hours of labor are not curtailed. . . .

All that [New York's legislature] could properly do has been done by it with regard to the conduct of bakeries [in numerous other sections of the act establishing requirements designed to ensure that bakeries are clean and healthy workplaces.] These various sections . . . go to the full extent of providing for the cleanliness and the healthiness, so far as possible, of the quarters in which bakeries are to be conducted. . . .

It was further urged on the argument that restricting the hours of labor in the case of bakers was valid because it tended to cleanliness on the part of the workers, as a man was more apt to be cleanly when not overworked, and if cleanly then his 'output' was also more likely to be so. What has already been said applies with equal force to this contention. We do not admit the reasoning to be sufficient to justify the claimed right of such interference. The state in that case would assume the position of a supervisor, or *pater familias*, over every act of the individual, and its right of governmental interference with his hours of labor, his hours of exercise, the character thereof, and the extent to which it shall be carried would be recognized and upheld. In our judgment it is not possible in fact to discover the connection between the number of hours a baker may work in the bakery and the healthful quality of the bread made by the workman. The connection, if any exist, is too shadowy and thin to build any argument for the interference of the legislature. If the man works ten hours a day it is all right, but if ten and a half or eleven his health is in danger and his bread may be unhealthy, and, therefore, he shall not be permitted to do it. This, we think, is unreasonable and entirely arbitrary.

When assertions such as we have adverted to become necessary in order to give, if possible, a plausible foundation for the contention that the law is a "health law," it gives rise to at least a suspicion that there was some other motive dominating the legislature than the purpose to subserve the public health or welfare.

This interference on the part of the legislatures of the several states with the ordinary trades and occupations of the people seems to be on the increase. . . . It is impossible for us to shut our eyes to the fact that many of the laws of this character, while passed under what is claimed to be the police power for the purpose of protecting the public health or welfare, are, in reality, passed from other motives. We are justified in saying so when, from the character of the law and the subject upon which it legislates, it is apparent that the public health or welfare bears but the most remote relation to the law. The purpose of a statute must be determined from the natural and legal effect of the language employed; and whether it is or is not repugnant to the Constitution of the United States must be determined from the natural effect of such statutes when put into operation, and not from their proclaimed purpose. The court looks beyond the mere letter of the law in such cases. *Yick Wo v. Hopkins* (1886).

It is manifest to us [that we cannot regard] the section as really a health law. It seems to us that the real object and purpose were simply to regulate the hours of labor between the master and his employees (all being men, *sui juris*), in a private business, not dangerous in any degree to morals, or in any real and substantial degree to the health of the employees. Under such circumstances the freedom of master and employee to contract with each other in relation to their employment, and in defining the same, cannot be prohibited or interfered with, without violating the Federal Constitution. . . .

MR. JUSTICE HARLAN (with whom MR. JUSTICE WHITE and MR. JUSTICE DAY concurred) dissenting:

. . . I take it to be firmly established that what is called the liberty of contract may, within certain limits, be subjected to regulations designed and calculated to promote the general welfare, or to guard the public health, the public morals, or the public safety. ". . . There are manifold restraints to which every person is necessarily subject for the common good." *Jacobson v. Massachusetts* (1905).

Granting, then, that there is a liberty of contract which cannot be violated even under the sanction of direct legislative enactment, but assuming, as according to settled law we may assume, that such liberty of contract is subject to such regulations as the state may reasonably prescribe for the common good and the well-being of society, what are the conditions under which the judiciary may declare such regulations to be in excess of legislative authority and void? Upon this point there is no room for dispute; for the rule is universal that a legislative enactment, Federal or state, is never to be disregarded or held invalid unless it be, beyond question, plainly and palpably in excess of legislative power. . . . If there be doubt as to the validity of the statute, that doubt must therefore be resolved in favor of its validity, and the courts must keep their hands off, leaving the legislature to meet the responsibility for unwise legislation. If the end which the legislature seeks to accomplish be one to which its power extends, and if the means employed to that end, although not the wisest or best, are yet not plainly and palpably unauthorized by law, then the court cannot interfere. In other words, when the validity of a statute is questioned, the burden of proof, so to speak, is upon those who assert it to be unconstitutional. *M'Culloch v. Maryland* (1819).

Let these principles be applied to the present case. . . . It is plain that this statute was enacted in order to protect the physical well-being of those who work in bakery and confectionery establishments. It may be that the statute had its origin, in part, in the belief that employers and employees in such establishments were not upon an equal footing, and that the necessities of the latter often compelled them to submit to such exactions as unduly taxed their strength. Be this as it may, the statute must be taken as expressing the belief of the people of New York that, as a general rule, and in the case of the average man, labor in excess of sixty hours during a week in such establishments may endanger the health of those who thus labor.

Whether or not this be wise legislation it is not the province of the court to inquire. Under our systems of government the courts are not concerned with the wisdom or policy of legislation. So that, in determining the question of power to interfere with liberty of contract, the court may inquire whether the means devised by the state are germane to an end which may be lawfully accomplished and have a real or substantial relation to the protection of health, as involved in the daily work of the persons, male and female, engaged in bakery and confectionery establishments. But when this inquiry is entered upon I find it impossible, in view of common experience, to say that there is here no real or substantial relation between the means employed by the state and the end sought to be accomplished by its legislation. . . . Therefore I submit that this court will transcend its functions if it assumes to annul the statute of New York.

It must be remembered that this statute does not apply to all kinds of business. It applies only to work in bakery and confectionery establishments, in which, as all know, the air constantly breathed by workmen is not as pure and healthful as that to be found in some other establishments or out of doors.

Professor Hirt in his treatise on the "Diseases of the Workers" has said:

> The labor of the bakers is among the hardest and most laborious imaginable, because it has to be performed under conditions injurious to the health of those engaged in it. It is hard, very hard, work, not only because it requires a great deal of physical exertion in an over-heated workshop and during unreasonably long hours, but more so because of the erratic demands of the public, compelling the baker to perform the greater part of his work at night, thus depriving him of an opportunity to enjoy the necessary rest and sleep—a fact which is highly injurious to his health.

Another writer says:

> The constant inhaling of flour dust causes inflammation of the lungs and of the bronchial tubes. The eyes also suffer through this dust, which is responsible for the many cases of running eyes among the bakers. The long hours of toil to which all bakers are subjected produce rheumatism, cramps, and swollen legs. The intense heat in the workshops induces the workers to resort to cooling drinks, which, together with their habit of exposing the greater part of their bodies to the change in the atmosphere, is another source of a number of diseases of various organs. . . .

> The average age of a baker is below that of other workmen; they seldom live over their fiftieth year, most of them dying between the ages of forty and fifty. During periods of epidemic diseases the bakers are generally the first to succumb to the disease, and the number swept away during such periods far exceeds the number of other crafts in comparison to the men employed in the respective industries. . . .

In the Eighteenth Annual Report by the New York Bureau of Statistics of Labor it is stated that among the occupations involving exposure to conditions that interfere with nutrition is that of a baker. In that Report it is also stated that, "from a social point of view, production will be increased by any change in industrial organization which diminishes the number of idlers, paupers, and criminals. Shorter hours of work, by allowing higher standards of comfort and purer family life, promise to enhance the industrial efficiency of the wage-working class—improved health, longer life, more content and greater intelligence and inventiveness."

Statistics show that the average daily working time among workingmen in different countries is, in Australia, eight hours; in Great Britain, nine; in the United States, nine and three-quarters; in Denmark, nine and three-quarters; in Norway, ten; Sweden, France, and Switzerland, ten and one-half; Germany, ten and one-quarter; Belgium, Italy, and Austria, eleven; and in Russia, twelve hours.

We judicially know that the question of the number of hours during which a workman should continuously labor has been, for a long period, and is yet, a subject of serious consideration among civilized peoples, and by those having special knowledge of the laws of health. Suppose the statute prohibited labor in bakery and confectionery establishments in excess of eighteen hours each day. No one, I take it, could dispute the power of the state to enact such a statute. But the statute before us does not embrace extreme or exceptional cases. It may be said to occupy a middle ground in respect of the hours of labor. . . .

We also judicially know that the number of hours that should constitute a day's labor in particular occupations involving the physical strength and safety of workmen has been the subject of enactments by Congress and by nearly all of the states. Many, if not most, of those enactments fix eight hours as the proper basis of a day's labor.

I do not stop to consider whether any particular view of this economic question presents the sounder theory. What the precise facts are it may be difficult to say. It is enough for the determination of this case, and it is enough for this court to know, that the question is one about which there is room for debate and for an honest difference of opinion. There are many reasons of a weighty, substantial character, based upon the experience of mankind, in support of the theory that, all things considered, more than ten hours' steady work each day, from week to week, in a bakery or confectionery establishment, may endanger the health and shorten the lives of the workmen, thereby diminishing their physical and mental capacity to serve the state and to provide for those dependent upon them.

If such reasons exist that ought to be the end of this case, for the state is not amenable to the judiciary, in respect of its legislative enactments, unless such enactments are plainly, palpably, beyond all question, inconsistent with the Constitution of the United States. . . .

The judgment, in my opinion, should be affirmed.

Mr. Justice Holmes dissenting:

I regret sincerely that I am unable to agree with the judgment in this case, and that I think it my duty to express my dissent.

This case is decided upon an economic theory which a large part of the country does not entertain. If it were a question whether I agreed with that theory, I should desire to study it further and long before making up my mind. But I do not conceive that to be my duty, because I strongly believe that my agreement or disagreement has nothing to do with the right of a majority to embody their opinions in law.

It is settled by various decisions of this court that state constitutions and state laws may regulate life in many ways which we as legislators might think as injudicious, or if you like as tyrannical, as this, and which, equally with this, interfere with the liberty to contract. Sunday laws and usury laws are ancient examples. A more modern one is the prohibition of lotteries. The liberty of the citizen to do as he likes so long as he does not interfere with the liberty of others to do the same, which has been a shibboleth for some well-known writers, is interfered with by school laws, by the Post Office, by every state or municipal institution which takes his money for purposes thought desirable, whether he likes it or not. The 14th Amendment does not enact Mr. Herbert Spencer's Social Statics.

The other day we sustained the Massachusetts vaccination law. *Jacobson v. Massachusetts* (1905). United States and state statutes and decisions cutting down the liberty to contract by way of combination are familiar to this court. *Northern Securities Co. v. United States* (1904). Two years ago we upheld the prohibition of sales of stock on margins, or for future delivery, in the Constitution of California. *Otis v. Parker* (1903). The decision sustaining an eight-hour law for miners is still recent. *Holden v. Hardy* (1898). Some of these laws embody convictions or prejudices which judges are likely to share. Some may not. But a Constitution is not intended to embody a particular economic theory, whether of paternalism and the organic relation of the citizen to the state or of *laissez faire*. It is made for people of fundamentally differing views, and the accident of our finding certain opinions natural and familiar, or novel, and even shocking, ought not to conclude our judgment upon the question whether statutes embodying them conflict with the Constitution of the United States.

General propositions do not decide concrete cases. The decision will depend on a judgment or intuition more subtle than any articulate major premise. But I think that the proposition just stated, if it is accepted, will carry us far toward the end. Every opinion tends to become a law. I think that the word "liberty," in the 14th Amendment, is perverted when it is held to prevent the natural outcome of a dominant opinion, unless it can be said that a rational and fair man necessarily would admit that the statute proposed would infringe fundamental principles as they have been understood by the traditions of our people and our law. It does not need research to show that no such sweeping condemnation can be passed upon the statute before us. A reasonable man might think it a proper measure on the score of health. Men whom I certainly could not pronounce unreasonable would uphold it as a first instalment of a general regulation of the hours of work. Whether in the latter aspect it would be open to the charge of inequality I think it unnecessary to discuss.

In general, the branch of substantive due process doctrine epitomized by *Lochner* required the courts to perform a significant independent assessment of economic regulation, casting suspicion on any statute that seemed either foolish or directed at redistribution simpliciter. But do not make the mistake of thinking that most economic regulations during this period were invalidated. To the contrary, the vast majority were upheld; see, for example, the impressive array of cases cited by the majority in *Nebbia v. New York* (1934).

 CROSS REFERENCE *Nebbia* is presented in Chapter I, at pp. 206–213.

It is difficult or impossible to state accurate doctrinal lines for the decisions during this period, because the decisions were not consistent and tended to be driven by the ideology of the justices. So, for example, a dozen years after *Lochner* the Supreme Court upheld, by a 5–3 vote, an Oregon law that set a maximum work day of 10 hours for any person working in "any mill, factory or manufacturing establishment" in the state, with some exceptions and an allowance for overtime at one and one-half times the regular wage. *Bunting v. Oregon* (1917). Gee, you might ask, isn't that inconsistent with *Lochner*? After all, the law upheld in *Bunting* was much broader than the one rejected in *Lochner*. So how did the *Bunting* Court handle *Lochner*? It never even cited the case!

Nevertheless, it is possible to spot some tendencies in the cases, and each of the next two cases will highlight one of them. First, the Court tended to look askance at price regulations, unless they were of a business that it characterized as "affected with a public interest." (One may wonder whether this term was much more than a conclusory label attached when the Court decided to uphold the regulation.) Second, labor regulations had a better chance of being upheld if they protected groups deemed particularly vulnerable; recall how the *Lochner* majority went to some length to deny that bakers needed special protection.

Munn v. Illinois

Supreme Court of the United States, 1877.
94 U.S. 113.

MR. CHIEF JUSTICE WAITE delivered the opinion of the court.

The question to be determined in this case is whether the general assembly of Illinois can, under the limitations upon the legislative power of the States imposed by the Constitution of the United States, fix by law the maximum of charges for the storage of grain in warehouses at Chicago . . . "in which grain is stored in bulk, and in which the grain of different owners is mixed together." . . .

Every statute is presumed to be constitutional. The courts ought not to declare one to be unconstitutional, unless it is clearly so. If there is doubt, the expressed will of the legislature should be sustained. . . .

When one becomes a member of society, he necessarily parts with some rights or privileges which, as an individual not affected by his relations to others, he might retain. . . . This does not confer power upon the whole people to control rights which are purely and exclusively private, but it does authorize the establishment of laws requiring each citizen to so conduct himself, and so use his own property, as not unnecessarily to injure another. . . . From this source come the police powers, which, as was said by Mr. Chief Justice Taney in the *License Cases* (1847), "are nothing more or less than the powers of government inherent in every sovereignty, . . . that is to say, . . . the power to govern men and things."

Under these powers the government regulates the conduct of its citizens one towards another, and the manner in which each shall use his own property, when such regulation becomes necessary for the public good. In their exercise it has been customary in England from time immemorial, and in this country from its first colonization, to regulate ferries, common carriers, hackmen, bakers, millers, wharfingers, innkeepers, &c., and in so doing to fix a maximum of charge to be made for services rendered, accommodations furnished, and articles sold. To this day, statutes are to be found in many of the States upon some or all these subjects; and we think it has never yet been successfully contended that such legislation came within any of the constitutional prohibitions against interference with private property. . . .

From this it is apparent that, down to the time of the adoption of the Fourteenth Amendment, it was not supposed that statutes regulating the use, or even the price of the use, of private property necessarily deprived an owner of his property without due process of law. Under some circumstances they may, but not under all. The amendment does not change the law in this particular: it simply prevents the States from doing that which will operate as such a deprivation.

This brings us to inquire as to the principles upon which this power of regulation rests, in order that we may determine what is within and what without its operative effect. Looking, then, to the common law, from whence came the right which the Constitution protects, we find that when private property is "affected with a public interest, it ceases to be *juris privati* only." This was said by Lord Chief Justice Hale more than two hundred years ago, in his trea-

WORTH NOTING

Sir Matthew Hale (1609-1676) was an influential and prolific jurist. The essay in question, on ports of the sea, was published in 1787, more than 100 years after his death.

tise *De Portibus Maris,* and has been accepted without objection as an essential element in the law of property ever since. Property does become clothed with a public interest when used in a manner to make it of public consequence, and affect the community at large. When, therefore, one devotes his property to a use in which the public has an interest, he, in effect, grants to the public an interest in that use, and must submit to be controlled by the public for the common good, to the extent of the interest he has thus created. He may withdraw his grant by discontinuing the use; but, so long as he maintains the use, he must submit to the control. . . .

Thus, as to ferries, . . . [and] to wharves and wharfingers, . . . [Lord Hale says they] "are affected with a public interest, and they cease to be *juris privati* only; as if a man set out a street in new building on his own land, it is now no longer bare private interest, but is affected by a public interest." . . . And the same has been held as to warehouses and warehousemen. . . . Upon this point Lord Ellenborough said:

> There is no doubt that the general principle is favored, both in law and justice, that every man may fix what price he pleases upon his own property, or the use of it; but if for a particular purpose the public have a right to resort to his premises and make use of them, and he have a monopoly in them for that purpose, if he will take the benefit of that monopoly, he must, as an equivalent, perform the duty attached to it on reasonable terms. . . .

. . . From the same source comes the power to regulate the charges of common carriers, which was done in England as long ago as the third year of the reign of William and Mary, and continued until within a comparatively recent period. . . . Common carriers exercise a sort of public office, and have duties to perform in which the public is interested. Their business is, therefore, "affected with a public interest". . . .

But we need not go further. Enough has already been said to show that, when private property is devoted to a public use, it is subject to public regulation. It remains only to ascertain whether the warehouses of these plaintiffs in error, and the business which is carried on there, come within the operation of this principle. . . .

For this purpose we accept as true the statements of fact contained in the elaborate brief of one of the counsel of the plaintiffs in error. From these it appears that

> the great producing region of the West and North-west sends its grain by water and rail to Chicago, where the greater part of it is shipped by vessel for transportation to the seaboard by the Great Lakes, and some of it is forwarded by railway to the Eastern ports. . . . Vessels, to some extent, are loaded in the Chicago harbor, and sailed through the St. Lawrence directly to Europe. . . . The quantity [of grain] received in Chicago has made it the greatest grain market in the world. . . .

In this connection it must also be borne in mind that . . . nine business firms controlled [the grain warehouses in Chicago], and that the prices charged and received for storage were such "as have been from year to year agreed upon and established by the different elevators or warehouses in the city of Chicago. . . ." Thus it is apparent that all the elevating facilities through which these vast productions "of seven or eight great States of the West" must pass on the way "to four or five of the States on the seashore" may be a "virtual" monopoly.

Under such circumstances it is difficult to see why, if the common carrier, or the miller, or the ferryman, or the innkeeper, or the wharfinger, or the baker, or the cartman, or the hackney-coachman, pursues a public employment and exercises "a sort of public office," these plaintiffs in error do not. They stand, to use again the language of their counsel, in the very "gateway of commerce," and take toll from all who pass. Their business most certainly "tends to a common charge, and is become a thing of public interest and use." Every bushel of grain for its passage "pays a toll, which is a common charge," and, therefore, according to Lord Hale, every such warehouseman "ought to be under public regulation, viz., that he . . . take but reasonable toll." Certainly, if any business can be clothed "with a public interest, and cease to be *juris privati* only," this has been. It may not be made so by the operation of the Constitution of Illinois or this statute, but it is by the facts. . . .

Neither is it a matter of any moment that no precedent can be found for a statute precisely like this. It is conceded that the business is one of recent origin, that its growth has been rapid, and that it is already of great importance. . . [T]his statute simply extends the law so as to meet this new development of commercial progress. . . .

It matters not in this case that these plaintiffs in error had built their warehouses and established their business before the regulations complained of were adopted. What they did was from the beginning subject to the power of the body politic to require them to conform to such regulations as might be established by the proper authorities for the common good. They entered upon their business and provided themselves with the means to carry it on subject to this condition. If they did not wish to submit themselves to such interference, they should not have clothed the public with an interest in their concerns. . . .

We know that this is a power which may be abused; but that is no argument against its existence. For protection against abuses by legislatures the people must resort to the polls, not to the courts. . . .

Mr. Justice Field and Mr. Justice Strong dissented.

Mr. Justice Field, dissenting.

. . . By the term "liberty," as used in the [Due Process Clause of the Fourteenth Amendment], something more is meant than mere freedom from physical restraint or the bounds of a prison. It means freedom to go where one may choose, and to act in such manner, not inconsistent with the equal rights of others, as his judgment may dictate for the promotion of his happiness; that is, to pursue such callings and avocations as may be most suitable to develop his capacities, and give to them their highest enjoyment. The same liberal construction which is required for the protection of life and liberty, in all particulars in which life and liberty are of any value, should be applied to the protection of private property.

If the legislature of a State, under pretence of providing for the public good, or for any other reason, can determine, against the consent of the owner, the uses to which private property shall be devoted, or the prices which the owner shall receive for its uses, it can deprive him of the property as completely as by a special act for its confiscation or destruction. If, for instance, the owner is prohibited from using his building for the purposes for which it was designed, it is of little consequence that he is permitted to retain the title and possession; or, if he is compelled to take as compensation for its use less than the expenses to which he is subjected by its ownership, he is, for all practical purposes, deprived of the property, as effectually as if the legislature had ordered his forcible dispossession. . . .

It requires no comment to point out the radical differences between the cases of public mills and interest on money, and that of the warehouses in Chicago. No prerogative or privilege of the crown to establish warehouses was ever asserted at the common law. The business of a warehouseman was, at common law, a private business, and is so in its nature. It has no special privileges connected with it, nor did the law ever extend to it any greater protection than it extended to all other private business. No reason can be assigned to justify legislation interfering with the legitimate profits of that business, that would not equally justify an intermeddling with the business of every man in the community, so soon, at least, as his business became generally useful.

I am of opinion that the judgment of the Supreme Court of Illinois should be reversed.

Mr. Justice Strong.

When the judgment in this case was announced by direction of a majority of the court, it was well known by all my brethren that I did not concur in it. It had been my purpose to prepare a dissenting opinion, but I found no time for the preparation, and I was reluctant to dissent in such a case without stating my reasons. Mr. Justice Field has now stated them as fully as I can, and I concur in what he has said.

Recall that *Lochner* specifically distinguished *Holden v. Hardy* (1898), which upheld a law limiting the working hours of miners except in certain emergencies. One factor supporting the law in *Holden* was the perception that the employees in that case were particularly vulnerable to exploitation. That same consideration also supported laws regulating the labor of children and, as the next case indicates, that of women.

Muller v. Oregon

Supreme Court of the United States, 1908.
208 U.S. 412.

Mr. Justice Brewer delivered the opinion of the court:

On February 19, 1903, the legislature of the state of Oregon passed an act, the first section of which is in these words:

> Sec. 1. That no female [shall] be employed in any mechanical establishment, or factory, or laundry in this state more than ten hours during any one day. . . .

Sec. 3 made a violation of the provisions of the prior sections a misdemeanor subject to a fine of not less than $10 nor more than $25.

[Defendant Curt Muller,] "being the owner of a laundry, known as the Grand Laundry," [was charged with] "unlawfully . . . requir[ing] a female, to wit, one Mrs. E. Gotcher, to work more than ten hours in said laundry on [the] 4th day of September, A. D. 1905. . . ." A trial resulted in a verdict against the defendant, who was sentenced to pay a fine of $10. . . . The single question is the constitutionality of the statute under which the defendant was convicted, so far as it affects the work of a female in a laundry. [Defendant contends that] "[b]ecause the statute attempts to prevent persons *sui juris* from making their own contracts," [it] "thus violates the provisions of the 14th Amendment. . . ."

. . . *Lochner v. New York* . . . is invoked by plaintiff in error as decisive of the question before us. But this assumes that the difference between the sexes does not justify a different rule respecting a restriction of the hours of labor. . . .

It may not be amiss, in the present case, before examining the constitutional question, to notice the course of legislation, as well as expressions of opinion from other than judicial sources. In the brief filed by Mr. Louis D. Brandeis for the defendant in error is a very copious collection of all these matters, an epitome of which is found in the margin.[1]

The legislation and opinions referred to in the margin may not be, technically speaking, authorities, and in them is little or no discussion of the constitutional question presented to us for determination, yet they are significant of a widespread belief that woman's physical structure, and the functions she performs in consequence thereof, justify special legislation restricting or qualifying the conditions under which she should be permitted to toil. Constitutional questions, it is true, are not settled by even a consensus of present public opinion, for it is the peculiar value of a written constitution that it places in unchanging form limitations upon legislative action, and thus gives a permanence and stability to popular government which otherwise would be lacking. At the same time, when a question of fact is debated and debatable, and the extent to which a special constitutional limitation goes is affected by the truth in respect to that fact, a widespread and long continued belief concerning it is worthy of consideration. We take judicial cognizance of all matters of general knowledge. . . .

---

[1]   [The Court cited a long list of "legislation of the states [that impose] restriction in some form or another upon the hours of labor that may be required of women," as well as a list of foreign statutes cited by future Justice Louis Brandeis, who represented Oregon at the Supreme Court. Also submitted were] extracts from over ninety reports of committees, bureaus of statistics, commissioners of hygiene, inspectors of factories, both in this country and in Europe, to the effect that long hours of labor are dangerous for women, primarily because of their special physical organization. . . . Following them are extracts from similar reports discussing the general benefits of short hours from an economic aspect of the question. . . . Perhaps the general scope and character of all these reports may be summed up in what an inspector for Hanover says: "The reasons for the reduction of the working day to ten hours—(a) the physical organization of women, (b) her maternal functions, (c) the rearing and education of the children, (d) the maintenance of the home—are all so important and so far reaching that the need for such reduction need hardly be discussed."

That woman's physical structure and the performance of maternal functions place her at a disadvantage in the struggle for subsistence is obvious. This is especially true when the burdens of motherhood are upon her. Even when they are not, by abundant testimony of the medical fraternity continuance for a long time on her feet at work, repeating this from day to day, tends to injurious effects upon the body, and, as healthy mothers are essential to vigorous offspring, the physical well-being of woman becomes an object of public interest and care in order to preserve the strength and vigor of the race.

Still again, history discloses the fact that woman has always been dependent upon man. . . . As minors, though not to the same extent, she has been looked upon in the courts as needing especial care that her rights may be preserved. Education was long denied her, and while now the doors of the schoolroom are opened and her opportunities for acquiring knowledge are great, yet even with that and the consequent increase of capacity for business affairs it is still true that in the struggle for subsistence she is not an equal competitor with her brother. Though limitations upon personal and contractual rights may be removed by legislation, [as they had been in Oregon,] there is that in her disposition and habits of life which will operate against a full assertion of those rights. She will still be where some legislation to protect her seems necessary to secure a real equality of right.

Doubtless there are individual exceptions, and there are many respects in which she has an advantage over him; but looking at it from the viewpoint of the effort to maintain an independent position in life, she is not upon an equality. . . . [L]egislation designed for her protection may [therefore] be sustained, even when like legislation is not necessary for men, and could not be sustained. . . . [H]er physical structure and a proper discharge of her maternal functions—having in view not merely her own health, but the well-being of the race—justify legislation to protect her from the greed as well as the passion of man. . . .

For these reasons, and without questioning in any respect the decision in *Lochner v. New York*, we are of the opinion that it cannot be adjudged that the act in question is in conflict with the Federal Constitution, so far as it respects the work of a female in a laundry, and the judgment of the Supreme Court of Oregon is affirmed.

The Court's reasoning in *Muller* did not always carry the day, even with respect to statutes focused on protecting women. In *Adkins v. Children's Hospital* (1923), for example, the Court struck down the District of Columbia's minimum wage for women workers by a vote of 5–4. But the stage was set for larger change.

b.   Economic Liberty—Anything Goes

The so-called *Lochner* era came to a close in the 1930s—around the same time that the Supreme Court also stepped back from policing strict limitations on federal legislation under the Commerce Clause. As a doctrinal matter, the critical case was *Nebbia v. New York* (1934), a 5–4 decision in which the Court upheld a state regulation on the price of milk. After a lengthy review of the Court's precedents on economic liberty, Justice Roberts declared for the majority that "there is no closed class or category of businesses affected with a public interest. . . . The phrase 'affected with a public interest' can, in the nature of things, mean no more than that an industry, for adequate reason, is subject to control for the public good."

 CROSS REFERENCE The Commerce Clause cases are presented at pp. 427–443 and *Nebbia* at pp. 206–213.

Milk prices were one thing; much more important politically was the constitutionality of minimum wage laws. Given the forcefulness and breadth of his *Nebbia* opinion upholding government price regulation, Justice Roberts might have been expected to vote for the constitutionality of a minimum wage law like the one rejected in *Adkins v. Children's Hospital of District of Columbia* (1923). But in *Morehead v. New York ex rel. Tipaldo* (1936)—for reasons that remain mysterious and appear to have been guided at least in part by procedural considerations—he joined the Court's four conservative members in adhering to *Adkins*. The Court's decision in *Tipaldo* was massively unpopular. Just months later, in October 1936, Roberts voted to take up the following case, and in December he voted with the four more liberal members of the Court to uphold a minimum-wage law and make clear that the *Lochner* era was over.

West Coast Hotel Co. v. Parrish

Supreme Court of the United States, 1937.
300 U.S. 379.

MR. CHIEF JUSTICE HUGHES delivered the opinion of the Court.

This case presents the question of the constitutional validity of the minimum wage law of the state of Washington. The act, entitled "Minimum Wages for Women," authorizes the fixing of minimum wages for women and minors. . . .

The appellant conducts a hotel. The appellee Elsie Parrish was employed as a chambermaid and (with her husband) brought this suit to recover the difference between the wages paid her and the minimum wage fixed [by an administrative agency] pursuant to the state law. The minimum wage was $14.50 per week of 48 hours. The appellant challenged the act as repugnant to the due process clause of the Fourteenth Amendment of the Constitution of the United States. . . .

The appellant relies upon the decision of this Court in *Adkins v. Children's Hospital* (1923), which held invalid the District of Columbia Minimum Wage Act which was attacked under the due process clause of the Fifth Amendment. . . . [This case thus] demands on our part a re-examination of the *Adkins* Case. . . .

The principle which must control our decision is not in doubt. The constitutional provision invoked is the due process clause of the Fourteenth Amendment governing the states, as the due process clause invoked in the *Adkins* Case governed Congress. In each case the violation alleged by those attacking minimum wage regulation for women is deprivation of freedom of contract. What is this freedom? The Constitution does not speak of freedom of contract. It speaks of liberty and prohibits the deprivation of liberty without due process of law. In prohibiting that deprivation, the Constitution does not recognize an absolute and uncontrollable liberty. Liberty in each of its phases has its history and connotation. But the liberty safeguarded is liberty in a social organization which requires the protection of law against the evils which menace the health, safety, morals, and welfare of the people. Liberty under the Constitution is thus necessarily subject to the restraints of due process, and regulation which is reasonable in relation to its subject and is adopted in the interests of the community is due process. . . .

This power under the Constitution to restrict freedom of contract has had many illustrations. That it may be exercised in the public interest with respect to contracts between employer and employee is undeniable. Thus statutes have been sustained limiting employment in underground mines and smelters to eight hours a day; in requiring redemption in cash of store orders or other evidences of indebtedness issued in the payment of wages; in forbidding the payment of seamen's wages in advance; in making it unlawful to contract to pay miners employed at quantity rates upon the basis of screened coal instead of the weight of the coal as originally produced in the mine; in prohibiting contracts limiting liability for injuries to employees; in limiting hours of work of employees in manufacturing establishments; and in maintaining workmen's compensation laws. In dealing with the relation of employer and employed, the Legislature has necessarily a wide field of discretion in order that there may be suitable protection of health and safety, and that peace and good order may be promoted through regulations designed to insure wholesome conditions of work and freedom from oppression.

The point that has been strongly stressed that adult employees should be deemed competent to make their own contracts was decisively met nearly forty years ago in *Holden v. Hardy* (1898), where we pointed out the inequality in the footing of the parties. [As we explained,] the fact "that both parties are of full age, and competent to contract, does not necessarily deprive the state of the power to interfere, where the parties do not stand upon an equality, or where the public heath demands that one party to the contract shall be protected against himself." . . . It is manifest that this established principle is peculiarly applicable in relation to the employment of women in whose protection the state has a special interest. *Muller v. Oregon* (1908). . . .

Those principles have been reenforced by our subsequent decisions. . . . In *Nebbia v. New York*, dealing with the New York statute providing for minimum prices for milk, the general subject of the regulation of the use of private property and of the making of private contracts received an exhaustive examination, and we again declared that if such laws "have a reasonable relation to a proper legislative purpose, and are neither arbitrary nor discriminatory, the requirements of due process are satisfied"; that "with the wisdom of the policy adopted, with the adequacy or practicability of the law enacted to forward it, the courts are both incompetent and unauthorized to deal"; that "times without number we have said that the Legislature is primarily the judge of the necessity of such an enactment, that every possible presumption is in favor of its validity, and that though the court may hold views inconsistent with the wisdom of the law, it may not be annulled unless palpably in excess of legislative power."

With full recognition of the earnestness and vigor which characterize the prevailing opinion in the *Adkins* Case, we find it impossible to reconcile that ruling with these well-considered declarations. What can be closer to the public interest than the health of women and their protection from unscrupulous and overreaching employers? And if the protection of women is a legitimate end of the exercise of state power, how can it be said that the requirement of the payment of a minimum wage fairly fixed in order to meet the very necessities of existence is not an admissible means to that end?

The Legislature of the state was clearly entitled to consider the situation of women in employment, the fact that they are in the class receiving the least pay, that their bargaining power is relatively weak, and that they are the ready victims of those who would take advantage of their necessitous circumstances. The Legislature was entitled to adopt measures to reduce the evils of the "sweating system," the exploiting of workers at wages so low as to be insufficient to meet the bare cost of living, thus making their very helplessness the occasion of a most injurious competition. The Legislature had the right to consider that its minimum wage requirements would be an important aid in carrying out its policy of protection. The adoption of similar requirements by many states evidences a deep seated conviction both as to the presence of the evil and as to the means adapted to check it. Legislative response to that conviction cannot be regarded as arbitrary or capricious and that is all we have to decide. Even if the wisdom of the policy be regarded as debatable and its effects uncertain, still the Legislature is entitled to its judgment. . . .

There is an additional and compelling consideration which recent economic experience has brought into a strong light. The exploitation of a class of workers who are in an unequal position with respect to bargaining power and are thus relatively defenseless against the denial of a living wage is not only detrimental to their health and well being, but casts a direct burden for their support upon the community. . . . We may take judicial notice of the unparalleled demands for relief which arose during the recent period of depression and still continue to an alarming extent despite the degree of economic recovery which has been achieved. It is unnecessary to cite official statistics to establish what is of common knowledge through the length and breadth of the land. . . . The community is not bound to provide what is in effect a subsidy for unconscionable employers.

The community may direct its law-making power to correct the abuse which springs from their selfish disregard of the public interest.

The argument that the legislation in question constitutes an arbitrary discrimination, because it does not extend to men, is unavailing. This Court has frequently held that the legislative authority, acting within its proper field, is not bound to extend its regulation to all cases which it might possibly reach. The Legislature "is free to recognize degrees of harm and it may confine its restrictions to those classes of cases where the need is deemed to be clearest."

Our conclusion is that the case of *Adkins v. Children's Hospital* should be, and it is, overruled. The judgment of the Supreme Court of the state of Washington is affirmed.

Affirmed.

Mr. Justice Sutherland[, dissenting].

Mr. Justice Van Devanter, Mr. Justice McReynolds, Mr. Justice Butler, and I think the judgment of the court below should be reversed. The principles and authorities relied upon to sustain the judgment were considered in *Adkins v. Children's Hospital* and *Morehead v. New York ex rel. Tipaldo*, and their lack of application to cases like the one in hand was pointed out. . . .

It is urged that the question involved should now receive fresh consideration, among other reasons, because of "the economic conditions which have supervened"; but the meaning of the Constitution does not change with the ebb and flow of economic events. We frequently are told in more general words that the Constitution must be construed in the light of the present. If by that it is meant that the Constitution is made up of living words that apply to every new condition which they include, the statement is quite true. But to say, if that be intended, that the words of the Constitution mean today what they did not mean when written—that is, that they do not apply to a situation now to which they would have applied then—is to rob that instrument of the essential element which continues it in force as the people have made it until they, and not their official agents, have made it otherwise. . . . The judicial function is that of interpretation; it does not include the power of amendment under the guise of interpretation. . . .

By the mid-twentieth century, it was clear that the Supreme Court would leave economic policy completely to the political branches, subject only to rational basis review—and perhaps not even to that.

The next case is a canonical statement of the doctrine that emerged, with Justice Black's absolutism prevailing (in this context) over Justice Harlan's more calibrated response.

Ferguson v. Skrupa

Supreme Court of the United States, 1963.
372 U.S. 726.

MR. JUSTICE BLACK delivered the opinion of the Court.

In this case . . . we are asked to review . . . a Kansas statute making it a misdemeanor for any person to engage "in the business of debt adjusting" except as an incident to "the lawful practice of law in this state." The statute defines "debt adjusting" as "the making of a contract, express, or implied with a particular debtor whereby the debtor agrees to pay a certain amount of money periodically to the person engaged in the debt adjusting business who shall for a consideration distribute the same among certain specified creditors in accordance with a plan agreed upon."

The complaint, filed by appellee Skrupa . . . , alleged that Skrupa was engaged in the business of "debt adjusting" as defined by the statute, that his business was a "useful and desirable" one. . . . The three-judge court heard evidence by Skrupa tending to show the usefulness and desirability of his business and evidence by the state officials tending to show that "debt adjusting" lends itself to grave abuses against distressed debtors. . . . [The three-judge court] concluded, one judge dissenting, that the Act . . . was an unreasonable regulation of a "lawful business," which the court held amounted to a violation of the Due Process Clause of the Fourteenth Amendment. The court accordingly enjoined enforcement of the statute. . . .

[T]he District Court . . . adopted the philosophy . . . that it is the province of courts to draw on their own views as to the morality, legitimacy, and usefulness of a particular business in order to decide whether a statute bears too heavily upon that business and by so doing violates due process. Under the system of government created by our Constitution, it is up to legislatures, not courts, to decide on the wisdom and utility of legislation. There was a time when the Due Process Clause was used by this Court to strike down laws which were thought unreasonable, that is, unwise or incompatible with some particular economic or social philosophy. In this manner the Due Process Clause was used, for example, to nullify laws prescribing maximum hours for work in bakeries, *Lochner v. New York* (1905). . . .

The doctrine that prevailed in *Lochner* . . . has long since been discarded. We have returned to the original constitutional proposition that courts do not substitute their social and economic beliefs for the judgment of legislative bodies, who are elected to pass laws. As this Court stated in a unanimous opinion in 1941, "We are not concerned . . . with the wisdom, need, or appropriateness of the legislation." [*Olsen v. Nebraska ex rel. Western Reference & Bond Assn.* (upholding a limit on fees charged by private employment agencies).] Legislative bodies have broad scope to experiment with economic problems, and this Court does not sit to "subject the state to an intolerable supervision hostile to the basic principles of our government and wholly beyond the protection which the general clause of the Fourteenth Amendment was intended to secure." . . .

In the face of our abandonment of the use of the "vague contours" of the Due Process Clause to nullify laws which a majority of the Court believed to be economically unwise, . . . [w]e conclude that the Kansas Legislature was free to decide for itself that legislation was needed to deal with the business of debt adjusting. Unquestionably, there are arguments showing that the business of debt adjusting has social utility, but such arguments are properly addressed to the legislature, not to us. We refuse to sit as a "superlegislature to weigh the wisdom of legislation," and we emphatically refuse to go back to the time when courts used the Due Process Clause "to strike down state laws, regulatory of business and industrial conditions, because they may be unwise, improvident, or out of harmony with a particular school of thought." . . . Whether the legislature takes for its textbook Adam Smith, Herbert Spencer, Lord Keynes, or some other is no concern of ours. The Kansas debt adjusting statute may be wise or unwise. But relief, if any be needed, lies not with us but with the body constituted to pass laws for the State of Kansas. . . .

Reversed.

MR. JUSTICE HARLAN concurs in the judgment on the ground that this state measure bears a rational relation to a constitutionally permissible objective. See *Williamson v. Lee Optical Co.* (1955)....

4. SDP: Privacy, Dignity, and Autonomy

We have seen that in the matter of incorporation, Justice Black won a practical victory, even if not a clean theoretical one: Most of the provisions of the Bill of Rights have been incorporated against the states, one by one. With respect to economic liberty, *Skrupa* likewise indicates that, at least as a practical matter, the doctrine conforms to Justice Black's vision of the Fourteenth Amendment: The judiciary will impose only light scrutiny of laws that restrict economic activity but do not conflict with some constitutional text more specific than the Due Process Clauses.

If we step outside that area, however, we find a very different situation. Accordingly, we begin this section with excerpts from Justice Harlan's opinion in *Poe v. Ullman* (1961), which has gained a great deal of favor in recent decades.

COURSE THEME The Supreme Court has sometimes been willing—always in the face of considerable controversy—to recognize unenumerated constitutional rights of privacy, dignity, and personal autonomy in areas of fundamental moral concern. Although the Court occasionally did so during the *Lochner* era, its tendency to do so gained force beginning just about the time of *Skrupa*. In this realm, it is the second Justice Harlan's open-ended constitutional vision—completely at odds with that of Justice Black—that has largely prevailed.

Poe was a challenge to a Connecticut law that purported to ban the use of contraceptives. The Court held that the plaintiffs lacked standing because there was absolutely no realistic prospect that the law would be enforced. Justice Harlan dissented from that conclusion, and then went on to give reasons why he thought the law was unconstitutional. He began his due process analysis with a discussion of general principles:

> It is but a truism to say that this provision of both [the Fifth and Fourteenth] Amendments is not self-explanatory.... It is important to note, however, that two views of the [Fourteenth] Amendment have not been accepted by this Court as delineating its scope. One view, which was ably and insistently argued in response to what were

felt to be abuses by this Court of its reviewing power, sought to limit the provision to a guarantee of procedural fairness.... The other view which has been rejected would have it that the Fourteenth Amendment, whether by way of the Privileges and Immunities Clause or the Due Process Clause, applied against the States only and precisely those restraints which had, prior to the Amendment, been applicable merely to federal action. However, "due process," in the consistent view of this Court, has even been a broader concept than the first view, and more flexible than the second.

Were due process merely a procedural safeguard, it would fail to reach those situations where the deprivation of life, liberty or property was accomplished by legislation which by operating in the future could, given even the fairest possible procedure in application to individuals, nevertheless destroy the enjoyment of all three. . . . Thus the guaranties of due process, though having their roots in Magna Carta's *per legem terrae* ["by the law of the land"] and considered as procedural safeguards "against executive usurpation and tyranny," have in this country "become bulwarks also against arbitrary legislation." *Hurtado v. California* (1884).

However, it is not the particular enumeration of rights in the first eight Amendments which spells out the reach of Fourteenth Amendment due process, but rather, as was suggested in another context long before the adoption of that Amendment, those concepts which are considered to embrace those rights "which are . . . fundamental; which belong . . . to the citizens of all free governments," *Corfield v. Coryell* (C.C.E.D. Pa. 1823), for "the purposes (of securing) which men enter into society," *Calder v. Bull* (1798). Again and again, this Court has resisted the notion that the Fourteenth Amendment is no more than a shorthand reference to what is explicitly set out elsewhere in the Bill of Rights. *The Slaughter-House Cases* (1873); . . . *Hurtado*; . . . *Palko v. Connecticut* (1937). Indeed, the fact that an identical provision limiting federal action is found among the first eight Amendments, applying to the Federal Government, suggests that due process is a discrete concept which subsists as an independent guaranty of liberty and procedural fairness, more general and inclusive than the specific prohibitions. . . .

Due process has not been reduced to any formula; its content cannot be determined by reference to any code. The best that can be said is that, through the course of this Court's decisions, it has represented the balance which our Nation, built upon postulates of respect for the liberty of the individual, has struck between that liberty and the demands of organized society. If the supplying of content to this constitutional concept has of necessity been a rational process, it certainly has not been one where judges have felt free to roam where unguided speculation might take them. The balance of which I speak is the balance struck by this country, having regard to what history teaches are the traditions from which it developed as well as the traditions from which it broke. That tradition is a living thing. A decision of this Court which radically departs from it could not long survive, while a decision which builds on what has survived is likely to be sound. No formula could serve as a substitute, in this area, for judgment and restraint.

It is this outlook which has led the Court continuingly to perceive distinctions in the imperative character of constitutional provisions, since that character must be discerned from a particular provision's larger context. And inasmuch as this context is one not of words, but of history and purposes, the full scope of the liberty guaranteed by the Due Process Clause cannot be found in or limited by the precise terms of the specific guarantees elsewhere provided in the Constitution. This "liberty" is not a series of isolated points pricked out in terms of the taking of property; the freedom of speech, press, and religion; the right to keep and bear arms; the freedom from unreasonable searches and seizures; and so on. It is a rational continuum which, broadly speaking, includes a freedom from all substantial arbitrary impositions and purposeless restraints, see *Allgeyer v. Louisiana* (1897); *Holden v. Hardy* (1898); . . . *Nebbia v. New York* (1934); *Skinner v. Oklahoma* (1942) (concurring opinion) . . . , and which also recognizes, what a reasonable and sensitive judgment must, that certain interests require particularly careful scrutiny of the state needs asserted to justify their abridgment. . . .

Each new claim to constitutional protection must be considered against a background of constitutional purposes, as they have been rationally perceived and historically developed. Though we exercise limited and sharply restrained judgment, yet there is no "mechanical yard-stick," no "mechanical answer." The decision of an apparently novel claim must depend on grounds which follow closely on well accepted principles and criteria. The new decision must take "its place in relation to what went before and further [cut] a channel for what is to come." *Irvine v. California* (1954) (dissenting opinion [by Frankfurter, J.]). . . .

As we will soon see, the Court eventually did address the constitutionality of a contraceptive ban. As one would expect, Justice Black expressed a very different constitutional vision. *Griswold v. Connecticut* (1965), infra pp. 1394–1406.

a.   SDP—Family and Relationships

The remaining sections in this part explore how the Court has further engaged with the various strands of privacy, dignity, and autonomy interests that have prompted particular judicial solicitude. The first among them is a special constitutional protection for the creation, direction, and nurturing of family and other close relationships.

Meyer v. Nebraska

Supreme Court of the United States, 1923.
262 U.S. 390.

MR. JUSTICE MCREYNOLDS delivered the opinion of the Court.

Plaintiff in error was tried and convicted in the district court for [violating] . . . "An act relating to the teaching of foreign languages in the state of Nebraska," approved April 9, 1919, which [prohibited instruction in schools *in* any language other than English and prohibited instruction *of* any language other than English to students who had not completed the eighth grade.]

The Supreme Court of the state affirmed the judgment of conviction. It declared the offense charged and established was "the direct and intentional teaching of the German language as a distinct subject to a child who had not passed the eighth grade," in the parochial school maintained by Zion Evangelical Lutheran Congregation, a collection of Biblical stories being used therefore. . . .

The problem for our determination is whether the statute as construed and applied unreasonably infringes the liberty guaranteed to the plaintiff in error by the Fourteenth Amendment: "No state . . . shall deprive any person of life, liberty or property without due process of law."

While this court has not attempted to define with exactness the liberty thus guaranteed, the term has received much consideration and some of the included things have been definitely stated. Without doubt, it denotes not merely freedom from bodily restraint but also the right of the individual to contract, to engage in any of the common occupations of life, to acquire useful knowledge, to marry, establish a home and bring up children, to worship God according to the dictates of his own conscience, and generally to enjoy those privileges long recognized at common law as essential to the orderly pursuit of happiness by free men. [See, *e.g.*] *Slaughter-House Cases* (1873); *Yick Wo v. Hopkins* (1886); *Allegeyer v. Louisiana* (1897); *Lochner v. New York* (1905); *Adkins v. Children's Hospital* (1923). The established doctrine is that this liberty may not be interfered with, under the guise of protecting the public interest, by legislative action which is arbitrary or without reasonable relation to some purpose within the competency of the state to effect. Determination by the Legislature of what constitutes proper exercise of police power is not final or conclusive but is subject to supervision by the courts.

The American people have always regarded education and acquisition of knowledge as matters of supreme importance which should be diligently promoted. The [Northwest] Ordinance of 1787 declares:

> Religion, morality and knowledge being necessary to good government and the happiness of mankind, schools and the means of education shall forever be encouraged.

Corresponding to the right of control, it is the natural duty of the parent to give his children education suitable to their station in life; and nearly all the states, including Nebraska, enforce this obligation by compulsory laws.

. . . Mere knowledge of the German language cannot reasonably be regarded as harmful. Heretofore it has been commonly looked upon as helpful and desirable. Plaintiff in error taught this language in school as part of his occupation. His right thus to teach and the right of parents to engage him so to instruct their children, we think, are within the liberty of the amendment. . . .

It is said the purpose of the legislation was to promote civic development by inhibiting training and education of the immature in foreign tongues and ideals before they could learn English and acquire American ideals, and "that the English language should be and become the mother tongue of all children reared in this state." It is also affirmed that the foreign born population is very large, that certain communities commonly use foreign words, follow foreign leaders, move in a foreign atmosphere, and that the children are thereby hindered from becoming citizens of the most useful type and the public safety is imperiled.

That the state may do much, go very far, indeed, in order to improve the quality of its citizens, physically, mentally and morally, is clear; but the individual has certain fundamental rights which must be respected. The protection of the Constitution extends to all, to those who speak other languages as well as to those born with English on the tongue. Perhaps it would be highly advantageous if all had ready understanding of our ordinary speech, but this cannot be coerced by methods which conflict

 WORTH NOTING If Justice McReynolds's opinion in *Meyer* strikes you as a model of an inclusive approach to American life, note an irony: He was a notorious racist and anti-Semite. See, *e.g.*, Jeffrey Lord, *Two Presidents and the Court: When Bigotry Takes the Bench,* The American Spectator, July 14, 2009.

with the Constitution—a desirable end cannot be promoted by prohibited means. . . .

The desire of the Legislature to foster a homogeneous people with American ideals prepared readily to understand current discussions of civic matters is easy to appreciate. Unfortunate experiences during the late war and aversion toward every character of truculent adversaries were certainly enough to quicken that aspiration. But the means adopted, we think, exceed the limitations upon the power of the state and conflict with rights assured to plaintiff in error. The interference is plain enough and no adequate reason therefor in time of peace and domestic tranquility has been shown.

The power of the state to compel attendance at some school and to make reasonable regulations for all schools, including a requirement that they shall give instructions in English, is not questioned. Nor has challenge been made of the state's power to prescribe a curriculum for institutions which it supports. . . . No emergency has arisen which renders knowledge by a child of some language other than English so clearly harmful as to justify its inhibition with the consequent infringement of rights long freely enjoyed. We are constrained to conclude that the statute as applied is arbitrary and without reasonable relation to any end within the competency of the state.

As the statute undertakes to interfere only with teaching which involves a modern language, leaving complete freedom as to other matters, there seems no adequate foundation for the suggestion that the purpose was to protect the child's health by limiting his mental activities. It is well known that proficiency in a foreign language seldom comes to one not instructed at an early age, and experience shows that this is not injurious to the health, morals or understanding of the ordinary child.

The judgment of the court below must be reversed and the cause remanded for further proceedings not inconsistent with this opinion.

MR. JUSTICE HOLMES, dissenting.

WORTH NOTING

Justice Holmes's dissent applied to this case and to *Bartels v. Iowa*, a companion case that also reviewed statutes from Iowa and Ohio.

We all agree, I take it, that it is desirable that all the citizens of the United States should speak a common tongue, and therefore that the end aimed at by the statute is a lawful and proper one. The only question is whether the means adopted deprive teachers of the liberty secured to them by the Fourteenth Amendment. It is with hesitation and unwillingness that I differ from my brethren with regard to a law like this, but I cannot bring my mind to believe that, in some circumstances, and circumstances existing it is said in Nebraska, the statute might not be regarded as a reasonable or even necessary method of reaching the desired result. . . .

Youth is the time when familiarity with a language is established and if there are sections in the state where a child would hear only Polish or French or German spoken at home I am not prepared to say that it is unreasonable to provide that in his early years he shall hear and speak only English at school. But, if it is reasonable, it is not an undue restriction of the liberty either of teacher or scholar. No

WORTH NOTING

Justice Holmes indicated that he did regard a "special proviso against the German language" in the Ohio statute as unconstitutional.

one would doubt that a teacher might be forbidden to teach many things, and the only criterion of his liberty under the Constitution that I can think of is "whether, considering the end in view, the statute passes the bounds of reason and assumes the character of a merely arbitrary fiat." *Purity Extract & Tonic Co. v. Lynch* (1912). I think I appreciate the objection to the law, but it appears to me to present a question upon which men reasonably might differ, and therefore I am unable to say that the Constitution of the United States prevents the experiment's being tried.

MR. JUSTICE SUTHERLAND concurs in this opinion.

The Court returned to the intersection of education and family in the next case, decided two years later.

Pierce v. Society of the Sisters of the Holy Names of Jesus and Mary

Supreme Court of the United States, 1925.
268 U.S. 510.

MR. JUSTICE MCREYNOLDS delivered the opinion of the Court.

These appeals [challenge the Oregon Compulsory Education Act (1922), which] requires every parent, guardian, or other person having control or charge or custody of a child between 8 and 16 years to send him "to a public school for the period of time a public school shall be held during the current year" in the district where the child resides; and failure so to do is declared a misdemeanor. There are exemptions—not specially important here—for children who are not normal, or who have completed the eighth grade, or whose parents or private teachers reside at considerable distances from any public school, or who hold special permits from the county superintendent. The manifest purpose is to compel general attendance at public schools by normal children, between 8 and 16, who have not completed the eight grade. And without doubt enforcement of the statute would seriously impair, perhaps destroy, the profitable features of appellees' business and greatly diminish the value of their property.

SUMMARY OF THE FACTS

The Society of Sisters maintained orphanages, primary and high schools, and junior colleges. In addition to instruction in the secular subjects taught by Oregon's public schools, the Society of Sisters also featured "[s]ystematic religious instruction and moral training according to the tenets of the Roman Catholic Church." Another appellee, Hill Military Academy, conducted a for-profit school for boys between the ages of 5 and 21.

No question is raised concerning the power of the state reasonably to regulate all schools, to inspect, supervise and examine them, their teachers and pupils; to require that all children of proper age attend some school, that teachers shall be of good moral character and patriotic disposition, that certain studies plainly essential to good citizenship must be taught, and that nothing be taught which is manifestly inimical to the public welfare.

The inevitable practical result of enforcing the act under consideration would be destruction of appellees' primary schools, and perhaps all other private primary schools for normal children within the state of Oregon. Appellees are engaged in a kind of undertaking not inherently harmful, but long regarded as useful and meritorious. Certainly there is nothing in the present records to indicate that they have failed to discharge their obligations to patrons, students, or the state. And there are no peculiar circumstances or present emergencies which demand extraordinary measures relative to primary education.

Under the doctrine of *Meyer v. Nebraska*, we think it entirely plain that the Act of 1922 unreasonably interferes with the liberty of parents and guardians to direct the upbringing and education of children under their control. As often heretofore pointed out, rights guaranteed by the Constitution may not be abridged by legislation which has no reasonable relation to some purpose within the competency of the state. The fundamental theory of liberty upon which all governments in this Union repose excludes any general power of the state to standardize its children by forcing them to accept instruction from public teachers only. The child is not the mere creature of the state; those who nurture him and direct his destiny have the right, coupled with the high duty, to recognize and prepare him for additional obligations. . . .

The decrees below are affirmed.

Recall that in *Loving v. Virginia* (1967), the Supreme Court invalidated
a Virginia statutory scheme that, with narrow exceptions, prohibited a white
person from marrying anyone be-
sides another white person. Most of
the Court's analysis was under the
Equal Protection Clause. But the
Court also held the Virginia laws in-

 CROSS REFERENCE The *Loving* decision's equal protection analysis is presented at pp. 1008–1012.

valid as a matter of due process. Here is Chief Justice Warren's brief discussion
on that point:

> These statutes also deprive the Lovings of liberty without due
> process of law in violation of the Due Process Clause of the Four-
> teenth Amendment. The freedom to marry has long been recognized
> as one of the vital personal rights essential to the orderly pursuit of
> happiness by free men.
>
> Marriage is one of the "basic civil rights of man," fundamental
> to our very existence and survival. *Skinner v. State of Oklahoma* (1942).
> *See also Maynard v. Hill* (1888). To deny this fundamental freedom
> on so unsupportable a basis as the racial classifications embodied in
> these statutes, classifications so directly subversive of the principle
> of equality at the heart of the Fourteenth Amendment, is surely to
> deprive all the State's citizens of liberty without due process of law.
> The Fourteenth Amendment requires that the freedom of choice to
> marry not be restricted by invidious racial discriminations. Under our
> Constitution, the freedom to marry, or not marry, a person of another
> race resides with the individual and cannot be infringed by the State.

 As You READ The next case invokes *Meyer, Pierce,* and *Loving* in support of its conclusion that a city zoning ordinance unconstitutionally interfered with
the plaintiff's protected interest in preserving her family unit. Do you
find its use of those precedents persuasive?

Moore v. City of East Cleveland

Supreme Court of the United States, 1977.
<u>431 U.S. 494</u>.

Mr. Justice Powell announced the judgment of the Court, and delivered an opinion in which Mr. Justice Brennan, Mr. Justice Marshall, and Mr. Justice Blackmun joined.

East Cleveland's housing ordinance, like many throughout the country, limits occupancy of a dwelling unit to members of a single family. But the ordinance contains an unusual and complicated definitional section that recognizes as a "family" only a few categories of related individuals. Because her family, living together in her home, fits none of those categories, appellant stands convicted of a criminal offense. The question in this case is whether the ordinance violates the Due Process Clause of the Fourteenth Amendment.

Appellant, Mrs. Inez Moore, lives in her East Cleveland home together with her son, Dale Moore Sr., and her two grandsons, Dale, Jr., and John Moore, Jr. The two boys are first cousins rather than brothers; we are told that John came to live with his grandmother and with the elder and younger Dale Moores after his mother's death. In early 1973, Mrs. Moore received a notice of violation from the city, stating that John was an "illegal occupant" and directing her to comply with the ordinance. When she failed to remove him [despite repeated complaints from the city over the next sixteen months, Mrs. Moore was prosecuted, convicted, and] sentenced to five days in jail and a $25 fine. . . .

The city argues that our decision in *Village of Belle Terre v. Boraas* (1974), requires us to sustain the ordinance attacked here. Belle Terre, like East Cleveland, imposed limits on the types of groups that could occupy a single dwelling unit. . . . [W]e sustained the Belle Terre ordinance on the ground that it bore a rational relationship to permissible state objectives.

But one overriding factor sets this case apart from *Belle Terre*. The ordinance there affected only unrelated individuals. It expressly allowed all who were related by "blood, adoption, or marriage" to live together, and in sustaining the ordinance we were careful to note that it promoted "family needs" and "family values." East Cleveland, in contrast, has chosen to regulate the occupancy of its housing by slicing deeply into the family itself. This is no mere incidental result of the ordinance. On its face it selects certain categories of relatives who may live together and declares that others may not. In particular, it makes a crime of a grandmother's choice to live with her grandson in circumstances like those presented here.

When a city undertakes such intrusive regulation of the family, neither *Belle Terre* nor *Euclid v. Ambler Realty Co.* (1926) governs; the usual judicial deference to the legislature is inappropriate. "This Court has long recognized that freedom of personal choice in matters of marriage and family life is one of the liberties protected by the Due Process Clause of the Fourteenth Amendment." A host of cases, tracing their lineage to *Meyer v. Nebraska* (1923) and *Pierce v. Society of Sisters* (1925), have consistently acknowledged a "private realm of family life which the state cannot enter." *Prince v. Massachusetts* (1944). See, e.g., *Roe v. Wade* (1973); *Wisconsin v. Yoder* (1972) [(holding that Amish parents had a constitutional right not to send their children to school past the eighth grade)]; *Griswold v. Connecticut* (1965); *Poe v. Ullman* (1961); cf. *Loving v. Virginia* (1967); *Skinner v. Oklahoma ex rel. Williamson* (1942). Of course, the family is not beyond regulation. But when the government intrudes on choices concerning family living arrangements, this Court must examine carefully the importance of the governmental interests advanced and the extent to which they are served by the challenged regulation.

WORTH NOTING

Euclid upheld a zoning ordinance against an argument that, by restricting the lawful uses of a tract of land, the ordinance destroyed most of the tract's value and so violated due process.

When thus examined, this ordinance cannot survive. The city seeks to justify it as a means of preventing overcrowding, minimizing traffic and parking congestion, and avoiding an undue financial burden on East Cleveland's school system. Although these are legitimate goals, the ordinance before us serves them marginally, at best. For example, the ordinance permits any family consisting only of husband, wife, and unmarried children to live together, even if the family contains a half dozen licensed drivers, each with his or her own car. At the same time it forbids an adult brother and sister to share a household, even if both faithfully use public transportation. The ordinance would permit a grandmother to live with a single dependent son and children, even if his school-age children number a dozen, yet it forces Mrs. Moore to find another dwelling for her grandson John, simply because of the presence of his uncle and cousin in the same household. We need not labor the point. Section 1341.08 has but a tenuous relation to alleviation of the conditions mentioned by the city.

The city would distinguish the cases based on *Meyer* and *Pierce*. It points out that none of them "gives grandmothers any fundamental rights with respect to grandsons," and suggests that any constitutional right to live together as a family extends only to the nuclear family essentially a couple and their dependent children.

To be sure, these cases did not expressly consider the family relationship presented here. They were immediately concerned with freedom of choice with respect to childbearing, *e.g., Roe v. Wade; Griswold*, or with the rights of parents to the custody and companionship of their own children, *Stanley v. Illinois* (1972) [see p. 1203], or with traditional parental authority in matters of child rearing and education. *Wisconsin v. Yoder* (1972); *Pierce; Meyer*. But unless we close our eyes to the basic reasons why certain rights associated with the family have been accorded shelter under the Fourteenth Amendment's Due Process Clause, we cannot avoid applying the force and rationale of these precedents to the family choice involved in this case. . . .

Substantive due process has at times been a treacherous field for this Court. . . . That history counsels caution and restraint. But it does not counsel abandonment, nor does it require what the city urges here: cutting off any protection of family rights at the first convenient, if arbitrary boundary the boundary of the nuclear family. Appropriate limits on substantive due process come not from drawing arbitrary lines but rather from careful "respect for the teachings of history [and] solid recognition of the basic values that underlie our society" *Griswold v. Connecticut* (Harlan, J., concurring). Our decisions establish that the Constitution protects the sanctity of the family precisely because the institution of the family is deeply rooted in this Nation's history and tradition. It is through the family that we inculcate and pass down many of our most cherished values, moral and cultural.

Ours is by no means a tradition limited to respect for the bonds uniting the members of the nuclear family. The tradition of uncles, aunts, cousins, and especially grandparents sharing a household along with parents and children has roots equally venerable and equally deserving of constitutional recognition. Over the years millions of our citizens have grown up in just such an environment, and most, surely, have profited from it. Even if conditions of modern society have brought about a decline in extended family households, they have not erased the accumulated wisdom of civilization, gained over the centuries and honored throughout our history, that supports a larger conception of the family. Out of choice, necessity, or a sense of family responsibility, it has been common for close relatives to draw together and participate in the duties and the satisfactions of a common home. Decisions concerning child rearing, which *Yoder, Meyer, Pierce* and other cases have recognized as entitled to constitutional protection, long have been shared with grandparents or other relatives who occupy the same household indeed who may take on major responsibility for the rearing of the children. Especially in times of adversity, such as the death of a spouse or economic need, the broader family has tended to come together for mutual sustenance and to maintain or rebuild a secure home life. This is apparently what happened here.

Whether or not such a household is established because of personal tragedy, the choice of relatives in this degree of kinship to live together may not lightly be denied by the State. *Pierce* struck down an Oregon law requiring all children to attend the State's public schools, holding that the Constitution "excludes any general power of the State to standardize its children by forcing them to accept instruction from public teachers only." By the same token the Constitution prevents East Cleveland from standardizing its children and its adults by forcing all to live in certain narrowly defined family patterns.

Reversed.

MR. JUSTICE BRENNAN, with whom MR. JUSTICE MARSHALL joins, concurring.

. . . I write only to underscore the cultural myopia of the arbitrary boundary drawn by the East Cleveland ordinance. . . . The line drawn by this ordinance displays a depressing insensitivity toward the economic and emotional needs of a very large part of our society. In today's America, the "nuclear family" is the pattern so often found in much of white suburbia. The Constitution cannot be interpreted, however, to tolerate the imposition by government upon the rest of us of white suburbia's preference in patterns of family living. The "extended family" that provided generations of early Americans with social services and economic and emotional support in times of hardship, and was the beachhead for successive waves of immigrants who populated our cities, remains not merely still a pervasive living pattern, but under the goad of brutal economic necessity, a prominent pattern—virtually a means of survival—for large numbers of the poor and deprived minorities of our society. For them compelled pooling of scant resources requires compelled sharing of a household. . . .

Mr. Justice Stevens, concurring in the judgment.

In my judgment the critical question presented by this case is whether East Cleveland's housing ordinance is a permissible restriction on appellant's right to use her own property as she sees fit. . . . Under that standard, East Cleveland's unprecedented ordinance constitutes a taking of property without due process and without just compensation.

WORTH NOTING Chief Justice Burger dissented without reaching the constitutional issue, on the ground that the appellant had not sufficiently exhausted her administrative remedies.

Mr. Justice Stewart, with whom Mr. Justice Rehnquist joins, dissenting.

. . . In my view, the appellant's claim that the ordinance in question invades constitutionally protected rights of association and privacy is in large part answered by the *Belle Terre* decision. . . . To be sure, the ordinance involved in *Belle Terre* did not prevent blood relatives from occupying the same dwelling, and the Court's decision in that case does not, therefore, foreclose the appellant's arguments based specifically on the ties of kinship present in this case. Nonetheless, I would hold, for the reasons that follow, that the existence of those ties does not elevate either the appellant's claim of associational freedom or her claim of privacy to a level invoking constitutional protection.

To suggest that the biological fact of common ancestry necessarily gives related persons constitutional rights of association superior to those of unrelated persons is to misunderstand the nature of the associational freedoms that the Constitution has been understood to protect. . . .

Several decisions of the Court have identified specific aspects of what might broadly be termed "private family life" that are constitutionally protected against state interference. See, *e.g.*, *Roe v. Wade* (woman's right to decide whether to terminate pregnancy); *Loving v. Virginia* (freedom to marry person of another race); *Griswold v. Connecticut* (right to use contraceptives); *Pierce v. Society of Sisters* (parents' right to send children to private schools); *Meyer v. Nebraska* (parents' right to have children instructed in foreign language). Although the appellant's desire to share a single-dwelling unit also involves "private family life" in a sense, that desire can hardly be equated with any of the interests protected in the cases just cited. The ordinance about which the appellant complains did not impede her choice to have or not to have children, and it did not dictate to her how her own children were to be nurtured and reared. The ordinance clearly does not prevent parents from living together or living with their unemancipated offspring.

But even though the Court's previous cases are not directly in point, the appellant contends that the importance of the "extended family" in American society requires us to hold that her decision to share her residence with her grandsons may not be interfered with by the State. This decision, like the decisions involved in bearing and raising children, is said to be an aspect of "family life" also entitled to substantive protection under the Constitution. Without pausing to inquire how far under this argument an "extended family" might extend, I cannot agree.[7] When the Court has found that the Fourteenth Amendment placed a substantive limitation on a State's power to regulate, it has been in those rare cases in which the personal interests at issue have been deemed " 'implicit in the concept of ordered liberty.' " See *Roe v. Wade.* The interest that the appellant may have in permanently sharing a single kitchen and a suite of contiguous rooms with some of her relatives simply does not rise to that level. To equate this interest with the fundamental decisions to marry and to bear and raise children is to extend the limited substantive contours of the Due Process Clause beyond recognition. . . .

For these reasons, I think the Ohio courts did not err in rejecting the appellant's constitutional claims. Accordingly, I respectfully dissent.

MR. JUSTICE WHITE, dissenting.

The emphasis of the Due Process Clause is on "process." . . . Although the Court regularly proceeds on the assumption that the Due Process Clause has more than a procedural dimension, we must always bear in mind that the substantive content of the Clause is suggested neither by its language nor by preconstitutional history; that content is nothing more than the accumulated product of judicial interpretation of the Fifth and Fourteenth Amendments. This is not to suggest, at this point, that any of these cases should be overruled, or that the process by which they were decided was illegitimate or even unacceptable, but only to underline Mr. Justice Black's constant reminder to his colleagues that the Court has no license to invalidate legislation which it thinks merely arbitrary or unreasonable. . . .

---

[7]   The opinion of Mr. Justice Powell and Mr. Justice Brennan's concurring opinion both emphasize the traditional importance of the extended family in American life. But I fail to understand why it follows that the residents of East Cleveland are constitutionally prevented from following what Mr. Justice Brennan calls the "pattern" of "white suburbia," even though that choice may reflect "cultural myopia." In point of fact, East Cleveland is a predominantly Negro community, with a Negro City Manager and City Commission.

. . . The Judiciary, including this Court, is the most vulnerable and comes nearest to illegitimacy when it deals with judge-made constitutional law having little or no cognizable roots in the language or even the design of the Constitution. Realizing that the present construction of the Due Process Clause represents a major judicial gloss on its terms, as well as on the anticipation of the Framers, and that much of the underpinning for the broad, substantive application of the Clause disappeared in the conflict between the Executive and the Judiciary in the 1930's and 1940's, the Court should be extremely reluctant to breathe still further substantive content into the Due Process Clause so as to strike down legislation adopted by a State or city to promote its welfare. Whenever the Judiciary does so, it unavoidably preempts for itself another part of the governance of the country without express constitutional authority. . . .

. . . The present claim is hardly one of which it could be said that "neither liberty nor justice would exist if [it] were sacrificed." *Palko v. Connecticut*. . . . Mrs. Moore's interest in having the offspring of more than one dependent son live with her qualifies as a liberty protected by the Due Process Clause; but, because of the nature of that particular interest, the demands of the Clause are satisfied once the Court is assured that the challenged proscription is the product of a duly enacted or promulgated statute, ordinance, or regulation and that it is not wholly lacking in purpose or utility.

The cases so far in this section have all involved family relationships in a traditional sense of the word: parent and child; husband and wife; grandparent and grandchild. In this light, consider for a moment the important relationships you have with people who you don't think of as family—at least not in an official sense. The next case explores the question whether the idea of a specially protected zone of intimate association might extend to such relationships as well.

Roberts v. United States Jaycees

Supreme Court of the United States, 1984.
468 U.S. 609.

JUSTICE BRENNAN delivered the opinion of the Court.

This case requires us to address a conflict between a State's efforts to eliminate gender-based discrimination against its citizens and the constitutional
freedom of association asserted by members of a private organization. In the
decision under review, the Court of Appeals for the Eighth Circuit concluded that, by requiring the United States Jaycees to admit women as full voting
members, the Minnesota Human Rights Act violates the First and Fourteenth
Amendment rights of the organization's members. We noted probable jurisdiction, and now reverse.

I

The United States Jaycees (Jaycees), founded in 1920 as the Junior Chamber
of Commerce, is a nonprofit membership corporation, incorporated in Missouri
with national headquarters in Tulsa, Okla. The objective of the Jaycees, as set
out in its bylaws, is to pursue

> such educational and charitable purposes as will promote and foster
> the growth and development of young men's civic organizations in
> the United States, designed to inculcate in the individual member-
> ship of such organization a spirit of genuine Americanism and civic
> interest, and as a supplementary education institution to provide them
> with opportunity for personal development and achievement and an
> avenue for intelligent participation by young men in the affairs of
> their community, state and nation, and to develop true friendship
> and understanding among young men of all nations.

. . . In 1974 and 1975, respectively, the Minneapolis and St. Paul chapters
of the Jaycees began admitting women as regular members. . . . As a result,
the two chapters have been in violation of the national organization's bylaws
for about 10 years. . . . In December 1978, the president of the national organization advised both chapters that a motion to revoke their charters would be
considered at a forthcoming meeting of the national board of directors in Tulsa.

Shortly after receiving this notification, members of both chapters filed
charges of discrimination with the Minnesota Department of Human Rights.

[The Department] concluded that the Jaycees organization is a "place of public accommodation" within the [meaning of the Minnesota Human Rights] Act and that it had engaged in an unfair discriminatory practice by excluding women from regular membership. [It] ordered the national organization to cease and desist from discriminating against any member or applicant for membership on the basis of sex and from imposing sanctions on any Minnesota affiliate for admitting women. . . . [The Eighth Circuit held that both this order and the Minnesota Human Rights Act violated the Fourteenth Amendment.]

II

. . . The Court has long recognized that, because the Bill of Rights is designed to secure individual liberty, it must afford the formation and preservation of certain kinds of highly personal relationships a substantial measure of sanctuary from unjustified interference by the State. *E.g., Pierce v. Society of Sisters* (1925); *Meyer v. Nebraska* (1923). Without precisely identifying every consideration that may underlie this type of constitutional protection, we have noted that certain kinds of personal bonds have played a critical role in the culture and traditions of the Nation by cultivating and transmitting shared ideals and beliefs; they thereby foster diversity and act as critical buffers between the individual and the power of the State. [Citing eight cases.] Moreover, the constitutional shelter afforded such relationships reflects the realization that individuals draw much of their emotional enrichment from close ties with others. Protecting these relationships from unwarranted state interference therefore safeguards the ability independently to define one's identity that is central to any concept of liberty. [Citing another seven cases.]

The personal affiliations that exemplify these considerations, and that therefore suggest some relevant limitations on the relationships that might be entitled to this sort of constitutional protection, are those that attend the creation and sustenance of a family—marriage, e.g., *Zablocki v. Redhail* (1978); childbirth, *e.g., Carey v. Population Services International* (1977); the raising and education of children, *e.g., Smith v. Organization of Foster Families* (1977); and cohabitation with one's relatives, *e.g., Moore v. East Cleveland* (1977). Family relationships, by their nature, involve deep attachments and commitments to the necessarily few other individuals with whom one shares not only a special community of thoughts, experiences, and beliefs but also distinctively personal aspects of one's life. Among other things, therefore, they are distinguished by such attributes as relative smallness, a high degree of selectivity in decisions to begin and maintain the affiliation, and seclusion from others in critical aspects of the relationship. As a general matter, only relationships with these sorts of qualities are likely to reflect the considerations that have led to an understanding of freedom of association as an intrinsic element of personal liberty. Conversely, an association lacking these qualities—such as a large business enterprise—seems remote from the concerns giving rise to this constitutional protection. Accordingly, the Constitution undoubtedly imposes constraints on the State's power to control the selection of one's spouse that would not apply to regulations affecting the choice of one's fellow employees.

Between these poles, of course, lies a broad range of human relationships that may make greater or lesser claims to constitutional protection from particular incursions by the State. Determining the limits of state authority over an individual's freedom to enter into a particular association therefore unavoidably entails a careful assessment of where that relationship's objective characteristics locate it on a spectrum from the most intimate to the most attenuated of personal attachments. We need not mark the potentially significant points on this terrain with any precision. We note only that factors that may be relevant include size, purpose, policies, selectivity, congeniality, and other characteristics that in a particular case may be pertinent. In this case, however, several features of the Jaycees clearly place the organization outside of the category of relationships worthy of this kind of constitutional protection.

The undisputed facts reveal that the local chapters of the Jaycees are large and basically unselective groups. At the time of the state administrative hearing, the Minneapolis chapter had approximately 430 members, while the St. Paul chapter had about 400. Apart from age and sex, neither the national organization nor the local chapters employ any criteria for judging applicants for membership, and new members are routinely recruited and admitted with no inquiry into their backgrounds. . . . Furthermore, despite their inability to vote, hold office, or receive certain awards, women affiliated with the Jaycees attend various meetings, participate in selected projects, and engage in many of the organization's social functions. . . .

In short, the local chapters of the Jaycees are neither small nor selective. Moreover, much of the activity central to the formation and maintenance of the association involves the participation of strangers to that relationship. Accordingly, we conclude that the Jaycees chapters lack the distinctive characteristics that might afford constitutional protection to the decision of its members to exclude women. . .

The judgment of the Court of Appeals is reversed.

JUSTICE REHNQUIST concurs in the judgment.

WORTH NOTING

Justice O'Connor, concurring in part and concurring in the judgment, disagreed with the Court's analysis of various First Amendment issues not presented in this excerpt. With respect to the issue presented here, she wrote: "Whatever the precise scope of the rights recognized in [prior] cases, they do not encompass associational rights of a 295,000-member organization whose activities are not 'private' in any meaningful sense of that term."

THE CHIEF JUSTICE and JUSTICE BLACKMUN took no part in the decision of this case.

As You READ

The next case explores a different constitutional problem that arises in the context of certain close relationships: what happens when family members disagree about what is in a child's best interests—or when they have incompatible visions of what the family relationship even is?

Troxel v. Granville

Supreme Court of the United States, 2000.
530 U.S. 57.

JUSTICE O'CONNOR announced the judgment of the Court and delivered an opinion, in which THE CHIEF JUSTICE, JUSTICE GINSBURG, and JUSTICE BREYER join.

. . . Tommie Granville and Brad Troxel shared a relationship that ended in June 1991. The two never married, but they had two daughters, Isabelle and Natalie. Jenifer and Gary Troxel are Brad's parents, and thus the paternal grandparents of Isabelle and Natalie. After Tommie and Brad separated in 1991, Brad lived with his parents and regularly brought his daughters to his parents' home for weekend visitation. Brad committed suicide in May 1993. Although the Troxels at first continued to see Isabelle and Natalie on a regular

basis after their son's death, Tommie Granville informed the Troxels in October 1993 that she wished to limit their visitation with her daughters to one
short visit per month.

In December 1993, the Troxels commenced the present action by filing
. . . a [state court] petition to obtain visitation rights with Isabelle and Natalie.
[They invoked Rev. Code § 26.10.160(3), which authorized the grant of visitation rights to "[a]ny person" whenever "visitation may serve the best interest of
the child." The court found that the Troxels were "part of a large, central, loving family, all located in this area," and that they could "provide opportunities
for the children in the areas of cousins and music." The court therefore ordered
visitation of one weekend per month, one week during the summer, and four
hours on both of the petitioning grandparents' birthdays.]

[While Granville's appeal of the trial court's visitation order was pending, she married, and her husband adopted the girls. The Washington Supreme
Court eventually decided that the federal Constitution barred the Troxels
from obtaining any visitation rights at all, on the ground that] § 26.10.160(3)
unconstitutionally infringes on the fundamental right of parents to rear their
children. We granted certiorari, and now affirm the judgment.

II

The demographic changes of the past century make it difficult to speak of
an average American family. The composition of families varies greatly from
household to household. While many children may have two married parents
and grandparents who visit regularly, many other children are raised in single-parent households. . . . Understandably, in these single-parent households,
persons outside the nuclear family are called upon with increasing frequency
to assist in the everyday tasks of child rearing. In many cases, grandparents
play an important role. . . .

The nationwide enactment of nonparental visitation statutes is assuredly
due, in some part, to the States' recognition of these changing realities of the
American family. Because grandparents and other relatives undertake duties
of a parental nature in many households, States have sought to ensure the welfare of the children therein by protecting the relationships those children form
with such third parties. . . .

The liberty interest at issue in this case—the interest of parents in the care,
custody, and control of their children—is perhaps the oldest of the fundamental

liberty interests recognized by this Court. *Meyer v. Nebraska* (1923); *Pierce v. Society of Sisters* (1925); *Stanley v. Illinois* (1972); *Wisconsin v. Yoder* (1972). . . .

Section 26.10.160(3), as applied to Granville and her family in this case, unconstitutionally infringes on that fundamental parental right. The Washington nonparental visitation statute is breathtakingly broad. According to the statute's text, "*[a]ny person* may petition the court for visitation rights *at any time*," and the court may grant such visitation rights whenever "visitation may serve *the best interest of the child*." § 26.10.160(3) (emphases added). That language effectively permits any third party seeking visitation to subject any decision by a parent concerning visitation of the parent's children to state-court review.

Once the visitation petition has been filed in court and the matter is placed before a judge, a parent's decision that visitation would not be in the child's best interest is accorded no deference. Section 26.10.160(3) contains no requirement that a court accord the parent's decision any presumption of validity or any weight whatsoever. Instead, the Washington statute places the best-interest determination solely in the hands of the judge. Should the judge disagree with the parent's estimation of the child's best interests, the judge's view necessarily prevails. Thus, in practical effect, in the State of Washington a court can disregard and overturn *any* decision by a fit custodial parent concerning visitation whenever a third party affected by the decision files a visitation petition, based solely on the judge's determination of the child's best interests. . . .

Turning to the facts of this case, the record reveals that the Superior Court's order was based on precisely the type of mere disagreement we have just described and nothing more. The Superior Court's order was not founded on any special factors that might justify the State's interference with Granville's fundamental right to make decisions concerning the rearing of her two daughters. To be sure, this case involves a visitation petition filed by grandparents soon after the death of their son—the father of Isabelle and Natalie—but the combination of several factors here compels our conclusion that § 26.10.160(3), as applied, exceeded the bounds of the Due Process Clause.

. . . [T]he Troxels did not allege, and no court has found, that Granville was an unfit parent. That aspect of the case is important, for there is a presumption that fit parents act in the best interests of their children. . . . Accordingly, so long as a parent adequately cares for his or her children (*i.e.,* is fit), there will normally be no reason for the State to inject itself into the private realm of the family to further question the ability of that parent to make the best decisions concerning the rearing of that parent's children.

The problem here is not that the Washington Superior Court intervened, but that when it did so, it gave no special weight at all to Granville's determination of her daughters' best interests. More importantly, it appears that the Superior Court applied exactly the opposite presumption. In reciting its oral ruling after the conclusion of closing arguments, the Superior Court judge explained:

> The burden is to show that it is in the best interest of the children to have some visitation and some quality time with their grandparents. I think in most situations a commonsensical approach [is that] it is normally in the best interest of the children to spend quality time with the grandparent, unless the grandparent, *[sic]* there are some issues or problems involved wherein the grandparents, their lifestyles are going to impact adversely upon the children. That certainly isn't the case here from what I can tell.

The judge's comments suggest that he presumed the grandparents' request should be granted unless the children would be "impact[ed] adversely." In effect, the judge placed on Granville, the fit custodial parent, the burden of *disproving* that visitation would be in the best interest of her daughters. The judge reiterated moments later: "I think [visitation with the Troxels] would be in the best interest of the children and I haven't been shown it is not in [the] best interest of the children."

The decisional framework employed by the Superior Court directly contravened the traditional presumption that a fit parent will act in the best interest of his or her child. . . . In an ideal world, parents might always seek to cultivate the bonds between grandparents and their grandchildren. Needless to say, however, our world is far from perfect, and in it the decision whether such an intergenerational relationship would be beneficial in any specific case is for the parent to make in the first instance. And, if a fit parent's decision of the kind at issue here becomes subject to judicial review, the court must accord at least some special weight to the parent's own determination.

Finally, we note that there is no allegation that Granville ever sought to cut off visitation entirely. Rather, the present dispute originated when Granville informed the Troxels that she would prefer to restrict their visitation with Isabelle and Natalie to one short visit per month and special holidays. . . .

Because we rest our decision on the sweeping breadth of § 26.10.160(3) and the application of that broad, unlimited power in this case, we do not consider the primary constitutional question passed on by the Washington Supreme Court—whether the Due Process Clause requires all nonparental visitation statutes to include a showing of harm or potential harm to the child as a condition precedent to granting visitation. . . . Because much state-court adjudication in this context occurs on a case-by-case basis, we would be hesitant to hold that specific nonparental visitation statutes violate the Due Process Clause as a *per se* matter. . . .

Accordingly, the judgment of the Washington Supreme Court is affirmed.

JUSTICE SOUTER, concurring in the judgment.

. . . Our cases, it is true, have not set out exact metes and bounds to the protected interest of a parent in the relationship with his child, but *Meyer's* repeatedly recognized right of upbringing would be a sham if it failed to encompass the right to be free of judicially compelled visitation by "any party" at "any time" a judge believed he "could make a 'better' decision" than the objecting parent had done. The strength of a parent's interest in controlling a child's associates is as obvious as the influence of personal associations on the development of the child's social and moral character. Whether for good or for ill, adults not only influence but may indoctrinate children, and a choice about a child's social companions is not essentially different from the designation of the adults who will influence the child in school. Even a State's considered judgment about the preferable political and religious character of schoolteachers is not entitled to prevail over a parent's choice of private school. *Pierce*. It would be anomalous, then, to subject a parent to any individual judge's choice of a child's associates from out of the general population merely because the judge might think himself more enlightened than the child's parent. . . .

JUSTICE THOMAS, concurring in the judgment.

[Reserving the issue of whether] the original understanding of the Due Process Clause precludes judicial enforcement of unenumerated rights under that constitutional provision . . . I agree with the plurality that this Court's recognition of a fundamental right of parents to direct the upbringing of their children resolves this case. . . .

Because the state supreme court had held the statute invalid on its face, Justice Stevens thought the Court should remand the case rather than conduct its own assessment of whether statute could be constitutionally applied here. "The task of reviewing a trial court's application of a state statute to the particular facts of a case," he argued, "is one that should be performed in the first instance by the state appellate courts."

JUSTICE SCALIA, dissenting.

. . . Only three holdings of this Court rest in whole or in part upon a substantive constitutional right of parents to direct the upbringing of their children—two of them from an era rich in substantive due process holdings that have since been repudiated. See *Meyer v. Nebraska* (1923); *Pierce v. Society of Sisters* (1925); *Wisconsin v. Yoder* (1972). . . . While I would not now overrule those earlier cases (that has not been urged), neither would I extend the theory upon which they rested to this new context.

Judicial vindication of "parental rights" under a Constitution that does not even mention them requires (as Justice Kennedy's opinion rightly points out) not only a judicially crafted definition of parents, but also—unless, as no one believes, the parental rights are to be absolute—judicially approved assessments of "harm to the child" and judicially defined gradations of other persons (grandparents, extended family, adoptive family in an adoption later found to be invalid, long-term guardians, etc.) who may have some claim against the wishes of the parents. If we embrace this unenumerated right, I think it obvious . . . that we will be ushering in a new regime of judicially prescribed, and federally prescribed, family law. I have no reason to believe that federal judges will be better at this than state legislatures; and state legislatures have the great advantages of doing harm in a more circumscribed area, of being able to correct their mistakes in a flash, and of being removable by the people.

For these reasons, I would reverse the judgment below.

JUSTICE KENNEDY, dissenting.

. . . [T]here is a beginning point that commands general, perhaps unanimous, agreement in our separate opinions: As our case law has developed, the custodial parent has a constitutional right to determine, without undue interference by the state, how best to raise, nurture, and educate the child. . . .

The State Supreme Court sought to give content to the parent's right by announcing a categorical rule that third parties who seek visitation must always prove the denial of visitation would "harm" the child. . . . "[S]hort of preventing harm to the child," the court considered the "best interests" of the child to be "insufficient to serve as a compelling state interest overruling a parent's fundamental rights." While it might be argued as an abstract matter that in some sense the child is always harmed if his or her best interests are not considered, the law of domestic relations, as it has evolved to this point, treats as distinct the two standards, one harm to the child and the other the best interests of the child. . . .

[The state supreme court's] holding seems to proceed from the assumption that the parent or parents who resist visitation have always been the child's primary caregivers and that the third parties who seek visitation have no legitimate and established relationship with the child. That idea, in turn, appears influenced by the concept that the conventional nuclear family ought to establish the visitation standard for every domestic relations case. As we all know, this is simply not the structure or prevailing condition in many households. See, *e.g.*, *Moore v. East Cleveland* (1977). Cases are sure to arise—perhaps a substantial number of cases—in which a third party, by acting in a caregiving role over a significant period of time, has developed a relationship with a child which is not necessarily subject to absolute parental veto. Some pre-existing relationships, then, serve to identify persons who have a strong attachment to the child with the concomitant motivation to act in a responsible way to ensure the child's welfare. . . .

In the design and elaboration of their visitation laws, States may be entitled to consider that certain relationships are such that to avoid the risk of harm, a best interests standard can be employed by their domestic relations courts in some circumstances. Indeed, contemporary practice should give us some pause before rejecting the best interests of the child standard in all third-party visitation cases, as the Washington court has done. The standard has been recognized for many years as a basic tool of domestic relations law in visitation proceedings. Since 1965 all 50 States have enacted a third-party visitation statute of some sort. Each of these statutes, save one, permits a court order to issue in certain cases if visitation is found to be in the best interests of the child. . . .

It should suffice in this case to reverse the holding of the State Supreme Court that the application of the best interests of the child standard is always unconstitutional in third-party visitation cases. Whether, under the circumstances of this case, the order requiring visitation over the objection of this fit parent violated the Constitution ought to be reserved for further proceedings. . . .

b. SDP—Bodily Integrity and Medical Autonomy

In *Buck v. Bell* (1927), over the silent dissent of Justice Butler, the Court upheld a state law providing for compulsory sterilization in certain defined circumstances, including hereditary "imbecility." Writing for the majority, Justice Holmes infamously proclaimed:

> We have seen more than once that the public welfare may call upon the best citizens for their lives. It would be strange if it could not call upon those who already sap the strength of the State for these lesser sacrifices, often not felt to be such by those concerned, in order to prevent our being swamped with incompetence. It is better for all the world, if instead of waiting to execute degenerate offspring for crime, or to let them starve for their imbecility, society can prevent those who are manifestly unfit from continuing their kind. The principle that sustains compulsory vaccination is broad enough to cover cutting the Fallopian tubes. *Jacobson v. Massachusetts* (1905). Three generations of imbeciles are enough.

The *Buck v. Bell* litigation appears to have been a shockingly collusive test case arranged by putatively opposing lawyers who were actually working together to secure the constitutionality of eugenics policies. Carrie Buck, the teenage girl challenging the constitutionality of the sterilization act, did not even meet the statutory requirements on their face:

WORTH NOTING

> Several of Carrie's own teachers could have attested, with supporting documentation, that Carrie was not mentally deficient. School records indicate that Carrie was a normal child: In the five years that she attended school, she was promoted to the sixth grade. In fact, the year before she left school, her teacher entered the comment "very good—deportment and lessons" and recommended her for promotion.

Paul A. Lombardo, *Three Generations, No Imbeciles: New Light on Buck v. Bell*, 60 N.Y.U. L. Rev. 30 (1985). One historian concludes that Carrie was targeted as part of what the state's expert in the case called a "'shiftless, ignorant and worthless class of anti-social whites,'" and that she had been committed to the institution by her guardians in an effort "to remove the embarrassment of a pregnant but unwed girl from their home" after she had been raped by their nephew. *Id.*

In *Skinner v. Oklahoma* (1942), however, the Court took a markedly different view with respect to Oklahoma's Habitual Criminal Sterilization Act, which provided for forced sterilization of those convicted of two or more crimes involving "moral turpitude." Though Justice Douglas's opinion for the Court concluded that the law violated equal protection—Skinner was convicted repeatedly of robbery, but if he had embezzled the same amount he would not have been subjected to sterilization—its language and logic had significant implications beyond cases of apparent discrimination:

> We are dealing here with legislation which involves one of the basic civil rights of man. Marriage and procreation are fundamental to the very existence and survival of the race. The power to sterilize, if exercised, may have subtle, far reaching and devastating effects. In evil or reckless hands it can cause races or types which are inimical to the dominant group to wither and disappear. There is no redemption for the individual whom the law touches. Any experiment which the State conducts is to his irreparable injury. He is forever deprived of a basic liberty. We mention these matters not to reexamine the scope of the police power of the States. We advert to them merely in emphasis of our view that strict scrutiny of the classification which a State makes in a sterilization law is essential, lest unwittingly or otherwise invidious discriminations are made against groups or types of individuals in violation of the constitutional guaranty of just and equal laws.

Note the conjunction of the term "strict scrutiny" with the concept that there are some (unenumerated) rights that are deemed "fundamental" and so worthy of particular constitutional protection. Thus arose the "fundamental rights" branch of strict scrutiny, dependent not on the use of a "suspect classification" but on a perception that the interest at stake was a fundamental one. *E.g., Kramer v. Union Free School Dist. No. 15* (1969) (invalidating a statute that allowed only owners or lessees of taxable realty (or their spouses) and parents or guardians of children in public schools to vote in certain school district elections); *Shapiro v. Thompson* (1969) (holding unconstitutional, as against the right of interstate movement, state laws denying welfare assistance to residents who had not resided within the state for at least one year immediately preceding their applications).

 For more detail, see subchapter B.5.

Rochin v. California

Supreme Court of the United States, 1952.
342 U.S. 165.

MR. JUSTICE FRANKFURTER delivered the opinion of the Court.

Having "some information that [the petitioner here] was selling narcotics," three deputy sheriffs of the County of Los Angeles, on the morning of July 1, 1949, made for the two-story dwelling house in which Rochin lived with his mother, common-law wife, brothers and sisters. Finding the outside door open, they entered and then forced open the door to Rochin's room on the second floor. Inside they found petitioner sitting partly dressed on the side of the bed, upon which his wife was lying.

On a "night stand" beside the bed the deputies spied two capsules. When asked "Whose stuff is this?" Rochin seized the capsules and put them in his mouth. A struggle ensued, in the course of which the three officers "jumped upon him" and attempted to extract the capsules. The force they applied proved unavailing against Rochin's resistance. He was handcuffed and taken to a hospital. At the direction of one of the officers a doctor forced an emetic solution through a tube into Rochin's stomach against his will. This "stomach pumping" produced vomiting. In the vomited matter were found two capsules which proved to contain morphine.

Rochin was brought to trial before a California Superior Court, sitting without a jury, on the charge of possessing "a preparation of morphine" in violation of the California Health and Safety Code. Rochin was convicted and sentenced to sixty days' imprisonment. The chief evidence against him was the two capsules. They were admitted over petitioner's objection, although the means of obtaining them was frankly set forth in the testimony by one of the deputies, substantially as here narrated. . . .

This Court granted certiorari because a serious question is raised as to the limitations which the Due Process Clause of the Fourteenth Amendment imposes on the conduct of criminal proceedings by the States. . . .

Regard for the requirements of the Due Process Clause "inescapably imposes upon this Court an exercise of judgment upon the whole course of the proceedings [resulting in a conviction] in order to ascertain whether they offend those canons of decency and fairness which express the notions of justice

1392 DOCTRINE AND PRACTICE SERIES: CONSTITUTIONAL LAW

of English-speaking peoples even toward those charged with the most heinous offenses." These standards of justice are not authoritatively formulated anywhere as though they were specifics. Due process of law is a summarized constitutional guarantee of respect for those personal immunities which, as Mr. Justice Cardozo twice wrote for the Court, are "so rooted in the traditions and conscience of our people as to be ranked as fundamental," *Snyder v. Commonwealth of Massachusetts* (1934), or are "implicit in the concept of ordered liberty," *Palko v. State of Connecticut* (1937). . . .

Due process of law . . . is not to be derided as resort to a revival of "natural law." To believe that this judicial exercise of judgment could be avoided by freezing "due process of law" at some fixed stage of time or thought is to suggest that the most important aspect of constitutional adjudication is a function for inanimate machines and not for judges, for whom the independence safeguarded by Article III of the Constitution was designed and who are presumably guided by established standards of judicial behavior. Even cybernetics has not yet made that haughty claim. To practice the requisite detachment and to achieve sufficient objectivity no doubt demands of judges the habit of self-discipline and self-criticism, incertitude that one's own views are incontestable and alert tolerance toward views not shared. But these are precisely the presuppositions of our judicial process. . . .

Applying these general considerations to the circumstances of the present case, we are compelled to conclude that the proceedings by which this conviction was obtained do more than offend some fastidious squeamishness or private sentimentalism about combatting crime too energetically. This is conduct that shocks the conscience. Illegally breaking into the privacy of the petitioner, the struggle to open his mouth and remove what was there, the forcible extraction of his stomach's contents—this course of proceeding by agents of government to obtain evidence is bound to offend even hardened sensibilities. They are methods too close to the rack and the screw to permit of constitutional differentiation.

. . . [Recent cases holding that convictions may not be based on confessions obtained by coercion] are only instances of the general requirement that States, in their prosecutions, respect certain decencies of civilized conduct. . . . Due process of law, as a historic and generative principle, precludes defining, and thereby confining, these standards of conduct more precisely than to say that convictions cannot be brought about by methods that offend "a sense of justice." It would be a stultification of the responsibility which the course of constitutional history has cast upon this Court to hold that in order to convict a man the police cannot extract by force what is in his mind but can extract what is in his stomach. . . .

On the facts of this case the conviction of the petitioner has been obtained by methods that offend the Due Process Clause. The judgment below must be reversed.

FOR DISCUSSION Exactly when was the Due Process Clause violated in *Rochin*? When police officers manhandled the defendant? When medical technicians forcibly pumped his stomach? When the trial judge admitted the morphine pills into evidence?

Mr. Justice Minton took no part in the consideration or decision of this case.

WORTH NOTING Justices Black and Douglas each concurred on the ground that Rochin had a right under the Fifth Amendment, made enforceable against the state by the Fourteenth, not "to be a witness against himself." (The Court had not yet held that this right was incorporated.) Most of Justice Black's opinion attacked "the majority's philosophy," which he said was marked by "evanescent standards" and "accordion-like qualities." Justice Douglas pointed out that the evidence in question would be held admissible in most states that had addressed the issue. Accordingly, he disagreed with the majority that the rule applied by those states violated the "decencies of civilized conduct": "It is a rule formulated by responsible courts with judges as sensitive as we are to the proper standards for law administration."

Consider also *Washington v. Harper*, 494 U.S. 210 (1990), in which the Court, per Justice Kennedy, held that, "that, given the requirements of the prison environment, the Due Process Clause permits the State to treat a prison inmate who has a serious mental illness with antipsychotic drugs against his will, if the inmate is dangerous to himself or others and the treatment is in the inmate's medical interest." Justice Stevens, joined by Justices Brennan and Marshall, agreed with the rest of the justices that the case was not rendered moot by the fact that the state was no longer administering the drugs against Harper's will, but dissented on the merits. He believed that Harper had a "substantive liberty interest to refuse psychotropic drugs, regardless of his medical interests," that the state had "sacrifice[d] . . . to institutional and administrative concerns."

Griswold v. Connecticut

Supreme Court of the United States, 1965.
381 U.S. 479.

Mr. Justice Douglas delivered the opinion of the Court.

Appellant Griswold is Executive Director of the Planned Parenthood League of Connecticut. Appellant Buxton is a licensed physician and a professor at the Yale Medical School who served as Medical Director for the League at its Center in New Haven—a center open and operating from November 1 to November 10, 1961, when appellants were arrested. They gave information, instruction, and medical advice to *married persons* as to the means of preventing conception. They examined the wife and prescribed the best contraceptive device or material for her use. Fees were usually charged, although some couples were serviced free.

The statutes whose constitutionality is involved in this appeal . . . provide[ ]:

> Any person who uses any drug, medicinal article or instrument for the purpose of preventing conception shall be fined not less than fifty dollars or imprisoned not less than sixty days nor more than one year or be both fined and imprisoned.
>
> Any person who assists, abets, counsels, causes, hires or commands another to commit any offense may be prosecuted and punished as if he were the principal offender.

The appellants were found guilty as accessories and fined $100 each, against the claim that the accessory statute as so applied violated the Fourteenth Amendment. . . .

We think that appellants have standing to raise the constitutional rights of the married people with whom they had a professional relationship. . . . Certainly the accessory should have standing to assert that the offense which he is charged with assisting is not, or cannot constitutionally be a crime. This case is [akin to] *Barrows v. Jackson* (1953), where a white defendant, party to a racially restrictive covenant, who was being sued for damages by the covenantors because she had conveyed her property to Negroes, was allowed to raise the issue that enforcement of the covenant violated the rights of prospective

Negro purchasers to equal protection, although no Negro was a party to the suit. The rights of husband and wife, pressed here, are likely to be diluted or adversely affected unless those rights are considered in a suit involving those who have this kind of confidential relation to them.

Coming to the merits, we are met with a wide range of questions that implicate the Due Process Clause of the Fourteenth Amendment. Overtones of some arguments suggest that *Lochner v. State of New York* (1905) should be our guide. But we decline that invitation as we did in *West Coast Hotel Co. v. Parrish* (1937) [and] *Williamson v. Lee Optical Co* (1955). We do not sit as a super-legislature to determine the wisdom, need, and propriety of laws that touch economic problems, business affairs, or social conditions.

This law, however, operates directly on an intimate relation of husband and wife and their physician's role in one aspect of that relation. The association of people is not mentioned in the Constitution nor in the Bill of Rights. The right to educate a child in a school of the parents' choice—whether public or private or parochial—is also not mentioned. Nor is the right to study any particular subject or any foreign language. Yet the First Amendment has been construed to include certain of those rights.

By *Pierce v. Society of Sisters* (1925), the right to educate one's children as one chooses is made applicable to the States by the force of the First and Fourteenth Amendments. By *Meyer v. State of Nebraska* (1923), the same dignity is given the right to study the German language in a private school. In other words, the State may not, consistently with the spirit of the First Amendment, contract the spectrum of available knowledge. The right of freedom of speech and press includes not only the right to utter or to print, but the right to distribute, the right to receive, the right to read and freedom of inquiry, freedom of thought, and freedom to teach—indeed the freedom of the entire university community. [Case citations omitted.] Without those peripheral rights the specific rights would be less secure. And so we reaffirm the principle of the *Pierce* and the *Meyer* cases.

In *NAACP v. State of Alabama* (1958) we protected the "freedom to associate and privacy in one's associations," noting that freedom of association was a peripheral First Amendment right. Disclosure of membership lists of a constitutionally valid association, we held, was invalid "as entailing the likelihood of a substantial restraint upon the exercise by petitioner's members of their right to freedom of association." In other words, the First Amendment has a penumbra where privacy is protected from governmental intrusion.

In like context, we have protected forms of "association" that are not political in the customary sense but pertain to the social, legal, and economic benefit of the members. . . . Those cases involved more than the "right of assembly"—a right that extends to all irrespective of their race or ideology. The right of "association," like the right of belief, is more than the right to attend a meeting; it includes the right to express one's attitudes or philosophies by membership in a group or by affiliation with it or by other lawful means. Association in that context is a form of expression of opinion; and while it is not expressly included in the First Amendment its existence is necessary in making the express guarantees fully meaningful.

The foregoing cases suggest that specific guarantees in the Bill of Rights have penumbras, formed by emanations from those guarantees that help give them life and substance. Various guarantees create zones of privacy. The right of association contained in the penumbra of the First Amendment is one, as we have seen. The Third Amendment in its prohibition against the quartering of soldiers "in any house" in time of peace without the consent of the owner is another facet of that privacy. The Fourth Amendment explicitly affirms the "right of the people to be secure in their persons, houses, papers, and effects, against unreasonable searches and seizures." The Fifth Amendment in its Self-Incrimination Clause enables the citizen to create a zone of privacy which government may not force him to surrender to his detriment. The Ninth Amendment provides: "The enumeration in the Constitution, of certain rights, shall not be construed to deny or disparage others retained by the people."

The Fourth and Fifth Amendments were described in *Boyd v. United States* (1886) as protection against all governmental invasions "of the sanctity of a man's home and the privacies of life." * We recently referred in *Mapp v. Ohio*

---

*   The Court said in full about this right of privacy:

The principles laid down in this opinion (by Lord Camden in [the English case] *Entick v. Carrington*, [5 E.R. 807 (K.B. 1765)]) affect the very essence of constitutional liberty and security. They reach further than the concrete form of the case then before the court, with its adventitious circumstances; they apply to all invasions on the part of the government and its employés of the sanctity of a man's home and the privacies of life. It is not the breaking of his doors, and the rummaging of his drawers, that constitutes the essence of the offense; but it is the invasion of his indefeasible right of personal security, personal liberty and private property, where that right has never been forfeited by his conviction of some public offense—it is the invasion of this sacred right which underlies and constitutes the essence of Lord Camden's judgment. Breaking into a house and opening boxes and drawers are circumstances of aggravation; but any forcible and compulsory extortion of a man's own testimony, or of his private papers to be used as

(1961) to the Fourth Amendment as creating a "right to privacy, no less im-

portant than any other right carefully and particularly reserved to the people." See Beaney, *The Constitutional Right to Privacy*, 1962 Sup. Ct. Rev. 212; Griswold, *The Right to be Let Alone*, 55 Nw. U. L. Rev. 216 (1960). We have had many controversies over these penumbral rights of "privacy and repose." See, *e.g.*, *Skinner v. State of Oklahoma* (1942) (holding the

WORTH NOTING

Entick v. Carrington, the old English case cited by the *Boyd* Court in support of this "sanctity of a man's home" language (see the footnote), set out limits on executive power in the absence of legislative authorization; it did not purport to limit legislative power.

compulsory sterilization of criminals unconstitutional). These cases bear witness that the right of privacy which presses for recognition here is a legitimate one.

The present case, then, concerns a relationship lying within the zone of privacy created by several fundamental constitutional guarantees. And it concerns a law which, in forbidding the use of contraceptives rather than regulating their manufacture or sale, seeks to achieve its goals by means having a maximum destructive impact upon that relationship. Such a law cannot stand in light of the familiar principle, so often applied by this Court, that a "governmental purpose to control or prevent activities constitutionally subject to state regulation may not be achieved by means which sweep unnecessarily broadly and thereby invade the area of protected freedoms." Would we allow the police to search the sacred precincts of marital bedrooms for telltale signs of the use of contraceptives? The very idea is repulsive to the notions of privacy surrounding the marriage relationship.

We deal with a right of privacy older than the Bill of Rights—older than our political parties, older than our school system. Marriage is a coming together for better or for worse, hopefully enduring, and intimate to the degree of being sacred. It is an association that promotes a way of life, not causes; a harmony in living, not political faiths; a bilateral loyalty, not commercial or social projects. Yet it is an association for as noble a purpose as any involved in our prior decisions.

Reversed.

---

evidence to convict him of crime, or to forfeit his goods, is within the condemnation of that judgment. In this regard the fourth and fifth amendments run almost into each other.

MR. JUSTICE GOLDBERG, whom THE CHIEF JUSTICE and MR. JUSTICE BREN-
NAN join, concurring.

I agree with the Court that Connecticut's birth-control law unconstitutionally intrudes upon the right of marital privacy, and I join in its opinion and
judgment. Although I have not accepted the view that "due process" as used in
the Fourteenth Amendment incorporates all of the first eight Amendments, I
do agree that the concept of liberty protects those personal rights that are fundamental, and is not confined to the specific terms of the Bill of Rights. My
conclusion that the concept of liberty is not so restricted and that it embraces
the right of marital privacy though that right is not mentioned explicitly in the
Constitution[1] is supported both by numerous decisions of this Court, referred to
in the Court's opinion, and by the language and history of the Ninth Amendment. In reaching the conclusion that the right of marital privacy is protected,
as being within the protected penumbra of specific guarantees of the Bill of
Rights, the Court refers to the Ninth Amendment. I add these words to emphasize the relevance of that Amendment to the Court's holding.

The Court stated many years ago that the Due Process Clause protects
those liberties that are "so rooted in the traditions and conscience of our people
as to be ranked as fundamental." *Snyder v. Com. of Massachusetts* (1934) [(holding that felony defendants are constitutionally entitled to be present during the
trial)]. . . . And, in *Meyer v. State of Nebraska* (1923), the Court, referring to the
Fourteenth Amendment, stated:

> While this Court has not attempted to define with exactness the
> liberty thus guaranteed, the term has received much consideration
> and some of the included things have been definitely stated. Without
> doubt, it denotes not merely freedom from bodily restraint but also
> (for example,) the right . . . to marry, establish a home and bring up
> children. . . .

---

[1]   My Brother Stewart dissents on the ground that he "can find no . . . general right of privacy in the Bill of
Rights, in any other part of the Constitution, or in any case ever before decided by this Court." He would require
a more explicit guarantee than the one which the Court derives from several constitutional amendments. This
Court, however, has never held that the Bill of Rights or the Fourteenth Amendment protects only those rights
that the Constitution specifically mentions by name. See, *e.g.*, *Bolling v. Sharpe* (1954) [(equal protection as against
the federal government)]; *NAACP v. Alabama* (1958)[(anonymous association)]; *Pierce v. Society of Sisters* (1925)
[(send a child to private school)]; *Meyer v. State of Nebraska* (1923) ([educate a child in a foreign language]). To
the contrary, this Court, for example, in *Bolling v. Sharpe*, while recognizing that the Fifth Amendment does not
contain the "explicit safeguard" of an equal protection clause, nevertheless derived an equal protection principle
from that Amendment's Due Process Clause. . . .

This Court, in a series of decisions, has held that the Fourteenth Amendment absorbs and applies to the States those specifics of the first eight amendments which express fundamental personal rights. The language and history of the Ninth Amendment reveal that the Framers of the Constitution believed that there are additional fundamental rights, protected from governmental infringement, which exist alongside those fundamental rights specifically mentioned in the first eight constitutional amendments.

The Ninth Amendment . . . is almost entirely the work of James Madison. It was introduced in Congress by him and passed the House and Senate with little or no debate and virtually no change in language. It was proffered to quiet expressed fears that a bill of specifically enumerated rights could not be sufficiently broad to cover all essential rights and that the specific mention of certain rights would be interpreted as a denial that others were protected. [Justice Goldberg here quotes James Madison acknowledging that the enumeration of some rights might possibly be taken to disparage the existence of others, and presenting the proposed Ninth Amendment as a means by which this danger might be "guarded against."] These statements . . . make clear that the Framers did not intend that the first eight amendments be construed to exhaust the basic and fundamental rights which the Constitution guaranteed to the people.

While this Court has had little occasion to interpret the Ninth Amendment,[6] "[i]t cannot be presumed that any clause in the constitution is intended to be without effect." *Marbury v. Madison* (1803). In interpreting the Constitution, "real effect should be given to all the words it uses." *Myers v. United States* (1925). The Ninth Amendment to the Constitution may be regarded by some as a recent discovery and may be forgotten by others, but since 1791 it has been a basic part of the Constitution which we are sworn to uphold. To hold that a right so basic and fundamental and so deep rooted in our society as the right of privacy in marriage may be infringed because that right is not guaranteed in so many words by the first eight amendments to the Constitution is to ignore the Ninth Amendment and to give it no effect whatsoever. Moreover, a judicial construction that this fundamental right is not protected by the Constitution because it is not mentioned in explicit terms by one of the first eight amendments or elsewhere in the Constitution would violate the Ninth Amendment, which

---

6   This Amendment has been referred to as "The Forgotten Ninth Amendment," in a book with that title by Bennett B. Patterson (1955). . . . As far as I am aware, until today this Court has referred to the Ninth Amendment only in *United Public Workers v. Mitchell* (1945); *Tennessee Electric Power Co. v. TVA* (1939); and *Ashwander v. TVA* (1936). See also *Calder v. Bull* (1798)[, presented at pp. 1306–1310].

specifically states that "[t]he enumeration in the Constitution, of certain rights shall not be construed to deny or disparage others retained by the people." . . .

Nor am I turning somersaults with history in arguing that the Ninth Amendment is relevant in a case dealing with a State's infringement of a fundamental right. While the Ninth Amendment—and indeed the entire Bill of Rights—originally concerned restrictions upon federal power, the subsequently enacted Fourteenth Amendment prohibits the States as well from abridging fundamental personal liberties. And, the Ninth Amendment, in indicating that not all such liberties are specifically mentioned in the first eight amendments, is surely relevant in showing the existence of other fundamental personal rights, now protected from state, as well as federal, infringement. In sum, the Ninth Amendment simply lends strong support to the view that the "liberty" protected by the Fifth and Fourteenth Amendments from infringement by the Federal Government or the States is not restricted to rights specifically mentioned in the first eight amendments. . . .

I agree fully with the Court that . . . the right of privacy is a fundamental personal right, emanating "from the totality of the constitutional scheme under which we live." . . .

The logic of the dissents would sanction federal or state legislation that seems to me even more plainly unconstitutional than the statute before us. Surely the Government, absent a showing of a compelling subordinating state interest, could not decree that all husbands and wives must be sterilized after two children have been born to them. Yet by their reasoning such an invasion of marital privacy would not be subject to constitutional challenge because, while it might be "silly," no provision of the Constitution specifically prevents the Government from curtailing the marital right to bear children and raise a family. While it may shock some of my Brethren that the Court today holds that the Constitution protects the right of marital privacy, in my view it is far more shocking to believe that the personal liberty guaranteed by the Constitution does not include protection against such totalitarian limitation of family size, which is at complete variance with our constitutional concepts. . . .

Finally, it should be said of the Court's holding today that it in no way interferes with a State's proper regulation of sexual promiscuity or misconduct. As my Brother Harlan so well stated in his dissenting opinion in *Poe v. Ullman* (1961):

Adultery, homosexuality and the like are sexual intimacies which the State forbids . . . but the intimacy of husband and wife is necessarily an essential and accepted feature of the institution of marriage, an institution which the State not only must allow, but which always and in every age it has fostered and protected. It is one thing when the State exerts its power either to forbid extra-marital sexuality . . . or to say who may marry, but it is quite another when, having acknowledged a marriage and the intimacies inherent in it, it undertakes to regulate by means of the criminal law the details of that intimacy.

. . .

Mr. Justice Harlan, concurring in the judgment.

I fully agree with the judgment of reversal, but find myself unable to join the Court's opinion. The reason is that it seems to me to evince an approach to this case very much like that taken by my Brothers Black and Stewart in dissent, namely: the Due Process Clause of the Fourteenth Amendment does not touch this Connecticut statute unless the enactment is found to violate some right assured by the letter or penumbra of the Bill of Rights. . . . For me this is just as unacceptable constitutional doctrine as is the use of the "incorporation" approach to impose upon the States all the requirements of the Bill of Rights as found in the provisions of the first eight amendments. . . .

In my view, the proper constitutional inquiry in this case is whether this Connecticut statute infringes the Due Process Clause of the Fourteenth Amendment because the enactment violates basic values "implicit in the concept of ordered liberty," *Palko v. State of Connecticut* (1937). For reasons stated at length in my dissenting opinion in *Poe v. Ullman* (1960), I believe that it does. While the relevant inquiry may be aided by resort to one or more of the provisions of the Bill of Rights, it is not dependent on them or any of their radiations. The Due Process Clause of the Fourteenth Amendment stands, in my opinion, on its own bottom. . . .

A further observation seems in order respecting the justification of my Brothers Black and Stewart for their "incorporation" approach to this case. Their approach [rests] on the thesis that by limiting the content of the Due Process Clause of the Fourteenth Amendment to the protection of rights which can be found elsewhere in the Constitution, in this instance in the Bill of Rights, judges will thus be confined to "interpretation" of specific constitutional provisions, and will thereby be restrained from introducing their own notions of constitutional right and wrong into the "vague contours of the Due Process Clause."

While I could not more heartily agree that judicial "self restraint" is an indispensable ingredient of sound constitutional adjudication, I do submit that the formula suggested for achieving it is more hollow than real. "Specific" provisions of the Constitution, no less than "due process," lend themselves as readily to "personal" interpretations by judges whose constitutional outlook is simply to keep the Constitution in supposed "tune with the times." Need one go further than to recall last Term's reapportionment cases, *Wesberry v. Sanders* and *Reynolds v. Sims* (1964), where a majority of the Court "interpreted" "by the People" (Art. I, § 2) and "equal protection" (Amdt. 14) to command "one person, one vote," an interpretation that was made in the face of irrefutable and still unanswered history to the contrary?

Judicial self-restraint . . . will be achieved in this area, as in other constitutional areas, only by continual insistence upon respect for the teachings of history, solid recognition of the basic values that underlie our society, and wise appreciation of the great roles that the doctrines of federalism and separation of powers have played in establishing and preserving American freedoms. Adherence to these principles will not, of course, obviate all constitutional differences of opinion among judges, nor should it. Their continued recognition will, however, go farther toward keeping most judges from roaming at large in the constitutional field than will the interpolation into the Constitution of an artificial and largely illusory restriction on the content of the Due Process Clause.

Mr. Justice White, concurring in the judgment.

. . . [Our previous] decisions affirm that there is a "realm of family life which the state cannot enter" without substantial justification. *Prince v. Massachusetts* (1944). . . . There is no serious contention [in this case] that Connecticut thinks the use of artificial or external methods of contraception immoral or unwise in itself, or that the anti-use statute is founded upon any policy of promoting population expansion. Rather, the statute is said to serve the State's policy against all forms of promiscuous or illicit sexual

WORTH NOTING Though it cited *Meyer* and *Pierce*, the *Prince* decision ultimately recognized broad state authority to regulate in the best interests of children, in that case by prohibiting them from selling literature on the streets.

relationships, be they premarital or extramarital, concededly a permissible and legitimate legislative goal.

Without taking issue with the premise that the fear of conception operates as a deterrent to such relationships in addition to the criminal proscriptions Connecticut has against such conduct, I wholly fail to see how the ban on the use of contraceptives by married couples in any way reinforces the State's ban on illicit sexual relationships. Connecticut does not bar the importation or possession of contraceptive devices; they are not considered contraband material under state law, and their availability in that State is not seriously disputed. The only way Connecticut seeks to limit or control the availability of such devices is through its general aiding and abetting statute whose operation in this context has been quite obviously ineffective and whose most serious use has been against birth-control clinics rendering advice to married, rather than unmarried, persons. . . . Moreover, it would appear that the sale of contraceptives to prevent disease is plainly legal under Connecticut law.

In these circumstances one is rather hard pressed to explain how the ban on use by married persons in any way prevents use of such devices by persons engaging in illicit sexual relations and thereby contributes to the State's policy against such relationships. . . . I find nothing in this record justifying the sweeping scope of this statute, with its telling effect on the freedoms of married persons, and therefore conclude that it deprives such persons of liberty without due process of law.

MR. JUSTICE BLACK, with whom MR. JUSTICE STEWART joins, dissenting.

. . . In order that there may be no room at all to doubt why I vote as I do, I feel constrained to add that the law is every bit as offensive to me as it is to my Brethren of the majority and my Brothers Harlan, White and Goldberg who, reciting reasons why it is offensive to them, hold it unconstitutional. There is no single one of the graphic and eloquent strictures and criticisms fired at the policy of this Connecticut law either by the Court's opinion or by those of my concurring Brethren to which I cannot subscribe—except their conclusion that the evil qualities they see in the law make it unconstitutional. . . .

The Court talks about a constitutional "right of privacy" as though there is some constitutional provision or provisions forbidding any law ever to be passed which might abridge the "privacy" of individuals. But there is not. There are, of course, guarantees in certain specific constitutional provisions which are designed in part to protect privacy at certain times and places with respect to certain activities. Such, for example, is the Fourth Amendment's guarantee against "unreasonable searches and seizures." But I think it belittles that Amendment to talk about it as though it protects nothing but "privacy." . . .

One of the most effective ways of diluting or expanding a constitutionally guaranteed right is to substitute for the crucial word or words of a constitutional guarantee another word or words, more or less flexible and more or less restricted in meaning. This fact is well illustrated by the use of the term "right of privacy" as a comprehensive substitute for the Fourth Amendment's guarantee against "unreasonable searches and seizures." "Privacy" is a broad, abstract and ambiguous concept which can easily be shrunken in meaning but which can also, on the other hand, easily be interpreted as a constitutional ban against many things other than searches and seizures. I have expressed the view many times that First Amendment freedoms, for example, have suffered from a failure of the courts to stick to the simple language of the First Amendment in construing it, instead of invoking multitudes of words substituted for those the Framers used.

For these reasons I get nowhere in this case by talk about a constitutional "right of privacy" as an emanation from one or more constitutional provisions.[1] I like my privacy as well as the next one, but I am nevertheless compelled to admit that government has a right to invade it unless prohibited by some specific constitutional provision. For these reasons I cannot agree with the Court's judgment and the reasons it gives for holding this Connecticut law unconstitutional. . . .

I have no doubt that the Connecticut law could be applied in such a way as to abridge freedom of speech and press and therefore violate the First and Fourteenth Amendments. My disagreement with the Court's opinion holding that there is such a violation here is a narrow one, relating to the application of the First Amendment to the facts and circumstances of this particular case. But my disagreement with Brothers Harlan, White and Goldberg is more basic. I think that if properly construed neither the Due Process Clause nor the Ninth Amendment, nor both together, could under any circumstances be a

---

[1] The phrase "right to privacy" appears first to have gained currency from an article written by Messrs. Warren and (later Mr. Justice) Brandeis in 1890 which urged that States should give some form of tort relief to persons whose private affairs were exploited by others. *The Right to Privacy*, 4 Harv. L. Rev. 193. Largely as a result of this article, some States have passed statutes creating such a cause of action, and in others state courts have done the same thing by exercising their powers as courts of common law. . . . [T]oday this Court, which I did not understand to have power to sit as a court of common law, now appears to be exalting a phrase which Warren and Brandeis used in discussing grounds for tort relief, to the level of a constitutional rule which prevents state legislatures from passing any law deemed by this Court to interfere with "privacy."

proper basis for invalidating the Connecticut law. I discuss the due process and Ninth Amendment arguments together because on analysis they turn out to be the same thing—merely using different words to claim for this Court and the federal judiciary power to invalidate any legislative act which the judges find irrational, unreasonable or offensive.

The due process argument which my Brothers Harlan and White adopt here is based, as their opinions indicate, on the premise that this Court is vested with power to invalidate all state laws that it considers to be arbitrary, capricious, unreasonable, or oppressive, or on this Court's belief that a particular state law under scrutiny has no "rational or justifying" purpose, or is offensive to a "sense of fairness and justice." If these formulas based on "natural justice," or others which mean the same thing,[4] are to prevail, they require judges to determine what is or is not constitutional on the basis of their own appraisal of what laws are unwise or unnecessary. . . . Such an appraisal of the wisdom of legislation is an attribute of the power to make laws, not of the power to interpret them. . . .

The Due Process Clause with an "arbitrary and capricious" or "shocking to the conscience" formula was liberally used by this Court to strike down economic legislation in the early decades of this century, threatening, many people thought, the tranquility and stability of the Nation. See, *e.g., Lochner v. State of New York.* That formula, based on subjective considerations of "natural justice," is no less dangerous when used to enforce this Court's views about personal rights than those about economic rights. I had thought that we had laid that formula, as a means for striking down state legislation, to rest once and for all in cases like *West Coast Hotel Co. v. Parrish* (1937) and many other opinions. See also *Lochner v. New York* (Holmes, J., dissenting). . . . Apparently my Brethren have less quarrel with state economic regulations than former Justices of their persuasion had. But any limitation upon their using the natural law due process

---

[4]   A collection of the catchwords and catch phrases invoked by judges who would strike down under the Fourteenth Amendment laws which offend their notions of natural justice would fill many pages. Thus it has been said that this Court can forbid state action which "shocks the conscience" . . . . It has been urged that States may not run counter to the "decencies of civilized conduct," or "some principle of justice so rooted in the traditions and conscience of our people as to be ranked as fundamental," or to "those canons of decency and fairness which express the notions of justice of English-speaking peoples," or to "the community's sense of fair play and decency." . . . States, under this philosophy, cannot act in conflict with "deeply rooted feelings of the community" or with "fundamental notions of fairness and justice." See also, *e.g. Wolf v. People of State of Colorado* (1949) ("rights . . . basic to our free society"); *Hebert v. State of Louisiana* (1926) ("fundamental principles of liberty and justice"); *Adkins v. Children's Hospital* (1923) ("arbitrary restraint of . . . liberties"); *Betts v. Brady* (1942) ("denial of fundamental fairness, shocking to the universal sense of justice"); *Poe v. Ullman* (1961) (dissenting opinion) ("intolerable and unjustifiable"). Perhaps the clearest, frankest and briefest explanation of how this due process approach works is the statement in another case handed down today that this Court is to invoke the Due Process Clause to strike down state procedures or laws which it can "not tolerate." *Linkletter v. Walker* (1965).

philosophy to strike down any state law, dealing with any activity whatever, will obviously be only self-imposed. [Justice Black here quotes from Justice Iredell's opinion in *Calder v. Bull* (1798); see pp. 1306–1310.]

MR. JUSTICE STEWART, whom MR. JUSTICE BLACK joins, dissenting.

Since 1879 Connecticut has had on its books a law which forbids the use of contraceptives by anyone. I think this is an uncommonly silly law. As a practical matter, the law is obviously unenforceable, except in the oblique context of the present case. As a philosophical matter, I believe the use of contraceptives in the relationship of marriage should be left to personal and private choice, based upon each individual's moral, ethical, and religious beliefs. As a matter of social policy, I think professional counsel about methods of birth control should be available to all, so that each individual's choice can be meaningfully made. But we are not asked in this case to say whether we think this law is unwise, or even asinine. We are asked to hold that it violates the United States Constitution. And that I cannot do.

In the course of its opinion the Court refers to no less than six Amendments to the Constitution: the First, the Third, the Fourth, the Fifth, the Ninth, and the Fourteenth. But the Court does not say which of these Amendments, if any, it thinks is infringed by this Connecticut law. . . . What provision of the Constitution, then, does make this state law invalid? The Court says it is the right of privacy "created by several fundamental constitutional guarantees." With all deference, I can find no such general right of privacy in the Bill of Rights, in any other part of the Constitution, or in any case ever before decided by this Court. . . .

It is the essence of judicial duty to subordinate our own personal views, our own ideas of what legislation is wise and what is not. If, as I should surely hope, the law before us does not reflect the standards of the people of Connecticut, the people of Connecticut can freely exercise their true Ninth and Tenth Amendment rights to persuade their elected representatives to repeal it. That is the constitutional way to take this law off the books.

In *Eisenstadt v. Baird* (1972), the Court extended *Griswold* to bar a narrower state law that prohibited distribution of contraceptives to unmarried persons. Justice Brennan's opinion for a 6–1 majority reflected a remarkable change of attitude since 1964, when *McLaughlin v. Florida* (1964), p. 1012, had assumed that a state had a valid interest in prohibiting sexual intercourse outside of marriage:

> If under *Griswold* the distribution of contraceptives to married persons cannot be prohibited, a ban on distribution to unmarried persons would be equally impermissible. It is true that in *Griswold* the right of privacy in question inhered in the marital relationship. Yet the marital couple is not an independent entity with a mind and heart of its own, but an association of two individuals each with a separate intellectual and emotional makeup. If the right of privacy means anything, it is the right of the individual, married or single, to be free from unwarranted governmental intrusion into matters so fundamentally affecting a person as the decision whether to bear or beget a child.

Anti-contraception laws were not common in this era, or actively enforced. Laws governing consensual conduct were common, but also not often enforced. *Griswold* and *Eisenstadt* were not particularly controversial decisions outside legal circles. By contrast, abortion decisions have created deep controversy, both inside and outside those circles, for nearly half a century.

c.   SDP—Abortion

Many different threads of substantive due process doctrine converge in the abortion context: family, bodily integrity, autonomy, and perhaps others too. See how well you think the precedents on which *Roe v. Wade* is grounded support its recognition of a constitutional right to abortion. How much does the answer to that question depend on the legitimacy of reasoning by analogy in constitutional adjudication?

Roe v. Wade

Supreme Court of the United States, 1973.
410 U.S. 113.

MR. JUSTICE BLACKMUN delivered the opinion of the Court.

This Texas federal appeal . . . present[s] constitutional challenges to state criminal abortion legislation. The Texas statutes under attack here are typical of those that have been in effect in many States for approximately a century. . . .

We forthwith acknowledge our awareness of the sensitive and emotional nature of the abortion controversy, of the vigorous opposing views, even among physicians, and of the deep and seemingly absolute convictions that the subject inspires. One's philosophy, one's experiences, one's exposure to the raw edges of human existence, one's religious training, one's attitudes toward life and family and their values, and the moral standards one establishes and seeks to observe, are all likely to influence and to color one's thinking and conclusions about abortion. In addition, population growth, pollution, poverty, and racial overtones tend to complicate and not to simplify the problem.

Our task, of course, is to resolve the issue by constitutional measurement, free of emotion and of predilection. We seek earnestly to do this, and, because we do, we have inquired into, and in this opinion place some emphasis upon, medical and medical-legal history and what that history reveals about man's attitudes toward the abortion procedure over the centuries. We bear in mind, too, Mr. Justice Holmes' admonition in his now-vindicated dissent in *Lochner v. New York* (1905): "[The Constitution] is made for people of fundamentally differing views. . . ."

I

The Texas statutes . . . make it a crime to "procure an abortion," as therein defined, or to attempt one, except with respect to "an abortion procured or attempted by medical advice for the purpose of saving the life of the mother." Similar statutes are in existence in a majority of the States. . . .

II

Jane Roe,[4] a single woman who was residing in Dallas County, Texas, instituted this federal action in March 1970 against the District Attorney of the county. She sought a declaratory judgment that the Texas criminal abortion statutes were unconstitutional on their face, and an injunction restraining the defendant from enforcing the statutes.

Roe alleged that she was unmarried and pregnant; that she wished to terminate her pregnancy by an abortion "performed by a competent, licensed physician, under safe, clinical conditions"; that she was unable to get a "legal" abortion in Texas because her life did not appear to be threatened by the continuation of her pregnancy; and that she could not afford to travel to another

---

4   The name is a pseudonym.

jurisdiction in order to secure a legal abortion under safe conditions. She claimed that the Texas statutes were unconstitutionally vague and that they abridged her right of personal privacy, protected by the First, Fourth, Fifth, Ninth, and Fourteenth Amendments. . . .

IV

We are . . . confronted with issues of justiciability [and] standing. . . . Ha[s] Roe . . . established that "personal stake in the outcome of the controversy," *Baker v. Carr* (1962), that insures that "the dispute sought to be adjudicated will be presented in an adversary context and in a form historically viewed as capable of judicial resolution"? . . .

The usual rule in federal cases is that an actual controversy must exist at stages of appellate or certiorari review, and not simply at the date the action is initiated. But when, as here, pregnancy is a significant fact in the litigation, the normal 266-day human gestation period is so short that the pregnancy will come to term before the usual appellate process is complete. If that termination makes a case moot, pregnancy litigation seldom will survive much beyond the trial stage, and appellate review will be effectively denied.

Our law should not be that rigid. Pregnancy often comes more than once to the same woman, and in the general population, if man is to survive, it will always be with us. Pregnancy provides a classic justification for a conclusion of nonmootness. It truly could be "capable of repetition, yet evading review." *Southern Pacific Terminal Co. v. ICC* (1911). We, therefore, agree with the District Court that Jane Roe had standing to undertake this litigation, that she presented a justiciable controversy, and that the termination of her 1970 pregnancy has not rendered her case moot. . . .

V

The principal thrust of appellant's attack on the Texas statutes is that they improperly invade a right, said to be possessed by the pregnant woman, to choose to terminate her pregnancy. Appellant would discover this right in the concept of personal "liberty" embodied in the Fourteenth Amendment's Due Process Clause; or in personal marital, familial, and sexual privacy said to be protected by the Bill of Rights or its penumbras, see *Griswold v. Connecticut* (1965); *Eisenstadt v. Baird* (1972); or among those rights reserved to the people by the Ninth Amendment, *Griswold v. Connecticut* (Goldberg, J., concurring). Before addressing this claim, we feel it desirable briefly to survey, in several aspects, the history of abortion, for such insight as that history may afford us, and then to examine the state purposes and interests behind the criminal abortion laws.

VI

It perhaps is not generally appreciated that the restrictive criminal abortion laws in effect in a majority of States today are of relatively recent vintage. Those laws, generally proscribing abortion or its attempt at any time during pregnancy except when necessary to preserve the pregnant woman's life, are not of ancient or even of common-law origin. Instead, they derive from statutory changes effected, for the most part, in the latter half of the 19th century. . . .

WORTH NOTING Here, the Court reviewed the ancient history of abortion; abortion was allowed in most ancient societies. The Hippocratic Oath forbade doctors to perform abortions, but the Court concluded that this reflected a minority view through most of antiquity.

    3. The common law. It is undisputed that at common law, abortion performed before "quickening"—the first recognizable movement of the fetus *in utero*, appearing usually from the 16th to the 18th week of pregnancy—was not an indictable offense. The absence of a common-law crime for pre-quickening abortion appears to have developed from a confluence of earlier philosophical, theological, and civil and canon law concepts of when life begins.

    These disciplines variously approached the question in terms of the point at which the embryo or fetus became "formed" or recognizably human, or in terms of when a "person" came into being, that is, infused with a "soul" or "animated." A loose consensus evolved in early English law that these events occurred at some point between conception and live birth. This was "mediate animation." Although Christian theology and the canon law came to fix the point of animation at 40 days for a male and 80 days for a female, . . . there was otherwise little agreement about the precise time of formation or animation. There was agreement, however, that prior to this point the fetus was to be regarded as part of the mother, and its destruction, therefore, was not homicide. Due to continued uncertainty about the precise time when animation occurred, to the lack of any empirical basis for the 40–80 day view, and perhaps to Aquinas' definition of movement as one of the two first principles of life, [the English treatise writer] Bracton focused upon quickening as the critical point.

The significance of quickening was echoed by later common-law scholars and found its way into the received common law in this country.

Whether abortion of a quick fetus was a felony at common law, or even a lesser crime, is still disputed. Bracton, writing early in the 13th century, thought it homicide. But the later and predominant view, following the great common-law scholars, has been that it was, at most, a lesser offense. In a frequently cited passage, [the 17th-century jurist Edward] Coke took the position that abortion of a woman "quick with childe" is "a great misprision, and no murder." Blackstone followed, saying that while abortion after quickening had once been considered manslaughter (though not murder), "modern law" took a less severe view. A recent review of the common-law precedents argues, however, that those precedents contradict Coke and that even post-quickening abortion was never established as a common-law crime. [Means, *The Phoenix of Abortional Freedom*, 17 N.Y.L.F. 335 (1971).] This is of some importance because while most American courts ruled, in holding or dictum, that abortion of an unquickened fetus was not criminal under their received common law, others followed Coke in stating that abortion of a quick fetus was a "misprision," a term they translated to mean "misdemeanor." . . .

4.   *The English statutory law.* England's first criminal abortion statute, Lord Ellenborough's Act, came in 1803. It made abortion of a quick fetus a capital crime, but it provided lesser penalties for the felony of abortion before quickening, and thus preserved the "quickening" distinction. . . .

5.   *The American law.* In this country, the law in effect in all but a few States until mid-19th century was the pre-existing English common law. Connecticut, the first State to enact abortion legislation, adopted in 1821 that part of Lord Ellenborough's Act that related to a woman "quick with child." The death penalty

WORTH NOTING The Court goes on to discuss further developments in English law, down to the Abortion Act of 1967, which allowed abortion under certain restrictive circumstances—primarily if continued pregnancy would threaten the life or health of the mother, or if there was a substantial risk that the child would be "seriously handicapped."

was not imposed. Abortion before quickening was made a crime in that State only in 1860. In 1828, New York enacted legislation that, in two respects, was to serve as a model for early anti-abortion statutes[:]

- First, while barring destruction of an unquickened fetus as well as a quick fetus, it made the former only a misdemeanor, but the latter second-degree manslaughter.

- Second, it incorporated a concept of therapeutic abortion by providing that an abortion was excused if it "shall have been necessary to preserve the life of such mother, or shall have been advised by two physicians to be necessary for such purpose."

By 1840, when Texas had received the common law, only eight American States had statutes dealing with abortion. It was not until after the War Between the States that legislation began generally to replace the common law. Most of these initial statutes dealt severely with abortion after quickening but were lenient with it before quickening. Most punished attempts equally with completed abortions. While many statutes included the exception for an abortion thought by one or more physicians to be necessary to save the mother's life, that provision soon disappeared and the typical law required that the procedure actually be necessary for that purpose.

Gradually, in the middle and late 19th century the quickening distinction disappeared from the statutory law of most States and the degree of the offense and the penalties were increased. By the end of the 1950's a large majority of the jurisdictions banned abortion, however and whenever performed, unless done to save or preserve the life of the mother. The exceptions, Alabama and the District of Columbia, permitted abortion to preserve the mother's health. Three States permitted abortions that were not "unlawfully" performed or that were not "without lawful justification," leaving interpretation of those standards to the courts. In the past several years, however, a trend toward liberalization of abortion statutes has resulted in adoption, by about one-third of the States, of less stringent laws, most of them patterned after the ALI Model Penal Code, § 230.3.

It is thus apparent that at common law, at the time of the adoption of our Constitution, and throughout the major portion of the 19th century, abortion was viewed with less disfavor than under most American statutes currently in effect. Phrasing it another way, a woman enjoyed a substantially broader right to terminate a pregnancy than she does in most States today. At least with respect to the early stage of pregnancy, and very possibly without such a limitation, the opportunity to make this choice was present in this country well into the

19th century. Even later, the law continued for some time to treat less punitively an abortion procured in early pregnancy. . . .

VII

Three reasons have been advanced to explain historically the enactment of criminal abortion laws in the 19th century and to justify their continued existence.

It has been argued occasionally that these laws were the product of a Victorian social concern to discourage illicit sexual conduct. Texas, however, does not advance this justification in the present case, and it appears that no court or commentator has taken the argument seriously.

WORTH NOTING

The Court also examined at length the evolving positions of the American Medical Association, the American Public Health Association, and the American Bar Association, each of which had very recently—in the 1970s—taken positions in favor of making abortion services available, at least early in pregnancy. As late as 1967, the AMA had passed a resolution opposing abortion except in very restrictive circumstances.

The appellants and amici contend, moreover, that this is not a proper state purpose at all and suggest that, if it were, the Texas statutes are overbroad in protecting it since the law fails to distinguish between married and unwed mothers.

A second reason is concerned with abortion as a medical procedure. When most criminal abortion laws were first enacted, the procedure was a hazardous one for the woman. This was particularly true prior to the development of antisepsis. Antiseptic techniques, of course, were based on discoveries by Lister, Pasteur, and others first announced in 1867, but were not generally accepted and employed until about the turn of the century. Abortion mortality was high. Even after 1900, and perhaps until as late as the development of antibiotics in the 1940's, standard modern techniques such as dilation and curettage were not nearly so safe as they are today. Thus, it has been argued that a State's real concern in enacting a criminal abortion law was to protect the pregnant woman, that is, to restrain her from submitting to a procedure that placed her life in serious jeopardy.

Modern medical techniques have altered this situation. Appellants and various amici refer to medical data indicating that abortion in early pregnancy, that is, prior to the end of the first trimester, although not without its risk, is now relatively safe. Mortality rates for women undergoing early abortions, where the procedure is legal, appear to be as low as or lower than the rates for normal childbirth. Consequently, any interest of the State in protecting the woman from an inherently hazardous procedure, except when it would be equally dangerous for her to forgo it, has largely disappeared.

Of course, important state interests in the areas of health and medical standards do remain. The State has a legitimate interest in seeing to it that abortion, like any other medical procedure, is performed under circumstances that insure maximum safety for the patient. This interest obviously extends at least to the performing physician and his staff, to the facilities involved, to the availability of after-care, and to adequate provision for any complication or emergency that might arise. The prevalence of high mortality rates at illegal "abortion mills" strengthens, rather than weakens, the State's interest in regulating the conditions under which abortions are performed. Moreover, the risk to the woman increases as her pregnancy continues. Thus, the State retains a definite interest in protecting the woman's own health and safety when an abortion is proposed at a late stage of pregnancy.

The third reason is the State's interest—some phrase it in terms of duty—in protecting prenatal life. Some of the argument for this justification rests on the theory that a new human life is present from the moment of conception. The State's interest and general obligation to protect life then extends, it is argued, to prenatal life. Only when the life of the pregnant mother herself is at stake, balanced against the life she carries within her, should the interest of the embryo or fetus not prevail. Logically, of course, a legitimate state interest in this area need not stand or fall on acceptance of the belief that life begins at conception or at some other point prior to live birth. In assessing the State's interest, recognition may be given to the less rigid claim that as long as at least potential life is involved, the State may assert interests beyond the protection of the pregnant woman alone. . . .

It is with these interests, and the weight to be attached to them, that this case is concerned.

VIII

The Constitution does not explicitly mention any right of privacy. In a line of decisions, however, . . . the Court has recognized that a right of personal privacy, or a guarantee of certain areas or zones of privacy, does exist under the Constitution. In varying contexts, the Court or individual Justices have, indeed, found at least the roots of that right in the First Amendment, *Stanley v. Georgia* (1969); in the Fourth and Fifth Amendments, *Terry v. Ohio* (1968), *Katz v. United States* (1967); in the penumbras of the Bill of Rights, *Griswold v. Connecticut*; in the Ninth Amendment, *id.* (Goldberg, J., concurring); or in the concept of liberty guaranteed by the first section of the Fourteenth Amendment, see *Meyer v. Nebraska* (1923). These decisions make it clear that only personal rights that can be deemed "fundamental" or "implicit in the concept of ordered liberty," *Palko v. Connecticut* (1937), are included in this guarantee of personal privacy. They also make it clear that the right has some extension to activities relating to marriage, *Loving v. Virginia* (1967); procreation, *Skinner v. Oklahoma* (1942); contraception, *Eisenstadt v. Baird* (1972); family relationships, *Prince v. Massachusetts* (1944); and child rearing and education, *Pierce v. Society of Sisters* (1925), *Meyer v. Nebraska*.

This right of privacy, whether it be founded in the Fourteenth Amendment's concept of personal liberty and restrictions upon state action, as we feel it is, or, as the District Court determined, in the Ninth Amendment's reservation of rights to the people, is broad enough to encompass a woman's decision whether or not to terminate her pregnancy. The detriment that the State would impose upon the pregnant woman by denying this choice altogether is apparent. Specific and direct harm medically diagnosable even in early pregnancy may be involved. Maternity, or additional offspring, may force upon the woman a distressful life and future. Psychological harm may be imminent. Mental and physical health may be taxed by child care. There is also the distress, for all concerned, associated with the unwanted child, and there is the problem of bringing a child into a family already unable, psychologically and otherwise, to care for it. In other cases, as in this one, the additional difficulties and continuing stigma of unwed motherhood may be involved. All these are factors the woman and her responsible physician necessarily will consider in consultation.

On the basis of elements such as these, appellant and some *amici* argue that the woman's right is absolute and that she is entitled to terminate her pregnancy at whatever time, in whatever way, and for whatever reason she alone chooses. With this we do not agree. Appellant's arguments that Texas either has no valid interest at all in regulating the abortion decision, or no interest strong enough to support any limitation upon the woman's sole determination, are unpersuasive. The Court's decisions recognizing a right of privacy also acknowledge that some state regulation in areas protected by that right is appropriate. As noted above, a State may properly assert important interests in safeguarding health, in maintaining medical standards, and in protecting potential life. At some point in pregnancy, these respective interests become sufficiently compelling to sustain regulation of the factors that govern the abortion decision. The privacy right involved, therefore, cannot be said to be absolute. In fact, it is not clear to us that the claim asserted by some *amici* that one has an unlimited right to do with one's body as one pleases bears a close relationship to the right of privacy previously articulated in the Court's decisions. The Court has refused to recognize an unlimited right of this kind in the past. *Jacobson v. Massachusetts* (1905) (vaccination); *Buck v. Bell* (1927) (sterilization).

We, therefore, conclude that the right of personal privacy includes the abortion decision, but that this right is not unqualified and must be considered against important state interests in regulation.

We note that those federal and state courts that have recently considered abortion law challenges have reached the same conclusion. A majority, in addition to the District Court in the present case, have held state laws unconstitutional. . . . Others have sustained state statutes. . . . Although the results are divided, most of these courts have agreed that the right of privacy, however based, is broad enough to cover the abortion decision; that the right, nonetheless, is not absolute and is subject to some limitations; and that at some point the state interests as to protection of health, medical standards, and prenatal life, become dominant. We agree with this approach.

Where certain "fundamental rights" are involved, the Court has held that regulation limiting these rights may be justified only by a "compelling state interest," and that legislative enactments must be narrowly drawn to express only the legitimate state interests at stake. *Griswold v. Connecticut*. . . .

IX

. . . Appellant, as has been indicated, claims an absolute right that bars any state imposition of criminal penalties in the area. Appellee argues that the State's determination to recognize and protect prenatal life from and after conception constitutes a compelling state interest. As noted above, we do not agree fully with either formulation.

A.   The appellee and certain amici argue that the fetus is a "person" within the language and meaning of the Fourteenth Amendment. In support of this, they outline at length and in detail the well-known facts of fetal development. If this suggestion of personhood is established, the appellant's case, of course, collapses, for the fetus' right to life would then be guaranteed specifically by the

Amendment. The appellant conceded as much on reargument. On the other hand, the appellee conceded on reargument that no case could be cited that holds that a fetus is a person within the meaning of the Fourteenth Amendment.

The Constitution does not define "person" in so many words. Section 1 of the Fourteenth Amendment contains three references to "person." The first, in defining "citizens," speaks of "persons born or naturalized in the United States." The word also appears both in the Due Process Clause and in the Equal Protection Clause. "Person" is used in other places in the Constitution: in the listing of qualifications for Representatives and Senators, Art. I, § 2, cl. 2, and § 3, cl. 3; in the Apportionment Clause, Art. I, § 2, cl. 3;[53] in the Migration and Importation provision, Art. I, § 9, cl. 1; in the Emolument Clause, Art. I, § 9, cl. 8; in the Electors provisions, Art. II, § 1, cl. 2, and the superseded cl. 3; in the provision outlining qualifications for the office of President, Art. II, § 1, cl. 5; in the Extradition provisions, Art. IV, § 2, cl. 2, and the superseded Fugitive Slave Clause 3; and in the Fifth, Twelfth, and Twenty-second Amendments, as well as in §§ 2 and 3 of the Fourteenth Amendment. But in nearly all these instances, the use of the word is such that it has application only postnatally. None indicates, with any assurance, that it has any possible prenatal application.[54]

All this, together with our observation, *supra*, that throughout the major portion of the 19th century prevailing legal abortion practices were far freer than they are today, persuades us that the word "person," as used in the Fourteenth Amendment, does not include the unborn. . . . This conclusion, however, does not of itself fully answer the contentions raised by Texas, and we pass on to other considerations.

B. The pregnant woman cannot be isolated in her privacy. She carries an embryo and, later, a fetus, if one accepts the medical definitions of the developing young in the human uterus. The situation therefore is inherently different from marital intimacy, or bedroom possession of obscene material, or marriage, or procreation, or education, with which *Eisenstadt* and *Griswold*, *Stanley*, *Loving*, *Skinner* and *Pierce* and *Meyer* were respectively concerned. As

---

53 We are not aware that in the taking of any census under this clause, a fetus has ever been counted.

54 When Texas urges that a fetus is entitled to Fourteenth Amendment protection as a person, it faces a dilemma. Neither in Texas nor in any other State are all abortions prohibited. Despite broad proscription, an exception always exists. . . . But if the fetus is a person who is not to be deprived of life without due process of law, and if the mother's condition is the sole determinant, does not the Texas exception appear to be out of line with the Amendment's command? . . . Further, the penalty for criminal abortion [under Texas law] is significantly less than the maximum penalty for murder . . . . If the fetus is a person, may the penalties be different?

we have intimated above, it is reasonable and appropriate for a State to decide that at some point in time another interest, that of health of the mother or that of potential human life, becomes significantly involved. The woman's privacy is no longer sole and any right of privacy she possesses must be measured accordingly.

Texas urges that, apart from the Fourteenth Amendment, life begins at conception and is present throughout pregnancy, and that, therefore, the State has a compelling interest in protecting that life from and after conception. We need not resolve the difficult question of when life begins. When those trained in the respective disciplines of medicine, philosophy, and theology are unable to arrive at any consensus, the judiciary, at this point in the development of man's knowledge, is not in a position to speculate as to the answer.

It should be sufficient to note briefly the wide divergence of thinking on this most sensitive and difficult question. There has always been strong support for the view that life does not begin until live birth. This was the belief of the Stoics. It appears to be the predominant, though not the unanimous, attitude of the Jewish faith. It may be taken to represent also the position of a large segment of the Protestant community, insofar as that can be ascertained; organized groups that have taken a formal position on the abortion issue have generally regarded abortion as a matter for the conscience of the individual and her family. As we have noted, the common law found greater significance in quickening. Physicians and their scientific colleagues have regarded that event with less interest and have tended to focus either upon conception, upon live birth, or upon the interim point at which the fetus becomes "viable," that is, potentially able to live outside the mother's womb, albeit with artificial aid. Viability is usually placed at about seven months (28 weeks) but may occur earlier, even at 24 weeks. The Aristotelian theory of "mediate animation," that held sway throughout the Middle Ages and the Renaissance in Europe, continued to be official Roman Catholic dogma until the 19th century, despite opposition to this "ensoulment" theory from those in the Church who would recognize the existence of life from the moment of conception. The latter is now, of course, the official belief of the Catholic Church. As one brief *amicus* discloses, this is a view strongly held by many non-Catholics as well, and by many physicians. Substantial problems for precise definition of this view are posed, however, by new embryological data that purport to indicate that conception is a "process" over time, rather than an event, and by new medical techniques such as menstrual extraction, the "morning-after" pill, implantation of embryos, artificial insemination, and even artificial wombs.

In areas other than criminal abortion, the law has been reluctant to endorse any theory that life, as we recognize it, begins before live birth or to accord legal rights to the unborn except in narrowly defined situations and except when the rights are contingent upon life birth. For example, the traditional rule of tort law denied recovery for prenatal injuries even though the child was born alive. That rule has been changed in almost every jurisdiction. In most States, recovery is said to be permitted only if the fetus was viable, or at least quick, when the injuries were sustained, though few courts have squarely so held. In a recent development, generally opposed by the commentators, some States permit the parents of a stillborn child to maintain an action for wrongful death because of prenatal injuries. Such an action, however, would appear to be one to vindicate the parents' interest and is thus consistent with the view that the fetus, at most, represents only the potentiality of life. Similarly, unborn children have been recognized as acquiring rights or interests by way of inheritance or other devolution of property, and have been represented by guardians *ad litem.* Perfection of the interests involved, again, has generally been contingent upon live birth. In short, the unborn have never been recognized in the law as persons in the whole sense.

X

In view of all this, we do not agree that, by adopting one theory of life, Texas may override the rights of the pregnant woman that are at stake. We repeat, however, that the State does have an important and legitimate interest in preserving and protecting the health of the pregnant woman, whether she be a resident of the State or a non-resident who seeks medical consultation and treatment there, and that it has still another important and legitimate interest in protecting the potentiality of human life. These interests are separate and distinct. Each grows in substantiality as the woman approaches term and, at a point during pregnancy, each becomes "compelling."

With respect to the State's important and legitimate interest in the health of the mother, the "compelling" point, in the light of present medical knowledge, is at approximately the end of the first trimester. This is so because of the now-established medical fact . . . that until the end of the first trimester mortality in abortion may be less than mortality in normal childbirth. It follows that, from and after this point, a State may regulate the abortion procedure to the extent that the regulation reasonably relates to the preservation and protection of maternal health. Examples of permissible state regulation in this area are requirements as to the qualifications of the person who is to perform the abortion; as to the licensure of that person; as to the facility in which the procedure is to be performed, that is, whether it must be a hospital or may be a clinic or some other place of less-than-hospital status; as to the licensing of the facility; and the like.

This means, on the other hand, that, for the period of pregnancy prior to this "compelling" point, the attending physician, in consultation with his patient, is free to determine, without regulation by the State, that, in his medical judgment, the patient's pregnancy should be terminated. If that decision is reached, the judgment may be effectuated by an abortion free of interference by the State.

With respect to the State's important and legitimate interest in potential life, the "compelling" point is at viability. This is so because the fetus then presumably has the capability of meaningful life outside the mother's womb. State regulation protective of fetal life after viability thus has both logical and biological justifications. If the State is interested in protecting fetal life after viability, it may go so far as to proscribe abortion during that period, except when it is necessary to preserve the life or health of the mother.

Measured against these standards, Art. 1196 of the Texas Penal Code, in restricting legal abortions to those "procured or attempted by medical advice for the purpose of saving the life of the mother," sweeps too broadly. The statute makes no distinction between abortions performed early in pregnancy and those performed later, and it limits to a single reason, "saving" the mother's life, the legal justification for the procedure. The statute, therefore, cannot survive the constitutional attack made upon it here. . . .

XI

To summarize and to repeat: . . .

(a)   For the stage prior to approximately the end of the first trimester, the abortion decision and its effectuation must be left to the medical judgment of the pregnant woman's attending physician.

(b)   For the stage subsequent to approximately the end of the first trimester, the State, in promoting its interest in the health of the mother, may, if it chooses, regulate the abortion procedure in ways that are reasonably related to maternal health.

(c)   For the stage subsequent to viability, the State in promoting
       its interest in the potentiality of human life may, if it chooses,
       regulate, and even proscribe, abortion except where it is neces-
       sary, in appropriate medical judgment, for the preservation of
       the life or health of the mother. . . .

This holding, we feel, is consistent with the relative weights of the respective interests involved, with the lessons and examples of medical and legal
history, with the lenity of the common law, and with the demands of the profound problems of the present day. The decision leaves the State free to place
increasing restrictions on abortion as the period of pregnancy lengthens, so
long as those restrictions are tailored to the recognized state interests. The
decision vindicates the right of the physician to administer medical treatment
according to his professional judgment up to the points where important state
interests provide compelling justifications for intervention. Up to those points,
the abortion decision in all its aspects is inherently, and primarily, a medical
decision, and basic responsibility for it must rest with the physician. If an individual practitioner abuses the privilege of exercising proper medical judgment,
the usual remedies, judicial and intra-professional, are available.

XII

Our conclusion that Art. 1196 is unconstitutional means, of course, that
the Texas abortion statutes, as a unit, must fall. . . .

It is so ordered.

MR. CHIEF JUSTICE BURGER, concurring.

I agree that, under the
Fourteenth Amendment to the
Constitution, the abortion statute
. . . [of] Texas impermissibly limit[s]
the performance of abortions necessary to protect the health of pregnant
women, using the term health in
its broadest medical context. I am
somewhat troubled that the Court

WORTH NOTING

Roe was decided
along with a compan-
ion case from Georgia,
Doe v. Bolton, de-
scribed on p. 1427.
The Chief Justice's
opinion, as well as those of Justices
Douglas, White, and Rehnquist, applied to both cases.

has taken notice of various scientific and medical data in reaching its conclusion; however, I do not believe that the Court has exceeded the scope of judicial
notice accepted in other contexts. . . .

I do not read the Court's holdings today as having the sweeping consequences attributed to them by the dissenting Justices; the dissenting views discount the reality that the vast majority of physicians observe the standards of their profession, and act only on the basis of carefully deliberated medical judgments relating to life and health. Plainly, the Court today rejects any claim that the Constitution requires abortions on demand.

Mr. Justice Stewart, concurring.

In 1963, this Court, in *Ferguson v. Skrupa*, purported to sound the death knell for the doctrine of substantive due process, a doctrine under which many state laws had in the past been held to violate the Fourteenth Amendment. As Mr. Justice Black's opinion for the Court in *Skrupa* put it: "We have returned to the original constitutional proposition that courts do not substitute their social and economic beliefs for the judgment of legislative bodies, who are elected to pass laws."[1]

Barely two years later, in *Griswold v. Connecticut*, the Court held a Connecticut birth control law unconstitutional. In view of what had been so recently said in *Skrupa*, the Court's opinion in *Griswold* understandably did its best to avoid reliance on the Due Process Clause of the Fourteenth Amendment as the ground for decision. Yet, the Connecticut law did not violate any provision of the Bill of Rights, nor any other specific provision of the Constitution. So it was clear to me then, and it is equally clear to me now, that the *Griswold* decision can be rationally understood only as a holding that the Connecticut statute substantively invaded the "liberty" that is protected by the Due Process Clause of the Fourteenth Amendment. As so understood, *Griswold* stands as one in a long line of pre-*Skrupa* cases decided under the doctrine of substantive due process, and I now accept it as such.

"In a Constitution for a free people, there can be no doubt that the meaning of 'liberty' must be broad indeed." *Board of Regents v. Roth* (1972). The Constitution nowhere mentions a specific right of personal choice in matters of marriage and family life, but the 'liberty' protected by the Due Process Clause of the Fourteenth Amendment covers more than those freedoms explicitly named in the Bill of Rights. [Justice Stewart here cites a string of ten cases, including *Meyer* and *Pierce*.] . . . Several decisions of this Court make clear that freedom of personal choice in matters of marriage and family life is one of the liberties

---

[1]	Only Mr. Justice Harlan failed to join the Court's opinion.

protected by the Due Process Clause of the Fourteenth Amendment. . . . As recently as last Term, in *Eisenstadt v. Baird*, we recognized "the right of the individual, married or single, to be free from unwarranted governmental intrusion into matters so fundamentally affecting a person as the decision whether to bear or beget a child." That right necessarily includes the right of a woman to decide whether or not to terminate her pregnancy. . . .

Clearly, therefore, the Court today is correct in holding that the right asserted by Jane Roe is embraced within the personal liberty protected by the Due Process Clause of the Fourteenth Amendment. [Justice Stewart concludes that the state's interests in protecting "the health and safety of the pregnant woman" and "the potential future human life within her" were "amply sufficient" to support some regulation, but not "the broad abridgement of personal liberty worked by the existing Texas law."]

MR. JUSTICE DOUGLAS, concurring.

While I join the opinion of the Court, I add a few words. . . .

The Ninth Amendment obviously does not create federally enforceable rights. It merely says, "The enumeration in the Constitution, of certain rights, shall not be construed to deny or disparage others retained by the people." But a catalogue of these rights includes customary, traditional, and time-honored rights, amenities, privileges, and immunities that come within the sweep of "the Blessings of Liberty" mentioned in the preamble to the Constitution. Many of them, in my view, come within the meaning of the term "liberty" as used in the Fourteenth Amendment.

First is the autonomous control over the development and expression of one's intellect, interests, tastes, and personality. These are rights protected by the First Amendment and, in my view, they are absolute, permitting of no exceptions. The Free Exercise Clause of the First Amendment is one facet of this constitutional right. The right to remain silent as respects one's own beliefs, is protected by the First and the Fifth. The First Amendment grants the privacy of first-class mail. All of these aspects of the right of privacy are rights "retained by the people" in the meaning of the Ninth Amendment.

Second is freedom of choice in the basic decisions of one's life respecting marriage, divorce, procreation, contraception, and the education and upbringing of children. These rights, unlike those protected by the First Amendment, are subject to some control by the police power. Thus, the Fourth Amendment speaks only of "unreasonable searches and seizures" and of "probable cause." These rights are "fundamental," and we have held that in order to support legislative action the statute must be narrowly and precisely drawn and that a "compelling state interest" must be shown in support of the limitation.

The liberty to marry a person of one's own choosing, *Loving v. Virginia*, the right of procreation, *Skinner v. Oklahoma*, the liberty to direct the education of one's children, *Pierce v. Society of Sisters*, and the privacy of the marital relation, *Griswold v. Connecticut*, are in this category. . . . This right of privacy was called by Mr. Justice Brandeis the right "to be let alone." *Olmstead v. United States* (dissenting opinion). That right includes the privilege of an individual to plan his own affairs, for, "outside areas of plainly harmful conduct, every American is left to shape his own life as he thinks best, do what he pleases, go where he pleases."

Third is the freedom to care for one's health and person, freedom from bodily restraint or compulsion, freedom to walk, stroll, or loaf. These rights, though fundamental, are likewise subject to regulation on a showing of "compelling state interest." We stated in *Papachristou v. City of Jacksonville* (1972) that walking, strolling, and wandering "are historically part of the amenities of life as we have known [them]." . . . In *Meyer v. Nebraska*, the Court said:

> Without doubt, [liberty] denotes not merely freedom from bodily restraint but also the right of the individual to contract, to engage in any of the common occupations of life, to acquire useful knowledge, to marry, establish a home and bring up children, to worship God according to the dictates of his own conscience, and generally to enjoy those privileges long recognized at common law as essential to the orderly pursuit of happiness by free men.

The [relevant] statute is at war with the clear message of these cases—that a woman is free to make the basic decision whether to bear an unwanted child. Elaborate argument is hardly necessary to demonstrate that childbirth may deprive a woman of her preferred lifestyle and force upon her a radically different and undesired future. For example, rejected applicants under the Georgia statute are required to endure the discomforts of pregnancy; to incur the pain, higher mortality rate, and aftereffects of childbirth; to abandon educational plans; to sustain loss of income; to forgo the satisfactions of careers; to tax further mental and physical health in providing child care; and, in some cases, to bear the lifelong stigma of unwed motherhood, a badge which may haunt, if not deter, later legitimate family relationships. . . .

Such a reasoning is, however, only the beginning of the problem. The State has interests to protect. . . . While childbirth endangers the lives of some women, voluntary abortion at any time and place regardless of medical standards would impinge on a rightful concern of society. The woman's health is part of that concern; as is the life of the fetus after quickening. These concerns justify the State in treating the procedure as a medical one. . . . [But] I agree with the Court that endangering the life of the woman or seriously and permanently injuring her health are standards too narrow for the right of privacy that is at stake. . . .

MR. JUSTICE WHITE, with whom MR. JUSTICE REHNQUIST joins, dissenting.

At the heart of the controversy in these cases are those recurring pregnancies that pose no danger whatsoever to the life or health of the mother but are, nevertheless, unwanted for any one or more of a variety of reasons—convenience, family planning, economics, dislike of children, the embarrassment of illegitimacy, etc. The common claim before us is that for any one of such reasons, or for no reason at all, and without asserting or claiming any threat to life or health, any woman is entitled to an abortion at her request if she is able to find a medical advisor willing to undertake the procedure.

The Court for the most part sustains this position: During the period prior to the time the fetus becomes viable, the Constitution of the United States values the convenience, whim, or caprice of the pregnant woman more than the life or potential life of the fetus; the Constitution, therefore, guarantees the right to an abortion as against any state law or policy seeking to protect the fetus from an abortion not prompted by more compelling reasons of the mother.

With all due respect, I dissent. I find nothing in the language or history of the Constitution to support the Court's judgments. The Court simply fashions and announces a new constitutional right for pregnant women and, with scarcely any reason or authority for its action, invests that right with sufficient substance to override most existing state abortion statutes. The upshot is that the people and the legislatures of the 50 States are constitutionally disentitled to weigh the relative importance of the continued existence and development of the fetus, on the one hand, against a spectrum of possible impacts on the mother, on the other hand. As an exercise of raw judicial power, the Court perhaps has authority to do what it does today; but in my view its judgment is an improvident and extravagant exercise of the power of judicial review that the Constitution extends to this Court.

The Court apparently values the convenience of the pregnant woman more than the continued existence and development of the life or potential life that she carries. Whether or not I might agree with that marshaling of values, I can in no event join the Court's judgment because I find no constitutional warrant for imposing such an order of priorities on the people and legislatures of the States. In a sensitive area such as this, involving as it does issues over which reasonable men may easily and heatedly differ, . . . [the] issue, for the most part, should be left with the people and to the political processes the people have devised to govern their affairs. . . .

Mr. Justice Rehnquist, dissenting.

. . . I have difficulty in concluding, as the Court does, that the right of "privacy" is involved in this case. Texas, by the statute here challenged, bars the performance of a medical abortion by a licensed physician on a plaintiff such as Roe. A transaction resulting in an operation such as this is not "private" in the ordinary usage of that word. Nor is the "privacy" that the Court finds here even a distant relative of the freedom from searches and seizures protected by the Fourth Amendment to the Constitution, which the Court has referred to as embodying a right to privacy.

If the Court means by the term "privacy" no more than that the claim of a person to be free from unwanted state regulation of consensual transactions may be a form of "liberty" protected by the Fourteenth Amendment, there is no doubt that similar claims have been upheld in our earlier decisions on the basis of that liberty. I agree with the statement of Mr. Justice Stewart in his concurring opinion that the "liberty," against deprivation of which without due process the Fourteenth Amendment protects, embraces more than the rights found in the Bill of Rights. But that liberty is not guaranteed absolutely against deprivation, only against deprivation without due process of law.

The test traditionally applied in the area of social and economic legislation is whether or not a law such as that challenged has a rational relation to a valid state objective. *Williamson v. Lee Optical Inc.* (1955). The Due Process Clause of the Fourteenth Amendment undoubtedly does place a limit, albeit a broad one, on legislative power to enact laws such as this. If the Texas statute were to prohibit an abortion even where the mother's life is in jeopardy, I have little doubt that such a statute would lack a rational relation to a valid state objective under the test stated in *Williamson*. But the Court's sweeping invalidation of any restrictions on abortion during the first trimester is impossible to justify under that standard, and the conscious weighing of competing factors that the Court's opinion apparently substitutes for the established test is far more appropriate to a legislative judgment than to a judicial one. . . .

While the Court's opinion quotes from the dissent of Mr. Justice Holmes in *Lochner v. New York* (1905), the result it reaches is more closely attuned to the majority opinion of Mr. Justice Peckham in that case. As in *Lochner* and similar cases applying substantive due process standards to economic and social welfare legislation, the adoption of the compelling state interest standard will inevitably require this Court to examine the legislative policies and pass on the wisdom of these policies in the very process of deciding whether a particular state interest put forward may or may not be "compelling." The decision here to break pregnancy into three distinct terms and to outline the permissible restrictions the State may impose in each one, for example, partakes more of judicial legislation than it does of a determination of the intent of the drafters of the Fourteenth Amendment.

The fact that a majority of the States reflecting, after all, the majority sentiment in those States, have had restrictions on abortions for at least a century is a strong indication, it seems to me, that the asserted right to an abortion is not "so rooted in the traditions and conscience of our people as to be ranked as fundamental." . . .

WORTH NOTING

Justice Rehnquist points out that in 1868, when the Fourteenth Amendment was adopted, abortion limitations were in effect in 36 states and territories—including Texas, which had not substantially changed its law since enactment in 1857—and there was apparently no question concerning their validity.

The decision in *Roe v. Wade* had many effects. One, beginning immediately with the companion case of *Doe v. Bolton* (1973) and continuing to the present day, was the development of a large and contentious body of caselaw determining which abortion regulations are acceptable and which are not. (In *Doe*, the Court invalidated several Georgia regulations, one of which required that the abortion be performed in an accredited hospital.) Another was a powerful and durable political backlash, especially from the political right. Though five of the seven justices in the *Roe* majority had been appointed by Republicans, by 1984, the Republican Party platform provided that "the unborn child has a fundamental individual right to life which cannot be infringed," called for "legislation to make clear that the Fourteenth Amendment's protections apply to unborn children," and promised "the appointment of judges at all levels of the judiciary who respect traditional family values and the sanctity of innocent human life."

On the backdrop of this political focus on judicial nominations, Republican presidents were able to replace three members of the *Roe* majority who retired from 1988 to 1991. Many expected the new justices—Anthony Kennedy, David Souter, and Clarence Thomas—to form the heart of a voting bloc that would overrule *Roe v. Wade*. That expectation was put to the test in *Planned Parenthood v. Casey* (1992), which seemed a plausible vehicle for a decision overruling *Roe* and abandoning the constitutional protection of abortion rights.

As you read the opinions in *Casey*, try to decide whether the expectations for fundamental change in abortion doctrine were dashed or fulfilled.

Planned Parenthood of Southeastern Pennsylvania v. Casey

Supreme Court of the United States, 1992.
505 U.S. 833.

JUSTICE O'CONNOR, JUSTICE KENNEDY, and JUSTICE SOUTER announced the judgment of the Court and delivered the opinion of the Court with respect to Parts I, II, III, V-A, V-C, and VI . . . , and an opinion with respect to Parts IV [and] V-B. . . .

I

Liberty finds no refuge in a jurisprudence of doubt. Yet 19 years after our holding that the Constitution protects a woman's right to terminate her pregnancy in its early stages, *Roe v. Wade* (1973), that definition of liberty is still questioned. Joining the respondents as *amicus curiae*, the United States, as it has done in five other cases in the last decade, again asks us to overrule *Roe*.

[Various provisions of the Pennsylvania Abortion Control Act of 1982 were at issue in the case. The excerpts presented here focus on the following:] The Act requires that a woman seeking an abortion give her informed consent prior to the abortion procedure, and specifies that she be provided with certain information at least 24 hours before the abortion is performed. . . . Another provision of the Act requires that, unless certain exceptions apply, a married woman seeking an abortion must sign a statement indicating that she has notified her husband of her intended abortion. The Act exempts compliance with these . . . requirements in the event of a "medical emergency," which is defined in § 3203 of the Act. . . . Each provision was challenged as unconstitutional on its face. . . .

[W]e acknowledge that our decisions after *Roe* [have] cast doubt upon the meaning and reach of its holding. . . . After considering the fundamental constitutional questions resolved by *Roe*, principles of institutional integrity, and the rule of *stare decisis*, we are led to conclude this: the essential holding of *Roe v. Wade* should be retained and once again reaffirmed.

It must be stated at the outset and with clarity that *Roe*'s essential holding, the holding we reaffirm, has three parts. First is a recognition of the right of the woman to choose to have an abortion before viability and to obtain it without undue interference from the State. Before viability, the State's interests are not strong enough to support a prohibition of abortion or the imposition of a substantial obstacle to the woman's effective right to elect the procedure. Second is a confirmation of the State's power to restrict abortions after fetal viability, if the law contains exceptions for pregnancies which endanger the woman's life or health. And third is the principle that the State has legitimate interests from the outset of the pregnancy in protecting the health of the woman and the life of the fetus that may become a child. These principles do not contradict one another; and we adhere to each.

II

. . . The controlling word in the cases before us is "liberty." . . . It is tempting, as a means of curbing the discretion of federal judges, to suppose that liberty encompasses no more than those rights already guaranteed to the individual against federal interference by the express provisions of the first eight Amendments to the Constitution. See *Adamson v. California* (1947) (Black, J., dissenting). But of course this Court has never accepted that view. It is also tempting, for the same reason, to suppose that the Due Process Clause protects only those practices, defined at the most specific level, that were protected against government interference by other rules of law when the Fourteenth Amendment was ratified. See *Michael H. v. Gerald D.* (1989) (opinion of Scalia, J.). But such a view would be inconsistent with our law.

It is a promise of the Constitution that there is a realm of personal liberty which the government may not enter. We have vindicated this principle before. . . . Neither the Bill of Rights nor the specific practices of States at the time of the adoption of the Fourteenth Amendment marks the outer limits of the substantive sphere of liberty which the Fourteenth Amendment protects. See U.S. Const., Amdt. 9. . . . It is settled now, as it was when the Court heard arguments in *Roe v. Wade,* that the Constitution places limits on a State's right to interfere with a person's most basic decisions about family and parenthood [citing the standard cases, including *Meyer, Pierce, Griswold,* and *Eisenstadt*] as well as bodily integrity [citing three other standard cases].

The inescapable fact is that adjudication of substantive due process claims may call upon the Court in interpreting the Constitution to exercise that same capacity which by tradition courts always have exercised: reasoned judgment. Its boundaries are not susceptible of expression as a simple rule. That does not mean we are free to invalidate state policy choices with which we disagree; yet neither does it permit us to shrink from the duties of our office. . . .

. . . Men and women of good conscience can disagree, and we suppose some always shall disagree, about the profound moral and spiritual implications of terminating a pregnancy, even in its earliest stage. Some of us as individuals find abortion offensive to our most basic principles of morality, but that cannot control our decision. Our obligation is to define the liberty of all, not to mandate our own moral code. . . .

Our law affords constitutional protection to personal decisions relating to marriage, procreation, contraception, family relationships, child rearing, and education. . . . These matters, involving the most intimate and personal choices a person may make in a lifetime, choices central to personal dignity and autonomy, are central to the liberty protected by the Fourteenth Amendment. At the heart of liberty is the right to define one's own concept of existence, of meaning, of the universe, and of the mystery of human life. Beliefs about these matters could not define the attributes of personhood were they formed under compulsion of the State.

These considerations begin our analysis of the woman's interest in terminating her pregnancy but cannot end it, for this reason: though the abortion decision may originate within the zone of conscience and belief, it is more than a philosophic exercise. Abortion is a unique act. It is an act fraught with consequences for others: for the woman who must live with the implications of her decision; for the persons who perform and assist in the procedure; for the spouse, family, and society which must confront the knowledge that these procedures exist, procedures some deem nothing short of an act of violence against innocent human life; and, depending on one's beliefs, for the life or potential life that is aborted.

Though abortion is conduct, it does not follow that the State is entitled to proscribe it in all instances. That is because the liberty of the woman is at stake in a sense unique to the human condition and so unique to the law. The mother who carries a child to full term is subject to anxieties, to physical constraints, to pain that only she must bear. That these sacrifices have from the beginning of the human race been endured by woman with a pride that ennobles her in the eyes of others and gives to the infant a bond of love cannot alone be grounds for the State to insist she make the sacrifice. Her suffering is too intimate and personal for the State to insist, without more, upon its own vision of the woman's role, however dominant that vision has been in the course of our history and our culture. The destiny of the woman must be shaped to a large extent on her own conception of her spiritual imperatives and her place in society.

It should be recognized, moreover, that in some critical respects the abortion decision is of the same character as the decision to use contraception, to which *Griswold v. Connecticut, Eisenstadt v. Baird,* and *Carey v. Population Services International* (1977) afford constitutional protection. We have no doubt as to the correctness of those decisions. . . . As with abortion, reasonable people will have differences of opinion about these matters. One view is based on such reverence for the wonder of creation that any pregnancy ought to be welcomed and carried to full term no matter how difficult it will be to provide for the child and ensure its well-being. Another is that the inability to provide for the nurture and care of the infant is a cruelty to the child and an anguish to the parent. These are intimate views with infinite variations, and their deep, personal character underlay our decisions in *Griswold, Eisenstadt,* and *Carey.* The same concerns are present when the woman confronts the reality that, perhaps despite her attempts to avoid it, she has become pregnant.

It was this dimension of personal liberty that *Roe* sought to protect, and its holding invoked the reasoning and the tradition of the precedents we have discussed. . . . [T]he reservations any of us may have in reaffirming the central holding of *Roe* are outweighed by the explication of individual liberty we have given combined with the force of *stare decisis*. We turn now to that doctrine.

III

A

The obligation to follow precedent begins with necessity, and a contrary necessity marks its outer limit. With Cardozo, we recognize that no judicial system could do society's work if it eyed each issue afresh in every case that raised it. See B. Cardozo, *The Nature of the Judicial Process* (1921). . . . At the other extreme, a different necessity would make itself felt if a prior judicial ruling should come to be seen so clearly as error that its enforcement was for that very reason doomed.

Even when the decision to overrule a prior case is not, as in the rare, latter instance, virtually foreordained, it is common wisdom that the rule of *stare decisis* is not an "inexorable command," and certainly it is not such in every constitutional case. Rather, when this Court reexamines a prior holding, its judgment is customarily informed by a series of prudential and pragmatic considerations designed to test the consistency of overruling a prior decision with the ideal of the rule of law, and to gauge the respective costs of reaffirming and overruling a prior case. . . .

So in this case we may enquire whether *Roe*'s central rule has been found unworkable; whether the rule's limitation on state power could be removed without serious inequity to those who have relied upon it or significant damage to the stability of the society governed by it; whether the law's growth in the intervening years has left *Roe*'s central rule a doctrinal anachronism discounted by society; and whether *Roe*'s premises of fact have so far changed in the ensuing two decades as to render its central holding somehow irrelevant or unjustifiable in dealing with the issue it addressed. . . .

1

Although *Roe* has engendered opposition, it has in no sense proven "unworkable," see *Garcia v. San Antonio Metropolitan Transit Authority* (1985), representing as it does a simple limitation beyond which a state law is unenforceable. While *Roe* has, of course, required judicial assessment of state laws affecting the exercise of the choice guaranteed against government infringement, and although the need for such review will remain as a consequence of today's decision, the required determinations fall within judicial competence.

2

The inquiry into reliance counts the cost of a rule's repudiation as it would fall on those who have relied reasonably on the rule's continued application. . . . While neither respondents nor their *amici* in so many words deny that the abortion right invites some reliance prior to its actual exercise, one can readily imagine an argument stressing the dissimilarity of this case to one involving property or contract. Abortion is customarily chosen as an unplanned response to the consequence of unplanned activity or to the failure of conventional birth control, and except on the assumption that no intercourse would have occurred but for *Roe's* holding, such behavior may appear to justify no reliance claim. Even if reliance could be claimed on that unrealistic assumption, the argument might run, any reliance interest would be *de minimis*. This argument would be premised on the hypothesis that reproductive planning could take virtually immediate account of any sudden restoration of state authority to ban abortions.

To eliminate the issue of reliance that easily, however, one would need to limit cognizable reliance to specific instances of sexual activity. But to do this would be simply to refuse to face the fact that for two decades of economic and social developments, people have organized intimate relationships and made choices that define their views of themselves and their places in society, in reliance on the availability of abortion in the event that contraception should fail. The ability of women to participate equally in the economic and social life of the Nation has been facilitated by their ability to control their reproductive lives. The Constitution serves human values, and while the effect of reliance on *Roe* cannot be exactly measured, neither can the certain cost of overruling *Roe* for people who have ordered their thinking and living around that case be dismissed.

3

No evolution of legal principle has left *Roe's* doctrinal footings weaker than they were in 1973. No development of constitutional law since the case was decided has implicitly or explicitly left *Roe* behind as a mere survivor of obsolete constitutional thinking. . . . [S]ubsequent constitutional developments have [not] disturbed . . . the scope of recognized protection accorded to the liberty relating to intimate relationships, the family, and decisions about whether or not to beget or bear a child. . . . [A]nd our cases since *Roe* accord with *Roe*'s view that a State's interest in the protection of life falls short of justifying any plenary override of individual liberty claims. . . .

4

We have seen how time has overtaken some of *Roe*'s factual assumptions: advances in maternal health care allow for abortions safe to the mother later in pregnancy than was true in 1973, and advances in neonatal care have advanced viability to a point somewhat earlier. But these facts go only to the scheme of time limits on the realization of competing interests, and the divergences from the factual premises of 1973 have no bearing on the validity of *Roe*'s central holding, that viability marks the earliest point at which the State's interest in fetal life is constitutionally adequate to justify a legislative ban on nontherapeutic abortions. The soundness or unsoundness of that constitutional judgment in no sense turns on whether viability occurs at approximately 28 weeks, as was usual at the time of *Roe*, at 23 to 24 weeks, as it sometimes does today, or at some moment even slightly earlier in pregnancy, as it may if fetal respiratory capacity can somehow be enhanced in the future. Whenever it may occur, the attainment of viability may continue to serve as the critical fact, just as it has done since *Roe* was decided; which is to say that no change in *Roe*'s factual underpinning has left its central holding obsolete, and none supports an argument for overruling it.

5

The sum of the precedential enquiry to this point shows *Roe*'s underpinnings unweakened in any way affecting its central holding. . . . Within the bounds of normal *stare decisis* analysis, then, and subject to the considerations on which it customarily turns, the stronger argument is for affirming *Roe*'s central holding, with whatever degree of personal reluctance any of us may have, not for overruling it.

B

In a less significant case, *stare decisis* analysis could, and would, stop at the point we have reached. But the sustained and widespread debate *Roe* has provoked calls for some comparison between that case and others of comparable dimension that have responded to national controversies and taken on the impress of the controversies addressed. Only two such decisional lines from the past century present themselves for examination, and in each instance the result reached by the Court accorded with the principles we apply today.

The first example is that line of cases identified with *Lochner v. New York* (1905), which imposed substantive limitations on legislation limiting economic autonomy in favor of health and welfare regulation, adopting, in Justice Holmes's view, the theory of laissez-faire. *Id.* (dissenting opinion). . . .

 CROSS REFERENCE *Lochner* is presented at pp. 1334–1346.

Fourteen years later, *West Coast Hotel Co. v. Parrish* (1937), signaled the demise of *Lochner* by overruling *Adkins v. Children's Hospital of District of Columbia* (1923)[, which had struck down a statutory minimum wage for women]. In the meantime, the Depression had come and, with it, the lesson that seemed unmistakable to most people by 1937, that the interpretation of contractual freedom protected in *Adkins* rested on fundamentally false factual assumptions about the capacity of a relatively unregulated market to satisfy minimal levels of human welfare. . . . The facts upon which the earlier case had premised a constitutional resolution of social controversy had proven to be untrue, and history's demonstration of their untruth not only justified but required the new choice of constitutional principle that *West Coast Hotel* announced. . . .

The second comparison that 20th century history invites is with the cases employing the separate-but-equal rule for applying the Fourteenth Amendment's equal protection guarantee. They began with *Plessy v. Ferguson* (1896), [which] reject[ed] the argument that racial separation enforced by the legal machinery of American society treats the black race as inferior. . . . But this understanding of the facts and the rule it was stated to justify were repudiated in *Brown v. Board of Education* (1954) (*Brown I*). . . . The Court in *Brown* addressed these facts of life by observing that whatever may have been the understanding in *Plessy's* time of the power of segregation to stigmatize those who were segregated with a "badge of inferiority," it was clear by 1954 that legally sanctioned segregation had just such an effect, to the point that racially separate public educational facilities were deemed inherently unequal. Society's understanding of the facts upon which a constitutional ruling was sought in 1954 was thus fundamentally different from the basis claimed for the decision in 1896. . . .

West Coast Hotel and *Brown* each rested on facts, or an understanding of facts, changed from those which furnished the claimed justifications for the earlier constitutional resolutions. . . . As the decisions were thus comprehensible they were also defensible, not merely as the victories of one doctrinal school over another by dint of numbers (victories though they were), but as applications of constitutional principle to facts as they had not been seen by the Court before. In constitutional adjudication as elsewhere in life, changed circumstances may impose new obligations. . . .

[T]he cases before us present no such occasion. . . . Because neither the factual underpinnings of *Roe's* central holding nor our understanding of it has changed (and because no other indication of weakened precedent has been shown), the Court could not pretend to be reexamining the prior law with any justification beyond a present doctrinal disposition to come out differently from the Court of 1973. . . .

C

[Thus, in *West Coast Hotel* and *Brown*, a] terrible price . . . would have been paid if the Court had not overruled as it did[, but here] the terrible price would be paid for overruling. . . . As Americans of each succeeding generation are rightly told, the Court cannot buy support for its decisions by spending money and, except to a minor degree, it cannot independently coerce obedience to its decrees. The Court's power lies, rather, in its legitimacy, a product of substance and perception that shows itself in the people's acceptance of the Judiciary as fit to determine what the Nation's law means and to declare what it demands. . . . The Court must take care to speak and act in ways that allow people to accept its decisions on the terms the Court claims for them, as grounded truly in principle, not as compromises with social and political pressures having, as such, no bearing on the principled choices that the Court is obliged to make. . . .

In two circumstances . . . the Court would almost certainly fail to receive the benefit of the doubt in overruling prior cases. There is, first, a point beyond which frequent overruling would overtax the country's belief in the Court's good faith. . . . [At some point,] disturbance of prior rulings would be taken as evidence that justifiable reexamination of principle had given way to drives for particular results in the short term. The legitimacy of the Court would fade with the frequency of its vacillation.

[The second] circumstance is to the point here and now. Where, in the performance of its judicial duties, the Court decides a case in such a way as to resolve the sort of intensely divisive controversy reflected in *Roe* and those rare, comparable cases, its decision has a dimension that the resolution of the normal case does not carry. It is the dimension present whenever the Court's interpretation of the Constitution calls the contending sides of a national controversy to end their national division by accepting a common mandate rooted in the Constitution.

The Court is not asked to do this very often, having thus addressed the Nation only twice in our lifetime, in the decisions of *Brown* and *Roe*. But when the Court does act in this way, its decision requires an equally rare precedential force to counter the inevitable efforts to overturn it and to thwart its implementation. . . . [To] surrender to political pressure, and [to] overrule under fire in the absence of the most compelling reason to reexamine a watershed decision would subvert the Court's legitimacy beyond any serious question. . . .

Like the character of an individual, the legitimacy of the Court must be earned over time. So, indeed, must be the character of a Nation of people who aspire to live according to the rule of law. Their belief in themselves as such a people is not readily separable from their understanding of the Court invested with the authority to decide their constitutional cases and speak before all others for their constitutional ideals. If the Court's legitimacy should be undermined, then, so would the country be in its very ability to see itself through its constitutional ideals. . . .

The Court's duty in the present cases is clear. . . . A decision to overrule *Roe*'s essential holding under the existing circumstances would address error, if error there was, at the cost of both profound and unnecessary damage to the Court's legitimacy, and to the Nation's commitment to the rule of law. It is therefore imperative to adhere to the essence of *Roe*'s original decision, and we do so today.

IV

From what we have said so far it follows that it is a constitutional liberty of the woman to have some freedom to terminate her pregnancy. We conclude that the basic decision in *Roe* was based on a constitutional analysis which we cannot now repudiate. The woman's liberty is not so unlimited, however, that from the outset the State cannot show its concern for the life of the unborn, and at a later point in fetal development the State's interest in life has sufficient force so that the right of the woman to terminate the pregnancy can be restricted.

That brings us, of course, to the point where much criticism has been directed at *Roe*, a criticism that always inheres when the Court draws a specific rule from what in the Constitution is but a general standard. We conclude, however, that the urgent claims of the woman to retain the ultimate control over her destiny and her body, claims implicit in the meaning of liberty, require us to perform that function. Liberty must not be extinguished for want of a line that is clear. And it falls to us to give some real substance to the woman's liberty to determine whether to carry her pregnancy to full term.

We conclude the line should be drawn at viability, so that before that time the woman has a right to choose to terminate her pregnancy. We adhere to this principle for two reasons. First, as we have said, is the doctrine of *stare decisis*. Any judicial act of line-drawing may seem somewhat arbitrary, but *Roe* was a reasoned statement, elaborated with great care. We have twice reaffirmed it in the face of great opposition. See *Thornburgh v. American College of Obstetricians and Gynecologists* (1986) [(affirming decision to enjoin enforcement of a statute that imposed a 24-hour waiting period and required the provision of information, apparently designed to discourage abortion, as part of the "informed consent" process)]; *Akron v. Akron Center for Reproductive Health, Inc.* (1983) (*Akron I*) [(striking down similar provisions among others, including one requiring abortions after the first trimester to be performed in a hospital)]. Although we must overrule those parts of *Thornburgh* and *Akron I* which, in our view, are inconsistent with *Roe*'s statement that the State has a legitimate interest in promoting the life or potential life of the unborn, the central premise of those cases represents an unbroken commitment by this Court to the essential holding of *Roe*. It is that premise which we reaffirm today.

The second reason is that the concept of viability, as we noted in *Roe*, is the time at which there is a realistic possibility of maintaining and nourishing a life outside the womb, so that the independent existence of the second life can in reason and all fairness be the object of state protection that now overrides the rights of the woman. . . . The viability line also has, as a practical matter, an element of fairness. In some broad sense it might be said that a woman who fails to act before viability has consented to the State's intervention on behalf of the developing child.

The woman's right to terminate her pregnancy before viability is the most central principle of *Roe v. Wade*. It is a rule of law and a component of liberty we cannot renounce.

On the other side of the equation is the interest of the State in the protection of potential life. . . . [I]t must be remembered that *Roe v. Wade* speaks with clarity in establishing not only the woman's liberty but also the State's "important and legitimate interest in potential life." That portion of the decision in *Roe* has been given too little acknowledgment and implementation by the Court in its subsequent cases. Those cases decided that any regulation touching upon the abortion decision must survive strict scrutiny, to be sustained only if drawn in narrow terms to further a compelling state interest. See, *e.g.*, *Akron I*. Not all of the cases decided under that formulation can be reconciled with the holding in *Roe* itself that the State has legitimate interests in the health of the woman and in protecting the potential life within her. In resolving this tension, we choose to rely upon *Roe*, as against the later cases.

Roe established a trimester framework to govern abortion regulations. Under this elaborate but rigid construct, almost no regulation at all is permitted during the first trimester of pregnancy. . . . A framework of this rigidity was unnecessary. . . . Though the woman has a right to choose to terminate or continue her pregnancy before viability, it does not at all follow that the State is prohibited from taking steps to ensure that this choice is thoughtful and informed. Even in the earliest stages of pregnancy, the State may enact rules and regulations designed to encourage her to know that there are philosophic and social arguments of great weight that can be brought to bear in favor of continuing the pregnancy to full term and that there are procedures and institutions to allow adoption of unwanted children as well as a certain degree of state assistance if the mother chooses to raise the child herself. " '[T]he Constitution does not forbid a State or city, pursuant to democratic processes, from expressing a preference for normal childbirth.' " *Webster v. Reproductive Health Services* (1989). . . .

We reject the trimester framework, which we do not consider to be part of the essential holding of *Roe*. Measures aimed at ensuring that a woman's choice contemplates the consequences for the fetus do not necessarily interfere with the right recognized in *Roe*, although those measures have [in some of this Court's subsequent cases] been found to be inconsistent with the rigid trimester framework announced in that case. A logical reading of the central holding in *Roe* itself, and a necessary reconciliation of the liberty of the woman and the interest of the State in promoting prenatal life, require, in our view, that we abandon the trimester framework as a rigid prohibition on all previability regulation aimed at the protection of fetal life. The trimester framework suffers from these basic flaws: in its formulation it misconceives the nature of the pregnant woman's interest; and in practice it undervalues the State's interest in potential life, as recognized in *Roe*.

As our jurisprudence relating to all liberties save perhaps abortion has recognized, not every law which makes a right more difficult to exercise is, *ipso facto*, an infringement of that right. An example clarifies the point. We have held that not every ballot access limitation amounts to an infringement of the right to vote. . . . The abortion right is similar. Numerous forms of state regulation might have the incidental effect of increasing the cost or decreasing the availability of medical care, whether for abortion or any other medical procedure. The fact that a law which serves a valid purpose, one not designed to strike at the right itself, has the incidental effect of making it more difficult or more expensive to procure an abortion cannot be enough to invalidate it. Only where state regulation imposes an undue burden on a woman's ability to make this decision does the power of the State reach into the heart of the liberty protected by the Due Process Clause. . . .

. . . Because we set forth a standard of general application to which we intend to adhere, it is important to clarify what is meant by an undue burden.

A finding of an undue burden is a shorthand for the conclusion that a state regulation has the purpose or effect of placing a substantial obstacle in the path of a woman seeking an abortion of a nonviable fetus. A statute with this purpose is invalid because the means chosen by the State to further the interest in potential life must be calculated to inform the woman's free choice, not hinder it. And a statute which, while furthering the interest in potential life or some other valid state interest, has the effect of placing a substantial obstacle in the path of a woman's choice cannot be considered a permissible means of serving its legitimate ends. . . .

Some guiding principles should emerge. What is at stake is the woman's right to make the ultimate decision, not a right to be insulated from all others in doing so. Regulations which do no more than create a structural mechanism by which the State . . . may express profound respect for the life of the unborn are permitted, if they are not a substantial obstacle to the woman's exercise of the right to choose. Unless it has that effect on her right of choice, a state measure designed to persuade her to choose childbirth over abortion will be upheld if reasonably related to that goal. Regulations designed to foster the health of a woman seeking an abortion are valid if they do not constitute an undue burden.

Even when jurists reason from shared premises, some disagreement is inevitable. That is to be expected in the application of any legal standard which must accommodate life's complexity. We do not expect it to be otherwise with respect to the undue burden standard. We give this summary:

(a) To protect the central right recognized by *Roe v. Wade* while at the same time accommodating the State's profound interest in potential life, we will employ the undue burden analysis as explained in this opinion. An undue burden exists, and therefore a provision of law is invalid, if its purpose or effect is to place a substantial obstacle in the path of a woman seeking an abortion before the fetus attains viability.

(b) We reject the rigid trimester framework of *Roe v. Wade*. To promote the State's profound interest in potential life, throughout pregnancy the State may take measures to ensure that the woman's choice is informed, and measures designed to advance this interest will not be invalidated as long as their purpose is to persuade the woman to choose childbirth over abortion. These measures must not be an undue burden on the right.

(c) As with any medical procedure, the State may enact regulations to further the health or safety of a woman seeking an abortion. Unnecessary health regulations that have the purpose or effect of presenting a substantial obstacle to a woman seeking an abortion impose an undue burden on the right.

(d) Our adoption of the undue burden analysis does not disturb the central holding of *Roe v. Wade*, and we reaffirm that holding. Regardless of whether exceptions are made for particular circumstances, a State may not prohibit any woman from making the ultimate decision to terminate her pregnancy before viability.

(e) We also reaffirm *Roe*'s holding that "subsequent to viability, the State in promoting its interest in the potentiality of human life may, if it chooses, regulate, and even proscribe, abortion except where it is necessary, in appropriate medical judgment, for the preservation of the life or health of the mother."

These principles control our assessment of the Pennsylvania statute, and we now turn to the issue of the validity of its challenged provisions.

V

. . . We now consider the separate statutory sections at issue.

A

Because it is central to the operation of various other requirements, we begin with the statute's definition of medical emergency. Under the statute, a medical emergency is

> [t]hat condition which, on the basis of the physician's good faith clinical judgment, so complicates the medical condition of a pregnant woman as to necessitate the immediate abortion of her pregnancy to avert her death or for which a delay will create serious risk of substantial and irreversible impairment of a major bodily function.

Petitioners argue that the definition is too narrow, contending that it forecloses the possibility of an immediate abortion despite some significant health risks. If the contention were correct, we would be required to invalidate the restrictive operation of the provision, for the essential holding of *Roe* forbids a State to interfere with a woman's choice to undergo an abortion procedure if continuing her pregnancy would constitute a threat to her health.

The District Court found that there were three serious conditions which would not be covered by the statute: preeclampsia, inevitable abortion, and premature ruptured membrane. Yet, as the Court of Appeals observed, it is undisputed that under some circumstances each of these conditions could lead to an illness with substantial and irreversible consequences. While the definition could be interpreted in an unconstitutional manner, the Court of Appeals construed the phrase "serious risk" to include those circumstances. . . . [W]e have said that we will defer to lower court interpretations of state law unless they amount to "plain" error. This " 'reflect[s] our belief that district courts and courts of appeals are better schooled in and more able to interpret the laws of their respective States.' "

We adhere to that course today, and conclude that, as construed by the Court of Appeals, the medical emergency definition imposes no undue burden on a woman's abortion right.

B

We next consider the informed consent requirement. Except in a medical emergency, the statute requires that at least 24 hours before performing an abortion a physician inform the woman of the nature of the procedure, the health risks of the abortion and of childbirth, and the "probable gestational age of the unborn child." The physician or a qualified nonphysician must inform the woman of the availability of printed materials published by the State describing the fetus and providing information about medical assistance for childbirth, information about child support from the father, and a list of agencies which provide adoption and other services as alternatives to abortion. An abortion may not be performed unless the woman certifies in writing that she has been informed of the availability of these printed materials and has been provided them if she chooses to view them.

Our prior decisions establish that as with any medical procedure, the State may require a woman to give her written informed consent to an abortion. In this respect, the statute is unexceptional. Petitioners challenge the statute's definition of informed consent because it includes the provision of specific information by the doctor and the mandatory 24-hour waiting period. . . .

[T]he undue burden standard adopted in this opinion require[s] us to overrule in part some of the Court's past decisions, decisions driven by the trimester framework's prohibition of all previability regulations designed to further the State's interest in fetal life. In *Akron I*, [for example,] we invalidated an ordinance which required that a woman seeking an abortion be provided by her physician with specific information "designed to influence the woman's informed choice between abortion or childbirth." . . . To the extent *Akron I* and *Thornburgh* find a constitutional violation when the government requires, as it does here, the giving of truthful, nonmisleading information about the nature of the procedure, the attendant health risks and those of childbirth, and the "probable gestational age" of the fetus, those cases go too far, are inconsistent with *Roe*'s acknowledgment of an important interest in potential life, and are overruled.

. . . It cannot be questioned that psychological well-being is a facet of health. Nor can it be doubted that most women considering an abortion would deem the impact on the fetus relevant, if not dispositive, to the decision. In attempting to ensure that a woman apprehend the full consequences of her decision, the State furthers the legitimate purpose of reducing the risk that a woman may elect an abortion, only to discover later, with devastating psychological consequences, that her decision was not fully informed. If the information the

State requires to be made available to the woman is truthful and not misleading, the requirement may be permissible.

We also see no reason why the State may not require doctors to inform a woman seeking an abortion of the availability of materials relating to the consequences to the fetus, even when those consequences have no direct relation to her health. An example illustrates the point. We would think it constitutional for the State to require that in order for there to be informed consent to a kidney transplant operation the recipient must be supplied with information about risks to the donor as well as risks to himself or herself. . . . [I]nformed choice need not be defined in such narrow terms that all considerations of the effect on the fetus are made irrelevant.

As we have made clear, we depart from the holdings of *Akron I* and *Thornburgh* to the extent that we permit a State to further its legitimate goal of protecting the life of the unborn by enacting legislation aimed at ensuring a decision that is mature and informed, even when in so doing the State expresses a preference for childbirth over abortion. In short, [these provisions are] a reasonable measure to ensure an informed choice, one which might cause the woman to choose childbirth over abortion. This requirement cannot be considered a substantial obstacle to obtaining an abortion, and, it follows, there is no undue burden. . . .

Our analysis of Pennsylvania's 24-hour waiting period between the provision of the information deemed necessary to informed consent and the performance of an abortion under the undue burden standard requires us to reconsider the premise behind the decision in *Akron I* invalidating a parallel requirement. . . . The idea that important decisions will be more informed and deliberate if they follow some period of reflection does not strike us as unreasonable, particularly where the statute directs that important information become part of the background of the decision. The statute, as construed by the Court of Appeals, permits avoidance of the waiting period in the event of a medical emergency and the record evidence shows that in the vast majority of cases, a 24-hour delay does not create any appreciable health risk. In theory, at least, the waiting period is a reasonable measure to implement the State's interest in protecting the life of the unborn, a measure that does not amount to an undue burden.

Whether the mandatory 24-hour waiting period is nonetheless invalid because in practice it is a substantial obstacle to a woman's choice to terminate her pregnancy is a closer question. The findings of fact by the District Court indicate that because of the distances many women must travel to reach an abortion provider, the practical effect will often be a delay of much more than a day because the waiting period requires that a woman seeking an abortion make at least two visits to the doctor. The District Court also found that in many instances this will increase the exposure of women seeking abortions to "the harassment and hostility of anti-abortion protestors demonstrating outside a clinic." As a result, the District Court found that for those women who have the fewest financial resources, those who must travel long distances, and those who have difficulty explaining their whereabouts to husbands, employers, or others, the 24-hour waiting period will be "particularly burdensome."

These findings are troubling in some respects, but they do not demonstrate that the waiting period constitutes an undue burden. We do not doubt that, as the District Court held, the waiting period has the effect of "increasing the cost and risk of delay of abortions," but the District Court did not conclude that the increased costs and potential delays amount to substantial obstacles. . . .

We also disagree with the District Court's conclusion that the "particularly burdensome" effects of the waiting period on some women require its invalidation. A particular burden is not of necessity a substantial obstacle. Whether a burden falls on a particular group is a distinct inquiry from whether it is a substantial obstacle even as to the women in that group. And the District Court did not conclude that the waiting period is such an obstacle even for the women who are most burdened by it. Hence, on the record before us, and in the context of this facial challenge, we are not convinced that the 24-hour waiting period constitutes an undue burden. . . .

C

Section 3209 of Pennsylvania's abortion law provides, except in cases of medical emergency, that no physician shall perform an abortion on a married woman without receiving a signed statement from the woman that she has notified her spouse that she is about to undergo an abortion. The woman has the option of providing an alternative signed statement certifying that her husband is not the man who impregnated her; that her husband could not be located; that the pregnancy is the result of spousal sexual assault which she has reported; or that the woman believes that notifying her husband will cause him or someone else to inflict bodily injury upon her. A physician who performs an abortion on a married woman without receiving the appropriate signed statement will have his or her license revoked, and is liable to the husband for damages. . . .

[Medical and social science research, as well as the] District Court's findings reinforce what common sense would suggest. In well-functioning marriages, spouses discuss important intimate decisions such as whether to bear a child. But there are millions of women in this country who are the victims of regular physical and psychological abuse at the hands of their husbands. Should these women become pregnant, they may have very good reasons for not wishing to inform their husbands of their decision to obtain an abortion. Many may have justifiable fears of physical abuse, but may be no less fearful of the consequences of reporting prior abuse to the Commonwealth of Pennsylvania. Many may have a reasonable fear that notifying their husbands will provoke further instances of child abuse; these women are not exempt from § 3209's notification requirement. Many may fear devastating forms of psychological abuse from their husbands, including verbal harassment, threats of future violence, the destruction of possessions, physical confinement to the home, the withdrawal of financial support, or the disclosure of the abortion to family and friends. These methods of psychological abuse may act as even more of a deterrent to notification than the possibility of physical violence, but women who are the victims of the abuse are not exempt from § 3209's notification requirement. . . .

The spousal notification requirement is thus likely to prevent a significant number of women from obtaining an abortion. It does not merely make abortions a little more difficult or expensive to obtain; for many women, it will impose a substantial obstacle. We must not blind ourselves to the fact that the significant number of women who fear for their safety and the safety of their children are likely to be deterred from procuring an abortion as surely as if the Commonwealth had outlawed abortion in all cases.

Respondents attempt to avoid the conclusion that § 3209 is invalid by pointing out that it imposes almost no burden at all for the vast majority of women seeking abortions. They begin by noting that only about 20 percent of the women who obtain abortions are married. They then note that of these women about 95 percent notify their husbands of their own volition. Thus, respondents argue, the effects of § 3209 are felt by only one percent of the women who obtain abortions. Respondents argue that since some of these women will be able to notify their husbands without adverse consequences or will qualify for one of the exceptions, the statute affects fewer than one percent of women seeking abortions. For this reason, it is asserted, the statute cannot be invalid on its face. We disagree with respondents' basic method of analysis.

The analysis does not end with the one percent of women upon whom the statute operates; it begins there. Legislation is measured for consistency with the Constitution by its impact on those whose conduct it affects. For example, we would not say that a law which requires a newspaper to print a candidate's reply to an unfavorable editorial is valid on its face because most newspapers would adopt the policy even absent the law. The proper focus of constitutional inquiry is the group for whom the law is a restriction, not the group for whom the law is irrelevant. . . .

Section 3209's real target is . . . married women seeking abortions who do not wish to notify their husbands of their intentions and who do not qualify for one of the statutory exceptions to the notice requirement. The unfortunate yet persisting conditions we document above will mean that in a large fraction of the cases in which § 3209 is relevant, it will operate as a substantial obstacle to a woman's choice to undergo an abortion. It is an undue burden, and therefore invalid.

This conclusion is in no way inconsistent with our decisions upholding parental notification or consent requirements. Those enactments, and our judgment that they are constitutional, are based on the quite reasonable assumption that minors will benefit from consultation with their parents and that children will often not realize that their parents have their best interests at heart. We cannot adopt a parallel assumption about adult women.

We recognize that a husband has a "deep and proper concern and interest . . . in his wife's pregnancy and in the growth and development of the fetus she is carrying." With regard to the children he has fathered and raised, the Court has recognized his "cognizable and substantial" interest in their custody. If these cases concerned a State's ability to require the mother to notify the father before taking some action with respect to a living child raised by both, therefore, it would be reasonable to conclude as a general matter that the father's interest in the welfare of the child and the mother's interest are equal. Before birth, however, the issue takes on a very different cast. It is an inescapable biological fact that state regulation with respect to the child a woman is carrying will have a far greater impact on the mother's liberty than on the father's. The effect of state regulation on a woman's protected liberty is doubly deserving of scrutiny in such a case, as the State has touched not only upon the private sphere of the family but upon the very bodily integrity of the pregnant woman.

The Court has held that "when the wife and the husband disagree on this decision, the view of only one of the two marriage partners can prevail. Inasmuch as it is the woman who physically bears the child and who is the more directly and immediately affected by the pregnancy, as between the two, the balance weighs in her favor." *Planned Parenthood of Central Missouri v. Danforth* (1976). . . . The Constitution protects individuals, men and women alike, from unjustified state interference, even when that interference is enacted into law for the benefit of their spouses.

There was a time, not so long ago, when a different understanding of the family and of the Constitution prevailed. In *Bradwell v. State* (1873), three Members of this Court reaffirmed the common-law principle that "a woman had no legal existence separate from her husband, who was regarded as her head and representative in the social state.["] These views, of course, are no longer consistent with our understanding of the family, the individual, or the Constitution.

. . . For the great many women who are victims of abuse inflicted by their husbands, or whose children are the victims of such abuse, a spousal notice requirement enables the husband to wield an effective veto over his wife's decision. Whether the prospect of notification itself deters such women from seeking abortions, or whether the husband, through physical force or psychological pressure or economic coercion, prevents his wife from obtaining an abortion until it is too late, the notice requirement will often be tantamount to the veto found unconstitutional in *Danforth*. The women most affected by this law—those who most reasonably fear the consequences of notifying their husbands that they are pregnant—are in the gravest danger. . . . Women do not lose their constitutionally protected liberty when they marry. . . .

JUSTICE STEVENS, concurring in part and dissenting in part.

The portions of the Court's opinion that I have joined are more important than those with which I disagree. I shall therefore first comment on significant areas of agreement, and then explain the limited character of my disagreement.

I

The Court is unquestionably correct in concluding that the doctrine of *stare decisis* has controlling significance in a case of this kind, notwithstanding an individual Justice's concerns about the merits.[1] The central holding of *Roe v. Wade* has been a "part of our law" for almost two decades. It was a natural sequel to the protection of individual liberty established in *Griswold v. Connecticut* (1965). The societal costs of overruling *Roe* at this late date would be enormous. *Roe* is an integral part of a correct understanding of both the concept of liberty and the basic equality of men and women. . . .

I also accept what is implicit in the Court's analysis, namely, a reaffirmation of *Roe*'s explanation of *why* the State's obligation to protect the life or health of the mother must take precedence over any duty to the unborn. The Court in *Roe* carefully considered, and rejected, the State's argument "that the fetus is a 'person' within the language and meaning of the Fourteenth Amendment." . . . Accordingly, an abortion is not "the termination of life entitled to Fourteenth Amendment protection." From this holding, there was no dissent; indeed, no Member of the Court has ever questioned this fundamental proposition. Thus, as a matter of federal constitutional law, a developing organism that is not yet a "person" does not have what is sometimes described as a "right to life." This has been and, by the Court's holding today, remains a fundamental premise of our constitutional law governing reproductive autonomy.

II

My disagreement with the joint opinion begins with its understanding of the trimester framework established in *Roe*. . . .

Weighing the State's interest in potential life and the woman's liberty interest, I agree with the joint opinion that the State may "expres[s] a preference for normal childbirth," that the State may take steps to ensure that a woman's choice "is thoughtful and informed," and that "States are free to enact laws to provide a reasonable framework for a woman to make a decision that has such profound and lasting meaning." Serious questions arise, however, when a State attempts to "persuade the woman to choose childbirth over abortion." Decisional autonomy must limit the State's power to inject into a woman's most personal deliberations its own views of what is best. The State may promote its preferences by funding childbirth, by creating and maintaining alternatives to

---

[1]   It is sometimes useful to view the issue of *stare decisis* from a historical perspective. In the last 19 years, 15 Justices have confronted the basic issue presented in *Roe v. Wade* (1973). Of those, 11 have voted as the majority does today: Chief Justice Burger, Justices Douglas, Brennan, Stewart, Marshall, and Powell, and Justices Blackmun, O'Connor, Kennedy, Souter, and myself. Only four—all of whom happen to be on the Court today—have reached the opposite conclusion.

abortion, and by espousing the virtues of family; but it must respect the individual's freedom to make such judgments. . . .

Under these principles, [some of the informed consent requirements] are unconstitutional. Those sections require a physician or counselor to provide the woman with a range of materials clearly designed to persuade her to choose not to undergo the abortion. While the Commonwealth is free . . . to produce and disseminate such material, the Commonwealth may not inject such information into the woman's deliberations just as she is weighing such an important choice.

Under this same analysis, [other elements of the informed consent requirements] are constitutional. Those sections, which require the physician to inform a woman of the nature and risks of the abortion procedure and the medical risks of carrying to term, are neutral requirements comparable to those imposed in other medical procedures. Those sections indicate no effort by the Commonwealth to influence the woman's choice in any way. If anything, such requirements *enhance,* rather than skew, the woman's decisionmaking.

III

The 24-hour waiting period required by . . . the Pennsylvania statute raises even more serious concerns. Such a requirement arguably furthers the Commonwealth's interests in two ways, neither of which is constitutionally permissible.

First, it may be argued that the 24-hour delay is justified by the mere fact that it is likely to reduce the number of abortions, thus furthering the Commonwealth's interest in potential life. But such an argument would justify any form of coercion that placed an obstacle in the woman's path. The Commonwealth cannot further its interests by simply wearing down the ability of the pregnant woman to exercise her constitutional right.

Second, it can more reasonably be argued that the 24-hour delay furthers the Commonwealth's interest in ensuring that the woman's decision is informed and thoughtful. But there is no evidence that the mandated delay benefits women or that it is necessary to enable the physician to convey any relevant information to the patient. The mandatory delay thus appears to rest on outmoded and unacceptable assumptions about the decisionmaking capacity of women. . . .

In the alternative, the delay requirement may be premised on the belief that the decision to terminate a pregnancy is presumptively wrong. This premise is illegitimate. . . . No person undertakes such a decision lightly—and States may not presume that a woman has failed to reflect adequately merely because her conclusion differs from the State's preference. . . .

Part of the constitutional liberty to choose is the equal dignity to which each of us is entitled. A woman who decides to terminate her pregnancy is entitled to the same respect as a woman who decides to carry the fetus to term. The mandatory waiting period denies women that equal respect.

IV

In my opinion, a correct application of the "undue burden" standard leads to the same conclusion concerning the constitutionality of these requirements. A state-imposed burden on the exercise of a constitutional right is measured both by its effects and by its character: A burden may be "undue" either because the burden is too severe or because it lacks a legitimate, rational justification.[6] . . .

Accordingly, while I disagree with Parts IV, V-B, and V-D of the joint opinion, I join the remainder of the Court's opinion.

JUSTICE BLACKMUN, concurring in part, concurring in the judgment in part, and dissenting in part.

I join Parts I, II, III, V-A, V-C, and VI of the joint opinion of Justices O'Connor, Kennedy, and Souter. . . . I do not underestimate the significance of today's joint opinion. Yet I remain steadfast in my belief that the right to reproductive choice is entitled to the full protection afforded by this Court [under the strict scrutiny standard]. And I fear for the darkness as four Justices anxiously await the single vote necessary to extinguish the light.

I

. . . [W]hile I believe that the joint opinion errs in failing to invalidate the other regulations [apart from the spousal notification requirement], I am pleased that the joint opinion has not ruled out the possibility that these regulations may be shown to impose an unconstitutional burden. The joint opinion makes clear that its specific holdings are based on the insufficiency of the record before it. I am confident that in the future evidence will be produced to show that "in a large fraction of the cases in which [these regulations are] relevant,

---

[6] The meaning of any legal standard can only be understood by reviewing the actual cases in which it is applied. For that reason, I discount both Justice Scalia's comments on past descriptions of the standard, see *post*, and the attempt to give it crystal clarity in the joint opinion. . . .

[they] will operate as a substantial obstacle to a woman's choice to undergo an abortion." *Ante.*

II

Today, no less than yesterday, the Constitution and decisions of this Court require that a State's abortion restrictions be subjected to the strictest of judicial scrutiny. . . . Under this standard, the Pennsylvania statute's provisions requiring content-based counseling [and] a 24-hour delay . . . must be invalidated.

. . . State restrictions on abortion violate a woman's right of privacy in two ways. First, compelled continuation of a pregnancy infringes upon a woman's right to bodily integrity by imposing substantial physical intrusions and significant risks of physical harm. . . . [R]estrictive abortion laws force women to endure physical invasions far more substantial than those this Court has held to violate the constitutional principle of bodily integrity in other contexts. See, *e.g., Winston v. Lee* (1985) (invalidating surgical removal of bullet from murder suspect); *Rochin v. California* (1952) (invalidating stomach pumping). [Second], when the State restricts a woman's right to terminate her pregnancy, it . . . has no less an impact on a woman's life than decisions about contraception or marriage. Because motherhood has a dramatic impact on a woman's educational prospects, employment opportunities, and self-determination, restrictive abortion laws deprive her of basic control over her life. For these reasons, "the decision whether or not to beget or bear a child" lies at "the very heart of this cluster of constitutionally protected choices."

A State's restrictions on a woman's right to terminate her pregnancy also implicate constitutional guarantees of gender equality. State restrictions on abortion compel women to continue pregnancies they otherwise might terminate. By restricting the right to terminate pregnancies, the State conscripts women's bodies into its service, forcing women to continue their pregnancies, suffer the pains of childbirth, and in most instances, provide years of maternal care. The State does not compensate women for their services; instead, it assumes that they owe this duty as a matter of course. This assumption—that women can simply be forced to accept the "natural" status and incidents of motherhood—appears to rest upon a conception of women's role that has triggered the protection of the Equal Protection Clause. See, *e.g., Mississippi Univ. for Women v. Hogan* (1982); *Craig v. Boren* (1976).[4] The joint opinion recognizes that these assumptions about women's place in society "are no longer consistent with our understanding of the family, the individual, or the Constitution."

The Court has held that limitations on the right of privacy are permissible only if they survive "strict" constitutional scrutiny. . . . *Griswold v. Connecticut* (1965). . . . Application of the strict scrutiny standard results in the invalidation of all the challenged provisions. . . .

* * *

In one sense, the Court's approach is worlds apart from that of the Chief Justice. . . . And yet, in another sense, the distance between the two approaches is short—the distance is but a single vote. I am 83 years old. I cannot remain on this Court forever, and when I do step down, the confirmation process for my successor well may focus on the issue before us today. That, I regret, may be exactly where the choice between the two worlds will be made.

CHIEF JUSTICE REHNQUIST, with whom JUSTICE WHITE, JUSTICE SCALIA, and JUSTICE THOMAS join, concurring in the judgment in part and dissenting in part.

The joint opinion, following its newly minted variation on *stare decisis*, retains the outer shell of *Roe v. Wade* (1973), but beats a wholesale retreat from the substance of that case. We believe that *Roe* was wrongly decided, and that it can and should be overruled consistently with our traditional approach to *stare decisis* in constitutional cases. We would . . . uphold the challenged provisions of the Pennsylvania statute in their entirety. . . .

In *Roe v. Wade*, the Court recognized a "guarantee of personal privacy" which "is broad enough to encompass a woman's decision whether or not to terminate her pregnancy." We are now of the view that, in terming this right fundamental, the Court in *Roe* read the earlier opinions upon which it based its decision much too broadly. Unlike marriage, procreation, and contraception, abortion "involves the purposeful termination of a potential life." The abortion decision must therefore "be recognized as *sui generis*, different in kind from the others that the Court has protected under the rubric of personal or family privacy and autonomy." *Thornburgh v. American College of Obstetricians and Gynecologists* (1986) (White, J., dissenting). One cannot ignore the fact that a

---

[4]   A growing number of commentators are recognizing this point. See, *e.g.,* L. Tribe, *American Constitutional Law* (1988); MacKinnon, *Reflections on Sex Equality Under Law*, 100 Yale L.J. 1281 (1991).

woman is not isolated in her pregnancy, and that the decision to abort necessarily involves the destruction of a fetus. See *Michael H. v. Gerald D.* (1989) ('To
look "at the act which is assertedly the subject of a liberty interest in isolation
from its effect upon other people [is] like inquiring whether there is a liberty
interest in firing a gun where the case at hand happens to involve its discharge
into another person's body").

Nor do the historical traditions of the American people support the view
that the right to terminate one's pregnancy is "fundamental." The common
law which we inherited from England made abortion after "quickening" an
offense. At the time of the adoption of the Fourteenth Amendment, statutory
prohibitions or restrictions on abortion were commonplace; in 1868, at least 28
of the then-37 States and 8 Territories had statutes banning or limiting abortion. By the turn of the century virtually every State had a law prohibiting or
restricting abortion on its books. By the middle of the present century, a liberalization trend had set in. But 21 of the restrictive abortion laws in effect in
1868 were still in effect in 1973 when *Roe* was decided, and an overwhelming
majority of the States prohibited abortion unless necessary to preserve the life
or health of the mother. On this record, it can scarcely be said that any deeply
rooted tradition of relatively unrestricted abortion in our history supported the
classification of the right to abortion as "fundamental" under the Due Process
Clause of the Fourteenth Amendment.

We think, therefore, both in view of this history and of our decided cases
dealing with substantive liberty under the Due Process Clause, that the Court
was mistaken in *Roe* when it classified a woman's decision to terminate her
pregnancy as a "fundamental right" that could be abridged only in a manner
which withstood "strict scrutiny." . . .

II

The joint opinion of Justices O'Connor, Kennedy and Souter cannot bring
itself to say that *Roe* was correct as an original matter. . . . Instead of claiming
that *Roe* was correct as a matter of original constitutional interpretation, the
opinion therefore contains an elaborate discussion of *stare decisis*.

This discussion of the principle of *stare decisis* appears to be almost entirely dicta, because the joint opinion does not apply that principle in dealing
with *Roe*. *Roe* decided that a woman had a fundamental right to an abortion.
The joint opinion rejects that view. *Roe* decided that abortion regulations were
to be subjected to "strict scrutiny" and could be justified only in the light of

"compelling state interests." The joint opinion rejects that view. *Roe* analyzed abortion regulation under a rigid trimester framework, a framework which has guided this Court's decisionmaking for 19 years. The joint opinion rejects that framework.

Stare decisis is defined in Black's Law Dictionary as meaning "to abide by, or adhere to, decided cases." Whatever the "central holding" of *Roe* that is left after the joint opinion finishes dissecting it is surely not the result of that principle. While purporting to adhere to precedent, the joint opinion instead revises it. *Roe* continues to exist, but only in the way a storefront on a western movie set exists: a mere facade to give the illusion of reality. Decisions following *Roe*, such as *Akron v. Akron Center for Reproductive Health, Inc.* (1983), and *Thornburgh v. American College of Obstetricians and Gynecologists* (1986), are frankly overruled in part under the "undue burden" standard expounded in the joint opinion. . . .

The end result of the joint opinion's paeans of praise for legitimacy is the enunciation of a brand new standard for evaluating state regulation of a woman's right to abortion—the "undue burden" standard. As indicated above, *Roe v. Wade* adopted a "fundamental right" standard under which state regulations could survive only if they met the requirement of "strict scrutiny." While we disagree with that standard, it at least had a recognized basis in constitutional law at the time *Roe* was decided. The same cannot be said for the "undue burden" standard, which is created largely out of whole cloth by the authors of the joint opinion. . . .

The sum of the joint opinion's labors in the name of *stare decisis* and "legitimacy" is this: *Roe v. Wade* stands as a sort of judicial Potemkin Village, which may be pointed out to passers-by as a monument to the importance of adhering to precedent. But behind the facade, an entirely new method of analysis, without any roots in constitutional law, is imported to decide the constitutionality of state laws regulating abortion. Neither *stare decisis* nor "legitimacy" are truly served by such an effort.

We have stated above our belief that the Constitution does not subject state abortion regulations to heightened scrutiny. Accordingly, we think that the correct analysis is that . . . [a] woman's interest in having an abortion is a form of liberty protected by the Due Process Clause, but States may regulate abortion procedures in ways rationally related to a legitimate state interest. *Williamson v. Lee Optical of Oklahoma, Inc.* (1955). With this rule in mind, . . .

each of the challenged provisions of the Pennsylvania statute is consistent with the Constitution. . . .

Justice Scalia, with whom The Chief Justice, Justice White, and Justice Thomas join, concurring in the judgment in part and dissenting in part.

My views on this matter are unchanged from [previous cases]. . . . A State's choice between two positions on which reasonable people can disagree is constitutional even when (as is often the case) it intrudes upon a "liberty" in the absolute sense. Laws against bigamy, for example—with which entire societies of reasonable people disagree—intrude upon men and women's liberty to marry and live with one another. But bigamy happens not to be a liberty specially "protected" by the Constitution.

That is, quite simply, the issue in these cases: not whether the power of a woman to abort her unborn child is a "liberty" in the absolute sense; or even whether it is a liberty of great importance to many women. Of course it is both. The issue is whether it is a liberty protected by the Constitution of the United States. I am sure it is not. I reach that conclusion not because of anything so exalted as my views concerning the "concept of existence, of meaning, of the universe, and of the mystery of human life." Rather, I reach it for the same reason I reach the conclusion that bigamy is not constitutionally protected—because of two simple facts: (1) the Constitution says absolutely nothing about it, and (2) the longstanding traditions of American society have permitted it to be legally proscribed. . . .

[A]pplying the rational basis test, I would uphold the Pennsylvania statute in its entirety. . . .

The emptiness of the "reasoned judgment" that produced *Roe* is displayed in plain view by the fact that, after more than 19 years of effort by some of the brightest (and most determined) legal minds in the country, after more than 10 cases upholding abortion rights in this Court, and after dozens upon dozens of *amicus* briefs submitted in these and other cases, the best the Court can do to explain how it is that the word "liberty" *must* be thought to include the right to destroy human fetuses is to rattle off a collection of adjectives that simply decorate a value judgment and conceal a political choice. The right to abort, we are told, inheres in "liberty" because it is among "a person's most basic decisions"; it involves a "most intimate and personal choic[e]"; it is "central to personal dignity and autonomy"; it "originate[s] within the zone of conscience and belief"; it is "too intimate and personal" for state interference; it reflects

"intimate views" of a "deep, personal character"; it involves "intimate relationships" and notions of "personal autonomy and bodily integrity"; and it concerns
a particularly " 'important decisio[n].' "

But it is obvious to anyone applying "reasoned judgment" that the same
adjectives can be applied to many forms of conduct that this Court . . . has held
are *not* entitled to constitutional protection—because, like abortion, they are
forms of conduct that have long been criminalized in American society. Those
adjectives might be applied, for example, to homosexual sodomy, polygamy,
adult incest, and suicide, all of which are equally "intimate" and "deep[ly] personal" decisions involving "personal autonomy and bodily integrity," and all of
which can constitutionally be proscribed because it is our unquestionable constitutional tradition that they are proscribable. It is not reasoned judgment that
supports the Court's decision; only personal predilection. . . .

If, indeed, the "liberties" protected by the Constitution are, as the Court
says, undefined and unbounded, then . . . confirmation hearings for new Justices *should* deteriorate into question-and-answer sessions in which Senators go
through a list of their constituents' most favored and most disfavored alleged
constitutional rights, and seek the nominee's commitment to support or oppose them. Value judgments, after all, should be voted on, not dictated; and if
our Constitution has somehow accidentally committed them to the Supreme
Court, at least we can have a sort of plebiscite each time a new nominee to
that body is put forward. Justice Blackmun not only regards this prospect with
equanimity, he solicits it. . . .

* * *

. . . We should get out of this area, where we have no right to be, and where
we do neither ourselves nor the country any good by remaining.

In *Stenberg v. Carhart* (2000), a five-justice majority applied *Casey*'s undue
burden standard to strike down a Nebraska statute that provided a flat prohibition on "partial birth abortions," which the statute defined as abortions in
which the physician "partially delivers vaginally a living unborn child before
killing the unborn child and completing the delivery." While such methods are
sometimes used for relatively late-term abortions, this case concerned pre-viabil-
ity abortions. Justice O'Connor, who was in the majority, found it critical that
the statute lacked any exception for cases where the technique is necessary for

the health of the mother. Justice Kennedy dissented along with the remaining three members of the four-justice bloc that would have overruled *Roe* in *Casey*.

Congress then passed the Partial-Birth Abortion Ban Act of 2003, providing criminal penalties for "[a]ny physician who, in or affecting interstate or foreign commerce, knowingly performs a partial-birth abortion and thereby kills a human fetus." The statute included a finding that "[a] moral, medical, and ethical consensus exists that the practice of performing a partial-birth abortion . . . is a gruesome and inhumane procedure that is never medically necessary and should be prohibited." In *Gonzales v. Carhart* (2007), a five-justice majority upheld the Act, with Justice Kennedy writing the majority decision and Justice Alito—who had replaced Justice O'Connor—helping to form the five-judge majority. Justices Stevens, Souter, Ginsburg, and Breyer dissented.

Justice Ginsburg's dissent was particularly notable in suggesting a path toward grounding abortion jurisprudence in equal protection values:

> As *Casey* comprehended, at stake in cases challenging abortion restrictions is a woman's "control over her [own] destiny." . . . Women, it is now acknowledged, have the talent, capacity, and right "to participate equally in the economic and social life of the Nation." Their ability to realize their full potential, the Court recognized, is intimately connected to "their ability to control their reproductive lives." Thus, legal challenges to undue restrictions on abortion procedures do not seek to vindicate some generalized notion of privacy; rather, they center on a woman's autonomy to determine her life's course, and thus to enjoy equal citizenship stature. . . .

> [T]he Court invokes an antiabortion shibboleth for which it concededly has no reliable evidence: Women who have abortions come to regret their choices, and consequently suffer from "[s]evere depression and loss of esteem." Because of women's fragile emotional state and because of the "bond of love the mother has for her child," the Court worries, doctors may withhold information about the nature of the intact D & E procedure. . . . This way of thinking reflects ancient notions about women's place in the family and under the Constitution—ideas that have long since been discredited. . . .

See also Ruth Bader Ginsburg, *Some Thoughts on Autonomy and Equality in Relation to* Roe v. Wade, 63 U.N.C. L. Rev. 375 (1985).

The Supreme Court returned to these issues in *Whole Women's Health v. Hellerstedt* (2016), which resulted in a 5–3 opinion invalidating two provisions of a Texas abortion law. The first of these required a physician performing an abortion to have admitting privileges at a hospital within 30 miles. The second required that abortion facilities satisfy the requirements of state law for ambulatory surgical centers.

Writing for the majority, Justice Breyer concluded that "neither of these provisions confers medical benefits sufficient to justify the burdens upon access that each imposes." He thus emphasized that courts must "consider the burdens a law imposes on abortion access together with the benefits those laws confer." He relied heavily on findings by the district court on both sides of the calculus. And in doing so, he expressed disagreement with a statement by the court of appeals that "medical uncertainty underlying a statute is for resolution by legislatures, not the courts." "Instead," he wrote, "the Court, when determining the constitutionality of laws regulating abortion procedures, has placed considerable weight upon evidence and argument presented in judicial proceedings."

With respect to the burden, Justice Breyer pointed to findings that each of the provisions would cause the closure of a substantial number of facilities—bringing the total number in the state from 40 down to seven or eight—so that many more women would have to travel great distances to secure an abortion. With respect to the medical benefits, Justice Breyer went through extensive analysis on both provisions. A key point with respect to both was that in the rare instances in which a serious complication results from an abortion, it is almost always after the patient has left the facility. Neither admitting privileges nor the surgical-center requirement would help in those cases. In addition, these requirements are not imposed for various procedures that are more dangerous than abortions, such as colonoscopies and vasectomies.

Justice Ginsburg, while concurring in Justice Breyer's opinion, wrote a one-paragraph concurrence. The subtext might have been that the case did not bear the extensive analysis Justice Breyer gave it. She said explicitly that it was "beyond rational belief" that the law would protect women's health, and certain that it would make it more difficult for them to obtain abortions.

Justice Alito, joined by the Chief Justice and Justice Thomas, dissented, principally on the ground that the action should have been precluded by prior litigation. He complained about the Court's "patent refusal to apply well-established law in a neutral way." Justice Thomas wrote a more broad-ranging dissent. He also contended that the Court was "bend[ing] the rules" in favor of abortion: The decision, he said, "creates an abortion exception to ordinary rules of res judicata, ignores compelling evidence that Texas' law imposes no unconstitutional burden, and disregards basic principles of the severability doctrine." Furthermore, he argued, the majority "eviscerate[d three] important features of [the undue burden] test to return to a regime like the one that *Casey* repudiated": First, the Court now required consideration of the benefits of restrictions together with the burdens they impose; second, the Court declined to defer to legislative assessments of the justifications for abortion restrictions; and third, even if a law imposes no substantial restriction on access to abortion, the Court now required more than a reasonable relation to a legitimate state interest.

Four years later, *June Medical Services L.L.C. v. Russo* (2020) presented the Court with a Louisiana statute that had an admitting-privileges requirement almost identical to Texas's—but now Justice Gorsuch filled the seat that was vacant at the time of *Whole Women's Health*, and Justice Kavanagh had replaced Justice Kennedy, who had been a member of the *Whole Women's Health* majority. This time, however, Chief Justice Roberts joined the four remaining members of the *Whole Women's Health* majority to yield a 5–4 decision invalidating the law. Justice Breyer wrote for the foursome; he intensely examined the evidence, doctor by doctor, of what the impact of the law would be. The Chief Justice wrote separately. He based his opinion largely on *stare decisis*, saying that he thought the Court needed to adhere to *Whole Women's Health*— but at the same time, he contended that the Court should apply a test that was rejected in that case, under which the Court, having determined that the law served a legitimate objective, would not balance benefits against burdens. Each of the dissenters wrote an opinion, raising a variety of issues—among others, objections to the standing of abortion providers and disagreement with Justice Breyer as to what the evidence showed. Justice Thomas's dissent included an argument that "[t]he Constitution does not constrain the States' ability to regulate or even prohibit abortion."

d.   SDP—a Right to Die?

Washington v. Glucksberg

Supreme Court of the United States, 1997.
521 U.S. 702.

CHIEF JUSTICE REHNQUIST delivered the opinion of the Court.

The question presented in this case is whether Washington's prohibition against "caus[ing]" or "aid[ing]" a suicide offends the Fourteenth Amendment to the United States Constitution. We hold that it does not.

It has always been a crime to assist a suicide in the State of Washington. [But] Washington's Natural Death Act, enacted in 1979, states that the "withholding or withdrawal of life-sustaining treatment" at a patient's direction "shall not, for any purpose, constitute a suicide."[2]

 WORTH NOTING In a companion decision also authored by Chief Justice Rehnquist, the Supreme Court held that New York did not violate the Equal Protection Clause by banning assisted suicide but allowing terminally ill patients to direct the withdrawal of life-support systems. *Vacco v. Quill* (1997).

Petitioners in this case are the State of Washington and its Attorney General. Respondents . . . are physicians who practice in Washington. These doctors occasionally treat terminally ill, suffering patients, and declare that they would assist these patients in ending their lives if not for Washington's assisted-suicide ban. In January 1994, respondents, along with three gravely ill, pseudonymous plaintiffs who have since died and Compassion in Dying, a nonprofit organization that counsels people considering physician-assisted suicide, sued in the United States District Court, seeking a declaration that [the assisted-suicide ban] is, on its face, unconstitutional. . . .[4]

---

[2]   . . . In Washington, "[a]ny adult person may execute a directive directing the withholding or withdrawal of life-sustaining treatment in a terminal condition or permanent unconscious condition," and a physician who, in accordance with such a directive, participates in the withholding or withdrawal of life-sustaining treatment is immune from civil, criminal, or professional liability.

[4]   John Doe, Jane Roe, and James Poe, plaintiffs in the District Court, were then in the terminal phases of serious and painful illnesses. They declared that they were mentally competent and desired assistance in ending their lives.

I

We begin, as we do in all due process cases, by examining our Nation's history, legal traditions, and practices. In almost every State—indeed, in almost every western democracy—it is a crime to assist a suicide. The States' assisted-suicide bans are not innovations. Rather, they are longstanding expressions of the States' commitment to the protection and preservation of all human life. Indeed, opposition to and condemnation of suicide—and, therefore, of assisting suicide—are consistent and enduring themes of our philosophical, legal, and cultural heritages. See generally New York State Task Force on Life and the Law, *When Death is Sought: Assisted Suicide and Euthanasia in the Medical Context* (May 1994) (hereinafter New York Task Force).

More specifically, for over 700 years, the Anglo-American common-law tradition has punished or otherwise disapproved of both suicide and assisting suicide. In the 13th century, Henry de Bracton, one of the first legal-treatise writers, observed that "[j]ust as a man may commit felony by slaying another so may he do so by slaying himself." The real and personal property of one who killed himself to avoid conviction and punishment for a crime were forfeit to the King; however, thought Bracton, "if a man slays himself in weariness of life or because he is unwilling to endure further bodily pain . . . [only] his movable goods [were] confiscated." . . . For the most part, the early American Colonies adopted the common-law approach. . . .

Over time, however, the American Colonies abolished these harsh common-law penalties. . . . Zephaniah Swift, who would later become Chief Justice of Connecticut, wrote in 1796:

> There can be no act more contemptible, than to attempt to punish an offender for a crime, by exercising a mean act of revenge upon lifeless clay, that is insensible of the punishment. There can be no greater cruelty, than the inflicting [of] a punishment, as the forfeiture of goods, which must fall solely on the innocent offspring of the offender. . . . [Suicide] is so abhorrent to the feelings of mankind, and that strong love of life which is implanted in the human heart, that it cannot be so frequently committed, as to become dangerous to society. There can of course be no necessity of any punishment.

This statement makes it clear, however, that the movement away from the common law's harsh sanctions did not represent an acceptance of suicide; rather, as Chief Justice Swift observed, this change reflected the growing consensus that it was unfair to punish the suicide's family for his wrongdoing. Nonetheless, although States moved away from Blackstone's treatment of suicide, courts continued to condemn it as a grave public wrong. . . .

That suicide remained a grievous, though nonfelonious, wrong is confirmed by the fact that colonial and early state legislatures and courts did not retreat from prohibiting assisting suicide. Swift, in his early 19th-century treatise on the laws of Connecticut, stated that "[i]f one counsels another to commit suicide, and the other by reason of the advice kills himself, the advisor is guilty of murder as principal." This was the well-established common-law view. . . . The earliest American statute explicitly to outlaw assisting suicide was enacted in New York in 1828, and many of the new States and Territories followed New York's example. . . .

Though deeply rooted, the States' assisted-suicide bans have in recent years been reexamined and, generally, reaffirmed. Because of advances in medicine and technology, Americans today are increasingly likely to die in institutions, from chronic illnesses. Public concern and democratic action are therefore sharply focused on how best to protect dignity and independence at the end of life, with the result that there have been many significant changes in state laws and in the attitudes these laws reflect. Many States, for example, now permit "living wills," surrogate health-care decisionmaking, and the withdrawal or refusal of life-sustaining medical treatment. At the same time, however, voters and legislators continue for the most part to reaffirm their States' prohibitions on assisting suicide. . . . Thus, the States are currently engaged in serious, thoughtful examinations of physician-assisted suicide and other similar issues. . . .

Attitudes toward suicide itself have changed since Bracton, but our laws have consistently condemned, and continue to prohibit, assisting suicide. Despite changes in medical technology and notwithstanding an increased emphasis on the importance of end-of-life decisionmaking, we have not retreated from this prohibition. Against this backdrop of history, tradition, and practice, we now turn to respondents' constitutional claim.

II

The Due Process Clause guarantees more than fair process, and the "liberty" it protects includes more than the absence of physical restraint. *Collins v. Harker Heights* (1992) (Due Process Clause "protects individual liberty against 'certain government actions regardless of the fairness of the procedures used to implement them' "). The Clause also provides heightened protection against government interference with certain fundamental rights and liberty interests.

In a long line of cases, we have held that, in addition to the specific freedoms protected by the Bill of Rights, the "liberty" specially protected by the Due Process Clause includes the rights to marry, *Loving v. Virginia* (1967); to have children, *Skinner v. Oklahoma ex rel. Williamson* (1942); to direct the education and upbringing of one's children, *Meyer v. Nebraska* (1923); *Pierce v. Society of Sisters* (1925); to marital privacy, *Griswold v. Connecticut* (1965); to use contraception, *Eisenstadt v. Baird* (1972); to bodily integrity, *Rochin v. California* (1952), and to abortion, *Planned Parenthood v. Casey* (1992). We have also assumed, and strongly suggested, that the Due Process Clause protects the traditional right to refuse unwanted lifesaving medical treatment. *Cruzan v. Director, Mo. Dept. of Health* (1990) [(permitting state to require clear and convincing evidence of a patient's intention regarding the removal of life support)].

But we "ha[ve] always been reluctant to expand the concept of substantive due process because guideposts for responsible decisionmaking in this unchartered area are scarce and open-ended." By extending constitutional protection to an asserted right or liberty interest, we, to a great extent, place the matter outside the arena of public debate and legislative action. We must therefore "exercise the utmost care whenever we are asked to break new ground in this field," lest the liberty protected by the Due Process Clause be subtly transformed into the policy preferences of the Members of this Court.

Our established method of substantive-due-process analysis has two primary features: First, we have regularly observed that the Due Process Clause specially protects those fundamental rights and liberties which are, objectively "deeply rooted in this Nation's history and tradition," *Moore v. East Cleveland* (plurality opinion); *Snyder v. Massachusetts* (1934) ("so rooted in the traditions and conscience of our people as to be ranked as fundamental"), and "implicit in the concept of ordered liberty," such that "neither liberty nor justice would exist if they were sacrificed," *Palko v. Connecticut* (1937). Second, we have required in substantive-due-process cases a "careful description" of the asserted fundamental liberty interest. *Cruzan.* Our Nation's history, legal traditions, and practices thus provide the crucial "guideposts for responsible decisionmaking" that direct and restrain our exposition of the Due Process Clause. As we stated recently in *Reno v. Flores* (1993), the Fourteenth Amendment "forbids the government to infringe . . . 'fundamental' liberty interests *at all*, no matter what process is provided, unless the infringement is narrowly tailored to serve a compelling state interest."

Justice Souter, relying on Justice Harlan's dissenting opinion in *Poe v. Ullman* (1961), would largely abandon this restrained methodology, and instead ask "whether [Washington's] statute sets up one of those 'arbitrary impositions' or 'purposeless restraints' at odds with the Due Process Clause of the Fourteenth Amendment," *post* (quoting *Poe* (Harlan, J., dissenting)). In our view, however, the development of this Court's substantive-due-process jurisprudence . . . has been a process whereby the outlines of the "liberty" specially protected by the Fourteenth Amendment—never fully clarified, to be sure, and perhaps not capable of being fully clarified—have at least been carefully refined by concrete examples involving fundamental rights found to be deeply rooted in our legal tradition. This approach tends to rein in the subjective elements that are necessarily present in due-process judicial review. In addition, by establishing a threshold requirement—that a challenged state action implicate a fundamental right—before requiring more than a reasonable relation to a legitimate state interest to justify the action, it avoids the need for complex balancing of competing interests in every case.

Turning to the claim at issue here, . . . respondents assert a "liberty to choose how to die" and a right to "control of one's final days," and describe the asserted liberty as "the right to choose a humane, dignified death," and "the liberty to shape death." As noted above, we have a tradition of carefully formulating the interest at stake in substantive-due-process cases. For example, although *Cruzan* is often described as a "right to die" case, we were, in fact, more precise: We assumed that the Constitution granted competent persons a "constitutionally protected right to refuse lifesaving hydration and nutrition." *Cruzan.* . . .

According to respondents, our liberty jurisprudence, and the broad, individualistic principles it reflects, protects the "liberty of competent, terminally ill adults to make end-of-life decisions free of undue government interference." The question presented in this case, however, is whether the protections of the Due Process Clause include a right to commit suicide with another's assistance. With this "careful description" of respondents' claim in mind, we turn to *Planned Parenthood v. Casey* (1992) [(reaffirming *Roe v. Wade*'s recognition of a constitutional right to abortion)]. . . .

The Court of Appeals, like the District Court, found *Casey* " 'highly in-structive' " and " 'almost prescriptive' " for determining " 'what liberty interest may inhere in a terminally ill person's choice to commit suicide' ":

> Like the decision of whether or not to have an abortion, the deci-sion how and when to die is one of "the most intimate and personal choices a person may make in a lifetime," a choice "central to personal dignity and autonomy."

Similarly, respondents emphasize the statement in *Casey* that:

> At the heart of liberty is the right to define one's own concept of existence, of meaning, of the universe, and of the mystery of human life. Beliefs about these matters could not define the attributes of personhood were they formed under compulsion of the State.

By choosing this language, the Court's opinion in *Casey* described, in a gen-eral way and in light of our prior cases, those personal activities and decisions that this Court has identified as so deeply rooted in our history and traditions, or so fundamental to our concept of constitutionally ordered liberty, that they are protected by the Fourteenth Amendment. . . . That many of the rights and liberties protected by the Due Process Clause sound in personal autonomy does not warrant the sweeping conclusion that any and all important, intimate, and personal decisions are so protected, and *Casey* did not suggest otherwise.

The history of the law's treatment of assisted suicide in this country has been and continues to be one of the rejection of nearly all efforts to permit it. That being the case, our decisions lead us to conclude that the asserted "right" to assistance in committing suicide is not a fundamental liberty interest pro-tected by the Due Process Clause. The Constitution also requires, however, that Washington's assisted-suicide ban be rationally related to legitimate gov-ernment interests. This requirement is unquestionably met here. As the court below recognized, Washington's assisted-suicide ban implicates a number of state interests.[21]

First, Washington has an "unqualified interest in the preservation of human life." *Cruzan.* . . . [A]ll admit that suicide is a serious public-health problem, especially among persons in otherwise vulnerable groups. . . . Those

---

[21] Respondents also admit the existence of these interests, but contend that Washington could better promote and protect them through regulation, rather than prohibition, of physician-assisted suicide. Our inquiry, how-ever, is limited to the question whether the State's prohibition is rationally related to legitimate state interests.

who attempt suicide—terminally ill or not—often suffer from depression or other mental disorders. Research indicates, however, that many people who request physician-assisted suicide withdraw that request if their depression and pain are treated. . . . Thus, legal physician-assisted suicide could make it more difficult for the State to protect depressed or mentally ill persons, or those who are suffering from untreated pain, from suicidal impulses.

The State also has an interest in protecting the integrity and ethics of the medical profession. . . . [T]he American Medical Association, like many other medical and physicians' groups, has concluded that "[p]hysician-assisted suicide is fundamentally incompatible with the physician's role as healer." American Medical Association, Code of Ethics § 2.211 (1994). . . .

Next, the State has an interest in protecting vulnerable groups—including the poor, the elderly, and disabled persons—from abuse, neglect, and mistakes. . . . We have recognized . . . the real risk of subtle coercion and undue influence in end-of-life situations. *Cruzan*. . . . The State's interest here goes beyond protecting the vulnerable from coercion; it extends to protecting disabled and terminally ill people from prejudice, negative and inaccurate stereotypes, and "societal indifference." The State's assisted-suicide ban reflects and reinforces its policy that the lives of terminally ill, disabled, and elderly people must be no less valued than the lives of the young and healthy, and that a seriously disabled person's suicidal impulses should be interpreted and treated the same way as anyone else's.

Finally, the State may fear that permitting assisted suicide will start it down the path to voluntary and perhaps even involuntary euthanasia. . . . This concern is further supported by evidence about the practice of euthanasia in the Netherlands. The Dutch government's own study . . . suggests that, despite the existence of various reporting procedures, euthanasia in the Netherlands has not been limited to competent, terminally ill adults who are enduring physical suffering, and that regulation of the practice may not have prevented abuses in cases involving vulnerable persons, including severely disabled neonates and elderly persons suffering from dementia. . . .

We need not weigh exactly the relative strengths of these various interests. They are unquestionably important and legitimate, and Washington's ban on assisted suicide is at least reasonably related to their promotion and protection. We therefore hold that Wash. Rev. Code § 9A.36.060(1) does not violate the Fourteenth Amendment, either on its face or[, in the words of the

Court of Appeals,] "as applied to competent, terminally ill adults who wish to hasten their deaths by obtaining medication prescribed by their doctors." . . .

Justice O'Connor, concurring.

Death will be different for each of us. For many, the last days will be spent in physical pain and perhaps the despair that accompanies physical deterioration and a loss of control of basic bodily and mental functions. Some will seek medication to alleviate that pain and other symptoms.

. . . I join the Court's opinions because I agree that there is no generalized right to "commit suicide." . . . The parties and *amici* agree that in [Washington] a patient who is suffering from a terminal illness and who is experiencing great pain has no legal barriers to obtaining medication, from qualified physicians, to alleviate that suffering, even to the point of causing unconsciousness and hastening death. In this light, even assuming that we would recognize such an interest, I agree that the State's interests in protecting those who are not truly competent or facing imminent death, or those whose decisions to hasten death would not truly be voluntary, are sufficiently weighty to justify a prohibition against physician-assisted suicide.

Every one of us at some point may be affected by our own or a family member's terminal illness. There is no reason to think the democratic process will not strike the proper balance between the interests of terminally ill, mentally competent individuals who would seek to end their suffering and the State's interests in protecting those who might seek to end life mistakenly or under pressure. . . .

In sum, there is no need to address the question whether suffering patients have a constitutionally cognizable interest in obtaining relief from the suffering that they may experience in the last days of their lives. There is no dispute that dying patients in Washington . . . can obtain palliative care, even when doing so would hasten their deaths. The difficulty in defining terminal illness and the risk that a dying patient's request for assistance in ending his or her life might not be truly voluntary justifies the prohibitions on assisted suicide we uphold here.

Justice Stevens, concurring in the judgments.

. . . Today, the Court decides that Washington's statute prohibiting assisted suicide is not invalid "on its face," that is to say, in all or most cases in which it might be applied. That holding, however, does not foreclose the possibility that some applications of the statute might well be invalid. . . . There remains room for vigorous debate about the outcome of particular cases that are not necessarily resolved by the opinions announced today. How such cases may be decided will depend on their specific facts. In my judgment, however, it is clear that the so-called "unqualified interest in the preservation of human life," is not itself sufficient to outweigh the interest in liberty that may justify the only possible means of preserving a dying patient's dignity and alleviating her intolerable suffering.

JUSTICE SOUTER, concurring in the judgments.

. . . I conclude that the statute's application to the doctors has not been shown to be unconstitutional, but I write separately to give my reasons for analyzing the substantive due process claims as I do, and for rejecting this one. . . .

II

. . . [W]e are dealing with a claim to one of those rights sometimes described as rights of substantive due process and sometimes as unenumerated rights, in view of the breadth and indeterminacy of the "due process" serving as the claim's textual basis. The doctors accordingly arouse the skepticism of those who find the Due Process Clause an unduly vague or oxymoronic warrant for judicial review of substantive state law, just as they also invoke two centuries of American constitutional practice in recognizing unenumerated, substantive limits on governmental action. . . .

Before the ratification of the Fourteenth Amendment, substantive constitutional review resting on a theory of unenumerated rights occurred largely in the state courts applying state constitutions that commonly contained either due process clauses like that of the Fifth Amendment (and later the Fourteenth) or the textual antecedents of such clauses, repeating Magna Carta's guarantee of "the law of the land." On the basis of such clauses, or of general principles untethered to specific constitutional language, state courts evaluated the constitutionality of a wide range of statutes. . . .

[I]ts most salient instance in this Court before the adoption of the Fourteenth Amendment was, of course, the case that the Amendment would in due course overturn, *Dred Scott v. Sandford* (1857). . . . *Dred Scott* was textually based on a Due Process Clause (in the Fifth Amendment, applicable to the National Government), and it was in reliance on that Clause's protection of property that the Court invalidated the Missouri Compromise. . . . The ensuing judgment of history needs no recounting here.

After the ratification of the Fourteenth Amendment, with its guarantee of due process protection against the States, interpretation of the words "liberty" and "property" as used in Due Process Clauses became a sustained enterprise, with the Court generally describing the due process criterion in converse terms of reasonableness or arbitrariness. . . . Although this principle was unobjectionable, what followed for a season was, in the realm of economic legislation, the echo of *Dred Scott. . . . Lochner v. New York* (1905), and the era to which that case gave its name, [are] famous now for striking down as arbitrary various sorts of economic regulations that post-New Deal courts have uniformly thought constitutionally sound. [W]hile the cases in the *Lochner* line routinely invoked a correct standard of constitutional arbitrariness review, they harbored the spirit of *Dred Scott* in their absolutist implementation of the standard they espoused.

Even before the deviant economic due process cases had been repudiated, however, the more durable precursors of modern substantive due process were reaffirming this Court's obligation to conduct arbitrariness review, beginning with [a series of cases involving non-economic interests. See, *e.g., Meyer v. Nebraska* (1923); *Pierce v. Society of Sisters* (1925); *Skinner v. Oklahoma ex rel. Williamson* (1942)]; *Palko v. Connecticut* (1937) ("[E]ven in the field of substantive rights and duties the legislative judgment, if oppressive and arbitrary, may be overridden by the courts." "Is that [injury] to which the statute has subjected [the appellant] a hardship so acute and shocking that our polity will not endure it? Does it violate those fundamental principles of liberty and justice which lie at the base of all our civil and political institutions?"). . . .

For two centuries American courts, and for much of that time this Court, have thought it necessary to provide some degree of review over the substantive content of legislation under constitutional standards of textual breadth. The obligation was understood before *Dred Scott* and has continued after the repudiation of *Lochner*'s progeny, most notably on the subjects of segregation in public education, interracial marriage, marital privacy and contraception, abortion, personal control of medical treatment, and physical confinement. This enduring tradition of American constitutional practice is . . . nothing more than what is required by the judicial authority and obligation to construe constitutional text and review legislation for conformity to that text. See *Marbury v. Madison* (1803). . . .

III

My understanding of unenumerated rights in the wake of [Justice Harlan's dissent in *Poe v. Ullman* (1961)] and subsequent cases avoids the absolutist failing of many older cases without embracing the opposite pole of equating reasonableness with past practice described at a very specific level. . . .

After the *Poe* dissent, as before it, this enforceable concept of liberty would bar statutory impositions even at relatively trivial levels when governmental restraints are undeniably irrational as unsupported by any imaginable rationale. See, *e.g.*, *United States v. Carolene Products Co.* (1938) (economic legislation "not . . .

CROSS REFERENCE Here, Justice Souter quotes the full paragraph from Justice Harlan's *Poe* dissent arguing that Due Process cannot be "reduced to any formula" and that it reflects a balance built on the organic traditions of liberty. See pp. 1363–1365.

unconstitutional unless . . . facts . . . preclude the assumption that it rests upon some rational basis"). Such instances are suitably rare. The claims of arbitrariness that mark almost all instances of unenumerated substantive rights are those resting on "certain interests requir[ing] particularly careful scrutiny of the state needs asserted to justify their abridgment[";] that is, interests in liberty sufficiently important to be judged "fundamental." In the face of an interest this powerful a State may not rest on threshold rationality or a presumption of constitutionality, but may prevail only on the ground of an interest sufficiently compelling to place within the realm of the reasonable a refusal to recognize the individual right asserted.[8]

This approach calls for a court to assess the relative "weights" or dignities of the contending interests, and to this extent the judicial method is familiar to the common law. Common-law method is subject, however, to two important constraints in the hands of a court engaged in substantive due process review. First, such a court is bound to confine the values that it recognizes to those truly deserving constitutional stature, either to those expressed in constitutional text, or those exemplified by "the traditions from which [the Nation] developed," or revealed by contrast with "the traditions from which it broke." *Poe* (Harlan, J., dissenting). " 'We may not draw on our merely personal and private notions

---

[8]   We have made it plain, of course, that not every law that incidentally makes it somewhat harder to exercise a fundamental liberty must be justified by a compelling counterinterest. See *Casey* (joint opinion of O'Connor, Kennedy, and Souter, JJ.).

and disregard the limits . . . derived from considerations that are fused in the whole nature of our judicial process. . . .' " *Id.*

The second constraint, again, simply reflects the fact that constitutional review, not judicial lawmaking, is a court's business here. The weighing or valuing of contending interests in this sphere is only the first step, forming the basis for determining whether the statute in question falls inside or outside the zone of what is reasonable in the way it resolves the conflict between the interests of state and individual. It is no justification for judicial intervention merely to identify a reasonable resolution of contending values that differs from the terms of the legislation under review. It is only when the legislation's justifying principle, critically valued, is so far from being commensurate with the individual interest as to be arbitrarily or pointlessly applied that the statute must give way. Only if this standard points against the statute can the individual claimant be said to have a constitutional right. . . .

Although the *Poe* dissent disclaims the possibility of any general formula for due process analysis (beyond the basic analytic structure just described), Justice Harlan of course assumed that adjudication under the Due Process Clauses is like any other instance of judgment dependent on common-law method, being more or less persuasive according to the usual canons of critical discourse. See also *Casey* ("The inescapable fact is that adjudication of substantive due process claims may call upon the Court in interpreting the Constitution to exercise that same capacity which by tradition courts always have exercised: reasoned judgment"). When identifying and assessing the competing interests of liberty and authority, for example, the breadth of expression that a litigant or a judge selects in stating the competing principles will have much to do with the outcome and may be dispositive. . . . So the Court in *Dred Scott* treated prohibition of slavery in the Territories as nothing less than a general assault on the concept of property.

. . . It is here that the value of common-law method becomes apparent, for the usual thinking of the common law is suspicious of the all-or-nothing analysis that tends to produce legal petrification instead of an evolving boundary between the domains of old principles. Common-law method tends to pay respect instead to detail, seeking to understand old principles afresh by new examples and new counterexamples. The "tradition is a living thing," albeit one that moves by moderate steps carefully taken. "The decision of an apparently novel claim must . . . take its place in relation to what went before and further

[cut] a channel for what is to come." *Poe* (Harlan, J., dissenting). Exact analysis and characterization of any due process claim are critical to the method and to the result. . . .[11]

The same insistence on exactitude lies behind questions, in current terminology, about the proper level of generality at which to analyze claims and counterclaims, and the demand for fitness and proper tailoring of a restrictive statute is just another way of testing the legitimacy of the generality at which the government sets up its justification. . . . [H]ere we are faced with an individual claim not to a right on the part of just anyone to help anyone else commit suicide under any circumstances, but to the right of a narrow class to help others also in a narrow class under a set of limited circumstances. And the claimants are met with the State's assertion, among others, that rights of such narrow scope cannot be recognized without jeopardy to individuals whom the State may concededly protect through its regulations.

IV

A

. . . I do not understand [respondents'] argument to rest on any assumption that rights either to suicide or to assistance in committing it are historically based as such. Respondents, rather, [rely on a] different, traditionally cognizable claims to autonomy in deciding how their bodies and minds should be treated. . . . This liberty interest in bodily integrity was phrased in a general way by then-Judge Cardozo when he said, "[e]very human being of adult years and sound mind has a right to determine what shall be done with his own body" in relation to his medical needs. The familiar examples of this right derive from the common law of battery and include the right to be free from medical invasions into the body, as well as a right generally to resist enforced medication. . . .

---

[11] Thus . . . the task of determining whether the concrete right claimed by an individual in a particular case falls within the ambit of a more generalized protected liberty requires explicit analysis when what the individual wants to do could arguably be characterized as belonging to different strands of our legal tradition requiring different degrees of constitutional scrutiny. See also Tribe & Dorf, *Levels of Generality in the Definition of Rights,* 57 U. Chi. L. Rev. 1057 (1990) (abortion might conceivably be assimilated either to the tradition regarding women's reproductive freedom in general, which places a substantial burden of justification on the State, or to the tradition regarding protection of fetuses, as embodied in laws criminalizing feticide by someone other than the mother, which generally requires only rationality on the part of the State). Selecting among such competing characterizations demands reasoned judgment about which broader principle, as exemplified in the concrete privileges and prohibitions embodied in our legal tradition, best fits the particular claim asserted in a particular case.

It is, indeed, in the abortion cases that the most telling recognitions of the importance of bodily integrity and the concomitant tradition of medical assistance have occurred. . . . The analogies between the abortion cases and this one are several. Even though the State has a legitimate interest in discouraging abortion, the Court recognized a woman's right to a physician's counsel and care. Like the decision to commit suicide, the decision to abort potential life can be made irresponsibly and under the influence of others, and yet the Court has held in the abortion cases that physicians are fit assistants. . . . [And] just as the decision about abortion is not directed to correcting some pathology, so the decision in which a dying patient seeks help is not so limited. The patients here sought not only an end to pain . . . but an end to their short remaining lives with a dignity that they believed would be denied them by powerful pain medication, as well as by their consciousness of dependency and helplessness as they approached death. . . .

In my judgment, the importance of the individual interest here, as within that class of "certain interests" demanding careful scrutiny of the State's contrary claim, cannot be gainsaid. Whether that interest might in some circumstances, or at some time, be seen as "fundamental" to the degree entitled to prevail is not, however, a conclusion that I need draw here, for I am satisfied that the State's interests described in the following section are sufficiently serious to defeat the present claim that its law is arbitrary or purposeless.

B

. . . The State claims interests in protecting patients from mistakenly and involuntarily deciding to end their lives, and in guarding against both voluntary and involuntary euthanasia. Leaving aside any difficulties in coming to a clear concept of imminent death, mistaken decisions may result from inadequate palliative care or a terminal prognosis that turns out to be error; coercion and abuse may stem from the large medical bills that family members cannot bear or unreimbursed hospitals decline to shoulder. Voluntary and involuntary euthanasia may result once doctors are authorized to prescribe lethal medication in the first instance. . . . The argument is that a progression would occur, obscuring the line between the ill and the dying, and between the responsible and the unduly influenced, until ultimately doctors and perhaps others would abuse a limited freedom to aid suicides by yielding to the impulse to end another's suffering under conditions going beyond the narrow limits the respondents propose. . . .

The State . . . argue[s] that dependence on the vigilance of physicians will not be enough. First, the lines proposed here (particularly the requirement of a knowing and voluntary decision by the patient) would be more difficult to draw than the lines that have limited other recently recognized due process rights. . . . [T]he trimester measurements of *Roe* and the viability determination of *Casey* were easy to make with a real degree of certainty. But the knowing and responsible mind is harder to assess. Second, this difficulty could become the greater by combining with another fact within the realm of plausibility, that physicians simply would not be assiduous to preserve the line. . . . [T]he barrier between assisted suicide and euthanasia could become porous, and the line between voluntary and involuntary euthanasia as well.

The case for the slippery slope is fairly made out here, not because recognizing one due process right would leave a court with no principled basis to avoid recognizing another, but because there is a plausible case that the right claimed would not be readily containable by reference to facts about the mind that are matters of difficult judgment, or by gatekeepers who are subject to temptation, noble or not. . . .

It is assumed in this case, and must be, that a State's interest in protecting those unable to make responsible decisions and those who make no decisions at all entitles the State to bar aid to any but a knowing and responsible person intending suicide, and to prohibit euthanasia. How, and how far, a State should act in that interest are judgments for the State, but the legitimacy of its action to deny a physician the option to aid any but the knowing and responsible is beyond question. . . . The Court should accordingly stay its hand to allow reasonable legislative consideration. While I do not decide for all time that respondents' claim should not be recognized, I acknowledge the legislative institutional competence as the better one to deal with that claim at this time.

JUSTICE GINSBURG, concurring in the judgments.

I concur in the Court's judgments in these cases substantially for the reasons stated by Justice O'Connor in her concurring opinion.

JUSTICE BREYER, concurring in the judgments.

I believe that Justice O'Connor's views, which I share, have greater legal significance than the Court's opinion suggests. I join her separate opinion, except insofar as it joins the majority. And I concur in the judgments. I shall briefly explain how I differ from the Court. . . .

Were the legal circumstances different—for example, were state law to prevent the provision of palliative care, including the administration of drugs as needed to avoid pain at the end of life—then the law's impact upon serious and otherwise unavoidable physical pain (accompanying death) would be more directly at issue. And as Justice O'Connor suggests, the Court might have to revisit its conclusions in these cases.

5.   SDP: Discrimination and Fundamental Rights

In our substantive due process cases so far, heightened scrutiny has been triggered by an across-the-board restriction on an unenumerated right that is in some sense constitutionally fundamental. There is also a parallel line of cases that involves a more complicated intersection of constitutional interests. Sometimes, the court has struck down a *discriminatory* restriction on some right even though (i) the discriminatory classification isn't sufficiently suspicious to prompt heightened scrutiny, and (ii) the restricted right isn't sufficiently fundamental to warrant its own special constitutional protection.

Now, given that we're talking about discrimination, you might well ask, "Aren't these really equal protection cases rather than due process ones?" Well, as a strict matter of doctrinal lines, maybe yes; we briefly described this line of cases—in which the Supreme Court sometimes says that strict scrutiny is invoked by discriminatory restrictions on a fundamental right—at the end of the last chapter. But we're putting these cases here, partly because they're better understood after studying due process and partly because sometimes it's debatable whether the Court should be relying on equal protection concepts or due process ones. (Does that mean we shouldn't have separated out equal protection and due process so sharply in organizing these chapters? That's something for you to think about when you do your own Con Law book.)

WORTH NOTING

While this line of cases basically hit a doctrinal dead end by the 1980s, the holdings that emerged continue to apply to some important rights, like voting. Moreover, the nexus between not-quite-suspicious classifications and not-quite-fundamental substantive due process has re-emerged in the LGBTQ+ cases that we'll see in the final section of this chapter.

Skinner v. State of Oklahoma ex rel. Williamson

Supreme Court of the United States, 1942.
316 U.S. 535.

Mr. Justice Douglas delivered the opinion of the Court.

This case touches a sensitive and important area of human rights. Oklahoma deprives certain individuals of a right which is basic to the perpetuation of a race—the right to have offspring. . . .

The statute involved is Oklahoma's Habitual Criminal Sterilization Act. That Act defines an "habitual criminal" as a person who, having been convicted two or more times for crimes "amounting to felonies involving moral turpitude" either in an Oklahoma court or in a court of any other State, is thereafter convicted of such a felony in Oklahoma and is sentenced to a term of imprisonment in an Oklahoma penal institution. § 173. Machinery is provided for the institution by the Attorney General of a proceeding against such a person in the Oklahoma courts for a judgment that such person shall be rendered sexually sterile. . . . [Section 195 of the Act] provides that "offenses arising out of the violation of the prohibitory laws, revenue acts, embezzlement, or political offenses, shall not come or be considered within the terms of this Act."

Petitioner was convicted in 1926 of the crime of stealing chickens and was sentenced to the Oklahoma State Reformatory. In 1929 he was convicted of the crime of robbery with fire arms and was sentenced to the reformatory. In 1934 he was convicted again of robbery with firearms and was sentenced to the penitentiary. He was confined there in 1935 when the Act was passed. In 1936 the Attorney General instituted proceedings against him. . . . A judgment directing that the operation of vasectomy be performed on petitioner was affirmed by the Supreme Court of Oklahoma by a five to four decision.

. . . [T]here is a feature of the Act which clearly condemns it. That is its failure to meet the requirements of the equal protection clause of the Fourteenth Amendment.

We do not stop to point out all of the inequalities in this Act. A few examples will suffice. In Oklahoma . . . [a] clerk who appropriates over $20 from his employer's till and a stranger who steals the same amount are . . . both guilty of felonies. If the latter repeats his act and is convicted three times, he may be sterilized. But the clerk is not subject to the pains and penalties of the

Act no matter how large his embezzlements nor how frequent his convictions. A person who enters a chicken coop and steals chickens commits a felony; and he may be sterilized if he is thrice convicted. If, however, he is a bailee of the property and fraudulently appropriates it, he is an embezzler. Hence no matter how habitual his proclivities for embezzlement are and no matter how often his conviction, he may not be sterilized. . . .

It was stated in *Buck v. Bell* (1927) that the claim that state legislation violates the equal protection clause of the Fourteenth Amendment is "the usual last resort of constitutional arguments." Under our constitutional system the States in determining the reach and scope of particular legislation need not provide "abstract symmetry." . . . It was in that connection that Mr. Justice Holmes . . .

CROSS REFERENCE *Bell*, which held constitutional a state law providing for coercive sterilization of those "afflicted with hereditary forms of insanity, imbecility, &c," is presented briefly on p. 1389.

stated, "We must remember that the machinery of government would not work if it were not allowed a little play in its joints." Only recently we reaffirmed the view that the equal protection clause does not prevent the legislature from recognizing "degrees of evil". . . . Thus, if we had here only a question as to a State's classification of crimes, such as embezzlement or larceny, no substantial federal question would be raised. . . .

But the instant legislation runs afoul of the equal protection clause, though we give Oklahoma that large deference which the rule of the foregoing cases requires. We are dealing here with legislation which involves one of the basic civil rights of man. Marriage and procreation are fundamental to the very existence and survival of the race. The power to sterilize, if exercised, may have subtle, far-reaching and devastating effects. In evil or reckless hands it can cause races or types which are inimical to the dominant group to wither and disappear. There is no redemption for the individual whom the law touches. Any experiment which the State conducts is to his irreparable injury. He is forever deprived of a basic liberty. We mention these matters not to reexamine the scope of the police power of the States. We advert to them merely in emphasis of our view that strict scrutiny of the classification which a State makes in a sterilization law is essential, lest unwittingly or otherwise invidious discriminations are made against groups or types of individuals in violation of the constitutional guaranty of just and equal laws. . . .

When the law lays an unequal hand on those who have committed intrinsically the same quality of offense and sterilizes one and not the other, it has made as an invidious a discrimination as if it had selected a particular race or nationality for oppressive treatment. . . .

Reversed.

MR. CHIEF JUSTICE STONE concurring.

I concur in the result, but I am not persuaded that we are aided in reaching it by recourse to the equal protection clause. If Oklahoma may resort generally to the sterilization of criminals on the assumption that their propensities are transmissible to future generations by inheritance, I seriously doubt that the equal protection clause requires it to apply the measure to all criminals in the first instance, or to none.

. . . I think the real question we have to consider is not one of equal protection, but whether the wholesale condemnation of a class to such an invasion of personal liberty, without opportunity to any individual to show that his is not the type of case which would justify resort to it, satisfies the demands of due process.

There are limits to the extent to which the presumption of constitutionality can be pressed, especially where the liberty of the person is concerned (see *United States v. Carolene Products Co.* n.4) and where the presumption is resorted to only to dispense with a procedure which the ordinary dictates of prudence would seem to demand for the protection of the individual from arbitrary action. Although petitioner here was given a hearing to ascertain whether sterilization would be detrimental to his health, he was given none to discover whether his criminal tendencies are of an inheritable type. Undoubtedly a state may, after appropriate inquiry, constitutionally interfere with the personal liberty of the individual to prevent the transmission by inheritance of his socially injurious tendencies. *Buck v. Bell.* But until now we have not been called upon to say that it may do so without giving him a hearing and opportunity to challenge the existence as to him of the only facts which could justify so drastic a measure. . . .

A law which condemns, without hearing, all the individuals of a class to so harsh a measure as the present because some or even many merit condemnation, is lacking in the first principles of due process. And so, while the state may protect itself from the demonstrably inheritable tendencies of the individual which are injurious to society, the most elementary notions of due process would seem to require it to take appropriate steps to safeguard the liberty of the individual by affording him, before he is condemned to an irreparable injury in his person, some opportunity to show that he is without such inheritable tendencies. The state is called on to sacrifice no permissible end when it is required to reach its objective by a reasonable and just procedure adequate to safeguard rights of the individual which concededly the Constitution protects. . . .

WORTH NOTING Justice Jackson concurred, noting that he thought the statute violated both equal protection and due process.

The endemic inequality of American primary education is a national disgrace. It has also been called a constitutional problem—but on what basis? Is the idea that education is a fundamental right, or that poverty is a suspect class? The following decision rejects both arguments.

San Antonio Independent School District v. Rodriguez

Supreme Court of the United States, 1973.
411 U.S. 1.

MR. JUSTICE POWELL delivered the opinion of the Court.

This suit attacking the Texas system of financing public education was initiated by Mexican-American parents whose children attend the elementary and secondary schools in the Edgewood Independent School District, an urban school district in San Antonio, Texas. They brought a class action on behalf of schoolchildren throughout the State who are members of minority groups or who are poor and reside in school districts having a low property tax base. . . .

I

The first Texas State Constitution, promulgated upon Texas' entry into the Union in 1845, provided for the establishment of a system of free schools. Early in its history, Texas adopted a dual approach to the financing of its schools, relying on mutual participation by the local school districts and the State. . . . Until recent times, Texas was a predominantly rural State and its population and property wealth were spread relatively evenly across the State. Sizable differences in the value of assessable property between local school districts became increasingly evident as the State became more industrialized and as rural-to-urban population shifts became more pronounced. . . . These growing disparities in population and taxable property between districts were responsible in part for increasingly notable differences in levels of local expenditure for education. . . .

Edgewood is one of seven public school districts in the metropolitan area. Approximately 22,000 students are enrolled in its 25 elementary and secondary schools. The district is situated in the core-city sector of San Antonio in a residential neighborhood that has little commercial or industrial property. The residents are predominantly of Mexican-American descent: approximately 90% of the student population is Mexican-American and over 6% is Negro. . . . [Drawing on a combination of district, state, and federal funds, the district school system has a budget of] $356 per pupil.

Alamo Heights is the most affluent school district in San Antonio. Its six schools, housing approximately 5,000 students, are situated in a residential community quite unlike the Edgewood District. The school population is predominantly "Anglo," having only 18% Mexican-Americans and less than 1% Negroes. [Also supported by district, state, and federal funds, the district school system has a budget of] $594 per pupil. . . .

Despite . . . recent increases [in state funding], substantial interdistrict disparities in school expenditures found by the District Court to prevail in San Antonio and in varying degrees throughout the State still exist. And it was these disparities, largely attributable to differences in the amounts of money collected through local property taxation, that led the District Court to conclude that Texas' dual system of public school financing violated the Equal Protection Clause. The District Court held that the Texas system discriminates on the basis of wealth in the manner in which education is provided for its people. Finding that wealth is a "suspect" classification and that education is a "fundamental" interest, the District Court held that the Texas system could be sustained only if the State could show that it was premised upon some compelling state interest. . . .

Texas virtually concedes that its historically rooted dual system of financing education could not withstand the strict judicial scrutiny that this Court has found appropriate in reviewing legislative judgments that interfere with fundamental constitutional rights or that involve suspect classifications. . . .

This, then, establishes the framework for our analysis. We must decide, first, whether the Texas system of financing public education operates to the disadvantage of some suspect class or impinges upon a fundamental right explicitly or implicitly protected by the Constitution, thereby requiring strict judicial scrutiny. If so, the judgment of the District Court should be affirmed. If not, the Texas scheme must still be examined to determine whether it rationally furthers some legitimate, articulated state purpose and therefore does not constitute an invidious discrimination in violation of the Equal Protection Clause of the Fourteenth Amendment.

II

. . . In concluding that strict judicial scrutiny was required, [the District Court] relied on decisions dealing with the rights of indigents to equal treatment in the criminal trial and appellate processes, and on cases disapproving wealth restrictions on the right to vote. Those cases, the District Court concluded, established wealth as a suspect classification. Finding that the local property tax system discriminated on the basis of wealth, it regarded those precedents as controlling. It then reasoned, based on decisions of this Court affirming the undeniable importance of education, that there is a fundamental right to education and that, absent some compelling state justification, the Texas system could not stand.

We are unable to agree that this case, which in significant aspects is sui generis, may be so neatly fitted into the conventional mosaic of constitutional analysis under the Equal Protection Clause. Indeed, for the several reasons that follow, we find neither the suspect-classification not the fundamental-interest analysis persuasive.

A

The wealth discrimination discovered by the District Court in this case, and by several other courts that have recently struck down school-financing laws in other States, is quite unlike any of the forms of wealth discrimination heretofore reviewed by this Court. Rather than focusing on the unique features of the alleged discrimination, the courts in these cases have virtually assumed their findings of a suspect classification through a simplistic process of analysis: since, under the traditional systems of financing public schools, some poorer people receive less expensive educations than other more affluent people, these systems discriminate on the basis of wealth. This approach largely ignores the hard threshold questions, including whether it makes a difference for purposes of consideration under the Constitution that the class of disadvantaged "poor" cannot be identified or defined in customary equal protection terms, and whether the relative—rather than absolute—nature of the asserted deprivation is of significant consequence. . . .

The Texas system of school financing might be regarded as discriminating (1) against "poor" persons whose incomes fall below some identifiable level of poverty or who might be characterized as functionally "indigent," or (2) against those who are relatively poorer than others or (3) against all those who, irrespective of their personal incomes, happen to reside in relatively poorer school districts. . . .

The individuals, or groups of individuals, who constituted the class discriminated against in our prior cases shared two distinguishing characteristics: because of their impecunity they were completely unable to pay for some desired benefit, and as a consequence, they sustained an absolute deprivation of a meaningful opportunity to enjoy that benefit. In *Griffin v. Illinois* (1956) and its progeny the Court invalidated state laws that prevented an indigent criminal defendant from acquiring a transcript, or an adequate substitute for a transcript, for use at several stages of the trial and appeal process. The payment requirements in each case were found to occasion *de facto* discrimination against those who, because of their indigency, were totally unable to pay for transcripts. And the Court in each case emphasized that no constitutional violation would have been shown if the State had provided some "adequate substitute" for a full stenographic transcript. Likewise, in *Douglas v. California* (1963), a decision establishing an indigent defendant's right to court-appointed counsel on direct appeal, the Court dealt only with defendants who could not pay for counsel from their own resources and who had no other way of gaining representation. *Douglas* provides no relief for those on whom the burdens of paying for a criminal defense are relatively speaking, great but not insurmountable. Nor does it deal with relative differences in the quality of counsel acquired by the less wealthy. . . .

Only appellees' first possible basis for describing the class disadvantaged by the Texas school-financing system—discrimination against a class of defineably "poor" persons—might arguably meet the criteria established in these prior cases. Even a cursory examination, however, demonstrates that neither of the two distinguishing characteristics of wealth classifications can be found here. First, . . . appellees have made no effort to demonstrate that [the system] operates to the peculiar disadvantage of any class fairly definable as indigent, or as composed of persons whose incomes are beneath any designated poverty level. Indeed, there is reason to believe that the poorest families are not necessarily clustered in the poorest property districts. . . . [A] Connecticut study found, not surprisingly, that the poor were clustered around commercial and industrial areas—those same areas that provide the most attractive sources of property tax income for school districts. Whether a similar pattern would be discovered in Texas is not known, but there is no basis on the record in this case for assuming that the poorest people—defined by reference to any level of absolute impecunity—are concentrated in the poorest districts.

Second, . . . unlike each of the foregoing cases, lack of personal resources has not occasioned an absolute deprivation of the desired benefit. The argument here is not that the children in districts having relatively low assessable property values are receiving no public education; rather, it is that they are receiving a poorer quality education than that available to children in districts having more assessable wealth. Apart from the unsettled and disputed question whether the quality of education may be determined by the amount of money expended for it, a sufficient answer to appellees' argument is that, at least where wealth is involved, the Equal Protection Clause does not require absolute equality or precisely equal advantages. Nor indeed, in view of the infinite variables affecting the educational process, can any system assure equal quality of education except in the most relative sense. . . .

For these two reasons—the absence of any evidence that the financing system discriminates against any definable category of "poor" people or that it results in the absolute deprivation of education—the disadvantaged class is not susceptible of identification in traditional terms. . . .

We thus conclude that the Texas system does not operate to the peculiar disadvantage of any suspect class. But in recognition of the fact that this Court has never heretofore held that wealth discrimination alone provides an adequate basis for invoking strict scrutiny, appellees have not relied solely on this contention. They also assert that the State's system impermissibly interferes with the exercise of a "fundamental" right and that accordingly the prior decisions of this Court require the application of the strict standard of judicial review. . . .

B

In *Brown v. Board of Education* (1954), a unanimous Court recognized that "education is perhaps the most important function of state and local governments." . . . This theme, expressing an abiding respect for the vital role of education in a free society, may be found in numerous opinions of Justices of this Court writing both before and after *Brown* was decided. *Wisconsin v. Yoder* (1971); *Pierce v. Society of Sisters* (1925); *Meyer v. Nebraska* (1923).

. . . We are in complete agreement with the conclusion of the three-judge panel below that "the grave significance of education both to the individual and to our society" cannot be doubted. But the importance of a service performed by the State does not determine whether it must be regarded as fundamental for purposes of examination under the Equal Protection Clause. . . . [T]he key to discovering whether education is "fundamental" is not to be found in comparisons of the relative societal significance of education as opposed to subsistence or housing. Nor is it to be found by weighing whether education is as important as the right to travel. Rather, the answer lies in assessing whether there is a right to education explicitly or implicitly guaranteed by the Constitution.

Education, of course, is not among the rights afforded explicit protection under our Federal Constitution. Nor do we find any basis for saying it is implicitly so protected. . . . It is appellees' contention, however, that education is distinguishable from other services and benefits provided by the State because it bears a peculiarly close relationship to other rights and liberties accorded protection under the Constitution. Specifically, they insist that education is itself a fundamental personal right because it is essential to the effective exercise of First Amendment freedoms and to intelligent utilization of the right to vote. . . .

We need not dispute any of these propositions. The Court has long afforded zealous protection against unjustifiable governmental interference with the individual's rights to speak and to vote. Yet we have never presumed to possess either the ability or the authority to guarantee to the citizenry the most effective speech or the most informed electoral choice. . . . These are indeed goals to be pursued by a people whose thoughts and beliefs are freed from governmental interference. But they are not values to be implemented by judicial instruction into otherwise legitimate state activities. . . .

[T]he logical limitations on appellees' nexus theory are difficult to perceive. How, for instance, is education to be distinguished from the significant personal interests in the basics of decent food and shelter? Empirical examination might well buttress an assumption that the ill-fed, ill-clothed, and ill-housed are among the most ineffective participants in the political process, and that they derive the least enjoyment from the benefits of the First Amendment. If so, appellees' thesis would cast serious doubt on the authority of *Dandridge v.*

Williams (1970) [(rejecting claim that equal protection was violated by a cap on subsistence welfare payments)]. . . .

C

It should be clear, for the reasons stated above and in accord with the prior decisions of this Court, that this is not a case in which the challenged state action must be subjected to the searching judicial scrutiny reserved for laws that create suspect classifications or impinge upon constitutionally protected rights.

. . . This case represents far more than a challenge to the manner in which Texas provides for the education of its children. We have here nothing less than a direct attack on the way in which Texas has chosen to raise and disburse state and local tax revenues. . . . [W]e are urged to direct the States either to alter drastically the present system or to throw out the property tax altogether in favor of some other form of taxation. No scheme of taxation, whether the tax is imposed on property, income, or purchases of goods and services, has yet been devised which is free of all discriminatory impact. In such a complex arena in which no perfect alternatives exist, the Court does well not to impose too rigorous a standard of scrutiny lest all local fiscal schemes become subjects of criticism under the Equal Protection Clause. . . .

The foregoing considerations buttress our conclusion that Texas' system of public school finance is an inappropriate candidate for strict judicial scrutiny. These same considerations are relevant to the determination whether that system, with its conceded imperfections, nevertheless bears some rational relationship to a legitimate state purpose. It is to this question that we next turn our attention.

III

. . . In its reliance on state as well as local resources, the Texas system is comparable to the systems employed in virtually every other State. . . . As articulated by [one commentator]: "The history of education since the industrial revolution shows a continual struggle between two forces: the desire by members of society to have educational opportunity for all chil-

WORTH NOTING Texas has authorized local property taxes for education since at least 1883; as disparities in local resources grew, however, it began to invest considerable state funds in education.

dren, and the desire of each family to provide the best education it can afford for its own children."

The Texas system of school finance is responsive to these two forces. While assuring a basic education for every child in the State, it permits and encourages a large measure of participation in and control of each district's schools at the local level. In an era that has witnessed a consistent trend toward centralization of the functions of government, local sharing of responsibility for public education has survived. . . .

The persistence of attachment to government at the lowest level where education is concerned reflects the depth of commitment of its supporters. In part, local control means . . . the freedom to devote more money to the education of one's children. Equally important, however, is the opportunity it offers for participation in the decisionmaking process that determines how those local tax dollars will be spent. Each locality is free to tailor local programs to local needs. Pluralism also affords some opportunity for experimentation, innovation, and a healthy competition for educational excellence. An analogy to the Nation-State relationship in our federal system seems uniquely appropriate. Mr. Justice Brandeis identified as one of the peculiar strengths of our form of government each State's freedom to "serve as a laboratory; and try novel social and economic experiments." . . .

Appellees suggest that local control could be preserved and promoted under other financing systems that resulted in more equality in education expenditures. . . . The people of Texas may be justified in believing that . . . along with increased control of the purse strings at the state level will go increased control over local policies. . . .

In sum, to the extent that the Texas system of school financing results in unequal expenditures between children who happen to reside in different districts, we cannot say that such disparities are the product of a system that is so irrational as to be invidiously discriminatory. Texas has acknowledged its shortcomings and has persistently endeavored—not without some success—to ameliorate the differences in levels of expenditures without sacrificing the benefits of local participation. The Texas plan is not the result of hurried, ill-conceived legislation. It certainly is not the product of purposeful discrimination against any group or class. On the contrary, it is rooted in decades of experience in Texas and elsewhere, and in major part is the product of responsible studies by qualified people. . . .

The constitutional standard under the Equal Protection Clause is whether the challenged state action rationally furthers a legitimate state purpose or interest. We hold that the Texas plan abundantly satisfies this standard. . . .

MR. JUSTICE STEWART, concurring.

The method of financing public schools in Texas, as in almost every other State, has resulted in a system of public education that can fairly be described as chaotic and unjust. It does not follow, however, and I cannot find, that this system violates the Constitution of the United States. I join the opinion and judgment of the Court because I am convinced that any other course would mark an extraordinary departure from principled adjudication under the Equal Protection Clause of the Fourteenth Amendment. The unchartered directions of such a departure are suggested, I think, by the imaginative dissenting opinion my Brother Marshall has filed today. . . .

MR. JUSTICE WHITE, with whom MR. JUSTICE DOUGLAS and MR. JUSTICE BRENNAN join, dissenting.

. . . The Equal Protection Clause permits discriminations between classes but requires that the classification bear some rational relationship to a permissible object sought to be attained by the statute. . . . If the State aims at maximizing local initiative and local choice, by permitting school districts to resort to the real property tax if they choose to do so, it utterly fails in achieving its purpose in districts with property tax bases so low that there is little if any opportunity for interested parents, rich or poor, to augment school district revenues. . . . In my view, the parents and children in Edgewood, and in like districts, suffer from an invidious discrimination violative of the Equal Protection Clause. . . .

WORTH NOTING

In a brief separate dissent, Justice Brennan "disagree[d] with the Court's rather distressing assertion that a right may be deemed 'fundamental' only if it is explicitly or implicitly guaranteed in the Constitution." To the contrary, he said, " 'fundamentality' is, in large measure, a function of the right's importance in terms of the effectuation of those right which are in fact constitutionally guaranteed."

MR. JUSTICE MARSHALL, with whom MR. JUSTICE DOUGLAS concurs, dissenting.

The Court today decides, in effect, that a State may constitutionally vary the quality of education which it offers its children in accordance with the amount of taxable wealth located in the school districts within which they reside. . . . More unfortunately, though, the majority's holding can only be seen as a retreat from our historic commitment to equality of educational opportunity and as unsupportable acquiescence in a system which deprives children in their earliest years of the chance to reach their full potential as citizens. The Court does this despite the absence of any substantial justification for a scheme which arbitrarily channels educational resources in accordance with the fortuity of the amount of taxable wealth within each district.

In my judgment, the right of every American to an equal start in life, so far as the provision of a state service as important as education is concerned, is far too vital to permit state discrimination on grounds as tenuous as those presented by this record. . . .

The appellants [contend] that whatever the differences in per-pupil spending among Texas districts, there are no discriminatory consequences for the children of the disadvantaged districts. . . . In my view, though, even an unadorned restatement of this contention is sufficient to reveal its absurdity. Authorities concerned with educational quality no doubt disagree as to the significance of variations in per-pupil spending. . . . We sit, however, not to resolve disputes over educational theory but to enforce our Constitution.

It is an inescapable fact that if one district has more funds available per pupil than another district, the former will have greater choice in educational planning than will the latter. In this regard, I believe the question of discrimination in educational quality must be deemed to be an objective one that looks to what the State provides its children, not to what the children are able to do with what they receive. That a child forced to attend an underfunded school with poorer physical facilities, less experienced teachers, larger classes, and a narrower range of courses than a school with substantially more funds—and thus with greater choice in educational planning—may nevertheless excel is to the credit of the child, not the State. Indeed, who can ever measure for such a child the opportunities lost and the talents wasted for want of a broader, more enriched education? Discrimination in the opportunity to learn that is afforded a child must be our standard. . . .

. . . I must once more voice my disagreement with the Court's rigidified approach to equal protection analysis. The Court apparently seeks to establish today that equal protection cases fall into one of two neat categories which dictate the appropriate standard of review—strict scrutiny or mere rationality.

But this Court's decisions in the field of equal protection defy such easy categorization. A principled reading of what this Court has done reveals that it has
applied a spectrum of standards in reviewing discrimination allegedly violative
of the Equal Protection Clause. This spectrum clearly comprehends variations
in the degree of care with which the Court will scrutinize particular classifications, depending, I believe, on the constitutional and societal importance
of the interest adversely affected and the recognized invidiousness of the basis
upon which the particular classification is drawn. . . .

    I therefore cannot accept the majority's labored efforts to demonstrate that
fundamental interests, which call for strict scrutiny of the challenged classification, encompass only established rights which we are somehow bound to
recognize from the text of the Constitution itself. . . . The majority is, of course,
correct when it suggests that the process of determining which interests are fundamental is a difficult one. But I do not think the problem is insurmountable. . . .

    . . . It is true that this Court has never deemed the provision of free public
education to be required by the Constitution. . . . Nevertheless, the fundamental importance of education is amply indicated by the prior decisions of this
Court, by the unique status accorded public education by our society, and by
the close relationship between education and some of our most basic constitutional values. . . .

    [I]t is [also] essential to recognize that an end to the wide variations in
taxable district property wealth inherent in the Texas financing scheme would
entail none of the untoward consequences suggested by the Court or by the
appellants. [It] would hardly sound the death knell for local control of education. It would mean neither centralized decisionmaking nor federal court
intervention in the operation of public schools. Clearly, this suit has nothing
to do with local decisionmaking with respect to educational policy or even educational spending. It involves only a narrow aspect of local control—namely,
local control over the raising of educational funds. . . .

San Antonio v. Rodriguez held that wealth is not a suspect classification,
and that education is not a fundamental right. The Court therefore subjected the
Texas school funding scheme to rational basis review and found it constitutional.
If that seems pretty straightforward as a matter of analytical structure (whatever you may think of the conclusions), then how do you explain the outcome

in the following case? Does it rest on the identification of a suspect class? Or a fundamental right? Or some combination of the two?

Plyler v. Doe

Supreme Court of the United States, 1982.
457 U.S. 202.

JUSTICE BRENNAN delivered the opinion of the Court.

The question presented by these cases is whether, consistent with the Equal Protection Clause of the Fourteenth Amendment, Texas may deny to undocumented school-age children the free public education that it provides to children who are citizens of the United States or legally admitted aliens.

I

Since the late 19th century, the United States has restricted immigration into this country. Unsanctioned entry into the United States is a crime, and those who have entered unlawfully are subject to deportation. But despite the existence of these legal restrictions, a substantial number of persons have succeeded in unlawfully entering the United States, and now live within various States, including the State of Texas.

In May 1975, the Texas Legislature revised its education laws to withhold from local school districts any state funds for the education of children who were not "legally admitted" into the United States. The 1975 revision also authorized local school districts to deny enrollment in their public schools to children not "legally admitted" to the country. Tex. Educ. Code Ann. § 21.031. These cases involve constitutional challenges to those provisions.

[This case] is a class action . . . on behalf of certain school-age children of Mexican origin residing in Smith County, Tex., who could not establish that they had been legally admitted into the United States. The action complained of the exclusion of plaintiff children from the public schools of the Tyler Independent School District. . . .

The District Court held that . . . § 21.031 violated [the Equal Protection] Clause. Suggesting that "the state's exclusion of undocumented children from its public schools . . . may well be the type of invidiously motivated state action for which the suspect classification doctrine was designed," the court held that it was unnecessary to decide whether the statute would survive a "strict scrutiny" analysis because, in any event, the discrimination embodied in the statute was not supported by a rational basis. The District Court also concluded that the Texas statute violated the Supremacy Clause.[5] The Court of Appeals for the Fifth Circuit upheld the District Court's injunction. . . .

II

. . . Appellants argue at the outset that undocumented aliens, because of their immigration status, are not "persons within the jurisdiction" of the State of Texas [within the meaning of the Fourteenth Amendment], and that they therefore have no right to the equal protection of Texas law. We reject this argument. Whatever his status under the immigration laws, an alien is surely a "person" in any ordinary sense of that term. Aliens, even aliens whose presence in this country is unlawful, have long been recognized as "persons" guaranteed due process of law by the Fifth and Fourteenth Amendments. Indeed, we have clearly held that the Fifth Amendment protects aliens whose presence in this country is unlawful from invidious discrimination by the Federal Government. *Mathews v. Diaz* (1976). . . .

. . . The Equal Protection Clause was intended to work nothing less than the abolition of all caste-based and invidious class-based legislation. That objective is fundamentally at odds with the power the State asserts here to classify persons subject to its laws as nonetheless excepted from its protection. . . .

Use of the phrase "within its jurisdiction" thus does not detract from, but rather confirms, the understanding that the protection of the Fourteenth Amendment extends to anyone, citizen or stranger, who *is* subject to the laws of a State, and reaches into every corner of a State's territory. That a person's initial entry into a State, or into the United States, was unlawful, and that he may for that reason be expelled, cannot negate the simple fact of his presence within the State's territorial perimeter. Given such presence, he is subject to the full range of obligations imposed by the State's civil and criminal laws. And until he leaves the jurisdiction—either voluntarily, or involuntarily in accordance with the Constitution and laws of the United States—he is entitled to the equal protection of the laws that a State may choose to establish. . . .

---

[5]　The court found § 21.031 inconsistent with the scheme of national regulation under the Immigration and Nationality Act, and with federal laws pertaining to funding and discrimination in education.

III

The Equal Protection Clause directs that "all persons similarly circumstanced shall be treated alike." But so too, "[t]he Constitution does not require things which are different in fact or opinion to be treated in law as though they were the same." The initial discretion to determine what is "different" and what is "the same" resides in the legislatures of the States. A legislature must have substantial latitude to establish classifications that roughly approximate the nature of the problem perceived, that accommodate competing concerns both public and private, and that account for limitations on the practical ability of the State to remedy every ill. In applying the Equal Protection Clause to most forms of state action, we thus seek only the assurance that the classification at issue bears some fair relationship to a legitimate public purpose.

But we would not be faithful to our obligations under the Fourteenth Amendment if we applied so deferential a standard to every classification. The Equal Protection Clause was intended as a restriction on state legislative action inconsistent with elemental constitutional premises. Thus we have treated as presumptively invidious those classifications that disadvantage a "suspect class,"[14] or that impinge upon the exercise of a "fundamental right." . . . We turn to a consideration of the standard appropriate for the evaluation of § 21.031.

A

Sheer incapability or lax enforcement of the laws barring entry into this country, coupled with the failure to establish an effective bar to the employment of undocumented aliens, has resulted in the creation of a substantial "shadow population" of illegal migrants—numbering in the millions—within our borders. This situation raises the specter of a permanent caste of undocumented resident aliens, encouraged by some to remain here as a source of cheap labor, but nevertheless denied the benefits that our society makes available to citizens

---

[14]   Several formulations might explain our treatment of certain classifications as "suspect." Some classifications are more likely than others to reflect deep-seated prejudice rather than legislative rationality in pursuit of some legitimate objective. Legislation predicated on such prejudice is easily recognized as incompatible with the constitutional understanding that each person is to be judged individually and is entitled to equal justice under the law. Classifications treated as suspect tend to be irrelevant to any proper legislative goal. See *Hirabayashi v. United States* (1943). Finally, certain groups, indeed largely the same groups, have historically been "relegated to such a position of political powerlessness as to command extraordinary protection from the majoritarian political process." *San Antonio Independent School Dist. v. Rodriguez* (1973); *Graham v. Richardson* (1971); see *United States v. Carolene Products Co.* n. 4 (1938). . . . Legislation imposing special disabilities upon groups disfavored by virtue of circumstances beyond their control suggests the kind of "class or caste" treatment that the Fourteenth Amendment was designed to abolish.

and lawful residents.[18] The existence of such an underclass presents most difficult problems for a Nation that prides itself on adherence to principles of equality under law.[19]

The children who are plaintiffs in these cases are special members of this underclass. Persuasive arguments support the view that a State may withhold its beneficence from those whose very presence within the United States is the product of their own unlawful conduct. These arguments do not apply with the same force to classifications imposing disabilities on the minor *children* of such illegal entrants. . . . Their "parents have the ability to conform their conduct to societal norms," and presumably the ability to remove themselves from the State's jurisdiction; but the children who are plaintiffs in these cases "can affect neither their parents' conduct nor their own status." *Trimble v. Gordon* (1977). Even if the State found it expedient to control the conduct of adults by acting against their children, legislation directing the onus of a parent's misconduct against his children does not comport with fundamental conceptions of justice. . . .

Of course, undocumented status is not irrelevant to any proper legislative goal. Nor is undocumented status an absolutely immutable characteristic since it is the product of conscious, indeed unlawful, action. But § 21.031 is directed against children, and imposes its discriminatory burden on the basis of a legal characteristic over which children can have little control. It is thus difficult to conceive of a rational justification for penalizing these children for their presence within the United States. Yet that appears to be precisely the effect of § 21.031.

Public education is not a "right" granted to individuals by the Constitution. *San Antonio Independent School Dist. v. Rodriguez* (1973). But neither is it merely some governmental "benefit" indistinguishable from other forms of social welfare legislation. Both the importance of education in maintaining our

---

[18]   As the District Court observed . . . , the confluence of Government policies has resulted in "the existence of a large number of employed illegal aliens, such as the parents of plaintiffs in this case, whose presence is tolerated, whose employment is perhaps even welcomed, but who are virtually defenseless against any abuse, exploitation, or callous neglect to which the state or the state's natural citizens and business organizations may wish to subject them."

[19]   We reject the claim that "illegal aliens" are a "suspect class." No case in which we have attempted to define a suspect class has addressed the status of persons unlawfully in our country. Unlike most of the classifications that we have recognized as suspect, entry into this class, by virtue of entry into this country, is the product of voluntary action. Indeed, entry into the class is itself a crime. In addition, it could hardly be suggested that undocumented status is a "constitutional irrelevancy." With respect to the actions of the Federal Government, alienage classifications may be intimately related to the conduct of foreign policy, to the federal prerogative to control access to the United States, and to the plenary federal power to determine who has sufficiently manifested his allegiance to become a citizen of the Nation. . . .

basic institutions, and the lasting impact of its deprivation on the life of the child, mark the distinction. . . . *Meyer v. Nebraska* (1923). . . . "[A]s . . . pointed out early in our history, . . . some degree of education is necessary to prepare citizens to participate effectively and intelligently in our open political system if we are to preserve freedom and independence." *Wisconsin v. Yoder* (1972). . . . In addition, education provides the basic tools by which individuals might lead economically productive lives to the benefit of us all. In sum, education has a fundamental role in maintaining the fabric of our society. We cannot ignore the significant social costs borne by our Nation when select groups are denied the means to absorb the values and skills upon which our social order rests.

In addition to the pivotal role of education in sustaining our political and cultural heritage, denial of education to some isolated group of children poses an affront to one of the goals of the Equal Protection Clause: the abolition of governmental barriers presenting unreasonable obstacles to advancement on the basis of individual merit. Paradoxically, by depriving the children of any disfavored group of an education, we foreclose the means by which that group might raise the level of esteem in which it is held by the majority. . . . The inability to read and write will handicap the individual deprived of a basic education each and every day of his life. The inestimable toll of that deprivation on the social economic, intellectual, and psychological well-being of the individual, and the obstacle it poses to individual achievement, make it most difficult to reconcile the cost or the principle of a status-based denial of basic education with the framework of equality embodied in the Equal Protection Clause. . . .

B

These well-settled principles allow us to determine the proper level of deference to be afforded § 21.031. Undocumented aliens cannot be treated as a suspect class because their presence in this country in violation of federal law is not a "constitutional irrelevancy." Nor is education a fundamental right; a State need not justify by compelling necessity every variation in the manner in which education is provided to its population. See *San Antonio Independent School Dist. v. Rodriguez.* But more is involved in these cases than the abstract question whether § 21.031 discriminates against a suspect class, or whether education is a fundamental right. Section 21.031 imposes a lifetime hardship on a discrete class of children not accountable for their disabling status. The stigma of illiteracy will mark them for the rest of their lives. By denying these children a basic education, we deny them the ability to live within the structure of our civic institutions, and foreclose any realistic possibility that they will contribute in even the smallest way to the progress of our Nation. In determining the rationality of § 21.031, we may appropriately take into account its costs to the Nation and to the innocent children who are its victims. In light of these countervailing costs, the discrimination contained in § 21.031 can hardly be considered rational unless it furthers some substantial goal of the State. . . .

V

Appellants argue that the classification at issue furthers an interest in the "preservation of the state's limited resources for the education of its lawful residents." Of course, a concern for the preservation of resources standing alone can hardly justify the classification used in allocating those resources. *Graham v. Richardson* (1971). The State must do more than justify its classification with a concise expression of an intention to discriminate. Apart from the asserted state prerogative to act against undocumented children solely on the basis of their undocumented status—an asserted prerogative that carries only minimal force in the circumstances of these cases—we discern three colorable state interests that might support § 21.031.

First, appellants appear to suggest that the State may seek to protect itself from an influx of illegal immigrants. While a State might have an interest in mitigating the potentially harsh economic effects of sudden shifts in population, § 21.031 hardly offers an effective method of dealing with an urgent demographic or economic problem. There is no evidence in the record suggesting that illegal entrants impose any significant burden on the State's economy. To the contrary, the available evidence suggests that illegal aliens underutilize public services, while contributing their labor to the local economy and tax money to the state fisc. The dominant incentive for illegal entry into the State of Texas is the availability of employment; few if any illegal immigrants come to this country, or presumably to the State of Texas, in order to avail themselves of a free education. Thus, even making the doubtful assumption that the net impact of illegal aliens on the economy of the State is negative, we think it clear that "[c]harging tuition to undocumented children constitutes a ludicrously ineffectual attempt to stem the tide of illegal immigration," at least when compared with the alternative of prohibiting the employment of illegal aliens.

Second, . . . appellants suggest that undocumented children are appropriately singled out for exclusion because of the special burdens they impose on the State's ability to provide high-quality public education. But the record in no way supports the claim that exclusion of undocumented children is likely to improve the overall quality of education in the State. As the District Court . . . noted, the State failed to offer any "credible supporting evidence that a proportionately small diminution of the funds spent on each child [which might result from devoting some state funds to the education of the excluded group] will have a grave impact on the quality of education." . . . Of course, even if improvement in the quality of education were a likely result of barring some *number* of children from the schools of the State, the State must support its selection of *this* group as the appropriate target for exclusion. In terms of educational cost and need, however, undocumented children are "basically indistinguishable" from legally resident alien children.

Finally, appellants suggest that undocumented children are appropriately singled out because their unlawful presence within the United States renders them less likely than other children to remain within the boundaries of the State, and to put their education to productive social or political use within the State. Even assuming that such an interest is legitimate, it is an interest that is most difficult to quantify. The State has no assurance that any child, citizen or not, will employ the education provided by the State within the confines of the State's borders. In any event, the record is clear that many of the undocumented children disabled by this classification will remain in this country indefinitely, and that some will become lawful residents or citizens of the United States. It is difficult to understand precisely what the State hopes to achieve by promoting the creation and perpetuation of a subclass of illiterates within our boundaries, surely adding to the problems and costs of unemployment, welfare, and crime. It is thus clear that whatever savings might be achieved by denying these children an education, they are wholly insubstantial in light of the costs involved to these children, the State, and the Nation.

VI

If the State is to deny a discrete group of innocent children the free public education that it offers to other children residing within its borders, that denial must be justified by a showing that it furthers some substantial state interest. No such showing was made here. Accordingly, the judgment of the Court of Appeals in each of these cases is

Affirmed.

JUSTICE MARSHALL, concurring.

While I join the Court's opinion, I do so without in any way retreating from my opinion in *San Antonio Independent School District v. Rodriguez* (1973) (dissenting opinion). I continue to believe that an individual's interest in education is fundamental, and that this view is amply supported "by the unique status accorded public education by our society, and by the close relationship between education and some of our most basic constitutional values." . . . It continues to be my view that a class-based denial of public education is utterly incompatible with the Equal Protection Clause of the Fourteenth Amendment.

JUSTICE BLACKMUN, concurring.

. . . [In *San Antonio Independent School District v. Rodriguez*, this Court articulated] a firm rule: fundamental rights are those that "explicitly or implicitly [are] guaranteed by the Constitution." It therefore squarely rejected the notion that "an ad hoc determination as to the social or economic importance" of a given interest is relevant to the level of scrutiny accorded classifications involving that interest. . . .

With all this said, however, I believe the Court's experience has demonstrated that the *Rodriguez* formulation does not settle every issue of "fundamental rights" arising under the Equal Protection Clause. Only a pedant would insist that there are *no* meaningful distinctions among the multitude of social and political interests regulated by the States, and *Rodriguez* does not stand for quite so absolute a proposition. To the contrary, *Rodriguez* implicitly acknowledged that certain interests, though not constitutionally guaranteed, must be accorded a special place in equal protection analysis. Thus, the Court's decisions long have accorded strict scrutiny to classifications bearing on the right to vote in state elections, and *Rodriguez* confirmed the "constitutional underpinnings of the right to equal treatment in the voting process." Yet "the right to vote, *per se*, is not a constitutionally protected right." See *Harper v. Virginia Board of Elections* (1966). Instead, regulation of the electoral process receives unusual scrutiny because "the right to exercise the franchise in a free and unimpaired manner is preservative of other basic civil and political rights." *Reynolds v. Sims* (1964). . . .

Because I believe that the Court's carefully worded analysis recognizes the importance of the equal protection and preemption interests I consider crucial, I join its opinion as well as its judgment.

JUSTICE POWELL, concurring.

I join the opinion of the Court, and write separately to emphasize the unique character of the cases before us.

The classification in question severely disadvantages children who are the victims of a combination of circumstances. Access from Mexico into this country, across our 2,000-mile border, is readily available and virtually uncontrollable. Illegal aliens are attracted by our employment opportunities, and perhaps by other benefits as well. . . . Perhaps because of the intractability of the problem, Congress—vested by the Constitution with the responsibility of protecting our borders and legislating with respect to aliens—has not provided effective leadership in dealing with this problem. It therefore is certain that illegal aliens will continue to enter the United States and, as the record makes clear, an unknown percentage of them will remain here. I agree with the Court that their children should not be left on the streets uneducated.

Although the analogy is not perfect, our holding today does find support in decisions of this Court with respect to the status of illegitimates. In *Weber v. Aetna Casualty & Surety Co.* (1972)[(applying strict scrutiny to discrimination against children of unmarried parents)], we said: "[V]isiting . . . condemnation on the head of an infant" for the misdeeds of the parents is illogical, unjust, and "contrary to the basic concept of our system that legal burdens should bear some relationship to individual responsibility or wrongdoing." . . .

In reaching this conclusion, I am not unmindful of what must be the exasperation of responsible citizens and government authorities in Texas and other States similarly situated. . . . But it hardly can be argued rationally that anyone benefits from the creation within our borders of a subclass of illiterate persons many of whom will remain in the State, adding to the problems and costs of both State and National Governments attendant upon unemployment, welfare, and crime.

CHIEF JUSTICE BURGER, with whom JUSTICE WHITE, JUSTICE REHNQUIST, and JUSTICE O'CONNOR join, dissenting.

. . . In a sense, the Court's opinion rests on such a unique confluence of theories and rationales that it will likely stand for little beyond the results in these particular cases. Yet the extent to which the Court departs from principled constitutional adjudication is nonetheless disturbing.

I have no quarrel with the conclusion that the Equal Protection Clause of the Fourteenth Amendment *applies* to aliens who, after their illegal entry into this country, are indeed physically "within the jurisdiction" of a state. However, as the Court concedes, this "only begins the inquiry." . . .

The Court acknowledges that, except in those cases when state classifications disadvantage a "suspect class" or impinge upon a "fundamental right," the Equal Protection Clause permits a state "substantial latitude" in distinguishing between different groups of persons. Moreover, the Court expressly—and correctly—rejects any suggestion that illegal aliens are a suspect class, or that education is a fundamental right. Yet by patching together bits and pieces of what might be termed quasi-suspect-class and quasi-fundamental-rights analysis, the Court spins out a theory custom-tailored to the facts of these cases. In the end, we are told little more than that the level of scrutiny employed to strike down the Texas law applies only when illegal alien children are deprived of a public education. If ever a court was guilty of an unabashedly result-oriented approach, this case is a prime example. . . .

Once it is conceded—as the Court does—that illegal aliens are not a suspect class, and that education is not a fundamental right, our inquiry should focus on and be limited to whether the legislative classification at issue bears a rational relationship to a legitimate state purpose. . . .

Without laboring what will undoubtedly seem obvious to many, it simply is not "irrational" for a state to conclude that it does not have the same responsibility to provide benefits for persons whose very presence in the state and this country is illegal as it does to provide for persons lawfully present. By definition, illegal aliens have no right whatever to be here. . . . In the absence of a constitutional imperative to provide for the education of illegal aliens, the State may "rationally" choose to take advantage of whatever savings will accrue from limiting access to the tuition-free public schools to its own lawful residents, excluding even citizens of neighboring States.

Denying a free education to illegal alien children is not a choice I would make were I a legislator. Apart from compassionate considerations, the long-range costs of excluding any children from the public schools may well outweigh the costs of educating them. But that is not the issue; the fact that there are sound *policy* arguments against the Texas Legislature's choice does not render that choice an unconstitutional one. . . .

6. LGBTQ+ Rights and the (Re-)Intersection of Due Process and Equality

We have seen that the law of Equal Protection and Due Process has a complex structure, one that sometimes breeds more confusion than clarity. A Due Process claim can invoke heightened scrutiny if the law infringes on a fundamental right. An Equal Protection claim can invoke heightened scrutiny if the law discriminates on the basis of a suspect classification, or if it discriminates in allocation of a right that might be deemed fundamental (though not sufficiently fundamental to justify a Due Process claim), or perhaps if it discriminates on the basis of a not-quite-suspect classification in the allocation of a not-quite-fundamental right. If heightened scrutiny is applied, the claim will probably succeed. But even if heightened scrutiny is not appropriate, either a Due Process or Equal Protection claim might yet succeed if the court is persuaded that the law is not reasonably related to a legitimate governmental goal.

COURSE THEME

The assertion of LGBTQ rights can bring into play all of these branches of doctrine. These cases—like those concerning, say, contraception, abortion, and choice in dying—address intimate aspects of how individuals conduct their lives, and so claimants contend that their fundamental rights are at stake. At the same time, they also involve claims of discrimination against groups that have certainly been subject to hatred and contempt, and so claimants contend that the classifications in question are suspect. But both of these contentions have been vigorously resisted by some government actors.

Until relatively recently, the Supreme Court treated same-sex orientation, when it considered it at all, as almost axiomatically a deviance not meriting constitutional protection. The case of *Baker v. Nelson* (1972) presented a gay couple's appeal of a Minnesota state court's rejection of their petition for an injunction requiring the local clerk to issue a marriage certificate to them. The Supreme Court denied their appeal on the merits in a decision that consisted in its entirety of the one-sentence formula used by the Court to signal that litigants had a right of appeal but no meritorious claims: "The appeal is dismissed for want of a substantial federal question."

WORTH NOTING

Recall that in his celebrated dissent in *Poe v. Ullman* (1961), the second Justice Harlan referred to "homosexuality" along with "adultery . . . and the like" as forbidden sexual intimacies. In one 1966 case, the Court spoke casually of "criminal, homosexual, treasonable, or other infamous conduct." *Linn v. United Plant Guard Workers of America, Local 114* (1966). In another case that year, the Court referred in passing to homosexuality as "deviant," *Ginzburg v. United States* (1966), and in a third it contrasted "relatively normal heterosexual relations" with "such deviations as sadomasochism, fetishism, and homosexuality." *Mishkin v. New York* (1966).

By 1986, public attitudes had changed so considerably that the Supreme Court could no longer treat such questions as obviously foreclosed. In *Bowers v. Hardwick* (1986), the Court rejected a gay man's challenge to Georgia's sodomy statute—but only by a 5–4 vote. The political liberalization on such questions continued, and in 1992, presidential candidate Bill Clinton advocated ending regulations that banned gay people and lesbians from the military. In a defense authorization act passed in 1993, however, Congress responded to Clinton's election by insisting that the military adhere to the regulations. The Clinton Administration then issued a directive prescribing that applicants for the military were not to be asked about their sexual orientation or about prior same-sex intimate conduct; this was the "Don't Ask, Don't Tell" policy (which lasted until passage of the Don't Ask, Don't Tell Repeal Act of 2011 ended the ban on openly gay and lesbian service members).

Also in 1993, the Hawaii Supreme Court ruled that the refusal to issue marriage licenses to same-sex couples was subject to strict scrutiny under the state constitution. In 1996, a state trial court judge determined that the state's refusal to issue marriage licenses to otherwise qualified same-sex couples could not pass constitutional muster under this test. By the time the case reached the state supreme court again, the state had by referendum adopted a constitutional amendment authorizing the legislature "to reserve marriage to opposite-sex couples," and so eliminating the challengers' claim under the state constitution.

Meanwhile, in 1996, largely in response to the 1993 Hawaii decision and with President Clinton's approval, Congress passed the Defense of Marriage Act (DOMA). Section 2 of DOMA, invoking Congress's power under the Full Faith and Credit Clause, provided that no state would be compelled to recognize a same-sex marriage performed under the laws of another state. (Some opponents of the bill argued that the provision was unnecessary because states could already take advantage of a "public policy" exception to the Clause and decline to recognize same-sex marriages from other states.) The other principal provision was § 3, which provided:

> In determining the meaning of any Act of Congress, or of any ruling, regulation, or interpretation of the various administrative bureaus and agencies of the United States, the word "marriage" means only a legal union between one man and one woman as husband and wife, and the word "spouse" refers only to a person of the opposite sex who is a husband or a wife.

In the same year that Congress passed DOMA, the Supreme Court issued *Romer v. Evans* (1996), which held invalid under the Equal Protection Clause the following amendment to the Colorado constitution, adopted by referendum:

> *No Protected Status Based on Homosexual, Lesbian or Bisexual Orientation.* Neither the State of Colorado, through any of its branches or departments, nor any of its agencies, political subdivisions, municipalities or school districts, shall enact, adopt or enforce any statute, regulation, ordinance or policy whereby homosexual, lesbian or bisexual orientation, conduct, practices or relationships shall constitute or otherwise be the basis of or entitle any person or class of persons to have or claim any minority status, quota preferences, protected status or claim of discrimination. This Section of the Constitution shall be in all respects self-executing.

Justice Kennedy's majority opinion formally analyzed the amendment under rational-basis review. (*Romer* is thus often thought of as an important illustration of "rational-basis plus.") He declared that

> the amendment imposes a special disability upon those persons alone. Homosexuals are forbidden the safeguards that others enjoy or may seek without constraint. . . . Its sheer breadth is so discontinuous with the reasons offered for it that the amendment seems inexplicable by anything but animus toward the class that it affects; it lacks a rational relationship to legitimate state interests. . . . It identifies persons by a single trait and then denies them protection across the board. The resulting disqualification of a class of persons from the right to seek specific protection from the law is unprecedented in our jurisprudence.

Justice Scalia dissented, joined by Chief Justice Rehnquist and Justice Thomas. He began his opinion by writing:

> The Court has mistaken a Kulturkampf for a fit of spite. The constitutional amendment before us here is not the manifestation of a " 'bare . . . desire to harm' " homosexuals, but is rather a modest attempt by seemingly tolerant Coloradans to preserve traditional sexual mores against the efforts of a politically powerful minority to revise those mores through use of the laws.

Question

Does the amendment involved in *Romer* deny the benefits of the political process to LGBTQ+ people—or does it does just reflect the fact they were on the losing end of this particular debate?

The stage was set for a more wide-ranging challenge to discrimination on the basis of sexual orientation.

Lawrence v. Texas

Supreme Court of the United States, 2003.
539 U.S. 558.

JUSTICE KENNEDY delivered the opinion of the Court.

Liberty protects the person from unwarranted government intrusions into a dwelling or other private places. In our tradition the State is not omnipresent in the home. And there are other spheres of our lives and existence, outside the home, where the State should not be a dominant presence. Freedom extends beyond spatial bounds. Liberty presumes an autonomy of self that includes freedom of thought, belief, expression, and certain intimate conduct. The instant case involves liberty of the person both in its spatial and in its more transcendent dimensions.

I

The question before the Court is the validity of a Texas statute making it a crime for two persons of the same sex to engage in certain intimate sexual conduct. In Houston, Texas, officers of the Harris County Police Department were dispatched to a private residence in response to a reported weapons disturbance. They entered an apartment where one of the petitioners, John Geddes Lawrence, resided. The right of the police to enter does not seem to have been questioned. The officers observed Lawrence and another man, Tyron Garner, engaging in

WORTH NOTING

The Texas statute criminalized the act of "deviate sexual intercourse with another individual of the same sex."

a sexual act. The two petitioners were arrested, held in custody overnight, and charged and convicted before a Justice of the Peace. . . . The petitioners were adults at the time of the alleged offense. Their conduct was in private and consensual.

II

We conclude the case should be resolved by determining whether the petitioners were free as adults to engage in the private conduct in the exercise of their liberty under the Due Process Clause of the Fourteenth Amendment to the Constitution. For this inquiry we deem it necessary to reconsider the Court's holding in *Bowers v. Hardwick* (1986) [(approving the constitutionality of a criminal prohibition on same-sex sodomy)].

There are broad statements of the substantive reach of liberty under the Due Process Clause in earlier cases, including *Pierce v. Society of Sisters* (1925), and *Meyer v. Nebraska* (1923); but the most pertinent beginning point is our decision in *Griswold v. Connecticut* (1965). In *Griswold*[, t]he Court described the protected interest as a right to privacy and placed emphasis on the marriage relation and the protected space of the marital bedroom. After *Griswold* it was established that the right to make certain decisions regarding sexual conduct extends beyond the marital relationship. In *Eisenstadt v. Baird* (1972), the Court [held that] "[i]f the right of privacy means anything, it is the right of the *individual,* married or single, to be free from unwarranted governmental intrusion into matters so fundamentally affecting a person as the decision whether to bear or beget a child." [I]n *Roe v. Wade* (1973)[, the] Court cited cases that protect spatial freedom and cases that go well beyond it[, and] recognized the right of a woman to make certain fundamental decisions affecting her destiny. . . .

This was the state of the law with respect to some of the most relevant cases when the Court considered *Bowers v. Hardwick*.

The facts in *Bowers* had some similarities to the instant case. A police officer, whose right to enter seems not to have been in question, observed Hardwick, in his own bedroom, engaging in intimate sexual conduct with another adult male. The conduct was in violation of a Georgia statute making it a criminal offense to engage in sodomy. One difference between the two cases is that the Georgia statute prohibited the conduct whether or not the participants were of the same sex, while the Texas statute, as we have seen, applies only to participants of the same sex. Hardwick was not prosecuted, but he brought an action in federal court to declare the state statute invalid. He alleged he was a

practicing homosexual and that the criminal prohibition violated rights guaranteed to him by the Constitution. The Court, in an opinion by Justice White,
sustained the Georgia law. . . .

> The Court began its substantive discussion in *Bowers* as follows:
>
> The issue presented is whether the Federal Constitution confers a
> fundamental right upon homosexuals to engage in sodomy and hence
> invalidates the laws of the many States that still make such conduct
> illegal and have done so for a very long time.

That statement, we now conclude, discloses the Court's own failure to appreciate the extent of the liberty at stake. To say that the issue in *Bowers* was simply
the right to engage in certain sexual conduct demeans the claim the individual
put forward, just as it would demean a married couple were it to be said marriage is simply about the right to have sexual intercourse. The laws involved in
Bowers and here are, to be sure, statutes that purport to do no more than prohibit a particular sexual act. Their penalties and purposes, though, have more
far-reaching consequences, touching upon the most private human conduct,
sexual behavior, and in the most private of places, the home. The statutes do
seek to control a personal relationship that, whether or not entitled to formal
recognition in the law, is within the liberty of persons to choose without being
punished as criminals.

This, as a general rule, should counsel against attempts by the State, or a
court, to define the meaning of the relationship or to set its boundaries absent
injury to a person or abuse of an institution the law protects. It suffices for us
to acknowledge that adults may choose to enter upon this relationship in the
confines of their homes and their own private lives and still retain their dignity
as free persons. When sexuality finds overt expression in intimate conduct with
another person, the conduct can be but one element in a personal bond that is
more enduring. The liberty protected by the Constitution allows homosexual
persons the right to make this choice.

Having misapprehended the claim of liberty there presented to it, and
thus stating the claim to be whether there is a fundamental right to engage in
consensual sodomy, the *Bowers* Court said: "Proscriptions against that conduct
have ancient roots." In academic writings, and in many of the scholarly *amicus*
briefs filed to assist the Court in this case, there are fundamental criticisms of
the historical premises relied upon by the majority and concurring opinions
in *Bowers*. Brief for Cato Institute as *Amicus Curiae*; Brief for American Civil

Liberties Union as *Amici Curiae*; Brief for Professors of History as *Amici Curiae*. We need not enter this debate in the attempt to reach a definitive historical judgment, but the following considerations counsel against adopting the definitive conclusions upon which *Bowers* placed such reliance.

At the outset it should be noted that there is no longstanding history in this country of laws directed at homosexual conduct as a distinct matter. Beginning in colonial times there were prohibitions of sodomy derived from the English criminal laws passed in the first instance by the Reformation Parliament of 1533. The English prohibition was understood to include relations between men and women as well as relations between men and men. Nineteenth-century commentators similarly read American sodomy, buggery, and crime-against-nature statutes as criminalizing certain relations between men and women and between men and men. The absence of legal prohibitions focusing on homosexual conduct may be explained in part by noting that according to some scholars the concept of the homosexual as a distinct category of person did not emerge until the late 19th century. Thus early American sodomy laws were not directed at homosexuals as such but instead sought to prohibit nonprocreative sexual activity more generally. This does not suggest approval of homosexual conduct. It does tend to show that this particular form of conduct was not thought of as a separate category from like conduct between heterosexual persons. . . .

Laws prohibiting sodomy do not seem to have been enforced against consenting adults acting in private. A substantial number of sodomy prosecutions and convictions for which there are surviving records were for predatory acts against those who could not or did not consent, as in the case of . . . . relations between men and minor girls or minor boys, relations between adults involving force, relations between adults implicating disparity in status, or relations between men and animals. [Various problems of evidentiary proof] may explain in part the infrequency of these prosecutions. In all events that infrequency makes it difficult to say that society approved of a rigorous and systematic punishment of the consensual acts committed in private and by adults.

[F]ar from possessing "ancient roots," *Bowers*, American laws targeting same-sex couples did not develop until the last third of the 20th century. The reported decisions concerning the prosecution of consensual, homosexual sodomy between adults for the years 1880–1995 are not always clear in the details, but a significant number involved conduct in a public place. It was not until the 1970's that any State singled out same-sex relations for criminal prosecution, and only nine States have done so. [The Court cites statutes from Arkansas, Kansas, Kentucky, Missouri, Montana, Nevada, Tennessee, and Texas, and an Oklahoma decision.] Post-*Bowers* even some of these States did not adhere to the policy of suppressing homosexual conduct. Over the course of the last decades, States with same-sex prohibitions have moved toward abolishing them. [The Court cites decisions from Arkansas, Kentucky, Montana, and Tennessee, and a Nevada statute.]

In summary, the historical grounds relied upon in *Bowers* are more complex than the majority opinion and the concurring opinion by Chief Justice Burger indicate. Their historical premises are not without doubt and, at the very least, are overstated.

It must be acknowledged, of course, that the Court in *Bowers* was making the broader point that for centuries there have been powerful voices to condemn homosexual conduct as immoral. The condemnation has been shaped by religious beliefs, conceptions of right and acceptable behavior, and respect for the traditional family. For many persons these are not trivial concerns but profound and deep convictions accepted as ethical and moral principles to which they aspire and which thus determine the course of their lives. These considerations do not answer the question before us, however. The issue is whether the majority may use the power of the State to enforce these views on the whole society through operation of the criminal law. . . .

In all events we think that our laws and traditions in the past half century are of most relevance here. These references show an emerging awareness that liberty gives substantial protection to adult persons in deciding how to conduct their private lives in matters pertaining to sex. "[H]istory and tradition are the starting point but not in all cases the ending point of the substantive due process inquiry." *County of Sacramento v. Lewis* (1998) (Kennedy, J., concurring). This emerging recognition should have been apparent when *Bowers* was decided. In 1955 the American Law Institute promulgated the Model Penal Code and made clear that it did not recommend or provide for "criminal penalties for consensual sexual relations conducted in private." Model Penal Code § 213.2, Comment 2 (1980). . . . In 1961 Illinois changed its laws to conform to the Model Penal Code. Other States soon followed.

In *Bowers* the Court referred to the fact that before 1961 all 50 States had outlawed sodomy, and that at the time of the Court's decision 24 States and the District of Columbia had sodomy laws. Justice Powell pointed out [in his dissent] that these prohibitions often were being ignored, however. Georgia, for instance, had not sought to enforce its law for decades. . . .

[References by judges in the *Bowers* majority] to the history of Western civilization and to Judeo-Christian moral and ethical standards did not take account of other authorities pointing in an opposite direction. A committee advising the British Parliament recommended in 1957 repeal of laws punishing homosexual conduct. Parliament enacted the substance of those recommendations 10 years later. Sexual Offences Act 1967. Of even more importance, almost five years before *Bowers* was decided the European Court of Human Rights . . . . held that the laws proscribing [same sex sodomy] were invalid under the European Convention on Human Rights. *Dudgeon v. United Kingdom*, 45 Eur. Ct. H.R. (1981). Authoritative in all countries that are members of the Council of Europe (21 nations then, 45 nations now), the decision is at odds with the premise in *Bowers* that the claim put forward was insubstantial in our Western civilization.

In our own constitutional system the deficiencies in *Bowers* became even more apparent in the years following its announcement. The 25 States with laws prohibiting the relevant conduct referenced in the *Bowers* decision are reduced now to 13, of which 4 enforce their laws only against homosexual conduct. In those States where sodomy is still proscribed, whether for same-sex or heterosexual conduct, there is a pattern of nonenforcement with respect to consenting adults acting in private. The State of Texas admitted in 1994 that as of that date it had not prosecuted anyone under those circumstances. *State v. Morales.*

Two principal cases decided after *Bowers* cast its holding into even more doubt. [The Court here quotes the passage from *Casey*, supra p. 1430, asserting that "the most intimate and personal choices a person may make in a lifetime, choices central to personal dignity and autonomy, are central to the liberty protected by the Fourteenth Amendment," and that "[a]t the heart of liberty is the right to define one's own concept of existence, of meaning, of the universe, and of the mystery of human life."] Persons in a homosexual relationship may seek autonomy for these purposes, just as heterosexual persons do. The decision in *Bowers* would deny them this right.

The second post-Bowers case of principal relevance is *Romer v. Evans* (1996). . . . *Romer* invalidated [under the Equal Protection Clause] an amendment to Colorado's Constitution which named as a solitary class persons who were homosexuals, lesbians, or bisexual either by "orientation, conduct, practices or relationships," and deprived them of protection under state antidiscrimination laws. We concluded that the provision was "born of animosity toward the class of persons affected" and further that it had no rational relation to a legitimate governmental purpose.

As an alternative argument in this case, counsel for the petitioners and some *amici* contend that *Romer* provides the basis for declaring the Texas statute invalid under the Equal Protection Clause. That is a tenable argument, but we conclude the instant case requires us to address whether *Bowers* itself has continuing validity. Were we to hold the statute invalid under the Equal Protection Clause, some might question whether a prohibition would be valid if drawn differently, say, to prohibit the conduct both between same-sex and different-sex participants. Equality of treatment and the due process right to demand respect for conduct protected by the substantive guarantee of liberty are linked in important respects, and a decision on the latter point advances both interests. If protected conduct is made criminal and the law which does so remains unexamined for its substantive validity, its stigma might remain even if it were not enforceable as drawn for equal protection reasons. . . .

The central holding of *Bowers* has been brought in question by this case, and it should be addressed. Its continuance as precedent demeans the lives of homosexual persons. The stigma this criminal statute imposes, moreover, is not trivial. The offense, to be sure, is but a class C misdemeanor, a minor offense in the Texas legal system. Still, it remains a criminal offense with all that imports for the dignity of the persons charged. . . . Furthermore, the Texas criminal conviction carries with it the other collateral consequences always following a conviction, such as notations on job application forms, to mention but one example.

The foundations of *Bowers* have sustained serious erosion from our recent decisions in *Casey* and *Romer*. When our precedent has been thus weakened, criticism from other sources is of greater significance. In the United States criticism of *Bowers* has been substantial and continuing, disapproving of its reasoning in all respects, not just as to its historical assumptions. See, *e.g.*, C. Fried, Order and Law: Arguing the Reagan Revolution—A Firsthand Account (1991); R. Posner, Sex and Reason (1992). The courts of five different States have declined to follow it in interpreting provisions in their own state constitutions parallel to the Due Process Clause of the Fourteenth Amendment. . . . [The Court cites decisions from Arkansas, Georgia, Montana, Tennessee, and Kentucky.]

The doctrine of *stare decisis* is essential to the respect accorded to the judgments of the Court and to the stability of the law. It is not, however, an inexorable command. . . . The holding in *Bowers* . . . has not induced detrimental reliance comparable to some instances where recognized individual rights are involved. Indeed, there has been no individual or societal reliance on *Bowers* of the sort that could counsel against overturning its holding once there are compelling reasons to do so. *Bowers* itself causes uncertainty, for the precedents before and after its issuance contradict its central holding.

The rationale of *Bowers* does not withstand careful analysis. In his dissenting opinion in *Bowers*, Justice Stevens [noted]: "[The fact] that the governing majority in a State has traditionally viewed a particular practice as immoral is not a sufficient reason for upholding a law prohibiting the practice; neither history nor tradition could save a law prohibiting miscegenation from constitutional attack. . . ." Justice Stevens' analysis, in our view, should have been controlling in *Bowers* and should control here. *Bowers* was not correct when it was decided, and it is not correct today. It ought not to remain binding precedent. *Bowers v. Hardwick* should be and now is overruled.

The present case does not involve minors. It does not involve persons who might be injured or coerced or who are situated in relationships where consent might not easily be refused. It does not involve public conduct or prostitution. It does not involve whether the government must give formal recognition to any relationship that homosexual persons seek to enter. The case does involve two adults who, with full and mutual consent from each other, engaged in sexual practices common to a homosexual lifestyle. The petitioners are entitled to respect for their private lives. The State cannot demean their existence or control their destiny by making their private sexual conduct a crime. Their right to liberty under the Due Process Clause gives them the full right to engage in their conduct without intervention of the government. "It is a promise of the Constitution that there is a realm of personal liberty which the government may not enter." *Casey*. The Texas statute furthers no legitimate state interest which can justify its intrusion into the personal and private life of the individual.

Had those who drew and ratified the Due Process Clauses of the Fifth Amendment or the Fourteenth Amendment known the components of liberty in its manifold possibilities, they might have been more specific. They did not presume to have this insight. They knew times can blind us to certain truths and later generations can see that laws once thought necessary and proper in fact serve only to oppress. As the Constitution endures, persons in every generation can invoke its principles in their own search for greater freedom.

The judgment of the Court of Appeals for the Texas Fourteenth District is reversed, and the case is remanded for further proceedings not inconsistent with this opinion. . . .

JUSTICE O'CONNOR, concurring in the judgment.

. . . I joined *Bowers*, and do not join the Court in overruling it. Nevertheless, I agree with the Court that Texas' statute banning same-sex sodomy is unconstitutional. . . . I base my conclusion on the Fourteenth Amendment's Equal Protection Clause. . . .

Laws such as economic or tax legislation that are scrutinized under rational basis review normally pass constitutional muster. . . . We have consistently held, however, that some objectives, such as "a bare . . . desire to harm a politically unpopular group," are not legitimate state interests. *Department of Agriculture v. Moreno* (1973). See also *Cleburne v. Cleburne Living Center* (1985); *Romer v. Evans* (1996). When a law exhibits such a desire to harm a politically unpopular group, we have applied a more searching form of rational basis review to strike down such laws under the Equal Protection Clause. We have been most likely to apply rational basis review to hold a law unconstitutional under the Equal Protection Clause where, as here, the challenged legislation inhibits personal relationships. [Justice O'Connor here discusses *Department of Agriculture v. Moreno, Eisenstadt v. Baird* (1972), *City of Cleburne v. Cleburne Living Center,* and *Romer v. Evans*.]

The statute at issue here makes sodomy a crime only if a person "engages in deviate sexual intercourse with another individual of the same sex." Sodomy between opposite-sex partners, however, is not a crime in Texas. That is, Texas treats the same conduct differently based solely on the participants. Those harmed by this law are people who have a same-sex sexual orientation and thus are more likely to engage in behavior prohibited by [the statute]. The Texas statute makes homosexuals unequal in the eyes of the law by making particular conduct—and only that conduct—subject to criminal sanction. . . .

Texas attempts to justify its law, and the effects of the law, by arguing that the statute satisfies rational basis review because it furthers the legitimate governmental interest of the promotion of morality. . . . This case raises a different issue than *Bowers:* whether, under the Equal Protection Clause, moral disapproval is a legitimate state interest to justify by itself a statute that bans homosexual sodomy, but not heterosexual sodomy. It is not. Moral disapproval of this group, like a bare desire to harm the group, is an interest that is insufficient to satisfy rational basis review under the Equal Protection Clause. See, *e.g., Department of Agriculture v. Moreno; Romer v. Evans.* Indeed, we have never held that moral disapproval, without any other asserted state interest, is a sufficient rationale under the Equal Protection Clause to justify a law that discriminates among groups of persons. . . . And because Texas so rarely enforces its sodomy law as applied to private, consensual acts, the law serves more as a statement of dislike and disapproval against homosexuals than as a tool to stop criminal behavior. . . .

Texas argues, however, that the sodomy law does not discriminate against homosexual persons. Instead, the State maintains that the law discriminates only against homosexual conduct. While it is true that the law applies only to conduct, the conduct targeted by this law is conduct that is closely correlated with being homosexual. Under such circumstances, Texas' sodomy law is targeted at more than conduct. It is instead directed toward gay persons as a class. . . .

A State can of course assign certain consequences to a violation of its criminal law. But the State cannot single out one identifiable class of citizens for punishment that does not apply to everyone else, with moral disapproval as the only asserted state interest for the law. . . .

Whether a sodomy law that is neutral both in effect and application, see *Yick Wo v. Hopkins* (1886), would violate the substantive component of the Due Process Clause is an issue that need not be decided today. I am confident, however, that so long as the Equal Protection Clause requires a sodomy law to apply equally to the private consensual conduct of homosexuals and heterosexuals alike, such a law would not long stand in our democratic society. In the words of Justice Jackson[,] "there is no more effective practical guaranty against arbitrary and unreasonable government than to require that the principles of law which officials would impose upon a minority be imposed generally. . . ." *Railway Express Agency, Inc. v. New York* (1949) (concurring opinion).

That this law as applied to private, consensual conduct is unconstitutional under the Equal Protection Clause does not mean that other laws distinguishing between heterosexuals and homosexuals would similarly fail under rational basis review. Texas cannot assert any legitimate state interest here, such as national security or preserving the traditional institution of marriage. Unlike the moral disapproval of same-sex relations—the asserted state interest in this case—other reasons exist to promote the institution of marriage beyond mere moral disapproval of an excluded group. . . .

JUSTICE SCALIA, with whom THE CHIEF JUSTICE and JUSTICE THOMAS join, dissenting.

. . . Most of . . . today's opinion has no relevance to its actual holding—that the Texas statute "furthers no legitimate state interest which can justify" its application to petitioners under rational-basis review. Though there is discussion of "fundamental proposition[s]" and "fundamental decisions," nowhere does the Court's opinion declare that homosexual sodomy is a "fundamental right" under the Due Process Clause; nor does it subject the Texas law to the standard of review that would be appropriate (strict scrutiny) if homosexual sodomy *were* a "fundamental right." . . . Instead the Court simply describes petitioners' conduct as "an exercise of their liberty"—which it undoubtedly is—and proceeds to apply an unheard-of form of rational-basis review that will have far-reaching implications beyond this case.

I

. . . Countless judicial decisions and legislative enactments have relied on the ancient proposition that a governing majority's belief that certain sexual behavior is "immoral and unacceptable" constitutes a rational basis for regulation. See, *e.g., Williams v. Pryor* (11th Cir. 2001) (citing *Bowers* in upholding Alabama's prohibition on the sale of sex toys). . . . State laws against bigamy, same-sex marriage, adult incest, prostitution, masturbation, adultery, fornication, bestiality, and obscenity are likewise sustainable only in light of *Bowers'* validation of laws based on moral choices.

Every single one of these laws is called into question by today's decision; the Court makes no effort to cabin the scope of its decision to exclude them from its holding. See *ante* (noting "an emerging awareness that liberty gives substantial protection to adult persons in deciding how to conduct their private lives *in matters pertaining to sex*" (emphasis added)). The impossibility of distinguishing homosexuality from other traditional "morals" offenses is precisely why *Bowers* rejected the rational-basis challenge. "The law," it said, "is constantly based on notions of morality, and if all laws representing essentially moral choices are to be invalidated under the Due Process Clause, the courts will be very busy indeed." . . .

II

Texas Penal Code Ann. § 21.06(a) undoubtedly imposes constraints on liberty. So do laws prohibiting prostitution, recreational use of heroin, and, for that matter, working more than 60 hours per week in a bakery. . . . Our opinions applying the doctrine known as "substantive due process" hold that the Due Process Clause prohibits States from infringing *fundamental* liberty interests, unless the infringement is narrowly tailored to serve a compelling state interest. *Washington v. Glucksberg.* We have held repeatedly, in cases the Court today does not overrule, that *only* fundamental rights qualify for this so-called "heightened scrutiny" protection—that is, rights which are " 'deeply rooted in this Nation's history and tradition.' " All other liberty interests may be abridged or abrogated pursuant to a validly enacted state law if that law is rationally related to a legitimate state interest. . . .

The Court today does not overrule this holding. Not once does it describe homosexual sodomy as a "fundamental right" or a "fundamental liberty interest," nor does it subject the Texas statute to strict scrutiny. Instead, having failed to establish that the right to homosexual sodomy is " 'deeply rooted in this Nation's history and tradition,' " the Court concludes that the application of Texas's statute to petitioners' conduct fails the rational-basis test, and overrules *Bowers'* holding to the contrary. . . .

I shall address that rational-basis holding presently. First, however, I address some aspersions that the Court casts upon *Bowers'* conclusion that homosexual sodomy is not a "fundamental right"—even though, as I have said, the Court does not have the boldness to reverse that conclusion.

III

[The Court's historical discussion] in no way casts into doubt the "definitive [historical] conclusio[n]," on which *Bowers* relied: that our Nation has a long-standing history of laws prohibiting *sodomy in general*—regardless of whether it was performed by same-sex or opposite-sex couples. . . .

. . . Whether homosexual sodomy was prohibited by a law targeted at same-sex sexual relations or by a more general law prohibiting both homosexual and heterosexual sodomy, the only relevant point is that it *was* criminalized—which suffices to establish that homosexual sodomy is not a right "deeply rooted in our Nation's history and tradition." The Court today agrees that homosexual sodomy was criminalized and thus does not dispute the facts on which *Bowers actually* relied.

Next the Court makes the claim, again unsupported by any citations, that "[l]aws prohibiting sodomy do not seem to have been enforced against consenting adults acting in private." . . . I do not know what "acting in private" means; surely consensual sodomy, like heterosexual intercourse, is rarely performed on stage. If all the Court means by "acting in private" is "on private premises, with the doors closed and windows covered," it is entirely unsurprising that evidence of enforcement would be hard to come by. . . . Surely that lack of evidence would not sustain the proposition that consensual sodomy on private premises with the doors closed and windows covered was regarded as a "fundamental right," even though all other consensual sodomy was criminalized. [In any event, t]here are 203 prosecutions for consensual, adult homosexual sodomy reported in the West Reporting system and official state reporters from the years 1880–1995. There are also records of 20 sodomy prosecutions and 4 executions during the colonial period.

Bowers' conclusion that homosexual sodomy is not a fundamental right "deeply rooted in this Nation's history and tradition" is [thus] utterly unassailable. Realizing that fact, the Court instead says:

> [W]e think that our laws and traditions in the past half century are of most relevance here. These references show *an emerging awareness* that liberty gives substantial protection to adult persons in deciding how to conduct their private lives *in matters pertaining to sex.*

. . . [A]n "emerging awareness" is by definition not "deeply rooted in this Nation's history and tradition[s]," as we have said "fundamental right" status requires. Constitutional entitlements do not spring into existence because some States choose to lessen or eliminate criminal sanctions on certain behavior. Much less do they spring into existence, as the Court seems to believe, because *foreign nations* decriminalize conduct. . . . The Court's discussion of these foreign views (ignoring, of course, the many countries that have retained criminal prohibitions on sodomy) is therefore meaningless dicta. Dangerous dicta, however, since "this Court . . . should not impose foreign moods, fads, or fashions on Americans." *Foster v. Florida* (2002) (Thomas, J., concurring in denial of certiorari).

IV

I turn now to the ground on which the Court squarely rests its holding: the contention that there is no rational basis for the law here under attack. This proposition is so out of accord with our jurisprudence—indeed, with the jurisprudence of *any* society we know—that it requires little discussion.

The Texas statute undeniably seeks to further the belief of its citizens that certain forms of sexual behavior are "immoral and unacceptable," *Bowers*—the same interest furthered by criminal laws against fornication, bigamy, adultery, adult incest, bestiality, and obscenity. *Bowers* held that this *was* a legitimate state interest. The Court today reaches the opposite conclusion. The Texas statute, it says, "furthers *no legitimate state interest* which can justify its intrusion into the personal and private life of the individual" (emphasis added). The Court embraces instead Justice Stevens' declaration in his *Bowers* dissent, that " 'the fact that the governing majority in a State has traditionally viewed a particular practice as immoral is not a sufficient reason for upholding a law prohibiting the practice.' " This effectively decrees the end of all morals legislation. If, as the Court asserts, the promotion of majoritarian sexual morality is not even a *legitimate* state interest, none of the above-mentioned laws can survive rational-basis review.

V

Finally, I turn to petitioners' equal-protection challenge, which no Member of the Court save Justice O'Connor embraces.

On its face § 21.06(a) applies equally to all persons. Men and women, heterosexuals and homosexuals, are all subject to its prohibition of deviate sexual intercourse with someone of the same sex. To be sure, § 21.06 does distinguish between the sexes insofar as concerns the partner with whom the sexual acts are performed: men can violate the law only with other men, and women only with other women. . . . The objection is made, however, that the antimiscegenation laws invalidated in *Loving v. Virginia* (1967), similarly were applicable to whites and blacks alike, and only distinguished between the races insofar as the *partner* was concerned. In *Loving*, however, we correctly applied heightened scrutiny, rather than the usual rational-basis review, because the Virginia statute was "designed to maintain White Supremacy." . . . No purpose to discriminate against men or women as a class can be gleaned from the Texas law, so rational-basis review applies. . . .

Justice O'Connor argues that the discrimination in this law which must be justified is not its discrimination with regard to the sex of the partner but its discrimination with regard to the sexual proclivity of the principal actor. . . . Of course the same could be said of any law. A law against public nudity targets "the conduct that is closely correlated with being a nudist," and hence "is targeted at more than conduct"; it is "directed toward nudists as a class." But be that as it may. Even if the Texas law *does* deny equal protection to "homosexuals as a class," that denial *still* does not need to be justified by anything more than a rational basis, which our cases show is satisfied by the enforcement of traditional notions of sexual morality. . . .

* * *

Today's opinion is the product of a Court, which is the product of a law-profession culture, that has largely signed on to the so-called homosexual agenda, by which I mean the agenda promoted by some homosexual activists directed at eliminating the moral opprobrium that has traditionally attached to homosexual conduct. . . . Many Americans do not want persons who openly engage in homosexual conduct as partners in their business, as scoutmasters for their children, as teachers in their children's schools, or as boarders in their home. They view this as protecting themselves and their families from a lifestyle that they believe to be immoral and destructive. The Court views it as "discrimination" which it is the function of our judgments to deter.

So imbued is the Court with the law profession's anti-anti-homosexual culture, that it is seemingly unaware that the attitudes of that culture are not obviously "mainstream"; that in most States what the Court calls "discrimination" against those who engage in homosexual acts is perfectly legal; that proposals to ban such "discrimination" under Title VII have repeatedly been rejected by Congress; that in some cases such "discrimination" is *mandated* by federal statute, see 10 U.S.C. § 654(b)(1) (mandating discharge from the Armed Forces of any service member who engages in or intends to engage in homosexual acts); and that in some cases such "discrimination" is a constitutional right, see *Boy Scouts of America v. Dale* (2000). . . .

It is indeed true that "later generations can see that laws once thought necessary and proper in fact serve only to oppress"; and when that happens, later generations can repeal those laws. But it is the premise of our system that those judgments are to be made by the people, and not imposed by a governing caste that knows best.

One of the benefits of leaving regulation of this matter to the people rather than to the courts is that the people, unlike judges, need not carry things to their logical conclusion. . . . At the end of its opinion—after having laid waste the foundations of our rational-basis jurisprudence—the Court says that the present case "does not involve whether the government must give formal recognition to any relationship that homosexual persons seek to enter." Do not believe it. . . . If moral disapprobation of homosexual conduct is "no legitimate state interest" for purposes of proscribing that conduct, . . . what justification could there possibly be for denying the benefits of marriage to homosexual couples exercising "[t]he liberty protected by the Constitution"? Surely not the encouragement of procreation, since the sterile and the elderly are allowed to marry. This case "does not involve" the issue of homosexual marriage only if one entertains the belief that principle and logic have nothing to do with the decisions of this Court. Many will hope that, as the Court comfortingly assures us, this is so. . . .

JUSTICE THOMAS, dissenting.

I join Justice Scalia's dissenting opinion. I write separately to note that the law before the Court today "is . . . uncommonly silly." *Griswold v. Connecticut* (1965) (Stewart, J., dissenting). If I were a member of the Texas Legislature, I would vote to repeal it. Punishing someone for expressing his sexual preference through noncommercial consensual conduct with another adult does not appear to be a worthy way to expend valuable law enforcement resources. Notwithstanding this, I recognize that as a Member of this Court I am not empowered to help petitioners and others similarly situated. . . .

Justice Scalia predicted that the logic of *Lawrence* would require the court to extend "the benefits of marriage" to same sex-couples. Developments were in fact breathtakingly fast. Less than five months later, the Massachusetts Supreme Judicial Court held by a 4–3 majority that the state constitution guaranteed same-sex couples the right to marry. *Goodridge v. Department of Public Health* (2003). The court gave the legislature 180 days to rectify the existing marriage ban, and the state senate responded by enacting a bill allowing same-sex couples to enter into civil unions, with all the incidents of marriage but not the name. In an advisory opinion, *In re Opinions of the Justices to the Senate* (2004), the court held by the same 4–3 vote that this was inadequate; the senate bill would establish "an unconstitutional, inferior, and discriminatory status for same-sex couples."

In the years right after the Massachusetts *Goodridge* decision (and at least partly in response to it) some thirty states adopted constitutional amendments affirmatively banning same-sex marriages, and sometimes even civil unions; most of these were adopted through referenda, and often by heavy majorities. But the tide soon turned, and decisively. Courts in several states followed the lead of *Goodridge* and held that there was a right to same-sex marriage under the state constitution. Beginning in 2009, legislatures in eight states approved same-sex marriages. And in the 2012 general election, same-sex marriage won at the ballot box in Maryland, Washington, and Maine.

The U.S. Supreme Court entered the arena in *United States v. Windsor* (2013), which invalidated § 3 of the 1996 Defense of Marriage Act (DOMA) by a 5–4 vote. That portion of the act provided, in essence, that even if a same-sex couple lived in a state that recognized their marriage, the federal government could not recognize it. *Windsor* did not decide the ultimate issue of whether same-sex couples have a federal constitutional right to marry.

By the time the Supreme Court addressed that issue in the following case, about 20 states had given same-sex couples the ability to marry, by legislation, by voter initiative, or by decision of state courts interpreting state constitutions; federal judicial decisions under the United States Constitution required an additional 20 states or so (depending on how you count) to license same-sex marriages. The Court of Appeals for the Sixth Circuit took a different view, and so the Supreme Court resolved the conflict.

Obergefell v. Hodges

Supreme Court of the United States, 2015.
576 U.S. 644.

JUSTICE KENNEDY delivered the opinion of the Court.

. . . These cases come from Michigan, Kentucky, Ohio, and Tennessee, States that define marriage as a union between one man and one woman. The petitioners are 14 same-sex couples and two men whose same-sex partners are deceased. The respondents are state officials responsible for enforcing the laws in question. The petitioners claim the respondents violate the Fourteenth Amendment by denying them the right to marry or to have their marriages, lawfully performed in another State, given full recognition. . . .

II

Before addressing the principles and precedents that govern these cases, it is appropriate to note the history of the subject now before the Court.

A

From their beginning to their most recent page, the annals of human history reveal the transcendent importance of marriage. The lifelong union of a man and a woman always has promised nobility and dignity to all persons, without regard to their station in life. Marriage is sacred to those who live by their religions and offers unique fulfillment to those who find meaning in the secular realm. Its dynamic allows two people to find a life that could not be found alone, for a marriage becomes greater than just the two persons. Rising from the most basic human needs, marriage is essential to our most profound hopes and aspirations.

The centrality of marriage to the human condition makes it unsurprising that the institution has existed for millennia and across civilizations. Since the dawn of history, marriage has transformed strangers into relatives, binding families and societies together. Confucius taught that marriage lies at the foundation of government. This wisdom was echoed centuries later and half a world away by Cicero, who wrote, "The first bond of society is marriage; next, children; and then the family." There are untold references to the beauty of marriage in religious and philosophical texts spanning time, cultures, and faiths, as well as in art and literature in all their forms. It is fair and necessary to say these references were based on the understanding that marriage is a union between two persons of the opposite sex.

That history is the beginning of these cases. The respondents say it should be the end as well. To them, it would demean a timeless institution if the concept and lawful status of marriage were extended to two persons of the same sex. Marriage, in their view, is by its nature a gender-differentiated union of man and woman. This view long has been held—and continues to be held—in good faith by reasonable and sincere people here and throughout the world.

The petitioners acknowledge this history but contend that these cases cannot end there. Were their intent to demean the revered idea and reality of marriage, the petitioners' claims would be of a different order. But that is neither their purpose nor their submission. To the contrary, it is the enduring importance of marriage that underlies the petitioners' contentions. This, they say, is their whole point. Far from seeking to devalue marriage, the petitioners seek it for themselves because of their respect—and need—for its privileges and responsibilities. And their immutable nature dictates that same-sex marriage is their only real path to this profound commitment. . . .

B

The ancient origins of marriage confirm its centrality, but it has not stood in isolation from developments in law and society. The history of marriage is one of both continuity and change. That institution—even as confined to opposite-sex relations—has evolved over time.

For example, marriage was once viewed as an arrangement by the couple's parents based on political, religious, and financial concerns; but by the time of the Nation's founding it was understood to be a voluntary contract between a man and a woman. As the role and status of women changed, the institution further evolved. Under the centuries-old doctrine of coverture, a married man and woman were treated by the State as a single, male-dominated legal entity. As women gained legal, political, and property rights, and as society began to understand that women have their own equal dignity, the law of coverture was abandoned. These and other developments in the institution of marriage over the past centuries were not mere superficial changes. Rather, they worked deep transformations in its structure, affecting aspects of marriage long viewed by many as essential.

These new insights have strengthened, not weakened, the institution of marriage. Indeed, changed understandings of marriage are characteristic of a Nation where new dimensions of freedom become apparent to new generations, often through perspectives that begin in pleas or protests and then are considered in the political sphere and the judicial process. . . .

III

. . . The fundamental liberties protected by [the Due Process] Clause include most of the rights enumerated in the Bill of Rights. In addition these liberties extend to certain personal choices central to individual dignity and autonomy, including intimate choices that define personal identity and beliefs.

The identification and protection of fundamental rights is an enduring part of the judicial duty to interpret the Constitution. That responsibility, however, "has not been reduced to any formula." *Poe v. Ullman* (1961) (Harlan, J., dissenting). Rather, it requires courts to exercise reasoned judgment in identifying interests of the person so fundamental that the State must accord them its respect. That process is guided by many of the same considerations relevant to analysis of other constitutional provisions that set forth broad principles rather than specific requirements. History and tradition guide and discipline this inquiry but do not set its outer boundaries. See *Lawrence v. Texas* (2003). That method respects our history and learns from it without allowing the past alone to rule the present.

The nature of injustice is that we may not always see it in our own times. The generations that wrote and ratified the Bill of Rights and the Fourteenth Amendment did not presume to know the extent of freedom in all of its dimensions, and so they entrusted to future generations a charter protecting the right of all persons to enjoy liberty as we learn its meaning. When new insight reveals discord between the Constitution's central protections and a received legal stricture, a claim to liberty must be addressed.

Applying these established tenets, the Court has long held the right to marry is protected by the Constitution. In *Loving v. Virginia* (1967), which invalidated bans on interracial unions, a unanimous Court held marriage is "one of the vital personal rights essential to the orderly pursuit of happiness by free men." The Court reaffirmed that holding in *Zablocki v. Redhail* (1978), which held the right to marry was burdened by a law prohibiting fathers who were behind on child support from marrying. The Court again applied this principle in *Turner v. Safley* (1987), which held the right to marry was abridged by regulations limiting the privilege of prison inmates to marry. Over time and in other contexts, the Court has reiterated that the right to marry is fundamental under the Due Process Clause. . . .

It cannot be denied that this Court's cases describing the right to marry presumed a relationship involving opposite-sex partners. The Court, like many institutions, has made assumptions defined by the world and time of which it is a part. This was evident in *Baker v. Nelson* (1971), a one-line summary decision issued in 1972, holding the exclusion of same-sex couples from marriage did not present a substantial federal question.

Still, there are other, more instructive precedents. This Court's cases have expressed constitutional principles of broader reach. In defining the right to marry these cases have identified essential attributes of that right based in history, tradition, and other constitutional liberties inherent in this intimate bond. And in assessing whether the force and rationale of its cases apply to same-sex couples, the Court must respect the basic reasons why the right to marry has been long protected.

This analysis compels the conclusion that same-sex couples may exercise the right to marry. The four principles and traditions to be discussed demonstrate that the reasons marriage is fundamental under the Constitution apply with equal force to same-sex couples.

A first premise of the Court's relevant precedents is that the right to personal choice regarding marriage is inherent in the concept of individual autonomy. This abiding connection between marriage and liberty is why *Loving* invalidated interracial marriage bans under the Due Process Clause. Like choices concerning contraception, family relationships, procreation, and childrearing, all of which are protected by the Constitution, decisions concerning marriage are among the most intimate that an individual can make. See *Lawrence.* Indeed, the Court has noted it would be contradictory "to recognize a right of privacy with respect to other matters of family life and not with respect to the decision to enter the relationship that is the foundation of the family in our society." *Zablocki.*

Choices about marriage shape an individual's destiny. . . . The nature of marriage is that, through its enduring bond, two persons together can find other freedoms, such as expression, intimacy, and spirituality. This is true for all persons, whatever their sexual orientation. There is dignity in the bond between two men or two women who seek to marry and in their autonomy to make such profound choices.

A second principle in this Court's jurisprudence is that the right to marry is fundamental because it supports a two-person union unlike any other in its importance to the committed individuals. This point was central to *Griswold.* [See also *Turner v. Safley.*] The right to marry thus dignifies couples who "wish to define themselves by their commitment to each other." *Windsor.* Marriage responds to the universal fear that a lonely person might call out only to find no one there. It offers the hope of companionship and understanding and as-surance that while both still live there will be someone to care for the other.

As this Court held in *Lawrence*, same-sex couples have the same right as opposite-sex couples to enjoy intimate association. . . . But while *Lawrence* confirmed a dimension of freedom that allows individuals to engage in inti-mate association without criminal liability, it does not follow that freedom stops there. Outlaw to outcast may be a step forward, but it does not achieve the full promise of liberty.

A third basis for protecting the right to marry is that it safeguards chil-dren and families and thus draws meaning from related rights of childrearing, procreation, and education. See *Pierce v. Society of Sisters* (1925); *Meyer v. Ne-braska* (1923). The Court has recognized these connections by describing the varied rights as a unified whole: "[T]he right to 'marry, establish a home and bring up children' is a central part of the liberty protected by the Due Process Clause." *Zablocki*. Under the laws of the several States, some of marriage's pro-tections for children and families are material. But marriage also confers more profound benefits. By giving recognition and legal structure to their parents' relationship, marriage allows children "to understand the integrity and close-ness of their own family and its concord with other families in their community and in their daily lives." *Windsor*. Marriage also affords the permanency and stability important to children's best interests.

As all parties agree, many same-sex couples provide loving and nurtur-ing homes to their children, whether biological or adopted. And hundreds of thousands of children are presently being raised by such couples. Most States have allowed gays and lesbians to adopt, either as individuals or as couples, and many adopted and foster children have same-sex parents. This provides pow-erful confirmation from the law itself that gays and lesbians can create loving, supportive families.

Excluding same-sex couples from marriage thus conflicts with a central premise of the right to marry. Without the recognition, stability, and pre-dictability marriage offers, their children suffer the stigma of knowing their families are somehow lesser. They also suffer the significant material costs of being raised by unmarried parents, relegated through no fault of their own to a more difficult and uncertain family life. The marriage laws at issue here thus harm and humiliate the children of same-sex couples. See *Windsor*.

That is not to say the right to marry is less meaningful for those who do not or cannot have children. An ability, desire, or promise to procreate is not and has not been a prerequisite for a valid marriage in any State. In light of precedent protecting the right of a married couple not to procreate, it cannot be said the Court or the States have conditioned the right to marry on the capacity or commitment to procreate. The constitutional marriage right has many aspects, of which childbearing is only one.

Fourth and finally, this Court's cases and the Nation's traditions make clear that marriage is a keystone of our social order. . . . This idea has been reiterated even as the institution has evolved in substantial ways over time, superseding rules related to parental consent, gender, and race once thought by many to be essential. Marriage remains a building block of our national community.

For that reason, just as a couple vows to support each other, so does society pledge to support the couple, offering symbolic recognition and material benefits to protect and nourish the union. Indeed, while the States are in general free to vary the benefits they confer on all married couples, they have throughout our history made marriage the basis for an expanding list of governmental rights, benefits, and responsibilities. These aspects of marital status include: taxation; inheritance and property rights; rules of intestate succession; spousal privilege in the law of evidence; hospital access; medical decisionmaking authority; adoption rights; the rights and benefits of survivors; birth and death certificates; professional ethics rules; campaign finance restrictions; workers' compensation benefits; health insurance; and child custody, support, and visitation rules. Valid marriage under state law is also a significant status for over a thousand provisions of federal law. See *Windsor.* The States have contributed to the fundamental character of the marriage right by placing that institution at the center of so many facets of the legal and social order.

There is no difference between same- and opposite-sex couples with respect to this principle. Yet by virtue of their exclusion from that institution, same-sex couples are denied the constellation of benefits that the States have linked to marriage. This harm results in more than just material burdens. Same-sex couples are consigned to an instability many opposite-sex couples would deem intolerable in their own lives. As the State itself makes marriage all the more precious by the significance it attaches to it, exclusion from that status has the effect of teaching that gays and lesbians are unequal in important respects. It demeans gays and lesbians for the State to lock them out of a central institution of the Nation's society. Same-sex couples, too, may aspire to the transcendent purposes of marriage and seek fulfillment in its highest meaning.

The limitation of marriage to opposite-sex couples may long have seemed natural and just, but its inconsistency with the central meaning of the fundamental right to marry is now manifest. With that knowledge must come the recognition that laws excluding same-sex couples from the marriage right impose stigma and injury of the kind prohibited by our basic charter.

Objecting that this does not reflect an appropriate framing of the issue, the respondents refer to *Washington v. Glucksberg* (1997), which called for a " 'careful description' " of fundamental rights. They assert the petitioners do not seek to exercise the right to marry but rather a new and nonexistent "right to same-sex marriage." *Glucksberg* did insist that liberty under the Due Process Clause must be defined in a most circumscribed manner, with central reference to specific historical practices. Yet while that approach may have been appropriate for the asserted right there involved (physician-assisted suicide), it is inconsistent with the approach this Court has used in discussing other fundamental rights, including marriage and intimacy. *Loving* did not ask about a "right to interracial marriage"; *Turner* did not ask about a "right of inmates to marry"; and *Zablocki* did not ask about a "right of fathers with unpaid child support duties to marry." Rather, each case inquired about the right to marry in its comprehensive sense, asking if there was a sufficient justification for excluding the relevant class from the right. See also *Glucksberg* (Souter, J., concurring in judgment).

That principle applies here. If rights were defined by who exercised them in the past, then received practices could serve as their own continued justification and new groups could not invoke rights once denied. This Court has rejected that approach, both with respect to the right to marry and the rights of gays and lesbians. See *Loving*; *Lawrence*. . . .

The right of same-sex couples to marry that is part of the liberty promised by the Fourteenth Amendment is derived, too, from that Amendment's guarantee of the equal protection of the laws. The Due Process Clause and the Equal Protection Clause are connected in a profound way, though they set forth independent principles. Rights implicit in liberty and rights secured by equal protection may rest on different precepts and are not always co-extensive, yet in some instances each may be instructive as to the meaning and reach of the other. . . .

The Court's cases touching upon the right to marry reflect this dynamic. In *Loving* the Court invalidated a prohibition on interracial marriage under both the Equal Protection Clause and the Due Process Clause. . . . The reasons why marriage is a fundamental right became more clear and compelling from a full awareness and understanding of the hurt that resulted from laws barring interracial unions. . . . The synergy between the two protections is illustrated further [by] *Lawrence*[, where] the Court acknowledged the interlocking nature of these constitutional safeguards in the context of the legal treatment of gays and lesbians. Although *Lawrence* elaborated its holding under the Due Process Clause, it acknowledged, and sought to remedy, the continuing inequality that resulted from laws making intimacy in the lives of gays and lesbians a crime against the State. . . .

This dynamic also applies to same-sex marriage. It is now clear that the challenged laws burden the liberty of same-sex couples, and it must be further acknowledged that they abridge central precepts of equality. Here the marriage laws enforced by the respondents are in essence unequal: same-sex couples are denied all the benefits afforded to opposite-sex couples and are barred from exercising a fundamental right. Especially against a long history of disapproval of their relationships, this denial to same-sex couples of the right to marry works a grave and continuing harm. The imposition of this disability on gays and lesbians serves to disrespect and subordinate them. And the Equal Protection Clause, like the Due Process Clause, prohibits this unjustified infringement of the fundamental right to marry.

These considerations lead to the conclusion that the right to marry is a fundamental right inherent in the liberty of the person, and under the Due Process and Equal Protection Clauses of the Fourteenth Amendment couples of the same-sex may not be deprived of that right and that liberty. The Court now holds that same-sex couples may exercise the fundamental right to marry. No longer may this liberty be denied to them. *Baker v. Nelson* must be and now is overruled, and the State laws challenged by Petitioners in these cases are now held invalid to the extent they exclude same-sex couples from civil marriage on the same terms and conditions as opposite-sex couples.

IV

. . . Of course, the Constitution contemplates that democracy is the appropriate process for change, so long as that process does not abridge fundamental rights. . . . But . . . [t]he dynamic of our constitutional system is that individuals need not await legislative action before asserting a fundamental right.

. . . The respondents also argue allowing same-sex couples to wed will harm marriage as an institution by leading to fewer opposite-sex marriages. This may occur, the respondents contend, because licensing same-sex marriage severs the connection between natural procreation and marriage. . . . Decisions about whether to marry and raise children are based on many personal, romantic, and practical considerations; and it is unrealistic to conclude that an opposite-sex couple would choose not to marry simply because same-sex couples may do so. The respondents have not shown a foundation for the conclusion that allowing same-sex marriage will cause the harmful outcomes they describe. Indeed, with respect to this asserted basis for excluding same-sex couples from the right to marry, it is appropriate to observe these cases involve only the rights of two consenting adults whose marriages would pose no risk of harm to themselves or third parties. . . .

* * *

No union is more profound than marriage, for it embodies the highest ideals of love, fidelity, devotion, sacrifice, and family. In forming a marital union, two people become something greater than once they were. As some of the petitioners in these cases demonstrate, marriage embodies a love that may endure even past death. It would misunderstand these men and women to say they disrespect the idea of marriage. Their plea is that they do respect it, respect it so deeply that they seek to find its fulfillment for themselves. Their hope is not to be condemned to live in loneliness, excluded from one of civilization's oldest institutions. They ask for equal dignity in the eyes of the law. The Constitution grants them that right.

The judgment of the Court of Appeals for the Sixth Circuit is reversed. . . .

CHIEF JUSTICE ROBERTS, with whom JUSTICE SCALIA and JUSTICE THOMAS join, dissenting.

. . . Supporters of same-sex marriage have achieved considerable success persuading their fellow citizens—through the democratic process—to adopt their view. That ends today. Five lawyers have closed the debate and enacted their own vision of marriage as a matter of constitutional law. Stealing this issue from the people will for many cast a cloud over same-sex marriage, making a dramatic social change that much more difficult to accept.

The majority's decision is an act of will, not legal judgment. The right it announces . . . invalidates the marriage laws of more than half the States and orders the transformation of a social institution that has formed the basis of human society for millennia, for the Kalahari Bushmen and the Han Chinese, the Carthaginians and the Aztecs. Just who do we think we are? . . .

Understand well what this dissent is about: It is not about whether, in my judgment, the institution of marriage should be changed to include same-sex couples. It is instead about whether, in our democratic republic, that decision should rest with the people acting through their elected representatives, or with five lawyers who happen to hold commissions authorizing them to resolve legal disputes according to law. The Constitution leaves no doubt about the answer.

I

Petitioners and their *amici* base their arguments on the "right to marry" and the imperative of "marriage equality." There is no serious dispute that, under our precedents, the Constitution protects a right to marry and requires States to apply their marriage laws equally. The real question in these cases is what constitutes "marriage," or—more precisely—*who decides* what constitutes "marriage"?

The majority largely ignores these questions, relegating ages of human experience with marriage to a paragraph or two. Even if history and precedent are not "the end" of these cases, I would not "sweep away what has so long been settled" without showing greater respect for all that preceded us.

As the majority acknowledges, marriage "has existed for millennia and across civilizations." For all those millennia, across all those civilizations, "marriage" referred to only one relationship: the union of a man and a woman. . . . This universal definition of marriage as the union of a man and a woman is no historical coincidence. Marriage did not come about . . . . as a result of a prehistoric decision to exclude gays and lesbians. It arose in the nature of things to meet a vital need: ensuring that children are conceived by a mother and father committed to raising them in the stable conditions of a lifelong relationship.

The premises supporting this concept of marriage are so fundamental that they rarely require articulation. The human race must procreate to survive. Procreation occurs through sexual relations between a man and a woman. When sexual relations result in the conception of a child, that child's prospects are generally better if the mother and father stay together rather than going their separate ways. Therefore, for the good of children and society, sexual relations that can lead to procreation should occur only between a man and a woman committed to a lasting bond. Society has recognized that bond as marriage. And by bestowing a respected status and material benefits on married couples, society encourages men and women to conduct sexual relations within marriage rather than without. . . .

As the majority notes, some aspects of marriage have changed over time. Arranged marriages have largely given way to pairings based on romantic love. States have replaced coverture, the doctrine by which a married man and woman became a single legal entity, with laws that respect each participant's separate status. Racial restrictions on marriage, which "arose as an incident to slavery" to promote "White Supremacy," were repealed by many States and ultimately struck down by this Court. *Loving.*

The majority observes that these developments "were not mere superficial changes" in marriage, but rather "worked deep transformations in its structure." They did not, however, work any transformation in the core structure of marriage as the union between a man and a woman. If you had asked a person on the street how marriage was defined, no one would ever have said, "Marriage is the union of a man and a woman, where the woman is subject to coverture." The majority may be right that the "history of marriage is one of both continuity and change," but the core meaning of marriage has endured. . . .

II

Petitioners first contend that the marriage laws of their States violate the Due Process Clause. The Solicitor General of the United States, appearing in support of petitioners, expressly disowned that position before this Court. The majority nevertheless resolves these cases for petitioners based almost entirely on the Due Process Clause. . . .

B

The majority['s] aggressive application of substantive due process breaks sharply with decades of precedent and returns the Court to the unprincipled approach of *Lochner.*

1

. . . When the majority turns to the law, it relies primarily on precedents discussing the fundamental "right to marry." These cases do not hold, of course, that anyone who wants to get married has a constitutional right to do so. They instead require a State to justify barriers to marriage as that institution has always been understood. . . . None of the laws at issue in those cases purported to change the core definition of marriage as the union of a man and a woman. . . . Removing racial barriers to marriage . . . did not change what a marriage was any more than integrating schools changed what a school was. As the majority admits, the institution of "marriage" discussed in every one of these cases "presumed a relationship involving opposite-sex partners."

In short, the "right to marry" cases stand for the important but limited proposition that particular restrictions on access to marriage *as traditionally defined* violate due process. These precedents say nothing at all about a right to make a State change its definition of marriage, which is the right petitioners actually seek here. Neither petitioners nor the majority cites a single case or other legal source providing any basis for such a constitutional right. None exists, and that is enough to foreclose their claim.

2

The majority suggests that "there are other, more instructive precedents" informing the right to marry. Although not entirely clear, this reference seems to correspond to a line of cases discussing an implied fundamental "right of privacy." . . .

Neither *Lawrence* nor any other precedent in the privacy line of cases supports the right that petitioners assert here. Unlike criminal laws banning contraceptives and sodomy, the marriage laws at issue here involve no government intrusion. They create no crime and impose no punishment. Same-sex couples remain free to live together, to engage in intimate conduct, and to raise their families as they see fit. No one is "condemned to live in loneliness" by the laws challenged in these cases—no one. At the same time, the laws in no way interfere with the "right to be let alone." . . .

[T]he privacy cases provide no support for the majority's position, because petitioners do not seek privacy. Quite the opposite, they seek public recognition of their relationships, along with corresponding government benefits. Our cases have consistently refused to allow litigants to convert the shield provided by constitutional liberties into a sword to demand positive entitlements from the State. See *DeShaney v. Winnebago County Dept. of Social Servs.* (1989); *San Antonio Independent School Dist. v. Rodriguez* (1973). Thus, although the right to privacy recognized by our precedents certainly plays a role in protecting the intimate conduct of same-sex couples, it provides no affirmative right to redefine marriage and no basis for striking down the laws at issue here.

3

Perhaps recognizing how little support it can derive from precedent, the majority goes out of its way to jettison the "careful" approach to implied fundamental rights taken by this Court in *Glucksberg*. It is revealing that the majority's position requires it to effectively overrule *Glucksberg*, the leading modern case setting the bounds of substantive due process. At least this part of the majority opinion has the virtue of candor. Nobody could rightly accuse the majority of taking a careful approach. Ultimately, only one precedent offers any support for the majority's methodology: *Lochner v. New York*. . . .

One immediate question invited by the majority's position is whether States may retain the definition of marriage as a union of two people. Cf. *Brown v. Buhman* (D. Utah 2013). Although the majority randomly inserts the adjective "two" in various places, it offers no reason at all why the two-person element of the core definition of marriage may be preserved while the man-woman element may not. Indeed, from the standpoint of history and tradition, a leap from opposite-sex marriage to same-sex marriage is much greater than one from a two-person union to plural unions, which have deep roots in some cultures around the world. If the majority is willing to take the big leap, it is hard to see how it can say no to the shorter one.

WORTH NOTING

The district court in *Buhman* had struck down Utah's criminal prohibition on polygamy, which was defined to include cohabitation as well as formal marriages. After *Obergefell* was decided, the 10th Circuit vacated the district court's ruling on the ground that—because there was no showing the ban was actually enforced absent other crimes—the *Buhman* plaintiffs did not have standing.

It is striking how much of the majority's reasoning would apply with equal force to the claim of a fundamental right to plural marriage. . . . If a same-sex couple has the constitutional right to marry because their children would otherwise "suffer the stigma of knowing their families are somehow lesser," why wouldn't the same reasoning apply to a family of three or more persons raising children? If not having the opportunity to marry "serves to disrespect and subordinate" gay and lesbian couples, why wouldn't the same "imposition of this disability" serve to disrespect and subordinate people who find fulfillment in polyamorous relationships?

I do not mean to equate marriage between same-sex couples with plural marriages in all respects. There may well be relevant differences that compel different legal analysis. But if there are, petitioners have not pointed to any. . . .

4

Near the end of its opinion, the majority offers perhaps the clearest insight into its decision. Expanding marriage to include same-sex couples, the majority insists, would "pose no risk of harm to themselves or third parties." This argument again echoes *Lochner*. . . . Then and now, this assertion of the "harm principle" sounds more in philosophy than law. . . . As Judge Henry Friendly once put it, echoing Justice Holmes's dissent in *Lochner*, the Fourteenth Amendment does not enact John Stuart Mill's On Liberty any more than it enacts Herbert Spencer's Social Statics. And it certainly does not enact any one concept of marriage. . . .

III

. . . The majority does not seriously engage with [the Equal Protection Clause] claim. Its discussion is, quite frankly, difficult to follow. The central point seems to be that there is a "synergy between" the Equal Protection Clause and the Due Process Clause, and that some precedents relying on one Clause have also relied on the other. Absent from this portion of the opinion, however, is anything resembling our usual framework for deciding equal protection cases. . . .

In any event, the marriage laws at issue here do not violate the Equal Protection Clause, because distinguishing between opposite-sex and same-sex couples is rationally related to the States' "legitimate state interest" in "preserving the traditional institution of marriage." *Lawrence* (O'Connor, J., concurring in judgment). . . .

IV

. . . By deciding this question under the Constitution, the Court removes it from the realm of democratic decision. There will be consequences to shutting down the political process on an issue of such profound public significance. Closing debate tends to close minds. People denied a voice are less likely to accept the ruling of a court on an issue that does not seem to be the sort of thing courts usually decide. As a thoughtful commentator observed about another issue, "The political process was moving . . . , not swiftly enough for advocates of quick, complete change, but majoritarian institutions were listening and acting. Heavy-handed judicial intervention was difficult to justify and appears to have provoked, not resolved, conflict." Ruth Bader Ginsburg, *Some Thoughts on Autonomy and Equality in Relation to Roe v. Wade*, 63 N.C. L. Rev. 375 (1985).

Indeed, however heartened the proponents of same-sex marriage might be on this day, it is worth acknowledging what they have lost, and lost forever: the opportunity to win the true acceptance that comes from persuading their fellow citizens of the justice of their cause. And they lose this just when the winds of change were freshening at their backs. . . . If you are among the many Americans—of whatever sexual orientation—who favor expanding same-sex marriage, by all means celebrate today's decision. Celebrate the achievement of a desired goal. Celebrate the opportunity for a new expression of commitment to a partner. Celebrate the availability of new benefits. But do not celebrate the Constitution. It had nothing to do with it.

JUSTICE SCALIA, with whom JUSTICE THOMAS joins, dissenting.

. . . Today's decree says that my Ruler, and the Ruler of 320 million Americans coast-to-coast, is a majority of the nine lawyers on the Supreme Court. . . . But what really astounds is the hubris reflected in today's judicial Putsch. . . . Of course the opinion's showy profundities are often profoundly incoherent. . . . The world does not expect logic and precision in poetry or inspirational pop-philosophy; it demands them in the law. The stuff contained in today's opinion has to diminish this Court's reputation for clear thinking and sober analysis. . . .

JUSTICE THOMAS, with whom JUSTICE SCALIA joins, dissenting.

. . . Perhaps recognizing that these cases do not actually involve liberty as it has been understood, the majority goes to great lengths to assert that its decision will advance the "dignity" of same-sex couples. The flaw in that reasoning, of course, is that the Constitution contains no "dignity" Clause, and even if it did, the government would be incapable of bestowing dignity.

Human dignity has long been understood in this country to be innate. When the Framers proclaimed in the Declaration of Independence that "all men are created equal" and "endowed by their Creator with certain unalienable Rights," they referred to a vision of mankind in which all humans are created in the image of God and therefore of inherent worth. That vision is the foundation upon which this Nation was built.

The corollary of that principle is that human dignity cannot be taken away by the government. Slaves did not lose their dignity (any more than they lost their humanity) because the government allowed them to be enslaved. Those held in internment camps did not lose their dignity because the government confined them. And those denied governmental benefits certainly do not lose their dignity because the government denies them those benefits. The government cannot bestow dignity, and it cannot take it away. . . .

Justice Alito, with whom Justice Scalia and Justice Thomas join, dissenting.

. . . Today's decision . . . . will be used to vilify Americans who are unwilling to assent to the new orthodoxy. In the course of its opinion, the majority compares traditional marriage laws to laws that denied equal treatment for African-Americans and women. The implications of this analogy will be exploited by those who are determined to stamp out every vestige of dissent. . . . I assume that those who cling to old beliefs will be able to whisper their thoughts in the recesses of their homes, but if they repeat those views in public, they will risk being labeled as bigots and treated as such by governments, employers, and schools. . . .

Today's decision will also have a fundamental effect on this Court and its ability to uphold the rule of law. If a bare majority of Justices can invent a new right and impose that right on the rest of the country, the only real limit on what future majorities will be able to do is their own sense of what those with political power and cultural influence are willing to tolerate. Even enthusiastic supporters of same-sex marriage should worry about the scope of the power that today's majority claims. . . .

Evancho v. Pine-Richland School District

Federal District Court for the Western District of Pennsylvania, 2017.
237 F. Supp. 3d 267.

MARK R. HORNAK, UNITED STATES DISTRICT JUDGE.

The three high school student Plaintiffs are each transgender, and all are in their senior year at Pine-Richland (Pa.) High School. Two of them, Juliet Evancho and Elissa Ridenour, each over eighteen years old, had "male" listed on their birth certificates when they were born.[1] That of the third Plaintiff, A.S. (also a high school senior, but not yet eighteen years old), said "female." For some time, Juliet Evancho and Elissa Ridenour have lived all facets of their lives as girls, and A.S. has done so as a boy.

The Defendant School District does not dispute that Plaintiffs identify as transgender, which means, among other things, that their gender identities are at odds with the sexes listed on their original birth certificates and with their external sex organs. It is undisputed that in all respects, the Plaintiffs have—at least for their high school years—lived every facet of their in-school and out-of-school lives consistently with their respective gender identities rather than their "assigned sexes."[3] Their teachers, school administrators, fellow students and others have treated the Plaintiffs consistently with their gender identities as they have lived and expressed them rather than according to their assigned sexes. According to the District, the Plaintiffs, except for purposes of excretory functions, are of the gender with which they identify, and the District treats the Plaintiffs' gender identities as their "sex" in all other interactions with the District.

The central issue now before the Court is whether the District acted in accord with federal law when it limited, by formal School Board Resolution 2, the common school bathrooms that these Plaintiffs may use to either (a) single-user bathrooms or (b) the bathrooms labeled as matching their assigned sexes. The Plaintiffs argue that the District's application of Resolution 2 to prevent them from continuing to use common student restrooms that conform

---

[1]   The Commonwealth of Pennsylvania has re-issued a birth certificate for Plaintiff Evancho that lists her sex as "female."

[3]   Solely for simplicity of reference, and because it is the focus of all of the arguments advanced by the Defendants, the Court will use the term "assigned sex" to refer to the physical characteristics of the external sex organs of a person being referenced. . . .

to their gender identities violates . . . the Equal Protection Clause of the Fourteenth Amendment, . . . by impermissibly treating them differently than other District students based on their gender identities, and therefore their sexes. . . .

The Court concludes that the Plaintiffs have a reasonable likelihood of success on the merits of their Equal Protection claim. . . . The Court will therefore grant in part the Plaintiffs' Motion for a Preliminary Injunction. . . .

I.

. . . Plaintiff Juliet Evancho began to change her appearance and dress to that typically associated with a girl at around age 12 or 13. She began medically supervised hormone treatment at around age 16, and in 2015, at age 17, she publicly began living as a girl. During the 2015–16 school year, Ms. Evancho and her parents met with school officials regarding her gender identity as a girl, and those school officials were fully on board with treating her consistently with that identity. She says that the passage of Resolution 2 and its implementation as to her have caused her serious emotional and other distress, making her feel unsafe, depressed, marginalized and stigmatized by, among other things, the School's requirement that she use only either the boys restrooms or the single-user restrooms at the High School. Ms. Evancho's photo, which shows that her appearance is completely consistent only with the gender identity that she lives every day, is in the record. . . .

Plaintiff Elissa Ridenour began to live her life as a girl at age 14, and she likewise began medically supervised hormonal therapy thereafter. In 2012, while in 8th grade, she and her parents met with school officials to advise them that she was living her life in all respects as a girl. The District officials stated that they would engage with her in that fashion. Ms. Ridenour is treated by the High School community as a girl, and—at least prior to the passage of Resolution 2—was fully accepted as a girl. She reports that Resolution 2 had essentially the same impact on her as does Ms. Evancho. Plaintiff Ridenour's photo, which shows that her appearance is consistent only with the gender identity that she lives every day, is in the record. . . .

Plaintiff A.S. and his parents met with school counselors in 2015 and advised them that he lived as a boy. The school counselors advised him that he would be treated as a boy within the school community, and he was. Beginning in his junior year at the High School, A.S. started using the "boys" restroom with no issues, and he was widely accepted as a boy by the school community. In 2016, he too began receiving medically-directed hormonal treatment, and he has now legally changed his given name to one traditionally used by boys. A.S. also asserts the same sorts of actual harm from the implementation of Resolution 2 as do the other Plaintiffs. . . .

As to the High School restroom facilities themselves, the parties agree that the student restrooms at the High School are well-maintained, well-lit, and provide locking doors for the toilets in both the girls and boys restrooms. There are partitions on the urinals in the boys rooms. . . . The parties agree that the nearly one dozen single-user restrooms arrayed around the High School are now open to any student at any time, including to any student that has a particularized privacy concern.

Until early 2016, there were no institutional issues with the participation of the Plaintiffs in any facet of daily life at the High School. The District, its educational staff, and apparently their fellow students, treated each of them in the very same way that their own families did—that is, consistently with their gender identities. . . . The most distinctive and illustrative evidence of this is that Juliet Evancho ran for Homecoming Queen in 2016, and she was elected by her peers to the "Homecoming Court" of finalists for that honor. . . .

[In 2016, the matter became a subject of public contention at Board meetings.] According to the declarations submitted by the individual Board Members, a (if not *the*) prevailing concern raised by both those who spoke in favor of Resolution 2 and Board proponents alike was that a student would in essence masquerade as being transgender, and would then use a designated student restroom inconsistent with their assigned sex. This would all occur in an effort to visually examine the sex organs of other restroom users or to engage in some other blatant and malicious invasion of bodily privacy of those simply using the restrooms for their intended purposes. Board members also expressed concern that the partially clothed body of a student of a given assigned sex would be observed in a restroom by a student of the opposite assigned sex. No explanations were provided as to the circumstances of how or when that has, or would, actually happen. And the record of these discussions . . . does not reveal that any such episode involving an imposter has ever occurred at the High School or in the District, nor was any reported episode in another school advanced to the Board.

At the end of its process, the Board in a 5–4 vote passed Resolution 2, reversed how things had been happening for the past several years, and directed, among other things, that students must use either unisex bathrooms or the school bathrooms of their "biological sex." . . .

The parties agree that other than perhaps one report received by the High School principal in October 2015 from a student that "there was a boy" in the girls bathroom (apparently in reference to Plaintiff Evancho), followed by a parent inquiry along the same lines in early 2016, there have been no reports of "incidents" where the use of a common restroom by any one of the Plaintiffs has caused any sort of alarm to any other student, nor of any actual or actually threatened impermissible conduct by or toward any student. . . . And the District appeared to agree that its existing codes of student conduct would proscribe and as necessary punish any student that engaged in such maliciously improper conduct. Certainly the statutory law of Pennsylvania would appear to do so. . . .

III.

. . . As a preliminary matter, the Court concludes that on the record now before it, the Plaintiffs have shown that the District is treating them differently from other students who are similarly situated on the basis of their transgender status. The Plaintiffs are being distinguished by governmental action from those whose gender identities are congruent with their assigned sex. The Plaintiffs are the only students who are not allowed to use the common restrooms consistent with their gender identities. [U]nlike every other student, the Plaintiffs would have to use restrooms where they are wholly unlike everyone else in appearance, manner, mode of living, and treatment at school. Resolution 2 therefore discriminates[29] based on transgender status. . . .

Given that the classification at hand is the Plaintiffs' transgender status, the parties dispute which Equal Protection standard should apply. The District says that the lowest Equal Protection bar applies, that is the rational basis test. . . . The Plaintiffs in turn . . . . contend that the rational basis test is not the test to be applied to the classification enacted by Resolution 2. They say that a heightened standard, known as "intermediate scrutiny," which is applied to classifications based on sex, should apply here. . . . [I]ntermediate scrutiny requires that differential treatment be supported by an exceedingly persuasive reason, advance an important governmental interest and have a direct relationship to the important governmental interest furthered by it.

---

[29] The Court uses the term "discrimination" to mean a choice by the District among and between groups of people. . . . Not all "discrimination" is unlawful, as that word means at its core the process of choosing. Whether that "choice" is legally permissible is the issue joined in this case.

The Supreme Court uses the following four factors to determine whether a "new" classification requires heightened scrutiny: (1) whether the class has been historically "subjected to discrimination," *Lyng v. Castillo* (1986); (2) whether the class has a defining characteristic that "frequently bears no relation to ability to perform or contribute to society," *City of Cleburne v. Cleburne Living Ctr.* (1985); (3) whether the class exhibits "obvious, immutable, or distinguishing characteristics that define them as a discrete group," *Lyng*; and (4) whether the class is "a minority or politically powerless." *Lyng*.

Against that backdrop, the Court concludes that an intermediate standard of Equal Protection review applies in this case. The record before the Court reflects that transgender people as a class have historically been subject to discrimination or differentiation; that they have a defining characteristic that frequently bears no relation to an ability to perform or contribute to society; that as a class they exhibit immutable or distinguishing characteristics that define them as a discrete group; and that as a class, they are a minority with relatively little political power. . . . [A]s a class of people, transgender individuals make up a small (according to all parties, less than 1%) proportion of the American population. As to these Plaintiffs, their transgender characteristics are inherent in who they are as people, which is not factually contested by the District. As to these Plaintiffs, and more generally as to transgender individuals as a class, that characteristic bears no relationship to their ability to contribute to our society. More precisely, the record reveals that the Plaintiffs are in all respects productive, engaged, contributing members of the student body at the High School. Thus, all of the indicia for the application of the heightened intermediate scrutiny standard are present here.

Moreover, as to these Plaintiffs, gender identity is entirely akin to "sex" as that term has been customarily used in the Equal Protection analysis. It is deeply ingrained and inherent in their very beings. Like "sex," as to these Plaintiffs, gender identity is neither transitory nor temporary. Further, what buttresses that conclusion is the fact that the school community as a whole treats these Plaintiffs in all other regards consistently with their stated gender identities, along with the reality that these Plaintiffs live all facets of their lives in a fashion consistent with their stated and experienced gender identities. . . .

. . . [T]he Court concludes that the Plaintiffs have a reasonable likelihood of success on the merits of their claim that the District has not demonstrated

DOCTRINE AND PRACTICE SERIES: CONSTITUTIONAL LAW

that applying Resolution 2 to Plaintiffs' restroom use actually furthers an important governmental interest. . . .

First, such an application of Resolution 2 would not appear to be necessary to quell any actual or incipient threat, disturbance or other disruption of school activities by the Plaintiffs. There is no record of any such thing. Any arguable disruption to the daily activities of the District that is the result of the passage of Resolution 2 (or the discussions leading up to or resulting from it) would not be attributable to the Plaintiffs, and there is no record evidence of such. . . .

Second, Resolution 2 would appear to do little to address any actual privacy concern of any student that is not already well addressed by the physical layout of the bathrooms. The District has stated that Resolution 2 is necessary to protect the privacy of students (presumably including the Plaintiffs), by which the District has stated it means the sanctity of excretory functions. The record simply does not reveal any actual risk (or even an actual risk of a risk) in such regards. The Court readily recognizes that the law acknowledges the existence of a generalized privacy interest and that the District has an obligation to protect the legitimate privacy interests of all students. . . . But [a]lthough the record reveals some specific concerns driven by the reputed presence (and presence alone) of a Plaintiff in a restroom matching her gender identity, there is no record evidence that this actually imperiled or risked imperiling any privacy interest of any person. And . . . given the actual physical layout of the student restrooms at the High School, it would appear to the Court that anyone using the toilets or urinals at the High School is afforded actual physical privacy from others viewing their external sex organs and excretory functions. Conversely, others in the restrooms are shielded from such views.[37]

FOR DISCUSSION Does the logic of the court's discussion suggest that the case would have come out differently if plaintiff's classmates and teachers had been less accepting of plaintiff's gender identity? Imagine, for example, that the school district was able to collect affidavits from students willing to state under oath that plaintiff's presence in the "wrong" bathroom was so upsetting as to cause them emotional trauma and harm the educational environment. What if affidavits like that were submitted by five students? By 100 students?

---

[37]   Put directly, everyone using the toilets in the "girls room" is doing so in an enclosed stall with a locking door, and everyone using the toilets in the "boys room" is doing the same or is using a urinal with privacy screens.

Third, Resolution 2 would not appear to have been necessary in order to fill some gap in the District's code of student conduct or the positive law of Pennsylvania in order to proscribe unlawful malicious "peeping Tom" activity by anyone pretending to be transgender. There is no evidence of such a gap. The existing disciplinary rules of the District and the laws of Pennsylvania would address such matters. And as noted above, there is no record evidence of an actual or threatened outbreak of other students falsely or deceptively declaring themselves to be "transgender" for the purpose of engaging in untoward and maliciously improper activities in the High School restrooms.

Fourth, such application of Resolution 2 also would not appear to be supported by any actual need for students to routinely use the corners of the restrooms for changing into athletic gear from street clothes. Even if pressed by such theoretical possibilities, it would appear to the Court that the dozen or so single-user restrooms sprinkled around the High School would easily fit the bill for private changing. There is also no record evidence that any student uses, has used, or will use any common restroom outside of its structurally privacy-protected areas in any state of undress or for "excretory functions," which the District advised was the focus of Resolution 2.

. . . [T]he Court must next examine the express rationales set forth by the District for applying Resolution 2 to the Plaintiffs' restroom use.

. . . [S]ome of [the Board members] received word that several parents had, and others would, move their children to other schools if the Board did not enact a policy akin to Resolution 2. . . . Additionally, the record reflects that there were members of the community who attended one or more Board meetings and voiced support for Resolution 2. The Court is certainly in no position to conclude that a school board should be inattentive to the expressed educational preferences of parents and students—they plainly should consider such matters. . . . But [if] adopting and implementing a school policy or practice based on those individual determinations or preferences of parents—no matter how sincerely held—runs counter to the legal obligations of the District, then the District's and the Board's legal obligations must prevail. . . . The Equal Protection Clause of the Fourteenth Amendment is neither applied nor construed by popular vote. . . .

[T]he District [also] asserts that there should not be an issue here because any student may use the single-user restrooms sprinkled around the High School. The District has proposed that those single-user bathrooms therefore provide a "safety valve" of sorts for the Plaintiffs. . . . Given that settled precedent provides that impermissible distinctions by official edict cause tangible Constitutional harm, the law does not impose on the Plaintiffs the obligation to use single-user facilities in order to "solve the problem." . . . It is no answer under the Equal Protection Clause that those impermissibly singled out for differential treatment can, and therefore must, themselves "solve the problem" by further separating themselves from their peers.

This all leads to the conclusion that under the intermediate scrutiny standard, the Plaintiffs have established a reasonable likelihood of success on their Equal Protection claim. . . .

WORTH NOTING

The district court's decision permitted the case to proceed towards trial. About six months later, the parties announced that they had reached a settlement. Under the terms of the resulting consent decree, the school district was "enjoined from enforcing Resolution 2 or any policy, practice, or custom . . . that denies transgender students the access and use of restrooms that match a student's consistently and uniformly asserted gender identity."

TEST YOUR KNOWLEDGE: To assess your understanding of the material in this chapter, **click here** to take a quiz.

Index